W9-AWJ-596

Frommer's®
Ireland

My Ireland
by Christi Daugherty

I USED TO DREAM ABOUT IRELAND. I DON'T KNOW WHY; MY ANCESTORS

haven't lived there for more than a century. And yet as a young girl I felt the country was mine. It took a succession of visits to realize that others had laid claim to it *long* before me.

Few would agree today with the poet Patrick Kavanagh, who called Dublin "the cruelest city on Earth," or with James Joyce, who once said, "An Irishman needs three things: silence, cunning, and exile." Ireland has changed in the last 2 decades. Membership in the European Union has brought wealth; mutual understanding between Catholics and Protestants has forged a hopeful peace. Emigrants have flooded home to find new jobs, the resurgence of an old (Celtic) language, and a new love for the country they were forced by hardship to leave.

As they have returned, so have I. I will continue coming back to this place my great-grandparents knew, to this country I find so magical, where greens are greener, where fine white horses graze along crumbling old castle walls, where people know that only on a misty day can you see forever. I feel a pang, because none of this is mine. But my sense of loss is my connection to Ireland.

Whenever I return, I try to visit some of the places featured in the photos below. I think they'll find a special place in your heart, too.

KILKENNY (left) This regal and colorful little town, with its cobbled streets and distinctively medieval atmosphere, is one of my favorites in all of Ireland. When I visit, I tend to wander with no particular goal in mind, taking in its venerable buildings and chatting with its friendly residents. If you tire of wandering, Kilkenny Castle has stood here since Strongbow invaded Ireland and is well worth a visit.

CLIFFS OF MOHER (above) At 228m (760 ft.) tall and 8km (5 miles) long, the steep, striated limestone Cliffs of Moher plunge violently into the sea surrounding remote County Clare. There's nothing subtle about them—they are brutal and firm, and, frankly, you don't want to get too close to the edge. But birdwatchers will be tempted enough by the avian activity to lean out over the cliffs for a better view.

BOOK OF KELLS (left) The ancient Book of Kells is one of Ireland's most impressive literary achievements. This magnificent, hand-illustrated copy of the four Gospels dates from around A.D. 800 and was created by early Christian monks in the town of Kells, north of Dublin. Since the 19th century, it's been on permanent public view at Trinity College in Dublin. All of the craftwork is remarkable, but because of the book's fragile nature, only parts of it can be seen.

POULNABRONE DOLMEN (above) The mysterious stone table of Poulnabrone Dolmen dates back to 2500 B.C and was originally used as an ancient tomb. Its name "Poulnabrone" translates as "the hole of sorrows," a name that ably describes the feeling of this sad, desolate place in central Burren. Today, the dolmen is one of Ireland's most photographed ancient monuments, as tourists continue to marvel at the burial ground and ponder why and how ancient dwellers built such a massive marker.

DRINKING AROUND IRELAND To literally drink in the auld sod, head for **BUSHMILLS DISTILLERY (left)**, where whiskey is brewed the old-fashioned way and distilled in giant copper kettles to create the smoothest blend. Of course, you might have to taste it several times to be sure they've done it right . . . Purists say it takes more than 3 minutes to pour a proper pint of Guinness, and at the **GUINNESS STOREHOUSE (below right)** in Dublin, you can learn why it tastes better when it has been allowed to settle to the blackest black and the creamiest white. And no trip to Ireland is complete without a visit to an atmospheric pub like **MURPHY'S (above right)** or **DAN FOLEY'S (below)** in Dingle. Few regulars will deny that they enjoy a drink or two, but these are really local meetinghouses, where the atmosphere is less about drinking than about gathering together and entertaining one another. Guests are always welcome.

DUNGUAIRE CASTLE (above) Castle remains dominate the Irish landscape—they crop up in horse paddocks, in sheep pastures, and at the edge of ancient towns. County Galway's dramatic skyline and rocky coast, as well as the views of nearby Burren and Galway Bay, make Dunguaire Castle a standout. A restored example of a Norman "safe house," supposedly built on the site of a 6th-century royal palace, Dunguaire Castle holds summer banquets where you can revel in medieval food and entertainment.

GIANT'S CAUSEWAY (right) Yes, the Giant's Causeway has been discovered by tourists, but walking here is still like walking on the moon. William Thackeray once wrote of it, "When the world was moulded and fashioned out of formless chaos, this must have been the bit left over." He was right, in a way—the walkway was created by unusual volcanic activity. Locals have given the formations fanciful but fitting names like the Honeycomb, the Wishing Well, and the Giant's Granny.

KERRY ON HORSEBACK (below) I've never done it on horseback, but there looks to be no better way to explore County Kerry's miles of rolling green hills. The countryside here is rich with ancient ruins, including Staigue Fort, one of the best preserved of all ancient Irish structures, located in the Ring of Kerry. Once the homes of royalty and wealthy landowners, most of these ruins now provide shelter for cattle and sheep—'tis a lesson in humility if ever there was one.

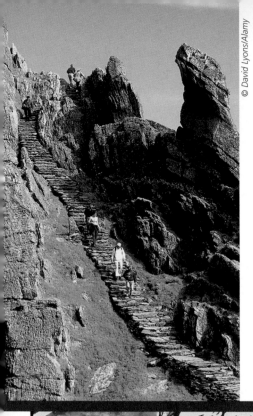

SKELLIG MICHAEL (left) Skellig Michael is one of those rare, astonishing places where man and nature have worked together to create something unforgettable. Rising sharply 214m (714 ft.) out of the Atlantic, this stunning crag of rock is dedicated to the Archangel Michael. Hidden in the velvety grass, among the craggy stones, sits a monastery dating to the 6th century. From the summit, visitors can spot the colorful puffins that raise their families here, 8 miles off-shore of the Iveragh Peninsula.

BELFAST MURAL (below) After years of religious warfare, Belfast is emerging as a vibrant city that's putting its troubled history behind it. It's got great sightseeing, fabulous nightlife, and wonderful places to eat, drink, and stay. All that, and it's also a pleasingly walkable city. Still, its famous street murals, like the one shown here, offer the greatest reminder that Belfast is a grand old city in transition, and that now is a great time to visit and see the changes firsthand.

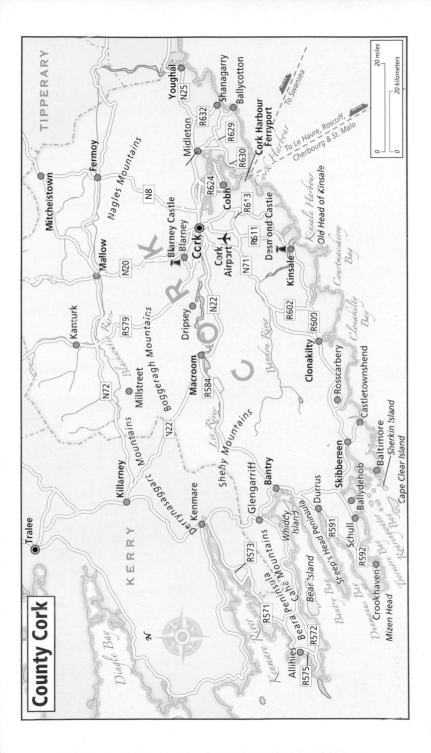

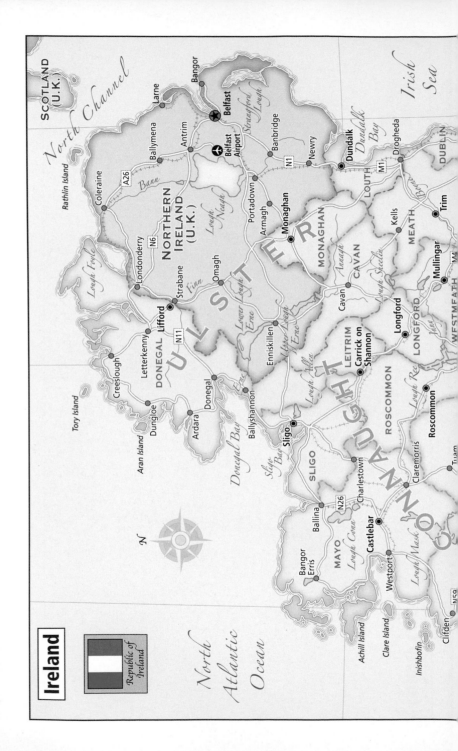

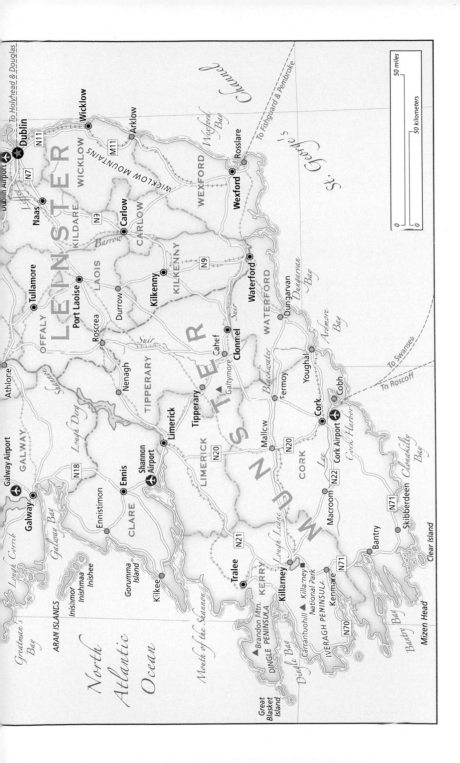

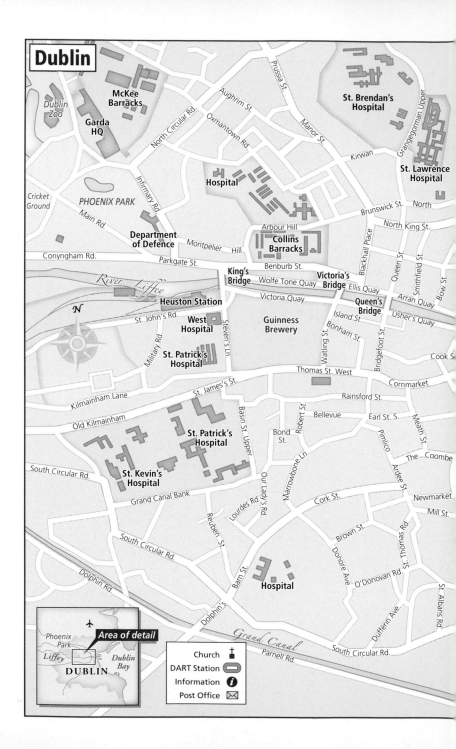

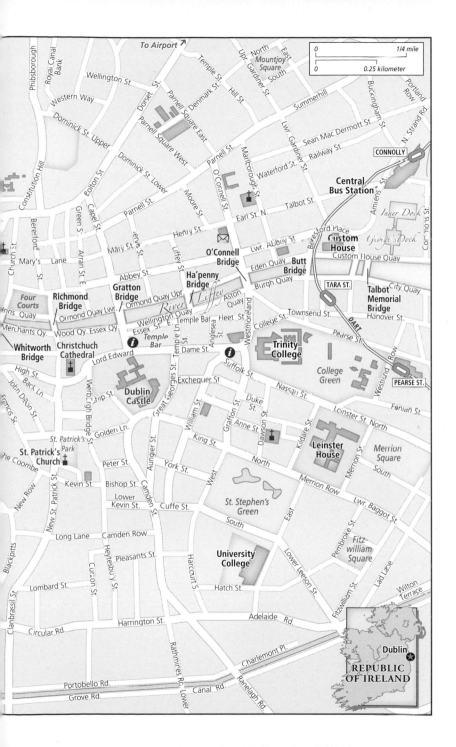

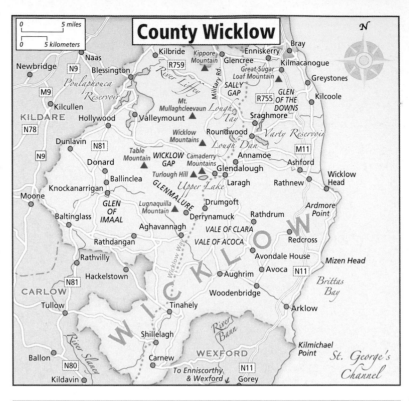

County Wicklow

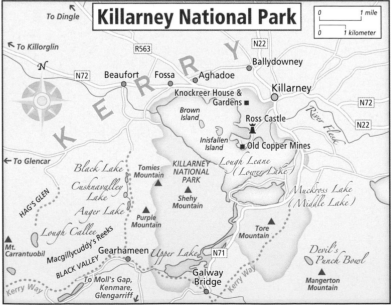

Killarney National Park

Frommer's®
Ireland 2009

by Christi Daugherty & Jack Jewers

Here's what the critics say about Frommer's:

"Amazingly easy to use. Very portable, very complete."
—BOOKLIST

"Detailed, accurate, and easy-to-read information for all price ranges."
—GLAMOUR MAGAZINE

"Hotel information is close to encyclopedic."
—DES MOINES SUNDAY REGISTER

"Frommer's Guides have a way of giving you a real feel for a place."
—KNIGHT RIDDER NEWSPAPERS

WILEY

Wiley Publishing, Inc.

Published by:

Wiley Publishing, Inc.

111 River St.
Hoboken, NJ 07030-5774

ISBN: 978-0-470-38749-8
Editor: Michael Kelly, with Kathleen Warnock
Production Editor: Lindsay Conner
Cartographer: Roberta Stockwell
Photo Editor: Richard Fox
Production by Wiley Indianapolis Composition Services

Front cover photo: County Galway, Connemara
Back cover photo: Irish Dancers at Craft Village

For information on our other products and services or to obtain technical support, please contact our Customer Care Department within the U.S. at 800/762-2974, outside the U.S. at 317/572-3993 or fax 317/572-4002.

Wiley also publishes its books in a variety of electronic formats. Some content that appears in print may not be available in electronic formats.

Manufactured in the United States of America

5   4   3   2

CONTENTS

4 SUGGESTED IRELAND ITINERARIES 78

5 IRELAND OUTDOORS 93

6 DUBLIN 106

7 OUT FROM DUBLIN 187

8 THE SOUTHEAST 219

9 CORK CITY 269

10 OUT FROM CORK 286

11 COUNTY KERRY 312

12 COUNTIES LIMERICK & CLARE 352

13 GALWAY CITY 390

LIST OF MAPS

ABOUT THE AUTHORS

Christi Daugherty is an expat American. A former journalist, she's the author of several travel books including *Frommer's Ireland 2008* and *Frommer's Paris Day by Day.* She also co-wrote *Frommer's MTV Ireland* and *Frommer's MTV Europe.* She learned everything she knows about Ireland accidentally, while getting lost repeatedly over the course of many years. She likes to think that she gets lost so you don't have to. On a recent trip, she stumbled across the ruins of the castle her family left behind when they fled Ireland in the 17th century, with the English hot on their trail. There wasn't much left of it. In her spare time she writes unpublished mystery novels.

Jack Jewers has directed films for the BBC, reviewed publications for *Time Out,* and contributed to several guidebooks, including previous editions of *Frommer's Ireland.* This is his first as co-author. He's also co-writing *Frommer's Ireland Day-by-Day.* Jack grew up listening to his great aunt's tales about living in Dublin during the Civil War. She once leaned out of a window during a late-night battle to tell the gunmen to keep the noise down—people were trying to sleep. Born and raised in England, Jack proposed to his Irish-American wife at a spa in County Kerry. It gets a great review in this book.

AN INVITATION TO THE READER

In researching this book, we discovered many wonderful places—hotels, restaurants, shops, and more. We're sure you'll find others. Please tell us about them, so we can share the information with your fellow travelers in upcoming editions. If you were disappointed with a recommendation, we'd love to know that, too. Please write to:

Frommer's Ireland 2009
Wiley Publishing, Inc. • 111 River St. • Hoboken, NJ 07030-5774

Other Great Guides for Your Trip:

Pauline Frommer's Ireland

Dublin Day by Day

Ireland For Dummies

Frommer's Ireland's Best-Loved Driving Tours

Frommer's Europe

Europe For Dummies

AN ADDITIONAL NOTE

Please be advised that travel information is subject to change at any time—and this is especially true of prices. We therefore suggest that you write or call ahead for confirmation when making your travel plans. The authors, editors, and publisher cannot be held responsible for the experiences of readers while traveling. Your safety is important to us, however, so we encourage you to stay alert and be aware of your surroundings. Keep a close eye on cameras, purses, and wallets, all favorite targets of thieves and pickpockets.

FROMMER'S STAR RATINGS, ICONS & ABBREVIATIONS

Every hotel, restaurant, and attraction listing in this guide has been ranked for quality, value, service, amenities, and special features using a **star-rating system**. In country, state, and regional guides, we also rate towns and regions to help you narrow down your choices and budget your time accordingly. Hotels and restaurants are rated on a scale of zero (recommended) to three stars (exceptional). Attractions, shopping, nightlife, towns, and regions are rated according to the following scale: zero stars (recommended), one star (highly recommended), two stars (very highly recommended), and three stars (must-see).

In addition to the star-rating system, we also use **seven feature icons** that point you to the great deals, in-the-know advice, and unique experiences that separate travelers from tourists. Throughout the book, look for:

(Finds	Special finds—those places only insiders know about
(Fun Facts	Fun facts—details that make travelers more informed and their trips more fun
(Kids	Best bets for kids, and advice for the whole family
(Moments	Special moments—those experiences that memories are made of
(Overrated	Places or experiences not worth your time or money
(Tips	Insider tips—great ways to save time and money
(Value	Great values—where to get the best deals

The following **abbreviations** are used for credit cards:

AE	American Express	DISC	Discover	V	Visa
DC	Diners Club	MC	MasterCard		

FROMMERS.COM

Now that you have this guidebook to help you plan a great trip, visit our website at **www.frommers.com** for additional travel information on more than 4,000 destinations. We update features regularly to give you instant access to the most current trip-planning information available. At Frommers.com, you'll find scoops on the best airfares, lodging rates, and car rental bargains. You can even book your travel online through our reliable travel booking partners. Other popular features include:

- Online updates of our most popular guidebooks
- Vacation sweepstakes and contest giveaways
- Newsletters highlighting the hottest travel trends
- Podcasts, interactive maps, and up-to-the-minute events listings
- Opinionated blog entries by Arthur Frommer himself
- Online travel message boards with featured travel discussions

What's New in Ireland

As this book was going to press, the Irish economy had fallen down the rabbit hole. The economy was crumbling around the edges and the Irish Republic insured all personal and corporate bank accounts in an attempt to avoid panic.

With its vast inflationary bubble evidently bursting at last, Ireland is in a state of transition. House prices plummeted 30% in Dublin in 2008, but new five-star hotels continued to open around the country, regardless of the national and international economic chaos.

After 10 years of prices spiraling out of control, this is a very expensive place to visit—particularly when it comes to hotels and restaurants. A 2008 study by the banking giant UBS identified Dublin as the world's fourth most expensive city behind only Oslo, London, and Copenhagen. Inflation helped the city leap up the charts rapidly—in 2006, it was in 13th place. How the economic changes now happening in Ireland will impact prices is yet to be seen, but hoteliers seem to be holding their breath.

Still, trips to Ireland remain prohibitively expensive for U.S. visitors, and that is taking its toll on the number of Americans heading here and the amount of time they're willing to spend in the country. In 2008, the number of U.S. visitors to Ireland dropped by an estimated 15%.

Still, the Irish tourism industry can't quite believe the boom is over; they're looking to Europe and China to fill the gap left by Americans, thus allowing them to keep their prices floating in the stratosphere.

Nonetheless, there are some signs that prices might begin to come down. In 2008, many hoteliers—who normally raise their prices substantially from one year to the next—held prices steady, and some of the most overpriced establishments even lowered charges slightly, albeit reluctantly. Sights also have a habit of raising prices by 10% to 20% every year. In 2008, most major sights didn't dare to do so.

But the facts are stark: When it costs the equivalent of $12 just to park your car at the Cliffs of Moher—a natural wonder in County Cork—and when a light lunch in a country pub costs $20 a person, there is an awfully long way to go before this country becomes affordable again for many travelers.

GETTING THERE Expanding Dublin Airport The first phase of Dublin Airport's expansion has now opened, to the relief of travelers who have had the misfortune to arrive in Dublin during one of the airport's busy times. A second terminal—dubbed T2—is now well underway, and scheduled to open for business in 2010. This follows the expansion of the airport's runways, and the addition of new services and shops for travelers.

By the time all the construction is finished, it is expected that the airport will see as many as 30 million passengers pass through its terminals each year.

In order for that to be viable, though, the government acknowledged that certain problems will have to be addressed, including the congestion on the M50—the key route to and from the airport, and really, the de facto gateway to Ireland. Plans are also underway to connect the airport to the city center by rail, which could make a tremendous difference for those who come to Ireland solely to visit Dublin.

Shannon Airport Changes to the rules regarding flights to Ireland from North America meant that fewer flights were forced to land at Shannon Airport (something that was once required even when most of the passengers were really heading to Dublin), and many thought the plucky little airport on Ireland's west coast might be quietly mothballed. Both American Airlines and Air Canada announced that they would cut back or end flights to Shannon, and even the Irish airline Aer Lingus dropped its regular flights to Shannon from London's Heathrow airport.

Those moves were worrying enough to have regional tourism authorities spending millions of dollars marketing the usefulness of the so-called "Shannon Gateway." It turned out it was far too early to write Shannon off. American and Air Canada never had many flights to Shannon to begin with, and in recent years the British budget airline, Ryanair, has made Shannon a hub. US Airways, Continental, and Delta still have regularly scheduled flights to the airport from major cities in the U.S.

Now many people see the expansion of Dublin Airport as a threat to Ireland's regional airports. But for those traveling to the country's west coast, avoiding a drive of several hours cross-country remains a fairly substantial draw. So it seems hard to believe the airport's future is truly in doubt. Time will tell.

GALWAY The entertaining and talented group known as Siamsa in Galway (or Siamsa na Gaillimhe), which worked to preserve and promote traditional Irish music, theater, and dance, closed in 2008, and many believe that it may not reopen.

Although touristy, its blend of traditional Irish music, clothes, dance, and folk drama was a window into the country's cultural heritage. However, the similarly named Siamsa Tíre, based in Tralee, remains open and busy.

ENNIS Problems with water quality in the bustling town of Ennis remained an issue as this book was going to press. In 2005, the town's water supply was found to be tainted with *Cryptosporidium,* a parasite that causes intestinal illness, and everybody who visited the town was advised to drink only bottled water.

A new water plant is being built, and is expected to open in 2009, but be sure and ask around if you're visiting the area before drinking anything that comes out of the tap.

Worryingly, water supplies in Dingle, Killarney, and Spiddal have also been found to have less-than-perfect water quality, so you might want to approach the Irish water with caution right now, particularly if you are elderly or traveling with young children.

SLIGO Dunfore Farmhouse—a charming, affordable guesthouse with beautiful art and lovely views, has closed its doors to guests, after its energetic and friendly host developed health problems. The family hopes to reopen as an art gallery in the coming years, though, so look for an update next year.

Also, Lough Rynn House and Gardens outside Mohill is no longer accepting visitors to explore the house, and is operating purely as a hotel now.

NORTHERN IRELAND While the Irish Republic has been flirting with the doldrums recently, the North has been dancing on the edge of a tourism miniboom of sorts.

Travelers are being drawn by its unspoiled atmosphere—its not-yet-over-run-by-tour-groups ambience. The lure of its scenic beauty is increasingly stronger than the lingering hesitation caused by years of very valid safety concerns. Travelers are emboldened to head north as the area's peace treaty holds and the political situation takes on an air of stability.

In 2007, the British army pulled out of Northern Ireland after 38 years, which many see as a sign that peace here may have some permanence.

Some visitors are lured by the natural beauty of the Antrim coastline and the wonder of the Giant's Causeway, both of which can often be explored in relative peace, without the roar of tour buses and the crush of crowds.

Others are so-called "political tourists," who head to Belfast and Derry to photograph the strident wall murals and explore the scene of the Troubles. But, for tourists at least, those troubles seem far behind us now. Even the July "Orangeman's Day" marches (marking the anniversary of the Battle of the Boyne, when the Protestant King William defeated the Catholic King James) that once sparked riots now attract international tourists who stand on the sidelines to photograph the banners and watch the parades.

Some hotels, such as the Malmaison Belfast, decorate their walls with photos of the city's notorious wall murals, and help to arrange "Black Cab tours" to the areas in west Belfast where much of the struggle took place.

The Best of Ireland

For visitors, Ireland is an ideal country to traverse, and with its varied and extensive offerings within a compact frame, it's visually addictive. Within a few miles, you can travel from rugged coastline to smooth pastureland to towering mountains to gloomy peat bog. You can spend the night in ancient castles or modern spa hotels, dine on fine Irish cuisine or skimp on fish and chips. The sheer number of sights, villages, charming pubs, and adorable restaurants and shops is overwhelming—you always feel that you might be missing something. The country's varied offerings can be a bit dazzling, so it's nice to have somebody help you focus. That's why we've put together this list of some of our favorite places and things in Ireland. We hope that while you're here, you'll find a few of your own.

1 THE BEST PICTURE-POSTCARD TOWNS

- **Dalkey** (County Dublin): This charming south-coast Dublin suburb has just enough glorious freedom from that city's traffic snarls and frenzy. With a castle, a mountaintop folly, and lovely beaches, there's a lot to enjoy. Dalkey is an upscale bedroom community for Ireland's rich, so it's unsurprising that it also has fine restaurants and welcoming pubs. This is a tempting town to settle into. See chapter 6.
- **Carlingford** (County Louth): Up in quiet, lazy Louth, little Carlingford is a draw. A tiny medieval village with castle ruins on the bay, its pedestrian-friendly lanes are filled with colorful shops, cafes, and pubs, and its other draws include a scattering of good eateries. See chapter 7.
- **Inistioge** (County Kilkenny): Nestled in the Nore River Valley, surrounded by undulating hills, this riverfront village with two spacious greens and a host of pubs cries out to be photographed. Its rivers and lakes are swimming with fish and attract hosts of anglers. See chapter 8.
- **Kinsale** (County Cork): Kinsale's narrow streets all lead to the sea, dropping steeply from the hills around the harbor, although the crowds of visitors teeming on the sidewalks every summer attest to the fact that the Kinsale secret is out. The walk from Kinsale through Scilly to Charles Fort and Frower Point is breathtaking. Kinsale has the added benefit of being a foodie town, with no shortage of good restaurants. See chapter 10.
- **Dingle/An Daingean** (County Kerry): Dingle is a charming hilltop medieval town. Its stone buildings ramble up and down hills, and its small population is relaxed about visitors. It has lots of little diners and picturesque pubs, and a lovely, historic church. See chapter 11.
- **Kenmare** (County Kerry): If you're driving the Ring of Kerry, this is the best base you could wish for at the mouth of the River Roughty on Kenmare Bay. The town is picture-perfect, with stone cottages, colorful gardens, and flowers overflowing from window boxes. See chapter 11.
- **Athlone** (County Westmeath): Sitting at the edge of the River Shannon, its streets curving around a sturdy, fortresslike castle, Athlone is a charmer. Houses are painted in bright hues, and with its small, funky boutiques and spirit of fun,

it has the feel of a busy university town. Good restaurants and lively pubs add to its charms. See chapter 14.

- **Ardara** (County Donegal): On the southwest coast of County Donegal, the tiny town of Ardara looks as if it were carved out of a solid block of granite. Its streets undulate up and down the rocky hills, and are lined with little boutiques and charming arts shops, many selling clothes made of the famed Donegal wool. You can wander its entirety in a few minutes. It's a bite-size place. See chapter 16.

2 THE BEST NATURAL WONDERS

- **MacGillycuddy's Reeks** (County Kerry): A mountain range on the Iveragh Peninsula, MacGillycuddy's Reeks not only has the best name of any mountain range in Ireland, but also the highest mountain on the island, Carrantuohill (1,041m/3,414 ft.). The Reeks are among Ireland's greatest spectacles. See p. 330.
- **The Slieve Bloom Way** (County Laois): Slieve Bloom, Ireland's largest and most unspoiled blanket bog, rises gently above the peat fields. Its beauty—gentle slopes, glens, rivers, waterfalls, and bog lands—is subtle but persistent, and it is comparatively untouched. You can have it more or less to yourself, apart from its deer and foxes, and an occasional frolicking otter. See p. 374.
- **The Burren** (County Clare): We can guarantee this: The Burren is one of the strangest landscapes you're likely to see. Its vast limestone grassland is spread with a quilt of wildflowers from as far afield as the Alps, all softening the stark stones jutting out of the ground. Its inhabitants include nearly every species of butterfly found in Ireland. See p. 380.
- **Cliffs of Moher** (County Clare): Rising from Hag's Head to the south, these magnificent sea cliffs reach their full height of 214m (702 ft.) just north of O'Brien's Tower. The views of the open sea, of the Aran Islands, and of the Twelve Bens mountains of Connemara (see below) are spectacular. A walk south along the cliff edge at sunset makes a perfect end to any day. See p. 385.

- **The Twelve Bens** (County Galway): Amid Connemara's central mountains, bogs, and lakes, the rugged Twelve Bens range crowns a spectacular landscape. Some of the peaks are bare and rocky, others clothed in peat. The loftiest, Benbaun, in Connemara National Park, reaches a height of 719m (2,395 ft.). See p. 413.
- **Croagh Patrick** (County Mayo): Rising steeply 750m (2,460 ft.) above the coast, Croagh Patrick is seen as a holy mountain, where the saint is said to have retreated in penance. Traditionally, barefoot pilgrims climb it the last Sunday of July, but in recent years, hundreds of Nike-shod tourists have been making the ascent daily. The view from above can be breathtaking or nonexistent—the summit is often wrapped in clouds. See p. 434.
- **Slieve League** (County Donegal): The Slieve League peninsula stretches for 48km (30 miles) into the Atlantic. Its wonderfully pigmented bluffs rise to startlingly high sea cliffs. They can also be walked along, if you dare. See p. 472.
- **Giant's Causeway** (County Antrim): At the foot of a cliff by the sea, this mysterious mass of dark, tightly packed, naturally occurring hexagonal basalt columns are nothing short of astonishing. This volcanic wonder, formed 60 million years ago, looks marvelous from above, even better when negotiated (cautiously) on foot. See p. 526.

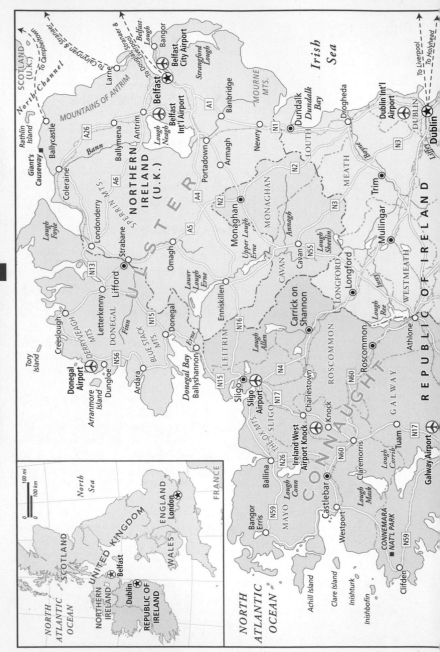

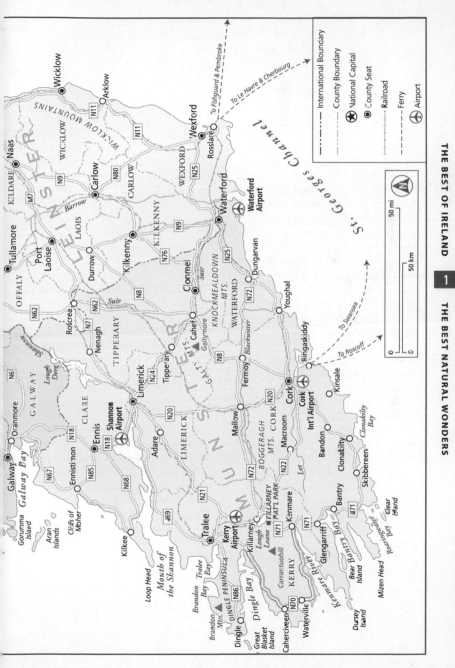

3 THE BEST CASTLES

- **Trim Castle** (County Meath): Trim, also called King John's Castle, restored as a "preserved ruin," is a massive Anglo-Norman structure. It was all but impregnable for 4 centuries (late 12th to mid-17th). Until it was abandoned and collapsed in the 17th century, it never underwent any significant alteration. For anyone with imagination, Trim is a visual gateway into medieval Ireland. See p. 213.

- **Cahir Castle** (County Tipperary): One of the largest of Ireland's medieval fortresses, this castle is in an extraordinary state of preservation. Tours explain some fascinating features of the military architecture, and then you're free to roam through a maze of tiny chambers, spiral staircases, and dizzying battlements. See p. 249.

- **Kilkenny Castle** (County Kilkenny): Although parts of the castle date from the 13th century, the existing structure has the feel of an 18th-century palace. There have been many modifications since medieval times, including the addition of colorful landscaping, and the old stables now hold numerous art galleries and shops. See p. 258.

- **Blarney Castle** (County Cork): Despite the mobs of tourists who besiege it daily, this majestic tower house is worth a visit. While you're there, check out the Badger Cave and dungeons at the tower's base, as well as the serpentine paths that wind through the castle gardens. Need we mention the Blarney Stone? You sidle in under the upper wall with your head hanging over a 10-story drop. You kiss it. It's a thing people do. See p. 280.

- **Charles Fort** (County Cork): On a promontory in Kinsale Harbor, this fortress's massive walls enclose a complex of buildings in varying states of repair. At the entrance you're handed a map and left to explore, discover, and almost certainly get lost in the maze of courtyards, passages, walls, and barracks. See p. 288.

- **Bunratty Castle and Folk Park** (County Clare): This grand old castle has been well restored and filled with a curious assortment of medieval furnishings, offering a glimpse into the life of its past inhabitants. This is the first stop for many arrivals from Shannon, so expect crowds. See p. 367.

- **Doe Castle** (County Donegal): This picturesque tower house is surrounded on three sides by the waters of Sheep Haven Bay and on the fourth by a moat carved into the bedrock that forms its foundation. It has a remote waterfront setting and sweeping views of the nearby hills. See p. 477.

- **Carrickfergus Castle** (County Antrim): This well-preserved Norman fortress on the bank of Belfast Lough is huge and impressive, with an imposing tower house and a high wall punctuated by corner towers. See p. 515.

- **Dunluce Castle** (County Antrim): These castle ruins surmount a razor-sharp promontory jutting into the sea. This was a highly defensible setting, and the castle wasn't abandoned until a large section collapsed and fell into the breakers. See p. 526.

4 THE BEST OF ANCIENT IRELAND

- **Hill of Tara** (County Meath): Of ritual significance from the Stone Age to the Christian period, Tara has seen it all

and kept it all a secret. This was the traditional center and seat of Ireland's high kings. Although the hill is only

154m (512 ft.) above sea level, from here you can see each of Ireland's four Celtic provinces on a clear day. The site is mostly unexcavated and tells its story in whispers. It's a place to be walked slowly. See p. 210.

- **Newgrange** (County Meath): Poised atop a low hill north of the River Boyne, Newgrange is the centerpiece of a megalithic cemetery dating back 5,000 years. The massive mound and passage tomb were constructed, it seems, as a communal vault to house cremated remains. The tomb's passage is so perfectly aligned with the solstice sun that the central chamber, deep within the mound, is illuminated for several days at the winter solstice. See p. 212.

- **Loughcrew** (County Meath): At this little-known site, not far from Newgrange, a series of cruciform passage tombs crown two hills. On the east hill, a guide unlocks the door to one of the domed tombs, answering your questions with a personal touch not possible at the larger sites. More rewarding, however, is a hike up the west hill to a second, more solitary series of tombs where you can make your own imaginative reconstruction. See p. 212.

- **Lough Gur** (County Limerick): This lakefront site will convince you that the Neolithic farmers of Ireland had an estimable sense of real estate. Inhabited for more than 4,000 years, the ancient farming settlement offers a number of prehistoric remains. The most impressive of

these is the largest surviving stone circle in Ireland, made up of 113 stones. See p. 361.

- **Dún Aengus** (County Galway): No one knows who built this massive stone fort, or when. The eminent archaeologist George Petrie called Dún Aengus "the most magnificent barbaric monument in Europe." Facing the sea, where its three stone rings meet steep 90m (295-ft.) cliffs, Dún Aengus still stands guard today over the southern coast of the island of Inishmore, the largest of the Aran Islands. See "Side Trips from Galway City," in chapter 13.

- **Carrowmore and Carrowkeel** (County Sligo): These two megalithic cities of the dead (Europe's largest) may have once contained more than 200 passage tombs. The two together—one in the valley and the other atop a nearby mountain—convey an unequaled sense of the scale and wonder of the ancient peoples' reverence for the dead. Carrowmore is well presented and interpreted, while Carrowkeel is left to itself and to those who seek it out. See p. 449.

- **Navan Fort** (County Antrim): There is no longer much remaining here to reflect the great past of this fort, though it was once the ritual and royal seat of Ulster. Thankfully, the interpretive center here is nothing short of remarkable, and it offers a great introduction to the myth and archaeology of the fort, known in Irish as Emain Macha. See p. 523.

5 REMNANTS OF THE GOLDEN AGE: THE BEST EARLY CHRISTIAN RUINS

- **Glendalough** (County Wicklow): Nestled in "the glen of the two lakes," this atmospheric monastic settlement was founded in the 6th century by St. Kevin, who was looking for seclusion and certainly found it here. The setting is endlessly scenic, with lakes and forests

surrounding it. Although quite remote, Glendalough suffered assaults from the Vikings and English forces, and eventually faded away. Today its stone ruins collude with the countryside to create one of the loveliest spots in Ireland. See p. 190.

- **The Rock of Cashel** (County Tipperary): In name and appearance, "the Rock" suggests a citadel, a place designed more for power than prayer. In fact, Cashel (or Caiseal) means "fortress." The rock is a huge outcropping—or an *up*cropping—of limestone topped with spectacularly beautiful ruins, including what was formerly the country's finest Romanesque chapel. This was the seat of clerics and kings, a power center to rival Tara. Now, however, the two sites vie only for the attention of tourists. See p. 249.

- **Jerpoint Abbey** (County Kilkenny): Jerpoint is the finest representative of the many Cistercian abbeys whose ruins dot the Irish landscape. Somehow, hundreds of years of rain and wind have failed to completely wipe away medieval carvings, leaving us a rare chance for a glimpse of how magnificent these abbeys once were. The splendid, richly carved cloister is the best place to spot the carvings, particularly at the top of the many columns. See p. 260.

- **Skellig Michael** (County Kerry): Thirteen kilometers (8 miles) offshore of the Iveragh Peninsula, rising sharply 214m (702 ft.) out of the Atlantic, this is a remote rocky crag dedicated to the archangel Michael. In flight from the world, early Irish monks in pursuit of "white martyrdom" chose this spot to build their austere hermitage. Today the journey to Skellig, across choppy seas, and the arduous climb to its summit are challenging and unforgettable. See "The Skellig Islands" under "The Iveragh Peninsula" in chapter 11.

- **Clonmacnois** (County Offaly): This was once one of Ireland's most important religious, artistic, and literary centers, a place of pilgrimage and culture. Founded in the mid–5th century at the axis of the River Shannon and the medieval east-west thoroughfare known as the Eiscir Riada, Clonmacnois thrived for centuries until its prime riverfront location brought repeated violent raids that proved its undoing. Even in ruins, Clonmacnois remains a place of peculiar serenity. See p. 426.

- **Inishmurray** (County Sligo): This uninhabited island off the Sligo coast holds another striking monastic ruin, this one surrounded by what appears to be the walls of an even more ancient stone fort. Despite its remoteness, the Vikings sought out this outpost of peace-seeking monks for destruction in A.D. 807. Today its circular walls and the surrounding sea create a stunning view, well worth the effort required to reach it. See "Exploring the Surrounding Countryside" under "Sligo & Yeats Country" in chapter 15.

6 THE BEST LITERARY SPOTS

- **Dublin Writers Museum:** With Joyce's typewriter, handwritten letters from Brendan Behan to friends back home, and early flyers from the Abbey Theatre when it was run by Lady Gregory and Yeats, this museum is heaven for bookish types. You can spend hours reading the memorabilia and marveling at the trivia. The only thing it lacks is a good shop. See p. 146.

- **Glasnevin Cemetery** (County Dublin): Besides being the setting for part of *Ulysses,* this is the resting place of James Joyce's parents and other members of his family. The English-born poet Gerard Manley Hopkins is buried here, in the Jesuit plot. Maud Gonne, the Irish nationalist and longtime Dublin resident who is said to have inspired Yeats's play *Cathleen ní Houlihan,* is buried in the Republican plot. The writer, drinker, and Irish Republican Brendan Behan is also buried here. See p. 153.

- **Davy Byrnes Pub:** In *Ulysses* Joyce describes the main character, Leopold Bloom, stopping in at this Dublin pub for a Gorgonzola sandwich and a glass of burgundy. "He raised his eyes and met the stare of a bilious clock. Two. Pub clock five minutes fast. Time going on. Hands moving. Two. Not yet." Today the clock is said to be kept 5 minutes fast, in honor of Bloom and Joyce. See p. 171.

- **James Joyce Museum:** At the edge of the sea in the Dublin suburb of Sandycove, this Martel tower was home to Joyce for a short time, but he based a character on his host, Oliver St. John Gogarty, described in *Ulysses* perfectly as "stately, plump Buck Mulligan." The museum was opened in 1962, and its interior has been restored to look as it did when Joyce was here, along with plenty of memorabilia, including Joyce's walking stick and guitar. See p. 180.

- **St. Patrick's Cathedral** (County Dublin): Jonathan Swift tickled and horrified the world with his vicious wit. He shook up political establishments with his sarcasm, and nauseated the English-speaking world with his suggestion that people should dine on Irish babies. While kicking up such a stir, he was dean of St. Patrick's Cathedral, which sponsored and supported him through it all. He is buried here alongside his longtime companion, Stella. See p. 148.

- **County Sligo:** With its many connections to the beloved poet W. B. Yeats, this county is a pilgrimage destination for Yeats fans. The poet's writing was shaped by the landscape and people in this farming region, and many of its monuments—including Lough Gill, Glencar Lake, Ben Bulben Mountain, and Maeve's tomb—appear in his poetry. There are also several museums housing first editions, photographs, and other memorabilia, and Yeats's dark and somber grave is in Drumcliff. See chapter 15.

7 THE BEST GARDENS

- **Powerscourt Gardens** (County Wicklow): This grandiose Irish garden is set amid the natural splendor of the Wicklow Hills just outside of Dublin. The sprawling, manicured gardens and the wild beauty of the Powerscourt waterfall make this a great day's outing, and a respite from the noise and congestion of the city. See p. 191.

- **Japanese Gardens** (County Kildare): On the grounds of the National Stud, this peaceful enclave is based on the traditional designs of Japanese gardens. A Japanese specialist planned the structure and its symbolism, and most of the plants and stones were imported from Japan. See p. 204.

- **Ilnacullin** (County Cork): A ferry conveys visitors from a rhododendron-framed bay in the town of Glengarriff to Garinish Island, the unlikely site of a fine Italianate garden. The formal garden, with the Casita at its center, is linked to a "wild garden" that showcases a collection of rhododendrons, azaleas, and rare trees. See p. 300.

- **Glenveagh National Park** (County Donegal): A castle and its gardens stretch across a strangely barren valley high in the hills of Donegal, along the banks of Lough Veagh. The sprawling park contains a grand statuary garden, a walled garden, and a rhododendron-lined path that leads to a stunning view of the castle and lake. See p. 477.

- **Mount Stewart House Gardens** (County Down): Built upon an elaborate plan, the Mount Stewart house has several gardens of distinctive character. The Ards Peninsula provides a climate conducive to cultivating many subtropical species. The statuary, topiary, and planting designs reflect a touch of whimsy. See p. 517.

8 THE BEST FAMILY ACTIVITIES

- **Dublin Zoo in the Phoenix Park** (Dublin): Kids love this sympathetically designed zoo, with its wild creatures, animal-petting corners, and train ride. The surrounding park has room to run, picnic, and explore. See p. 158.
- **Irish National Heritage Park** (County Wexford): Nearly 9,000 years of Irish history come alive here in ways that will fascinate visitors of all ages. The whole family will be captivated by the story of ancient Ireland, from its first inhabitants to its Norman conquerors. See p. 224.
- **Fota Island Wildlife Park** (County Cork): In this wildlife park, rare and endangered animals roam freely. You'll see everything from giraffes and zebras to kangaroos, flamingos, penguins, and monkeys wandering the grassland. Add in a small amusement park for toddlers, a tour train, picnic tables, and a gift shop and you have the makings of a wonderful family outing. See p. 295.
- **Muckross House and Gardens** (Killarney, County Kerry): This huge Victorian mansion with its exquisite gardens is also home to skilled artisans at work. Nearby are a series of reconstructed traditional farms, with animals and docents, providing a gateway to rural Ireland as it was for centuries. See p. 325.
- **Fungie the Dolphin Tours** (Dingle, County Kerry): Every day, fishing boats ferry visitors out into the nearby waters to see Fungie, the friendliest dolphin you're ever likely to meet. Fungie swims right up to the boat, and the boatmen stay out long enough for ample sightings. You can also arrange an early-morning dolphin swim. See p. 338.
- **Bunratty Castle and Folk Park** (County Clare): Kids are enthralled by this well-restored medieval castle and re-created 19th-century village. It's complete with a school and loaded with active craftspeople. See p. 367.
- **Marble Arch Caves** (Marlbank, County Fermanagh): Adventurous families are guided by boat through well-lit underground waterways to explore caves and view amazing stone formations. See p. 561.

9 THE BEST ACTIVE VACATIONS

- **Sailing Ireland's West Coast:** Spectacular coastal scenery, interesting harbor towns, and an abundance of islands make the west coast a delight for cruising sailors. See "Sailing," in chapter 5.
- **Horseback Riding in Donegal:** The wild and woolly coast of Donegal offers the perfect scenic backdrop for trail riding, and as varied a terrain—beaches, countryside, mountains—as you'll find anywhere. See chapter 16.
- **Sea Kayaking in West Cork:** In Castletownbere on the dramatic, rugged Beara Peninsula, Beara Outdoor Pursuits specializes in accompanied trips out and around Bere Island and as far as Glengarriff. You can play it as safe or as rough as you want. See p. 303.
- **Bicycling in the Southwest:** The peninsulas and islands of Cork and Kerry are perfect for cycling, with an abundance of beautiful places to visit. Roycroft's Stores in Skibbereen, County

Cork, rent bikes that are a notch above the usual rental equipment. See the "Sports & Outdoor Pursuits" sections in chapters 10 and 11.

- **Walking the Donegal Coast:** The rugged headlands of Donegal are the most spectacular in Ireland, and the best way to explore them is on foot. Among the finest walks are Slieve League, Malin Head, and Horn Head. See "The Donegal Bay Coast," in chapter 16.

10 THE BEST LUXURY ACCOMMODATIONS

- **The Clarence** (Dublin; ✆ 01/407-0800; www.theclarence.ie): Owned by members of the band U2, the Clarence is a perfect mixture of sleek sophistication and coolness. Everything here is designed for subtle elegance, from the soft, neutral color schemes, to the luxurious bed linens and huge beds, to the helpful staff. The Octagon Bar is a relaxing hangout, while the Tea Room restaurant is one of the best eateries in town. The new spa will pummel and facial you into relaxation, while the staff members hurry off to find your favorite red wine. Staying here is a real treat. See p. 120.

- **BrookLodge Hotel** (County Wicklow; ✆ 0402/36444; www.brooklodge.com): This place keeps getting better and better. Rooms have firm king-size four-poster beds, wood-paneled window seats, deep bathtubs, quality linens, and contemporary furnishings. The latest addition to this holistic oasis is the Wells, a gorgeous spa with Finnish baths, mud baths, hot tubs, Jacuzzis, indoor and outdoor pools, a *hammam* (Turkish bath), and a flotation room in which you're sure to relax. See p. 196.

- **Park Hotel Kenmare** (County Kerry; ✆ 800/323-5463 in the U.S., or 064/41200; www.parkkenmare.com): In a palm-tree-lined garden beside Kenmare Bay, this imposing 19th-century hotel is grand and luxurious. In the high-ceilinged sitting rooms, fires crackle in the open fireplaces, oil paintings decorate the walls, and there's a full set of armor at the top of the grand staircase surrounded by tapestries and rare antiques. Guest rooms have Georgian and Victorian furnishings and peaceful waterfront or mountain views. The guest-only, in-house spa is extraordinary. See p. 318.

- **Glin Castle** (County Limerick; ✆ 068/34173; www.glincastle.com): This beautifully restored 18th-century castle guesthouse near the mouth of the Shannon is a peaceful and elegant place to pass an evening or two. Owned for centuries by the knights of Glin, it is all very well done, with multiple parlors warmed by crackling fires, walled gardens, and beautiful grounds to explore. Rooms are huge and gorgeously appointed with antiques, and the staff is friendly and helpful. It offers class without snobbery. See p. 361.

- **Gregans Castle Hotel** (County Clare; ✆ 800/323-5463 in the U.S., or 065/707-7005; www.gregans.ie): Not a castle at all, but an ivy-covered, stone manor house, this small, family-run hotel is filled with light, and it has lovely views of the Burren and Galway Bay. The drawing room and expansive hallways are filled with heirlooms, and the walls are decorated with Raymond Piper's mural paintings of the Burren. Guest rooms are spacious and elegantly decorated in muted colors with antique pieces, and all have expansive views of the spectacular countryside. Dinners here are outstanding, and eating in is worth every penny. See p. 382.

- **Delphi Lodge** (County Galway; ✆ 095/42222; www.delphilodge.ie): This was once the country hideaway for the marquis of Sligo, and now it can be yours. Inside, the emphasis is on clean, bright simplicity and perfect taste; the grounds and environs are spectacular.

"Tranquillity," "comfort," and, well, "fishing" are the operative words here. You will want to stay longer than you'd planned—and by renting one of the cottages for a week or more, you can make the indulgence more affordable. See p. 421.

11 THE BEST MODERATELY PRICED ACCOMMODATIONS

- **Moy House** (County Clare; ✆ 065/708-2800; www.moyhouse.com): This unusual 19th-century tower house atop a hill overlooking the sea is beautiful inside and out. Rooms have comfortable, modern beds covered in crisp Irish linens, and are decorated with original paintings and period antiques. Bathrooms are beautifully designed to combine modern conveniences with the building's old architecture (a glass panel in one room provides a look down into an old well). Downstairs, the small, attractive dining room serves up excellent food and has a sea view. It's a snug, warm, friendly place to visit. See p. 387.

- **The Bastion** (County Westmeath; ✆ 090/649-4954; www.thebastion. net): This simple and peaceful guesthouse in the heart of colorful Athlone is a find. Run by brothers Vinny and Anthony McCay, it has a minimalist approach, with clean white walls and crisp white linens contrasted with dark polished wood. The big, rambling house is comfortable, friendly, and perfectly located for touring Athlone or as a base for exploring the surrounding countryside. See p. 429.

- **The Bervie** (County Mayo; ✆ 098/43114; www.bervieachill.com): Views really don't get any better than this—right at the edge of the sea, overlooking the cliffs across the bay. This cozy retreat is an ideal place to stay for those exploring Ireland's wild west coast. Owners Elizabeth and John Barrett are charming hosts who greet you with fresh scones and will cook you a delightful dinner if you wish. The house is a former coast guard station—as solid as a rock, and as comforting as a security blanket. This is one of our favorite places in Ireland. See p. 441.

- **Temple House** (County Sligo; ✆ 071/918-3329; www.templehouse.ie): Roderick and Helena Perceval's grand Victorian manor house is an extraordinary place where ceilings soar to the stratosphere, marble stays solidly underfoot, and the family's working farm stretches out for miles around you. A Templar castle lies in ruins on the banks of their lake, well stocked with fish. To spend a few days here is to experience a different world. See p. 452.

- **Bruckless House** (County Donegal; ✆ 074/973-7071): This mid-18th-century farmhouse, restored with impeccable taste, has many charms, including award-winning gardens and a stable of Connemara ponies. Spacious, welcoming, and comfortable, Bruckless House feels like home (or better) after only a very short time. See p. 474.

- **Rathmullan House** (County Donegal; ✆ 800/223-6510 in the U.S., or 074/915-8188 in Ireland; www.rathmullan house.com): This getaway lies at the end of a long private drive on the banks of the mirrorlike waters of Lough Swilly. Rooms are big and beautifully detailed, with a soft color scheme, claw-foot tubs, and private patios. There are half a dozen drawing rooms in which you can relax on big leather sofas by open fires. The staff is friendly and open, and the atmosphere is one of pure rural rest and relaxation. See p. 480.

- **Ross Castle and House** (County Cavan; ℂ 043/81286): A tower room in a centrally heated, haunted castle awaits you at Ross Castle. It won't take too big a bite out of your wallet, either.

It might not be elegant, but it is unquestionably memorable. Warm, comfortable Ross Castle and nearby Ross House are great places to relax beside Lough Sheelin, a noteworthy source of trout and pike. See p. 326.

- **Slieve Croob Inn** (County Down; ℂ 028/4377-1412): Whether you want to drop anchor and set up a home away from home in a self-catering cottage or just spend a night in a stunning landscape, you'll adore this tasteful hideaway in the magical Mournes. See p. 537.

12 THE BEST RESTAURANTS

- **Locks** (County Dublin; ℂ 01/454-3391): This effortlessly elegant place on the Grand Canal has a great country-chic style. Its white, tongue-in-groove walls and fresh floors set the stage for French-influenced cuisine. Try the cider-braised pork with celeriac *boulangere*, girolles, and confit savoy cabbage. Desserts are inspired. See p. 131.

- **L'Gueuleton** (County Dublin; ℂ 01/675-3708): This place is worth the effort you'll have to put in to book a table well in advance. The cozy dining room is all candlelight, exposed brick walls, flagstone floors, polished wood beams, and Prada clad clientele. It's an elegant Irish-French bistro. The menu changes constantly, but includes warming options such as whole roast sea bass with new potatoes and chive beurre blanc, or venison casserole with juniper and organic root vegetables. See p. 136.

- **Chapter One** (County Dublin; ℂ 01/873-2266): Arguably the city's most atmospheric restaurant, this remarkable eatery fills the vaulted basement space of the Dublin Writers Museum. Artfully lighted and tastefully decorated, it offers a menu with local, organic ingredients, all cleverly used in dishes like

the ravioli with Irish goat cheese and warm asparagus. Fabulous! See p. 140.

- **The Chart House** (County Kerry; ℂ 066/915-2255): In this inviting bistro, everyone comes for Laura Boyce's confident, simple cooking. Think wonderful comfort food with a flair—the kind of food you never tire of. And the service is, as the Irish would say, "spot on." See p. 344.

- **The Wild Geese** (County Limerick; ℂ 061/396451): After spending years making other people's restaurants fabulous, owner-chef David Foley created a gem of his own in Limerick. The cooking is complex, exquisitely flavorful, and refined. See p. 363.

- **Cromleach Lodge** (County Sligo; ℂ 071/916-5155): In this lovely country house with panoramic views of Lough Arrow and environs, Christy and Moira Tighe have created a culinary destination with few peers. The menu, Irish in focus, changes daily. The eight-course gourmet menu is the ultimate indulgence. See p. 453.

- **James Street South** (County Antrim; ℂ 028/9043-4310; www.jamesstreet south.co.uk): This is the table of the moment in Belfast. This place is a hit because of the terrific cooking, which delivers modern classics with an Irish twist. The lamb is always excellent, and shouldn't be missed. Portions are generous, the wine list very good, the crowd rapturous. See p. 510.

- **The Narrows** (County Down; ℂ **028/4272-8148**): Who'd have thought that

the sleepy little waterside hamlet of Portaferry would have a restaurant like this? Danny Millar is one of the hottest young chefs on this island—just ask *Food & Wine* magazine—and his complex, yet earthy, cooking is worth going out of your way for. See p. 520.

13 THE BEST PUBS

- **Brazen Head** (County Dublin): Nearly qualifying as one of Ireland's ancient sites, the Brazen Head, commissioned by Charles II, is more than 300 years old, but its stout is as fresh as it comes. Among its illustrious alumni are Wolfe Tone, Daniel O'Connell, and Robert Emmet, who planned the Dublin rising of 1803 under the Head's low timbers. See p. 172.

- **Abbey Tavern** (County Dublin): A short distance from Dublin center, the Abbey Tavern is the perfect place to recover and refuel after spending a day exploring Dublin. The Abbey is known far and wide for its ballads as well as its brew. See p. 176.

- **The Long Valley** (County Cork): For anyone who knows and loves Cork, this is a place of pilgrimage. There's one endless, low-slung room with a bar running its full length, doors taken from an ocean liner, barmen in white butchers' coats, and a selection of delectable sandwiches. It's a slice of heaven. See p. 284.

- **McGann's** (County Clare): Doolin, a dot of a town on the Clare Coast, is a magnet for traditional Irish musicians—and a wonderful spot to hear impromptu

sessions of Irish music. Gus O'Connor's, down the road, is more famous (but also thicker with tourists); McGann's remains the genuine article without the hype. See p. 389.

- **Moran's Oyster Cottage** (County Galway): Famed for its seafood, this centuries-old thatched-cottage pub on the weir also draws a perfect pint. This may well be the oyster capital of Ireland. It's 19km (12 miles) out of Galway and well worth the drive—or the walk, for that matter. See p. 407.

- **Smuggler's Creek** (County Donegal): This place is worth a stop if only for its spectacular cliff-top views of Donegal Bay. Stone walls, beamed ceilings, open fires, excellent fare, and the brew that's true are among the charms that proprietor Conor Britton has on tap. See p. 471.

- **Crown Liquor Saloon** (County Antrim): This National Trust pub, across from the Grand Opera House in Belfast, is a Victorian gem. Your mouth will drop open at its antique publican splendor even before you lift your first pint. See p. 512.

14 THE BEST WEBSITES

- **Dublin Tourist Office** (www.visitdublin.com): This site is the most comprehensive resource for visiting the capital. We especially like the new last-minute

booking service, which lets you find out which hotels and guesthouses have immediate availability, as well as which are offering the best discounts.

- **Irelandhotels.com** (www.irelandhotels. com): What catapults this accommodations database ahead of the raft of hotel-finding sites is its "search by facility" function. Gotta have a gym? Need to find a babysitter? Want an in-room dataport for your laptop? No problem. Plug in your requirements and you'll get a list of hotels and guesthouses that fit the bill.

- **Irish Tourist Board** (www.discover ireland.ie): Bord Fáilte's site is both easy to navigate and extremely informative. It's an excellent place to start gathering ideas for your trip.

- **AA Roadwatch** (www.aaroadwatch.ie): Planning on driving? The route-planning feature of the Irish Automobile Association's site is brilliantly simple. Plug in a starting point and destination and you'll get a detailed, no-brainer set of directions from A to B.

- **Entertainment Ireland** (www. entertainment.ie): This handy, exhaustive, searchable database includes just about every event in Ireland, from museum exhibitions and rock concerts to new plays and nightclub theme nights—and there are well-written reviews of them all.

- **Irish Family History Foundation** (www. irishroots.net): This new, comprehensive genealogy resource contains documentation from all 32 counties. Much of the archived information is free for your perusal, or you can avail yourself of researchers.

- **Newshound** (www.nuzhound.com): Hands down, this is the best single resource for keeping up-to-date on Northern Ireland. It's a searchable library of news articles about developments in the North, including a terrific timeline of key events in the Troubles. In addition, there are articles on the Republic, as well as travel and dining reviews.

2

Ireland in Depth

At first glance, Ireland presents a familiar face to American visitors. The language is the same, only more lyrical; the faces are familiar, the food recognizable; and even the beer is well known. Many visitors, notably Irish-Americans, experience it as a kind of homecoming. It takes a while for this superficial impression to wear off, but it will, because this is a unique country in its own right, a fact that becomes clearer the longer you stay here. The impenetrable Gaelic language is increasingly prevalent, and in some counties, road signs are exclusively in that language. This creates a kind of distance, a feeling of foreignness, that it seems many Irish do not mind cultivating. This chapter offers a bit of insight into just what kind of country Ireland is trying to be, at the same time that it tries to preserve and maintain what it has been over its long, long history.

1 IRELAND TODAY

Proving wrong those who said the Irish boom economy of the late 1990s was a short-lived bubble has been one of Ireland's great pleasures in recent years. The economy was dubbed "the Celtic Tiger" in the international press, and other nations looked on enviously as Ireland decided what to do with its newfound wealth. It verged on silly money, as the E.U. lavished one of its poorest members with subsidies so vast that, at times, the Irish government seemed not to know what to do with it all. Sometimes politicians made bad decisions—building bridges, statues, and clocks while traffic in Dublin and Galway City ground to a standstill, brought to inertia by roads too old and narrow to handle the modern traffic. Hospitals crumbled, and parents put their children in private schools to save them from the inadequacies of the state-funded versions.

In recent years, though, the country seemed to get a handle on its new situation and poured money into infrastructure—developing a new tram system in Dublin and widening roads around the country. Today, the dump truck seems to be the national symbol of Ireland, as the huge vehicles trundle along by the dozen, each carrying tons of gravel and sand to be used for all the construction: building new roads, widening old roads; building new houses, expanding old houses; building structures in ugly, boxlike shapes helter-skelter along the edges of old villages, towns, and suburbs that seem to be free of the pesky limitations of zoning ordinances. The chatter of jackhammers forms a constant aural background in virtually every town in the Republic. The sound of hammer hitting nail has replaced the bodhran and tin whistle.

It is, we suppose, the sound of success and progress. But it is changing Ireland rapidly—has changed Ireland already. Every time we visit a part of the country we haven't seen in a few months, we are astonished by the new apartment complexes and businesses thrown up in the meantime—so many of them with no character or charm. One worries that architects go begging in Ireland today, as construction companies flourish.

All of this doesn't come cheap, and housing prices in Ireland are shocking. You would pay hundreds of thousands of euros for even the most isolated, unrenovated cottage. To peruse the property pages in the *Irish Times* is to marvel that anybody can afford to own a home, and many cannot. Property prices have made millions of people millionaires on paper, while making it virtually impossible for young people to buy homes or to live in city centers.

Those who didn't own property before the boom cannot afford to buy now, particularly in Dublin and Galway, where most of the workers come into town every day from small homes in the distant suburbs. This has led to a paradoxical situation familiar to many "wealthy" nations—wealth has been accompanied by rising crime, drug abuse, and urban homelessness—but new to Ireland, and it has come as a shock.

Added to this is a worrying growth in overall inflation, which of late has been exceeding the inflation rate in other European nations such as Germany and Britain. Property prices (combined with soaring fuel costs) were primarily to blame. Has the Irish economic bubble yet to burst? Or has the Celtic Tiger only just hit its stride?

Only time will tell.

Still, it's not all bad news. While the Irish find themselves adjusting to the problems of having, to some extent, too much wealth, they've also relished the biggest side effect of a strong economy—peace.

In recent years, the violence in the North has calmed, and a recognizable democratic debate grips the land. There is much disagreement still between those who think it should stay as it is—with Northern Ireland still under U.K. control, and the Republic fully independent and part of the European Union of nations—and those who believe it should be united.

There is also still tension between Catholics and Protestants, who are learning not to greet each other's divergent religious views with violence, but who still whisper the words "Catholic" and "Protestant" when talking in a public place. With all the changes and recent peace, this is still the kind of place where you look over your shoulder when you talk, even in the most inoffensive terms, about religion or Irish politics.

But that is something the Irish themselves seem not even to notice. To them, looking over their shoulders when talking about religion is nothing compared to the past, when they waited for bullets to fly or bombs to explode. For them, this is real democratic peace. There is so much joy in the Republic of Ireland right now about its prosperity—and a kind of intense pride not seen in this country in some time, about its independence, its strong economy, and its place within the E.U.—that the North could be forgiven for feeling a bit of jealousy about that. For while the Republic has grown richer, the North has stayed—at least economically—the same.

At the moment both the North and the Republic are working through these growing pains, and even when the Irish complain about the changes in their country over the last few years, they do so with a kind of heartwarming pride—heartwarming because, for so very long, there was little to be proud of in an Ireland torn apart by violence, and perennially threatened by its own intrinsic inability to ever give way, even to itself.

Now the Irish have learned what you will find out for yourself on any visit here, and that is that the new Ireland is not yet incompatible with the old. The country has thus far maintained and preserved its beautiful old buildings and quiet country lanes, while also growing and changing into a place that *it* can love. It is a difficult—even tense—balancing act. Modern new supermarkets stand beside Georgian town houses, and many of the old Irish shops have been replaced by European and British chain stores. But the Irish always find a way to sell their wares in small boutiques and shops around the country, and to make the old new again. (One of the most popular Irish chains—Avoca Weavers—uses old methods to make intensely modern products from Irish wool and clay.)

Yes, the old Irish spirit is still here, beneath its new facade, behind the coffee shops, the juice bars, the pricey restaurants, and expensive cars. You'll find it in the pubs, and when walking in the hills, sharing a laugh with someone in the post office, or as you stand under an awning in the rain.

2 LOOKING BACK AT IRELAND

THE FIRST SETTLERS With some degree of confidence, we can place the date of the first human habitation of the island somewhere after the end of the last ice age, around the late 8000s B.C.

Ireland's first colonizers, Mesolithic Homo sapiens, walked, waded, or floated across the narrow strait from what is now Britain in search of flint and, of course, food.

The next momentous prehistoric event was the arrival of Neolithic farmers and herders, sometime around 3500 B.C. The Neolithic "revolution" was the first of many to come to Ireland a bit late, at least 5,000 years after its inception in the ancient Near East. The domestication of the human species—settled life, agriculture, animal husbandry—brought with it a radically increased population, enhanced skills, stability, and all the implications of leisure. Unlike Ireland's Mesolithic hunters, who barely left a trace, this second

wave of colonizers began to transform the island at once. They came with stone axes that could fell a good-size elm in less than an hour. Ireland's hardwood forests receded to make room for tilled fields and pastureland. Villages sprang up, and more permanent homes, planked with split oak, appeared at this time.

Far more striking, though, was the appearance of massive megalithic monuments, including court cairns, dolmens (stone tables), round subterranean passage tombs, and wedge tombs. There are thousands of these scattered around Ireland, and to this day only a small percentage of them have been excavated. These megalithic monuments speak volumes about the early Irish. To visit Newgrange and Knowth in the Boyne Valley and Carrowmore in County Sligo is to marvel at the mystical practices of the early Irish. Even today little is known about the meaning of these mysterious stone remnants of their lives.

DATELINE

- **c. 8000 B.C.** Earliest known human settlers arrive in Ireland.
- **2000 B.C.** First metalworkers come to Ireland.
- **c. 700 B.C.** Celtic settlement of Ireland begins.
- **c. A.D. 100** The Gaels arrive in Ireland, naming one of their biggest settlements "Dubhlinn."
- **A.D. 432** Traditional date of St. Patrick's return to Ireland as a Christian missionary.
- **500–800** Ireland becomes one of the largest centers of Christianity in Europe—often referred to as the "golden age."
- **795** First Viking invasion.
- **841** Vikings build a sea fort in the area of modern-day Dublin.
- **853** Danes take possession of the Norse settlement.
- **1014** Battle of Clontarf. High king of Ireland, Brian Boru, defeats the Vikings.
- **1167–71** Forces of English King Henry II seize Dublin and surrounding areas.
- **1204** Dublin Castle becomes center of English power.
- **1297** First parliamentary sessions in Dublin.
- **1300s** First great plague kills a third of the population of Dublin.

Early Celtic inhabitants of the island assumed that the tremendous stones and mounds were raised by giants. They called them the people of the *sí*, who eventually became the Tuatha Dé Danann, and, finally, faeries. Over many generations of oral tradition, the mythical people were downsized into "little people," who were believed to have led a magical life, mostly underground, in the thousands of *raths,* or earthwork structures, coursing the island like giant mole works. All of these sites were believed to be protected by the fairies, and to tamper with them was believed to bring great bad luck, so nobody ever touched them. Thus they have lasted to this day—ungraffitied, undamaged, unprotected by any visible fences or wires, but utterly safe.

THE CELTS Of all the successive waves of outsiders who have, over the years, shaped, cajoled, and pockmarked the timeline of Irish history, none have made quite such a deep-seated impact as that of the Celts. They came in waves, the first perhaps as early as the 6th century B.C. and continuing until the end of the first millennium. They fled from the Roman invasion and clung to the edge of Europe—Ireland being, at the time, about as far as you could go to elude a Roman force. In time, they controlled the island and absorbed into their culture everyone they found there. Their ways—and their genes—dominated. They brought iron weapons; chariots; cults and contests; and poetry, music, and other forms of artistic genius, all of which took root and flourished in Irish soil.

Despite their cultural potency, however, the Celts developed little in the way of centralized government, existing instead in a near-perpetual state of division and conflict with one another. The island was divided among as many as 150 tribes, grouped under alliances to one of five provincial kings. The provinces of Munster, Leinster, Ulster, and Connaught date from this period. They fought fiercely among themselves over cattle (their "currency" and standard of wealth), land, and women. None among them ever ruled the entire island, though not for lack of trying. One of the most impressive monuments from the time of the warring Celts is the stone fortress of Dún Aengus, on the wind-swept hills of the Aran Islands.

THE COMING OF CHRISTIANITY The Celtic chiefs neither warmly welcomed nor violently resisted the Christians who came ashore beginning in the 5th century A.D. Although threatened, the pagan Celts settled for a bloodless rivalry with this new religion. In retrospect, this may have been a mistake.

Not the first, but eventually the most famous, of these Christian newcomers was

- **1500s** English rule consolidated across Ireland. Henry VIII proclaims himself king of Ireland.
- **1534–52** Henry VIII begins suppression of Catholic Church in Ireland.
- **1558–1603** Reign of Elizabeth I. Ireland proclaimed an Anglican country. The "plantation" of Munster divides Ireland into counties.
- **1591** Trinity College founded.

- **1607** The flight of the Irish earls, marking the demise of the old Gaelic order.
- **1641** Irish Catholic revolt in Ulster led by Sir Phelim O'Neill ends in defeat.
- **1649** Oliver Cromwell invades and begins the reconquest of Ireland.
- **1690** The forces of King James II, a Catholic, are defeated at the Battle of the Boyne, consolidating Protestant order in England.

- **1691** Patrick Sarsfield surrenders Limerick. He and some 14,000 Irish troops, the "Wild Geese," flee to the Continent.
- **1704** Enactment of first Penal Laws. Apartheid comes to Ireland.
- **1778** The Penal Laws are progressively repealed.
- **1782** The Irish Parliament is granted independence.

continues

a man called Maewyn Succat, a young Roman citizen torn from his Welsh homeland in a Celtic raid and brought to Ireland as a slave, where he was forced to work in a place called the forest of Foclut (thought to be around modern County Antrim). He escaped on a ship bound for France, where he spent several years as a priest before returning to Ireland as a missionary. He began preaching at sacred Celtic festivals, a tactic that frequently led to confrontations with religious and political leaders, but eventually he became such a popular figure with the people of Ireland that after his death in 461, a dozen clan chiefs fought over the right to bury him. His lasting legacy was, of course, the establishment in Ireland of one of the strongest Christian orthodoxies in Europe—an achievement for which he was later beatified as St. Patrick.

Ireland's conversion to Christianity was a somewhat negotiated process. The church at the time of St. Patrick was, like the man who brought it, Roman. To Ireland, an island then still without a single proper town, the Roman system of dioceses and archdioceses was mysterious and pointless. So the Irish adapted the church to their own situation. They built isolated monasteries with extended monastic "families," each more or less autonomous. The pope, like an Irish high king, was to them like an ordained prizefighter—he was expected to defend his title, one challenge after another, or lose it.

Ireland flourished in this fashion for several centuries, and became a center of monastic learning and culture. Monks and scholars were drawn to it in droves, and they were sent out in great numbers as well, to Britain and the Continent as emissaries for the island's way of thinking and praying.

As the historian Thomas Cahill wrote in *How the Irish Saved Civilization,* "Wherever they went the Irish brought with them their books, many unseen in Europe for centuries and tied to their waists as signs of triumph, just as Irish heroes had once tied to their waists their enemies' heads." And they worked with a fervor; in fact, they worked so hard that the Irish penned more than half the biblical commentaries written worldwide between A.D. 650 and 850.

Like their megalithic ancestors, these monks left traces of their lives behind, and these have become enduring monuments to their spirituality. Early monastic sites such as gorgeous Glendalough in County Wicklow, wind-swept Clonmacnois in County Offaly, and isolated Skellig Michael off the Kerry coast give you an idea of how they lived, while striking examples of their work can be seen at Trinity College (which houses the Book of Kells) and at the Chester Beatty museum at Dublin Castle.

- **1791** Wolfe Tone founds the Society of the United Irishmen.
- **1796–97** Wolfe Tone launches an invasion from France, fails, is taken captive, and commits suicide.
- **1798** "The Year of the French." A French invasion force is defeated at Killala Bay. General Humbert surrenders to Cornwallis.
- **1801** The Irish Parliament is induced to dissolve itself.

Ireland becomes part of the United Kingdom.
- **1803** Twenty-five-year-old Robert Emmet is hanged after his uprising of fewer than 100 men is a tragic failure.
- **1829** Daniel O'Connell secures passage of the Catholic Emancipation Act. He is later named lord mayor of Dublin.
- **1845–48** The Great Famine. An estimated 2 million Irish

either die or emigrate, mostly to the U.S.
- **1848** The revolt of the Young Irelanders ends in failure.
- **1858** The Irish Republican Brotherhood, a secret society known as the Fenians, is founded in New York.
- **1866** In an imaginative publicity stunt, a minuscule army of Fenians attempts to invade Canada.

THE VIKING INVASIONS The monastic city-states of early medieval Ireland might have continued to lead the world's intellectual process, but the Vikings came along and ruined everything. After centuries of relative peace, the first wave of Viking invaders arrived in A.D. 795. The wealthy nonviolent Irish monasteries were among their first targets. Unprepared and unprotected, the Irish monasteries, which had amassed collections of gold, jewels, and art from followers and thinkers around the world, were decimated. The round towers to which the monks retreated for safety were neither high enough nor strong enough to protect them and their treasures from the onslaught.

Once word spread of the wealth to be had on the small island, the Scandinavian invaders just kept on coming, but much as they were experts in the arts of pillage and plunder, one thing of which they had no knowledge was literature. They didn't know how to read. Therefore, they paid scant attention to the magnificent books they came across, passing them over for more obvious riches. This fortunate quirk of history allowed the monks some means of preserving their dying culture—and their immeasurably valuable work—for the benefit of future generations.

Of course, the Vikings did more than hit and run. They settled down and took over much of the country—securing every major harbor on Ireland's east coast with a fortified town. These were the first real towns in Ireland: In addition to Dublin, they also founded Cork, Waterford, and the river city of Limerick. They had plundered the country fairly thoroughly by the time the Irish, always disinclined to unite, did so at last, and managed to push out the Vikings after a decisive military campaign lead by the army of Brian Boru in 1014. When the Vikings departed, they left their towns behind, forever altering the Irish landscape. The legacy of the Vikings in Ireland is complex, and a visit to Dublin's Wood Quay and the city walls of Waterford is a good introduction to their influence.

With the Vikings gone, Ireland enjoyed something of a renewal in the 11th and 12th centuries. Its towns grew, its regional kings made successive unsuccessful bids to unite the country under a single high kingship, and its church came under increased pressure to conform to the Vatican's rules. All of these factors would play a part in ripening Ireland for the next invasion.

The Vikings may have been gone, but prosperous and factionalized Ireland made attractive prey to other nations, and it was, tragically, an Irish king who opened the door to the next predator. Diarmait Mac Murchada, king of Leinster, whose ambition was to be king of all of Ireland, decided he could do it, with a little help.

- **1879** Michael Davitt founds the National Land League to support the claims of tenant farmers.
- **1879–82** The "land war" forces the enactment of reform. The tenant system unravels; land returns to those who work it.
- **1886 and 1894** Bills for home rule are defeated in Parliament.

- **1893** The Gaelic League is founded to revive the Irish language.
- **1904** The Abbey Theatre opens in Dublin.
- **1905–08** Founding of Sinn Fein ("We Ourselves") with close links to the Irish Republican Brotherhood.
- **1912** Third home rule bill passes in the House of Commons and is defeated by the House of Lords.

- **1916** Patrick Pearse and James Connolly lead an armed uprising on Easter Monday to proclaim the Irish Republic. Defeat is followed by the execution of 15 leaders of the revolt.
- **1918** Sinn Fein wins a landslide election victory against the Irish Parliamentary Party.
- **1919** Sinn Fein, led by Eamon de Valera, constitutes

continues

So he called on Henry II, the Norman king of England. Diarmait offered Henry a series of incentives in return for military aid: Not only did he bequeath his eldest daughter to whoever led the army, but he also offered them overlordship of the Kingdom of Leinster. To put it bluntly, he made Henry an offer he couldn't refuse. So it was that an expeditionary force, led by the earl of Pembroke, Richard de Clare—better known as Strongbow—was sent to Diarmait's aid. After the successful invasion and subsequent battles in which Strongbow emerged victorious, he remained in Ireland as governor, and thus gave the English their first foothold in Ireland. What Diarmait did not realize, of course, was that they would never leave.

THE NORMAN INVASION In successive expeditions from 1167 to 1169, the Normans, who had already conquered Britain, crossed the Irish Sea from England with crushing force. The massive Norman fortifications at Trim are a powerful reminder of the sheer power the invaders brought with them. During the next century, the Norman-English settled in, consolidating their power in new towns and cities. Indeed, many settlers grew attached to the island, and did their best to integrate with the local culture. Marriages between the native Irish and the invaders became commonplace. Over the next couple of centuries, they became more Irish and less English in their loyalties.

In 1314 Scotland's Robert the Bruce defeated the English at Bannockburn and set out to fulfill his dream of a united Celtic kingdom. He installed his brother Edward on the Irish throne, but the constant state of war took a heavy toll. Within 2 years, famine and economic disorder had eroded any public support Edward might have enjoyed. By the time he was defeated and killed at Dundalk in 1317, few were prepared to mourn him.

Over the next 2 centuries, attempts to rid Ireland of its English overlords fell short. Independent Gaelic lords in the north and west continued to maintain their territories. By the close of the 15th century, English control of the island was effectively limited to the Pale, a walled and fortified cordon around what is now greater Dublin. (The phrase "beyond the pale" comes from this—meaning anything that is uncontrollable or unacceptable.)

ENGLISH POWER & THE FLIGHT OF THE EARLS During the reign of the Tudor monarchs in England (1485–1603), the brutal reconquest of Ireland was set in motion. Henry VIII was the first to proclaim himself king of all Ireland—something even his warlike ancestors had stopped short of doing—but it wasn't until later that century that the claim was

itself as the first Irish Dáil and declares independence.

■ **1919–21** The Irish War of Independence. Michael Collins commands the Irish forces.

■ **1921** Anglo-Irish Treaty. Ireland is partitioned. Twenty-six counties form the Free State; the other six remain a part of the U.K. The Free State adopts its first constitution a year later.

■ **1922–23** The Irish civil war, between the government of the Free State and those who opposed the Anglo-Irish treaty. Michael Collins is assassinated by the IRA, who saw the treaty as a sellout.

■ **1932** Eamon de Valera leads Fianna Fáil to victory and becomes head of government.

■ **1937** The Free State adopts a new constitution, abandoning membership of the British Commonwealth and changing the country's official name to Eire.

■ **1939** Dublin is bombed by Germany at start of World War II, but Ireland remains neutral.

■ **1948** The Republic of Ireland Act. Ireland severs its last constitutional links with Britain.

■ **1955** Ireland is admitted into the United Nations.

backed up by force. Elizabeth I, Henry's daughter, declared that all Gaelic lords in Ireland must surrender their lands to her, with the dubious promise that she would immediately grant them all back again—unsurprisingly, the proposition was hardly welcomed in Ireland, and a rebel army was raised by Hugh O'Neill and "Red" Hugh O'Donnell, two Irish chieftains.

Despite significant victories early on in their decade-long campaign, most notably over a force led by the earl of Essex, whom Elizabeth had personally sent to subdue them, by 1603 O'Neill was left with few allies and no option but to surrender, which he did on March 23, the day before Elizabeth died. O'Neill had his lands returned, but constant harassment by the English prompted him, along with many of Ireland's other Gaelic lords, to sail for Europe on September 14, 1607, abandoning their lands and their aspirations for freedom.

THE COMING OF CROMWELL   By the 1640s, Ireland was effectively an English plantation. Family estates had been seized and foreign (Scottish) labor brought in to work them. A systematic persecution of Catholics, which began with Henry VIII's split from Rome but did not die with him, barred Catholics from practicing their faith. Resentment against the English and their punitive laws led to fierce uprisings in

Ulster and Leinster in 1641, and by early 1642 most of Ireland was again under Irish control. Unfortunately for the rebels, any hope of extending the victories was destroyed by internal disunion and by the eventual decision to support the Royalist side in the English civil war. In 1648 King Charles I of England was beheaded, and the victorious commander of the parliamentary forces, Oliver Cromwell, was installed as ruler. Soon his supporters were taking on his enemies in Ireland. A year later, the Royalists' stand collapsed in defeat at Rathmines, just south of Dublin.

Defeat for the Royalist cause did not, however, mean the end of the war. Cromwell became paranoid that Ireland would be used to launch a French-backed insurgency if it was not brought to heel, and he detested the country's Catholic beliefs. So it was that as the hot, sticky summer of 1649 drew to a close, Cromwell set sail for Dublin, bringing with him an army of 12,000 men, and a battle plan so ruthless that, to paraphrase another dark chapter in the history of warfare, it would live forever in infamy.

In the town of Drogheda, over 3,552 Irish soldiers were slaughtered in a single night. When a large group of men sought sanctuary in the local church, Cromwell ordered them to be burned alive, an act of such monstrosity that some of his own

- **1963** U.S. President John F. Kennedy visits Dublin.
- **1969** Violence breaks out in Northern Ireland. British troops are called in.
- **1972** In Derry a peaceful rally turns into "Bloody Sunday." The Northern Irish Parliament is dissolved, and direct rule imposed from Britain.
- **1973** Ireland joins the European Community.

- **1986** The Anglo-Irish Agreement gives the Republic a say in the government of Northern Ireland.
- **1990** Mary Robinson is elected Ireland's first female president.
- **1994** The IRA announces a cease-fire, and the Protestant paramilitaries follow suit. Commencement of peace talks.
- **1995** The British and Irish governments issue "A New

Framework for Agreement," and U.S. President Bill Clinton makes a historic visit to Ireland, speaking to large crowds in Belfast and Derry. He is received with enthusiasm in the Republic.
- **1996** The IRA breaks its cease-fire. An IRA bomb in Omagh kills 29. The North sees the worst rioting in 15 years.

continues

men risked a charge of mutiny and refused the order. On another day, in Wexford, over 2,000 were murdered, many of them civilians. The trail of destruction rolled on, devastating counties Galway and Waterford. When asked where the Irish citizens could go to be safe from him, Cromwell famously suggested they could go "to hell or Connaught"—the latter being the most far-flung, rocky, and unfarmable part of Ireland.

After a rampage that lasted 7 months, Cromwell finally left Ireland and its shattered administration in the care of his lieutenants and returned to England. His memory lingers painfully in Ireland. In certain parts of the country, people still spit at the mention of Cromwell's name.

THE PENAL LAWS Cromwell died in 1658, and 2 years later the English monarchy was restored, but the anti-Catholic oppression continued apace. In 1685, though, something quite remarkable happened. Contrary to the efforts of the English establishment, the new king, James II, refused to relinquish his Catholic faith after ascending to the throne. It looked for a while as if things could change in Ireland, and that the Catholics might have found a new ally in the unlikeliest of quarters. However, such hopes were dashed 3 years later, when James was ousted from power, and the Protestant William of Orange installed in his place.

James fled to France to raise support for a rebellion, then sailed to Ireland to launch his attack. He struck first at Derry, to which he laid siege for 15 weeks before finally being defeated by William's forces at the Battle of the Boyne. The battle effectively ended James's cause, and with it, the hopes of Catholic Ireland for the best part of a century.

After James's defeat, English power was once more consolidated across Ireland. Protestant landowners were granted full political power, while laws were enacted to effectively immobilize the Catholic population. Being a Catholic in late-17th-century Ireland was not exactly illegal per se, but in practice life was all but impossible for those who refused to convert to Protestantism. Catholics could not purchase land, and existing landholdings were split up unless the families who owned them became Protestants; Catholic schools were banned, as were priests and all forms of public worship. Catholics were barred from holding any office of state, practicing law, or joining the army. Those who still refused to relinquish their faith were forced to pay a tax to the Anglican church, and by virtue of not being able to own land, the few who previously had been allowed to vote certainly were not anymore.

- **1997** The IRA declares a new cease-fire. Sinn Fein enters inclusive all-party peace talks designed to bring about a comprehensive settlement.
- **1998** The all-party peace talks conclude with the so-called Good Friday Agreement, later strongly supported in referendums held on the same day in the Republic and the North. John Hume and David Trimble are awarded the Nobel Peace Prize.
- **1999** The implementation of the agreement is blocked by a Unionist demand—"in the spirit" but contrary to the letter of the Good Friday Agreement—that IRA decommissioning precede the appointment of a new Northern Ireland executive. The peace process stalls until November, when the new power-sharing Northern Ireland Executive is established.
- **2000** The IRA issues a statement saying it will decommission its arms. In May, power is restored to the institutions established by the Good Friday Agreement.
- **2001** David Trimble threatens to resign as Ulster Unionist party leader if the IRA does not decommission as promised. The IRA doesn't; Trimble resigns in June.

The new British landlords settled in, planted crops, made laws, and sowed their own seeds. Inevitably, over time, the "Anglos" became the Anglo-Irish. Hyphenated or not, they were Irish, and their loyalties were increasingly unpredictable. After all, an immigrant is only an immigrant for a generation; whatever the birthright of the colonists, their children would be Irish-born and bred. And so it was that an uncomfortable sort of stability set in for a generation or three, albeit of a kind that was very much separate and unequal. There were the haves—the wealthy Protestants—and the have-nots—the deprived and disenfranchised Catholics.

A kind of unhappy peace held for some time. But by the end of the 18th century, the appetite for rebellion was whetted again. To understand why, one need look no further than the intellectual hotbed that flourished among the coffee shops and lecture halls of Europe's newest boomtown: Dublin.

WOLFE TONE, THE UNITED IRISHMEN & THE 1798 REBELLION By the 1770s, Dublin was thriving like never before. As a center for culture and learning, it was rivaled only by Paris and London; thanks to the work of such architects as Henry Gratton (who designed Custom House, the Kings Inns, and the Four Courts), its very streets were

being remodeled in a grand, neoclassical style that was more akin to the great cities of southern Italy than of southern Ireland.

However, while the urban classes reveled in their newfound wealth, the stringent penal laws that had effectively cut off the Catholic workers from their own countryside forced many of them to turn to the city for work. Into Dublin's buzzing intellectual scene were poured rich seams of political dissent, and even after a campaign by Irish politicians led to many of the penal laws being repealed in 1783, all the ingredients were there to make Dublin a breeding ground for radical thinking and political activism. The results were explosive.

When war broke out between Britain and France in the 1790s, the United Irishmen—a nonviolent society formed to lobby for admission of Catholic Irishmen to the Irish Parliament—sent a secret delegation to persuade the French to intervene on Ireland's behalf against the British. Their emissary in this venture was a Dublin lawyer named Wolfe Tone. In 1796 Tone sailed with a French force bound for Ireland and determined to defeat forces loyal to the English crown, but they were turned back by storms.

In 1798, though, full-scale insurrection led by the United Irishmen did spread across much of Ireland, particularly the southwestern counties of Kilkenny and

Following a surge of feeling in the wake of the September 11 terrorist attacks on the U.S., IRA decommissioning begins.

- **2002** The peace process continues amid sectarian violence on both sides.
- **2004** Irish government passes smoking ban in all public indoor spaces. U.S. President George W. Bush arrives for E.U.-U.S. Summit

and is greeted with anti–Iraq War protests.

- **2005** David Trimble loses his parliamentary seat, but hardline parties Sinn Fein and the DUP do extremely well. The IRA decommissioning process is officially declared complete, and the IRA disbands as a paramilitary unit.
- **2006** Peace holds, but the North has rarely been more polarized. The Gaeltacht

movement spreads, and larger regions of the country are declared, in essence, Gaelic language only.

- **2007** A power-sharing executive is put into place in Northern Ireland, bringing together lifelong enemies DUP leader Ian Paisley and Sinn Fein leader Gerry Adams.

"An Bhfuil Gaeilge Agat?" ("Do You Speak Irish?")

Ireland has two official languages, Irish Gaelic and English. Today English is still the first and most commonly spoken language for the vast majority of the Irish people. In 1835 the Irish-speaking population of Ireland was reckoned at four million. The language was suppressed by Britain for many years, and gradually its use waned. When the 2002 census was taken, just under 60,000 Irish residents said they spoke Gaelic.

There is a huge and emotional pro-Irish-language movement underway in Ireland right now—one that is disproportionate to the actual number of Irish speakers (although the popularity of the language is growing, particularly among the young, as all children now learn Gaelic in school).

Still, the vast majority of Irish residents do not speak Gaelic; yet all Irish citizens are entitled by law to conduct any official business with the state (legal proceedings, university interviews, and filing taxes, for example) in Gaelic. Increasingly, street signs are in both Gaelic and English, and many towns are reverting to their Gaelic names (which often bear no resemblance to their old English names).

Areas of the country (counties Kerry, Galway, and Donegal in particular) where Gaelic is widely spoken are Gaelic protection zones called Gaeltacht, and in those areas all English words have been removed from road signs, warning signs, and street signs. This has got cartographers moving as rapidly as possible (which, unfortunately, isn't *that* fast) to rewrite maps in order to keep up, but the simple fact is you're likely to have a map that still calls the Dingle "Dingle," rather than the name that all the street signs now call it: "An Daingean." And even the cartographers won't tell you the Gaelic word for "Caution."

The growing Gaeltacht movement in Ireland is increasingly aggressive, with a bit of a nationalistic bent, and its proponents want to make no exceptions to the strict anti-English rules on signage for the millions of tourists who visit the island every year. This means that visitors are more likely to find themselves utterly lost—clutching a map in which the town's names are all in English, and standing in a town in which all street names are in Gaelic. Should this happen to you, don't hesitate to ask for help—all Irish residents who speak Gaelic also speak English, and most are very sympathetic to the plight of nonresidents who do not know this complex, ancient language.

Wexford, where a tiny republic was briefly declared in June. But it was crushed by loyalist forces, which then went on a murderous spree, killing tens of thousands of men, women, and children, and burning towns to the ground. The nadir of the rebellion came when Wolfe Tone, having raised another French invasion force, sailed into Lough Swilley in Donegal, but was promptly captured by the British. At his trial, wearing a French uniform, Tone requested that he be shot, in accordance with the rights of a foreign soldier, but when the request was refused, he suffered a rather more gruesome end. While waiting for the gallows, he slit his own throat in jail; however, he missed the jugular vein, instead severing his windpipe, leading to a

Impressions

You cannot conquer Ireland. You cannot extinguish the Irish passion for freedom. If our deed has not been sufficient to win freedom, then our children will win it by a better deed.

—Patrick Pearse

slow and painful death 8 days later. His last words were reputed to have been: "It appears, sir, that I am but a bad anatomist."

The rebellion was over. In the space of 3 weeks, more than 30,000 Irish had been killed. As a final indignity in what became known as "The Year of the French," the British tricked the Irish Parliament into dissolving itself, and Ireland reverted to strict British rule.

A CONFLICT OF CONFLICTS In 1828 a Catholic lawyer named Daniel O'Connell, who had earlier formed the Catholic Association to represent the interests of tenant farmers, was elected to the British Parliament as Member of Parliament for Dublin. Public opinion was so solidly behind him that he was able to persuade the British prime minister that the only way to avoid a civil war in Ireland was to force the Catholic Emancipation Act through Parliament. He remained an MP until 1841, when he was elected lord mayor of Dublin, a platform he used to push for repeal of the direct rule imposed from London after the 1798 rebellion. O'Connell organized enormous rallies (nicknamed "monster meetings") attended by hundreds of thousands, and provoked an unresponsive conservative government to such an extent that it eventually arrested him on charges of seditious conspiracy. The charges were dropped, but the incident—coupled with growing impatience toward his nonviolent approach of protest and reform—led to the breakdown of his power base. "The Liberator," as he had been known, faded, his health failed, and he died on a trip to Rome.

THE GREAT FAMINE Even after the anti-Catholic legislation began to recede, the vast majority of farmland available to the poor, mostly Catholic population of the countryside was harsh, and difficult to cultivate. One of the few crops that could be grown reliably was the potato, which effectively became the staple diet of the rural poor. So when, in 1845, a fungus destroyed much of the potato crop of Ireland, it is not difficult to understand the scale of the devastation this caused. However, to label the Great Irish Famine of 1845 to 1861 as a "tragedy" would be an incomplete description. It was, of course, tragic—undeniably, overwhelmingly so—but at the same time, the word implies a randomness to the whole sorry, sickening affair that fails to capture its true awfulness. The fact is that what started out as a disaster was turned into a devastating crisis by the callous response of an uninterested British establishment.

As the potato blight worsened, it became apparent to many landlords that their farm tenants would be unable to pay rent. In order to offset their financial losses, they continued to ship grain overseas, in lieu of rent from their now-starving tenants. The British Parliament, meanwhile, was reluctant to send aid, putting the reports of a crisis down to, in the words of Prime Minister Robert Peel, "the Irish tendency to exaggerate."

Of course, as people started to die by the thousands, it became clear to the government that something had to be done, and emergency relief was sent to Ireland in the form of cheap, imported Indian corn-meal. However, this contained virtually no nutrients, and ultimately contributed to the spread of such diseases as typhus and cholera, which were to claim more victims than starvation itself.

To make matters worse, the cornmeal was not simply given to those in need of it. Fearful that handouts would encourage laziness among a population they viewed as prone to that malaise, the British government forced people to work for their food. Entirely pointless make-work projects were initiated, just to give the starving men something to do for their cornmeal; roads were built that led nowhere, for instance, and elaborate follies constructed that served no discernible purpose, some of which still litter the countryside today, memorials to cruelty and ignorance.

One of the most difficult things to comprehend a century and a half later is the sheer futility of it all. For behind the statistics, the memorials, and the endless personal anguish, lies perhaps the most painful truth of all: that the famine was easily preventable. Enormous cargoes of imported corn sat in Irish ports for months, until the British government felt that releasing them to the people would not adversely affect market rates. Meanwhile, huge quantities of meat and grain were exported from Ireland. (Indeed, in 1847, cattle exports went up 33% from the previous year.)

Given the circumstances, it is easy to understand why so many chose to leave Ireland. More than a million emigrated over the next decade, about three-quarters of them to America, the rest to Britain or Europe. They drained the country. In 1841, Ireland's population was 8 million; by 1851 it was 6.5 million.

THE STRUGGLE FOR HOME RULE

As the famine waned and life returned to something like normality, the Irish independence movement gained new momentum. New fronts opened up in the struggle for home rule, both violent and nonviolent, and, significantly, the Republicans now drew considerable support from overseas—particularly from America. There, groups such as the Fenians fundraised and published newspapers in support of the Irish cause, while more audacious schemes, such as an 1866 "invasion" of Canada with fewer than 100 men, amounted to little more than publicity stunts, designed to raise awareness for the cause.

Back home in Ireland, partial concessions were won in Parliament, and by the 1880s, nationalists such as the MP for Meath, Charles Stewart Parnell, were able to unite various factions of Irish nationalists (including the Fenian Brotherhood in America) to fight for home rule. In a tumultuous decade of legislation, he came close, but revelations about his long affair with Kitty O'Shea, the wife of a supporter, brought about his downfall as a politician.

By 1912, a bill to give Ireland home rule was passed through the British House of Commons, but was defeated in the House of Lords. Many felt that the political process was still all but unstoppable, and that it was only a matter of time before the bill passed fully into law and effective political independence for Ireland would be secured. However, when the onset of World War I in 1914 forced the issue onto the back burner once again, many in the home rule movement grew tired of the political process.

THE EASTER REBELLION On Easter Monday 1916, a group of nationalists occupied the General Post Office in the heart of Dublin, from which they proclaimed the foundation of an Irish Republic. Inside were 1,500 fighters, led by schoolteacher and Gaelic League member Patrick Pearse and Socialist leader James Connolly.

The British, nervous at an armed uprising on its doorstep while it fought a massive war in Europe, responded with overwhelming force. Soldiers were sent in, and a battle raged in the streets of Dublin for 6 days before the leaders of the rebellion were captured and imprisoned. There are still bullet holes in the walls of the post office and the buildings and statues up and down O'Connell Street. Pearse, Connolly, and 12 other leaders were imprisoned, secretly tried, and speedily executed.

Ultimately, though, the British reaction was as counterproductive as it was harsh. The totality with which those involved in organizing the rebellion were pursued and dispatched acted as a lightning rod for many of those who had been undecided about the effectiveness of a purely political struggle. Indeed, a fact that has become somewhat lost in the ensuing hundred or so years since Patrick Pearse stood on the steps of the post office early on that cold Monday morning, reading a treatise on Irish independence, is that a great many Irish didn't support the rebellion at the time. Many either believed that the best course of action was to lie low until the war had ended, when concessions would be won as a result, or that it was simply the wrong thing to do, as long as sons of Ireland were sacrificing their lives in the trenches of Europe.

The aftermath of 1916 all but guaranteed, for better or for worse, that Ireland's future would be decided by the gun.

REBELLION A power vacuum was left at the heart of the nationalist movement after the Easter Rising, and it was filled by two men: Michael Collins and Eamon de Valera. On the surface, both men had much in common; Collins was a Cork man who had returned from Britain in order to join the Irish Volunteers (later to become the Irish Republican Army, or IRA), while de Valera was an Irish-American math teacher who came back to Ireland to set up a new political party, Sinn Fein.

When de Valera's party won a landslide victory in the general election of 1918, its MPs refused to sit in London, instead proclaiming the first Dáil, or independent parliament, in Dublin. De Valera went to rally support for the cause in America, while Collins stayed to concentrate on his work as head of the Irish Volunteers. Tensions escalated into violence, and for the next 2 years, Irish nationalists fought a tit-for-tat military campaign against the British in Ireland.

The low point of the struggle came in 1920, when Collins ordered 14 British operatives to be murdered in their beds, in response to which British troops opened fire on the audience at a football game at Croke Park in Dublin, randomly killing 12 innocent people. A truce was eventually declared on July 9, 1921, and 6 months later, the Anglo-Irish treaty was signed in London, granting legislative independence to 26 Irish counties (known together as the Irish Free State). The compromise through which that freedom was won, though, was that six counties in the north would remain part of the United Kingdom. Collins knew that compromise would not be accepted by the more strident members of his rebel group. And he knew they would blame him for agreeing to it in the first place. When he signed the treaty he told the people present, "I am signing my own death warrant."

As he feared, nationalists were split between those who accepted the treaty as a platform on which to build, and those, led by the nationalist de Valera, who saw it as a betrayal, and would accept nothing less than immediate and full independence at any cost. Even the withdrawal of British troops from Dublin for the first time in nearly 800 years did not quell their anger. The result was an inexorable slide into civil war. The flashpoint came in April 1922, when violence erupted around the streets of the capital, and rolled on for 8 days until de Valera's supporters were forced to surrender.

The government of the fledgling free state ordered that Republicans be shot on sight, leading to the deaths of 77 people. And Collins had been right about his own fate: 4 months later he was assassinated while on a visit to his childhood home.

The fallout from the civil war dominated Irish politics for the next decade. De Valera split from the Republicans to form another party, Fianna Fáil ("the Warriors of Ireland"), which won the election of 1932 and governed for 17 years. Despite his continuing dedication to the Republican ideal, however, de Valera was not to be the one who finally declared Ireland a republic, in 1948; ironically, that distinction went to a coalition led by de Valera's opponent, Douglas Hyde, whose victory in the election of 1947 was attributed to the fact that de Valera had become too obsessed with abstract Republican ideals to govern effectively.

STUCK IN NEUTRAL One of the more controversial, not to say morally ambiguous, decisions that Eamon de Valera made while in office was to stay neutral during World War II, despite the best efforts of Winston Churchill and Franklin Roosevelt to persuade him otherwise. The basis for his decision—a combination of Ireland's size and economic weakness, and the British presence in Northern Ireland—may have made sense to some extent, but it left Ireland in the peculiar position of openly favoring one side in the war, but refusing to help it. His reticence didn't find much favor among the Irish population, and as many as 300,000 Irish men found ways to enlist in the British or U.S. armies. In the end, more than 50,000 Irish soldiers died in the war their country never joined.

TROUBLE ON THE WAY After the war, 2 decades passed without violence in Ireland, until the late 1960s once more saw the outbreak of sectarian conflict in the North. What started out as a civil rights movement, to demand greater equality for Catholics within Northern Ireland, soon escalated into a cycle of violence that lasted for 30 years.

It would be a terrible oversimplification to say that the Troubles were merely a clear-cut struggle between those who wanted to complete the process of Irish

unification and those who wanted to remain part of the United Kingdom, although that was, of course, the crux of the conflict. Factors such as organized crime and terrorism, together with centuries-old conflicts over religious, land, and social issues, make the conflict even harder for outsiders to understand.

The worst of the Troubles came in the 1970s. In 1972, British troops inexplicably opened fire on a peaceful demonstration in Derry, killing 12 people—many of whom were shot while they tended to the wounds of the first people injured. The IRA took advantage of the mood of public outrage to begin a civilian bombing campaign on the British mainland. The cycle of violence continued for 20 years, inexorably and depressingly, while all the while, none of the myriad sides in the conflict would talk to each other. Finally, in the early 1990s, secret talks were opened between the British and the IRA, leading to an IRA cease-fire in 1994 (although the cease-fire held only shakily—an IRA bomb in Omagh 4 years later killed 29, the most to die in any single incident of the Troubles).

The peace process continued throughout the 1990s, helped significantly by the mediation efforts of U.S. President Bill Clinton, who arguably became more involved in Irish affairs than any president before him until, eventually, on Good Friday 1998, a peace accord was finally signed in Belfast. The agreement committed all sides to a peaceful resolution of the conflict in Northern Ireland, and included the reinstatement of full self-government for the region in a power-sharing administration. It stopped short of resolving the territorial issue once and for all—in other words, Northern Ireland is still part of the U.K., and will be for the foreseeable future. On the contrary, to some extent the conflicts rage more bitterly and more divisively than ever before, the difference being that, with notable exceptions, they are fought through the ballot box, rather than the barrel of a gun. As a coda, in 2005 the IRA fully decommissioned its weapons, and officially dissolved itself as a paramilitary unit.

While Northern Ireland is still struggling to recover from years of conflict, the Republic of Ireland continues to flourish. The 1990s brought unprecedented wealth and prosperity to the country, thanks in part to European Union subsidies, and partly to a thriving economy, which acquired the nickname "the Celtic Tiger" for its new global strength. It has also become a more socially liberal country over the last 20 years or so—although it has to be said, Ireland is still a long way behind much of the western world over attitudes toward divorce, homosexuality, and abortion.

---

3 IRELAND IN POPULAR CULTURE

BOOKS
Fiction
Ireland is one of the most written-about places in the world. You've probably been reading about it all your life. If you're especially ambitious, you could bite off James Joyce's *Ulysses,* a classic to be certain, but a famously impenetrable one. Some Joycean classics that are a bit easier to dip into include *Dubliners,* a book of short stories about the titular city, and *A Portrait of the Artist as a Young Man.*

Dive into the absorbing books and plays of Brendan Behan by finding a copy of *Borstal Boy,* his breakthrough semi-autobiographical book about growing up as a member of the IRA. Also good is his play *Quare Fellow.*

If you're headed out into the Irish countryside, you might want to pick up a copy of W. B. Yeats's *Collected Poems,* since the view you're about to see is the same one that inspired him.

Of modern writers, among the best loved are Maeve Binchy *(Dublin 4),* J. P. Donleavy (whose book, *The Ginger Man,* about a drunken Trinity College student, was banned by the Catholic Church); Roddy Doyle (whose book *The Commitments,* about aspiring Irish musicians, became a top-grossing film); and Jennifer Johnston, who addressed the tension between Protestants and Catholics in *How Many Miles to Babylon?* There are also Edna O'Brien *(The Country Girls)* for bawdy laughs, Flann O'Brien *(At-Swim-Two-Birds)* for hilarious writing about writing, and Liam O'Flaherty, whose *The Informer* is a tense thriller about a veteran of the civil war.

Nonfiction
Two excellent books by Tim Pat Coogan, *The Irish Civil War* (Seven Dials, 2001) and *The Troubles: Ireland's Ordeal 1966–1996 and the Search for Peace* (National Book Network, 1997), are essential reading for anyone wanting to understand the complexities of 21st-century Ireland. For a look at modern Ireland, try John Ardagh's *Ireland and the Irish,* or F. S. Lyons's *Ireland Since the Famine.* To understand more about the famine, try Cecil Woodham-Smith's *The Great Hunger.* It's viewed as the definitive, dispassionate examination of what really happened.

FILM
Although lots of movies have been made about Ireland, not very many *good* movies have been made about Ireland. Here are a few exceptions. *Michael Collins* (Neil Jordan, 1996) is a fine biopic about the Irish rebel, filmed largely on location. *Maeve* (John Davis/Pat Murphy, 1982) is widely viewed as one of Ireland's first proper independent films. It addresses the lives of the

young amid sectarian violence. *Veronica Guerin* (Joel Schumacher, 2003) is a dark, fact-based film with Cate Blanchett about a troubled investigative reporter on the trail of a drugs boss. In a cheerier vein, *Wild About Harry* (2000) is a romantic comedy about a philandering TV host, while *Intermission* (2003) is a lively romance featuring Colin Farrell talking in his own accent. *The Commitments* (1990) may be the most famous Irish musical yet made, but *Once* (2007) is a touching, Oscar-winning portrait of two struggling young musicians busking on the streets of Dublin.

MUSIC

Music is inescapable in Ireland, and if you hear a band play in a bar and you like them, we strongly advise you to buy a CD from them, as you'll be happy you did when you get home. Here are a few top Irish bands you're not likely to see playing in a bar anytime soon. Damien Rice *(O)* did play in bars until he became a superstar a couple of years ago. The Irish folk singer Christy Moore *(Live at the Point)* is still widely viewed as one of the greatest ever. Barry McCormack has been winning accolades from critics for his *We Drank Our Tears.* David Kitt is one of Dublin's top songwriters, and you cannot go wrong with his *The Big Romance.* The Frames have been playing on the Dublin scene for years, and you can join their devoted followers by buying *Cost.* Finally, Adrian Crowley's *When You Are Here, You Are Family,* is a warm and delightful folksy album well worth having in your collection

4 EATING & DRINKING IN IRELAND

RESTAURANTS

Restaurants in Ireland have become surprisingly expensive in recent years, and it's getting harder to find good places that do not charge an average of €25 ($40) for a main course. On the plus side, restaurants are varied and interesting here—settings range from old-world hotel dining rooms, country mansions, and castles to sky-lit terraces, shop-front bistros, riverside cottages, thatched-roof pubs, and converted houses. Lately, appreciation has grown for creative cooking here, with an emphasis on locally grown produce and meat.

Before you book a table, here are a few things you should know.

RESERVATIONS Except for self-service eateries, informal cafes, and some popular seafood spots, most restaurants encourage reservations, and most expensive restaurants require them. In the most popular eateries, Friday and Saturday nights are often booked up a week or more in advance, so have a few options in mind if you're booking at the last minute and want to try out the hot spots in town.

Tip: If you stop into or phone a restaurant and find that it is booked from 8 or 8:30pm onward, ask if you can dine early (at 6:30 or 7pm), with a promise to leave by 8pm. You will sometimes get a table.

PRICES Meal prices at restaurants include taxes (13.5% VAT in the Republic of Ireland and a 17.5% VAT in Northern Ireland). Many restaurants include the tip as a service charge added automatically to the bill (it's usually listed at the bottom, just before the bill's total). It ranges from 10% to 15%, usually hovering around 12%. When no service charge is added, tip up to 15% depending on the quality of the service. But do check your bill, as some unscrupulous restaurants do not make it clear that you have actually already tipped, thus encouraging you to accidentally do so twice.

The price categories used in this book are based on the price of a complete

(Value) **Dining Bargains**

Restaurant prices in Ireland have gone up dramatically—in many cases by 20% to 25%—in recent years. Nobody is more aware of this than the Irish themselves, who are furious. Some people blame the price hikes on the changeover from the punt to the euro, some blame general inflation, and still others cite bald-faced greed on the part of restaurateurs. But there are some strategies you can use to keep your meal costs down.

If you want to try a top-rated restaurant but can't afford dinner, have your main meal there in the middle of the day by trying the set-lunch menu. You'll experience the same great cuisine at half the price of a nighttime meal.

Try an inexpensive lunch in a cafe or pub. Pub food is usually a lot better than its name suggests; the menu usually includes a mix of sandwiches and traditional Irish food, including stews and meat pies. In recent years, many pubs have converted or expanded into restaurants, serving excellent, unpretentious meals at (somewhat) reasonable prices.

dinner (or lunch, if dinner is not served) for one person, including tax and tip, but not wine or alcoholic beverages:

Very Expensive   €50 ($80) and up
Expensive   €35 to €50 ($56–$80)
Moderate   €17 to €34 ($27–$54)
Inexpensive   Under €17 ($27)

DINING TIPS   Don't be surprised if you are not ushered to your table as soon as you arrive at some upscale restaurants. This is not a delaying tactic—many of the better dining rooms carry on the old custom of seating you in a lounge while you sip an aperitif and peruse the menu. Your waiter then comes to discuss the choices and to take your order. You are not called to the table until the first course is about to be served. You are not under an obligation to have a cocktail, of course. It's perfectly fine to order a soft drink or sparkling water.

PUBS

The pub continues to be a mainstay of Irish social life. There are pubs in every city, town, and hamlet, on every street, and at every turn. Most people have a "local"—a favorite pub near home—where

they go for a drink and some conversation with neighbors, family, and friends. Pubs are not bars—they are more about socializing than drinking, and many people you see in the pub are just having a soft drink (lime and soda water is a particular favorite, or orange juice and lemonade). So feel free to go to the pub, even if you don't drink alcohol. It's a good way to meet locals.

PUB HOURS   The Republic of Ireland's drinking hours were extended a couple of years ago, a mere 2 centuries after they were introduced. Gone are the days when all pubs closed at 11pm. Now pubs set their own hours. Most close by midnight, but some stay open until 2am, and most stay open throughout the day (laws previously required pubs to close from 2–4pm). After normal pub hours, there are always nightclubs and discos, which stay open to the wee hours.

You'll notice that when the dreaded "closing time" comes, nobody clears out of the pub. That's because the term is a misnomer. The "closing time" is actually the time when the barmen must stop serving alcohol, so expect to hear a shout for "Last orders!" or, occasionally, the marvelous but antiquated "Time, gentlemen, please!" Anyone who wants to order his or her last drink does so at that point, and the bars don't actually shut their doors for another 20 to 30 minutes. When the time comes to really close, the bartenders will shout "Time to leave!" and people make their way to the doors.

In the North, the laws have also changed recently to allow them to stay open later, although most still close at 11pm on Monday to Thursday. On Friday and Saturday nights, many pubs stay open until midnight or 1am, and a few even later than that—particularly in large towns and cities.

3

Planning Your Trip to Ireland

Chances are you've been looking forward to your trip to Ireland for some time. You've probably set aside a significant amount of hard-earned cash; taken time off from work, school, or other commitments; and now want to make the most of your holiday. To accomplish that, you'll need to plan carefully.

The aim of this chapter is to provide you with the information you need, and to answer any questions you might have on lots of topics, including: When to go? How to get there? Should you book a tour or travel independently? What should you pack? How much will it cost? You'll find all the necessary resources, along with addresses, phone numbers, and websites here.

For additional help in planning your trip and for more on-the-ground resources in Ireland, please see the "Fast Facts, Toll-Free Numbers & Websites" appendix on p. 565.

1 VISITOR INFORMATION

When you're first getting started, contact your local offices of the Irish Tourist Board and the Northern Ireland Tourist Board. They are eager to answer your questions and have stacks of helpful information, mostly free of charge.

After you've perused the brochures, check the appropriate websites for more information.

IN THE UNITED STATES

• **Tourism Ireland,** 345 Park Ave., New York, NY 10154 (© **800/223-6470** in the U.S., or 212/418-0800; fax 212/371-9052; www.discoverireland.com/us).

IN CANADA

• **Tourism Ireland,** 2 Bloor St. W., Ste. 1501, Toronto, ON M4W 3E2 (© **800/223-6470** or 416/925-6368; fax 416/929-6783; www.discoverireland.com/ca-en).

IN THE UNITED KINGDOM

• **Tourism Ireland,** Nation's House, 103 Wigmore St., London W1U 1QS (© **020/7518-0800;** fax 020/7493-9065; www.discoverireland.com/gb).

IN AUSTRALIA

• **Tourism Ireland,** 36 Carrington St., 5th Level, Sydney, NSW 2000 (© **02/9299-6177;** fax 02/9299-6323; www.discoverireland.com/au).

IN NEW ZEALAND

• **Tourism Ireland,** Dingwall Building, Second Floor, 87 Queen St., Auckland (© **0064-9/379-8720;** fax 0064-9/302-2420; www.discoverireland.com/nz).

IN IRELAND

• **Tourist Board/Bord Fáilte,** Baggot Street Bridge, Dublin 2 (© **01/602-4000;** fax 01/602-4100; www.discoverireland.ie).

- **Northern Ireland Tourist Board,** 16 Nassau St., Dublin 2 (© **01/679-1977;** fax 01/679-1863; www.discovernorthern ireland.com).

IN NORTHERN IRELAND

- **Northern Ireland Tourist Board,** St. Anne's Court, 59 North St., Belfast BT1 1NB (© **028/9023-1221;** www. discovernorthernireland.com).

2 ENTRY REQUIREMENTS

PASSPORTS

For information on how to get a passport, see "Passports" in the "Fast Facts, Toll-Free Numbers & Websites" appendix at the end of this book—the websites listed provide downloadable passport applications as well as the current fees for processing passport applications. For an up-to-date, country-by-country listing of passport requirements around the world, go to the International Travel Web page of the U.S. State Department at http://travel.state.gov (click on the "International Travel for U.S. Citizens" link).

VISAS

For citizens of the United States, Canada, Australia, and New Zealand entering the Republic of Ireland for a stay of up to 3 months, no visa is necessary, but a valid passport is required.

For entry into Northern Ireland, the same conditions apply.

For citizens of the United Kingdom, when traveling on flights originating in Britain, the same rules apply as they would for travel to any other member state of the European Union (E.U.).

MEDICAL REQUIREMENTS

For information on medical requirements and recommendations, see "Health," p. 59.

CUSTOMS
What You Can Bring into Ireland

Ireland and Northern Ireland Customs are mainly concerned with two categories of goods: (1) items bought duty-paid and value-added-tax-paid (VAT-paid) in other E.U. countries and (2) goods bought under duty-free and VAT-free allowances at duty-free shops.

The first case normally applies to Irish citizens, visitors from Britain, and travelers from other E.U. countries. If the goods are for personal use, you won't need to pay additional duty or VAT. The limits for goods in this category are 800 cigarettes, 10 liters of spirits, 90 liters of wine, and 110 liters of beer.

The second category pertains primarily to overseas visitors, such as U.S. and Canadian citizens. The limit on duty-free and VAT-free items that may be brought into the E.U. for personal use is 200 cigarettes, 1 liter of liquor, 2 liters of wine, and other goods (including beer, gifts, and souvenirs) not exceeding the value of €175 ($280) per adult. You can enter Ireland with up to €10,000 ($16,000) of currency without needing to make a Customs declaration.

Regardless of whether you arrive in the Republic or Northern Ireland, the Customs system is the same, operating on a green, red, and blue format. If you're coming from the United States or another non-E.U. country, follow the green signs as long as you don't exceed the duty-free allowances, and the red signs if you have extra goods to declare. If you are like most visitors, bringing in only your own clothes and personal effects, use the Green Channel. The lanes marked with blue signs are for passengers with E.U. passports.

Cut to the Front of the Airport Security Line as a Registered Traveler

In 2003, the **Transportation Security Administration** (**TSA**; www.tsa.gov) approved a pilot program to help ease the time spent in line for airport security screenings. In exchange for information and a fee, persons can be prescreened as registered travelers, granting them a front-of-the-line position when they fly. The program (available only to U.S. citizens and permanent foreign residents in the U.S.) is run through private firms—the largest and most well known is Steven Brill's **Clear** (www.flyclear.com), and it works like this: Travelers complete an online application providing specific points of personal information including name, addresses for the previous 5 years, birth date, Social Security number, driver's license number, and a valid credit card (you're not charged the **$128 fee** until your application is approved). Print out the completed form and take it, along with proper ID, with you to an "enrollment station" (these can be found in 20 participating airports—with more to be added—and in a growing number of American Express offices around the country, for example). It's at this point where it gets seemingly sci-fi. At the enrollment station, a Clear representative will record your biometrics necessary for clearance; in this case, your fingerprints and your irises will be digitally recorded.

Once your application has been screened against no-fly lists, outstanding warrants, and other security measures, you'll be issued a clear plastic card that holds a chip containing your information. Each time you fly through participating airports (and the numbers are steadily growing), go to the Clear pass station located next to the standard TSA screening line. Here you'll insert your card into a slot and place your finger on a scanner to read your print—when the information matches up, you're cleared to cut to the front of the security line. You'll still have to follow all the procedures of the day like removing your shoes and walking through the X-ray machine, but Clear promises to cut 30 minutes off your wait time at the airport.

In addition to your luggage, you may bring in sports equipment for your own recreational use or electronic equipment for your own business or professional use. Prohibited goods include firearms, ammunition, and explosives; narcotics; meat, poultry, plants, and their byproducts; and domestic animals from outside the United Kingdom.

What You Can Take Home from Ireland:
U.S. Citizens

Onboard the flight back to the United States, you'll be given a Customs declaration to fill out. Returning **U.S. citizens** who have been away for at least 48 hours are allowed to bring back, once every 30 days, $800 worth of merchandise duty-free. You'll be charged a flat rate of duty on the next $1,000 worth of purchases. Any dollar amount beyond that is dutiable at whatever rates apply. On mailed gifts, the duty-free limit is $200. Be sure to have your receipts or purchases handy to expedite the declaration process. *Note:* If you owe duty, you are required to pay on your arrival in the United States, either by cash, personal check, government or traveler's check, or money order, and in some locations, a Visa or MasterCard.

To avoid having to pay duty on foreign-made personal items you owned before you left on your trip, bring along a bill of sale, insurance policy, jeweler's appraisal, or receipts of purchase. Or you can register items—think laptop computers, cameras, and CD players—with Customs before you leave. Take the items to any Customs office or register them with Customs at the airport from which you're departing. You'll receive, at no cost, a certificate of registration, which allows duty-free entry for the life of the item.

With some exceptions, you cannot bring fresh fruits and vegetables into the United States. For specifics on what you can bring back and corresponding fees, download the invaluable free pamphlet *Know Before You Go* online at **www.cbp. gov.** (Click on "Travel," and then click on "Know Before You Go.") Or contact the **U.S. Customs & Border Protection (CBP),** 1300 Pennsylvania Ave. NW, Washington, DC 20229 (✆ **877/287-8667**) and request the pamphlet.

Canadian Citizens

For a clear summary of Canadian rules, write for the booklet *I Declare,* issued by the **Canada Border Services Agency** (✆ **800/461-9999** in Canada, or 204/983-3500; www.cbsa-asfc.gc.ca). Canada allows its citizens a C$750 exemption and you're allowed to bring back duty-free 1 carton of cigarettes, 1 can of tobacco, 40 imperial ounces of liquor, 200 cigarettes, and 50 cigars per adult. In addition, you're allowed to mail gifts to Canada valued at less than C$60 once a day, provided they're unsolicited and don't contain alcohol or tobacco (write on the package "Unsolicited gift, under $60 value"). All valuables should be declared on the Y-38 form before departure from Canada, including serial numbers of valuables you already own, such as expensive foreign

cameras. *Note:* The C$750 exemption can only be used once a year and only after an absence of 7 days.

U.K. Citizens

Citizens of the U.K. who are **returning from a European Union (E.U.) country** will go through a separate Customs exit (called the "Blue Exit"). In essence, there is no limit on what you can bring back from an E.U. country, as long as the items are for personal use (this includes gifts), and you have already paid the necessary duty and tax. However, Customs law sets out guidance levels. If you bring in more than these levels, you may be asked to prove that the goods are for your own use. Guidance levels on goods bought in the E.U. for your own use are 3,200 cigarettes, 200 cigars, 400 cigarillos, 3 kilograms of smoking tobacco, 10 liters of spirits, 90 liters of wine, 20 liters of fortified wine (such as port or sherry), and 110 liters of beer. For information, contact **HM Customs & Excise** at ✆ **0845/010-9000** in the U.K., or 020/8929-0152, or consult their website at www.hmce.gov.uk.

Australian Citizens

The duty-free allowance in **Australia** is A$900 or, for those 17 and under, A$450 (including gifts given to you or intended for others). Citizens can bring in 250 cigarettes or 250 grams of loose tobacco, and 2.25 liters of alcohol. If you're returning with valuables you already own, such as foreign-made cameras, you should file form B263. A helpful brochure available from Australian consulates or Customs offices is *Know Before You Go.* For more information, call the **Australian Customs Service** at ✆ **1300/363-263,** or log on to www.customs.gov.au.

New Zealand Citizens

The duty-free allowance for **New Zealand** is NZ$700. Citizens 18 and over can bring in 200 cigarettes, 50 cigars, or 250 grams of tobacco (or a mixture of all three if their combined weight doesn't exceed

250g); plus 4.5 liters of wine and beer, or 1.125 liters of liquor. New Zealand currency does not carry import or export restrictions. Fill out a certificate of export, listing the valuables you are taking out of the country; that way, you can bring them back without paying duty. Most questions are answered in a free pamphlet available at New Zealand consulates and Customs offices: *New Zealand Customs Guide for Travellers, Notice no. 4.* For more information, contact **New Zealand Customs,** the Customhouse, 17–21 Whitmore St., Box 2218, Wellington (© **04/473-6099** or 0800/428-786; www.customs.govt.nz).

3 WHEN TO GO

WEATHER

In Ireland you will often hear the phrase, "Today we can expect showers, followed by periods of rain." In fact, rain is the one constant in Irish weather, although a bit of sunshine is usually just around the corner. The best of times and the worst of times are often only hours, or minutes, apart. It can be quite chilly when it rains, even in the summer, so think *layers* when you dress to travel.

Winters can be brutal, as the wind blows in off the Atlantic with numbing constancy, and gales are common. But deep snow is rare, and temperatures rarely drop much below freezing. In fact, Ireland is a fairly temperate place: January and February bring frosts but seldom snow, and July and August are very warm, but rarely hot. The Irish consider any temperature over 68°F (20°C) to be "roasting," and below 34°F (1°C) as bone chilling. For a complete online guide to Irish weather, consult **www.ireland.com/weather**.

Average Monthly Temperatures in Dublin

	Jan	Feb	Mar	Apr	May	June	July	Aug	Sept	Oct	Nov	Dec
Temp (°F)	36–46	37–48	37–49	38–52	42–57	46–62	51–66	50–65	48–62	44–56	39–49	38–47
Temp (°C)	2–8	3–9	3–9	3–11	6–14	8–17	11–19	10–18	9–17	7–13	4–9	3–8

HIGH & LOW SEASONS

A visit to Ireland in the summer and in the winter are two different things. Apart from climatic considerations, there are the issues of cost, closures, and crowds.

Generally speaking, in summer, transatlantic airfares, car-rental rates, and hotel prices are highest and crowds at their most intense. But the days are long (6am sunrises and 10pm sunsets), the weather is warm, and every sightseeing attraction and B&B is open.

In winter, you can get rock-bottom prices on airfare and hotels, especially if you book a package through a good travel agent or Aer Lingus (see "Getting There & Getting Around," later in this chapter).

But it will rain and the wind will blow, and many rural sights and a fair proportion of the rural B&Bs and restaurants will be closed.

All things considered, the best time to visit is in spring and fall, when weather falls in between bad and good, but you get lower-than-high-season prices and the crowds have yet to descend.

HOLIDAYS

The Republic observes the following national holidays: New Year's Day (Jan 1), St. Patrick's Day (Mar 17), Easter Monday (variable), May Day (May 1), first Mondays in June and August (summer bank holidays), last Monday in October (autumn bank holiday), Christmas (Dec

25), and St. Stephen's Day (Dec 26). Good Friday (the Fri before Easter) is mostly observed, but not statutory.

In the North, the schedule of holidays is the same as in the Republic, with some exceptions: the North's summer bank holidays fall on the last Mondays of May and August; the Battle of the Boyne is celebrated on Orangeman's Day (July 12); and Boxing Day (Dec 26) follows Christmas.

In both Ireland and Northern Ireland, holidays that fall on weekends are celebrated the following Monday.

IRELAND CALENDAR OF EVENTS

This sampling of events is drawn from 2008 schedules. Many events had not set their 2009 dates at the time this book is being written. The most up-to-date listings of events can be found at **www.discoverireland.ie** and **www.entertainment.ie** for Ireland, and **www.eventguide.ie** and **www.visitdublin.com** for Dublin.

JANUARY

Funderland. Royal Dublin Society, Ballsbridge, Dublin 4. An annual indoor funfair, complete with white-knuckle rides, carnival stalls, and family entertainment (✆ 061/419988; www.funfair.ie). December/January.

Yeats Winter School. Sligo Park Hotel, Sligo Town. This event offers a weekend of relaxation, lectures, and a tour of Yeats Country (✆ 071/42693; fax 071/42780; www.yeats-sligo.com). Late January.

FEBRUARY

Six Nations Rugby Tournament. Lansdowne Road, Ballsbridge, County Dublin. This annual international tourney includes Ireland, England, Scotland, Wales, France, and Italy—and it's coming here in 2009. Big games scheduled at this writing include Ireland versus France on February 7 and Ireland versus England on February 28. It's a brilliant atmosphere, be it at Lansdowne Road or a neighborhood pub. Contact **Irish Rugby Football Union,** 10–12 Lansdowne Rd., Dublin 4 (✆ 01/647-3800; fax 01/647-3801; wwwirishrugby.ie). Early February to April.

Dublin International Film Festival. Irish Film Centre, Temple Bar, Dublin 2, and various cinemas in Dublin. More than 100 films are featured, with screenings of the best in Irish and world cinema, plus seminars and lectures on filmmaking (✆ 01/672-8861; www.dubliniff.com). Late February.

MARCH

St. Patrick's Dublin Festival. Held around St. Patrick's Day itself, this massive 4-day festival is open, free, and accessible to everyone. Street theater, carnival acts, sports, music, fireworks, and other festivities culminate in Ireland's grandest parade, with marching bands, drill teams, floats, and delegations from around the world (✆ 01/676-3205; fax 01/676-3208; www.stpatricksday.ie). On and around March 17.

St. Patrick's Day Parades. In celebration of Ireland's patron saint. All over Ireland, north and south. March 17.

Samhlaíocht Chiarrai/Kerry Arts Festival. A spring festival of music, drama, film, dance, literature, craft, and visual art (✆ 066/712-9934; fax 066/712-0934; www.samhlaiocht.com). March/April.

APRIL

Pan Celtic Festival. County Donegal. For 5 days, the wider Celtic family (including Cornwall, Isle of Man, Scotland, Wales, and Brittany) unites for culture, song, dance, sports, and parades with marching bands and pipers. There are also lots of fringe events, from

nature walks to poetry readings (www.
panceltic.ie). March/April.

World Irish Dancing Championships.
Waterfront Hotel, Belfast. The premier
international competition in Irish dancing features more than 4,000 contend-
ers from as far away as New Zealand
(℮ **01/475-2220;** fax 01/475-1053;
www.clrg.ie). April.

MAY

County Wicklow Gardens Festival. In
the county known as the "garden of
Ireland," stately heritage properties and
gardens open their gates to visitors on
selected dates. Contact Wicklow County
Tourism (℮ **0404/20070;** www.visit
wicklow.ie). Entire summer, starting in
May.

Wicklow Arts Festival. The county's
other big offering in May, held over 5
days in Wicklow Town. There are dozens of music, theater, art, and literary
events, many of which are free (www.
wicklowartsfestival.ie). Early May.

Belfast City Marathon. An epic 42km
(26-mile) race of 6,000 international
runners through the city. It starts and
finishes at Mayfield Leisure Centre
(℮ **028/9060-5944;** www.belfastcity
marathon.com). Early May.

May Day Races. Down Royal Racecourse, Maze, Lisburn, County Antrim.
One of the major events on the horse-
racing calendar (℮ **028/9262-1256;**
www.downroyal.com). Early May.

Diversions Temple Bar. Dublin 2. This
is an all-free, all-outdoor, all-ages cultural program, featuring a combination
of day and night performances in dance,
film, theater, music, and visual arts.
Beginning in May and lasting throughout summer, the Diversions program
includes live music, open-air films,
and a circus (℮ **01/677-2255;** fax 01/
677-2525; www.temple-bar.ie). May to
August.

Waterford Maritime Festival. Quays
of Waterford City. The highlight of this
4-day celebration over the June bank
holiday weekend is an international
round-trip powerboat race from Waterford to Swansea, Wales. Other events
include close-to-shore kayak races,
open-air concerts, and family entertainment. Representatives from Irish, British, French, and Dutch naval fleets sail
in Waterford Harbour (℮ **051/873511**).
Late May/early June.

**Murphy's Cat Laughs Comedy Festi-
val.** Various venues in Kilkenny Town.
Past performers at this international
festival of stand-up comedy include
American comics Bill Murray, George
Wendt, and Emo Phillips, and Ireland's
Ardal O'Hanlon (℮ **056/776-3837;**
www.thecatlaughs.com). Late May/early
June.

Music Festival in Great Irish Houses.
Various venues throughout counties
Dublin, Wicklow, and Kildare. This
10-day festival of classical music performed by leading Irish and world-
renowned international artists is
intimately set in the receiving rooms of
stately buildings and mansions (℮/fax
01/664-2822; www.musicgreatirish
houses.com). Early June.

Taste of Ireland. Iveagh Gardens, Dublin. Visitors to this 4-day celebration of
all things food-related can sample dishes
prepared by some of the country's top
chefs. It's best to book in advance as the
event is usually a sellout—and consider
wearing elastic pants (℮ **01/210-9290;**
fax 01/288-0379; www.tastefestivals.ie).
Mid-June.

Bloomsday Festival. Various venues in
Dublin. This unique day of festivity
celebrates Leopold Bloom, the central
character of James Joyce's *Ulysses.* Every
aspect of the city, including the menus
at restaurants and pubs, duplicates the

aromas, sights, sounds, and tastes of Joyce's fictitious Dublin on June 16, 1904, the day when all of the action in *Ulysses* takes place. Ceremonies are held at the James Joyce Tower and Museum, and there are guided walks of Joycean sights. Contact the James Joyce Centre, 35 N. Great George's St., Dublin 1 (✆ **01/ 878-8547;** fax 01/878-8488; www. jamesjoyce.ie). June 16.

Cork Midsummer Arts Festival. Emmet Place, Cork City. The program includes musical performances and traditional Irish *céilí* bands, and always has a strong literary content. Bonfire nights are particularly popular (✆ **021/421-5131;** fax 021/421-5193; www.corkfestival. com). Mid-June to early July.

Killarney SummerFest. Fitzgerald Stadium, Killarney, County Kerry. This (mainly rock) music festival gets bigger every year and is one of the highlights of the Irish summer of music. Past performers have included Bryan Adams and Sheryl Crow. Fringe events include street entertainment and art workshops (✆ **064/71560;** www.killarneysummer fest.com). June/July.

Dubai Duty Free Irish Derby. The Curragh, County Kildare. It's one of the richest horse races in Europe, and widely accepted as the definitive European middle-distance classic. This is Ireland's version of the Kentucky Derby or Royal Ascot and is a fashionable gathering (**hint:** jackets for men, posh hats for women) of racing fans from all over the world. Booking recommended (✆ **045/ 441205;** fax 045/441442). June 28.

JULY

Battle of the Boyne Commemoration. Belfast and other cities. This annual event, often called Orangeman's Day, recalls the historic battle between two 17th-century kings. It's a national day of parades by Protestants all over Northern Ireland. Contact the House of

Orange, 65 Dublin Rd., Belfast BT2 7HE (✆ **028/9032-2801**). July 12.

Oxegen. Punchestown Racecourse, County Kildare. This (mainly rock) music festival is now one of Europe's premier summer music fests, with nearly 100 acts playing on five stages over the duration of a weekend. Previous headliners have included Coldplay and Counting Crows. For tickets, contact **www.ticketmaster.ie** or **www. oxegen.ie.** Early July.

Galway Arts Festival and Races. Galway City and Racecourse. This 2-week fest is a shining star on the Irish arts scene, featuring international theater, big-top concerts, literary evenings, street shows, arts, parades, music, and more. The famous Galway Races follow, with 5 more days of racing and merriment, music, and song (✆ **091/ 566577;** fax 091/562655; www.galway artsfestival.ie). Mid- to late July.

Lughnasa Fair. Carrickfergus Castle, County Antrim. A spectacular revival with a 12th-century Norman castle and its grounds, this event features people in period costumes, medieval games, traditional food, entertainment, and crafts (✆ **028/4336-6455**). Late July.

AUGUST

Fáilte Ireland Horse Show. RDS Showgrounds, Ballsbridge, Dublin 4. This is the most important equestrian and social event on the Irish national calendar. Aside from the dressage and jumping competitions each day, highlights include a fashionable ladies' day, formal hunt balls each evening, and the awarding of the Aga Khan Trophy and the Nation's Cup (✆ **01/668-0866;** fax 01/ 660-4014; www.dublinhorseshow.ie or www.rds.ie). Early August.

Kilkenny Arts Festival. Kilkenny Town. This weeklong event has it all, from classical and traditional music to plays, one-person shows, readings, films, poetry, and art exhibitions (© **056/775-2175;** fax 056/775-1704; www.kilkenny arts.ie). August.

Puck Fair. Killorglin, County Kerry. Each year the residents of this tiny Ring of Kerry town capture a wild goat and enthrone it as "king" over 3 days of merrymaking that include open-air concerts, horse fairs, parades, and fireworks. This is one of Ireland's oldest festivals (©/fax **066/976-2366;** www. puckfair.ie). Early August.

Rose of Tralee International Festival. Tralee, County Kerry. A gala atmosphere prevails at this 5-day event, with a full program of concerts, street entertainment, horse races, and a beauty-and-talent pageant leading up to the televised selection of the "Rose of Tralee" (© **066/712-1322;** fax 066/22654; http://roseoftralee.ie). Late August.

Lisdoonvarna Matchmaking Festival. Lisdoonvarna, County Clare. Still the biggest and best singles' event after all these years, this traditional "bachelor" festival carries on in the lovely spa town of Lisdoonvarna, with lots of wonderful music and dance (© **065/707-4005;** fax 065/707-4406; www.matchmaker ireland.com). August/September.

SEPTEMBER

National Heritage Week. More than 400 events are held throughout the country—walks, lectures, exhibitions, music recitals, and more (© **01/647-2455;** www.heritageireland.ie). Early September.

All-Ireland Hurling and Gaelic Football Finals. Croke Park, Dublin 3. The finals of Ireland's most beloved sports, hurling and Gaelic football, are Ireland's equivalent of the Super Bowl. If you can't be at Croke Park, experience this in the full bonhomie of a pub. You can find information at www.gaa.ie, or obtain tickets through Ticketmaster at

www.ticketmaster.ie (© **01/836-3222;** fax 01/836-6420). September.

Fleadh Cheoil na hÉireann. Tullamore, County Offaly. This has been Ireland's premier summer festival of traditional music since 1951, with competitions held to select the all-Ireland champions in all categories of instruments and singing (© **057/932-5704;** fax 057/932-5706; www.fleadh2009. com). Late August/early September.

International Puppet Festival. Lambert Puppet Theatre, Monkstown, County Dublin. (© **01/280-0974;** fax 01/280-4772; www.lambertpuppet theatre.com). Mid-September.

Irish Antique Dealers' Fair. RDS Showgrounds, Ballsbridge, Dublin 4. Ireland's premier annual antiques fair, with hundreds of dealers from all over the island (© **01/679-4147;** www.iada. ie). Late September.

Galway International Oyster Festival. Galway and environs. Find out why London's *Sunday Times* put it on its "Top 12 World's Best Event List." A haven for oyster aficionados from across the globe, its highlights include the World Oyster Opening Championship, a golf tournament, a yacht race, an art exhibition, a gala banquet, traditional music, and, of course, lots of oyster eating (© **091/ 522066;** fax 091/527282; www.galway oysterfest.com). Late September.

Dublin Theatre Festival. Theaters throughout Dublin. Showcases for new plays by every major Irish company (including the Abbey and the Gate), plus a range of productions from abroad (© **01/677-8899;** fax 01/679-7709; www.dublintheatrefestival.com). Late September to mid-October.

OCTOBER

Kinsale International Gourmet Festival. Kinsale, County Cork. The foodie capital of Ireland hosts this well-respected annual fest, featuring special menus in all the restaurants and plenty of star chefs in town from abroad. Tickets may be purchased from **Maria O Mahony Finishing Services** (© 021/477-3571) or online at www.kinsalerestaurants. com. October.

Murphy's Cork International Film Festival. Cinemas throughout Cork. Ireland's oldest and biggest film festival offers a plethora of international features, documentaries, short films, and special programs (© 021/427-1711; fax 021/427-5945; www.corkfilmfest. org). Mid-October.

Baboró International Arts Festival for Children. Galway. A fun-filled, educational festival geared to kids 3 to 12 years of age, with theater, music, dance, museum exhibitions, and literary events (© 091/562667; fax 091/562642; www.baboro.ie). Late October.

Wexford Festival Opera. Theatre Royal, Wexford City. Now in its 55th year, this is not your average stuffy opera festival. Famous as much for the jubilant, informal atmosphere as for the acclaimed productions of lesser known 18th- and 19th-century operatic masterpieces, the festival also offers classical music concerts, recitals, and more (© 053/912-2144; www.wexfordopera. com). Late October/early November.

Guinness Cork Jazz Festival. Cork City. Ireland's number-two city stages a first-rate festival of jazz, with an international lineup of live acts playing in hotels, concert halls, and pubs (© 021/427-8979; fax 021/427-0463; www. corkjazzfestival.com). Late October.

Kinsale Jazz Festival. Meanwhile, not to be outdone, nearby Kinsale plays host to its own concurrent fringe jazz festival (© 021/477-2234; www.kinsale.ie/ kinsjazz.htm). Late October.

Belfast Festival at Queens. Queens University, Belfast. Ireland's largest arts festival attracts enormous crowds each year for its stellar program of drama, opera, music, and film (© 028/9097-1197; fax 028/9066-5577; www.belfast festival.com). There's also a concurrent fringe festival in the Cathedral Quarter (© 028/9027-0466). October/November.

Dublin City Marathon. On the last Monday in October, more than 5,000 runners from both sides of the Atlantic and the Irish Sea participate in this popular run through the streets of the capital (© 01/623-2250; www.dublin citymarathon.ie). Late October.

DECEMBER

Limerick Christmas Racing Festival. Limerick Racecourse, Greenpark, Limerick. Four days of holiday horse racing (© 061/320000; fax 061/355766; www.limerick-racecourse.com). Late December.

Woodford Mummers Feile. Woodford, County Galway. This festival offers traditional music, song, dance, and mime performed in period costume. A formal competition is held on the second day (© 0509/49248). Late December.

Leopardstown National Hunt Festival. Leopardstown Racecourse, Foxrock, Dublin 18. This festival offers 3 days of winter racing for thoroughbreds (© 01/289-0500; www.leopardstown. com). Late December.

For an exhaustive list of events beyond those listed here, check http://events. frommers.com, where you'll find a searchable, up-to-the-minute roster of what's happening in cities all over the world.

4 GETTING THERE & GETTING AROUND

GETTING TO IRELAND

By Plane

About half of all visitors from North America arrive in Ireland on direct transatlantic flights to **Dublin Airport** (© 1/ 814-1111; www.dublinairport.com), **Shannon Airport** (© 061/712000; www. shannonairport.com), or **Belfast International Airport** (© 028/9448-4848; www. belfastairport.com). The other half fly first into Britain or Europe, then "backtrack" into Ireland by air or sea.

In the Republic, there are seven smaller regional airports, all of which offer service to Dublin and several of which receive some European traffic. They are Cork, Donegal, Galway, Kerry, Knock, Sligo, and Waterford. In Northern Ireland, the secondary airports are Belfast City Airport and Derry City Airport. Services and schedules are always subject to change, so be sure to consult your preferred airline or travel agent as soon as you begin to sketch your itinerary. The routes and carriers listed below are provided to suggest the range of possibilities for air travel to Ireland.

From the United States & Canada

The Irish national carrier, **Aer Lingus** (© 800/474-7424 in the U.S., or 0818/ 365-000 in Ireland; www.aerlingus.ie) provides transatlantic flights to Ireland with scheduled, nonstop flights from New York (JFK), Boston, Chicago, Los Angeles, and Baltimore to Dublin, Shannon, and Belfast international airports.

American Airlines (© 800/433-7300; www.aa.com) flies directly from New York (JFK), Boston, and Chicago to Dublin and Shannon. **Delta Airlines** (© 800/ 241-4141; www.delta.com) flies directly from Atlanta and New York (JFK) to Dublin and Shannon. **Continental Airlines** (© 800/231-0856; www.continental.

com) offers nonstop service to Dublin, Shannon, and Belfast from Newark.

From Canada, **Air Canada** (© 888/ 247-2262 in the U.S. and Canada, or 0180/ 070-0900 in Ireland; www.aircanada.com) runs frequent direct flights to Dublin from major Canadian cities.

It's possible to save money by booking your air tickets through a consolidator (also known as a bucket shop) who works with the airlines to sell off their unsold air tickets at a cut price. But note that the savings generally range from minuscule in the high season to substantial in the off season. **UK Air** (© 888/577-2900; www. ukair.com) sells tickets to Britain, Ireland, and the rest of Europe on regular Delta, British Airways, and Continental flights.

From London

The London-Dublin and London-Shannon routes are two of the busiest flight paths in Europe, and competition is stiff— which means that you can often get a fantastic deal.

The following carriers offer direct flights from London: **British Airways** (© 800/247-9297 in the U.S., or 087/ 085-9850 in Britain; www.ba.com); **Aer Lingus** (© 800/474-7424 in the U.S., or 0818/365-000 in Ireland; www.aerlingus. ie); **bmibaby** (© 800/788-0555 in the U.S., or 01/242-0794 in Ireland; www. bmibaby.com); **CityJet** (© 01/605-0383 in Ireland, or 0870/142-4343 in Britain; www.cityjet.com); and **Ryanair** (© 0818/ 30-30-30 in Ireland; 0871/246-0000 in Britain; www.ryanair.com).

British Airways flies directly from Britain to Belfast.

From the Continent

Major direct flights into Dublin from the Continent include service from Amsterdam on **KLM** (© 800/374-7747 in the U.S.; www.klm.com); Madrid and Barcelona on **Iberia** (© 800/772-4642 in the

U.S.; www.iberia.com); Brussels on **Ryanair** (www.ryanair.com); Copenhagen on **Aer Lingus** and **SAS** (© **800/221-2350** in the U.S.; www.scandinavian.net); Frankfurt on **Aer Lingus** and **Lufthansa** (© **800/645-3880** in the U.S.; www.lufthansa.com); Paris on **Aer Lingus** and **Air France** (© **800/237-2747** in the U.S.; www.airfrance.com); Prague on **CSA Czech Airlines** (© **1800/223-2365** in the U.S.; http://usa.czechairlines.com); and Rome on **Aer Lingus.**

Quite recently, **Cork Airport** (© **021/ 431-3131;** www.cork-airport.com) passed Shannon to become the second-ranked airport in Ireland, though it offers no nonstop transatlantic service. **Aer Lingus, KLM,** and **Ryanair** are among the airlines flying into Cork from Great Britain and the Continent (see above for their contact info). Direct service to Shannon from the Continent includes **Aer Lingus** from Düsseldorf, Frankfurt, Paris, and Zurich.

There are no direct flights from New Zealand or Australia to Ireland; if you're coming from there, you'll most probably transfer in London.

Staying Comfortable on Long-Haul Flights

- Your choice of airline and airplane will definitely affect your legroom. Find more details about U.S. airlines at **www.seatguru.com**. For international airlines, the research firm Skytrax has posted a list of average seat pitches at **www.airlinequality.com**.

- Emergency exit seats and bulkhead seats typically have the most legroom. Emergency exit seats are usually left unassigned until the day of a flight (to ensure that someone able-bodied fills the seats); it's worth checking in online at home (if the airline offers that option) or getting to the ticket counter early to snag one of these spots for a long flight. Many passengers find that bulkhead seating offers more legroom, but keep in mind that bulkhead seats have no storage space on the floor in front of you.

- To have two seats for yourself in a three-seat row, try for an aisle seat in a center section toward the back of coach. If you're traveling with a companion, book an aisle and a window seat. Middle seats are usually booked last, so chances are good you'll end up with three seats to yourselves. And in the event that a third passenger is assigned the middle seat, he or she will probably be more than happy to trade for a window or an aisle.

- To sleep, avoid the last row of any section or the row in front of an emergency exit, as these seats are the least likely to recline. Avoid seats near highly trafficked toilet areas. Avoid seats in the back of many jets—these can be narrower than those in the rest of coach. Or reserve a window seat so you can rest your head and avoid being bumped in the aisle.

- Get up, walk around, and stretch every 60 to 90 minutes to keep your blood flowing. This helps avoid **deep vein thrombosis,** or "economy-class syndrome." See the box "Avoiding 'Economy-Class Syndrome,'" p. 60.

- Drink water before, during, and after your flight to combat the lack of humidity in airplane cabins. Avoid caffeine and alcohol, which will dehydrate you.

By Ferry

If you're traveling to Ireland from Britain or the Continent, especially if you're behind the wheel of a car, a ferry can get you there. Several car and passenger ferries offer reasonably comfortable furnishings, cabin berths (for longer crossings), restaurants, duty-free shopping, and lounges.

Prices fluctuate seasonally and depend on your route, your time of travel, and whether you're on foot or in a car. It's best to check with your travel agent for up-to-date details, but just to give you an idea,

(Tips) Coping with Jet Lag

Jet lag is a pitfall of traveling across time zones. If you're flying north-south and you feel sluggish when you touch down, your symptoms will be the result of dehydration and the general stress of air travel. When you travel east-west or vice versa, your body becomes confused about what time it is, and everything from your digestive system to your brain is knocked for a loop. Traveling east is more difficult on your internal clock than traveling west because most peoples' bodies are more inclined to stay up late than to fall asleep early.

Here are some tips for combating jet lag:

- **Reset your watch** to your destination time before you board the plane.
- **Drink lots of water** before, during, and after your flight. Avoid alcohol.
- **Exercise and sleep well** for a few days before your trip.
- If you have trouble sleeping on planes, **fly eastward on morning flights.**
- **Daylight** is the key to resetting your body clock. At the website for **Outside In** (www.bodyclock.com), you can get a customized plan of when to seek and avoid light.

the lowest one-way adult fare in high season on the cruise ferry from Holyhead to Dublin starts at around €30 ($48). Add your car, and the grand total could be four or five times that. The Irish Sea has a reputation for rough crossings, so it's always a good idea to consider an over-the-counter pill or patch to guard against seasickness. (Be sure to take any pills *before* you set out; once you're underway, it's generally too late.)

The websites given below have regularly updated schedules and prices.

From Britain

Irish Ferries operates from Holyhead, Wales, to Dublin, and from Pembroke, Wales, to Rosslare, County Wexford. For reservations, call **Scots-American Travel** (© 800/247-7268 in the U.S.; www.scotsamerican.com) or **Irish Ferries** (© 0870/517-1717 in the U.K., 0818/300-400 in the Republic of Ireland, or 00353/818-300-400 in Northern Ireland; www.irishferries.com). **Stena Line** (© 01/204-7777; www.stenaline.com) sails from Holyhead to Dùn Laoghaire, 13km (8 miles) south of Dublin; from Fishguard, Wales, to Rosslare; and from Stranraer, Scotland, to Belfast, Northern Ireland.

Brittany Ferries (© 021/427-7801 in Cork; www.brittany-ferries.com) operates from Holyhead to Dublin; from Fishguard and Pembroke to Rosslare; and from Stranraer to Belfast. **P&O Irish Sea Ferries** (© 561/563-2856 in the U.S., 0870/242-4777 in Britain, or 01/638-3333 in Ireland; www.poirishsea.com) operates from Liverpool to Dublin and from Cairnryan, Scotland, to Larne, County Antrim, Northern Ireland.

From Continental Europe

Destinations are changeable, but at the moment **Irish Ferries** sails from Roscoff and Cherbourg, France, to Rosslare. For reservations, call Scots-American Travel (© 800/247-7268 in the U.S.; www.scotsamerican.com) or **Irish Ferries** (© 0870/517-1717 in the U.K., 0818/300-400 in the Republic of Ireland, or 00353/818-300-400 in Northern Ireland; www.irishferries.com). **P&O Irish Sea Ferries** (© 561/563-2856 in the U.S., 0870/242-4777 in Britain, or 01/638-3333 in Ireland, www.poirishsea.com) operates from Cherbourg, France, to Rosslare. **Brittany Ferries** (© 021/427-7801 in Cork; www.brittany-ferries.com) connects Roscoff, France, to Cork.

Note to Eurailpass holders: Because Irish Ferries is a member of the Eurail system, you can travel free between Rosslare and Roscoff or Cherbourg.

GETTING AROUND
By Plane
Because Ireland is such a small country, it's unlikely you'll be flying from place to place. If you do need to get somewhere very quickly, the main domestic carrier is **Aer Arann** (© 011/353-81821-0210 in the U.S., 818/210-210 in Ireland, or 0800/587-23-24 in the U.K.; www.aer arann.com). It operates flights between Dublin and Belfast, Cork, Derry, Donegal, Galway, Kerry, Knock, and Sligo, as well as from Galway to the Aran Islands.

By Car
Although Ireland has a reasonably extensive network of public transportation, there are advantages to having your own car. Mainly, you'll be unhampered by imposed schedules and have the freedom to explore anywhere serendipity leads you—a real plus in a country like Ireland, where small-town doings can be the highlight of your day, or even of your entire trip. In a nutshell, if you want to see the "real Ireland" outside the major cities, you'll want a car.

The disadvantages begin with the cost of rental and continue with each refueling. In high season, weekly rental rates on a manual-transmission compact vehicle begin at around $250 (and that's if you've shopped around) and ascend steeply—but it's at the pump that you're likely to go into shock. Irish gas prices can be triple what you pay in the United States. And while Ireland is a tiny country by comparison, and distances between places are relatively short, the roads in the countryside can be so narrow and winding that getting from A to B can take considerably longer than it looks.

Another potential pitfall is that rental cars in Ireland are almost always equipped with standard transmissions—you can rent an automatic, but it will cost substantially more (about $200 per week). Driving on the left side of the road and shifting gears with your left hand can take some getting used to. Then consider that another fact of life in Ireland is cramped roads. Even the major Irish motorways are surprisingly narrow, with lanes made for the tiniest cars—just the kind you'll wish you had rented once you're underway. Off the motorways, it's rare to find a road with a hard shoulder—leaving little maneuvering space when a bus or truck is coming from the opposite direction. So think small when you pick out your rental car. The choice is yours: room in the car or room on the road.

Unless your stay in Ireland extends beyond 6 months, your own valid U.S. or Canadian driver's license (provided you've had it for at least 6 months) is all you need to drive in Ireland. Rules and restrictions for car rental vary slightly and correspond roughly to those in the United States, with two important distinctions. Most rental-car agencies in the Republic won't rent to you (1) if you're 24 and under or 75 and over (there's no upper age limit in the North) or (2) if your license has been valid for less than a year.

Note: Double-check your credit card's policy on picking up the insurance on rental cars. Almost none of the American-issued cards—including gold cards—cover the collision damage waiver (CDW) on car rentals in Ireland anymore.

Driving Laws, Tips & Warnings
Highway safety has become a critical issue in Ireland during the past several years. The number of highway fatalities is shocking for such a small nation, and Ireland is ranked as the second-most dangerous country in Europe in which to drive (second only to Greece). In the past year, the Irish government has initiated a penalty

Road Rules in a Nutshell

1. Drive on the left side of the road.
2. Road signs are in kilometers, except in Northern Ireland, where they are in miles.
3. On motorways, the left lane is the traveling lane. The right lane is for passing (though many drivers just use it as the "fast lane").
4. Everyone must wear a seat belt by law. Children must be in age-appropriate child seats.
5. Children 11 and under are not allowed to sit in the front seat.
6. When entering a roundabout (traffic circle), give way to traffic coming from the right.
7. The speed limits are 50kmph (31 mph) in built-up areas; 80kmph (50 mph) on regional and local roads, sometimes referred to as non-national roads; 100kmph (62 mph) on national roads, including divided highways (called dual carriageways); and 120kmph (75 mph) on freeways (called motorways).

points system similar to that in most U.S. states and in Britain in an effort to rein in the Irish drivers, who seem to value speed above lives. Some particularly hideous fatal accidents in 2006 and 2007—one that took the lives of five young people from a wedding party—seemed to have had some impact on the government's attitude toward the country's traditionally reckless drivers. While visitors won't have points added to their licenses, they may still be penalized with fines if they speed or commit driving infractions.

Since 2005, all distances and speed limits on road signs in the Republic of Ireland have been changed to **kilometers,** while in Northern Ireland they are still given in **miles.** Take extra care if you're driving around the borderlands—the border is unmarked, so you can cross over from one side to the other without knowing it. There are no plans to harmonize the situation in the near future, and it's easy to get confused, particularly since the border is so ill-defined.

In light of Ireland's unfortunate highway statistics, every precaution is in order. Try to avoid driving after dark, or around

pub-closing time (generally from 11pm–2am); get off the road when driving conditions are compromised by rain, fog, or excessive holiday traffic. Getting used to left-side driving, left-handed stick shift, narrow roads, and a new landscape are enough for the driver to manage, not to mention having to find his or her way to a destination, so it's helpful if you can have somebody along as a navigator. (Alternatively, you could rent a GPS navigation device with your car—most major rental firms now offer them.) Consider driving only an hour or two on the day you arrive, just far enough to get to a nearby hotel or bed-and-breakfast and to get a feel for the roads.

Traffic in Dublin provides its own frustration. Don't even think about renting a car for your time in Dublin. The pace of traffic in the capital's city center is around 8kmph (about 5 mph) due to heavy congestion. In addition, a recent change has replaced many of the large English-language street signs with small, hard-to-read bilingual signs in which the Gaelic words are easier to read than the English (much to the annoyance of the local population, as well as visitors). Add in all the one-way streets and dire lack of parking, and you're probably better off on foot.

Roundabouts (what Americans call traffic circles or rotaries) are found on most major roads and take a little getting used to. Remember always to yield to traffic on the right as you approach a roundabout and follow the traffic to the left, signaling before you exit the circle.

One signal that could be misleading to U.S. drivers is a flashing amber light at a pedestrian traffic light. This almost always follows a red light and it means yield to pedestrians, but proceed when the crossing is clear.

There are relatively few types of roads in the Republic. **National (N)** roads link major cities on the island. Though these are the equivalent of U.S. highways, they are rarely more than two lanes in each direction, and are sometimes as small as one U.S.-size lane. Most pass directly through towns, making cross-country trips longer than you'd expect. **Regional (R)** roads have one lane of traffic traveling in each direction, and generally link smaller cities and towns. Last are the rural or unclassified roads, often the most scenic back roads. These can be poorly signposted, very narrow, and a bit rough, but travel through beautiful countryside.

In the North, there are two **Major Motorways (M),** equivalent to interstates, as well as a network of lesser A- and B-level roads. Speed limits are posted.

Both the North and the Republic have severe laws against drunk driving, even more so than in the U.S., and they will enforce them. The general rule is: Don't drink and drive, or you could find yourself in a lot of trouble. Both countries also enforce the mandatory use of seat belts in the front seat, and the North extends that to rear-seat passengers. It is against the law in the Republic for any child 11 and under to sit in the front seat.

Rentals

Try to make car-rental arrangements well in advance of your departure. Leaving such arrangements until the last minute—or, worse, until your arrival in Ireland—can mean you wind up either walking, or wishing you were. Ireland is a small country, and in high season it can completely run out of rental cars—but before it does, it runs out of *affordable* rental cars. Discounts are common in the off season, of course, but it's also possible to negotiate a decent deal for July and August if you put in enough time and effort.

Major international car-rental firms are represented at airports and cities throughout Ireland and Northern Ireland. They include **Alamo-Treaty** (© 800/462-5266 in the U.S.; www.goalamo.com), **Auto-Europe** (© 888/223-5555 in the U.S.; www.autoeurope.com), **Avis** (© 800/230-4898 in the U.S.; www.avis.com), **Budget** (© 800/527-0700 in the U.S.; www.budget.com), **Hertz** (© 800/654-3001 in the U.S.; www.hertz.com), **Murrays Europcar** (© 800/800-6000 in the U.S.; www.europcar.ie), **National** (© 800/227-7368 in the U.S.; www.nationalcar.com), and **Payless/Bunratty** (© 800/729-5377 in the U.S.; www.paylesscarrental.com).

In addition, a variety of Ireland-based companies have desks at the major airports and full-service offices in city or town locations. The leader among the Irish-based firms is **Dan Dooley/Kenning Rent-a-Car** (© 800/331-9301 in the U.S.; www.dan-dooley.ie).

When comparing prices, always ask if the quoted rate includes the 13.5% government tax (VAT), the €15 ($24) airport pickup fee (assuming you pick up your car right upon arrival), CDW (collision damage waiver), or theft insurance. If you have your own auto insurance, you may be covered; check your existing policy before you pay for additional coverage you may not need. If you rent a car in the Republic, it is best to return it to the Republic, and if you rent it in the North, return it in the North. (Most firms charge extra for cross-border drop-offs.)

A sticky, and expensive, caveat about car rentals: If you rent with a credit card that claims to provide free protection, be sure to call your card's customer service line to make certain there are no restrictions on that coverage in Ireland. Visa *does not* offer insurance protection for car rentals in Ireland. And MasterCard and American Express—even gold cards—have limited their protection on Irish rentals. Be certain that your information is current. Always confirm the details of your coverage when you charge your car rental to your credit card. If you are renting a car in the Republic and taking it into the North (or vice versa), be sure to ask the car-rental firm if the CDW and theft insurance covers cross-border transport. If not, you may be required to buy extra insurance.

Parking

Rule number one: Not to beat a dead horse, but you're better off without a car in Dublin. Traffic, a shortage of parking places, and one-way streets conspire to make you regret having wheels. Cork is nearly as bad.

Rule number two: Never park in bus lanes or next to a curb with double yellow lines. Dublin, in particular, cracks down hard on offenders by booting or towing delinquent cars. It will cost you around €85 ($136) to have your car unclamped, or a whopping €165 ($264) to reclaim a towed car—so be extra vigilant.

In Dublin, virtually all streets are pay to park. Look for signs directing you to ticket machines; there should be one each block or so. Some larger towns also have multi-story car parks; in central Dublin they average about €2.30 ($3.70) per hour and €20 ($32) for 24 hours. Night rates are about €6.50 to €9.50 ($10–$15) per hour. In central Dublin, you'll find parking lots on Kildare Street, Lower Abbey Street, Marlborough Street, and St. Stephen's Green West.

Parking in most villages and small towns is easy and usually free. Look out for public parking lots—they're often free and are clearly marked at the edge of town centers.

In Belfast and other large cities in the North, certain security measures are still in place from the bad old days. Control zone signs indicate that no unattended vehicle can be left there at any time. That means if you are a single traveler, you cannot leave your car; if you are a twosome, one person must remain in the car while it's parked. Also, unlocked cars anywhere in the North are subject to a fine, for security reasons.

BY TRAIN

Iarnród Éireann (Irish Rail) (© **1850/366222** or 01/836-6222; www.irishrail.ie) operates the train services in Ireland. With the exception of flying, train travel is the fastest way to get around the country. Most lines radiate from Dublin to other principal cities and towns. From Dublin, the journey time to Cork is 3 hours; to Belfast, 2 hours; to Galway, 3 hours; to Limerick, 2¹/₄ hours; to Killarney, 4 hours; to Sligo, 3¹/₄ hours; and to Waterford, 2³/₄ hours.

(Tips) **Ticket Talk**

When buying travel tickets—air, ferry, or train—ask for either a "single" (one-way) or a "return" (round-trip).

ⓥValue   Money-Saving Rail & Bus Passes

For extensive travel by public transport, you can save money by purchasing a rail/bus pass or a rail-only pass. The options include the following:

- **Eurailpass:** Of the dozens of different Eurailpasses available, some are valid for unlimited rail travel in 17 European countries—but none include Britain or Northern Ireland. Other passes let you save money by selecting fewer countries. In the Irish Republic, the Eurailpass is good for travel on trains, Expressway coaches, and the Irish Continental Lines ferries between France and Ireland. For passes that let you travel throughout continental Europe and the Republic of Ireland, first-class passes begin at €503 ($805) for 15 consecutive days of travel; youth passes (passengers must be 25 years old and under) begin at €327 ($523) for 15 consecutive days of travel in second class. The pass must be purchased 21 days before departure for Europe by a non–European Union resident. For further details or for purchase, call **Rail Pass Express** (ⓒ 800/722-7151; www.eurail.com). It's also available from **STA Travel** (ⓒ 800/781-4040; www.sta.com) and other travel agents. You can also find more information online at www.eurail.com.

- **BritRail Pass + Ireland:** Includes all rail travel throughout the United Kingdom and Ireland, including a round-trip ferry crossing on Stena Line. A pass good for any 5 days of unlimited travel within a 30-day period costs $601 first class, $408 second class; 10 days of unlimited travel within a 30-day period costs $1,059 first class, $711 second class. It must be purchased before departure for Ireland or the United Kingdom, and is available from **BritRail** (ⓒ 866/BRITRAIL [274-8724]; www.britrail.com).

Iarnród Éireann also offers an enticing array of weekend-to-weeklong holiday packages or **RailBreaks** to practically every corner of Ireland, north as well as south.

In addition to the Irish Rail service between Dublin and Belfast, **Translink** (ⓒ 028/9066-6630; www.nirailways.co.uk) operates routes from Belfast that include Coleraine and Derry, in addition to virtually all 21 localities in Northern Ireland. The same organization runs the Belfast city service, called **Citybus.**

By Bus

Bus Éireann (ⓒ 01/830-2222; www.buseireann.ie) operates an extensive system of express bus service, as well as local service, to nearly every town in Ireland. Express routes include Dublin to Donegal (4¼ hr.), Killarney to Limerick (2½ hr.), Limerick to Galway (2 hr.), and Limerick to Cork (2 hr.). The Bus Éireann website provides the latest timetables and fares for bus service throughout Ireland. Bus travel is usually affordable, reliable, and comfortable. See **Translink** for detailed information on services within Northern Ireland (ⓒ 028/9066-6630; www.nirailways.co.uk/atulsterbus.asp).

5 MONEY & COSTS

CURRENCY

The Republic of Ireland uses the single European currency known as the **euro.** In this guide, the € sign symbolizes the euro. In converting prices to U.S. dollars, we used the rate €1 = $1.60.

Euro notes come in denominations of €5, €10, €20, €50, €100, €200, and €500. The euro is divided into 100 cents; coins come in denominations of €2, €1, 50¢, 20¢, 10¢, 5¢, 2¢, and 1¢.

So far, the United Kingdom has resisted the euro and retained its traditional currency, the **pound sterling.** Northern Ireland, as part of the United Kingdom, uses the British pound. In this guide, the £ sign symbolizes the British pound. The British pound is not legal tender in the Republic, and the euro is not legal tender in the North—if you're traveling in both parts of Ireland, you'll need some of both currencies, although shops right on the border tend to accept both. For those traveling between Great Britain and Northern Ireland, although the pounds issued in Northern Ireland are legal tender in Great Britain and vice versa, the paper money actually *looks* different, and you may find that cabdrivers and small business owners in the North won't accept bills issued in Great Britain and vice versa. In that case, you can change the money into locally issued versions at any large, central bank,

free of charge. In converting prices for this guide, we used the rate £1 = $2.

The British currency used in Northern Ireland has notes in denominations of £5, £10, £20, £50, and £100. Coins are issued in £2, £1, 50p, 20p, 10p, 5p, 2p, and 1p denominations.

As a general rule, when converting prices to U.S. dollars, if the U.S. price is less than $10, we round it to the nearest nickel; if more than $10, to the nearest dollar.

Note for U.S. travelers: The value of the U.S. dollar has been fluctuating a great deal lately, so it is best to begin checking exchange rates well in advance of your visit to get a feel for where they will stand for your trip.

ATMS

The easiest and best way to get cash away from home is from an ATM (automated teller machine), sometimes referred to as a "cash machine" or a "cashpoint." The **Cirrus** (© **800/424-7787;** www.mastercard. com) and **PLUS** (© **800/843-7587,** or 1800/558-002 toll-free in Ireland; www. visa.com) networks span the globe; look at the back of your bank card to see which network you're on, then call or check online for ATM locations at your destination. Be sure you know your personal identification number (PIN) and daily withdrawal limit before you depart. *Note:*

What Things Cost in Ireland	Euro €	US$
Cup of coffee	2.25	3.60
Pint of beer	3.50	5.60
Movie ticket	8.50	13.60
Bus fare	1.20	1.90
Moderate three-course meal for one	30.00	48.00
Gallon of gas	4.20	6.70

Remember that many banks impose a fee every time you use a card at another bank's ATM, and that fee can be higher for international transactions (up to $5 or more) than for domestic ones (where they're rarely more than $2). In addition, the bank from which you withdraw cash may charge its own fee. For international withdrawal fees, ask your bank.

Large towns usually have an ATM linked to a network that includes your home bank. However, out in rural counties—especially Galway, Clare, and Limerick—ATMs can be few and far between. We once drove 50 miles looking for an ATM in Clare before finally finding one, so stock up on cash if you're headed out to the countryside.

Most Republic and Northern Ireland ATMs accept PINs of four to six digits. One hiccup, however, is that they often don't have alphanumeric keypads. If your PIN features letters (for example: STAN37), use a telephone dial to figure out the numeric equivalents (or better yet, memorize it before you leave home).

CREDIT CARDS

Credit cards are another safe way to carry money. They also provide a convenient record of all your expenses, and they generally offer relatively good exchange rates. You can withdraw cash advances from your credit cards at banks or ATMs, provided you know your PIN. Keep in mind that you'll pay interest from the moment of your withdrawal, even if you pay your monthly bills on time. Also, note that many banks now assess a 1% to 3% "transaction fee" on **all** charges you incur abroad (whether you're using the local currency or your native currency). Visa and MasterCard are the most widely accepted credit cards in Ireland. American Express and Diners Club are accepted by most major hotels, but are less commonly accepted elsewhere. Cards are widely accepted at shops and restaurants, although small rural businesses and some B&Bs do not accept them.

TRAVELER'S CHECKS

Traveler's checks are not widely accepted in Ireland. You'll probably have to change the checks at a bank and pay a fee for the privilege.

The most popular traveler's checks are offered by **American Express** (© **800/807-6233**, or 800/221-7282 for cardholders—this number accepts collect calls, offers service in several foreign languages, and exempts Amex gold and platinum cardholders from the 1% fee); **Visa** (© **800/732-1322**, or 1800-411-055 toll-free in Ireland)—AAA members can obtain Visa checks for a $9.95 fee (for checks up to $1,500) at most AAA offices or by calling © **866/339-3378**; and **MasterCard** (© **800/622-7747**).

Tips   **Dear Visa: I'm Off to Killarney!**

Some credit card companies recommend that you notify them of any impending trip abroad or they may become suspicious when the card is used numerous times in a foreign destination and they'll block your charges. If you don't call your credit card company in advance, you should carry the card's toll-free emergency number (see "Lost & Found" in this book's appendix) with you, so that you can get in touch if a charge is refused. But perhaps the most important lesson here is to carry more than one card on your trip; a card might not work for any number of reasons, so having a backup is actually quite important.

> **ⓘps   Easy Money**
>
> You'll avoid lines at airport ATMs by exchanging at least some money—just enough to cover airport incidentals and transportation to your hotel—before you leave home.
>
> When you change money, ask for some small bills or loose change. Petty cash will come in handy for tipping and public transportation. Consider keeping the change separate from your larger bills, so that it's readily accessible and you'll be less of a target for theft.

American Express, Thomas Cook, Visa, and **MasterCard** offer **foreign currency traveler's checks,** which are sometimes accepted at locations where dollar checks may not be.

If you carry traveler's checks, keep a record of their serial numbers separate from your checks in the event that they are stolen or lost. You'll get a refund faster if you know the numbers.

6 HEALTH

STAYING HEALTHY

As a rule, no health documents or vaccinations are required to enter Ireland or Northern Ireland from the United States, Canada, the United Kingdom, Australia, New Zealand, or most other countries. If, however, you have visited areas in the previous 14 days where a contagious disease is prevalent, proof of immunization may be required.

General Availability of Healthcare

Healthcare in Ireland is comparable to that in the U.S., and it is a similar system in which private doctors and hospitals provide care and patients purchase healthcare insurance.

Contact the **International Association for Medical Assistance to Travelers (IAMAT)** (© **716/754-4883,** or 416/652-0137 in Canada; www.iamat.org) for tips on travel and health concerns in Ireland, and for lists of English-speaking doctors. The United States **Centers for Disease Control and Prevention** (© **800/311-3435;** www.cdc.gov) provides up-to-date information on health hazards by region

or country and offers tips on food safety. The website **www.tripprep.com,** sponsored by a consortium of travel medicine practitioners, may also offer helpful advice on traveling abroad. You can find listings of reliable clinics overseas at the **International Society of Travel Medicine** (www.istm.org).

WHAT TO DO IF YOU GET SICK AWAY FROM HOME

If you require the services of a physician, dentist, or other health professional during your stay in Ireland, your accommodations host may be in the best position to recommend someone local. Otherwise, contact the **embassy or consulate** of your home country (see "Embassies & Consulates" in this book's appendix) or the **Irish Medical Council,** Lynn House, Portobello Court, Lower Rathmines Road, Dublin 6 (© **01/498-3100**), for a referral.

Depending on the severity of your illness, you may need to be treated at the emergency room of a local hospital. If your problem is less severe, some hospitals also have walk-in clinics for cases that are

Avoiding "Economy-Class Syndrome"

Deep vein thrombosis, or as it's known in the world of flying, "economy-class syndrome," is a blood clot that develops in a deep vein. It's a potentially deadly condition that can be caused by sitting in cramped conditions—such as an airplane cabin—for too long. During a flight (especially a long-haul flight), get up, walk around, and stretch your legs every 60 to 90 minutes to keep your blood flowing. Other preventative measures include frequent flexing of the legs while sitting, drinking lots of water, and avoiding alcohol and sleeping pills. If you have a history of deep vein thrombosis, heart disease, or another condition that puts you at high risk, some experts recommend wearing compression stockings or taking anticoagulants when you fly; always ask your physician about the best course for you. Symptoms of deep vein thrombosis include leg pain or swelling, or even shortness of breath.

not life-threatening. We list **hospitals** and **emergency numbers** under "Fast Facts" sections in most of the individual chapters/town sections.

If you suffer from a chronic illness, consult your doctor before your departure. Pack **prescription medications** in your carry-on luggage, and carry them in their original containers, with pharmacy labels—otherwise they won't make it through airport security. Carry the generic

name of prescription medicines, in case a pharmacist is unfamiliar with the brand name.

For travel abroad, you may have to pay all medical costs upfront and be reimbursed later. See "Medical Insurance," under "Travel Insurance," in the appendix.

We list **emergency numbers** in the "Fast Facts, Toll-Free Numbers & Websites" appendix.

7 SAFETY

STAYING SAFE

By U.S. standards, Ireland is very safe, but, particularly in the cities, it's not safe enough to warrant carelessness. Travelers should take normal precautions to protect their belongings from theft and themselves from harm.

In the countryside, you're unlikely to encounter any problems with crime. In Dublin and Belfast, you'll need to be wary of the usual tourists' plague: pickpockets, purse snatchers, and car thieves. Also, in recent years, some of Dublin's busiest thoroughfares have been the scenes of brutal attacks at night. To alert visitors to potential dangers, the Dublin Police (called the

Garda) publish a small leaflet, *A Short Guide to Tourist Security,* which is available at tourist offices and other public places. The booklet advises you not to carry large amounts of money or important documents like your passport or airline tickets when strolling around.

Most advice is standard for travel anywhere: Do not leave cars unlocked or cameras, binoculars, or other expensive equipment unattended. Be alert and aware of your surroundings, and do not wander alone in isolated areas.

Take special care if you'll be out in Dublin late at night when the pubs and nightclubs close. Ask at your hotel which

> ⓘ **Tips**   **Worrisome Water Supply**
>
> In 2005, the water supply in Ennis in County Clare was found to be tainted with *Cryptosporidium*, a parasite that causes intestinal illness. Everybody in the town (including visitors) is presently advised to boil water for cooking and to drink bottled water until a new water plant is built—which at this writing was scheduled for May 2009. Worryingly, a 2007 report by the Irish Environmental Protection Agency found that harmful carcinogens had been discovered in the water supply of several other towns—including Dingle, Killarney, and Spiddal—at levels that will be illegal after a planned law change in December 2008. Although Ennis is the only town in which special procedures currently apply, you may want to err on the side of caution throughout Ireland, particularly when it comes to young children, the elderly, and those vulnerable to infection. For more information see **www.epa.ie/whatwedo/enforce/pa/drink**.

areas are safe and which are not. Take a taxi back to your hotel if you're out after about 11pm.

In Northern Ireland, safety has tended to be a somewhat greater concern because of the political unrest that has prevailed there for the past 30 years, but violence has diminished since the Good Friday Agreement. Occasionally, though, flare-ups do happen, especially during the Orange marching season in the late summer. Still, visitors rarely, if ever, have problems with sectarian strife, since they are simply not the target of it.

Note for U.S. travelers: These are tense times in the world politically, and while few Americans encounter hostility or anti-Americanism when visiting Ireland, it can happen. According to the U.S. State Department: "Several Americans have reported incidents of verbal abuse, and one reported a physical assault apparently in reaction to U.S. policy on the war on terrorism. As elsewhere in Europe, there have been public protests, which for the most part are peaceful and well policed. Americans are advised, nonetheless, to avoid public demonstrations in general and to monitor local media when protests occur."

If you have any questions or concerns, contact the **U.S. State Department** to obtain the latest safety recommendations (ⓒ **202/647-5225;** http://travel.state.gov).

8 SPECIALIZED TRAVEL RESOURCES

TRAVELERS WITH DISABILITIES

Most disabilities shouldn't stop anyone from traveling. There are more options and resources out there than ever before.

One of the best Irish-based online resources is **www.disability.ie**. Click on the "Holidays" link for good advice on traveling in Ireland with a disability and for companies that specialize in helping travelers with disabilities.

The **Irish Wheelchair Association,** Áras Chúchulainn, Blackheath Drive, Clontarf, Dublin 3 (ⓒ **01/818-6400;** www.iwa.ie), loans free wheelchairs to travelers in Ireland. A donation is appreciated. Several branch offices are located in Carlow, Clare, Cork, Donegal, Dublin, Galway, Kavan, Kerry, Kildare, Kilkenny,

Laois, Leitrim, Limerick, Longford, Louth, Mayo, Meath, Offaly, Roscommon, Sligo, Tipperary, Waterford, Westmeath, Wexford, and Wicklow.

If you plan to travel by train in Ireland, be sure to check out Iarnród Éireann's website (**www.irishrail.ie**), which includes services for travelers with disabilities. A mobility-impaired liaison officer (© **01/703-2634**) can arrange assistance for travelers with disabilities if given 24-hour notice prior to the departure time.

For advice on travel to Northern Ireland, contact **Disability Action,** Portside Business Park, 189 Airport Rd. W., Belfast BT3 9ED (© **028/9029-7880;** www.disabilityaction.org). The Northern Ireland Tourist Board also publishes a helpful annual *Information Guide to Accessible Accommodation,* available from any of its offices worldwide.

Finding accessible lodging can be tricky in Ireland. As a historic country, where many of the buildings are hundreds of years old, older hotels, small guesthouses, and landmark buildings still have steps outside and in. The **National Rehabilitation Board of Ireland,** 24–25 Clyde Rd., Ballsbridge, Dublin 4 (© **01/608-0400**), publishes several guides, the best of which is *Guide to Accessible Accommodations in Ireland.* Also, **O'Mara Travel** (disability@omara-travel.com), in association with the Disability.ie website (see above), often offers special deals on accommodations to travelers with disabilities.

Many travel agencies offer customized tours and itineraries for travelers with disabilities. Among them are **Flying Wheels Travel** (© **507/451-5005;** www.flyingwheelstravel.com), **Access-Able Travel Source** (© **303/232-2979;** www.access-able.com), and **Accessible Journeys** (© **800/846-4537** or 610/521-0339; www.disabilitytravel.com).

Organizations that offer assistance to travelers with disabilities include **Moss-Rehab** (www.mossresourcenet.org), the

American Foundation for the Blind (AFB) (© **800/232-5463;** www.afb.org), and **SATH** (Society for Accessible Travel & Hospitality) (© **212/447-7284;** www.sath.org). **AirAmbulanceCard.com** is now partnered with SATH and allows you to preselect top-notch hospitals in case of an emergency.

Also check out the quarterly magazine *Emerging Horizons* (www.emerginghorizons.com) and *Open World* magazine, published by SATH.

For more about organizations that offer resources to travelers with disabilities, go to Frommers.com.

GAY & LESBIAN TRAVELERS

Ireland has come a long way since homosexuality was legalized in 1993 (1982 in the North), but gay and lesbian visitors should be aware that this is still a deeply conservative country. With rare exceptions, gay communities are relatively low-key, and even in such ostensibly liberal places as Dublin and Galway, gay bashing is not unheard of. Things have improved light-years over the last decade, but this is still not New York or San Francisco. Proceed with caution.

That said, there's a burgeoning gay community in Dublin. The *Gay Community News (GCN)* is a monthly free newspaper of comprehensive Irish gay-related information, available in gay venues and bookshops. *In Dublin,* the city's leading event listings guide, dedicates several pages to gay events, club info, and a helpful directory. Two mini-magazines have recently emerged—*Free!* and *Scene City*—and both contain city maps with gay venues highlighted.

Among the best resources on the Web are **Gay Ireland Online** (www.gay-ireland.com) and **Outhouse** (www.outhouse.ie). These include events listings, advice sections, useful contacts, and discussion forums.

The following is a selection of organizations and help lines, staffed by knowledgeable and friendly people:

- **Outhouse Community & Resource Centre,** 105 Capel St., Dublin 1 (*©* 01/873-4999; fax 01/865-0900; www.outhouse.ie).
- **National Lesbian and Gay Federation (NLGF),** 2 Scarlet Row, Dublin 2 (*©* 01/671-0939; fax 01/671-3549; www.nlgf.ie).
- **Gay Switchboard Dublin,** Carmichael House, North Brunswick Street, Dublin 7 (*©* 01/872-1055; fax 01/873-5737; www.gayswitchboard.ie), Monday to Friday 7:30 to 9:30pm and Saturday 3:30 to 6pm.
- **Lesbian Line Dublin,** Carmichael Centre, North Brunswick Street, Dublin 7 (*©* 01/872-1055), Thursday 7 to 9pm.
- **LOT (Lesbians Organizing Together),** the umbrella group of the lesbian community, has a drop-in cafe at 5 Capel St., Dublin 1 (*©*/fax 01/872-7770), open Monday to Thursday 10am to 6pm and Friday 10am to 4pm. LOT also sponsors LEA (Lesbian Education Awareness) (*©*/fax 01/872-0460; home.indigo.ie).
- **AIDS Helpline Dublin** (*©* 1800/549-549 toll-free), Monday to Friday 7 to 9pm and Saturday 3 to 5pm, offers assistance with HIV/AIDS prevention, testing, and treatment. Branches are also located in **Belfast** (*©* 0800/137-437), **Galway** (*©* 091/562213), **Cork** (*©* 021/2766/6), **Limerick** (*©* 061/316661), and **Donegal** (*©* 074/25500).

The **International Gay and Lesbian Travel Association (IGLTA)** (*©* 800/448-8550 or 954/776-2626; www.iglta.org) is the trade association for the gay and lesbian travel industry, and offers an online directory of gay- and lesbian-friendly travel businesses; go to its website and click on "Travelers."

Many agencies offer tours and travel itineraries specifically for gay and lesbian travelers. Among them are **Above and Beyond Tours** (*©* 800/397-2681; www.abovebeyondtours.com); **Now, Voyager** (*©* 800/255-6951; www.nowvoyager.com); and **Olivia Cruises & Resorts** (*©* 800/631-6277; www.olivia.com).

Gay.com Travel (*©* 800/929-2268 or 415/644-8044; www.gay.com/travel or www.outandabout.com) is an excellent online successor to the popular *Out & About* print magazine. It provides regularly updated information about gay-owned, gay-oriented, and gay-friendly lodging, dining, sightseeing, nightlife, and shopping establishments in every important destination worldwide.

The following travel guides are available at many bookstores, or you can order them from any online bookseller: *Spartacus International Gay Guide* (Bruno Gmünder Verlag; www.spartacusworld.com/gayguide); *Odysseus: The International Gay Travel Planner* (Odysseus Enterprises Ltd.); and the *Damron* guides (www.damron.com), with separate, annual books for gay men and lesbians.

SENIOR TRAVEL

One of the benefits of age is that travel often costs less. If possible, always carry photo ID with you, especially if you've kept that youthful glow (although for security reasons, a driver's license or something similar is better than a passport, unless you're actually traveling).

Mention the fact that you're a senior when you first make your travel reservations—although most of the major U.S. airlines have canceled their senior discount and coupon book programs, many hotels still offer discounts for seniors. In most cities, people over the age of 60 qualify for reduced admission to theaters, museums, and other attractions.

Seniors, known throughout Ireland as **OAPs** (old-age pensioners), enjoy a variety of discounts and privileges. Native OAPs ride the public transport system free of charge, but the privilege does not extend to tourists. Visiting seniors can avail themselves of other discounts, though, particularly on admission to attractions and theaters. Always ask about an OAP discount if special rates are not posted.

The Irish Tourist Board is helpful, and can offer advice on how to find the best accommodations, travel, and so forth. It publishes lists of reduced-rate hotel packages for seniors; contact it for details (see "Visitor Information," earlier in this chapter).

Members of **AARP** (formerly known as the American Association of Retired Persons), 601 E St. NW, Washington, DC 20049 (© **888/687-2277;** www.aarp.org), get discounts on hotels, airfares, and car rentals. AARP offers members a wide range of benefits, including *AARP The Magazine* and a monthly newsletter. Anyone 50 and over can join. Similarly, **SAGA Tours** (© **800/343-0273** or 617/ 262-2262) operates tours to Ireland specifically geared to seniors or anyone 50 and over.

Many reliable agencies and organizations target the 50-plus market. **Elderhostel** (© **877/426-8056;** www.elderhostel. org) arranges study programs for those aged 55 and over. **ElderTreks** (© **800/ 741-7956;** www.eldertreks.com) offers small-group tours to off-the-beaten-path or adventure-travel locations, restricted to travelers 50 and older.

Recommended publications offering travel resources and discounts for seniors include the quarterly magazine *Travel 50 & Beyond* (www.travel50andbeyond.com); *Travel Unlimited: Uncommon Adventures for the Mature Traveler* (Avalon); *101 Tips for Mature Travelers,* available from Grand Circle Travel (© **800/959-0405;** www.gct.com); and *Unbelievably Good Deals and Great Adventures That You Absolutely Can't Get Unless You're Over 50* (McGraw-Hill), by Joan Rattner Heilman.

FAMILY TRAVEL

With its castles, parks, zoos, and playgrounds, rural Ireland is ideal for family travel. The big cities—Dublin and Belfast—are slightly less hospitable, if only because of a scattering of child-unfriendly hotels, limited kid-oriented activities, and high prices. Out in the country, though, most hotels and guesthouses have family rooms, most restaurants welcome children (children are even allowed in family pubs—those that serve meals—during the day), and there's plenty of space for them to run off a bit of energy. Throughout the book, we've noted kid-friendly attractions, and we've also listed good places to rent cottages by the week—ideal for families.

Your first goal will be to find truly child-friendly places to stay. Hotels that *say* they welcome small children and hotels that really provide for them are, sadly, not always the same. To sort the wheat from the chaff, one of the most helpful websites is **www.irelandhotels.com**. Click on "Detailed Search," then "Browse Properties" to search using a wide range of options (including kids' meals, day nurseries, and so on).

Given 24-hour advance notice, most airlines can arrange for a special children's menu. If you're renting a car, be sure to reserve car seats if your kids are small—don't assume that the car-rental companies will have extras on hand. Throughout the island, entrance fees and tickets on public transportation are often reduced for children 11 and under. Family rates for parents with children are also commonplace. In this guide, a "family" rate, unless otherwise stated, is for two adults with two children. Additional charges are often made for larger families.

Some hotels, guesthouses, and B&Bs provide babysitting, and many others can arrange it. (Although, just like back home, don't assume this can be done immediately.)

To locate accommodations, restaurants, and attractions that are particularly kid-friendly, refer to the "Kids" icon throughout this guide.

Familyhostel (© 800/733-9753; www.hihostels.com/web/family.en.htm) takes the whole family, including kids ages 8 to 15, on moderately priced U.S. and international learning vacations. Lectures, field trips, and sightseeing are guided by a team of academics.

Recommended family travel websites include **Family Travel Forum** (www.familytravelforum.com), **Family Travel Network** (www.familytravelnetwork.com), **Traveling Internationally with Your Kids** (www.travelwithyourkids.com), and **Family Travel Files** (www.thefamilytravelfiles.com).

WOMEN TRAVELERS

Women should expect few if any problems traveling in Ireland. The country's views on women are much more advanced now than they were a couple of decades ago. Women are accepted traveling alone or in groups in virtually every environment, and gone are the days when women were expected to order half-pints of beer in pubs, while men were allowed to order the bigger, more cost-effective pints of ale. In fact, the only time you're likely to attract any attention at all is if you eat alone in a restaurant at night—a sight that is still relatively uncommon in Ireland outside of the major cities. Even then, you'll not be hassled. If you drink in a pub on your own, though, expect all kinds of attention, as a woman drinking alone is still considered to be on the market—even if she's reading a book, talking on her cellphone to her fiancé, or doing a crossword puzzle. So be prepared to fend them off. Irish men almost always respond well to polite rejection, though.

In cities, as ever, take a cab home at night, and follow all the usual advice of caution you get when you travel anywhere. Essentially, don't do anything in Ireland that you wouldn't do at home.

Check out the award-winning website **Journeywoman** (www.journeywoman.com), a "real-life" women's travel-information network where you can sign up for a free e-mail newsletter and get advice on everything from etiquette and dress to safety; or the travel guide *Safety and Security for Women Who Travel* by Sheila Swan and Peter Laufer (Travelers' Tales, Inc.), offering sensible tips on safe travel.

STUDENT TRAVEL

Considering the sheer number of language schools, business colleges, and universities in Dublin alone, it's not surprising the country's student population is considerable. If you're interested in studying here, contact your university to find out if it has a partnership program in Ireland. To get basic info on whether or not you need a student visa and how to get one, get in touch with the Irish Department of Foreign Affairs Visa Section, Hainault House, 69–71 St. Stephen's Green, Dublin (© 01/408-2374). U.S. firms offering educational travel programs to Ireland include Academic Travel Abroad (© 800/556-7896 or 202/785-9000; www.academictravel.com) and North American Institute for Study Abroad (© 570/275-5099 or 275-1644).

If you do spend a semester or two in Ireland, contact the Union of Students in Ireland Travel (© 02/602-1906; www.usit.ie). It's great for arranging travel from and around Ireland at the cheapest rates. Its notice boards are filled with flat shares, language classes, jobs, and cheap flights.

If you're looking for less structured knowledge, try spending a week in Glencolmcille, County Donegal, studying the Irish (Gaelic) language, dancing, archaeology, Celtic pottery, or tapestry weaving at Oideas Gael (© 074/973-0248; www.oideas-gael.com).

If you're traveling internationally, you'd be wise to arm yourself with an **International Student Identity Card (ISIC)**, which offers substantial savings on rail passes, plane tickets, and entrance fees. It also provides you with basic health and life insurance and a 24-hour help line. The card is available from **STA Travel** (*℃* **800/ 781-4040** in North America; www.sta. com or www.statravel.com, or www.sta travel.co.uk in the U.K.), the biggest student travel agency in the world. If you're no longer a student but are still age 25 or under, you can get an **International Youth**

Travel Card (IYTC) from the same people, which entitles you to some discounts (but not on museum admissions). **Travel CUTS** (*℃* **800/592-2887** from the U.S. or **1866/246-9762** from Canada; www. travelcuts.com) offers similar services for both Canadians and U.S. residents. Irish students may prefer to turn to **USIT** (*℃* **01/602-1906;** www.usit.ie), an Ireland-based specialist in student, youth, and independent travel.

9 SUSTAINABLE TOURISM

Sustainable tourism is conscientious travel. It means being careful with the environments you explore, and respecting the communities you visit. Two overlapping components of sustainable travel are **eco-tourism** and **ethical tourism.** The **International Ecotourism Society** (TIES) defines eco-tourism as responsible travel to natural areas that conserves the environment and improves the well-being of local people. TIES suggests that eco-tourists follow these principles:

- Minimize environmental impact.
- Build environmental and cultural awareness and respect.
- Provide positive experiences for both visitors and hosts.
- Provide direct financial benefits for conservation and for local people.
- Raise sensitivity to host countries' political, environmental, and social climates.
- Support international human rights and labor agreements.

You can find some eco-friendly travel tips and statistics, as well as touring companies and associations—listed by destination under "Travel Choice"—at the **TIES** website, www.ecotourism.org. Also check out **Ecotravel.com,** which lets you search for sustainable touring companies in several categories (water-based, land-based, spiritually oriented, and so on).

While much of the focus of eco-tourism is about reducing impacts on the natural environment, ethical tourism concentrates on ways to preserve and enhance local economies and communities, regardless of location. You can embrace ethical tourism by staying at a locally owned hotel or shopping at a store that employs local workers and sells locally produced goods.

Responsible Travel (www.responsible travel.com) is a great source of sustainable travel ideas; the site is run by a spokesperson for ethical tourism in the travel industry. **Sustainable Travel International** (www.sustainabletravelinternational.org) promotes ethical tourism practices, and manages an extensive directory of sustainable properties and tour operators around the world.

In the U.K., **Tourism Concern** (www. tourismconcern.org.uk) works to reduce social and environmental problems connected to tourism. The **Association of Independent Tour Operators (AITO)** (www.aito.co.uk) is a group of specialist operators leading the field in making holidays sustainable.

Volunteer travel has become increasingly popular among those who want to venture beyond the standard group-tour experience to learn languages, interact with locals, and make a positive difference while on vacation. Volunteer travel usually

(Tips) It's Easy Being Green

Here are a few simple ways you can help conserve fuel and energy when you travel:

- Each time you take a flight or drive a car greenhouse gases release into the atmosphere. You can help neutralize this danger to the planet through "carbon offsetting"—paying someone to invest your money in programs that reduce your greenhouse gas emissions by the same amount you've added. Before buying carbon offset credits, just make sure that you're using a reputable company, one with a proven program that invests in renewable energy. Reliable carbon offset companies include **Carbonfund** (www.carbonfund.org), **TerraPass** (www.terrapass.org), and **Carbon Neutral** (www.carbonneutral.org).
- Whenever possible, choose nonstop flights; they generally require less fuel than indirect flights that stop and take off again. Try to fly during the day—some scientists estimate that nighttime flights are twice as harmful to the environment. And pack light—each 15 pounds of luggage on a 5,000-mile flight adds up to 50 pounds of carbon dioxide emitted.
- Where you stay during your travels can have a major environmental impact. To determine the green credentials of a property, ask about trash disposal and recycling, water conservation, and energy use; also question if sustainable materials were used in the construction of the property. The website **www.greenhotels.com** recommends green-rated member hotels around the world that fulfill the company's stringent environmental requirements. Also consult **www.environmentallyfriendlyhotels.com** for more green accommodations ratings.
- At hotels, request that your sheets and towels not be changed daily. (Many hotels already have programs like this in place.) Turn off the lights and air conditioner (or heater) when you leave your room.
- Use public transport where possible—trains, buses, and even taxis are more energy-efficient forms of transport than driving. Even better is to walk or cycle; you'll produce zero emissions and stay fit and healthy on your travels.
- If renting a car is necessary, ask the rental agent for a hybrid, or rent the most fuel-efficient car available. You'll use less gas and save money at the tank.
- Eat at locally owned and operated restaurants that use produce grown in the area. This contributes to the local economy and cuts down on greenhouse gas emissions by supporting restaurants where the food is not flown or trucked in across long distances.

doesn't require special skills—just a willingness to work hard—and programs vary in length from a few days to a number of weeks. Some programs provide free housing and food, but many require volunteers to pay for travel expenses, which can add up quickly.

For general info on volunteer travel, visit **www.volunteerabroad.org** and **www.idealist.org**.

Frommers.com: The Complete Travel Resource

Planning a trip or just returned? Head to **Frommers.com,** voted Best Travel Site by *PC Magazine*. We think you'll find our site indispensable before, during, and after your travels—with expert advice and tips; independent reviews of hotels, restaurants, attractions, and preferred shopping and nightlife venues; vacation giveaways; and an online booking tool. We publish the complete contents of over 135 travel guides in our **Destinations** section, covering over 4,000 places worldwide. Each weekday, we publish original articles that report on **Deals and News** via our free **Frommers.com Newsletters.** What's more, **Arthur Frommer** himself blogs 5 days a week, with cutting opinions about the state of travel in the modern world. We're betting you'll find our **Events** listings an invaluable resource; it's an up-to-the-minute roster of what's happening in cities everywhere—including concerts, festivals, lectures, and more. We've also added weekly **podcasts, interactive maps,** and hundreds of new images across the site. Finally, don't forget to visit our **Message Boards,** where you can join in conversations with thousands of fellow Frommer's travelers and post your trip report once you return.

Before you commit to a volunteer program, it's important to make sure any money you're giving is truly going back to the local community, and that the work you'll be doing will be a good fit for you.

Volunteer International (www.volunteer international.org) has a helpful list of questions to ask to determine the intentions and the nature of a volunteer program.

10 PACKAGES FOR THE INDEPENDENT TRAVELER

Package tours are simply a way to buy the airfare, accommodations, and other elements of your trip (such as car rentals, airport transfers, and sometimes even activities) at the same time and often at discounted prices.

One good source of package deals is the airlines themselves. Most major airlines offer air/land packages, including **American Airlines Vacations** (© 800/321-2121; www.aavacations.com), **Delta Vacations** (© 800/221-6666; www.deltavacations. com), **Continental Airlines Vacations**

(© 800/301-3800; www.covacations. com), and **United Vacations** (© 888/854-3899; www.unitedvacations.com). Several big **online travel agencies**—Expedia, Travelocity, Orbitz, and Lastminute.com—also do a brisk business in packages.

Travel packages are also listed in the travel section of your local Sunday newspaper. Or check ads in the national travel magazines such as *Arthur Frommer's Budget Travel Magazine, Travel + Leisure, National Geographic Traveler,* and *Condé Nast Traveler.*

(Tips) Ask Before You Go

Before you invest in a package deal or an escorted tour:

- Always ask about the **cancellation policy.** Can you get your money back? Is a deposit required?
- Ask about the **accommodations choices and prices** for each. Then look up the hotels' reviews in a Frommer's guide and check their rates online for your specific dates of travel. Also find out what types of rooms are offered.
- Request a complete **schedule** (escorted tours only).
- Ask about the **size** and demographics of the group (escorted tours only).
- Discuss what is included in the **price** (transportation, meals, tips, airport transfers, and so on; escorted tours only).
- Finally, look for **hidden expenses.** Ask whether airport departure fees and taxes, for example, are included in the total cost—they rarely are.

11 ESCORTED GENERAL-INTEREST TOURS

Escorted tours are structured group tours, with a group leader. The price usually includes everything from airfare to hotels, meals, tours, admission costs, and local transportation.

Despite the fact that escorted tours require big deposits and predetermine hotels, restaurants, and itineraries, many people derive security and peace of mind from the structure they offer. Escorted tours—whether they're navigated by bus, motorcoach, train, or boat—let travelers sit back and enjoy the trip without having to drive or worry about details. They take you to the maximum number of sights in the minimum amount of time with the least amount of hassle. They're particularly convenient for people with limited mobility and they can be a great way to make new friends.

On the downside, you'll have little opportunity for serendipitous interactions with locals. The tours can be jampacked with activities, leaving little room for individual sightseeing, whim, or adventure—plus they often focus on the heavily touristed sites, so you miss out on many a lesser known gem.

12 SPECIAL-INTEREST TRIPS

HISTORY & ARCHITECTURE TOURS

The Dublin bus company, **Dublin Bus** (© 01/873-4222; www.dublinbus.ie), operates several tours focusing on Irish history and architecture, all of which depart from the Dublin Bus office at 59 Upper O'Connell St., Dublin 1. You can buy your ticket from the bus driver or book in advance at the Dublin Bus office or at the Dublin Tourism ticket desk on Suffolk Street.

Gray Line (© 01/605-7705; www.irishcitytours.com) offers a range of full-day and multiple-day excursions from

Dublin, to the historic monastic site at Glendalough, as well as to the prehistoric remains at Newgrange, and the architecturally significant Powerscourt.

The national bus company, **Bus Éireann** (© 091/562000; www.buseireann.ie), provides a good range of tours throughout Ireland. You can tour Dublin and around to Glendalough or Newgrange by bus, or travel by boat to Waterford, and it also offers good tours of Galway, taking in the Maam Cross, Recess, Roundstone, and Clifden.

For a more historical, intellectual approach to Ireland's famous history, try **Mary Gibbons Tours** (© 01/283-9973; www.newgrangetours.com), which leads absorbing, in-depth tours of Dublin and Glendalough.

WILDERNESS TRIPS

For touring the Wicklow Mountains and Glendalough, try **Discover Dublin** (© 01/280-1899; www.discoverdublin.ie), which offers a tour it has dubbed the "Wild Wicklow Tour." Wild might be too strong a word, but it is certainly lively and enjoyable, and includes visits to the mountainous area around Avoca and the scenic Sally Gap.

POLITICAL TOURS

The best tours in Belfast are the extraordinary **Black Taxi Tours** ★ (© 0800/052-3914 or 0289/064-2264; www.belfast tours.com), which take you through the areas where the Troubles had the most impact, and explain it all in intelligent, compassionate, unbiased, firsthand terms.

13 STAYING CONNECTED

TELEPHONES

In the Republic, the telephone system is known as Eircom; in Northern Ireland, it's British Telecom. Every effort has been made to ensure that the numbers and information in this guide are accurate at the time of writing. **Overseas calls** from Ireland can be quite costly, whether you use a local phone card or your own calling card. If you think you will want to call home regularly while in Ireland, you may want to open an account with **Vartec Telecom Ireland** in Ireland (© 1800/411-0077; www.vartec.ie). Its rates represent a considerable savings, not only from Ireland to the United States but vice versa (handy for planning your trip as well as keeping in touch afterward).

To call Ireland from home: Dial the international access code (011 from the U.S., 00 from the U.K., 0011 from Australia, or 0170 from New Zealand). Then dial the country code (353 for the Republic, 44 for the North).

Next, dial the local number, remembering to omit the initial 0, which is for use only within Ireland (for example, to call the County Kerry number 066/12345 from the United States, you'd dial 011-353-66/12345).

To make local calls: To dial a local number within an area code, drop the initial 0. To dial a number within Ireland, but in a different area code, use the initial 0. Local calls from a phone booth require a Callcard (in the Republic) or Phonecard (in the North). Both are prepaid computerized cards that you insert into the phone instead of coins. They can be purchased in a range of denominations at phone company offices, post offices, and many retail outlets (such as newsstands). There's a local and international phone center at the General Post Office on O'Connell Street in Dublin.

To make international calls from within Ireland, first dial 00 and then the country code (U.S. or Canada 1, U.K. 44, Australia 61, New Zealand 64). Next you dial the area code and local number. For example, to call the U.S. number 212/000-0000, you'd dial © 00-1-212/000-0000. The toll free international access code for **AT&T** is 🕿 1-800-550-000, for **Sprint** it's 🕿 1-800-552-001, and for **MCI** it's 🕿 1-800-55-1001. ***Note:*** To dial direct to Northern Ireland from the Republic, simply replace the 028 prefix with 048.

For directory assistance, dial the toll-free number 🕿 **11811** if you're looking for a number inside Ireland. In Northern Ireland, try 🕿 **118888.** From the United States, the (toll) number to call is 🕿 **00353-91-770220.**

CELLPHONES

The three letters that define much of the world's wireless capabilities are GSM (Global System for Mobiles), a big, seamless network that makes for easy cross-border cellphone use throughout Europe and dozens of other countries worldwide. In the U.S., T-Mobile and AT&T Wireless use this quasi-universal system; in Canada, Microcell and some Rogers customers are GSM, and all Europeans and most Australians use GSM. If your cellphone is on a GSM system, and you have a world-capable multiband phone such as many Sony Ericsson, Motorola, or Samsung models, you can make and receive calls across civilized areas around much of the globe. Just call your wireless operator and ask for "international roaming" to be activated on your account. Unfortunately, per-minute charges can be high—usually $1 to $1.50 in western Europe and up to $5 in places like Russia and Indonesia.

For many, **renting** a phone is a good idea. While you can rent a phone from any number of overseas sites, including kiosks at airports and at car-rental agencies, we suggest renting the phone before you leave home.

North Americans can rent one before leaving home from **InTouch USA** (🕿 **800/ 872-7626;** www.intouchglobal.com) or **RoadPost** (🕿 **888/290-1616** or 905/272-5665; www.roadpost.com). InTouch will also, for free, advise you on whether your existing phone will work overseas; simply call 🕿 **703/222-7161** between 9am and 4pm EST, or go to **http://intouchglobal. com/travel.htm.**

One handy option is **Cellular Abroad** (🕿 **800/287-5072;** www.cellularabroad. com), which allows you to rent a phone for your journey before you leave, and prices start at $30. Another, similar firm is **Mind Logic** (🕿 **800/815-9380** in the U.S.; www.mindlogic.com), where rates start at $30 and all incoming calls are free.

There's a Vodafone shop in Dublin airport where you can purchase an Irish SIM card for your own phone—this allows you to pay in-country rather than international rates for calls you receive while you're there. They also rent and sell mobile phones.

Buying a phone can be economically attractive, as many nations have cheap prepaid phone systems. Once you arrive at your destination, stop by a local cellphone shop and get the cheapest package; you'll probably pay less than $100 for a basic phone and a starter calling card. Local calls may be as low as 10¢ per minute, and in Ireland incoming calls are free.

Most car-rental companies also rent phones, although their rates can be higher than those of the burgeoning Internet cellphone industry.

VOICE-OVER INTERNET PROTOCOL (VOIP)

If you have Web access while traveling, consider a broadband-based telephone service (in technical terms, **Voice over Internet Protocol,** or **VoIP**) such as Skype (www.skype.com) or Vonage (www. vonage.com), which allow you to make free international calls from your laptop or in a cybercafe. Neither service requires the people you're calling to also have that service (though there are fees if they do not). Check the websites for details.

Online Traveler's Toolbox

Veteran travelers usually carry some essential items to make their trips easier. Following is a selection of handy online tools to bookmark and use.

- **Airplane food** (www.airlinemeals.net)
- **Airplane seating** (www.seatguru.com and www.airlinequality.com)
- **Disabilities issues** (www.disability.ie)
- **Events and attractions** (www.discoverireland.ie)
- **What's up in the North** (www.discovernorthernireland.com)
- **Maps** (www.mapquest.com)
- **Travel warnings** (http://travel.state.gov, www.fco.gov.uk/travel, or www.voyage.gc.ca)
- **Universal currency converter** (www.xe.com/ucc)
- **Visa ATM locator** (www.visa.com), **MasterCard ATM Locator** (www.mastercard.com)
- **Weather** (www.intellicast.com or www.weather.com)

INTERNET & E-MAIL
With Your Own Computer

Wi-Fi (wireless fidelity) is not nearly as widespread in Ireland and the U.K. as it is in the U.S. In fact, it's still relatively rare to come across hotels that offer it, and virtually no coffee shops outside of inner-city Starbucks do at this time. Most business-class hotels do have broadband now in rooms now, though, which is a major improvement for those who wish to stay connected.

If you haven't got a laptop equipped for broadband, major Internet service providers (ISPs) have **local access numbers** around the world, allowing you to go online by placing a local call. The **iPass** network also has dial-up numbers around the world. You'll have to sign up with an iPass provider, who will then tell you how to set up your computer for your destination(s). For a list of iPass providers, go to www.ipass.com and click on "Individuals Buy Now." One solid provider is **i2roam** (© **866/811-6209** or 920/235-0475; www.i2roam.com).

Wherever you go, bring a **connection kit** of the right power and phone adapters, a spare phone cord, and a spare Ethernet network cable—or find out whether your hotel supplies them to guests. You might want to purchase a phone cord converter at the airport so that you can plug your phone cable into the wall using the U.K./Ireland-style plug, which is flatter than the U.S. and Canadian phone plugs.

Without Your Own Computer

Most major airports have **Internet kiosks** that provide basic Web access for a per-minute fee that's usually higher than cybercafe prices. Check out copy shops like **Kinko's** (FedEx Kinkos), which offers computer stations with fully loaded software (as well as Wi-Fi).

For help locating cybercafes and other establishments where you can go for Internet access, see "Internet Access" in this book's appendix.

Ireland offers a remarkable array of accommodations, some quite affordable and others outrageously lavish. There is something for everyone, from families on a budget to lovers on the splurge of a lifetime. Here's a sketch of what's out there.

HOTELS & GUESTHOUSES

Be Our Guest, a comprehensive guide to the hotels, country houses, castles, and inns of Ireland, is published by the Irish Hotel Federation and is available from the Irish Tourist Board. It's also online at **www.irelandhotels.com**, which is a particularly handy, searchable site, with options to sort hotels by feature (TV in all rooms, elevators, crèche [day care/babysitting], and so on). Hotels and guesthouses, depending on their size and scope, offer a good deal more than a bed and a meal—everything from nightclubs to children's playrooms to golf courses. Some were historic buildings in a former life and others have been elegant hotels from birth, but there are plenty that are nondescript. If you're traveling with a well-padded wallet, **Ireland's Blue Book** (www.irelands-blue-book.ie) is a collection of upscale manor house hotels and castles.

The governments of the Republic and of the North inspect and rate all approved hotels and guesthouses. In the Republic, hotels can aspire to five stars, but guesthouses can reach no higher than four. In the North, hotels receive one to four stars, and guesthouses are either grade A or grade B.

In this guide, however, we use a system of zero to three stars for rating places to stay, based on quality of amenities, atmosphere, and the most elusive, overall value for money. Cost is only a factor inasmuch as it affects value. For example, an expensive hotel may rate only one star, while a moderately priced guesthouse rates two stars if it delivers an exceptional experience

for the money. See the "Where to Stay" sections throughout this book for recommendations.

BED & BREAKFASTS

Throughout Ireland, in cities and countryside, a huge number of private homes are open to lodgers, by the night or longer. A warm bed and a substantial Irish breakfast can be expected, and other meals are negotiable. While most B&Bs are regulated and inspected by Tourism Quality Services (look for the shamrock seal of approval), approximately 12,000 premises are under no external supervision. Regulated or not, they are all different, as are your hosts. *Note:* Establishments without governmental supervision or approval are not necessarily inferior to those stamped with the green shamrock. Approval involves an annual fee, as well as specific restrictions that some proprietors prefer not to accept.

For a modest fee, the Irish Tourist Board will send you a detailed listing of roughly 2,000 approved B&Bs, complete with a color photo of each. Or, you can follow the recommendations in this book. Needless to say, you receive a personal touch when you stay in someone's home, and more often than not, this is a real bonus. For anyone on a budget who is touring the country and spending only a night or two in each location, B&Bs are often hard to beat.

In high season it's a good idea to make your reservation at least 24 hours in advance; your room will ordinarily be held until 6pm. In a moderately priced B&B, the average cost for a room with private bathroom is roughly €45 ($72) per person per night. Obviously, some B&Bs charge less than this, and some charge more. *Note:* More and more B&Bs accept credit cards, but many still do not—ask in advance.

In the North, the Northern Ireland Tourist Board inspects each of its recommended

B&Bs annually. Its *Information Guide to Bed & Breakfast* is available free from the NITB. The NITB also sells a useful comprehensive annual listing titled *Where to Stay in Northern Ireland.*

THE HIDDEN IRELAND

The Hidden Ireland is essentially a collection of very upscale B&Bs—think *Town & Country* with a brogue. These are private houses offering visitors the opportunity to sample upscale B&Bs, in a style not usually experienced by the ordinary tourist. The properties include some of Ireland's oldest and grandest buildings, many of particular architectural merit and character. A B&B for two people generally runs €120 to €345 ($192–$552). To explore this option, contact The Hidden Ireland, P.O. Box 31, Westport, County Mayo (✆ **800/688-0299** in the U.S., or 01/662-7166; fax 01/662-7144; www.hidden-ireland.com).

FARMHOUSE ACCOMMODATIONS

Many of Ireland's small, family-run farms offer an attractive alternative to hotels and guesthouses, especially for families with small children. The **Irish Farm Holidays Association** (www.irishfarmholidays.com) produces an annual guide to farmhouse accommodations.

SELF-CATERING

If you want to stay awhile and establish a base, you might want to consider renting an apartment, town house, cottage, or castle. Self-catering is a huge business in Ireland, and the range of available accommodations is impressive. The minimum rental period is usually 1 week, although shorter periods are negotiable in the off season. Families and small groups often find self-catering works out to be less expensive than staying in hotels. In the high season, in both the Republic and the North, a cottage sleeping seven could cost anywhere from $350 to more than $2,000 per week. Both the Irish Tourist Board and the Northern Ireland Tourist Board prepare helpful annual guides to self-catering cottages.

Among the self-catering companies worth checking out are **Trident Holiday Homes,** 15 Irishtown Rd., Irishtown, Dublin 4 (✆ **01/201-8440;** www.thh.ie). For alluring seaside properties in west County Cork, try **Cashelfean Holiday Houses,** Durrus, County Cork (✆ **027/62000;** fax 027/62012; www.cashelfean.com). In the west of Ireland a selection of traditional Irish cottages, fully equipped to meet modern expectations, is offered by **Rent an Irish Cottage PLC,** 85 O'Connell St., Limerick, County Limerick (✆ **061/411109;** fax 061/314821; www.rentacottage.ie). If you're interested in sampling the rural lifestyle, **Irish Country Holidays,** Discovery Centre, Rearcross, County Tipperary (✆ **067/27790;** fax 067/27791; www.country-holidays.ie), has properties all over Ireland.

Finally, for self-catering in any of Northern Ireland's areas of outstanding natural beauty, there is one surefire recommendation: **Rural Cottage Holidays Ltd.,** St. Anne's Court, 59 North St., Belfast BT1 1NB (✆ **0870/236-1630;** fax 028/9044-1530; www.ruralcottageholidays.com).

YOUTH HOSTELS

Ordinarily, youth hostels are not included in this book. You should be aware, however, that some Irish hostels are broadening their scope and redesigning to attract travelers of all ages, as well as families. Many have private rooms and, although they cost a fraction of even a modest bed-and-breakfast, quite a few are attractive and in extraordinarily beautiful locations.

An Óige, the Irish Youth Hostel Association, 61 Mountjoy St., Dublin 7 (✆ **01/830-4555;** fax 01/830-5808; www.anoige.ie), runs dozens of exquisitely located hostels in rural Ireland. Most are in drop-dead-gorgeous spots of natural beauty and housed in buildings of real character. Before you dismiss this option, explore the website and see if you can believe the views and the prices.

In the North, **YHANI** (Youth Hostels Association of Northern Ireland), 22–32 Donegall Rd., Belfast BT12 5JN (*©* **028/9032-4733;** fax 028/9043-9699; www.hini.org.uk), runs similar hostels of real character.

BOTTOM LINE ON BEDS

RATES Room charges quoted in this guide include 13.5% government tax (value-added tax, or VAT) in the Republic of Ireland and 17.5% VAT in Northern Ireland. They do not (unless otherwise noted) include service charges, which are usually between 10% and 15%. Most hotels and guesthouses automatically add the service charge onto your final bill, although in recent years many family-run or limited-service places have begun the practice of not charging for service, leaving it as an option for the guest. Home-style B&Bs do not ordinarily charge for service.

The price categories used throughout this guide indicate the cost of a double room for two per night, including tax but not service charges:

> **Very Expensive** €275 ($440) and up
> **Expensive** €200 to €275 ($320–$440)
> **Moderate** €100 to €200 ($160–$320)
> **Inexpensive** Under €100 ($160)

Note: Many accommodations span more than one of these categories, and in those cases, we've done our best to assign each to the category that best represents its characteristic rates in high season.

Ordinarily, the Irish list prices per person, but since we find that confusing, in this guide we've used the price a double room would cost for two people spending 1 night. Children staying in their parent's room are usually charged at 20% to 50% of the adult rate. If you're traveling on your own, there is often a single surcharge.

TERMINOLOGY The Irish use the phrase "en suite" to indicate a room with private bathroom. A "double" has a double bed, and a "twin" has two single beds. An "orthopedic" bed has an extra-firm mattress. Queen- and king-size beds are not common except in large, deluxe hotels.

RESERVATIONS If you are traveling from the U.S., you should always have at least your first night's room booked, as you will be required to give an address for where you're staying at Immigration when you arrive at the airport. That's just as well, since having rooms booked in advance is always a good idea. For properties that do not have a U.S. reservation number, the fastest way to reserve is by calling ahead or via the Internet (check the property's website anyway, as that's often where the best prices and last-minute deals are posted).

If you arrive in Ireland without a room reservation for some nights of your stay, head straight to the local tourist office, which can help with their computerized reservation service known as **Gulliver.** In Ireland or Northern Ireland, you can also call the Gulliver line directly (*©* **00800/668-668-66**). This is a nationwide and cross-border "free-phone" facility for credit card bookings, operated 8am to 11pm from Monday to Friday, and 8am to 10pm weekends. Gulliver is also accessible from the United States (*©* **011-800/668-668-66**) and on the Web at **www.gulliver.ie**.

QUALITY & VALUE Despite the various systems of approval, regulation, and ratings, accommodations in Ireland are quite uneven in quality and cost. Often these variations are due to location; a wonderful, budget B&B in an isolated area of countryside can be dirt-cheap, while a mediocre guesthouse in Dublin or Cork can cost much more.

In any given lodging, the size and quality of the rooms can vary considerably, often without any corresponding variation in cost. This is particularly true of single rooms, which can approach Victorian boardinghouse standards even in semiluxurious hotels. Don't be discouraged by this, but know what you're getting into so you're not disappointed. If you have complaints, state them at once and unambiguously—doing so may bring an immediate resolution (ask for a lower rate or a better room).

Note: Many lodgings close for a few days or more on and around Christmas, even when they announce that they are open year-round. If you plan to visit Ireland during the Christmas holidays, double-check that the hotels, restaurants, and attractions you're counting on will be open.

SAVING ON YOUR HOTEL ROOM

The **rack rate** is the maximum rate that a hotel charges for a room. Hardly anybody pays this price, however, except in high season or on holidays. To lower the cost of your room:

- **Ask about special rates or other discounts.** You may qualify for corporate, student, military, senior, frequent flyer, trade union, or other discounts.
- **Dial direct.** When booking a room in a chain hotel, you'll often get a better deal by calling the individual hotel's reservation desk rather than the chain's main number.
- **Book online.** Many hotels offer Internet-only discounts, or supply rooms to Priceline, Hotwire, or Expedia at rates much lower than the ones you can get through the hotel itself.
- **Remember the law of supply and demand.** Resort hotels are most crowded and therefore most expensive on weekends, so discounts are usually available for midweek stays. Business hotels in downtown locations are busiest during the week, so you can expect big discounts over the weekend. Many hotels have high-season and low-season prices, and booking even 1 day after

high season ends can mean big discounts.

- **Look into group or long-stay discounts.** If you come as part of a large group, you should be able to negotiate a bargain rate. Likewise, if you're planning a long stay (at least 5 days), you might qualify for a discount. As a general rule, expect 1 night free after a 7-night stay.
- **Avoid excess charges and hidden costs.** When you book a room, ask whether the hotel charges for parking. Use your own cellphone, pay phones, or prepaid phone cards instead of dialing direct from hotel phones, which usually have exorbitant rates. And don't be tempted by the room's minibar offerings. Finally, ask about local taxes and service charges, which can increase the cost of a room by 15% or more.
- **Carefully consider your hotel's meal plan.** If you enjoy eating out and sampling the local cuisine, it makes sense to choose a **Continental Plan (CP),** which includes breakfast only, or a **European Plan (EP),** which doesn't include any meals and allows you maximum flexibility. If you're more interested in saving money, opt for a **Modified American Plan (MAP),** which includes breakfast and one meal, or the **American Plan (AP),** which includes three meals. If you must choose a MAP, see if you can get a free lunch at your hotel if you decide to do dinner out.
- **Book an efficiency.** A room with a kitchenette allows you to shop for groceries and cook your own meals. This is a big money saver, especially for families on long stays.
- **Consider enrolling in hotel "frequent-stay" programs,** which are upping the ante lately to win the loyalty of repeat customers. Frequent guests can now accumulate points or credits to earn free hotel nights, airline miles, in-room

3

(Moments) Keys to the Castle

Dream of spending your vacation like a king or queen? Two companies specialize in self-catering accommodations in Ireland's historic and architecturally significant properties—including elegant Georgian manor houses, stately country mansions, lighthouses, and castles. The **Irish Landmark Trust,** 25 Eustace St., Dublin 2 ((C) **01/670-4733;** fax 01/670-4887; www.irishlandmark.com), rescues historic but neglected properties all over the island and restores them into fabulous hideaways, complete with period furnishings. It's a not-for-profit institution, so prices are hard to beat. **Elegant Ireland,** 15 Harcourt St., Dublin 2 ((C) **01/473-2505;** fax 01/473-2430; www.elegant.ie), can put you up in anything from an upscale seaside bungalow to a medieval castle that sleeps 20. As most properties are privately owned, they are priced according to what the market will bear. Bargains are harder to come by, and deals are more likely in the off season.

amenities, merchandise, tickets to concerts and events, discounts on sporting facilities—and even credit toward stock in the participating hotel, in the case of the Jameson Inn hotel group. Perks are awarded not only by many chain hotels and motels (Hilton HHonors, Marriott Rewards, Wyndham ByRequest, to name a few), but individual inns and B&Bs. Many chain hotels partner with other hotel chains, car-rental firms, airlines, and credit card companies to give consumers additional incentive to do repeat business.

LANDING THE BEST ROOM

Somebody has to get the best room in the house. It might as well be you. You can start by joining the hotel's frequent-guest program, which may make you eligible for upgrades. A hotel-branded credit card usually gives its owner "silver" or "gold" status in frequent-guest programs for free. Always ask about corner rooms. They're often larger and quieter, with more windows and light, and they often cost the same as standard rooms. When you make your reservation, ask if the hotel is renovating; if it is, request a room away from the construction. Ask about nonsmoking rooms; rooms with views; rooms with twin, queen-, or king-size beds. If you're a light sleeper, request a quiet room away from vending machines, elevators, restaurants, bars, and discos. Ask for a room that has been most recently renovated or redecorated.

If you aren't happy with your room when you arrive, ask for another one. Most lodgings will be willing to accommodate you.

Suggested Ireland Itineraries

Ireland is such a small island that you can cover a lot of ground in a week, and feel quite at home within two, but even with the best of intentions and all the energy in the world, you'll never see it all on a short visit.

To get the most out of it, you need to know, at least in part, what you want to see, and that will decide how you should travel. If your ideal Ireland involves wandering through the countryside, visiting small villages, climbing castle walls, hailing history from a ruined abbey, or finding yourself alone on a rocky beach—you simply cannot do those things without a car. Out of the main towns, public transportation exists, but it's slow and limiting. Every major town has car-rental agencies, so give strong consideration to renting a car.

The next step is deciding where to start. That decision can be made for you by where your flight terminates. If you're flying into Shannon Airport, then it makes good geographic sense to start out on the west coast. If you're flying into Dublin, you might as well explore that city first, then either head up to the North and the ruggedly beautiful Antrim coast, or head south down to the Wicklow Mountains, Kilkenny, and the crystal land of Waterford.

Still, even if you fly into Dublin but your heart is in Galway, no worries. You can traverse the width of the country in a few hours (once you get out of Dublin's stultifying sprawl), so if you start early enough, it's doable. Just bear in mind that rural roads are not well lighted or well signposted, so driving at night should be avoided. It's too stressful, and being lost in unfamiliar territory, where it can be many miles between villages, is no fun at all. This is more of an issue in the winter, when it can get dark as early as 4pm, than in the summer, when it often stays light until after 10pm.

So taking all of these factors into consideration, the question remains: *Where do you want to go?* We can't answer that question for you, but we can give you some itineraries that we have used ourselves, which you might enjoy, depending upon your interests.

These might help you focus on ways in which you can orchestrate your journey so that you can get the most out of it with the fewest scheduling worries—the last thing you want to do on vacation is to spend the whole time looking at your watch.

If you've never visited Ireland, Dublin is a good place to start, and the surrounding area holds plenty to keep you busy. If you have been here before, and Dublin and Galway are old hat, you might consider heading north, through County Mayo, County Sligo, and on to the exotic wilds of Donegal and the Antrim Coast.

Take what you find here, and pick and choose the parts that appeal to you, add in your own favorite shopping or scenic drives, and turn it all into a holiday custom-made for yourself.

The island is divided into two major political units—Northern Ireland, which, along with England, Scotland, and Wales, forms the United Kingdom, and the Republic of Ireland. Of Ireland's 32 counties, 26 are in the Republic.

Ireland divided into two separate countries in 1922, when the British government that had occupied Ireland agreed to allow the Republic to become a free state, with the exception of the six northern counties that remained part of the U.K.

The line between north and south is no longer marked, and the only indication on many roads that you've crossed into a different nation is the road signs, which change from metric distances in the Republic to imperial in Northern Ireland.

The ancient Gaelic regions into which Ireland was once divided are still used in conversation and directions: Ulster is north, Munster is south, Leinster is east, and Connaught is west. Each region is divided into counties:

In Ulster (to the north): Cavan, Donegal, and Monaghan in the Republic; Antrim, Armagh, Derry, Down, Fermanagh, and Tyrone in Northern Ireland.

In Munster (to the south): Clare, Cork, Kerry, Limerick, Tipperary, and Waterford.

In Leinster (to the east): Dublin, Carlow, Kildare, Kilkenny, Laois, Longford, Louth, Meath, Offaly, Westmeath, Wexford, and Wicklow.

In Connaught (to the west): Sligo, Mayo, Galway, Roscommon, and Leitrim.

DUBLIN & ENVIRONS With 40% of the Republic's population living within 97km (61 miles) of Dublin, the capital is the center of the profound, high-speed changes that have transformed Ireland into a prosperous and increasingly European country. Within an hour's drive of Dublin are Dalkey, Dùn Laoghaire, and many other engaging coastal towns, as well as the rural beauty of the Wicklow Mountains, and the prehistoric ruins in County Meath.

THE SOUTHEAST The southeast offers sandy beaches, Waterford's city walls and crystal works, Kilkenny and Cahir castles, the Rock of Cashel, the Irish National Heritage Park at Ferrycarrig, and Ireland's largest bird sanctuary, on the Saltee Islands.

CORK & ENVIRONS Cork, Ireland's second-largest city, feels like a buzzy university town, and provides a congenial gateway to the south and west of the island. Within arm's reach are the Blarney Castle (and its famous stone), the culinary and scenic delights of Kinsale, the Dromberg Stone Circle, Sherkin and Clear islands, and Mizen Head. Also in this region is the dazzling landscape of West Cork.

THE SOUTHWEST The once-remote splendor of County Kerry has long since ceased to be a secret, so at least during the high season, be prepared to share the view in this gorgeous section. Highlights are the Dingle Peninsula, and two sets of islands: the Skelligs and the Blaskets. Killarney is surrounded by natural beauty, but is synonymous with souvenir shops and tour buses. The Ring of Kerry (less glamorously known as highways N70 and N71) encircling the Iveragh Peninsula is the most visited attraction in Ireland after the Book of Kells. That's both a recommendation and a warning. Killarney National Park provides a stunning haven from buses.

THE WEST The west of Ireland offers a first taste of Ireland's wild beauty and striking diversity for those who fly into

Shannon Airport. County Limerick has an array of impressive castles: Knappogue, Bunratty, King John's, Ashrod, and (just over the county line in Galway) Dunguaire. County Clare's natural offerings—the Cliffs of Moher and the lunar landscape of the Burren—are unforgettable. Farther up the coast to the north, past Galway, County Mayo is the home of the sweet town of Westport on Clew Bay. Achill Island, Ireland's largest, has beaches and stunning cliff views, and is accessible by car.

GALWAY & ENVIRONS Galway just may be the perfect small city. It is vibrant, colorful, and funky—a youthful, prospering port and university city, and the self-proclaimed arts capital of Ireland with theater, music, dance, and an exciting street life. County Galway is the gateway to Connemara's moody, melancholy, magical landscapes. Here are the Twelve Bens mountains, Kylemore Abbey, and the charming town of Clifden. Offshore lie the mysterious Aran Islands—Inishmore, Inishmaan, and Inisheer—with their irresistible desolation.

THE NORTHWEST In Ireland it's easy to become convinced that isolated austerity is beautiful, and nowhere is this more true than Donegal, with its jagged, desolate coastline that, if you don't mind the cold, offers some of the finest surfing in the world. Inland, the Glenveagh National Park has as much wilderness as you could want. County Sligo inspired the poetry of

W. B. Yeats with its dense collection of megalithic sites: stone circles, passage tombs, dolmens, and cairns at Carrowmore, Knocknarea, and Carrowkeel.

THE MIDLANDS The lush center of Ireland, bisected by the lazy River Shannon, is a land of pastures, rivers, lakes, woods, and gentle mountain slopes, a lush antidote to the barren beauty of Connemara and a retreat, in high season, from the throngs of tourists who crowd the coasts. The shores and waters of the Shannon and Lough Derg and of their many lesser cousins provide much of the lure. Outdoor pursuits—cycling, boating, fishing, and hiking—are the heart of the matter here. The midlands also hold remarkable sites—Birr Castle and its splendid gardens, and Clonmacnois, the evocative ruins of a famous Irish monastic center.

NORTHERN IRELAND Across the border, Northern Ireland's six counties are undergoing a time of intense change, as peace has held there for nearly a decade. Still one of the most underrated parts of the island, the stunning Antrim coast (particularly between Ballycastle and Cushendun); the bizarre, octagonal basalt columns of the Giant's Causeway; and the Glens of Antrim are unforgettable. The loveliness of the Fermanagh Lake District is written in a minor key. The old city walls of Derry, the past glory of Carrickfergus Castle, and Belfast's elaborate political murals make a trip across the border worthwhile.

2 THE BEST OF IRELAND IN 1 WEEK

We love to fly into Dublin, knowing that the compact, laid-back city awaits a few miles down the road, with its old-fashioned pubs, its modern restaurants, and its absorbing sights all laid out for walking. If you've never been here, a couple of days in Dublin make for a quick primer on Ireland. It's just enough time to do some shopping on **Grafton Street,** head up O'Connell Street to the **General Post Office,** and discover the Georgian beauty of **St. Stephen's Green** and **Merrion Square.** It's not nearly enough time, but you can give the surface of the city a good brush in a couple of days, and then head south to **Kilkenny** and **Wicklow,** on to **Waterford, Cork,** and **Kerry,** and up to **Clare** for a quick

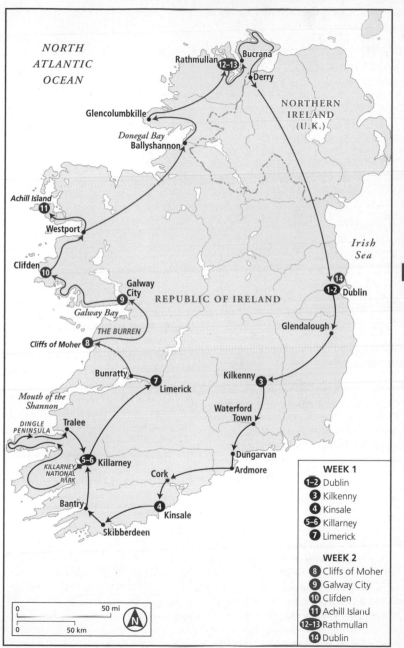

NORTH
ATLANTIC
OCEAN

Rathmullan
Bucrana
12–13
Derry

Glencolumbkille

NORTHERN
IRELAND
(U.K.)

Donegal Bay
Ballyshannon

Achill Island
11

Westport

Clifden
10

Galway
City
9
Galway Bay
THE BURREN

REPUBLIC OF IRELAND

Irish
Sea

14
1–2 Dublin

Glendalough

Cliffs of Moher 8

Bunratty

7
Limerick

Kilkenny
3

Mouth of the
Shannon

Waterford
Town

DINGLE
PENINSULA

Tralee

Dungarvan
Ardmore

5–6 Killarney

KILLARNEY
NATIONAL
PARK

Cork

Bantry

4
Kinsale

Skibberdeen

0 ____ 50 mi
0 ____ 50 km

N

WEEK 1
1–2 Dublin
3 Kilkenny
4 Kinsale
5–6 Killarney
7 Limerick

WEEK 2
8 Cliffs of Moher
9 Galway City
10 Clifden
11 Achill Island
12–13 Rathmullan
14 Dublin

glance before the clock runs out. It is only hitting the high points but, as high points go, they're not bad. This kind of trip will require at least four rolls of film and is quite high energy, but it's not completely exhausting.

Days ❶ & ❷: Arrive in Dublin ★★★

Check into your hotel, take advantage of any scones and tea offered, take a minute to relax, and then head out on foot. Get a map from your hotel to augment the ones in this book, and then just start walking. Stay south of the River Liffey, and head down Dame Street to **Dublin Castle** (p. 146), which holds the magical **Chester Beatty Library** (p. 142) with its vast collection of gorgeous illuminated manuscripts. Later take in **St. Patrick's Cathedral** (p. 148) and the vibrant green quadrangles of **Trinity College** (p. 149), before heading down to Merrion Square, with its impressive granite architecture and the ancient gold on display at the **National Museum** (p. 148). It's a short stroll from here down to **St. Patrick's Green,** where you can rest your weary toes and soak up the floral view, before strolling up **Grafton Street** for a last bit of shopping before collapsing in your hotel.

On **Day 2,** have a hearty breakfast in your hotel before striking out for **Temple Bar.** Stroll down Parliament Street to the river, then take a right, and walk along the noisy, vibrant waterfront to the effervescent arc of the **Ha'penny Bridge.** Head across and down to O'Connell Street and walk on up past its many statues to the bullet-ridden columns of the **General Post Office** (p. 154), where the 1916 Easter Rising was based. After exploring its displays, head farther up O'Connell Street to the **Dublin Writers Museum** (p. 146), which bookish types will love for its extensive display of memorabilia. It's a few doors down from the small but mighty **Hugh Lane Gallery** (p. 147), where you can marvel that such a strong collection of classical pieces was ever owned by one man.

Day ❸: South to Wicklow & Kilkenny ★★★

It takes less than 2 hours to drive from the hustle and traffic of Dublin to the peace and quiet of the **Wicklow Mountains** (p. 194), and it's well worth the trip. Drive through the town of Enniskerry to the great estate of **Powerscourt** (p. 191) on the south end of the village. After lunching in its Avoca Café, head on to **Glendalough** (p. 190) and feel your soul relax in the pastoral mountain setting of this ancient monastic retreat. From there drive on to the colorful village of **Kilkenny,** where you can spend the rest of the day shopping in its pottery and crafts shops and exploring noble **Kilkenny Castle** (p. 258). This is a good place to spend your first night outside of Dublin.

Day ❹: West to Waterford & Cork ★★

Set off west to the coastal fishing villages of County Waterford, looking out along the way for the charming village of **Dunmore East** and the alluring beaches of **Ardmore.** Stop in for a little shopping at the **Waterford Crystal Factory** (p. 240) in **Waterford Town,** and after lunch head on to Cork. If castles entice you, stop at **Dungarvan,** midway between Waterford and Cork, and spend some time wandering through the sturdy walls of **King John's Castle** (p. 215). From there, head on to explore the delightful Cork coast. Introduce yourself to busy Cork City and smaller, quieter Kinsale, either one of which would make a perfect place to spend the night.

Days ❺ & ❻: From Cork to Kerry ★★

Start Day 5 by heading west to the wilder section of Cork. It's a sprawling, political, complex area, and well worth taking some time to understand. Consider taking a tour of the area in the morning (several good ones are listed in the Cork chapter), to get a more in-depth look at it, although foodies might prefer to indulge in a half-day cooking class at **Ballymaloe Cookery School** (p. 294). Walkers might want to add a day to their journey, in order to spend some time exploring the countryside on foot. There's plenty to do, and even touristy **Blarney Castle** (p. 280), where you're bound to end up starring in a thousand Japanese home movies, is interesting to explore.

At your own pace, move on into County Kerry, at the southwest tip of the island. Here the most popular place to explore—and the most popular tourist spot in Ireland—is the **Ring of Kerry** (see "The Ring of Kerry," in chapter 11). It is a beautiful drive, but because of the preponderance of tourist buses, not everybody will want to make it. Others will brave the masses to see extraordinary countryside. If it's quiet you're after, skip the Ring and head instead to the bucolic peace of **Killarney National Park** (p. 325), where you can indulge in a buggy ride around its lake

and leave only your footsteps. Golfers with a bit of money to burn will want to play a round at the **Waterville Golf Links** (p. 317), surrounded by soft sand dunes at the edge of the sea. You can spend the afternoon shopping in Killarney if you're bored with the car by now, or drive around the **Dingle Peninsula.**

Day ❼: County Clare
Time is short now, so you won't be able to see as much of Clare as it deserves. But make a promise to yourself to come back someday, and head for the perilously tall **Cliffs of Moher** (p. 385) where the view seems to stretch all the way to America (although the price to park will make you shiver). You can lunch in the town of **Ennis,** and then decide whether you'd rather spend the rest of the day exploring the touristy but interesting offerings at **Bunratty Castle** (p. 367) or marveling at the otherworldly landscape of the **Burren** (see "The Burren," in chapter 12). If it's the latter, strike out for the R480 road, which offers the best immediate gratification, as it winds its way through the extraordinary limestone landscape. What a way to end your trip!

3 THE BEST OF IRELAND IN 2 WEEKS

With 2 weeks, your visit to Ireland will be much more relaxed. You can stretch out a bit more in your travels, heading to less crowded counties, with more time to meet the locals. In your second week, head up to Galway, Mayo, and Donegal, taking time to smell the heather along the way.

Days ❶ through ❼
Follow "The Best of Ireland in 1 Week" itinerary, as outlined above.

Day ❽: County Clare
After spending Day 7 exploring Clare, you'll discover that you need more time to really get the most out of this big, varied place. Wander the castles of Clare—**Bunratty,**

Dromoland, and **Knappogue** (p. 367, 374, and 372)—and consider indulging in one of their medieval banquets held nightly in summer. They're unsurprisingly expensive, but also good fun. Abbey lovers should take the time for the mile-long walk to the exquisite **Corcomroe Abbey** (p. 382).

Day ❾: County Clare to Galway City

This morning, drive up from Clare to Galway City (it will take around an hour), and spend a relaxing day walking the delightful streets of this artsy, vibrant town. Shop for stemware at the **Galway Irish Crystal Heritage Centre** (p. 399), and wander the waterfront. Spend the afternoon relaxing and shopping for locally made arts and crafts, or lingering over pints at the sunny **Front Door** pub (p. 403). If you don't need the rest, and you want to stay busy, take a cruise out to the misty **Aran Islands** (see "The Aran Islands," in chapter 13), or head down to explore Yeats's old country home, **Thoor Ballylee** (p. 407).

Day ❿: County Galway

Start early, and strike out for the tiny R336, the best road for exploring the craggy Galway coastline. Stop by the pretty little town of **Spiddal,** where plentiful adorable little shops sell Aran sweaters and other Irish knits—our favorite shop is **Standún** (p. 410). Follow signs to the cliff-top town of **Clifden,** which has spectacular views and lots of good restaurants and pubs, making it a good place to break for lunch, and a spot of crafts shopping at **Fuchsia Craft** (p. 416). We love to see the countryside from horseback, and **Cleggan Riding Centre** (p. 418) offers great horseback tours.

Day ⓫: County Mayo

Driving up from Galway, the scenery stays spectacular in Mayo, where the rocky shoreline plunges to the cobalt sea in glorious fashion. Head to the south Mayo town of **Westport,** which sits at the edge of a picturesque river, and is a delightful, peaceful place to wander. From there, drive across the flatlands, a strangely empty landscape, toward **Achill Island;** the drive along the coast and out across a bridge to the island is slow and windy, but the views are fantastic. Spend a relaxing afternoon

and evening exploring the island, before climbing into a comfortable bed at the **Bervie,** where the sea is right outside the door.

Day ⓬: County Mayo to Donegal

Drive up through Mayo and the quiet farmland of Sligo to the rugged landscape of Donegal. Head up the coast past Donegal Town until you catch the N15 road, and then follow it around the breathtaking coastline to the busy hill town of **Ballyshannon,** which has excellent crafts shops and glorious views from the top of the hill. The adventurous can explore the **Catsby Cave** (p. 468), a picturesque grotto at the edge of the Abbey River. But here the drive is really the thing, so drive on to the darling town of Glencolumbkille. There's an excellent folk park here that's well worth an hour of your time before you head on to the stone-cut town of Ardara at the foot of a steep hill—it's wall-to-wall arts-and-crafts shops, and is a pleasure to explore. From there it's around an hour's drive to the Fanad, a scenic drive around Lough Swilly. Follow it around to Rathmullan, a quiet, lakefront village, and spend the night there at relaxing **Rathmullan House** (p. 480).

Day ⓭: Donegal

You've been traveling a great deal, so today is a rest day. Spend the morning walking along the lake, or take a horseback tour down its sandy beaches (Rathmullan House arranges excellent horseback treks for adults and pony treks for children). In the afternoon, after you've recharged your batteries, drive around the lake and explore the little villages: **Rathmelton** is a picturesque town with stone cottages mirrored in the glassy lake, while **Dunfanaghy** is adorable and has an excellent beach—perfect for an afternoon swim.

Day ⓮: Heading Home

If your flight leaves late, you could rise early and spend the morning driving up to

Malin Head, the northernmost tip of Ireland; a wild and woolly place just a couple of hours' drive from Rathmullan. From there, expect the drive to the airport to take at least 4 hours, but allow plenty of time in case of traffic backups around Dublin—they're virtually constant.

4 THE BEST OF IRELAND FOR FAMILIES

Traveling with children is always a bit of an adventure, and you'll want all the help you can get. Luckily Ireland—with its vast open countryside, farm hotels, and castles—is a fairy-tale playground for kids. You'll have trouble finding babysitters outside the major towns, but just take the kids with you—most restaurants, sights, and even pubs (during the day) welcome children. The best part of the country for those traveling with kids is arguably Cork and Kerry, where everything seems to be set up for families, so here's a sample itinerary to give you some ideas.

Day ❶: Cork City
Start with a stroll through the city on foot. You can pick and choose what your kids will like best. There's a pleasantly scary exhibition at the old **Cork City Gaol** (p. 278), where lifelike figures still await their release in the jail cells. Afterward, you can all go shopping at the **Coal Quay Market** (p. 278)—a flea market where you never quite know what to expect amid its colorful stalls. Next, pack a picnic lunch and head outside the city to the **Blarney Castle** (p. 280), where you can easily fill an entire afternoon kissing rocks, climbing castle walls, and exploring Badger Cave and the castle's gloomy dungeons. The sprawling grounds make a perfect place to dine alfresco. If money is no object, spend the night at the **Hayfield Manor Hotel** (p. 273), where the kids will get cookies and milk before bedtime.

Day ❷: Eastern County Cork
In the morning head to the star-shaped **Charles Fort** (p. 288), where the kids can clamber around the ancient walls while you bone up on a little history. You can head for more ancient wall climbing at **Desmond Castle** (p. 288), or, if the kids have had enough historic buildings, indulge them at the **Fota Island Wildlife Park** (p. 295), a zoo without borders, where rare and endangered animals have the run of the place—only cheetahs are behind conventional fencing. You can have another picnic here, as picnic tables are ready and waiting. Spend the night at the **Barnabrow Country House** (p. 297), which is set up for families with everything from babysitters on call to cribs.

Day ❸: Western County Cork
Take the kids on an unforgettable ride in a wooden cable car out to **Dursey Island** (p. 298), which you can easily explore on foot while taking in the sweeping views. Back on the mainland there are plenty of little colorful towns, including Ballydehob, where all the signs for local shops and pubs are done in pictures rather than words. Take them to the **Dromberg Stone Circle** (p. 299) to learn about ancient religions; its strange beauty will bewitch even younger travelers. Take a ferry out to Ilnacullin—just for the ride—or go swimming off Barleycove Beach, where the sand is white and soft. Spend the night at **Baltimore Harbour Hotel** (p. 306), which has a kids' club in the summer to keep them busy while you relax.

Day ❹: Kenmare
After driving along a coastal route through a number of tiny beachfront villages, the

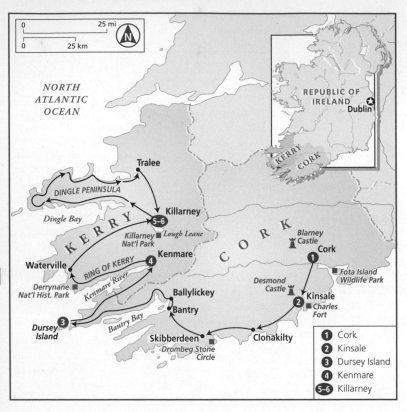

kids will be ready to hit the water themselves. You can either drive down the Ring of Kerry to the idyllic beach resort of **Waterville,** where you can spend an afternoon swimming, sunbathing, and picnicking, or stop at Kenmare for a seal-watching trip with **Seafari Eco-nature Cruises** (p. 316). The kids will spot everything from frolicking sea otters to sleepy gray seals on the way.

Day ❺: Killarney
Welcome to Ireland's ideal town for families: You could keep the kids busy in Killarney for days. Head straight for the gorgeous **Killarney National Park** (p. 325), stopping first at **Muckross House** (p. 325),

where you can get a good park map and a helpful explanation of all of its myriad offerings. Set yourself up near the lakes and spend a relaxing morning rowing out to the **islands,** which hold medieval ruins ripe for exploration. Bring a picnic lunch and relax on the shore, or dine in one of the island cafes. In the afternoon, pack the kids into one of the many **buggies** that traverse the park, or head off to **Kennedy's Pet Farm** (p. 326) for some hands-on learning about traditional farming.

Day ❻: The Dingle Peninsula
It's back to the seafront today to get up close and personal with sea life. In the morning, introduce the kids to Fungie the

Dolphin on a **Fungie Tour** (p. 338)—the town mascot is playful and personable, and has a disarming affinity for humans. Boats go out throughout the day to her favorite play area, and she'll swim right up to you. In the afternoon, there's a chance to play with rays, mollusks, and other sea creatures in the hands-on displays in the **Oceanworld Aquarium** (p. 338).

Day ❼: Heading Home

If you have the time, in the morning head to the little town of Blennerville to see its huge working **windmill** (p. 346). If you go inside, you can see it doing its stuff—grinding wheat into flour as it has done for more than 200 years. It's a beautiful way to end your tour of Kerry. From here expect a drive to Shannon Airport to take less than 2 hours, and a drive to Dublin Airport to take 3 to 4 hours.

5 DISCOVERING THE NORTH

Years of turmoil made the North of Ireland a no-go zone for many tourists, and justifiably so. There was a time when, whatever your perspective on the Troubles, driving around here could be a bit nerve-racking. But times have changed, and peace has taken hold here, giving you a perfect opportunity to discover this complex region. It is, perhaps, the most untouched section of Ireland, since for decades it's been protected from the tourist hordes by its political problems. Even today you can explore the restless beauty of the **Antrim Coast** in relative peace, and walk the **Giant's Causeway** alone at sunset. But do it quickly, because word is getting out.

Day ❶: Belfast

Spend the morning getting your bearings, something that is best done by getting out on the street and walking. You can easily see most of Belfast's central sights—tour the grand **City Hall** (p. 499), shop on the small medieval arcades, stop to view the extraordinary ceiling mosaics at the **Belfast Cathedral** (p. 499). Have lunch at **White's Tavern** (p. 512), a 300-year-old pub where you can get traditional Irish stews, and bangers and mash (sausages and mashed potatoes) in a historic setting. In the afternoon, take a "Black Cab" tour of the Falls and Shankill roads—these one-on-one tours of the areas where the Troubles were the most destructive are an unforgettable chance to hear what happened from those who were there.

Day ❷: Carrickfergus & the Antrim Coast

The noble Norman castle of **Carrickfergus** (p. 515) stands guard about a 15-minute

drive from Belfast, and if you head there first thing in the morning, and strike out northward on the A2 road from there, you'll be amid peaceful coastal scenery in about 20 minutes—look out for sweeping views of craggy coastline just after the town of Ballygawley. Stop in the little town of **Glenarm** to explore its castle walls and take in its stone buildings, then head on to **Carnlough,** where you can walk to a waterfall before having a traditional Irish lunch at the **Londonderry Arms** (p. 531). Next, drive on to **Cushendun,** to photograph its little stone cottages and have a cup of tea. From there, if you're not afraid of heights, follow signs for the **Torr Head Scenic Road** to **Murlough Bay** for the most spectacular views of the day from the top of a rocky cliff so high that clouds swirl around your ankles. Spend the night at **Whitepark House** (p. 529) overlooking the white crescent of **White Park Bay.**

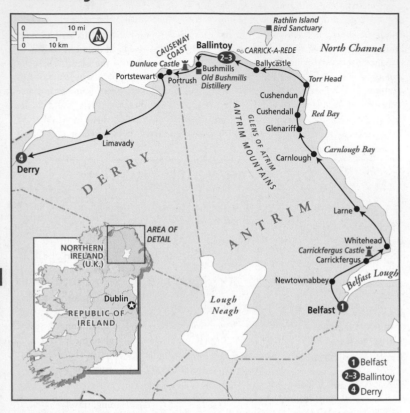

Day ❸: Ballintoy & the Headlands

After a soul-affirming breakfast, take a brisk walk down the steep hill to **White Park Bay,** and explore for fossils and seashells while soaking up the sea air, then backtrack a few miles on the A2 to the **Carrick-A-Rede Rope Bridge** (but cross it only if you're fine with heights; p. 525). Heading northwest again, follow signs to the **Giant's Causeway** (p. 526), and spend an hour or so exploring its dramatic octagonal pillars. Lunch in **Ballintoy** (or have a picnic on the beach at White Park Bay), then either relax in the countryside or take an afternoon tour of the **Old Bushmills Distillery** (p. 527) in Bushmills. Spend another night at Whitepark House.

Day ❹: Derry

Head inland along the A37 to the busy waterfront town of Derry—about a 40-minute drive. Spend the morning wandering its 17th-century city **walls,** taking in the views and history, and have a pub lunch at **Badger's** (p. 551). In the afternoon, indulge in some shopping in the old city (especially in the **Derry Craft Village;** p. 547), and then take time to explore the **Tower Museum** (p. 546) and the **Cathedral of St. Columb** (p. 545), where a 17th-century mortar shell still sits on the porch. In the evening, feast on steaks at **O'Brien's** (p. 551), then meet the locals and catch a traditional Irish band at **Mullan's Bar** (p. 552).

6 EXPLORING ANCIENT IRELAND

Unique among European nations, Ireland has treasured and protected its ancient past, and its mysterious stone circles, cairns, and huge stone tables called dolmens are still to be found, perfectly preserved, in pastures and on hillsides all over the island. These are precious connections to our own long-lost pasts, as they provide a window through which we can catch a hazy glimpse of what life was like very long ago. Some of the oldest tombs predate the Egyptian pyramids by centuries, and, in many cases, the sites are preserved but their meaning has long since disappeared, making them intriguing and elusive in equal measures. Exploring these rocky symbols can be the most memorable part of any trip to Ireland.

Day ❶: Knowth & the Boyne Valley

After an early breakfast, head north to the rich rolling Boyne Valley, about an hour's drive north of Dublin off the N2, to the Brú na Bóinne Visitor Centre—the essential center of an extensive Neolithic burial ground. This huge necropolis holds numerous sites, with three open to visitors—**Newgrange** (p. 212), **Knowth** (p. 210), and **Dowth.** Register at the center to tour Newgrange first—a tour here, early in the day before it gets crowded, is spectacular. Next tour the burial ground at Knowth, with its extensive collection of passage-grave art. In the afternoon, head down the N3 to the **Hill of Tara** (p. 210), where mounds and passage graves date to the Bronze Age.

Day ❷: Céide Fields

It will take a couple of hours to drive to the remote location in north County Mayo, but your efforts will be rewarded at this extraordinary ancient site (p. 435) that holds the stony remains of an entire prehistoric farming village on top of a cliff with breathtaking views of the sea and surrounding countryside. Spend the day exploring the 5,000-year-old site, and lunch in the excellent visitor center.

Day ❸: County Sligo

In the morning, drive east to County Sligo. On the N4, south of Sligo Town, visit the **Carrowkeel Passage Tomb Cemetery** (p. 449), on a hilltop overlooking

Lough Arrow. It has wide, sweeping views, and its 14 cairns and dolmens are often very quiet early in the day—with luck you might have it all to yourself. Then head on to Sligo Town, and follow signs to **Carrowmore Megalithic Cemetery** (p. 449). This extraordinary site has 60 stone circles, passage tombs, and dolmens scattered across acres of green pastures, and is believed to predate Newgrange by nearly a millennium. In the afternoon, if you're feeling energetic, climb to the hilltop cairn of **Knocknarea** nearby—it's believed to be the grave of folklore fairy Queen Maeve.

Day ❹: Inishmurray Island

After a relaxing morning, travel by boat to the island of **Inishmurray** (see "Exploring the Surrounding Countryside" in chapter 15) off the coast of Sligo. There you can spend the day wandering the impressively complete remains of the early monastic settlement founded in the 6th century. You can still make out its chapels and churches, its beehive cells and altars. If the weather is fine, pack a picnic lunch, and eat on the sunny beach.

Day ❺: Skellig Michael

Right after breakfast, head south to County Kerry, where this starkly beautiful island sits 13km (8 miles) offshore, standing sternly as a kind of memorial to the hardy souls who once eked out a living amid its formidable cliffs and stony mountains (see "The Ring of Kerry" in chapter

4

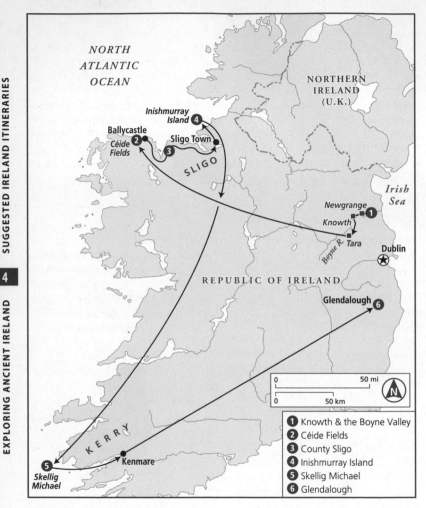

1 Knowth & the Boyne Valley
2 Céide Fields
3 County Sligo
4 Inishmurray Island
5 Skellig Michael
6 Glendalough

11). Deeply observant early Christian monks punished their bodies by living here in miserable conditions, and spent their days carving 600 steps into the unyielding stone, so that their walk up to their beehive huts and icy chapels could be made somewhat safer. Today it is an unforgettable landscape, and the ruins of their homes are deeply evocative and profoundly moving. A trip out here by boat, and an afternoon's exploration, will take up much of the day. Once you return to the mainland, reward yourself with a relaxing evening in Kenmare.

Day 6: Glendalough

Drive east today to County Wicklow, where the evocative ruins of the monastery at **Glendalough** (p. 190) are so large and sprawling, spread around two peaceful lakes on the side of a mountain, that they can fill your entire day. Get a map and information from the visitor center before beginning your exploration of the round towers, chapels, and huts dotted around the wooded site. Don't miss the ancient chapel known as **St. Kevin's Kitchen.** If the weather is warm, bring your lunch and picnic by the lake.

7 THE BEST DUBLIN PUB-CRAWL

Dublin has a collection of some of the world's best pubs, tucked away on side streets, quietly minding their own business. James Joyce theorized that it was impossible to walk across the city without passing one, and you'd be hard-pressed to do it today. Many of these places have been offering pints of ale to weary travelers for centuries, so touring them is a refreshing way to look at Dublin's history. In a few hours of pub hopping you can take in a lot of city sights, while also taking advantage of the opportunity to meet (and drink with) locals on their home turf. Start in the afternoon and take your time. Make it a relaxing walking tour of central Dublin, stopping for drinks and conversation. Who knows who you'll meet along the way?

Pub ❶: Doheny and Nesbitt

Long popular with politicians, journalists, and (oddly) economists, this pub makes a great start to any stout-based tour of Dublin. Founded in 1850, it's just around the corner from the government buildings. It's said that the seeds of Ireland's current economic success were planted here, where a band of politicians, civil servants, and economists regularly met and drank in the 1980s. Journalists dubbed them "the Doheny and Nesbitt School of Economics." 5 Lower Baggot St., Dublin 2.

Pub ❷: Grogan's Castle Lounge

With its old, wood-paneled walls lined with a rag-tag collection of art, this pub is known as one of the city's friendlier joints. It's a favorite with writers and journalists, so it's a great place to eavesdrop on political gossip or hear the latest jokes. Open a newspaper, sit conspicuously near the bar, order a pint of Guinness, and somebody will surely come ask your opinion about something. 15 William St. S., Dublin 2.

Pub ❸: The Long Hall

Many locals believe this is the city's most handsome pub, and it's easy to see why. Its rich ceiling of red oak, and the titular long bar stretching the length of the building, make it a uniquely atmospheric place in which to sip a pint. The regulars are a mixed group of local professionals and tourists, and the bar staff are friendly. The clock behind the bar mysteriously promising "Correct Time" can be easily ignored, as many a visitor has come for a quick pint but stayed for hours. 51 S. Great George's St., Dublin 2.

Pub ❹: McDaid's

Just off Grafton Street, McDaid's is one of those rare establishments—able to be all things to all people. Founded in 1779, it's a charming old pub with a long literary history. It was the writer Brendan Behan's favorite pub, and its fame still brings in crowds of tourists, but that doesn't stop the locals from coming, and the colorful mix of Irish regulars and wide-eyed tourists looking for an authentic experience makes for a lively evening. It's packed to the rafters every night, so it's a good thing you've come here late in the afternoon. 3 Harry St., off Grafton Street, Dublin 2.

Pub ❺: The Porterhouse

After all that pub-crawling, it's time to put some food in your stomach. The

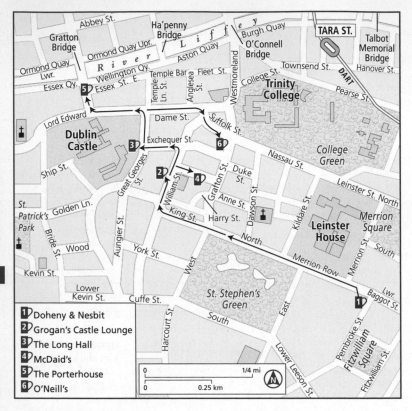

1 Doheny & Nesbit
2 Grogan's Castle Lounge
3 The Long Hall
4 McDaid's
5 The Porterhouse
6 O'Neill's

Porterhouse is a microbrewery, and it specializes in traditional Irish pub food. You can have a hearty plate of sausages and mash, or a big bowl of Irish stew, and a small half-pint (known just as a "half") of one of their seasonal tasty ales. This is a big, modern pub, with wood floors and lots of tables, so you're likely to get a seat, and you can sit and think about where to go next while filling up on some affordable, quality pub food. 16–18 Parliament St., Dublin 2.

Pub 6: O'Neill's

If you've made it this far, then you deserve to finish your night in O'Neill's. This big,

blowsy barn of a pub is a lively place to spend an evening. Outside it's a grand, historic Victorian building; inside it's a big, busy place with a lively atmosphere. Bands play most nights, so it's a good place to hear traditional and modern Irish music. It has a band of fiercely loyal regulars who will talk your ear off if you let them. It's a great place to sit back and people-watch into the small hours—but it's certainly not a relaxing place. 2 Suffolk St., Dublin 2.

5

Ireland Outdoors

Ireland is a satisfyingly wild place, where foxes and hares wander in and out of city limits, otters frolic in the rivers, seals bark on the beaches, and wildflowers blanket the countryside in spring like someone has spilled the paint. It has spaces of extreme isolation—in Donegal and County Mayo you can drive for long stretches on empty highways and walk for hours along a coastal headland without meeting another human. It can almost be unnerving. But you have to get out of the city to do it.

About a third of Ireland's 3.8 million residents live in Dublin and its sprawling suburbs—and almost half its entire population live within 60 miles. Apart from a few other small cities, the remaining population spreads thinly across the rest of the island, putting very few demands on the environment. As a result, there are remarkably intact bird and wildlife habitats.

That's the way the locals like it—they love the outdoors and spend as much of their time in it as possible. So what if it rains? That doesn't stop the Irish from golfing, hiking, fishing, and cycling. You're not made of sugar—get outside.

1 BICYCLING

Bicycling is an ideal way to explore the Irish landscape. The distances are quite manageable, and in a week or two on a bike, you can travel through several of the regions described in this guide or explore one in greater detail. Hostels, B&Bs, and hotels are abundantly available for touring cyclists who don't want to deal with the extra weight of a tent and sleeping bag. Even if you're not game to undertake a full-fledged bike tour, day trips on two wheels are a great way to stretch your legs after spending too much time in the car.

Roads in Ireland are categorized as **M** (Motorway), **N** (National), or **R** (Regional); some still bear the older **T** (Trunk) and **L** (Link) designations. For reasons of scenery as well as safety, you probably want to avoid motorways and national roads. The R and L roads are always suitable for cycling, as are the N roads in outlying areas where there isn't too much traffic. The biggest disadvantage of the smaller roads in remote areas is that they often are not signposted, so you should have a good map and compass. In some areas of the west and northwest, *only* the N roads are consistently signposted.

If you're going to hook up with a cycling outfitter (see below), you probably won't need to bring your own gear. But if you're planning on going it alone, ask your airline how much it will cost to stow your bike in the baggage hold. Be forewarned that airlines are increasingly charging additional fees for "oddly" shaped and bulky items, such as golf bags and bicycles.

Even if you'll be renting a bike, you'll still want to consider bringing a few of your own items. Helmets are only sporadically available, and you have a poor chance of finding one that fits, so bring one with you. Rental panniers (saddlebags) are often on the flimsy side. If you have cycling shoes and good pedals, you can easily attach them to the rental bike and make your trip immeasurably more enjoyable. With advance notice, most rental shops can outfit a bike with toe clips, bar ends, and water-bottle holders; an advance booking can also improve your chances of reserving the right size bike. Many rental outfits can also arrange a one-way rental over a short distance (up to 161km/100 miles or so). The national companies, such as Eurotrek Raleigh and Ireland Rent-A-Bike (see below), are set up for one-way rentals throughout the country.

Anyone cycling in Ireland should be prepared for two inevitable obstacles: wind and hills. Outside the midlands, there are hills just about everywhere, and those on the back roads can have thigh-burning grades. Road engineering is rather primitive—instead of having switchbacks on a steep slope, roads often climb by the most direct route.

> (Tips) **Biking Tip**
>
> If you'll be biking in the west, plan your route from south to north—the same direction as the prevailing winds.

Cyclists have long favored the coastal roads of the southwest, west, and northwest. The quiet roads and rugged scenery of the Beara Peninsula (see chapter 10) make it perfect for a cycling tour, along with the nearby Dingle Peninsula (see chapter 11). The spectacular Causeway Coast and the Glens of Antrim in the North (see chapter 17) are just made for cycling, with quiet roads and dazzling views. Donegal (see chapter 16) is one of the hilliest regions and rewards the energetic cyclist with some of the country's most spectacular coastal and mountain scenery.

Ireland's many islands provide further cycling options—you can bring your bike on all passenger ferries, often for no extra charge, and roads out on the islands have little or no traffic. Some of the best islands with accommodations are Cape Clear, County Cork (see chapter 10); Great Blasket Island, County Kerry (see chapter 11); the Aran Islands, County Galway (see chapter 13); and Achill and Clare islands, County Mayo (see chapter 15).

BICYCLING OUTFITTERS & RESOURCES

If you're booking from the United States, **Backroads** (© **800/462-2848** or 510/527-1555; www.backroads.com) and **VBT** (© **800/245-3868;** www.vbt.com) are both well-regarded companies offering all-inclusive bicycle trips in Ireland. Included are bikes, gear, luggage transportation via a support van, good food, and accommodations in local inns and hotels of character—everything bundled into one price.

If you want to design your own itinerary and bike independently, several rental agencies with depots nationwide permit one-way rental. They include **Eurotrek Raleigh** (Ireland's largest), Longmile Road, Dublin 12 (© **01/465-9659;** www.raleigh.ie); and **Emerald Cycles/Ireland Rent-A-Bike,** Roches Street, Limerick, County Limerick (© **061/416983;** www.irelandrentabike.com). Mountain and cross-country bike rental rates average €20 ($32) per day, €80 ($128) per week, and €100 ($160) for a one-way rental. You'll also have to fork up a refundable deposit of €50 to €100 ($80–$160) per bike.

If you want your cycling trip to be orchestrated and outfitted by affable local experts, consider **Irish Cycling Safaris,** Belfield Bike Shop, Belfield House, University College Dublin, Dublin 4 (© **01/260-0749;** fax 01/716-1168; www.cyclingsafaris.com). It offers trips to practically every part of Ireland suitable for two wheels.

For independent cycling adventures in the Southeast of Ireland, contact **Celtic Cycling,** Lorum Old Rectory, Bagenalstown, County Carlow (© **059/977-5282;** fax 059/977-5455; www.celticcycling.com). On the opposite side of the island, **Irish Cycling Tours,** Derrynasliggaun, Leenane, Connemara, County Galway, Ireland (© **095/43411;** fax 095/42314; www.irishcyclingtours.com) offers guided and self-guided tours in the

> **Tips Biking Tip**
>
> Don't wait until you arrive in Ireland to reserve your bike. Many outfitters have gone out of business in the past few years due to skyrocketing insurance costs. The only way to guarantee you'll have a bike is to prebook.

west—specifically Kerry and Connemara—for everyone from honeymooners and families to seniors and singles.

2 WALKING

Hiking is a relatively new sport in Ireland, but one that is growing fast. Since 1982, the network of long-distance, marked trails has grown from 1 to 25, covering some 2,414km (1,500 miles). The first to open was the **Wicklow Way,** which begins just outside Dublin and proceeds through rugged hills and serene pastures on its 132km (82-mile) course. Others include the **Beara Peninsula** (see chapter 10), the **Kerry Way** (see chapter 11), the **Dingle Way** (see chapter 11), and the **Ulster Way** (see chapter 17). Most trails are routed so that meals and accommodations—B&Bs, hostels, or hotels—are never more than a day's walk apart. Routes are generally uncrowded, and lots of people tend to walk just part of the trails' lengths.

Though long-distance routes are the best-marked trails in Ireland, the signposting is surprisingly random and inadequate, and a map is an absolute necessity. Markers are frequently miles apart and often seem to be lacking at crucial crossroads. Because trees on Irish hillsides rarely impede visibility, a post or cairn on each summit usually indicates the way between two peaks. A compass becomes crucial when a fog blows in and all landmarks quickly disappear. **Be warned:** This can happen quite unexpectedly, and the safest strategy when you can't see your way is to stay exactly where you are until the fog clears.

The walks listed in this guide are on clearly marked trails whenever possible, and otherwise indicated if sections are without markings. We can't give you all the information you need for the walks, of course, so you should consult the local tourist office for advice before setting out. Bear in mind that walking, or rambling as it's called in the U.K., is not as popular here as it is in Britain. There, walkers have the right of way across private property, and fences that cross public paths must have places for walkers to pass through. Here the laws are in favor of the property owners, and farmers are passionate about the privacy of their land. Stay on marked paths, or face the unmitigated wrath of an angry Irish sheep farmer.

For inland hillwalking, try the Wicklow Way (see chapter 7), the Galtee Mountains (see chapter 8), or Glenveagh National Park (see chapter 16). For coastal walks, the best-known kind in this island country, try the Beara Peninsula (see chapter 10), the Inishowen Peninsula (see chapter 16), the Dingle Peninsula (see chapter 11), the Western Way in Connemara (see chapter 14), and the Donegal Bay Coast (see chapter 16).

Ireland's National Parks

Ireland's six **national parks** offer up some of the most spectacular scenery and best walking in the country, and all have free admission.

- The **Burren National Park,** Mullaghmore, County Clare (www.burren nationalpark.ie), holds fascinating landscapes—a series of limestone beds eroded during the Ice Age to form a barren, lunarlike landscape. The Burren is of particular interest to botanists, since it's the only place in the world where Arctic, Mediterranean, and Alpine species of wildflowers grow side by side in the fissures of the rock.

- **Connemara National Park,** Letterfrack, County Galway (www.connemara nationalpark.ie), is a rugged, heather-clad landscape of blanket bog and wet heath, encompassing some of the Twelve Bens mountain range. There are nature trails with accompanying map/booklets (guided walks are available in summer) and a visitor center at Letterfrack.

- **Glenveagh National Park,** near Gweedore, County Donegal (www.glenveagh nationalpark.ie), is Ireland's largest national park and also its remotest wilderness—103,600 sq. km (40,000 sq. miles) of mountains, lakes, and natural woodlands that are home to a large red deer population. From the visitor center, you can grab a ride on a minibus along the shores of Lough Veagh to Glenveagh Castle, notable for its outstanding gardens. There are also a self-guided nature trail and a summer program of guided walks.

- **Killarney National Park,** Killarney, County Kerry (www.killarneynational park.ie), contains nearly 64,750 sq. km (25,000 sq. miles) of spectacular lake and mountain scenery. There are four self-guided trails, a visitor center with a restaurant, and two small lodges with tearooms.

- **Ballycroy National Park,** Ballycroy, County Mayo (www.ballycroynational park.ie), is the newest of the parks, centered in the Owenduff-Nephinbeg area. It features gorgeous bog landscapes. Along with a visitor center in Ballycroy, there are nature trails galore.

- **Wicklow Mountains National Park,** Glendalough, County Wicklow (www. wicklowmountainsnationalpark.ie), is the only park of the six that's not on the west coast. At over 129,500 sq. km (50,000 sq. miles), it contains picturesque woodlands, moors, and mountains, and includes the atmospheric Glendalough monastic site and the Glenealo Valley. There is a park information office at the Upper Lake, near the Glendalough car park.

In addition to national parks, there are 12 **forest reserve parks,** several of which were former private estates. Among the most enchanting is Lough Key Forest Park in County Roscommon, which features a bog-garden, fairy bridge, and archaeological monuments. Contact the Irish Tourist Board (see "Visitor Information" in chapter 3) for more information on Ireland's park system.

| Impressions

Our greatest glory is not in never falling, but in rising every time we fall.

—Oliver Goldsmith |

WALKING RESOURCES

Start your research on the Web. An excellent online resource with plenty of recommended walks is **www.gowalkingireland.com**. The **Mountaineering Council of Ireland,** which oversees hillwalking on the island, can be visited at **www.mountaineering.ie**.

Before leaving home, you can order maps and guidebooks, including details of available accommodations en route, from **EastWest Mapping** (℗/fax **053/937-7835;** www.eastwestmapping.ie). You can buy maps and guidebooks in local bookshops and outdoor-gear shops across Ireland. Guides can also be obtained from **An Óige,** the Irish Youth Hostel Association, 61 Mountjoy St., Dublin 1 (℗ **01/830-4555;** www.anoige.ie), or in the North from **Hostelling International Northern Ireland,** 22–32 Donegall Rd., Belfast BT12 5JN (℗ **028/9032-4733;** www.hini.org.uk).

Ordnance survey maps are available in several scales; the most helpful to the walker is the 1:50,000, or 1¼-inches-to-1-mile, scale. This series is currently available for all of Northern Ireland and a limited number of locations in the Republic. A half-inch-to-1-mile series covers the whole country in 25 maps, available in most shops. These indicate roads, major trails, and historic monuments in some detail, but are too small in scale to be very useful. For ordnance survey maps, contact **Ordnance Survey Ireland,** Phoenix Park, Dublin 8 (℗ **01/802-5300;** www.osi.ie), or **Ordnance Survey of Northern Ireland,** Colby House, Stranmillis Court, Belfast BT9 5BJ (℗ **028/9025-5755;** www.osni.gov.uk). The Irish Tourist Board's booklet *Walking Ireland* and the Northern Ireland Tourist Board's *An Information Guide to Walking* are both very helpful. Other excellent resources include *Best Irish Walks,* edited by Joss Lynam (Passport Books, 1995), and *Irish Long Distance Walks: A Guide to All the Way-Marked Trails,* by Michael Fewer (Gill and Macmillan, 1993).

Hidden Trails (℗ **888/9-TRAILS** [987-2457]; www.hiddentrails.com) offers 7-day guided and self-guided hiking tours of six regions in Ireland, including the Wicklow Mountains, West Cork, the Burren, and Connemara. The tours are graded easy, moderate, or challenging, and include lodging, meals (breakfast, picnic lunch, and dinner), and luggage transport to and from the trail heads. Rates average €325 ($520) per person, double occupancy, for a week.

In the west of Ireland, there's a wide selection of guided walks in the Burren, from 1 day to a week or more. Contact **Burren Walking Holidays,** with the Carrigann Hotel, Lisdoonvarna (℗ **065/707-4036;** fax 065/707-4567). In the southwest, contact **South-WestWalks Ireland,** 28 The Anchorage, Tralee, County Kerry (℗ **066/712-8733;** fax 066/712-8762; www.southwestwalksireland.com). For a full walking holiday package to County Kerry or County Clare and Connemara, consult **Backroads,** 801 Cedar St., Berkeley, CA, 94710 (℗ **800/462-2848;** www.backroads.com).

On the Northern Ireland Tourist Board's website (**www.discovernorthernireland.com/walking**), a walking and hiking page lists self-guided tours, short hikes along the Ulster Way, and names and addresses of organizations offering guided walks throughout the North.

3 BIRD-WATCHING

Ireland is of great interest to birders because of its position on the migration routes of many passerines and seabirds, which find the isle a convenient stopping point on their Atlantic journeys. Opportunities for birding abound, particularly in the 71 **National Nature Reserves.** The network of reserves covers woodlands, bog lands, grasslands, sand dune systems, bird sanctuaries, coastal heath lands, and marine areas.

Most of the important nesting colonies for seabirds are on the west coast, the western-most promontory of Europe; exceptions are Lambey Island, near Dublin, and Great Saltee in County Wexford. Sandy beaches and tidal flats on the east and west coasts are nesting grounds for large populations of winter waders and smaller, isolated tern colonies. In the North, the largest seabird colony is on Rathlin Island, off the North Antrim coast.

Until recently, rural Ireland was home to large numbers of a small bird known as the **corncrake** *(Crex crex),* whose unusual cry during breeding season was a common feature of the early summer night. Sadly, the introduction of heavy machinery for cutting silage has destroyed the protective high-grass environment in which the mother corncrake lays her eggs. (The period for cutting silage coincides with the corncrake breeding period.) Ireland now has only a few areas where the corncrake still breeds. One is the **Shannon Callows ★**, where the bird's cry, which now seems quite mournful, can often be heard in the quiet of nightfall.

In the **winter,** Ireland's lakes and wetlands serve as a wintering ground for great num-bers of wildfowl from the Arctic and northern Europe. From Greenland, Iceland, and Canada come waders such as knot, golden plover, and black-tailed godwit; flocks of brent, barnacle, and white-fronted geese; and thousands of whooper swans. Every year, as many as 10,000 Greenland white-fronted geese winter on the north shores of Wexford Harbor, making it a mecca for birders. Flooded fields, or "callows," provide habitats for wigeons, whooping swans, and plover; the callows of the Shannon and the Blackwater are especially popular with birders. One of the best winter bird-watching sites is the Wexford Wildfowl Reserve (see chapter 8).

From March onward, mild **spring** weather invites Irish birds to begin nesting early, and their songs fill the woods and hedgerows. The arrival of migrants from Africa can be observed in April and May all along the south coast. Rathlin Island reserve (see chapter 17), home to Northern Ireland's largest seabird colony, is best visited in May and June.

Summer is the time to head to the west of Ireland, where seaside cliffs are an ideal place for large seabird colonies such as puffins and gannets. Some of the best summer birding sites are Great Saltee Island (see chapter 8), Cape Clear Island (see chapter 10), the Skellig Islands (see chapter 11), and Loop Head (see chapter 12).

Autumn is a particularly attractive time for bird-watchers in Ireland, when many rare American waders—mainly sandpipers and plovers—arrive when blown across the Atlan-tic. A spectacular avian event is the annual fall migration of brent geese. On the shores of Strangford Lough in County Down—Europe's premier brent-watching site—you might see as many as 3,000 on a single day.

BIRD-WATCHING RESOURCES

One of the best sources of information is the **Irish Birding** website (**www.irishbirding. com**), which features links on birding events, sites, and news. Another excellent resource is **BirdWatch Ireland,** Rockingham House, Newcastle, County Wicklow (© **01/281-9878;** www.birdwatchireland.ie), an organization devoted to bird conservation in the Republic of Ireland. An equivalent organization in Northern Ireland is the **Royal Society for the Protection of Birds,** Belvoir Park Forest, Belfast BT8 7QT (© **048/9049-1547;** www.rspb.org.uk/nireland).

Wexford Wildfowl Reserve, North Slob, Wexford (© **053/912-3129;** fax 053/912-4785), has a visitor center with information on local bird-watching sites. The reserve's full-time warden, Chris Wilson, can direct you to other places corresponding to your areas of interest.

The **Altamount Garden,** Tullow, County Wicklow (© **059/915-9444**), offers weekend courses in ornithology. See chapter 7 for more information.

On **Cape Clear Island,** there is a bird observatory at the North Harbour, with a warden in residence from March to November and accommodations for bird-watchers. **Ciarán and Mary O'Driscoll** (© **028/39153**), who operate a B&B on the island, also run boat trips for bird-watchers around the island and have a keen eye for vagrants and rarities.

Northern Ireland has two first-class nature centers for bird enthusiasts, both ideal for families. **Castle Espie,** Ballydrain Road, Comber, County Down BT23 6EA (© **028/9187-4146**), is home to a large collection of ducks, geese, and swans. The **Lough Neagh Discovery Centre,** Oxford Island, Craigavon, County Armagh (© **028/3832-2205**), is in the outstanding Oxford Island National Nature Reserve. For all-inclusive bird-watching packages in the North, contact **Murphy's Wildlife Tours,** 12 Belvoir Close, Belfast BT8 7PL (© **048/9069-3232;** fax 028/9064-4681).

4 GOLF

Golf is the single biggest sporting attraction in Ireland, with over 200,000 visitors traveling here specifically to play. Thus, the country holds more than 380 courses—including scores of championship courses. The Irish landscape and climate, like those of Scotland, seem almost custom-designed for scenic links, fair fairways, green greens, and dramatic traps—and there is never a shortage of 19th holes. In short, Ireland is a place of golfing pilgrimage.

Best of all, golfing is not confined to those with an Olympian income. Membership fees do not require mortgages, and greens fees for walk-ins are often quite modest, especially on weekdays and at off-peak hours.

See "Sports & Outdoor Pursuits" in each of the sightseeing chapters for a recommended selection of each region's top courses.

GOLF RESOURCES

The **Irish Tourist Board** has a dedicated golf website with numerous links and contacts at **www.golf.ireland.ie**.

A host of U.S. companies offer package golf tours. Among them are **AtlanticGolf** (© **800/542-6224** or 203/363-1003; fax 203/363-1006; www.atlanticgolf.com), **Golf International** (© **800/833-1389** or 212/986-9176; www.golfinternational.com), and **Wide World of Golf** (© **800/214-4653;** www.wideworldofgolf.com).

5 HORSEBACK RIDING

Ireland is a horse-loving country, with a plethora of stables and equestrian centers offering trail rides and instruction. The **Association of Irish Riding Establishments** (www. aire.ie) is the regulatory body that accredits stables, ensuring adequate safety standards and instructor competence. Riding prices range from €20 to €40 ($32–$64) per hour; expect to pay €25 ($40) on average. A list of accredited stables throughout the country is available from the Irish Tourist Board (see "Visitor Information" in chapter 3).

A variety of riding options can be found to suit different interests and levels of experience. Pony trekking caters primarily to beginners, and you don't need experience. Trail riding over longer distances requires the ability to trot for extended periods, and can be exhausting for the novice. Several establishments have accommodations and offer packages that include meals, lodging, and riding. Post-to-post trail riding allows a rider to stay at different lodgings each night, riding on trails all day.

RIDING RESOURCES

The **Irish Tourist Board** has a dedicated horseback-riding website with numerous links and contacts at www.equestrian.ireland.ie.

Equestrian Holidays Ireland (www.ehi.ie) is a collection of some 37 riding centers, each registered with the Association of Irish Riding Establishments, offering a wide variety of accommodations and holiday riding experiences. EHI properties include **Dingle Horse Riding,** Ballinaboula, Dingle, County Kerry (© **066/915-2199;** www.dingle horseriding.com), and **Drumindoo Stud & Equestrian Centre,** Knockranny, Westport, County Mayo (© **098/25616**).

In Dublin, you can go trail riding through Phoenix Park with **Ashtown Riding Stables** (© **01/838-3807**). They're in the village of Ashtown adjoining the park and only 10 minutes by car or bus (no. 37, 38, 39, or 70) from the city center. Among the other riding centers within easy reach of downtown Dublin are **Calliaghstown Riding Centre,** Calliaghstown, Rathcoole, County Dublin (© **01/458-8322**), and **Carrickmines Equestrian Centre,** Glenamuck Road, Foxrock, Dublin 18 (© **01/295-5990**).

If you want to try hunting Irish-style, you can go leaping across the hedges with the **Broomfield Riding School,** Broomfield, Tinahely, County Wicklow (© **0402/38117**), which offers access to the hunt for those who can demonstrate adequate equestrian skills, especially jumping. The riding school is open year-round for lessons and trail rides.

You can see the beaches of Connemara from horseback on a trek with the **Cleggan Riding Centre,** Cleggan, County Galway (© **095/44746;** www.clegganridingcentre. com). The center offers beach and mountain treks, and the most popular is a 3-hour ride to Omey Island at low tide.

(Tips **Horseback-Riding Tip**

Always phone ahead to make sure any particular equestrian center is still offering rides. Many have discontinued this service in the past few years due to skyrocketing insurance costs.

6 FISHING

What makes Ireland such a great fishing destination? A coastline of more than 5,603km (3,472 miles), thousands of lakes and ponds, countless creeks, rills, streams, and rivers—those certainly don't hurt. Ireland's temperate climate and low pollution also encourage a high fish population, and low human density has put little pressure on that. It all adds up to fairly ideal fishing conditions.

The sport of fishing—referred to by the Irish as **angling**—is a cherished tradition. Festivals and competitions celebrate the many forms of this sport; for dates and locations, contact the Irish Tourist Board (see "Visiting Information" in chapter 3); you have to sign up well in advance to participate in most of the competitions. Among the festivals are Killybegs International Sea Angling Festival in July, the Baltimore Deep Sea Angling Festival in August, and the Cobh International Deep Sea Angling Festival in September.

In the west and northwest, Killybegs (see chapter 16) is a center for sea angling, while Lough Corrib (see chapters 13 and 14) offers much to entice the freshwater angler. The Killarney area (see chapter 11) is a popular angling destination, as are the Blackwater River near Cork (see chapter 9) and Kinsale (see chapter 10) for sea angling. Also consider the Shannon River and its lakes, especially Lough Derg (see chapter 12).

FISHING RESOURCES

Fishing seasons are as follows: salmon, January 1 to September 30; brown trout, February 15 to October 12; sea trout, June 1 to September 30; coarse fishing and sea angling, all year. A license is required only for salmon and sea trout angling; the cost is €34 ($54) for a day, €48 ($77) for 21 days, or €128 ($205) annually. For all private salmon and sea trout fisheries, a permit is required in addition to the license, and it can be considerably more expensive. Prices vary greatly, from €10 to €200 ($16–$320) per rod per day (depending on the venue and provider), although most permits run €30 to €40 ($48–$64).

The Irish Tourist Board has websites dedicated to fishing at **www.discoverireland. com/us/ireland-things-to-see-and-do/activities/fishing**. A helpful brochure, *Angling in Ireland*, detailing what fish can be caught where, is available from the Angling Information Office at the **Central Fisheries Board,** Balnagowan House, Mobhi Boreen, Glasnevin, Dublin 9 (© **01/884-2600;** fax 01/836-0060; www.cfb.ie). Another helpful resource, *The Angler's Guide,* is published by the Irish Tourist Board. Permits, licenses, and specific information can be obtained from local outfitters or the Central Fisheries Board.

Many hotels have exclusive access to lakes and ponds, and will rent boats, gear, and *ghillies* (fishing guides) to their guests. Nearly two dozen such hotels have formed the **Great Fishing Houses of Ireland** (www.irelandfishing.com). Examples include Adare Manor in Limerick (p. 361); the Delphi Lodge in County Galway (p. 421); and Newport House Hotel and Enniscoe House, both in Mayo (p. 440).

In Northern Ireland, you must get a rod license from the **Fisheries Conservancy Board,** 1 Mahon Rd., Portadown, Craigavon, County Armagh (© **028/3833-4666;** www.fcbni.com), or in the Derry area from the **Foyle Carlingford Irish Lights Commission,** 22 Victoria Rd., Derry BT47 2AB (© **028/7134-2100;** www.loughs-agency. org). A permit may also be required; you can obtain information from local outfitters or the **Department of Culture, Arts and Leisure,** Interpoint Centre, York Street, Belfast BT4 3PW (© **028/9025-8825;** fax 028/9025-8906; www.dcalni.gov.uk). A rod license costs £4 to £24 ($8–$48), depending on the license provider and duration of license; permits run upwards of £5 ($10) for 3 days or £15 ($30) for 14 days. You can find a wealth of information and contacts in *An Information Guide to Game Fishing,* available from any office of the Northern Ireland Tourist Board (see "Visitor Information" in chapter 3).

7 KAYAKING

This sport has always been popular with the natives—and no wonder, considering the island's 5,603km (3,472 miles) of coastline, plus its numerous lakes and rivers.

In particular, the coastline provides year-round superb sea-kayaking waters, some of which are remote, with spectacular scenery. In a sea kayak, the wonders of the Irish coast can be investigated up close. You'll find caves, tiny inlets, out-of-the-way cliffs, and reefs inhabited by abundant seabirds, colorful crustaceans, seals, and the occasional dolphin. Many islands are within easy reach of the mainland, and with experience and good conditions, a sea kayaker can reach any of Ireland's island outposts.

A number of adventure centers offer kayaking lessons, and a few schools are devoted solely to kayaking. For those new to the sport or unfamiliar with the Irish coast, a guided excursion is the best option.

KAYAKING RESOURCES

For a rich source of information about kayaking in Ireland, visit the **Irish Canoe Union** website at www.canoe.ie.

Courses and day trips for all levels of experience are available from **Deep Blue Sea Kayaking** (*©* 01/276-0263; www.deepblueseakayaking.com) and **Shearwater Sea Kayaking** (*©* 086/836-8736 or 087/988-5658; www.shearwaterseakayaking.ie). Although kayaking is mainly a summer activity, the latter also runs special winter excursions to the Skerries and Lambay Island in Dublin Bay. Kayaking vacations are also available at **Delphi Adventure Company,** Leenane, County Galway (*©* 095/42208; www.delphimountain resort.com).

8 SAILING

Whether by cruising from port to port or dinghy sailing on the lakes, many regions of Ireland can best be experienced from the water. The craggy and indented coastline has plenty of safe havens for overnight stops—there are more than 140 between Cork Harbor and the Dingle Peninsula alone. This region of West Cork and Kerry is the most popular coastline for cruising, and several companies offer yacht charters.

Some of the harbors in the southwest that are most popular with sailors include Cork, Kinsale, Glandore, Baltimore, and Bantry. On the **west coast,** Killary Harbour, Westport, and Sligo have sailing clubs and are in areas of great beauty. There are also several sailing clubs and yacht-charter companies in the Dublin area.

A Bit of Adventure

If you're looking for more from your Ireland trip than just a bit of golf or hiking, you might want to try one of the country's adventure centers. These lively, youthful facilities offer a range of guided activities—from rappelling to kite surfing—in some of the country's most remote and beautiful settings, along with accommodations, food, and all you need for a holiday with like-minded folk.

The **Delphi Adventure Company,** Leenane, County Galway (© **095/42208;** www.delphimountainresort.com), is a popular option deep in the mountains of County Galway. There is almost nothing you can't do here; the resort offers courses in kayaking, windsurfing, and sailing, as well as mountaineering, rappelling, hiking, and pony trekking. Everything is reasonably priced, and the atmosphere is laid-back and friendly.

Another option is the **Killary Adventure Company,** Leenane, County Galway (© **095/43411;** www.killary.com), which will take you on Hobie Cat sailing trips, or guide you through an exploration of the countryside by kayak, waterskis, or on foot on hill and coastal walking tours, straight up on rock climbing expeditions, and more.

Deep in the Wicklow Mountains outside Dublin, the Blessington Lakes are a playground of tranquil, clean, speedboat-free water where the **Blessington Adventure Centre,** Blessington, County Wicklow (© **045/857844**), offers all you need to get going canoeing, kayaking, sailing, or windsurfing, as well as everything required for archery, orienteering, and pony trekking.

SAILING RESOURCES

Sailing schools hold courses for sailors at all levels of experience, and sometimes offer day sailing as well. Ireland also has more than 120 yacht and sailing clubs along the coast and lakes. The best sources for information are the Irish Tourist Board (see "Visitor Information" in chapter 3); the **Irish Sailing Association,** 3 Park Rd., Dun Laoghaire, County Dublin (© **01/280-0239;** fax 01/280-7558; www.sailing.ie); and *East and North Coasts of Ireland Sailing Directions* and *South and West Coasts of Ireland Sailing Directions* (both published by Imray, Laurie, Norie & Wilson Ltd. of Wych House) from the Irish Cruising Club (www.irishcruisingclub.com). The directions guides give information on harbors, port facilities, tides, and other topics of interest. They are available in bookshops in Ireland or online at www.imray.com.

The **International Sailing Schools Association** is an excellent resource for finding a sailing school; you can find links to members at www.sailingschools.org. **Sailing Holidays in Ireland** (www.sailingireland.com) lists many sailing schools and yacht-charter companies throughout the Republic. One of the best-known schools, **Glenans Irish Sailing Club,** 5 Lower Mount St., Dublin 2 (© **01/661-1481;** fax 01/676-4249; www.gisc.ie), has two locations in West Cork and one in Mayo, and offers classes at all levels (see chapter 10). Day sailing is available during the summer at the West Cork location.

Sail Ireland Charters, Trident Hotel Marina, Kinsale, County Cork (© **021/477-2927;** fax 021/774170; www.sailireland.com; see chapter 10), is the largest charter firm in Ireland and also offers sailing holidays. Yacht charters are also available at **Sporting Tours Ireland,** 71 Main St., Kinsale, County Cork ((©/fax **021/477-4727;** www.sporting toursireland.ie), and **Shannon Sailing Ltd.,** New Harbor, Dromineer, Nenagh, County Tipperary ((© **067/24499;** www.shannonsailing.com).

9 DIVING

With visibility averaging 15m (49 ft.) and occasionally reaching 29m (95 ft.), and many wrecks to explore, the west coast of Ireland may be cold, but it's still a pretty good place for divers.

The Irish dive season generally starts in March and ends in October, although specific dates depend on your comfort zone. Outside these months, weather and ocean conditions could make jumping into the sea unappealing. The PADI open-water diver certification is the minimum requirement for all dives; most schools also offer introductory dives for novices.

The rocky coast of West Cork and Kerry is great for diving, with centers in Baltimore (see chapter 10) and Dingle (see chapter 11). On the west coast, there are many great locations, one of which is the deep, sheltered Killary Harbour. Northern Ireland offers many interesting dives, with more than 400 named wrecks off the coast and many in the Irish Sea and in Belfast Lough.

DIVING RESOURCES

The **Irish Underwater Council (CFT,** or **Comhairle Fo-Thuinn**), 78A Patrick St., Dun Laoghaire, County Dublin ((© **01/284-4601;** fax 01/284-4602; www.cft.ie), is an association of more than 70 Irish diving clubs. Its website lists information on diving and snorkeling, dive centers, and dive hotels (no pun intended) throughout the Republic and publishes the *CFT Guide to Dive Sites* and other information on exploring the Emerald Isle's emerald waters. The CFT operates under the aegis of the CMAS (Confédération Mondiale des Activités Subaquatiques), the world diving federation.

Sign up for certified level-one and level-two instruction and equipment rental for kayaking, sailing, and windsurfing at the **Surfdock Centre,** Grand Canal Dock Yard, Ringsend, Dublin 4 ((© **01/668-3945;** fax 01/668-1215; www.surfdock.ie). Dublin Bay is filled with sea life and old wrecks, making it ideal for cold-water diving. To try it out, get in touch with **Oceantec Adventures** in Dun Laoghaire ((© **01/280-1083,** or toll-free within Ireland 1800/272-822). It offers a five-star PADI diving school and arranges dive vacations on the west coast.

The **UK Diving** website, **www.ukdiving.co.uk,** features information on diving in the North, including a wreck database you can access either through a conventional listing or by pinpointing on a map.

Irish dive centers and schools include the **National Diving School,** Malahide Marina Village, County Dublin ((© **01/845-2000;** natdive@indigo.ie); **Oceantec Adventures,** Dun Laoghaire, County Dublin ((© **01/280-1083**); **Baltimore Diving Centre,** Baltimore, County Cork ((©/fax **028/20300;** www.baltimorediving.com); and **Scubadive West,** Renvyle, County Galway ((© **095/43922;** fax 095/43923; www.scubadivewest.com).

10 WINDSURFING

Windsurfing is increasingly popular in Ireland, and some spots play host to vast flotillas of colorful sails and wet-suited windsurfers when conditions are good. Some of the best locations are in remote areas of the west coast, and those spots are rarely crowded. Windsurfing schools with boards for rent can be found in most regions of the country, with the greatest concentration on the southeast and southwest coasts.

In Dublin the most popular spot is Dollymount Beach; Salthill, behind Dun Laoghaire Harbour, is another good choice. In the Southeast, try Brittas Bay (County Wicklow), Cahore (County Wexford), and Rosslare (County Wexford). Dunmore East (County Waterford), Dungarvan (County Waterford), and Cobh (County Cork) are good in the south. The most challenging waves and winds are in the west, at Brandon Bay on the Dingle Peninsula, Roundstone in Galway, Achill Island in Mayo, and Magheroarty and Rossnowlagh in Donegal.

Because even skilled windsurfers spend a sizable portion of their time in the water, the water quality is surely a concern. Ireland has 27 designated European Union Blue Flag beaches and marinas, and Northern Ireland has 12. To find a complete listing or to check out a particular beach in advance, go to **www.blueflag.org**.

WINDSURFING RESOURCES

Equipment rental and lessons are widely available on Ireland's coasts and lakes. Try the following centers: the **Surfdock Centre,** Grand Canal Dock Yard, Ringsend, Dublin 4 (© **01/668-3945;** fax 01/668-1215; www.surfdock.ie); the **Dunmore East Adventure Centre,** Dunmore East, County Waterford (© **051/383783;** fax 051/383786; www.dunmoreadventure.com); the **Oysterhaven Centre,** Oysterhaven, Kinsale, County Cork (© **021/477-0738;** fax 021/770776; www.oysterhaven.com); and, in the North, **Craigavon Watersports Centre,** 1 Lake Rd., County Armagh (© **028/3834-2669;** fax 028/3834-6018; www.craigavon.gov.uk).

If kite surfing is your thing, check out the website **www.kitesurfing.ie**. It offers advice on where to buy or rent boards, the best locations, and weather conditions, and it also hooks you up with other kite surfers.

Dublin

Low slung, gray, and solid, Ireland's premier city can look surprisingly dark and gloomy at first glance. Its appearance—the result of its 19th-century architecture of Irish stone and granite—is deceptive. The town itself is anything but gloomy, and it's not the stodgy, old-fashioned city of the late 20th century. Behind all those sturdy columns and beneath all that gray is the real, modern, Euro-Dublin—an affluent buzzing city with all the trendy coffee shops, organic juice bars, pricey five-star restaurants, and designer boutiques that entails. The last few years changed Ireland from top to toe, and Dublin most of all—this historic town has been catapulted from the early 20th century, where it had lingered too long, into the 21st, where it revels in its own success.

Gone are the days when many visitors to Ireland chose to skip Dublin altogether. Nowadays, a weekend in Dublin is one of the hottest city breaks in Europe, as people pile into its old pubs and modern bars, shop in its thriving markets and malls, and relax in its trendy cafes. Because of all of this, Dublin's population has swollen to 1.5 million; more than a third of the Irish population lives in this city, which, while good news for the economy, has residual side effects of overcrowding, high property prices, and gridlocked traffic. This is also one of the world's most youthful cities—an estimated 50% of its population is under 30 years old.

It is a contrary, amusing, complex small city, and our advice to those who haven't been here in a while, or who have never been here is this: The first thing you should do is leave your preconceptions behind. Then you can see this historic, modern, flawed, charming, and entertaining city for what it really is.

1 ORIENTATION

222km (138 miles) NE of Shannon Airport, 258km (160 miles) NE of Cork, 167km (104 miles) S of Belfast, 309km (192 miles) NE of Killarney, 219km (136 miles) E of Galway, 237km (147 miles) SE of Derry, 142km (88 miles) N of Wexford

ARRIVING

BY PLANE   Aer Lingus, Ireland's national airline, operates regularly scheduled flights into Dublin International Airport from Chicago; Boston; Los Angeles; Washington, D.C.; San Francisco; and New York's JFK. **American Airlines** flies to Dublin from Chicago, **Delta Airlines** from Atlanta and New York, **Continental Airlines** from Newark, and **US Airways** from Philadelphia. (This book's appendix has the contact information for the above airlines.) Charters operate from a number of U.S. and Canadian cities. You can also fly from the United States to London or other European cities and backtrack to Dublin (see "Getting There & Getting Around" in chapter 3).

Dublin International Airport (© 01/814-1111; www.dublin-airport.com) is 11km (6³⁄₄ miles) north of the city center. A travel information desk in the arrivals concourse provides information on public bus and rail services throughout the country.

An excellent airport-to-city shuttle bus service called **AirCoach** operates 24 hours a day, making runs at 15-minute intervals. Its buses run direct from the airport to Dublin's city center and south side, stopping at O'Connell Street, St. Stephen's Green, Fitzwilliam Square, Merrion Square, Ballsbridge, and Donnybrook—that is, all the key hotel and business districts. The fare is €7 ($11) one-way or €12 ($19) round-trip (children 11 and under travel free); buy your ticket from the driver. Although AirCoach is slightly more expensive than the Dublin Bus (see below), it makes fewer intermediary stops, so it is faster (the journey to the city center takes about 45 min.), and it brings you right into the hotel districts. To confirm AirCoach departures and arrivals, call ☎ **01/844-7118** or find it on the Web at **www.aircoach.ie**.

If you need to connect with the Irish bus or rail service, the **Airlink Express Coach** (☎ **01/844-4265**) provides express coach services from the airport into central Dublin and beyond. Routes 747 and 748 go to the city's central bus station, **Busáras,** on Store Street, and on to **Connolly** railway station, and route 748 makes an additional stop at **Heuston** railway station. Service runs daily from 5:45am until 11:30pm (Sun 7:15am–11:30pm), with departures every 20 to 30 minutes. One-way fare is €6 ($9.60) for adults and €3 ($4.80) for children 11 and under.

Finally, **Dublin Bus** (☎ **01/872-0000;** www.dublinbus.ie) runs daily connections between the airport and the city center from 6am to 11:30pm. The one-way trip takes about 30 minutes, and the fare is €6 ($9.60). Nos. 16a, 41, 41b, 46x, 230, 746, 747, or 748 all serve the city center from Dublin Airport. Consult the travel information desk in the arrivals concourse to figure out which bus takes you closest to your hotel.

For speed and ease—especially if you have a lot of luggage—a **taxi** is the best way to get directly to your hotel or guesthouse. Depending on your destination in Dublin, fares average between €20 and €30 ($32–$48). Surcharges include €.50 (80¢) for each additional passenger and for each piece of luggage. Depending on traffic, a cab should take between 20 and 45 minutes to get into the city center. A 10% tip is standard. Taxis are lined up at a first-come, first-served taxi stand outside the arrivals terminal.

Major international and local car-rental companies operate desks at Dublin Airport. For a list of companies, see "Getting Around," later in this chapter.

BY FERRY   Passenger and car ferries from Britain arrive at the **Dublin Ferryport** (☎ **01/855-2222**), on the eastern end of the North Docks, and at the **Dún Laoghaire Ferryport** (☎ **01/842-8864**). Call **Irish Ferries** (☎ **0818/300-400;** www.irishferries.ie), **P&O Irish Sea** (☎ **01/800-409-049;** www.poirishsea.com), or **Stena Line** (☎ **01/204-7777;** www.stenaline.com) for bookings and information. There is bus and taxi service from both ports.

BY TRAIN   **Irish Rail** (☎ **01/850-366222;** www.irishrail.ie), also called Iarnród Éireann, operates daily train service to Dublin from Belfast, Northern Ireland, and all major cities in the Irish Republic, including Cork, Galway, Limerick, Killarney, Sligo, Wexford, and Waterford. Trains from the south, west, and southwest arrive at **Heuston Station,** Kingsbridge, off St. John's Road; from the north and northwest at **Connolly Station,** Amiens Street; and from the southeast at **Pearse Station,** Westland Row, Tara Street.

BY BUS   **Bus Éireann** (☎ **01/836-6111;** www.buseireann.ie) operates daily express coach and local bus service from all major cities and towns in Ireland into Dublin's central bus station, **Busáras,** Store Street.

BY CAR   If you are arriving by car from other parts of Ireland or on a car ferry from Britain, all main roads lead into the heart of Dublin and are well signposted to An Lar

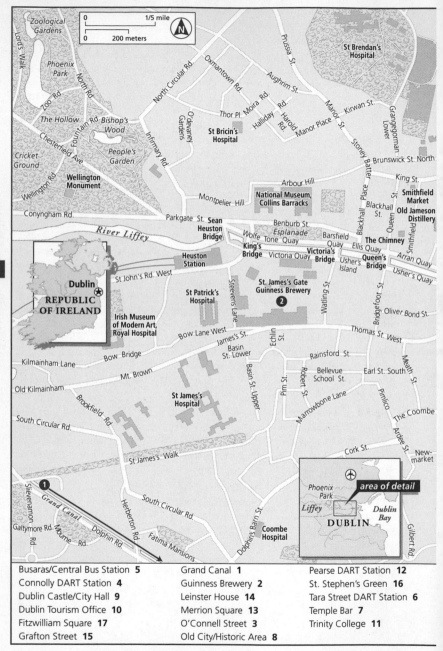

Busaras/Central Bus Station **5**	Grand Canal **1**	Pearse DART Station **12**
Connolly DART Station **4**	Guinness Brewery **2**	St. Stephen's Green **16**
Dublin Castle/City Hall **9**	Leinster House **14**	Tara Street DART Station **6**
Dublin Tourism Office **10**	Merrion Square **13**	Temple Bar **7**
Fitzwilliam Square **17**	O'Connell Street **3**	Trinity College **11**
Grafton Street **15**	Old City/Historic Area **8**	

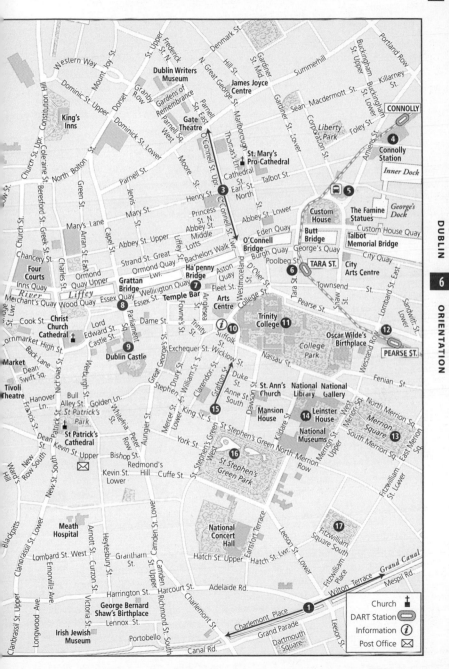

(City Centre). To bypass the city center, the East Link (toll bridge €1.90/$3.05) and West Link are signposted, and M50 circuits the city on three sides.

VISITOR INFORMATION

Dublin Tourism operates six walk-in visitor centers in greater Dublin that are open every day except Christmas. The principal center is on Suffolk Street, Dublin 2, open from June to August Monday to Saturday from 9am to 8:30pm, Sunday and bank holidays 10:30am to 3pm, and the rest of the year Monday to Saturday 9am to 5:30pm, Sunday and bank holidays 10:30am to 3pm. The Suffolk Street office has a currency exchange counter, a car-rental counter, an accommodations-reservations service, bus and rail information desks, a gift shop, and a cafe. For accommodations reservations throughout Ireland by credit card, contact Dublin Tourism at © 01/605-7700 or www.visitdublin.com.

The five other centers are in the **arrivals concourse** of Dublin Airport; **Exclusively Irish,** O'Connell Street, Dublin 1; **Baggot Street Bridge,** Baggot Street, Dublin 2; the **Square Towncentre,** Tallaght, Dublin 24; and the ferry terminal at **Dún Laoghaire Harbor** (all telephone inquiries should be directed to the number listed above). All centers are open year-round with at least the following hours: Monday to Friday 9am to 5:30pm and Saturday 9am to 5pm.

For information on Ireland outside of Dublin, call **Bord Fáilte** (© 1850/230330 in Ireland; www.ireland.ie).

At any of these centers you can pick up the free *Tourism News.* The free *Event Guide,* a biweekly entertainment guide, is online at **www.eventguide.ie.** *InDublin,* a biweekly arts-and-entertainment magazine selling for €3 ($4.80), is available at most newsstands, or online at www.indublin.ie.

CITY LAYOUT

The city is neatly divided down the middle by the curves of the River Liffey, which empties into the sea at the city's farthest edge. To the north and south, the city center is encircled by canals: The Royal Canal arcs across the north and the Grand Canal through the south. Traditionally, the area south of the river has been Dublin's buzzing, prosperous hub. It still holds most of the best hotels, restaurants, shops, and sights, but the Northside is on the upswing, with hip new bars and trendy hotels making it the new place to be. Both north and south, Dublin is compact and easily walked in an hour. In fact, a 45-minute walk from the bucolic peace of St. Stephen's Green, up Grafton Street, and across the Liffey to the top of O'Connell Street offers a good overview of the city's prosperous present and troubled past.

The most interesting suburban towns tend to be along Dublin Bay—these include (heading north along the bay) Drumcondra, Glasnevin, Howth, Clontarf, and Malahide; and (heading south along the bay) Ballsbridge, Blackrock, Dún Laoghaire, Dalkey, Killiney, Rathgar, and Rathmines.

MAIN ARTERIES, STREETS & SQUARES   In the town center just south of the river, Dame Street, which changes its name to College Green, Westmoreland Street, and Lord Edward Street at various points, is the main east-west artery connecting Trinity College with Dublin Castle and Christ Church Cathedral. On one side of Dame Street are the winding medieval lanes of Temple Bar, which, with its many pubs and bars, is Dublin's party central. On the other side of Dame Street are lots of tributary streets lined with shops and cafes; the best of these is Great St. George's Street, which arcs off toward the south. Where Dame turns into College Green, the sturdy gray stone walls of Trinity College make an excellent landmark as you get your bearings, and at its southwest corner is

---

Fun Facts **A Toll Tale**

Built in 1816 as one of the earliest cast-iron bridges in Britain and Ireland, the graceful pedestrians-only Ha'penny Bridge (pronounced *Hay*-penny) is the prettiest of Dublin's bridges. Though officially named the Liffey Bridge, it's far better known by the toll once charged to cross it: half a penny. The turnstiles were removed in 1919, when passage was made free.

---

the top of Grafton Street—a lively pedestrianized shopping lane crowded with tourists, musicians, and artists, which leads to the bucolic, statue-filled peace of St. Stephen's Green. From there, heading back up via Kildare Street will take you past Leinster House, where the Irish Parliament meets, and a turn to the right brings you to Merrion Square, another of Dublin's extraordinarily well-preserved Georgian squares.

To get to the Northside, most visitors choose to walk across the eminently photographable arch of the Ha'penny Bridge (see "A Toll Tale," above), but most locals take the less attractive O'Connell Bridge nearby. You can be different and cross via the Ha'penny's sleekly modern neighbor, the Millennium Bridge, which is beautifully illuminated after dark. The O'Connell Bridge leads directly onto O'Connell Street, a wide, statue-lined boulevard that is the north's main thruway. O'Connell Street runs north to **Parnell Square,** which holds a couple of marvelous museums and marks the edge of central Dublin. From the bottom to the top, O'Connell Street is lined with statues, starting with an absurdly ornate representation of the titular politician Daniel O'Connell surrounded by angels (which still have bullet holes left from the Easter Rising). The street running along the Liffey's embankment is called the North Quays by all, though its name changes on virtually every block, reflecting the long-gone docks that once lined it.

In the older section of the city, **High Street** is the gateway to medieval and Viking Dublin, from the city's two medieval cathedrals to the old city walls and nearby Dublin Castle. The other noteworthy street in the older part of the city is **Francis Street,** Dublin's antiques row.

DUBLIN NEIGHBORHOODS IN BRIEF

Trinity College Area On the south side of the River Liffey, Trinity College is an Ivy League–style university with shady quadrangles and atmospheric stone buildings. It's virtually the dead center of the city, and is surrounded by bookstores, shops, and noisy traffic. This area lies in the Dublin 2 postal code.

Temple Bar Wedged between Trinity College and the Old City, this is Dublin's party hub, packed with bars, discos, and pubs. During the day it's quieter

and quaint, with good shops, two worthwhile art galleries, recording studios, and theaters. But at night, this is largely the stamping ground of young tourists looking for lots of alcohol, and it's easy to feel over the hill here if you're 25. This area lies in the Dublin 2 and Dublin 8 postal codes.

Old City Dating from Viking and medieval times, the cobblestone enclave of the historic Old City includes Dublin Castle, the remnants of the city's original walls, and Christ Church and St. Patrick's cathedrals. Recently, Old City has also gained cachet for its hip boutiques where local designers sell their clothes. It encompasses the Dublin 8 and 2 zones.

Liberties Adjacent to Old City, the Liberties district takes its name from the fact that it was once just outside the city walls, and, therefore, exempt from Dublin's jurisdiction. Although it prospered in its early days, Liberties fell on hard times in the 17th and 18th centuries and is only now feeling a touch of urban renewal. Its main claim to fame is the Guinness Brewery. Most of this area is in the Dublin 8 zone.

St. Stephen's Green/Grafton Street Area The biggest tourist draw in town, this district is home to Dublin's finest hotels, restaurants, and shops. The neighborhood is filled with impressive Georgian architecture, and is primarily a business and shopping zone. It is part of Dublin 2.

Fitzwilliam & Merrion Square These two little square parks between Trinity College and St. Stephen's Green are surrounded by grand Georgian town houses. Some of Dublin's most famous citizens once lived here; today many of the houses are offices for doctors, lawyers, and government agencies. This area is part of the Dublin 2 zone.

O'Connell Street (North of the Liffey) The epicenter of Dublin's stormy political struggles, the north was once a fashionable area, but it lost much of its charm as it decayed in the 20th century. Happily, it is now rebounding with high-profile hotels, plenty of shops, and a few top-rated restaurants. With four theaters in walking distance of O'Connell Street, this is Dublin's theater district. It is mostly in Dublin 1.

North Quays (the Liffey riverbanks on the Northside) Once the center of Dublin's shipping industry, this is now an increasingly trendy address for hotels, bars, and clubs. The quays are actually a series of streets named after the wharves that once stood at water's edge. The quays start near the mouth of the Liffey and end in the green peace of Phoenix Park. This area is mostly in Dublin 1.

Ballsbridge/Embassy Row Immediately south of the Grand Canal, this upscale suburb is just barely within walking distance of the city center. Primarily a prestigious residential area, it is also home to hotels, restaurants, and embassies, including the U.S. embassy. This area is part of the Dublin 4 zone.

2 GETTING AROUND

While driving in the city is intimidating, getting around Dublin is not at all daunting, in general. Public transportation is good and getting better, taxis are plentiful and reasonably priced, and your own two feet can easily carry you from one end of town to the other. In fact, with its current traffic and parking problems, it's a city where the foot is mightier than the wheel. If you can avoid it, don't use a car while you're in Dublin.

BY BUS Dublin Bus operates a fleet of green double-deckers and single-deckers, as well as minibuses (the latter charmingly called "imps"). Most originate on or near O'Connell Street, Abbey Street, and Eden Quay on the Northside, and at Aston Quay, College Street, and Fleet Street on the south side. Bus stops, which resemble big blue or green lollipops, are located every few blocks on main thoroughfares. To tell where the bus is going, look at the destination street and bus number above its front window; those heading for the city center indicate that with an odd mix of Gaelic and Latin: VIA AN LAR.

Bus service runs daily throughout the city, starting at 6am (10am on Sun), with the last bus at 11:30pm. On Thursday, Friday, and Saturday nights, **Nitelink** service runs from the city center to the suburbs from midnight to 3am. Buses operate every 10 to 15 minutes for most runs; schedules are posted on revolving notice boards at bus stops.

Inner-city fares are based on distances traveled. The minimum fare is €1.05 ($1.70); the maximum fare for journeys in the city center is €2 ($3.20). The Nitelink fare is a flat €5 ($8). Buy your tickets from the driver as you enter the bus. Following a rise in robberies of bus drivers in Dublin, all buses now use an "Autofare" machine. This means that fares must be paid with coins directly into a fare box next to the driver's cab. Bills are not accepted and no change is given. If you have to pay more than the cost of the ticket, the driver will issue you a refund ticket, which must be presented along with your travel ticket at the Dublin Bus office on Upper O'Connell Street to claim a refund for the difference. Inevitably, this is rarely worth the effort.

If you plan to travel quite a bit by bus, consider purchasing a **bus pass.** Discounted 1-day, 3-day, 5-day, and 7-day passes are available in advance. The 1-day bus-only pass costs €6 ($9.60); the 3-day pass costs €11.50 ($18); the 5-day pass goes for €18.50 ($30). For more information, contact **Dublin Bus,** 59 Upper O'Connell St., Dublin 1 (© 01/ 873-4222; www.dublinbus.ie).

BY DART   While Dublin has no subway in the strict sense, there is an electric rapid-transit train, known as the **DART (Dublin Area Rapid Transit).** It travels mostly at ground level or on elevated tracks, linking the city-center stations at **Connolly Station, Tara Street,** and **Pearse Street** with suburbs and seaside communities as far as Malahide to the north and Greystones to the south. Service operates roughly every 10 to 20 minutes Monday to Saturday from 7am to midnight and Sunday from 9:30am to 11pm. Typical adult fares cost around €1.60 ($2.55) for a single journey; combination rail-and-bus tickets, valid all day within the "short hop" zone of the city center, start from €9 ($14) adults. One-day, 3-day, and 10-trip passes, as well as student and family tickets, are available at reduced rates from ticket windows in stations. For further information, contact DART, Dublin Pearse Station (© 01/703-3592; www.dart.ie).

BY TRAM   The newest addition to Dublin's public transportation network, the sleek light-rail tram system known as **LUAS** opened in the summer of 2004. With trams traveling at a maximum speed of 70kmph (45 mph) and departing every 5 minutes in peak hours, LUAS has been popular enough to make at least a small impact on Dublin's appalling traffic congestion. Services run from 5:30am to 12:30am Monday to Friday, 6:30am to 12:30am Saturday, and 7am to 11:30pm on Sunday. The lines link the city center at **Connolly Station** and **St. Stephen's Green** with the suburbs of Tallaght in the southwest and Dundrum and Sandyford to the south. For visitors, one of the handiest reasons to use the LUAS is to get between Connolly and Heuston stations. The one-way fare within the city center is €1.50 ($2.40) adults, €.80 ($1.30) children. One-day and multiple-day passes are also available. For further information, contact LUAS (© 01/ 800-300-604; www.luas.ie).

ON FOOT   Marvelously compact, Dublin is ideal for walking, as long as you remember to look right and then left (and in the direction opposite your instincts if you're from the U.S. or Canada) before crossing the street. Pedestrians have the right of way at specially marked, zebra-striped crossings (there are usually two flashing lights at these intersections). For some walking-tour suggestions, see "Seeing the Sights," later in this chapter.

BY TAXI   It's very difficult to hail a taxi on the street; instead, they line up at taxi stands (called "ranks") outside major hotels, at bus and train stations, and on prime thoroughfares such as Upper O'Connell Street, College Green, and the north side of St. Stephen's Green.

You can also phone for a taxi. Some of the companies that operate a 24-hour radio-call service are **Co-Op** (✆ **01/676-6666**), **NRC** (✆ **01/708-9222**), and **VIP/ACE Taxis** (✆ **01/478-3333**). If you need a wake-up call, VIP offers that service, along with especially courteous dependability.

Taxi rates are fixed by law and posted in each vehicle. The following are typical travel costs in the city center: The starting fare for the first kilometer (²/₃ mile) is €3.80 ($6.10) by day and €4.10 ($6.55) at night. For the next 14km (8²/₃ miles) the fare is €.95 ($1.50) per kilometer by day, €1.25 ($2) by night, rising to a maximum of €1.65 ($2.65) per kilometer thereafter. It costs an extra €2 ($3.20) if you order a cab by phone. *Be warned:* At some hotels, staff members will tack on as much as €5 ($8) for calling you a cab, although this practice violates city taxi regulations. Ask before you request a taxi if you'll be charged.

BY CAR   As mentioned earlier, if you plan to spend all of your time in Dublin, it is very unlikely you'll need to rent a car. In fact, getting around the city and its environs is much easier without one.

If you must drive in Dublin, remember to keep to the *left-hand side of the road,* and don't drive in bus lanes. The speed limit within the city is 50kmph (31 mph)—falling to 30kmph (19 mph) in certain areas—although it's very unlikely you'll ever reach it. Seat belts must be worn at all times by driver and passengers.

Most major international **car-rental firms** are represented in Dublin, as are many Irish-based companies. They have desks at the airport, full-service offices downtown, or both. Rates vary greatly according to company, season, type of car, and duration of rental. In high season, the average weekly cost of a subcompact starts at around €200 ($320); you'll get the best price if you've made car-rental arrangements well in advance from home. (Also see "By Car" under "Getting There & Getting Around" in chapter 3.)

International firms represented in Dublin include **Avis,** 35–39 Old Kilmainham, Dublin 8, and at Dublin Airport (✆ 01/605-7500; www.avis.ie); **Budget,** 151 Lower Drumcondra Rd., Dublin 9 (✆ 01/837-9611; www.budget.ie), and at Dublin Airport (✆ 01/844-5150); **Hertz,** 151 S. Circular Rd., Dublin 8 (✆ 01/709-3060; www.hertz.ie), and at Dublin Airport (✆ 01/844-5466); and **Murray's Europcar,** Baggot Street Bridge, Dublin 4 (toll-free ✆ 1/614-2888; www.europcar.ie), and at Dublin Airport (✆ 01/812-0410).

During normal business hours, free parking on Dublin streets is nonexistent. Never park in bus lanes, cycle lanes, or along a curb with double yellow lines. City officials will either clamp ("boot") or tow errant vehicles. To get your car declamped, the fee is around €90 ($144), and if your car is towed away, it costs €165 ($265) to reclaim it.

Throughout Dublin, you'll find multibay meters and "pay and display" **parking.** If you park on the street, look around for a meter (there's usually one on every block). You insert coins into the machine for however many hours you expect to be there, retrieve a ticket, and then stick that ticket in the front window of your car to prove you've done it. Expect to pay around €2 ($3.20) per hour. The best places to park are surface parking lots and multistory car parks in central locations such as Kildare Street, Lower Abbey Street, Marlborough Street, and St. Stephen's Green West. Expect to pay €1.90 ($3.05) per hour and €20 ($32) for 24 hours.

BY BICYCLE   The steady flow of Dublin traffic rushing down one-way streets may be a little intimidating for most cyclists, but there are many opportunities for more relaxed

pedaling in residential areas and suburbs, along the seafront, and around Phoenix Park.
The Dublin Tourism office can supply you with bicycle touring information and suggested routes.

Bicycle rental averages from upwards of €20 ($32) per day, or €100 ($160) per week, with a €70 ($112) deposit. In the downtown area, bicycles can be rented from the **Bike Store,** 58 Lower Gardiner St., Dublin 1 (☎ **01/8725399**).

Ⓕast Facts   Dublin

For countrywide information, see this book's Appendix, "Fast Facts, Toll-Free Numbers & Websites."

American Express There is no full-service **American Express** office in Dublin. Keith Prowse Travel, Lower Abbey Street, Irish Life Mall, Dublin 1 (☎ **01/878-3500**), offers limited services to cardholders. It is open Monday to Friday 9:30am to 5:30pm.

Banks Nearly all banks are open Monday to Friday 10am to 4pm (to 5pm Thurs) and have ATMs that accept Cirrus network cards as well as MasterCard and Visa. Convenient locations include the **Bank of Ireland,** at 2 College Green, Dublin 2, and 6 O'Connell St., Dublin 1, and the **Allied Irish Bank,** at 100 Grafton St., Dublin 2, and 87 N. Strand, Dublin 3.

Business Hours **Museums and sights** are generally open 10am to 5pm Tuesday to Saturday, and 2 to 5pm Sunday. **Shops** generally open 9am to 6pm Monday to Friday, with late opening on Thursday until 7 or 8pm. In the city center most department stores and many shops are open noon to 6pm on Sunday.

Currency Exchange Currency-exchange services, signposted as BUREAU DE CHANGE, are in most Dublin banks and at many branches of the Irish post office system, known as **An Post.** A bureau de change operates daily during flight arrival and departure times at Dublin Airport; a foreign-currency note-exchanger machine is also available on a 24-hour basis in the arrivals concourse. Some hotels and travel agencies offer bureau de change services, although the best rate of exchange is usually when you use your bank card at an ATM.

Dentists For dental emergencies, contact the **Eastern Health Board Headquarters,** Parkgate Street Business Centre, Dublin 8 (☎ **01/635-2500**), or try **Molesworth Clinic,** 2 Molesworth Place, Dublin 2 (☎ **01/661-5544**). See also "Dental Surgeons" in the Golden Pages (Yellow Pages) of the telephone book. The American Embassy (see "Embassies & Consulates," below) can provide a list of dentists in the city. Expect to be charged upfront for services.

Doctors If you need to see a physician, most hotels and guesthouses will contact a house doctor for you. The **American Embassy** (see "Embassies & Consulates," below) can provide a list of doctors in the city, and you should contact them first. Otherwise, you can call either the **Eastern Health Board Headquarters,** Parkgate St. Business Centre, Dublin 8 (☎ **01/635-2500**), or the **Irish Medical Organization** (a doctors' union) at 10 Fitzwilliam Place, Dublin 2 (☎ **01/676-7273**). As with dentists, expect to pay for treatment upfront, and contact your insurance company when you return home to find out whether you are eligible for reimbursement.

Embassies & Consulates The **American Embassy** is at 42 Elgin Rd., Ballsbridge, Dublin 4 (© **01/668-8777;** http://dublin.usembassy.gov); the **Canadian Embassy** is at 7–8 Wilton Terrace, 3rd Floor, Dublin 2 (© **01/234-4000;** www.canada.ie); the **British Embassy** is at 29 Merrion Rd., Dublin 2 (© **01/205-3700;** www. britishembassy.ie); and the **Australian Embassy** is at Fitzwilton House, Wilton Terrace, 7th Floor, Dublin 2 (© **01/664-5300;** www.ireland.embassy.gov.au). In addition, there is an **American Consulate** at 223 Stranmillis Rd., Belfast BT9 5GR (© **028/9038-6100**).

Emergencies For police, fire, or other emergencies, dial © **999.**

GLBT Resources Contact the **Gay Switchboard Dublin,** Carmichael House, North Brunswick Street, Dublin 7 (© **01/872-1055;** fax 01/873-5737); the **National Lesbian and Gay Federation (NLGF),** Unit 2, Scarlet Row, Temple Bar Dublin 8 (© **01/671-0939;** www.nlgf.ie); or the **LOT** (Lesbians Organizing Together), 5 Capel St., Dublin 1 (© **01/872-7770**). For more complete listings, see "Specialized Travel Resources" in chapter 3.

Hospitals For emergency care, two of the most modern hospitals in Dublin are **St. Vincent's University Hospital,** Elm Park (© **01/221-4000**), on the south side of the city, and **Beaumont Hospital,** Beaumont (© **01/837-7755**), on the Northside.

Hot Lines In Ireland, hot lines are called "helplines." For **emergencies, police, or fire,** dial © **999; Alcoholics Anonymous** (© **01/453-8998,** or after hours 01/679-5967); **Narcotics Anonymous** (© **01/672-8000**); **Rape Crisis Centre** (© **01/661-4911** or 1800/778-888); and for people suffering from depression, **Samaritans** (© **01/872-7700** or 1850/609-090).

Information For directory assistance, dial © **11811** or 11850. For visitor information offices, see "Orientation," earlier in this chapter.

Internet Access Internet access is everywhere in Dublin; look for signs in cafes, pubs, shopping malls, hotels, and hostels. Like all of Dublin's public libraries, the **Central Library,** in the ILAC Centre, off Henry Street, Dublin 1 (© **01/873-4333**), has a bank of PCs with free Internet access. Centrally located cybercafes are **Planet Cyber Café,** 13 St. Andrews St., Dublin 2 (© **01/670-5183**), and the **Central Cybercafe,** 6 Grafton St., Dublin 2 (© **01/677-8298**), which also offers a left-luggage service. A half-hour online averages €3 ($4.80).

Magazines The leading magazines for upcoming events and happenings are *InDublin,* published every 2 weeks and available at newsstands; *The Dubliner,* published monthly; *Hot Press,* also published every 2 weeks with excellent event listings; *JMI (The Journal of Music in Ireland)* for music information (www.thejmi. com); and the free biweekly *Event Guide* (**www.eventguide.ie**).

Pharmacies Centrally located drugstores—known as pharmacies or chemist shops—include **Dame Street Pharmacy,** 14 Dame St., Dublin 2 (© **01/670-4523**). A late-night chemist shop is **Hamilton Long & Co.,** 5 Lower O'Connell St. (© **01/874-8456**), and its sister branch, **Hamilton Long Byrnes,** 4 Merrion Rd., Dublin 4 (© **01/668-3287**). Both branches close at 9pm on weeknights and 6pm on Saturday.

Police Dial (C) **999** in an emergency. The metropolitan headquarters for the **Dublin Garda Siochana (Police)** is in Phoenix Park, Dublin 8 ((C) **01/666-0000**).

Post Office The Irish post office is best known by its Gaelic name, **An Post.** The **General Post Office (GPO)** is located on O'Connell Street, Dublin 1 ((C) **01/705-7000;** www.anpost.ie). Hours are Monday to Saturday 8am to 8pm. Branch offices, identified by the sign OIFIG AN POST/POST OFFICE, are open Monday to Saturday only, 9am to 5pm.

Weather Phone (C) **1550/122113,** or check the Web at **www.ireland.com/weather**.

Yellow Pages The classified section of the telephone book is called the Golden Pages (**www.goldenpages.ie**), but the online version doesn't seem to work terribly well.

---

3 WHERE TO STAY

With a healthy mix of plush, modern hotels and grand old guesthouses, Dublin excels in providing a place to rest your head at the end of a day. Prices are not cheap, but there are good off-season deals to be had if you book early, particularly in the luxury category—keep an eye on the hotel websites in the months before your trip.

In this guide, we give each hotel zero to three stars, based on overall value. As a result, a fine but expensive hotel may get one star, while an excellent budget choice may get two.

In general, hotel rates in Dublin do not vary as much seasonally as they do in the countryside, although some hotels charge slightly higher prices during special events, such as St. Patrick's Day and the Dublin Horse Show. The money savings here comes by the day of the week: If you're looking for the best deal, some hotels cut their rates by as much as 50% on Friday and Saturday nights, when business traffic is low. On the other hand, some hotels offer midweek specials.

It usually pays to book hotels well in advance. Many hotels can be booked through toll-free numbers from North America, and the quoted prices offered can be appreciably (as much as 40%) lower than those offered at the door. Even better, book online—many hotels offer Web-only special deals.

If you arrive in Ireland without a reservation, don't despair. One of the best sources of last-minute rooms (often at a discount) is **www.visitdublin.com**. The website lets you view hotels and guesthouses with immediate availability.

Another option is to arrive in person at the nearest **tourist office.** Alternatively, phone them at (C) **066/979-2030.** This is a nationwide and cross-border "free-phone" facility for credit card bookings, which operates daily from 8am to 11pm (Ireland time). You can access it from North America ((C) **011-66/979-2030**) and on the Web at **www.gulliver.ie**.

Most luxury hotels are on the south side of the river in Temple Bar and around Trinity College, but some are springing up on the Northside. Places like the boutique, U2-owned **Clarence** hotel in Temple Bar are stylish indicators of how far Dublin has come, while the celebrity hangout **Morrison** hotel just across the river from it proves that the north bank is on the upswing. There are lots of excellent midrange hotels around St. Stephen's Green, where the small but perfectly formed **Number 31** leads the way. Most budget

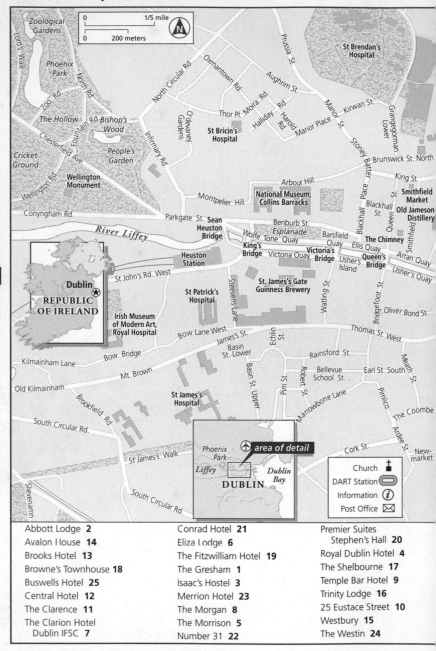

Abbott Lodge **2**
Avalon House **14**
Brooks Hotel **13**
Browne's Townhouse **18**
Buswells Hotel **25**
Central Hotel **12**
The Clarence **11**
The Clarion Hotel
  Dublin IFSC **7**

Conrad Hotel **21**
Eliza Lodge **6**
The Fitzwilliam Hotel **19**
The Gresham **1**
Isaac's Hostel **3**
Merrion Hotel **23**
The Morgan **8**
The Morrison **5**
Number 31 **22**

Premier Suites
  Stephen's Hall **20**
Royal Dublin Hotel **4**
The Shelbourne **17**
Temple Bar Hotel **9**
Trinity Lodge **16**
25 Eustace Street **10**
Westbury **15**
The Westin **24**

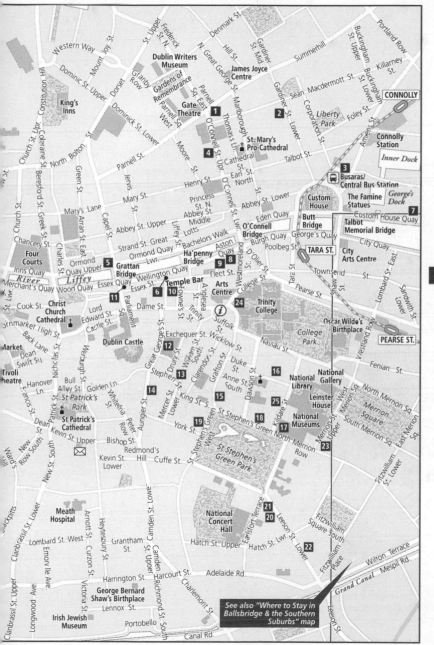

hotels are in the north, where affordable guesthouses like the **Abbott Lodge** cluster around funky Lower Gardiner Street.

HISTORIC OLD CITY & TEMPLE BAR/ TRINITY COLLEGE AREA

Temple Bar is the youngest, most vibrant niche in a young, vibrant town. Stay here and you'll be on the doorstep of practically anywhere you'd want to go. That said, it can get *very* noisy at night, so request a room on a top floor or at the rear of the establishment if you want some shut-eye.

Very Expensive

The Clarence ★★★ This has been the most famous hotel in Dublin since 1992, when U2's Bono and the Edge bought it. For some, knowing that a hotel is owned by rock stars might actually be a strike against the place, but don't be put off—this is one of the most sophisticated hotels in the city. The mid-19th-century, Regency-style building was beautifully renovated, keeping the best of its antique charm, but adding layers of contemporary elegance. Rooms are designed with lush fabrics in neutral tones of oatmeal and chocolate, light Shaker-style oak furniture, and exceptionally comfortable, firm, king-size beds. The cheery staff are on top of things, and always seem to remember who you are. The elegant **Tea Room** restaurant (p. 134) is one of the best in town for contemporary Irish cuisine. The **Octagon Bar** (p. 175) has a good buzz, and the **Study,** which has the feel of an old-style gentleman's club, is a relaxing place to read the papers and sip a glass of wine. The Clarence is business-friendly, with big, well-lighted desks and interactive TV/DVD/broadband Internet systems in each room. There's also a well-equipped fitness room and health spa, which offers a range of massage treatments starting from about €100 ($160) for an hour. Please note that it's possible a planned expansion of the hotel in 2009 could close it down for a period of months. Keep an eye out for midweek specials, which drop the price from "Very Expensive" to just "Expensive."

6–8 Wellington Quay, Dublin 2. © **01/407-0800.** Fax 01/407-0820. www.theclarence.ie. 47 units. €350–€380 ($560–$608) double; €720 ($1,152) 1-bedroom suite; €930 ($1,488) 2-bedroom suite. Full Irish breakfast €28 ($45). AE, DC, MC, V. Valet parking €25 ($40). Bus: 51B, 51C, 68, 69, or 79. **Amenities:** Restaurant (eclectic Continental); bar; gym; spa; concierge; salon; 24-hr. room service; babysitting; laundry service; dry cleaning; nonsmoking rooms; foreign-currency exchange; study. *In room:* A/C, interactive TV/DVD/broadband system, minibar, hair dryer, safe.

The Westin ★★ The Westin makes good use of this building's grand, 19th-century facade (the building was once a bank)—it promises real luxury and the interior easily fulfills it. The elegant lobby is lined with big marble columns and decorated with exquisite plasterwork; one entrance leads down a great hall of mirrors. The spacious rooms

---

ⓘ Tips   A Parking Note

Many Dublin hotels do not offer parking; if you have a car, you'll have to find (and pay for) street parking. In this section, we've provided parking information only for the few hotels that do offer parking arrangements or discounts for guests. The more expensive hotels can charge as much as €25 ($40) per night to park, so ask about this hidden charge before you book.

have a real sense of modern sophistication, with decor in shades of mahogany and cream, comfortable beds, and soft linens; many have sweeping views of the city. The hotel's bar, the **Mint,** is in the old vaults, and the **Exchange** restaurant is bright and modern. Well worth a splurge.

College Green, Dublin 2. ✆ **01/645-1000.** Fax 01/645-1234. www.westin.com/dublin. 163 units. €260–€485 ($416–$776) double. AE, DC, MC, V. Parking €20 ($32). Bus: All An Lar (cross-city) buses. **Amenities:** Restaurant (Continental); lounge; bar; gym; concierge; business services; conference facilities; 24-hr. room service; babysitting; laundry service; nonsmoking floors. *In room:* A/C, TV, Wi-Fi, minibar, iron, safe.

Expensive

The Morgan ★★   Sitting coolly amid Temple Bar's revelry, this trendy boutique hotel has a bit of a cult following among those in the fashion and music industries, so you never know who might sit next to you on one of the lobby's fashionably uncomfortable chairs. It's easy to see what attracts guests: Rooms are airy and minimalist, with light beechwood furnishings, crisp, white bedspreads, and creamy neutral walls. The color scheme is enlivened with colorful paintings by Irish artists. The effect is understated elegance with a modern, luxurious twist. But the attraction here goes beyond mere good looks. Every detail—from the classy cutlery to the pillows on the beds—is designed within an inch of its life. Bring your best Fendi bag.

10 Fleet St., Dublin 2. ✆ **01/643-7000.** Fax 01/643-7060. www.themorgan.com. 121 units. €160–€200 ($256–$320) double. AE, DC, MC, V. Bus: 78A or 78B. **Amenities:** Cafe; bar; fitness center; room service; aromatherapy/masseuse; babysitting; laundry service; dry cleaning; video/CD library. *In room:* A/C (deluxe rooms only), TV/VCR, CD player, Wi-Fi, tea/coffeemaker, iron, garment press, safe, voice mail.

Moderate

Buswells Hotel ★   This traditional hotel has a wonderful sense of class that saves it from feeling stuffy. The spacious, slightly masculine rooms are spread throughout three Georgian buildings. The fact that the hotel is so sprawling can make it feel a bit idiosyncratic, and finding your room can be a challenge after a few pints of Guinness. But it's worth the wandering, as it has great style and a unique ambience, in part because its location near the Irish government buildings makes its bar and restaurant hotbeds of political intrigue.

23–25 Molesworth St., Dublin 2. ✆ **01/614-6500.** Fax 01/676-2090. www.buswellshotel.com. 69 units. €140–€190 ($224–$304) double. AE, DC, MC, V. DART: Pearse. Bus: 10, 11, 13, or 46A. **Amenities:** Restaurant; bar; gym; concierge; business services; conference facilities; 24-hr. room service; babysitting; laundry service; nonsmoking floors; foreign-currency exchange. *In room:* TV, Wi-Fi, iron, trouser press.

Eliza Lodge ★   This hotel opened a few years ago right beside the Liffey and embodies all the exuberance and zest of Temple Bar. The reception rooms aren't much to write home about, but guest rooms are simple and attractive, done up in neutral creams and blond woods, with big floor-to-ceiling windows—the better to take in the riverside vistas. At the top end, executive rooms have Jacuzzi tubs and bay windows looking out over the quay. But a better-value splurge is the smaller penthouse doubles that have balconies overlooking the river for €190 ($304). *Note:* The windows are not soundproof, and rooms on the lower floors can get a lot of street noise. Take your breakfast (included in the room rate) in the Liffey-view **Eliza Blues** restaurant.

23–24 Wellington Quay, Dublin 2. ✆ **01/671-8044.** Fax 01/671-8362. www.dublinlodge.com. 18 units. €125–€150 ($200–$240) double. AE, MC, V. Bus: 51B, 51C, 68, 69, or 79. **Amenities:** Restaurant; bar; Wi-Fi (downstairs only); nonsmoking rooms. *In room:* A/C, TV, tea/coffeemaker, hair dryer, iron, safe, Jacuzzi tubs in executive rooms.

(Fun Facts) **What's in a Name?**

The "Bar" in Temple Bar has nothing to do with a pub or the law. "Bar" was a Viking word meaning "street," and Dublin was occupied for many of its early years by Viking invaders. Temple Bar, the district, came to be the name for the area around a street that the Irish called Temple.

Temple Bar Hotel   It may be twice as big and half as stylish as the Morgan, but this is still a trendy option. The five-story hotel was developed from a former bank building, and great care was taken to preserve the brick facade and Victorian mansard roof. Guest rooms are not so fancy and are quite plain, if comfortable. The orthopedic beds are firm, although the smallish rooms are a bit cramped. **Buskers,** the hotel's nightclub, is very popular and loud. Bear that in mind before you book—if you're looking for peace and quiet, this is probably not the place for you, at least on the weekend. Midweek, rooms are quieter and frequently cheaper.

Fleet St., Temple Bar, Dublin 2. ☎ **01/612-9200.** Fax 01/677-3088. www.templebarhotel.com. 129 units. €145–€200 ($232–$320) double. Rates include full Irish breakfast. AE, MC, V. DART: Tara St. Bus: 78A or 78B. **Amenities:** Restaurant (contemporary Irish); 2 bars; access to a nearby health club; concierge; room service; babysitting; laundry service; dry cleaning; foreign-currency exchange. *In room:* TV, tea/coffee-maker, hair dryer, garment press.

Self-Catering

25 Eustace Street (Finds)   This wonderfully restored Georgian town house, dating from 1720, has an enviable location in the heart of Temple Bar. It is a showcase property for the Irish Landmark Trust, whose mission is to rescue neglected historic buildings and restore them, and that it does with aplomb. The three-story house has been faithfully restored, with a superb timber-paneled staircase, fireplaces in every room, mahogany furniture, and brass beds. There's a huge drawing room with a baby grand piano, full dining room, equipped galley kitchen, and three bedrooms (a double, a twin, and a triple). There are two bathrooms, one with a cast-iron claw-foot tub placed dead center. Bookshelves have been thoughtfully stocked with classics by Irish novelists. As with all ILT properties, there is no TV. All this, and Temple Bar at your doorstep. Some readers have reported that the house is a little too close for comfort to Temple Bar's party scene and the noise can be a bit much on weekends.

25 Eustace St., Dublin 2. Contact the Irish Landmark Trust ☎ **01/670-4733.** Fax 01/670-4887. www.irishlandmark.com. 1 apt. From €1,742 ($2,787) or €2,016 ($3,226) per week during peak months. Weekly bookings only July–Aug; rest of year 3- or 4-night stays. AE, MC, V. Bus: Any An Lar (cross-city) bus. **Amenities:** Full kitchen. *In room:* No phone.

ST. STEPHEN'S GREEN/GRAFTON STREET AREA

St. Stephen's Green may be only a 10-minute walk from the hustle and bustle of Temple Bar and Trinity College, but it's infinitely calmer and less harried. This is a good area if you're looking for a little peace and quiet.

Very Expensive

Conrad Hotel ★★   This modern, glass-walled hotel, which sits on one corner of St. Stephen's Green, is a favorite of the international and Irish business travelers, so it has all of the fast Internet connections, big desks, and fax machines you would expect. Bedrooms are nicely done in neutral colors with big windows, with individual temperature controls for the air-conditioning and big, modern bathrooms. The gym is hypermodern, and reduced rates are available for the nearby K Club golf course. The **Alex** restaurant is a sleek, Continental place geared to those with comfortable expense accounts.

Earlsfort Terrace, Dublin 2. ℂ **01/602-8900.** Fax 01/676-5424. www.conradhotels.com. 198 units. €295–€495 ($472–$792) double. AE, DC, MC, V. Parking €10 ($16). Bus: 10, 11, 13, 14, 15, 44, 46A, 47, 48, or 86. **Amenities:** Restaurant (Continental); cocktail bar; pub; gym; concierge; car service; business services; conference facilities; salon; 24-hr. room service; babysitting; laundry service; nonsmoking floors; foreign-currency exchange. *In room:* A/C, TV w/pay movies, high-speed Internet, minibar, iron, trouser press, safe.

The Fitzwilliam Hotel ★★★ Take an unbeatable location with sweeping views over the green, add a Michelin-starred restaurant, throw in contemporary design by Terence Conran, and you have a hit on your hands. Conran has a knack for easygoing sophistication, and in the Fitzwilliam he uses clean lines and only a few neutral colors (white, beige, gray) throughout the public rooms and guest rooms. The beauty is in the detail here—even the staff uniforms are custom-made by Irish designers Marc O'Neill and Cuan Hanly. Rooms are simply done in neutral tones with stripped-down furniture. **Thornton's,** the hotel restaurant, is very good, or you could try the more casual **Citron,** or linger over a pint at the **Inn on the Green** bar.

109 St. Stephen's Green, Dublin 2. ℂ **01/478-7000.** Fax 01/478-7878. www.fitzwilliamhotel.com. 130 units. €300–€375 ($480–$600) double. Breakfast €22 ($35). AE, DC, MC, V. DART: Pearse. Bus: 10, 11A, 11B, 13, or 20B. **Amenities:** 2 restaurants (French, international); bar; concierge; room service; babysitting; laundry service; dry cleaning; nonsmoking rooms; foreign-currency exchange; roof garden. *In room:* A/C, TV/VCR, CD player, fax, high-speed Internet, minibar, tea/coffeemaker, hair dryer, garment press, voice mail, fresh flowers.

The Shelbourne ★★★ One of the city's true *grande dame* hotels, the Shelbourne has been a Dublin landmark since 1824. The hotel has played a significant role in Irish history—the Irish constitution was drafted here in 1922, in room no. 112—and it still attracts Irish politicians, especially to its bars and restaurants. To Dubliners, the Shelbourne symbolizes history and politics, and nothing—not even getting swallowed up and fully renovated by the Marriott Group—can change that. Rooms are air-conditioned and decorated in grand, traditional style, with subtle yellows and pinks. The hotel claims to have "Ireland's most luxurious beds," with 300-thread-count Egyptian cotton linens wrapped around feather mattresses. Rooms also have international power sockets, so your curling iron shouldn't explode. The bars, restaurant, and lobby are still warmed by fireplaces and lighted by elegant Waterford chandeliers, and the **Lord Mayor's Lounge** is still ideal for afternoon tea. Unsurprisingly, prices have risen since the face-lift. If you have an Irish name and you're staying here, ask the in-house **genealogy butler** to explore your family history.

27 St. Stephen's Green, Dublin 2. ℂ **1-888/236-2427** in the U.S., or 01/663-4500. Fax 01/661-6006. www.marriott.co.uk. 190 units. €285–€475 ($456–$760) double. Breakfast €20–€26 ($32–$42). AE, DC, MC, V.

DUBLIN

6

WHERE TO STAY

Ⓣips **Service Charges**

A reminder: Unless otherwise noted, room rates don't include service charges (usually 10%–15% of your bill).

Limited free self-parking; valet parking €25 ($40). DART: Pearse. Bus: 10, 11A, 11B, 13, or 20B. **Amenities:** 2 restaurants (modern Irish, oyster bar); 2 bars; fitness center; beauty and spa treatments; concierge; barbershop; room service; babysitting; laundry service; dry cleaning; foreign-currency exchange; safe-deposit boxes; video library. *In room:* A/C, TV, radio, dataport, minibar.

Westbury ★   This upscale hotel straddles the line between traditional and modern, trying to offer a little something for everyone just off the bustling shopping hub of Grafton Street. The understated guest rooms have luxurious touches, like minibars stocked with Waterford crystal; the lobby is spacious with a restaurant, cafe terrace, and bar—a favorite of Dublin's beautiful people. But there are significant flaws to the look of the rooms in particular—there is a cheapness to its design and furniture choices. This is not the most lavish hotel in the city at that price.

Grafton St., Dublin 2. *©* **01/679-1122.** Fax 01/679-7078. www.jurysdoyle.com. 204 units. €210–€500 ($336–$800) double. Full Irish breakfast €30 ($48). AE, DC, MC, V. Parking €20 ($32). Bus: All An Lar (cross-city) buses. **Amenities:** 2 restaurants (international, casual); bar; concierge; 24-hr. room service; babysitting; laundry service; dry cleaning; nonsmoking rooms. *In room:* A/C, interactive TV/DVD/broadband system, minibar, hair dryer, safe.

Expensive

Brooks Hotel ★   This sophisticated hotel has recently undergone a full makeover that brightened the hotel lobby, with its friendly restaurant and bar, cushy sofas, and sooth-ingly elegant furnishings. The relatively small guest rooms have been redone in a muted gold-and-purple color scheme that won't appeal to everyone. Superior and executive rooms are more spacious and have DVD players and radios. The oak-paneled drawing room is a restful oasis for a cup of tea or a glass of sherry while you peruse the *Irish Times.*

59–62 Drury St., Dublin 2. *©* **01/670-4000.** Fax 01/670-4455. www.brookshotel.ie. 98 units. €225–€300 ($360–$480) double. AE, DC, MC, V. Discounted overnight parking at adjacent parking lot. DART: Tara St. or Pearse. Bus: 10, 11A, 11B, 13, 14, 15, 15A, 15B, 20B, or 46A. **Amenities:** Restaurant (international); bar; minigym; concierge; secretarial services; room service; babysitting; laundry service; dry cleaning; non-smoking floors; foreign-currency exchange; video library. *In room:* A/C, TV, VCR/DVD player (in superior rooms and up), fax, dataport, minibar, hair dryer, iron, garment press, safe.

Browne's Townhouse ★★   If you love luxury but hate big chain hotels, look no further than this sumptuously restored Georgian town house right on St. Stephen's Green. Originally a gentleman's club, it is now a small, classy boutique hotel. Downstairs is all Georgian splendor: comfy wingback chairs, rich upholstery, ornate ceiling plaster-work. The 11 guest rooms come in all shapes and sizes, and are sumptuously decorated with period furnishings, marble bathrooms, and unique architectural details. If you splurge on the Thomas Leighton suite, you'll sleep on a magnificent king-size mahogany bed that once belonged to Marilyn Monroe. Downstairs, the elegant brasserie serves up excellent French fare.

22 St. Stephen's Green, Dublin 2. *©* **01/638-3939.** Fax 01/638-3900. www.brownesluxuryhotel.com. 11 units. €180–€280 ($288–$448) double. Breakfast €13–€20 ($21–$32). MC, V. DART: Pearse. Bus: 10, 11A, 11B, 13, or 20B. **Amenities:** Restaurant (French). *In room:* A/C, TV, fax, dataport, tea/coffeemaker, hair dryer.

Number 31 ★   A discreet plaque outside an elegant locked gate on a tiny side street is your only clue that what lies beyond is an award-winning guesthouse. It's actually two converted buildings—one a grand Georgian town house, the other a more modern coach house—with nice touches, like a sunken living room where seating is arranged around a peat-burning fireplace. In the main house, rooms are large and simply decorated, while in the coach house rooms are elegant and modern. Handmade beds are enveloped in natural linens. Unfortunately, the rack rate doesn't reflect what's on offer—there's no restaurant, no bar, no room service, and no air-conditioning. Breakfast here is some consolation—cooked to order for you, with organic, seasonal ingredients, and choices ranging from mushroom frittatas to fresh-baked cranberry bread. And keep an eye out for discounted rates.

31 Leeson Close, Lower Leeson St., Dublin 2. ℂ **01/676-5011.** Fax 01/676-2929. www.number31.ie. 21 units. €150–€320 ($240–$500) double. Rates include breakfast. AE, MC, V. Free parking. Bus: 11, 11A, 11B, 13, 13A, or 13B. *In room:* TV, hair dryer.

Trinity Lodge   In an enormous Georgian town house that feels miles away from the anonymous chain hotels in the city center, the Trinity is a classy option a few blocks off Grafton Street. The gray stone building dates to 1785, and its 10 large guest rooms are brightly decorated in keeping with that period, some with paintings by the respected Irish artist Graham Knuttel. The breakfast room downstairs is warmly designed in country-house style. There's a second building across the street where six large rooms have a more contemporary edge. These buildings are protected historical structures, so there's no elevator access to their four levels—ask for a ground-floor room if you have mobility problems.

12 S. Frederick St., Dublin 2. ℂ **01/617-0900.** Fax 01/617-0999. www.trinitylodge.com. 16 units. €180–€235 ($288–$376) double. Rates include breakfast. MC, V. Bus: All An Lar (cross-city) buses. **Amenities:** Bar; restaurant; room service (7:30–10am); nonsmoking rooms. *In room:* A/C (some), TV, Wi-Fi, safe.

Moderate

Central Hotel   This charming, rambling, eccentric old hotel makes up in personality for what it lacks in style. The public areas have a pleasantly cluttered, Victorian atmosphere enhanced by a collection of original Irish art. Faded floral fabrics and busy carpet patterns are everywhere, and guest rooms look a bit battered and cheap, but they have nice historical touches, including high ceilings and carved cornices. The atmospheric **Library Bar** is a real find—a low-key haven for a cup of tea or a pint and a bit of calm.

1–5 Exchequer St. (at the corner of Great Georges St.), Dublin 2. ℂ **01/679-7302.** Fax 01/679-7303. www.centralhotel.ie. 70 units. €115–€200 ($184–$320) double. Rates include service charge and full Irish breakfast. AE, DC, MC, V. Discounted parking in nearby public lot. Bus: 22A. **Amenities:** Restaurant (Irish/Continental); lounge; bar; room service; nonsmoking rooms. *In room:* TV, minibar, tea/coffeemaker, hair dryer, iron, garment press, voice mail.

Premier Suites Stephen's Hall (Value)   How suite it is. Well located on the southeast corner of St. Stephen's Green in a handsome Georgian town house, this all-suite hotel offers a bit of value for families, visitors who plan an extended stay, or folks who want to entertain or do their own cooking. The building recently underwent a full renovation, which renewed each suite in tasteful modern style. Each apartment contains a sitting room, dining area, fully equipped kitchenette, tiled bathroom, and bedroom, and the smallest apartment is just under 150 sq. m (1,615 sq. ft.).

14–17 Lower Leeson St., Dublin 2. ℂ **01/638-1111.** Fax 01/638-1122. www.stephens-hall.com. 30 units. €140–€180 ($224–$288) 1-bedroom suite. AE, DC, MC, V. Parking €10 ($16). DART: Pearse. Bus: 11, 11A, 11B, 13, 13A, or 13B. **Amenities:** Concierge; nonsmoking floor; safe-deposit boxes. *In room:* TV, fax, Wi-Fi.

Inexpensive

Avalon House (Value)   This warm and friendly hostel in a beautiful old redbrick building is well known among those who travel to Dublin on a budget. Its pine floors, high ceilings, and open fireplace make it a pleasant place in which to relax, and its cafe is a popular hangout for international travelers. Most accommodations are in dorms of varying sizes, with a few single and twin bedded rooms available, too. It's not exactly the Clarence, but it's got all you really need—clean, cheerful rooms in a safe location at a cheap price. This is one of the best budget options in town.

55 Aungier St., Dublin 2. © **01/475-0001.** Fax 01/475-0303. www.avalon-house.ie. 12 units. €15–€38 ($24–$61) per person double with private bathroom. Rates include light continental breakfast. AE, MC, V. Bus: 16, 16A, 19, 22, or 155. No curfew but passes must be shown on entry after 9pm. **Amenities:** Cafe; game room; Wi-Fi; nonsmoking rooms; TV lounge; foreign-currency exchange; cooking facilities; 24-hr. security; luggage storage; safe.

FITZWILLIAM SQUARE/MERRION SQUARE AREA

This elegant Georgian neighborhood feels and looks much like nearby St. Stephen's Green, but its streets are less busy and commercialized, and its hotels marginally less expensive. Fitzwilliam Square and Merrion Square are small parks surrounded by Georgian town houses. Many of the houses are offices for doctors, lawyers, and government agencies.

Very Expensive

Merrion Hotel ★   Housed in four restored Georgian houses, the Merrion is a deeply feminine, traditionally elegant hotel. Downstairs the lobby and lounges have formal furniture and fires glowing in hearths—the kinds of places where proper afternoon tea seems called for. The impressive contemporary art on the walls is part of one of the country's largest private collections. Service is discreetly omnipresent, and the spacious rooms overlook either the government buildings or the hotel's 18th-century-inspired gardens of acacia and lilac. Pamper yourself in the **Tethra Spa.** Stretch your credit card's limit at the Michelin-starred **Restaurant Patrick Guilbaud** or save a few pennies at the somewhat cheaper and more atmospheric **Cellar** restaurant.

Upper Merrion St., Dublin 2. © **01/603-0600.** Fax 01/603-0700. www.merrionhotel.com. 142 units. €470–€495 ($752–$792) double. Breakfast €27 ($43). AE, DC, MC, V. Parking €20 ($32) per night. DART: Pearse. Bus: 10, 13, or 13A. **Amenities:** 2 restaurants (Continental); 2 bars; pool; gym; spa; concierge; car service; business services; conference facilities; salon; 24-hr. room service; babysitting; laundry service. *In room:* A/C, TV w/DVD, high-speed Internet, minibar, iron, safe.

O'CONNELL STREET AREA NORTH OF THE LIFFEY

The newly hip Northside has much to offer in the way of hotels. With the grand Gresham and the trendy Morrison (see below) leading the way, it's growing in popularity as a place to stay. Best of all, not only is it very central and within walking distance of all the major sights and shops, but hotel rates tend to be lower than they are just across the bridge.

Very Expensive

The Morrison ★★   This is really an oversize boutique hotel, with an ideal location just across the Liffey from Temple Bar. Fashion fans will surely have no trouble pegging the design as the work of designer John Rocha, who is responsible for everything from the crushed velvet bed throws in blood red to the Waterford crystal vases. Rocha uses a palette of neutral colors—cream, chocolate, and black—to achieve a kind of warm minimalism in the guest rooms, which have stereos, Egyptian-cotton linens, and cool Portuguese limestone in the bathrooms. The stylish atrium-style restaurant, **Halo,** is one of the most talked-about in town. A recent expansion has added a new wing of 48 bedrooms, significantly increasing the hotel's capacity.

Lower Ormond Quay, Dublin 1. ℂ **01/887-2400.** Fax 01/874-4031. www.morrisonhotel.ie. 138 units. €220–€450 ($352–$720) double. AE, DC, MC, V. DART: Connolly. Bus: 70 or 80. **Amenities:** Restaurant (fusion); 2 bars; concierge; room service; babysitting; dry cleaning; video/CD library. *In room:* A/C, CD player, iPod docking station, high-speed Internet, minibar, hair dryer, safe, voice mail.

Expensive
The Clarion Hotel Dublin IFSC ★
All smooth straight lines and extra touches, this relaxing, modern hotel is a good option for business travelers. The comfortable rooms are softened by Egyptian cotton bedding, and filled with the latest electronic gadgets, including high-speed Internet and PlayStation units. However, some rooms are starting to look a bit scuffed. The stylish bar and restaurant are workaday but useful. However, this hotel's best offering is arguably its state-of-the-art health club, with its gorgeous low-lit pool that urges you to exercise. There are yoga and aerobics classes for the energetic. Happily, the sauna, steam room, and whirlpool require no physical exertion at all. Rooms at the front have a gorgeous view of the Liffey and Dublin skyline.

International Financial Services Centre, Dublin 1. ℂ **01/433-8800.** Fax 01/433-8811. www.clarionhotelifsc. com. 163 units. €150–€300 ($240–$480) double. AE, DC, MC, V. Parking €12 ($19). Dart: Connolly. Bus: All An Lar (cross-city) buses. **Amenities:** Restaurant; bar; swimming pool; gym; spa; concierge; room service; babysitting; laundry service; dry cleaning; nonsmoking floors; foreign-currency exchange. *In room:* A/C, TV (satellite/DVD), high-speed Internet, minibar, hair dryer, safe.

The Gresham ★★
Along with the Shelbourne, this is one of Dublin's two most historic hotels, and it has welcomed visitors for 200 years. With a row of flags out front and its grand, up-lighted facade, this hotel stands out, and the vast lobby is one of the best places in the city to have a cup of tea or a cocktail in elegant but relaxed surroundings. A lengthy renovation lasting several years has recently been completed, giving it all a badly needed makeover, and redesigned rooms are coolly done in neutral tones, with big, firm beds and huge windows. It has a friendly, modern bar, and a handy restaurant serving European cuisine.

23 Upper O'Connell St., Dublin 1. ℂ **01/874-6881.** Fax 01/878 7175. www.gresham-hotels.com. 289 units. €155–€290 ($248–$464) double. AE, DC, MC, V. Parking €14 ($22) per night. Bus: 11 or 13. **Amenities:** Restaurant (contemporary French); 2 bars; concierge; room service; babysitting; laundry; service; dry cleaning; nonsmoking floors. *In room:* A/C, TV, high-speed Internet, fridge, hair dryer, safe, U.S. voltage plug sockets (some rooms).

Moderate
Royal Dublin Hotel
This five-story Best Western–owned property, near Parnell Square at the north end of Dublin's main thoroughfare, is within walking distance of all the main theaters and Northside attractions. The contemporary sky-lit lobby sits next to the historic, attractive lounges that were part of the original 1752 building. Guest rooms are, by comparison, quite plain, featuring light woods, plaid bedspreads, and windows overlooking a busy street below. If you can get one of its frequent Internet bargain rates, this can be a well-priced option, but at full rack rate, it's not a great deal.

40 Upper O'Connell St., Dublin 1. ℂ **800/528-1234** in the U.S., or 01/873-3666. Fax 01/873-3120. www. royaldublin.com. 120 units. €130–€225 ($208–$360) double. Rates include service charge, full Irish breakfast, and VAT. AE, DC, MC, V. Free parking. DART: Connolly. Bus: 36A, 40A, 40B, 40C, or 51A. **Amenities:** Restaurant (brasserie); lounge; bar; concierge; room service; babysitting; laundry; foreign-currency exchange. *In room:* TV, radio, tea/coffeemaker, hair dryer.

Abbott Lodge (Value) Historic Abbott Lodge has long been one of Dublin's most popular guesthouses, and for good reason. The rooms are simply decorated, but many have high ceilings or architectural details like original cornices, and nice touches like mahogany beds. The staff is genuinely friendly and will happily fill you in on the neighborhood's offerings, including the best pubs and restaurants nearby. This place is good to know about if you're traveling on a budget. Rooms facing the street can be noisy, so ask for a room at the back if you're a light sleeper.

87–88 Lower Gardiner St., Dublin 1. ℂ **01/836-5548.** Fax 01/836-5549. www.abbott-lodge.com. 17 units. €90–€120 ($144–$192) double. Rates include full Irish breakfast and VAT. MC, V. Parking €10 ($16) per night. DART: Connolly. Bus: All An Lar (cross-city) buses. **Amenities:** Lounge. *In room:* TV.

Isaac's Hostel (Value) This friendly guesthouse takes the backpacker concept of humble frugality and turns it right on its head. Calling itself "Dublin's first V.I.P. hostel," it has the usual mix of bunk beds, lockers, and TV rooms. But it also has a heady cocktail of extras, including polished wood floors, a full restaurant, and an attractive sauna. It's a thoughtful hybrid hostel, with Internet access, a kitchen for guests' use, pool tables, and a friendly and relaxing atmosphere. Prices are liable to rise during "event" weekends, such as when big sports matches are on, but it's definitely one of the best options for those traveling on a tight budget.

2–5 Frenchman's Lane, Dublin 1. ℂ **01/855-6215.** Fax 01/855-6574. www.isaacs.ie. 54 units. €14–€24 ($22–$38) dormitory (per person); €40 ($64) double. Rates include light breakfast. MC, V. DART: Connolly. Bus: All An Lar (cross-city) buses. **Amenities:** Restaurant; deli; sauna; game room; Internet lounge; laundry service; foreign-currency exchange; cooking facilities; TV lounge.

BALLSBRIDGE & THE SOUTHERN SUBURBS

This is the most prestigious Dublin residential neighborhood, south of the canal, coveted for its leafy streets and historic buildings. Beautiful though it is, the downside is that it's a good 20- or 30-minute walk to most sights and shops.

Very Expensive

Four Seasons ★★★ (Kids) If money is no object, the Four Seasons lures you like a De Beers diamond draws a socialite. The beauty is in the details here: The indoor pool and whirlpool overlook a sunken garden; the lobby and guest rooms are equally smart and plush; the spa is outstanding and the restaurants elegant. This is an excellent option for families, as there are complimentary cribs, child-proof bedrooms, and a babysitting service. A menu of children's activities will keep the kids occupied while you have a romantic meal or just kick back for some quiet meditation (the better to prepare yourself for the bill). Always check the website's rates before booking; online discounts can be very good.

Simmonscourt Rd., Ballsbridge, Dublin 4. ℂ **800/819-5053** in the U.S., or 01/665-4000. Fax 01/665-4099. www.fourseasons.com/dublin. 259 units. €295–€445 ($472–$712) double. Breakfast €25 ($40). AE, DC, MC, V. Valet parking €14 ($22). DART: Sandymount (5-min. walk). Bus: 7, 7A, 7X, 8, or 45. **Amenities:** 2 restaurants (modern Continental, cafe); lobby lounge; bar; indoor pool; health club/spa; whirlpool; salon services; children's programs; concierge; room service; babysitting; laundry service; dry cleaning; non-smoking rooms. *In room:* TV/VCR, CD player available, radio, dataport, minibar, hair dryer, safe, voice mail.

Expensive

The Dylan ★ The latest incredibly trendy hotel in increasingly hip Dublin, this place puts its cards on the table the moment you walk in the door—here, only two things

DUBLIN

6

WHERE TO STAY

matter: how big your wallet is, and how good you look. Chanel bag? Prada skirt? $500 shoes? Welcome to your new home! This determinedly glamorous boutique hotel has transformed the former Royal Hospital Nurses' Home with vivid colors, bright carpets and curtains, Murano glass chandeliers, studded leather wallpaper, and lime-green sofas. Guest rooms are quite small, and the decor is disco chic, with Frette linens and 7th Heaven beds. Service here is excellent, but beauty's in the eye of the beholder, so this very hip, very adult hotel is certainly not for everyone. Families in particular might find its party-hearty atmosphere a bit off-putting (it has a signature cocktail—vanilla vodka with crème de banana—as well as a thumping club soundtrack). But 20-somethings line up to spend the night.

Eastmoreland Place, Ballsbridge, Dublin 4. ℂ **01/660-3000.** Fax 01/660-3005. www.dylan.ie. 44 units. €220–€300 ($352–$480) double. Breakfast €20 ($32). AE, MC, V. Valet parking €20 ($32). Bus: 10, 46A, 46B, 63, or 84. **Amenities:** Restaurant (Continental); lounge; bar; nightclub; concierge; salon; room service; laundry service; nonsmoking rooms; foreign-currency exchange. *In room:* Plasma TV, CD player, radio, dataport, minibar, hair dryer, garment press, safe, bathrobes, voice mail.

Moderate

Anglesea Town House ★ Everyone who stays at this 1903 Edwardian-style B&B raves about the same thing: the extraordinary breakfasts served by host Helen Kirrane. From freshly squeezed orange juice to homemade fruit compote, yogurt, and baked fruit, you can move on to home-baked cereals, then bacon, eggs, and sausages or a smoked salmon omelet. There's always a decadent dessert (the profiteroles are divine) and gallons of brewed coffee. The place is full of old-world comforts—rocking chairs, settees, a sun deck, and flowering plants—and guest rooms are attractive and comfortable.

63 Anglesea Rd., Ballsbridge, Dublin 4. ℂ **01/668-3877.** Fax 01/668-3461. 7 units. €130 ($208) double. Rates include full breakfast. AE, MC, V. DART: Lansdowne Rd. Bus: 10, 46A, 46B, 63, or 84. **Amenities:** Babysitting. *In room:* TV, hair dryer.

Butlers Town House ★★ ⓥalue This beautifully restored Victorian town house feels like a gracious family home. The atmosphere is elegant but comfortable; rooms are richly furnished with four-poster or half-tester beds, draped in luxurious fabrics in rich colors. The gem here is the Glendalough Room, with a lovely bay window and small library; it requires booking well in advance. Free tea and coffee are on offer all day, and breakfast and afternoon tea are served in the atrium dining room.

44 Lansdowne Rd., Ballsbridge, Dublin 4. ℂ **01/667-4022.** Fax 01/667-3960. www.butlers-hotel.com. 20 units. €110–€196 ($176–$314) double. Rates include full breakfast. AE, DC, MC, V. Free parking. Closed Dec 23–Jan 10. DART: Lansdowne Rd. Bus: 7, 7A, 8, or 45. **Amenities:** Breakfast room; room service; babysitting; laundry service; dry cleaning. *In room:* A/C, TV, dataport, hair dryer.

Waterloo House ★ This classy guesthouse is charming in an old-world kind of way, with classical music wafting through the elegant, high-ceilinged drawing room where you can linger over the morning papers. Guest rooms are large (some have two double beds), but it's hard to decide whether the patterned carpet and box-pleated bedspreads are reassuringly traditional or just dated. The varied breakfast menu offers more than the usual fried eggs. Like many small establishments in Dublin, Waterloo House raises its prices during special events, such as major sports matches.

8–10 Waterloo Rd., Ballsbridge, Dublin 4. ℂ **01/660-1888.** Fax 01/667-1955. www.waterloohouse.ie. 17 units. €80–€200 ($128–$320) double. Rates include full breakfast. MC, V. Free parking. Closed Christmas week. DART: Lansdowne Rd. Bus: 5, 7, or 8. **Amenities:** Breakfast room. *In room:* TV, tea/coffeemaker, hair dryer, garment press.

4 WHERE TO DINE

Dublin's restaurant scene is a bit of a good news/bad news situation: The good news is that the economic upswing over the last decade has brought with it a new generation of international, sophisticated eateries. The bad news is that prices are considerably more than you'd pay in a comparable U.S. city, or even in Paris or London.

A combination of high taxes (the VAT on wine is 21%, and on restaurant meals it's 13.5%) and a bit of nouveau riche overenthusiasm among restaurateurs has the effect of

How to Eat Without Breaking the Bank

Prices on food in Dublin are sky-high these days, so if money is an object, you're going to have to be creative.

You can get a cost break in the city's many cafes and tearooms, which offer sandwiches, scones, soup, and hot platters at reasonable prices. Or you could have your lunch in a pub, where you can get a hearty lunch for around €10 ($16). The pub option is for lunch only, though, as most pubs don't serve food after 3pm.

If it's summer, cut costs by buying a sandwich at one of the city's many sandwich shops—or even in grocery chains like Tesco and Londis—and having a picnic in a city square. Store-bought sandwiches are better and fresher here than in North America, and they only cost a few euros.

In the winter, though, getting out of the cold can be a priority, so consider popping into a coffee shop and grabbing a sandwich there—usually no more than €4 ($6.40).

Alternatively, you can make lunch your main meal—most restaurants have good lunch deals—and just pick up a sandwich to have later as a light dinner in your hotel room.

Take advantage of free breakfasts if your hotel offers them, as that's the best deal on food you're going to get in Dublin.

making dining out memorably expensive. But the quality is good, and splurging once or twice while you're in town can be a real treat.

HISTORIC OLD CITY/LIBERTIES & AROUND
Expensive

Locks ★★ FRENCH One of the hottest restaurants of the moment in Dublin, this effortlessly elegant place on the Grand Canal has a great country-chic style. Its white, tongue-in-groove walls and fresh floors set the stage for French-influenced cuisine, made with artisan cheeses and local, organic meats and produce. Try the cider-braised pork with celeriac *boulangere*, girolle mushrooms, and confit savoy cabbage, or the monkfish and mussel cassoulet with Morteau sausage. Desserts are inspired. Book in advance or you'll never get a seat.

1 Windsor Terrace, Portobello, Dublin 8. © **01/454 3391**. Reservations required. Main courses €21–€39 ($34–$62). AE, DC, MC, V. Mon–Fri 12:30–2:30pm and 7:30–10:30pm; Sat 7:15–11pm. Bus: Any An Lar.

Lord Edward ★★★ SEAFOOD Established in 1890 in the heart of the Old City opposite Christ Church Cathedral, this cozy upstairs dining room claims to be Dublin's oldest seafood restaurant. A dozen versions of sole, including au gratin and Veronique, are available. There are also many variations of prawns, from thermidor to Provençal, and fresh lobster is prepared au naturel or in sauces. Fresh fish—from salmon and sea trout to plaice and turbot—is served grilled, fried, meunière, or poached. Vegetarian dishes are also available. At lunch, the bar sells simpler fare.

23 Christ Church Place, Dublin 8. © **01/454-2420**. Reservations required. Main courses €16–€30 ($26–$48); fixed-price dinner €35 ($56). AE, DC, MC, V. Mon–Thurs 10:30am–11:30pm; Fri–Sat 10:30am–12:30am; Sun noon–11pm. Closed Dec 24–Jan 3. Bus: 50, 54A, 56A, 65, 65A, 77, 77A, 123, or 150.

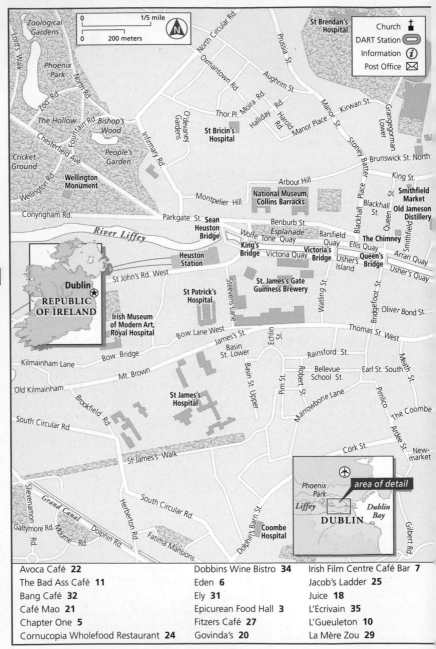

Avoca Café **22**	Dobbins Wine Bistro **34**	Irish Film Centre Café Bar **7**
The Bad Ass Café **11**	Eden **6**	Jacob's Ladder **25**
Bang Café **32**	Ely **31**	Juice **18**
Café Mao **21**	Epicurean Food Hall **3**	L'Ecrivain **35**
Chapter One **5**	Fitzers Café **27**	L'Gueuleton **10**
Cornucopia Wholefood Restaurant **24**	Govinda's **20**	La Mère Zou **29**

DUBLIN

6

WHERE TO DINE

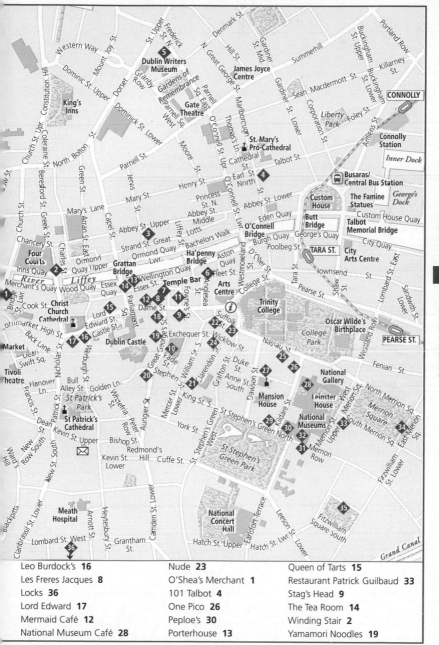

Leo Burdock's **16**	Nude **23**	Queen of Tarts **15**
Les Freres Jacques **8**	O'Shea's Merchant **1**	Restaurant Patrick Guilbaud **33**
Locks **36**	101 Talbot **4**	Stag's Head **9**
Lord Edward **17**	One Pico **26**	The Tea Room **14**
Mermaid Café **12**	Peploe's **30**	Winding Stair **2**
National Museum Café **28**	Porterhouse **13**	Yamamori Noodles **19**

Govinda's VEGETARIAN The motto of this Hare Krishna–run establishment is healthy square meals on square plates for very good prices. The meals are generous, belly-warming concoctions of vegetables, cheese, rice, and pasta. Every day, 10 main courses are offered cafeteria-style. Some are Indian, others are a variety of mainstream staples such as lasagna or macaroni and cheese. Veggie burgers are prepared to order. For dessert, try a rich wedge of carrot cake with a dollop of cream or homemade ice cream.

4 Aungier St., Dublin 2. ✆ **01/475-0309.** Main courses €10 ($16). MC, V. Mon–Sat noon–9pm. Closed Dec 24–Jan 2. Bus: 16, 16A, 19, or 22.

Leo Burdock's FISH AND CHIPS Established in 1913, this quintessential Irish take-away shop across from Christ Church Cathedral is a cherished Dublin institution. Cabinet ministers, university students, and Hollywood stars alike (Tom Cruise and Liam Neeson are both fans) can be found at the counter waiting for fish bought fresh that morning and good Irish potatoes, both cooked in "drippings" (none of that modern cooking oil!). There's no seating, but you can sit on a nearby bench or stroll down to the park at St. Patrick's Cathedral.

2 Werburgh St., Dublin 8. ✆ **01/454-0306.** Main courses €6–€8 ($9.60–$13). No credit cards. Mon–Sat noon–midnight; Sun 4pm–midnight. Bus: 21A, 50, 50A, 78, 78A, or 78B.

Queen of Tarts ★★ TEA SHOP This tiny tearoom is one of our favorite places to blow a diet on decadent cakes and cookies, with a pot of tea on the side to make it all legal. The cake counter is dizzying—we challenge you to come here and not order something sweet, like the luscious blackberry pie or the rich chocolate cake, with cream bursting from its seams. The scones are tender and light, dusted with powdered sugar, and served with tiny pots of jam. Delicious, hearty breakfasts and light lunches are also served.

4 Corkhill, Dame St., Dublin 2. ✆ **01/670-7499.** Baked goods and cakes €1.25–€4 ($2–$6.40); breakfast €3–€7 ($4.80–$11); lunch €5–€8 ($8–$13). No credit cards. Mon–Fri 7:30am–7pm; Sat 9am–6pm; Sun 10am–6pm. Bus: Any city-center bus.

TEMPLE BAR/TRINITY COLLEGE AREA

Very Expensive

Les Frères Jacques ★★ FRENCH/SEAFOOD The business crowd loves this friendly, upmarket French restaurant, which brings a touch of haute cuisine to the lower edge of the trendy Temple Bar district. The menu offers such entrees as Irish beef in pastry or roasted magret (breast) of duckling. The chef is talented with shellfish and seafood as well, so don't overlook the Irish lobster, fresh from the tank, flamed in Irish whiskey.

74 Dame St., Dublin 2. ✆ **01/679-4555.** www.lesfreresjacques.com. Reservations recommended. Main courses €30–€38 ($48–$61); fixed-price lunch €18–€23 ($29–$37); 4-course dinner €38 ($61). AE, DC, MC, V. Mon–Fri 12:30–2:30pm and 7:30–10:30pm; Sat 7:15–11pm. Closed Dec 24–Jan 4. Bus: 50, 50A, 54, 56, or 77.

The Tea Room ★★★ INTERNATIONAL This ultrasmart restaurant, ensconced in the U2-owned Clarence hotel, is guaranteed to deliver one of your most memorable meals in Ireland. This gorgeous room's soaring yet understated lines are the perfect back-drop for the complex but controlled cooking that takes form in dishes such as filet of John Dory with wild mushroom and razor clams, or red-leg partridge with juniper-fla-vored *jus*. A fixed-price Market Dinner menu offering more straightforward fare is avail-able during all dinner hours Sunday through Thursday, and from 7 to 8pm on Friday and Saturday.

In the Clarence, 6–8 Wellington Quay, Dublin 2. (☎) **01/407-0813.** Reservations required. Main courses
€30–€40 ($48–$64); fixed-price dinner €39 ($62). AE, MC, V. Mon–Fri 12:30–2pm; daily 6:30–9:45pm. Bus:
51B, 51C, 68, 69, or 79.

Expensive

Eden ★★ INTERNATIONAL/MEDITERRANEAN   This is one of Temple Bar's
hippest eateries, a cool minimalist space with an open-plan kitchen overlooking Meeting
House Square. The food is influenced by the global village, with a special penchant for
Mediterranean flavors and local seafood, so homey smoked haddock will appear on the
menu alongside exotic Moroccan lamb tagine with couscous. *Tip:* The fixed-price lunch
is a particularly good value.

Meeting House Sq. (entrance on Sycamore St.), Dublin 2. (☎) **01/670-5372.** www.edenrestaurant.ie. Main
courses €19–€30 ($30–$48); fixed-price 2-course lunch €22 ($35). AE, DC, MC, V. Daily 12:30–3pm; Mon–
Sat 6–10:30pm; Sun 6–10pm. Bus: 51B, 51C, 68, 69, or 79.

Jacob's Ladder ★★ (**Value**) MODERN IRISH   Inspired cooking by chef-owner
Adrian Roche and a stylish dining room with great views over Trinity College tend to
keep this place booked. Roche's forte is taking old Irish stalwarts and updating them into
sublime signature dishes. You can start with a rich prawn bisque with sautéed spinach
and move on to roast loin of wild boar with *tarte fine* of red onions. Service is terrific.

4–5 Nassau St., Dublin 2. (☎) **01/670-3865.** www.jacobsladder.ie. Reservations required. Main courses
€21–€34 ($34–$54); fixed-price dinner €44 ($70). AE, DC, MC, V. Tues–Sat 12:30–2:30pm; Tues–Fri
6–10pm; Sat 7–10pm. Closed Dec 24–Jan 4. DART: Pearse. Bus: 7, 8, 10, 11, or 46A.

Mermaid Café ★★ MODERN   Owned by a chef and an artist, this popular eatery is a
mixture of good restaurant and classy hangout. This place is a lunchtime favorite of local
professionals, and a good place to take a date in the evening. Dishes often found on the frequently changing menu range from the likes of slow-roasted pork belly to an array of excellent
seafood dishes, including a rich seafood casserole. The popular weekend brunch can give you
a good idea of the menu at a less wallet-denting price than going for an evening meal.

69–70 Dame St., Dublin 2. (☎) **01/670-8236.** www.mermaid.ie. Reservations required. Main courses lunch
€13–€20 ($21–$32), dinner €20–€30 ($32–$48); Sunday brunch €11–€17 ($18–$27). MC, V. Mon–Sat 12:30–
2:30pm and 6–11pm; Sun 12:30–3:30pm (brunch) and 6–9pm. Bus: 50, 50A, 54, 56A, 77, 77A, or 77B.

(**Tips**)   **Outdoors Is the New Indoors (for a Smoke)**

While Ireland has a reputation as a hard-drinking, heavy-smoking place, it is not
above American-style health laws, and thus it has a sweeping antismoking law.
Smoking is banned in virtually all public spaces, including restaurants, bars, hotel
lobbies—you name it. Therefore, there will be no smoking at the table, and not
even any nipping into the bar for a quick drag. It's out into the cold and wet if
you need to indulge.

The Irish are not entirely unsympathetic to the addicted among us, and most
restaurants and bars have created lavish patios and gardens, usually covered and
heated, where smokers can puff away in relative comfort. In fact, one unintended
outcome of the antismoking legislation is that Dublin has become more of an
outdoor city than ever before, as outdoors is the new indoors, and the smoking
patio is often the place to see and be seen.

Juice VEGETARIAN   If nobody told you this place was vegetarian, you'd probably never notice, so interesting is the menu and so tasty is the food. It's a lovely looking place, with soaring 9m (30-ft.) ceilings softened by a suspended sailcloth and muted lighting. Brunch is classic here, with pancakes, huevos rancheros, and French toast topped with fresh fruit or organic maple syrup. The rest of the day, you can sample the homemade dips—hummus, baba ghanouj, tapenade, roasted carrot pâté—with crudités and pita-bread strips. True to its name, there are about 30 kinds of juices and smoothies on offer.

Castle House, 73–83 S. Great Georges St., Dublin 2. (C) **01/475-7856.** www.juicerestaurant.ie. Reservations recommended Fri–Sat. Main courses €12–€14 ($19–$22). AE, MC, V. Daily 11am–11pm. Bus: 50, 54, 56, or 77.

L'Gueuleton ★★ FRENCH   Rated by local critics as one of the best restaurants in Dublin, L'Gueuleton is worth the effort you'll have to put in to book it well in advance. The cozy dining room is all candlelight, exposed brick walls, flagstone floors, polished wood beams, and Prada-clad clientele. It's an elegant, Irish-French bistro. The menu changes constantly, but includes warming options like whole roast sea bass with new potatoes and chive beurre blanc, or venison casserole with juniper and organic root vegetables.

1 Fade St., Dublin 2. (C) **01/675-3708.** www.lgueuleton.com. Reservations required. Main courses €15–€25 ($24–$40). AE, DC, MC, V. Mon–Sat 12:30–3pm and 6–10pm. Bus: Any An Lar.

Yamamori Noodles JAPANESE   This place has such a casually exuberant atmosphere that you may just be startled by how good the food is. Prices range from bargain to splurge for dishes such as chili chicken ramen or the *yamamori yaki soba* with its mound of wok-fried noodles, piled high with prawns, squid, chicken, and roast pork. Vegetarians aren't overlooked, as there are plenty of veggie options. Lunch specials are outstanding here.

71–72 S. Great George's St., Dublin 2. (C) **01/475-5001.** www.yamamorinoodles.ie. Reservations only for parties of 4 or more. Main courses €15–€22 ($24–$35). MC, V. Sun–Wed 12:15–11pm; Thurs–Sat 12:15–11:30pm. Bus: 50, 50A, 54, 56, or 77.

Inexpensive

Avoca Café ★★ (Finds) MODERN IRISH   Who would think that one of the best places to have lunch in all of Dublin is on the third floor of a shop? It's true! This polished, casual cafe is perched above the vibrant pinks and reds of the knitted wools and painted doodads in the charming Avoca shop near Trinity College. If you can tear yourself away from the shopping, there are thick homemade soups, fresh salads, and big sandwiches to keep you going in the buzzing cafe.

11–13 Suffolk St., Trinity College, Dublin 2. (C) **01/672-6019.** www.avoca.ie. Main courses €10–€15 ($16–$24). MC, V. Mon–Wed and Fri 10am–6pm; Thurs 10am–8pm; Sat 10am–6:30pm; Sun 11am–6pm. Bus: 50, 54, or 56.

The Bad Ass Café AMERICAN   This loud, bright restaurant has been packing in tourists and local families since 1983. The draw is the approachable menu with the familiar burgers, pasta, steaks, salads, and fajitas that you'll recognize from back home. The drawback is that it can all be just a bit touristy for some, and a bit noisy for others. Still, it's cheap, and it has an entertaining system for placing orders, wherein waitstaff clip your order to a wire above your head and it whizzes off to the kitchen. Apparently, Sinéad O'Connor used to wait tables here, for what it's worth.

9–11 Crown Alley, Temple Bar, Dublin 2. ℰ **01/671-2596.** www.badasscafe.com. Main courses €10–€18 ($16–$29). MC, V. Daily 11:30am–late. Bus: 50, 54, or 56.

Irish Film Centre Cafe Bar IRISH/INTERNATIONAL   A trendy drinking spot in Temple Bar, the hip Cafe Bar (in the lobby of the city's coolest place to watch a movie) features an excellent, affordable menu that changes daily. A vegetarian and Middle Eastern menu is available for both lunch and dinner. The weekend entertainment usually includes music or comedy.

6 Eustace St., Temple Bar, Dublin 2. ℰ **01/677-8788.** www.irishfilm.ie. Lunch and dinner €9–€12 ($14–$19). MC, V. Mon–Fri 12:30–3pm; Sat–Sun 1–3pm; daily 6–9pm. Bus: 21A, 78A, or 78B.

Nude VEGETARIAN   This small chain with sleek little outlets all around town is an excellent place to grab lunch or a snack without blowing your diet. The emphasis here is on healthy, from the freshly squeezed juices down to the wraps (chickpea and chili is a longtime favorite), sandwiches, soups, salads, and sweets. The prices are practically reasonable! Other branches are at 103 Lower Leeson St., 38 Upper Baggot St., and 28 Grafton St.

21 Suffolk St., Trinity College, Dublin 2. ℰ **01/677-4804.** Main courses €4–€6 ($6.40–$9.60). No credit cards. Mon–Sat 7:30am–9pm; Sun 9:30am–7pm. Bus: 50, 54, or 56.

ST. STEPHEN'S GREEN/GRAFTON STREET AREA
Very Expensive
One Pico ★★ MODERN EUROPEAN   About a 5-minute walk from Stephen's Green, on a wee lane off Dawson Street, this is a sophisticated, grown-up, classy place, with excellent service and fantastic food. The food is a mixture of European influences in a menu that changes daily. If you're lucky, you might find the duck confit with red cabbage and beet-root chiffonade, or the roast pheasant with red-wine risotto. For dessert, a caramelized lemon tart is the end to a near-perfect meal.

5–6 Molesworth Place, Schoolhouse Lane, Dublin 2. ℰ **01/676-0300.** www.onepico.com. Reservations required. Main courses lunch €19–€28 ($30–$45), dinner €30–€37 ($48–$59). AE, DC, MC, V. Mon–Sat 12:30–2:30pm and 6–11pm. DART: Pearse. Bus: 10, 11A, 11B, 13, or 20B.

Expensive
La Mère Zou ★★ FRENCH   Imagine a country house in Provence where you could get superb Gallic cooking *en famille.* Chef Eric Tydgdat has created a warm, comfortable, basement-level bistro in which to savor his fresh French country specialties. The emphasis is on perfectly cooked food accompanied by persuasive but "unarmed" sauces served in an unpretentious manner. Mussels are a house specialty, in an irresistible tomato gratin sauce. Other dishes, like the duck confit or the pot-roast pork, are all lavished with the same attention. Unsurprisingly, the excellent wine list favors French wines, with several reasonably priced options.

22 St. Stephen's Green, Dublin 2. ℰ **01/661-6669.** www.lamerezou.ie. Reservations recommended. Main courses €19–€32 ($30–$51). AE, DC, MC, V. Mon–Fri 12:30–2:30pm; Mon Thurs 6–10:30pm; Fri–Sat 6–11pm; Sun 6–9:30pm. DART: Pearse. Bus: 10, 11A, 11B, 13, or 20B.

Peploe's ★ MODERN IRISH   In the vast basement of a Georgian building, this wine bar and restaurant is at the top of the charts for Dublin's nouveau riche, business-suit crowd, and it's easy to see why. It's all so chic even the waitstaff is nattily attired. Food is a bit on the traditional side, and features local meats and produce—in the fall try the venison loin with balsamic *jus.* Prices are a bit eyebrow raising, but you can get a good deal at lunchtime.

(Tips) How to Eat Like an Irishman

If you've come to Dublin expecting to find plenty of restaurants still serving traditional Irish food, you're going to be disappointed. Dublin is far too chic, and Dubliners far too sophisticated, for the Irish stew, soda bread, and shepherd's pie they grew up eating. The very food you cannot escape in the Irish countryside, you cannot find in Dublin restaurants.

A number of pricey restaurants do modern, upscale interpretations on Irish cooking; places like **Chapter One** (p. 140) and **Restaurant Patrick Guilbaud** (p. 139) use only Irish ingredients in their complex dishes, for which you will pay a premium. But the simple, basic food that the Irish are known for is not really represented.

Still, you can get around this, as long as you don't mind eating in a pub. Several of the city's traditional pubs still serve plain, hearty Irish food, and as an added benefit, it's certainly much cheaper than what you'll find in the high-and-mighty restaurants. Your best options include the **Porterhouse** microbrewery on Parliament Street in Temple Bar (p. 172), which is an excellent place for a midweek lunch of dishes such as Irish stew with brown bread, or bubble-and-squeak. Not too far away, **O'Shea's Merchant** (12 Bridge St. Lower; © 01/679-3797) and the **Stag's Head** pub (p. 172) are among the best places in town for real Irish food. Both offer home-cooked, traditional food in pleasant surroundings (just don't try to eat there on busy weekend nights when it's too crowded for comfort).

16 St. Stephen's Green, Dublin 2. © **01/676-3144.** Reservations recommended. Main courses lunch €13–€17 ($21–$27), dinner €19–€30 ($30–$48). AE, DC, MC, V. Daily noon–11pm; small plates only 3:30–6pm and 10:30–11pm. DART: Pearse. Bus: 10, 11A, 11B, 13, or 20B.

Moderate

Café Mao ★ ASIAN   This is where to go when you feel like some Asian cooking with an exhilarating attitude. The exposed kitchen lines one entire wall, and the rest of the space is wide open—great for people-watching. The menu reads like a Best of Asia list: Thai fish cakes, *nasi goreng*, chicken hoisin, salmon ramen. Everything is delicious—you can't go wrong. There's a branch in the Pavilion in Dún Laoghaire as well (© **01/214-8090**).

2 Chatham Row, Dublin 2. © **01/670-4899.** www.cafemao.com. Reservations recommended. Main courses €10–€19 ($16–$30). AE, MC, V. Mon–Wed noon–10:30pm; Thurs noon–11pm; Fri–Sat noon–11:30pm; Sun noon–10pm. DART: Pearse. Bus: 10, 11A, 11B, 13, or 20B.

Fitzers Café INTERNATIONAL   This is one branch of a chain of winning cafes that serve up excellent, up-to-date, and reasonably priced food. Nestled on a street known for its bookshops, this bright, airy Irish-style bistro is a bright space with lots of windows and modern decor. Menu options range from chicken breast with hot chili-cream sauce or brochette of lamb tandoori with mild curry sauce, to gratin of smoked cod. There are also tempting vegetarian dishes made from organic produce. Fitzers has two other Dublin locations: just a few blocks away at the National Gallery (© **01/670-6577**), Merrion Square West (© **01/661-4496**), and at Temple Bar Square (© **01/679-0440**).

51 Dawson St., Dublin 2. (📞) **01/677-1155.** www.fitzers.ie. Dinner main courses €15–€25 ($24–$40). AE, DC, MC, V. Daily 11:30am–11:30pm. Closed Dec 24–27 and Good Friday. DART: Pearse. Bus: 10, 11A, 11B, 13, or 20B.

Inexpensive

Cornucopia Wholefood Restaurant (Value) VEGETARIAN This little cafe just off Grafton Street is one of the best vegetarian restaurants in the city, and also serves wholesome meals for people on various restricted diets (vegan, nondairy, low sodium, low fat). Soups are particularly good here, as are the salads and the hot dishes, like the Moroccan chickpea tagine. This place is a delicious healthy alternative.

19 Wicklow St., Dublin 2. (📞) **01/677-7583.** www.cornucopia.ie. Main courses €11–€13 ($18–$21). MC, V. Mon–Sat 8:30am–8pm; Sun noon–7pm. Bus: Any city-center bus.

FITZWILLIAM SQUARE/MERRION SQUARE AREA

Very Expensive

L'Ecrivain ★★ FRENCH This is one of Dublin's truly exceptional restaurants, from start to finish. The atmosphere is relaxed, welcoming, and unpretentious, and chef Derry Clarke's food is extraordinary. Most dishes consist of Irish ingredients, prepared without dense sauces. You might find, on the constantly changing menu, seared wild Irish venison loin with caramelized pear, or seared Bere Island scallops with lobster strudel.

109 Lower Baggot St., Dublin 2. (📞) **01/661-1919.** www.lecrivain.com. Reservations required. Fixed-price 2-course lunch €35 ($56); dinner main courses €44–€45 ($70–$72). 10% service charge. AE, DC, MC, V. Mon–Fri 12:30–2pm; Mon–Sat 7–10:30pm. Bus: 10.

Restaurant Patrick Guilbaud ★★ FRENCH/IRISH Ireland's most award-winning restaurant (including two Michelin stars) holds court in elegant quarters at the equally elegant Merrion Hotel. The menu is lavish; roast loin of Wicklow lamb with eggplant caviar and black sole with creamed brown morels are two representative options. This is one of the most absurdly priced restaurants in Dublin—several dishes are more than €90 ($144) each—so this place is not for everyone.

In the Merrion Hotel, 21 Upper Merrion St., Dublin 2. (📞) **01/676-4192.** www.restaurantpatrickguilbaud. ie. Reservations required. Fixed-price 2-course lunch €38 ($61), 3-course lunch €50 ($80); dinner main courses €42–€100 ($67–$160). AE, DC, MC, V. Tues–Sat 12:30–2:15pm and 7–10:15pm. DART: Westland Row. Bus: 10, 11A, 11B, 13, or 20B.

Expensive

Bang Café ★ ORGANIC IRISH This chic dining room serves up innovative cuisine in a candlelit, masculine room with slick leather seats and oxblood walls. It's known for its dedication to organic meat and produce (its menu lists the organic Irish farms it buys from), and for the trendiness of its regular crowd. Wear your Jimmy Choos to come dine on the loin of veal with sweetbreads, crushed potatoes, and sage *jus*, or the rare peppered tuna with organic herb salad. It also has a lovely bar, where you can linger over a martini before dinner, as well as a new outdoor terrace, with seating for an additional 30-plus diners.

11 Merrion Row, Dublin 2. (📞) **01/676-0898.** www.bangrestaurant.com. Reservations recommended. Dinner main courses €15–€29 ($24–$46). AE, DC, MC, V. Mon–Sat 12:30–3pm and 6–10:30pm. Bus: 7, 7A, 8, 10, 11, or 13.

Dobbins Wine Bistro ★ BISTRO Almost hidden in a lane between Upper and Lower Mount streets, this hip, friendly bistro is a haven for inventive Continental cuisine. A major refurbishment in 2008 replaced the once self-consciously kitsch decor with a sleek modern look—neutral fabrics and snazzy leather banquettes. The menu changes often, but usually includes such items as duckling with orange-and-port sauce; steamed *paupiette* of black sole with salmon, crab, and prawn filling; pan-fried veal kidneys in pastry; and filet of beef topped with crispy herb bread crumbs with shallot and Madeira sauce.

15 Stephen's Lane (off Upper Mount St.), Dublin 2. © **01/676-4679.** Reservations recommended. Dinner main courses €15–€24 ($24–$38). AE, DC, MC, V. Mon–Fri 12:30–2:30pm; Tues–Sat 7:30–10:30pm. DART: Pearse. Bus: 5, 7A, 8, 46, or 84.

Ely ★ ORGANIC IRISH   This cosmopolitan, clever place does everything right. The owners get the organic produce from their family farm in County Clare, so everything is absurdly fresh. The food is simple but expertly prepared versions of Irish favorites, the service attentive and helpful. Think gourmet "bangers and mash" (wild boar sausages and mashed spuds), fresh Clare oysters, rich Irish stew, and a vast selection of artisan cheeses. Factor in a smashing wine list and you've got a winner. There are two other Ely venues in town: Ely Chq in Customs House Quay, and Ely Hq on Hanover Quay.

22 Ely Place (off Merrion Row), Dublin 2. © **01/676-8986.** www.elywinebar.ie. Reservations recommended. Dinner main courses €15–€29 ($24–$46). AE, DC, MC, V. Mon–Sat noon–3pm and 6–10:30pm. Bus: 7, 7A, 8, 10, 11, or 13.

Inexpensive

National Museum Café CAFETERIA   This is a great place to step out of the rain, warm yourself, and then wander among the nation's treasures. The cafe is informal, but has a certain elegance, thanks to an elaborate mosaic floor, marble tabletops, and tall windows that look across a cobbled yard. Everything is made fresh: beef salad, chicken salad, quiche, an abundance of pastries. The soup of the day is often vegetarian, and quite good. Admission to the museum is free, so you can visit without worry.

National Museum of Ireland, Kildare St., Dublin 2. © **01/677-7444.** Soup €3 ($4.80); lunch main courses under €8 ($13). MC, V. Tues–Sat 10am–5pm; Sun 2–5pm. Bus: 7, 7A, 8, 10, 11, or 13.

O'CONNELL STREET AREA/NORTH OF THE LIFFEY
Very Expensive

Chapter One ★★ MODERN IRISH   Arguably the city's most atmospheric restaurant, this remarkable eatery fills the vaulted basement space of the Dublin Writers Museum. Artfully lighted and tastefully decorated, it's one of the best restaurants in town, although prices are very high for what's on offer. Meals are prepared with local, organic ingredients, all cleverly used in dishes like the rabbit with smoked bacon and asparagus, and the shoulder of suckling pig with carrot and cumin.

18–19 Parnell Sq., Dublin 2. © **01/873-2266.** www.chapteronerestaurant.com. Reservations recommended. Main courses €32–€38 ($51–$61); 3-course fixed-price lunch/pretheater menu €38 ($61). AE, DC, MC, V. Tues–Fri 12:30–2pm and 6–11pm; Sat 6–11pm. Bus: 27A, 31A, 31B, 32A, 32B, 42B, 42C, 43, or 44A.

Moderate

101 Talbot ★ INTERNATIONAL   This modest, second-floor eatery above a shop may be unassuming, but don't be fooled—it's actually a bright beacon of good cooking on the Northside. The menu features light, healthy food, with a strong emphasis on vegetarian dishes. Dishes change regularly, but mains might include seared filet of tuna, roast duck breast, and Clare salmon with shellfish and chorizo. The dining room is casually funky, with contemporary Irish art and big windows. The staff are endlessly friendly, making it a pleasure to visit.

101 Talbot St. (at Talbot Lane near Marlborough St.), Dublin 1. © **01/874-5011.** Reservations recommended. Dinner main courses €15–€22 ($24–$35). AE, MC, V. Tues–Sat 5–11pm. DART: Connolly. Bus: 27A, 31A, 31B, 32A, 32B, 42B, 42C, 43, or 44A.

Winding Stair ★★ MODERN IRISH This long-beloved bookstore cafe was recently reworked into a sleek, gorgeous restaurant with wood floors, big windows, and stunning river view. It's still in a lovely old bookstore (you can pick up some Joyce on your way to dinner), but it's definitively modern in its cooking style. Dishes are clever interpretations of Irish favorites: steamed mussels and homemade fries with aioli; boiled Irish bacon collar with buttered organic cabbage and mashed potatoes; or seafood chowder with chorizo and treacle bread. The wine list is brilliantly chosen; the atmosphere is pure elegant sophistication. This place isn't trendy, it's classy.

40 Lower Ormond Quay, Dublin 1. © **01/872-7320.** www.winding-stair.com. Reservations recommended. Main courses €19–€24 ($30–$38). AE, DC, MC, V. Daily 12:30–3:30pm; Mon–Sat 6–10:30pm; Sun 6–9:30pm. Bus: 90, 92, or 151.

Inexpensive
Epicurean Food Hall GOURMET FOOD COURT This wonderful food hall houses a wide variety of artisan produce, delicious local Irish meats, and regional specialties. Favorites include **Caviston's,** Dublin's premier deli, for smoked salmon and seafood; **Itsabagel,** for its delicious bagels, imported from H&H Bagels in New York City; **Crème de la Crème,** for its French-style pastries and cakes; **Missy and Mandy's,** for its American-style ice cream; **Nectar,** for its plethora of healthy juice drinks; and **Christophe's Café,** for its delicious gourmet sandwiches, wraps, and panini. There is some seating, but this place gets jammed during lunchtime midweek, so visit at off-peak times if possible.

Middle Abbey St., Dublin 1. © **01/878-7016.** All items €3–€15 ($4.80–$24). No credit cards. Mon–Sat 10am–6pm. Bus: 70 or 80.

BALLSBRIDGE/EMBASSY ROW AREA
Expensive
Roly's Bistro IRISH/INTERNATIONAL This two-story, shop-front restaurant is a local institution, beloved for providing the kind of reliably good, tummy-warming food you never get tired of: roasted breast of chicken with orzo pasta and wild mushrooms, or braised shank of lamb with root vegetable purée and rosemary *jus,* to name just two. The bright and airy main dining room can be noisy when the house is full, but there's also an enclave of booths for those who prefer a quiet tête-à-tête.

7 Ballsbridge Terrace, Dublin 4. © **01/668-2611.** www.rolysbistro.ie. Reservations required. Main courses €20–€30 ($32–$48); 3-course set-price lunch €23 ($37), dinner €43 ($69). AE, DC, MC, V. Daily noon–3pm and 6–9:45pm. DART: Lansdowne Rd. Station. Bus: 5, 6, 7, 8, 18, or 45.

Moderate
The French Paradox ★ WINE BAR This is just what Dublin needed: a price-conscious, darling little bistro and wine bar that endears itself to everyone. The wine's the thing here, so relax with a bottle of bordeaux or Côte du Rhône and nibbles from the menu. There's a lovely cheese plate named for West Cork cheesemaker Bill Hogan, superb Iberico hams from Spain, or, if you prefer, the small dining menu offers bistro favorites such as gravad lax and blinis, or scrambled eggs with truffle butter.

53 Shelbourne Rd., Dublin 4. © **01/660-4068.** www.thefrenchparadox.com. Reservations recommended. All items €10–€20 ($16–$32). AE, MC, V. Mon–Fri noon–3pm and 6pm–midnight; Sat noon–midnight. DART: Lansdowne Rd. Bus: 5, 6, 7, 8, or 18.

5 SEEING THE SIGHTS

Wandering Dublin—just walking down its Georgian streets with a map only in case you get really lost—is one of the great pleasures of any visit here. There's almost no way you can go wrong. One minute, you're walking along a quiet leafy street and suddenly the Irish Parliament appears before you. A few minutes later, it's gorgeous Merrion Square. Then, the granite buildings of Trinity College—and on and on. So get a sturdy pair of shoes and have your umbrella at the ready, and head out to discover this rewarding city.

THE TOP ATTRACTIONS

Aras an Uachtaráin (The Irish President's House)
Áras an Uachtaráin was once the Viceregal Lodge, the summer retreat of the British viceroy, whose main digs were in Dublin Castle. From what were never humble beginnings, the original 1751 country house was expanded several times, gradually accumulating splendor. President Mary McAleese opened the house to visitors; guided tours originate at the Phoenix Park Visitors Centre every Saturday. After an introductory historical film, a bus brings visitors to and from Áras an Uachtaráin. The focus of the tour is the state reception rooms. The entire tour lasts 1 hour. Only 525 tickets are given out, first-come, first-served; arrive before 1:30pm, especially in summer.

Note: For security reasons, no backpacks, travel bags, strollers, buggies, cameras, or mobile phones are allowed on the tour.

In Phoenix Park Visitor Centre, Dublin 8. ℂ **01/670-9155.** Free admission. Summer Sat 10am–5pm; winter Sat 10:30am–4pm. Closed Dec 24–26. Same-day tickets issued at Phoenix Park (p. 148). Bus: 10, 37, or 39.

The Book of Kells ★
This extraordinary hand-drawn manuscript of the four Gospels, dating from the year 800, is one of Ireland's jewels, and with elaborate scripting and colorful illumination, it is undeniably magnificent. It is displayed, along with another early Christian manuscript, at Trinity College's Old Library. Unfortunately, the need to protect the books for future generations means that there's little for you to actually see. The volumes are very small and displayed inside a wooden cabinet shielded by bullet-proof glass. So all you really see here are the backs of a lot of tourists, leaning over a small table trying to get a peek at two pages of the ancient books. It's quite anticlimactic, but the Library's Long Room goes some way toward making up for that, at least for biblio-philes. The grand, chained library holds many rare works on Irish history and has fre-quently changing displays of rare works. Still, it's hard to say that it's all worth the rather large admission fee.

College Green, Dublin 2. ℂ **01/608-2320.** www.tcd.ie/about/trinity/bookofkells. Admission €8 ($13) adults, €7 ($11) seniors/students, free for children 11 and under. Combination tickets for the Library and Dublin Experience also available. Mon–Sat 9:30am–5pm; Sun noon–4:30pm (opens at 9:30am June–Sept). Bus: Any An Lar (cross-city) bus.

Chester Beatty Library ★★★ (Finds)
Sir Alfred Chester Beatty was an American of Irish heritage who made a fortune in the mining industry and collected rare manu-scripts. In 1956, he bequeathed his extensive collection to Ireland, and this fascinating museum inside the grounds of Dublin Castle was the ultimate result of his largesse. The breathtaking array of early illuminated gospels and religious manuscripts outshines the Book of Kells, and there are endless surprises here: ancient editions of the Bible and other religious books, beautiful copies of the Koran, and endless icons from Western, Middle

Eastern, and Far Eastern cultures. Best of all: It's free. The Library's **Silk Road Café** is an award-winning restaurant that has a devoted local following, offering a menu that features Mediterranean and Near Eastern cuisine.

Clock Tower Building, Dublin Castle, Dublin 2. © **01/407-0750.** www.cbl.ie. Free admission. Tues–Fri 10am–5pm (Mon–Fri May–Sept); Sat 11am–5pm; Sun 1–5pm. Free guided tours Wed and Sat 2:30pm. Closed Dec 24–26, Jan 1, and holidays. DART: Sandymount. Bus: 5, 6, 6A, 7A, 8, 10, 46, 46A, 46B, or 64.

Christ Church Cathedral ★

This magnificent cathedral was designed to be seen from the river, so walk to it from the riverside in order to truly appreciate its size. It dates from 1038, when Sitric, Danish king of Dublin, built the first wooden Christ Church here. In 1171, the original foundation was extended into a cruciform and rebuilt in stone by the Norman warrior Strongbow. The present structure dates mainly from 1871 to 1878, when a huge restoration took place—the work done then remains controversial to this day, as much of the building's old detail was destroyed in the process. Still, magnificent stonework and graceful pointed arches survive. There's also a statue of Strongbow inside, and some believe his tomb is here as well, although historians are not convinced. Look out for a heart-shaped iron box in the southeast chapel, which is believed to contain the heart of St. Laurence O'Toole. The best way to get a glimpse of what the original building must have been like is to visit the crypt, which is original to the 12th-century structure.

Christ Church Place, Dublin 8. © **01/677-8099.** Admission €6 ($9.60) adults, €4 ($6.40) students and children 14 and under. June–Aug daily 9am–6pm; Sept–May daily 9:45am–5:30pm. Closed Dec 26. Bus: 21A, 50, 50A, 78, 78A, or 78B.

Collins Barracks

Collins Barracks is a splendidly restored, early-18th-century military building, but only worth visiting if you're a fan of the decorative arts, as it's been converted into part of the Irish National Museum. Until the acquisition of this vast space, only a fraction of the National Museum's collection could be displayed, but that is changing, and more and more treasures find their way here. Most notable among the collection is the display of Irish silver and furniture. It is a prime site for touring exhibitions, so consult the *Event Guide* for details.

Benburb St., Dublin 7. © **01/677-7444.** Free admission. Tours (hours vary) €2 ($3.20) adults, free for seniors and children. Tues–Sat 10am–5pm; Sun 2–5pm. Bus: 34, 70, or 80.

Dublin Castle

This 13th-century structure was the center of British power in Ireland for more than 7 centuries, until the new Irish government took it over in 1922. You can walk the grounds for free, although this is largely municipal office space now and is disappointingly dominated by parking lots. Still, it's worth a wander; highlights include the 13th-century Record Tower; the State Apartments, once the residence of English viceroys; and the Chapel Royal, a 19th-century Gothic building with particularly fine plaster decoration and carved-oak gallery fronts and fittings. If they're open, check out the Undercroft, an excavated site on the grounds where an early Viking fortress stood, and the Treasury, built in the early 18th century. There are also a vaguely interesting on-site craft shop, heritage center, and restaurant.

Palace St. (off Dame St.), Dublin 2. © **01/677-7129.** Admission €4.50 ($7.20) adults (€3.50/$5.60 when State Apartments not available), €3.25 ($5.20) seniors and students, €2 ($3.20) children 11 and under. Mon–Fri 10am–4:45pm; Sat–Sun and holidays 2–4:45pm. Guided tours every 20–25 min. Bus: 50, 50A, 54, 56A, 77, 77A, or 77B.

Dublinia (Kids)

This museum aims to teach the little ones about the medieval history of Dublin through a series of interactive exhibits. With visual effects, background sounds

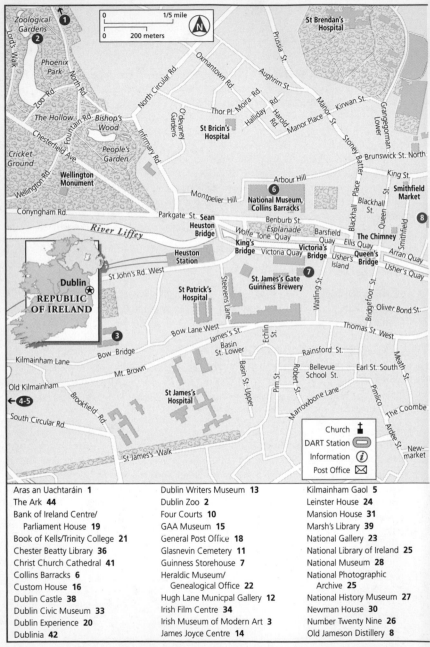

Zoological Gardens **1**

Dublin Zoo **2**

St Brendan's Hospital

Prussia St.

Oxmantown Rd.

Aughrim St.

North Circular Rd.

Manor St.

Kirwan St.

Grangegorman Lower

Lord's Walk

Phoenix Park

North Rd.

Zoo Rd.

Thor Pl. Moira Rd.

Harold Rd.

Halliday Rd.

Manor Place

Stoney Batter

Brunswick St. North

The Hollow

Fountain Rd.

Bishop's Wood

O'devaney Gardens

Infirmary Rd.

St Bricin's Hospital

King St.

Chesterfield Ave.

People's Garden

Arbour Hill

Blackhall Place

Blackhall St.

Queen St.

Smithfield

Smithfield Market **8**

Cricket Ground

Wellington Rd.

Wellington Monument

Montpelier Hill

National Museum, Collins Barracks **6**

Conyngham Rd.

Parkgate St. **Sean Heuston Bridge**

Benburb St.

Esplanade

Barsfield Quay

The Chimney

King's Place

River Liffey

Wolfe Tone Quay

King's Bridge

Ellis Quay

Arran Quay

Heuston Station

Victoria Quay

Victoria's Bridge

Usher's Island

Queen's Bridge

Usher's Quay

St John's Rd. West

Dublin

REPUBLIC OF IRELAND

St James's Gate Guinness Brewery **7**

Steevens Lane

St Patrick's Hospital

Watling St.

Bridgefoot St.

Oliver Bond St.

3

Bow Lane West

James's St.

Echlin St.

Thomas St. West

Kilmainham Lane

Bow Bridge

Mt. Brown

Basin St. Lower

Rainsford St.

Meath St.

Old Kilmainham

4-5

Brookfield Rd.

Basin St. Upper

Pim St.

Robert St.

Bellevue School St.

Earl St. South

Pimlico

South Circular Rd.

St James's Hospital

Marrowbone Lane

The Coombe

Ardee St.

St James's Walk

Newmarket

Church ✝

DART Station ⬭

Information ⓘ

Post Office ✉

Aras an Uachtaráin **1**	Dublin Writers Museum **13**	Kilmainham Gaol **5**
The Ark **44**	Dublin Zoo **2**	Leinster House **24**
Bank of Ireland Centre/ Parliament House **19**	Four Courts **10**	Mansion House **31**
	GAA Museum **15**	Marsh's Library **39**
Book of Kells/Trinity College **21**	General Post Office **18**	National Gallery **23**
Chester Beatty Library **36**	Glasnevin Cemetery **11**	National Library of Ireland **25**
Christ Church Cathedral **41**	Guinness Storehouse **7**	National Museum **28**
Collins Barracks **6**	Heraldic Museum/ Genealogical Office **22**	National Photographic Archive **25**
Custom House **16**	Hugh Lane Municpal Gallery **12**	National History Museum **27**
Dublin Castle **38**	Irish Film Centre **34**	Newman House **30**
Dublin Civic Museum **33**	Irish Museum of Modern Art **3**	Number Twenty Nine **26**
Dublin Experience **20**	James Joyce Centre **14**	Old Jameson Distillery **8**
Dublinia **42**		

Our Lady of Mount Camel **37**	St. Michan's Church **9**	Shaw Birthplace **29**
St. Audoen's Church **43**	St. Patrick's Cathedral **40**	Temple Bar Gallery **35**
St. Mary's Pro Cathedral **17**	St. Teresa's Church **32**	War Memorial Gardens **4**

Should You Purchase a Dublin Pass?

If you're planning a lot of sightseeing in Dublin, the tourism board would like you to consider purchasing its **Dublin Pass,** which offers free admission to most of the city's major sights, as well as free travel from the airport on the AirCoach shuttle, and discounts at a number of shops, bars, and restaurants.

Unfortunately, the pass is a bit pricey, given that so many of Dublin's sights are free, and the Dublin Pass website muddies the water by including free museums (such as the Chester Beatty Library and the national museums) among fee-charging sights you'll have free access to with the pass. Our advice is this: Buy the pass, but plan carefully how best to use it. For example, consider buying a pass good for 1 or 2 days, and then see all of the city's most expensive sights (the Guinness Storehouse, Kilmainham Gaol, and so forth) on those days. On the other days of your trip, you can devote your time to the museums, parks, and galleries that charge no entrance fee.

An adult pass costs €31 ($50) for 1 day, €49 ($78) for 2 days, and €59 ($94) for 3 days. A child's pass costs €17 ($27) for 1 day, €29 ($46) for 2 days, and €34 ($54) for 3 days.

You can purchase a pass at any Dublin Tourism office, or online at **www. dublinpass.ie.**

(some on an annoying loop seem to follow you around repeating the same phrase over and over, until you can still hear it in your sleep 2 weeks later), and aromas ostensibly from that time, it's designed to stimulate, but will probably bore anybody over the age of 14. Still, you and the kids can dress up in medieval garb, receive papal pardons, and put yourselves in the town stocks. This seems to be one of those museums largely directed at kids on school field trips.

St. Michael's Hill, Christ Church, Dublin 8. (℃ **01/679-4611.** www.dublinia.ie. Admission €6.25 ($10) adults, €3.75 ($6) children. Apr–Sept daily 10am–5pm; Oct–Mar Mon–Fri 11am–4pm, Sat–Sun and holidays 10am–4:30pm. Closed Dec 23–26 and Mar 17. Bus: 50, 78A, or 123.

Dublin Writers Museum ★★ (Moments) This is an excellent little museum that represents the best of what literary galleries can be, and lovers of Irish literature will find it hard to tear themselves away. The attraction is more than just seeing Joyce's typewriter or reading early playbills for the Abbey Theatre when Yeats was involved in running it. The draw is also long letters from Brendan Behan talking about parties he was invited to with the Marx Brothers in Los Angeles after he hit the big time, and scrawled notes from Behan, Joyce, and Beckett about work, life, and love. This museum opens a window and lets in light on Ireland's rich literary heritage, and it is wonderful to walk in that glow. There's a good gift shop with writing-related souvenirs and a selection of books by many classic and modern Irish writers.

18–19 Parnell Sq. N., Dublin 1. (℃ **01/872-2077.** www.writersmuseum.com. Admission €7.25 ($12) adults, €6.10 ($9.75) seniors and students, €4.55 ($7.30) children, €21 ($34) families (2 adults and up to 4 children). Combined ticket with James Joyce Museum or Shaw Birthplace €13 ($20). Mon–Sat 10am–5pm (until 6pm June–Aug); Sun and holidays 11am–5pm. DART: Connolly Station. Bus: 11, 13, 16, 16A, 22, or 22A.

The Tortured Tale of the Hugh Lane Gallery

Hugh Lane was a millionaire and exuberant collector of art. In the early 20th century, he opened his own gallery in Dublin on Harcourt Street, but he soon tired of running it, and offered to donate the whole thing—millions of pounds worth of Impressionist paintings—to the city. His only condition was that the city should build an appropriate structure to hold it all. Dublin agreed, and all seemed well. However, months later, having failed to find a suitable structure, and caught up in wrangling over the cost, the city withdrew from the deal. Lane was furious and, in a temper, made an agreement with the National Gallery in London to give that vast art museum his collection instead.

To the rescue came W. B. Yeats, who was so infuriated by the government's ineptitude that he wrote a series of angry poems lambasting it for its failure to find a place to house such magnificent works. Inspired, in part, by Yeats's fervor, Lane changed his mind, and decided to leave his collection to Dublin after all. He ordered his will changed, but had not yet had it signed and witnessed when he was killed in 1915 aboard the ocean liner *Lusitania* when it was torpedoed by a German U-boat.

So began a legal stalemate in which the National Gallery and the city of Dublin struggled for the ownerships of the Monets, Courbets, and Manets that, a few months earlier, Dublin wasn't even sure it wanted.

To an extent, the issue is still unresolved 90 years later, but luckily an agreement is in place by which the main works in the collection are displayed at different times by both galleries. The Hugh Lane Gallery now has a gorgeous home in the classical Charlemont House on Parnell Square.

Mr. Lane would surely approve.

Hugh Lane Municipal Gallery of Modern Art ★   This little gallery, which celebrated its 100-year anniversary during 2008, has a strong collection of Impressionist works led by Degas's *Sur la Plage* and Manet's *La Musique aux Tuileries,* and also holds sculptures by Rodin, a marvelous collection of Harry Clarke stained glass, and numerous works by modern Irish artists. One room holds the maddeningly cluttered studio of the Irish painter Francis Bacon, which the gallery purchased from London and moved to Dublin piece by piece, where it was reconstructed behind glass. Everything was moved, right down to the dust. It's an excellent, compact art museum, and a great place to spend an afternoon.

Parnell Sq. N., Dublin 1. (© **01/222-5550.** Fax 01/872-2182. www.hughlane.ie. Free admission. Tues–Thurs 10am–6pm; Fri–Sat 10am–5pm; Sun 11am–5pm. DART: Connolly or Tara stations. Bus: 3, 10, 11, 13, 16, or 19.

Kilmainham Gaol Historical Museum ★★★   This is a key sight for anyone interested in Ireland's struggle for Independence from British rule. Within these walls, political prisoners were incarcerated, tortured, and killed from 1796 until 1924. The leaders of the 1916 Easter Rising were executed here, along with many others. Future *taoiseach* (prime minister) Eamon de Valera was its final prisoner. To walk along these corridors, through the grim exercise yard, or into the walled compound is a moving experience that lingers in your memory.

Kilmainham, Dublin 8. © **01/453-5984.** www.heritageireland.ie. Guided tour €5.30 ($8.50) adults, €3.70 ($5.90) seniors, €2.10 ($3.35) children, €12 ($19) families. Apr–Sept daily 9:30am–4:45pm; Oct–Mar Mon–Fri 9:30am–4pm, Sun 10am–4:45pm. Bus: 51B, 78A, or 79.

National Gallery of Ireland ★   This museum houses Ireland's national art collection, as well as a collection of European art spanning the 14th to the 20th centuries. Every major European school of painting is represented, including selections by Italian Renaissance artists (especially Caravaggio's *The Taking of Christ*), French Impressionists, and Dutch 17th-century masters. The highlight of the Irish collection is the room dedicated to the mesmerizing works of Jack B. Yeats, brother of the poet W. B. Yeats. All public areas are wheelchair accessible. The museum has a shop and an excellent self-service **cafe.**

Merrion Sq. W., Dublin 2. © **01/661-5133.** Fax 01/661-5372. www.nationalgallery.ie. Free admission. Mon–Sat 9:30am–5:30pm (Thurs until 8:30pm); Sun noon–5:30pm. Closed Dec 24–26 and Good Friday. Free guided tours (meet in the Shaw Room) Sat 3pm and Sun 2, 3, and 4pm. DART: Pearse. Bus: 5, 6, 7, 7A, 8, 10, 44, 47, 47B, 48A, or 62.

National Museum of Ireland ★★   Established in 1890, this museum is a reflection of Ireland's heritage from 2000 B.C. to the present. It is the home of many of the country's greatest historical finds, ranging from an extensive collection of Irish Bronze Age gold and the Ardagh Chalice, Tara Brooch, and Cross of Cong. Other highlights include the artifacts from the Wood Quay excavations of the Old Dublin Settlements. The only place where it falls flat is on interactive exhibits, which are well thought out and *could* be excellent, but which have not been, on our visits, well maintained. The museum has a shop and a cafe (p. 140). *Note:* The National Museum encompasses two other attractions, Collins Barracks (p. 143) and the Natural History Museum (which is closed until at least 2010).

Kildare St. and Merrion St., Dublin 2. © **01/677-7444.** www.museum.ie. Free admission. Tues–Sat 10am–5pm; Sun 2–5pm. Closed Dec 25 and Good Friday. DART: Pearse. Bus: 7, 7A, 8, 10, 11, or 13.

Phoenix Park ★ (Kids)   The vast green expanses of Phoenix Park are Dublin's playground, and it's easy to see why. This is a well-designed, user-friendly park crisscrossed by a network of roads and quiet pedestrian walkways that make its 704 hectares (1,739 acres) easily accessible. Avenues of oaks, beech trees, pines, and chestnut trees are shady hideaways, or you can sun yourself in broad expanses of grassland. It's a relaxing place to spend a restful afternoon, but there's plenty to do here should you feel active. The home of the Irish president (p. 142) is in the park, as is the Dublin Zoo (p. 158). Livestock graze peacefully on pasturelands, deer roam the forested areas, and horses romp on polo fields. The visitor center, adjacent to Ashtown Castle, has information about all the park has to offer. The cafe/restaurant is open 10am to 5pm weekdays, 10am to 6pm weekends. Free car parking is adjacent to the center. The park is 3km (2 miles) west of the city center on the north bank of the River Liffey.

Phoenix Park, Dublin 8. © **01/677-0095.** www.heritageireland.ie. Free admission. Apr–Sept daily 10am–6pm; Jan–Mar and Nov–Dec daily 10am–5pm; Oct daily 10am–5:30pm. Bus: 37, 38, or 39.

St. Patrick's Cathedral ★   This is the largest church in Ireland, and one of the best-loved churches in the world. The present cathedral dates from 1190, but because of a fire and 14th-century rebuilding, not much of the original foundation remains. It is mainly

Hard to Love: Jonathan Swift

For all his cynicism, the sardonic writer Jonathan Swift loved Dublin and its residents. While dean of St. Patrick's Cathedral from 1713 to 1745, he wrote many of his most controversial works, and he knew that he owed the church and the city a great deal for supporting him when, given that they were often the targets of his barbed wit, they could hardly have been blamed for throwing him out. Heaven knows the English wouldn't have wanted him—he'd already written such sharp polemics about English governmental corruption that he was infamous in that country. In his own way, Swift understood the Irish and the English a bit too well for their comfort. But the Irish kept him on, even after he published his infamous essay "A Modest Proposal," in which he advocated (sarcastically) that the English should eat Irish babies in order to solve Ireland's famine problems.

One of Swift's biggest causes was humane treatment for the mentally ill, which, in his time, was unheard of. When he died, he bequeathed much of his estate to found St. Patrick's Hospital for the mentally ill.

Typically, though, he couldn't just leave it at that. Instead, he wrote one last caustic verse, as if seeking to guarantee that no Irish person would ever leave flowers on his grave:

"He left the little wealth he had
To build a house for fools and mad;
Showing in one satiric touch
No nation needed it so much."

early English in style. A square medieval tower with an 18th-century spire houses the largest ringing peal bells in Ireland. The 90m-long (295-ft.) interior allows for sweeping perspectives of soaring vaulted ceilings and the vast nave. The church is much older than the current building, as there were religious structures here as early as the 5th century. Consecrated by its namesake, it acts as a memorial to Irish war dead (represented in banners and flags throughout the building, some literally rotting away on their poles), and holds a memorial to the Irish soldiers who died fighting in the two world wars (although Ireland was neutral in World War II, an estimated 50,000 Irish soldiers died fighting with the British army in that war). St. Patrick's is closely associated with the writer Jonathan Swift, who was dean here from 1713 to 1745, and he is buried here alongside his long-time partner, Stella. St. Patrick's is the national cathedral of the Church of Ireland.

21–50 Patrick's Close, Patrick St., Dublin 8. © 01/475-4817. Fax 01/454-6374. www.stpatrickscathedral. ie. Admission €5.50 ($8.80) adults, €4.20 ($6.70) students and seniors, €15 ($24) families. Year-round Mon–Fri 9am–6pm; Nov–Feb Sat 9am–5pm, Sun 10–11am and 12:45–3pm; Mar–Oct Sat 9am–6pm, Sun 9–11am, 12:45–3pm, and 4:15–6pm. Closed except for services Dec 24–26. Bus: 65, 65B, 50, 50A, 54, 54A, 56A, or 77.

Trinity College ★★ The oldest university in Ireland, Trinity was founded in 1592 by Queen Elizabeth I to offer an education to the children of the upper classes and protect them from the "malign" Catholic influences elsewhere in Europe. Its purpose has changed with the ages, and now it is simply the most well-respected university in Ireland.

Among its alumni are Bram Stoker, Jonathan Swift, Oscar Wilde, and Samuel Beckett, as well as an array of rebels and revolutionaries who helped create the Republic of Ireland. The poet and wit Oliver Goldsmith also attended, and his statue stands near the main entrance at College Green, near the statue of the philosopher and fellow Trinity alumnus Robert Burke. The campus spreads across central Dublin just south of the River Liffey, with cobbled squares, gardens, a picturesque quadrangle, and buildings dating from the 17th to the 20th centuries. This is also where you'll find the Book of Kells (p. 142).

College Green, Dublin 2. ℂ **01/896-1000.** www.tcd.ie. Free admission.

MORE ATTRACTIONS
Art Galleries & Art Museums
Irish Film Centre   This art-house film institute is a hip hangout for cinephiles in Dublin's artsy Temple Bar district. It houses two cinemas, the Irish Film Archive, a library, a small but comprehensive bookshop, and a good cafe (p. 137) that makes a good place for a cup of coffee on a cold afternoon. There's also a busy bar that does banner business. The cinemas show arty, ground-breaking films and are the main attraction here, bar or no bar.

6 Eustace St., Dublin 2. ℂ **01/679-5744,** or 679-3477 for cinema box office. www.irishfilm.ie. Free admission; cinema tickets €7–€10 ($11–$16). Centre daily 10am–11pm; cinemas daily 2–11pm; cinema box office daily 1:30–9pm. Bus: 21A, 78A, or 78B.

> ### Impressions
>
> *It was a bold man who first swallowed an oyster.*
>
> —Jonathan Swift

Irish Museum of Modern Art (IMMA)
In the splendidly restored, 17th-century edifice known as the Royal Hospital, the IMMA is frequently used as a venue for theatrical and musical events. The small permanent collection contains mostly works by Irish artists, and the big draws are the numerous temporary exhibitions that pass through. Outside, the formal gardens have been restored to stellar condition.

Military Rd., Kilmainham. ℂ **01/612-9900.** www.modernart.ie. Free admission. Tues and Thurs–Sat 10am–5:30pm; Wed 10:30am–5:30pm; Sun and holidays noon–5:30pm. Bus: 79 or 90.

Temple Bar Gallery and Studios   Founded in 1983 in the heart of Dublin's "Left Bank," this is one of the largest studio and gallery complexes in Europe. More than 30 Irish artists work here at a variety of contemporary visual arts, including sculpture, painting, printing, and photography. Only the gallery section is open to the public, but you can make an appointment in advance to view individual artists at work. The Studios hosts free talks and discussion panels, featuring the great and the good of the Irish arts scene. Call for details.

5–9 Temple Bar, Dublin 2. ℂ **01/671-0073.** Fax 01/677-7527. www.templebargallery.com. Free admission. Tues–Wed 11am–6pm; Thurs 11am–7pm; Sun 2–6pm. Bus: 21A, 46A, 46B, 51B, 51C, 68, 69, or 86.

Breweries/Distilleries
Guinness Storehouse ★   Founded in 1759, the Guinness Brewery is one of the world's most famous breweries, producing a distinctive dark stout. You can explore the Guinness Hopstore, tour a converted 19th-century four-story building housing the World of Guinness Exhibition, and view a film showing how the stout is made; then move on to the Gilroy Gallery, dedicated to the graphic design work of John Gilroy; and last but not

(Fun Facts) **Monumental Humor**

Dublin boasts countless public monuments, some modest, others boldly evident. The Irish make a sport of naming them, giving their irrepressible wit and ridicule yet another outlet. A sampler:

Poor **Molly Malone,** who, in song, "wheeled her wheelbarrow through streets broad and narrow," appears with her cockles and mussels at the intersection of Nassau and Grafton streets, across from Trinity College. Due to her ample bosom and plunging neckline, this statue is called "the Tart with the Cart."

Just around the corner from Molly on Dame Street stands another sculpture, a silent frenzy of **trumpeters** and streaming columns of water, proclaiming "You're a nation again"—popularly transliterated as "urination again."

The city's newest monument is the **Millennium Spire,** a 120m-high (394-ft.) needle thrusting upward in the middle of traffic on O'Connell Street. Made of stainless steel and designed by London architect Ian Ritchie, the spire is intended to reflect the Dublin of the 21st century. (It replaced Nelson's Pillar, a statue of the British Admiral Horatio Nelson, erected under British rule and blown up by the IRA in 1966, on the 50th anniversary of the Easter Rising. Nelson's head was all that survived, and it is now in the Dublin Civic Museum.) Dubliners have had great fun coming up with a suitable nickname for the spire. The favorite is simply "the Spike," although another front-runner is "the Stiletto in the Ghetto."

Then there's the statue of Ireland's great patriot, **Wolfe Tone.** Born at 44 Stafford St. in 1763 and graduated from Trinity College, Tone went on to spark a revolutionary fervor among the Irish. He is commemorated in thoroughly modern fashion on the north side of St. Stephen's Green by a semicircle of rough-hewed columns locally known as "Tonehenge."

The best renamed statue, though, is no more. Until a few years ago, **Anna Livia,** James Joyce's mythical personification of the River Liffey, could be found cast in bronze on O'Connell Street across from the General Post Office. The unattractive, hard-to-like statue reclining in streaming water was widely reviled—you'd be hard-pressed to find anybody who didn't hate it. It was nicknamed "the Floozy in the Jacuzzi." Due to her intense unpopularity, she has been removed.

least, stop in at the breathtaking Gravity Bar, where you can sample a glass of the famous brew in the glass-enclosed bar 60m (197 ft.) above the ground, with 360-degree views of the city.

St. James's Gate, Dublin 8. *(C)* **01/408-4800.** www.guinness-storehouse.com. Admission €14 ($22) adults, €9.50 ($15) seniors and students, €5 ($8) children 6–12, €30 ($48) families. Daily 9:30am–5pm. Guided tours every half-hour. Bus: 51B, 78A, or 123.

The Old Jameson Distillery ★ This museum illustrates the history of Irish whiskey, known in Irish as *uisce beatha* (the water of life). Learn as much as you can bear from the film, whiskey-making exhibitions, and right-in-front-of-your-eyes demonstrations.

At the conclusion of the tour, you can sip a little firewater and see what you think. A couple of lucky people on each tour are selected to be "tasters" and sample different Irish, Scotch, and American whiskeys.

Bow St., Smithfield Village, Dublin 7. © **01/807-2355.** www.whiskeytours.ie. Admission €13 ($20) adults, €9 ($14) students and seniors. Daily 9:30am–6pm (last tour at 5pm). Closed Good Friday and Christmas holidays. Bus: 67, 67A, 68, 69, 79, or 90.

Cathedrals & Churches

St. Patrick's Cathedral and Christ Church Cathedral are listed earlier in this chapter, under "The Top Attractions."

St. Audeon's Church   Near the only remaining gate of the Old City walls (dating from 1214), this church is said to be the only surviving medieval parish in Dublin. Although it is partly in ruins, significant parts have survived, including the west doorway, which dates from 1190, and the 13th-century nave. It's a Church of Ireland property, but nearby is another St. Audeon's Church, this one Catholic and dating from 1846. It was in the latter church that Father "Flash" Kavanagh used to say the world's fastest Mass so that his congregation was out in time for the football matches. Since 1999, entrance to the ancient church is through a visitor center. The center's exhibition, relating the history of St. Audeon's, is self-guided; visits to the church itself are by guided tour, and it is only open in high summer.

Cornmarket (off High St.), Dublin 8. © **01/677-0088.** Free admission. June–Sept daily 9:30am–5:30pm. Last admission 45 min. before closing. Bus: 21A, 78A, or 78B.

St. Mary's Pro-Cathedral   It may be tucked away on a rather unimpressive back street, but St. Mary's is the heart of the city's Northside. It was built between 1815 and 1825 in Greek Revival Doric style. The exterior portico is modeled on the Temple of Theseus in Athens, with six Doric columns, while the Renaissance-style interior is patterned after the Church of Saint-Philippe du Roule of Paris. The church is noted for its awe-inspiring Palestrina Choir, which sings a Latin Mass every Sunday at 11am.

Cathedral and Marlborough sts., Dublin 1. © **01/874-5441.** www.procathedral.ie. Free admission. Mon–Fri 7:30am–6:45pm; Sat 7:30am–7:15pm; Sun 9am–1:45pm and 5:30pm–7:45pm. DART: Connolly. Bus: 28, 29A, 30, 31A, 31B, 32A, 32B, or 44A.

St. Michan's Church   Built on the site of an early Danish chapel (1095), this 17th-century edifice has fine interior woodwork and an organ (dated 1724) on which Handel is said to have played his *Messiah*. A unique (and, let it be noted, macabre) feature of this church is the underground burial vault. Because of the dry atmosphere, bodies have lain for centuries without showing signs of decomposition. It is said that Bram Stoker was inspired to write *Dracula* in part by having visited the vaults as a child. *Note:* The church is wheelchair accessible, but the vaults are not.

Church St., Dublin 7. © **01/872-4154.** Free admission. Guided tour of church and vaults €4 ($6.40) adults, €3.50 ($5.60) seniors and students, €3 ($4.80) children 11 and under. Nov–Mar 16 Mon–Fri 12:30pm–3:30pm; Mar 17–Oct Mon–Fri 10am–12:45pm and 2–4:30pm; year-round Sat 10am–12:45pm. Bus: 134 (from Abbey St.).

St. Teresa's Church   The foundation stone was laid for this building in 1793, and the church was opened in 1810 by the Discalced Carmelite Fathers. After continuous enlargement, it reached its present form in 1876. After years of anti-Catholic legislation, this was the first Catholic church to be legally and openly erected in Dublin, following the Catholic Relief Act of 1793. Among the artistic highlights are John Hogan's *Dead*

Christ, a sculpture displayed beneath the altar, and Phyllis Burke's seven beautiful stained-glass windows.

Clarendon St., Dublin 2. (*C*) **01/671-8466.** Free admission; donations welcome. Daily 8am–8pm or longer. Bus: 16, 16A, 19, 19A, 22, 22A, 55, or 83.

Whitefriar Street Carmelite Church This 19th-century Byzantine-style church is unexpectedly one of the city's most romantic spots. Lovers are drawn here because the church holds the relics of St. Valentine. The pieces of bone are believed to be authentic, and they were given to the church by Pope Gregory XVI. They're kept in a casket on an altar to the right of the main altar. The church also holds an icon known as Our Lady of Dublin, a 15th-century woodcarving that was rescued from a nearby farm where it had been used as a pig trough.

56 Aungier St., Dublin 2. (*C*) **01/475-8821.** Free admission. Mon and Wed–Fri 8am–6:30pm; Tues 8am–9:30pm; Sat 8am–7pm; Sun 8am–7:30pm. Bus: 16, 16A, 19, 19A, 83, 122, or 155.

A Cemetery

Glasnevin Cemetery North of the city center, the Irish national cemetery was founded in 1832 and covers more than 50 hectares (124 acres). Most people buried here were ordinary citizens, but there are also many famous names on the headstones, ranging from former Irish *taoiseach* (prime minister) Eamon de Valera to other political heroes and rebels including Michael Collins, Daniel O'Connell, Roger Casement, and Charles Stewart Parnell. Literary figures also have their place here, such as writers Christy Brown (immortalized in the film *My Left Foot*) and Brendan Behan (at whose funeral, in 1964, the coffin was escorted by an IRA honor guard from the church to its burial spot). A heritage map, on sale in the flower shop at the entrance, serves as a guide to who's buried where, or you can take a free 2-hour guided tour.

Finglas Rd., Dublin 11. (*C*) **01/830-1133.** www.glasnevin-cemetery.ie. Free admission. Daily 8am–4pm. Free guided tours Wed and Fri 2:30pm from main gate. Map €3.50 ($5.60). Bus: 19, 19A, 40, 40A, 40B, or 40C.

More Historic Buildings

It's not open to the public, but it's worth lingering outside **Mansion House,** Dawson Street, if only because of its fascinating history. The Queen Anne–style building has been the official residence of Dublin's lord mayors since 1715. In 1919, the first Dáil Éireann (House of Representatives) assembled here to adopt Ireland's Declaration of Independence and ratify the Proclamation of the Irish Republic.

Bank of Ireland Centre/Parliament House ★ This building was built in 1729 to house the Irish Parliament, and it did so for less than a century. Then, in 1797, the British Prime Minister William Pitt became convinced that the only way to bring an end to religious violence in Ireland was to close the Irish Parliament and merge it with the English. However, since the Parliament members had purchased their seats at great expense, it was difficult to convince them to agree, so Pitt bought them off with a combination of cash, titles, and promises that anti-Catholic rules would be ended if they only voted themselves out of existence. In 1801 they agreed—the only Parliament ever to do so—and passed the so-called "Act of Union." However, King George III disagreed with Pitt's plans to end the anti-Catholic laws and forced Pitt to resign before any such legislation could be passed. The Irish lost their independent government and got nothing in return. After standing empty for 2 years, the building was sold in 1803; the bill of sale required that it be physically altered so that it could never again be used for governmental gatherings. Today it's a bank, but it still has many architectural elements dating from its heyday. Highlights include the windowless front portico, built to avoid distractions from the outside when Parliament was in session, and the grand House of Lords chamber with its Irish oak woodwork, 18th-century tapestries, golden mace, and a sparkling crystal chandelier.

This is also the home of the **Bank of Ireland Arts Centre** (*©* **01/671-1488**), accessible via the entrance on Foster Place. It hosts art exhibitions, concerts, and literary readings. Entry to readings, lunchtime recitals, and exhibitions is free.

2 College Green, Dublin 2. *©* **01/661-5933,** ext. 2265. Free admission. Mon–Wed and Fri 10am–4pm; Thurs 10am–5pm. Guided 45-min. tours of House of Lords chamber Tues 10:30am, 11:30am, and 1:45pm (except holidays). DART: Tara St. Bus: Any city-center bus.

Custom House   The Custom House, which sits prominently on the Liffey's north quays (to the right of the O'Connell Street Bridge if you're coming from the South Bank), is a fine Georgian building. Completed in 1791, it is beautifully proportioned, with a long classical facade of graceful pavilions, arcades, and columns, and a central dome topped by a statue of Commerce. The 14 keystones over the doors and windows are known as the Riverine Heads, because they represent the Atlantic Ocean and the 13 principal rivers of Ireland. Although it burned to a shell in 1921, the building has been masterfully restored, and its bright Portland stone was recently cleaned. The exterior is the main attraction here, and most of the interior is closed to the public, but if you're very interested in learning more, there's a visitor center with exhibitions and an audiovisual presentation telling the story of its reconstruction.

Custom House Quay, Dublin 1. *©* **01/888-2538.** Admission to Visitor's Centre €1 ($1.60). Mid-Mar to Oct Mon–Fri 10am–12:30pm, Sat–Sun 2–5pm; Nov to mid-Mar Wed–Fri 10am–12:30pm, Sun 2–5pm. DART: Tara St.

Four Courts   Home to the Irish law courts since 1796, this fine 18th-century building overlooks the north bank of the Liffey on Dublin's west side. With a sprawling 132m (433-ft.) facade, it was designed by James Gandon (who also designed the Custom House) and is distinguished by its graceful Corinthian columns, massive dome (192m/630 ft. in diameter), and exterior statues of Justice, Mercy, Wisdom, and Moses (sculpted by Edward Smyth). The building was at the center of the fighting during the civil war of 1922 and was badly damaged in the battle, but it was later artfully restored. The public is admitted only when court is in session.

Inns Quay, Dublin 8. *©* **01/872-5555.** Free admission. Mon–Fri 11am–1pm and 2–4pm, but only if court is in session. Bus: 34, 70, or 80.

General Post Office (GPO) ★   Don't be fooled by the nondescript name: With a facade of Ionic columns and Greco-Roman pilasters 60m long (197 ft.) and 17m high (56 ft.), this is more than a post office—it is the symbol of Irish freedom. Built between 1815 and 1818, it was the main stronghold of the Irish Volunteers during the Easter Rising. On Easter Sunday, 1916, Patrick Pearse stood on its steps and read a proclamation declaring a free Irish Republic, which began, "In every generation the Irish people have asserted their right to national freedom and sovereignty." Then he and an army of supporters barricaded themselves inside the post office. A siege ensued that ultimately involved much of the north of the city, and before it was over, the building was all but destroyed. It had barely been restored before the civil war broke out in 1922 and it was heavily damaged again. After that, it remained closed until 1929. You can put your fingers into the bullet holes that riddle its columns, lingering reminders of the Irish struggle.

To this day, its steps are a rallying point for demonstrations and protests. In the vast, somber interior, a series of paintings tell the tale of the Easter Rising. An impressive bronze statue of Cúchulainn, the legendary knight of the Red Branch who is used as a symbol by both Loyalist and Republican paramilitary groups, stands proudly amid it all.

O'Connell St., Dublin 1. ℰ **01/705-8833.** www. anpost.ie. Free admission. Mon–Sat 8am–8pm; Sun 10:30am–6:30pm. DART: Connolly. Bus: 25, 26, 34, 37, 38A, 39A, 39B, 66A, or 67A.

> ## Impressions
>
> *You cannot conquer Ireland. You cannot extinguish the Irish passion for freedom. If our deed has not been sufficient to win freedom, then our children will win It by a better deed.*
>
> —Patrick Pearse

Leinster House The home of the Dáil (Irish House of Representatives) and Seanad (Irish Senate), which together constitute the Oireachtas (National Parliament), this is the center of Irish government. Dating from 1745 and originally known as Kildare House, the building is said to have been the model for Irish-born architect James Hoban's design for the White House in Washington, D.C. It was sold in 1815 to the Royal Dublin Society, which developed it as a cultural center. The National Museum, Library, and Gallery all surround it. The Irish Free State government acquired it in 1924. Tickets are available for guided tours when the Dáil is in session (Oct–May Tues–Thurs); tours must be arranged in advance from the Public Relations Office (ℰ **01/618-3066**).

Kildare St. and Merrion Sq., Dublin 2. ℰ **01/618-3000.** Free admission. By appointment only, Oct–May Mon and Fri 10am–4:30pm. DART: Pearse. Bus: 5, 7A, or 8.

Newman House ★ These fine Georgian town houses on the south side of St. Stephen's Green are the historic seat of the Catholic University of Ireland. Named for Cardinal John Henry Newman, the 19th-century writer, theologian, and the first rector of the university, the buildings date from 1740 and are decorated with outstanding Palladian and rococo plasterwork, marble tiled floors, and wainscot paneling. No. 85 has a somber exterior, but inside it has been magnificently restored to its original splendor, with one exception—when the Catholic University took over the buildings in 1865, the fathers must have been put off by the luscious rococo nudes carved into the elaborate plasterwork, for they had all the female forms painted over. Most have been blessedly returned to their natural shape, but a figure of Juno is still hidden by a very conservative tunic. *Note:* Every other Sunday, Newman House hosts an antiques-and-collectibles fair, where dealers from throughout Ireland sell a wide range of items, including silver, rare books, paintings and prints, coins, stamps, and so forth.

85–86 St. Stephen's Green, Dublin 2. ℰ **01/706-7422.** Fax 01/706-7211. Guided tours €5 ($8) adults; €4 ($6.40) seniors, students, and children 11 and under. June–Aug Tues–Fri noon–5pm; Oct–May by appointment only. Bus: 10, 11, 13, 14, 14A, 15A, or 15B.

Libraries
Marsh's Library This caged library, founded in 1701, is the real thing. Unlike Trinity College's Long Room, which is largely for show these days, Marsh's Library is still functioning. Its walls are lined with scholarly volumes, chiefly on theology, medicine, ancient history, maps, and Hebrew, Greek, Latin, and French literature. Wire cages, in which readers would be locked in with the more valuable tomes, still stand anachronistically. The interior—a magnificent example of a 17th-century scholar's library—has remained

much the same for 3 centuries. The excellent collection of books by and about Jonathan Swift includes books with his editing comments in the borders.

St. Patrick's Close, Upper Kevin St., Dublin 8. ✆ **01/454-3511.** www.marshlibrary.ie. Donation of €2.50 ($4) adults, €1.25 ($2) seniors and students requested. Mon and Wed–Fri 10am–1pm and 2–5pm; Sat 10:30am–1pm. Bus: 50, 54A, or 56A.

National Library of Ireland If you're coming to Ireland to research your roots, this library should be one of your first stops (along with the Heraldic Museum; see below). It has thousands of volumes and records that yield ancestral information. Open at this location since 1890, this is the principal library of Irish studies. It's particularly noted for its collection of first editions and the papers of Irish writers and political figures, such as W. B. Yeats, Daniel O'Connell, and Patrick Pearse. It also has an unrivaled collection of maps of Ireland.

Kildare St., Dublin 2. ✆ **01/603-0200.** www.nli.ie. Free admission. Mon–Wed 9:30am–9pm; Thurs–Fri 9:30am–5pm; Sat 9:30am–1pm. DART: Pearse. Bus: 10, 11A, 11B, 13, or 20B.

National Photographic Archive The newest member of the Temple Bar cultural complex, this archive houses the extensive (with more than 300,000 items) photo collection of the National Library, and serves as its photo exhibition space. It's an excellent space, and photos are rotated out regularly, so there's always something new to see. In addition to the exhibition area, there are a library and a small gift shop.

Meeting House Sq., Temple Bar, Dublin 2. ✆ **01/603-0374.** www.nli.ie. Free admission. Mon–Fri 10am–5pm; Sat 10am–2pm. DART: Tara St. Bus: 21A, 46A, 46B, 51B, 51C, 68, 69, or 86.

Literary Landmarks

See also "Libraries," above, and the listing for the Dublin Writers Museum (p. 146). You might also be interested in the James Joyce Museum, in nearby Sandycove (p. 180).

James Joyce Centre Just beyond the top of O'Connell Street on the city's Northside, near the Dublin Writers Museum, the Joyce Centre is a small, idiosyncratic gallery in a restored 1784 Georgian town house. There are pros and cons to this place—there's not much in the way of real memorabilia related to Joyce, save for a writing table Joyce used in Paris when he was working on *Finnegan's Wake,* and there are early copies of his work, including a copy of *Ulysses* inscribed by a mischievous Brendan Behan ("I wish that I had written it"). Overall, it's best to come here if an interesting speaker is scheduled. True Joyce fans, of course, will be in heaven here. Call about the James Joyce walking tours.

35 N. Great George's St., Dublin 1. ✆ **01/878-8547.** www.jamesjoyce.ie. Admission €5 ($8) adults; €4 ($6.40) seniors, students, and children 9 and under. Separate fees for walking tours and events. Tues–Sat 10am–5pm. Closed Dec 24–26. DART: Connolly. Bus: 3, 10, 11, 11A, 13, 16, 16A, 19, 19A, 22, or 22A.

Shaw Birthplace This simple, two-story terraced house near the Grand Canal on the south side was the birthplace in 1856 of George Bernard Shaw, author of *Pygmalion, Man and Superman,* and *John Bull's Other Island,* among many others. Shaw, one of Dublin's three winners of the Nobel Prize for literature, lived here until 1876, when he moved to London. Recently restored, it has been furnished in Victorian style to re-create the atmosphere of Shaw's early days. Rooms on view are the kitchen, the maid's room, the nursery, the drawing room, and a couple of bedrooms, including young Bernard's. The house is a 15-minute walk from St. Stephen's Green.

33 Synge St., Dublin 2. ✆ **01/475-0854.** Admission €7 ($11) adults, €6 ($9.60) seniors and students, €4.40 ($7.05) children, €29 ($46) families. Discounted combination ticket with Dublin Writers Museum

More Museums

See also "Art Galleries & Art Museums," earlier in this chapter. The National Gallery, the National Museum, the Dublin Writers Museum, and Kilmainham Gaol Historical Museum are all listed earlier in this chapter, in "The Top Attractions."

Dublin Civic Museum In the old City Assembly House, a fine 18th-century Georgian structure next to the Powerscourt Townhouse Centre, this museum focuses on the history of the Dublin area from medieval to modern times. In addition to old street signs, maps, and prints, you can see Viking artifacts, wooden water mains, coal covers—and even the head from the statue of Lord Nelson, which stood in O'Connell Street until it was blown up by the IRA in 1966.

58 William St. S., Dublin 2. (✆ **01/679-4260.** Free admission. Tues–Sat 10am–6pm; Sun 11am–2pm. Bus: 10, 11, or 13.

GAA Museum On the grounds of Croke Park, principal stadium of the Gaelic Athletic Association, this museum dramatically presents the athletic heritage of Ireland. The Gaelic Games (Gaelic football, hurling, handball, and *camogie*) have long been contested on an annual basis between teams representing the various regions of Ireland. Test your skills with interactive exhibits, and peruse the extensive video archive of football finals dating from 1931.

Croke Park, Dublin 3. (✆ **01/819-2323.** Fax 01/819-2324. http://museum.gaa.ie. Admission €5.50 ($8.80) adults, €4 ($6.40) students, €3.50 ($5.60) children 11 and under, €15 ($24) families. Mon–Sat 9:30am–5pm (July–Aug until 6pm); Sun noon–5pm. Bus: 3, 11, 11A, 16, 16A, 51A, or 123.

Heraldic Museum/Genealogical Office This museum is an excellent resource for families trying to track down their Irish heritage. Exhibits on display include shields, banners, coins, paintings, porcelain, and stamps depicting Irish coats of arms. In-house searches by the office researcher are billed at the rate of €56 ($90) per hour.

2 Kildare St., Dublin 2. (✆ **01/603-0200.** Fax 01/676-6690. Free admission. Mon–Wed 10am–8:30pm; Thurs–Fri 10am–4:30pm; Sat 10am–12:30pm. DART: Pearse. Bus: 5, 7A, 8, 9, 10, 14, or 15.

Number Twenty Nine (Finds) This little museum in a typical town house on one of the fashionable Georgian streets on Dublin's south side re-creates the lifestyle of a middle-class family from 1790 to 1820. The exhibition is designed to be authentic all the way from the artifacts and artwork of the time to the carpets, curtains, plasterwork, and bell pulls. Tables are set with period dishes and the nursery is filled with toys from the time. It's both educational and particularly beautiful.

29 Lower Fitzwilliam St., Dublin 2. (✆ **01/702-6165.** www.esb.ie/numbertwentynine. Tours only, €6 ($9.60) adults, €3 ($4.80) seniors and students. Free for children 15 and under. Tues–Sat 10am–5pm; Sun 2–5pm. Closed 2 weeks at Christmas. DART: Pearse. Bus: 7, 8, 10, or 45.

ESPECIALLY FOR KIDS

The Ark: A Cultural Centre for Children ★★★ (Kids) Every year, more than 20,000 children visit this unique cultural center where they are the makers, thinkers, doers, listeners, and watchers. Age-specific programs are geared to small groups of kids from 4 to 14 years old. There are organized minicourses (1–2 hr. long) designed around themes in music, visual arts, and theater, as well as workshops in photography, instrument making, and the art of architecture. The custom-designed arts center has three

(Kids) Family Favorites

As with any big(ish) city, Dublin can seem a little kid-unfriendly, but never fear—there's more than enough to do here to keep the little ones happy.

If the weather's fine, Dublin's many parks give families on the go a respite from the city's ruckus. Right in the center at **Merrion Square** and **St. Stephen's Green,** there are lawns for picnicking, ducks to feed, playgrounds for swinging, and gardens for dashing around madly. If you feel like splurging, the whole family can take a carriage ride around the parks (see "Organized Tours," below).

West of Dublin's city center, the vast **Phoenix Park** is paradise for children on a sunny day (p. 148). It holds the **Dublin Zoo** (see below) as well as sports fields, playgrounds, and herds of free-roaming deer. Ice-cream vendors and teahouses are on hand to help keep you going. Those weary of walking can take a trail ride through the park from the **Ashtown Riding Stables** (see section 6, "Sports & Outdoor Pursuits").

For a lively tour of Dublin's Viking history (well, it's a gentle brush across the surface of Dublin's Viking history, to be honest), the **Viking Splash Tour,** in a reconditioned World War II amphibious "duck" vehicle (see "Organized Tours," below), is more about fun than history.

If they need a little artistic stimulation, the **Ark** (see above) offers arts classes and cultural experiences ranging from painting and drawing to theater, while the **Lambert Puppet Theatre** (see below) offers good, clean, old-fashioned fun.

At the edge of town in the suburbs, fresh air, ocean breezes, and castles await their wondering eyes. North of the city is the **Malahide Castle** (p. 183), with a grand, rambling old stone castle, acres of parks and playgrounds, and the incongruous additions of the **Fry Model Railway** exhibit and **Tara's Palace,** filled with antique dollhouses and toys.

modern floors that house a theater, a gallery, and a workshop for hands-on learning sessions. Weekdays are often booked for school groups, but Saturdays (and sometimes Sun) are kept open for families. Check the current themes and schedule on the Ark's very helpful website and book well ahead.

11a Eustace St., Temple Bar, Dublin 2. (C) **01/670-7788.** www.ark.ie. Individual activities start at around €6.50 ($10) per child. Daily 10am–4pm. Closed mid-Aug to mid-Sept. DART: Tara St. Bus: 37, 39, 51, or 51B.

Dublin Zoo ★★★ (Kids)   Sprawling across 24 hectares (59 acres) of bucolic Phoenix Park on the north bank of the Liffey, this modern, humane zoo provides a naturally landscaped habitat for more than 235 species of wild animals and tropical birds. Highlights for youngsters include the Children's Pets Corner and a train ride around the zoo. Self-explanatory exhibits include "African Plains," "Fringes of the Arctic," and the "World of Primates." There are playgrounds and gift shops throughout the zoo. A downside: The restaurants within the zoo serve only fast food, but there are plenty of picnic areas for folks who want to bring their own meals.

The towns south of Dublin are best explored by DART light rail from the city center. You might stop in Monkstown to see a puppet show at the **Lambert Puppet Theatre and Museum** (Clifton Lane; ✆ 01/280-0974; www.lambert puppettheatre.com), or, if the kids need a little seaside adventure, go on a few more stops to the charming heritage village of Dalkey. The **Ferryman** of Coliemore Harbour, just a 10-minute walk from the train, can take the family out to explore **Dalkey Island** and return you safely to shore a few hours later. After your adventure, reward yourself with a creamy soft-serve ice-cream cone in the village. The park at the top of **Dalkey Hill** offers a memorable view of the town and bay beyond, but it's a very steep climb.

One stop after Dalkey on the DART lies the long pebbled beach of **Killiney.** This is just the place to find the perfect stone for your family collection or to take a beachcombing stroll along the strand. Farther on down the line is the seaside resort town of **Bray,** where Irish water creatures, from starfish to sharks, can be found in the **National Sea Life Centre** (p. 191). Along with the aquarium, Bray has arcades, games, and other family amusements along its boardwalk. If you get to Bray with energy and daylight to spare, the hike up **Bray Head** will give you a spectacular view of the Dublin coastline; in summer, it's covered in purple heather and yellow gorse.

Even with so much out there for families to do together, there may be some events—a romantic dinner, perhaps?—to which you'd rather not bring the kids. So where do you turn for a babysitter? Dublin parents swear by **Minder Finders** (www.minderfinders.ie), a clued-in agency that uses only certified child minders (many are former nannies or teachers) who arrive armed with a bag full of kid-friendly activities. Each sitter is matched with your kids' ages and interests in mind, to alleviate any "new babysitter" jitters.

Phoenix Park, Dublin 8. ✆ 1800/924-848. www.dublinzoo.ie. Admission €15 ($24) adults; €12 ($19) seniors and students; €9 ($14) children 3–16; free for children 2 and under; €40–€49 ($64–$78) families, depending on number of children. Summer Mon–Sat 9:30am–6pm, Sun 10:30am–6pm; winter Mon–Sat 9:30am–dusk, Sun 10:30am–dusk. Bus: 10, 25, or 26.

ORGANIZED TOURS
Bus Tours
The city bus company, **Dublin Bus** (✆ 01/873-4222; www.dublinbus.ie), operates several tours of Dublin, all of which depart from the Dublin Bus office at 59 Upper O'Connell St., Dublin 1. You can buy your ticket from the bus driver or book in advance at the Dublin Bus office or at the Dublin Tourism ticket desk on Suffolk Street. The following are the best options.

The 75-minute guided **Dublin City Tour** operates on a hop-on, hop-off basis, connecting 10 major points of interest, including museums, art galleries, churches and cathedrals, libraries, and historic sites. Rates are €15 ($24) for adults, €13 ($21) seniors and students, €6 ($9.60) for children 15 and under. Tours operate daily from 9:30am to 6:30pm.

Horse-Drawn-Carriage Tours

You can tour Dublin in style in a handsomely outfitted horse-drawn carriage with a driver who will comment on the sights as you travel the city's streets and squares. To arrange a ride, consult one of the drivers stationed with carriages at the Grafton Street side of St. Stephen's Green. Rides range from a short swing around the green to an extensive half-hour Georgian tour or an hour-long Old City tour. It's slightly touristy, but kids (and romantics) love it.

Rides are available on a first-come, first-served basis from approximately April to October (weather permitting) and will run you between €20 and €50 ($32–$80) for one to four passengers.

The 2¹/₄-hour **Dublin Ghost Bus** is a spooky evening tour run by Dublin Bus, departing Monday to Thursday at 8pm, Friday at 8 and 8:30pm, and Saturday and Sunday at 7 and 9:30pm. The tour addresses Dublin's history of felons, fiends, and phantoms. You'll see haunted houses, learn of Dracula's Dublin origins, and even get a crash course in body snatching. It's properly scary, though, and not recommended for children who do not have "teen" in their age. Fares are €25 ($40) for adults only (not recommended for those 13 and under).

The 3-hour **Coast and Castle Tour** departs daily at 10am and 2pm traveling up the north coast to Malahide and Howth. Fares are €25 ($40) for adults, €12 ($19) for children 13 and under. Visiting Malahide Castle will require an additional charge.

The 3³/₄-hour **South Coast Tour** departs daily at 11am and 2pm, traveling south through the seaside town of Dún Laoghaire, through the upscale "Irish Riviera" villages of Dalkey and Killiney, and farther south to visit the vast Powerscourt Estate. Fares are €25 ($40) for adults, €12 ($19) for children 13 and under.

Gray Line (© 01/605-7705; www.irishcitytours.com) operates its own hop-on, hop-off city tour, covering all the same major sights as the Dublin Bus's "Dublin City Tour." The first tours leave at 10am from 14 Upper O'Connell St., and run every 10 to 15 minutes thereafter. The last departures are at 4:30pm. You can also join the tour at any of a number of pickup points along the route and buy your ticket from the driver. Gray Line's Dublin city tour costs €16 ($26) for adults, €13 ($21) for seniors and students, €7 ($11) for children, and €38 ($61) families.

Gray Line also offers a range of full-day excursions from Dublin to such nearby sights as Glendalough, Newgrange, and Powerscourt. Adult fares for their other tours range from €20 to €40 ($32–$64).

Land & Water Tours

The immensely popular **Viking Splash Tour** ★★ (© 01/707-6000; www.vikingsplash. ie) is an unusual way for kids to see Dublin. Aboard a reconditioned World War II amphibious landing craft, or "duck," this tour starts on land (from Bull Alley St. beside St. Patrick's Cathedral) and eventually splashes into the Grand Canal. Passengers wear horned Viking helmets (a reference to the original settlers of the Dublin area) and are encouraged to issue war cries at appropriate moments. One of the ducks even has bullet holes as evidence of its military service. Tours depart roughly on the half-hour every day 9:30am to 5pm and last an hour and 15 minutes. It costs €20 ($32) for adults, €10 ($16) for children 12 and under, €18 ($29) seniors and students, and €60 ($96) for a family of five.

Walking Tours

Walking Tours

Small and compact, Dublin was made for walking. If you prefer to set off on your own, the **Dublin Tourism** office, St. Andrew's Church, Suffolk Street, Dublin 2, has maps for four tourist trails signposted throughout the city: Old City, Georgian Heritage, Cultural Heritage, and the "Rock 'n Stroll" music tour.

However, if you'd like more guidance, historical background, or just some company, you might want to consider one of the following.

Historical Walking Tours of Dublin ★★ (Value) Tours with this award-winning outfit are like 2-hour primers on Dublin's historic landmarks, from medieval walls and Viking remains around Wood Quay, to the architectural splendors of Georgian Dublin, to highlights of Irish history. Guides are historians, and participants are encouraged to ask questions. Tours assemble just inside the front gate of Trinity College; no reservations are needed.

From Trinity College. ✆ **01/688-9412.** www.historicalinsights.ie. Tickets €12 ($19) adults, €10 ($16) seniors and students, free for children 13 and under. May–Sept daily 11am and 3pm; Apr and Oct Fri–Sun 11am; Nov–March Fri–Sun 11am.

Literary Pub Crawl ★ Walking in the footsteps of Joyce, Behan, Beckett, Shaw, Kavanagh, and other Irish literary greats, this tour visits Dublin's most famous pubs and explores their deep, literary connections. Actors provide humorous performances and commentary between stops. Throughout the night, you can join in a literary quiz—if you win, you'll get a prize. The tour begins at the Duke Pub on Duke Street (off Grafton St.).

The Duke Pub, 9 Duke St., Dublin 2. ✆ **01/670-5602.** www.dublinpubcrawl.com. Tickets €12 ($19) adults, €10 ($16) students. Apr–Nov daily 7:30pm; Dec–Mar Thurs–Sun 7:30pm.

1916 Rebellion Walking Tour ★ Dublin was profoundly changed by the rebellion early in the 20th century that became known as the Easter Rising. This tour takes you into the heat of the action at the General Post Office, explaining how the anger rose until the rebellion exploded on Easter Sunday in 1916. The tour is well thought out and run by local historians who wrote a book on the events of that year. Their vast knowledge of the history of Dublin shines through, making this an absorbing tour.

The International Bar, 23 Wicklow St., Dublin 2. ✆ **086/858-3847.** www.1916rising.com. Tickets €12 ($19) per person. Mar 1–Oct 30 Mon–Sat 11:30am; Sun 1pm. No tours Mar 17 or Good Friday. Phone or check the website for the winter schedule.

Traditional Irish Musical Pub Crawl ★★ This tour explores and samples the traditional music scene, and the price includes a songbook. Two professional musicians, who sing as you make your way from one famous pub to another in Temple Bar, lead the tour. The evening is touristy, but the music is good. It lasts 2½ hours.

Leaves from Oliver St. John Gogarty pub and restaurant (upstairs), 57–58 Fleet St. (at Anglesea St.), Temple Bar. ✆ **01/475-3313.** Tickets €12 ($19) adults, €10 ($16) students and seniors. Apr–Oct daily 7:30pm; Nov–Mar Thurs–Sat 7:30pm. Tickets on sale at 7pm or in advance from Dublin Tourist Office.

Walk Macabre ★ The Trapeze Theatre Company offers this 90-minute walk past the homes of famous writers around Merrion Square, St. Stephen's Green, and Merrion Row, while reconstructing scenes of past murders and intrigue. The tour includes reenactments from some of the darker pages of Yeats, Joyce, Bram Stoker, and Oscar Wilde. This one would be rated "R" for violent imagery, so it's not for children or light sleepers. Advance booking is essential. Tours leave from the main gates of St. Stephen's Green.

✆ **087/677-1512** or 271-1346. Tickets €12 ($19) adults, €10 ($16) students. Daily 7:30pm.

6 SPORTS & OUTDOOR PURSUITS

BEACHES   Plenty of fine beaches are accessible by city bus or DART, which follows the coast from Howth, north of the city, to Bray, south of the city in County Wicklow. Some popular beaches include **Dollymount,** 5km (3 miles) away; **Sutton,** 11km (6³/₄ miles) away; **Howth,** 15km (9¹/₃ miles) away; and **Portmarnock** and **Malahide,** each 11km (6³/₄ miles) away. In addition, the southern suburb of **Dún Laoghaire,** 11km (6³/₄ miles) away, offers a beach (at Sandycove) and a long bayfront promenade ideal for strolling in the sea air. For more details, inquire at the Dublin Tourism office.

BIRD-WATCHING   The many estuaries, salt marshes, sand flats, and islands near Dublin Bay provide a varied habitat for a number of species. **Rockabill Island,** off the coast at Skerries, is home to an important colony of roseate terns; there is no public access to the island, but the birds can be seen from the shore. **Rogerstown and Malahide estuaries,** on the Northside of Dublin, are wintering grounds for large numbers of brent geese, ducks, and waders. **Sandymount Strand,** on Dublin's south side, has a vast intertidal zone; around dusk in July and August, you can often see large numbers of terns, including visiting roseate terns from Rockabill Island.

But your all-around best bet is a bird sanctuary called Bull Island, also known as the **North Bull,** just north of Dublin city harbor at the suburb of Clontarf. It's not an island at all, but a 3km (2-mile) spit of marshland connected to the mainland by a bridge. It was created by Captain William Bligh, of *Mutiny on the Bounty* fame. Early in the 19th century, he was head of the Port and Docks Board, and he ordered the construction of a harbor wall at the mouth of the River Liffey, in an effort to stop the bay from silting up. In fairly short order, the shifting sands created this small landmass. Its dunes, salt marsh, and extensive intertidal flats provide a unique environment that attracts thousands of seabirds. Hundreds of species have been recorded here, and 40,000 birds shelter and nest here. In winter, these figures are boosted by tens of thousands of visiting migrants from the Arctic Circle, as well as North American spoonbills, little egrets, and sandpipers. Together, they all make a deafening racket. A visitor center is open daily 10:15am to 4:30pm.

FISHING   There are plenty of opportunities for freshwater angling on local rivers, reservoirs, and fisheries. A day's catch might include perch, rudd, pike, salmon, sea trout, brown trout, or freshwater eel. The **Irish Tourist Board** operates a good website dedicated to fishing (**www.discoverireland.ie/what-to-do/activities/angling.aspx**). Options for anglers include fishing for brown trout with the River Dodder Anglers' Club (© **01/ 298-2112**) in southwest County Dublin, and sea fishing on Charles Weston's 36-foot ketch (© **01/843-6239**) off the shores of Malahide, just north of the city. In addition, the **Dublin Angling Initiative,** Balnagowan, Mobhi Boreen, Glasnevin, Dublin 9 (© **087/ 674-0214**), offers a guide—the *Dublin Freshwater Angling Guide,* available for €2 ($3.20)—to tell you everything you'll need to know about local fishing.

GOLF   Dublin is one of the world's great golfing capitals. A quarter of Ireland's courses—including 5 of the top 10—lie within an hour's drive of the city. Visitors are welcome, but phone ahead and make a reservation. The following four courses—two parkland and two links—are among the best 18-hole courses in the Dublin area.

Elm Park Golf & Sports Club ★, Nutley Lane, Donnybrook, Dublin 4 (© **01/269-3438;** www.elmparkgolfclub.ie), is in the residential, privileged south side of Dublin. The beautifully manicured parkland, par-69 course is especially popular with visitors because it is within 6km (3³/₄ miles) of the city center and close to the Jurys, Berkeley

Court, and Four Seasons hotels. Greens fees are €80 ($128) on weekdays, €100 ($160) on weekends.

Portmarnock Golf Club ★★★, Portmarnock, County Dublin (☏ **01/846-2968;** www.portmarnockgolfclub.ie), is respected as one of the finest links courses in Europe. About 16km (10 miles) from the city center on Dublin's Northside, on a spit of land between the Irish Sea and a tidal inlet, this course opened in 1894. Over the years, the par-72 championship course has been the scene of leading tournaments, including the Dunlop Masters (1959, 1965), Canada Cup (1960), Alcan (1970), St. Andrews Trophy (1968), and many an Irish Open. You won't be surprised, then, to find out that fees are a bit pricey. Greens fees are €180 ($288) on weekdays, €215 ($344) on weekends.

Royal Dublin Golf Club ★★, Bull Island, Dollymount, Dublin 3 (☏ **01/833-6346;** www.theroyaldublingolfclub.com), is often compared to St. Andrews. The century-old, par-73 championship seaside links is on an island in Dublin Bay, 4.8km (3 miles) northeast of the city center. Like Portmarnock, it has been rated among the world's top courses and has played host to several Irish Opens. The home base of Ireland's legendary champion Christy O'Connor, Sr., the Royal Dublin is well known for its fine bunkers, close lies, and subtle trappings. Greens fees are €170 ($272).

St. Margaret's Golf & Country Club ★, Skephubble, St. Margaret's, County Dublin (☏ **01/864-0400;** www.stmargaretsgolf.com), is a stunning, par-72 parkland course 4.8km (3 miles) west of Dublin Airport. Though one of Dublin's newest championship golf venues, St. Margaret's has already hosted three international tournaments, including the Irish Open in 2004. Greens fees are around €75 ($120) Monday to Thursday, €90 ($144) Friday to Sunday.

HORSEBACK RIDING   Plenty of riding stables are within easy reach of central Dublin, and prices average about €30 ($48) an hour, with or without instruction. Many stables offer guided trail riding, as well as courses in show jumping, dressage, prehunting, eventing, and cross-country riding. For trail riding through Phoenix Park, **Ashtown Riding Stables** (☏ **01/838-3807**) is ideal. They're in the village of Ashtown, adjoining the park and only 10 minutes by car or bus (no. 37, 38, 39, or 70) from the city center. Among the other riding centers within easy reach of downtown Dublin are **Calliaghstown Riding Centre,** Calliaghstown, Rathcoole, County Dublin (☏ **01/458-8322;** www.calliaghstownriding centre.com), and **Carrickmines Equestrian Centre,** Glenamuck Road, Foxrock, Dublin 18 (☏ **01/295-5990;** www.carrickminesequestrian.ie).

WALKING   For casual walking, the Royal Canal and Grand Canal, which skirt the north and south city centers, respectively, are ideal for seeing the area. Both are marked trails, so you can't get lost, and because they stick to the towpaths of the canals, the paths are flat and easy. Both routes pass a range of small towns and villages that can be used as starting or stopping points.

The walk from Bray (the southern terminus of the DART) to Greystones along the rocky promontory of **Bray Head** is a great excursion, with beautiful views back toward Killiney Bay, Dalkey Island, and Bray. Follow the beachside promenade south through Bray; at the outskirts of town, the promenade turns left and up, beginning the ascent of Bray Head. Shortly after the ascent begins, a trail branches to the left—this is the cliff-side walk, which continues another 5km (3 miles) along the coast to Greystones. From the center of Greystones, a train will take you back to Bray. This is an easy walk, about 2 hours each way. Don't attempt this walk in bad weather or strong winds, as the cliff-side path will be quite treacherous.

Dalkey Hill and **Killiney Hill** drop steeply into the sea and command great views of Killiney Bay, Bray Head, and Sugarloaf Mountain. To get there, leave the Dalkey DART station, head into the center of Dalkey and then south on Dalkey Avenue (at the post office). About 1km (half a mile) from the post office, you'll pass a road ascending through fields on your left—this is the entrance to the Dalkey Hill Park. From the parking lot, climb a series of steps to the top of Dalkey Hill; from here you can see the expanse of the bay, the Wicklow Hills in the distance, and the obelisk topping nearby Killiney Hill. If you continue on to the obelisk, there is a trail leading from there down the seaward side to Vico Road, another lovely place for a seaside walk. It's about 1km (¹/₂ mile) from the parking lot to Killiney Hill.

WATERSPORTS   Certified level-one and level-two instruction and equipment rental for three watersports—kayaking, sailing, and windsurfing—are available at the **Surfdock Centre,** Grand Canal Dock Yard, Ringsend, Dublin 4 (© **01/668-3945;** www.surfdock. ie). The center has 17 hectares (42 acres) of enclosed fresh water for its courses. It's open from June to September.

7 SPECTATOR SPORTS

GAELIC SPORTS   If your schedule permits, try to get to a **Gaelic football** or **hurling** match—the only indigenously Irish games and two of the fastest-moving sports in the world. Gaelic football is vaguely a cross between soccer and American football; you can move the ball with either your hands or feet. **Hurling** is a lightning-speed game in which 30 men use heavy sticks to fling a hard leather ball called a *sliotar*—think field hockey meets lacrosse. Both amateur sports are played every weekend throughout the summer at various local fields, culminating in September with the **All-Ireland Finals,** the Irish version of the Super Bowl. For schedules and admission fees, phone the **Gaelic Athletic Association,** Croke Park, Jones Road, Dublin 3 (© **01/836-3222;** www.gaa.ie).

GREYHOUND RACING   Races are held throughout the year at **Shelbourne Park Greyhound Stadium,** Southlotts Road, Dublin 4 (© **01/668-3502**), and **Harold's Cross Stadium,** 151 Harold's Cross Rd., Dublin 6 (© **01/497-1081**). For a complete schedule and details for races throughout Ireland, contact **Bord na gCon (Greyhound Board),** Limerick (© **061/316788;** www.igb.ie).

HORSE RACING   The closest racecourse to the city center is the **Leopardstown Race Course,** off the Stillorgan road (N11), Foxrock, Dublin 18 (© **01/289-0500;** www. leopardstown.com). This modern facility with all-weather, glass-enclosed spectator stands is 9.7km (6 miles) south of the city center. Racing meets—mainly steeplechases, but also a few flats—are scheduled throughout the year, two or three times a month.

POLO   With the Dublin Mountains as a backdrop, polo is played from May to mid-September on the green fields of Phoenix Park, on Dublin's west side. Matches take place on Wednesday evenings and Saturday and Sunday afternoons. Admission is free. For full details, contact the **All Ireland Polo Club,** Phoenix Park, Dublin 8 (© **01/677-6248**), or check the sports pages of the newspapers.

8 SHOPPING

In recent years, Dublin has surprised everyone by becoming a good shopping town. You'll find few bargains, but for your money you will get excellent craftsmanship in the form of hand-woven wool blankets and clothes in a vivid array of colors, Belleek china and Waterford crystal, and chic clothes from the seemingly limitless line of Dublin designers.

While the hub of mainstream shopping south of the Liffey is **Grafton Street,** crowned by the city's most fashionable department store, Brown Thomas (known as BT), and the jeweler Weirs. There's much better shopping on the smaller streets radiating out from Grafton, such as **Duke, Dawson, Nassau,** and **Wicklow.** On these streets you'll find small, interesting shops that specialize in books, handicrafts, jewelry, gifts, and clothing. For clothes, look out for tiny **Cow's Lane,** off Lord Edward Street—it is popular with those in the know for its excellent clothing boutiques selling the works of local designers. Also in Grafton's penumbra are **William Street South, Castle Market,** and **Drury Street,** all of which have smart boutiques and irresistible tiny shops. On William Street South, look out for the **Powerscourt Townhouse Centre,** a small, elegant shopping center in a grand Georgian town house. It has relaxing cafes, antiques shops, shoe shops, and the top-floor Design Centre, which sells works by some of Ireland's top designers. Not far away, the **George's Street Arcade** is a marvelous clutter of bohemian jewelry, used books, and vintage clothes.

Generally, Dublin shops are open from 9am to 6pm Monday to Saturday, and Thursday until 9pm. Many of the larger shops have Sunday hours from noon to 6pm.

Major department stores include, on the Northside, **Arnotts,** 12 Henry St., Dublin 1 (© **01/805-0400**), and the marvelously traditional **Clerys,** Lower O'Connell Street, Dublin 1 (© **01/878-6000**); and, on the south side, **Brown Thomas,** 15–20 Grafton St., Dublin 2 (© **01/605-6666**).

Dublin also has several clusters of shops in **multistory malls** or ground-level **arcades,** ideal for indoor shopping on rainy days. On the Northside, these include the **ILAC Centre,** off Henry Street, Dublin 1, and the **Jervis Shopping Centre,** off Henry Street, Dublin 1. On the south side, there's the **Royal Hibernian Way,** 49–50 Dawson St., Dublin 2; **St. Stephen's Green Centre,** at the top of Grafton Street, Dublin 2; and the aforementioned **Powerscourt Townhouse Centre,** 59 William St. S., Dublin 2.

ART

Combridge Fine Arts In business for more than 100 years, this shop features works by modern Irish artists, as well as quality reproductions of classic Irish art. 17 William St. S., Dublin 2. © **01/677-4652.** www.cfa.ie. DART: Pearse. Bus: 15A, 15B, 15C, 55, or 83.

Davis Gallery One block north of the Liffey, this shop offers a wide selection of Irish watercolors and oil paintings, with emphasis on Dublin scenes, wildlife, and flora. 11 Capel St., Dublin 1. © **01/872-6969.** Bus: 34, 70, or 80.

Green on Red This gallery behind Pearse Street DART station is a little off the tourist track, but it's worth the effort, for some say it's Dublin's finest contemporary art gallery. The gallery represents top local and international contemporary artists including Fergus Feehily, Martin & Hobbs, Gerard Byrne, and Bridget Riley. 26–28 Lombard St., Dublin 2. © **01/671-3414.** www.greenonredgallery.com. DART: Pearse.

Greene's Bookshop Ltd. Established in 1843, this shop near Trinity College is one of Dublin's treasures for scholarly bibliophiles. It's chock-full of new and secondhand books on every topic from religion to the modern novel. The catalog of Irish-interest books is issued five to six times a year. 16 Clare St., Dublin 2. ℭ **01/676-2554.** www.greenesbookshop.com. DART: Pearse. Bus: 5, 7A, 8, or 62.

Hodges Figgis This enormous bookstore has books on virtually every topic and is Dublin's go-to store for absolutely everything literary. It's so big you can practically get lost in it. It's well worth an afternoon's wander. 56–58 Dawson St., Dublin 2. ℭ **01/677-4754.** DART: Pearse. Bus: 10, 11A, 11B, 13, or 20B.

CERAMICS

Louis Mulcahy The ceramic creations of Louis Mulcahy are internationally renowned. For years he has been exporting his work throughout Ireland and the rest of the world from his studio on the Dingle Peninsula. This modest shop across from the Shelbourne hotel gives him a base in Dublin. In addition to pottery, he designs furniture, lighting, and hand-painted silk and cotton lampshades. 46 Dawson St., Dublin 2. ℭ **01/670-9311.** www.louismulcahy.com. DART: Pearse. Bus: 10, 11A, 11B, 13, or 20B.

CHINA & CRYSTAL

If you're specifically looking for Waterford crystal, don't bother shopping around because it has fixed pricing. You'll find the best selections at **Brown Thomas** (Grafton St., Dublin 2), **Weirs** (Grafton St., Dublin 2), and **House of Ireland** (Nassau St., Dublin 2). If brand names aren't important, check out other native crystal makers, including Galway, Tipperary, Cavan, and Tyrone. Don't forget to get your cash-back forms if you want to reclaim the VAT.

CRAFT STORES

Avoca Handweavers This place is a wonderland of vivid colors, soft, intricately woven fabrics, blankets, throws, light woolen sweaters, children's clothes, and toys, all in a delightful shopping environment spread over three floors near Trinity College. All the fabrics are woven in the Vale of Avoca in the Wicklow Mountains. There's also pottery, jewelry, art, food, and adorable little things you really don't need, but can't live without. Hands down, this is one of the best stores in Dublin. The top-floor **cafe** is a great place for lunch (p. 136). 11–13 Suffolk St., Dublin 2. ℭ **01/677-4215.** www.avoca.ie. Bus: All An Lar (cross-city) buses.

Powerscourt Townhouse Centre Housed in a restored 1774 town house, this four-story complex consists of a central sky-lit courtyard and more than 60 boutiques, craft shops, art galleries, snack bars, wine bars, and restaurants. The wares include all kinds of crafts, antiques, paintings, prints, ceramics, leatherwork, jewelry, clothing, hand-dipped chocolates, and farmhouse cheeses. 59 William St. S., Dublin 2. ℭ **01/671-7000.** www.powerscourtcentre.com. Bus: 10, 11A, 11B, 13, 16A, 19A, 20B, 22A, 55, or 83.

Tower Craft Design Centre Alongside the Grand Canal, this beautifully restored 1862 sugar refinery now houses a nest of craft workshops where you can watch the artisans at work. The merchandise ranges from fine-art greeting cards and hand-marbled stationery to pewter, ceramics, pottery, knitwear, hand-painted silks, copperplate etchings, all-wool wall hangings, silver and gold Celtic jewelry, and heraldic gifts. Pearse St. (off Grand Canal Quay), Dublin 2. ℭ **01/677-5655.** Limited free parking. DART: Pearse. Bus: 2 or 3.

Whichcraft If you're serious about taking home quality, contemporary crafts, this is an essential stop for the best contemporary art from around Ireland. All kinds of crafts are represented, from wooden bowls, hand-woven baskets, and rocking horses to pottery, jewelry, and ironwork. 4 Cow's Lane, Dublin 2. ℂ **01/671-3469.** Bus: 50, 54A, 56A, 65, 65A, 77, 77A, 123, or 150.

FASHION
See also "Knitwear," below.

Men's Fashion
Alias Tom This was Dublin's best small, men's designer shop until BT2 opened. The emphasis is Italian (Gucci, Prada, Armani), but the range covers other chic designers from the rest of Europe and America. Prices are exorbitant. Duke House, Duke St., Dublin 2. ℂ **01/671 5443.** DART: Pearse. Bus: 10, 11A, 11B, 13, or 20B.

BT2 This offshoot of Brown Thomas, the high-end department store, which is across the street on Grafton, is the best shop in Dublin for the hippest designer labels for both men and women. The look is sportier, more casual, and geared to the younger, hopelessly cool set. The prices are nearly as crazy as in BT. Grafton St., Dublin 2. ℂ **01/605-6666.** Bus: All An Lar (cross-city) buses.

Kevin & Howlin For more than a half-century, this has been the best place in town for hand-woven Donegal tweed garments. The selection includes suits, overcoats, jackets, scarves, vests, and myriad hats—everything from Patch caps and Gatsby fedoras to Sherlock Holmes–style deerstalkers and the ubiquitous Paddy hats. 31 Nassau St., Dublin 2. ℂ **01/677-0257.** www.kevinandhowlin.com. DART: Pearse. Bus: 7, 8, 10, 11, or 46A.

Women's Fashion
BT2 Brown Thomas's sister shop, located across the street, is the best place in town for A-list designer labels. BT2 targets a younger but no less label-conscious crowd than BT—think style-obsessed Trustifarians and yuppies and you've got the clientele in a nutshell. Grafton St., Dublin 2. ℂ **01/605-6666.** Bus: All An Lar (cross-city) buses.

Claire Garvey The brightest luminary in Old City is a 34-year-old Dublin native with a talent for creating romantic, dramatic, and feminine clothing with Celtic flair. A favorite designer of Irish divas Enya and Sinéad O'Connor, Garvey transforms hand-dyed velvet and silk into sumptuous garments that beg to be worn on special occasions. Her one-of-a-kind bijou handbags are a white-hot fashion accessory. 6 The Music Hall, Cow's Lane, Dublin 2. ℂ **01/671-7287.** www.clairegarvey.com. Bus: 50, 54A, 56A, 65, 65A, 77, 77A, 123, or 150.

Design Centre This is the city's best one-stop shop if you want to find all of Ireland's hottest contemporary designers—including Louise Kennedy, Mary Gregory, Karen Millen, Mary Grant, and Sharon Hoey—under one roof. Prices are generally high, but there are good bargains to be had during sale seasons and on the seconds rack. Powerscourt Townhouse Centre, Dublin 2. ℂ **01/679-5718.** DART: Pearse. Bus: 10, 11A, 11B, 13, or 20B.

Jenny Vander This is where actresses and supermodels come to find extraordinary and stylish antique clothing. There are plenty of jeweled frocks, vintage day wear, and stunning costume jewelry filling the clothing racks and display cases. Overall, it's a fabulous place to shop for one-of-a-kind pieces. 20 Market Arcade, S. Great Georges St., Dublin 2. ℂ **01/677-0406.** DART: Pearse. Bus: 10, 11A, 11B, 13, or 20B.

Louise Kennedy This glamorous and sophisticated designer is a longtime favorite of Meryl Streep, former British first lady Cherie Blair, and Carol Vorderman. Dublin native and popstress/actress/model Samantha Mumba has signed on to be the body and face of Kennedy's sumptuous collection. Her elegant showroom carries her clothing, accessories, and home collections, as well as Philip Treacy hats, Lulu Guinness handbags, Lindley furniture, and other items of perfect taste. 56 Merrion Sq., Dublin 2. ℭ **01/662-0056.** DART: Pearse. Bus: 5, 7A, or 8.

Tulle This place is small but mighty when it comes to contemporary clothing designs. It's filled with works by hot new designers like Joanne Hynes and international designers like Pink Soda and Stella Forest. 28 George's St. Arcade, Dublin 2. ℭ **01/679-9115.** Bus: 10, 11A, 11B, or 13.

JEWELRY

Costelloe & Costelloe This charming little shop is filled with irresistible little trinkets, handbags, colorful wraps, and jewelry, much of which is heartwarmingly affordable. 14A Chatham St., Temple Bar, Dublin 2. ℭ **01/671-4209.** www.costelloeandcostelloe.com. DART: Tara St. Bus: 68, 69, or 86.

DESIGNyard This beautiful emporium showcases exquisite, often affordable work from the best contemporary Irish jewelry designers. All exhibited pieces are for sale, and you may also make an appointment to commission an original work of Irish applied art and design. Cow's Lane, Temple Bar, Dublin 8. ℭ **01/474-1011.** Bus: All An Lar (cross-city) buses.

Rhinestones This shop glitters, but don't be fooled—the reasonable prices let you know it's not really gold. Vivien Walsh is considered Ireland's top designer of costume jewelry, and the shop is a seductive place where her contemporary jewelry with an antique feel shines. 18 Andrews St., Dublin 2. ℭ **01/475-5031.** Bus: All An Lar (cross-city) buses.

Weir and Sons Established in 1869, this is the granddaddy of Dublin's fine jewelry shops. It sells new and antique jewelry as well as silver, china, and crystal. There is a second branch at the ILAC Centre, Henry Street (ℭ **01/872-9588**). 96 Grafton St., Dublin 2. ℭ **01/677-9678.** www.weirandsons.ie. DART: Pearse. Bus: 10, 11A, 11B, 13, or 20B.

KNITWEAR

Blarney Woollen Mills This branch of the successful Cork-based enterprise stands opposite the south side of Trinity College. Known for its competitive prices, it stocks a wide range of woolen knitwear made in Blarney, as well as Irish-made crystal, china, pottery, and souvenirs. 21–23 Nassau St., Dublin 2. ℭ **01/671-0068.** www.blarney.ie. DART: Pearse. Bus: 5, 7A, 8, 15A, 15B, 46, 55, 62, 63, 83, or 84.

Dublin Woollen Mills Since 1888, this shop has been a leading source of Aran sweaters, vests, hats, jackets, and scarves, as well as lamb's-wool sweaters, kilts, ponchos, and tweeds at competitive prices. The shop is on the Northside next to the Ha'penny Bridge. 41–42 Lower Ormond Quay, Dublin 1. ℭ **01/828-0301.** www.woollenmills.com. Bus: 70 or 80.

Monaghan's Established in 1960 and operated by two generations of the Monaghan family, this store is a prime source of cashmere sweaters for men and women. It has a good selection of colors, sizes, and styles. There are also Aran knits, lamb's wool, crochet, and Shetland wool products. There's another store at 4–5 Royal Hibernian Way, off Dawson Street (ℭ **01/679-4451**). 15–17 Grafton Arcade, Grafton St., Dublin 2. ℭ **01/677-0823.** DART: Pearse. Bus: 10, 11A, 11B, 13, or 20B.

(Tips) **Going to Market**

The traditional Dublin method of buying virtually everything has always been the weekly market. There were weekly vegetable markets, bread markets, meat markets, fish markets . . . in fact, there was a time when there was almost no need to go to the store at all. Look around sleek, modern, retail-loving, credit card–wielding Dublin, and it appears that things have changed, but don't be fooled. Just underneath that facade the truth can be found—Dubliners still love a good market. In fact, there are great markets around, if you know where to look.

There are workaday markets like the **Moore Street Market,** where fruit, vegetables, fish, and bread are sold every weekday from 10am to 2pm, on Moore Street on the Northside. Then there are more upscale, gourmet markets, like the **Temple Bar Food Market** every weekend from 10am to 5pm in Meeting House Square. This is where to go for farmhouse cheeses and fresh, home-made breads, jams, and chutneys. For books, try the **Temple Bar Book Market,** weekends in Temple Bar Square from 11am to 4pm—every imaginable topic is wrapped in its pages, and prices are very good.

If you're looking for antiques at reasonable prices, head south of the city center to the **Blackberry Fair** (42 Rathmines Rd., south of the Grand Canal). This market every weekend from 10am to 2pm gathers equal amounts of discoveries and discardables, and weeding through it all is half the fun.

Finally, if it's all about fashion for you, try the **Cow's Lane Market** on Cow's Lane in the Old City. Here local designers try out their work on a savvy crowd, who pack in knowing they'll get the clothes at much lower prices than in a boutique. It's held every Saturday from 10am to 4pm.

TRADITIONAL IRISH MUSIC

The Celtic Note Second only to Claddagh Records (below), this is a terrific source of recorded Irish music in Dublin. The staff is experienced and helpful, and you can listen to a CD before purchasing it. You'll pay full price here, but you're likely to find what you're looking for. 12 Nassau St., Dublin 2. ℂ **01/670-4157.** DART: Pearse. Bus: 5, 7A, 15A, 15B, 46, 55, 62, 63, 83, or 84.

Claddagh Records Renowned among insiders in traditional Irish music circles, this is where to find "the genuine article" in traditional music and perhaps discover a new favorite. Not only is the staff knowledgeable and enthusiastic about new artists, but they're also able to tell you which venues and pubs are hosting the best music sessions that week. Dame St., Dublin 2. ℂ **01/677-8943.** www.claddaghrecords.com. Bus: 50, 50A, 54, 56, or 77.

9 DUBLIN AFTER DARK

Nightlife in Dublin is a mixed bag of traditional old pubs, where the likes of Joyce and Behan once imbibed and where traditional Irish music is often reeling away, and cool modern bars, where the repetitive rhythms of techno now fill the air and the crowd

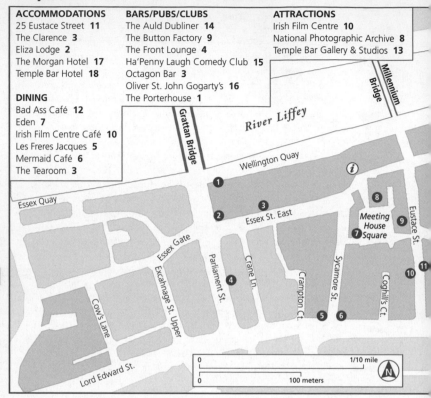

ACCOMMODATIONS
25 Eustace Street **11**
The Clarence **3**
Eliza Lodge **2**
The Morgan Hotel **17**
Temple Bar Hotel **18**

DINING
Bad Ass Café **12**
Eden **7**
Irish Film Centre Café **10**
Les Freres Jacques **5**
Mermaid Café **6**
The Tearoom **3**

BARS/PUBS/CLUBS
The Auld Dubliner **14**
The Button Factory **9**
The Front Lounge **4**
Ha'Penny Laugh Comedy Club **15**
Octagon Bar **3**
Oliver St. John Gogarty's **16**
The Porterhouse **1**

ATTRACTIONS
Irish Film Centre **10**
National Photographic Archive **8**
Temple Bar Gallery & Studios **13**

knows more about Prada than the Pogues. There's little in the way of crossover, although there are a couple of quieter bars and a few with a rock music angle, so you take your pick. Aside from the eternal elderly pubs, things change rapidly on the nightlife scene, so pick up a copy of *InDublin* and the *Event Guide* at local cafes and shops if you're looking for the latest club scene. Both have good listings.

The award-winning website of the *Irish Times* (**www.ireland.com**) offers a "what's on" daily guide to cinema, theater, music, and whatever else you're up for. The **Dublin Events Guide,** at www.dublinevents.com, also provides a comprehensive listing of the week's entertainment possibilities.

Advance bookings for most large concerts, plays, and so forth can be made through **Ticketmaster Ireland** (② **01/648-6060;** www.ticketmaster.ie), with ticket centers in most HMV music stores, as well as at the Dublin Tourism Centre, Suffolk Street, Dublin 2.

THE PUB SCENE

In *Ulysses,* James Joyce referred to the puzzle of trying to cross Dublin without passing a pub; his characters quickly abandoned the quest as fruitless, preferring to stop and sample a few instead. You may want to do the same, so here are some of the city's most distinctive.

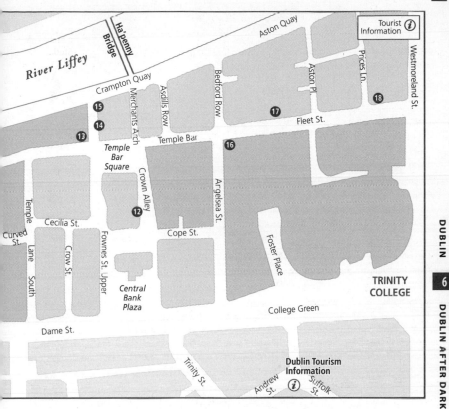

Pubs for Conversation & Atmosphere

Davy Byrnes   In *Ulysses*, Leopold Bloom describes this place as a "moral pub," and stops in for a Gorgonzola sandwich and a glass of burgundy. It has drawn poets, writers, and readers ever since. It dates from 1873, when Davy Byrnes first opened the doors—he presided over it for more than 50 years, and visitors can still see his likeness on one of the turn-of-the-20th-century murals hanging over the bar. 21 Duke St. (off Grafton St.), Dublin 2. ✆ 01/677-5217. www.davybyrnes.com.

Doheny and Nesbitt   Competition is stiff, but this may well be the best-looking traditional pub in town. The Victorian bar houses two fine old "snugs"—small rooms behind the main bar where women could have a drink out of sight of men in days of old—and a restaurant that's good for traditional Irish food. 5 Lower Baggot St., Dublin 2. ✆ 01/676-2945.

Grogan's Castle Lounge   This eclectic place is a bit run down around the edges, but it's a proper local pub, not heavily frequented by tourists. Its crowd includes local writers and artists, as well as people who just live around the corner. It's a good place to get in touch with local nightlife. 15 William St. S., Dublin 2. ✆ 01/677-9320.

---

172 **Kehoe's** This tiny traditional bar is best during the day when it's not too crowded and you can take in its old-fashioned character, eavesdrop on its chatty regulars, and settle in for a pint or two in its comfortable snugs. 9 S. Anne St., Dublin 2. ℭ 01/677-8312.

The Long Hall This is Doheny and Nesbitt's main competition in the "Prettiest Pub" contest. With a beautiful Victorian decor of filigree-edged mirrors, polished dark woods, and traditional snugs, this place is like a theater of beer. The atmosphere is great and bartenders pour a good pint. 51 S. Great George's St., Dublin 2. ℭ 01/475-1590.

Impressions

I formed a new group called Alcoholics Unanimous. If you don't feel like a drink, you ring another member and he comes over to persuade you.
—Richard Harris

McDaid's This was Brendan Behan's favorite hangout—well, one of them at least; he had so many—back in his Dublin drinking days, and it still has a literary bent. It's well on the tourist track these days, and thus has lost some of its cool cache. Still, it's got a good atmosphere. 3 Harry St., off Grafton St., Dublin 2. ℭ 01/679-4395.

Neary's Adjacent to the back door of the Gaiety Theatre, this celebrated enclave is a favorite with stage folk and theatergoers. Its pink-and-gray marble bar and Victorian touches, like the brass hands that support the globe lanterns by the entrance, give it a touch of class. 1 Chatham St., Dublin 2. ℭ 01/677-8596.

O'Neill's This friendly place is the pub equivalent of quicksand—you walk in for a quick pint, and before you know it, it's midnight and you've got 20 new best friends. It's big and noisy, but it's made up of a series of smaller rooms and that makes it a pleasant place for conversation. It gets a bit boisterous on the weekends, though. 2 Suffolk St., Dublin 2. ℭ 01/679-3656. www.oneillsbar.com.

The Porterhouse This is Dublin's first microbrewery pub and it's well worth a visit. Right in the middle of the action in Temple Bar, it offers a constantly changing range of its own ales, lagers, and stouts in a laid-back folksy atmosphere with plenty of room to sit. With a good menu of Irish food (Irish stew, bangers and mash, steak pie) it makes a reasonably priced choice for lunch as well. 16–18 Parliament St., Dublin 2. ℭ 01/679-8847. www.porterhousebrewco.com.

Stag's Head Mounted stags' heads and eight stag-themed stained-glass windows dominate the decor in this grand old Victorian pub, but it doesn't stop there. There are also wrought-iron chandeliers, polished Aberdeen granite, old barrels, and ceiling-high mirrors. Look for the stag sign inlaid into the sidewalk. This place is a classic. 1 Dame Court (off Dame St.), Dublin 2. ℭ 01/679-3687.

Pubs for Traditional & Folk Music

The Auld Dubliner This is a good pub for people who don't normally go to pubs. It's in Temple Bar, so it's central. It's completely relaxed, with bands playing traditional music upstairs, Irish stew on the stove, and quiet pints at the downstairs pub. 24–25 Temple Bar, Dublin 2. ℭ 01/677-0527.

Brazen Head In its time, revolutions were plotted in this brass-filled, lantern-lit pub. The Head was first licensed in 1661, which makes it one of the oldest pubs in Ireland. Nestled on the south bank of the River Liffey, it is at the end of a cobblestone courtyard and was once the meeting place of rebels Robert Emmet and Wolfe Tone. A full a la carte

DUBLIN

6

DUBLIN AFTER DARK

(Tips) **Listen to the Music . . .**

When you're out for a night of traditional Irish/folk music, you should know that some pubs charge and some do not; if the band is playing informally in the main bar, as often happens, there's no charge, although they will probably pass a hat at some point, and everybody should toss in a few euros. If there is a charge, the music usually happens in a separate room from the main pub, and the charge will be noted on the door; usually it's €5 to €7 ($8–$11), and you pay as you go in, cash only.

Tipping and buying CDs happens in exactly the same fashion as in the U.S. There will be a big jar or an open guitar case with change already in it as an enticement, so you toss in a few coins, and they nod. If they're selling CDs they'll make sure you know about it! (They'll probably autograph them too, after the set. Maybe the band *won't* be the next U2, but you never know!)

menu is offered and traditional music sessions start at 9:30pm nightly. 20 Lower Bridge St., Dublin 8. (C) **01/679-5186.**

The Cobblestone This is the most Irish of Irish pubs, with a musicians' corner downstairs where traditional Irish music is played for free and a proper music hall upstairs where you have to buy tickets, but the bands are top-notch. It's one of the places where the locals go to hear music, so expect to find none of what they call "paddy-whackery." 77 King St. N., Dublin 7. (C) **01/872-1799.**

O'Donoghue's (Overrated) Tucked between St. Stephen's Green and Merrion Street, this enclave is widely heralded as the granddaddy of traditional-music pubs. A spontaneous session is likely to erupt at almost any time of the day or night, but it's become very touristy, and we don't consider it local or authentic in terms of clientele. They put on a show for tourists, and it's a bit dull compared to some of the more authentic places. 15 Merrion Row, Dublin 2. (C) **01/676-2807.** www.odonoghues.ie.

Oliver St. John Gogarty In the heart of Temple Bar and named for one of Ireland's literary greats, this pub has an inviting old-world atmosphere, with shelves of empty bottles, stacks of dusty books, a horseshoe-shaped bar, and old barrels for seats. There are traditional-music sessions almost every night from 9 to 11pm, as well as Saturday at 4:30pm, and Sunday from noon to 2pm. 58–59 Fleet St., Dublin 2. (C) **01/671-1822.** www. gogartys.ie.

BARS & NIGHTCLUBS

Over the last few years, cocktail bars and nightclubs have been springing up around Dublin like daffodils in spring. The nightclub scene is confoundingly complex. One club could be a gay fetish scene one night and techno-pop dance the next, so you have to stay on your toes. The first rule is to get the latest listings from local sources (see the introduction to "Dublin After Dark" above for options).

The hottest clubs have a "strict" (read: unfriendly) door policy of admitting only "regulars." Your chances of getting past the door increase if you're female and wear your hippest clothes.

> **(Tips) Staying Up Late**
>
> Traditionally, pubs close quite early in Ireland (at 11pm in winter, 11:30pm in summer), and for many, that's just too soon to call it a night. If you're in that group, you might want to crawl to one of the city's many late-night pubs and bars. These boozers have received legal permission to remain open after hours, usually until 2 or 3am.
>
> One popular late-nighter for the 18-to-25 set is the **Capitol,** 2 Aungier St., Dublin 2 (℡ **01/475-7166**).
>
> After-hours pubs that attract the young and hip but are still congenial for those over 25 include **Whelan's,** 25 Wexford St., Dublin 2 (℡ **01/478-0766**), and the second-oldest pub in Dublin, the **Bleeding Horse,** 24–25 Camden St., Dublin 2 (℡ **01/475-2705**).
>
> For the over-30 late crowd, try **Major Tom's,** South King Street, Dublin 2 (℡ **01/478-3266;** www.majortoms.com), or **Sinnotts,** South King Street, Dublin 2 (℡ **01/478-4698**).

Cover charges tend to fluctuate from place to place and from night to night and even from person to person (some people can't buy their way in, while others glide in gratis). Cover charges range from nothing to €20 ($32) and vary from one night to the next.

Bars for Mixing, Mingling & Chatting

These are modern cocktail bars, where the kind of financially successful, under-40 person who wouldn't be caught dead in a pub goes for a drink.

Ba Mizu   This bar draws the young, glamorous set. The clientele includes a regular smattering of models (both male and female) and trendy urbanites. Powerscourt Townhouse Centre, William St. S., Dublin 2. ℡ 01/674-6712. www.bamizu.com.

The Bank on College Green   As the name implies, this bar is in a converted bank building, and that is somehow appropriate, given that the crowd is made up largely of professionals in very expensive shoes. It's got a good reputation, and it's a gorgeous, vast space. 20–22 College Green, Dublin 2. ℡ 01/677-0677. www.bankoncollegegreen.com.

Bruxelles   This is one of Dublin's late-night bars, staying open until 2:30am on weekends, and its crowd tends to be well lubricated and therefore overly friendly. It's not a beautiful place, but it's very popular with locals. 7–8 Harry St., off Grafton St., Dublin 2. ℡ 01/677-5362.

Café en Seine   This vast bar packs in thousands of young, well-dressed, well-paid local professionals, and yet it never seems crowded. It's a gorgeous turn-of-the-20th-century building, with plenty of architectural detail, but nobody who comes here regularly cares. They're here for the booze and each other. 40 Dawson St., Dublin 2. ℡ 01/677-4567.

Cocoon   This is a small space with lots of straight lines and open spaces, and with big windows designed so that those outside can admire your new outfit. The color scheme is chocolate and cream; it's filled with low tables, tiny candles, and leather stools; and it's all about how good you look. Duke Lane, off Grafton St., Dublin 2. ℡ 01/679-6259. www.cocoon.ie.

The Market Bar   This is what they call around here a "superpub," but it's not really a pub at all, just a big, laid-back bar, with a soaring ceiling, gorgeous design, a good beer and wine list, and friendly bar staff. This is the kind of place where you could sit in the late afternoon and have a solitary pint and nobody would bother you. Its no-music policy means that it's quiet enough to hear yourself drink. 14a Fade St., off S. Great George's St., Dublin 2. © 01/613-9094. www.marketbar.ie.

Octagon Bar   This incredibly trendy bar on the ground floor of the Clarence hotel is one of the hottest places in town. It's got an eight-sided bar, which the bartenders handle with aplomb, and you don't have to be rich or beautiful to get in the door. There's a quieter back room and prices are not as high as they might be. It's a favorite celebrity hangout in Dublin. The Clarence Hotel, 6–8 Wellington Quay, Dublin 2. © 01/407-0800. www. theclarence.ie.

Dance Clubs

Lillie's Bordello   Open more than a decade and still the hippest of them all, Lillie's breaks the rule that you've got to be new to be hot. Paintings of nudes hanging on whorehouse-red walls is the look that's made Lillie's a surprisingly unraunchy icon of kitsch. It has a well-deserved reputation for posers and boy-band celebrities, and the door policy can best be described as callous, except on Sundays. If you don't feel like dancing, head for "the Library," whose floor-to-ceiling bookcases and well-worn leather Chesterfields evoke a Victorian gentlemen's club. Open daily from 11pm to 3am. Adam Court, off Grafton St., Dublin 2. © 01/679-9204. www.lilliesbordello.ie.

Rí-Rá   The name means "uproar" in Irish, and it's appropriate. Though trendy, Rí-Rá has a friendlier door policy than most of its competition, so this may be the place to try first. Open nightly from 11:30pm to 4am or later. Dame Court, Dublin 2. © 01/671-1220. www.rira.ie.

Spy Club   Fashionable 30-somethings love this lounge bar, where the emphasis is off dance and firmly on socializing. The look begins with a classical, 18th-century town house with mile-high, corniced ceilings. Next, add Greco-Roman friezes and pared-down, contemporary furnishings. Need more drama? The VIP room's focal point is a photo of a woman in the buff riding a tiger pelt—an in-your-face wink at the Celtic tiger. Saturday is electric pop night; Sunday is gay night. Open nightly from 7pm to 3am. Powerscourt Townhouse Centre, William St. S., Dublin 2. © 01/677-0014.

Traffic   Opposite Arnott's department store, this urban-cool bar and club covers three floors. Music is provided by a mix of Dublin DJs and international talent. By day, the mood is fresh and funky; after hours, things get hotter. 54 Middle Abbey St., Dublin 1. © 01/873-4800.

Voodoo Lounge   Partly owned by New York's Fun Lovin' Criminals, this hip Northside joint is a hard-core music and dance bar, and a popular late-night hangout for those who are not into the normal techno-pop mix. Given its roots, it's unsurprising that the music here is the latest and best stuff around, with an emphasis on hip-hop and R&B. This place isn't pretty, but it's cool. 38 Arran Quay, Dublin 7. © 01/873-6013.

COMEDY CLUBS

Besides the favorite clubs listed below, **Vicar Street** (see the box, "Smaller Concert Venues," below) tends to get many of the international comics. As always, check the latest listings in magazines for details. Admission ranges from €5 to €20 ($8–$32) depending on the act and the night.

Ha'Penny Laugh Comedy Club Ha'Penny plays host to some of Ireland's funniest people, many of whom are in theater. "The Battle of the Axe" is a weekly show in which comedians, singers, songwriters, musicians, actors, and others storm the open mic in pursuit of the Lucky Duck Award. Ha'penny Bridge Inn, Merchant's Arch, 42 Wellington Quay, Dublin 2. ℂ 01/677-0616.

International Bar This virtually legendary bar hosts comedy clubs 3 nights a week: Thursdays and Saturdays, it's Murphy's International Comedy Club, and Wednesdays, it's the Comedy Cellar (which, you'll be unsurprised to learn, is held upstairs). While Murphy's International has more established comedians, the Cellar has the young and unpredictable ones. 23 Wicklow St., Dublin 2. ℂ 01/677-9250.

DINNER SHOWS & TRADITIONAL IRISH ENTERTAINMENT

Abbey Tavern After you've ordered an a la carte dinner, the show—authentic Irish ballad music, with its blend of fiddles, pipes, tin whistles, and spoons—costs €20 ($32), which includes an Irish coffee. The price of a full dinner and show starts at around €60 ($96). The box office is open Monday to Saturday from 9am to 5pm. Dinner is at 7pm, and shows start at 9pm. There are shows nightly in the summer; in the off season, call ahead to find out the show nights. Abbey Rd., Howth, County Dublin. ℂ 01/839-0307.

Cultúrlann na hÉireann This is the home of Comhaltas Ceoltoiri Éireann, an Irish cultural organization that has been the prime mover in encouraging Irish traditional music. The programs include *céilí* dances, informal recitals, and full-blown music festivals. They also hold regular "tempo sessions" (jam sessions) every Tuesday at 9:15pm, which musicians of all abilities are free to join in (so long as you can hold a tune!). No reservations are necessary for any of the events. 32 Belgrave Sq., Monkstown, County Dublin. ℂ 01/280-0295. www.comhaltas.com. Tickets for céilís average €5–€10 ($8–$16), informal music €2.50 ($4), shows €20 ($32). DART: Monkstown. Bus: 7, 7A, or 8.

THE GAY & LESBIAN SCENE

The gay scene in Dublin has expanded by leaps and bounds in the last decade, from absolutely nothing at all, to small but sturdy. Due to the country's traditional conservatism, it's unlikely this will ever be an Ibiza-level gay zone, but at least there are high-quality gay bars and regular gay nights at local dance clubs. Hotels accept same-sex couples without raising an eyebrow, unlike in years past. However, the aforementioned conservatism means that it's not a great idea for same-sex couples to hold hands or cuddle on the street, and keeping a low profile when wandering with your gay friends from restaurant to bar isn't a bad idea. Think small-town America, and you'll get the zeitgeist. The tolerance here only goes so far.

Cover charges range from €5 to €20 ($8–$32), depending on the club or venue, with discounts for students and seniors.

Check the *Gay Community News* (www.gcn.ie) or **Gay Ireland Online** (www.gay-ireland.com) to find out what's going to on during your stay. You can also try **Ireland's Pink Pages** (www.pink-pages.org) to find specific businesses. Folks on the help line **Gay Switchboard Dublin** (ℂ 01/872-1055) can direct you to activities of particular interest.

Since 1994, LGBTQ people have been stopping by the **Outhouse** (105 Capel St.; 01/873-4932; www.outhouse.ie) for information, advice, and a cup of tea or coffee. There's a handy cafe, meeting rooms (groups from AA to Gay Trekkies meet here), a library, and free Internet access, as well as endless information and a referral service. It's open 7 days a week, and is a vital resource in gay Dublin.

The Dragon ★   This is the biggest, shiniest gay bar in Dublin. It's a two-level affair with a raucous first floor, complete with dance floor and all-ages crowd shouting to be heard over the thumping music, and a quieter upstairs area with lots of cozy nooks for whispering sweet nothings. It has a more upscale crowd than its funkier sister-bar, the George (see below). S. Great Georges St, Dublin 2. ℂ 01/478-1590.

The Front Lounge   This modern bar sprawls across several levels, with wide windows overlooking the hustle and bustle of Temple Bar. The crowd is a friendly, mixed gay/straight clientele. The look here is nice shoes, just the right amount of stubble, and expensive hair gel. 33–34 Parliament St., Temple Bar, Dublin 2. ℂ 01/670-4112.

The George   This is Dublin's most established gay bar, and it tends to be packed most nights with a laid-back, cheerful crowd, mixing mostly locals with savvy tourists. It's a quiet haven during the day, and a good place to sit and have a coffee, but late at night there's a DJ, and tables are pushed back for dancing. If you're gay and visiting Dublin, this is the place you're looking for. 89 S. Great George's St., Dublin 2. ℂ 01/478-2983. www.capitalbars.com.

GUBU   This mixed gay/straight Northside dance club, with an emphasis on gay, is filled to bursting most nights, with a casually but beautifully dressed, laid-back, enthusiastic crowd drawn by its party-pop music and "it's-a-gay-thing" attitude. 7–8 Capel St., Dublin 1. ℂ 01/874-0710. www.gubu.ie.

Panti Bar   This casual joint is run by Pandora "Panti" Bliss, a drag queen with great affection for Dolly Parton. It's a smallish place, with a sort of rec room in the basement, and with ongoing events ranging from Panti's search for a new assistant to a crafts night called "Make and Do Do." 7–8 Capel St., Dublin 1. ℂ 01/874-0710.

THE PERFORMING ARTS
Theater

With a heritage extending from the likes of George Bernard Shaw, Dublin has a venerable and vital theatrical tradition. Homegrown talent has kept the many theaters here alive, whether it's actors like Colin Farrell or writers like the currently very hot Marina Carr *(By the Bog of Cats)* and Marie Jones *(Stones in His Pockets)*. Complementing the talent are beautiful, historic theaters so vaingloriously gilded that they make every performance an event. Most theaters are within the city's Northside, not far off the river.

The online booking site **Ticketmaster** (www.ticketmaster.ie) is an excellent place to get a quick look at what's playing where and also to buy tickets. In addition to the major theaters listed below, other venues present fewer, although on occasion quite impressive, productions. They also book music and dance performances. They include the **Focus Theatre,** 12 Fade St., Dublin 2 (ℂ 01/671-2417); the **Olympia,** 72 Dame St., Dublin 2 (ℂ 01/679-3323); **Project: Dublin,** 39 E. Essex St., Dublin 2 (ℂ 01/679-6622; www.project.ie); and the **Tivoli,** 135–138 Francis St., opposite Iveagh Market, Dublin 8 (ℂ 01/454-4472; www.tivoli.ie).

Abbey Theatre   Since 1903, the Abbey has been the national theater of Ireland. The original theater, destroyed by fire in 1951, was replaced in 1966 by the current functional, although uninspired, 600-seat house. The Abbey's artistic reputation in Ireland has risen and fallen many times, but is reasonably strong at present. Lower Abbey St.,

Dublin 1. ✆ **01/878-7222**. www.abbeytheatre.ie. Tickets €15–€30 ($24–$48). Senior, student, and children's discounts available Mon–Thurs evening and Sat matinee. Bus: 130, 142, or 33.

Andrews Lane Theatre   This relatively new venue has a rising reputation for fine theater. It consists of a 220-seat main theater where contemporary work from home and abroad is presented, and a 76-seat studio geared for experimental productions. 9–17 St. Andrews Lane, Dublin 2. ✆ **01/679-5720**. www.andrewslane.com. Tickets €15–€24 ($24–$38).

Gaiety   The elegant little Gaiety holds a varied array of performances, including everything from opera to classical Irish plays to Broadway-style musicals and variety acts. King St. S., Dublin 2. ✆ **01/677-1717**. www.gaietytheatre.com. Tickets €13–€75 ($21–$120). LUAS: St. Stephen's Green.

The Gate   Just north of O'Connell Street off Parnell Square, this recently restored 370-seat theater was founded in 1928 by Hilton Edwards and Michael MacLiammoir to provide a venue for a broad range of plays. That policy prevails today, with a program that includes a blend of modern works and the classics. Although less known by visitors, the Gate is easily as distinguished as the Abbey. 1 Cavendish Row, Dublin 1. ✆ **01/874-4045**. www.gate-theatre.ie. Tickets €22–€30 ($35–$48).

The Peacock   In the same building as the Abbey, this 150-seat theater features contemporary plays and experimental works. It books poetry readings and one-person shows, as well as plays in the Irish language. Lower Abbey St., Dublin 1. ✆ **01/878-7222**. www. abbeytheatre.ie. Tickets €20 ($32) adults, €14 ($22) children and students. Discounts for seniors are only available to those resident in Ireland.

Concerts

On any given night, you can find almost anything—rock, pop, jazz, blues, traditional Irish, country, or folk—in this town, so check listings magazines to find out what's on and where. Music and dance concerts take place in a range of venues—theaters, churches, clubs, museums, sports stadiums, castles, parks, and universities. While you're probably more likely to choose your entertainment based on the performer rather than the venue, these institutions stand out.

Smaller Concert Venues

If you prefer more intimate settings, below are some of the best small venues in Dublin. The Village is the newest and hottest; Whelan's and the Vicar are the old favorites. Check local listings, or the individual websites, to find out what's on when you're in town:

- **Button Factory,** Temple Bar, Dublin 2 (✆ **01/670-9202;** www.tbmc.ie)
- **Vicar Street,** 58–59 Thomas St., Dublin 8 (✆ **01/454-5533;** www.vicarstreet. com)
- **Whelan's,** 25 Wexford St., Dublin 2 (✆ **01/478-0766;** www.whelanslive.com)
- **Eamonn Doran's,** 3A Crown Alley, Temple Bar, Dublin 2 (✆ **01/679-9114**)
- **The Village,** 26 Wexford St., Dublin 2 (✆ **1890/200-078;** www.thevillage venue.com)

The Helix   This massive auditorium at University College Dublin hosts many concerts throughout the year. The box office is open Monday to Saturday 10am to 6pm. Collins Ave., Glasnevin, Dublin 9. *C* **01/700-7077**. www.helix.ie. Tickets €10–€60 ($16–$96). Bus: 11, 11A, 11B, 13, 13A, or 19A.

National Concert Hall   This 1,200-seat hall is home to the National Symphony Orchestra and Concert Orchestra, and it hosts dozens of international orchestras and performing artists. In addition to classical music, there are Broadway-style musicals, opera, jazz, and recitals. The box office is open Monday to Friday from 10am to 3pm and from 6pm to close of concert. Open weekends 1 hour before concerts. Parking is available on the street. Earlsfort Terrace, Dublin 2. *C* **01/417-0000**. www.nch.ie. Tickets €10–€40 ($16–$64). Lunchtime concerts €10–€15 ($16–$24). DART: Pearse St. Bus: 10, 11, 13, 14, 15, 27C, 44, 46A, 46B, 48A, or 86.

The Point Depot   With a seating capacity of 3,000, the Point is one of Dublin's larger indoor theater/concert venues, attracting Broadway-caliber shows and international stars such as Justin Timberlake and Tom Jones. It was renovated in 2008 to give it a shiny new look. The box office is open Monday to Saturday 10am to 6pm. Parking is €4 ($6.40) per car. East Link Bridge, North Wall Quay. *C* **01/836-3633**. Tickets €20–€100 ($32–$160). Bus: 53.

---

10 SIDE TRIPS FROM DUBLIN

Dublin's suburbs stretch out for miles along the coastline of Dublin Bay. Within a 15- to 20-minute DART ride or a 30-minute drive from the city center, they have fresh ocean breezes and sweeping views of the striking rocky coastline. They also have lots to see, including castles, museums, and literary sights. If all else fails, you can always spend an afternoon playing in the sand.

DUBLIN'S SOUTHERN SUBURBS

Heading southward along the bay, the bustling harbor town of **Dún Laoghaire** (pronounced *Dun* Leary) is quickly followed by the more upscale seaside towns of **Dalkey** ★ and **Killiney.** All have been collectively nicknamed "Bel Eire" for their beauty and for the density of Irish celebrity residents. You could spend an afternoon wandering all three, or just pick one and linger there for a day. Dún Laoghaire has lots of shopping, as well as a long promenade and a bucolic park. Killiney has a picturesque, cliff-backed expanse of beach. Pretty little Dalkey is a heritage town with two tiny castle towers, a lovely medieval streetscape, and lots of charming pubs, gourmet restaurants, and pricey little boutiques.

If you're looking for a quick break from the big city, these are good options, since all three have fine places to stay, many with sea views. On the top of a hillside overlooking the bay just outside of Dalkey, you can stay in a manor house hotel that looks, for all the world, like a pastel-tinged castle—Fitzpatrick Castle (see below).

If you're traveling to Ireland by ferry from Holyhead, Wales, your first glimpse of Ireland will be the port of Dún Laoghaire. Many people decide to base themselves here and commute into downtown Dublin each day.

Seeing the Sights

Dalkey Castle and Heritage Centre   Housed in a little 16th-century tower house, the center tells the history of this venerable town in a few sweet, if unsophisticated, displays. There are tours, in which guides tell the tale, but they're unpredictable—the level of detail can be a bit more than you need to know, and on one tour, there was an inexplicable interpretive dancer halfway through it, which baffled all of us. If you prefer to go your own way, you can climb the battlements and take in the view. Adjoining the center is a medieval graveyard and the Church of St. Begnet, Dalkey's patron saint, whose foundations date back to Ireland's early Christian period. *Note:* Prices have risen steeply here recently, and it's hard to say the little castle tower offers enough to make it worthwhile. Malahide Castle (p. 183) is infinitely more impressive.

Castle St., Dalkey, County Dublin. ⓒ **01/285-8366.** www.dalkeycastle.com. Admission €6 ($9.60) adults, €5 ($8) seniors and students, €4 ($6.40) children. Mon–Fri 9:30am–5pm; Sat–Sun and public holidays 11am–5pm. Closed Christmas Day. DART: Dalkey. Bus: 8.

James Joyce Museum ★   Sitting on the edge of the bay at the little suburb of Sandycove, this 12m (39-ft.) Martello tower was one of a series of stone structures built in the early 19th century to guard the island against an anticipated invasion by Napoleon's troops. When the threat passed, many of the towers were converted into homes. James Joyce lived here in 1904 as a guest of Oliver Gogarty, who rented the tower from the army for an annual fee of IR£8 (€10/$16). Joyce put the tower in the first chapter of *Ulysses* and it has been known as Joyce's Tower ever since. Its collection of Joycean memorabilia includes letters, documents, first and rare editions, personal possessions, and photographs.

Sandycove, County Dublin. ⓒ **01/280-9265.** Admission €6.50 ($10) adults, €5.50 ($8.80) seniors and students, €4 ($6.40) children. Apr–Oct Mon–Sat 10am–1pm and 2–5pm; Sun 2–6pm. DART: Sandycove. Bus: 8.

Where to Stay

Fitzpatrick Castle Hotel ★   With a fanciful Victorian facade of turrets, towers, and battlements, this restored 1741 gem is an ideal choice for those who have always wanted to live in a castle. A 15-minute drive from the center of the city, it is between the villages of Dalkey and Killiney, amid hilltop grounds with clear views of Dublin Bay. It's a marvelous, rambling old building, with a wandering lobby that seems to go on forever, filled with comfortable sofas, a piano, and working fireplaces. There's an excellent bar, with leather chairs to sink into, and two good restaurants—**P.J.'s** for upscale dining, and downstairs, the casual and very good **Dungeon Restaurant,** for less formal meals. The color of the building changes yearly—one year it's blue, the next it's pink, at the moment it's red. Book online if possible, as good deals are often available. If you prefer more privacy, ask about their guesthouses.

Killiney Hill Rd., Killiney, County Dublin. ⓒ **01/230-5400.** Fax 01/230-5430. www.fitzpatrickcastlehotel. com. 113 units. €190–€250 ($304–$400) double. Breakfast €20 ($32). AE, DC, MC, V. DART: Dalkey. Bus: 59. **Amenities:** 2 restaurants (Continental, grill); bar; indoor swimming pool; guest privileges at nearby 18-hole golf course; gym; saunas; concierge; salon; room service; laundry service; nonsmoking rooms. *In room:* TV, tea/coffeemaker, hair dryer, garment press.

Where to Dine
Expensive
Hartleys INTERNATIONAL   This incredibly popular restaurant sits squarely in the bustle of Dún Laoghaire's busy seafront. Elegantly converted from the old Kingstown terminal building, it packs in crowds for a varied menu of pasta, salads, steaks, and grilled seafood. The food can be hit-or-miss here, but the atmosphere is unbeatable, and that's what seems to draw in most people.

Balbriggan○

Bernageagh Bay

⑤

R127

⑥

⑦ *St. Patrick's Island*

Skerries

⑧

Shenick's Island

N1

R127

R128

Area of detail

Dublin

REPUBLIC
OF IRELAND

R100

R126

⑨ Donabate

Lambay Island

Swords○

R106

Malahide

⑩⑪⑫

Irish Sea

R106

R122

N1

Dublin
Airport ✈ M1

○ Portmarnock

Ireland's Eye

R104

R107

R105

Sutton ○ **Howth** ⑭

N2 **3**

2 R103 **4**

1

○ Clontarf

⑬ ▲ *Ben of Howth*

North Bull Island

N3

DUBLIN

Dublin Bay

R119

N4 ✪ **DUBLIN**

Liffey

N7

Royal Canal

N11

R117

R112 **Dun Laoghaire**

Sandycove ○

⑮⑯

⑰ ⑱ ⑲

Dalkey Island

R113

Dalkey ○

Dalkey Hill ▲

Killiney Hill ▲

⑳

22 ㉑

Killiney

To Shankill
↓

DINING ◆
Abbey Tavern **14**
Bon Appetit **12**
Brasserie na Mara **15**
Caviston's **16**
Hartleys **17**
Nosh **20**
PD Woodhouse **19**
The Red Bank **8**

ATTRACTIONS ●
Ardgillan Castle **5**
Casino Marino **4**
Dalkey Castle **21**
The Fry Model Railway **10**
Howth Castle Rhododendron
   Gardens **13**
James Joyce Museum **18**
Malahide Castle **11**
National Botanic Gardens **2**
Newbridge House **9**
Skerries Mills **6**

ACCOMMODATIONS ■
Clontarf Castle Hotel **1**
Egan's House **3**
Fitzpatrick Castle Hotel **22**
Red Bank House **7**

1 Harbour Rd., Dún Laoghaire, County Dublin. ℂ **01/280-6767.** Reservations required. Main courses €19–€38 ($30–$61). AE, DC, MC, V. Mon–Fri 12:30–2:30pm; Mon–Sat 6:30–10pm. DART: Dún Laoghaire. Bus: 7, 7A, 8, or 46A.

Moderate

Caviston's ★★ SEAFOOD   Fresh, fresh fish is the hallmark of this tiny lunch spot in Sandycove, run by the Caviston family, whose neighboring fish shop is legendary. The menu changes daily, but might include roast monkfish with pasta in a saffron-and-basil sauce, chargrilled salmon with béarnaise, or marinated red mullet with roasted red peppers. The three lunchtime sittings can make for frantic service, so your best bet is to arrive at noon sharp, before things get too hectic.

59 Glasthule Rd., Sandycove, County Dublin. ℂ **01/280-9120.** www.cavistons.com. Reservations recommended. Main courses €15–€29 ($24–$46). DC, MC, V. Tues–Sat 3 sittings noon–6pm. DART: Dún Laoghaire.

Nosh ★★ INTERNATIONAL   This light, bright, and buzzing restaurant is so laid-back that it has plastic chairs, and yet it delivers the sort of hit-the-spot food that you wish you could get every day: French toast with bacon, bananas, and maple syrup; wonderful soups; and big club sandwiches or salads. For dinner, there's grilled plaice with crabmeat, and wine from the short-but-sweet list. Weekend brunch is simply fabulous here.

111 Coliemore Rd., Dalkey, County Dublin. ℂ **01/284-0666.** www.nosh.ie. Reservations recommended. Main courses €17–€27 ($27–$43). MC, V. Tues–Sun noon–4pm and 6–10pm. DART: Dalkey.

Pubs

P. McCormack and Sons   The main bar at this popular pub has an old-world feel, with globe lamps, stained-glass windows, books, and jugs on the shelves, and lots of nooks and crannies for a quiet drink. In the sky-lit, plant-filled conservatory area, classical music fills the air, and outdoors you'll find a festive courtyard beer garden. The pub grub here is top-notch, with a varied buffet table of lunchtime salads and meats. 67 Lower Mounttown Rd. (off York Rd.), Dún Laoghaire, County Dublin. ℂ **01/280-5519.** DART: Dún Laoghaire.

The Purty Kitchen   Housed in a building that dates from 1728, this old pub has a homey atmosphere, with an open brick fireplace, cozy alcoves, a large fish mural, and pub poster art on the walls. There's always something going on—be it a session of Irish traditional music in the main bar area, blues upstairs in the Loft, or a DJ spinning dance music. The food is great here as well. Call ahead for entertainment details. Old Dunleary Rd., Dún Laoghaire, County Dublin. ℂ **01/284-3576.** No cover for traditional music; cover €6–€10 ($9.60–$16) for blues in the Loft.

DUBLIN'S NORTHERN SUBURBS

Dublin's northern suburbs make a convenient base for travelers via **Dublin International Airport,** and there's much to do here, with a delightful assortment of castles, historic buildings, gardens, and the beach to keep you busy. The towns of **Drumcondra** and **Glasnevin** have good hotels.

Just north of Dublin, the picturesque suburbs of **Howth** and **Malahide** offer panoramic views of Dublin Bay, beautiful hillside gardens, and many fine seafood restaurants. Best of all, they are easily reached on the DART. Farther north along the coast, but only 20 minutes from Dublin Airport, lies the bustling and attractive harbor town of **Skerries ★.** Skerries is a convenient and appealing spot to spend your first or last night in Ireland; or stay longer and explore all this area has to offer, including a resident colony of gray seals.

Ardgillan Castle and Demesne ★ Between Balbriggan and Skerries, this 18th-century castellated country house sits on the coastline on sumptuously manicured lawns. The house was built in 1738 and contains some fine period furnishings and antiques. But the real draw is the setting, at the edge of the wild Irish Sea, with miles of walking paths and coastal views, as well as a rose garden and an herb garden. Behind the lavish rose garden, there's a nice cafe for a quick bite or some ice cream.

Balbriggan, County Dublin. ✆ **01/849-2212.** Admission to house €7 ($11) adults, €5 ($8) seniors and students, €15 ($24) families. Castle Oct–Dec and Feb–Mar Tues–Sun 11am–4:30pm; Apr–Sept Tues–Sun 11am–6pm. Park daily dawn–dusk. Closed Jan. Free parking. Signposted off N1. Bus: 33.

Casino Marino In the town of Marino, just off the Malahide Road, this charming structure was designed by Sir William Chambers as a pleasure house. A garden amusement it might have been, but it is a fine 18th-century neoclassical structure. The tiny Casino (meaning "small house") somehow manages to contain 16 finely decorated rooms.

Malahide Rd., Marino, Dublin 3. ✆ **01/833-1618.** Admission €3 ($4.80) adults, €2.10 ($3.35) seniors and group members, €1.30 ($2.10) students and children, €7.40 ($12) families. Feb–Apr and Nov Sun and Thurs noon–4pm; May and Oct daily noon–5pm; June–Sept daily 10am–6pm. Bus: 20A, 20B, 27, 27A, 27B, 42, 42B, or 42C.

The Fry Model Railway (Kids) On the grounds of Malahide Castle (see below), this is an exhibit of handmade models of more than 300 Irish trains. The trains were built in the 1920s and 1930s by Cyril Fry, a railway engineer and draftsman. The complex includes items of Irish railway history dating from 1834, and models of stations, bridges, trams, buses, barges, boats, the River Liffey, and the Hill of Howth.

Malahide, County Dublin. ✆ **01/846-3779.** Admission €7.25 ($12) adults, €6.10 ($9.75) seniors and students, €4.60 ($7.35) children, €21 ($34) families. Apr–Sept Mon–Sat 10am–5pm; Sun and public holidays 2–6pm. Tours closed for lunch 1–2pm. Suburban rail to Malahide. Bus: 42.

Howth Castle Rhododendron Gardens On a steep slope about 13km (8 miles) north of downtown, this 12-hectare (30-acre) garden was first planted in 1875 and is best known for its 2,000 varieties of rhododendrons. Peak bloom time is in May and June. *Note:* The castle and its private gardens are not open to the public.

Howth, County Dublin. ✆ **01/832-2624.** Free admission. Apr–June daily 8am–sunset. DART: Howth. Bus: 31.

Malahide Castle ★★★ (Kids) This crenelated and towered stone castle is satisfyingly complete. Most castles still open to the public in Ireland are ruins, but this one stands so solidly, you get the picture—it's what a castle should be. Founded in the 12th century by Richard Talbot, it was occupied by his descendants until 1973. The fully restored interior is furnished with Irish antiques from the 17th to the 19th centuries. One-of-a-kind historical portraits and tableaux on loan from the National Gallery line the walls. After touring the house, explore the vast estate, with prized **gardens** filled with more than 5,000 species of plants and flowers—it's the perfect place for a picnic on a sunny day. The Malahide grounds also contain the **Fry Model Railway** museum (see above) and **Tara's Palace,** an antique dollhouse and toy collection.

Malahide, County Dublin. ✆ **01/846-2184.** www.malahidecastle.com. Admission €7.25 ($12) adults, €6.10 ($9.75) students and seniors, €4.60 ($7.35) children 11 and under, €21 ($34) families; gardens free. Combination tickets with Fry Model Railway, Joyce Birthplace, Shaw Birthplace, and Newbridge House available. AE, MC, V. Year-round Mon–Sat 10am–5pm; Apr–Sept Sun and public holidays 10am–6pm; Oct–Mar Sun and public holidays 11am–5pm; gardens May–Sept daily 2–5pm. Castle closed for lunch 12:45–2pm (restaurant remains open). DART: Malahide. Bus: 42.

National Botanic Gardens ★★   Established by the Royal Dublin Society in 1795 on a rolling 20-hectare (49-acre) expanse of land north of the city center, this is Dublin's horticultural showcase. The attractions include more than 20,000 different plants and cultivars, the Great Yew Walk, a bog garden, a water garden, a rose garden, and an herb garden. A variety of Victorian-style glass houses are filled with tropical plants and exotic species. Remember this spot when you suddenly crave refuge from the bustle of the city. It's a quiet, lovely haven, within a short walk of Glasnevin Cemetery. All but the rose garden is wheelchair accessible. There's free roadside parking outside the garden gates.

Botanic Rd., Glasnevin, Dublin 9. ✆ **01/804-0300.** www.heritageireland.ie. Free admission. Guided tour €2 ($3.20). Mid-Feb to mid-Nov daily 9am–6pm; mid-Nov to mid-Feb daily 9:30am–4:30pm. Bus: 13, 19, or 134.

Newbridge House and Park ★★★ (Kids)   This country mansion 19km (12 miles) north of Dublin dates from 1740 and was once the home of Dr. Charles Cobbe, an archbishop of Dublin. Occupied by the Cobbe family until 1984, the house is a showcase of family memorabilia: hand-carved furniture, portraits, daybooks, and dolls, as well as a museum of objects collected on world travels. The Great Drawing Room, in its original state, is one of the finest Georgian interiors in Ireland. The house sits on 140 hectares (346 acres), laid out with picnic areas and walking trails. The grounds also include a working Victorian farm, as well as a craft shop and a coffee shop. There's a terrific, up-to-the-minute playground where children can let off some steam.

Donabate, County Dublin. ✆ **01/843-6534.** Admission €6.50 ($10) adults, €5.50 ($8.80) seniors and students, €3.70 ($5.90) children 11 and under, €18 ($29) families. Apr–Sept Tues–Sat 10am–1pm and 2–5pm, Sun and public holidays 2–6pm; Oct–Mar Sat–Sun and public holidays noon–5pm. Suburban rail to Donabate. Bus: 33B.

Skerries Mills   Originally part of an Augustinian Priory, the mill has had many lives (and deaths). Last known as the Old Mill Bakery, providing loaves to the local north coast, it suffered a devastating fire in 1986 and lay in ruins until it was reborn as Skerries Mills in 1999. An ambitious restoration project brought two windmills and a water mill back into operation. There's even an adjoining field of grains—barley, oats, and wheat, all that's needed for the traditional brown loaf—sown, harvested, and threshed using traditional implements and machinery. The result is not only the sweet smell of fresh bread, but also an intriguing glimpse into the past, brought to life by guided tours and the chance to put your hand to the stone and grind flour. If you've worked up an appetite, there's a lovely tearoom and a fine gift shop of Irish crafts.

Skerries, County Dublin. ✆ **01/849-5208.** www.skerriesmills.org. Admission €6 ($9.60) adults; €4.50 ($7.20) seniors, students, and children; €12 ($19) families. Apr–Sept daily 10:30am–6pm; Oct–Mar daily 10:30am–4:30pm. Closed Dec 20–Jan 1. Suburban rail to Skerries. Bus: 33. Skerries town and the Mills signposted north of Dublin off the N1.

Where to Stay
Very Expensive
Clontarf Castle Hotel ★   If you want to be within striking distance of Dublin airport (8km/5 miles away), this handsome castle hotel in Clontarf is a good option as it's about 10 minutes' drive away. The Norman stone castle that forms the hotel's center dates to 1172, although most of the building is modern. In the 1600s, the castle was given to one of Oliver Cromwell's crew and his family retained ownership for 300 years. There's still a regal quality to the magnificent entrance hall and lobby, which are draped with tapestries and hold a huge fireplace. Guest rooms are in the modern portion of the

building, but are nicely done with a mixture of contemporary furniture and antique **185** touches. Some rooms have four-poster beds. It's a popular conference center and entertainment venue, so is not really the place for a peaceful getaway.

Castle Ave., Clontarf, Dublin 3. (© **01/833-2321.** Fax 01/833-0418. www.clontarfcastle.ie. 111 units. €400 ($640) double. Breakfast €22 ($35). AE, DC, MC, V. Free parking. Bus: 130. **Amenities:** Restaurant (international); 2 bars; gym; room service; babysitting; laundry service; nonsmoking rooms. *In room:* A/C, TV, radio, dataport, tea/coffeemaker, hair dryer, garment press, voice mail.

Inexpensive

Egan's House　This two-story, red-brick Victorian guesthouse is in the center of a pleasant residential neighborhood. It's within walking distance of the botanic gardens; facilities for various sports, including tennis and swimming; and a gym. Operated by Pat and Monica Finn, it has bright if basic rooms in a variety of sizes and styles. The comfortable public rooms feature traditional dark woods, brass fixtures, and antiques.

7/9 Iona Park (btw. Botanic and Lower Drumcondra roads), Glasnevin, Dublin 9. (© **01/830-3611.** Fax 01/830-3312. www.eganshouse.com. 23 units. €60–€130 ($96–$208) double. 50% reduction for children 5 and under sharing with 2 adults. Rates include full breakfast. MC, V. Limited free parking available. Bus: 3, 11, 13, 13A, 16, 19, 19A, 41, 41A, or 41B. **Amenities:** Dining room; lounge; nonsmoking rooms. *In room:* TV, tea/coffeemaker, hair dryer.

Red Bank House ★★ Ⓥalue　This comfortable nook in the heart of Skerries town is only 20 to 30 minutes by car from Dublin Airport, so it can provide a convenient first or last night's lodging for your Ireland holiday. Better yet, it virtually abuts the award-winning Red Bank restaurant (see below), so you are guaranteed a memorable introductory or farewell meal in the country. There's an invitingly simple, country style to the guest rooms—cream walls, dark woods, crisp white bedspreads, and floral drapes. The power showers are just the ticket after or before a long journey.

7 Church St. and Convent Lane, Skerries, County Dublin. (© **01/849-1005** or 849-0439. Fax 01/849-1598. www.redbank.ie. 18 units, several with shower only. €110 ($176) double. Rates include service and full Irish breakfast. 3-course dinner €50 ($80), 3-course value menu until 7pm, €30 ($48). Half-board (B&B and dinner) for 2 €200 ($320). AE, DC, MC, V. Parking on street and lane. Suburban rail to Skerries. Bus: 33. **Amenities:** Restaurant (seafood). *In room:* TV, dataport, tea/coffeemaker, hair dryer.

Where to Dine

Abbey Tavern　SEAFOOD/INTERNATIONAL　Well known for its nightly traditional-music ballad sessions, this 16th-century tavern also has a full-service restaurant upstairs. Although the menu changes by season, entrees might include scallops *ty ar mor* (with mushrooms, prawns, and cream sauce), *crepes fruits de mer* (seafood crepes), filet of sea bass, roast duckling with ginger and pineapple, or spinach and ricotta tortellini. After a meal, you might want to join the audience downstairs for some lively Irish traditional music, although you'll have to pay an extra €20 ($32) to join in the fun.

Abbey St., Howth, County Dublin. (© **01/839-0307.** www.abbeytavern.ie. Reservations necessary. Fixed-price dinner €38 ($61) 3 courses, €33 ($53) 2 courses. MC, V. Mon–Sat 7–11pm. DART: Howth. Bus: 31.

Bon Appetit ★ FRENCH　Walls covered in silk wallpaper, glittering crystal chandeliers, and cream linens hallmark this place as a formal dining extravaganza. Ingredients are just as luxurious: Try the seared filets of slow-roasted John Dory with banana shallots, crab soubise, and a veloute of crab; or spring lamb with braised shoulder herb crumb, red-pepper purée, and aubergine caviar. It's been earning top marks from local critics, and now has a Michelin star, so it's packing in the wealthy suburban crowd. Some say it has

DUBLIN

6

SIDE TRIPS FROM DUBLIN

fallen victim to its own success, and crowding people in on tiny tables, but can so many eager diners be wrong?

9 James Terrace, Malahide, County Dublin. ℭ **01/845-0314.** www.bonappetit.ie. Reservations required. Fixed-price 3-course dinner €67 ($107). AE, DC, MC, V. Tues–Sat 7–9:30pm; Friday lunch noon–2pm. Suburban rail to Malahide.

The Red Bank ★★ SEAFOOD   The hugely popular Red Bank restaurant has been winning friends, influencing people, and garnering awards for nearly 20 years. The mood here is charmingly old-fashioned and classy. The waiter takes your order in the cozy lounge, where you wait with a drink until the appetizers are ready and you're brought to a table. Chef Terry McCoy is an exuberant and inspired chef, who gets fresh seafood from local waters. This place is at its best with timeless icons, such as scallops in butter, cream, and white wine; or the divine lobster thermidor. Service is correct and respectfully old school, highlighted when the dessert cart is wheeled in, laden with a mouthwatering selection of confections.

7 Church St., Skerries, County Dublin. ℭ **01/849-1005.** www.redbank.ie. Reservations required. Dinner main courses €20–€40 ($32–$64); fixed-price dinner €50 ($80); value menu until 7pm €30 ($48). AE, DC, MC, V. Mon–Sat 6:30–9:30pm; Sun 12:30–4pm. Suburban rail to Skerries. Bus: 33.

Out from Dublin

The area immediately around Dublin is not the most dramatic or beautiful in the country, but if you get off the big, bland motorways, there are treasures in those hills. This region was the scene of some of Ireland's most dramatic history and some of its most vicious battles. The stretch of flat coastland between Dundalk and the Wicklow Mountains marks the greatest weakness in Ireland's natural defenses, made worse by the inviting estuaries of the Liffey and the Boyne. Thus it was frequently invaded over the years by Celts, Danes, Normans, and, last but certainly not least, English.

To the north of Dublin are the remnants of ancient civilizations, at prehistoric sites Newgrange and Knowth. A short distance away, the green hills around the Valley of the Boyne are where the Irish kings once reigned with a mixture of mysticism and force. To the south, the Wicklow Mountains create a landscape of hills and peaceful monastic sites. To the east, the plains of County Kildare form Ireland's horse country.

This may not be the greatest scenery Ireland has to offer, but it's a fantastic introduction.

1 COUNTY WICKLOW & COUNTY CARLOW

County Wicklow extends from Bray, 19km (12 miles) S of Dublin, to Arklow, 64km (40 miles) S of Dublin

Sitting at a seaside cafe in the cheerful suburban town of **Bray** ★, you can look off to the southern horizon and see the mountains of County Wicklow casting their shadow your way. Wicklow's northernmost border is just a dozen or so miles south of Dublin, making it one of the easiest day trips. The beauty of the mountains, with their peaceful **Vale of Avoca** and isolated, contemplative monastery site, **Glendalough,** makes this landscape one of the most rewarding views.

Bray is a stylish, upscale town, but it's also busy and bustling, so many people choose to head to County Wicklow by way of the sweet harbor town of **Greystones** ★, a place you might not tell your friends about, for fear of spoiling the secret. It has no special attractions except its charming self, and that's enough.

Beyond Greystones, a raised granite ridge runs through the county, peaking at two of the highest mountain passes in Ireland—the **Sally Gap** and the **Wicklow Gap.** Once you're among the mountains, the best way to soak up the scenery is to strike out on foot on the well-marked **Wicklow Way** walking path, which wanders for miles past mountain tarns and secluded glens. You can pick up a map at any tourism office, and then choose a stretch of the path to explore. If you're staying in the car, you'll want to track down the picturesque villages of **Roundwood, Laragh,** and **Aughrim.**

Just over the border of County Wicklow lies County Carlow, one of Ireland's smallest counties, bordered to the east by the **Blackstairs Mountains** and to the west by the fertile limestone land of the Barrow Valley and the Killeshin Hills. Its most prominent feature is the 5,000-year-old granite formation known as **Browne's Hill Dolmen.** Its capstone is believed to weigh a colossal 100 tons.

GETTING THERE   **Irish Rail** (© 01/836-6222; www.irishrail.ie) provides daily train service between Dublin and Bray and Wicklow.

Bus Éireann (© 01/836-6111; www.buseireann.ie) operates daily express bus service to Arklow, Bray, and Wicklow towns. Both Bus Éireann and **Discover Dublin** (© 01/ 280-1899; www.discoverdublin.ie) offer an excellent tour that they have dubbed the "Wild Wicklow Tour." It certainly is lively and enjoyable, and includes visits to Avoca and Sally Gap. Another tour option is the **Mary Gibbons Tours** (© 01/283-9973; www.newgrangetours.com), which does an absorbing, in-depth tour of Glendalough.

Still, arguably the best way to see Wicklow is by car, as that's the only way that you can take in all the little villages not well served by bus or train. The Dublin Tourist Office has excellent road maps for all of Ireland. Take the N11 south from Dublin City and follow turnoff signs for major attractions.

VISITOR INFORMATION   The **Wicklow Tourist Office,** Fitzwilliam Square, Wicklow Town, County Wicklow (© 0404/69117; www.visitwicklow.ie), is open Monday to Friday year-round, Saturday during peak season. The **Carlow Tourist Office,** Forester's Hall, College Street, Carlow Town, County Carlow (© 059/913-1554; www.carlow tourism.com), is open Monday to Friday year-round.

SEEING THE SIGHTS

Altamount Garden   The lush, colorful extravagance of Altamount is the result of decades of nurturing. A shadowy avenue of beech trees leads to bright lawns and flowers growing beneath ancient yew trees. Gravel walks weave around a lake, constructed as a famine-relief project. It's arguably at its best in late May, when spectacular displays of bluebells fill the forest floor on slopes overlooking the River Slaney.

Tullow, County Carlow. © **059/915-9444.** www.altamontgarden.com. Free admission. Apr–Oct Mon–Thurs 9am–5pm, Fri 9am–3:30pm, Sat–Sun 10am–6pm; Nov–Mar Mon–Thurs 9am–5pm, Fri 9am–3:30pm.

Avondale House & Forest Park ★ **Kids**   In a fertile valley between Glendalough and the Vale of Avoca, this is the former home of Charles Stewart Parnell (1846–91), one of Ireland's great political leaders. Built in 1779, the house is now a museum dedicated to his memory. The parkland around the house is beautiful, with wooded nature trails along a river, and more formal gardens near the house. There's a cute cafe serving tea and light lunches, as well as homemade breads and pastries, and there's also a playground for children, which should keep them busy for a while.

Off R752, Rathdrum, County Wicklow. © **0404/46111.** www.coillteoutdoors.ie. Admission €6 ($9.60) adults, €5.50 ($8.80) seniors and children 11 and under, €17.50 ($28) families. Mid-Mar to Oct 31 daily 11am–6pm. Parking €5 ($8).

Browne's Hill Dolmen   The purpose of this megalithic stone table has been the subject of conjecture for centuries, but nobody knows for certain. The tomb is an estimated 5,000 years old, and its massive size led earlier Irish residents to believe that it was built by giants. Archaeologists believe the capstone was rolled into place by way of an earthen ramp constructed for the process and then destroyed. It's likely the dolmen marks the burial place of a long-dead king, but it has been invested with a rich overlay of myth and legend.

Off Rathvilly Rd., Carlow, County Carlow. Free admission. Daily year-round. Access via car park and enclosed pedestrian pathway.

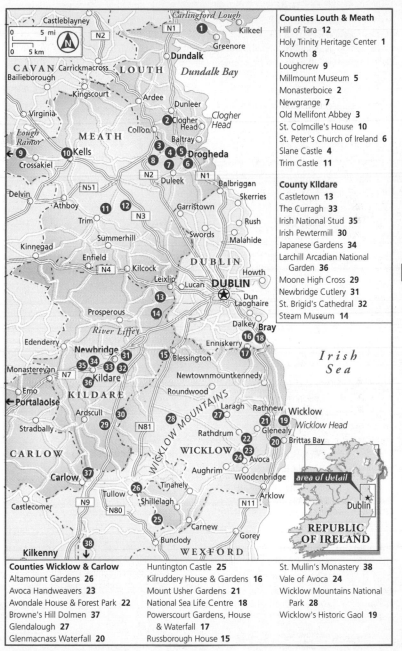

Counties Louth & Meath
Hill of Tara **12**
Holy Trinity Heritage Center **1**
Knowth **8**
Loughcrew **9**
Millmount Museum **5**
Monasterboice **2**
Newgrange **7**
Old Mellifont Abbey **3**
St. Colmcille's House **10**
St. Peter's Church of Ireland **6**
Slane Castle **4**
Trim Castle **11**

County Kildare
Castletown **13**
The Curragh **33**
Irish National Stud **35**
Irish Pewtermill **30**
Japanese Gardens **34**
Larchill Arcadian National
   Garden **36**
Moone High Cross **29**
Newbridge Cutlery **31**
St. Brigid's Cathedral **32**
Steam Museum **14**

Counties Wicklow & Carlow
Altamount Gardens **26**
Avoca Handweavers **23**
Avondale House & Forest Park **22**
Browne's Hill Dolmen **37**
Glendalough **27**
Glenmacnass Waterfall **20**

Huntington Castle **25**
Kilruddery House & Gardens **16**
Mount Usher Gardens **21**
National Sea Life Centre **18**
Powerscourt Gardens, House
   & Waterfall **17**
Russborough House **15**

St. Mullin's Monastery **38**
Vale of Avoca **24**
Wicklow Mountains National
   Park **28**
Wicklow's Historic Gaol **19**

Glendalough ★★★   This evocative, misty glen is a magical place. An old, abandoned monastery built around two dark lakes, surrounded by forests, it's a memorable sight. Its name is derived from the Irish *gleann da locha,* meaning "the glen of the two lakes." Things always seem to be in soft focus here as you wander the rocky paths beside the ancient chapels, and it exudes spirituality. The ruins date back to the 5th century, when a monk who became known as St. Kevin chose this secluded setting, which was already used as a Bronze Age tomb, for his home. For 7 years he fasted, prayed, slept on the hard ground, and ate only what he could catch or find. His self-deprivation and fervor gained attention from passing hunters and peddlers, and soon similarly devout followers found their way here. Over the next 4 centuries, Kevin's church became a center of religious learning, attracting thousands of students from all over Europe. Unfortunately, its success, as with so many early Irish religious sites, was its downfall, and Glendalough came to the attention of the Vikings, who pillaged it repeatedly between A.D. 775 and 1071. But it was always rebuilt, stronger than ever, until 1398, when it was virtually wiped out by English forces. Attempts were made to resuscitate it, and it limped on in some form until the 17th century as a shadow of its former greatness, and then was abandoned altogether.

The combination of so many years of history and such an evocative setting means that there's plenty to see here. Your first step should be to stop by the visitor center behind the Glendalough Hotel near the entrance to the valley, and pick up a map and learn a bit about the lay of the land. There are many walking trails, each one taking in different ruins, as the chapels and houses were scattered over miles around the glen. The oldest ruins, the **Teampall na Slellig,** can be seen across the lake at the foot of towering cliffs, but as there's no boat service, they cannot be visited. There's also a cave known as Kevin's Bed, which is believed to be where the saint lived when he first arrived at Glendalough. Follow the path from the upper lake to the lower lake and walk through the remains of the monastery complex. Although much of the monastic city is in ruins, there's a nearly perfect round tower, 31m (102 ft.) high and 16m (52 ft.) around the base, as well as hundreds of timeworn Celtic crosses and several chapels. One of these is St. Kevin's chapel, often called St. Kevin's Kitchen, a fine specimen of an early Irish barrel-vaulted oratory with a miniature round belfry rising from a stone roof. The only drawback of the whole place is that, once again, it's a victim of its own success, and in the summer it tends to be overrun with tourists, which rather defeats the purpose of visiting such a peaceful place. In the high season, it's best to arrive very early in the morning, or after 5pm (it stays light until 9pm at least) in order to see it at its best. (The visitor center closes at 5 or 6pm, but the grounds remain open).

County Wicklow (11km/6³/₄ miles east of Wicklow on T7 via Rathdrum). ✆ **0404/45325** or 45352. Admission €2.80 ($4.50) adults, €2.10 ($3.35) seniors, €1.30 ($2.10) students and children 11 and under, €7.40 ($12) families. Mid-Oct to mid-Mar daily 9:30am–5pm; mid-Mar to mid-Oct daily 9am–6pm.

Glenmacnass Waterfall ★   The River Glenmacnass flows south across the highest mountain in western Wicklow, Mt. Mullaghcleevaun (848m/2,781 ft.). At one point, it reaches the edge of a plateau and flows off the edge quite spectacularly. There's a parking lot near the top, and a path to the falls, but take care on the rocks, which can be treacherous.

Follow the Military rd. through the Sally Gap and Laragh to the top of Glenmacnass Valley, and then watch for signs to the waterfall. Free admission.

Huntington Castle ★   Built in 1621 on the site of an abbey, which was itself built in the 14th century on the site of a Druid temple, this rambling, crenelated manor house was originally the home of Lord Esmond (on whom the writer Thackeray based his novel *The History of Henry Esmond*). His descendants still occupy the main building. It's a rambling, lived-in old house, with vast grounds bounded by the rivers Derry and Slaney. The place is more than a little bit spooky. There's an old temple to the Goddess Isis in the dungeon (heaven knows why), and it's said to be one of the most haunted buildings in Ireland. It's an eccentric place, and both Stanley Kubrick and Mick Jagger have stayed here at one point or another (Kubrick filmed *Barry Lyndon* here). If you like it so much you can't bear to leave, you can rent one wing of the castle—if you're brave enough—with space for up to five people, from €195 to €425 ($312–$680) a week, depending on the season.

Clonegal, County Carlow (off N80, 6.5km/4 miles from Bunclody). © **053/937-7552.** Guided tour €6 ($9.60) adults, €4 ($6.40) seniors and children 7 and older, free for children 6 and under. June–Aug daily 2–6pm; other times by appointment. Accommodations booked through www.shamrockcottages.co.uk.

Killruddery House & Gardens This estate has been the seat of the earl of Meath since 1618. The original part of its mansion, dating from 1820, features a frilly Victorian conservatory modeled on the long-gone Crystal Palace in London. The gardens are a highlight, with a lime avenue, a sylvan theater, foreign trees, exotic shrubs, twin canals, and a fountain-filled, round pond edged with beech hedges.

Killruddery, Bray, County Wicklow (off the N11). © **0404/46024.** www.killruddery.com. House and garden tour €10 ($16) adults, €8 ($13) seniors and students, €3 ($4.80) children 12 and under, €18 ($29) families; gardens only €6 ($9.60) adults, €5 ($8) seniors and students, €2 ($3.20) children 12 and under. House May–June and Sept daily 1–5pm; gardens Apr Sat–Sun 1–5pm, May–Sept daily 1–5pm.

Mount Usher Gardens ★ Spreading out on 8 hectares (20 acres) at the edge of the River Vartry, this peaceful site was once an ancient lake. These days, it's a garden, designed in a distinctively informal style. Fiery rhododendrons, fragrant eucalyptus trees, giant Tibetan lilies, and snowy camellias compete for your attention. Informal and responsive to their natural setting, these gardens have an almost untended feel—a sort of floral woodland. A spacious tearoom overlooks the river and gardens. The courtyard at the entrance to the gardens contains an interesting assortment of shops that are open year-round.

Ashford, County Wicklow (off the N11). © **0404/40116.** www.mountushergardens.ie. Admission €7 ($11) adults; €6 ($9.60) seniors and students, €3 ($4.80) children 5–16, free for children 4 and under. Mid-Mar to late Oct daily 10:30am–6pm; cafe and shops year-round.

National Sea Life Centre (Kids) This cleverly designed aquarium at the water's edge in coastal Bray provides a kid-centric introduction to sea life. A labyrinthine path through the aquarium begins with a rock tunnel carved by a winding freshwater stream; from there, you follow the water's course toward the open sea, from freshwater river to tidal estuary to storm-pounded harbor and finally to the briny deep. Along the way, kids use "magic" glasses to read coded questions and find the answers. In the ocean portion of the center, the emphasis is on scary critters, like sharks (of course) and the blue-ringed octopus. It's well done, and good family fun, but it's a bit pricey considering its size.

Strand Rd., Bray, County Wicklow. © **01/286-6939.** www.sealife.ie. Admission €11 ($18) adults, €9 ($15) seniors and students, €7.90 ($13) children 12 and under, €34–€40 ($54–$64) families. Mar–Oct daily 10am–5pm; Nov–Feb Mon–Fri 11am–4pm, Sat–Sun 10am–5pm.

Powerscourt Gardens, House Exhibition, and Waterfall ★★★ (Kids) On a 400-hectare (988-acre) estate less than 19km (12 miles) south of Dublin city, Powerscourt has magnificent gardens, designed by the Irish landscaper Daniel Robertson between 1745 and 1767. Between the gardens, the shops, and the surrounding countryside, there's enough to do here to keep you busy all day long. The gardens are filled with brilliant touches—splendid Greek- and Italian-inspired statuary everywhere, a shady grotto made of petrified moss, a Japanese garden, and an over-the-top fountain from which statues of winged horses rise. Stories have it that Robertson, afflicted with gout, was pushed around the grounds in a wheelbarrow to oversee the work.

The house, on the other hand, has a sad tale to tell. You can see just by looking at its exterior that it once was magnificent—it was designed in the 18th century by Richard Cassels (also called Richard Castle), the architect of Russborough House (see below) and Dublin's Parliament building. The same family lived in the building for 350 years, until the 1950s. By the time they moved out and donated it to the public, it was very run down. Its renovation was painstaking and troubled with financial shortages, and 2 decades passed before it was completed. In 1974, on the day before the building was scheduled to open to the public at long last, it was gutted by fire. After that, the building was closed for more than 30 years, with another achingly slow renovation underway, but a few rooms are now open, including an exhibition room telling the Powerscourt history and a grand ballroom sometimes used for weddings.

There's a garden center where you can learn all there is to learn about the plants that thrive here, and pick up seeds to take home (if your home country's Customs laws permit it—the U.S. doesn't). There are also a playground for the kids and plenty of gift shops. The cafe at Powerscourt is run by the Avoca chain, and serves up rich cakes, hot soups and stews, and healthy salads, along with a breathtaking view. If you feel energetic, follow the well-marked path over 7km (4¹/₃ miles) to the picturesque Powerscourt Waterfall—the highest in Ireland (121m/397 ft.). If you're not feeling energetic, you can drive, following signs from the estate.

Enniskerry, County Wicklow (off the N11). ✆ **01/204-6000.** www.powerscourt.ie. Gardens €8 ($13) adults, €7 ($11) seniors and students, €5 ($8) children 5–16, free for kids 4 and under; waterfall €5 ($8) adults, €4.50 ($7.20) seniors and students, €3.50 ($5.60) children 2–16, free for kids 1 and under. Gardens and house exhibition daily 9:30am–5:30pm (gardens close at dusk in winter); closed Dec 25–26. Ballroom and Garden Rooms year-round Sun 9:30am–1:30pm; May–Sept Tues 9:30am–1:30pm. Waterfall Mar–Apr and Sept–Oct daily 10:30am–5:30pm, May–Aug daily 9:30am–7pm, Nov–Feb daily 10:30am–4pm; closed mid-Dec to Dec 26.

Russborough House ★★

This impressive Palladian villa was built between 1741 and 1751, designed by the great Richard Cassels, who also designed the ill-fated Powerscourt House. In the 1950s, the house was purchased by Sir Alfred Beit, a member of the De Beers diamond family. He had inherited a massive collection of art and wanted someplace to keep it, and thought this rural mansion was just the spot. Thus began one of the most exquisite small rural collections you're likely to find, including paintings by Vernet, Vermeer, Guardi, Goya, Gainsborough, and Rubens. You can see the house only by guided tour, and there is certainly a lot to see—stucco ceilings by the Lafranchini brothers, huge marble mantelpieces, inlaid floors, and lavish use of mahogany in doors and staircase, as well as fine displays of silver, porcelain, and fine furniture.

Blessington, County Wicklow (off N81). ✆ **045/865239.** www.russborough.ie. Admission to main rooms €6 ($9.60) adults, €4.50 ($7.20) seniors and students, €3 ($4.80) children 11 and under. May–Sept daily 10am–5pm; Easter–Apr and Oct Sun and bank holidays 10am–5pm. Tours given on the hour. Closed Nov–Easter, except by appointment.

St. Mullin's Monastery (Finds)

This little gem is a well-kept secret. On a sunny day, its idyllic setting—in a sleepy hamlet beside the River Barrow, ringed by soft carpeted

Russsborough House: A Life of Crime

Russborough House sits in a quiet stretch of countryside on a sprawling estate, miles from anywhere in deepest County Wicklow. Given its location, and its low-key reputation (many visitors to Ireland don't even know it's there), you might think that its collection of paintings by Vermeer, Goya, Gainsborough, and Rubens couldn't be safer. You'd be wrong. There have been three major robberies here over the last 30 years in which millions of dollars worth of art have been stolen, damaged, and lost forever. It all started in 1976 when members of the IRA stole 16 paintings in a sort of crime-based fundraising effort. All of the works were eventually recovered and peace descended, but 10 years later it happened again. That time, a Dublin gangster, Martin Cahill, ordered a number of paintings to be stolen from Russborough to enhance the riches of loyalist paramilitary groups. Only some of those were ever recovered, and many were badly damaged.

In 1988, the owners gave up on the expensive losing game of trying to protect the small but precious collection, and Dublin's National Gallery began managing the collection. Again, all was calm until 2001. This time, thieves smashed a car through the front of the house and drove off with two paintings, including a Gainsborough that had already been stolen twice before. Both were recovered, but security here is now tighter than ever. Thus, you can expect to be followed around by anxious-looking staff, but persevere, as it's a marvelous setting in which to take in the artwork. Just don't try to take it home with you!

hills—is reason enough for a visit. Besides that, this is a fascinating spot, an outdoor museum of sorts, spanning Irish history from the early Christian period to the present, over the course of a few acres. There are the ruins of a monastery founded by St. Moling (Mullin) in roughly A.D. 614. Plundered again and again by the Vikings in the 9th and 10th centuries, it was annexed in the 12th century by a nearby Augustinian abbey. Here, too, are a steep grassy *motte* (grove) and the outline of a bailey (the outer wall or court of a castle) constructed by the Normans in the 12th century. In the Middle Ages, the monastery ruins were a popular destination, especially during the height of the Black Death in 1348, when pilgrims would cross the river barefoot, circle the burial spot of St. Mullin nine times in prayer, adding small stones to the cairn marking the spot, and drink from the healing waters of the saint's well. These ruins and waters are still the subject of an annual pilgrimage near or on July 25.

Adjoining the monastery buildings is an ancient cemetery still in use, where, contrary to common practice, Protestants and Catholics have long lain side by side. A number of rebels from the 1798 Rising are buried here, including Gen. Thomas Cloney. If the Heritage Centre is closed (it opens at the discretion of the caretaker, Seamus Fitzgerald), there's a map and brief history at the entrance to the cemetery.

On the Barrow Dr., 12km (7½ miles) north of New Ross, St. Mullins, County Carlow. Free admission.

Vale of Avoca ★ Basically a peaceful riverbank, the Vale of Avoca was immortalized in the writings of 19th-century poet Thomas Moore. It's here at the "Meeting of the

Waters" that the Avonmore and Avonbeg rivers join to form the Avoca River. It's said that the poet sat under "Tom Moore's Tree" looking for inspiration and penned the lines, "There is not in the wide world a valley so sweet as the vale in whose bosom the bright waters meet. . . ." The tree itself is a sorry sight—it's been picked almost bare by callous souvenir hunters (please don't emulate them!)—but the place is still worth a visit.

Rte. 755, Avoca, County Wicklow.

Wicklow Mountains National Park ★★★

Nearly 20,000 hectares (49,400 acres) of County Wicklow make up this national park. The core area surrounds Glendalough, including the Glendalough Valley and Glendalough Wood Nature Reserves. *Hikers note:* The most mountainous stretch of the Wicklow Way cuts through this park (**www.walkireland.ie** or **www.irishways.com**). You'll find an information station at the Upper Lake at Glendalough. Information is available on hiking in the Glendalough Valley and surrounding hills, including maps and descriptions of routes. (See "Walking" under "Sports & Outdoor Pursuits," below, for suggestions.) The closest parking is at Upper Lake, where you'll pay €2 ($3.20) per car; or, just walk up from the Glendalough Visitor Centre, where the parking is free.

Glendalough, County Wicklow. ℭ **0404/45425.** www.wicklowmountainsnationalpark.ie. Information office free admission. Monastic City Visitor Centre admission €2.90 ($4.65) adults, €2.10 ($3.35) seniors, €1.30 ($2.10) students and children, €7.50 ($12) families. May–Sept daily 10am–5:30pm; Oct–Apr Sat–Sun 10am–5:30pm.

Wicklow's Historic Gaol ★

Given the archaic look of the place, it's impossible to believe that this old jail operated until 1924, the end of a terrifying career that spanned 2 centuries. A visit here is creative and interactive—after passing under the hanging beam, visitors are lined up against the wall of the "day room" and confronted with some dark facts of prison life in 1799, when more than 400 prisoners, most of them rebels, occupied the jail's 42 cells. After years of being fed once every 4 days and allowed to walk in the prison yard for 15 minutes a month, prisoners must have warmed to the idea of the hangman's noose. Within the main cellblock, you can roam the cells and visit informative exhibitions. The impact of these stories is immediate and powerful for children as well as for adults, because this jail held both. Many prisoners were sent from here to penal colonies in Australia and Tasmania; that story, too, is told here, with the help of a stage-set wharf and prison ship. There's an in-house cafe, but if you've still got an appetite after that, you're doing better than us. A more lively, nighttime tour of the Gaol takes place on the last Friday of every month, although this is unsuitable for children.

Kilmantin Hill, Wicklow Town, County Wicklow. ℭ **0404/61599.** www.wicklowshistoricgaol.com. Tour €7.30 ($12) adults, €5.50 ($8.80) seniors and students, €4.25 ($6.80) children 5–15, €19 ($30) families with up to 3 children, free for children 4 and under. Apr 17–Sept daily 10am–6pm (last admission at 5pm). Night tours last Fri of every month 6:30–8:30pm €15 ($24), includes glass of wine. Children 15 and under not admitted on night tours.

SHOPPING

Wicklow and Carlow offer a wide array of wonderful craft centers and workshops. Here is a small sampling:

Avoca Handweavers Inside this picturesque cluster of 18th-century whitewashed stone, workers produce the Avoca chain's distinctively bright and cheerful wool throws, scarves, dainty knitwear, and colorful accessories. You can watch the craftspeople weave strands of yarn (made from Irish wool) into desirable throws and blankets, or just head straight to the shops or the excellent cafe (p. 202). There are other branches throughout

Ireland, including one on the N11 at Kilmacanogue, Bray, County Wicklow (© **01/286-**
7466), open daily 9am to 6pm. Avoca, County Wicklow. © **0402/35105.** www.avoca.ie.

Bergin Clarke Studio In this little workshop, Brian Clarke hand-fashions silver jewelry and giftware, and Yvonne Bergin knits stylish, colorful apparel using local yarns. Open May to September daily 10am to 8pm; October to April Monday to Saturday 10am to 5:30pm. The Old Schoolhouse, Ballinaclash, Rathdrum, County Wicklow. © **0404/46385.**

The Woollen Mills Glendalough This long-established crafts shop in a converted farmhouse offers handicrafts from all over Ireland, such as Bantry Pottery and Penrose Glass from Waterford. Books, jewelry, and a large selection of hand-knits from the area are also sold. Open daily 9:30am to 6:30pm. Laragh, County Wicklow. © **0404/45156.** www. glendaloughwoollenmills.com.

SPORTS & OUTDOOR PURSUITS

CYCLING The Lorum Old Rectory (p. 198) is also the base for **Celtic Cycling** (© **097/977-5282;** www.celticcycling.com), which offers a variety of 1- and 2-week cycling tours, or you can hire the gear you need from them and go it alone. In the summer, this area, with its rolling hills (although things get a bit steep in Wicklow) and gentle breezes, is great cycling country, and this outfit will help you make the most of it. Also, **Cycling Safaris** (© **01/260-0749;** www.cyclingsafaris.com) offers a weeklong tour of the area for €630 ($1,008) per person, including accommodations and food.

FISHING During brown-trout season (Mar 15–Sept 30), you'll find lots of angling opportunities on the Aughrim River (contact Arie Van Derwel; © **0402/36753** or 087/920-2751) and on the Avonmore River (contact Peter Driver in Rathdrum; © **087/ 978-7040**). The Dargle River flows from Enniskerry to the sea at Bray and offers great sea-trout fishing in season from February 1 to October 12 (contact Hugh Duff in Enniskerry; © **01/286-8652**). Shore angling is hugely popular from beaches along the coast; contact the **Irish Federation of Sea Anglers** (© **01/280-6873;** www.ifsa.ie) for information on how to obtain permits. *Note:* Lovely though it is, the Avoca River south of the Meeting of the Waters is polluted by copper mines and is unsuitable for fishing.

GOLF If you're looking for cachet, head to the championship **Druids Glen Golf Club,** Newtonmountkennedy (© **01/287-3600;** www.druidsglen.ie), an inland beauty of a course that bears more than a fleeting resemblance to Augusta and was European Golf Course of the Year in 2000. Greens fees are €190 ($304) daily if you arrive after 9am; early-bird greens fees, from 7:30 to 8:50am, are €80 ($128). It also has a partner course nearby: **Druid's Heath.** It's arguably just as nice, and is slightly cheaper. It can be reached at the same phone number. Special rates that include breakfast or a five-course dinner are available at both. For a more affordable day out, try the parkland **Glenmalure Golf Club,** Greenane, Rathdrum (© **0404/46679;** www.glenmalure.com), where greens fees are €25 ($40) weekdays and €35 ($56) weekends. Lessons are also available for €50 ($80) per person, per hour. The **Arklow Golf Club** (© **0402/32492;** www.arklowgolflinks. com), a seaside par-68 course, charges fees of €45 ($72).

HORSEBACK RIDING The hillside paths of Wicklow are perfect for horseback riding. More than a dozen stables and equestrian centers offer horses for hire and instructional programs. Rates for horse hire average around €30 to €50 ($48–$80) per hour. Among the leading venues are **Broomfield Riding School,** Broomfield, Tinahely (© **0402/ 38117**), and **Brennanstown Riding School,** Hollybrook, Kilmacanogue (© **01/286-3778**). At the **Paulbeg Riding School,** Shillelagh (© **053/942-9100**), experienced riders can explore the surrounding hills, and beginners can receive expert instruction from Sally Duffy, who gives an enthusiastic introduction to the sport.

HUNTING   The **Broomfield Riding School,** Broomfield, Tinahely (© 0402/38117), offers access to the hunt for those who can demonstrate adequate equestrian skills, including jumping. The riding school is open year-round for lessons and trail rides.

WALKING   Loved by hikers and ramblers for its peace, isolation, and sheer beauty, the **Wicklow Way** is a 132km (82-mile) signposted walking path that follows forest trails, sheep paths, and country roads from the suburbs south of Dublin, up into the Wicklow Mountains, and down through country farmland to Clonegal, where the path ends. It takes about 5 to 7 days to walk its entirety, with overnight stops at B&Bs and hostels along the route. Most people choose to walk sections as day trips.

You can pick up information and maps at the Wicklow National Park center at Glendalough, or at any local tourist office. Information on less strenuous walks can be found in the *Wicklow Trail Sheets,* also from tourist offices. It provides a map and route description for several good short walks along the path.

The most spectacular places to walk in Wicklow are in the north and central parts of the county, and it is traversed by the Wicklow Way and numerous short trails. One lovely walk on the Way begins at the **Deerpark parking lot** near the Dargle River and continues to Luggala, passing Djouce Mountain; the next section, between Luggala and Laragh, traverses some wild country around Lough Dan.

St. Kevin's Way, an ancient pilgrims' route more than 1,000 years old, has recently been restored. The path runs for 30km (19 miles) through scenic countryside from Hollywood to Glendalough, following the route taken by pilgrims who visited the ancient monastic site, and winds its way through roads, forest paths, and open mountainside. It takes in many of the historical sites associated with St. Kevin, who traveled the route in search of a mountain hermitage, as well as areas of geological interest and scenic beauty.

Folks who prefer less strenuous walking can follow the paths around the lakes at **Glendalough,** or join the southern section of the **Wicklow Way,** through Tinahely, Shillelagh, and Clonegal. Not as rugged as the terrain in central Wicklow, the gentle hills roll through peaceful glens. Through much of this section, the path follows country roads chosen for their lack of traffic.

WATERSPORTS & ADVENTURE SPORTS   Deep in the Wicklow Mountains, the Blessington Lakes are a 2,000-hectare (4,940-acre) playground of tranquil, clean, speedboat-free water. Less than an hour's drive from Dublin center, and signposted on the N81, the **Blessington Lakes Leisure,** Blessington, County Wicklow (© 045/857844 or 900890), provides all you need for canoeing, kayaking, sailing, and windsurfing, as well as land-based sports such as archery, orienteering, tennis, and pony trekking. Some representative prices per hour for adults are €20 ($32) for canoeing and kayaking, and €30 ($48) for sailing, windsurfing, and pony trekking. Full- and half-day multiactivity prices are also available, and lower children's prices are available. Open daily 10am to 5pm.

WHERE TO STAY
Very Expensive
BrookLodge Hotel & Wells Spa ★★★   BrookLodge is a revolutionary idea—not so much a hotel as a planned village with accommodations scattered around the property amid restaurants, pubs, an award-winning spa, a chapel, a bakery, and a number of shops selling wines, homemade jams, crafts, and the like. The entire property offers a comfortable kind of luxury—rooms have firm king-size beds, deep tubs, soft linens, and contemporary

> **Tips** **Service Charges**
>
> *A reminder:* Unless otherwise noted, room rates don't include service charges (usually 10%–15% of your bill).

furnishings. Service is excellent—the personal touch extends to a decidedly Irish nightly turndown service: chocolates on your pillow and a hot-water bottle between the sheets. The primary restaurant is the **Strawberry Tree**—a gourmet destination eatery with a passionate dedication to organic cuisine (p. 201). Lately the hotel's lavish spa, the **Wells,** has been making headlines as word spreads about its Finnish baths, mud baths, hot tubs, indoor and outdoor pools, flotation room, and innovative therapies and skin treatments. You can often get good discounts by booking online.

Macreddin Village (btw. Aughrim and Aghavannagh), County Wicklow. ☎ **0402/36444.** Fax 0402/36580. www.brooklodge.com. 54 units. €250–€360 ($400–$576) double; €330–€390 ($528–$624) suite; €330–€420 ($528–$672) double with dinner in the Strawberry Tree restaurant. Rates include service charge and full Irish breakfast. Fixed-price 4-course dinner €65 ($104). AE, DC, MC, V. **Amenities:** 3 restaurants (organic, Southern Italian, cafe); 2 pubs; full-service spa; laundry service. *In room:* TV, hair dryer.

Rathsallagh House Hotel & Golf Club ★★ Converted from Queen Anne stables in 1798, this long, brick, ivy-covered country house sits amid 212 hectares (524 acres) of parkland, which is, in turn, surrounded by Rathsallagh Golf Course (greens fees €50–€75/$80–$120). This is a cheerful place, with log fires roaring in the lounge, and a reviving cup of tea available whenever you need it. Return guests request their favorite rooms by name—the Buttercup, the Romantic, the Over Arch, or the Yellow Room. Rooms are priced according to size, starting with standard rooms, which are rather tiny, and rising to superior rooms, which offer plenty of space. Most rooms have sitting areas, and some have Jacuzzis. Children 11 and under are not allowed here.

Dunlavin, County Wicklow. ☎ **800/323-5463** in the U.S., or 045/403112. Fax 045/403343. www.rathsallaghousehotel.com. 31 units. €270–€320 ($432–$512) double. Rates include full breakfast. Fixed-course menus €50–€80 ($80–$128). AE, DC, MC, V. Closed Dec 23–31. **Amenities:** Restaurant (modern Continental); lounge/bar; small indoor pool; 18-hole championship golf course; tennis court; sauna; steam room; archery; billiards; croquet. *In room:* TV, VCR, video library, dataport, tea/coffeemaker, hair dryer.

Tinakilly Country House & Restaurant ★★ Tinakilly is designed to spoil you with luxurious rooms, sweeping views, and an award-winning restaurant. The building dates from the 1870s when it was the home of a sea captain—its central staircase is said to be the twin of the one on his ship. Rooms are done in Victorian style; most have either four-poster or canopy beds. The Captain's Suites are quite grand (with enormous bathrooms), while standard doubles are small but well decorated, albeit with tiny bathrooms. The restaurant (p. 201) is highly rated, so gourmets will want to dine in, rather than heading to the nearby village of Rathnew. Breakfasts here earn raves.

On R750, off the Dublin-Wexford rd. (N11), Rathnew, County Wicklow. ☎ **800/525-4800** in the U.S., or 0404/69274. Fax 0404/67806. www.tinakilly.ie. 51 units. €250–€320 ($400–$512) double; €420–€640 ($672–$1,024) suite. Rates include full breakfast and VAT. AE, DC, MC, V. **Amenities:** Restaurant (modern country house); lounge. *In room:* TV, radio, hair dryer.

Expensive

Clone House ★★ Built in the 1600s, then burned down in the 1798 rebellion and rebuilt in 1805, Clone House has had a rough history, but today Jeff and Carla Watson run the place with panache. Carla was raised in Tuscany and has given the house a bit of Mediterranean elegance. The guest rooms have an Italianate feel, with king-size beds, polished wood floors, and richly colored fabrics. Small luxuries like thick cotton towels, chocolates, and fresh fruit make you feel pampered. The best room, the Vale of Avoca, has a working fireplace. Carla is a superb cook, and you can book in advance for her memorable five-course dinners.

Aughrim, County Wicklow. © **0402/36121.** Fax 0402/36029. www.clonehouse.com. 7 units, all with private bathroom. €140–€200 ($224–$320) double. Rates include full breakfast. Dinner €55–€65 ($88–$104). MC, V. **Amenities:** Bar; small gym; sauna. *In room:* Tea/coffeemaker, hair dryer.

Kilgraney Country House ★★ A striking mix of old and new give this lovely stone building its flavor. In the public areas, solid, Irish-made antiques are balanced with vivid works of contemporary art and pieces of modern furniture. Rooms are soothing and minimalist, with lots of creative touches and pieces of modern art. Dinner, served on a long communal table of black Kilkenny marble, is also a fusion of the exotic and the traditional, and the conversation it inspires can last well into the night. Breakfasts are satisfying—perhaps raisin-and-orange pancakes as a first course, and more standard second-course offerings of scrambled eggs with salmon.

Just off the R705 (L18), 5.6km (3¹/₂ miles) from Bagenalstown on the Borris rd., Bagenalstown, County Carlow. © **059/977-5283.** Fax 059/977-5595. www.kilgraneyhouse.com. 6 units, all with private bathroom, 4 with shower only. €130–€240 ($208–$384) double; €240 ($384) suites. Rates include full breakfast. Dinner €48–€56 ($77–$90). AE, MC, V. Closed Nov–Feb. Children 11 and under not accepted. **Amenities:** Full-service spa; lounge; nonsmoking rooms. *In room:* TV, hair dryer.

Moderate

The Lord Bagenal Inn ★ Ⓕⁱⁿᵈˢ This storybook country inn begs to be photographed, with its old stone archway and lovely setting at the leafy edge of the Barrow River. Inside it's just as cute, with prim rooms neatly decorated with chic country fabrics. At night, the award-winning restaurant delivers French-influenced classics created with fresh local produce. Overall, this is a great address to know about when you want to unwind and be comforted.

Main St., Leighlinbridge, County Carlow. © **059/972-1668.** Fax 059/972-2629. www.lordbagenal.com. 12 units. €110–€125 ($176–$200) double. Rates include full breakfast. MC, V. **Amenities:** Restaurant (modern country); pub; boat hire. *In room:* TV, tea/coffeemaker, hair dryer.

Lorum Old Rectory ★ Set well back from the road and surrounded by undulating pastures in the serene Barrow Valley, the Old Rectory is a weathered and welcoming place. The bedrooms are spacious and comfortable with big four-poster and canopy beds. Most rooms have calming views of the lush Carlow countryside. There's a small gift shop just for guests, displaying the work of local artisans. This is a nonsmoking hotel.

Just off the R705 (L18), 7km (4¹/₃ miles) from Bagenalstown on the Borris rd., Bagenalstown, County Carlow. © **059/977-5282.** Fax 059/977-5455. www.lorum.com. 5 units, all with private bathroom with shower only. €150–€160 ($240–$256) double. Rates include full breakfast. Dinner (must be booked by noon) €45 ($72). AE, MC, V. Closed Dec–Feb. **Amenities:** Drawing room. *In room:* TV, tea/coffeemaker, hair dryer.

Summerhill House Hotel ★ This atmospheric country mansion south of Enniskerry makes an excellent base for exploring the mountains. Surrounded by manicured grounds, the serene 19th-century house offers a peaceful getaway to the countryside. Its lobby makes you feel as if you've walked into a comfortable country home. Rooms are spacious and well appointed, with views of the countryside. Guests can use the fitness center at the more modern Esplanade Hotel a few minutes away.

Enniskerry, County Wicklow. © **01/286-7928.** Fax 01/286-7929. www.summerhillhousehotel.com. 57 units. €150–€180 ($240–$288) double. Rates include full breakfast. MC, V. **Amenities:** Lounge; nonsmoking rooms; sitting room. *In room:* TV, tea/coffeemaker, hair dryer, iron.

Inexpensive

An Óige Glendaloch International Hostel ★
Location, location—this An Óige (Irish Youth Hostel Association) hostel has a prime location right near the Glendalough ruins and lakes, with spectacular views. It was renovated a few years ago, so everything's clean and comfortable, if a tad sterile, and there's no curfew. Doors are locked between noon and 5pm. A full breakfast is available for €7.50 ($12), packed lunch for €6 ($9.60) and three-course dinner for €13 ($21); if you'd rather cook for yourself, you'll have to head to Laragh, a mile away, for groceries. The Irish Writers' Centre of Dublin hosts traditional music and poetry sessions here three times a week during the summer months, and there's live music in the bar every Saturday year-round. It's got a great vibe, attracting people of all ages, and it's very big with hikers.

Glendalough (follow the signs for Glendalough; the hostel is on the road to the upper lake). © **0404/ 45342.** www.anoige.ie. €19–€25 ($30–$40) per person dorms; €49–€54 ($78–$86) per room double, twin. No credit cards. **Amenities:** Restaurant; laundry; Internet; kitchen; foreign-currency exchange.

Derrybawn Mountain Lodge
This elegant, comfortable fieldstone manor house surrounded by parkland has picturesque views of the surrounding hills. Rooms here are spacious, bright, tastefully furnished, and outfitted with comfortable orthopedic beds. Just outside Laragh village, Derrybawn is close to prolific fishing streams and excellent hiking trails (including the Wicklow Way), and a great place from which to explore Wicklow's natural wonders.

Laragh, County Wicklow © **0404/45493.** Fax 0404/45645. http://homepage.eircom.net/~derrymore. 8 units. €80–€100 ($128–$160) double. Rates include full breakfast. MC, V. **Amenities:** Recreation/billiards room; nonsmoking rooms; sitting room. *In room:* TV, VCR, video library.

Sherwood Park House
This big, grand, 18th-century Georgian country house looms four stories high and has memorable views of the green countryside from every window. Its four guest rooms are all spacious—two on the second floor also have small, adjoining twin rooms, making them perfect for families. Rooms have four-poster and half-tester beds done up in well-chosen fabrics. A peat fire warms the attractive sitting room, with its old piano in the corner. Dinner is served in the high-ceilinged dining room, and conversation tends to be lively as everyone sits together at one long polished table.

Kilbride, Ballon, County Carlow (off the N80, 3km/2 miles south of Ballon). © **059/915-9117.** Fax 059/ 915-9355. www.sherwoodparkhouse.ie. 4 units. €100 ($160) double. Ask about discount for children. Dinner €40 ($64). AE, MC, V. **Amenities:** Sitting room. *In room:* TV.

Tudor Lodge
Well located on the slopes of the Wicklow Mountains, this guesthouse makes a good base for ramblers and a peaceful getaway for those who are simply looking to escape the noise of ordinary life. The whitewashed decor is clean and crisp, and most bedrooms are spacious and all are simply decorated—each has a small desk, as well as both a double and a single bed (this makes the smaller rooms a bit of a squeeze). The dining room and living room have large windows overlooking green meadows and mountains. In the summer, you can relax on the generous stone terrace or riverside patio.

There is an appetizing array of breakfast choices, and the restaurants and pubs of Laragh are a short and scenic walk away.

Laragh, County Wicklow. ©/fax **0404/45554.** www.tudorlodgeireland.com. 6 units, all with private bathroom, shower only. €90 ($144) double. MC, V. **Amenities:** Nonsmoking rooms; living room; sunroom; Wi-Fi; 4 rooms are wheelchair accessible. *In room:* TV, tea/coffeemaker, hair dryer.

Self-Catering

Fortgranite   Fortgranite is—and has been for centuries—a working farm in the rolling foothills of the Wicklow Mountains, and it's an unusual and restful place to stay. Three rustic stone cottages, once home to farm workers, have been refurbished with care into guesthouses, available for rent by the week. Two gatehouses each have one double bedroom fully equipped with all essentials, while a lodge sleeps four. All have open fireplaces, and each has its own garden. Those in search of luxury might be disappointed here, but those looking for character will be thrilled. Golf, fishing, hiking, and horseback riding can all be found nearby. Smoking is discouraged.

Baltinglass, County Wicklow (4.8km/3 miles southeast of Baltinglass on R747). © **059/648-1396.** Fax 059/647-3510. 3 cottages. €350–€950 ($560–$1,520) per week. AE, MC, V. *In room:* TV, kitchen, no phone.

Manor Kilbride   This grand Wicklow manor house and its manicured grounds form a kind of peaceful haven across two small lakes and along a stretch of the River Brittas. There are four stone cottages available for rent: two courtyard cottages and a river lodge that each sleep four, as well as a gate lodge perfect for a couple. All the cottages are cleverly designed with every modern amenity beneath their old beamed ceilings. The owners leave a lavish welcome basket for each guest, helping you to settle smoothly into your new temporary home.

N. Blessington, County Wicklow (on N81 6.5km/4 miles north of Blessington, take Kilbride/Sally Gap turn, then left at sign for Sally Gap). © **01/458-2105.** Fax 01/458-2607. 4 cottages. €520–€760 ($832–$1,216) per week year-round. AE, MC, V. *In room:* TV, kitchen, microwave, washing machine.

Tynte House ★ (Kids)   This lovingly preserved, 19th-century family farm complex near the tiny town of Dunlavin in western Wicklow has a good mix of rooms, apartment units, and self-catering stone cottages. All are cleverly designed for both efficiency and taste. They have bright, tasteful color schemes, light-pine furniture, and spacious tiled bathrooms. The no. 3 mews house and the open-plan apartment are favorites, but none will disappoint. This place is great for families, with a grassy play area and treehouse, a barbecue grill and picnic tables, tennis courts, and a game room with Ping-Pong and pool tables. Prices depend on the season and the size of the cottage. Short stays and weekend discounts are available in the off season.

Dunlavin center, County Wicklow. © **045/401561.** Fax 045/401586. www.tyntehouse.com. 7 units, 4 homes, 4 apts, 4 cottages. B&B €90 ($144) double; self-catering units €245–€530 ($392–$848) per week. Dinner €25 ($40). Packed lunches €8 ($13). AE, MC, V. *In room:* TV, kitchen, dishwasher, microwave, washer/dryer.

Wicklow Head Lighthouse ★★ (Finds)   This 18th-century lighthouse on rocky Wicklow Head makes an unusual getaway. The Irish Landmark Trust (ILT), whose mission is to rescue neglected historic buildings, has transformed the old lighthouse into a kind of coastal show home. The interior is chic rustic with whitewashed walls, pine furniture, brass beds, and well-chosen nautical memorabilia. Each of the six floors holds one octagonal unit with two double bedrooms, one bathroom, one sitting room, and the kitchen. Every window has a dazzling ocean view, and the sitting room comes complete with a telescope—great for watching seals frolicking below. As with all ILT properties, there is no TV. *Note:* The spiral staircase that corkscrews up the tower is not suitable for people with mobility problems, or for children 4 and under.

Wicklow, County Wicklow. Contact the Irish Landmark Trust (✆ **01/670-4733.** Fax 01/670-4887. www. irishlandmark.com. €495 ($792) for 4 nights in low season, sliding up to €1,575 ($2,520) per week in high season. MC, V. **Amenities:** Kitchen.

WHERE TO DINE
Expensive
Hungry Monk Wine Bar (Overrated) IRISH   Once a good, well-priced option, this restaurant has sadly converted into another pricey, French-influenced Irish fine-dining option for those with money to burn. The food is fine, with the usual big-night-out menu choices—butter-rich duck and chicken dishes, roasted meats, and so forth. But the look and feel of the place doesn't reflect the new-money prices charged.

Church Rd., Greystones, County Wicklow. (✆ **01/287-5759.** www.thehungrymonk.ie. Main courses €25–€38 ($40–$61). MC, V. Mon–Sat 5–11pm; Sun 4–9pm.

The Strawberry Tree ★★★ GOURMET ORGANIC   Winner of the Irish *Food & Wine*'s Best Restaurant award in 2003, this place has gone from innovative to iconic in a few years. Only wild and organic foods are the ingredients in the memorable meals served in the chic dining room. Starters might include purple sprouting broccoli soup or carrot-and-orange sorbet. Then there could be beef filet with beet root, in a balsamic *jus;* or wild guinea fowl with dried fruit compote. If you're feeling sociable, ask to be seated on the "big table," where dishes (from a special, set menu) are presented "feast style" for you and up to 40 other diners to share. From Rathdrum, follow signs for Aughrim and then 3km (2 miles) to Macreddin Village and the BrookLodge Hotel.

Macreddin Village (btw. Aughrim and Aghavannagh), County Wicklow. (✆ **0402/36444.** Fax 0402/36580. www.brooklodge.com. Reservations required. Fixed-price dinner €65 ($104); Sun lunch €40 ($64). MC, V. Mon–Sat 7–9:30pm; Sun 1:30–3:30pm and 7–9pm.

Tinakilly Country House Hotel ★★ MODERN COUNTRY   This excellent restaurant, which *Bon Appétit* magazine once called "a beacon to restore hope to the traveler's heart," has won as many accolades as the hotel to which it belongs (p. 197). The table d'hôte menu changes daily and is confidently balanced—sophisticated without being fussy. The service, too, is precise and intuitive. Dishes can include pan-fried salmon and John Dory with chili sauce and crème fraiche, or supreme of chicken with gratin potato–and-tarragon *jus.* If dinner here is out of your budget, consider coming for a light lunch (1–3pm) or afternoon tea (3–5pm).

In Tinakilly Country House, Rathnew, County Wicklow (on R750, off the N11). (✆ **0404/69274.** Reservations recommended. Dinner main courses €28–€34 ($45–$54). AE, DC, MC, V. Tues–Sat 7:30–9pm; Sun 1–8pm.

Moderate
Poppies Country Cooking IRISH   As the name implies, this is a friendly, casual place to get a bite to eat in Enniskerry. The food is simple fare (stews, sandwiches, soups, and meat pies), but is homemade and a cut above most such fare. The cakes are excellent, so it's worth stopping in for a cup of tea in the afternoon. A second branch of Poppies has recently opened in the Dundrum Town Center, County Dublin ((✆ **01/296-0629**).

The Square, Enniskerry, County Wicklow. (C) **01/282-8869.** www.poppies.ie. Main courses €13–€20 ($21–$32). MC, V. Daily 8:30am–6pm.

Roundwood Inn ★ IRISH/CONTINENTAL   Let this lovely old 18th-century coaching inn act as a lure to draw you to Roundwood, a place of unspoiled mountain beauty. In keeping with the setting, this place has an old-world atmosphere, with open log fireplaces and antique furnishings. Nearly everything is home baked or locally grown—from steaks and sandwiches to Irish stew, fresh lobster and salmon, and seafood pancakes. In good weather, there's seating in a secluded garden. There's outstanding pub grub in the bar between mealtimes.

Main St. (R755), Roundwood, County Wicklow. (C) **01/281-8107.** Reservations recommended for dinner. Main courses €9–€18 ($14–$29). MC, V. Wed–Fri 7:30–9:30pm; Sat–Sun 1–2:30pm.

Rugantino's River Café SEAFOOD   This riverside restaurant is as attractive for its setting beside the water in Wicklow Town as it is for the fresh fish and shellfish served. Excellent grilled and sautéed dishes fresh off the boat are the main offerings. Items on the wine list are half price until 9pm if dinner is ordered before 7:30pm.

Schooner House, South Quay, Wicklow Town, County Wicklow. (C) **0404/61900.** Reservations not accepted. Main courses €15–€25 ($24–$40). MC, V. Mon–Thurs 7:30–10pm; Fri–Sat 7:30–11pm.

Inexpensive

Avoca Handweavers Tea Shop ★ BISTRO/VEGETARIAN   Forget for a moment that this is an informal cafeteria—at a tourist magnet, no less. It is a great place to eat and it delivers a good, healthy meal. The menu changes frequently, but starters might include pea-and-mint soup or a crisp Caesar salad. Main courses could be sesame-glazed chicken, honey-roasted ham, Mediterranean sweet frittata, or smoked Wicklow trout. The tea shop attracts a loyal local clientele with its perfect pastries.

Avoca, County Wicklow. (C) **0402/35105.** Lunch €5–€12 ($8–$19). AE, DC, MC, V. Daily 9am–5:30pm (5pm in winter).

PUBS

The Coach House   Adorned with hanging flowerpots, this Tudor-style inn is marvelously sweet, surrounded by mountains in picturesque Roundwood. The 18th-century pub is full of local memorabilia, and makes a pleasant stop for pub food and a drink. Main St., Roundwood, County Wicklow. (C) **01/281-8157.** www.thecoachhouse.ie.

Harbour Bar   This is a terrific pub near the seafront in Bray—it's essentially two places in one: one half is a traditional pub with a stone floor and an eclectic collection of memorabilia. The other half is a kind of 1970s lounge, with velvet curtains and wall hangings (including one donated by Peter O'Toole, an occasional regular). The crowd is laid-back, bohemian locals. There are free traditional Irish music shows every other Saturday. Seapoint Rd., Bray, County Wicklow. (C) **01/286-2274.** www.harbourbarbray.com.

Johnnie Fox's   This attractive pub in little Glencullen is endlessly popular—as much for its seafood as for nightly sessions of traditional Irish music. It can get quite crowded on weekends, but the food is good and the crowd is friendly. Main St., Rathdrum, County Wicklow. (C) **01/295-5647.** www.jfp.ie.

The Meetings   This quaint country-cottage pub stands idyllically at the "Meeting of the Waters" in the Vale of Avoca. Good pub grub is served daily, with traditional Irish music from April to October, every Sunday afternoon (4–6pm) and weekend nights all year. Avoca, County Wicklow. (C) **0402/35226.**

2 COUNTY KILDARE: IRELAND'S HORSE COUNTRY

24 to 48km (15–30 miles) W of Dublin

The flatlands of Kildare are rich in more ways than one. The soil is lush and fertile, producing miles of green pastures perfect for raising horses, and the population is one of the most affluent in the country, with plenty of cash for buying horses. Driving through the smooth rolling hills, dotted with the sleekest horses in Ireland, you'll notice a similarity to the green grass of Kentucky—in fact, the county is twinned with Lexington, Kentucky. This is the home of the Curragh, the racetrack where the Irish Derby is held, and of smaller tracks at Naas and Punchestown.

Once the stronghold of the Fitzgerald Clan, Kildare comes from the Irish *cill dara,* or "Church of the Oak Tree," a reference to St. Brigid's monastery, which once sat in the county, surrounded by oak trees. Brigid was a bit ahead of her time as an early exponent for women's equality—she founded her coed monastery in the 5th or 6th century.

ESSENTIALS

GETTING THERE **Irish Rail** (© 01/836-6222; www.irishrail.ie) provides daily train service to Kildare.

Bus Éireann (© 01/836-6111; www.buseireann.ie) operates daily express bus service to Kildare.

By car, take the main Dublin-Limerick road (N7) west of Dublin from Kildare, or the main Dublin-Galway road (N4) to Celbridge, turning off on local road R403.

VISITOR INFORMATION Contact the **Wicklow Tourist Office,** Wicklow Town (© 0404/69117). It's open year-round Monday to Friday, and Saturday during peak season. There is also a seasonal (mid-May to Sept) information office on The Square, Kildare Town, County Kildare (© 045/530672).

SEEING THE SIGHTS

Castletown ★★ Designed by Italian architect Alessandro Galilei for the then-speaker of the Irish House of Commons William Connolly (1662–1729), this is a spectacular Palladian-style mansion. The elaborate style of the grand facade was much imitated across Ireland over the centuries. The fully restored interior is worth the price of admission, as are the two glorious follies on the grounds—both commissioned by William Connolly's wife, Louisa, as make-work for the starving population during the famine. One is a graceful obelisk, the other is the extraordinarily playful barn, created as a slightly crooked inverted funnel, around which winds a stone staircase. Its name, appropriately enough, is the "Wonderful Barn."

R403, off main Dublin-Galway rd. (N4), Celbridge, County Kildare. © 01/628-8252. Admission (guided tour only) €4 ($6.40) adults; €2 ($3.20) seniors, students, and children; €10 ($16) families. No cameras. Mid-July to Nov daily 10am–6pm.

The Curragh ★★ This is the country's best-known racetrack, majestically placed at the edge of Ireland's central plain, and home to the **Irish Derby,** held every spring. Races are on at least one Saturday a month from March to October. The track has rail links with all major towns, and Irish Rail runs directly to it from Dublin (Heuston Station) for around €15 ($24), including courtesy coach to the main entrance. There's also a

"Racing Bus" from Dublin (Busáras) each race day. Call Bus Éireann for details (② **01/836-6111;** www.buseireann.ie).

Dublin-Limerick rd. (N7), Curragh, County Kildare. ② **045/441205.** www.curragh.ie. Admission €15–€20 ($24–$32) for most days of racing; €25–€150 ($40–$240) on derby days. AE, DC, MC, V. Hours vary; 1st race usually 2pm, but check newspaper sports pages.

Irish National Stud with Japanese Gardens & St. Fiachra's Garden ★★ Some of Ireland's fastest horses have been bred on the grounds of this government-sponsored stud farm. Horse lovers and racing fans will be in heaven walking around the 383-hectare (946-acre) grounds watching the well-groomed horses being trained. A converted groom's house has exhibits on racing, steeplechase, hunting, and show jumping, plus a rather macabre display featuring the skeleton of Arkle, one of Ireland's most famous horses.

There's a peaceful **Japanese garden ★** dating from 1906, with pagodas, ponds, and trickling streams. There's also a beautifully designed visitor center with a restaurant and shop. The Commemorative Garden of St. Fiachra, in a natural setting of woods, wetlands, lakes, and islands, opened in 1999. The reconstructed hermitage has a Waterford crystal garden of rocks, ferns, and delicate glass orchids.

Off the Dublin-Limerick rd. (N7), Tully, Kildare, County Kildare. ② **045/522963.** www.irish-national-stud. ie. Admission €11 ($18) adults, €8 ($13) seniors and students, €6 ($9.60) children 5–16, €27 ($43) families, free for children 4 and under. MC, V. Mid-Feb to mid-Nov daily 9:30am–5pm; mid-Nov to Dec 23rd daily 10am–5pm. Last admission 3:30pm; car park locked at 6:30pm sharp. Bus: From Busáras, Dublin, each morning, returning each evening.

The Irish Pewtermill In an 11th-century mill originally constructed for the nunnery of St. Moling, Ireland's oldest pewter mill makes for a nice diversion. Six skilled craftsmen cast pewter in antique molds, some of which are 300 years old. Casting takes place most days, usually in the morning. The showroom has a wide selection of high-quality, hand-cast pewter gifts for sale, from bowls to brooches, at reasonable prices. There's a set of excellent reproductions of the principal panels from Moone High Cross (see the listing below), with explanatory plaques. They're helpful in further understanding and appreciating the ancient carvings.

Timolin-Moone (signposted off N9 in Moone), County Kildare. ② **059/862-4164.** Free admission. Mon–Fri 10am–4:30pm; Sat–Sun 11am–4pm.

Larchill Arcadian Garden ★ (Kids) (Finds) This unusual farm garden is the only surviving "ornamental farm" in Europe and it was nearly lost forever—it had fallen into decay in the 1970s and 1980s, but was restored in the late 1990s. Products of the Romantic Movement, these hybrid farms were popular throughout Europe in the 18th century. Larchill is a marvelous example of art for art's sake, as all around the working farm are little things of beauty: a lake dotted with delightful Gothic follies; miles of wooded nature trails; meadows stocked with emus and llamas; a walled garden filled with goats, geese, and peacocks. There's even a resident ghost haunting a medieval tower. Kids will not be completely bored here, as there's an adventure trail with traditional games, a playground, a sand pit, and guinea pigs and rabbits to pet. Snacks and ice cream are available in the tearoom.

Kilcock, County Kildare (signposted off N4 near Maynooth). ② **01/628-7354.** www.larchill.ie. Admission €7.50 ($12) adults, €5.50 ($8.80) children, €28 ($45) families. May (holiday weekends only, including Mon) and Sept Sat–Sun noon–6pm; June–Aug Thurs–Sun (holiday weekends Sat–Mon) noon–6pm.

Moone High Cross ★ Amid the picturesque ruins of Moone Abbey, this magnificent high cross is nearly 1,200 years old. The abbey, established by St. Columba in the 6th century, is in evocative ruins around it. The cross features finely crafted Celtic designs as well as biblical scenes: the temptation of Adam and Eve, the sacrifice of Isaac, and Daniel in the lions' den. Among the carvings are several surprises, such as a carving of a Near Eastern fish that reproduces when the male feeds the female her own eggs, which eventually hatch from her mouth.

Moone, County Kildare (signposted off N9 on southern edge of Moone village).

Newbridge Cutlery For 60 years, this has been Ireland's leading manufacturer of fine silverware. The visitor center has displays of place settings, bowls, candelabras, trays, frames, and one-of-a-kind items; and if you like it all too much to leave it behind, you can stock up at the shop.

Off Dublin-Limerick rd. (N7), Newbridge, County Kildare. © **045/431301.** Free admission. Mon–Fri 9am–5:15pm; Sat 11am–5:15pm; Sun 11am–5pm.

St. Brigid's Cathedral This 13th-century church stands on the site of St. Brigid's monastery, which was founded in the 5th century. The church, which dominates central Kildare, is a beautiful building with exquisite stained-glass windows portraying Ireland's three great saints: Patrick, Colmcille, and Brigid. The round tower on the grounds dates to the 10th century, and is the second tallest in the country (33m/108 ft.). Somewhere down the line, its pointed roof was replaced by a Norman turret. If the groundskeeper is in, you can climb the stairs to the top for €4 ($6.40). There's a strange-looking stone with a hole at the top near the tower; it's known as the "wishing stone"—according to lore, if you put your arm through the hole and touch your shoulder when you make a wish, then your wish will come true.

Market Sq., Kildare Town, County Kildare. © **045/521229.** Suggested donation €1.50 ($2.40); admission to round tower €4 ($6.40). May–Sept Mon–Sat 10am–1pm and 2–5pm; Sun 2–5pm.

Steam Museum Celebrating the age of steam, this museum contains two collections: The Richard Guinness Hall has prototypical locomotive engines dating from the 18th century, and the Power Hall has rare industrial stationary engines. The engines are turned on fairly regularly—if you're interested, call ahead to find out times. The museum is inside an old church, outside of which an 18th-century walled garden wanders through several verdant spaces to a delightful rose garden. The shop stocks a variety of recent books and videos on the Irish Railway.

Straffan, County Kildare (signposted off N7 at Kill Village). © **01/627-3155.** www.steam-museum.com. Admission to museum and gardens €7.50 ($12) adults; €5 ($8) seniors, children, and students; €20 ($32) families. June–Aug and public holidays Wed–Sun 2–6pm; May–Sept by arrangement.

SPORTS & OUTDOOR PURSUITS

CYCLING Kildare's flat-to-rolling landscape is perfect for gentle cycling. Sadly, most organized tours bypass Kildare for regions with more diverse scenery, but you can always plan your own route.

GOLF The flat plains here create excellent parkland layouts, including two 18-hole championship courses. If your wallet is padded, the Arnold Palmer–designed, par-72 **Kildare Hotel & Country Club** (also known as the **K Club**), Straffan (© **01/601-7200;** www.kclub.com), has two courses, with greens fees ranging from €124 to €380 ($198–$608) for nonresidents in high season, €88 to €165 ($141–$264) in low season.

St. Brigid: Early Feminist

Feminists have embraced this 5th-century saint for decades. Brigid was a head-strong girl who fought against the oppressive rules of her time. When her father picked a husband for her, she refused to marry him. Legend holds that when her father insisted that the wedding should go forward, she pulled out her own eye to prove she was strong enough to resist his plans. He backed down, and the mutilated girl joined a convent, but when she took her vows the bishop accidentally ordained her as a bishop rather than a nun. It is said that, as soon as that happened, she was miraculously made beautiful again.

As she grew older, Brigid remained a rebel. She founded a monastery in Kildare, but insisted that it be open to both nuns and monks—something that was extraordinary at that time. Unsurprisingly, word of the monastery, and of its unusual abbess, soon spread throughout Europe and she became a powerful figure in European Christianity. Her followers marked their homes with a plain cross woven from river reeds, and you'll still find crosses, made in precisely that way, in many Irish homes.

One of Brigid's strangest rules for her monastery was that there should always be a fire kept burning, day and night, tended by 20 virgins. Long after she died, the fire at St. Brigid's burned constantly, tended as she said it should be. This continued as late as 1220, when the bishop of Dublin insisted that the tradition, which he viewed as pagan, be stopped. But there is still a fire pit at St. Brigid's Cathedral, and a fire is lit in it every February 1, on St. Brigid's feast day.

For a less costly game, the par-70 **Kilkea Castle Golf Club,** Castledermot (© **059/914-5555;** www.kilkeacastle.ie), charges €40 ($64) Monday to Thursday, €50 ($80) Friday to Sunday. Kilkea also has a golf and four-course meal package for €55 ($88) Monday to Thursday, €60 ($96) Friday to Sunday. Or try the par-72 championship course at the **Curragh Golf Club,** Curragh (© **045/441896;** www.curraghgolf.com), with greens fees of €35 ($56) weekdays, €45 ($72) weekends; it is closed to nonmembers on Tuesdays.

HORSEBACK RIDING   Visitors can expect to pay an average of €25 ($40) per hour for trekking or trail riding in the Kildare countryside. To arrange a ride, contact the **Kill International Equestrian Centre,** Kill (© **045/877-3333;** www.killinternational.ie), or the **Abbeylands Equestrian Centre,** Clane (© **045/868188**).

WALKING   The way-marked **Grand Canal Way** is a long-distance walking path that cuts through part of Kildare. Its flatness makes it ideal for beginners and for walkers who lack ambition. The canal passes through plenty of scenic towns, such as Sallins, Robertstown, and Edenderry, where you can find a room and stock up on provisions. For more information, contact the tourist office.

WHERE TO STAY
Very Expensive
Kildare Hotel & Country Club ★   The darling of the affluent, sporty set, Kildare is most famous for its 18-hole Arnold Palmer–designed golf course that hosted the Ryder

Cup in 2006 (see above). A 45-minute drive from Dublin, this 132-hectare (326-acre), no-expense-spared resort makes a luxurious base from which to visit Dublin and the sights of Kildare. The surroundings are gorgeous and the service excellent, but the atmosphere here is more formal and less relaxed than at some of Ireland's other manor hotels. A Georgian mansion serves as the main hotel, although guest rooms are spread out among several buildings—all sumptuously appointed with luxurious fabrics. The main restaurant, the **Byerley Turk,** is formal (and a tad snooty) and features rich French food. You can adjourn for drinks in the library—it's a showcase for an extraordinary collection of Jack B. Yeats paintings.

Straffan, County Kildare. ✆ **800/221-1074** in the U.S., or 01/601-7200. Fax 01/601-7297. www.kclub. com. 95 units. €350–€625 ($560–$1,000) double; €575–€825 ($920–$1,320) 2-bedroom suite. AE, DC, DISC, MC, V. **Amenities:** 3 restaurants (Irish, Asian, bistro); pub; indoor swimming pool; 18-hole golf course; 2 indoor and 2 outdoor tennis courts; squash courts; gym; beauty treatments; sauna; concierge; room service; massage; babysitting; laundry; library; private access to salmon and trout fishing; solarium; clay pigeon shooting; horse riding. *In room:* A/C, TV/VCR, minibar, hair dryer.

Kilkea Castle Hotel & Golf Club ★★ Nestled beside the River Greese and surrounded by striking formal gardens, this stern, stone castle was built around 1180. Given such a long history, it's not particularly surprising that it's said to be haunted, in this case by the 11th earl of Kildare, who is said to gallop around the castle walls every 7 years. The hotel's owners know perfectly well what its attraction is, so it's filled with all the suits of armor and medieval banners your heart could desire. About a third of the guest rooms are in the original castle building, with the rest in a courtyard addition, but all are fairly large and have a similar decor with dark wood, beds surrounded in flowing fabric, and gilt-framed paintings. The **Geraldine Bar** is atmospheric with its original stone walls, stained-glass windows, and a huge fireplace. Even if you're not staying here, it's worth having a stroll to check out the castle building. Look out for the evil-eye stone high up on the wall at the back of the structure—it's believed to date from the 13th century and features a monster-headed man and woman.

Castledermot, County Kildare. ✆ **059/914-5156.** Fax 059/914-5187. www.kilkeacastle.ie. 40 units. €230–€360 ($368–$576) double. Rates include service charge and full Irish breakfast. AE, DC, MC, V. **Amenities:** Restaurant (Continental); bar; indoor swimming pool; 18-hole golf course; exercise room; spa pool; sauna; concierge; room service; babysitting; laundry. *In room:* TV, hair dryer.

Expensive

Barberstown Castle ★★ This sturdy castle has overlooked Kildare for more than 750 years. Its five segments—constructed in the 13th, 16th, 18th, 20th, and 21st centuries—somehow form a coherent and pleasing whole. Each luxurious guest room is named after one of the castle's former lords or proprietors. They begin with Nicholas Barby, who constructed the battlemented rectangular keep in the 13th century, and include the guitarist Eric Clapton, who once owned it. The latest extension to this magnificent castle in 2004 added 36 luxurious bedrooms. All the rooms are warm and cozy, with sitting areas, four-poster beds, antiques, and spacious bathrooms. Two-bedroom family spaces are available, as is a room designed for guests with disabilities.

Straffan, County Kildare. ✆ **800/323-5463** in the U.S., or 01/628-8157. Fax 01/627-7027. www. barberstowncastle.ie. 58 units. €240 ($384) double; €280 ($448) 4-poster double bed. Rates include full Irish breakfast. AE, DC, MC, V. Closed Jan–Feb. From Dublin, drive south on N7, take turn for Straffan at Kill; from west on N4, then turn for Straffan at Maynooth. **Amenities:** Restaurant (Continental); lounge; laundry service; nonsmoking rooms. *In room:* TV, hair dryer, garment press.

Very Expensive

Moyglare Manor ★★ FRENCH   A half-hour's drive on the Dublin-Galway road (N4) delivers you to this grand Georgian mansion and inn, where the lavishly decorated, candlelit restaurant is surprisingly intimate. Elegance is the operative word here, and dishes tend to be rich and delicious: roast quail, baked plaice stuffed with shrimp, grilled sea trout, and steaks, all with fresh vegetables from the manor's garden, and are all memorable. Service is excellent, and the desserts are worth saving room for. Rooms in this grand mansion (€250/$400 double) are as luscious as the food.

Maynooth, County Kildare. ℂ 01/628-6351. www.moyglaremanor.ie. Reservations required. Fixed-price 4-course dinner €65 ($104). AE, DC, MC, V. Daily 12:30–3pm and 7–9pm. Closed Good Friday and Dec 25–27.

Moderate

Ballymore Inn INTERNATIONAL   Don't judge this book by its cover. It may look like a modest country restaurant, but the inspired cooking means each dish is a thing of beauty. The menu is varied yet unpretentious—typical mains might include organic chicken with roasted vegetables and walnut balsamic, or Clare Island salmon with ginger salsa. The pizzas are often the most adventurous thing on the menu, with toppings such as Greek lamb with yogurt and mint definitely winning points for originality. If all this sounds too adventurous there's a more limited menu on offer in the bar.

Ballymore Eustace, County Kildare (off the N81, southeast of Blessington). ℂ 045/864585. www.ballymore inn.com. Reservations required. Main courses €18–€36 ($29–$58). MC, V. Restaurant daily 12:30–3pm and 6–9pm. Bar menu Mon–Fri 3–9pm; Sat 2–9pm; Sun 12:30–9pm.

Silken Thomas GRILL   This historic inn is an old-world pub and an atmospheric restaurant with wooden floors and fires crackling in the hearth. The menu offers a good selection of soups, sandwiches, burgers, and salads, as well as steaks, roasts, mixed grills, and fresh seafood platters. **Chapter 16,** an upscale restaurant adjoining the lounge bar, is one of a growing list of side ventures at the Silken Thomas (along with a nightclub and an alcohol-free teen disco). Bookings can be made on the main reservations number, but we haven't yet paid a visit.

The Square, Kildare, County Kildare. ℂ 045/522232. www.silkenthomas.com. Reservations recommended for dinner. Main courses €14–€28 ($22–$45). AE, MC, V. Mon–Sat 12:30–2:30pm and 6–10pm; Sun 12:30–3pm and 6–9pm.

PUBS

The George Inn   The back room of this pub is what makes it special. It was probably the kitchen of the original cottage, which would explain the huge fireplace with warm inglenooks and a brass-and-leather horse harness hanging over the mantel. Seating is random at a hodgepodge of cozy pine tables and chairs, and the atmosphere is welcoming and local. Prosperous, County Kildare. ℂ 045/861041.

The Moone High Cross Inn   This big, 18th-century pub is ideal for a pit stop. There's genuine hospitality and excellent pub food—toasted sandwiches, shepherd's pie, all the classics—not to mention an open fire, finely pulled pints, and convivial conversation. Moone, County Kildare. No phone.

3 COUNTIES MEATH & LOUTH/THE BOYNE RIVER VALLEY

48 to 80km (30–50 miles) N and W of Dublin

Less than 48km (30 miles) north of Dublin along Ireland's east coast runs the River Boyne, surrounded by the rich, fertile countryside of counties Meath and Louth. More than any other river in the country, this meandering body of water has been at the center of Irish history.

The banks of the Boyne hold reminders of Ireland's ancient past in the extraordinary and mysterious prehistoric passage tombs of Newgrange and the storied Hill of Tara, once the seat of the High Kings. This was the setting for the infamous Battle of the Boyne, when in July 1690, King William III defeated the exiled King James II for the crown of England.

Today its historic treasures are tucked away among miles of farmland, smooth, rolling hills, and modern Dublin suburbs.

ESSENTIALS

GETTING THERE **Irish Rail** (© 01/836-6222; www.irishrail.ie) provides daily train service between Dublin and Drogheda.

Bus Éireann (© 01/836-6111; www.buseireann.ie) operates daily express bus service to Slane and Navan in County Meath, and Collon and Drogheda in County Louth. Bus Éireann and **Gray Line Tours** (© 01/605-7705; www.guidefriday.com) offer seasonal sightseeing tours to Newgrange and the Boyne Valley.

By car, take the N1 north from Dublin City to Drogheda, then the N51 west to Boyne Valley; the N2 northwest to Slane and east on the N51 to Boyne Valley; or the N3 northwest via Hill of Tara to Navan, and then east on the N51 to Boyne Valley.

VISITOR INFORMATION Contact the **Dundalk Tourist Office,** Jocelyn Street, County Louth (© 042/933-5484); the **Drogheda Tourist Office,** Mayoralty Street, Drogheda, County Meath (© 041/983-7070); or the **Bru na Boinne Center,** Newgrange, Donore, County Meath (© 041/988-0300).

COUNTY MEATH: THE ROYAL COUNTY

The verdant pastures and low hills of Meath are Dublin's closest northern neighbor. The farmland here is so rich that there's an old Irish saying that a farm in Meath is worth two in any other county. With sheep grazing peacefully in green fields, Meath may look ordinary, but it holds remnants of Ireland's mysterious past. It is also the site of the **Hill of Tara**—the Olympus of early Ireland where the kings of Ireland ruled.

By then, though, the county was already very old. Meath's rich soil has attracted settlers for more than 8,000 years, and archaeologists have uncovered fascinating burial grounds and settlements that give some insight into where and how they lived. The most intriguing of these is **Newgrange,** with its mysterious carvings and huge stone passage tombs. Nearby, the Hill of Slane, a lofty 150m (492-ft.) mound, overlooks one of the loveliest parts of the Boyne Valley. On this hill, tradition has it, Patrick lit the Christian paschal fire in direct defiance of the Irish King Laoghaire, throwing down the gauntlet for a confrontation between Ireland's old and new religious orders.

The chief town of County Meath is **Navan,** but nearby **Kells** is better known to the traveler because of its association with the famous Book of Kells, the hand-illustrated gospel manuscript on display at Trinity College in Dublin (see chapter 6). The town of Kells, known in Gaelic as *Ceanannus Mor* ("Great Residence"), was originally the site of an important 6th-century monastic settlement founded by St. Colmcille. The monastery was dissolved in 1551, and today only ruins and crosses survive.

Less than 40km (25 miles) southeast of Kells, beside the River Boyne, stand the alluring ruins of **Bective Abbey**, a Cistercian monastery founded in 1147. Today it feels more like a castle than a monastery; it is a great ruin, with myriad staircases, passageways, and chambers—a favorite hide-and-seek venue for local children, and perfect for a family picnic.

Even though Meath is primarily an inland county, it is also blessed with a stretch of coastline and two fine sandy beaches, **Bettystown** and **Laytown.** History pops up everywhere in County Meath, even on the beach: The Tara Brooch was found at Bettystown in 1850. Often copied in modern jewelry designs, the brooch is one of Ireland's finest pieces of early Christian gold-filigree work, embellished with amber and glass. It's on view at the National Museum in Dublin.

Seeing the Sights

Hill of Tara ★   This hill is a sentimental lure to the Irish diaspora, drawn by legends and folklore that place it at the center of early Irish history. Something about this nondescript green hill has always attracted people for reasons of spiritualism. Ancient tombs have been discovered on the hill that date back to the Stone Age. Pagans believed that the goddess Maeve lived and reigned from here. By the 3rd century, it was home to the most powerful men in Ireland—the high kings. They had a ceremonial residence on the hill, and ruled as much by myth as by military strength. Every 3 years, a *feis* (a banquet reaching the proportions of a great national assembly) was held. It's said that more than 1,000 princes, poets, athletes, priests, druids, musicians, and jesters celebrated for a week. A *feis* wasn't all fun and games: Laws were passed, disputes settled, and matters of defense decided. The last *feis* was held in A.D. 560, and thereafter, Tara went into a decline as the power and popularity of Christianity rose. What's left of all of this is not physically impressive—grassy mounds, some ancient pillar stones, and depressions where the Iron Age ring forts stood. All the wooden halls rotted long ago, so you'll have to rely on your imagination. But it's still a magnificent spot, with the hill rising 90m (295 ft.) above the surrounding countryside, and beautiful views. A visitor center, with exhibits and a stirring film, is in the old church beside the entrance to the archaeological area. There's no picnicking, but there is a coffee shop/tearoom.

Off the main Dublin rd. (N3), Navan, County Meath. ✆ **046/902-5903.** Admission €2.10 ($3.35) adults, €1.30 ($2.10) seniors, €1.10 ($1.75) students and children, €5.80 ($9.30) families. Mid-May to mid-Sept daily 10am–6pm.

Knowth ★★   There is some debate over whether this site is more historically important than Newgrange. Both are Stone Age burial grounds, with complex passage tombs. Knowth's tomb was closed to the public for many years as archaeologists explored its depths, but is now open, at least in part. It is a massively long passage—at 34m (112 ft.), it is longer than the one at Newgrange. Then, in 1968, archaeologists discovered a second passage tomb on the opposite side of the mound that was 6m (20 ft.) longer. In the mound itself, scientists found the largest collection of passage tomb art uncovered thus far in Europe, as well as a number of underground chambers and 300 carved slabs. The mound itself is surrounded by 17 satellite graves in a complex pattern. The meaning of it all remains shadowed in mystery, and even now, all of Knowth's secrets have not been

Threatening Tara

Ireland's insatiable hunger for construction, highways, and speed is heading for a head-on collision with its ancient history. Plans to build an expanded M3 motorway smack-dab in the middle of the historic Tara-Skryne Valley has shocked even this nouveau riche, couldn't-care-less-about-a-bunch-of-rocks country, and brought calls for a long-needed national debate about the long-term price of overdevelopment.

The highway, which will smooth the commute for residents of bedroom communities in leafy County Meath to their offices in Dublin, has been called an "act of governmental vandalism" by opponents, but the government in question has shown no interest in backing down on its plans to speed up the movement of the Irish through Ireland at what sometimes seems like any cost.

This kind of heedless development has seemed, in recent years, to be paving the country over with little thought for what this means to everything that has long defined this nation. But Tara—the seat of the ancient kings, the site of the Battle of the Boyne, arguably the heart of Ireland—had always seemed to be sacred.

Now it seems nothing is sacred in Ireland, anymore.

The Tara valley is riddled with ceremonial monuments virtually as old as the land itself. The vast majority are yet to be explored by scientists. Archaeologists believe one of them—known as the Mound of the Hostages—dates back to 3000 B.C., making it as old as the pyramids.

The area also has political significance to modern Ireland, as it was to Tara that Daniel O'Connell—the "Great Liberator"—came, to speak to a million people, urging the repeal of the Act of Union between Britain and Ireland and the restoration of the Irish Parliament.

But in 2007, Ireland's minister for transportation dug a ceremonial shovel of earth at a groundbreaking for the motorway, right through the middle of it all.

Within weeks, an unknown ancient archaeological site was discovered directly in the road's planned path. Many thought that this would surely stop the government's plans, but it didn't. It turned out that in 2004 the government amended the National Monuments Act to allow for the demolition of national monuments when the government sees fit.

Protests of the road building have been virtually nonstop since work began, but the government has been undaunted.

You can learn the latest before your visit at **www.tarawatch.org**.

uncovered—excavation work is quite constant here, and you may get a chance to see the archaeologists at work. All tickets are issued at the visitor center. Combined tickets with Newgrange are available.

Drogheda, County Meath (1.6km/1 mile northwest of Newgrange, btw. Drogheda and Slane). (✆) **041/ 988-0300**. www.knowth.com. Admission to Knowth and Bru na Boinne Centre €4.50 ($7.20) adults, €2.90 ($4.65) seniors, €1.60 ($2.55) students and children 7 and over, €11 ($18) families. Combined ticket with Newrange €10 ($16) adults, €7.40 ($12) seniors, €4.50 ($7.20) children, €26 ($42) families. Nov–Feb daily

9:30am–5pm; Mar–Apr and Oct daily 9:30am–5:30pm; May daily 9am–6:30pm; June to mid-Sept daily 9am–7pm; mid- to late Sept daily 9am–6:30pm.

Loughcrew ★   The 30 passage tombs of Loughcrew, also known as Slieve na Cal-liaghe or "The Hill of the Witch," crown three hilltops in western Meath. From their summits, the views of the plains of Meath and the lake lands of Cavan are spectacular on a clear day. Two of the cairns—ornamented with Neolithic carvings—can be entered with a key. Guided tours of the eastern cairn are offered from mid-June to mid-September, and a key is available at the office for the western tomb (in many ways the more interesting of the two). A €25 ($40) deposit is required for the key. From October to May, the keys to both cairns are available from Mrs. Basil Balfe (✆ **049/854-1256**), whose home is the first house on your right after turning into the Loughcrew drive. There are gardens on-site for a fee, but admission is a bit steep. The cairns, however, are still free.

Outside Oldcastle, County Meath. ✆ **049/854-1356.** www.loughcrew.com. Cairns free, admission to gardens €7 ($11) adults, €5 ($8) seniors and students, €3.50 ($5.60) children, €20 ($32) families. Apr–Sept daily 10am–6pm; year-round Sun and bank holidays only 1–5pm. Key is available at other times (see above). From N3, take R195 through Oldcastle toward Mullingar. 2.4km (1½ miles) out of Oldcastle, look for a signposted left turn. The next left turn into Loughcrew is also signposted.

Newgrange ★★★   Ireland's best-known prehistoric monument is one of the archaeological wonders of western Europe. Built as a burial mound more than 5,000 years ago—long before the Egyptian pyramids or Stonehenge—it sits atop a hill near the Boyne, massive and mysterious. The mound is 11m (36 ft.) tall, and approximately 78m (256 ft.) in diameter. It consists of 200,000 tons of stone, a 6-ton capstone, and other stones weighing up to 16 tons each, many of which were hauled from as far away as County Wicklow and the Mountains of Mourne. Each stone fits perfectly in the overall pattern, and the result is a watertight structure, an amazing feat of engineering. The question remains, though: Who was it for? Even as archaeologists found more elaborate carvings in the stones—spirals, diamonds, and concentric circles—they got no clues as to whether it was for kings, political leaders, or for a long-lost ritual. Inside, a passage 18m (59 ft.) long leads to a central burial chamber that sits in pitch darkness all year, except for 5 days in December. During the winter solstice (Dec 19–23), a shaft of sun-light travels down the arrow-straight passageway for 17 minutes, until it hits the back wall of the burial chamber. You can register for a lottery to be in the tomb for this extraordinary event. As part of the tour, you can walk down the passage, past elaborately carved stones and into the chamber, which has three sections, each with a basin stone that once held cremated human remains.

Tips: Admission to Newgrange is by guided tour only. It's 3.2km (2 miles) east of Slane. Get there early. All tickets are issued at the visitor center, Bru na Boinne. Com-bined tickets with Knowth, another nearby megalithic passage tomb, are available. Because of the great numbers of visitors, especially in the summer, expect delays; access is not guaranteed. The last tour is given at 4:30pm.

Off N51, Slane, County Meath. ✆ **041/988-0300.** Fax 041/982-3071. www.knowth.com/newgrange.htm. Guided tour and admission to Bru na Boinne Centre €5.80 ($9.30) adults, €4.50 ($7.20) seniors, €2.90 ($4.65) students and children over 6, €15 ($24) families. Combined ticket with Knowth €10 ($16) adults, €7.40 ($12) seniors, €4.50 ($7.20) children, €26 ($42) families. Nov–Feb daily 9:30am–5pm; Mar–Apr and Oct daily 9:30am–5:30pm; May and mid-late Sept daily 9am–6:30pm; June to mid-Sept daily 9am–7pm.

Newgrange Farm (Kids)   After all that history, the kids will thank you for bringing them here to this busy 133-hectare (329-acre) farm where farmer Willie Redhouse and his family will take them on a 1½-hour tour of their farm. You can feed the ducks, groom a calf, and bottle-feed the lambs and kid goats. Children can hold a newborn chick, pet a pony, and play with the pigs. In the aviaries are pheasants and rare birds. The high point of the week (for kids, anyway) occurs at roughly 3pm every Sunday when the sheep take to the track with teddy bear jockeys for the weekly derby. Demonstrations of sheepdogs working, threshing, and horseshoeing are regularly underway, while in the herb garden you can get a lesson in picking edible plants and herbs. There is a coffee shop and plenty of picnic space.

Off N51, 3.2km (2 miles) east of Slane (signposted off N51 and directly west of Newgrange monument), County Meath. ℂ 041/982-4119. www.newgrangefarm.com. Admission €8 ($13) per person, €24 ($38) families. Daily 10am–5pm. Closed Sept to Good Friday.

St. Colmcille's House

Sitting incongruously in a row of modern houses, like a memory of Ireland's past, St. Colmcille's House is all that's left of an old monastic settlement that once stood where modern homes are now built. Most of the building is 10th century, although the oldest parts predate that by a century. Precisely what the house was built for is unknown, although some experts believe it was once a scriptorium—where monks wrote and illuminated books. The first-floor room still contains the traces of an ancient fireplace and entryway. A narrow metal staircase ascends 4.5m (15 ft.) to a dark vault just under the roof. The small two-chambered space has both a structural and mythical dimension. It is thought to help reinforce the stone arch of the oratory roof and—though this is more conjectural—is also said to be the place where the Book of Kells was completed.

About 180m (about 590 ft.) northwest of St. Columba's Church, Church Lane, Kells, County Meath. Free admission. Mon–Sat 10am–5pm. Ask for key from caretaker Mrs. B. Carpenter, next door to the oratory on Church Lane.

Slane Castle

This 18th-century castle is best known within Ireland for the open-air rock and pop concerts held here in the summertime. For tourists, the big draw is the building itself, a Gothic Revival structure by James Wyatt. The design of the building was made grander in the early 19th century in advance of a visit by the English King George IV to Lady Conyngham, who is believed to have been his mistress (in fact, the Irish claim that the road from Dublin to Slane was built to ease George's journeys to her home). A fire in 1991 burned most of the castle's extensive collection of art and antiques. After extensive renovations, the castle is now open again for visits.

Just west of Slane (signposted off the Navan rd.), County Meath. ℂ 041/988-4400. www.slanecastle.ie. Admission €7 ($11) adults; €5 ($8) seniors, students, and children; €20 ($32) families. May–Aug Sun–Thurs noon–5pm.

Trim Castle ★

This massive Anglo-Norman edifice is a magnificent sight. The Norman lord Hugh de Lacy occupied the site in 1172 and built the enclosed cruciform keep. In the 13th century, his son Walter enlarged the keep, circled it with a many-towered curtain wall, and added a great hall as an upgraded venue for courts, parliaments, and feasts. After the 17th century, it was abandoned and lay in ruins for centuries. Few paid much attention to it until Mel Gibson chose to use it as a setting for the film *Braveheart*. Since then, it's generally overrun with curious visitors in the summertime. The Irish Heritage Service restored it as a "preserved ruin," leaving much of its historic integrity. It's a skeletal reminder of the once-great Anglo-Norman clout. You can take the guided tour, but you'll have to arrive early. It's usually a sellout, but can't be booked in advance. Note that this tour is unsuitable for small or unruly children, and for anyone unable to climb steep climbs or afraid of formidable heights.

Gruesome Find at Trim Castle

In 1971 when excavation work was underway at Trim Castle, workers made a macabre discovery. While digging to the south of the central keep, they uncovered the remains of 10 headless men. Historians believe that the bodies date from the 15th century. During a time of high crime in 1465, King Edward IV ordered that all robbers should be beheaded, and their heads displayed on spikes to intimidate those who might be thinking of a career in crime. Presumably, these men had all suffered that fate.

Trim, County Meath. ℂ **046/943-8619.** Admission to grounds and tour of keep €3.70 ($5.90) adults, €1.60 ($2.55) seniors, €2.30 ($3.70) students and children, €8.70 ($14) families; admission to grounds only €1.60 ($2.55) adults, €1.10 ($1.75) seniors, €1 ($1.60) children and students, €4.50 ($7.20) families. Easter–Oct daily 10am–6pm; Nov–Easter weekends only 10am–5pm. Tours every 30 min. starting at 10:15am; last admission 1 hr. before closing.

Shopping

Mary McDonnell Craft Studio Textile artist Mary McDonnell welcomes visitors to watch as she creates leather items, ceramics, jewelry, and quilts. Her shop stocks the works of local artisans inspired by ancient Celtic designs. Open Tuesday to Saturday from 10:30am to 6pm, Sunday from 3 to 6pm. 4 Newgrange Mall, Slane, County Meath. ℂ **041/982-4722.**

Sports & Outdoor Pursuits

CYCLING You can rent bikes by the day from **Clarke's Sports Den** at the back of the Navan Indoor Market (39 Trimgate St.; ℂ **046/902-1130**). Rates are around €14 ($22) per day.

GOLF The **Headfort Golf Club,** Kells (ℂ **046/924-0146;** www.headfortgolfclub.ie), has two courses and its greens fees are €40 to €50 ($64–$80) weekdays, €55 to €70 ($88–$112) weekends. Even more reasonably priced is the par-73 **County Meath Golf Club,** Trim (ℂ **046/943-1463;** www.countymeathgolfclubtrim.ie), with greens fees of €30 ($48) weekdays, €35 ($56) weekends. If you prefer links courses, the **Laytown and Bettystown Golf Club,** Bettystown (ℂ **041/982-8793;** www.landb.ie), charges greens fees of €60 ($96) weekdays, €75 ($120) weekends.

HORSEBACK RIDING Visitors can expect to pay an average of €25 ($40) per hour for trekking or trail riding in the countryside. To arrange a ride, contact the **Kells Equestrian Centre,** Kells (ℂ **046/924-6998;** www.kellsequestrian.com).

Where to Stay
Moderate

Conyngham Arms Hotel This three-story stone building dates from 1850 and has been run by the same family for more than 60 years. These days, it balances old-world charm with 21st-century conveniences. The guest rooms have classic dark-wood furnishings—some with sturdy four-poster beds—and a traditional look that is getting a bit dated in places. Good bar food is available all day in the lounge, while an excellent dinner is served in the adjacent restaurant. *Note:* The bar can be noisy at night, so ask for a room on the top floor.

Main St., Slane, County Meath. ℂ **800/44-UTELL** (448-8355) in the U.S., or 041/988-4444. Fax 041/982-4205. www.conynghamarms.com. 16 units. €115–€175 ($184–$280) double. Rates include full breakfast. DC, MC, V. Free parking. **Amenities:** Bar/lounge; babysitting. *In room:* TV, hair dryer.

Glebe House ★   This is a beautifully maintained, ivy-covered country house, about
a 15-minute drive from Drogheda, and close to all the major sights in County Meath.
It's a peaceful, isolated place, and the rooms are big and distinctively decorated, many
with log-burning fireplaces. Breakfast is big enough to keep you going all day.

Dowth, County Meath. ℭ **041/983-6101.** Fax 041/984-3469. www.theglebehouse.ie. 9 units. €120
($192) double. Rates include breakfast. MC, V. **Amenities:** Lounge. *In room:* Hair dryer.

Inexpensive

Tara Guesthouse ★   The main attraction at this friendly, well-maintained guesthouse is its location at the edge of the sea. Tara Guesthouse sits so close to the water that
sand might blow into your room. It's affordable, rooms are attractively designed, and the
sea breezes are endlessly refreshing. Breakfast is not included in the room price.

Beachfront, Laytown, County Meath. ℭ **041/982-7239.** 10 units. €80 ($128) double. No credit cards.
Amenities: Lounge. *In room:* TV, hair dryer.

Where to Dine

Vanilla Pod ★   MODERN IRISH   In this modern, creative little restaurant in the
center of Kells, fresh local ingredients are the center of attention. The menu features light
dishes prepared with fresh herbs and local poultry and meat, and it's all served up in a
cheerful dining room, with a friendly touch.

At the Headfort Arms Hotel, John St., Kells, County Meath. ℭ **046/924-0084.** Reservations not needed.
Main courses €19–€24 ($30–$38). MC, V. Mon–Thurs 5:30–10pm; Fri–Sat 5:30–11pm; Sun noon–3pm and
5–10pm. Early-bird specials until 7:30pm.

COUNTY LOUTH/CUCHULAINN COUNTRY

Blink and you'll miss it—to the north and east of Meath, little Louth is Ireland's tiniest
county at only 824 sq. km (318 sq. miles), and even its largest towns (**Drogheda** and
Dundalk) are quite small. The heritage town of **Carlingford** ★★ is easily the prettiest,
sitting on a spur of the Cooley Mountains, overlooking glassy Carlingford Lough—a
photo just waiting to happen. Established by the Vikings, Carlingford still follows its
medieval street patterns, and is overseen by a massive 13th-century castle. On the heights
above the town, the ancient Irish folk hero Cúchulainn is said to have single-handedly
defeated the armies of Ulster in an epic battle.

Aside from Carlingford, Louth is not a place of outstanding scenic beauty, and most
visitors move on in fairly short order, leaving it in peace.

Seeing the Sights

Holy Trinity Heritage Centre   In a beautifully restored medieval church, this center
details Carlingford's history from its Norman origins. If you book ahead, your visit can
include a free guided walking tour of the town and a look at King John's Castle, the Mint,
the Tholsel (the sole surviving, though altered, gate to the old medieval town), and a
Dominican friary.

Carlingford, County Louth. ℭ **042/9373454.** Admission €3 ($4.80) adults; €1.50 ($2.40) seniors, students, and children. Sept–May Sat–Sun noon–5pm; June–Aug daily 10am–4:30pm.

Mellifont Abbey ★   Founded in the 12th century, this was the first Cistercian monastery on the island, and ultimately became the most spectacular. Enough is left of the abbey
buildings just a few miles north of Drogheda to give you an idea of what Mellifont was like
in its day, when it was the center of Cistercian faith in Ireland, with more than 400 monks
living and working within its walls. You can see the outline of the cross-shaped nave, as well

High Crosses

You see them all over Ireland, often in the most picturesque rural surroundings, standing alone like sentries, high Celtic crosses with faded stories carved into every inch of space. They are extraordinary—mournful and unforgettable—but when they were created, they served a useful purpose: They were books, of sorts, in the days when books were rare and precious. Think of the carvings, which inevitably explain the stories of the Bible, as illustrations acting sort of like cartoons explaining the Bible to the uneducated population. When they were created, the crosses were probably brightly painted as well, but the paint has been lost to the wind and rain.

The **Muiredach Cross** ★ at Monasterboice has carvings telling, from the bottom up, the stories of Adam and Eve, Cain and Abel, David and Goliath, and Moses, as well as the wise men bringing gifts to the baby Jesus. At the center of the old cross, the carving is thought to be of Revelation, while, at the top, St. Paul stands alone in the desert. The western side of the cross tells the stories of the New Testament, with, from the top down, a figure praying, the Crucifixion, St. Peter, Doubting Thomas, and, below that, Jesus' arrest. On the base of the cross is an inscription of the sort found often carved on stones in ancient Irish monasteries. It reads in Gaelic, "A prayer for Muiredach for whom the cross was made." Muiredach was the abbot at Monasterboice until 922, so the cross was probably made as a memorial shortly after his death.

Another excellent example of a carved high cross is to be found at the monastery of Cloncmanoise near Shannonbridge.

as the remains of the cloister, refectory, and warming room, which, because the monks lived lives of suffering, would have been the only part of the monastery with heating. The octagonal washing room, or lavabo, is widely viewed as one of the best surviving pieces of Cistercian architecture in the country. Mellifont was closed in the 16th century during the English dissolution, and a manor house was soon built on the site for an English landlord, using the abbey's stones. A century later, that house would be the last place where Hugh O'Neill, the final Irish chief, stayed before surrendering to the English and then fleeing to Europe in 1607, in the "flight of the Earls." There's a good visitor center next door where you can find out more about the monastery and its complex and lengthy history.

Off the R168, Tullyallen, County Louth. ✆ **041/982-6459.** www.mellifontabbey.ie. Admission €2.10 ($3.35) adults; €1.30 ($2.10) seniors, students, and children; €5.80 ($9.30) families. June–Sept daily 9:30am–6:30pm; Oct–May daily 10am–5pm.

Millmount Museum and Martello Tower ★   In the courtyard of 18th-century Millmount Fort, this eclectic little museum tells the history of Drogheda and the Boyne Valley. The collection includes Bronze Age finds, medieval tiles, and a large collection of 19th-century trades-union banners, which the staff will enthusiastically talk your ear off about if business is slow. The mishmash display also includes random domestic items: looms, brewing equipment, gramophones, and, strangely, mousetraps. A geological exhibit contains specimens of stone from every county in Ireland, every country in Europe, and beyond.

Admission museum and tower €5.50 ($8.80) adults, €3 ($4.80) seniors and children, €4 ($6.40) students, €12 ($19) families; tower only €3 ($4.80) adults, €2 ($3.20) seniors and children, €2.50 ($4) students, €6 ($9.60) families. Mon–Sat 10am–5:30pm; Sun and bank holidays 2–5pm. Last tour 1 hr. before closing.

Monasterboice ★   This interesting ancient monastic site holds a peaceful cemetery, one of the tallest round towers in Ireland, ancient church ruins, and two excellent high crosses. The atmosphere here is dreamy, and you get the sense that it was once a peaceful place of prayer. The original site is said to have been founded in the 4th century by a follower of St. Patrick named St. Buithe. The name "Buithe" was corrupted to Boyne over time, and thus the whole region is named after him. The small monastic community thrived here for centuries, until it was seized and occupied by Vikings in the 10th century, but the Vikings were, in turn, defeated by the Irish high king of Tara, Donal, who is said to have single-handedly killed 300 of them. Today there's only a little left, but the Muiredeach's High Cross is worth the trip all on its own. Dating from 922, the near-perfect cross is carved with elaborate scenes from the Old and New Testaments. Two other high crosses are more faded, and one was smashed by Cromwell's forces.

Off the main Dublin rd. (N1), 9.7km (6 miles) northwest of Drogheda, near Collon, County Louth. Free admission. Daily dawn–dusk.

Old Mellifont Abbey   "Old Mellifont" (distinct from "New Mellifont," a Cistercian monastery several miles away) was established in 1142 by St. Malachy of Armagh. Although little more than foundations survive, this tranquil spot is worth a visit for a few moments of quiet. Remnants of a 14th-century chapter house, an octagonal lavabo dating from around 1200, and several Romanesque arches remain. A visitor center contains sculpted stones from the excavations.

On the banks of the Mattock River, 9.7km (6 miles) west of Drogheda, off T25, Collon, County Louth. © **041/982-6459.** www.mellifontabbey.com. Admission €2.10 ($3.35) adults, €1.30 ($2.10) seniors, €1.10 ($1.75) students and children, €5.80 ($9.30) families. May–Oct daily 10am–6pm.

St. Peter's Church of Ireland   This church dating from the 18th century is the latest in a series of churches on this site. It's a low-key but lovely place, approached through frilly, wrought-iron gates. Inside the simple, peaceful nave are several heavily carved tombs, including one spooky carving featuring skeletons wearing shrouds. Some have associated it with the Black Death. St. Peter's is notorious for an incident that occurred here during the battle of Drogheda in 1641. A group of Irish men, fleeing the losing battle, sought refuge in this Protestant church. When Cromwell's forces invaded the church, the men climbed into the steeple. Cromwell used the pews as timber to start a fire, and the men were burned alive. This is the second reincarnation of St. Peter's since that infamous event.

William St., Drogheda, County Louth. No phone. Free admission. Daily 10am–3pm.

Shopping
Celtic Clays   This little pottery shop sells the work of Ciaran O'Conboirne. He uses Celtic motifs and rich, earthy tones to create distinctive, collectible pieces that look and feel Irish. Every item is handmade and makes a superb souvenir. Open Monday to Friday 9am to 5:30pm, Sunday noon to 6pm. 2 Riverlane, Carlingford, County Louth. © **042/938-3996.** www.celticclays.com.

Where to Stay & Dine
Ballymascanlon House Hotel   This 19th-century Victorian mansion was formerly the home of Baron Plunkett. The house has been enlarged several times with astounding

lack of sympathy for the beauty and symmetry of the original building. If you can ignore the unattractiveness of some of the modern structures, you can enjoy the award-winning gardens and grounds forming a peaceful oasis 5km (3 miles) south of the Northern Ireland border. Rooms vary in size, but all are decorated with antiques. The Cellar Bar offers traditional Irish music on weekends.

Off the Dublin-Belfast rd. (N1), Dundalk, County Louth. ✆ **042/935-8200.** Fax 042/937-1598. www. ballymascanlon.com. 90 units. €370 ($592) double; €590 ($944) suite. Rates include full breakfast. AE, DC, MC, V. **Amenities:** Restaurant (Continental); pub; swimming pool; golf course; tennis courts; gym; sauna; solarium. *In room:* TV, hair dryer.

Boyne Valley Hotel & Country Club ★

Belonging to the Best Western chain, this modern, well-designed hotel has sunny public areas and huge guest rooms, many with gorgeous views of the vast manicured grounds and the river running through it all. It's virtually impossible to be bored here: The hotel has its own tennis courts, and a modern fitness center with an indoor swimming pool; it will also arrange for horseback rides on the beach, fishing trips, and other activities. Situated within an hour of six separate courses, this hotel is popular with golfers. The owners are happy to book sessions on behalf of guests.

Off the Dublin rd. (N1), Drogheda, County Louth. ✆ **041/983-7737.** www.bestwestern.com or www. boyne-valley-hotel.ie. 72 units. €140–€170 ($224–$272) double. AE, DC, MC, V. **Amenities:** Restaurant (Continental); bar; swimming pool; tennis court; gym; sauna; crèche. *In room:* TV, tea/coffeemaker, hair dryer.

Ghan House ★★

This 18th-century country house makes a beautiful and quiet retreat at the foot of Slieve Foy and overlooking the glassy waters of Carlingford Lough. Some guest rooms are in the main house, while others are in an atmospheric converted dairy next door—all rooms are spacious and have a charmingly old-fashioned feel, with antique beds, floral fabric, and wingback chairs. Little touches—bathrobes, homemade cookies left out in your room, bottled water—convey a small sense of luxury. Dinner in the acclaimed restaurant is worth catching, and if you like what you eat, there are periodic cooking courses for those who want to learn the tricks. There are also eight-course "gourmet nights" on 7 nights each year, and if you're coming in the winter months you might even be able to catch one of their extremely festive Georgian-themed nights, complete with full costume and authentic food, but these generally need to be booked well in advance.

Coast Rd., Carlingford, County Louth. ✆ **042/937-3682.** Fax 042/937-3772. www.ghanhouse.com. 12 units. €190–€250 ($304–$400) double. Rates include full breakfast. 5-course fixed-price dinner €55 ($88); 8-course gourmet nights €75 ($120). Georgian-themed nights €75 ($120) usually twice yearly, Feb/Mar and Nov (call for details). AE, MC, V. **Amenities:** Restaurant (Continental). *In room:* TV, tea/coffeemaker, hair dryer.

McKevitts Village Hotel

This is a pleasant hotel for unwinding and taking long walks along the shores of Carlingford Lough. Its vintage two-story property has been updated and refurbished in recent years. Guest rooms vary in size and shape, but all have sturdy, Irish-made furnishings and are comfortable, with nice views of the town. A discounted rate is available for over-55s.

Market Sq., Carlingford, County Louth. ✆ **800/447-7462** in the U.S., or 042/937-3116. Fax 042/937-3144. www.mckevittshotel.com. 17 units. €110–€198 ($176–$317) double. Rates include full breakfast. AE, DC, MC, V. **Amenities:** Restaurant (seafood); bar. *In room:* TV.

The Southeast

Wexford, Waterford, South Tipperary, and Kilkenny combine to form a green, bucolic, easily traversed, and only slightly touristy region just a few hours' drive from Dublin. The local accent down here is particularly musical, almost hypnotic, and it makes even a boring shopping transaction disproportionately memorable.

Expect to do a lot of driving, as there's plenty of space between sights and little in the way of public transportation, and you'll want to see it all—from the breakable world of the Waterford Crystal Factory to the sturdy Viking streets of Wexford, and from the majestic Rock of Cashel to Kilkenny's mysterious medieval remains.

1 COUNTY WEXFORD

Wexford Town: 142km (88 miles) S of Dublin, 63km (39 miles) E of Waterford, 90km (56 miles) S of Wicklow, 187km (116 miles) E of Cork, 214km (133 miles) SE of Shannon Airport

County Wexford is most remarkable for the long stretches of pristine beach that line its coast, and for the evocative historic monuments in Wexford Town and on the Hook Peninsula. The Blackstairs Mountains dominate the western border of the county and provide excellent hillwalking, while bird-watchers can find plenty of fluttering action at the Wexford Wildfowl Reserve and Great Saltee Island.

The modern English name of Wexford evolved from *Waesfjord*, which is what the Viking sea-rovers called it when they settled here in the 9th century. It means "the Harbor of the Mud Flats." The Normans captured the town at the end of the 12th century, and you can still see remnants of their fort at the Irish National Heritage Park.

The next significant conqueror was Cromwell, who arrived in the mid–17th century and found that the county stood up to him. There was a bitter battle and he won, as usual, by basis of overwhelming force. Afterward, he handled victory with his usual largesse—gathering together 1,500 of the town's 2,000 residents and slaughtering them. Among the dead were all of the area's Franciscan friars. After the massacre, Wexford became a center of Irish resistance for centuries, and, in 1798, another bloody uprising would again leave thousands dead here.

With a population of about 10,000, Wexford Town is a hardworking Irish harbor community with a surprisingly sophisticated social calendar, highlighted by the opera festival in late October.

WEXFORD TOWN ESSENTIALS

GETTING THERE   Irish Rail (© **1850/366222**; www.irishrail.ie) provides daily train service to Wexford and Rosslare Pier. It serves **O'Hanrahan Station,** Redmond Square, Wexford.

Bus Éireann operates daily bus service to Wexford and Rosslare, into O'Hanrahan Station and Bus Depot, Redmond Square, Wexford (© **053/33114;** www.buseireann.ie).

If you're driving from Dublin and points north, take the N11 or N80 to Wexford; if you're coming from the west, take the N25 or N8. Two bridges lead into Wexford from

Nenagh

N7

N7

Silvermines

Templemore

Templetuohy

LAOIS

Rathdowney

N77

Castlecomer

N78

Ballyragget

Johnstown

Freshford

15

Borrisoleigh

Urlingford

Thurles

N8

Thurles

Milestone

Kilkenny City

N700

Holycross

Ballingarry

Bennettsbridge

Cappamore

Killenaule

Stoneyford

13

N10

Caherconlish

Cappawhite

N24

Rock of Cashel

1

TIPPERARY

N76

Callan

14

Herbertstown

2

Cashel

3

Knocktophet

Tipperary Town

N74

Fethard

Windgap

R697

N9

4

N688

Slievenamon Mountain

Knocklong

Glen of Aherlow

Ahenny

12

Kilfinane

Galty Mountains

Cahir

6

5

N24

Clonmel

11

Ballylanders

N8

Carrick-on-Suir

N24

IMERICK

Burncourt

R678

Portlaw

R665

Clogheen

R671

R. Suir

N73

Mitchelstown

R676

R677

Kildorrery

Ballyporeen

R626

WATERFORD

N25

N8

Knockmealdown Mountains

10

Kilmacthomas

N72

Ballyduff

N25

N72

R666

7

Cappoquin

R672

Lemybrien

Bunmahon

R675

Fermoy

N72

R672

8

Dungarvan

Rathcormac

R628

Lismore

N72

Annestown

Tallow

Dungarvan

Clonea Strand

Ballyknock

R634

R671

Ring

R614

Watergrasshill

N25

N8

R626

R627

9

Cork

Cork

Ardmore

Midleton

N25

Youghal

N71

REPUBLIC OF IRELAND

Cobh

Dublin ★

CORK

area of detail

Ballycotton

To St. Malo & Roscoff

To Swansea →

Ballyknock

Ahenny High Crosses **12**	Ferns Castle **29**	Mount Leinster **28**
Ardmore High Cross **9**	Jerpoint Abbey **14**	National 1798 Visitor
Athassel Priory **4**	John F. Kennedy Arboretum **20**	Centre **27**
Ballyhack Castle **21**	JFK Trust Dunbrody **19**	Ormond Castle **11**
Bolton Library **3**	Johnstown Castle Gardens &	Raven Nature Reserve **27**
Brú Ború Heritage Centre **2**	Irish Agricultural Museum **25**	The Rock of Cashel **1**
Cahir Castle **5**	Kells Priory **13**	St. Mullin's Monastery **18**
Duiske Abbey **16**	Kilfane Glen and Waterfall **17**	Saltee Islands **23**
Dunmore Cave **15**	Lismore Castle **8**	Swiss Cottage **6**
Enniscorthy Castle/	Lismore Heritage Centre **7**	Tintern Abbey **22**
Wexford County Museum **27**	Mahon Falls **10**	Yola Farmstead **24**

the north—the Ferrycarrig Bridge from the main Dublin road (N11) and the Wexford Bridge from R741. The Ferrycarrig Bridge takes you into town from the west. The Wexford Bridge leads right to the heart of town along the quays.

Ferries from Britain run to Rosslare Harbour, 19km (12 miles) south of Wexford Town. **Stena Line** (© **053/916-1555;** www.stenaline.com) handles service from Fishguard, Wales. **Irish Ferries** (© **0818/300400;** www.irishferries.com) has a route between Rosslare and Pembroke, Wales. (Irish Ferries also provides service from Le Havre and Cherbourg, France.)

If you're traveling between County Wexford and County Waterford, there's a waterborne shortcut. The **Passage East Car Ferry Ltd.,** Barrack Street, Passage East, County Waterford (© **051/382488;** http://homepage.eircom.net/~passferry), operates a car-ferry service across Waterford Harbour. It links Passage East, about 16km (10 miles) east of Waterford, with Ballyhack, about 32km (20 miles) southwest of Wexford. The shortcut saves about an hour's driving time between the cities. Crossing time averages 10 minutes. It offers continuous drive-on, drive-off service, with no reservations required. Fares are €7 ($11) one-way and €10 ($16) round-trip for car and passengers; €2 ($3.20) single trip for foot passengers and €2.50 ($4) round-trip; and €3 ($4.80) one-way and €4 ($6.40) round-trip for cyclists. It operates April to September Monday to Saturday 7am to 10pm, Sunday 9:30am to 10pm; and October to March Monday to Saturday 7am to 8pm, Sunday 9:30am to 8pm.

VISITOR INFORMATION   The **Wexford Tourist Office** is on Crescent Quay, Wexford (© **053/912-3111**); the **Rosslare Harbour Tourist Office** is at the Ferry Terminal in Rosslare Harbour (© **053/913-3232**), or you can visit the website at **www.wexford tourism.com**. The Wexford office is open year-round Monday to Saturday 9am to 6pm. The Rosslare Harbour office is open daily to coincide with ferry arrivals. **Seasonal offices,** open April to September, are found in Enniscorthy town center (© **053/923-7596**) and at New Ross town center (© **051/421857**).

TOWN LAYOUT   At the edge of the River Slaney, Wexford is a busy, compact town with quaint narrow streets—successors of the 9th-century market trails—lined with 18th-century houses and workaday shop fronts. Four quays (Custom House, Commercial, Paul, and the semicircular Crescent) run beside the water. Crescent Quay marks the center of town. One block inland, Main Street is a long, narrow thoroughfare that you can easily walk. Wexford's shops and businesses are on Main Street and the many smaller streets that fan out from it.

GETTING AROUND   Wexford Town is so small that it has no public transportation. **Bus Éireann** (© **01/703-3232;** www.buseireann.ie) operates daily service between Wexford and Rosslare. Other local services operate on certain days only to Kilmore Quay, Carne, and Gorey.

The best way to see the town is to walk it. Park your car along the quays; you'll probably need to pay to park, so look for parking meters on the street (marked with big blue P signs) and have some coins ready. You pay in and get a receipt to put in your car window ("pay and display"). There is free parking off Redmond Square, beside the train and bus station. You'll need a car to reach most attractions out of town.

If you need to rent a car, contact **Budget** at the Rosslare Harbour, Wexford (© **051/843747**), or Waterford Airport, Waterford (© **051/843747**); **Murrays Europcar,** Rosslare Ferryport, Rosslare (© **053/33634**); or **Hertz,** Ferrybank, Wexford (© **053/52500**), or Rosslare Harbour, Wexford (© **053/33238**).

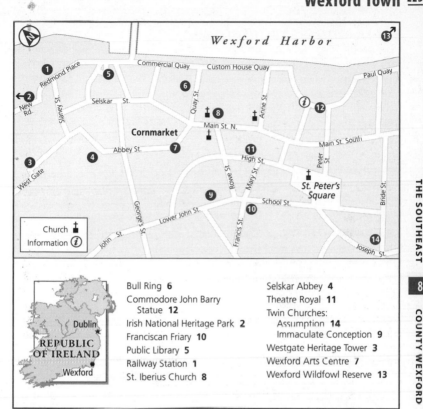

Wexford Harbor

Commercial Quay Custom House Quay Paul Quay

Redmond Place

New Rd.

Slaney St.

Selskar St.

Cornmarket

Abbey St.

West Gate

George's St.

John St.

Lower John St.

Quay St.

Main St. N.

High St.

Rowe St.

Mary St.

Francis St.

School St.

Anne St.

Main St. South

Peter St.

St. Peter's Square

Bride St.

Joseph St.

Church ✝
Information ⓘ

Dublin ★

REPUBLIC OF IRELAND

Wexford

Bull Ring **6**
Commodore John Barry Statue **12**
Irish National Heritage Park **2**
Franciscan Friary **10**
Public Library **5**
Railway Station **1**
St. Iberius Church **8**

Selskar Abbey **4**
Theatre Royal **11**
Twin Churches:
 Assumption **14**
 Immaculate Conception **9**
Westgate Heritage Tower **3**
Wexford Arts Centre **7**
Wexford Wildfowl Reserve **13**

THE SOUTHEAST

8

COUNTY WEXFORD

If you want a cab, call **Wexford Cabs** (☎ **053/23123**) or **Wexford Taxi** (☎ **053/ 53999**).

FAST FACTS If you need a drugstore, try **John Fehily/The Pharmacy,** 28 S. Main St., Wexford (☎ **053/23163**); **Sherwood Chemist,** 2 N. Main St., Wexford (☎ **053/22875**); or **Fortune's Pharmacy,** 82 N. Main St., Wexford (☎ **053/42354**).

In an emergency, dial ☎ **999.** The **Garda Station** (police) is on Roches Road, Wexford (☎ **053/22333**). **Wexford General Hospital** is on Richmond Terrace, Wexford (☎ **053/42233**).

Like most towns in Ireland, Wexford offers free Internet access in its **public library** (☎ **053/21637**), which is in Selskar House, off Redmond Square just in from Commercial Quay. Its hours are Tuesday 1 to 5:30pm, Wednesday 10am to 4:30pm and 6 to 8pm, Thursday and Friday 10am to 5:30pm, and Saturday 10am to 1pm. The demand is so great, however, that it's advisable to call in advance to reserve time on a PC. Otherwise, Monday to Saturday between 9am and 5pm, you can go to the **Westgate Computer Centre,** Westgate (☎ **053/46291**), next to the Heritage Tower, offering Internet access for €3 ($4.80) per 30 minutes online.

The weekly *Wexford People* covers town and county events and entertainment.

The **General Post Office** on Anne Street, Wexford (✆ **053/22587**), is open Monday to Saturday 9am to 5:30pm.

EXPLORING WEXFORD TOWN

Get started exploring by walking the length of Main Street, both north and south, taking time to detour up and down the alleys and lanes that crisscross it. The tourist office can supply you with a free map if you want some guidance. You may want to start out by visiting the Westgate Heritage Tower (see below), which will provide you with valuable context and background information before you explore the rest of the city.

The Bull Ring In 1798, the first declaration of an Irish republic was made here, and a statue memorializes the Irish pikemen who fought for the cause. Earlier, in the 17th century, the town square was a venue for bull baiting, a sport introduced by the butcher's guild. Tradition maintained that after a match, the hide of the ill-fated bull was presented to the mayor and the meat was used to feed the poor. Today, activity at the ring is much tamer: a weekly outdoor market, open Friday and Saturday from 10am to 4:30pm.

Off N. Main St., Wexford, County Wexford. Free admission.

Cornmarket Until a century ago, this central marketplace buzzed with the activity of cobblers, publicans, and more than 20 other businesses. Today it's just a wide street dominated by the Wexford Arts Centre, a structure dating from 1775.

Off Upper George's St., Wexford, County Wexford.

Irish National Heritage Park ★ (Kids) This 14-hectare (35-acre) living-history park on the banks of the River Slaney outside of Wexford Town provides an ideal introduction for visitors of all ages to life in ancient Ireland, from the Stone Age to the Norman invasion. Each reconstructed glimpse into Irish history is well crafted and has its own natural setting and wildlife. The tour led by head guide Jimmy O'Rourke is great for families with kids—he's a master in bringing each site to life, captivating children. There's also a nature trail and interpretive center, complete with gift shop and cafe. Plan to spend several hours in the park.

Off the Dublin-Wexford rd. (N11), Ferrycarrig, County Wexford. ✆ **053/20733.** www.inhp.com. Admission €8 ($13) adults, €6.50 ($10) seniors and students, €4.50 ($7.20) youths 13–16, €4 ($6.40) children 4–12. Mar–Oct daily 9:30am–6:30pm (last admission 5pm).

John Barry Monument This bronze statue, a gift from the American people in 1956, faces out to the sea as a tribute to the titular Mr. Barry, a favorite son who became the father of the American navy. Born at Ballysampson, Tacumshane, 16km (10 miles) southeast of Wexford Town, Barry emigrated to the colonies while in his teens and volunteered to fight in the American Revolution. One of the U.S. Navy's first commissioned

---

(Tips) Phone Number Changes in Wexford

As this book was going to press, phone numbers were changing in County Wexford, expanding from five digits to seven. Not all the new numbers were in place, so some phone numbers in this book might not work when you travel. Either your hotel or the local tourism office should be able to help you contact any facilities that have changed their numbers since this book was published.

officers, he became captain of the *Lexington*. In 1797 George Washington appointed him commander in chief of the U.S. Navy.

Crescent Quay, Wexford, County Wexford.

St. Iberius Church   Erected in 1660, St. Iberius was built on hallowed ground—the land has been used for houses of worship since Norse times. The church has a lovely Georgian facade and an interior known for its superb acoustics. Free guided tours are given according to demand.

N. Main St., Wexford, County Wexford. ℭ **053/43013.** Free admission; donations welcome. May–Sept daily 10am–5pm; Oct–Apr Tues–Sat 10am–3pm.

Selskar Abbey   This abbey dates from the early 12th century, and it has often been the scene of synods and parliaments. The first Anglo-Irish treaty was signed here in 1169, and it's said that Henry II spent Lent 1172 at the abbey doing penance for having Thomas à Becket beheaded. Although the abbey is mostly in ruins, its choir is part of a Church of Ireland edifice, and a portion of the original tower is a vesting room. The adjoining graveyard has suffered a disturbing amount of vandalism over the years. The entrance most likely to be open is to the left of Westgate.

Off Temperance Row at Westgate St., Wexford, County Wexford. Free admission.

The Twin Churches: Church of the Assumption and Church of the Immaculate Conception   These twin Gothic structures (1851–58) were designed by architect Robert Pierce, a pupil of Augustus Pugin. Their 69m (226-ft.) spires dominate Wexford's skyline. Mosaics on the main doors of both churches give a good bit of local history.

Bride and Rowe sts., Wexford, County Wexford. ℭ **053/22055.** Free admission; donations welcome. Daily 8am–6pm.

Westgate Heritage Tower   This ancient tollgate once guarded the western entrance of Wexford Town. Sir Stephen Devereux had it built in the 13th century on instructions from King Henry. Like other town gates, it consisted of a toll-taking area, cells for offenders, and rooms for guards. Fully restored as a heritage center, it presents artifacts uncovered around the town, and offers a rather long (nearly 30 min.) informational film, which provides an arguably overly informative look at Wexford's complex and turbulent history.

Westgate St., Wexford, County Wexford. ℭ **053/46506.** Audiovisual show €3.20 ($5.10) adults, €1.75 ($2.80) children and students. May–Aug Mon–Fri 10am–6pm, Sat–Sun noon–6pm; Sept–Apr Mon–Fri 10am–5pm.

Wexford Wildfowl Reserve ★   This national nature reserve is part of the unfortunately named North Slob, adjacent to Wexford Harbour, 5km (3 miles) east of Wexford Town. About 10,000 Greenland white-fronted geese—more than one-third of the world's population—winter here, as do brent geese, Bewick's swans, and wigeons. The area is immensely attractive to other wildfowl and birds, and more than 240 species have been spotted. The reserve has a visitor center, the inevitable informational film, a new exhibition hall, and an observation tower and blinds.

North Slob, Wexford, County Wexford. ℭ **053/23129.** Free admission. Apr 16–Sept daily 9am–6pm; Oct–Apr 15 daily 10am–5pm.

Sightseeing Tours

Walking Tours of Wexford   Proud of their town's ancient streets and vintage buildings, the people of Wexford began giving tours to visitors more than 30 years ago.

A Trip through History: Exploring the Ring of Hook

The **Hook Peninsula** in southwest County Wexford is a picturesque place of rocky headlands and secluded beaches between Bannow Bay and Waterford Harbour. These were significant inlets in medieval times for travelers from Britain to Ireland, and the abundance of archaeological remains reflects that. The end of the peninsula, with its sturdy old lighthouse, is popular with birders as a site for watching the spring and fall passerine migration. The route described below will guide you through a driving or biking tour, and hikers can see most of the places listed from the Wexford Coastal Pathway.

Start your exploration of the peninsula at the town of **Wellington Bridge.** Just west of town on R733 is a roadside stop on the left by a cemetery; from here you can look across Bannow Bay to the ruins of **Clonmines**—a Norman village established in the 13th century. It's a fine example of a walled medieval settlement, with remains of two churches, three tower houses, and an Augustinian priory. You can drive to the ruins—just follow R733 another mile west to a left turn posted for the Wicklow Coastal Pathway, and continue straight on this road where the pathway turns right. The ruins are on private land, so you should ask permission at the farmhouse at the end of the road.

Continuing west on R733, turn left on R734 at the sign for the Ring of Hook, and turn right at the sign for **Tintern Abbey** (p. 230). The abbey was founded by the monks of Tintern in South Wales in the 13th century, but it has been much altered over the centuries. The grounds are beautiful and contain a restored stone bridge that spans a narrow sea inlet.

At **Baginbun Head,** a fine beach nestles against the cliffs, from which you can see the outline of the Norman earthwork fortifications on the head. Here the Norman presence in Ireland was first established with the victory of Norman forces over the Irish at the Battle of Baginbun.

The **tip of the peninsula,** with its line of low cliffs, eroded in places for blowholes, has been famous for shipwrecks since Norman times. There has long been a **lighthouse** on this site; the present structure consists of a massive base, built in the early 13th century, and a narrower top dating from the 19th.

The Ring of Hook road returns along the western side of the peninsula, passing the beaches at **Booley Bay** and **Dollar Bay.** On a promontory overlooking the town of Duncannon is a **fort** built in 1588 to protect Waterford Harbour from the Spanish Armada. Just north of Duncannon, along the coast at the village of **Ballyhack,** a ferry runs to County Waterford, and a Knights Hospitallers castle (see Ballyhack Castle, below) stands on a hill.

A visit to the Hook Peninsula wouldn't be complete without a stop at **Dunbrody Abbey,** in a field beside the road about 6.5km (4 miles) north of Duncannon. The abbey, founded in 1170, is a magnificent ruin and one of the largest Cistercian abbeys in Ireland. Despite its grand size, it bears remarkably little ornamentation. Tours are sometimes available; inquire at the visitor center across the road.

Eventually organized as the Old Wexford Society, the local folk have developed a real expertise over the years, and continue to give tours on a regular basis. All tours depart from Westgate Heritage Tower.

c/o Seamus Molloy, "Carmeleen," William St., Wexford, County Wexford. ℭ **053/22663**. €2.50 ($4) adults, free for children. Individual tours arranged when you call.

Attractions Farther Afield in County Wexford

The rounded granite form of **Mount Leinster,** the highest in Wexford, is a landmark throughout the region. This is a popular hang-gliding spot as the summit is always windy. On a clear day, views are sweeping. To get there, follow signs for the Mount Leinster Scenic Drive from the sleepy town of **Kiltealy** on the eastern slopes of the mountain. Soon you will begin climbing the exposed slopes; don't get too distracted by the views, because the road is twisting and quite narrow in places. There's a parking area at the highest point of the auto road, and a paved access road (closed to cars) continues for over 2km (1¼ miles) to the summit. From the top you can scramble along the ridge to the east, known as Black Rock Mountain. To return, continue along the Scenic Drive, which ends a few miles outside the town of Bunclody.

Ballyhack Castle   On a steep slope overlooking the Waterford estuary, about 32km (20 miles) west of Wexford, this large tower house was built around 1450 by the Knights Hospitallers of St. John, one of the two great military orders of the Crusades. The castle has been restored and turned into a heritage information center, with displays on the Crusader knights, medieval monks, and Norman nobles.

Off R733, Ballyhack, County Wexford. ℭ **051/389468**. www.heritageireland.ie. Admission €1.80 ($2.90) adults; €1 ($1.60) seniors, students, and children; €4.50 ($7.20) families. June–Sept daily 9am–6pm.

Enniscorthy Castle/Wexford County Museum   Overlooking the River Slaney at Enniscorthy, 24km (15 miles) north of Wexford Town, this castle tower was built by the Prendergast family in the 13th century. It's said that the poet Edmund Spenser once owned it briefly. Remarkably well preserved, it's now home to the Wexford County Museum, which focuses on the area's history and traditions. Displays include an old Irish farm kitchen, early modes of travel, and items connected with Wexford's role in Ireland's struggle for independence, especially the 1798 and 1916 risings.

Castle Hill, Enniscorthy, County Wexford. ℭ **054/35926**. Admission €4.50 ($7.20) adults, €3.50 ($5.60) seniors and students, €1 ($1.60) children, €11 ($17) families. June–Sept daily 10am–6pm; Oct–Nov and Feb–May daily 2–5:30pm; Dec–Jan Sun 2–5pm.

Ferns Castle   These atmospheric ruins are all that's left of a once-grand castle built in 1221. Sitting at the north end of the village of Ferns, the castle is believed to have been the old fortress of Dermot MacMurrough. There's still a moat and walls, as well as a tower that has excellent views from the top. If you do climb up, notice the hole at the top just to the left of the door. This was a murder hole, through which defenders could pour hot oil or drop heavy stones onto invaders below. The castle was destroyed in the mid–17th century by Parliamentarians led by Sir Charles Coote, who also ordered the deaths of almost all of the local residents.

Ferns, County Wexford. Free admission. Daily dawn–dusk.

Irish Agricultural Museum and Famine Exhibition ★   The importance of farming in Wexford's history is the focus of this museum, on the Johnstown Castle Demesne 6km (3¾ miles) southwest of Wexford Town. In historic farm buildings,

The Rising (and Falling) of Vinegar Hill

Of the many rebel groups that took hold in the late 18th century, the Society of United Irishmen, founded in 1791, was most ahead of its time. Led by Wolfe Tone, it welcomed Catholics, Protestants, and dissenters alike in its effort to free Ireland from England's yoke. The British were deeply suspicious of the group's motives, not least because Tone was not shy about involving the French, England's enemy. In fact, in 1796, the French government sent 14,000 soldiers to join a United Irishmen uprising, but poor weather forced the boats back.

In 1798, the group tried again. Battles were fought in Kildare, Carlow, Wicklow, and Meath, and quickly won by English forces. In Wexford, though, feelings were very high, and the rebels were victorious. A detachment of 100 English-led soldiers was cut down at Oulart, and the city of Wexford burned. Wexford became the center of the battle in part because of the behavior of English-led forces. Throughout that spring there had been fury in Wexford because of torture of residents, and house burnings conducted by the loyalist North Cork Militia. Once the rebellion began, Wexford residents heard of summary executions of suspected United Irishmen in Wicklow and at the edge of Wexford. In the end, they knew they were fighting for their lives.

On May 29, led by Father John Murphy, a priest who reluctantly agreed to take over the leadership of the group, insurgents headed to Wexford Town. The group, armed with muskets and pikes, gathered size as it moved, and by the time it reached the town it had 15,000 fighters. The town fell quickly. Exhilarated, the group attempted to take the entire county, but its efforts to take other towns failed in places like Arklow and New Ross.

the museum contains exhibits on planting and the diverse activities of the farm household. There are also extensive displays on dairying, crafts, and Irish country furniture. Large-scale replicas illustrate the workshops of the blacksmith, cooper, wheelwright, harness maker, and basket maker. Sadly, the 19th-century Gothic Revival castle on the grounds is not open to the public beyond the entrance hall, which holds an information booth. Still, the grounds are perfect for picnics.

Johnstown Castle, Bridgetown Rd., off Wexford-Rosslare rd. (N25), Wexford, County Wexford. ② 053/918-4671. www.irishagrimuseum.ie. Admission to museum €5.50 ($8.80) adults, €3.50 ($5.60) students and children, €15 ($24) families; gardens €2.50 ($4) adults, €.50 (80¢) children and students, or €4 ($6.40) by the car. Museum June–Aug Mon–Fri 9am–5pm, Sat–Sun 11am–5pm; Apr–May and Sept–Nov Mon–Fri 9am–12:30pm and 1:30–5pm, Sat–Sun 2–5pm; Dec–Mar Mon–Fri 9am–12:30pm and 1:30–5pm. Gardens year-round daily 9am–5:30pm.

John F. Kennedy Arboretum Dedicated to the memory of the 35th U.S. president, this 240-hectare (593-acre) arboretum is about 32km (20 miles) west of Wexford and overlooks the simple thatched cottage where JFK's great-grandfather was born. The whole thing was initiated with financial help from a group of Irish Americans, although the Irish government funds it now. Plants and trees from five continents grow here. There are play and picnic areas, and there's a small miniature railway as a sort of payback to the kids who must find it all a bit dull. A hilltop observation point (at 266m/872 ft.) presents

The English were shocked by the rebels' success at Wexford Town, but were soon emboldened by their subsequent failures, and they marched out to take them on. The troops arrived at the rebel encampment, on Vinegar Hill at the edge of Enniscorthy, on June 21. The rebels knew they were coming, and they prepared to take them on. Battle began at dawn, and lasted less than 2 hours. The rebels were mercilessly shelled, and their poor weapons were no match for the English artillery. More than 500 died in the battle, but that was nothing compared to what happened next.

Weeks of murder and atrocities followed, as loyalist troops raped and pillaged ruthlessly, killing an estimated 25,000 men, women, and children. Protestant leaders of the rebellion were beheaded, and their heads mounted on spikes outside the courthouse in Wexford town. Father Murphy was stripped, flogged, hanged, and beheaded. His corpse was burned in a barrel. His head was spiked outside the local Catholic church, and Catholics in town were forced to open their windows so that they could smell his body burn.

The horrific massacre became a rallying cry for all subsequent Irish rebellions, and Wexford is forever associated with sacrifice and violence.

Vinegar Hill is at the east end of Enniscorthy, and although there's little there to memorialize the rebellion, it's a peaceful place with beautiful views. You reach it by crossing the bridge in town, and taking the first right after Treacy's Hotel, then following the signs. There's also an excellent hour-long walking tour that includes the 1798 history, with lots of fascinating details. Contact **Castle Hill Crafts** ((✆ **054/36800**) for details.

a sweeping view of County Wexford and five neighboring counties, the Saltee Islands, the Comeragh Mountains, and parts of the rivers Suir, Nore, and Barrow.

Off Duncannon rd. (R733), New Ross, County Wexford. ✆ 051/388171. Admission €3 ($4.80) adults, €2.30 ($3.70) seniors, €1.50 ($2.40) students and children, €8 ($13) families. Apr and Sept daily 10am–6:30pm; May–Aug daily 10am–8pm; Oct–Mar daily 10am–5pm.

JFK Trust Dunbrody Housed in twin 18th-century grain mills, this intelligent, absorbing center tells the story of the Irish Diaspora, beginning with the monks who went to Europe in the 6th century and continuing to the present day, using a variety of interactive and live-action methods. It is an interesting and sometimes heartbreaking tale. A section of the center is devoted to John F. Kennedy, who was (in case you haven't noticed yet) descended from a County Wexford family.

The magnificent tall ship *Dunbrody*—458 tons and 174 feet—is also here, moored on the New Ross quays as a floating exhibition center.

The Quay, New Ross, County Wexford. ✆ 051/425239. Fax 051/425240. www.dunbrody.com. Admission €7 ($11) adults, €4.50 ($7.20) seniors, €4 ($6.40) students and children, €18 ($29) families. Sept–June Mon–Fri 10am–5pm, Sat–Sun noon–5pm; July–Aug daily 9am–6pm.

The National 1798 Visitor Centre (Kids) Just south of Enniscorthy Castle, this visitor center, dedicated to the 1798 rebellion and its aftermath, uses interactive displays to give insight into the birth of modern democracy in Ireland. It's largely geared to youths, although it's not so childish that adults will find it completely dull. Computers, a dramatic film about the uprising, and an array of artifacts help bring the events home in an interesting way. There is also a small tearoom and a tiny gift shop.

Millpark Rd., Enniscorthy, County Wexford. (☎ 054/923-7596. www.iol.ie/~98com. Admission €6 ($9.60) adults, €3.50 ($5.60) seniors and students, €16 ($26) families. Mon–Fri 9:30am–6pm; Sat–Sun 11am–6pm.

SS *Dunbrody* Emigrant Ship   A full-scale reconstruction of a ship built in 1845 and ultimately used to carry emigrants to the U.S. at the height of the Great Famine, this is an interesting way to step back into that turbulent history. There's a visitor center on board that explains the ship and the story of the mass migration in which it took part. There's also a database of Irish immigration to the U.S., and you can look your family up.

On the quay, New Ross, County Wexford. (☎ 051/425239. Admission €6 ($9.60) adults, €3.50 ($5.60) seniors and students, €16 ($26) families. Apr–Sept daily 9am–5pm; Oct–Mar daily noon–5pm.

Tintern Abbey ★   In a lovely rural setting overlooking Bannow Bay, Tintern Abbey was founded in the 12th century by William Marshall, the earl of Pembroke, as thanks to God after he nearly died at sea. The early monks were Cistercians from Tintern in South Wales (hence the name). The parts that remain—nave, chancel, tower, chapel, and cloister—date from the early 13th century, though they have been much altered since then. The grounds are extraordinarily beautiful and include a stone bridge spanning a narrow sea inlet. There's a small coffee shop on the premises if the caffeine situation gets desperate.

Saltmills, New Ross, County Wexford. (☎ 051/562650. Admission €2.20 ($3.50) adults, €1.40 ($2.25) seniors, €1.20 ($1.90) students and children, €6 ($9.60) families. Mid-May to mid-Oct daily 10am–6pm. Signposted 19km (12 miles) south of New Ross off of R733.

Yola Farmstead   A voluntary community project, this theme park depicts a Wexford farming community as it would have been 200 or more years ago. There are plenty of quaint thatched-roof buildings; bread and butter making are demonstrated; and craftspeople can be seen at work blowing and hand-cutting crystal at Wexford Heritage Crystal, a glass-production enterprise. It's quite touristy, but can be interesting. The **Genealogy Center** (☎ 053/31177; fax 053/32612) is open daily 9am to 5pm. Consultation or one name search costs €25 ($40).

16km (10 miles) south of Wexford Town, 2.4km (1½ miles) from Rosslare Ferryport, Wexford-Rosslare rd. (N25), Tagoat, County Wexford. (☎ 053/913-2610. Admission €6 ($9.60) adults, €4.50 ($7.20) seniors and students, €3 ($4.80) children, €15 ($24) families. May–Oct daily 10am–6pm; Mar–Apr and Nov Mon–Fri 10am–4:30pm.

SHOPPING

Shops in Wexford are open Monday to Thursday 9am to 5:30pm, and Friday and Saturday 9am to 6pm; some shops stay open until 8pm on Friday.

Barkers   Established in 1848, this shop has an admirable selection of Waterford crystal, Belleek china, and Royal Irish Tara china, as well as Irish linens and international products such as Aynsley, Wedgwood, and Lladró. 36–40 S. Main St., Wexford, County Wexford. (☎ 053/23159.

Byrne's Bookstore & World of Wonder   This extensive and bustling emporium—spread out across three levels—offers much more than books, as the self-aggrandizing name implies. There's a long wall full of magazines and newspapers, a selection of stationery, and a slew of toys. 31 N. Main St., Wexford, County Wexford. ✆ 053/22223.

Westgate Design　Original Irish art, including paintings, drawings, and photographs, as well as a variety of locally made crafts fill this popular shop. 22 N. Main St., Wexford, County Wexford. ✆ 053/23787.

Wexford Silver　Pat Dolan and his sons create gold, silver, and bronze pieces by hand using traditional tools and techniques. They trace their silversmithing connections back to 1647. A second workshop is in Kinsale (p. 289). 115 N. Main St., Wexford, County Wexford. ✆ 053/21933.

SPORTS & OUTDOOR PURSUITS

BEACHES　County Wexford's beaches at **Courtown, Curracloe, Duncannon,** and **Rosslare** are ideal for walking, jogging, and swimming.

BICYCLING　You can rent mountain bikes in Wexford Town at **Hayes Cycle Shop,** 108 S. Main St. (✆ 053/22462). From Wexford, the road north up the coast through Curracloe to Blackwater is a scenic day trip. For complete 1- or 2-week cycling holidays in the Southeast, contact Bobbie Smith or Bill Passmore at **Celtic Cycling,** Lorum Old Rectory, Bagenalstown (✆ 059/977-5282).

BIRD-WATCHING　A good starting place for bird-watching in the region is the **Wexford Wildfowl Reserve** (p. 225); warden Chris Wilson can direct you to other places of interest.

　　The **Great Saltee Island** is excellent for watching seabirds, especially during May, June, and July, when it's mobbed with nesting parents and their young. Like something out of a Hitchcock feature, the cliffs on the island's southernmost point are packed to overflowing with raucous avian residents. You can get up close and personal with puffins, which nest in underground burrows, or graceful guillemots. Other species include cormorants, kittiwakes, gannets, and Manx shearwaters. The island is privately owned, but visitors are welcome on the condition that they do nothing to disturb the bird habitat and the island's natural beauty. From April to September, weather permitting, **Declan Bates** (✆ 053/29684) provides boat rides to the island and back from the town of Kilmore Quay (about 16km/10 miles south of Wexford Town). He charges €100 ($160) minimum for the boat, or €20 ($32) per person for groups of at least five people.

　　Hook Head is a good spot for watching the spring and autumn passerine migration—the lack of sizable cliffs means that it isn't popular with summer nesting seabirds. In addition to swallows, swifts, and warblers, look out for the less common cuckoos, turtledoves, redstarts, and blackcaps.

　　While driving south from Gorey toward Ballycanew on R741, keep an eye out for a reddish **cliff** on the left, about 2km (1¼ miles) out of Gorey; this is a well-known peregrine aerie, with birds nesting until the early summer. The land is private, but you can watch the birds from the road.

DIVING　The Kilmore Quay area, south of Wexford Town, offers some of the most spectacular diving in Ireland, especially around the Saltee Islands and Conningbeg rocks. For all your diving needs, consult the **Pier House Diving Centre** (✆ 053/29703).

GOLF　In recent years, Wexford has blossomed as a golfing venue. One of the newest developments is an 18-hole championship seaside par-72 course at **St. Helens Bay Golf Club,** Kilrane (✆ 053/913-3234; www.sthelensbay.com). Greens fees in high season are €40 ($64) on weekdays and €50 ($80) on weekends. Tennis courts and luxury cottages are available. The **Enniscorthy Golf Club,** Knockmarshall, Enniscorthy (© 054/923-3191; www.enniscorthygc.ie), is an inland par-70 course with greens fees of €30 ($48) on weekdays, €40 ($64) on weekends.

HORSEBACK RIDING   Horetown House, Foulksmills (© 051/565633), offers riding lessons by the hour or in a variety of packages that include meals and lodging. Refurbished in 2007, this is one of the better residential equestrian centers in Ireland; it caters particularly to families and children. For more experienced riders, lessons in jumping and dressage are available. Training in hunting and admission to the hunt can also be arranged. Riding costs around €25 ($40) per hour; accommodations start at €100 ($160) for a double room, including an all-organic breakfast.

SAILING/FISHING   The town of **Kilmore Quay,** south of Wexford Town on R739, is a center for sea angling in Wexford. The most popular rivers for fishing are the Barrow and the Slaney, where the sea trout travel upstream from mid-June to the end of August. **Blackwater Anglers** (© 053/912-7318) offer fishing on a lake stocked with rainbow and brown trout. Dick Hayes runs **Harbour Thrills** (© 053/912-9684), which offers numerous boat trips, including journeys to and from Kilmore Quay.

WALKING   Along the entire coastline, you'll see brown signs with a picture of a hiker on them. The signs mark the **Wexford Coastal Path,** along which you can walk the coast via pristine beaches and country lanes. Unfortunately, the roads are often too busy for it to be a good idea to walk the whole route—especially on the bypass around Wexford Town. The markers are handy, however, for shorter walks between Wexford's beaches. In the northern part of the county, the section of beach from Clogga Head (County Wicklow) to Tara Hill is especially lovely, as is the walk to the top of Tara Hill, which offers views across sloping pastures to the sea. Farther south, the path veers off the roads and sticks to the beach from Cahore Point south to Raven Point and from Rosslare Harbour to Kilmore Quay.

There's a lovely coastal walk near the town of Wexford in the **Raven Nature Reserve,** an area of forested dunes and uncrowded beaches. To get there, take R741 north out of Wexford, turn right on R742 to Curracloe just out of town, and in the village of Curracloe, turn right and continue for just over a mile to the beach parking lot. The nature reserve is to your right. You can get there by car, driving a half-mile south, or walk the distance along the beach. The beach extends another 5km (3 miles) to Raven Point, where at low tide you can see the remains of a shipwreck, half-buried in the sand.

On the border between counties Wexford and Carlow, the long, rounded ridge of peaks are the **Blackstairs Mountains,** which allow for plenty of walks in an area remarkably unspoiled by tourism. Get a guidebook and maps from any sizable Wexford tourist office.

WHERE TO STAY
Very Expensive
Marlfield House ★★   Formerly the principal residence of the earl of Courtown, this splendid Regency manor home, 65km (40 miles) north of Wexford Town, was built around 1850. The current owners, Ray and Mary Bowe, have transformed it into a top-notch country house and restaurant. Although the individually decorated rooms have every modern convenience and comfort, they haven't sacrificed old-world charm, so many have four-poster or canopied beds along with hand-carved furniture and luxurious fabrics. Bathrooms tend to be quite large, stocked with thick towels, bathrobes, and plenty of complimentary toiletries. The public rooms and lounge are appropriately posh, with crystal chandeliers and marble fireplaces. Marlfield is celebrated for its cuisine,

> **(Tips)**   **Service Charges**
>
> **A reminder:** Unless otherwise noted, room rates don't include service charges
> (usually 10%–15% of your bill).

which incorporates organically grown fruits and vegetables from the garden. It's served in the main dining area or in a fanciful sky-lit Victorian-style conservatory room.

Courtown Rd., Gorey, County Wexford. (℃) **800/323-5463** in the U.S., or 055/942-1124. Fax 055/942-1572. www.marlfieldhouse.com. 20 units. €255–€275 ($408–$440) double. Dinner from €55 ($88). Rates include full breakfast. AE, DC, MC, V. Closed mid-Dec to Jan. **Amenities:** Restaurant (local/French/Mediterranean); lounge; tennis court; nonsmoking rooms; croquet lawn. In room: TV, CD player, hair dryer, iron, garment press.

Expensive

Kelly's Resort Hotel ★★ (Kids)   Four generations of the Kelly family have turned this hotel into a popular family resort. It's been an honest-to-goodness pioneer in the country's hotel industry, being the first proper beachfront resort hotel; prices are all-inclusive for multiple-night stays, so you don't pay extra for meals or access to leisure facilities. It has plenty to keep you busy—an indoor swimming pool, spa, squash courts, and indoor tennis courts. In keeping with resort tradition, there's good dining at **La Marine** restaurant, and plenty of (sometimes cheesy) nighttime entertainment. Prices are a bit high, especially given that rooms are quite basic, if comfortable, but the all-inclusive factor is worth remembering.

Wexford–Rosslare Harbour rd. (N25), about 16km (10 miles) south of Wexford Town, Rosslare, County Wexford. (℃) **053/913-2114.** Fax 053/913-2222. www.kellys.ie. 116 units. €873–€940 ($1,397–$1,504) per person for 7 nights. Children's discounts available. AE, MC, V. **Amenities:** 2 restaurants (Continental, bistro); bar; 2 indoor swimming pools; indoor tennis; squash; gym; beauty/spa treatments; Jacuzzi; outdoor hot tub; sauna; steam room; children's playground; billiard room; miniature golf. In room: TV, radio, tea/coffeemaker, hair dryer.

Talbot Hotel ★   Beautifully decorated with lots of warm red tones and highly polished wood, this is a good option in Wexford. The lobby and dining room are comfortable places to relax, with thickly cushioned chairs and plenty of sunlight. Bedrooms are midsize and contemporary, with all the modern conveniences. There's a nicely designed leisure center inside an adjacent 100-year-old grain mill, with a pool, steam room, and sauna. Spa treatments are also available to work out the kinks, and there's a supervised children's play area so that you don't have to worry while you're getting a massage. Dinner in the restaurants or drinks in the bar are relaxing.

On the Quay, Wexford Town, County Wexford. (℃) **053/912-2566.** Fax 053/912-3377. www.talbothotel.ie. 132 units. €180–€220 ($288–$352) double. Rates include full breakfast. AE, MC, V. **Amenities:** 2 restaurants (Continental, seafood); bar; indoor swimming pool; gym; beauty/spa treatments; Jacuzzi; sauna; steam room; children's playroom. In room: TV, radio, tea/coffeemaker, hair dryer.

Moderate

Ballinkeele House ★★   This grand, 19th-century Irish manor B&B, built in 1840, is a wonderful place to appreciate Irish country-house living. As soon as you enter the majestic entrance hall with its Corinthian columns and fireplace, John and Margaret Maher see to it that you feel at home. Rooms are beautifully done in soft pastels, with heavy four-poster or half-tester beds and period touches everywhere. Dinner (book before noon) is served by candlelight in a chandeliered dining room, and it is excellent. Some 140 hectares (346 acres) of fields and woodlands surround the house, with gardens created around a pond, and strolling the grounds, you may encounter pheasants or foxes going about their business.

Signposted off the N11 north of Wexford at Oylgate, Ballymurn, Enniscorthy, County Wexford. © 053/ 913-8105. Fax 053/913-8468. www.ballinkeele.com. 5 units. €160–€180 ($256–$288) double. Rates include full breakfast. Dinner €40 ($64). MC, V. Closed Dec–Jan. **Amenities:** Dining room; lounge. *In room:* TV, hair dryer.

Riverside Park Hotel   Set on the green banks of the River Suir in the bustling market town of Enniscorthy, this contemporary hotel has a warm facade, a bold stone tower centerpiece, and a circular atrium lobby. A flower-fringed terrace lures you to dine and relax by the river's edge. Guest rooms may be a bit colorful for some, with bold print fabrics, bright carpets, and vivid curtains. Front-facing rooms have fine views from their own small balconies. This place makes a great base from which to explore the Blackstairs Mountains and Wexford Town.

At the junction of N11 and N30 on the south edge of town, The Promenade, Enniscorthy, County Wexford. © 053/923-7800. Fax 054/37900. www.riversideparkhotel.com. 60 units. €170 ($272) double. Rates include full Irish breakfast. AE, DC, MC, V. **Amenities:** 2 restaurants (international, Mexican); 2 bars; discounts at nearby leisure center and golf course; babysitting. *In room:* TV, tea/coffeemaker, hair dryer.

Woodbrook House ★★   Hidden away at the end of a long drive through farmland and rolling hills a few miles outside the historic town of Enniscorthy, this 17th-century country house looks as if it stepped out of a Jane Austen book. In the vast central hall, a gorgeous, wrought-iron "flying staircase" curves upward with no support save for its clever engineering. Walls are done with elegant paint washes and *trompe l'oeil* to give the place an intelligent sense of history. Heavy wooden furniture has been well chosen to fit in with this look. Owners Giles and Alexandra FitzHerbert run the place with calm skill, while also raising their four children. They know a great deal about the area, and can help you plan your outings to get the most of them.

Killanne, Enniscorthy, County Wexford. © 054/925-5114. www.woodbrookhouse.ie. 3 units. €150–€170 ($240–$272) double. Rates include full breakfast. Dinner €40 ($64). MC, V. Closed Nov–Apr, but stays can be arranged during this time by contacting the management. **Amenities:** Lounge w/fireplace. *In room:* Radio, hair dryer.

Inexpensive

Clonard House   Set on a hillside overlooking Wexford Town, Clonard House is a Georgian country home (1792) with high ceilings and lots of architectural detail. It's attractively furnished with period antiques, and has a marvelous historical feel. At night you can unwind over an Irish coffee in the elegant drawing room before retiring to one of the nine bedrooms, most of which have four-poster beds with orthopedic mattresses. Breakfast is served in the charming dining room with period features.

Clonard Great, Wexford Town, County Wexford. © 054/43141. 9 units. €90 ($144) double. Rates include full breakfast. MC, V. **Amenities:** Lounge. *In room:* TV, hair dryer.

Clone House   This 250-year-old farmhouse is furnished with handsome antiques. A courtyard opens onto a garden in back, and you can walk through the fields to the bank of the River Bann. The owners pride themselves on their knowledge of the area (both the local region and Ireland as a whole), and they're very helpful when it comes to planning touring or outdoor activities.

Ferns, Enniscorthy, County Wexford. © **054/936-6113.** Fax 054/66225. 7 units, 5 with bathroom. €85–
€110 ($136–$176) double. Rates include full breakfast. No credit cards. Closed Nov–Apr. **Amenities:**
Nonsmoking rooms. *In room:* TV in 3 rooms.

McMenamin's Townhouse At the western end of Wexford Town, opposite the
railroad station, this Victorian-style town house offers warm, hospitable accommodations at an affordable price. Guest rooms are nicely furnished with Irish antiques and
brass beds. McMenamin's is run by Seamus and Kay McMenamin, who formerly ran a
restaurant, and Kay puts her culinary skills to work by providing copious gourmet breakfasts complete with homemade breads and cereals. Not all rooms have televisions, so if
this is important to you, ask.

3 Auburn Terrace, Redmond Rd., Wexford, County Wexford. © **053/914-6442.** Fax 053/46442. www.
wexford-bedandbreakfast.com. 6 units. €90 ($144) double. Rates include full breakfast. MC, V. **Amenities:**
Babysitting; nonsmoking rooms. *In room:* TV in some rooms, tea/coffeemaker.

WHERE TO DINE
Moderate
Forde's Restaurant ★★ BISTRO This waterfront restaurant has become one of
Wexford Town's most in-demand restaurants. In many ways, it's a classic bistro, both in
looks and in terms of the menu: Dublin Bay prawns with garlic, beignets of fresh crabmeat with ginger and basil, and an excellent sirloin with garlic butter. The wine list is
well chosen and affordable, the crowd happy, the service professional.

The Crescent, Wexford, County Wexford. © **053/912-3832.** Reservations recommended. Main courses
€19–€29 ($30–$46). AE, MC, V. Daily 6–10:30pm.

Mange2 FRENCH FUSION This attractive restaurant does French cooking with a
global twist. The mix won't be for everybody, but many will love the roasted red pepper
and fennel samosa with baby beets, or the pine-nut fritter that accompanies the filets of
sole. The roast breast of chicken comes with thin strips of pan-fried chorizo and savoy
cabbage. Veggie side dishes begin with ingredients at the peak of freshness and arrive crisp
and steaming, wrapped in parchment packets. The wine list is modest and judicious.
Fusion continues on the dessert menu, which might feature baked passion-fruit ricotta
cake with orange ice cream.

Above the Crown Bar, Monck St., Wexford. © **053/914-4033.** Reservations recommended. Dinner main
courses €17–€24 ($27–$38). AE, MC, V. Tues–Sun 12:30–2:30pm and 5:30pm–late.

Inexpensive
Westgate Design DELI The restaurant inside this popular arts shop offers fresh-
made sandwiches, wraps, hot platters, soups, and salads at thoroughly reasonable prices.
The bread is made fresh, and you can eat your organic greens surrounded by original art.
This is an excellent place to take a break in the afternoon for tea and cake.

22 N. Main St., Wexford, County Wexford. © **053/23787.** All Items €2.50–€10 ($4–$16). MC, V. Daily
11am–5pm.

WEXFORD AFTER DARK
The Performing Arts
Opera fans troop to little Wexford each fall for the **Wexford Festival Opera** in October,
but you can catch interesting theatrical performances here all year-round. Wexford is a
town with a fine tradition of music and the arts. Sadly, in the name of progress the local

authorities have taken it upon themselves to demolish the historic Theatre Royal, built in 1832, and rebuild it as a multipurpose performance venue; no other details were available at time of writing. Still, the festival is a unique experience, and opera lovers will be in heaven. Booking for the festival (www.wexfordopera.com) opens in June each year. Tickets start at about €10 ($16) and go up to around €100 ($160).

There's always something interesting going on at the **Wexford Arts Centre,** Cornmarket, Wexford (℃ **053/23764**). Built as the market house in 1775, this building is a focal point for the arts in Wexford, and now houses three exhibition rooms and showcases a range of theatrical and artistic events. It's open year-round from 10am to 6pm daily.

To see professional Irish music and dancing, head 16km (10 miles) south of Wexford to the **Yola Farmstead,** Wexford-Rosslare road (N25), Tagoat, County Wexford (℃ **053/ 32610**). For groups, by prior arrangement, the Farmstead stages traditional Irish banquets and *céilí* evenings of Irish music, song, and dance. If you're on your own, you still might be able to join in if a performance is planned. The average cost is €32 ($51) per person.

Pubs

Antique Tavern   It's worth a 24km (15-mile) trip from Wexford City to Enniscorthy to see this Tudor-style pub, off the main Dublin-Wexford road (N11). True to the name, the walls are lined with memorabilia from the Wexford area—old daggers, pikes, and lanterns—and the mood is friendly. 14 Slaney St., Enniscorthy, County Wexford. ℃ **054/923-3428.** www.theantiquetavern.com.

The Crown Bar   Once a stagecoach inn, this tiny pub in the center of town has been in the Kelly family since 1841. Along with its historical overtones, it is known for its museum-like collection of antique weapons, including 18th-century dueling pistols and pikes from the 1798 rebellion. It's not always open during the day, so it's best to visit in the evening. Monck St., Wexford, County Wexford. ℃ **053/21133.**

Oak Tavern   More than 150 years old, this pub—originally a tollhouse—is 3km (2 miles) north of town, overlooking the River Slaney near the Ferrycarrig Bridge. There is a riverside patio for fine days, and traditional music sessions are held most evenings in the front bar. Wexford-Enniscorthy rd. (N11), Ferrycarrig, County Wexford. ℃ **053/20922.**

The Wren's Nest   Near the John Barry Memorial on the harbor, 5 minutes from the bus and train station, this is a traditional pub, right down to its wooden floors and ceilings. The varied pub menu includes Wexford mussel platters, house pâtés, soups, salads, and vegetarian entrees. There is free traditional Irish music on Tuesday and Thursday nights. Custom House Quay, Wexford, County Wexford. ℃ **053/912-2359.**

2 COUNTY WATERFORD

Waterford City: 65km (40 miles) W of Wexford, 53km (33 miles) W of Rosslare Harbour, 158km (98 miles) SW of Dublin, 126km (78 miles) E of Cork, 153km (95 miles) SE of Shannon Airport

Waterford City (pop. 42,500) is the main seaport of southeast Ireland. Its proximity to the ferocious Atlantic Ocean makes it Ireland's Windy City, as the sea breeze always blows here. Its location has a lot to do with the fact that it is Ireland's oldest city, founded by Viking invaders in the 9th century. In recent years, a major archaeological endeavor has excavated much of the ancient Viking city, and some of the more striking finds from these excavations can be seen in the **Waterford Treasures** exhibition at the Granary Museum.

Although the historic district around Reginald's Tower is intriguing, outside of that Waterford is largely a commercial center, dominated by its busy port. Because the rest of County Waterford is so beautiful, many travelers don't linger long in the capital city, though it is currently undergoing a wave of renewal and development, which could, over time, enhance its offerings.

Coastal highlights south of Waterford include **Dunmore East,** a picturesque fishing village and the charmingly old-fashioned **Portally Cove,** Ireland's only Amish-Mennonite community; **Dungarvan,** a major town with a fine harbor; **Ardmore,** an idyllic beach resort; and **Passage East,** a tiny seaport from which you can catch a ferry across the harbor and cut your driving time from Waterford to Wexford in half. Of all the coastal towns in County Waterford, Ardmore most stands out. It has an ancient monastic site, a pristine Blue Flag beach, a stunning cliff walk, a fine craft shop, an excellent restaurant, and comfortable seaside accommodations.

In northwest County Waterford, the **Comeragh Mountains** provide many opportunities for beautiful walks, including the short trek to Mahon Falls. These mountains also have highly scenic roads for biking. Farther west, there's great fishing on the **Blackwater estuary.**

WATERFORD CITY ESSENTIALS

GETTING THERE Little **Waterford Airport,** off R675, Waterford (© 051/846600; www.flywaterford.com), is served by **Aer Arran** (© 011/353-81821-0210 in the U.S., 818/210-210 in Ireland, or 0800/587-2324 in the U.K.; www.aerarann.com) from Manchester in northern England, and Luton in London.

Irish Rail offers daily service from Dublin and other points into Plunkett Station, at Ignatius Rice Bridge, Waterford (© 051/873401; www.irishrail.ie).

Bus Éireann operates daily service into Plunkett Station Depot, Waterford (© 051/879000; www.buseireann.ie), from Dublin, Limerick, and other major cities throughout Ireland.

Four major roads lead into Waterford: N25 from Cork and the south, N24 from the west, N19 from Kilkenny and points north, and N25 from Wexford.

The **Passage East Car Ferry Ltd.,** Barrack Street, Passage East, County Waterford (© 051/382480 or 382488; http://homepage.eircom.net/~passferry), operates a car-ferry service across Waterford Harbour. It links Passage East, about 16km (10 miles) east of Waterford, with Ballyhack, about 32km (20 miles) southwest of Wexford. This shortcut saves about an hour's driving time. The crossing time averages 10 minutes. It's continuous drive-on, drive-off service, with no reservations required. See "Wexford Town Essentials," earlier in this chapter, for fare and schedule information.

VISITOR INFORMATION The **Waterford Tourist Office** is at 41 The Quay, Waterford (© 051/875788; www.waterfordtourism.com). It's open April to September Monday to Saturday 9am to 6pm; October Monday to Saturday 9am to 5pm; and November to March Monday to Friday 9am to 5pm. The year-round office in the courthouse, off the Square in Dungarvan (© 058/41741), keeps comparable hours. The seasonal tourist office on the Square at Tramore (© 051/381572) is open from mid-June to August Monday to Saturday 10am to 6pm.

CITY LAYOUT Waterford is a commercial city focused on its waterfront. The city center sits on the south bank of the Suir. Traffic from the north, west, and east enters from the north bank over the Ignatius Rice Bridge and onto a series of quays (Grattan, Merchants, Meagher, and Parade), although most addresses simply say "The Quay."

Shops and attractions are concentrated near the quay area or on two thoroughfares that intersect it: The Mall and Barronstrand Street (changing their names to Broad, Michael, and John sts.). These streets were once rivers flowing into the Suir and, in fact, the original waterways continue to flow roughly 15m (49 ft.) beneath today's pavement.

GETTING AROUND Bus Éireann operates daily **bus service** within Waterford and its environs. The flat fare is €1.10 ($1.75). **Taxi** stands are outside Plunkett Rail Station and along the Quay opposite the Granville Hotel. If you need to call a taxi, try **Rapid Cabs** (✆ **051/858585**), **Metro Cabs** (✆ **051/857157**), or **Waterford Taxi Co-op** (✆ **051/877778**).

To see most of Waterford's sights (except the Waterford Crystal Factory), it's best to walk. You can park along the quays, and pay at the nearest machine. You'll need a car to reach the Waterford Crystal and County Waterford attractions outside of town.

To rent a car, contact **Budget Rent A Car,** Waterford Airport (✆ **051/873747**).

FAST FACTS If you need a drugstore, try **Gallagher's Pharmacy,** 29 Barronstrand St. (✆ **051/878103**), or **Mulligan's Chemists,** 40–41 Barronstrand St. (✆ **051/875211**).

In an emergency, dial ✆ **999. Garda Headquarters** (✆ **051/305300**) is the local police station. **Holy Ghost Hospital** is on Cork Road (✆ **051/374397**), and **Waterford Regional Hospital** is on Dunmore Road (✆ **051/848000**).

Among the resources for gay travelers is the **Gay and Lesbian Line Southeast** (✆ **051/879907**). The **Waterford Gay and Lesbian Resource Centre** is at the Youth Resources Centre, St. John's Park (✆ **087/638-7931**).

The **Voyager Internet Cafe,** 85 The Quay (✆ **051/843843**), isn't actually a cafe, but it does provide high-speed access with all the peripherals. Charges are €1.50 ($2.40) for 150 minutes. It's open Monday to Saturday 10am to 9pm.

The **General Post Office** on Parade Quay (✆ **051/317312**) is open Monday to Friday 9am to 5:30pm, and Saturday 9am to 1pm.

EXPLORING WATERFORD CITY

City Hall Headquarters of the local city government, this late-18th-century building houses local memorabilia, including the city's charter, granted in 1205. There's an absorbing display on the incredible life of Thomas Francis Meagher, a leader in an Irish insurrection in 1848; he was sentenced to death, but escaped to America. There he fought in the Civil War, earned the rank of brigadier general, and was eventually appointed governor of Montana. City Hall's other treasures include an 18th-century Waterford glass chandelier and priceless antique Waterford glasses.

The Mall, Waterford, County Waterford. ✆ **051/73501.** Free admission. Mon–Fri 9am–1pm and 2–5pm.

Garter Lane Arts Centre One of Ireland's largest arts centers, the Garter Lane occupies two buildings on O'Connell Street. No. 5, the site of the former Waterford Library, holds exhibition rooms and artists' studios, and no. 22a, the former Friends Meeting House, is home of the Garter Lane Theatre, with an art gallery and outdoor courtyard. The gallery showcases works by contemporary and local artists.

5 and 22a O'Connell St., Waterford, County Waterford. ✆ **051/55038.** Free admission to exhibitions. Gallery Tues–Sat noon–6pm.

Holy Trinity Cathedrals Waterford has two impressive cathedrals, one Catholic and the other Protestant, both built by one equal-opportunity architect, John Roberts. Roberts lived 82 years (1714–96), fathered 22 children with his beloved wife, and built nearly every

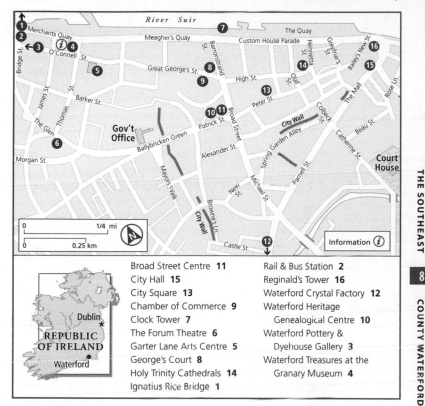

River Suir

Merchants Quay
Meagher's Quay
The Quay
Custom House Parade
O'Connell St.
Bridge St.
Barronstrand St.
Great George's St.
High St.
Henrietta St.
Greyfriar's St.
Bailey's New St.
Rose Ln.
Olaf St.
Peter St.
James St.
Thomas St.
Barker St.
The Glen
Gov't Office
Ballybricken Green
Patrick St.
Broad Street
City Wall
Colbeck St.
Spring Garden Alley
Beau St.
Catherine St.
The Mall
Morgan St.
Mayors Walk
Alexander St.
Parnell St.
Court House
Browne's Ln.
New St.
Michael St.
City Wall
Castle St.
Information ℹ

0 — 1/4 mi
0 — 0.25 km

REPUBLIC OF IRELAND
Dublin ★
Waterford

Broad Street Centre **11**	Rail & Bus Station **2**
City Hall **15**	Reginald's Tower **16**
City Square **13**	Waterford Crystal Factory **12**
Chamber of Commerce **9**	Waterford Heritage
Clock Tower **7**	Genealogical Centre **10**
The Forum Theatre **6**	Waterford Pottery &
Garter Lane Arts Centre **5**	Dyehouse Gallery **3**
George's Court **8**	Waterford Treasures at the
Holy Trinity Cathedrals **14**	Granary Museum **4**
Ignatius Rice Bridge **1**	

THE SOUTHEAST
8
COUNTY WATERFORD

significant 18th-century building in and around Waterford. Holy Trinity on Barronstrand is the only baroque cathedral in Ireland and has 10 unique Waterford crystal chandeliers. It's open daily 7:30am to 7pm. The Anglican or Church of Ireland Holy Trinity Cathedral (conveniently nicknamed Christ Church) on Henrietta Street has a most peculiar spire and only clear glass, because its first bishop and rector disliked stained glass.

Barronstrand and Henrietta sts., Waterford, County Waterford.

Reginald's Tower Circular, topped with a conical roof, and with walls 3m (10 ft.) thick, this mighty tower stands at the eastern end of the Quay beside the river. It's said to have been built in 1003 by a Viking governor named Reginald and has never fallen into ruin, which makes it Ireland's oldest standing building in continuous use. Still dominating the Waterford skyline, it's particularly striking at night when fully floodlit. Over the centuries, it's been a fortress, a prison, a military depot, a mint, an air-raid shelter, and now a museum.

The Quay, Waterford, County Waterford. ℂ **051/73501.** Admission €2.10 ($3.35) adults, €1.30 ($2.10) seniors, €1.10 ($1.75) children. Combined ticket with Waterford Treasures available. June–Aug daily 9:30am–9pm; May and Sept daily 9:30am–6pm; Oct–Apr daily 10am–5pm.

Waterford Crystal Factory and Visitor Centre ★★ For obvious reasons, this is Waterford's number-one attraction. Since it was founded in 1783, Waterford has been a byword for the crystal of connoisseurs. The devastating effects of the Irish famine forced the factory to close in 1851, but it was revived in 1947, and has since regained its prominence. The gallery contains a glittering display of crystal, with elaborate confections like trophies, globes, and chandeliers. In the shop, you can spend your way into the poorhouse in no time at all (don't look for any discounts at the factory—there are no seconds to be had; the main advantage in shopping here is simply the wide selection). True fans will take the excellent 35-minute tour of the factory to see the work firsthand.

Cork Rd., Waterford, County Waterford. ✆ **051/358398.** www.waterfordvisitorcentre.com. Tour €9 ($14) adults, €6.50 ($10) seniors and students, €4.50 ($7.20) groups, free for children 11 and under. Free admission to gallery. Tours Mar–Oct daily 8:30am–4:15pm; Nov–Feb Mon–Fri 9am–3:15pm. Reservations not required. Showrooms Mar–Oct daily 8:30am–6pm; Nov–Feb Mon–Fri 9am–5pm. Closed on St. Patrick's Day.

Waterford Heritage Genealogical Centre Did your ancestors come from Waterford? If so, follow the small lane between George's and Patrick streets to this historic building adjoining St. Patrick's and get the trained staff to trace your County Waterford ancestry. Church registers dating from 1655, surveys, rolls, and census lists are used as resources.

St. Patrick's Church, Jenkins Lane, Waterford, County Waterford. ✆/fax **051/876123.** www.waterford-heritage.ie. Free admission; basic search fee €90 ($144) by appointment only. Mon–Thurs 9am–5pm; Fri 9am–2pm.

Waterford Pottery and the Dyehouse Gallery Liz McCay is both the resident potter and the gallery director of this combined venue, which displays not only her own unique works, inspired by the black ceramic pottery discovered in local Viking excavations, but also contemporary paintings and prints by many of Ireland's leading visual artists. The gallery hosts seven or eight exhibitions per year.

Dyehouse Lane, Waterford, County Waterford. Pottery ✆ **051/878166.** Gallery ✆ **051/844770.** www.dyehouse-gallery.com. Free admission to exhibitions. Shop and gallery Mon–Sat 11am–6pm, or phone for appointment.

Waterford Treasures at the Granary Museum This impressive heritage center and museum, housed in a converted granary, unfolds Waterford's history from its earliest Viking origins. Along with an exceptional collection of Viking and medieval artifacts recovered in the region, there's also an ambitious state-of-the-art multimedia show including a three-dimensional film. There's so much to see and do that the exhibitions can seem like a circus with too many rings, more chaotic than enticing. If you move along at your own pace, however, there's a lot to see and learn. There's also a gift shop and cafe.

Merchant's Quay, Waterford, County Waterford. ✆ **051/304500.** www.waterfordtreasures.com. Admission €4 ($6.40) adults, €3 ($4.80) seniors and students, €2 ($3.20) children, €10 ($16) families. Combined ticket with Reginald's Tower available. June–Aug daily 9:30am–9pm; Apr–May and Sept daily 9:30am–6pm; Oct–Mar daily 10am–5pm.

Attractions Farther Afield in County Waterford

Ardmore High Cross ★ Ardmore (Irish for "the great height") is a very ancient Christian site—St. Declan, its founder, is said to have been a bishop in Munster as early as the mid–4th century, well before St. Patrick came to Ireland. Tradition has it that the small stone oratory in a cemetery high above Ardmore marks his burial site. St. Declan's

---

> ### (Tips) Walking Your Way Through Waterford
>
> The best way to begin your exploration of Waterford is to take a **Waterford City Walking Tour** ★. Jack Burtchaell, well versed in the history, folklore, and witty anecdotes of the city, conducts an engaging hour-long tour of the old city, leaving daily from the reception area of the Granville Hotel on the Quay. Tours are offered daily at noon and 2pm from March through October and cost €6 ($9.60) for adults. For more information, call Waterford Tourist Services at ✆ **051/873711**.

Oratory is one of several stone structures here composing the ancient monastic settlement. The most striking is the perfectly intact 30m-high (98-ft.) round tower. There are also ruins of a medieval cathedral and, nearby, St. Declan's well and church. For more in-depth exploration, pick up a copy of *The Pilgrim's Round of Ardmore, County Waterford*, at a local newspaper store for €3 ($4.80), or join the walking tour of ancient Ardmore, which leaves twice daily Monday to Saturday from the Tourist Information Office in the harbor. Contact the tourism office for times (see "Visitor Information," above).

Ardmore, County Waterford.

Lismore Castle ★   High above the River Blackwater, this turreted castle dates from 1185, when Prince John of England built a similar fortress on this site. Local lore says that Lismore Castle was once granted to Sir Walter Raleigh for IR£12 a year, although he never occupied it. One man who did live here was Richard Boyle, the first earl of Cork. He rebuilt the castle, including the thick defensive walls that still surround the garden, in 1626, but most of the present structure was rebuilt in the mid–19th century. You're free to wander the 3,200-hectare (7,904-acre) estate of gardens, forests, and farmland, but not the castle itself. It is the Irish seat of the duke and duchess of Devonshire, who won't let the general public in, though they're not above being entrepreneurs. In fact, if you've got the money, you can see it all, since the castle can be rented, complete with the duke's personal staff, to private groups for a minimum of €31,500 ($50,400) per week for up to 12 guests, during June through August. Included in the price are dinners, afternoon teas, and silver-service breakfasts. For booking information call ✆ **058/54424**, or 011/353 5854 424 from the U.S.

Lismore, County Waterford. ✆ **058/54424**. www.lismorecastle.com. Admission to gardens €6 ($9.60) adults, €3 ($4.80) children 15 and under. Mid–Apr to early Oct daily 1:45–4:45pm (June–Aug from 11am). From Cappoquin, take N72 6.5km (4 miles) west.

Lismore Heritage Centre   This interpretive center in the town's Old Courthouse tells the history of Lismore, a charming town founded by St. Carthage in the year 636. There's an interesting multimedia display on the town's unique treasures, including the Book of Lismore, which dates back 1,000 years, and the Lismore crosier (1116). Both were discovered hidden in the walls of Lismore Castle in 1814. The presentation also provides an excellent introduction to the surrounding area and its attractions. The center also offers several walking tours of the Lismore town and cathedral, leaving daily at 11am and 3pm.

Lismore, County Waterford. ✆ **058/54975**. www.discoverlismore.com. Admission €5 ($8) adults; €4 ($6.40) seniors, students, and children. May–Oct Mon–Fri 9:30am–5:30pm; Sat 10am–5:30pm; Sun noon–5:30pm.

(Finds) **A Walk to Mahon Falls**

Mahon Falls is in the Comeragh Mountains, on R676 between Carrick-on-Suir and Dungarvan. At the tiny village of Mahon Bridge, 26km (16 miles) south of Carrick-on-Suir, turn west on the road marked for Mahon Falls, then follow signs for the falls and the COMERAGH DRIVE. In about 5km (3 miles), you reach a parking lot along the Mahon River (in fact, just a tiny stream). The trail, indicated by two boulders, begins across the road. Follow the stream along the floor of the valley to the base of the falls. From here you can see the fields of Waterford spread out below you, and the sea a glittering mirror beyond. Walking time is about 30 minutes round-trip.

SHOPPING

Most come to Waterford for the crystal, but there are many other fine products in the shops and in the three multilevel enclosed shopping centers: **George's Court,** off Barronstrand Street, **Broad Street Centre,** on Broad Street, and **City Square,** off Broad Street. Hours are usually Monday to Saturday from 9 or 9:30am to 6 or 6:30pm. Some shops are open until 9pm on Thursday and Friday.

Aisling　Beside the Granville Hotel, this interesting shop offers an assortment of hand-made crafts, from quilts, tartans, and kilts to floral art, miniature paintings, and watercolors of Irish scenes and subjects. 61 The Quay, Waterford, County Waterford. © 051/873262.

The Book Centre　This huge, four-level bookstore has all the books, newspapers, and magazines you need, as well as useful maps and CDs. You can also make a photocopy here or zap off a fax. Barronstrand St., Waterford, County Waterford. © 051/873823.

Joseph Knox　This store has a large selection of Waterford crystal, particularly specialty items like chandeliers. 3 Barronstrand St., Waterford, County Waterford. © 051/875307.

Kelly's　Dating from 1847, this shop offers a wide selection of Waterford crystal, Aran knitwear, Belleek and Royal Tara china, Irish linens, and other souvenirs. 75–76 The Quay, Waterford, County Waterford. © 051/873557.

Penrose Crystal　Established in 1786 and revived in 1978, this is Waterford's other glass company, which turns out delicate hand-cut and engraved glassware carved with the stipple engraving process. A retail sales outlet is at Unit 8 of the City Square Shopping Centre. Both are open the usual hours, but the factory is also open Sunday 2 to 5:30pm from June to August. 32 John St., Waterford, County Waterford. © 051/876537.

SPORTS & OUTDOOR PURSUITS

BEACHES　There are wide sandy beaches at **Tramore, Ardmore, Clonea,** or **Dunmore East.**

BICYCLING　From Waterford City, you can ride 13km (8 miles) to Passage East and take the ferry (€3/$4.80 with a bicycle) to Wexford and the beautiful Hook Peninsula. Or continue on from Passage East to Dunmore East, a picturesque seaside village with a small beach hemmed in by cliffs. The road from there to Tramore and Dungarvan is quite scenic. For a complete 1- or 2-week biking vacation in the Southeast, contact Don Smith at **Celtic Cycling,** Lorum Old Rectory, Bagenalstown, County Carlow (©/fax **059/977-5282;** www.celticcycling.com). Prices start at €600 ($960) per person.

FISHING The Colligan River is excellent for sea trout and salmon. For permit information, contact **Gone Fishing,** 42 Lower Main St., Dungarvan (© **058/43514**). For sea angling, there are plenty of licensed charter-boat companies operating out of Kilmore Quay, roughly 24km (15 miles) southwest of Wexford. One such operation is **Dunmore East Angling Charters** (© **053/383397**). For landlubbers, the River Slaney, brimming with salmon and sea trout, can be fished from the old bridge in Enniscorthy.

GOLF County Waterford's golf venues include three 18-hole championship courses. **Waterford Castle Golf and Country Club,** The Island, Ballinakill, Waterford (© **051/ 871633;** www.waterfordcastle.com/golf), is a par-72 parkland course; greens fees are €50 to €55 ($80–$88) on weekdays, €55 to €65 ($88–$104) on weekends. **Faithlegg Golf Club,** Faithlegg House (© **051/380587;** www.faithlegg.com), a par-72 parkland course beside the River Suir, charges greens fees of €40 to €55 ($64–$88) Monday to Thursday, €60 to €69 ($96–$110) Friday to Sunday. **Dungarvan Golf Club,** Knocknagranagh, Dungarvan (© **058/41605;** www.dungarvangolfclub.com), a par-72 parkland course, has greens fees of €32 ($51) on weekdays, €44 ($70) on weekends. In addition, the 18-hole par-71 inland course at **Waterford Golf Club,** Newrath, Waterford (© **051/ 876748**), is 1.6km (1 mile) from the center of the city. Its greens fees are €40 ($64) on weekdays, €50 ($80) on weekends.

HORSEBACK RIDING Arrange to ride at **Killotteran Equitation Centre,** Killotteran, Waterford (© **051/384158**). Fees average around €25 ($40) per hour.

SAILING, WINDSURFING & SEA KAYAKING From May to September, the **Dunmore East Adventure Centre,** Dunmore East (© **051/383783**), offers courses of 1 to 4 days that cost €43 to €90 ($69–$140) per day, including equipment rental. Summer programs for children are also available. This is a great spot for an introductory experience, but there isn't much wave action for thrill-seeking windsurfers.

WHERE TO STAY
Very Expensive
Waterford Castle ★★ There's something magical about taking a boat back home to your castle at the end of the night. Dating back 800 years, this is a deeply secluded castle on a private island in the River Suir, surrounded by woodland and an 18-hole championship golf course. It's 3km (2 miles) south of Waterford, accessible only by the castle's private car ferry. With an original Norman keep and two Elizabethan wings, it is the real thing, with a leaded roof, mullioned windows, and fairy-tale turrets. Inside are oak-paneled walls, colorful tapestries, and huge stone fireplaces. The bedroom decor is a bit dated, and it could all use a bit of a makeover given the price charged, but four of the five suites are furnished with four-poster or canopied beds, and all rooms have firm mattresses and claw-foot bathtubs. The atmosphere is graciously informal; the staff is excellent and can help make arrangements for horseback riding, fishing, watersports, and other local activities.

The Island, Ballinakill, Waterford, County Waterford. © **051/878203.** Fax 051/879316. www.waterford castle.com. 19 units. €195–€450 ($312–$720) double. Breakfast €16–€20 ($26–$32). AE, MC, V. **Amenities:** Restaurant (international); bar; 18-hole championship golf course; tennis courts; concierge; room service; laundry and valet service. In room: TV, CD player, radio, hair dryer.

Moderate
Days Hotel Waterford With a location on the waterfront at the foot of the Ignatius Rice Bridge, this is one of the city's oldest hotels, but it was recently purchased by the

Days Hotel group and completely refurbished. Lounges and dining rooms are now sleek and modern with creamy walls, and guest rooms are similarly modern, with comfortable Hypnos beds. Rooms are spacious, with desks and chairs, and most are surprisingly quiet, given the busy location.

1 The Quay, Waterford, County Waterford. © **800/221-2222** in the U.S., or 051/877222. Fax 051/877229. www.dayshotelwaterford.com. 134 units. €100–€138 ($160–$221) double. Rates include service charge and full Irish breakfast. MC, V. **Amenities:** 2 restaurants (Continental, cafe); 2 bars; room service; babysitting. *In room:* TV, tea/coffeemaker, hair dryer.

Granville   Along the quay-side strip of Waterford's main business district, and looking out onto the south side of the River Suir, the Granville was originally a coaching inn. A past refurbishment of the hotel has preserved its architectural blend, although the rooms are nothing special—basic, contemporary, with somewhat garish covers on the orthopedic beds. As a saving grace, some front rooms look out onto the river.

Meagher Quay, Waterford, County Waterford. © **051/305555.** Fax 051/305566. www.granville-hotel.ie. 98 units. €110–€200 ($176–$320) double. Rates include full breakfast. AE, MC, V. Closed Dec 24–27. **Amenities:** Restaurant (international); bar; concierge; room service; laundry. *In room:* TV, radio, dataport, hair dryer, ironing board, garment press.

Inexpensive
An Bohreen ★★ Ⓥⁿˡᵘᵉ   This little B&B is sweetly done, with a gracious sitting room with a warming fire; charming guest rooms with pine furniture, polished wood floors, and white bed covers; and excellent food. In fact, whatever you do, don't miss dinner—you'll feast on Dungarvan Bay fish soup, prawns and crab on brown bread, mushrooms stuffed with crabmeat, rack of lamb, and homemade desserts. We can't think of another B&B in these parts that offers such value for the money.

Killineen West, Dungarvan, County Waterford. © **051/291010.** www.anbohreen.com. 4 units, all with private bathroom. €80–€90 ($128–$144) double. Rates include full breakfast. Dinner €38 ($61). AE, MC, V. **Amenities:** Sitting room. *In room:* Tea/coffeemaker.

Brown's Townhouse ★★ Ⓥⁿˡᵘᵉ   This friendly Victorian town-house B&B is within walking distance of the center of Waterford town. Leslie and Barbara Brown are keen collectors of Irish modern art, and their colorful paintings hang in every room. Bedrooms are spacious, with big windows and pleasant, old-fashioned decor. The best room has a roof garden terrace. Breakfast is a grand affair, with pancakes, homemade breads and preserves, fruit salad, and all the usual egg-and-bacon options.

29 S. Parade, Waterford, County Waterford. © **051/870594.** Fax 051/871923. 6 units. €110–€120 ($176–$192) double. Rates include full breakfast. MC, V. Closed Dec 25–Jan. **Amenities:** Nonsmoking rooms. *In room:* TV.

Foxmount Country House ★★ Ⓚⁱᵈˢ   This elegant, secluded, 17th-century country home is the perfect place to relax after a busy day of sightseeing. Rooms are attractively decorated, with soft colors and antique touches. Two adjacent guest rooms share a separate alcove—perfect for a family with kids. Four double rooms have private bathrooms. All have pastoral views. Margaret's breakfasts are bountiful affairs. The terrific Jack Meade pub (see below) is within walking distance.

Passage East rd., Waterford, County Waterford. © **051/874308.** Fax 051/854906. www.foxmountcountry house.com. 5 units. €110 ($176) double. 25% discount for children 11 and under. Rates include full breakfast. No credit cards. Closed Nov–Feb. *In room:* TV, hair dryer.

Glencairn Inn ★★ (Finds)   Formerly known as Buggy's, this intimate farmhouse B&B
has acquired a Gallic flavor since husband-and-wife team Stéphane and Fiona Tricot took
it over in 2006. Wisely, they have done little to tamper with its existing charms, and the
changes are subtle. Rooms are tastefully decorated with buttermilk-colored walls and
iron-and-brass beds, while the en suite bathrooms still have, big, old-fashioned tubs that
look like something out of a doll's house. However, it's in the restaurant where the new
owners have really made their stamp, and the excellent **Pastis Bistro,** serving predominantly French and Mediterranean cuisine, has become something of a local fixture. *Vive
la différence!*

Glencairn, County Waterford (4.8km/3 miles from Lismore). ℂ **058/56232.** www.glencairninn.com. 4
units. €95 ($152) double. Rates include full Irish breakfast. Dinner from €45 ($72). MC, V. Closed week of
Christmas. **Amenities:** Restaurant (bistro); bar; Wi-Fi; garden w/boules. *In room:* TV.

WHERE TO DINE
Expensive
Pastis Bistro ★★ FRENCH/MEDITERRANEAN   The jewel in the crown of
Stéphane and Fiona Tricot's successful takeover of the Glencairn Inn (see above) is this
exceptional little bistro, which has gathered quite a following among the diners of Waterford. Stéphane—who does most of the cooking himself—serves up an inventive combination of Mediterranean fare with a distinctly Irish accent, using ingredients sourced
locally where possible. Mains might include pan-fried hake or lobster, or steak *frites* with
a Jameson's whiskey–and-peppercorn sauce. The wine list is short, but every bit as well
selected as one would expect from such welcome French invaders.

In the Glencairn Inn, Lismore, County Waterford. ℂ **058/56232.** www.glencairninn.com. Reservations
recommended. Main courses €18–€26 ($29–$42). MC, V. Tues–Thurs 6:30–8:30pm; Fri–Sat 6:30–9:30pm;
Sun lunch 1–3pm.

The Tannery ★★ ECLECTIC EUROPEAN   Until 1995 this impressive stone
building on the quays was (as the name implies) a tannery in a former life; then it reap-
peared as a stylish contemporary restaurant and met instant success. The cuisine blends
unlikely ingredients to create interesting, creative dishes that seem impossible on paper,
but (at least for fusion fans) really work—a perfect plum-tomato soup, sea bream with
pepperoni and saffron-laced potatoes, French toast with baked apples and Chantilly
cream. It's not for all, but some will love it.

Quay St., Dungarvan, County Waterford (beside the library). ℂ **058/45420.** Reservations recommended.
Main courses €18–€28 ($29–$45). AE, DC, MC, V. Tues–Fri and Sun 12:30–2:30pm; Tues–Sat 6:30–9:30pm;
Sun 6:30–9pm (July–Aug only).

Moderate
Bodega! CONTINENTAL   If you're looking for the party place in Waterford, you've
just found it. This place draws a young (20-something) crowd for the great food, lack of
volume control, and convivial atmosphere. Choose from specials chalked onto the blackboard menu, which tends to be heavy on the fish and seafood. Everything's tasty, so just
go for what you like: There's sea bass with string beans and ratatouille, or a fish medley
of cod, salmon, crab ravioli, and mussels. The coffee and desserts are excellent, too, so
leave room to relax at the end of the meal with something sweet. One note of caution—
the restaurant is wheelchair accessible, but the toilets, unhelpfully, are not.

54 John St., Waterford, County Waterford. ℂ **051/844177.** Main courses lunch €5–€10 ($8–$16), dinner
€15–€26 ($24–$42). MC, V. Mon–Fri noon–5pm; Mon–Wed 5:30–10pm; Thurs–Sat 5:30–10:30pm; late
menu Fri–Sat 10:30pm–12:30am.

The Strand Seafood Restaurant ★★ SEAFOOD This intimate restaurant, attached to two pubs, has a well-deserved reputation for outstanding cuisine, and, if you can bring yourself to look up from your plate, the views of Waterford Harbour and the Celtic Sea are stunning. Daily seafood specials augment the excellent regular menu. Grilled wild salmon with green-gooseberry sauce sounds risky but generously rewards all takers, and lemon sole stuffed with seafood mousse is gorgeous. A vegetarian choice is provided each evening, and plates of crisp sautéed vegetables are liable to appear all by themselves. An alluring dessert cart awaits the end of your meal.

In the Strand Inn, Dunmore East, County Waterford. © 051/383174. Reservations recommended. Main courses €13–€15 ($21–$24). AE, MC, V. Daily 6:30–10pm.

The Wine Vault ★★ WINE BISTRO The food here is great, and the wines are excellent, but the real draw is that the place is so welcoming, with red-brick walls and wood paneling—like in your favorite trattoria. The herb-crusted salmon with peppered cucumber and cabernet sauvignon dressing is disarmingly simple and perfect, the marinated squid with garlic and ginger a memorable delicacy. Desserts, such as the Chocolate Nemesis and homemade lemon-curd ice cream, provide the perfect finish to a wonderful meal. The service here is exceptional—attentiveness without fuss, sophistication with warmth and humor.

High St., Waterford, County Waterford. © 051/853444. Reservations recommended. Main courses €12–€18 ($19–$29). AE, DC, MC, V. Mon–Sat 12:30–2:30pm and 5:30–10:30pm.

WATERFORD AFTER DARK

Waterford has two main entertainment centers. The 170-seat **Garter Lane Arts Centre Theatre,** 22a O'Connell St. (© 051/855038), presents the work of local production companies such as the Red Kettle and Waterford Youth Drama. Visiting troupes from all over Ireland also perform contemporary and traditional works here. Performances are usually Tuesday to Saturday, and tickets average €10 to €13 ($16–$21) for most events. There are also film screenings, which cost €6 ($9.60) for adults and €5 ($8) for children and seniors. The box office is open Tuesday to Saturday noon to 6pm, and accepts MasterCard and Visa.

When big-name Irish or international talents come to Waterford, they usually perform at the **Forum Theatre** at the Glen (© **051/871111;** www.forumwaterford.com), a 1,000-seat house off Bridge Street. Tickets average €10 to €25 ($16–$40), depending on the event. The box office is open Monday to Friday 11am to 1pm and 2 to 4pm. In addition to concerts, stand-up comedy, and theatrical productions, there are special indie club nights every Saturday and an '80s-themed disco on the first Friday of every month, price €10 ($16).

Otherwise, Waterford's nightlife is centered in the hotel lounges and in the city's interesting assortment of pubs.

Pubs

Jack Meade Waterford's most unusual pub is not in the city, but nestled beneath an old stone bridge in an area known as Halfway House, about 6km (3³/₄ miles) south. Dating from 1705, the pub is widely known by the locals as Meade's Under the Bridge. As a public house with a forge, it was once a stopping-off point for coach travelers between Waterford and Passage East. The facade and interior—wooden beams and open fireplaces—haven't changed much over the years. There's a playground for kids and ducks to feed, and in July and August there's music with singalong sessions on Wednesday nights. All year, impromptu evening sessions can spring up at a moment's notice. From May to September, bar food is served daily. Cheekpoint Rd., Halfway House, County Waterford. © 051/850950.

The Munster The flavor of old Waterford prevails in this 300-year-old building that is often referred to as Fitzgerald's (the name of the family that owns it). It is rich in etched mirrors, antique Waterford glass sconces, and dark-wood walls, some of which are fashioned out of timber from the old Waterford Toll Bridge. Among the many rooms are an original Men's Bar and a lively modern lounge that often features traditional Irish music on weekends. Bailey's New St., Waterford, County Waterford. © 051/874656.

T. & H. Doolan Once a stagecoach stop, this 170-year-old pub in the center of town is a favorite venue for evening sessions of ballad, folk, and traditional music. Lanterns light the whitewashed stone walls and a collection of old farm implements, crocks, mugs, and jugs. 32 George's St., Waterford, County Waterford. © 051/841504.

3 COUNTY TIPPERARY

Clonmel: 174km (108 miles) SW of Dublin, 182km (113 miles) SE of Galway, 79km (49 miles) SE of Limerick, 103km (64 miles) SE of Shannon Airport, 48km (30 miles) NW of Waterford, 145km (90 miles) E of Killarney

The southern section of County Tipperary is one of Ireland's best-kept secrets. Here, far from the tour buses and the clicking of camera shutters, you may just find the Ireland everyone is looking for: welcoming, unspoiled, and splendidly beautiful.

GETTING THERE   By Train   Irish Rail runs several trains a day into Clonmel from Limerick and Waterford. It serves Clonmel Station, Thomas Street, Clonmel, Tipperary (© 052/21982; www.irishrail.ie). The station is a 10-minute walk from the town center.

By Bus There are more **buses** than trains to Clonmel, and **Bus Éireann** operates daily bus service to Limerick, Wexford and Rosslare, into Clonmel Train Station, Thomas Street, Clonmel (© 052/21982; www.buseireann.ie).

By Car If you're driving from Dublin and points north, take the N7 or N76; if you're coming from the west, take the N24.

VISITOR INFORMATION The **Clonmel Tourist Office** is at 6 Sarsfield St., Clonmel (© 052/22960). It's open year-round Monday to Saturday 9:30am to 5:30pm. **Seasonal offices** are at Castle Street, Cahir (© 052/41453), open June to August Monday to Saturday 9:30am to 6pm, and at the Town Hall, Cashel (© 062/61333), open daily 9:30am to 5:30pm from March to October and Monday to Friday from November to February.

EXPLORING THE AREA

Clonmel, the capital of Tipperary, is the unassuming gateway to the region. A working town, largely unspoiled by tourism, Clonmel (whose name in Gaelic, Cluaín Meala, means "Meadows of Honey") makes a strategic, pleasant base in the Southeast. Looking at the pretty rural town, poised on the banks of the Suir, it's hard to believe that it once withstood a Cromwellian siege for 3 brutal months.

Whether you're staying in Clonmel or just passing through, several scenic drives converge here: the **Comeragh or Nire Valley Drive** deep into the Comeragh Mountains, which rise from the south banks of the Suir; the **Knockmealdown Drive,** through the historic village of Ardfinnan and the Vee Gap (see below); and the **Suir Scenic Drive.** All are signposted from Clonmel.

North of Clonmel and deep in the Tipperary countryside, **Cashel,** with its Rock of Cashel and cluster of monastic buildings in a dramatic setting, is not to be missed. Because it's on the main N8 road, most people pass through en route from Dublin to Cork. If your travels don't take you to Cashel, a side trip from Waterford is worth the drive. In particular, the following two scenic routes are well worth a detour.

At Cahir, head north through the scenic **Galtee Mountains** ★ to the Glen of Aherlow. The pristine 11km (7-mile) Glen of Aherlow is a secluded and scenic pass between the plains of counties Tipperary and Limerick.

If you're driving south into Waterford, you might want to travel via the **Vee Gap.** This 18km-long (11-mile) road winds through the Knockmealdown Mountains from Clogheen to Lismore and Cappoquin in County Waterford. It's a dramatic drive, which peaks at the Tipperary-Waterford border, where the two slopes of the pass converge to frame the patchwork fields of the Galtee Valley far below. At this point, numerous walking trails lead to the nearby peaks and down to the mountain lake of Petticoat Loose—named after a, shall we say, lady of flexible morals. A more edifying local character was Samuel Grubb, of Castle Grace, who so loved these slopes that he left instructions to be buried upright overlooking them. And so he was. The rounded stone cairn you might notice off the road between Clogheen and the Vee Gap is where he stands in place, entombed, facing the Golden Vale of Tipperary.

Ahenny High Crosses   You're likely to have this little-known and rarely visited site to yourself, except for the cows whose pasture you will cross to reach it. The setting is idyllic and, on a bright day, gorgeous. The well-preserved Ahenny high crosses date from the 8th or 9th century. Tradition associates them with seven saintly bishops, all brothers who were said to have been waylaid and murdered. Their unusual stone "caps," thought by some to be bishops' miters, more likely suggest the transition from wood crosses, which would have had small roofs to shelter them from the rain. Note, too, their intricate spiral and cable ornamentation in remarkably high relief, which may have been inspired by earlier Celtic metalwork.

Kil Crispeen Churchyard, Ahenny, County Tipperary. 8km (5 miles) north of Carrick-on-Suir, signposted off R697. Box for donations.

Athassel Priory   Although it is in ruins, many delightful details from the original medieval priory that once stood here still remain. This was an Augustinian priory, founded in the late 12th century, and it was once elaborately decorated. The main approach is over a low stone bridge and through a gatehouse. The church entrance is a beautifully carved doorway at its west end, while to the south of the church is the cloister, its graceful arches eroded by time. Look for a carved face protruding from the southwest corner of the chapel tower, about 9m (30 ft.) above ground level.

3km (2 miles) south of Golden, County Tipperary. Take signposted road from Golden, on the N74; the priory is in a field just east of the road.

The Bolton Library   In this library, you'll see the smallest book in the world, as well as other rare, antiquarian, and unusual books dating as far back as the 12th century. The works by Dante, Swift, Calvin, Newton, Erasmus, and Machiavelli are displayed alongside silver altarpieces from the cathedral on the Rock of Cashel.

On the grounds of St. John the Baptist Church, John St., Cashel, County Tipperary. ℂ **062/61944.** Admission €2 ($3.20), free for young children. Mon–Thurs 10am–4pm.

Brú Ború Heritage Centre ★　At the foot of the Rock of Cashel, this modern complex adds a musical element to the historic Cashel area. Operated by Comhaltas Ceoltoiri Éireann, Ireland's foremost traditional-music organization, Brú Ború presents daily performances of authentic Irish traditional music at an indoor theater. Many summer evenings feature concerts in the open-air amphitheater. A subterranean "Sounds of History" exhibition gives an audio tour of Ireland through the ages. A gift shop, restaurant, and self-service snack bar are also on hand.

Rock Lane, Cashel, County Tipperary. ✆ **062/61122.** Free admission to center; show €18 ($29) adults, €10 ($16) children; 7pm "Sounds of History" exhibition €5 ($8) adults, €3 ($4.80) children. Oct–Apr daily 9am–5:30pm; May–Sept daily 9am–5pm. Shows mid-June to mid-Sept Tues–Sat 9pm.

Cahir Castle ★★　On a rock in the middle of the River Suir, this medieval fortress can trace its history from the 3rd century, when a fort was first built on the rock—hence the town's Gaelic name, "City of the Fishing Fort." The present structure, which belonged to the Butler family for 600 years, 1375 to 1961, is Norman. It has a massive keep, high walls, spacious courtyards, and a great hall, all fully restored. The interpretive center has an engaging 20-minute video introduction to the region's major historic sites, as well as guided tours of the castle grounds. Take the time to walk through the castle buildings, which are not included in the tour.

Cahir, County Tipperary. ✆ **052/41011.** Admission €3 ($4.80) adults, €2.40 ($3.85) seniors, €1.50 ($2.40) students and children, €7.50 ($12) families. Mid-Mar to mid-June and mid-Sept to mid-Oct daily 9:30am–5:30pm; mid-June to mid-Sept daily 9am–7pm; mid-Oct to mid-Mar daily 9:30am–4:30pm.

Ormond Castle　The mid-15th-century castle built by Sir Edward MacRichard Butler on a strategic bend of the River Suir has lain in ruins for centuries. What still stands, attached to the ancient battlements, is the last surviving Tudor manor house in Ireland. Trusting that "if he built it, she would come," Thomas Butler constructed an extensive manor in honor of his most successful relation, Queen Elizabeth I—whose mother, Anne Boleyn, is rumored to have been born in Ormond Castle. He was wrong. Elizabeth never dropped by, but many others have, especially since the Heritage Service partially restored this impressive piece of Irish history. The manor's plasterwork, carvings, period furniture, and collection of original 17th- and 18th-century royal charters will make you glad you bothered to visit and wonder why Liz never did.

Signposted from the center of Carrick-on-Suir, Carrick-on-Suir, County Tipperary. ✆ **051/640787.** Admission €3 ($4.80) adults, €2.50 ($4) seniors, €1.30 ($2.10) students and children, €7 ($11) families. June–Sept daily 9:30am–6:30pm.

The Rock of Cashel ★★　When you're near the town of Cashel, the first thing you'll see is the extraordinary, dramatic outline of this craggy old abbey at the top of the hill at the town center. It dominates views for miles around. An outcrop of limestone reaching 60m (197 ft.) into the sky, "the Rock" tells the tales of 16 centuries. It was the castled seat of the kings of Munster at least as far back as A.D. 360, and it remained a royal fortress until 1101, when King Murtagh O'Brien granted it to the church. Among Cashel's many great moments was the legendary baptism of King Aengus by St. Patrick in 448. Remaining on the rock are the ruins of a two-towered chapel, a cruciform cathedral, a 28m (92-ft.) round tower, and a cluster of other medieval monuments. Inside the cathedral, ancient carvings survive in excellent condition. The views of and from the Rock are spectacular. Forty-five-minute guided tours are available on request.

Cashel, County Tipperary. ℭ **062/61437.** Admission €5.30 ($8.50) adults, €3.70 ($5.90) seniors, €2.10 ($3.35) students and children, €12 ($19) families. Mid-June to mid-Sept daily 9am–7pm; mid-Sept to mid-Mar daily 9am–4:45pm; mid-Mar to mid-June daily 9am–5:30pm. Last admission 45 min. before closing.

Swiss Cottage   The earls of Glengall used the Swiss Cottage as a hunting and fishing lodge as far back as 1812. It's a superb example of *cottage orné:* a rustic house embodying the ideal of simplicity that so appealed to the Romantics of the early 19th century. The thatched-roof cottage has extensive timberwork, usually not seen in Ireland, and is believed to have been designed by John Nash, a royal architect. The interior has some of the first wallpaper commercially produced in Paris. A guided tour (the only way to see the building) lasts approximately 40 minutes.

Off Dublin-Cork rd. (N8), Cahir, County Tipperary. ℭ **052/41144.** Guided tour €3 ($4.80) adults, €2.10 ($3.35) seniors, €1.30 ($2.10) students and children, €7.40 ($12) families. Late Mar and mid-Oct to Nov Tues–Sun 10am–1pm and 2–4:30pm; Apr Tues–Sun 10am–1pm and 2–6pm; May to mid-Oct daily 10am–6pm.

SPORTS & OUTDOOR PURSUITS

BICYCLING   For complete 1- or 2-week cycling holidays in the Southeast, contact Don Smith at **Celtic Cycling,** Lorum Old Rectory, Bagenalstown, County Carlow (ℭ/fax **059/977-5282;** www.celticcycling.com).

BIRD-WATCHING   As many as 15 species of Irish water birds—including mute swans, coots, gadwalls, and gray herons—can be seen at the **Marlfield Lake Wildfowl Refuge,** several miles west of Clonmel in Marlfield. On your way, you will pass signposts for **St. Patrick's Well,** less than a mile away, a tranquil spot with an effervescent pool of reputedly healing crystalline water. In the middle of the pool rises an ancient Celtic cross. The legend that Patrick visited here seems more solidly rooted than most such claims.

FISHING   The **River Suir,** from Carrick-on-Suir to Thurles, was once one of the finest salmon rivers in Europe, but recent excessive trawling at its mouth has threatened its stock. It's still a decent salmon river, especially in the February run and from June to September. Trout (brown and rainbow) are in abundance here in the summer. Here you'll find some of the least expensive game fishing in Ireland; single weekday permits cost €20 to €32 ($32–$51) for salmon, €7 ($11) for trout. They are available from **Kavanagh Sports,** Westgate, Clonmel, County Tipperary (ℭ/fax **052/21279**), as is everything else you'll need. Manager Declan Byrne can outfit you with all of the essentials and more. To orient yourself and to consider your options, pick up a copy of *Angling on the Suir,* a helpful pamphlet put out by the Tourist Office. The **River Nore** and the nearby **River Barrow** are also known for good salmon and trout fishing.

For sea fishing, picturesque Dunmore East, 13km (8 miles) south of Waterford, is a good bet. Contact **John O'Connor** (ℭ **051/383397**) to charter a boat for reef, wreck, and shark fishing. Boat charter rates are around €400 ($640) per day.

HORSEBACK RIDING   For trekking and trail riding on the slopes of the Comeragh Mountains, you can't do better than **Melodys Nire Valley Equestrian Centre,** Nire View, Ballycarbry, Clonmel (ℭ **052/36147**).

SWIMMING   If you're staying in the area, you're welcome to swim at the **Clonmel Civic Swimming Pool** (ℭ **052/21972**), near the Market Place, which also has a handy gym and sauna. It's open Monday to Friday 9am to 9:45pm, Saturday and Sunday 10am to 7:45pm. Call for specific public swimming hours.

TENNIS The courts of the **Hillview Sports Club,** Mountain Road, Clonmel (✆ 052/ 21805), may be used by visitors.

WALKING **R668** between Clogheen and Lismore is a scenic stretch of road, and some great walks begin at the **Vee Gap,** a dramatic notch in the Knockmealdown Mountains. About 2km (1¼ miles) north of R669 and R668, you reach the highest point in the gap; there is a parking lot, as well as a dirt road continuing down to a lake nestled into the slope below. This is Bay Lough, and the dirt road used to be the main thoroughfare over the gap; it now offers a fine walk to the shores of the lake, with outstanding views of the valley to the north. For a panoramic perspective of the region, start walking due east from the gap parking lot to the summit of Sugarloaf Hill; the hike is extremely steep, but well worth the effort—the views from the ridge are superb.

In the Clonmel area, there are excellent river and hill walks, some more challenging than others. The most spectacular is the ascent of famed **Slievenamon,** a mountain rich in myth. Inexpensive, detailed trail maps for at least a half-dozen walks are available at the Clonmel Tourist Office on Sarsfield Street, Clonmel. Also available is a free leaflet guide to the birds, butterflies, and flora of nearby **Wilderness Gorge.**

The **Galtee Mountains,** northwest of the Knockmealdowns, offer some great long and short walks. One beautiful route on a well-defined trail is the circuit of **Lake Muskry,** on the north side of the range. To get there, take R663 west out of Bansha, and follow signs for the town of Rossadrehid. To get to the trail, ask for directions in Rossadrehid; there are several turns, and the landmarks change frequently because of logging. The trail leads you up a glaciated valley to the base of a ring of cliffs where the crystalline waters of Lake Muskry lie; from here you can walk around the lake, take in the tremendous views of the valley, and return the way you came. Walking time to the lake and back is 3 hours.

Another option on this walk is to continue up past the lake to the top of the ridge, and from there along the ridge top to Galtymore, a prominent dome-shaped peak about 5km (3 miles) west of Lake Muskry. It is a beautiful but extremely demanding walk, about 6 hours to Galtymore and back. This is only one of many extraordinary walks in the Glen of Aherlow. Trail maps and all the information and assistance you need are available at the **Glen of Aherlow Fáilte Society,** Coach Road, Newtown (✆ **062/56331**). It's open daily June to October from 9:30am to 6pm.

WHERE TO STAY
Very Expensive
Cashel Palace Hotel Originally built in 1730 as a residence for Church of Ireland archbishops, this mammoth red-brick Palladian mansion has been a hotel for over 30 years. It has an ideal location right in the middle of Cashel town, yet within its own walled grounds, and recent owners have updated the property and filled it with antiques and designer fabrics. The house is a proud display of lofty, corniced ceilings, Corinthian pillars, mantelpieces of Kilkenny marble, and a paneled early Georgian staircase of red pine. Guest rooms have a warm, traditional look and vast bathrooms, while the 10 rooms in the Mews House are smaller and more modern. The **Bishop's Buttery** restaurant has splendid views of the floodlit Rock, while well-tended gardens hold mulberry bushes that were planted in 1702 to commemorate the coronation of Queen Anne.

Main St., Cashel, County Tipperary. ✆ **062/62707.** Fax 062/61521. www.cashel-palace.ie. 23 units. €250–€305 ($400–$488) double. €30 ($48) supplement for rooms with a view of the Rock of Cashel. Rates include service charge and full Irish breakfast. AE, MC, V. **Amenities:** Restaurant (international); bar; babysitting; drawing room. *In room:* TV, hair dryer.

Expensive

Hotel Minella ★★   The attractive centerpiece of this sprawling hotel complex along the River Suir was built in 1863, but there have been many additions since then. Its riverbank location and attractive landscaping provide an appeal beyond the somewhat incongruous mix of architectural styles. Once you're inside, its warm, welcoming atmosphere takes over. The standard guest rooms are furnished traditionally in dark wood and prints. As the name implies, the Jacuzzi suites have Jacuzzi tubs, while the steam room suites are especially spacious and luxuriant, with rich colors, big comfortable beds, and private steam rooms with showers. Perhaps the chief appeal of this hotel is its new, state-of-the-art **health and fitness club**—you could easily spend several days making use of the facilities.

1.6km (1 mile) east of Clonmel center on the south bank of the River Suir, Coleville Rd., Clonmel, County Tipperary. (℃) **052/22388.** Fax 052/24381. www.hotelminella.ie. 90 units. €160–€185 ($256–$296) double; €200–€250 ($320–$400) suite. Rates include service charge and full breakfast. AE, MC, V. **Amenities:** Restaurant (international); bar; 2 lounges; indoor swimming pool; outdoor hot tub; all-season tennis court; gym; indoor Jacuzzi; sauna; aromatherapy steam room; room service; massage; babysitting; laundry service; dry cleaning; nonsmoking rooms; foreign-currency exchange; therapy rooms. *In room:* TV, free broadband, tea/coffeemaker, iron, garment press.

Moderate

Dundrum House Hotel   Located 10km (6¼ miles) northwest of Cashel, this Georgian country manor is nestled in the fertile Tipperary countryside, surrounded by sprawling grounds and gardens. Originally built as a residence in 1730 by the earl of Montalt, it was later used as a convent school, and then transformed into a hotel in 1978. It is furnished with heirlooms, vintage curios, Victorian pieces, and reproductions. Each room is individually decorated with a traditional and slightly dated feel, some with four-poster beds or hand-carved headboards, armoires, vanities, and other traditional furnishings. Look for exceptional weekend specials on offer all year. The hotel's bar is especially appealing, in a former chapel with vivid stained-glass windows.

Dundrum, County Tipperary. (℃) **062/71116.** Fax 062/71366. www.dundrumhousehotel.com. 86 units. €160 ($256) double. Weekend discounts available. AE, MC, V. **Amenities:** Restaurant (Irish/Continental); bar; indoor pool; 18-hole championship golf course; gym; sauna; horseback riding; trout fishing privileges. *In room:* TV, radio, hair dryer.

Kilcoran Lodge Hotel   A former hunting lodge nestled amid wooded grounds, this old Victorian treasure is on a hillside set back from the main road a few miles west of Cahir. The public areas retain their old-world charm, with open fireplaces, grandfather clocks, antique tables and chairs, brass fixtures, and tall windows framing expansive views of the Suir Valley and Knockmealdown Mountains. Guest rooms are basically but comfortably appointed and have modern bathrooms. The bar is noted for its excellent daytime menu, which includes Irish stew, traditional boiled bacon and cabbage, homemade soups, and hot scones.

Dublin-Cork rd. (N8), Cahir, County Tipperary. (℃) **800/447-7462** in the U.S., or 052/41288. Fax 052/41994. www.kilcoranlodgehotel.com. 22 units. €130 ($208) double. Rates include service charge and full breakfast. AE, MC, V. **Amenities:** Restaurant (international); bar; lounge; indoor swimming pool; gym; Jacuzzi; sauna; solarium. *In room:* TV, radio, tea/coffeemaker, hair dryer, garment press.

Mobarnane House ★   This elegant, splendidly restored 18th-century farmhouse was opened in 2000 as a B&B and immediately became popular with discerning travelers in search of a period setting, tranquil surroundings, and warm hospitality. Richard Craik-White is a terrific chef, and his wife, Sandra, is a warm hostess. Dinner is a convivial affair, served at a communal table. Guest rooms are prettily decked out in cream or blue, furnished with mahogany pieces and antiques. The best two rooms have mountain views and their own sitting rooms; the other two face the lake and are equally pretty but not as large. The 24-hectare (59-acre) estate of woodlands, meadows, and gardens—with its own lake—makes this a wonderful base for walkers.

Fethard, County Tipperary. ✆/fax **052/31962.** www.mobarnanehouse.com. 4 units. €160–€190 ($256–$304) double. 4-course dinner €45 ($72). Rates include service charge and full breakfast. MC, V. Closed Nov–Feb. Not suitable for those with mobility problems. No young children. **Amenities:** Drawing room. *In room:* TV.

Inexpensive

Bansha House   The guest rooms in this small Georgian manor house are pleasant, with sturdy country furniture and, perhaps, a bit too much pink in the color scheme. However, through a cruel twist of fate, the largest rooms lack private bathrooms. The self-catering Primrose Cottage, which sleeps five, is perfect for families and folks who want to do their own cooking, although prices for the cottage have risen lately, making it less of a good deal. The town of Bansha sits at the base of the magnificent Galtee Mountains, which dominate the skyline on a clear day and make this an ideal base for walking, cycling, or just taking in the scenery. The adjacent Bansha House Stables are professional horse breeders.

Bansha, County Tipperary. ✆ **062/54194.** Fax 062/54215. www.tipp.ie/banshahs.htm. 8 units, 5 with private bathroom. €80–€90 ($128–$144) double. Rates include full breakfast. Cottage €500–€600 ($800–$960) per week. MC, V. Closed Dec 20–28. **Amenities:** Sitting room.

Kilmaneen Farmhouse (Finds)   This sweetly decorated, relaxing farmhouse B&B is a real find. Set amid a beautiful mountainous terrain, it's run with aplomb by Kevin and Ber O'Donnell. Those who love fishing love Kilmaneen, as you can cast for trout here, into either the Suir or the Tar, without any permit required. You will be provided with a fisherman's hut for tying flies, storing equipment, and waders. Kevin is trained in mountaineering and leads trekking and walking tours into the nearby Knockmealdowns, Comeraghs, or Galtee mountains. If you decide you want to stay a week, there's a fully equipped guest cottage, cozy enough for two and spacious enough for five. It rents for anywhere from €250 to €500 ($400–$800) per week, depending on the season and number of occupants. The main farmhouse can also be hired on a self-catering basis for €400 to €700 ($640–$1,120) per week. Finding your way here can be tricky, so call ahead and ask for detailed directions.

Newcastle, County Tipperary. ✆/fax **052/36231.** 3 units, 2 with shower only. €80 ($128) double. Rates include full breakfast. MC, V. *In room:* Tea/coffeemaker.

Mr. Bumbles (Value)   Above Declan Gavigan's Mr. Bumbles restaurant (see below), with their own exterior staircase, these four rooms are basic but bright. They are meticulously clean and have firm beds. The family room sleeps three. If you crave a night off from the social rituals of the standard B&B and want an excellent breakfast, this is the place. Better yet, it's possible to negotiate a B&B-and-dinner combination, which all but guarantees sweet dreams.

Richmond House, Kickham St., Clonmel, County Tipperary (top of Clonmel Market Place). ⓒ **052/29188.** Fax 052/29007. 4 units, all with shower only. €80 ($128) double; €90 ($144) family room. Rates include full breakfast. MC, V. **Amenities:** Restaurant (international). *In room:* TV.

Self-Catering

Coopers Cottage ★   This adorable Victorian cottage is perfect for a family wanting to explore the southeastern counties of Tipperary, Waterford, and Kilkenny. Stella and Eamonn Long have lovingly restored and renovated this 19th-century cooper's cottage, once Eamonn's family home, into a comfortable, tasteful hideaway. With exposed beams and polished wood floors, the Longs have created a house full of light, with spectacular views of the Galtee Mountains. The house, which has three bedrooms and sleeps six, comes with absolutely everything, and there's even a barbecue and a modest fenced-in garden, with a patio for sunny days.

1.6km (1 mile) off N24 at Bansha, Raheen, Bansha, County Tipperary. ⓒ **062/54027.** Fax 062/54027. www.dirl.com/tipperary/bansha/coopers.htm. 1 cottage. €400–€495 ($640–$792) per week. No credit cards. **Amenities:** Patio; barbecue. *In room:* TV, kitchen, wood-burning stove, microwave, dishwasher, dryer, washing machine.

WHERE TO DINE
Expensive

Chez Hans ★★ CONTINENTAL/SEAFOOD   In a former Gothic chapel in the shadow of the mighty Rock of Cashel, this restaurant's cathedral-style ceiling, stone walls, and candlelight create a perfect setting for a memorable meal. The menu draws from local produce and seafood for dishes such as Dublin Bay prawn bisque, cassoulet of seafood, roast sea scallops, succulent herb-crusted roast Tipperary lamb, and free-range duckling with honey and thyme. The flavors are luxurious, the portions generous, the crowd appreciative.

Rockside, Cashel, County Tipperary. ⓒ **062/61177.** Reservations required. Main courses €27–€33 ($43–$53). MC, V. Tues–Sat 6:30–10pm. Closed last 2 weeks in Jan and last 2 weeks in Sept.

Moderate

Mr. Bumbles ★★ INTERNATIONAL   With its natural woods, bright colors, and bistro feel, this split-level restaurant is inviting and the food first-rate. Many dishes are grilled or pan-seared with a Mediterranean slant to the spicing, and all are fresh. Wild sea trout, Tipperary sirloin, and Mediterranean vegetables are representative entrees. The presentation is nicely done, and portions are generous. The French house wines are fairly reasonable at roughly €14 ($22), and the French and Australian entries on the international wine list are particularly strong.

Richmond House, Kickham St., Clonmel, County Tipperary. ⓒ **052/29188.** Reservations recommended. Main courses €18–€27 ($29–$43). MC, V. Mon–Sat noon–2:30pm and 6–10pm; Sun noon–3pm and 6–9:30pm.

Inexpensive

Angela's Wholefood Restaurant ★★ Ⓥalue CAFETERIA   This laid-back, low-key cafe is a favorite with locals and budget travelers for its substantial fare at good prices. The blackboard menu might include breakfast omelets, spicy Moroccan lamb stew, savory tomato-and-spinach flan, homemade soups, sandwiches to order, and an array of crisp salads. The food is vibrant, fresh, and appreciated by the bustling patrons who line up with trays in hand, from barristers to babysitters.

14 Abbey St., Clonmel, County Tipperary. ℰ **052/26899.** Breakfast menu €2.50–€5 ($4–$8); lunch menu €2.50–€9 ($4–$14). No credit cards. Mon–Fri 9am–5:30pm; Sat noon–5pm.

PUBS

Gerry Chawkes   Chawkes is a Clonmel landmark, a shrine not so much to stout as to sport. A fanatic of hurling and racing (dogs and horses), Gerry Chawke has made his pub a cult place, lined with fascinating sports memorabilia. Athletic clubs from throughout Ireland make a point of stopping here, as do local politicians in recovery from council meetings. 3 Gladstone St. Upper, Clonmel, County Tipperary. ℰ **052/21149.**

Railway Bar (Finds)   You'll need on-the-ground directions to find Kitty's, which is what locals call this pub in a cul-de-sac behind the train station. Your efforts will be worthwhile, especially on weekends, when a traditional-music session is likely to break out. No one is paid or even invited to play here; they just show up. Often, there are so many musicians and so many wanting to hear them that the music spills outside, down the lane. No frills here—just the best Irish music around, and a pub out of the who-knows-when past. Clonmel, County Tipperary. No phone.

Tierney's   This place has been the Tipperary pub of the year so many times that we've lost count. It's a remarkably classy pub, with dark carved wood, shiny brass railings, and stained glass. It goes on and on from one level to another, with small lounges, big dining rooms, and little nooks. Upstairs, a full-service restaurant has several dining rooms, each with its own character, and outside there's a walled beer garden for times when the weather is kind. 13 O'Connell St., Clonmel, County Tipperary. ℰ **052/24467.**

---

4 COUNTY KILKENNY

Kilkenny City: 48km (30 miles) N of Waterford, 81km (50 miles) NW of Wexford, 121km (75 miles) SW of Dublin, 137km (85 miles) SE of Shannon Airport, 148km (92 miles) NE of Cork, 61km (38 miles) NE of Cashel

With its remarkable collection of well-preserved castles, churches, monastic sites, and winding narrow lanes, lovely **Kilkenny City** ★★ is a graceful medieval town. It's also a national hub for crafts and design, and its streets are dotted with shops selling pottery, woodwork, paintings, and jewelry. Its lively pub-and-entertainment circuit (including much-loved comedy festivals) make this a top weekend getaway for the Irish. Its many charms make it popular with travelers, and it's not untouched by tourism, but it's not as overrun as Kerry, and in the off season, it reverts to its normal, sleepy self (its normal population is just 11,000) and you can wander the streets in peace.

Like so many Irish towns, Kilkenny stands on the site of an old monastery from which it takes its name. A priory was founded here in the 6th century by St. Canice—in Gaelic, Cill Choinnigh means "Canice's church." As the monastery grew, the town sprang up around it and prospered. It owes its appearance to its success in the Middle Ages. Then it was a prosperous walled city, and it served as an important governmental center during the 14th century. Much of its medieval architecture has been skillfully preserved, and the basic town plan has not changed much in the last 600 years.

The oldest house in town may well be **Kyteler's Inn** on St. Kieran Street. It was once the home of Dame Alice Kyteler, a wealthy woman accused of witchcraft in 1324. Facing execution, she escaped and disappeared into the countryside, never to be seen again, but her maid Petronilla was burned at the stake. Her home is now a pub and restaurant, decorated with effigies of witches.

Another building that stands out on the streetscape is the **Tholsel,** on High Street, with its curious clock tower and front arcade. It was originally (in 1761) a tollhouse or exchange. Milk and sugar candy were sold here, and dances, bazaars, and political meetings were held here. Today, completely restored, it houses municipal archives.

The surrounding County Kilkenny countryside is dotted with rich river valleys, green pastures, hills, and picture-postcard villages. If you like monastic sites, take time to see the **Jerpoint Abbey,** on the River Nore just southwest of Thomaston on N9. It's an extraordinary Cistercian ruin that still has many elaborate medieval carvings on its walls; some even have traces of the original pigment. Also on the Nore is the picturesque village of **Inistioge** ★, about 24km (15 miles) southeast of Kilkenny City, with a tree-lined square and stone bridge with nine low arches spanning the river.

Abbey lovers will want to continue on to the tongue-twister town of Graiguenamanagh (its name means "village of the monks"), which holds the **Duiske Abbey.** Surrounded by peaceful views of Brandon Hill and the Blackstairs Mountains, Graiguenamanagh is at a bend of the River Barrow, about 32km (20 miles) southeast of Kilkenny City.

Kells, about 10km (6¼ miles) south of Kilkenny City (and not to be confused with the town of the same name in County Meath), is the only completely walled medieval town in Ireland. The thick city walls, seven towers, and some of the monastic buildings have all been well preserved.

KILKENNY CITY ESSENTIALS

GETTING THERE   **Irish Rail** provides daily service from Dublin into the Irish Rail McDonagh Station, Dublin Road, Kilkenny (✆ **056/772-2024;** www.irishrail.ie).

Bus Éireann, McDonagh Station, Dublin Road, Kilkenny (✆ **056/776-4933;** www.buseireann.ie), operates daily service from Dublin and all parts of Ireland.

Many roads pass through Kilkenny, including the N9/N10 from Waterford and Wexford, the N8 and N76 from Cork and the southwest, the N7 and N77 from Limerick and the west, and the N9 and N78 from Dublin and points north and east.

VISITOR INFORMATION   For information, maps, and brochures about Kilkenny and the area, contact the **Kilkenny Tourist Office,** Shee Alms House, Rose Inn Street, Kilkenny (✆ **056/775-1500**). It's open May to September Monday to Saturday 10am to 6pm; October to April, hours are Monday to Saturday 9:15am to 5pm.

CITY LAYOUT   The main business district sits on the west bank of the River Nore. High Street runs the length of the city north to south, changing its name to Parliament Street at midpoint. It starts at the Parade, on the south end near Kilkenny Castle, and continues through the city to St. Canice's Cathedral at the northern end. Most of the city's attractions are along this route or on cross streets such as Patrick, Rose Inn, Kieran, and John. The tourist office can supply you with a good street map.

GETTING AROUND   There is no bus service within Kilkenny. Local buses run to nearby towns on a limited basis, departing from the Parade. Check with **Bus Éireann** (✆ **056/776-4933;** www.buseireann.ie).

It's unlikely you will, but if you need a taxi, call **Nicky Power Taxi** (✆ 056/776-3000), **Billy Delaney Cabs** (✆ 056/772-2457), or **Kilkenny Taxi Service** (✆ 056/776-3017).

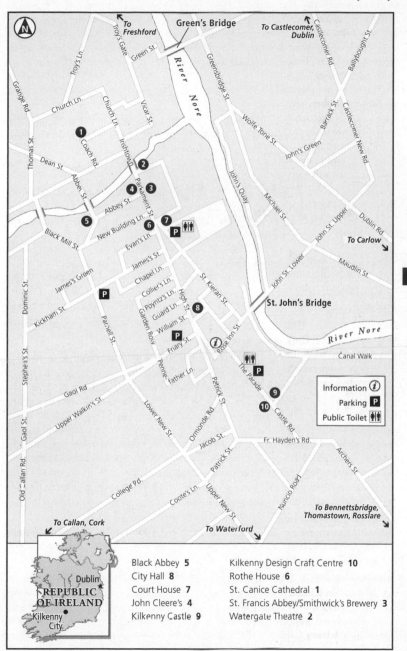

Black Abbey **5**

City Hall **8**

Court House **7**

John Cleere's **4**

Kilkenny Castle **9**

Kilkenny Design Craft Centre **10**

Rothe House **6**

St. Canice Cathedral **1**

St. Francis Abbey/Smithwick's Brewery **3**

Watergate Theatre **2**

It's best not to drive once you're in town—Kilkenny's narrow medieval streets are only really navigable by locals, and you'll almost certainly get stuck. Park at one of the designated parking areas at the Parade, at the rail station, or at one of the shopping centers. Some parking is free, and other spaces have coin-operated machines, usually for €1.20 ($1.90) per hour. There's also a central multistory car park on Ormonde Street. If you need to rent a car to see the surrounding countryside, call Barry Pender, Dublin Road, Kilkenny (© **056/776-5777**).

The best way to see Kilkenny City is on foot. Plot your own route or join a guided walking tour (see below).

FAST FACTS   If you need a drugstore, try **John Street Pharmacy,** 47 John St. (© **056/ 776-5971**); **John O'Connell,** 4 Rose Inn St. (© **056/772-1033**); or **White's Chemist,** 5 High St. (© **056/772-1328**).

In an emergency, dial © **999.** The local **Garda Station** is on Dominic Street (© **056/ 772-2222**).

If you need to access the Internet, try the **Kilkenny Library** at 6 John's Quay (© **056/ 779-4174**), open Tuesday to Saturday 10:30am to 1pm, Tuesday to Friday 2 to 5pm, and Tuesday and Wednesday 7 to 9pm. **Web-Talk,** Rose Inn Street (no phone), is an Internet cafe with ISDN Internet access; it's open Monday to Saturday 10am to 10pm and Sunday 2 to 8pm, and charges €1.50 ($2.40) every 10 minutes and €6.50 ($10) an hour.

For information on upcoming events and festivals, visit **www.kilkenny.ie** or **www. kilkennycityonline.com**. When you're in town, check out the weekly *Kilkenny People* (**www.kilkennypeople.ie**), which also covers local happenings. The **Kilkenny District Post Office,** 73 High St. (© **056/776-2327**), is open Monday to Friday 9:30am to 5:30pm, Saturday 9:30am to 1pm.

EXPLORING KILKENNY CITY

Black Abbey   Nobody is sure why this Dominican church, founded in 1225, is named Black Abbey. It may be because the Dominicans wore black capes over their white habits, or perhaps because the Black Plague claimed the lives of eight priests in 1348. The Black Abbey's darkest days came in 1650, when Oliver Cromwell used it as a courthouse before destroying it; by the time he left, all that remained was the walls. The abbey was rebuilt, and opened in 1816 as a church, a new nave was completed in 1866, and the entire building was fully restored in 1979. Among the elements remaining from the original abbey are an alabaster sculpture of the Holy Trinity that dates from 1400, and a pre-Reformation statue of St. Dominic carved in Irish oak, which is believed to be the oldest such piece in the world. The huge Rosary Window, a stained-glass work of nearly 45 sq. m (484 sq. ft.) that represents the 15 mysteries of the rosary, was created in 1892 by Mayers of Munich.

Abbey St. (off Parliament St.), Kilkenny, County Kilkenny. © **056/772-1279.** Free admission; donations welcome. Apr–Sept Mon–Sat 7:30am–7pm, Sun 9am–7pm; Oct–Mar Mon–Sat 7:30am–5:30pm. No visits during worship.

Kilkenny Castle ★★★   Standing majestically beside the River Nore on the south side of the city, this landmark medieval castle—built in the 12th century and remodeled in Victorian times—was the principal seat of the Butler family, whose members were the earls, marquesses, and dukes of Ormonde. In 1967, the castle was given to the Irish government to be restored to period splendor as an enduring national monument. From its sturdy corner towers to its battlements, Kilkenny Castle retains the imposing lines of an authentic fortress and sets the tone for the city. The exquisitely restored interior includes a fine collection of Butler family portraits, some from as far back as the 14th century. The old castle kitchen operates as a tearoom in the summer. The 20-hectare (49-acre) grounds include a riverside walk, extensive gardens, and a well-equipped children's playground. Access to the main body of the castle is by guided tour only, prefaced by an informative video on the rise, demise, and restoration of the structure. This is a very busy site, so arrive early (or quite late) to avoid waiting.

The Parade, Kilkenny, County Kilkenny. © **056/772-1450.** Admission €5.50 ($8.80) adults, €3.90 ($6.25) seniors, €2.20 ($3.50) children and students, €14 ($22) families. Apr–May daily 10:30am–5pm; June–Sept daily 10am–7pm; Oct–Mar Tues–Sat 10:30am–12:45pm and 2–5pm, Sun 10am–7pm.

Rothe House ★

This is a typical middle-class house from the Tudor period. Originally a merchant's home, built in 1594, it consists of three stone buildings divided by cobbled courtyards. It has an arcaded shop front and a remarkable timber ceiling. Purchased in 1961 by the Kilkenny Archeological Society, it was restored and opened to the public. Inside is a museum of sorts, filled with artifacts and period costumes. A family history research service for Kilkenny city and county has its offices here.

Parliament St., Kilkenny, County Kilkenny. © **056/772-2893.** Admission €3 ($4.80) adults, €2 ($3.20) seniors and students, €1 ($1.60) children, free for 11 and under. Combination tickets are available with St. Canice Cathedral (not including cathedral round tower). Apr–Oct Mon–Sat 10:30am–5pm, Sun 3–5pm; Nov–Mar Mon–Sat 10:30am–4:30pm. Closed Dec 24–Jan 3.

St. Canice Cathedral ★

At the northern end of the city, this is the church that gave Kilkenny its name, although the current structure is a relative newcomer—it was built in the 13th century on the site of a 6th-century church. The cathedral was built in early Gothic style, but has been much restored and altered over the years, not the least after Cromwell's gang defaced the building, using it as a stable for their horses. Restoration after that took more than a century to complete. It is noteworthy for its rich interior timber and stone carvings, its colorful glasswork, and the structure itself. Its roof dates from 1863, and its marble floor is composed of the four marbles of Ireland. On the grounds, amid the tombstones in the churchyard, is a massive round tower, 30m high (98 ft.) and 14m (46 ft.) in circumference; believed to be a relic of the ancient church (although its original conical top has been replaced by a slightly domed roof). If you want to climb to the tip of the tower, it will cost you €1.30 ($2.10) and more calories than you can count (it's a steep and very narrow climb that is not for the faint of heart or the unfit). The steps that lead to the cathedral were constructed in 1614, and the carvings on the wall at the top of the stairs date from medieval times. Combination tickets providing admission to the cathedral and Rothe House are available, but be aware that these do not include access to the cathedral round tower.

Coach Rd., Irishtown, Kilkenny, County Kilkenny. © **056/776-4971.** Admission to cathedral only €4 ($6.40) adults; €3 ($4.80) seniors, children, and students. Admission to cathedral and round tower €6 ($9.60) adults, €5.50 ($8.80) groups per person (no senior, child, or student discount). Combination tickets are available with Rothe House. Apr–May and Sept Mon–Sat 10am–1pm and 2–5pm, Sun 2–6pm; June–Aug Mon–Sat 9am–6pm, Sun 2–6pm; Oct–Mar Mon–Sat 10am–1pm and 2–4pm, Sun 2–4pm.

St. Francis Abbey Brewery ★

Established in 1710 by John Smithwick, the brewery occupies a site that originally belonged to the 12th-century Abbey of St. Francis. A popular local beer called Smithwick's is produced here, as are Budweiser and Land Kilkenny Irish beer. A video presentation and free samples are offered in the summer.

Parliament St., Kilkenny, County Kilkenny. © **056/772-1014.** Free admission. June–Aug Mon–Fri at 3pm.

> **Fun Facts** **The City of Marble**
>
> Kilkenny is sometimes known as the Marble City. That's because fine black marble was once quarried on the outskirts of town and, until 1929, some of the town's streets were paved in marble.

Organized Tours

Kilkenny City Sightseeing Tour   This 13-stop double-decker tour bus runs seven times daily from Kilkenny Castle. Tickets are valid for 24 hours, so you can hop on and off at will.

Kilkenny Castle, The Parade, County Kilkenny. © **01/458-0054.** Tickets €10 ($16) adults, €6 ($9.60) children, €8 ($13) seniors and students. Apr 23–Sept 24 departs 10:30 and 11:30am, and 12:30, 2, 3, and 4pm (also 5pm June–Aug).

Tynan's Walking Tours   Local historian Pat Tynan leads you through the streets and lanes of medieval Kilkenny, providing historical facts and anecdotes along the way. Tours depart daily from the tourist office, Rose Inn Street.

10 Maple Dr., Kilkenny, County Kilkenny. © **087/265-1745.** Tickets €6 ($9.60) adults, €3 ($4.80) children, €5.50 ($8.80) seniors and students. Mar–Oct Mon–Sat 9:15 and 10:30am, and 12:15, 1:30, 3, and 4:30pm; Sun 11am and 12:15, 3, and 4:30pm; Nov–Feb Tues–Sat 10:30am, 12:15pm, and 3pm.

Attractions Farther Afield in County Kilkenny

Duiske Abbey ★   Duiske Abbey (1204) is a fine example of an early Cistercian abbey. It was suppressed in 1536, but its monks continued to occupy the site for many years. In 1774 the tower of the abbey church collapsed. In 1813 the roof was replaced and religious services returned to the church, but the abbey didn't approach its former glory until the 1970s, when a group of local people mounted a reconstruction effort. Now, with its fine lancet windows and a large effigy of a Norman knight, the abbey is the pride of Graiguenamanagh. The adjacent visitor center has an exhibit of Christian art and artifacts.

Graiguenamanagh, County Kilkenny. © **0593/24238.** Free admission; donations welcome. Daily 8am–7:30pm.

Dunmore Cave   This gloomy series of chambers, formed over millions of years, contains some fine calcite formations. Known to humans for many centuries, the cave may have been the site of a Viking massacre in A.D. 928. Exhibits at the visitor center tell the story of the cave. It's about 11km (7 miles) from Kilkenny City.

Off Castlecomer rd. (N78), Ballyfoyle, County Kilkenny. © **056/776-7726.** Admission €3 ($4.80) adults, €2.30 ($3.70) seniors, €1.40 ($2.25) students and children. Mid-Mar to mid-June and mid-Sept to Oct daily 9:30am–5:30pm; mid-June to mid-Sept daily 9:30am–6:30pm; Nov to mid-Mar Fri–Sun and holidays 9:30am–5:30pm.

Jerpoint Abbey ★★   About 18km (11 miles) southeast of Kilkenny, this is an outstanding Cistercian monastery, founded in the latter half of the 12th century. Preserved in a peaceful country setting, one of the abbey's highlights is a sculptured cloister arcade. There is a splendid array of artifacts from medieval times, including unique stone carvings on ancient tombs and Romanesque architecture in the north nave. A tasteful interpretive center with an adjoining picnic garden makes this a perfect midday stop. Sheila

Walsh, who runs the front desk, is as friendly and knowledgeable as they come. She's also a font of information about the area.

On the N9, 2.4km (1¹/₂ miles) south of Thomastown, County Kilkenny. © **056/772-4623.** Admission €3 ($4.80) adults, €2.30 ($3.70) seniors, €1.50 ($2.40) children. Mar–May and mid-Sept to mid-Nov daily 9:30am–5pm; June to mid-Sept daily 9:30am–6pm; late Nov daily 10am–4pm.

Kells Priory ★★★   With its encompassing fortification walls and towers, as well as complex monastic ruins enfolded into the sloping south bank of the King's River, Kells is a glorious ruin. In 1193 Baron Geoffrey FitzRobert founded the priory and established a Norman-style town beside it. The current ruins date from the 13th to 15th centuries. The priory's wall has been carefully restored, and it connects seven towers, the remains of an abbey, and foundations of chapels and houses. You can tell by the thick walls that this monastery was well fortified, and those walls were built for a reason—it was frequently attacked. In the 13th century, it was the subject of two battles and burned to the ground. The priory is less than a half-mile from the village of Kells. If you have some time to spare, there's a footbridge behind it, which takes you across the river and intersects a riverside walk leading to a picturesque old mill.

Kells, County Kilkenny. Off N76 or N10. © **056/772-8255.** Tours by appointment. From N76 south of Kilkenny, follow signs for R699/Callan and stay on R699 until you see signs for Kells.

Kilfane Glen and Waterfall   The main place of interest in this small garden is the glen, created in true picturesque style, with an artificial waterfall and a rustic cottage. Views of the cottage and waterfall have been carefully composed, and the sound of water creates a counterpoint to the visual delights of the garden. An installation by the American artist James Turrell, *Air Mass,* is open to visitors, although the time of day it was intended to be seen—dusk—unfortunately doesn't correspond with the garden's hours in summer (the sun's still shining when they close at 6pm).

Thomastown, County Kilkenny. © **056/772-4558.** Admission €6 ($9.60) adults, €5.50 ($8.80) seniors, €5 ($8), students and children. July–Aug daily 11am–6pm. Other times by appointment.

SHOPPING

If you're an enthusiast of Irish crafts, Kilkenny City is well worth the trip. Its crafts scene is vibrant and lively, and it's difficult to leave empty-handed. The local tourist office provides a free **Craft Trail map** and information on local artisans.

Kilkenny shopping hours are normally Monday to Saturday 9am to 6pm; many shops stay open until 9pm on Thursday and Friday.

The newest major addition to the shopping scene is **Market Cross,** a shopping center off High/Parliament Street (© **056/52666**), with its own multistory parking lot.

The Book Centre   This shop offers a fine selection of books about Kilkenny and the area, as well as books of Irish interest. You can grab a quick daytime snack at the Pennefeather Cafe upstairs. 10 High St., Kilkenny, County Kilkenny. © **056/776-2117.**

Fallers Sweater Shop   As its name implies, this shop specializes in Aran hand-knit sweaters (of which it carries a large selection) and mohair, cotton, and linen knits. 75 High St., Kilkenny, County Kilkenny. © **056/564833.**

Kilkenny Crystal   Established in 1969, this is the retail shop for Kilkenny's hand-cut crystal enterprise. The factory is on Callan Road (© **056/772-5132**), 16km (10 miles) outside of town, and it welcomes visitors. 19 Rose Inn St., Kilkenny, County Kilkenny. © **056/772-1090.**

Kilkenny Design Craft Centre   The 18th-century coach house and stables of Kilkenny Castle have been wonderfully converted into shops and workshops for craftspeople. The center and the smaller shops collected nearby provide a showcase for handcrafted products—jewelry, glassware, pottery, clothing, linens, and furniture. There's also an excellent coffee shop and restaurant upstairs. Open Monday to Saturday from 10am to 7pm, and Sunday from 11am to 7pm (closed Sun Jan–Apr). Castle Yard, the Parade, Kilkenny, County Kilkenny. ℂ 056/22118. www.kilkennydesign.com.

Liam Costigan   This alumnus of the Kilkenny Design Centre produces fine handcrafted jewelry in gold and silver in this tiny studio. You can watch him work as you browse. Open Monday to Saturday 9am to 6pm. Colliers Lane, off High St., Kilkenny, County Kilkenny. ℂ 056/776-2408.

P. T. Murphy   This is Kilkenny's master jeweler. The shop is a very good source for Irish Claddagh and heraldic jewelry. 85 High St., Kilkenny, County Kilkenny. ℂ 056/772-1127.

Shopping Farther Afield in County Kilkenny

The Bridge Pottery   Recently moved to a new studio in Burnchurch, this quirky enterprise is a dazzling kaleidoscope of Mediterranean colors and warm, earthen tones. Jugs, mugs, bowls, tiles, plates, even drawer handles—there's something here for every taste and budget, with prices from €4 to €400 ($6.40–$640). Open Monday to Saturday from 10am to 5pm. Coalsfarm, Burnchurch, County Kilkenny. ℂ 056/772-9156. www.bridge pottery.com.

Jerpoint Glass Studio   At the last stop on the Craft Trail from Kilkenny to Stoneyford, you can witness the creation of Jerpoint glass, which you've probably been admiring in shops all across Ireland. The lines of the glasses, goblets, and pitchers are simple and fluid, highlighted with swirls of color. You can watch the glass being blown and then blow your budget next door at the shop, which includes an entire room of discounted seconds. The shop is open Monday to Saturday from 10am to 6pm and Sunday from noon to 5pm, while you can look in at the studio Monday to Thursday from 10am to 4:30pm, and Friday 10am to 2pm. Signposted from the N9 just south of Jerpoint Abbey, Stoneyford, County Kilkenny. ℂ 056/772-4350. www.jerpointglass.com.

Nicholas Mosse Pottery   In a former flour mill on the banks of the River Nore, this is the studio of Nicholas Mosse, a potter since age 7. Using hydropower from the river to fire the kilns, he produces colorful country-style earthenware from Irish clay, including jugs, mugs, bowls, vases, and plates. All are hand-slipped and hand-turned, then decorated by hand with cut sponges and brushes. An on-site museum displays antique Irish earthenware. There is also a cafe which closes an hour before the shop. Open year-round Monday to Saturday from 10am to 6pm, and also July and August Sunday from 1:30 to 5pm. The Mill, Bennettsbridge, County Kilkenny. ℂ 056/772-7105. www.nicholasmosse.com.

Stoneware Jackson   Here's another fine pottery studio in Bennettsbridge, fast becoming a one-stop village for some of Ireland's most beautiful earthenware. The pieces are hand-thrown, featuring two-color glazing and Celtic motifs. Open Monday to Saturday from 10am to 6pm. Bennettsbridge, County Kilkenny. ℂ 056/27175. www.stonewarejackson. com.

SPORTS & OUTDOOR PURSUITS

BICYCLING   For complete 1- or 2-week cycling holidays in the Southeast, contact Don Smith at **Celtic Cycling,** Lorum Old Rectory, Bagenalstown, County Carlow (ℂ/fax **059/977-5282;** www.celticcycling.com).

FISHING The **River Nore,** southeast of Kilkenny, is known for salmon and trout. For advice, permits, and supplies, visit the **Sports Shop,** 82 High St., Kilkenny (© 056/772-1517).

GOLF **Mount Juliet Golf and Country Club,** Thomastown, County Kilkenny (© 056/777-3000; www.mountjuliet.ie), is an excellent course 16km (10 miles) south of Kilkenny City. The 18-hole, par-72 championship course, designed by Jack Nicklaus, charges greens fees of €100 to €165 ($160–$264) on weekdays, and €150–€185 ($240–$296) on weekends. The price drops for Mount Juliet guests (see below), and reduced early and late rates are also available. Alternatively, try the 18-hole championship course at the **Kilkenny Golf Club,** Glendine, County Kilkenny (© 056/776-5400; www.kilkenny golfclub.com), an inland par-71 layout 1.6km (1 mile) from the city. Greens fees are €35 ($56) on weekdays, €45 ($72) on weekends.

WHERE TO STAY
Very Expensive
Mount Juliet Estate ★★★ A private 3km (2-mile) lane wends its way beside the pastures of the Ballylinch Stud Farm to this exclusive hotel, an 18th-century manor house set on a hillside overlooking the River Nore and surrounded by 600 walled hectares (1,482 acres) of parkland. Mount Juliet is most famous for its Jack Nicklaus–designed golf course, and is also the home of Ireland's oldest cricket club. Unsurprisingly, it's hugely popular with the affluent sporting set, drawn by the luxurious accommodations and extensive leisure possibilities. Guests can choose between the manor house, the Hunters Yard, and the Rose Garden lodges. Rooms are individually and sumptuously decorated with mahogany antiques and designer fabrics, and public areas are full of period pieces and original art.

The **Paddocks,** a cluster of 12 **self-catering luxury lodges** located between the 10th and 16th fairways, are also available. Each has a fully equipped kitchen, an elegantly furnished lounge/dining room, and bedrooms en suite. Weekly rentals start at €2,400 ($3,120) for a two-bedroom lodge.

Thomastown, County Kilkenny. © **056/777-3000.** Fax 056/777-3019. www.mountjuliet.ie. 32 units. €230–€350 ($368–$560) double; €450–€520 ($720–$832) 2-bedroom garden lodge. AE, DC, MC, V. **Amenities:** 3 restaurants (international, bistro, bar food); bar; indoor swimming pool; 18-hole golf course; tennis courts; squash; gym; beauty and spa treatments; Jacuzzi; sauna; concierge; room service; valet and laundry service; archery; clay target shooting; riding stables; salmon and trout fishing on exclusive 2.4km (1½-mile) stretch of River Nore. *In room:* A/C, TV, minibar, hair dryer, garment press.

Expensive
Hotel Kilkenny ★★ (Kids) Tucked away in a quiet residential neighborhood on the edge of town, this contemporary hotel is great for families. The whole place has been recently refurbished, and even the standard double rooms are big enough for a small family. Rooms may not be elegant, exactly, but they're very pleasant—decked out in a smart chocolate-and-cream palette—and there's good attention to detail (nice toiletries and bathrobes in the small but well-renovated bathrooms). There are lovely, well-tended gardens, and an excellent modern leisure center.

College Rd., Kilkenny, County Kilkenny. © **056/776-2000.** Fax 056/776-5984. www.griffingroup.ie. 138 units. €140–€300 ($224–$480) double. Rates include full breakfast. AE, MC, V. **Amenities:** Restaurant (international); bar; indoor swimming pool; gym; Jacuzzi; sauna; children's playroom/activities; babysitting; solarium. *In room:* TV, free broadband, hair dryer, iron.

Kilkenny Ormonde Hotel (Kids) This big hotel in the heart of Kilkenny town is a good option for families. Its central location means there are no scenic views, but rooms are big and modern. The emphasis is on open spaces—the halls are wide and full of light, and rooms are done in soft, warm colors. There's plenty of stress relief to be had next door at a state-of-the-art leisure club, connected to the hotel by an underground walkway. Deluxe rooms are spacious, with a queen-size bed and a single bed (great for families), as well as amenities including plush bathrobes. The service here could use improvement, however, and the breakfast will not win any awards as Ireland's best.

Ormonde St., Kilkenny, County Kilkenny. (C) **056/772-3900.** Fax 056/772-3977. www.kilkennyormonde. com. 118 units. €136–€212 ($218–$339) double. Rates include full breakfast and VAT. AE, MC, V. **Amenities:** 3 restaurants (international, cafe, bistro); 2 bars; indoor pool; kiddie pool; volcano pool; gym; Jacuzzi; sauna/steam room; children's playroom; concierge; room service; massage; laundry service; nonsmoking rooms; foreign-currency exchange; tanning bed. *In room:* TV, minibar, hair dryer, iron, garment press.

Moderate

Butler House ★ Built in 1770 by the 16th earl of Ormonde as an integral part of Kilkenny Castle, this elegant building with a series of conical rooftops has a front door facing busy Patrick Street and a backyard overlooking secluded 17th-century-style gardens. Converted into a guesthouse more than 20 years ago, it has a sweeping staircase, marble fireplaces, and modern guest rooms with peaceful views (some overlooking the castle), big bathrooms, and neutral color schemes with vivid splashes of bright color.

16 Patrick St., Kilkenny, County Kilkenny. (C) **056/776-5707.** Fax 056/776-5626. www.butler.ie. 13 units. €120–€180 ($192–$288) double. Rates include full breakfast. AE, MC, V. **Amenities:** Restaurant (international); bar; babysitting. *In room:* TV/VCR, tea/coffeemaker, hair dryer.

The Newpark Hotel ★ This useful hotel about 1.6km (1 mile) north of the city center is part of the Flynn Hotels chain. Set amid 20 hectares (49 acres) of gardens and parkland, it was opened as a small Victorian-style country hotel more than 35 years ago, but has been vastly modernized since then. It still has an elegant touch—rooms are done up in light wood with colorful Irish textiles, and the public areas have a stylish, contemporary look. Look for good-value off-season specials on the hotel's website.

Castlecomer Rd., Kilkenny, County Kilkenny. (C) **056/776-0500.** Fax 056/776-0555. www.newparkhotel. com. 129 units. €190–€220 ($304–$352) double. AE, MC, V. **Amenities:** Indoor swimming pool; kiddie pool; gym; beauty and spa treatments; Jacuzzi; sauna/steam room; solarium. *In room:* TV, free broadband, hair dryer, iron.

Inexpensive

Abbey House This attractive Georgian (ca. 1750) building alongside the Little Argile River was once part of the Jerpoint Abbey's estate. The front garden is a perfect spot to relax, and the sitting room, complete with piano and stacks of books, suits both quiet reading and a round of songs. Owner Helen Blanchfield serves you tea and scones when you arrive, and then directs you to one of the comfortable rooms, all of which have firm, orthopedic beds. Nearby, the village of Thomastown is charming.

Thomastown, County Kilkenny. On the N9, directly across from Jerpoint Abbey. (C) **056/772-4166.** Fax 056/772-4192. www.abbeyhousejerpoint.com. 7 units. €70–€110 ($111–$176) double. Rates include service charge and full Irish breakfast. AE, MC, V. Closed Dec 21–30. **Amenities:** Sitting room. *In room:* TV.

Ballyduff House ★★ This is a fine B&B, with big, comfortable rooms filled with sunlight and decorated with antiques. It's in a rambling old house beautifully done with an eye to period style. Owner Brede Thomas worked in the U.S. for 10 years, and has a marvelous relaxed approach—you're welcome to relax just about anywhere, although the library is the best place of all, with shelves filled with enticing books, and lots of soft sofas to sink into. The grounds have plenty of streams for fishing, and Brede will arrange pony rides for the kids.

Thomastown, County Kilkenny. On R700, 5km (3 miles) from New Ross. © 056/775-8488. www.ballyduff house.com. 4 units. €90 ($144) double. Rates include full breakfast. No credit cards. **Amenities:** Library; lounge; salmon and trout fishing.

Cullintra House ★   A slightly bohemian atmosphere is tangible at this historic country farmhouse, presided over by Patricia Cantlon, an accomplished artist and cook, and her several cats. The 92-hectare (227-acre) farm is a sanctuary for birds and all sorts of animals. As you would expect in a 200-year-old, ivy-clad farmhouse, each rustic guest room is charming and uniquely decorated. Morning brings a relaxed breakfast schedule (served 9:30am–noon) and perhaps a walk to Mount Brandon or the nearby cairn (prehistoric burial mound)—a trail departs from the back gate. Dinner begins around 9pm, announced by the sound of a gong, and guests sometimes don't depart from the candlelit dining room until the wee hours. Mrs. Cantlon is an enthusiastic hostess, and enjoys entertaining her guests and making them feel at home. This is a good bet if you like good food, candlelight, and cats.

The Rower, Inistioge, County Kilkenny. On R700, 9.7km (6 miles) from New Ross. © 051/423614. http://indigo.ie/~cullhse. 6 units, 3 with bathroom. €60–€100 ($96–$160) double. Minimum 2-night booking. 5-course dinner €35–€40 ($56–$64). Rates include full breakfast. No credit cards. **Amenities:** Conservatory.

Lawcus Farm Guesthouse ★   This fabulously rustic, 200-year-old stone cottage at the edge of the King's River near the village of Kells cries out to be photographed. Owner Mark Fisher bought the place years back to be near good fishing waters, and has gradually converted it into a relaxing, modern country lodge, with walls warmly paneled in polished wood, brass bedsteads, and endless green views. He's added on a deck now, so that you can relax outside with a glass of wine and watch the sun set over the fields. Mark knows the best places to hear traditional music, have a pint, or dine, and he's happy to share them. There are no TVs or outside distractions. For those looking to get away from it all, this just might be the place.

Stonyford, County Kilkenny. Off the N10 on the Kells Rd. © 056/772-8949. www.lawcusfarmguesthouse. com. 5 units. €100 ($160) double. Rates include full breakfast. No credit cards. **Amenities:** Lounge; dining room.

Self-Catering

Clomantagh Castle ★★ (Finds)   Yet another one-of-a-kind rental property from the nonprofit Irish Landmark Trust, this huge, rambling establishment sleeps 10 and is ideal for a large family or group. Around it, a complex of buildings includes the ruins of a 12th-century church and an early 15th-century crenelated tower house attached to an 18th-century farmhouse. There are four large double bedrooms in the farmhouse, with a staircase leading to a fifth wonderfully medieval double bedroom in the tower. The decor throughout is pleasingly rustic, with fine period pieces and brass beds. There are several reception rooms and an enormous, well-equipped country kitchen with a flagstone floor, timbered ceiling, and Stanley range. Like all Irish Landmark Trust properties, Clomantagh Castle has no TV. Although the setting is rural, Kilkenny City is only about a 20-minute drive away.

Freshford, County Kilkenny. Contact the Irish Landmark Trust © 01/670-4733. Fax 01/670-4887. www. irishlandmark.com. From €600 ($960) for 4 nights in low season, going up to €1,400 ($2,240) per week in high season. MC, V. **Amenities:** Kitchen; dishwasher; washing machine.

Expensive

Lacken House ★★ MODERN IRISH   With a stately Victorian house as its setting, this restaurant is exceptional, offering fixed-price meals cleverly created with local produce. The menu changes daily (there is no a la carte selection), but starters might include spring onion–and–red cheddar soup or smoked salmon on a bed of cucumber ribbons with homemade chive dressing. Main dishes might include roast leg of lamb, breast of chicken with blue cheese and bacon wrapped in phyllo pastry, or Asian pan-fried salmon in tomato vinaigrette. Roast crispy duckling in orange-and-star-anise sauce is a house specialty. There are modest rooms to rent here as well, if you cannot bear to leave (€170/ $272 for a double).

Dublin Rd., Kilkenny, County Kilkenny. © **056/776-1085.** www.lackenhouse.ie. Reservations required. Fixed-price 4-course dinner €60 ($96). MC, V. Tues–Sat 7–10:30pm.

Zuni ★★ MODERN INTERNATIONAL   Kilkenny Town has taken off as a trendy getaway for Dubliners, and Zuni has hitched its wagon to that star. With its sleek design—leather banquettes, dark polished wood, creamy walls—it's one of the reigning hot spots. The jet-setter menu features Moroccan lamb, tempura king prawns with sesame toast, and roast cod with Puy lentils. Upstairs are 13 chic guest rooms available for €130 to €220 ($208–$352) for a double. Ask about midweek and weekend good-value specials combining 2 nights at a B&B with one dinner.

26 Patrick St., Kilkenny, County Kilkenny. © **056/772-3999.** www.zuni.ie. Reservations required. Dinner main courses €16–€21 ($26–$34). AE, MC, V. Tues–Sat 12:30–2:30pm; Mon–Sat 6:30–9:30pm; Sun 1–3pm and 6–9pm.

Moderate

Café Sol ★★ SOUTHERN AMERICAN/MEDITERRANEAN   This bright cafe with light streaming in through floor-to-ceiling windows is a cheerful place in both cuisine and appearance. It's open all day, starting with homemade scones and biscuits at breakfast time, moving on to a lunch menu stocked with comfort foods for busy Kilkenny shoppers and business folk—mainly homemade soups, salads, sandwiches, and hot plates. But the place really comes into its own at dinnertime, when the menu comes alive with zestier options, like Louisiana crab cakes with tomato salsa, chicken and mozzarella wrapped in phyllo, and steamed mussels with wine and garlic.

6 William St. (opposite the Town Hall), Kilkenny, County Kilkenny. © **056/776-4987.** www.cafesol kilkenny.com. Reservations recommended for dinner. Main courses lunch €6–€12 ($9.60–$19), dinner €16–€29 ($26–$46). MC, V. Mon–Sat 11:30am–10pm; Sun noon–9pm.

The Motte ★★ MODERN CONTINENTAL   This is a pretty place—the intimate dining room shimmers with gilt and candlelight, each table crowned by a bouquet of field flowers. The menu is unusual—clearly, the chef experiments with mixing flavors. Take, for instance, the profiteroles filled with Cashel blue cheese and laced with chili-chocolate sauce. It shouldn't work, but it does. Main courses range from sirloin in burgundy-butter sauce to filets of plaice with lemon butter. Sorbet precedes an excellent choice of diet-busting desserts, like velvety-rich chocolate cardamom truffle cake served with custard and a drizzle of raspberry sauce. Book a table well in advance and surrender your evening to conversation and good food.

Plas Newydd Lodge, Inistioge, County Kilkenny. © **056/775-8655.** Reservations recommended. 3-course set menu €35 ($56). MC, V. Wed–Sat 7–9:30pm.

Kilkenny Design Restaurant ★★ CAFETERIA Above the Kilkenny Design shop, this self-service restaurant is a classy place, with whitewashed walls, circular windows, beamed ceilings, and fresh, delicious food. The ever-changing menu often includes local salmon, chicken-and-ham platters, salads, and homemade soups. The pastries and breads offer some unique choices, such as cheese and garlic scones.

Castle Yard, Kilkenny, County Kilkenny. ✆ **056/772-2118.** Main courses €13–€16 ($21–$26). AE, MC, V. Year-round Mon–Sat 9am–5pm; May–Dec Sun 10am–5pm.

Marble City Bar and Tea Rooms TEAROOM A brand-new tearoom has opened in the basement of this picture-perfect old pub, discreetly tucked away like a little fortress of gentility. It's a thoroughly civilized affair, serving tea, cakes, sandwiches, and light meals all day.

66 High St., Kilkenny, County Kilkenny. ✆ **056/776-2091.** Main courses €9 ($14). AE, DC, MC, V. Daily 9am–7pm.

The Water Garden TEAROOM Just outside Thomastown on the road to Kilkenny, this tearoom and small garden is operated by a local group that helps people with special needs or disabilities. The cafe serves lunch, tea, and baked goods; meals are prepared with organic vegetables and meats raised on the community farm. Lunches include sandwiches made with home-baked bread, soups, and a vegetable or meat pâté. Buy a ticket to the garden (admission €2.50/$4) and you can take a stroll along a trickling stream; there's also a garden shop.

Ladywell, Thomastown, County Kilkenny. ✆ **056/772-4690.** Garden admission €1.50 ($2.40). Lunch €4–€7 ($6.40–$11). No credit cards. Tues–Fri 10am–5pm; Sun 12:30–5pm. Closed Sun Christmas–Easter.

KILKENNY AFTER DARK

To find out what's going on around town, pick up a copy of the local weekly paper *Kilkenny People.* Kilkenny is home to the small-but-mighty **Watergate Theatre,** Parliament Street (✆ **056/776-1674**), a 328-seat venue for local talent and visiting troupes in classic and contemporary plays, concerts, and ballets. Ticket prices average €10 to €20 ($16–$32).

Across the street from the theater, **John Cleere's,** 28 Parliament St. (✆ **056/776-2573**), is a pub theater that's good for music and local productions.

For 2 weeks every August, the **Kilkenny Arts Festival** (✆ **056/775-2175;** www.kilkennyarts.ie) takes over the town. It is one of Ireland's largest and longest-running arts festivals, covering music, theater, dance, visual arts, literature, and film. There are also a variety of street theater performances on hand, so even if you don't plan to go to any of the scheduled events, you'll likely get caught up in the proceedings at some point. Check out the festival website for specific program details.

Pubs

Caislean Ui Cuain (The Castle Inn) A striking facade with a mural of old Kilkenny welcomes guests to this pub, founded in 1734 as a stagecoach inn. The interior is a pub lover's dream, with dark-wood furnishings and a paneled ceiling. Traditional music sessions—both scheduled and spontaneous—often start up, and many patrons and staff speak Irish. The Parade, Kilkenny, County Kilkenny. ✆ **056/776-5406.**

Eamon Langton's No self-respecting Irishman—or anyone, for that matter—would pass through Kilkenny without stopping for a pint. It's a classic traditional pub, with a lovely fireplace, etched mirrors, stained-glass windows, and burgundy-leather banquettes. On summer days, everyone heads to the back room—actually a lush, plant-filled conservatory with Gothic-style windows and a garden backed by the old city walls. Langton's has won plaudits for its pub grub, too, so bring your appetite. 69 John St., Kilkenny, County Kilkenny. ℂ 056/776-5133.

Kyteler's Inn This inn has served up spirits for over 650 years. The ground-floor restaurant and bar are done in cozy, contemporary pine, so if you are in a medieval mood, head downstairs to the cellar, where a deep-set window overlooks Kieran's Well, which predates the inn itself, and where the original stone pillars still reach from floor to ceiling. This was once the home of Dame Alice Kyteler, a colorful character who made the tavern into a den of merrymaking. She also laid four husbands to rest in the Kilkenny graveyard. She was tried for being a witch and condemned to burn at the stake, but escaped and was never heard from again. You may feel Alice's presence in the cellar, thanks to a life-size doll of her overseeing the proceedings. Kieran's St., Kilkenny, County Kilkenny. ℂ 056/772-1064. www.kytelersinn.com.

Marble City Bar and Tea Rooms This central pub has a marvelous facade of carved wood, wrought iron, and polished brass, with flower boxes overhead—and the interior is equally inviting. Even if you don't stop for a drink here, you'll certainly want to take a picture. For a more genteel experience, try the new tearooms downstairs—they're open every day from 9am to 7pm. If you choose to have lunch here, a main course will set you back about €9 ($14). 66 High St., Kilkenny, County Kilkenny. ℂ 056/776-1143.

Tynan's Bridge House (Finds) Before a man named Tynan turned it into a pub in 1919, this 225-year-old building was a pharmacy and grocery shop. Behind the horseshoe-shaped marble-top bar, side drawers marked CLOVES, ALMONDS, MACE, and CITRON are vestiges of those days, as is the 200-year-old scale with its little set of cup weights. It's all lit by nostalgic globe gas lamps, and adorned with brass fixtures and silver tankards. An intricate old clock chimes the hour. 2 Horseleap Slip, St. John's Bridge, Kilkenny, County Kilkenny. ℂ 056/772-1291.

Cork City

Cork City (pop. 125,000) is developing a reputation as a kind of Dublin South, and for good reason. It's far smaller than the capital, but Cork is a busy, attractive, artsy place that combines the conveniences of a city with an appreciation for rural life. For travelers, it offers plenty to see and do, and has the added attraction of a burgeoning restaurant scene that has been making headlines around Ireland.

Cork has had a long and rebellious history, which has been for centuries tied intrinsically to Ireland's struggle for independence. The city was founded by St. Finbarr in the 6th century, when he built a monastery on a swampy estuary of the River Lee. (It may have been built at the site of the current St. Finbarr's Cathedral.) He gave the place the rather generic Gaelic name of *Corcaigh*, which means "marsh." Over the next 600 years, the little piece of swamp would ultimately become the crown in the Kingdom of South Munster, but by the end of the 12th century, the English had asserted what they saw as their rightful ownership of the region. Over the following centuries, Cork would change ownership many times as the English and the Irish struggled for control. It resisted Cromwell's forces, only to lose to William of Orange.

Once firmly under English control, Cork thrived until the 18th century, when it was battered by the potato famine. The potato blight drained the region of its wealth and, ultimately, of its population.

The city earned its nickname, "Rebel Cork," because it was a center of the 19th-century Fenian movement, and also played an active part in Ireland's 20th-century battle for independence. The fighting here was long and ugly. Thomas MacCurtain, Cork's mayor, was killed by British forces in 1920. His successor, Terence Mac-Swiney, died in a London prison after a hunger strike lasting 75 days.

British forces in Cork were among the most repressive in Ireland, and many atrocities were attributed to the troops (which were called "Black and Tans" for the color of their uniforms). Much of the city center, including the library, the City Hall, and most of the buildings on St. Patrick's Street, were burned to the ground during the British occupation and the subsequent brutal civil war of the 1920s.

It was not until the last decades of the 20th century that Cork began to come into its own, and to find its feet as a university town with strong connections to Europe and a kind of gentle sophistication. It's certainly not a perfect place—it has severe traffic congestion, and can feel a bit gritty and crowded, but it has much to offer and is well worth a couple of days of your time.

1   ORIENTATION

Cork is 258km (160 miles) SW of Dublin, 206km (128 miles) SE of Galway, 101km (63 miles) S of Limerick, 122km (76 miles) S of Shannon Airport, 126km (78 miles) W of Waterford, and 87km (54 miles) E of Killarney

ARRIVING

GETTING THERE   **Aer Arann** (② **011/353-81821-0210** in the U.S., 818/210-210 in Ireland, or 0800/587-23-24 in the U.K.; www.acrarann.com) flies from Dublin and

Belfast to Cork Airport, Kinsale Road (🕻 **021/413-131;** www.cork-airport.com), 13km (8 miles) south of the city. Other airlines serving the city include **Aer Lingus** (🕻 **800/ 474-7424** in the U.S., or 0818/365-000 in Ireland; www.aerlingus.ie) with flights from London and Europe. **British Airways** (🕻 **800/247-9297** in the U.S., or 087/085-9850 in Britain; www.ba.com) offers flights to and from Manchester and the north of England. **Ryanair** (🕻 **0818/30-30-30** in Ireland, or 0871/246-0000 in Britain; www.ryanair. com) serves Cork from London Stansted and Liverpool, while **Easyjet** (🕻 **1890/923- 922;** www.easyjet.com) runs a daily service to London Gatwick, and **bmibaby** (🕻 **800/ 788-0555** in the U.S., or 01/242-0794 in Ireland; www.bmibaby.com) serves Cork from Manchester and Birmingham in the north of England.

There are **taxi** stands outside the arrivals hall of the airport. A journey to the city center should cost around €15 ($24).

Sky Link (🕻 **021/432-1020;** www.skylinkcork.com), with its distinctive bright-yellow buses, provides a shuttle service direct from Cork airport to the city center. It takes 10 to 15 minutes and costs €5 ($8) one-way, €8 ($13) round-trip. Departures are every 30 minutes from outside the arrivals hall.

Bus Éireann (🕻 **021/450-8188;** www.buseireann.ie) provides bus service from the airport to Parnell Place Bus Station in the city center; the fare is €4.10 ($6.55) one-way, €6.90 ($11) round-trip. The trip takes between 18 and 24 minutes, depending on time of day. Buses from all parts of Ireland arrive at **Bus Éireann's Passenger Depot,** Parnell Place, in the downtown area, 3 blocks from Patrick Street.

Iarnród Éireann (Irish Rail) (toll-free 🕻 **1850/366222** or 01/836-6222; www.irish rail.ie) operates the train services in Ireland. Trains from Dublin, Limerick, and other parts of Ireland arrive at **Kent Station,** Lower Glanmire Road, Cork (🕻 **021/450-6766**), on the city's eastern edge.

Ferry routes into Cork from Britain include service from Swansea on **Swansea/Cork Ferries** (🕻 **021/483-6000**), and from Roscoff on **Brittany Ferries** (🕻 **021/427-7801;** www.brittany-ferries.com). All ferries arrive at Cork's Ringaskiddy Ferryport.

If you're approaching Cork from the east, take the Carrigaloe-Glenbrook ferry from Cobh across Cork Harbour. This ferry can save you an hour's driving time around the edge of Cork Harbour, and you'll bypass the generally heavy Cork City traffic. The ferry runs from 7:15am to 12:30am. Cars cost €4.50 ($7.20) one-way, €6.50 ($10) round-trip. For cyclists, the fare is €1 ($1.60) one-way, €1.50 (2.40) round-trip. The trip lasts less than 5 minutes. For more information, contact Cross River Ferries Ltd., Westland House, Rushbrooke, Cobh (🕻 **021/481-1485;** www.scottcobh.ie).

Many main national roads lead into Cork, including N8 from Dublin, N25 from Waterford, N20 from Limerick, N22 from Killarney, and N71 from West Cork.

VISITOR INFORMATION

For brochures, maps, and other information, visit the **Cork Tourist Office,** Tourist House, 42 Grand Parade, Cork (🕻 **021/425-5100;** www.corkkerry.ie). Its hours are Monday to Saturday 9:15am to 5:30pm year-round. For online information, consult the **Cork Guide** (www.cork-guide.ie). For accommodations in Cork, consult our recommendations below, then try **www.booking.com.**

CITY LAYOUT

Cork's center is on an island, which lies between two branches of the River Lee. The city is divided into three sections:

CORK CITY

9

ORIENTATION

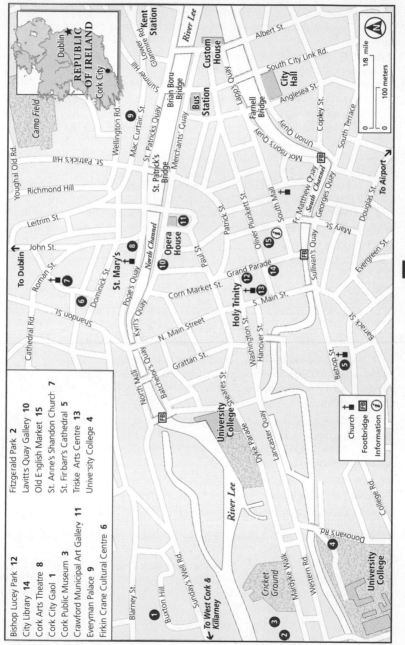

Bishop Lucey Park 12
City Library 14
Cork Arts Theatre 8
Cork City Gaol 1
Cork Public Museum 3
Crawford Municipal Art Gallery 11
Everyman Palace 9
Firkin Crane Cultural Centre 6

Fitzgerald Park 2
Lavitts Quay Gallery 10
Old English Market 15
St. Anne's Shandon Church 7
St. Firbarr's Cathedral 5
Triskel Arts Centre 13
University College 4

FLAT OF THE CITY The city's downtown core is bounded by channels of the River Lee, and its main thoroughfare is **St. Patrick Street,** a graceful avenue lined with shops. A favorite meeting place here is by the statue of 19th-century priest Father Theobald Matthew, a crusader against drink who is fondly called the "Apostle of Temperance." The statue stands at the point where Patrick Street reaches St. Patrick's Bridge.

Nearby, the **South Mall** is a wide tree-lined street with attractive Georgian architecture and a row of banks, insurance companies, and legal offices, while the **Grand Parade** is a spacious thoroughfare that blends 18th-century bow-fronted houses with the remains of the old city walls. It has lots of offices and shops as well as the **Bishop Lucey Park.**

NORTH BANK St. Patrick's Bridge leads over the river to the north side of the city, a hilly, terraced area where St. Patrick Street becomes **St. Patrick's Hill.** And is it ever a hill, with an incline so steep that it is nearly San Franciscan. If you climb the stepped sidewalks of St. Patrick's Hill, you will be rewarded with a sweeping view of the Cork skyline.

East of St. Patrick's Hill, **MacCurtain Street** is a commercial thoroughfare that runs east, leading to Summerhill Road and up into the Cork hills to the residential districts of St. Luke's and Montenotte. West of St. Patrick's Hill is one of the city's oldest neighborhoods, **St. Ann's Shandon Church,** and the city's original Butter Market building.

SOUTH BANK South of the River Lee, South Bank encompasses the grounds of St. Finbarr's Cathedral, the site of St. Finbarr's 6th-century monastery, and also includes 17th-century city walls, the remains of Elizabeth Fort, and the City Hall (built in 1936).

2 GETTING AROUND

BY PUBLIC TRANSPORTATION **Bus Éireann** operates bus service from Parnell Place Bus Station (*©* **021/450-8188;** www.buseireann.ie) to all parts of the city and its suburbs, including Blarney and Kinsale. The flat fare is €1.10 ($1.75). Buses run frequently from 7am to 11pm Monday to Saturday, with slightly shorter hours on Sunday.

BY TAXI Taxis are readily available throughout Cork. The main taxi ranks are along St. Patrick's Street, along the South Mall, and outside major hotels. To call for a taxi, try **ABC Cabs** (*©* **021/496-1961**), **Cork Taxi Co-Op** (*©* **021/427-2222**), or **Satellite Cabs** (*©* **1890/202020** or 021/431-9619).

BY CAR It's best to park and explore the city on foot or by public transport. Unless your hotel has a parking lot, it can be a hassle finding street parking. If you have to park in public areas, it costs upwards of €1.80 ($2.90) per hour, whether you park in one of the city's two multistory parking lots, at Lavitt's Quay and Merchant's Quay, or on the street, where you still must pay to park. There are plenty of ground-level parking lots throughout the city.

Many international car-rental firms maintain rental desks at Cork Airport, including **Alamo** (*©* 021/431-8623), **Avis** (*©* 021/432-7460), **Budget** (*©* 021/431-4000), **Hertz** (*©* 021/496-5849), and **Murray's Europcar** (*©* 021/491-7300).

ON FOOT Because of the limited parking, the best way to see Cork is on foot, but don't try to do it all in a day. The South Bank and the central part, or flat, of the city can easily take a day to explore; save the Cork Hills and the North Bank for another day. You might want to follow the signposted Tourist Trail to guide you to the major sights.

(Fast Facts) Cork City

Drugstores Try **Murphy's Pharmacy,** 48 N. Main St. (℃ **021/427-4121**) or **Deasy's Pharmacy,** 99 Shandon St. (℃ **021/430-4535**).

Emergencies Dial ℃ **999.**

Gay & Lesbian Resources For information and aid, call the **Southern Gay Health Project,** 8 S. Main St. (℃ **021/427-8471**). The **Gay Information** line (℃ **021/427-1087**) is open Wednesday 7 to 9pm and Saturday 3 to 5pm. The **Lesbian Line** (℃ **021/431-8318**) is open Thursday 8 to 10pm.

Hospitals Try **Cork University Hospital,** Wilton Road (℃ **021/454-6400**), or **Bon Secours Hospital,** College Road (℃ **021/454-2807**).

Information See "Visitor Information," under "Orientation," above.

Internet Access **Cork City Library,** 57 Grand Parade (℃ **021/492-4900**), has a bank of public Internet workstations available for €1 ($1.60) per half-hour. You can also try **Wired to the World,** 27 Washington St. (℃ **021/453-0383;** www. wiredtotheworld.ie). In addition to Internet access for €1 ($1.60) an hour, it also offers cheap international phone calls.

Library **Cork City Library,** 57 Grand Parade (℃ **021/492-4900**).

Police The local Garda Headquarters is on Anglesea Street (℃ **021/452-2000**).

Post Office The **General Post Office,** on Oliver Plunkett Street (℃ **021/485-1042**), is open Monday to Saturday 9am to 5:30pm.

3 WHERE TO STAY

VERY EXPENSIVE

Hayfield Manor Hotel ★★★ (Kids)   This is Cork's only true luxury hotel, with sky-high tariffs to prove it. Its period appearance and feel are false—it was built in 1996 and expanded in 1999. The entire hotel is decorated with a warm palette of apricots and ochers, including the magnificent foyer with marble columns and a grand mahogany staircase. Guest rooms are spacious and lend the feel of an elegant private manor home, with large windows and marble bathrooms. Although less than a mile from the city center and near Cork's University College, Hayfield Manor is quite secluded. The fully equipped conservatory/leisure center is inviting, and, for such a posh hotel, it is surprisingly welcoming to pampered children. It offers everything from babysitting service to miniature bathrobes and cookies and milk at bedtime.

Perrott Ave., College Rd., Cork, County Cork. ℃ **021/484-5900,** or 800/525-4800 in the U.S. for reservations through Small Luxury Hotels of the World. Fax 021/431-6839. www.hayfieldmanor.ie. 88 units. €230–€400 ($368–$640) double; €380–€450 ($608–$720) deluxe rooms; €560–€660 ($896–$1,056) executive suite; €1,030 ($1,648) master suite. Rates include service charge and full Irish breakfast. AE, DC, MC, V. Free parking. **Amenities:** 2 restaurants (Continental, bistro); bar; indoor swimming pool; spa; health and beauty treatments; Jacuzzi; steam room; concierge; room service; babysitting; laundry service; drawing room. *In room:* A/C, TV, CD player, hair dryer, garment press, orthopedic beds, American socket converter.

Tips **Service Charges**

A reminder: Unless otherwise noted, room rates don't include service charges (usually 10%–15% of your bill).

EXPENSIVE

The Gresham Metropole ★★   This elegant, historic hotel has been a local land-mark for 100 years. It was fully renovated a couple of years ago, and now it has all you need—comfortable rooms neatly designed with neutral decor, firm beds, and luxurious fabrics; an excellent bar and restaurant; and a full leisure center with pool, sauna, and steam room. The lobby and bar are pleasant places to relax at the end of a long day, and the food in the restaurant comes in handy when you're tired (as does room service).

MacCurtain St., Tivoli, Cork, County Cork. ✆ **021/464-3700.** Fax 021/450-6450. www.gresham-hotels. com. 113 units. €145–€260 ($232–$416) double. AE, DC, MC, V. **Amenities:** 2 restaurants (international, cafe); bar; indoor swimming pool; health club; gym; hot tub; sauna; steam room; free Wi-Fi; room service; laundry service; solarium. *In room:* TV, tea/coffeemaker, hair dryer, garment press.

The Imperial Hotel ★★   Since opening in 1845, the Imperial has played host to a number of renowned figures. Charles Dickens, Sir Walter Scott, and William Makepeace Thackeray have all been guests here, and the Irish revolution leader Michael Collins stayed in room no. 115 the night before his assassination. With Waterford crystal chan-deliers, marble floors, and brass fittings, the reception area and public rooms exude an aura of 19th-century grandeur. The guest rooms recently received an injection of much-needed attention, and are attractive enough with a warm, golden palette and dark-wood furniture. There are plenty of modern conveniences, and executive rooms have DVD players, dataports, minibars, and fax machines. The location couldn't be better either—right in the city center.

South Mall, Cork, County Cork. ✆ **800/44-UTELL** [448-8355] in the U.S., or 021/427-4040. Fax 021/427-5375. www.flynnhotels.com/Imperial_Hotel. 88 units. €160–€230 ($256–$368) double. Breakfast €15 ($24). AE, MC, V. Parking (designated spaces in Union Quay car park) €6 ($9.60) per day. **Amenities:** 2 restaurants (modern Irish, brasserie); bar; cafe; concierge; room service; laundry service. *In room:* TV, radio, broadband, tea/coffeemaker, iron, garment press, voice mail.

MODERATE

Garnish House ★★ **Finds**   This is the best B&B on the Western Road and, since B&Bs are wall-to-wall along the entire thoroughfare, that's saying something. Hansi Lucey is a wonderful innkeeper, the kind who makes a fuss about you as if you were a much-cherished friend. Fresh tea and scones await you upon arrival, and give an inkling of the excellent food you can expect at breakfast. Never content to rest on her laurels, a few years ago she added family suites and champagne breakfasts.

Western Rd., Cork, County Cork. ✆ 021/427-5111. Fax 021/427-3872. www.garnish.ie. 14 units. €90–€140 ($144–$224) double. AE, DC, MC, V. Free parking. **Amenities:** Lounge; nonsmoking rooms. *In room:* TV, hair dryer.

Hotel Isaac ★   This place has a kind of stripped-down chic—the furniture is not expen-sive, and the furnishings are not mahogany, but it uses what it has with class. Exposed brick walls, huge picture windows, and excellent use of light all combine to make you forget the tired upholstery and weary carpet. Bedrooms are comfortable with pine furniture and **275** individual decor. There's also an excellent restaurant, **Greenes** (p. 277), and a cozy bar.

48 MacCurtain St., Cork, County Cork. © 021/450-0011. Fax 021/450-6351. www.isaacs.ie. 47 units. €130–€150 ($208–$240) double. AE, DC, MC, V. Free parking. **Amenities:** Restaurant (international); bar; room service; nonsmoking rooms. *In room:* TV, tea/coffeemaker, hair dryer.

Lotamore House ★★ (Value)   Following a makeover, one of Cork's most trusted old standbys has gone from endearingly old-fashioned to elegantly chic. Overlooking the River Lee amid wooded grounds and gardens, 3km (2 miles) east of Cork City, this Georgian manor is impressive. But where it used to have a certain grandmotherly charm—sweeping staircase, ornate plasterwork, crystal chandeliers, and a fireplace dating from 1791—it now has been smartened up with matte, neutral colors, gorgeous mahogany beds, and soft linens. Breakfast is exceptional, with freshly squeezed juices, fresh fruit, and homemade scones all accompanying the traditional Irish options.

Lower Glanmire Rd. (Dublin-Waterford rd. N8/N25), Tivoli, Cork, County Cork. © 021/482-2344. Fax 021/482-2219. www.lotamorehouse.com. 20 units. €130–€180 ($208–$288) double. Rates include full breakfast. AE, MC, V. Free parking. Closed Dec 20–Jan 7. **Amenities:** Lounge; laundry service; nonsmoking rooms. *In room:* TV, tea/coffeemaker, hair dryer, garment press.

Silver Springs Hotel ★   On a hillside overlooking the River Lee 3km (2 miles) out of the city, this modern seven-story hotel is a popular choice for local wedding receptions. It's surrounded by 17 hectares (42 acres) of gardens, and has plenty of elegant touches. Each room, outfitted with handcrafted Irish furniture and designer fabrics, has lovely views of the river, city, or gardens, and there's an exterior glass elevator that overlooks the countryside.

Dublin Rd., Tivoli, Cork, County Cork. © 021/450-7533. Fax 021/450-7641. www.silverspringshotel.ie. 109 units. €130–€180 ($208–$288) double; €180–€220 ($288–$352) suite. Rates include service charge and full breakfast. AE, DC, MC, V. Free parking. **Amenities:** 2 restaurants (international, bistro); bar; indoor swimming pool; tennis courts; squash court; health club; Jacuzzi; sauna; steam room; concierge; room service; laundry service. *In room:* TV, tea/coffeemaker, hair dryer, garment press.

INEXPENSIVE

Jurys Cork Inn ★★ (Kids)   This comfortable if rather functional hotel overlooking the River Lee is an excellent choice for families traveling on a budget. The flat-rate room price covers up to three adults or two adults and two children—exceptional value for a city-center location. The brick facade and mansard-style roof blend in with Cork's older architecture, yet the interior is bright and modern, with contemporary light-wood furnishings.

Anderson's Quay, Cork, County Cork. © 800/44-UTELL [448-8355] in the U.S., or 021/494-3000. Fax 021/427-6144. www.jurys.com. 133 units. €139–€250 ($222–$400) per room. Breakfast €10 ($16). AE, DC, MC, V. Limited free parking. **Amenities:** Restaurant (international); bar; laundry service; nonsmoking rooms. *In room:* TV, tea/coffeemaker, hair dryer.

Maranatha Country House ★★ (Finds)   Olwen Venn is the energetic hostess at this 19th-century manor house tucked away in the forests outside Cork. Each room is uniquely designed—one room is fit for a princess, with a canopy of velvet and lavish florals; another evokes a cool forest; a third uses 365m (1,197 ft.) of fabric in its draperies alone. Traditional rules of decorating have been discarded in favor of whimsical effusiveness. The most luxurious quarters are in a huge ground-floor suite, which has a canopy bed and a large Jacuzzi. The breakfast conservatory houses an abundance of flowers, and the breakfast itself is plentiful and delicious.

Tower, Blarney, County Cork. ©/fax **021/438-5102.** www.maranathacountryhouse.com. 6 units, all with private bathroom, 5 with shower only, 1 with Jacuzzi. €70–€120 ($112–$192) double. Reduction for seniors and children 11 and under. Rates include full breakfast. MC, V. Free parking. Closed mid-Dec to mid-Feb. **Amenities:** Babysitting; nonsmoking rooms; TV lounge. *In room:* Hair dryer.

4 WHERE TO DINE

VERY EXPENSIVE

The Ivory Tower ★★ FUSION   With its unattractive exterior, the Tower can be off-putting, but true foodies will persevere. American-born Seamus O'Connell has made a name as a truly innovative chef. He uses the freshest ingredients—most from local markets—and adds layers of ingredients on top of that foundation. His style is unusual and iconoclastic, and his menu reads like a roster of unlikely flavor combinations: swordfish on banana ketchup? Hot smoked salmon with lemon geranium sauce? Kumquats in Rioja wine? This place is not for the faint of heart, but it has many devoted fans.

The Exchange Buildings, 35 Princes St. © **021/427-4665.** Reservations required. Fixed 5-course dinner €60 ($96); main courses €35–€40 ($56–$64). MC, V. Wed–Sat 6:30–11pm.

EXPENSIVE

Café Paradiso ★★ VEGETARIAN   This is not only the best vegetarian restaurant in Ireland but also one of the best of any kind. The menu features organic local produce, complemented by Irish farmhouse cheeses. Lunches are light fare—understated but tasty sandwiches and fresh soups. For dinner, you might begin your meal with vegetable sushi with tempura, before moving on to sweet chili-glazed pan-fried tofu with Chinese greens in a coconut broth, or a feta, pistachio, and couscous cake with citrus greens and hot-pepper relish. Dark-chocolate silk cake or poached rhubarb with an orange blossom–and-saffron parfait makes an ideal finish. The well-selected wine list offers a number of choices by the glass or half-bottle.

16 Lancaster Quay, Western Rd. (across from Jurys hotel). © **021/427-7939.** www.cafeparadiso.ie. Reservations recommended. Dinner main courses €24–€28 ($38–$45). AE, MC, V. Tues–Sat noon–3pm and 6:30–10:30pm. Closed Christmas week.

Jacques ★★ INTERNATIONAL   Cork adores the effortlessly contemporary creations of sisters Eithne and Jacqueline Barry. Lately, the menu is highly influenced by Mediterranean and Asian ingredients, as seen in main dishes such as monkfish on Rosscarbery pak choi with ginger and chili. There are also classics such as sirloin steak and a modern spin on duck à l'orange served with chard and Gubbeen bacon. The small dining room, with cheery lemon, tangerine, and green walls that are lined with modern artwork, is the perfect backdrop for the buzzy, fresh atmosphere.

9 Phoenix St. © **021/427-7387.** www.jacquesrestaurant.ie. Reservations recommended. Early-bird dinner (6–7pm) €22 ($35); dinner main courses €23–€29 ($37–$46). AE, MC, V. Mon–Fri noon–3pm and 6–10:30pm; Sat 6–10:30pm.

MODERATE

Crawford Gallery Cafe ★★ COUNTRY HOUSE   In a ground-floor room at the Crawford Art Gallery (p. 278), this popular bistro, decorated with oil paintings and statuary, is run by the Allen family of Ballymaloe House fame (p. 296). The dinner menu includes such traditional dishes as lamb braised with vegetables and rosemary, while the

lunch menu features delightful salads, seafood, and an excellent spinach-and-mushroom
crepe. All seafood is brought in fresh daily from Ballycotton Bay, and the fresh breads and
baked goods are from Ballymaloe kitchens.

Emmet Place. © **021/427-4415.** www.crawfordartgallery.com. Reservations recommended for parties
of 6 or more. Set lunch €25 ($40); main courses €10–€15 ($16–$24). MC, V. Mon–Fri 10am–5pm; Sat
10am–4:30pm.

Fenn's Quay Restaurant ★★ INTERNATIONAL Eilish and Pat O'Leary's
superbly restored 18th-century terrace house attracts a well-heeled clientele and is set to
be a long-distance runner among Cork's many excellent restaurants. Bold, creative dishes
furnish—but do not overwhelm—the menu, so that one may just as easily order an
aubergine (eggplant) Charlotte with Gubbeen cheese custard (pudding) as a locally
reared beef burger with tomato and horseradish ketchup and rough-cut fries. The place
gets jammed at lunchtime, when the prices offer good value, so be prepared to wait, or
better yet, go for a leisurely dinner.

5 Fenn's Quay. © **021/427-9527.** Reservations recommended. Early-bird dinners (6–7pm) 2-course €23
($37), 3-course €27 ($43); dinner main courses €17–€28 ($27–$45). AE, MC, V. Mon–Sat 10am–10pm.

Greenes ★★ INTERNATIONAL Inside the Hotel Isaacs in central Cork, this is a
beautiful and contemporary space, with soaring warehouse-style ceilings, exposed brick
walls, and big windows overlooking a waterfall. The attraction here is the modern, understated cuisine, with perfectly grilled meats and fish. Daily specials add to the variety.

Hotel Isaacs, 48 MacCurtain St. © **021/455-2279.** Reservations recommended. Early-bird dinners
(6–7pm) 3 courses €27 ($43); dinner main courses €18–€29 ($29–$46). AE, DC, MC, V. Mon–Thurs 6–10pm;
Fri–Sat 6–10:30pm; Sun 12:30–2:30pm and 6–9:30pm.

Jacob's on the Mall ★★ INTERNATIONAL Housed in what was once an old
bathhouse, this eatery is the talk of the town for its fresh ingredients and attention to
detail. Grilled mackerel comes with buttery new potatoes and the licorice-like hint of
fennel, crispy salmon is served with Chinese greens and noodles, and breast of chicken
comes with a dollop of lemon aioli. The place is lovely, with tall windows flooding the
dining room with light.

30A South Mall. © **021/425-1530.** Fax 021/425-1531. www.jacobsonthemall.com. Reservations recommended. Main courses €17–€32 ($27–$51). AE, MC, V. Mon–Sat 12:30–2:30pm and 6:30–10pm.

INEXPENSIVE

Idaho Cafe ★★ INTERNATIONAL This is a tiny place, with patrons squeezing in
like sardines, and the attraction is the reliably good food. Lunchtime specials feature such
items as Ummero bacon with minty new potatoes and cashews, or crabmeat and tuna
quesadillas. Everything is made from fresh ingredients by people who understand that a
bit of care in preparing even an inexpensive meal goes much appreciated. To find it, turn
off Patrick Street, directly behind the Brown Thomas department store.

19 Caroline St. © **021/427-6376.** Breakfast €2–€8 ($3.20–$13); main courses €9–€10 ($14–$16). No
credit cards. Mon–Fri 9am–9pm; Sat–Sun 9am–6pm.

Quay Co-op ★★ VEGETARIAN/CAFETERIA The ground floor of this insider
establishment is a whole-foods store that also sells fresh breads and cakes. The main
attraction is on the second floor, reached by a narrow, steep staircase. Don't be put off by
the inauspicious first impression—this self-service restaurant offers delicious hot and

cold dishes, including soups, pasta, chickpea burgers, and a variety of daily specials. There are also some vegan offerings on the menu.

24 Sullivan's Quay. ☎ **021/431-7026.** www.quaycoop.com. Dinner main courses €7–€10 ($11–$16). MC, V. Mon–Fri 9am–9pm; Sat–Sun 9am–6pm.

5 SEEING THE SIGHTS

IN TOWN

Coal Quay Market ⟨Overrated⟩ This is Cork's open-air flea market, a trove of second-hand clothes, old china, used books, memorabilia, and—well, to be truthful—a lot of junk. It all happens on a street, now a little ragged, that was once Cork's original outdoor market.

Cornmarket St. Free admission. Mon–Sat 9am–5pm.

Cork Butter Museum ★ Started in 1770, Cork's butter exchange became the largest exporter of salted butter in the world, exporting around 500,000 casks of the stuff each year by 1892. The exchange closed in 1924, and it now houses the Shandon Craft Centre and the Firkin Crane Centre, a hot venue for contemporary dance performances. This museum is an unusual celebration of butter and the role it has played in Irish life from medieval times to the present day. For dairy fans.

John Redmond St. ☎ **021/430-0600.** www.corkbutter.museum. Admission €3.50 ($5.60) adults, €2.50 ($4) seniors and students, €1.50 ($2.40) children 11 and under. Mar–Oct daily 10am–5pm; July–Aug daily 10am–6pm; rest of year by appointment only.

Cork City Gaol ★ Less than 2km (1¼ miles) west of the city center, this restored prison was infamous in the 19th century, when it housed many of Ireland's great patriots. Sound effects and lifelike characters inhabiting the cells re-create the social history of Cork. The "Radio Museum Experience," an exhibition drawn from the RTE Museum Collection, depicts a restored 6CK Radio Studio and an array of antique radio equipment and memorabilia.

Convent Ave., Sunday's Well. ☎ **021/430-5022.** www.corkcitygaol.com. Admission to gaol or exhibition €7.50 ($12) adults, €6.50 ($10) seniors and students, €4 ($6.40) children, €20 ($32) families. Mar–Oct daily 9:30am–5pm; Nov–Feb daily 10am–5pm. Last admission 1 hr. before closing.

Cork Public Museum ★ This museum occupies a magnificent Georgian building in a park on the western edge of the city. Exhibits include models depicting early medieval times; artifacts recovered from excavations in the city, some dating 4,000 years; and a working model of an early flour mill with an unusual horizontal water wheel. There's an archive of photographs and documents relating to Cork-born Irish patriots Terence McSwiney, Thomas MacCurtain, and Michael Collins. Antique Cork silver, glass, and lace are on display.

Fitzgerald Park. ☎ **021/427-0679.** Free admission. Year-round Mon–Fri 11am–1pm and 2:15–5pm; Apr–Sept Sun 3–5pm.

Crawford Municipal Art Gallery ★★★ The Crawford ranks among Ireland's best art galleries, with a strong collection led by works of Irish painters including Jack B. Yeats, Nathaniel Grogan, William Orpen, Sir John Lavery, James Barry, and Daniel Maclise. In the well-converted, 18th-century customs house, the gallery also holds sculptures and

handcrafted silver and glass pieces. A fine restaurant (p. 276) and bookstore are on the **279**
premises.

Emmet Place. ✆ **021/490-7855**. www.crawfordartgallery.com. Free admission. Mon–Sat 9am–5pm.

Lavitts Quay Gallery　Operated by the Cork Arts Society, this gallery, in an early-18th-century Georgian house overlooking the River Lee, promotes the area's contemporary arts scene. The ground floor presents works by established artists, and the upper floor showcases up-and-coming talent.

5 Father Matthew St. ✆ **021/427-7749**. Free admission. Mon–Sat 10:30am–6pm.

Mutton Lane Mural ★　In 2004, local artist Anthony Ruby painted a giant mural along the walls of Mutton Lane. It depicts musicians performing the traditional Pana Shuffle, and is a vivid and colorful evocation of peace and community spirit. In a sign of the times, however, the artist hand-painted a notice above it reading: "Dedicated to everyone except George Bush."

Mutton Lane, off Patrick St.

Old English Market ★★　Ireland's best food market dates from a charter of James I in 1610. The present building, finished in 1786, was damaged by fire in 1980 and then brilliantly refurbished. Inside food stands brim with meats, fish, vegetables, and fruit, and you'll also see such traditional Cork foods as hot buttered eggs, tripe (animal stomach), *crubeens* (pigs' feet), and *drisheens* (local blood sausage). The market's name is a holdover from the days of English rule.

Grand Parade; enter from Patrick St., Grand Parade, Oliver Plunkett St., or Princes St. Free admission. Mon–Sat 9am–6pm.

St. Anne's Church ★★ (Moments)　Cork's prime landmark, also known as Shandon Church, is famous for its giant pepper-pot steeple and its eight melodious bells. No matter where you stand in the downtown area, you can see the stone tower, crowned with a gilt ball and a unique fish weather vane. Until recently, due to a quirk of clockworks, it was known as "the four-faced liar" because each of its four clock faces showed a different time, except on the hour, when they all managed to synchronize. Somewhat sadly, that charming quirk has been fixed. Built in 1722, the steeple has red sandstone (south) and limestone (west) walls, from which the colors of the Cork hurling and football teams are taken. A climb to the belfry rewards with the chance to play a tune on the famous Shandon Bells. Consequently, you might hear the bells of Shandon ringing at all times of the day. Continue on a sometimes-precarious climb up past the bells and you'll be further rewarded with spectacular views.

Church St. ✆ **021/450-5906**. www.shandonbells.org. Admission €6 ($9.60) adults, €5 ($8) seniors and students. Easter–Oct Mon–Sat 9:30am–5:30pm; Nov–Easter Mon–Sat 10am–3pm.

St. Fin Barre's Cathedral ★　This Church of Ireland cathedral sits on the spot St. Finbarr chose in A.D. 600 for his church and school. The current building dates from 1880 and is a fine example of early French Gothic style; its three giant spires dominate the skyline. The interior is highly ornamented with unique mosaic work. The bells were inherited from the 1735 church that previously stood on this site.

Bishop St. ✆ **021/496-3387**. Admission €3 ($4.80) adults; €1.50 ($2.40) seniors, children, and students. Apr–Sept Mon–Sat 10am–5:30pm; Oct–Mar Mon–Sat 2–5:30pm.

CORK CITY

9

SEEING THE SIGHTS

The Gift of Gab (or is it Just Blarney?)

The much-beloved myth that being held upside down and backward from the top of a tall castle to kiss a rock brings you the ability to talk up a storm is actually quite new, although the Blarney association with the gift of gab goes back a long way. It is believed to have been Queen Elizabeth I who created it in the 16th century, in a fit of exasperation at the ability of then-Lord Blarney to prattle on at great length without actually ever agreeing to what she wanted. The custom of kissing the stone, though, is less than a century old. Nobody knows quite why it started, but around here they've got a thousand possible tales, some involving witches and others the crusaders, but don't believe them. It's all a bunch of . . .

University College, Cork (U.C.C.)   A component of Ireland's National University, with about 7,000 students, this center of learning is housed in a pretty quadrangle of Gothic Revival–style buildings. Colorful gardens and wooded grounds grace the campus. A tour of the grounds takes in the Crawford Observatory, the Harry Clarke stained-glass windows in the Honan Chapel, and the Stone Corridor, a collection of stones inscribed with the ancient Irish ogham style of writing.

Also at the university is the **Lewis Glucksman Museum** (© 021/490-1844; www.glucksman.org), a new public art gallery and cultural institute that also comprises a shop and riverside restaurant. The building itself has earned or been on the short list for several architectural awards, and is as much of an attraction as the eclectic program of modern art, which changes out roughly every quarter.

Western Rd. © 021/490-1876. http://visitorscentre.ucc.ie. University tours (by arrangement) €4 ($6.40), €15 ($24) families. Free admission to Glucksman Museum. Tues–Sat 10am–5pm (Thurs until 8pm); Sun noon–5pm.

Bus Tours

In July and August, **Bus Éireann,** Parnell Place Bus Station (© 021/450-8188), offers narrated half-day tours to Cork's major landmarks and buildings, including nearby Blarney. Fares start at €10 ($16), and tours leave at 10:30am daily.

Cork City Tours   These open-top buses let you hop on and hop off to explore the sights of Ireland's second city. They run all day in a loop from April through October, so when you see something you want to explore, just get off and rejoin the tour later. Or you can stay on the bus and use the tour to get oriented. Tour highlights include the Cork City Gaol, St. Ann's Church, and U.C.C. (University College, Cork). You can buy your ticket on the bus if you get on at any of these stops, or buy a ticket and board the bus at the tourist office. Further details are available from the Cork Tourist Office.

© 021/430-9090. Admission €13 ($21) adults, €11 ($18) seniors and students, €5 ($8) children. Apr–Oct daily, with hours and number of tours reflecting seasonal demand.

NEARBY: BLARNEY CASTLE & MORE

Blarney Castle and Stone ★★   While Blarney Castle is extremely touristy, it is still one of the most impressive castles in Ireland. It was once huge, and the massive square

tower that is all that remains of it has a parapet rising 25m (82 ft.). The famous Blarney
Stone itself is wedged far enough underneath the battlements to make it uncomfortable
to reach, but not far enough that countless tourists don't bend over backward, hang
upside down in a parapet, and kiss it in hopes of increased loquaciousness. It's customary
to tip the attendant who holds your legs (you might want to do it before he hangs you
over the edge).

After bypassing the stone, take a stroll through the gardens and a nearby dell beside
Blarney Lake. The Badger Cave and adjacent dungeons penetrating the rock at the base
of the castle can be explored by all but the claustrophobic with the aid of a flashlight.

R617, 8km (5 miles) northwest of Cork City, Blarney, County Cork. ℂ 021/438-5252. www.blarneycastle.
ie. Admission €10 ($16) adults, €8 ($13) seniors and students, €3.50 ($5.60) children 8–14, €24 ($38)
families. May and Sept Mon–Sat 9am–6:30pm, Sun 9:30am–5:30pm; June–Aug Mon–Sat 9am–7pm, Sun
9:30am–5:30pm; Oct–Apr Mon–Sat 9am–sundown, Sun 9:30am–sundown. Bus: Marked BLARNEY or TOWER
from bus station on Parnell Place, Cork City.

---

6 SPORTS & OUTDOOR PURSUITS

SPECTATOR SPORTS

GAELIC GAMES   Hurling and Gaelic football are both played on summer Sunday
afternoons at Cork's **Pairc Ui Chaoimh Stadium,** Marina Walk (ℂ **021/496-3311**).
Check the local newspapers for details or log on to the Gaelic Athletics Association's site
at www.gaa.ie.

GREYHOUND RACING   Go to the dogs, as they say in Cork, only now in distinctly
21st-century style, at the **Cork Greyhound Stadium,** Curraheen Park, Cork (ℂ **021/454-
3095**), on Wednesday, Thursday, and Saturday at 8pm. Admission is €10 ($16).

HORSE RACING   The nearest racetrack is **Mallow Race Track,** Killarney Road, Mallow (ℂ **022/50207**), approximately 32km (20 miles) north of Cork. Races are scheduled
year-round, but particularly in mid-May, early August, and early October. Admission is
€18 ($29) adults, €10 ($16) seniors and students, and free for children 13 and under.

OUTDOOR PURSUITS

BICYCLING   Although walking is probably the ideal way to get around Cork, you can
rent a bike at **Cyclescene,** 396 Blarney St. (ℂ **021/430-1183**; www.cyclescene.ie). It
costs €15 to €20 ($24–$32) per day or €80 ($128) per week, plus a refundable deposit
of €100 ($160). Open Monday to Saturday 8:30am to 5:45pm.

FISHING   The **River Lee,** which runs through Cork, the nearby **Blackwater River,**
and the many area lakes present fine opportunities. Salmon licenses, lake fishing permits,
tackle, and equipment can be obtained from **T. W. Murray,** 87 Patrick St. (ℂ **021/427-
1089**).

GOLF   Local clubs that welcome visitors are the **Cork Golf Club,** Little Island (ℂ **021/
435-3451**; www.corkgolfclub.ie), 8km (5 miles) east of Cork, with greens fees of €85
($136) weekdays, €95 ($152) weekends; **Douglas Golf Club,** Maryboro Hill, Douglas
(ℂ **021/489-5297**; www.douglasgolfclub.ie), 4.8km (3 miles) south of Cork, with
greens fees of €50 ($80) weekdays, €55 ($88) weekends; and **Harbour Point,** Little
Island (ℂ **021/435-3094**; www.harbourpointgolfclub.com), 6.5km (4 miles) east of
Cork, with greens fees of €37 ($59) weekdays, €45 ($72) weekends.

WALKING The **Old Railway Line** is a dismantled train route running from Cork to the old maritime town of Passage West. It is from here that Captain Roberts set out and crossed the Atlantic in the first passenger steamship, the *Sirius*. Following along the rails, a scenic walk affords the visitor excellent views of the inner harbor.

7 SHOPPING

Patrick Street is the main shopping thoroughfare, and many stores are scattered throughout the city on side streets and in lanes. In general, shops are open Monday to Saturday 9:30am to 6pm, unless indicated otherwise. In the summer many shops remain open until 9:30pm on Thursday and Friday, and some are open on Sunday.

Until recently, Cork had a lovely antiques quarter on Paul's Lane, but virtually all the shops that made the street unique have closed now, pushed out by higher rents and lack of local interest in anything old. It's all about the new now.

The main mall is **Merchant's Quay Shopping Centre,** Merchant's Quay and Patrick Street. This enclosed complex houses large department stores, such as **Marks and Spencer** (© 021/427-5555), as well as small specialty shops, such as **Laura Ashley** (© 021/427-4070).

Cork's best department store is **Brown Thomas,** 18 St. Patrick St. (© 021/480-5555). It has three floors of the upscale items found in its sister shop in Dublin.

BOOKS & MUSIC

The Living Tradition This small shop on the North Bank specializes in Irish folk and traditional music—CDs, books, videos, sheet music—as well as instruments. In addition, it stocks a good selection of recordings of musicians from around the world, along with handcrafted goods. 40 MacCurtain St. © 021/450-2564.

Mainly Murder Tucked between French Church and Academy streets, this tiny bookshop is a huge treasure-trove of whodunits for amateur sleuths. It stocks volumes on murder, mystery, and mayhem from Ireland, England, and many other English-speaking lands. 2A Paul St. © 021/427-2413.

Waterstone's Booksellers With entrances on two streets, this large branch of the British-owned chain is always busy. It has a good selection of books about Cork and of Irish interest, as well as U.S. and other international titles. 69 Patrick St. and 12 Paul St. © 021/427-6522.

CRAFTS

Crafts of Ireland Just a block off Patrick Street, this well-stocked shop presents an array of local crafts, including weavings, wrought iron, batik hangings, glass, graphics, pottery, toys, and Irish floral stationery. 11 Winthrop St. © 021/427-5864.

Meadows & Byrne This shop, with branches in many of Ireland's larger towns, offers attractive contemporary furniture, furnishings, and household items. It also has items of contemporary Irish design and crafts, including Jerpoint glass, Shanagarry and Jack O'Patsy pottery, and wrought-iron works by John Forkin. Academy St. © 021/427-2324.

Shandon Craft Centre Inside the Cork Butter Museum (p. 278), this is a general cooperative of local artisans. Sadly, their numbers have dwindled in recent years, but at the time of writing there were still a stained-glass worker, a jeweler, a ceramic restorer, a glass cutter, and a violin maker in residence. In the summer, folk, traditional, jazz, and classical musicians offer **free concerts** from 1 to 2pm. Cork Butter Museum, John Redmond St. For general information, call the museum: © 021/430-0600.

TWEEDS & WOOLENS

Blarney Woollen Mills   About 10km (6¹/₄ miles) northwest of Cork City, on the same grounds as the famous castle, this huge store (part of an Irish chain) in an 1824 mill is a one-stop source for Irish products: cashmere, crystal, wool—especially the distinctive Kelly green Blarney Castle–design wool sweaters, made on the premises. Best of all, it's open until 10pm every night in summer. The mills are on the grounds of Blarney Castle, so if you're going on a tour from Cork, you're already there! Blarney, County Cork. © 021/438-5280. www.blarney.ie.

Quills Woolen Market   For tweeds, woolens, and knits at the best prices, you might want to try this enterprise on Cork's busy main thoroughfare. It has branches in Killarney, Kenmare, and Sneem. 107 Patrick St. © 021/427-1717.

---

8 CORK AFTER DARK

PUBS

An Bodhran   There's Irish traditional music at this friendly pub every night starting at 9:30pm. The old-world decor includes stone walls, dark woods, and a huge stained-glass window. 42 Oliver Plunkett St. © 021/427-4544.

An Spailpin Fanac (The Migrant Worker)   Opposite the Beamish Brewery, this is another of the city's choice spots for traditional Irish music Sunday to Thursday, starting at 9:30pm. It dates from 1779, and is a lovely, soothing place with low ceilings, exposed brick walls, flagstone floors, open fireplaces, a simple wooden bar, and woven rush seats. 28–29 S. Main St. © 021/427-7949.

The Hibernian   This is a real insider's place, which everyone calls by its nickname, "the Hi-B." Located up a linoleum-covered flight of stairs (the entrance is beside the Minahan Chemist shop), it looks like a living room gone astray, with a mishmash of slightly threadbare upholstered armchairs and sofas strewn about at odd angles. The one-room bar is always crammed with a cross section of Cork—blue-collar types, students, artists, writers, eccentrics, and the beautiful, well-heeled set. 108 Oliver Plunkett St. (corner of Winthrop St.). © 021/427-2758.

Fun Facts   **Brewing Up Loyalty**

Ireland is known for its love of Guinness, but in Cork you're more likely to find locals drinking Murphy's or Beamish—the two locally brewed stouts. There is a definite sense of civic loyalty when it comes to drinking stout in this town. In fact, walk into any pub and order a "home and away" and you'll be presented with a pint of Murphy's and one of Guinness.

John Henchy & Sons   It's worth a walk up steep Summerhill Road, a northeast continuation of busy MacCurtain Street, to reach this classic pub near the Arbutus Lodge hotel. Established by John Henchy in 1884, it looks much the same as it did then, with leaded-glass windows, thick red curtains, and a small snug. The original Henchy family grocery store still operates adjacent to the pub. 40 St. Luke's. ✆ 021/450-7833.

The Long Valley Finds   This is one of those exceptional, family-run, old-fashioned bars that you fall in love with as soon as you enter—or even before you enter. To the left of the entrance hallway is a snug with etched-glass doors and chased-silver doorknobs. Those doors came from the *Celtic,* a White Star ocean liner that ran aground in Cork Harbor. Inside the main bar is one long, low-slung room with a polished wooden bar running its full length. The barmen wear white butchers' coats, Victorian-style, and provide a constant supply of pints to the laid-back, predominantly 30-something crowd. Winthrop St. ✆ 021/427-2144.

CLUBS: COMEDY, DANCE & MUSIC

You're likely to have the last laugh every Friday and Saturday night from 9:30pm at **City Limits Comedy Club,** 2 Coburg St. (✆ 021/450-1206; www.thecomedyclub.ie). You can purchase tickets in advance at **www.tickets.ie**. Ticket prices vary depending on the act.

Club FX   Starting at 11pm on Friday nights, there's "Planet of Sound" with four rooms of "delicious noise." In other words, you can expect retro, hip-hop, and two live bands. You'll find it down the lane opposite Jurys hotel on Washington Street. Lynch's St. ✆ 021/427-1120. Cover €6 ($9.60).

Half Moon   After the main stage empties, the Cork Opera House Bar, the Half Moon, swings into action. It schedules an ever-changing program of contemporary music, from blues and ragtime to pop and rock, with comedy gigs on occasion. Open Thursday to Sunday from 11:30pm to 3am. Cork Opera House, Emmet Place. ✆ 021/427-0022. Cover €8–€15 ($13–$24).

THE PERFORMING ARTS

Cork Opera House   Just off Lavitt's Quay along the River Lee, this is southwest Ireland's major venue for opera, drama, musicals, dance, and concerts. The original century-old opera house was completely gutted by a fire in 1955; this 1,000-seat replacement opened a decade later. Emmet Place. ✆ 021/427-0022. www.corkoperahouse.ie. Tickets €17–€50 ($27–$80); average €25 ($40).

Firkin Crane Cultural Centre   Dating from the 1840s, this unique rotunda was part of Cork's original Butter Exchange, and the building's name derives from Danish words pertaining to measures of butter. Although destroyed by fire in 1980, the site was rebuilt and opened as a cultural center in 1992. Today, it is dedicated to contemporary dance, and serves as a venue for new dance works and for touring national and international dance companies. Performances are occasional, with the best usually reserved for the Guinness Jazz Festival in October (see below). John Redmond St., Shandon. ✆ 021/450-7487. Tickets €15–€25 ($24–$40).

Guinness Jazz Festival ★★   Held every year since 1978, this is Ireland's biggest and most prestigious jazz festival. Big names such as Ella Fitzgerald, Oscar Peterson, and Stéphane Grappelli have played here over the years, and over a thousand performers from all over the world take part annually. It's held at various citywide venues in late October. Call ✆ 021/427-8979 or check **www.corkjazzfestival.com** for details. Tickets go on sale September 1; prices vary, some events are free.

Triskel Arts Centre This ever-growing arts center presents a variety of entertainment—drama, poetry readings, opera, and traditional music concerts. There is also a full curriculum of daytime art workshops and gallery talks as well. The in-house restaurant is a stylish place to have a light meal or a cappuccino. Tobin St., off S. Main St. © 021/427-2022. www.triskelart.com. Tickets €6–€20 ($9.60–$32); some performances are free.

THEATERS

Cork Arts Theatre Formerly based opposite the Opera House, this nonprofit theater moved to a new home in Carrolls Quay in late 2006, from where it presents contemporary dramas and musicals in an intimate, 100-seat performance space. Tickets cost around €6 to €15 ($9.60–$24), and occasionally there are such egalitarian initiatives as "pay what you want" previews. One of the benefits of the new venue is that it is now fully accessible to those with limited mobility. Camden Court, Carroll's Quay. © 021/450-5624. www.corkartstheatre.com.

Everyman Palace This elegant, historic theater 2 minutes from the bus and train station is well known as a showcase for quality new plays, both Irish and international. The Irish National Ballet also performs here regularly. 17 MacCurtain St. © 021/450-1673. www.everymanpalace.com. Tickets €15–€40 ($24–$64).

Out from Cork

The largest of the 32 Irish counties, and one of the most diverse, Cork offers a brief course in all things Irish. It has lively small cities, quiet country villages, rocky hills, picturesque beaches, and long stretches of flat, green farmland. Here, modern tourism (this is where you find the Blarney Castle, after all) meets workaday Irish life, and somehow they manage to exist peacefully, side by side.

West Cork is the county's most remote and wild region, with strikingly rugged coastal landscapes where long sandy beaches stretch out beneath sheer cliffs.

The county's capital, Cork (chapter 9), is a university town that keeps the population young and the arts scene ever evolving, and this also ensures that it has lots of affordable restaurants and interesting pubs and bars.

At the other end of the scale is lovely Kinsale, a small harbor town directly south of Cork City. It makes an ideal place to start any tour of this popular and endlessly absorbing county.

1 KINSALE & SOUTH CORK ★

Kinsale: 29km (18 miles) S of Cork, 87km (54 miles) SE of Killarney, 156km (97 miles) SE of Shannon Airport, 285km (177 miles) SW of Dublin, and 32km (20 miles) E of Clonakilty

Only 29km (18 miles) south of Cork City, **Kinsale** is a charming fishing village sitting on a picturesque harbor, surrounded by green hills. Considered the gateway to the western Cork seacoast, this artsy town of 3,000 residents supports dozens of little art galleries and craft shops filled with the work of regional artists. It also has also made a name for itself as a foodie town, home to award-winning restaurants and pubs. Kinsale draws food lovers year-round, particularly in October during the 4-day **Gourmet Festival.**

With its narrow, winding streets, well-kept 18th-century houses, imaginatively painted shop fronts, window boxes overflowing with colorful flowers, and a harbor full of sailboats, Kinsale is enchanting. The downside of all this is that the secret is out: This is a tourist town, so add parking problems, crowds, and tour buses to the list of qualities making up the city's ambience.

In 1601, this was the scene of the Battle of Kinsale, a turning point in Irish history. In September of that year, a Spanish fleet anchored at Kinsale and came under attack by English forces. An Irish army marched across virtually the whole of Ireland to reach and help the Spanish troops, but they were routed in a battle on Christmas Eve. In response to their support of the Spanish, Catholics were banned by English administrators from the town of Kinsale—a banishment that lasted for a century.

Just off the coast of the Old Head of Kinsale—about 8km (5 miles) west of the town—a German submarine sank the *Lusitania,* which was on its way from New York to Liverpool, in 1915. The attack, which killed 1,200, ultimately brought America into World War I. Some of the victims are buried in a local cemetery.

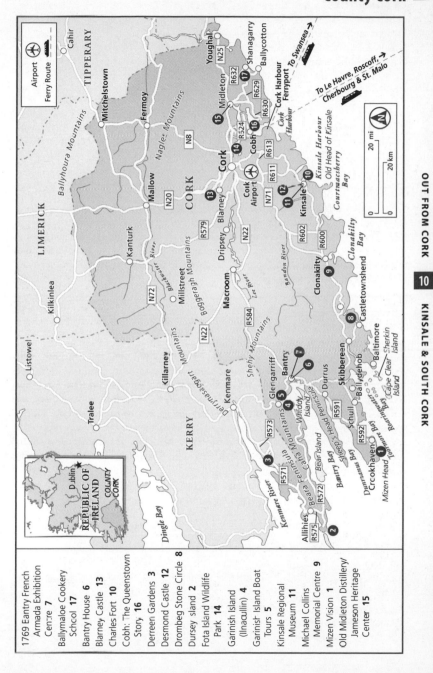

1769 Entry French
Armada Exhibition
Centre **7**

Ballymaloe Cookery
School **17**

Bantry House **6**

Blarney Castle **13**

Charles Fort **10**

Cobh: The Queenstown
Story **16**

Derreen Gardens **3**

Desmond Castle **12**

Drombeg Stone Circle **8**

Dursey sland **2**

Fota Island Wildlife
Park **14**

Garinish Island
(Ilnacullin) **4**

Garinish Island Boat
Tours **5**

Kinsale Regional
Museum **11**

Michael Collins
Memorial Centre **9**

Mizen Vision **1**

Old Mideton Distillery/
Jameson Heritage
Center **15**

GETTING THERE Bus Éireann (℘ 021/450-8188; www.buseireann.ie) operates regular daily service from Cork City to Kinsale. The arrival and departure point is the Esso gas station on Pier Road, opposite the tourist office.

Kinsale is 29km (18 miles) south of Cork City on the Airport Road; if you're coming by car from the west, use the N71. From East Cork, Cross River Ferries Ltd. provides regular service across Cork Harbour (see "East Cork," later in this chapter).

VISITOR INFORMATION The **Kinsale Tourist Office,** Pier Road, Kinsale (℘ 021/477-2234; www.kinsale.ie), is open March through November; call for hours.

GETTING AROUND Kinsale's streets are so narrow that walking is the best way to get around, and the town is so small that there is no local transport; if you need a taxi to outlying areas, call **Kinsale Cabs** (℘ 021/477-2642) or **Cabs 3000** (℘ 021/477-7126).

SEEING THE SIGHTS

Charles Fort ★ Southeast of Kinsale, at the head of the harbor, this coastal landmark dates from the late 17th century. A classic star-shaped fort, it was constructed to prevent foreign naval forces from entering the harbor of Kinsale, then an important trading town. Additions and improvements were made throughout the 18th and 19th centuries, and the fort remained garrisoned until 1921. Across the river is James Fort (1602). The complex includes an exhibition center and cafe.

Off the Scilly rd., Summer Cove, County Cork. ℘ 021/477-2263. Admission €3.70 ($5.90) adults, €2.60 ($4.15) seniors, €1.30 ($2.10) students and children, €8.70 ($14) families. Tours available on request. Mid-March to Oct daily 10am–6pm; Nov to mid-March daily 10am–5pm.

Desmond Castle ★ Built around 1500 as a customhouse by the earl of Desmond, this tower house has a dark history: Spanish troops occupied it during the battle of 1601, and the British later used it as a prison for captured American sailors during the War of Independence. Locally, it's known as "French Prison" because French prisoners were kept here during the mid–18th century. In a horrible accident, 54 French prisoners died here in a fire in 1747. During the Great Famine, the building was used as a workhouse for the starving populace. Now, in more peaceful times, the castle is at last benign. Today it is the home of the **International Museum of Wine,** celebrating the Irish emigrants who colonized the wine trade throughout the world after being forced to leave their own shores.

Cork St., Kinsale, County Cork. ℘ 021/477-4855. Admission €2.90 ($4.65) adults, €2.10 ($3.35) seniors, €1.30 ($2.10) students and children, €7.40 ($12) families. Mid-Apr to Oct daily 10am–6pm (last admission 45 min. before closing).

Kinsale Regional Museum This small but enthusiastic museum in the historic Market House (1600) tells the town's story from its earliest days, with paintings, photos, and memorabilia highlighting such events as the Battle of Kinsale in 1601 and the sinking of the *Lusitania* in 1915. It's all you ever wanted to know about Kinsale, and so much more.

Market Sq., Kinsale, County Cork. ℘ 021/477-7930. Admission €2.50 ($4) adults, €1.50 ($2.40) seniors and students, free for children. Apr–Sept daily 10am–6pm; Oct–Dec and Feb–Mar Mon–Fri 11am–1pm and 3–5pm.

SHOPPING

Boland's Kinsale Crafts This is a quality shop for made-in-Ireland goods, such as traditional Kinsale smocks, Aran sweaters, pottery, quilts, Irish leather belts, and jewelry. Pearse St., Kinsale, County Cork. (✆ **021/477-2161.** www.bolandkinsale.com.

Crackpots Pottery This shop holds a mix of functional and artistic pottery made by local artists. Some work is done on-site in the workshop; there are also a showroom and a good restaurant. 3 Cork St., Kinsale, County Cork. (✆ **021/477-2847.**

Granny's Bottom Drawer Traditional Irish linens and lace are the ticket here. It's well stocked with tablecloths, pillowcases, Victorian table runners, and hand-crocheted place mats. 53 Main St., Kinsale, County Cork. (✆ **021/477-4839.**

Jagoes Mill Pottery Just over 3km (2 miles) from Kinsale, Irene Gahan Ryle runs a small pottery workshop in an 18th-century mill. Her work has a good balance of practicality and beauty, and it is only sold from the studio workshop and selected galleries. Jagoes Mill, Kinsale, County Cork. (✆ **021/477-2771.**

Kinsale Crystal Started in 1991 by a former Waterford Crystal master craftsman, this small workshop produces traditional full-lead, mouth-blown, and hand-cut crystal. Visitors are welcome to watch the process and purchase the sparkling results, which are sold nowhere else in Ireland. Market St., Kinsale, County Cork. (✆ **021/477-4493.** www.kinsale crystal.ie.

Kinsale Silver Kinsale silver traces its origins back more than 300 years. The Dolan family runs this silversmith workshop, where you can watch as each piece is forged by hand, using traditional tools. Pearse St., Kinsale, County Cork. (✆ **021/477-4359.** www.kinsale silver.com.

SPORTS & OUTDOOR PURSUITS

BICYCLING Kinsale Harbour is perfectly designed for biking. To rent a bike, contact the **Hire Shop,** 18 Main St. ((✆ **021/477-4884**). Rentals average around €15 ($24) a day, €70 ($112) per week, depending on equipment. The shop is open weekdays from 8:30am to 6pm. In summertime, it's also open Saturday from 9am to 6pm and Sunday from 10:30am to 5:30pm.

FISHING Kinsale is one of the southern Irish coast's sea-angling centers. There are numerous shipwrecks in the area for wreck fishing (not the least of them the *Lusitania,* near the Old Head of Kinsale). **Kinsale Deep Sea Angling,** Pier Head ((✆ **021/477-8944**), arranges sea fishing from Kinsale Harbor, as well as whale-watching expeditions. Prices vary widely, so call or e-mail (willemvandijk@eircom.net) for more information.

   For fishing tackle or to rent a rod and other equipment, try the **Hire Shop** (see above).

GOLF Embraced by the sea on three sides, the nothing-short-of-spectacular **Old Head Golf Links** ((✆ **021/477-8444;** www.oldhead.com) is Tiger Woods's favorite Irish course. Named one of *Golf Magazine*'s "Top 100 Courses in the World," it is hauntingly beautiful, rain or shine. The course retains a resident environmentalist to ensure that crucial wildlife habitats are not disturbed. But golfing here costs big money: Greens fees are currently a whopping €295 ($472) for one 18-hole round. Caddy fees run €30 ($48) for a junior caddy or €50 ($80) for a senior caddy, and golf carts can be rented for €60 ($96).

OUT FROM CORK

10

KINSALE & SOUTH CORK

If that's too rich for your blood, there's a fine par-72 championship course at the **Fota Island Golf Club,** Carrigtwohill (© **021/488-3700;** www.fotaisland.ie), with greens fees of €90 ($144) on Monday, €100 ($160) Tuesday to Thursday, €115 ($184) on Friday, and €120 ($192) weekends.

Less expensive is the **Kinsale Golf Club,** Kinsale (© **021/477-4722;** www.kinsale golf.com), which has two courses, about 5km (3 miles) north of town. The 18-hole, par-71 Farrangalway course has greens fees of €35 ($56) Monday to Thursday, and €40 ($64) Friday to Sunday, while the smaller course at Ringenane charges €25 ($40) daily.

SAILING Yacht charters are available from **Sail Ireland Charters,** Trident Hotel, County Cork (© **021/477-2927;** www.sailireland.com). From Kinsale it is possible to sail to Bantry Bay and back on a 1-week charter, or to the Dingle Peninsula on a 2-week charter. Prices for a six-berth, 36-foot yacht run €1,595 to €2,750 ($2,552–$4,400) per week, not including outboard or skipper. A 10-berth, 49-foot yacht runs €2,850 to €3,375 ($4,560–$5,400) per week.

Sovereign Sailing (© **021/477-4145;** www.sovereignsailing.com) offers a full range of yacht sailing options for all ages and levels of experience. Between March and November, day- or half-day sails from Kinsale head out every day. Rates vary widely based on the kind of sailing you try.

TENNIS Court time can be had at the **Oysterhaven Activity Centre** (© **021/477-0738;** www.oysterhaven.com), 8km (5 miles) from Kinsale, for €15 ($24) per hour. It's open Monday to Thursday 10am to 9pm, Friday and Saturday 10am to 6pm, and Sunday 1 to 6pm.

WALKING The **Scilly Walk** is a signposted pedestrian path along the sea that runs from Scilly, the community across the harbor from Kinsale, all the way to Charles Fort. If you continue to walk south along the sea from Charles Fort, you'll find another path that follows the headland to the tip of **Frower Point,** which offers great views across the harbor to the Old Head of Kinsale. The complete walk from Kinsale to Frower Point is 8km (5 miles) each way, and every part of it is quite rewarding.

One of the most pleasant ways to spend an hour in these parts is to take local resident Don Herily's excellent walking tour—or **Historic Stroll,** as he prefers to call it—of Kinsale town. Don and his fellow guide, Barry Moloney, have been leading visitors around the main sights since the mid-1990s, and their local knowledge is second to none. Highlights include the 12th-century St. Multose Church; a walk past Desmond Castle; and the harbor, where the 17th-century Battle of Kinsale is recounted with an enthusiasm only found in people who really love their subject. The tour starts outside the tourist office at 11:15am every day from April to October and costs €7 ($11) adults, €1 ($1.60) children. For details, call © **021/477-2873** or 087/250-0731, or check out www.historicstrollkinsale.com.

WATERSPORTS The **Oysterhaven Activity Centre** (© **021/477-0738**), 8km (5 miles) from Kinsale, rents windsurfers, dinghies, and kayaks. It's open Monday to Thursday 10am to 9pm, Friday and Saturday 10am to 6pm, and Sunday 1 to 6pm.

WHALE-WATCHING Whale-watching is a popular activity in summer, and one of the best companies is **Whale of a Time** (© **086/328-3250;** www.whaleofatime.ie), which uses rigid inflatable boats to cause less disruption to the creatures of the deep. **Kinsale Deep Sea Angling** (see "Fishing," above) also offers dolphin-, whale-, and seal-watching trips, as does **Angling Kinsale** (© **021/477-8054;** www.anglingkinsale.com).

Expensive

The Blue Haven ★★ With a sophisticated design and a friendly attitude, this place is just about all a small inn should be. All the rooms are chic, with a creamy color scheme and a real sense of elegance. There's a highly rated—and very romantic—restaurant (see review below) here, as well as a sophisticated, relaxing bar, so you never have to leave the building if you don't want to. *Tip:* If you want a canopy bed, request one of the rooms in the new wing, as these have more traditional decor, with canopy beds, window seats, armoires, and brass fixtures.

3 Pearse St., Kinsale, County Cork. © **021/477-2209.** Fax 021/477-4268. www.bluehavenkinsale.com. 17 units. €160–€240 ($256–$384) double. Rates include full breakfast. AE, MC, V. **Amenities:** Restaurant (seafood); cafe; bar. *In room:* TV.

The Harbour Lodge ★ This wonderfully appointed guesthouse has a bright, contemporary decor and sweeping views of the water. All the rooms are nonsmoking, and furnished with brass beds, quilts in pastel hues, and modern art. The best five rooms have balconies facing the harbor—you could nearly swan dive right into the water—while the rest overlook the lush garden. There's a cozy, traditional parlor and a large sunlit conservatory with panoramic maritime views. Scilly, this part of Kinsale, is a 10-minute walk along the harbor from the bustling town center. Consequently, it's a quieter alternative to hotels in town, but also farther from the action.

Scilly, Kinsale, County Cork. © **021/477-2376.** Fax 021/477-2675. www.harbourlodge.com. 9 units. €198–€240 ($317–$384) double. Rates include full breakfast. AE, DC, MC, V. Free parking. **Amenities:** Conservatory; sitting room. *In room:* TV, tea/coffeemaker, hair dryer.

The Old Bank House ★★ This well-restored, waterside Georgian town house–turned-B&B is a calming place. It's got a kind of low-key luxury, as demonstrated in the well-chosen antiques and the plush, Egyptian cotton towels and bathrobes. Prices are a bit high for what you get, but the rooms and the views are lovely. Rooms at the front of the house overlook the sailboat-dotted harbor, and the views get significantly better the higher you go. The largest (and priciest) room is the new Collection Suite, with a lovely sitting room, open fireplace, and Jacuzzi bath. *Tip:* Prices drop nearly by half in the off season.

11 Pearse St. (next to post office), Kinsale, County Cork. © **021/477-4075.** Fax 021/477-4296. www. oldbankhousekinsale.com. 17 units. €200–€250 ($320–$400) double; €260–€330 ($416–$528) suite. Rates include full breakfast. AE, MC, V. **Amenities:** Concierge. *In room:* TV.

Moderate

Blindgate House ★ This small, contemporary hotel has a valuable combination of a central location and real sense of style. Its look is a good mix of contemporary dark-wood furnishings, natural fabrics in soothing neutral tones, polished wood floors, and serene lighting. Guest rooms are spacious and elegantly simple, while providing modern conveniences such as satellite TV and modem connections. All in all, you don't normally expect to find this level of designer savvy at this price level. It's a Zen haven amid the bustle of Kinsale town.

Blindgate, Kinsale, County Cork. © **021/477-7858.** Fax 021/477-7868. www.blindgatehouse.com. 11 units. €115–€170 ($184–$272) double. Rates include full breakfast. AE, MC, V. Free parking. Closed mid-Dec to mid-Mar. **Amenities:** Residents' lounge; babysitting; nonsmoking rooms. *In room:* TV, radio, dataport, tea/coffeemaker, hair dryer.

The Old Presbytery   Noreen McEvoy runs this little B&B with an eye for detail and a passion for hospitality. Set on a calm street, it is a labyrinth of half-staircases and landings, giving each room a private feel (though it can be tricky to find your way back if you leave for a while). Guest rooms are winningly decorated with brass and cast-iron beds, old armoires, and other antiques. There are also two self-catering apartments that are perfect for families or friends traveling together. Breakfasts here are fabulous.

43 Cork St., Kinsale, County Cork. (C) **021/477-2027.** Fax 021/477-2166. www.oldpres.com. 10 units. €110–€170 ($176–$272) double; €180 ($288) self-catering apt. Rates include full Irish breakfast. MC, V. Free parking. *In room:* Hair dryer.

Inexpensive

Walyunga (Value)   This sweet, modern B&B with ocean views sits in the peaceful countryside 5 minutes' drive outside Kinsale. The noisiest things around here are the birds. Inside, all the guest rooms are nonsmoking, comfortable, and decorated with soft bedspreads and neutral tones. The spacious living room is a good place to meet other guests, and breakfasts are great here. Rooms have no TVs, but there's a shared set in the lounge.

Sandycove, Kinsale, County Cork. (C) **021/477-4126.** www.walyunga.com. 5 units. €70–€80 ($112–$128) double. 25% discount for children 11 and under sharing room with parents. Rates include full Irish breakfast. MC, V. Closed Nov–Mar.

WHERE TO DINE

Expensive

The Blue Haven ★ SEAFOOD   Of all the restaurants in Kinsale, this hotel eatery has the biggest following, if only because there's something to suit most budgets and appetites. There are two places to eat: the atmospheric bar for first-rate bar food (seafood quiches, seafood pancakes, oak-smoked salmon) or the sky-lit restaurant for a full a la carte menu of fresh seafood, including salmon cooked slowly over oak chips. Other specialties include Irish beef filet with horseradish dauphinoise, Parmesan crumbled crab claws, and local venison (in season). The wines have Irish connections; they come from many of the French wineries that were started by Irish exiles.

3 Pearse St., Kinsale, County Cork. (C) **021/477-2209.** www.bluehavenkinsale.com. Reservations recommended. Main courses at the bar €10–€20 ($16–$32); fixed 3-course dinner €35 ($56); dinner main courses €20–€40 ($32–$64). AE, MC, V. Restaurant daily 7–10pm. Bar daily 12:15–3pm and 6:30–10pm.

Jim Edwards ★ CONTINENTAL   This classy, nautical "gastropub" is known as much for its refined menu as for its convivial atmosphere. Dishes are elegant: boneless duck with cassis and red-currant sauce, rack of lamb, king prawns in light basil-cream sauce, medallions of monkfish with fresh herbs, a variety of steaks, and a range of vegetarian dishes.

Market Quay, off Emmet Place, Kinsale, County Cork. (C) **021/477-2541.** www.jimedwardskinsale.com. Reservations recommended for dinner. Dinner main courses €16–€30 ($26–$48). AE, MC, V. Daily 12:30–11pm for bar food; lunch 12:30–3pm; dinner 6–10:30pm.

Max's Wine Bar Restaurant ★ MODERN IRISH   For more than 20 years, this old-world town house with outdoor dining space has been a local favorite. The fare ranges from light snacks to full meals—grilled mussels are a specialty. Other dishes include goat-cheese pastas, fresh soups, and roast lamb with lavender sauce.

Main St., Kinsale, County Cork. (C) **021/477-2443.** Reservations recommended. Fixed-price early-bird 3-course dinner €19 ($30); dinner main courses €18–€29 ($29–$46). MC, V. Mon and Wed–Sun 12:30–3pm and 6:30–10:30pm. Closed Nov–Feb.

Fishy Fishy Cafe ★★ SEAFOOD   This marvelous joint has it all—the food is outstanding, prices could be worse, and the only drawback is that it's only open for lunch. There's nothing complicated about it: fresh seafood from local sources (they'll even tell you the names of who caught what if asked), fresh vegetables, farmhouse cheeses, imaginative salads, and homemade breads. The cold dishes are wonderful, but its culinary talents shine with the seafood chowder, grilled John Dory, and tiger prawns with bacon. Be forewarned that the dozen or so tables are in demand, and you can wait 30 minutes. An early or late lunch beats the rush.

Guardwell (next to St. Multose Church in center of town), Kinsale, County Cork. ✆ **021/470-0415.** www. fishyfishy.ie. Reservations not accepted. Lunch average €16–€22 ($26–$35). MC, V. Daily noon–3:45pm.

The Little Skillet ★ IRISH   This popular place has a feel-good atmosphere, with its big open hearth and rough stone walls. The kitchen serves up tasty Irish food, with a smattering of international fare; porter and port beef casserole, Kinsale fish hot pot, and local pork and herb sausages share the menu with Cajun chicken, fajitas, and Thai vegetable stir-fry. When they're busy, you wait in the bar across the street and they call you when your table is ready. (You can even bring your pint back with you.) A warm and friendly place, it's perfect for a chilly day.

Main St., Kinsale, County Cork. ✆ **021/477-4202.** Reservations recommended. Main courses €18–€20 ($29–$32). MC, V. Daily 12:30–2:30pm and 6–10:30pm.

PUBS

The Bulman   About a mile along the quay in the direction of Fort Charles, this pub draws a sweater-and-Wellington-boot contingent of fishermen and yachtsmen. There's also a smattering of artists, students, and expats, all of whom come for the pints and the lovely location. Twilight is great here—you can take your drink outside, listen to the waves lap up against the wharf, and watch the gulls turn a shimmery orange as the sun sets. Summercove, Kinsale, County Cork. ✆ **021/477-2131.**

The Greyhound   Photographers are enchanted with the exterior of this pub, with its neat flower boxes, rows of stout barrels, and handmade signs. Inside it's cozy and known for hearty pub food—farmhouse soups, seafood pancakes, shepherd's pie, and Irish stew. Market Sq., Kinsale, County Cork. ✆ **021/477-2889.**

Lord Kingsale   A touch of elegance prevails at this handsome pub, decorated with polished horse brass. It takes its name from the first Anglo-Norman baron who took charge of this Irish port in 1223. You'll often find evening singalongs here, and the soup-and-sandwich pub food is very good. There is nightly live entertainment in the summer. Main St. and Market Quay, Kinsale, County Cork. ✆ **021/477-2371.**

1601   Named after the year of the Battle of Kinsale, this vintage pub is popular with locals and visitors alike. There are three sections: pub, restaurant, and coffeehouse. If you've come to have a pint, head into the back room, where there's a fireplace and seating for only about 50 people. Pearse St., Kinsale, County Cork. ✆ **021/477-2529.**

The Spaniard Inn (Finds)   High on Compass Hill overlooking the harbor, this atmospheric pub has picturesque whitewashed walls and a thatched roof, and if you have your pint outside while watching the sun set, somebody will probably take your picture. Inside, low ceilings create an intimate feel, and a fireplace warms the main room. Named for Don Juan de Aguila, who rallied his fleet with the Irish in an unsuccessful attempt to

OUT FROM CORK

10

KINSALE & SOUTH CORK

defeat the British, the pub has live music nightly in the summer and on weekends at other times of the year, and it tends to get very crowded. On Sunday year-round, there is a jazz-blues session at 5pm. Scilly, Kinsale, County Cork. *C* **021/477-2436.**

The White House With its Georgian facade, this is yet another pub that tempts many a visitor to take a photograph. Inside, along with the pub itself, there's a popular bistro, the Antibes Room, with bright decor and a comfortable bar. End of Pearse St., Kinsale, County Cork. *C* **021/477-2125.**

---

2 EAST CORK

Lying 24km (15 miles) east of Cork City, the harbor town of **Cobh** (pronounced *Cove,* meaning "haven" in Irish), was once Ireland's chief port of emigration, with three or four transatlantic liners calling each week. For thousands of Irish emigrants, particularly during the famine years and in the early part of the 20th century, Cobh was the last bit of Ireland they ever saw. It was also the last port of call for the Belfast-built RMS *Titanic* before it sank spectacularly in April 1912. Cobh is still a heavily industrialized port.

The county's major coastal town is **Youghal** (pronounced *Yawl*), near the Waterford border. A leading beach resort and fishing port, Youghal is loosely associated with Sir Walter Raleigh, who was once the mayor and is said to have planted Ireland's first potatoes here. From a tourist's-eye view, present-day Youghal is a moderately attractive, congested town with a grand stretch of beach just beyond the center.

ESSENTIALS

GETTING THERE If you're driving from Cork City, take the main Waterford road (N25) east. Exit at R624 for Fota and Cobh, or R632 for Shanagarry and Ballycotton. Midleton and Youghal have their own signposted exits. If you're coming from West Cork and want to bypass Cork City (a good idea during rush hour), take the car ferry operated by **Cross River Ferries Ltd.,** Atlantic Quay, Cobh (*C* **021/481-1485**). It links Carrigaloe, near Cobh, with Glenbrook, south of Cork City. Ferries run daily from 7:15am to 12:45am; average crossing time is 5 minutes. No reservations are necessary. Fares are payable on the ferry. Cars cost €4 ($6.40) one-way, €6 ($9.60) round-trip.

Irish Rail (*C* **021/450-64777;** www.irishrail.ie) operates daily train service between Cork City and Cobh via Fota Island. **Bus Éireann** (*C* **021/450-8188;** www.buseireann. ie) also provides daily service from Cork City to Cobh and other points in East Cork.

VISITOR INFORMATION The **tourist office** is open 9:30am to 5:30pm Monday through Friday, 1 to 5pm Saturday and Sunday, at the Old Yacht Club in the lower harbor at Cobh (*C* **021/481-3301**). **Seasonal tourist offices** operate at 4 Main St., Midleton (*C* **021/461-3702**), and Market Square, Youghal (*C* **024/20170**), from May or June through September. Hours are daily 9:30am to 5:30pm.

SEEING THE SIGHTS

Ballymaloe Cookery School ★ Professional and amateur cooks flock here from all over the world to sit near the whisk of Darina Allen. It all started with Darina's mother-in-law, Myrtle, whose evangelization of Ireland's bounty of fresh produce at Ballymaloe House restaurant (p. 296) elevated Irish "country house" cooking to gourmet status. The Allen family's success led to the founding of this cooking school, which offers dozens of courses ranging in length from a half-day to 12 weeks. Topics include bread making, tapas, sushi, vegetarian cuisine, family food, barbecue, and holiday cooking. Prices start at around €100 ($160) and rise to the stratosphere. The beautiful, extensive **gardens** ★ on the grounds are open to visitors from April to October. Admission to the gardens is €6 ($9.60) adults; family discounts available. The **Garden Café,** open Wednesday to Sunday 11am to 6pm, serves morning coffee, memorable light lunches, and afternoon tea.

Kinoith, Shanagarry, County Cork. ℂ **021/464-6785.** Fax 021/464-6909. www.cookingisfun.ie. Half-day courses €105 ($168); 1- to 5-day courses €175–€835 ($280–$1,336). Accommodations for students in self-catering cottages €28 ($45) sharing, 45 ($72) single per night extra. Open year-round; schedule varies.

Cobh: The Queenstown Story ★★   More than 2.5 million people from across Ireland departed from Cobh in the mid-1800s (it was then known as Queenstown) for new lives in the United States, Canada, and Australia, so the city became synonymous with farewells. This intelligent heritage center commemorates Cobh's heartbreaking history as the last port of call for emigrants, many of them doomed to take convict ships to Australia, coffin ships to America, and transatlantic liners like the ill-fated *Titanic* and *Lusitania*. In a beautifully restored Victorian railway station, the center tells the story of the city, its harbor, and the Irish exodus in a series of displays, films, and exhibits. The center also has a restaurant, a shop, and a genealogical referral service.

Cobh Railway Station, Cobh, County Cork. ℂ **021/481-3591.** Admission €7.10 ($11) adults, €6 ($9.60) seniors and students, €3 ($4.80) children 8–12, free for children 7 and under, €20 ($32) families. Daily 10am–6pm. Last admission 5pm. Closed Christmas week.

Fota Island Wildlife Park & Arboretum ★★★ (**Kids**)   Fota Wildlife Park is a modern, thoughtfully designed zoo, which takes away much of the guilt one often gets from visiting zoos. Wherever possible, the animals roam free with no obvious barriers, mixing and mingling with other species, and sometimes with human visitors. As with most zoos, it's got its fair share of rare and endangered zebras, ostriches, antelopes, and the like. Kangaroos, macaws, and lemurs have the run of 16 hectares (40 acres) of grassland. Only the cheetahs are behind conventional fencing. Admission includes entrance to the adjacent **Fota Arboretum.** First planted in the 1820s, it contains exotic trees and plants from temperate regions around the world. A coffee shop, a small amusement park for young children, a tour train, picnic tables, and gift shop are on the grounds.

Fota Island, Carrigtwohill (16km/10 miles east of Cork on Cobh Rd.), County Cork. ℂ **021/481-2678.** www.fotawildlife.ie. Admission €13 ($21) adults; €8.50 ($14) seniors, students, and children; €54 ($86) families. Mon–Sat 10am–6pm; Sun 11am–6pm. Rail: Cork-Cobh line from Cork City to Fota station. Closed Dec 25–26.

The Old Midleton Distillery/Jameson Heritage Centre ★   This is sort of a Willy Wonka factory of booze. In a brightly colored building, with a huge copper vat out front, shining in the sun, this distillery and visitor center are all about smooth Irish whiskey. It's all done in a modern factory now, but the center of production for Jameson Whiskey still holds many of the original 1825 structures, all meticulously preserved. For the truly interested, there's a film to watch in the visitor center as well as a whiskey-making demonstration, followed by a tasting after the tour.

Distillery Rd., off Main St., Midleton, County Cork. ℂ **021/461-3594.** www.jamesonwhiskey.com/omd. Admission €13 ($21) adults, €9 ($14) seniors, €9.50 ($15) children, €25 ($40) families. Daily 10am–6pm. Tours on request; last tour at 5pm.

Stephen Pearce Pottery   Potter Stephen Pearce creates his popular terra-cotta-and-white earthenware pieces in this sunny, sky-lit studio showroom. Downstairs is the workshop and upstairs is a shop with a desirable array of glass, jewelry, linens, and the entire range of Pearce's pottery. You can watch the team of potters at work and, whenever possible, children get a piece of clay to make their own masterpieces. The workshop is open Monday to Friday from 10am to 5pm, Saturday from 10am to 6pm, and Sunday from noon to 6pm. Shanagarry, County Cork. ✆ **021/464-6807.**

Youghal Pottery   This workshop offers a very good selection of pottery and ceramics in stoneware, earthenware, porcelain, and smoke-fired raku, all handmade on the premises. The shop also offers a selection of crafts, woolens, and textiles. On N25 to Waterford, 1km (²⁄₃ mile) from Youghal. ✆ **024/91222.**

WHERE TO STAY & DINE
Expensive

Aherne's Townhouse and Restaurant ★★   In the heart of a busy seaside resort, this cozy restaurant with rooms has been penned into many travelers' journals because of its first-rate seafood. Comfortable and stylishly furnished, the guest rooms are all quite large by Irish standards. Most are more like hotel suites than rooms—each with king-size beds, antiques, and designer fabrics. There are two bars and a library-style sitting room, but the main reason to stay here is to be near the classic seafood restaurant. The French-influenced cooking makes the most of the local catch—Blackwater salmon, giant prawn tails, rock oysters, and lobsters. Even the bar food is worth a detour—seafood pies, chowders, crab sandwiches, and crisp salads. Breakfasts here are a real indulgence, served in front of the fire.

163 N. Main St., Youghal, County Cork. ✆ **800/223-6510** in the U.S., or 024/92424. Fax 024/93633. www.ahernes.com. 12 units. €210–€280 ($336–$448) double. Bar lunch from €10 ($16); dinner main courses €25–€34 ($40–$54). Rates include full breakfast. AE, DC, MC, V. **Amenities:** Restaurant (seafood); 2 bars; nonsmoking rooms; library. *In room:* TV, hair dryer, garment press.

Ballymaloe House ★   Combining a Georgian farmhouse facade with the tower of a 14th-century castle, this ivy-covered enclave of hospitality run by the Allen family is on a working farm, complete with grazing sheep and cows. Ballymaloe is about 23km (14 miles) southeast of Cork City, less than 3km (2 miles) from Ballycotton Bay. Guest rooms are furnished in informal, comfortable, even rather rustic style. Make no mistake—the main attraction is the dining room, a pioneer of Ireland's "country house" culinary style. It is French-inspired and relies on local seafood and produce, accompanied by fresh vegetables from the garden. The kitchen's success has spawned an acclaimed **cooking school** (p. 294) and a shelf of Allen family cookbooks. If you're interested in Ballymaloe only for the food, consider staying at the more stylish Barnabrow Country House nearby (see below), and popping over here for dinner.

Shanagarry, Midleton, County Cork. ✆ **800/323-5463** in the U.S., or 021/465-2531. Fax 021/465-2021. www.ballymaloe.ie. 33 units. €220–€320 ($352–$512) double. Dinner averages €60 ($96). Rates include full breakfast. AE, DC, MC, V. **Amenities:** Restaurant (Country House); outdoor swimming pool; 9-hole golf course; tennis courts; sitting room. *In room:* Hair dryer.

Bayview Hotel ★   It's hard to imagine a more romantic location for a seaside hotel, overlooking miles of spectacular coastline stretching out from Ballycotton Harbour. This former manor house has certainly benefited from some TLC over the years, in the capable hands of owners John and Carnel O'Brien, who completely restored the place when they turned it into a hotel in the early 1990s. Rooms are bright and airy with modern furnishings and subtle, chocolate-and-cream tones. All have sea views. If you're in the mood to splurge, **Capricho** is one of the most imaginative restaurants in the area. Typical dishes (which can be served in the garden if the weather's good) include local salmon with mustard and champagne sauce, or maple and vanilla roast pork with parsnip-and-apple purée and white turnip gratin. Elaborate desserts include the spectacular "Rebel Yell," an iced parfait with Southern Comfort, caramelized orange, and cocoa sorbet. Oh my.

Ballycotton, County Cork. ☎ **021/464-6746**. Fax 021/464-6075. www.thebayviewhotel.com. 35 units. €100–€220 ($160–$352) double. Dinner main courses €28–€33 ($45–$53). Rates include full breakfast. AE, MC, V. **Amenities:** Restaurant (modern European); bar; babysitting; gardens. *In room:* TV.

Moderate

Barnabrow Country House ★★ (Kids) Geraldine O'Brien has created a completely original, highly romantic, and stylish place to stay in the rolling hills of East Cork. Guest rooms, in the main house and in stone buildings off the courtyard, are bathed in warm hues of terra cotta and cool pale blue, with polished hardwood floors, brass beds, and an eccentric collection of African furniture and crafts. Some of the bathrooms are huge, with big, claw-foot tubs. For families, this is that elusive (no, make that near-impossible) find: the truly family-friendly-style hotel. There are cots, cribs, babysitters, and special children's menus. Kids are safe to roam freely, and there are plenty of tame animals to meet and pet—donkeys, ducks, hens, geese, sheep, goats—plus a playground for letting off steam.

Cloyne, Midleton, County Cork. ☎ **021/465-2534**. www.barnabrowhouse.ie. 19 units. €130–€180 ($208–$288) double. Rates include full breakfast. AE, MC, V. **Amenities:** Restaurant (Continental); lounge; babysitting. *In room:* TV, hair dryer.

Harty's Restaurant ★ (Finds) CONTINENTAL In the little medieval village of Cloyne, this unfussy, whitewashed eatery is one of the best little restaurants you could ever hope to happen upon. Owner/chef Eamon Harty's food is straightforward—chargrilled steaks; wild salmon with a cool, cucumber sauce; and pan-fried fish cakes with lemon. As is true with all great chefs, Harty's success comes from choosing the freshest vegetables, ripest fruits, and highest-quality meats and fish, then knowing what to do with them. His homemade breads are heavenly, too.

Cloyne, near Midleton, County Cork. ☎ **021/465-2401**. Dinner main courses €16–€23 ($26–$37). MC, V. Daily 10:30am–9pm.

Self-Catering

Myrtleville Oceanside Retreat This timbered ocean-side retreat—a curiosity in Ireland, where most cottages are built of stone—offers a touch of Cape Cod and a lot more. It's right on the sea, with stunning views from the wraparound deck and living room. Convenient to Cork City, Kinsale, golfing, yachting, deep-sea fishing, and a sandy beach, it's on a small country road, facing the Atlantic at precisely the spot where Victor Hugo worked on *Les Misérables*. Although the house is 80 years old, its kitchen appliances are new, its decor graciously inviting. It sleeps six people comfortably.

Contact Elegant Ireland ☎ **01/475-1632**. Fax 01/475-1012. www.elegant.ie. 3 double bedrooms (1 with king-size bed, 2 with queen-size). €1,800–€2,500 ($2,880–$4,000) per week, including utilities. MC, V. **Amenities:** Babysitting (by prior arrangement). *In room:* Full kitchen, washer/dryer.

3 WEST CORK

For many, West Cork is Ireland's ultimate destination—not quite as crowded with tourists as Kerry, yet every bit as charming. It shares with Kerry a photo-friendly craggy topography and jagged coastline. It's impossible to make good time on the roads here, as they tend to be narrow and sinuous, twisting along rivers, through valleys, around mountains, and passing through lovely small towns. Those willing to slow down and go with the flow are amply rewarded. You'll probably come across at least one puzzling rural intersection that's completely unsignposted, and have to slow down for a herd of sheep slowly making its way down a country lane. In places, the public route that hugs the coast narrows to just one lane and delivers heart-stopping views. Over time, you may even come to think of the roads here as one of West Cork's great pleasures.

Some of the most beautiful coastal scenery (and severe weather) is on the islands. **Cape Clear ★**, home to a bird-watching observatory, is also a well-known Gaeltacht: Both schoolchildren and adults come here to work on their Gaelic skills each summer. **Dursey Island,** off the tip of the Beara Peninsula, is accessible by cable car. **Garinish Island** in Glengarriff is the site of Ilnacullin, an elaborate Italianate garden.

West Cork is known for its enticing and colorful towns. A cluster of artists gives **Bally-dehob** a creative flair. At the local butcher, colorful drawings of cattle, pigs, and chickens indicate what's available, and a mural on the outside wall of a pub depicts a traditional-music session. Other notable enclaves include the buzzy, seaside town of **Skibbereen** (meaning "Little Boat Harbor"), where impromptu traditional-music sessions are commonplace in its 22 pubs; the immaculate, flower box–on-every-sill town of **Clonakilty;** the yachting town **Schull;** and **Barleycove,** a remote, wind-swept resort that's the last stop before Mizen Head and the sheer cliffs at the island's southernmost tip.

ESSENTIALS

GETTING THERE   N71 is the main road into West Cork from north and south; from Cork and points east, N22 also leads to West Cork.

Bus Éireann (© **021/450-8188;** www.buseireann.ie) provides daily bus service to the principal towns in West Cork.

VISITOR INFORMATION   Contact the **Skibbereen Tourist Office,** North Street, Skibbereen, County Cork (© **028/21766**). It is open year-round Monday to Friday 9:15am to 5:30pm, with weekend and extended hours May through September. There are **seasonal tourist offices** in the Square, Bantry (© **027/50229**), and Rossa Street, Clonakilty (© **023/33226**), operating from May or June through August or September. The **Beara Tourism & Development Association,** the Square, Castletownbere (© **027/70054;** www.bearatourism.com), is also open during the summer.

EXPLORING THE REGION

There is a magnificent **Sheep's Head Loop** drive that begins outside Bantry along the Goat's Path to Kilcrohane, then back through Ahakista, and on to Durrus. The north side is all sheer cliffs and stark beauty (the sunsets are incredible) while the more lush south-side road runs right alongside the wondrous Dunmanus Bay.

You may also want to explore **Dursey Island,** a barren promontory extending into the sea at the tip of the Beara Peninsula. It offers no amenities for tourists, but the adventurous will find beautiful seaside walks and a memorable passage from the mainland via

Remembering Michael Collins

West Cork's most *and* least favorite son is the revolutionary Michael Collins (1890–1922), who was both born and assassinated in the county. Everyone here has an opinion about him. A hero to some, a traitor to others, Collins (who was immortalized in a movie starring Liam Neeson in 1996) was a larger-than-life, utterly charismatic man. The memory of Collins, sometimes referred to as "the Man Who Made Ireland," is preserved at the Michael Collins Memorial Centre and the ambush site near Macroom.

cable car. To get there, take R571 past Cahermore to its terminus. As you sway wildly in the wooden cable car, reading the text of Psalm 91 (which has kindly been posted to comfort the nervous), you might wonder whether a ferry would have been a wiser option. It wouldn't. Apparently the channel between the island and mainland is often too treacherous to permit regular crossing by boat. There is no lodging on the island, so be sure you know when the last cable car departs for the mainland; for schedule information, call © 027/73017.

Unfortunately a number of formerly reliable historical tours of the area have recently gone out of business or put up their prices so much that we can no longer recommend them. However, **Dolores and Tim Crowley** (© 023/46107) still run a wide variety of tours associated with Michael Collins and the civil war. Prices begin at around €6 ($9.60) per person.

SEEING THE SIGHTS

Bantry House ★★   On the edge of the town of Bantry, this Georgian house was built around 1750 for the earls of Bantry. It holds furniture and objets d'art from all over Europe, including Aubusson and Gobelin tapestries said to have been made for Marie Antoinette. The gardens, with original statuary, are beautifully kept—climb the steps behind the building for a panoramic view of the house, gardens, and Bantry Bay. The house also holds an informative exhibition on the ill-fated Spanish armada, which, led by the Irish rebel Wolfe Tone, attempted to invade the country near Bantry House in 1769. If you really love it, you can spend the night (€200–€300/$320–$480 double).

Bantry, County Cork. © 027/50047. www.bantryhouse.ie. Admission €10 ($16) adults, €8 ($13) students and seniors, free for children 13 and under. Mar 17–Oct daily 10am–6pm.

Derreen Gardens ★   The benign climate of West Cork and Kerry has made this informal garden a site of great natural beauty on the breathtaking north coast of the Beara Peninsula. In the late 19th century, the garden was planted with American species of conifer, many of which have become venerable giants. One path follows the sweep of the shoreline through tunnels of rhododendron, while others wind through the dense foliage of the promontory, opening occasionally to a view of the mountains or an entrancing rocky glen. The garden is home to several rarities, most notably the New Zealand tree ferns that flourish in a small glade, among giant blue gum and bamboo.

Signposted 1.6km (1 mile) off R571 in Lauragh, County Kerry. © 064/83588. Admission €5 ($8) adults; €2 ($3.20) seniors, students, and children. Apr–July and Sept–Oct daily 10am–6pm; Aug Fri–Sun 10am–6pm.

Drombeg Stone Circle ★★   This ring of 17 standing stones is the finest example of a megalithic stone circle in County Cork. Hills slope gently toward the sea nearby, and

Who Was Michael Collins?

Much of County Cork, and particularly the little town of Clonakilty, seems obsessed with Michael Collins, but when you learn a bit about him, you can understand why. Collins, also known as "the Big Fella," was one of the heroes of the Irish struggle for independence—the commander in chief of the army of the Irish Free State, which, under his command, won the Republic's independence from Britain in 1921.

Collins was born in 1890 and, along with his seven brothers and sisters, was raised on a farm in Sam's Cross, just outside Clonakilty. He emigrated to England at 15 and, like many other young Irish men, found work in London. In his 20s, he joined the Irish revolutionary group, the Irish Republican Brotherhood (I.R.B.). He first came to fame in 1916, as one of the planners and leaders of the Easter Rising, fighting alongside Patrick Pearse at the General Post Office in Dublin. It may have roused passions among the population, but the Rising was a military disaster, and Collins—young but clever—railed against its amateurism. He was furious about the seizure of prominent buildings—such as the GPO—that were impossible to defend, impossible to escape from, and difficult to get supplies into.

After the battle, Collins was arrested and sent to an internment camp in Britain, along with hundreds of other rebels. There his stature within the I.R.B. grew, and by the time he was released, he had become one of the leaders of the Republican movement. In 1918, he was elected a member of the British Parliament, but like many other Irish members, refused to go to London, instead announcing that he would sit only in an Irish parliament in Dublin. Most of the rebel Irish MPs (including Eamon de Valera) were arrested by British troops for their actions, but Collins avoided arrest, and later helped de Valera escape from prison. Over the subsequent years, de Valera and Collins worked together to create an Irish state.

the builders could hardly have chosen a more picturesque spot. The circle dates from 153 B.C., and little is known about its ritual purpose. Just west of the circle are the remains of two huts and a cooking place; it is thought that heated stones were placed in a water trough (which can be seen adjacent to the huts), and the hot water was used for cooking. The cooking place dates from between A.D. 368 and 608.

Off R597 btw. Rosscarbery and Glandore, County Cork.

Ilnacullin (Garinish Island) ★★ Officially known as Ilnacullin, but usually referred to as Garinish, this little island was once barren. In 1919 it was transformed into an elaborately planned Italianate garden, with classical pavilions and myriad unusual plants and flowers. It's said that George Bernard Shaw wrote parts of *St. Joan* under the shade of its palm trees. The island can be reached for a round-trip fee of approximately €11 ($18) per person on a covered ferry operated by **Blue Pool Ferry,** the Blue Pool, Glengarriff (© **027/63333**; www.bluepoolferry.com), or **Harbour Queen Ferries,** the Harbour, Glengarriff (© **027/63116**). Boats run back and forth every 30 minutes.

After lengthy negotiations and much bloodshed (Collins orchestrated an assassination that essentially wiped out the British secret service in Ireland), Collins was sent by de Valera in 1921 to negotiate a treaty with the British government. In the meeting, British Prime Minister Lloyd George agreed to allow Ireland to become a free republic, as long as that republic did not include the counties of Ulster. Those largely Protestant counties would join Great Britain, forming the United Kingdom. Knowing he could not get more at the time and hoping to renegotiate later, Collins reluctantly agreed to sign the treaty, deciding that it was time to stop the bloodshed. (Along with Lloyd George, Winston Churchill, then a government minister, also signed the treaty.) After signing the document Collins said, "I have just signed my death warrant."

As he'd expected, the plan tore the new Republic apart, dividing the group now known as the IRA into two factions—those who wanted to continue fighting for all of Ireland, and those who favored the treaty. Fighting soon broke out in Dublin, and the civil war was underway.

Collins had learned many lessons from the Easter debacle, and now his strategy was completely different. His soldiers operated as "flying columns," waging a guerrilla war against the enemy—suddenly attacking, and then just as suddenly withdrawing, thus minimizing their losses, and leaving the opposition never knowing what to expect next, but the battle stretched on for 10 months.

In August 1922, Collins was weary of the war, and was on a peace mission in his home county. After visiting various factions, and stopping at a pub near his mother's birthplace, he and his escort were on the road near Béal na mBláth when Collins was shot and killed. Precisely who killed him—whether it was his own men or the opposition—is not known. He had made, on his rapid rise to the top, too many enemies. He was 31 years old.

Glengarriff, County Cork. (✆) **027/63040.** Admission (gardens) €3.70 ($5.90) adults, €2.75 ($4.40) seniors, €1.50 ($2.40) students and children. Mar and Oct Mon–Sat 10am–4:30pm, Sun 1–5pm; Apr–June and Sept Mon–Sat 10am–6:30pm, Sun 1–7pm; July–Aug Mon–Sat 9:30am–6:30pm, Sun 11am–6:30pm. Last landing 1 hr. before closing.

Michael Collins Memorial Centre More a place of pilgrimage than a traditional attraction, the center is frequented by those who revere Collins rather than those who want to learn more about him. It's on the farm where he was born and raised—the old stone farmhouse in which Collins and his siblings were born still survives, although the larger farmhouse into which his family moved when Michael was 10 was burned to the ground in 1921 by the Black and Tans. The ambush site at Béal na mBláth, near Macroom, where he was assassinated, is kept as a shrine of sorts.

Signposted off N71, 5.6km (3¹/₂ miles) west of Clonakilty, Woodfield, County Cork.

Mizen Vision ★★★ At Mizen Head, the southernmost point in Ireland, the land falls precipitously into the Atlantic breakers in a procession of spectacular 210m (700-ft.)

sea cliffs. A suspension bridge permits access to the old signal station, now a visitor center, on a rock promontory, the southernmost point on the Irish mainland, with awe-inspiring views of the cliffs and the open sea. Whales, seals, dolphins, and seabirds contribute to the spectacle. No matter what the weather, it's worth a trip. On wild days, tremendous Atlantic waves assault the cliffs. On a clear day, seals bask on the rocks and gannets wheel over the sea and dive into the tranquil waters.

On the way out to Mizen Head, you'll pass Barleycove Beach, one of the most beautiful beaches in southwest Ireland and a great place to explore.

Mizen Head, County Cork. ℂ **028/35115.** Fax 028/35603. www.mizenhead.net. Admission €6 ($9.60) adults, €4.50 ($7.20) seniors and students, €3.50 ($5.60) children, free for children 4 and under, €18 ($29) families. Mid-Mar to May and Oct daily 10:30am–5pm; June–Sept daily 10am–6:30pm; Nov to mid-Mar Sat–Sun 11am–4pm. Take R591 to Goleen, and follow signs for Mizen Head.

SHOPPING

Bandon Pottery This attractive little shop, located behind artist Jane Forrester's home and studio, is full to bursting with colorful tableware, vases, bowls and ornaments, all of which are handmade on-site. It's lovely stuff, and very unique, but Jane opens the place by appointment only (normally Mon–Sat from 11am–6pm), so make sure you call ahead first. Ardkitt East, Enniskeane, County Cork. ℂ **023/47843.** www.bandonpottery.ie.

Courtmacsherry Ceramics Overlooking the sea, this studio and shop offers an array of porcelain animals and tableware, inspired by West Cork. Visitors are welcome to watch potter Peter Wolstenholme at work on new creations. Main St., Courtmacsherry, County Cork. ℂ **023/46239.**

Quills Woollen Market This family-run enterprise in a small village deep in West Cork's Gaelic-speaking region has handmade sweaters and garments made from wool and goatskins. Main St., Macroom, County Cork. ℂ **026/43910.**

Rossmore Country Pottery This family-run studio produces a lovely range of practical domestic stoneware and a colorful collection of earthenware decorated flowerpots. Rossmore, County Cork (11km/6¾ miles from Clonakilty on Bandon-Bantry rd.). ℂ **023/38875.**

SPORTS & OUTDOOR PURSUITS

BEACHES **Barleycove Beach** is a vast expanse of pristine sand with a fine view out toward the Mizen Head cliffs; despite the trailer park and holiday homes on the far side of the dunes, large parts of the beach never seem to get crowded. Take R591 to Goleen, and follow signs for Mizen Head. There is a public parking lot at the Barleycove Hotel.

Inchydoney Beach, on Clonakilty Bay, is famous for both its gorgeous beach and the salubrious **Inchydoney Lodge & Spa** (ℂ **023/33143**) that specializes in thalasso (seawater) treatments. For more information, visit **www.inchydoneyisland.com.**

BICYCLING The **Mizen Head, Sheep's Head,** and **Beara peninsulas** offer fine roads for cycling, with great scenery and few cars. The Beara Peninsula is the most spectacular; the other two are less likely to be crowded with tourists during peak season. The loop around Mizen Head, starting in Skibbereen, is a good 2- to 3-day trip, and a loop around the Beara Peninsula from Bantry, Glengarriff, or Kenmare takes at least 3 days at a casual pace.

In Skibbereen, 18- and 21-speed bicycles can be rented from **Roycroft's Stores** (ℂ **028/21235;** roycroft@iol.ie); expect to pay around €70 ($112) per week, depending on the season. If you call ahead, you can reserve a lightweight mountain bike with toe clips at no extra cost.

BIRD-WATCHING Cape Clear Island is the prime birding spot in West Cork, and one of the best places in Europe to watch seabirds (see the box "Southern Exposure: An Excursion to Cape Clear Island," below). The best time for seabirds is July to September, and October is the busiest month for migratory passerines (and for bird-watchers, who flock to the island). There is a bird observatory at the **North Harbour,** with a warden in residence from March to November, and accommodations for bird-watchers; to arrange a stay, write to **Kieran Grace,** 84 Dorney Court, Shankhill, County Dublin. **Ciarán O'Driscoll** (© **028/39153**), who operates a B&B on the island, also runs boat trips for bird-watchers and has a keen eye for vagrants and rarities.

DIVING The **Baltimore Diving & Watersports Centre,** Baltimore, County Cork (© **028/20300;** www.baltimorediving.com), provides equipment and boats to certified divers for exploring the many shipwrecks, reefs, and caves in this region. The cost starts at around €50 ($80) per dive with equipment. Various 2-hour to 15-day certified PADI courses are available for all levels of experience.

FISHING The West Cork coast is known for its many shipwrecks, making this one of the best places in Ireland for wreck fishing. **Mark and Patricia Gannon** of Woodpoint House, Courtmacsherry (© **023/46427**), offer packages that include bed-and-breakfast in their idyllic stone farmhouse and a day's sea angling aboard one of their two new Aquastar fishing boats. A day's fishing costs around €60 ($96) per person. Boats holding up to 12 people can also be chartered.

KAYAKING With hundreds of islands, numerous inviting inlets, and a plethora of sea caves, the coast of West Cork is a sea kayaker's paradise. **Lough Ine** offers warm, still waters for beginners, a tidal rapid for the intrepid, and access to a nearby headland riddled with caves that demand exploration. In Castletownbere on the dramatic and rugged Beara Peninsula, **Sea Kayaking West Cork** (© **086/309-8654** or 328-4182; www.sea kayakingwestcork.com) specializes in accompanied trips out and around Bere Island and as far as Glengarriff.

SAILING The **Glenans Irish Sailing Club** (www.gisc.ie) was founded in France and has two centers in Ireland, one of which is in Baltimore Harbour. The centers provide weeklong courses at all levels, using dinghies, cruisers, catamarans, or windsurfers; prices run from €350 to around €600 ($560–$960). The living facilities are spartan, with dorm-style accommodations, and you cook for yourself. The clientele is mostly middle-aged and younger, from Ireland and the Continent. Call © **01/661-1481** or fax 01/676-4249 for advance booking.

WALKING One of the most beautiful coastal walks in West Cork begins along the banks of **Lough Ine,** one of the largest saltwater lakes in Europe. Connected to the sea by a narrow isthmus, the lake is in a lush valley of exceptional beauty. To get there, follow signs for Lough Ine along R595 between Skibbereen and Baltimore; there is a parking lot at the northwest corner of the lake. The wide trail proceeds gradually upward from the parking lot through the woods on the west slope of the valley, with several viewpoints toward the lake and the sea beyond. Once you reach the hilltop, there is a sweeping view of the coast from Mizen Head to Galley Head. Walking time to the top and back is about 1 1/2 hours.

Near Lauragh on the Beara Peninsula is the abandoned town of **Cummingeera,** at the base of a cliff in a wild, remote valley. The walk to the village gives you a taste for the rough beauty of the Caha Mountains, and a sense for the lengths to which people in

(Moments) **Southern Exposure: An Excursion to Cape Clear Island**

Cape Clear Island, 13km (8 miles) off the mainland, is the southernmost inhabited point in Ireland. It can be bleak, with a craggy coastline and no trees to break the rush of sea wind, but that very barrenness appeals to many for its stark beauty, rough and irregular, but not without solace and grace. In early summer, wildflowers brighten the landscape, and in October, passerine migrants, some on their way from North America and Siberia, fill the air. Sea-birds are present in abundance during the nesting season, especially from July to September. At any time, Cape Clear is unforgettable.

The first step (obviously) is getting there. The *Naomh Ciarán II* offers passenger-only ferry service year-round, seas permitting. In the highest season (July–Aug), the *Naomh Ciarán II* leaves Baltimore Monday to Saturday at 11am, and 2:15, 5, and 7pm, and Sunday at noon, 2:15, 5, and 7pm; return service from Cape Clear departs Monday to Saturday at 9am and 6pm, and Sunday at 11am, and 1, 4, and 6pm. Service is always subject to the seas and is more limited off season. The passage takes 45 minutes, and a round-trip ticket costs €12 ($19) for adults, €6.50 ($10) for children, and €28 ($45) for families. For inquiries, contact **Cape Clear Island Ferry Service** ((C) **028/39135** or 086/282-4008). For the same price, there's also the *Karycraft* ((C) **028/28278**), departing Schull daily in June, July, and August at 10:30am, and 2:30 and 4:30pm; and departing Cape Clear at 11:30am, and 3:30 and 5:30pm. In September, service is limited to one crossing daily, departing Schull at 2:30pm and Cape Clear at 5:30pm.

Once you're on Cape Clear, there are a number of things to see, including birds galore, seals, dolphins, the occasional whale, and ancient "marriage stones."

There's also a lot to do apart from hiking and sightseeing. **Cléire Lasmuigh,** Cape Clear Island Adventure Centre ((C) **028/39198**), offers outdoor programs, from snorkeling and sea kayaking to hillwalking and orienteering. Coastal cruises—for sea angling, scuba diving, or bird-watching—are the specialty of **Ciarán O'Driscoll** ((C)/fax **028/39153**). There's no shopping mall, but local art, crafts, and books can be found in Harpercraft and the Back Room in Cotter's Yard, North Harbour. While you're at it, pick up a copy of Chuck Kruger's *Cape Clear Island Magic*. There's no better introduction to the wonder of this place.

Modest hostel, B&B, and self-catering accommodations are available by the day, week, or month. The island's **An Óige Youth Hostel** ((C) **028/39198**) at the Cape Clear Adventure Centre is open March through October. Most B&Bs are open year-round. They include **Fáilte** (contact Eleanór Uí Drisceoil, (C) **028/ 39153**) and **Ard na Gaoith** (contact Eileen Leonard, (C) **028/39160**). For self-catering cottages by the day or week, contact **Ciarán O'Driscoll** ((C) **028/39153**). You can't miss the town's three pubs and two restaurants, which will keep you well fortified. (Also, the fruit scones baked at Cistin Chléire on North Harbour are fabulous.)

Cape Clear has a helpful website at **www.oilean-chleire.ie**.

pre-famine Ireland would go to find a patch of arable land. To get to the start of the walk, take the road posted for Glanmore Lake south from R571; the road is just over 1km (0.6 mile) west of the turnoff for Healy Pass. Follow the Glanmore Lake road 1km (0.6 mile), then turn right at the road posted for "stone circle"; continue 2km (1.25 miles) to the point at which the road becomes dirt, and park on the roadside. From here, there is no trail—just walk up the valley to its terminus, about 2km (1.25 miles) away, where the ruins of a village hug the cliff's base. Where the valley is blocked by a headland, take the route around to the left, which is less steep. Return the way you came; the whole walk—4km (2.5 miles)—is moderately difficult and takes 2 hours.

An easy seaside walk on the **Beara Peninsula** begins at Dunboy Castle, just over a mile west of Castletownbere on R572, this stretch of trail is part of the O'Sullivan Beara trail, which may eventually extend from Castletownbere to Leitrim. You can park your car along the road, by the castellated gatehouse, or drive up to the castle. The castle is a ruined 19th-century manor house overlooking the bay, with some graceful marble arches spanning the grand central hall. Just down the road are the sparse ruins of a medieval fortress. Beyond, the trail continues to the tip of Fair Head through rhododendrons, with fine views across to Bere Island. A walk from the gatehouse parking lot to the tip of Fair Head and back takes about 2 hours.

The **Sheep's Head Way,** voted "Best Walk in Ireland" by *Country Walking* magazine, makes an 89km (55-mile) loop and incorporates numerous smaller day loops. The *Guide to the Sheep's Head Way,* available in most local stores and tourist offices, combines history, poetry, and topography in a fantastic introduction to the region. It is a rough place, and you won't find many tourists in its more remote reaches. There are treasures to be found, but you might have to work a little harder to unearth them here than in regions long since "discovered."

One of Ireland's most beautiful spots, **Gougane Barra** (which means "St. Finbarr's Cleft") is a still, dark, romantic lake a little northeast of the Pass of Keimaneigh, 24km (15 miles) northeast of Bantry off T64 (also well signposted on the Macroom-Glengarriff rd.). This is the source of the River Lee, where St. Finbarr founded a monastery in these deeply wooded mountains, supposedly on the small island connected by a causeway to the mainland. Though nothing remains of the saint's 6th-century community, the setting is idyllic, with rhododendrons spilling into the still waters where swans glide by. The island now holds an elfin chapel and eight small circular cells, dating from the early 1700s, as well as a modern chapel. Today Gougane Barra is a national forest park, and there are signposted walks and drives through the wooded hills. There's a small admission charge per car to enter the park.

WINDSURFING   Weeklong courses and equipment rental are available at the **Glenans Irish Sailing Club** (see "Sailing," above) in Baltimore. There is a sheltered beach in Courtmacsherry where beginners can get started and another nearby beach that's good for wave jumping.

WHERE TO STAY

Expensive

Ballylickey Manor House ★★   Hidden in rugged inlets with a stunning view of Bantry Bay, nestled amid sculpted lawns and gardens, and with a backdrop of mountains and moorlands, this 300-year-old manor house was built as a shooting lodge. It has five large suites, and seven spacious, well-decorated cottages clustered around the swimming pool. Throughout the house, the decor is country-style chic. This inn has an international ambience, thanks to the influence of its owners, the Franco-Irish Graves family, and a largely European clientele.

Bantry-Glengarriff rd. (N71), Ballylickey, County Cork. ℭ **800/323-5463** in the U.S., or 027/50071. Fax 027/50124. www.ballylickeymanorhouse.com. 14 units. €170–€350 ($272–$560) double. Rates include full breakfast. AE, DC, MC, V. Closed Nov–Feb. **Amenities:** Restaurant (Continental); outdoor heated swimming pool; 3 drawing rooms. *In room:* TV, hair dryer, garment press.

Longueville House Hotel ★★★ This is one of those rare places that is refined and yet charmingly rural, without a hint of pretense. The house is a palatial affair built in 1720 amid sprawling farmland, and with its own winery. All this grandeur is saved from pomposity by the laid-back O'Callaghan family, who keep things down-to-earth. Guest rooms are sumptuous without going overboard, furnished in old-world style, with family heirlooms and period pieces, and most have bucolic views of the gardens, grazing pastures, or vineyards. The beacon of Longueville is the Presidents' Restaurant, where William O'Callaghan continues to prove that he is a gifted chef. He sources produce and vegetables from the hotel's farm and gardens and from local markets, and transforms them into memorable dishes. In the summer, meals are also served in a gorgeous, sky-lit Victorian conservatory.

Killarney rd. (N72), Mallow, County Cork. ℭ **800/323-5463** in the U.S., or 022/47156. Fax 022/47459. www.longuevillehouse.ie. 20 units. €235–€260 ($376–$416) double. Rates include full breakfast. Dinner €55 ($88). AE, DC, MC, V. Closed mid-Feb to early Mar. **Amenities:** Restaurant (modern Continental); nonsmoking rooms; drawing rooms. *In room:* TV, hair dryer, garment press.

Moderate

Baltimore Harbour Hotel ★★ Kids Nearly every room in this harbor hotel has a lovely view. The public rooms—bar, garden room, and Clipper Restaurant—are fresh, bright, and inviting, with a contemporary nautical feel. The guest rooms are simply decorated but comfortable, with extraordinary views of the harbor. Room nos. 216 and 217 are especially spacious, at no extra cost. The hotel's 18 suites are ideal for families, as is the kids' club (for ages 4 and older) that offers activity programs in the summer and on Irish holiday weekends.

Signposted off R595 in Baltimore, County Cork. ℭ **028/20361.** Fax 028/20466. www.baltimore harbourhotel.ie. 64 units. €120–€168 ($192–$269) double. Rates include service charge and full Irish breakfast but may increase on Irish holiday weekends. Packages available. AE, DC, MC, V. **Amenities:** Restaurant (international); bar; indoor swimming pool; gym; Jacuzzi; steam room; nonsmoking rooms. *In room:* TV, tea/coffeemaker, hair dryer.

Rock Cottage ★ This new B&B offers a wonderfully secluded, relaxing retreat in what was once Lord Bandon's hunting lodge. The spacious guest rooms in the tastefully restored Georgian building combine ample shares of elegance and comfort. Here's the best news: Your hostess, Barbara Klötzer, is a former head chef, and is now able to focus her culinary wizardry on a handful of lucky guests.

Barnatonicane (11km/6³⁄₄ miles from Durrus on R591), Schull, County Cork. ℭ **028/35538.** www.rock cottage.ie. 3 units. €130 ($208) double. Rates include full breakfast. 3-course dinner €45 ($72). MC, V. Free parking. *In room:* TV, hair dryer.

Sea View House ★★ This handsome seaside hotel is homey and full of interesting heirlooms, fine antiques, and an utter disregard for fads and trends. Instead, it sticks to old-fashioned principles of good service. The cheerily decorated rooms are individually furnished in a manner Grandma would like, with dark woods, busy fabrics, and mattresses firm enough to bounce a penny on. Request a room in the front of the house for peek-a-boo views of Bantry Bay through the leafy trees. The hotel is best known for its award-winning cuisine, the sort of hearty comfort food that's reassuringly still devoted to using marvelously fattening dollops of fresh cream, real butter, a slug of booze now and then, and salt.

Bantry-Glengarriff rd. (N71), Ballylickey, County Cork. © **800/447-7462** in the U.S., or 027/50073. Fax 027/51555. www.seaviewhousehotel.com. 25 units. €150–€170 ($240–$272) double. Rates include full breakfast. AE, MC, V. Closed mid-Nov to mid-Mar. **Amenities:** Restaurant (Continental); bar; outdoor patio. *In room:* TV, hair dryer.

West Cork Hotel ★★ (Finds) This is the sort of comfy, old style hotel that has a bit of style despite itself. Everything is designed to induce contentment and familiarity, and it's a testimony to its success that the public areas—particularly the buzzy pub—always draw a local crowd. Guest rooms are relaxing in the old-fashioned Irish way, with lots of traditional dark woods and mismatched patterns. The handsome yellow building at the Kennedy bridge is the first thing you see if you enter Skibbereen from the west on N71, or the last as you leave town if you're heading in the opposite direction.

Ilen St., Skibbereen, County Cork. © **028/21277.** Fax 028/22333. www.westcorkhotel.com. 30 units. €110–€150 ($176–$240) double. Rates include full breakfast. AE, MC, V. Closed Dec 22–28. **Amenities:** Restaurant (Continental); bar. *In room:* TV.

Westlodge Hotel ★ (Kids) Though more than a little generic looking, this modern three-story hotel is handy for families. What separates it from the ho-hum pack is its excellent leisure center and a wide array of child-friendly amenities. The lobby and guest rooms are sunny and airy, enhanced by wide windows, blond-wood furnishings, and bright Irish fabrics. Westlodge specializes in family holidays and offers organized activities for children from June through August.

Off Bantry-Glengarriff rd. (N71), Bantry, County Cork. © **027/50360.** Fax 027/50438. www.westlodge hotel.ie. 95 units. €130–€140 ($208–$224) double. Rates include service charge and full breakfast. AE, DC, MC, V. **Amenities:** Restaurant (international); bar; indoor swimming pool; tennis; squash; gym; Jacuzzi; steam room; kids' playroom; babysitting; nonsmoking rooms. *In room:* TV, tea/coffeemaker.

Inexpensive

Ballinatona Farm ★ (Finds) Like the region that surrounds it, this working dairy farm is a little-known treasure, just far enough off the beaten track to be spared the crowds that congest much of the southwest during the summer. While the landscape isn't wild and rugged like that of the West Cork coast, its gentler beauty is still magnificent. The energetic hosts, Jytte Storm and Tim Lane, know the region well and their excitement over its hidden delights is infectious. A 15-minute walk brings you to the lovely valley that holds Coomeenatrush waterfall at its head. The house is tucked high onto the hillside at 240m (787 ft.) above sea level and commands magnificent views. The second-floor front room, reached by a spiral staircase, offers a breathtaking view, with glass walls on three sides.

4.8km (3 miles) out of Millstreet on the Macroom rd., Millstreet, County Cork. © **029/70213.** Fax 029/70940. www.irishfarmholidays.com. 6 units. €72–€80 ($115–$128) double. Rates include full breakfast. Discount for children 11 and under with parent. MC, V. Closed Dec 15–Jan 1. *In room:* TV, tea/coffeemaker, hair dryer.

Fortview House ★★   With pristine country-style rooms, antique pine furniture, wood floors, iron and brass beds, and crisp Irish linens, this place is a treasure. Beamed ceilings and a warm color palette add to the comfortable feeling, and the spacious, inviting sitting room completes the welcome. Violet Connell's breakfasts are legendary, with seven varieties of fresh-squeezed juices jostling for space on a menu that includes hot potato cakes, pancakes, kippers, and smoked salmon. If you prefer self-catering, there are two three-bedroom cottages (each sleeps six) on the Fortview grounds that rent for €400 ($640) per week in low season, rising to €950 ($1,520) per week in mid-summer.

On R591 from Durrus toward Goleen, Gurtyowen, Toormore, Goleen, County Cork. ℭ **028/35324.** www.fortviewhousegoleen.com. 5 units. €100 ($160) double. Rates include full breakfast. No credit cards. Closed Nov–Feb. **Amenities:** Sitting room. *In room:* TV.

Glebe Country House ★   Built in 1690 as a rectory, Glebe House is now a gracious guesthouse. The charming rooms, each comfortable and individually decorated, have views of the rose and herb gardens that wreath the house. The spacious dining room provides a lovely setting for candlelit five-course dinners partly drawn from the house's garden. Dinners cost €35 ($56); book before noon and bring your own wine. The enticing breakfast menu includes waffles, scrambled eggs with rosemary shortbread, and "cheesy French toast" (a Glebe House invention).

The Coach House apartments behind the main house offer comfortable self-catering accommodations. The ground floor, two-bedroom garden apartment sleeps five in two rooms. The ideal choice for families is the one-bedroom loft apartment that sleeps five, with a double and single bed in one room and a pullout sofa in the living room. Both apartments have linens, and each has a private patio-garden. A chalet in the garden, Beech Lodge, is available for up to six guests.

Balinadee (off Balinadee center), Bandon, County Cork. ℭ **021/477-8294.** Fax 021/477-8456. www.glebe countryhouse.ie. 4 units and 2 self-catering units. €90–€110 ($144–$176) double (rates include service charge and full Irish breakfast); €325–€570 ($520–$912) per week for self-catering units. MC, V. **Amenities:** Living room. *In room:* Tea/coffeemaker.

The Heron's Cove ★   Locals on the Mizen Head peninsula know the Heron's Cove as a terrific seafood restaurant (see below), but it's really what the Irish call a restaurant with rooms and a very inviting place to stay. Its three sea-view rooms, with balconies overlooking a beautiful, sheltered cove, are tremendously appealing. The rooms are simple but comfortable, and the atmosphere of the entire B&B is so friendly, it's almost familial. Enjoying a wonderful dinner with wine over sunset and then heading upstairs to your room for a moonlit view of the harbor is relaxing indeed.

Signposted in the center of Goleen, County Cork. ℭ **028/35225.** Fax 028/35422. www.heronscove.com. 5 units. €110 ($176) double. Rates include full breakfast. AE, MC, V. *In room:* TV, tea/coffeemaker, hair dryer.

Rolf's Country House   A long-established family-run guesthouse overlooking the harbor and the Mizen peninsula, Rolf's is an appealing complex of cut-stone buildings. All guests have access to the open self-catering kitchen, although it is unlikely to compete with Rolf's Cafe Art and Restaurant. The art on the walls is part of a rotating exhibit of contemporary Irish painting and sculpture. There are also a number of private little bungalows available.

.5km (¹/₃ mile) off R595, signposted just outside Baltimore center, Baltimore, County Cork. ℭ/fax **028/ 20289.** www.rolfsholidays.eu. €80–€100 ($128–$160) double; €500–€800 ($800–$1,280) per week bungalow. MC, V. **Amenities:** Restaurant (international). *In room:* Full kitchen, washing machine.

Self-Catering

Ahakista ★ Simplicity, charm, and an alluring location on the Sheep's Head Peninsula (the least touristy of Cork's three peninsulas) make this recently restored stone cottage a magnificent getaway. It's a short walk to the two-pub farming and fishing village of Ahakista. The old-fashioned cottage has low-slung ceilings and a traditional, narrow staircase as well as fine views of Dunmanus Bay. It's perfect for walkers, as it's surrounded by 97km (60 miles) of marked walking paths along the wild coastline. The two-bedroom cottage has one double bed and one twin bed.

Contact Elegant Ireland ℂ **01/475-1632.** Fax 01/475-1012. www.elegant.ie. 1 cottage. From €990 ($1,584) per week. MC, V. *In room:* TV, full kitchen, dishwasher, dryer, washing machine.

Anne's Grove Medieval Miniature Castle ★★ (Finds) What could be more romantic than a tiny Gothic castle just big enough for two? Designed by the distinguished architect Benjamin Woodward in 1853, this gate lodge of Anne's Grove Gardens was conceived as a medieval castle in miniature. It lay vacant and neglected from the 1940s to the 1990s, when the Irish Landmark Trust bought it and renovated it. Today, it is an enchanting place with a living room warmed by a fireplace, a well-equipped kitchen, one double bedroom, and a bathroom. There are hardwood floors throughout the lodge, and the furnishings are rustic and inviting. The architectural lines of the rooms—leaded windows, doorways, and ceilings all echo the classic Gothic arch. There is perhaps no more dreamy base from which to explore northwest Cork, and the price is downright unbeatable. One word of caution, though: The bedroom is accessed via a spiral staircase and so is unsuitable for people with limited mobility.

Castletownroach, County Cork. Contact the Irish Landmark Trust ℂ **01/670-4733.** Fax 01/670-4887. www.irishlandmark.com. 1 unit. €250–€400 ($400–$640) for 4 nights in low season, rising to €450–€1,106 ($720–$1,770) in high season. AE, MC, V at booking. *In room:* Kitchen, microwave.

Galley Head Lightkeeper's House ★★ (Finds) A recent addition to the wonderful stable of Irish Landmark Trust properties, this lighthouse keeper's house stands next to the lighthouse on the tip of breathtaking Galley Head, just south of Clonakilty. It's actually two connecting houses, which can be rented separately or together. The first house has a fully equipped kitchen, sitting room, and lounge (or bedroom) with bathroom downstairs, and two bedrooms (one double, one twin) and a bathroom upstairs. The second house has the same basic floor plan, minus the downstairs lounge and bathroom. Both houses have sturdy mahogany furnishings, oversize sofas and armchairs, and a fireplace in every room. Its location is as remote as you'd hope for, yet still only a 20-minute drive to bustling Clonakilty. As with all ILT properties, there is no TV. One of the property's best assets is its caretaker, Gerald Butler. He grew up in this house and is a marvelous storyteller and history buff and can give you a private tour of the lighthouse.

Galley Head, County Cork. Contact the Irish Landmark Trust ℂ **01/670-4733.** Fax 01/670-4887. www.irishlandmark.com. 2 units. €350–€500 ($560–$800) for 4 nights in low season, rising to €550–€1,106 ($880–$1,770) in high season. AE, MC, V at booking. *In room:* Kitchen, dishwasher, washing machine.

WHERE TO DINE
Expensive

Blairs Cove ★★ INTERNATIONAL This romantic restaurant has it all: a stone-walled, high-ceilinged dining room, open fireplaces, and windows overlooking majestic Dunmanus Bay. Owners Philip and Sabine de Mey have converted an old stone barn into one of the best dining experiences in southwest Ireland. You begin with the hors d'oeuvre buffet of cold starters (perhaps salmon fumé, prawns, oysters, or mousse) and then move on to the main course—perhaps rack of lamb or grilled rib of beef, or maybe monkfish filet flambéed in Pernod. For dessert, step up to the grand piano that doubles as a dessert cart. Don't look for cutting-edge, break-the-mold fusion; this place is all about classic dishes done in a familiar way, only better than you've probably had them elsewhere. There are also **rooms** available for nightly B&B, costing €150 to €260 ($240–$416) for a double, depending on the time of year. Apartments and cottages are available for rent, starting at around €500 ($800) per week.

Barley Cove Rd., Durrus, County Cork. ℂ **027/61127.** Fax 027/61487. www.blairscove.ie. Reservations required. Dinner with starter buffet €55 ($88). MC, V. Tues–Sat 7:15–9:30pm. Closed Nov to mid-Mar.

Casino House ★★ INTERNATIONAL The views of Courtmacsherry Bay from this lovely restaurant are exquisite, and the interior is charming—Nantucket meets Provence. The food is similarly fine; the menu changes with the seasons, but starters might include ricotta, vegetables, and tofu in phyllo pastry; cream of carrot soup served with caramelized walnuts; or terrine of quail with pistachio nuts and shiitake mushrooms. Main dishes might include roast duck with Madeira, or chef Michael Relja's melt-in-your-mouth sole with spring onions and wild rice. The international wine list includes many good-value options from Germany and Italy. Casino House also has a small self-catering cottage, starting at €85 ($136) per night.

16km (10 miles) from Kinsale on coast road (R600), Coulmain Bay, Kilbrittain, County Cork. ℂ **023/49944.** Reservations recommended. Main courses €20–€30 ($32–$48). MC, V. Tues–Sun 7–9pm; Sun 1–3pm. Closed Jan to mid-Mar.

Chez Youen ★★ SEAFOOD Overlooking the marina of this picturesque harbor town, the style of Frenchman Youen Jacob's restaurant evokes his native Brittany—with beamed ceilings, candlelight, and an open copper fireplace. Lobster is the specialty here, fresh from local waters, but the steaks, poached wild salmon, and leg of lamb are also very good. The owners also run the neighboring Baltimore Bay Guesthouse and the lower-priced bistro, La Jolie Brise.

The Pier, Baltimore, County Cork. ℂ **028/20136.** www.youenjacob.com/chez_youen. Reservations required. Fixed-price dinners €30–€40 ($48–$64); dinner main courses €26–€55 ($42–$88). AE, DC, MC, V. Mar–Oct daily 6pm–midnight; Sun noon–4pm.

The Heron's Cove ★ SEAFOOD This is a regular port of call for locals, who know they can count on it for excellent dining free of formality. The casual, modest dining room has a splendid view of a secluded cove, while the menu focuses on local seafood, with selections for vegetarians and carnivores alike. Typical dishes include Heron's Cove crab cakes with wasabi mayonnaise, or pan-fried filet of John Dory served with balsamic butter. For dessert, indulge in the Russian cheesecake, the house specialty. The cellar of 50 to 60 international wines is open for browsing, and you can discuss the wines with other diners.

Signposted in the center of Goleen, County Cork. ℂ **028/35225.** www.heronscove.com. Reservations recommended. Main courses €20–€28 ($32–$45). AE, DC, MC, V. May–Oct daily noon–10pm.

Moderate

The Customs House ★★ Finds SEAFOOD This restaurant offers excellently prepared fresh seafood dishes that are known around the county. The blackboard menu lists the day's choices, which might be red mullet with tapenade; grilled squid with hot salsa;

or John Dory with spinach, soy, and ginger. Desserts, like the poached pear with roasted almond ice cream, are elegant and simple. The dress code is smart casual, with the emphasis on smart. Children 11 and under would most likely feel like a fish out of . . . well, you know.

50m (164 ft.) from the pier (beside the Garda Station), Baltimore, County Cork. ⓒ **028/20200.** Reservations recommended. Fixed-price dinners €30–€40 ($48–$64). No credit cards. Wed–Sat 7–10pm. Closed Oct to mid-Mar.

Good Things Café ★★ (Finds) CAFE   This is one of our favorite restaurants in Cork. This tiny, unpretentious, bare-bones bistro uses the freshest local produce and artisan cheeses, breads, and foodstuffs to make simply perfect meals. You'll be amazed at how a humble omelet or salmon in puff pastry manages to be so memorable. For dessert, don't pass up on Murphy's Ice Cream, trucked in from County Kerry.

Ahakista Rd., Durrus, County Cork. ⓒ **027/61426.** www.thegoodthingscafe.com. Main courses lunch €8–€20 ($13–$32), dinner €15–€28 ($24–$45); lobster €38 ($61). MC, V. Wed–Mon 10:30am–5pm and 6:30–8:30pm.

Mary Ann's ★★ PUB GRUB   Dating from 1844, this rustic pub perched halfway up a hill is decorated with ships' wheels, lanterns, and bells—but you don't go to Mary Ann's for the cute decor. You go for the superlative pub menu of fresh seafood salads and West Cork cheese plates, as well as more ambitious dishes, such as scallops meunière or sirloin steak with garlic butter. On sunny days, sit outside in the attractive courtyard.

Castletownshend, Skibbereen, County Cork. ⓒ **028/36146.** Reservations recommended for dinner. Main dishes €15–€22 ($24–$35). MC, V. Daily 12:30–2pm and 6–9pm. Closed holidays.

County Kerry

With its softly rolling green fields, long, sweeping seascapes, and vibrant little towns, it's easy to see why so many tourists make a beeline for County Kerry, and more of them do so every year. Tourism figures for the county have jumped from fewer than 800,000 visitors per year a decade ago to nearly two million each year. Given that only 126,000 people live in the county, you can see how this could be problematic.

The influx has been great for Kerry businesses, but it has also turned the county into a strange hybrid place, where spectacular rural scenery coexists uncomfortably with crass tourism. In July and August, tour buses struggle to share narrow mountain roads with local traffic, and at the best vantage points, the view is often blocked by two or three of the behemoths. Given that, it's easy to feel like the whole place is on the verge of being overrun. Luckily, it's still easy to escape the crowds. If you're driving along the congested Ring of Kerry and the crowds are getting to you, simply turn off onto a small country lane and you'll find yourself virtually alone and in the peaceful Irish wilderness within seconds.

Of course, not everybody minds the inevitable clutter and cacophony of the tourism industry. Those who enjoy the conviviality of the international crowds can stay on the main roads and soak up all the hubbub. Only you can decide which Ireland you want to experience.

1 THE IVERAGH PENINSULA

Millions of tourists who come to County Kerry each year are dependent upon the turn of a bus driver's wheel for their tour of the Iveragh Peninsula—which means they see nothing save for the famed two-lane road known as the Ring of Kerry. There's certainly plenty to see there, but it's worth mentioning that the 178km (110-mile) road traces only the shores. In total, the peninsula is nearly 1,813 sq. km (700 sq. miles) of wild splendor, which you'll only see if you're able to get off the tourist strip. Admittedly, almost everyone who gets this far feels compelled to "do" the Ring of Kerry, so once it's done, why not take an unplanned turn, get a little lost, and let serendipity lead you to the unspoiled heart of Kerry?

ESSENTIALS

GETTING THERE　Bus Éireann (© 064/34777; www.buseireann.ie) provides limited daily service from Killarney to Cahersiveen, Waterville, Kenmare, and other towns on the Ring of Kerry. The best way to get to the Ring is by car, on N70 and N71. Several Killarney-based tour companies offer daily sightseeing tours of the Ring (see section 2, "Killarney," later in this chapter).

VISITOR INFORMATION　Stop in at the **Killarney Tourist Office,** Aras Fáilte, at the Town Centre Car Park, Beech Road, Killarney (© 064/31633; www.killarney.ie), before you explore the area. It's open October to May Monday to Saturday 9:15am to 5:15pm, June and September daily 9am to 6pm, and July to August daily 9am to 8pm. During

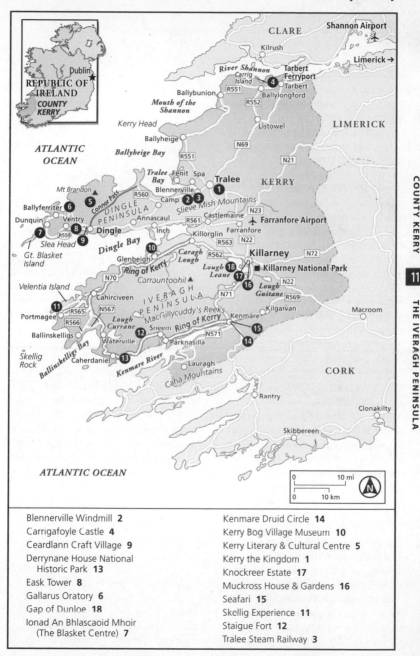

Blennerville Windmill **2**

Carrigafoyle Castle **4**

Ceardlann Craft Village **9**

Derrynane House National
   Historic Park **13**

Eask Tower **8**

Gallarus Oratory **6**

Gap of Dunloe **18**

Ionad An Bhlascaoid Mhoir
   (The Blasket Centre) **7**

Kenmare Druid Circle **14**

Kerry Bog Village Museum **10**

Kerry Literary & Cultural Centre **5**

Kerry the Kingdom **1**

Knockreer Estate **17**

Muckross House & Gardens **16**

Seafari **15**

Skellig Experience **11**

Staigue Fort **12**

Tralee Steam Railway **3**

low season, the office occasionally closes for lunch from 1 to 2pm. The **Kenmare Tourist Office,** Market Square, Kenmare (② **064/41233**), is open daily Easter through September from 9:15am to 5:30pm, with extended hours in July and August. The rest of the year (Oct–Easter), it's open Monday to Saturday. More information is available online at www.kerrytourist.com.

THE RING OF KERRY ★★★

Undoubtedly Ireland's most popular scenic drive, the Ring of Kerry is the name for the small highway that skirts the edges of the Iveragh Peninsula, passing along the way a panorama of rugged coastline, tall mountains, and pristine lakes. What you won't find, at least in the summertime, is much in the way of peace. Bicyclists avoid the route because of the scores of tour buses thundering down it from early morning until late in the day. Most people traveling the route start and finish at its largest hub, Killarney, but the town of Kenmare makes for a more charming (and certainly more quiet) base. *Tip:* You can go either way, but we recommend a counterclockwise route for the most spectacular views.

Originally called Neidin (pronounced Nay-*deen,* meaning "little nest" in Irish), **Kenmare** is indeed a little nest of verdant foliage and colorful buildings nestled between the River Roughty and Kenmare Bay. It's an enchanting little place with flower boxes at every window, sparkling clean sidewalks, and lots of restaurants and plenty of places to stay.

From Kenmare to busy **Killarney,** the Ring road takes you through a scenic mountain stretch known as **Moll's Gap.** Killarney is best known for its glorious surroundings, in particular the spectacular landscapes of **Killarney National Park,** which includes the **Killarney Lakes** and the scenic **Gap of Dunloe.** The town itself, though, while colorful and bustling, is a victim of its own success. Tourism is more in-your-face here than perhaps anywhere else in Kerry, with generic leprechaun-laden souvenir shops and overpriced restaurants on every corner. So, to avoid becoming jaded, head out of town and get back on the road as quickly as possible. Along the way, you'll pass the lovely seaside town of **Portmagee,** which is connected by a bridge to leafy **Valentia Island.**

Departing Killarney, follow the signs for **Killorglin,** a smallish town that lights up in mid-August when it has a traditional horse, sheep, and cattle fair. It's officially called the **Puck Fair,** because local residents capture a wild goat (symbolizing the *puka* or *puki,* a mischievous sprite in Celtic legend) from the mountains and enthrone it in the center of town as a sign of unrestricted merrymaking. There's a whimsical statue of a goat by the river in honor of this town's love of the *puka.*

Continue on the N70, and glimpses of Dingle Bay will soon appear on your right. **Carrantuohill,** at 1,041m (3,414 ft.) Ireland's tallest mountain, is to your left, and bleak views of open bog land constantly come into view.

The Ring winds around cliffs and the edges of mountains, with nothing but the sea below—another reason you will probably average only 50kmph (31 mph), at best. As you go along, you'll notice the remnants of many stone cottages dotting the fields along the way. Most date from the mid-19th-century Great Famine, when millions of people starved to death or were forced to emigrate. This area was hard hit, and the peninsula alone lost three-fourths of its population.

Glenbeigh is next on the Ring, and it's a sweet little seafront town with streets lined with palm trees and a sandy beach. It makes a good spot for a break, or you could continue along the sea's edge to **Cahersiveen,** where you can zip across to the little island of **Valentia.** In the 18th century, the Valentia harbor was notorious as a refuge for smugglers and privateers; it's said that John Paul Jones, the Scottish-born American naval officer in the War of Independence, also anchored here quite often.

From Valentia you can hop a ferry to arguably the most magical site of the Ring of Kerry, an island just off its shore: **Skellig Michael,** a rocky pinnacle towering over the sea, where medieval monks built a monastery in exquisite isolation. Today, the ruins of their church, reached by way of rambling stone staircases up the sides of cliffs at the edge of the cobalt sea, still convey a sense of deep spirituality. Seabirds nest here in abundance, and more than 20,000 pairs of gannets inhabit neighboring Little Skellig during the summer nesting season. The crossing to the island can be rough, so you'll want to visit on as clear and calm a day as possible.

Head next for **Waterville,** an idyllic beach resort between Lough Currane and Ballinskelligs Bay. For years it was a favorite retreat of Charlie Chaplin, and there's a statue of him near the beach.

If you follow the sea road north of town to the Irish-speaking village of **Ballinskelligs,** you'll see where the medieval monastery is slowly rotting away. There's a sandy Blue Flag beach just past the post office by Ballinskelligs Bay, and at the end of the beach are the remnants of a 16th-century castle.

Continuing on the N70, the next point of interest is **Derrynane,** at **Caherdaniel. Derrynane** is the former seat of the O'Connell clan and erstwhile home to Daniel O'Connell ("the Liberator" who freed Irish Catholics from the last of the English Penal Laws in the 19th c.).

From there, watch for signs to **Staigue Fort,** about 3km (2 miles) off the main road. This well-preserved ancient stone fort is constructed of rough stones without mortar of any kind. The walls are 4m (13 ft.) thick at the base. Historians are not certain what purpose it served—it may have been a fortress, or just a kind of prehistoric community center—but experts think it probably dates from around 1000 B.C.

Sneem, the next village on the circuit, is a colorful little hamlet, where houses are painted in vibrant shades. The colors—blue, pink, yellow, and orange—burst out on a rainy day, like a little touch of the Mediterranean.

From here, you're no distance at all from your starting point, and you've made your way around the Ring.

Seeing the Sights

Derrynane House National Historic Park ★

On a comfortable estate along the Ring of Kerry coast between Waterville and Caherdaniel, this manor house was once the seat of the O'Connells and is where Ireland's Great Liberator, Daniel O'Connell, lived for most of his life. The Irish government maintains the house as a museum, filled with documents, illustrations, and memorabilia related to O'Connell's life. Some pieces are more interesting than others—take, for example, the chariot in which he traveled triumphantly through Dublin after his release from prison in 1844.

Caherdaniel, County Kerry. ✆ **066/947-5113.** Admission €2.90 ($4.65) adults, €2.10 ($3.35) seniors, €1.50 ($2.40) students and children, €7.40 ($12) families. Nov–Mar Sat–Sun 1–5pm; Apr and Oct Tues–Sun 1–5pm; May–Sept Mon–Sat 9am–6pm, Sun 11am–7pm.

Kenmare Druid Circle ★ On a small hill near the central town market, this large Bronze Age druid stone circle is magnificently intact, with 15 standing stones arranged around a central boulder, which still bears signs (circular holes, a shallow dent at the center) of having been used in ceremonies. To find it, walk down to the market square and follow signs on the left side of the road.

Kenmare, County Kerry.

Kerry Bog Village Museum This little cluster of thatched-roof cottages effectively demonstrates what life was like in Kerry in the early 1800s. The museum village has a blacksmith's forge and house, turf cutter's house, laborer's cottage, thatcher's dwelling, and tradesman's house. Stacks of cut turf are piled high by the road.

Ring of Kerry rd. (N71), Ballycleave, Glenbeigh, County Kerry. ℭ **066/976-9184.** www.kerrybogvillage.ie. Admission €6 ($9.60) adults, €5 ($8) seniors and students, €4 ($6.40) children. AE, DC, MC, V. Mar–Nov daily 9am–6pm; Dec–Feb by appointment.

Seafari Eco-nature Cruises and Seal-Watching Trips Ⓚⁱᵈˢ This is a good option for families who want to interest their kids in Kenmare Bay—aboard a 49-foot covered boat. The 2-hour cruise covers 16km (10 miles) and is narrated by guides well versed in local history and wildlife, including dolphins, sea otters, and gray seals who frolic nearby. Boats depart from the pier next to the Kenmare suspension bridge. From May to October, as many as four cruises may depart daily, depending on demand. Reservations are recommended.

Kenmare Pier, Kenmare, County Kerry. ℭ **064/42059.** www.seafariireland.com. Tickets €20 ($32) adults, €18 ($29) students, €15 ($24) children 12–18, €13 ($21) children 11 and under, €60 ($96) families with children 11 and under, €65 ($104) families with children 12–16.

The Skellig Experience Just off the Ring of Kerry route (R765) on Valentia Island, this well-designed information center blends right into the terrain, its stark stone facade framed by grassy mounds based on the design of ancient archaeological sites. A series of displays tell the story of the lives of the monks who once existed in near total isolation on Skellig Rocks, Skellig Michael, and Little Skellig. There's a section on the geology of the area and an informative bit on the seabirds that are now the islands' main inhabitants. Finally, you can take a (pricey) boat tour around the islands.

Skellig Heritage Centre, Valentia Island, County Kerry. ℭ **066/947-6306.** www.skelligexperience.com. Exhibition and audiovisual €5 ($8) adults, €4 ($6.40) seniors and students, €3 ($4.80) children 11 and under, €14 ($22) families (2 adults and up to 4 children); exhibition, audiovisual, and sea cruise €28 ($45) adults, €25 ($40) seniors and students, €15 ($24) children 11 and under. Apr–Oct daily 10am–6pm.

Shopping

Many good craft and souvenir shops lie along the Ring of Kerry, but those in **Kenmare** offer the most in terms of variety and quality. Kenmare shops are open year-round, usually Monday to Saturday 9am to 6pm. From May to September, many shops remain open until 9 or 10pm, and some open on Sunday from noon to 5 or 6pm.

Avoca Handweavers at Moll's Gap High on a mountain pass (288m/945 ft. above sea level) between Killarney and Kenmare, this isolated shop is an outpost of the famed County Wicklow weavers. As in all Avoca shops, the stock here features colorful, hand-woven blankets and throws, delicate knitted clothing, and pottery and jewelry in vivid colors. The excellent cafe makes a great place to stop for lunch or afternoon tea and cake. Closed from November to mid-March. Ring of Kerry rd. (N71), Moll's Gap, County Kerry. ℭ **064/34720.**

The Skellig Islands

Craggy, inhospitable islands rising precipitously from the tumultuous sea, the **Skelligs** ★★★ look extraordinary, holding onto the earth where gray skies meet stormy horizons about 14km (8²/₃ miles) off the coast of the Iveragh Peninsula. Seen from the mainland, the islands appear impossibly steep and sharp angled. They must have seemed even more formidable in the 6th and 7th centuries, when simply getting to the islands would have been a dangerous prospect, and yet not only did a small community of devout monks build a community there, but they built it on the steepest, most wind-battered peaks of all. Over the course of many years, they carved 600 steps into the cliff face. Gradually they built monastic buildings amid the rocks hundreds of feet above the churning sea. There is something tragic and beautiful about the remains of the ancient oratories and beehive cells, the largest of which is about 4×4m (13×13 ft.). Historians know very little about these monks and how they lived, although they were apparently influenced by the Coptic Church founded by St. Anthony in Egypt, and, like the saint, sought intense isolation. Records relating to the Skelligs indicate that, even here, all but completely hidden, the Vikings found the monastery, and punished it as they did all the Irish monastic settlements. Monks were kidnapped and killed in attacks in the 8th century, but the settlement always recovered. To this day, nobody knows why the monks finally abandoned the rock in the 12th century.

The passage to the islands by boat takes about 45 minutes, while the ascent up the steps is also time-consuming and only for the fit.

Ferries from Valentia Island are run by **Des Lavelle** (© **066/947-6124;** http://indigo.ie/~lavelles), while those from Portmagee are run by **O'Keefe's** (© **066/947-7103**). The average cost is €40 ($64) per person.

De Barra Jewellery   Having taken over the family jewelry business a couple of years ago, talented young jeweler Shane de Barra has put his own stamp on things in this small, elegant shop on Kenmare's main street. His freshwater pearl concoctions in silver or gold and his restrained beautiful touch on gold rings and bangles mark this place as special. Best of all, prices are reasonable. Main St., Kenmare, County Kerry. © **064/41867.**

Kenmare Bookshop   This shop specializes in books on Ireland—biographies and books by Irish writers, as well as maps and guides to the surrounding area. This is a good place for hikers to find survey maps and walking and specialist guides, and for sailors to track down marine charts. Shelbourne St., Kenmare, County Kerry. © **064/41578.**

Quills Woolen Market   This shop has two locations, both of which are good for chunky, Aran hand knits, traditional Donegal tweed jackets, delicate Irish linen, Celtic jewelry, and hand-loomed knitwear. Market Sq. and Main St., Kenmare, County Kerry. © **064/32277.** South Sq., Sneem, County Kerry. © **064/45277.**

Sports & Outdoor Pursuits

GOLF   **Waterville Golf Links,** Waterville (© **066/947-4102;** www.watervillegolflinks. ie), sits at the edge of the Atlantic. On huge sand dunes, bounded on three sides by the sea, the 18-hole championship course is one of the longest in Ireland (7,184 yd.). Visitors are welcome. Greens fees start at €180 ($288) daily, cheaper for early birds.

Other challenging 18-hole courses on the Ring include **Dooks Golf Club,** Glenbeigh (© **066/976-8205;** www.dooks.com), a links par-70 course on the Ring of Kerry road, with greens fees of €85 ($136); and the expanded **Kenmare Golf Club,** Kenmare (© **064/41291;** www.kenmaregolfclub.com), a parkland par-71 course where greens fees run €50 ($80) weekdays and Saturdays, €55 ($88) on Sundays.

WALKING The low, long-distance path, the **Kerry Way,** traverses the extraordinary scenery of the Ring of Kerry. The first stage, from Killarney National Park to Glenbeigh, travels inland over rolling hills and past pastoral scenes. The second stage circles the Iveragh Peninsula via the towns of Cahersiveen, Waterville, Caherdaniel, Sneem, and Kenmare with a farther inland walk along the old Kenmare Road back to Killarney, for a total of 202km (125 miles). The route consists primarily of paths and "green roads" (old, unused roads built as make-work famine relief projects and now converted into walking paths). Maps outlining the route are available from the Killarney and Kenmare tourist offices (some are free, though the better ones cost a couple of euros), while good walking guides are available from bookstores in the area.

Where to Stay
Very Expensive
Park Hotel Kenmare ★★★ (Finds) Ensconced in a palm-tree-lined garden beside Kenmare Bay, this imposing 19th-century building was originally built by the Great Southern Railway for first-class train travelers. Some things never change, and it's still a grand, luxury hotel. In the high-ceilinged sitting rooms, fires crackle in the open fireplaces and original oil paintings decorate the walls. There's a full set of armor at the top of the grand staircase surrounded by tapestries and rare antiques. Guest rooms have exquisite Georgian and Victorian furnishings, and some have four-posters, all with firm mattresses, rich fabrics, and peaceful waterfront or mountain views. The hotel restaurant has a similarly romantic perspective, and is acclaimed for its modern Irish cuisine. The hotel spa, **Sámas,** is famed in Ireland for its creative use of the gorgeous, bucolic setting (the spa's heated pool fits in particularly well with the surroundings) to induce relaxation and for beauty treatments ranging from hot-stone massages to facials. Obviously, none of this comes cheap, but then you expected that.

Kenmare, County Kerry. © **800/323-5463** in the U.S., or 064/41200. Fax 064/41402. www.parkkenmare. com. 46 units. €364–€606 ($582–$970) double; €696–€846 ($1,114–$1,354) suites. AE, DC, MC, V. Closed Nov 30–Dec 22 and Jan 4–Feb 12. **Amenities:** Restaurant (Modern Irish); bar; 18-hole golf course; tennis court; spa and beauty treatments; concierge; room service; babysitting; laundry service; nonsmoking rooms; croquet lawn; drawing room; joggers' trail; salmon fishing. *In room:* TV, CD player, minibar, hair dryer, garment press.

Sheen Falls Lodge ★★★ Originally the 18th-century home of the earl of Kerry, this salubrious resort sits beside a natural waterfall amid vast, sprawling grounds filled with a mixture of smooth lawns and lush gardens. The public areas are decorated in lemony tones, with plenty of polished woodwork, open fireplaces, and original oil paintings. Reception staff members address guests by name, the bar feels like a drawing room, and the 1,000-volume library, with its green leather sofas and floor-to-ceiling bookshelves, is like an old-fashioned gentlemen's club. Guest rooms are spacious, decorated in rich, contemporary style; each overlooks the falls (stunning when floodlit at night) or the bay. There are also some self-catering cottages and villas available for those with deep pockets and a desire for privacy. It comes at a price, but this is the perfect Irish country-house atmosphere: elegant and yet relaxed.

Kenmare, County Kerry. (© **800/537-8483** in the U.S., or 064/41600. Fax 064/41386. www.sheenfalls lodge.ie. 66 units. €310–€455 ($496–$728) double. Full breakfast €24 ($38). AE, DC, MC, V. Closed Jan 2–Feb 1. **Amenities:** 2 restaurants (French, bistro); bar; indoor swimming pool; tennis; gym; spa; health and beauty treatments; Jacuzzi; concierge; room service; laundry service; dry cleaning; billiard room; croquet; library; helicopter pad; horseback riding; library; private salmon fishing. *In room:* A/C, TV/VCR, radio, minibar, hair dryer, garment press.

Moderate

Derrynane Hotel ★   Perched on a precipice between the mountainous coast and the open waters of the Atlantic, this contemporary hotel boasts one of the Ring's most dramatic and remote locations, next to the Derrynane National Park and midway between Waterville and Sneem. The guest rooms are basic, but you might forgive them for that once you take in the superb views. There are a few amenities, including an outdoor swimming pool, should the weather be accommodating enough for a swim. A local guide is available to take guests on weekend walking trips.

Off Ring of Kerry rd. (N71), Caherdaniel, County Kerry. (© **800/528-1234** or 066/947-5136. Fax 066/947-5160. www.derrynane.com. 70 units. €180–€200 ($288–$320) double. Rates include service charge and full Irish breakfast. AE, DC, MC, V. Closed early Oct to mid-Apr. **Amenities:** Restaurant (international); lounge; outdoor swimming pool; tennis court; gym; sauna/steam room; seaweed baths. *In room:* TV.

Iskeroon ★★ (Finds)   This is as good as it gets for this price. David and Geraldine Hare's charming B&B sits amid an arrestingly beautiful natural setting overlooking the sailboats of Derrynane Harbour and the Skelligs beyond. If the view and the exotic subtropical gardens aren't enough, just step inside. The Hares have renovated their villa (built in the 1930s) in a fresh, Cape Cod style, with flagstone floors and a deep blue palette, decorated with locally made furniture and tasteful art. There are plenty of extras, including portable DVD players and a vast DVD library. Breakfasts are exceptional, with homemade bread and free-range eggs and bacon. This place is a real find. They've changed the rules here recently to require a minimum 2-night stay, and recently added a self-catering cottage (€500/$800 per week) for those who would like a little more privacy.

Bunavalla (near pier), Caherdaniel, County Kerry. (© **066/947-5119.** Fax 066/947-5488. www.iskeroon.com. 2 units, all with private bathroom. €160 ($256) double. Rates include service charge and full Irish breakfast. MC, V. Closed Oct–Apr. **Amenities:** Lounge. *In room:* TV.

Kenmare Bay   This modern hotel on a hillside at the edge of Kenmare recently underwent a major renovation and expansion, and the changes are all for the better. Guest rooms have been spruced up, and given a sleeker look, with neutral paint and linens, and nicely modernized bathrooms. The lobby is brighter, more sophisticated and relaxing than before. New self-catering cottages have been built around the central building, offering more options for travelers. It has a handy restaurant and bar. Still, the big draw here is the sweeping views from nearly all of the large windows.

Sneem rd., Kenmare, County Kerry. (© **064/41300.** Fax 064/41541. www.kenmarebayhotel.com. 128 units. €140–€220 ($224–$352) double. Rates include service charge and full breakfast. AE, DC, MC, V. Closed Nov–Mar. **Amenities:** Restaurant (international); bar; gym. *In room:* TV.

Sallyport House ★★   This country-house B&B has many things going for it—a great location, a 2-minute walk into Kenmare, and its extensive manicured grounds. It's a handsome manor with a sophisticated, luxurious feel. The spacious guest rooms are furnished with well-chosen antiques and have grand bathrooms. The rooms are made even more desirable by their gorgeous views of the surrounding countryside.

Glengarriff rd., Kenmare, County Kerry. ✆ **064/42066.** Fax 064/42067. www.sallyporthouse.com. 5 units. €150–€170 ($240–$272) double. Rates include service charge and full breakfast. No children 11 and under. No credit cards. Closed Nov–Mar. **Amenities:** Lounge; nonsmoking rooms. *In room:* TV, hair dryer.

Shelburne Lodge ★★ This Georgian farmhouse has been transformed into one of the most original, stylish, and comfortable B&Bs in Killowen. Every room has polished wood parquet floors, quality antique furnishings, contemporary art, and a luxurious but homey feel. The guest rooms are all large and gorgeously appointed, and breakfasts are virtually decadent.

Killowen, Cork rd., Kenmare, County Kerry. ✆ **064/41013.** Fax 064/42067. www.shelburnelodge.com. 9 units. €100–€160 ($160–$256) double. Rates include service charge and full breakfast. MC, V. Closed Dec to mid-Mar. **Amenities:** Tennis court; drawing room. *In room:* TV.

Tahilla Cove ★ This grand country house sprawls along the edge of the water in a secluded cove near Sneem. Owned by the same family for decades now, this is a house of great character. The vast wooded acreage around the building gives it a feeling of seclusion, and the friendly Waterhouse family runs the place with unpretentious affability. The spacious bedrooms are comfortably and simply furnished and have private balconies, some with great views of Beara Peninsula (ask for a room with a sea view). You can borrow one of the boats and row out into the water, or go for a walk with the family's energetic spaniels—bring your own dog! This is a dog-friendly hotel. **Dinners** here are like house parties, and are well worth staying for.

On the N70, follow signs, Sneem, County Kerry. ✆ **064/45204.** Fax 064/4504. www.tahillacove.com. 9 units. €120–€150 ($192–$240) double. Rates include service charge and full breakfast. MC, V. Closed Dec to mid-Mar. **Amenities:** Drawing room; fishing; boating. *In room:* TV, tea/coffeemaker, hair dryer, iron.

Inexpensive

Hawthorn House ★ ⟨Value⟩ On a quiet side street in Kenmare, this town-house B&B is an excellent value and has a huge following. Mary O'Brien is a congenial hostess, and her guest rooms have a feminine feel with floral touches and pale walls. Rooms here may be slightly smaller than you'd find at rural B&Bs, but they are comfortable and attractive. Breakfasts are bountiful and delicious.

Shelbourne St., Kenmare, County Kerry. ✆ **064/41035.** Fax 064/41932. www.hawthornhousekenmare. com. 8 units. €80–€90 ($128–$144) double. Rates include service charge and full breakfast. MC, V. Closed Christmas. **Amenities:** Sitting room. *In room:* TV, hair dryer.

Where to Dine
Expensive

d'Arcy's Oyster Bar and Grill ★ CONTINENTAL In a two-story stone house at the top end of Kenmare, this restaurant has a homey atmosphere with a big open fireplace. The house specialty is Irish oysters, but there are plenty of other seafood options as well. The homemade breads and desserts are also excellent. There are also seven well-appointed rooms upstairs, for those who fall in love with the place (€140/$224 double).

Main St., Kenmare, County Kerry. ✆ **064/41589.** www.darcys.ie. Reservations recommended. Main courses €21–€31 ($34–$50). MC, V. Oyster bar daily noon–10pm. Grill daily 6–9:30pm. Closed Jan to mid-Mar.

Lime Tree ★★ MODERN IRISH Innovative cuisine is the focus at this Kenmare restaurant in an 1821 landmark renovated schoolhouse next to the Park Hotel. Paintings by local artists line the stone walls in the atmospheric dining room. The menu offers modern interpretations of classic Irish dishes and European cuisine in such dishes as the filet of beef with horseradish rösti and green-peppercorn cream, or falafel strudel with yogurt and dill oil. The restaurant shows a sense of humor in its variation on the Caesar salad, with fresh greens and capers—called the "Brutus salad."

Shelbourne Rd., Kenmare, County Kerry. ℰ **064/41225.** www.limetreerestaurant.com. Reservations recommended. Main courses €20–€26 ($32–$42). MC, V. Apr–Nov daily 6:30–10pm.

Mulcahy's MODERN/FUSION   A good example of why Kenmare has become one of Ireland's foodie towns, Mulcahy's is dedicated to imaginative fusion cooking. Starters might include anything from pea soup to sushi, and Asian influences come to bear on Irish dishes like the Kerry lamb with pistachio crust. Everything is done imaginatively, with a bit of restraint.

16 Henry St., Kenmare, County Kerry. ℰ **064/42383.** Reservations recommended. Main courses €18–€30 ($29–$48). MC, V. June–Sept daily 6–10pm, Sun noon–3pm; Oct–May Thurs–Mon 6:15–10pm. Closed 2 weeks in Nov.

Moderate

The Blue Bull TRADITIONAL IRISH   Sneem is so small that if you blink, you miss it. Yet it has several good pubs, and this one serves excellent food. There are three small rooms, each with an open fireplace, plus a sky-lit conservatory in the back. Time-honored Irish fare, like smoked salmon and Irish stew, shares the menu with such dishes as salmon stuffed with spinach and Valencia scallops in brandy—all served to a backdrop of traditional Irish music on most nights. According to the pub's owners, the Blue Bull also holds the dubious honor of being Andrew Lloyd Webber's favorite place to eat in Ireland.

South Sq., Ring of Kerry rd. (N70), Sneem, County Kerry. ℰ **064/45382.** www.sneem.com/bluebull.html. Reservations recommended. Main courses €10–€25 ($16–$40). AE, MC, V. Bar food year-round daily 11am–8pm. Restaurant Mar–Oct daily 6–10pm.

Packie's MODERN IRISH   If you're looking for a stylish place to have a great meal that won't break the bank, this is the place. There's always a buzz here, and the smart crowd fits in perfectly with the bistro look—colorful window boxes, slate floors, stone walls filled with contemporary art. Everyone comes for the food: tried-and-true favorites such as Irish lamb stew, crisp potato pancakes, seafood sausages, and crab claws in garlic butter. Desserts are terrific, too.

Henry St., Kenmare, County Kerry. ℰ **064/41508.** Reservations recommended. Main courses €15–€30 ($24–$48). MC, V. Mid-Mar to Dec Tues–Sat 6–10pm (also Mon 6–10pm in summer).

Inexpensive

Prego ★ Ⓥalue ITALIAN   When you're craving a break from all that heavy Irish food, head here for fresh, tasty Italian cuisine. The pasta is all homemade, and served with a light touch on the sauce. Salads are big and crisp, and the thin-crust pizzas are all made from scratch to order. All the classics are here and are well made.

Henry St., Kenmare, County Kerry. ℰ **064/42350.** All items €7–€15 ($11–$24). MC, V. Daily 9am–10:30pm.

Purple Heather ★ IRISH   This lovely little eatery is *the* place to lunch in Kenmare. The food consists of tearoom classics with a gourmet twist—wild smoked salmon or prawn salad; smoked trout pâté; vegetarian omelets; Irish cheese platters; and fresh, homemade soups.

Henry St., Kenmare, County Kerry. ℰ **064/41016.** www.kenmarerestaurants.com/purpleheather. All items €6–€18 ($9.60–$29). No credit cards. Mon–Sat 11am–7pm. Closed Sun, Christmas week, and bank holidays.

2 KILLARNEY

135km (84 miles) SW of Shannon, 309km (192 miles) SW of Dublin, 87km (54 miles) W of Cork, 111km (69 miles) SW of Limerick, 193km (120 miles) SW of Galway

Perhaps the busiest tourist hub in rural Ireland, Killarney's sidewalks are spacious enough in the winter, but in the summertime, they're absolutely packed, as the streets become one giant tour-bus traffic jam and horse-and-buggy drivers risk life and limb to push their way through. The locals are well practiced at dispensing a professional brand of Irish charm, even as they hike up the hotel and restaurant prices to capitalize on the hordes descending from the buses. It all feels a bit cynical, with a few too many cheesy leprechaun-heavy gift shops for its own good. It's a bit much for some people, and hardly the bucolic, gentle Ireland that many are looking for. Luckily, it's easy enough to resist Killarney's gravitational pull and spend your time exploring the quieter countryside around it. You can always sneak into town from time to time for dinner or a night out in the pub with lots of people from your home nation.

Ironically, Killarney's popularity has nothing to do with the town itself; the attraction is the valley in which it nestles—a verdant landscape of lakes and mountains so spectacular that Brendan Behan once said, "Even an ad man would be ashamed to eulogize it." Exploring its glories is certainly easy—just walk (or drive) from the town parking lot toward the cathedral and turn left. In a matter of minutes, you'll forget all that Killarney stress amid the quiet rural splendor of the 65-sq.-km (25-sq.-mile) **Killarney National Park.** Here the ground is a soft carpet of moss and the air is fragrant with wildflowers. Cars are banned from most of the ferny trails, so take a hike or hire a "jarvey," an old-fashioned horse-and-buggy available for hire at reasonable prices. Within the park's limits are two estates, **Muckross** and **Knockreer,** and the romantic remains of medieval abbeys and castles. At almost every turn, you'll see Killarney's own botanical wonder, the arbutus, or "strawberry tree," plus eucalyptus, redwoods, and native oak.

For many, the main attractions are the park's three lakes. The largest of these, the Lower Lake, is sometimes called Lough Leane or Lough Lein, which means "the lake of learning." It's more than 6km (3¾ miles) long and is dotted with 30 small islands. Nearby are the Middle Lake or Muckross Lake, and the smallest of the three, the Upper Lake. The most noteworthy of Killarney's islands, **Innisfallen,** seems to float peacefully in the Lower Lake. You can allegedly reach it by rowboat, available for rental at Ross Castle, but on a recent visit, the boathouse was unmanned all day, and trying to figure out just who was responsible for the boats proved impossible, so that franchise may be in flux. If you can get a boat and row yourself out, you can see what's left of the monastery St. Fallen, which was founded in the 7th century and flourished for 1,000 years. It's said that Brian Boru, the great Irish chieftain, and St. Brendan the Navigator were educated here. From 950 to 1320, the "Annals of Innisfallen," a chronicle of early Irish history, was written at the monastery; it's now in the Bodleian Library at Oxford University. Traces of an 11th-century church and a 12th-century priory can still be seen today.

ESSENTIALS

GETTING THERE **Aer Arann** (✆ 011/353-81821-0210 in the U.S., 818/210-210 in Ireland, or 0800/587-23-24 in the U.K.; www.aerarann.ie) offers regular flights from Dublin into Kerry County Airport, Farranfore, County Kerry (✆ 066/976-4644; www.kerryairport.ie), about 16km (10 miles) north of Killarney. **Ryanair** (www.ryanair.com) flies direct from London (Stansted) to Kerry.

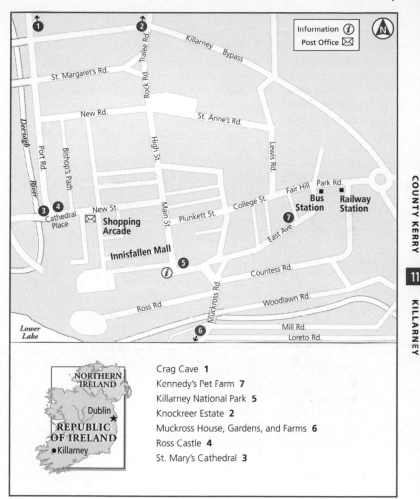

Crag Cave **1**
Kennedy's Pet Farm **7**
Killarney National Park **5**
Knockreer Estate **2**
Muckross House, Gardens, and Farms **6**
Ross Castle **4**
St. Mary's Cathedral **3**

Irish Rail trains from Dublin, Limerick, Cork, and Galway arrive daily at the **Killarney Railway Station** (✆ **064/31067;** www.irishrail.ie), Railway Road, off East Avenue Road.

Bus Éireann operates regularly scheduled service into Killarney from all parts of Ireland. The bus depot (✆ **064/34777;** www.buseireann.ie) is adjacent to the train station at Railway Road, off East Avenue Road.

Kerry folk like to say that all roads lead to Killarney, and at least a half-dozen major national roads do. They include N21 and N23 from Limerick, N22 from Tralee, N22 from Cork, N72 from Mallow, and N70 from the Ring of Kerry and West Cork.

VISITOR INFORMATION The **Killarney Tourist Office,** Aras Fáilte, is at the town center on Beech Road (© 064/31633). It's open October to May Monday to Saturday 9:15am to 5:15pm, June and September daily 9am to 6pm, and July to August daily 9am to 8pm. During low season, the office occasionally closes for lunch from 1 to 2pm. It offers many helpful booklets, including the *Tourist Trail* walking-tour guide and the *Killarney Area Guide,* with maps.

Useful local publications include ***Where: Killarney,*** a quarterly magazine distributed free at hotels and guesthouses. It is packed with current information on tours, activities, events, and entertainment.

TOWN LAYOUT Killarney is small, with a full-time population of approximately 7,000. The town is built around one central thoroughfare, Main Street, which changes its name to High Street at midpoint. The principal offshoots of Main Street are Plunkett Street, which becomes College Street, and New Street. The Deenagh River edges the western side of town and East Avenue Road edges the eastern side.

The busiest section of town is at the southern tip of Main Street, where it meets East Avenue Road. Here the road curves and heads southward out to the Muckross road and the entrance to Killarney National Park.

GETTING AROUND Killarney Town is so small and compact that there is no local bus service; the best way to get around is on foot. For a quick and easy tour, follow the signposted Tourist Trail for the highlights of the main streets. It takes less than 2 hours to complete. A booklet outlining the sights along the trail is available at the tourist office.

Taxi cabs line up at the rank on **College Square** (© 064/31331). You can also phone for a taxi from **Killarney Cabs** (© 064/37444), **Dero's Taxi Service** (© 064/31251), or **Euro Cabs** (© 064/35624).

There are a couple of large public parking lots near the town center, where parking costs upwards of €1 ($1.60) per hour. It's a good idea to leave your car in one of these unless you're heading out to Killarney National Park on the Muckross and Kenmare road (N71).

If you need to rent a car in Killarney, contact **Budget,** c/o International Hotel, Kenmare Place (© 064/34341; www.budget.ie), or **Randles Bros.,** Muckross road (© 064/31237). Alternatively, **Avis** has a branch at Kerry Airport (© 066/976-4499; www.avis.ie) and **Hertz** has branches at Cork Airport (© 021/496-5849) and Shannon Airport (© 061/471-369; www.hertz.ie).

Horse-drawn **buggies,** called "jarveys," line up at Kenmare Place in Killarney Town. They offer rides to Killarney National Park sites and other scenic areas. Depending on the time and distance, prices range from €16 to €45 ($26–$72) per ride (up to four persons). For details, see "Organized Tours," below.

FAST FACTS If you need a drugstore, try **O'Sullivans Pharmacy,** 81 New St. (© 064/35866), or **Donal Sheahan,** 34 Main St. (© 064/31113).

In an **emergency,** dial © **999.** The **Killarney District Hospital** is on St. Margaret's Road (© 064/31076). The **Killarney Garda (Police) Station** is on New Road (© 064/31222).

The **Killarney Public Library,** on Rock Road (© 064/32655), provides Internet access from its bank of computers.

If you need to do your laundry, head for the **Gleesons Launderette,** Brewery Lane, off College Square (© 064/33877).

The **Killarney Post Office,** New Street (© 064/31461), is open Monday and Wednesday to Friday 9am to 5:30pm, Tuesday 9:30am to 5:30pm, and Saturday 9am to 1pm.

The Top Attractions

There's access to **Killarney National Park** ★★ (✆ **064/31947;** www.killarneynational
park.ie) from several points along the Kenmare road (N71). The main entrance is at
Muckross House, where the little visitor center can give you maps for walking or driving,
as well as a good rundown on what to expect. There's also a pleasant cafe with indoor and
outdoor seating if you need sustenance before setting out. Admission is free, and it's open
in all daylight hours year-round.

Just outside of town, the winding, rocky **Gap of Dunloe** ★★ rises through mountains and wetlands about 10km (6¼ miles) west of Killarney. The route through the gap
passes craggy hills, meandering streams, and deep gullies, and it ends in the park at Upper
Lake. One of the best ways to explore the gap is by bicycle (see "Bicycling," under "Sports
& Outdoor Pursuits," below). Horse fanciers may want to take one of the excursions
offered by **Castlelough Tours,** Shillelagh House, Knockasartnett (✆ **064/32496;** www.
castlelough-tours.com); **Corcoran's Tours,** Kilcummin (✆ **064/36666;** www.corcoran
tours.com); or **Dero's Tours,** 22 Main St. (✆ **064/31251** or 31567; www.derostours.
com). Combination horse/boat tours cost around €20 to €25 ($32–$40) per person. If
you'd rather have someone else handle the horse, you can take an 11km (6¾-mile) buggy
tour. Excursions go from Kate Kearney's Cottage through the Gap of Dunloe to Lord
Brandon's Cottage and back.

Knockreer Estate ★ The grand old house that once stood here burned down years
ago, but the gardens are lovely, and 200-year-old trees mix with sweet wildflowers and
azaleas for an attractive effect. There are beautiful views of the lake and the valley, and a
pathway leads down to the River Deenagh. Main access to Knockreer is through Deenagh Lodge Gate, opposite the cathedral, in town.

Cathedral Place, off New St., Killarney, County Kerry. ✆ **064/31440.** Free admission to gardens. Daily
during daylight hours.

Muckross House and Gardens ★★ This rambling ivy-covered Victorian mansion
was built for a wealthy landowner in 1843 and donated to the state in the 1930s. It is
now a museum of sorts, of life in the county, showcasing locally made furniture, prints,
art, and needlework, although it mixes them with non-Irish items like Oriental screens,
Chippendale chairs, and Turkish carpets. But never mind, it's all an attractive international mixture and pleasant enough to explore. The gardens outside are lovely, and you
can wander to the on-site restaurant and workshops, where local artisans demonstrate
bookbinding, weaving, and pottery.

The ruin of the 15th-century **Muckross Abbey,** founded about 1448 and burned by
Cromwell's troops in 1652, is also near the house. The abbey's central feature is a vaulted
cloister around a courtyard that contains a huge yew tree, said to be as old as the abbey itself.
W. M. Thackeray once called it "the prettiest little bijou of a ruined abbey ever seen."

Kenmare rd. (N71), Killarney, County Kerry. ✆ **064/31440.** www.muckross-house.ie. Admission house
only €5.75 ($9.20) adults, €4.50 ($7.20) seniors, €2.45 ($3.90) students and children, €15 ($24) families.
Joint ticket with Muckross Traditional Farms (below) €10 ($16) adults, €8 ($13) seniors, €5 ($8) students
and children, €27 ($43) families. Mar–Apr and Oct Sat–Sun 1–6pm; May daily 1–6pm; June–Sept daily
10am–6pm.

Muckross Traditional Farms ★★ (Kids) Not far from the Muckross House estate, these
farms are designed to demonstrate what traditional farm life was like in previous centuries in
County Kerry. It's cleverly done—the farmhouses and barns are so authentically detailed that

you feel as if you've dropped in on real farms. Work really does go on here, so farmhands work the fields, while the blacksmith, carpenter, and wheelwright ply their trades. Women draw water from the wells and cook meals in historically accurate kitchens. Children get a kick out of the animals, and it's interesting enough to keep adults from getting bored as well. *Note:* A combination ticket allows you to visit Muckross House for a small extra fee.

Kenmare rd. (N71), Killarney, County Kerry. ✆ **064/31440.** www.muckross-house.ie. Admission €6.50 ($10) adults, €5 ($8) seniors, €3 ($4.80) students and children. Joint ticket with Muckross House (above) €10 ($16) adults, €8 ($13) seniors, €5 ($8) students and children, €27 ($43) families. Mid-Mar to Apr and Oct Sat–Sun 1–6pm; May daily 1–6pm; June–Sept daily 10am–7pm.

Ross Castle ★   Just outside of Killarney Town, this 15th-century fortress still guards the edge of the Lower Lake. Built by the O'Donoghue chieftains, the castle was the last stronghold in Munster to surrender to Cromwell's forces in 1652. But it could not withstand time as well as the English army, and all that remains is a tower house, surrounded by a fortified *bawn* (walled garden) with rounded turrets. The tower has been furnished in the style of the late 16th and early 17th centuries. While you can wander the grounds at will, you can only see inside the castle on a guided tour, and these tend to be a bit tedious, as the guides seem to scrounge around a bit for facts interesting enough to justify the ticket price. In good weather, the best way to reach it is via a lakeside walk (it's 3km/2 miles from Killarney to the castle). From the castle, you can take a boat tour of the lake, although these are not for those allergic to touristy things.

Ross Rd., off Kenmare rd. (N71), Killarney, County Kerry. ✆ **064/35851.** Admission €5.30 ($8.50) adults, €3.70 ($5.90) seniors, €2.10 ($3.35) students and children, €12 ($19) families. Mar–May and Sept to mid-Oct daily 9:30am–5:30pm; June–Aug daily 9:30am–6:30pm; mid-Oct to mid-Nov daily 9:30am–4:30pm. Last admission 45 min. before closing.

St. Mary's Cathedral   Officially known as the Catholic Church of St. Mary of the Assumption, this limestone cathedral is designed in the Gothic Revival style, in the shape of a cross. Construction began in 1842, was interrupted by the famine, and concluded in 1855, although the towering spire wasn't added until 1912.

Cathedral Place, off Port Rd., Killarney, County Kerry. ✆ **064/31014.** Free admission; donations welcome. Daily 10:30am–6pm.

More Attractions

Crag Cave ★   Although they are believed to be more than a million years old, these limestone caves were not discovered until 1983. Today, they're open for the wandering (via guided tour only, of course). The guides accompany you 3,753m (12,310 ft.) into the well-lit cave passage on a half-hour tour revealing massive stalactites and fascinating caverns. If you just can't bear not to shop, even here there's a crafts shop. There are also a children's play area and a cafe. It's very touristy, but interesting nonetheless.

Off Limerick rd. (N21), 24km (15 miles) from Killarney, Castleisland, County Kerry. ✆ **066/714-1244.** www.cragcave.com. Admission €12 ($19) adults, €8 ($13) seniors and students, €5 ($8) children, €30 ($48) families (up to 4 children). Mid-Mar to Oct daily 10am–5:30pm (until 6pm July–Aug).

Kennedy's Pet Farm ⓚⁱᵈˢ   At this 30-hectare (74-acre) dairy and sheep farm surrounded by mountain vistas, kids can watch cows being milked, piglets being fed, and peacocks strutting their stuff. Horse-drawn machinery is on display, and it's all good rural fun.

9.7km (6 miles) east of Killarney, off the main Cork rd. (N22), Glenflesk, Killarney, County Kerry. ✆ **064/54054.** www.killarneypetfarm.com. Admission €8 ($13). Price includes pony ride for children. Feb–Oct daily 10am–5pm.

Organized Tours

In addition to Killarney's main sights, some bus tours also venture into the two prime scenic areas nearby: the Ring of Kerry and Dingle Peninsula. From May to September, tours are offered daily; prices range from €18 to €23 ($29–$37) per person. This list is far from exhaustive, but the following companies take tours outside Killarney: **Bus Éireann,** Bus Depot, Railway Road, off East Avenue Road (© **064/34777;** www.buseireann. ie); **Castlelough Tours,** Shillelagh House, Knockasartnett (© **064/32496;** www.castlelough-tours.com); **Corcoran's Chauffeur Tours,** 8 College St. (© **064/36666;** www.corcoran tours.com); and **Dero's Tours,** 22 Main St. (© **064/31251** or 31567; www.derostours. com).

Bus Tours

To get your bearings of the Killarney environs, consider one of these sightseeing tours:

Dero's Tours   As well as showing off Killarney's lakes from the best vantage points, this 3-hour tour takes you to Aghadoe, the Gap of Dunloe, Ross Castle, Muckross House and Gardens, and Torc Waterfall.

7 Main St., Killarney, County Kerry. © **064/31251** or 31567. www.derostours.com. Tour €25 ($40). May–Sept daily 10:30am; schedules vary.

Gap of Dunloe   This tour takes you through the spectacularly scenic Gap of Dunloe and includes a boat tour of the Killarney lakes. For an extra €20 ($32) you can also take a picturesque (but bumpy) horse-and-cart ride through the Black Valley.

Gap of Dunloe Tours, 7 High St., Killarney, County Kerry. © **064/30200.** www.gapofdunloetours.com. Tour €30 ($48). May–Sept; call for hours and reservations.

Buggy Tours

The quaint horse-driven buggies known as "jaunting cars" or "jarveys" that constantly clip-clop down the lanes around the lakes are one of the most persistent and charming features of the Killarney landscape. If you decide to give them a try, note that jaunting-car rates are set and monitored by the Killarney Urban District Council, so if you're quoted a price that seems outlandish, pass on by and try the next one. Current rates (per person, based on four people to a jaunting car) run roughly from €12 ($19) for a basic tour to €25 ($40) for a tour including lake cruise. The buggies are arguably the best way to get around the national park, since cars are not allowed. The price depends on the destinations, which include Ross Castle, Muckross House and Gardens, Torc Waterfall, Muckross Abbey, Dinis Island, and Kate Kearney's Cottage, gateway to the Gap of Dunloe. You can hire a buggy at the park near Muckross House, or to arrange a tour in advance, contact **Tangney Tours,** 10B Muckross Close, Killarney (© **064/33358;** www. killarneyjauntingcars.com).

Boat Tours

MV Lily of Killarney Tours   Departing from the pier at Ross Castle, this enclosed water bus cruises the lakes for just over an hour. Make reservations.

Old Weir Lodge, Muckross rd., Killarney, County Kerry. © **064/31068.** Tour €10 ($16) adults, €5 ($8) children 11 and under, €25 ($40) families. Apr–Oct daily 10:30am, noon, 1:45, 3:15, 4:30 and 5:45pm.

MV Pride of the Lakes Tours   This enclosed boat offers daily sailings from the pier at Ross Castle. The trip lasts just over an hour, and reservations are suggested.

Scotts Gardens, Killarney, County Kerry. © **064/32638.** Tour €10 ($16) adults, €5 ($8) children 11 and under, €25 ($40) families. Apr–Oct daily 11am, 12:30, 2:30, 4, and 5pm.

Shopping hours are usually Monday to Saturday 9am to 6pm, but from May through September or October, most stores are open every day until 9 or 10pm. Although there are more souvenir and craft shops than you can shake a shillelagh at, here are a few of the best:

Brian de Staic   Brian de Staic specializes in Celtic jewelry, handcrafted and engraved with ancient Celtic symbols or the letters of the ogham alphabet, an ancient Irish form of writing. Hours are Monday to Saturday from 9am to 6pm. 18 High St., Killarney, County Kerry. © 064/33822. www.briandestaic.com.

Christy's Irish Stores   A branch of the highly successful County Cork–based enterprise, this large store on the corner of Plunkett Street in the center of town carries an array of wares ranging from cheesy leprechaun souvenirs to genuinely attractive hand-knit or hand-loomed sweaters, crystal, china, and pottery. Prices are reasonable. 10 Main St., Killarney, County Kerry. © 064/33222.

Frank Lewis Gallery   This gallery sells contemporary and traditional paintings, sculptures, and photographic work—much of it with a Kerry theme—by emerging artists. It's in a restored artisan's dwelling near the post office. 6 Bridewell Lane, Killarney, County Kerry. © 064/34843.

Killarney Art Gallery   This shop-front gallery features original paintings by leading Irish artists, from the Killarney area and elsewhere, as well as art supplies, Irish prints, and engravings. 4 Plunkett St., Killarney, County Kerry. © 064/34628.

Killarney Bookshop   Stop at this shop for books on the history, legends, and lore of Killarney and Kerry. It also has a good stock of maps and other books of Irish and international interest. 32 Main St., Killarney, County Kerry. © 064/34108.

Mucros Craft Centre   On the grounds of Muckross House, this art studio and shop carries on local craft traditions in its weaver's workshop and pottery studio. There is also a wide selection of quality crafts from all over the country. Muckross House, Muckross rd., Killarney, County Kerry. © 064/31440.

Quill's Woollen Market   This is one of the best spots in town for hand-knit sweaters of all colors and types, along with mohair and sheepskins. As well as this shop, there are branches in Sneem and Kenmare on the Ring of Kerry, in Cork City, and at Ballingeary, County Cork (the original shop). 1 High St., Killarney, County Kerry. © 064/32277.

Serendipity   The shelves of this tidy shop feature a wide range of unusual crafts from local artisans, such as hand-thrown pottery from the likes of Nicholas Mosse and Stephen Pearce, Jerpoint glass, and handcrafted jewelry. 15 College St., Killarney, County Kerry. © 064/31056.

SPORTS & OUTDOOR PURSUITS

BICYCLING   **Killarney National Park,** with its lakeside and forest pathways, trails, and roads, is a paradise for bikers. If you haven't brought your own wheels, you can rent whatever you need here, from 21-speed touring bikes to mountain bikes to tandems. Rental charges average €15 ($24) per day, €80 ($128) per week. Bicycles can be rented from **David O'Sullivan's Cycles,** Bishop Lane, New Street (© 064/31282). Most shops are open year-round daily 9am to 6pm, until 8 or 9pm in the summer.

One great ride beginning in Killarney takes you through the Gap of Dunloe along a dirt forest road, where you'll see some of the best mountain scenery in the area. It can be made into a 56km (35-mile) loop if you return on N71.

FISHING   Fishing for salmon and brown trout in Killarney's unpolluted lakes and rivers is a popular pastime around here. Brown-trout fishing is free on the lakes, but a permit is necessary for the rivers Flesk and Laune. A trout permit costs €5 to €15 ($8–$24) per day.

Salmon fishing anywhere in Ireland requires a license; the cost is €36 ($58) per day, €50 ($80) for 21 days. In addition, some rivers also require a salmon permit, which costs €10 to €15 ($16–$24) per day. Permits and licenses can be obtained at the Fishery Office at the **Knockreer Estate Office,** New Street (© **064/31246**).

For fishing tackle, bait, rod rental, and other fishing gear, as well as permits and licenses, try **O'Neill's,** 6 Plunkett St. (© **064/31970**). The shop also arranges the hire of boats and *ghillies* (fishing guides) for €80 ($128) per day on the Killarney Lakes, leaving from Ross Castle.

GOLF   Visitors are always welcome at the twin 18-hole championship courses of the **Killarney Golf & Fishing Club,** Killorglin Road, Fossa (© **064/31034;** www.killarney-golf.com), 5km (3 miles) west of the town center. Widely praised as one of the most scenic golf settings in the world, these courses, known as Killeen and Mahony's Point, have gorgeous lake and mountain settings. Greens fees are €60 to €120 ($96–$192) weekdays and €70 to €130 ($112–$208) weekends.

HORSEBACK RIDING   Many trails in the Killarney area are suitable for horseback riding. Hiring a horse costs about €25 ($40) per hour at **Killarney Riding Stables,** N72, Ballydowney (© **064/31686;** www.killarney-trail-riding.com), and **Rocklands Stables,** Rockfield, Tralee Road (© **064/32592**). Lessons and weeklong trail rides can also be arranged.

WALKING   There are four signposted nature trails in the **Killarney National Park.** The **Mossy Woods Nature Trail** starts near Muckross House, by Muckross Lake, and rambles 2.4km (1.5 miles) through yew woods along low cliffs. The **Old Boat House Nature Trail** begins at the 19th-century boathouse below Muckross Gardens and leads .8km (.5 mile) around a small peninsula by Muckross Lake. **Arthur Young's Walk** (4.8km/3 miles) starts on the road to Dinis, traverses natural yew woods, and then follows a 200-year-old road on the Muckross Peninsula. The **Blue Pool Nature Trail** (2.4km/1.5 miles) travels from Muckross village through woodlands and past a small peaceful lake known as the Blue Pool. Maps of the four trails are available at the park's visitor center.

Rising steeply from the south shore of Muckross Lake, **Torc Mountain** provides spectacular views of the Killarney Lakes and nearby **MacGillycuddy's Reeks,** a moody mountain range. Start at the **Torc Waterfall** parking lot, about 6km (3¾ miles) south of Killarney, and follow the trail to the top of the falls. At a T-intersection, turn left toward the top parking lot, and almost immediately turn right on the Old Kenmare Road, which follows a small stream along the south slopes of Torc Mountain. After leaving the woods, you will see Torc Mountain on your right. Look for a crescent-shaped gouge in the side of the road, about 9m (30 ft.) across, with a small cairn at its far edge. This is the beginning of the path to the ridge top, marked somewhat erratically by cairns along the way. Return the way you came; the whole trip is just under 10km (6.25 miles), takes about 4 hours, and is moderate in difficulty.

If you prefer a little guidance, you might prefer to take a guided walking tour of some length (from 1 day to a weekend to a full week). A number of walks and walking holidays are offered by **SouthWestWalks Ireland Ltd.,** 40 Ashe St., Tralee, County Kerry (© **066/712-8733;** www.southwestwalksireland.com), which has tours of varying lengths. Or you can arrange in advance to meet up with the **Wayfarers,** an international organization

> ### (Fun Facts) MacGillycuddy's Reeks
>
> This marvelously named range of mountains just west of Killarney is beautiful to look at—they were formed of red sandstone that was gradually shaved down by glaciers until they reached the gentle shape they hold today. The name, though, is a bit baffling. It turns out the mountains were named after an ancient clan that once predominated in this area—the Mac Gilla Machudas. The word *reek* is an old Irish term for a peaked hill. So these are the mountains of the Mac Gilla Machudas, just in case you were wondering.

of passionate pedestrians, who schedule 5-week-long footloose circuits of the Ring of Kerry each spring, summer, and fall. To receive a schedule, contact the **Wayfarers,** 172 Bellevue Ave., Newport, RI 02840 (② **800/249-4620;** www.thewayfarers.com).

For long-distance walkers, the 202km (125-mile) **Kerry Way** is a signposted walking route that extends from Killarney around the Ring of Kerry (see "Sports & Outdoor Pursuits," in section 1, earlier in this chapter).

SPECTATOR SPORTS

GAELIC GAMES   The people of Killarney are passionately devoted to the national sports of hurling and Gaelic football, and games are played almost every Sunday afternoon during the summer at **Fitzgerald Stadium,** Lewis Road (② **064/31700;** www.gaa. ie). For complete details, consult the local *Kerryman* newspaper or the Killarney Tourist Office.

HORSE RACING   Killarney has two annual horse-racing meets, in early May and mid-July. Each event lasts for 3 or 4 days and draws large crowds. For more information, contact the **Killarney Racecourse,** Ross Road (② **064/31125**), or the tourist office.

WHERE TO STAY

Very Expensive

Killarney Park Hotel ★★   With a handsome yellow neo-Georgian facade, this elegant four-story property is on the eastern edge of town near the tourist office. Public rooms are spacious and evoke a distinguished Victorian country house, with oil paintings, wainscot paneling, open fireplaces, and a sunlit conservatory-style lounge, as well as a high-end **spa.** The guest rooms have a traditional, conservative style, with quality provincial furnishings, designer fabrics, and marble-finished bathrooms.

Kenmare Place, Killarney, County Kerry. ② **064/35555.** Fax 064/35266. www.killarneyparkhotel.ie. 72 units. €340–€400 ($544–$640) double. Rates include full breakfast. AE, DC, MC, V. **Amenities:** Restaurant; bar; indoor swimming pool; gym; spa/beauty treatments; Jacuzzi; sauna/steam room; concierge; room service; massage; babysitting; laundry service; library. *In room:* TV, minibar, hair dryer, garment press.

Expensive

Aghadoe Heights Hotel & Spa ★★   A few miles outside of town, and with spectacular views of the lake, Aghadoe Heights is a jarringly modern structure sitting rudely by an ancient ruined church, but inside it's a five-star oasis of luxury. Rooms are spacious and calming in neutral tones, and they have big, orthopedic beds. Many rooms have breathtaking views of the lake and surrounding hills through floor-to-ceiling, wall-to-wall windows. The excellent **spa** is available at the push of a button. Guests can book a relaxing hour in the many steam rooms and saunas for €25 ($40). Breakfast is silver service, and the in-house **restaurant** specializes in modern Irish cuisine. You also can snack on a burger in the bar overlooking the lake. The hotel's Mercedes shuttle bus will take you into central Killarney for free.

Lakes of Killarney, Killarney, County Kerry. ℭ **064/31766.** Fax 064/31345. www.aghadoeheights.com. 74 units. €250–€450 ($400–$720) double. Rates include full breakfast. MC, V. Free parking. **Amenities:** Restaurant (modern Irish); bar; indoor pool; gym; full-service spa; salon; Internet room; free shuttle. *In room:* TV w/DVD, minibar, hair dryer, iron, safe.

Hotel Europe ★★   Part of the same group as the Dunloe Castle, this modern, five-story hotel has a picturesque setting right on the shores of the Lower Lake, adjacent to Killarney's two 18-hole championship golf courses and surrounded by mountain peaks. Views from lakeside rooms—all of which were renovated in 2005—are spectacular, and most rooms have private balconies. As this book went to press, the hotel was about to open a new full-service spa overlooking the sunken garden.

Spa Life, Irish-Style

In the last few years, spas have been sprouting up all over Ireland like clover in spring. Nowhere have more five-star spas been turning the smooth heads of Prada-clad ladies than in County Kerry. Spas here rate among the best in the world, and for good reason. They use exquisite natural settings to spectacular effect and borrow their treatments from the Irish countryside. Everything from Irish spring water to Irish peat mud and Irish river stones can be used to coax forth beauty from our tired, work-dulled skin and hair.

At the **Sámas** spa in the Park Hotel Kenmare (p. 318), which has won numerous awards for its unique design, you can soak in the warm spa pool while gazing out over the mountains nearby. If you indulge in the Sámas "Experience" for €150 ($240), you'll spend an hour relaxing in the thermal suite (rock sauna, ice fountain, tropical mist shower), before moving on to your facial, wrap, or massage, followed by an hour of indulgent relaxation.

All guests at the **Aghadoe Heights Hotel & Spa** (p. 330) outside Killarney are welcome to spend an hour in its exquisite thermal suite for a fairly small fee. With the wide array of steam rooms, saunas, tropical showers, cooling rooms, and hot tubs, it is a luxuriant 60 minutes. Once you're fully relaxed, you might sample one of the spa's numerous massages or facials, using Aveda products.

The spa at the **Sheen Falls Lodge** (p. 318) in Kenmare features a pool shaped like a flower—each petal forming a kind of private relaxation space. You can have a hot stone massage or facial and then float off in total relaxation.

The spa at the **Killarney Park Hotel** (see p. 330) is a modern, peaceful oasis, with a soothing pool and such exotic treatments as the Absolute Spa Ritual for €270 ($432) in which you are rubbed with coconut before being wrapped in a milk-and-lavender essence and then massaged. It cures jet lag, apparently.

So if you're headed to Kerry and are looking for relaxation, you're heading to the right place.

COUNTY KERRY

11

KILLARNEY

Off Killorglin rd., Fossa, Killarney, County Kerry. ℭ **800/221-1074** in the U.S., or 064/71300. Fax 064/32118. www.theeurope.com. 206 units. €240–€350 ($384–$560) double. Rates include full breakfast. V. Free parking. Closed Nov to mid-Mar. **Amenities:** 2 restaurants (international, cafe); bar; lounge; indoor pool; tennis; gym; saunas; salon; babysitting; boating; fishing; horseback riding. *In room:* TV, hair dryer.

Muckross Park Hotel ★★   Deep in the Killarney National Park, this hotel cleverly mixes new and old architecture. In the process of incorporating a much older structure into the modern building, a lovely space is created. Its history does stretch back—Queen Victoria once lunched here, and George Bernard Shaw spent a summer here writing *Pygmalion*. Recently awarded five-star status, the hotel is furnished in country-house style, with wood-paneled walls, open fireplaces, and oil paintings in the public areas, and stone walls and low ceilings in the restaurant and bar. Rooms, which vary in size, are done in creamy colors with luxurious fabrics and some four-poster and half-tester beds. The latest addition is the extraordinary Cloisters Spa, beautifully designed with arched marble ceilings, a stunning pool, lots of space, and a peaceful ambience.

Muckross village, N71, Killarney, County Kerry. ℭ 064/23400. Fax 064/31965. www.muckrosspark.com. 70 units. €220–€400 ($352–$640) double. Rates include full breakfast. AE, DC, MC, V. Free parking. Closed Nov–Feb. **Amenities:** Restaurant (Continental); bar; lounge; pool; full-service spa. *In room:* TV, hair dryer, garment press.

Moderate

Earl's Court House   A 5-minute walk from the town center, Earl's Court is the kind of genteel place where guests are greeted with tea and scones. The spacious guest rooms are tastefully furnished with Irish antiques, and have a distinct Victorian flair. Some have half-tester beds, others king-size beds and sitting areas, and nearly all have private balconies—the second-floor rooms, in particular, have clear mountain views. The breakfast menu has a range of selections, from apple crepes to kippers and tomatoes.

Signposted off N71, Woodlawn Junction, Muckross rd., Killarney, County Kerry. ℭ 064/34009. Fax 064/34366. www.killarney-earlscourt.ie. 24 units. €125–€175 ($200–$280) double. Rates include service charge and full Irish breakfast. MC, V. Free parking. Closed Nov 6–Feb 5. **Amenities:** Room service; non-smoking rooms. *In room:* TV, radio, dataport, hair dryer.

Fuchsia House   This modern house built in classic Victorian style is a darling guesthouse, beautifully run by Mary and Tommy Treacy. The owners are former teachers, and they've decorated the guest rooms in Provençal style, with wallpaper in delicate French designs, well-chosen fabrics in pastel colors, and classic prints on the walls. Families are welcome since most of the rooms are designed with space for both parents and children. Breakfast is served in a sunny conservatory, and the food is excellent.

Muckross rd., Killarney, County Kerry. ℭ 064/33743. Fax 064/36588. www.fuchsiaguesthouse.com. 9 units. €120–€130 ($192–$208) double. Rates include full breakfast. MC, V. **Amenities:** Lounge; nonsmoking rooms; conservatory. *In room:* TV, hair dryer.

Gleann Fia Country House   Although it's only 1.6km (1 mile) from town, this modern, Victorian-style guesthouse feels pleasantly secluded, with thick forests surrounding it like a blanket. The house has an airy conservatory where you can relax over a cup of tea or, in the morning, choose from the extensive breakfast menu. The house has been thoughtfully and tastefully constructed to evoke old-world charm, rather than purposely built to be your average guesthouse. Rooms are spacious and have firm, comfortable beds, but the main attraction is the great outdoors. You can enjoy nature walks through the woods, along with peace and quiet to soothe your soul. Cheaper rates are available by booking in advance, or in the off season.

Deerpark, Killarney, County Kerry. ✆ **064/35035.** Fax 064/35000. www.gleannfia.com. 19 units. €140–€180 ($224–$288) double. Rates include full breakfast. AE, MC, V. Free parking. **Amenities:** Lounge; nonsmoking rooms; conservatory. *In room:* TV.

Kathleen's Country House ★ About 1.6km (1 mile) north of town amid acres of sprawling gardens next to a dairy farm, this pleasant guesthouse is a two-story contemporary stone building with lots of big windows. Enthusiastic, efficient hostess Kathleen O'Regan-Sheppard has created attractive guest rooms with antique pine furniture and light floral fabrics, complemented by a collection of contemporary pastels and paintings. *Note:* The guesthouse is off a busy highway—ask for rooms at the back if you might be disturbed by road noise.

> **(Tips) Service Charges**
>
> *A reminder:* Unless otherwise noted, room rates don't include service charges (usually 10%–15% of your bill).

Madam's Height, Tralee rd. (N22), Killarney, County Kerry. ✆ **064/32810.** Fax 064/32340. www.kathleens. net. 17 units. €130–€140 ($208–$224) double. Rates include full breakfast. AE, MC, V. Free parking. Closed mid-Nov to mid-Mar. **Amenities:** Nonsmoking rooms; drawing room; sunroom. *In room:* TV, tea/coffeemaker, hair dryer, garment press.

Killarney Royal ★ This small hotel neatly crosses the line between historic guesthouse and modern hotel, with beautiful attention to detail. Owner Margaret Scally grew up in the hotel business, and when she inherited the Royal, she renovated it in elegant style, with lots of cream and ivory tones and nice touches like delicate, carved-wood chairs and luxurious fabrics in the guest rooms. All the modern accouterments (phones, broadband, televisions) are also present.

College St., Killarney, County Kerry. ✆ **064/31853.** Fax 064/34001. www.killarneyroyal.ie. 29 units. €100–€180 ($160–$288) double. Rates include full breakfast. AE, MC, V. Closed Nov–Feb. **Amenities:** Restaurant (Continental); lounge. *In room:* TV, broadband, hair dryer.

Killeen House Hotel With a sign reading PROPERTY PROTECTED BY KILLER LEPRECHAUNS, you get the impression right away that this place is going to be friendly and casual. Dating from 1838 and set on high ground overlooking Killarney's lakes and golf courses, this rambling Edwardian country manor house is all about golf. This is where golfers come to talk about golf after playing some golf. Surrounded by mature gardens in a quiet residential area just northwest of the town, it has a relaxed, down-home feel, with many of the comforts of a hotel. The guest rooms, which vary in size and decor, feature orthopedic beds and standard furniture. The pub is golf centric, the staff friendly and golf savvy.

Aghadoe, Killarney, County Kerry. ✆ **064/31711.** Fax 064/31811. www.killeenhousehotel.com. 23 units. €180–€240 ($288–$384) double. Rates include full breakfast. Fixed dinner €55 ($88). AE, DC, MC, V. Free parking. Closed Nov to mid-Apr. **Amenities:** Restaurant (Continental); bar; lounge. *In room:* TV, radio.

Randles Court ★ A former rectory dating from the early 20th century, this attractive yellow, gabled four-story house sits just outside Killarney Town on the road to Muckross House. With marble floors and chandeliers, and warmed by open fireplaces, the lounges and lobby are quite elegant. Rooms have traditional decor, including heavy armoires, antique desks, and vanities, and they're tastefully decorated in bright colors.

Muckross rd. (N71), Killarney, County Kerry. ✆ **800/4-CHOICE** [424-6423] in the U.S., or 064/35333. Fax 064/35206. www.randleshotels.com. 55 units. €180–€220 ($288–$352) double. Rates include service charge and full breakfast. AE, DC, MC, V. Free parking. **Amenities:** Restaurant (international); bar; swimming pool; fitness center; spa; limited room service; babysitting; laundry service. *In room:* TV, hair dryer.

WHERE TO DINE
Very Expensive
Gaby's Seafood Restaurant ★★ SEAFOOD   The walls at Gaby's are filled with commendations and awards, which could be a bit tacky if the food weren't so good. Gaby's is known for its succulent lobster, served grilled or in a house sauce of cream, cognac, and spices. Other choices include turbot with glazed pastry, black sole meunière, and a giant Kerry shellfish platter—a veritable feast of prawns, scallops, mussels, lobster, and oysters.

27 High St., Killarney, County Kerry. ⓒ **064/32519.** www.gabysireland.com. Reservations recommended. Main courses €25–€43 ($40–$69). AE, DC, MC, V. Mon–Sat 6–10pm. Closed late Feb to mid-Mar and Christmas week.

Moderate
Bricín ★ TRADITIONAL IRISH   Seafood dishes and old-time Kerry *boxty* (a traditional dish of potato pancakes filled with chicken, seafood, curried lamb, or vegetables) are the trademarks of this relaxed restaurant above a craft-and-book shop. Don't be put off by the fact that you enter through the shop—the building dates from the 1830s, and the dining room has a pleasant rustic feel, with wood-paneled walls, turf fireplaces, and wood floors. The seafood is excellent and the service is charming.

26 High St., Killarney, County Kerry. ⓒ **064/34902.** www.bricin.com. Reservations recommended for dinner. Fixed-price 2-course dinner €24 ($31); dinner main courses €17–€28 ($27–$45). AE, DC, MC, V. Year-round Tues–Sat 10am–4:30pm; Easter–Oct Mon–Sat 6–9:30pm.

Treyvaud's ★ IRISH   When this place opened a couple of years back, it immediately became one of the most popular lunch spots in town. Owned by two Irish brothers, it offers a clever mix of traditional Irish favorites for lunch (stews, steak pie, and sandwiches). For dinner, it raises the ante, focusing on fresh local ingredients (lamb, salmon, sea bass) creatively prepared. It all works and the crowds keep coming.

62 High St., Killarney, County Kerry. ⓒ **064/33062.** www.treyvaudsrestaurant.com. Reservations recommended. Dinner main courses €16–€25 ($26–$40). MC, V. Tues–Sat noon–10:30pm.

PUBS
Killarney Grand   This large bar has a big following for its traditional music, played nightly from 9 to 11pm. After that, louder bands tend to play, and the crowd gets a little younger as the night goes on. Admission is free until 11pm, and rates vary after that. Main St., Killarney, County Kerry. ⓒ **064/31159.**

The Laurels   One of the more popular "singsong" pubs in town, this place rings to the rafters with the lilt of Irish ditties. Ballad singers are booked nightly from April through October, starting at 9pm. Main St., Killarney, County Kerry. ⓒ **064/31149.**

Molly Darcy's   This is a delightful traditional pub, with a thatched roof, stone walls, an oak-beamed ceiling, open fireplaces, and lots of quirky touches (such as the public phones, which are in confessionals salvaged from a monastery). There's Irish dancing on Sunday evenings. Muckross village, Muckross rd., Killarney, County Kerry. ⓒ **064/34973.**

O'Connor's   This is a terrific place to have a pint and catch a performance with an Irish theme. Depending on the night, you could hear traditional music, Irish stand-up comedy, literary readings, or a play. Performances start at 9:15pm. 7 High St., Killarney, **335** County Kerry. ☎ 064/31115.

Tatler Jack   This traditional pub is a favorite gathering place for followers of Gaelic football and hurling. Traditional music or ballads are scheduled from June through September nightly from 9:30pm. Plunkett St., Killarney, County Kerry. ☎ 064/32361.

3 THE DINGLE PENINSULA

Dingle Town: 48km (30 miles) W of Tralee and 80km (50 miles) NW of Killarney

The quieter, smaller alternative to the Ring of Kerry, the Dingle Peninsula is a short drive away from Killarney. Locals say everything moves a little slower in Dingle, perhaps because everybody is taking in the extraordinary views. This is a unique place where all you can see for miles are undulating hills, craggy mountains, and a creamy shoreline curving at the edge of thick, fragrant woods. To call it "undiscovered" would be too generous—in the summer Dingle Town is packed with travelers—but it's not as ruthlessly jammed as the Ring of Kerry, and, from time to time, even in the high season, you can find yourself blissfully alone amid its natural beauty.

ESSENTIALS

GETTING THERE   Bus Éireann (☎ 066/712-3566; www.buseireann.ie) provides daily coach service to Dingle from all parts of Ireland. The boarding and drop-off point is on Upper Main Street.

If you're driving from Tralee to Dingle, follow R559, or take R561 from Castlemaine.

VISITOR INFORMATION   The **Dingle Tourist Office** is on Main Street, Dingle (☎ 066/915-1188). It is open seasonally, usually mid-April through October. Regular hours are Monday to Saturday 9am to 5pm (extended and Sun hours in peak summer season).

For extensive, detailed tourist information on the Dingle Peninsula, see **www.kerry-tourism.com** or **www.dingle-peninsula.ie**.

GETTING AROUND   Dingle Town has a population of only 1,200 and thus is too small for a local bus service. **Bus Éireann** (☎ 066/712-3566) provides service from Dingle to other towns on the peninsula. For local taxi or minibus service, contact **John Sheehy** (☎ 066/915-1301). The best way to get around little Dingle Town, with its narrow, winding, hilly streets, is to walk. The street along the waterfront is Strand Street, and aside from that, it has three other main streets—Green Street, John Street, and Main Street. Once you've figured those out, the rest will follow easily.

To see the sights beyond the town, drive west along R559 or take one of the sightseeing tours suggested below.

FAST FACTS   In an emergency, dial ☎ **999.** The **Dingle Hospital** is on Upper Main Street (☎ **066/915-1455** or 915-1172). The local **Garda Station** is at Holy Ground, Dingle (☎ **066/915-1522**).

The **O'Conchuir Padraig (Laundry)** is on Green Street (☎ **066/915-1837**).

The **Dingle District Library** is on Green Street, Dingle (☎ **066/915-1499**).

In & About Dingle Peninsula is a newspaper-style publication distributed free at hotels, restaurants, shops, and the tourist office. It lists events, attractions, activities, and more.

You Say "Dingle," I Say "An Daingean"

If you're planning on visiting the Dingle Peninsula in County Kerry, things might get a little confusing, given that, technically speaking, it no longer exists. The whole region has been embroiled in heated controversy after the Irish government ruled in 2005 that as it was in an Irish-language area, Dingle must have a Gaelic name. Since nobody could remember what Dingle's Irish name originally was, the government helpfully invented one for it. Cute little Dingle, it decreed, would now be called "An Daingean," which translates as "The Fortress."

Aside from being less than catchy, the new name caused an explosion of outrage among Dingle residents and business owners who had grown up in Dingle, lived in Dingle all their lives, and didn't want to live in An Daingean now.

Surveys found that more than 90% of An Daingean residents wanted to be Dingle residents. Meetings were held. Voices were raised. In a move clearly not decided to calm tempers, the government minister responsible for the name change threatened to kick Dingle out of the Gaeltacht (the government-supported Irish-language region) if it refused to change all road signs from "Dingle" to "An Daingean." It even forbade it to keep the word "Dingle" on any signs, no matter how tiny the print size. Being dropped from the Gaeltacht would cost Dingle millions in government support.

Given that the minister involved is Eamon O Cuiv, the grandson of Irish rebel and founding prime minister Eamon de Valera (also a vociferous supporter of the Irish language), it's possible that this all should have come as no surprise. But residents were still furious.

In 2006, road signs were changed, and Dingle disappeared from government maps, but virtually all private businesses kept the Dingle in their names. A local artist built a huge, wooden Hollywood-style sign on a hill above the town reading DINGLE. It was short-lived, but the battle was far from over. Locals called for a referendum, and it seemed that every window in Dingle Town had a sticker calling for both names to be represented on road signs and maps. In October 2006 a vote was held locally over whether to change the name back; the motion carried, with a grand total of just 81 votes against. But because it had no legal basis under Irish law, the government still refused to agree. Recently, locals have begun spray painting "Dingle" onto signs that only used the Irish name, only for it to be washed off—and then sprayed right on again.

So it seems that, at least for now, your kids will likely be visiting Fungie the An Daingean Dolphin during your visit.

EXPLORING THE TOWN

Dingle (An Daingean) is a charming, brightly colored little town at the foot of steep hills and on the edge of a gorgeous stretch of coast. There's not much to do here, but it has plenty of hotels and restaurants and makes a good base for exploring the region. The town's most famous resident is a dolphin that adopted the place years back and has been bringing in dolphin-loving tourists ever since. Its busiest time is in August, when the

Dingle Races bring in crowds from throughout the area to watch the horses run every other weekend. (The racetrack is just outside of town on the N86.) In the last week of August, the Dingle Regatta fills the harbor with traditional Irish currach boats in a vivid display of color and history.

When leaving Dingle, heading west takes you on the **Slea Head Drive,** a gorgeous stretch of road known for its collection of ancient sites. At any tourist information center, you can get a guide to the various ruined abbeys and old forts along the way. (*Note:* This is serious Gaeltacht territory, so under new Irish rules, all signs—even road hazard signs—are in Gaelic only.)

Not far from Dingle, **Gallarus Oratory** is a beautifully preserved, early Christian church building. With a shape much like an overturned boat, it's made of stone with no mortar and was so well constructed that it's completely watertight after more than 1,000 years. The oratory is signposted on the R559 near Ballyferriter. There's a visitor center that charges more than €2 ($3.20) for parking and has little to offer besides a short film, so if that doesn't interest you, skip the center, park elsewhere, and walk up to the oratory—access is free.

A few miles away, the village of **Ballyferriter (Baile an Fheirtearaigh)** is named after a local rebel named Piaras Ferriter. He was a poet and soldier who fought in the 1641 rebellion and ultimately became the last area commander to surrender to Oliver Cromwell's English troops. Just north of the village, you can follow signs to the moody ruins of the Dún an Oir Fort, where a massacre took place during an Irish rebellion against English rule in 1580. More than 600 members of an international group of rebel fighters (including Italian and Spanish volunteers as well as Irish) were summarily executed by English soldiers after losing a battle here.

The village of **Dunquin (Dún Chaion),** stunningly situated between Slea Head and Clogher Head, is where you catch ferries (© **066/915-6455**) to the **Blasket Islands (Na Blascaodaí).** Until they were evacuated in 1953, the islands were famous for having an entirely Gaelic-speaking population. These days it's inhabited only by seals and seabirds. If you're up to it, there's a 13km (8-mile) walk to the west end of Great Blasket and back, and it passes sea cliffs and beaches of ivory sand; you can stop along the way at the only cafe on the island.

Slea Head, at the southwestern edge of the peninsula, has pristine beaches, great walks, and extensive archaeological remains. **Dunbeg Fort** sits on a rocky promontory just south of Slea Head, its walls rising from the cliff edge. Although much of the fort has fallen into the sea, the place is well worth a visit at the bargain-basement rate of €3 ($4.80) per person.

COUNTY KERRY

11

THE DINGLE PENINSULA

Impressions

I walked up this morning along the slope from the east to the top of Sybil Head, where one comes out suddenly on the brow of a cliff with a straight fall of many hundreds of feet into the sea. It is a place of indescribable grandeur, where one can see Carrantuohill and the Skelligs and Loop Head and the full sweep of the Atlantic, and over all, the wonderfully tender and searching light that is seen only in Kerry. One wonders in these places why there is anyone left in Dublin, or London, or Paris, when it would be better, one would think, to live in a tent or hut with this magnificent sea and sky, and to breathe this wonderful air, which is like wine in one's teeth.

—John Millington Synge (1871–1909), Irish playwright

Back on the mainland and on the north side of the peninsula, **Castlegregory (Caislean an Ghriare)** is a seaside village with two wide, sandy beaches. It's known for its good diving waters, and scuba divers and watersports fans flock to the place in summer. It's a bit bustling for isolationists, who are better off heading to tiny **Cloghane (An Clochán)** on the southern edge of Brandon Bay. With a population of 270 and a lovely beach, it's got much to offer. It also is a good place for climbers interested in tackling nearby **Mount Brandon (Cnoc Bhréannain)**, which is Ireland's second-highest mountain (951m/3,120 ft.). The mountain is a good all-day climb and has gorgeous views, but don't try it without a map and compass and some experience scaling considerable heights.

Dingle's Oceanworld Aquarium (Kids)   This is a nicely designed aquarium, although it's quite small, given the ticket price. As is the norm at such places, there are lots of sea critters in creatively designed tanks. There's an aquarium tunnel you can walk through with the fish swimming above and around you, and members of the young staff carry around live lobsters, crabs, starfish, and other "inner space" creatures and introduce them up close to kids. This is a compact, hands-on, interactive place that is a good way of rewarding your kids for being so patient while you took pictures of a pile of rocks back up the road.

Dingle Harbour, Dingle, County Kerry. (✆) **066/915-2111.** www.dingle-oceanworld.ie. Admission €12 ($19) adults, €7 ($11) children, €32 ($51) families. MC, V. Daily 10am–5pm.

Eask Tower   Built in 1847 as a famine-relief project, this is a remarkable edifice, a 12m (39-ft.) tower built of solid stone nearly 5m (16 ft.) thick, with a wooden arrow pointing to the mouth of the harbor. It is certainly interesting to look at, but the main reason for making the 1.6km (1-mile) climb to the summit of Carhoo Hill is not to see the tower, but the incredible views of Dingle Harbour, Connor Pass, and, on the far side of the bay, the peaks of the Iveragh Peninsula. This is a great place to get your bearings, but save a trip here for a clear day.

Carhoo Hill, Dingle, County Kerry. (✆) **066/915-1850.** Admission €2 ($3.20). Daily 8am–10pm. From Dingle, follow Slea Head Rd. 3.2km (2 miles), turn left at road signposted for Coláiste Ide, and continue another 3.2km (2 miles).

Ionad An Bhlascaoid Mhoir/The Blasket Centre ★   On the westerly tip of the Dingle Peninsula, this visitor center is dedicated to the remote Blasket Islands. The largest of the islands, Great Blasket, was once an outpost of Irish civilization and a nurturing ground for Irish-language writers, but its inhabitants abandoned the island in 1953. The center explains in interesting style the cultural and literary traditions of the Blaskets and the history of Corca Dhuibhne, the Gaeltacht area. There's a bookshop specializing in local literature, and a handy cafe with views of the Blaskets.

Dunquin, County Kerry. (✆) **066/915-6444.** www.heritageireland.ie. Admission €3.70 ($5.90) adults, €2.60 ($4.15) seniors, €1.30 ($2.10) children and students, €8.70 ($14) families. Easter–May and Sept–Oct daily 10am–6pm; June–Aug daily 10am–7pm.

Sightseeing Tours

Fungie the Dolphin Tours ★ (Kids)   The story of Fungie is both strange and heart-warming. The bottlenose dolphin was first spotted by Dingle's lighthouse keeper in 1984, as it escorted fishing boats out to sea and then back again at the end of their voyages, day after day. The sailors named him and he became a harbor fixture. Fishermen took their children out to swim with him, and he seemed to love human contact. It is a rare case of a wild dolphin essentially domesticating itself. Now people come from miles around to have a few minutes' time with Fungie and the fishermen ferry them out to

meet him. Trips last about 1 hour and depart regularly, roughly every 2 hours in the low
season and as frequently as every half-hour in high season. Fungie swims right up to the boats, which stay out long enough for you to take in views of the picturesque bay. If you want to get closer and more personal with Fungie, you can also arrange an early-morning dolphin swim (see "Up Close with Fungie," below).

The Pier, Dingle, County Kerry. ℂ 066/915-2626 or 915-1967. Tour starting at €16 ($26) adults, €8 ($13) children 11 and under. Daily 10am–6pm, weather permitting.

Sciuird Archaeological Adventures　For real history buffs, these tours are a great opportunity to get deeper insight into ancient local history. Led by a local historian, these tours last about a half-day and involve a short bus journey and some easy walking. Four or five monuments, from the Stone Age to medieval times, are on the route. All tours, limited to 8 to 10 people, start from the top of the pier. Reservations are required.

Holy Ground, Dingle, County Kerry. ℂ **066/915-1606.** Tour €20 ($32) per person. May–Sept daily 10:30am and 2pm.

SHOPPING
Brandon Gallery　This gallery displays and sells the work of local artist Michael Flaherty. His oil paintings, in a bold impasto style, are influenced by the local landscape and much in demand. Open daily from 10am to 6pm. Clappagh Cross, Brandon, County Kerry. ℂ **066/713-8233.** www.michaelflaherty.net.

Greenlane Gallery　This art gallery holds a good selection of quality contemporary Irish paintings on its whitewashed walls—watercolors, sculpture, and ceramics. In summer, the shop is open from 10am to 9pm; in winter, hours are 11am to 5pm. Green St., Dingle, County Kerry. ℂ **066/915-2018.** www.greenlanegallery.com.

Holden Leathergoods　Talented leather craftsman Conor Holden creates exquisite handcrafted, silk-lined leather handbags, baggage, briefcases, and belts. Open Monday to Saturday from 8:30am to 6:30pm and Sunday 10:30am to 5pm (in low season, open Mon–Fri 9am–5pm). The Old School House, signposted 4.8km (3 miles) west of town on the Ventry rd. (R559), off the Slea Head Dr., Burnham, Dingle, County Kerry. ℂ **066/915-1796.** www.holdenleathergoods.com.

Louis Mulcahy Pottery　North of Dunquin, this is the studio where Louis Mulcahy produces a sophisticated range of pottery from local clay. The finished products include everything from unique tableware to teapots, platters, and lamps. Furniture and handmade silk lampshades are also available, as is a selection of Lisbeth Mulcahy's tapestries and weavings. The Mulcahys also have a shop and cafe in Ballyferriter Village, just down the road, with more distinctive painted housewares. Open daily from 10am to 6pm. Clogher, Ballyferriter, County Kerry. ℂ **066/915-6229.** www.louismulcahy.com.

The Weavers' Shop　Weaver Lisbeth Mulcahy creates fabrics and tapestries inspired by the local landscape. She uses wool, Irish linen, cotton, and alpaca in her scarves, throws, tapestries, and napkins. Everything is gorgeous and pricey. Open October to May Monday to Saturday from 9am to 6pm; June to September Monday to Saturday from 9am to 9pm, Sunday from 10am to 6pm. Green St., Dingle, County Kerry. ℂ **066/915-1688.**

SPORTS & OUTDOOR PURSUITS
BEACHES　The Dingle Peninsula has some of the most dramatic beaches in Ireland. The most famous is **Inch Strand**—a 5km-long (3-mile) creamy stretch of sand dunes in the town of Inch (Inse)—but one of the most striking is **Kilmurray Bay at Minard** ★★

where, in the shadow of Minard Castle, giant sandstone boulders form a beach unlike anything you've ever seen. It's definitely not safe for swimming, but ideal for a picnic.

Like Minard, **Trabeg Beach** confronts the southwest storms of the Atlantic head on. Here, during ebb tide, you will find exquisite wave-sculptured, maroon sandstone shapes below sheer rock cliffs, and small sea caves lined with veins of crystalline quartz. The beauty of the rock sculptures combined with the roar of the surf is magical.

Some of the calmest beaches in this area for swimming are east of Castlegregory, on the more protected west side of Tralee Bay. The beach at **Maherabeg** has a coveted European Blue Flag (meaning it is exceptionally unpolluted and environmentally safe), and the beaches of **Brandon Bay** are particularly scenic—great for walking and swimming.

BICYCLING　　Mountain bikes can be rented at the **Mountain Man,** Strand Street, Dingle (© **066/915-2400**), for €12 ($19) per day or €55 ($88) per week, or from **Foxy John Moriarty,** Main Street, Dingle (© **066/915-1316**), for essentially the same price. Workers at both shops know the area well, and can suggest a number of day trips or overnight touring options. Foxy John's has the added advantage of also being a pub, although you might want to save your pints until after your bike ride. One possible day trip is to take the road out to the tip of the peninsula past Slea Head and Clogher Head. The scenery is outrageously beautiful and the journey is hilly, but not ridiculously so.

BIRD-WATCHING　　In summer, the small, uninhabited islands surrounding Great Blasket attract flocks of nesting seabirds, including vast numbers of storm petrels. From Clogher Head north of Dunquin at the western extremity of the Dingle Peninsula, rare autumn migrants can sometimes be seen. Inch Peninsula, extending into Castlemaine Harbour south of Inch town, is a wintering ground for brent geese, which arrive in late August and move on in April; there is also a large wigeon population in the fall.

DIVING　　On the North Dingle Peninsula, **Harbour House,** The Maharees, Castlegregory, County Kerry (© **066/713-9292;** www.waterworld.ie), is a diving center that offers packages including diving, room, and board at good rates. Classes for beginners are available. The house is yards from the Scraggane Pier and a short boat ride from most of the diving sites. The much beloved **Dingle Dive Centre** (© **066/915-2789;** www.diving dingle.ie) runs a number of trips and courses out of Dingle Marina, including wreck dives.

GOLF　　Sixteen kilometers (10 miles) west of Dingle Town, on the western edge of the Dingle Peninsula, overlooking the Atlantic, the **Dingle Golf Club (Ceann Sibéal),** Ballyferriter (© **066/915-6255;** www.dinglelinks.com), welcomes visitors to play its 18-hole, par-72 course. Greens fees for 18 holes are €40 to €65 ($64–$104) Monday to Friday, and €45 to €75 ($72–$120) Saturday and Sunday, depending on the season.

HORSEBACK RIDING　　At **Dingle Horse Riding,** Ballinaboula House, Dingle (© **066/ 915-2199;** www.dinglehorseriding.com), rides are available along nearby beaches or through the mountains. A 1¹/₂-hour mountain ride starts at €25 ($40). Half-day, full-day, and 3- to 5-day packages including accommodations, meals, and riding can be arranged.

SAILING　　The **Dingle Sailing Centre,** c/o The Wood, Dingle (© **066/915-1984;** www.saildingle.com), offers an array of courses taught by experienced, certified instructors. Summer courses run €130 to €190 ($208–$304).

SEA ANGLING　　For packages and day trips, contact Nicholas O'Connor at **Angler's Rest,** Ventry (© **066/915-9947;** www.iol.ie/~avalon), or Seán O'Conchúir (© **066/915-5429**), representing the **Kerry Angling Association.**

Moments   **Up Close with Fungie**

It is extremely rare for a wild dolphin to choose voluntarily to live among people rather than with his own kind, but for more than 20 years, a dolphin named Fungie has chosen to live with Dingle's human population. In fact, he likes people so much that diving into the water to swim with him has become a popular local pastime, and one that he seems to enjoy as much as the human visitors. He can swim about 40kmph (25 mph), but he slows down to the pace of an Australian crawl when you're out there, and amuses himself by leaping over the human swimmers' heads. If you want to swim with Fungie, contact **John Brosnan** (© **066/915-1967**) to book a time. He'll rent you the necessary gear for the cold Irish waters (semi-dry suit, mask, snorkel, boots, and fins, all in one duffel—€25/$40 per person), and then ferry you out by boat. The 2-hour escorted swim also costs €25 ($40). For obvious reasons (it's out in the sea), only adults can swim with Dingle, although children will certainly enjoy watching.

WALKING   The **Dingle Way** begins in Tralee and circles the peninsula, covering 153km (95 miles) of gorgeous mountain and coastal landscape. The most rugged section is along Brandon Head, where the trail passes between Mount Brandon and the ocean. The views are tremendous, but the walk is long (about 24km/15 miles, averaging 9 hr.) and strenuous, and should be attempted only by experienced walkers and in good weather. The section between Dunquin and Ballyferriter (also 24km/15 miles) follows an especially lovely stretch of coast. For more information, see *The Dingle Way Map Guide*, available in local tourist offices and shops.

Another good walk is the ascent up **Mount Brandon.** The approach from the west is a more gradual climb, but the walk from the eastern, Cloghane side is far more interesting and passes the pastoral beauty of the Paternoster Lakes. The road to the trail head is signposted just past Cloghane on the road to Brandon town; drive about 5km (3 miles) on this road to a small parking lot and the Lopsided Tea House. Be sure to bring plenty of water and food, gear for wind and rain, and a good map. The trail climbs through fields, past an elaborate grotto, and along the slope of an open hillside where red-and-white poles clearly mark the way. As you round the corner of the high open hillside, the Paternoster Lakes and Brandon come into view. The walk through this glacial valley toward the base of the mountain is the most beautiful part—if the weather's bad, you won't have wasted your time if you turn around before reaching the summit.

The only seriously strenuous leg is the climb out of this valley to the ridge, a short but intense scramble over boulders and around ledges. Once you reach the ridge top, turn left and follow the trail another .4km (.25 mile) or so to the summit. You can return the way you came or continue south along the ridge, returning to Cloghane on the Pilgrim's Route, an old track that circumnavigates the Dingle Peninsula. Although this is a day hike (about 4 hr. to the summit and back), and very well marked, it shouldn't be taken too lightly—bring all necessary supplies and let someone know when you expect to return. Information on routes and weather conditions is available at the Cloghane visitor center.

Hidden Ireland Tours, Dingle (© **888/246-9026** in the U.S., or 087/221-4002; www.hiddenirelandtours.com), offers a week of easy to moderate guided hiking through some of Ireland's most beautiful scenery. It takes in parts of the Kerry Way, Killarney National Park, the Beara Peninsula in County Cork, Skellig Michael, and the Dingle Peninsula. The cost, including luggage transfers and accommodations, runs around €2,300 ($3,680) per person. Hikes are available April to September.

WINDSURFING The beaches around Castlegregory offer a variety of conditions for windsurfing. Those on the eastern side of the peninsula are generally calmer than those to the west. Equipment can be hired from **Jamie Knox Watersports,** Maharees, Castlegregory, County Kerry (© **066/713-9411;** www.jamieknox.com), on the road between Castlegregory and Fahamore. Kayaks can also be rented for €30 ($48) per hour.

WHERE TO STAY
Expensive
Dingle Skellig Hotel (Kids) This three-story hotel has an idyllic location next to Dingle Bay on the eastern edge of town. The look of the place is all polished pine and contemporary touches, most tastefully done. Most guest rooms are done in neutral colors with floral touches, although some have slightly lurid color combinations. Many have gorgeous views. This is a family hotel in the classic sense—in the summer, there are evening cabaret performances and children's entertainment.

Annascaul Rd., Dingle, County Kerry. © **066/915-0200.** Fax 066/915-1501. www.dingleskellig.com. 111 units. €250–€300 ($400–$480) double. Rates include full breakfast. AE, MC, V. Free parking. Closed Jan–Feb Mon–Thurs. **Amenities:** Restaurant (seafood); bar; lounge; indoor pool; gym; Jacuzzi; steam room; spa; health treatments; children's playroom; room service. *In room:* TV, radio, hair dryer.

Moderate
Benners Hotel One of the few hotels out here open year-round, Benners is right in the heart of town. The lovely Georgian doorway with a fanlight at the front entrance sets the tone for this old-world hostelry. The 250-year-old hotel blends traditional Irish charm with modern comforts. Its style is a bit old-fashioned, but rooms are comfortable and furnished with antiques, including some four-poster beds.

Main St., Dingle, County Kerry. © **066/915-1638.** Fax 066/915-1412. www.dinglebenners.com. 52 units. €190–€210 ($304–$336) double. Rates include service charge and full Irish breakfast. AE, DC, MC, V. **Amenities:** Restaurant (Continental); 2 bars. *In room:* TV, tea/coffeemaker, hair dryer.

Doyle's Townhouse Sister to the successful Doyle's restaurant (see below) next door, this three-story guesthouse is a handy hideaway. The attractive drawing room is warmed by a Victorian fireplace, and furnished with antiques. Period pieces and country pine predominate in the cozy guest rooms, along with firm beds and Italian marble bathrooms. The rooms at the back of the house have a balcony or patio and have peaceful mountain views in the background. The ground-floor rooms are fine for people who have difficulty with stairs. In addition, there are four little town houses a short distance away; each has its own entrance and a sitting room downstairs, with a bedroom and bathroom upstairs.

5 John St., Dingle, County Kerry. © **800/223-6510** in the U.S., or 066/915-1174. Fax 066/915-1816. www. doylesofdingle.com. 12 units. €160 ($256) double. Rates include full breakfast. DC, MC, V. Closed Christmas and mid-Jan to mid-Feb. **Amenities:** Drawing room. *In room:* TV, hair dryer.

Greenmount House ★★ This modern bungalow on a hill above Dingle isn't much to look at from the outside, but don't be fooled. Inside it's a stylish place, with lush colors and clever design. Each of the spacious guest rooms has its own sitting area and large bathroom—some are split-level, a few have balconies, and some have sea views. Breakfasts, ranging from smoked salmon omelets to ham-and-pineapple toasted sandwiches, have won awards for owners Mary and John Curran.

John St., Dingle, County Kerry. ℂ **066/915-1414.** Fax 066/915-1974. www.greenmount-house.com. 12 units. €100–€160 ($160–$256) double. Rates include full breakfast. MC, V. Closed Dec 20–26. **Amenities:** Nonsmoking rooms; conservatory; sitting room. *In room:* TV, tea/coffeemaker.

Milltown House Tucked away near a tidal inlet just outside of Dingle, Milltown House is a simple, white-and-black 19th-century house, but it's a good guesthouse to know about. The spacious guest rooms have sitting areas and orthopedic beds. Some have sea views and the others overlook the garden. Two rooms are wheelchair accessible. The nonsmoking sitting room—with easy chairs and an open fire—is comfortable, while the conservatory breakfast room (with a lavish breakfast menu) looks out on Dingle Bay. Film buffs might want to request room no. 2—it's where Robert Mitchum stayed while filming *Ryan's Daughter.*

Milltown (off Ventry Rd.), Dingle, County Kerry. ℂ **066/915-1372.** Fax 066/915-1095. www.milltown housedingle.com. 10 units. €130–€170 ($208–$272) double. Rates include full breakfast. MC, V. Closed mid-Nov to late Apr. **Amenities:** Conservatory; sitting room. *In room:* TV, tea/coffeemaker, hair dryer.

Pax Guest House ★ This former retirement home has been transformed into a comfortable B&B with homey touches. On a green hill overlooking Dingle Bay, Pax House's sunny balcony takes in sweeping views as far as Slea Head. The furniture is heavy pine (some four-poster beds), and the decor is bright and cheerful. This peaceful place is a real getaway.

Pax House is signposted on the N86, Dingle, County Kerry. ℂ **066/915-1518.** Fax 066/915-2461. www. pax-house.com. 12 units. €120–€160 ($192–$256) double. Rates include full breakfast. MC, V. Free parking. **Amenities:** Conservatory; sitting room. *In room:* TV, radio, tea/coffeemaker, hair dryer.

Inexpensive
The Captain's House ★ (Value) Jim and Mary Milhench own and run this dapper little B&B in the middle of Dingle. The name is inspired less by the location (the house is landlocked, except for a river running through the manicured yard) than by Jim's former career as a sea captain. It's a friendly place—when you arrive, you're offered tea with scones or a slice of rich cake and made to feel genuinely welcome. As in many town houses, the rooms here are a bit small, but it feels cozy rather than cramped. Returning guests often ask specifically to stay in room no. 10, which is tucked under the gables and has a sloping ceiling. Mary's breakfasts are excellent, with homemade muesli, baked ham, local cheeses, homemade honey, and fresh local eggs.

The Mall, Dingle, County Kerry. ℂ **066/915-1531.** Fax 066/915-1079. http://homepage.tinet.le/~captigh. 8 units. €100–€110 ($160–$176) double. Rates include full breakfast. AE, MC, V. Closed Dec–Jan. **Amenities:** Sitting room. *In room:* TV.

WHERE TO DINE
Expensive
Beginish ★ SEAFOOD Owner/chef Mrs. Pat Moore runs this delightful, small, unassuming Dingle restaurant with aplomb. A sunny conservatory overlooks the gardens and there are outdoor tables in summer. Although there are lamb and beef dishes and a vegetarian special each night, the emphasis is on fresh fish. Among the starters, the smoked salmon with capers and horseradish cream is perfect—nothing fancy, just excellent ingredients. You can't go wrong with any of the fish courses—monkfish with Provençal sauce or cod on thyme-scented potatoes. For dessert, Pat's rhubarb soufflé tart is legendary.

Green St., Dingle, County Kerry. © **066/915-1588.** Reservations recommended. Dinner main courses €16–€30 ($26–$48). MC, V. Tues–Sun 12:30–2:15pm and 6–10pm. Closed Dec–Feb.

Doyle's Seafood Bar SEAFOOD   This is a casual fish bar, so the atmosphere is homey, with stone walls and floors and traditional Irish *sugan* (straw) chairs. All the ingredients are local—from the sea, the gardens, or nearby farms. Even the smoked salmon is smoked here, in small batches. Dingle bay lobster is the house specialty, but there's plenty to choose from—Glenburgh oysters, salmon filet in puff pastry, rack of lamb, and a signature platter of seafood (sole, salmon, lobster, oysters, and crab claws).

4 John St., Dingle, County Kerry. © **066/915-1174.** www.doylesofdingle.com. Reservations required. Main courses €20–€32 ($32–$51). MC, V. Mon–Sat 6–9:30pm. Closed mid-Dec to mid-Feb.

Moderate

The Chart House ★★ MODERN COUNTRY   This popular restaurant (be sure to book ahead) has an inviting bistro atmosphere with lots of polished pine and warm, rose-colored walls. The cooking here is an ambitious blend of Irish dishes and outside influences. Main courses might include steak filet with black pudding mash, or pork with brandied apples. With unusual food and excellent service, it has carved out quite a reputation.

The Mall, Dingle, County Kerry. © **066/915-2255.** Reservations required. Dinner main courses €15–€28 ($24–$45). MC, V. Wed–Mon 6:30–10pm. Closed Jan 8–Feb 12.

Lord Bakers SEAFOOD/PUB GRUB   The ages-old decor in this pub restaurant combines a stone fireplace and cozy alcoves with a more modern, sunlit conservatory and a few Art Deco touches. The menu offers standard bar food, but juices it up with things like crab claws in garlic butter, Kerry oysters, seafood Mornay, and steaks. Dinner specialties are more elegant, including sole stuffed with smoked salmon and spinach in cheese sauce, lobster, and rack of lamb.

Main St., Dingle, County Kerry. © **066/915-1277.** Reservations recommended for dinner. Bar food €10–€15 ($16–$24); dinner main courses €16–€30 ($26–$48). AE, MC, V. Fri–Wed 12:30–2pm and 6–9:30pm.

Inexpensive

An Cafe Liteartha CAFE/TEAROOM   "The Literary Cafe" is a self-service cafe in an excellent bookstore. This is heaven for those interested in Irish history, literature, maps, and . . . scones. The cafe sells fresh soups, sandwiches, salads, seafood, and scones and cakes that melt in your mouth. It's an ideal spot for a quiet lunch or snack in the middle of town.

Dykegate St., Dingle, County Kerry. © **066/915-2204.** All items €3–€6 ($4.80–$9.60). No credit cards. Mon–Sat 9am–6pm (later in summer).

PUBS

An Driochead Beag/The Small Bridge   Sitting directly on a bridge, with a cool stone floor and a friendly rustic atmosphere, this pub draws crowds year-round for sessions of traditional Irish music, usually starting at 9:30pm. It's not very big, so arrive early if you want even standing room! Lower Main St., Dingle, County Kerry. © **066/915-1723.**

Dick Mack's   The titular Dick Mack (a much-loved Dingle character) died a few years ago, but his family carries on his name. Dick ran the place as a pub and shoeshine shop, and his small leather shop is still in its regular place. This is a favorite among locals, as its quirky nature has attracted celebrities such as Robert Mitchum, Timothy Dalton, and Paul Simon, whose names are commemorated with stars on the sidewalk just outside. Green St., Dingle, County Kerry. © **066/915-1960.**

O'Flaherty's   This big barn of a pub is true Dingle. Old posters and news clippings line the walls, alongside poems by local authors and favorite Gaelic phrases. In the evenings, excellent traditional-music sessions fill the place from wall to wall. Bridge St., Dingle, County Kerry. ✆ **066/915-1983.**

4 TRALEE

32km (20 miles) NW of Killarney

Forget the visions of bucolic splendor conjured up by its singsong name; with a population of 22,000, Tralee is three times the size of Killarney, and it feels like it. This is more a workaday town than a tourist center, and there's not much here for visitors to do. In fact, it can feel a bit rough at times—especially on weekend nights, when the town's many bars are packed, and walking the streets can feel a bit of a health hazard. However, it has quite a few good hotels, and it makes a handy base for exploring Kerry. Locals tend to outnumber visitors here most of the year, except during the **Rose of Tralee festival** in August. The town is the permanent home of the National Folk Theatre of Ireland, **Siamsa Tire,** which operates year-round, but is most active during July and August.

ESSENTIALS
GETTING THERE   **Aer Arann** (✆ **011/353-81821-0210** in the U.S., 818/210-210 in Ireland, or 0800/587-23-24 in the U.K.; www.aerarann.ie) offers regular flights from Dublin into **Kerry County Airport,** Farranfore, County Kerry (✆ **066/976-4644;** www.kerryairport.ie), about 24km (15 miles) south of Tralee. **Ryanair** (www.ryanair.com) flies direct from London (Stansted) to Kerry.

Buses from all parts of Ireland arrive daily at the **Bus Éireann Depot,** John Joe Sheehy Road (✆ **066/712-3566;** www.buseireann.ie).

Trains from major cities arrive at the **Irish Rail Station,** John Joe Sheehy Road (✆ **01850/366222;** www.irishrail.ie).

Four major national roads converge on Tralee: N69 and N21 from Limerick and the north, N70 from the Ring of Kerry and points south, and N22 from Killarney, Cork, and the east.

VISITOR INFORMATION   The **Tralee Tourist Office,** Ashe Memorial Hall, Denny Street (✆ **066/712-1288**), offers information on Tralee and the Dingle Peninsula. It is open year-round Monday through Friday 9am to 1pm and 2 to 5pm, with weekend and extended hours in the spring and summer. There is also a first-rate cafe on the premises. For Tralee tourist information online, explore **www.tralee.ie** and **www.tralee-insight.com.**

GETTING AROUND   The best way to get around Tralee's downtown area is to walk. If you prefer to take a taxi, call **Kingdom Cabs,** Boherbee (✆ **066/712-7828**), or **Tralee Radio Cabs,** Monavelley (✆ **066/712-5451**).

FAST FACTS   If you need a drugstore, try **Kelly's Pharmacy,** 9 The Mall (✆ **066/712-1302**), or **Costello's Pharmacy** Russel St. (✆ **066/712-1075**).

In an emergency, dial ✆ **999. Bon Secours Hospital** is on Strand Street (✆ **066/714-9800**). **Tralee General Hospital** is on Killarney road (N22; ✆ **066/718-4000**). The local **Garda Station** is off High Street (✆ **066/710-2300**).

Tralee is not really a pretty town, but it has some attractive Georgian architecture and a few sights worth seeing. Mostly, though, it's a good place to load up on supplies and gas up the car before heading into the countryside. A fairly short drive away, the town of **Listowel** is a neatly laid out Georgian town on the River Feale. It's also home to the **Kerry Literary and Cultural Center,** which is a small but interesting exhibit on local writers. Nearby, **Carrigafoyle Castle** stands its ground as it has for 500 years.

Blennerville Windmill ★ Just 5km (3 miles) west of Tralee and reaching 20m (66 ft.) into the sky, this must surely be the most photographed object in Tralee. This picturesque windmill at the edge of a river still works, and that makes it quite rare in this part of the world. Built in 1800, it flourished until 1850, when it was largely abandoned. After decades of neglect, it was restored, and is now fully operational, producing 5 tons of ground whole-meal flour per week. The visitor complex has an emigration exhibition center, an audiovisual theater, craft workshops, and a cafe.

R559, Blennerville, County Kerry. ℂ **066/712-1064.** Admission €5 ($8) adults, €4 ($6.40) seniors and students, €3 ($4.80) children over 5, €15 ($24) families. Apr–Oct daily 10am–6pm.

Carrigafoyle Castle ★ This rugged medieval castle entirely surrounded by water outside of Listowel dates from the 15th century. Its name comes from the Gaelic Carragain Phoill (or "Rock of the Hole"), and probably describes its location in the channel between the land and Carrig Island. It was once the seat of the O'Connor clan, who ruled most of the Kerry clan for a century or so—it was besieged by English forces in the late 16th century and taken again by Cromwell less than a century later. Today you can climb the stone staircase to the top of the tower for magnificent views.

2km (1¼ miles) west of Ballylongford, County Kerry. No phone. Free admission.

Kerry Literary & Cultural Centre Writer's Museum ★ This small museum is cleverly designed to draw attention to Kerry's rich literary history by introducing you to its impressive slate of writers, living and dead. There are all kinds of interactive displays, films to watch, and explanations of the works of writers such as the poet Brendan Kennelley and the novelist Maurice Walsh, who wrote *The Quiet Man.* There are regular literary readings held here (call ahead or check the website for listings) and lots of events in the summer. The museum hosts the prestigious Writers' Week literary festival each June, which attracts top writers from Europe and the Americas.

24 The Square, Listowel, County Kerry. ℂ **068/22212.** www.seanchai-klcc.com. Admission €5 ($8) adults; €4 ($6.40) seniors and students, €12 ($19) families. Apr–Sept daily 10am–6pm.

Kerry the Kingdom ★ (Kids) This is a sort of super visitor center—a large facility designed to give an in-depth look at 7,000 years of life in County Kerry. There are super-size versions of all the usual visitor center offerings: historic displays, photos, a film, mannequins in period garb—all the bases are covered. There's also the Kerry County Museum that chronologically examines Kerry music, history, legends, archaeology, and, um, football, through interactive and hands-on exhibits—complete with lighting effects and a theme park–style ride to "take you back in time." You couldn't ask for more from a visitor center.

Ashe Memorial Hall, Denny St., Tralee, County Kerry. ℂ **066/712-7777.** Admission €8 ($13) adults, €6.50 ($10) seniors and students, €5 ($8) children, €22 ($35) families. Jan–Mar Tues–Fri 10am–4:30pm; Apr–May and Sept–Dec Tues–Sat 9:30am–5:30pm; June–Aug daily 9:30am–5:30pm.

Rose of Tralee

A 19th-century song about a pretty local girl named Mary O'Connor is at the root of this now-famous beauty contest. William Mulchinock's tear-jerker of a song about the girl he was stopped by fate from marrying so caught the public's imagination that more than 100 years later, it is still performed in Irish pubs worldwide. Thus, in the 1960s was the idea born for a contest to find the prettiest girl in Tralee and crown her.

Every August, the town fills with pretty girls, those who make them beautiful, and those who want to look at them. The contest rules are fairly generous in terms of just who is Irish, not to mention Traleean—the rules require contestants to be of Irish birth *or ancestry,* so past winners have been from places as far flung as the U.S. and Australia. The festival lasts 5 days, during which time the entire town becomes somewhat obsessed with it—restaurants, pubs, and theaters all get involved in hosting events related to the Rose of Tralee.

If you want to join in the fun, or if you know a pretty girl with an Irish last name, contact the **Rose of Tralee Festival Office** (© **066/712-1322;** www.rose oftralee.ie).

Tralee-Blennerville Steam Train ★ This restored steam train rolls along for a short but scenic 3km (2 miles) from Tralee's Ballyard Station to Blennerville. It uses equipment that was once part of the Tralee and Dingle Light Railway (1891–1953), one of the world's most famous narrow-gauge railways. It's a trip back in time, although we have always found that steam trains are more interesting to watch than to ride on. *Note:* Near the end of every month, the trains are off track and serviced for a day or two; call before you visit.

Ballyard, Tralee, County Kerry. © **066/712-1064.** Round-trip fare €5 ($8) adults, €4 ($6.40) students and seniors, €2.50 ($4) children, €15 ($24) families. May–Oct daily. Trains depart Blennerville on the half-hour (1st departure 10:30am) and depart Tralee on the hour (last departure 5pm).

SPORTS & OUTDOOR PURSUITS

GOLF The **Tralee Golf Club,** Fenit/Churchill Road, West Barrow, Ardfert (© **066/ 713-6379;** www.traleegolfclub.com), overlooking the Atlantic 13km (8 miles) northwest of town, is an Arnold Palmer–designed course. One of Ireland's newer courses, it's expected in time to rank among the best in the world. Greens fees are €180 ($288).

About 40km (25 miles) north of Tralee in the northwest corner of County Kerry is Bill Clinton's favorite Irish course, the **Ballybunion Golf Club ★,** Ballybunion, County Kerry (© **068/27146;** www.ballybuniongolfclub.ie). This facility offers the chance to play on two challenging 18-hole seaside links, both on cliffs overlooking the Shannon River estuary and the Atlantic. Tom Watson has rated the Old Course one of the finest in the world, while the Cashen Course was designed by Robert Trent Jones, Sr. Greens fees are €110 to €180 ($176–$288) or €265 ($424) for golf on both courses within 1 week.

HORSEBACK RIDING If you'd like to see the Tralee sights from horseback, you can't do better than to hire a horse from **Eagle Lodge Equestrian Centre,** Gortatlea (© **066/ 37266**). Prices start at €25 ($40) per hour for 1- or 2-hour rides on the Slieve Mish Mountains and Queen Scotia's Glen.

DOG RACING   Greyhounds race year-round on Tuesday and Friday starting at 8pm at the **Kingdom Greyhound Racing Track,** Oakview, Brewery Road (☎ **066/712-4033**). Admission is €10 ($16) per person, including a program.

HORSE RACING   Horse racing takes place twice a year (in early June and late Aug) at **Tralee Racecourse,** Ballybeggan Park (☎ **066/713-6148,** or on race days 712-6188). Post time is usually 2:30pm. Admission starts at around €12 ($19) for adults, €6 ($9.60) for seniors and students, and is free for children 13 and under.

WHERE TO STAY
Moderate

Abbey Gate Hotel ★   This modern three-story hotel is ideally located within walking distance of Tralee's prime attractions, shops, and pubs. Its lobby and public rooms are sleek and contemporary, while guest rooms—though quite small—are tastefully decorated with comfortable beds and bright colors. The **bar,** with its polished paneling and open fireplace, is perhaps the best room in the place.

Maine St., Tralee, County Kerry. ☎ **066/712-9888.** Fax 066/712-9821. www.abbeygate-hotel.com. 100 units. €150–€180 ($240–$288) double. AE, DC, MC, V. Limited parking. **Amenities:** 2 restaurants (international, bistro); bar; room service; nonsmoking rooms. *In room:* TV, tea/coffeemaker, hair dryer.

Ballygarry House Hotel ★★   Just south of town, this country inn is surrounded by well-tended gardens and shaded by sheltering trees, making it feel like a real hideaway. The guest rooms vary in size; each is classically decorated with dark-wood reproductions and luxurious fabrics in neutral tones. The lobby and lounges are steeped in elegant comfort, with lots of big sofas and club chairs to sink down into. **Brooks** restaurant is a classy option for relaxing at the end of the day, and the new hotel spa, **Nádúr,** is a soothing, modern oasis. Guests have the run of the thermal suite, which soothes away the cares of your traveling day.

Tralee-Killarney rd., Leebrook, Tralee, County Kerry. ☎ **066/712-3322.** Fax 066/712-7630. www.ballygarry house.com. 46 units. €200–€220 ($320–$352) double. Rates include service charge and full Irish breakfast. AE, MC, V. Closed Dec 20–28. **Amenities:** Restaurant (international); bar; full-service spa. *In room:* TV, tea/coffeemaker, iron, bathrobes.

Ballyseede Castle Hotel ★   This 15th-century castle 3km (2 miles) east of Tralee comes complete with a live-in ghost and was once the chief garrison of the Fitzgeralds, the earls of Desmond. A hotel for 20 years, it has a marvelously regal look. The lobby has Doric columns and a hand-carved oak staircase, while drawing rooms have ornate plasterwork and marble fireplaces. Guest rooms are a mixed bag—some are elegantly appointed, others are a bit old-fashioned and faded. With wood paneling and a towering alcohol cabinet, the **Library Bar** is impressive. The **restaurant** is highly rated and known for its extensive wine cellar. Be warned, however, that the hotel has a punishing cancellation policy, and it can leave you paying for a room, even if you cancel weeks in advance.

Tralee-Killarney rd., Tralee, County Kerry. ☎ **066/712-5799.** Fax 066/712-5287. www.ballyseedecastle. com. 12 units. €180–€230 ($288–$368) double. MC, V. **Amenities:** Restaurant (modern Irish); bar. *In room:* TV, hair dryer, garment press.

Brandon Hotel   This is a dependable, modern hotel at the western edge of town. Its lobby and public rooms are nicely done, with polished wood floors and leather sofas, and the guest rooms are nice enough, if a bit old-fashioned, with pine furniture. Its leisure

center and indoor pool, restaurant, and bar make it a good option just a block from the
tourist office and strolling distance from shops and downtown restaurants.

Princes St., Tralee, County Kerry. ⓒ **800/44-UTELL** (448-8355) in the U.S., or 066/712-3333. Fax 066/712-5019. www.brandonhotel.ie. 182 units. €140–€250 ($224–$400) double. Rates include full breakfast. AE, DC, MC, V. Closed Dec 24–28. **Amenities:** Restaurant (international); bar; indoor pool; gym; sauna/steam room. *In room:* TV, tea/coffeemaker, hair dryer.

Manor West Hotel ★★ Your first sight of Manor West is not very promising—it sits at the edge of Tralee in a shopping center on a busy highway surrounded by parking lots. However, inside it's another story, as this modern, efficient, attractive hotel has plenty to offer. Rooms are contemporary, quiet, and comfortable with plenty of elegant touches (a few are fully accessible for those with mobility problems). The Walnut Room restaurant is very good, and ideal for a quiet dinner. The Harmony spa is small but offers marvelous treatments and covetable Elemis products, while the gym and swimming pool give you a place to work off the rich dinners. *Note:* It's a long walk or cab ride into the town center from Manor West if you haven't got a car.

Killarney Rd., Tralee, County Kerry. ⓒ **800/618-5343** in the U.S., or 066/719-4500. Fax 066/719-4545. www.manorwesthotel.ie. 77 units. €160–€240 ($256–$384) double. Rates include full breakfast. AE, DC, MC, V. **Amenities:** Restaurants (Irish and international); bar; indoor pool; gym; spa; sauna/steam room. *In room:* TV, broadband (free), minibar, tea/coffeemaker, hair dryer, safe.

Inexpensive

Barnagh Bridge Country Guesthouse ★ Perched on a hillside overlooking Tralee Bay, this handsome contemporary house sits on the quiet north side of the peninsula, and makes an ideal touring base for those who prefer a country setting to a town. The rooms have light pine furnishings and orthopedic beds, and most have views of the mountains and sea. Breakfast here is stellar, with plenty of fruit and homemade breads and scones, granola, and yogurt, as well as the option of eggs and meat.

Cappalough, Camp, County Kerry. ⓒ **066/713-0145.** Fax 066/713-0299. 5 units. €60–€90 ($96–$144) double. Rates include full breakfast. AE, MC, V. Closed Nov–Mar 15. **Amenities:** Lounge; nonsmoking rooms. *In room:* TV, tea/coffeemaker, hair dryer.

The Shores ★★ (Value) This modern house offers sweeping views of Tralee Bay from virtually every window. Inside, furnishings are eminently tasteful, with a creamy, light color scheme, and well-chosen antiques adding touches of simple beauty. One downstairs room has a private entrance and a fireplace. All rooms have firm orthopedic mattresses, with crisp white cotton and cream lace linen. There's a sun deck and a private beach for when the sun shines, and a guest library and video rentals for when it does not. Breakfast options are extensive, with smoked salmon and waffles as alternatives to the standard fried eggs. For those in search of additional privacy, there's also a self-catering cottage available for weekly rental.

.8km (½ mile) west of Stradbally on the Conor Pass Rd., Cappatigue, Castlegregory, County Kerry. ⓒ **066/713-9196.** www.theshorescountryhouse.com. 6 units. €70–€90 ($112–$144) double. Rates include full breakfast. Fixed-price dinner €35 ($56). MC, V. Closed Dec–Jan. **Amenities:** Nonsmoking rooms. *In room:* TV, tea/coffeemaker.

Self-Catering

Illauntannig Island Cottage (Moments) For those who really want to get away from it all, this cottage is perfectly located. Illauntannig is one of the seven Maharees Islands, about 1.6km (1 mile) offshore from Scraggane Bay, on the north shore of the Dingle

Peninsula. This is the only cottage on the island, and with its four bedrooms, one bathroom, a sitting room with fireplace, and a sunny kitchen, it feels like a snug, safe place. Make no mistake—you'll be roughing it, with oil lamps substituting for electric lighting and drinking water imported from the mainland. The basic necessities are provided, with gas-powered refrigeration and hot water, but your only companions will be seabirds and cows—the island's only year-round residents. Bob Goodwin, a venerable seaman with a wealth of knowledge on local birds and history, will check in on you every day by two-way radio, and can take you to the mainland as often as necessary for supplies. You can spend your days exploring the small island, which holds the evocative remains of a 6th-century monastery, but little else except exquisite wind-swept views of the deep blue sea.

Contact Bob Goodwin, Maharees, Castlegregory, County Kerry. ℂ/fax **066/713-9443.** 1 cottage. Starting at €630 ($1,008) per week. Rates include transport to and from the island, bedding, and all utilities. No credit cards. Closed Nov–Mar.

Kerry Cottages ★★ (Kids) Deep in the heart of Kerry, these 10 cottages are off a back road, a few minutes on foot to the beach and another 20 minutes or so to little Castlegregory village. All the cottages have polished pine furnishings, terra-cotta floors (carpeting upstairs), and whitewashed walls. The smallest is a cozy two-bedroom retreat with a small private garden; six cottages have three bedrooms and little backyards. The Sands is the largest house, with five bedrooms, each with a private bathroom. Second-story bedrooms in the larger cottages have great sea views. Each place is equipped with a washer-dryer and dishwasher, and the kitchens have all you need to prepare most meals. There's a small playground area for kids, with a swing set and slide. Rates vary seasonally; the cottages are an especially good value outside the summer season.

Castlegregory, Dingle Peninsula, County Kerry (1.6km/1 mile from Castlegregory). ℂ **01/284-4000.** Fax 01/284-4333. www.kerrycottages.com. Book through Kerry Cottages, 3 Royal Terrace W., Dun Laoghaire, County Dublin. 10 cottages. €295–€1,045 ($472–$1,672) per week for a 2- or 3- bedroom cottage; €900–€1,750 ($1,440–$2,800) for a 5-bedroom cottage. MC, V. *In room:* TV, kitchen, microwave, dishwasher, dryer, washing machine, no phone.

WHERE TO DINE

Restaurant David Norris ★★ MODERN CONTINENTAL Set in the pretty upstairs of Ivy House in the middle of Tralee, this restaurant has caused quite a stir in foodie circles for modern comfort food: homemade fettucine with wild mushrooms, chili-roasted pineapple-and-duck confit, and roasted Kerry beef with colcannon. Service is good and it's worth saving room for the desserts.

Ivy House, Ivy Terrace, Tralee, County Kerry. ℂ **066/718-5654.** Reservations necessary. Main courses €16–€28 ($26–$45). AE, MC, V. Tues–Fri 5–9:30pm; Sat 7–9:30pm.

The Tankard SEAFOOD Right on the water's edge, the restaurant's wide picture windows provide gorgeous views of the seafront amid a chic, contemporary decor. The menu focuses on local seafood—lobster, scallops, prawns, and black sole are all house specialties. It also includes local meat including rack of lamb, duck, quail, and steak. Bar food is available all day, but this restaurant is at its best in the early evening, especially at sunset.

10km (6¼ miles) northwest of Tralee, Kilfenora, Fenit, County Kerry. ℂ **066/713-6164.** Reservations recommended. Main courses €16–€32 ($26–$51). AE, DC, MC, V. Bar food daily 2–10pm. Restaurant daily noon–4pm and 6–10pm.

Siamsa Tire ★, the National Folk Theatre of Ireland, is at Town Park (© **066/712-3055**; www.siamsatire.com). Founded in 1974, Siamsa (pronounced *Sheem*-sha) offers a mixture of Irish music, dance, and mime. Its folk programs depict old folk tales and utilize farmyard activities, such as thatching a cottage roof, flailing sheaves of corn, and twisting a *sugan* rope. It also offers dramatic performances and musical concerts (traditional and classical) by amateur and professional companies. Admission averages €20 ($32) for adults, €14 ($22) for seniors, students, and children. Performances take place Monday, Tuesday, Thursday, and Saturday in May and from September to mid-October; Monday to Thursday and Saturday in June; and Monday to Saturday in July and August. Curtain time is 8:30pm. Call ahead for reservations.

Pubs

Harty's Lounge Bar   This pub—celebrated as the meetinghouse where the Rose of Tralee festival was born—is known for its good traditional pub food, such as steak and Guinness pie, shepherd's pie, and Irish stew. 30 Lower Castle St., Tralee, County Kerry. © **066/712-5385**.

Kirby's Olde Brogue Inn   This big barn of a pub is properly rustic, with decor heavy on farming implements. There's an excellent menu here, and traditional music and folk ballads when the right people show up. Rock St., Tralee, County Kerry. © **066/712-3221**.

Oyster Tavern   This tavern has the nicest location of any pub in the Tralee area, just 5km (3 miles) west of downtown, overlooking Tralee Bay. The pub grub includes seafood soups and platters. Fenit Rd., The Spa, Tralee, County Kerry. © **066/713-6102**.

Counties Limerick & Clare

If County Limerick and County Clare were ever to hold a beauty contest, Clare would win hands down (and then turn right around and lose in the semifinals to Galway, which would, in turn, be defeated by Donegal). That little fantasy aside, the fact remains that Limerick, despite its marvelous name and 50,000 bad jokes and dirty songs for which it can arguably be blamed, is a rather quiet, bucolic farmland that never bothers anyone and asks only not to be bothered in return. Clare, on the other hand, with its desolate Burren and majestic Cliffs of Moher, is just showing off.

So what we're saying, we suppose, is stop in at Limerick for a photo or two and then hurry on to Clare (and from there to Galway and Donegal) for the real show.

---

1 LIMERICK CITY & ENVIRONS

24km (15 miles) E of Shannon Airport, 198km (123 miles) SW of Dublin, 105km (65 miles) N of Cork, 111km (69 miles) NE of Killarney, 105km (65 miles) S of Galway

In such a tiny country, a population approaching 80,000 is enough to make gritty Limerick the third-largest city in the Republic. Strategically located on the banks of the River Shannon, the town was founded as a Viking settlement in the 10th century and grew in importance over the centuries. For many years, it struggled with endemic poverty, but today it is a busy place with a serious focus on business, and its shiny new office buildings stand as evidence. It is working hard to throw off the grim legacy bestowed by Frank McCourt's best-selling book *Angela's Ashes*, which described in excruciating detail a childhood spent there in abject poverty and unimaginable horribleness. Still, despite the effort to scrub itself up, Limerick City has long wrestled with a crime problem and struggles to control gang activity—so much so that the locals who wryly dubbed this place "stab city" have now started calling it "slab city." The tourist board is forever trying to put a positive spin on Limerick, but the reality is that it still feels like a rough old town, and the area where its most impressive sights are located—the riverside Medieval Heritage Precinct dominated by the 13th-century **King John's Castle**—is no exception. Frankly, this is the kind of area where we spend all our time worrying about whether somebody is breaking into our car. Given that major sights are few, there's little to keep you here unless you're doing business. However, should you find some hours to spare, you can peruse the scant offerings of the castle, or stop by the **Hunt Museum,** which houses a strong collection of Bronze Age, Celtic, and medieval treasures.

Happily, the countryside around Limerick City is less scary, and has a number of interesting sights. The picture-postcard village of Adare is definitely worth a visit (although you'll be parking at the end of a row of tour buses), as are Lough Gur and Rathkeale.

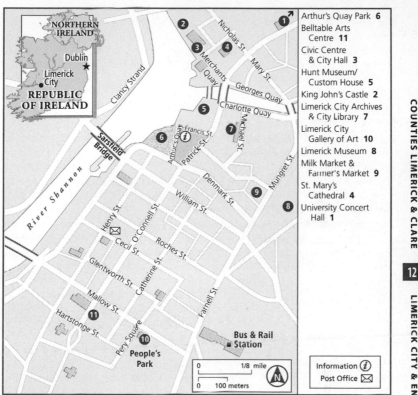

Arthur's Quay Park **6**
Belltable Arts Centre **11**
Civic Centre & City Hall **3**
Hunt Museum/ Custom House **5**
King John's Castle **2**
Limerick City Archives & City Library **7**
Limerick City Gallery of Art **10**
Limerick Museum **8**
Milk Market & Farmer's Market **9**
St. Mary's Cathedral **4**
University Concert Hall **1**

COUNTIES LIMERICK & CLARE

12

LIMERICK CITY & ENVIRONS

ESSENTIALS

GETTING THERE From the United States, American Airlines, Air France, Aer Lingus, Continental, Delta Airlines, and US Airways operate regularly scheduled flights into **Shannon Airport,** off the Limerick-Ennis road (N18), County Clare (© **061/712000;** www.shannonairport.com), 24km (15 miles) west of Limerick. Flights from Canada are on Air Transat, while domestic flights from Dublin and flights from Britain and the Continent are available from a range of carriers including Ryanair. (See "Getting There & Getting Around" in chapter 3 for airline details.) A taxi from the airport to the city center costs about €30 to €35 ($48–$56).

Bus Éireann (© **061/313333;** www.buseireann.ie) provides bus service from Shannon Airport to Limerick's Railway Station. The fare is approximately €5.60 ($8.95). Bus services from all parts of Ireland come into Limerick's **Colbert Station,** Parnell Street.

Irish Rail operates direct trains from Dublin, Cork, and Killarney, with connections from other parts of Ireland. They arrive at Limerick's **Colbert Station,** Parnell Street (© **061/315555;** www.irishrail.ie).

Limerick City can be reached on N7 from the east and north; N20, N21, N24, and N69 from the south; and N18 from the west and north.

VISITOR INFORMATION The **Limerick Tourism Centre** is on Arthur's Quay, Limerick (© **061/317522;** www.visitlimerick.com). It is open Monday to Friday 9:30am to 5:30pm, Saturday 9:30am to 1pm, with expanded and weekend hours in summer. Ask for a free copy of the *Shannon Region Visitors Guide,* which is packed with helpful information about activities and events.

There is another office in the **Adare Heritage Centre,** Main Street, Adare (© **061/ 396666;** www.adareheritagecentre.ie). It is open daily year-round (except Christmas, St. Stephen's Day [Dec 26], and New Year's Day) 9am to 1pm and 2 to 5pm (until 6pm and on Sun during the summer).

For good all-around visitor information on the Web, see **www.visitlimerick.com** or **www.limerick.com**.

GETTING AROUND Bus Éireann (© **061/313333**) operates local bus service around Limerick and its environs; fares start at €1.35 ($2.15). Buses depart from Colbert Station, Parnell Street.

Taxis line up outside Colbert Station, at hotels, and along Thomas and Cecil streets, off O'Connell Street. To reserve a taxi, call **Economy Cabs** (© **061/411411**), **Fixed Price Taxis** (© **061/313131**), or **Top Cabs** (© **061/417417**).

Driving around Limerick can be a little confusing because of the profusion of one-way streets—it's best to park your car and walk to see the sights. You might want to drive to King's Island for the Medieval Heritage Project, which includes King John's Castle and the other historic sights (there's a free parking lot opposite the castle). If you must park downtown, head for the lot at Arthur's Quay, which is convenient to sightseeing and shopping, and well signposted. Parking costs around €1.50 ($2.40) per hour.

If you need to rent a car in Limerick, contact **Irish Car Rental** (© **061/206088;** www.irishcarrentals.com). Most major international car-rental firms maintain desks at Shannon Airport (see the "County Clare" section, later in this chapter).

On foot, the city's streets are fairly easy to figure out, and the main central street has a changing name—it's Rutland Street in the north and O'Connell Street and Quinlan Street in the south. Most tourist sights are in the north on King's Island, which is the oldest part of the city, although some are to the south around Pery Square (where the architecture is grand Georgian buildings) and on the river's edge. A good way to hit the high points is to pick up a booklet outlining the Tourist Trail at the tourist office and in bookshops.

FAST FACTS If you need a drugstore, try **Hogan's Pharmacy,** 45 Upper William St. (© **061/415195**). After-hours service is available by calling © **088/526800.**

In an emergency, dial © **999. St. John's Hospital** is on St. John's Square (© **061/ 415822**). The local **Garda Headquarters** is on Henry Street (© **061/212400**).

The **General Post Office** is at 39 Upper William St. (© **061/409805**).

SEEING THE SIGHTS

Hunt Museum ★ Part of the reason to come to this museum is just to see the building—the grand, 18th-century Old Custom House, where the elegant Palladian facade is a copy of the Petit Trianon at Versailles. The museum's 2,000-work collection of ancient, medieval, and modern treasures—the finest outside of Dublin's National Museum—includes ancient Irish metalwork and medieval bronzes, ivories, and enamels. The collection was once privately owned by the late John and Gertrude Hunt, antiques dealers and consultants who willed their collection to Ireland in the 1970s. Free guided

There Once Was a Poet from Limerick . . .

To find out how a genre of bawdy pub poetry came to be associated with this unassuming Irish town requires looking back nearly 300 years. Nobody really knows who wrote the first sharply worded, five-line poem, but the style gained popularity in the 18th century and is credited to a group of poets who lived in the town of Croom in County Limerick. Known as the *Fili na Maighe*, or the "Gaelic poets of the Maigue," the poets wrote sardonic, quick-witted poems in Irish that soon became all the rage. Their style was adopted across the region, and within a century, everybody was doing it. Most anthologies on the subject list 42 poets and Irish scholars in the county in the 19th century, who were known for composing limericks, most with themes of romance, drinking, personal squabbles, and politics.

But it's possible that the true rise of the limerick came as a result of an 18th-century battle of wills between a poet and pub owner, Sean O'Tuama, and his friend Andrias MacCraith. Boyhood friends O'Tuama and MacCraith grew up in County Limerick and were well educated. The two fell out quite spectacularly (nobody remembers over what) and then wrote a series of castigating verses about each other. These became enormously popular, and the modern limerick was born. In retrospect, they're kind of cute, although the meter was sometimes a little stretched. As MacCraith once wrote:

> *O'Tuama! You boast yourself handy,*
> *At selling good ale and bright brandy*
> *But the fact is your liquor*
> *Makes everyone sicker,*
> *I tell you this, I, your good friend, Andy.*

tours are available (check at the front desk), and there are tours for kids as well. The in-house restaurant serves snacks and full meals.

The Custom House, Rutland St., Limerick. (C) **061/312833.** www.huntmuseum.com. Admission €7.75 ($12) adults, €6.25 ($10) seniors and students, €4 ($6.40) children, €18 ($29) families. Mon–Sat 10am–5pm; Sun 2–5pm.

King John's Castle (Overrated This stern riverside fortress is the centerpiece of Limerick's historic area. It dates from 1210, and may have been ordered built by King John of England. The low-slung gray-stone structure is a good example of medieval architecture, with distinctive rounded gate towers and thick curtain walls. Over the years, the castle has not always fared well, though. In an astonishing piece of historical vandalism, its ancient courtyard was filled up with cheap, modern houses during the mid–20th century. Happily they're gone now, and a recent €7-million restoration has put the castle back into better condition—but unfortunately, there's just not much to see here. Aside from a poorly explained archaeological excavation in the courtyard, the rest of the structure has little to offer. Access to the actual castle structure is limited, and what you can see is not well used. Worse, the big, modern visitor center serves mainly to ruin views of

the castle, and it justifies the high admission price with a sprawling display of mannequins in period costumes and one of the most overwrought and historically simplified
visitor center films you'll see on your Irish trip. The simple fact is—King John's Castle
costs more than it's worth.

Nicholas St., Limerick. ℂ **061/411201.** Admission €9 ($15) adults, €6.65 ($11) seniors and students,
€5.25 ($8.40) children, €21 ($34) families. May–Sept daily 9:30am–5:30pm; Mar–Apr and Oct daily
9:30am–5pm; Jan–Feb and Nov–Dec daily 10am–4:30pm. Last admission 1 hr. before closing.

Limerick City Gallery of Art   This gallery houses a permanent collection of 18th-,
19th-, and 20th-century art, including some fine paintings by the celebrated artist Jack
B. Yeats. It regularly hosts traveling contemporary-art exhibitions, including touring
exhibitions from the Irish Museum of Modern Art. The gallery building is the lovely
neo-Romanesque Carnegie Building (1903). On some evenings, there are literary readings or traditional or classical music concerts, so check local listings to see if one is
scheduled on your visit.

Pery Sq., on the corner of Mallow St. in the People's Park, Limerick. ℂ **061/310633.** www.limerickcity.ie/
lcga. Free admission. Mon–Wed and Fri 10am–6pm; Thurs 10am–7pm; Sat 10am–5pm; Sun 2–5pm.

Limerick Museum   This small museum is overshadowed by the Hunt Museum, but
for history buffs it's worth stopping in. It provides an insight into the town's background,
with displays on Limerick's archaeology, natural history, civic treasures, and traditional
crafts of lace, silver, furniture, and printing. Also on view are historical paintings, maps,
prints, and photographs, as well as the city's original charter, signed by Oliver Cromwell
and King Charles II, and a sword presented by Queen Elizabeth I.

Castle Lane, at Nicholas St., Limerick. ℂ **061/417826.** www.limerickcorp.ie/citymuseum. Free admission. Tues–Sat 10am–1pm and 2:15–7pm.

St. Mary's Cathedral   This cathedral sits on a site that was originally a palace belonging to one of the kings of Munster, Donal Mor O'Brien, who donated the land to the
church in 1172. The current building is much newer than that, but still contains a 12th-
century Romanesque doorway, a pre-Reformation stone altar, and a huge stone slab said
to be the coffin lid of Donal Mor O'Brien's grave. It also has original 15th-century **mise-
ricords** (supports for standing worshipers).

Bridge St., Limerick. ℂ **061/310293.** Donation €2 ($3.20). June–Sept Mon–Sat 9am–5pm; Oct–May
Mon–Sat 9am–4:30pm.

SHOPPING

Shopping hours in Limerick are Monday to Saturday 9:30am to 5:30pm. Many stores
also stay open until 9pm on Thursday and Friday.

At the corner of Ellen and Wickham streets, in the heart of Limerick's old Irishtown,
the old **Milk Market** is an informal bazaar selling everything from pottery to french fries.
It holds two weekly markets worth knowing about: a **Farmer's Market** Saturdays from
8am to 12:30pm, and an **Arts and Crafts Market** Fridays from 11am to 4pm.

Arthur's Quay Centre   This four-story shopping center overlooking Arthur's Quay
Park houses dozens of shops, including both workaday chains and small boutiques selling
handicrafts. Open Monday to Wednesday 9am to 7pm, Thursday and Friday 9am to
9pm, Saturday 9am to 6pm. Arthur's Quay, Limerick. ℂ **061/419888.**

Brown Thomas This is the Limerick branch of Ireland's native upscale department store. Its prices aren't the lowest, but it sells Waterford crystal, Aran knitwear, Donegal tweeds, and designer clothing. O'Connell St., Limerick. ℂ **061/417222.**

Cruises Street Shopping Centre The centerpiece of Limerick's downtown shopping district, this is a cleverly designed village-style mall on a pedestrianized street. There are plenty of stores for everyone here. Cruises St. (off Patrick St.), Limerick. No phone.

O'Mahoney's This quaint old bookshop has stood here for more than a century, and, along with all the latest hardbacks and paperbacks, it's also a good place to get information about Limerick and the countryside around it. 120 O'Connell St., Limerick. ℂ **061/418155.**

SPORTS & OUTDOOR PURSUITS

FISHING If you're looking for endless fish tales, an excellent guide, the best local tackle, and pure, all-around entertainment, it's hard to beat Paddy Guerin at the **Kingfisher Angling Centre** in nearby Castleconnell (15-min. drive from Limerick; ℂ **061/377407;** www.ireland360.com/kingfisher). He's even got a pub where you can tell your own tales at the end of the fishing day. In Limerick itself, get information, licenses, permits, and equipment at **Steve's Fishing and Shooting Store,** The Milk Market, Carr Street (ℂ **061/413484**). **Celtic Angling,** in nearby Ballingarry, Adare (ℂ **069/68202;** www.celticangling.com), can provide daylong salmon-fishing excursions on the Shannon, including pickup from Limerick City, equipment, licenses, and everything else you need. A day's fishing will cost on average €190 to €375 ($304–$600) for one person, plus €60 to €145 ($96–$232) for each additional person in a group.

GOLF The Limerick area has three 18-hole golf courses, including a championship par-72 parkland layout at the **Limerick County Golf & Country Club,** Ballyneety (ℂ **061/351881;** www.limerickcounty.com), 8km (5 miles) east of Limerick. It charges greens fees of €45 ($72) Monday to Friday, €55 ($88) weekends. The par-70 inland course at the **Limerick Golf Club,** Ballyclough (ℂ **061/415146;** www.limerickgolfclub. ie), 4.8km (3 miles) south of Limerick, has greens fees of €50 ($80) weekdays, €70 ($112) weekends. The par-71 inland course at **Castletroy Golf Club,** Castletroy, County Limerick (ℂ **061/335753;** www.castletroygolfclub.ie), 4.8km (3 miles) east of Limerick, charges greens fees of €50 ($80) Monday to Thursday, €60 ($96) Friday to Sunday.

HORSEBACK RIDING The county's fields provide good turf for horseback riding. Rates run about €25 to €30 ($40–$48) per hour. The **Clonshire Equestrian Centre,** Adare, County Limerick (ℂ **061/396770;** www.clonshire.com), offers riding for all levels, horsemanship classes, and instruction for cross-country riding, dressage, and jumping. Clonshire is also home to the Limerick Foxhounds; in the winter, it's a center for hunting in the area. Per-hour rates average upwards of €40 ($64) for adults, €30 ($48) for students and children 17 and under. Riding and board packages are available.

WHERE TO STAY
Moderate

Castle Oaks House ★★ This gracious, two-story Georgian manor house at the edge of the River Shannon was once a convent, and it still has a few touches, including stained-glass windows, although the old chapel is now used as a banquet hall. The comfortable guest rooms are quite feminine, furnished with soft pastel fabrics, and well-chosen antiques. There's also a three-bedroom house on the grounds available for €400

ⓘTips **Service Charges**

A reminder: Unless otherwise noted, room rates don't include service charges (usually 10%–15% of your bill).

to €850 ($640–$1,360) per week, depending on the season. The hotel will help you arrange activities, including fishing or horseback riding, during your stay.

9.7km (6 miles) east of Limerick City, off Dublin rd. (N7), Castleconnell, County Limerick. ☏ 800/223-6510 in the U.S., or 061/377666. Fax 061/377717. www.castleoaks.ie. 20 units. €100–€160 ($160–$256) double; €180–€200 ($288–$320) suite. Rates include full breakfast. AE, DC, MC, V. **Amenities:** Restaurant (Continental); bar; indoor pool; tennis court; gym; spa treatments; Jacuzzi; steam room. *In room:* TV, tea/coffeemaker.

Clarion Hotel Limerick ★★   Built in 2002, this is Limerick's sleekest modern hotel. Its white tower stands out amid the low-slung buildings—you won't have trouble finding it. It's a badly needed dose of modernity compared to Limerick's other, largely old-fashioned, hotels. Rooms are big and decorated in shades of coffee and cream, and those high up among its 17 floors have excellent views. It has all the latest accouterments, and does it all with great style. The restaurant has floor-to-ceiling windows overlooking the river, and the bar is deliciously trendy.

Steamboat Quay, Limerick, County Limerick. ☏ 061/444100. Fax 061/444101. www.clarionhotellimerick. com. 158 units. €100–€150 ($160–$240) double. AE, DC, MC, V. **Amenities:** Restaurant (Continental); bar; pool; gym; sauna. *In room:* TV, high-speed Internet access, minibar, tea/coffeemaker, hair dryer.

Inexpensive

Jurys Inn Limerick ★ ⓥValue   This hotel's riverfront location is appealing, and the river-facing rooms, especially on the upper floors, have splendid views. Rooms are tastefully contemporary, with firm beds, large bathtubs, desks, and ample shelf and wardrobe space—everything you need and very little you don't. All rooms are big enough to handle up to three adults or two adults and two children, and some are specially designed for those with mobility problems, including interconnecting rooms for caregivers.

Lower Mallow St., Limerick, County Limerick. ☏ 800/843-3311 in the U.S., or 061/207000. Fax 061/400966. www.jurys.com. 151 units. €70–€95 ($112–$152) double. AE, DC, MC, V. Discounted parking available at adjoining car park, €7.50 ($12). **Amenities:** Restaurant (international); pub; coffee bar; laundry service; nonsmoking rooms. *In room:* TV, dataport, tea/coffeemaker, hair dryer.

Sarsfield Bridge Hotel ★ ⓥValue   On the leafy banks of the Shannon across the Sarsfield Bridge, this contemporary, business traveler's hotel is a 3-minute walk from O'Connell Street in the thick of the action. The up-to-date guest rooms are practical, with conservative, mahogany-like furniture and views of the gardens and river. The hotel's bar is a popular place to watch sports on plasma-screen TVs. Like so many business hotels, this one does everything right, but lacks individuality.

Sarsfield Bridge Limerick, County Limerick. ☏ 061/317179. Fax 061/317182. www.tsbh.ie. 55 units. €100–€160 ($160–$256) double. Rates include full breakfast. AE, MC, V. Free parking. **Amenities:** Restaurant (international); bar; nonsmoking rooms. *In room:* TV, tea/coffeemaker.

WHERE TO DINE

Expensive

Freddy's Bistro ★ MODERN IRISH   The old coach house that holds this pleasant, upscale restaurant conveys a great sense of history, while the restaurant itself is reliably relaxed and friendly. The menu changes regularly here, but always combines local produce and meats with a creative touch. The steaks are particularly good, perfectly cooked, and served with inventive sauces.

Theatre Lane, Limerick. © 061/418749. www.freddysbistro.com. Reservations recommended. Main courses €22–€27 ($35–$43); early evening fixed-price menu €30 ($48), available 5:30–7pm (use code "early evening" when making reservation). AE, MC, V. Tues–Sat 5:30pm–closing.

Moderate

Copper and Spice ★ INDIAN/THAI   This good Indian restaurant is a refreshing change from all that Irish cuisine. The mod dining room sets a brilliant backdrop for Seema Conroy's superb cooking: terrific breads, tantalizing curries, wonderful veggie pakoras. All the usual favorites are on offer, in pleasant, modern surroundings, making this a good option.

2 Cornmarket Row, Limerick. © 061/313620. www.copperandspice.com. Reservations recommended. Main courses €14–€22 ($22–$35); fixed-price 3-course dinner €25 ($40), available 5–7pm. AE, MC, V. Tues–Sun 5–10:30pm.

Curragower Seafood Bar ★ (Finds) SEAFOOD   This place is stripped down to the bare bones, and its entire focus is on seafood. There are hearty seafood chowders in the winter, and crab claws on ice in the summer. Savor huge Irish oysters in season, and prawns and Atlantic salmon all the time. The restaurant's terrace has good views of the castle.

Clancy's Strand, Limerick. © 061/321788. Main courses €11–€23 ($18–$37). MC, V. Daily noon–11pm.

Piccola Italia ITALIAN   This traditional Italian restaurant is like any Italian restaurant in New York—the tables have red-and-white-checked tablecloths, while chianti baskets hang from the ceiling. The menu reads like the "best of Italy," with cannelloni, lasagna, fettuccine, pizza, and steak pizzaiola.

56 O'Connell St., Limerick. © 061/313899. Reservations recommended. Main courses €10–€22 ($16–$35). MC, V. Mon–Sat 6–11pm.

LIMERICK CITY AFTER DARK

Pubs

The Locke   Established in 1724 near the river, this is one of Limerick's oldest and most popular pubs. It's a lovely, rambling place, with open fires roaring, and nooks and crannies for quiet conversations over a pint. It's known for its traditional Irish music—played on Sunday and Tuesday year-round. It's a good place to come on a summer's evening, when there is outdoor seating and Japanese lanterns are strung along a cobbled walkway to lend a romantic, festive air. The pub also has a comfortable restaurant that serves Irish and Mediterranean cuisine. 2A–3 Georges Quay, Limerick. © 061/413733.

Vintage Club   In one of Limerick's older sections near the quays, this pub used to be a wine cellar, and the decor reflects it: barrel seats and tables, oak casks, dark-paneled walls, and a beer garden. It's not fancy, but it's good old-fashioned Limerick. 9 Ellen St., Limerick. © 061/410694.

W.M. South's This timeless old pub has a black-and-white-checkerboard floor; a high, white marble bar; and a succession of Victorian mahogany arches behind the bar, which frame bottles, mirrors, and curios. The pub's crowd is a mixture of locals and tourists, and they keep things buzzing here year-round. Quinlan St., Limerick. ℰ **061/318850.**

The Performing Arts

Belltable Arts Centre By day, the building is open for gallery exhibits of modern Irish artists, while at night, there's a mixture of local professional theatrical productions. There are also a popular bar and a coffee shop. Most shows run Monday to Saturday at 8pm, but call ahead to confirm showtimes. 69 O'Connell St., Limerick. ℰ 061/319866. www.belltable.ie. Tickets €10–€25 ($16–$40); "snatch-and-grab" tickets €7 ($11) at 7pm (cash only).

Dolan's Warehouse This is a popular venue for touring international rock bands, and a good place to see Irish bands as well. Everybody from Evan Dando to Kasabian has played here, and the eclectic lineup is well worth checking out. There are actually three venues here—**Dolan's Pub and Restaurant,** which has traditional Irish music by local or visiting bands every night; the Warehouse itself, where the big acts play; and a new bar and performance space upstairs—imaginatively called **Upstairs**—where there are comedy nights every Wednesday. 3 Dock Rd., Limerick. ℰ 061/314483. www.dolanspub.com. Tickets €7–€35 ($11–$56).

University Concert Hall On the grounds of the University of Limerick, this 1,000-seat hall offers a broad program of national and international solo stars, variety shows, and ballet. It also books the Irish Chamber Orchestra, RTE Concert Orchestra, University of Limerick Chamber Orchestra, Limerick Singers, and European Community Orchestra. A list of events is available from the tourist office. Most performances start at 8pm, but call ahead for details. University of Limerick, Plassey, County Limerick. ℰ 061/331549. www.uch.ie. Tickets €10–€35 ($16–$56).

SIDE TRIPS FROM LIMERICK CITY

If you're seduced by charming Irish villages, you'll want to head to the lovely village of **Adare** ★★, which is full of picturesque thatched-roof cottages, beautiful gardens, ivy-covered medieval churches, and lots and lots of tour buses. Yes, this place has been very seriously discovered, but it's still worth a stop—even though its peace has long since been shattered. It's a good place to break for lunch.

Adare Heritage Centre If you make it to Adare, drop by this small but friendly heritage center artfully tucked away in a stone building. It has a walk-through display on Adare's colorful history, as well as a small cafe and several crafts shops, with a fairly good selection of pottery and linen.

Main St., Adare, County Limerick. ℰ 061/396666. www.adareheritagecentre.ie. Daily 9am–6pm (closed at lunchtime).

Foynes Flying Boat Museum ★★ This one isn't just for aviation buffs—history fans will fall for it, too. This was the first Shannon Airport—predecessor to the modern runways of Shannon Airport in County Clare—restored as an absorbing museum. It commemorates an era begun on July 9, 1939, when Pan Am's luxury flying boat *Yankee Clipper* landed at Foynes, marking the first commercial passenger flight on the direct route between the United States and Europe. On June 22, 1942, Foynes was the departure point for the first nonstop commercial flight from Europe to New York. This is also where bartender Joe Sheridan invented Irish coffee in 1942. (At a festival each Aug, there's a contest to select the world Irish-coffee-making champion.) The complex includes a 1940s-style cinema and cafe, the original terminal building, and the radio and weather rooms with original transmitters, receivers, and Morse code equipment.

Foynes, County Limerick. ℂ **069/65416.** www.flyingboatmuseum.com. Admission €8 ($13) adults, €6 ($9.60) seniors and students, €5 ($8) children 5–13, €25 ($40) families, free for children 4 and under. MC, V. Mar–Oct daily 10am–6pm; Nov and Dec 1 daily 10am–4pm. 37km (23 miles) east of Limerick on N69.

Glin Castle ★★ Lilies of the valley and ivy-covered ash, oak, and beech trees line the driveway leading from the village of Glin to this gleaming-white castle, home to the knights of Glin for the past 700 years. The vast estate sprawls over 160 hectares (395 acres) of sloping lawns, gardens, farmlands, and forests. The centerpiece of it all is, naturally, the castle—which is really more of a Georgian house with added Gothic details—but it's not possible to see inside unless you love it enough to spend the night (see below).

Limerick-Tarbert rd. (N69), Glin, County Limerick. ℂ **068/34173.** www.glincastle.com. Free admission to gardens. Approx. 40km (25 miles) east of Limerick City.

Lough Gur Interpretive Centre ★ The lovely lake known as Lough Gur is surrounded by an unusual preponderance of ancient sites, most of which are well signposted on the R512, the drive that skirts around the lake's edge. There's much to see here, and it might be best to stop at the visitor center first for information and a map to the sites, although it's a little expensive for what it offers, so you may prefer to explore on your own. Lough Gur area was occupied continuously from the Neolithic period to late medieval times. Archaeologists have uncovered foundations of a small farmstead built around the year 900, a lake island dwelling built between 500 and 1000, a wedge-shaped tomb that was a communal grave around 2500 B.C., and the extraordinary Grange Stone Circle, which is a 4,000-year-old site with 113 upright stones forming the largest prehistoric stone circle in Ireland. The lake itself is a great place to explore and have a picnic.

11km (6¾ miles) SE of Limerick City on R512, Lough Gur, County Limerick. ℂ **061/385186.** Museum and audiovisual presentation €5 ($8) adults; €3 ($4.80) seniors, students, and children; €13 ($21) families. Visitor center mid-May to Sept daily 10am–6pm (last admission 5:30pm); site open year-round.

Where to Stay Around County Limerick
Very Expensive
Adare Manor ★★★ You usually wouldn't expect to find such an exclusive hotel in a village as tiny and secluded as Adare, but this 19th-century Tudor Gothic mansion, nestled on the banks of the River Maigue, is full of surprises. The former home of the earls of Dunraven, it has been masterfully restored and refurbished as a deluxe resort, with 15th-century carved doors; Waterford crystal chandeliers; ornate fireplaces; and spacious, antiques-filled guest rooms. Two- to four-bedroom garden town houses for families and larger groups are also available, and there is an excellent full-service spa. Outside is an 18-hole championship golf course that draws guests as much as does the incredibly relaxing atmosphere and fine restaurant cuisine. Virtually every known countryside activity, from horseback riding to salmon fishing to fox hunting, can be arranged.

Adare, County Limerick. ℂ **800/462-3273** in the U.S., or 061/605200. Fax 061/396124. www.adare manor.com. 63 units. €270–€445 ($432–$712) double; €385–€695 ($616–$1,112) staterooms; €200–€260 ($320–$416) carriage house rooms; €360–€670 ($576–$1,072) town houses; €643 ($1,029) villas. AE, DC, MC, V. **Amenities:** 2 restaurants (Continental, brasserie); bar; indoor swimming pool; 18-hole Robert Trent Jones, Sr., golf course; gym; spa treatments; sauna; concierge; room service; babysitting; laundry service; clay-pigeon shooting; nature trails; riding stables; salmon and trout fishing. In room: TV, minibar, hair dryer, garment press.

Glin Castle ★★★   This beautifully restored, 18th-century castle guesthouse has everything the aspiring lord and lady of the manor could dream of. Rooms are huge and gorgeously appointed with antiques, augmented with modern, orthopedic beds. Floor-to-ceiling windows overlook pristine manicured grounds. Bathrooms are the size of New York apartments, and claw-foot tubs are big enough for two to splash in. Downstairs are three sitting rooms where you can lounge by crackling fires; the friendly staff members wander by regularly to see if you need tea, coffee, or brandy. Breakfast is silver service with lots of options (the hot chocolate is recommended). To the rear of the castle is a charming walled garden where fresh fruit and vegetables are grown for the kitchen, and there are lovely views of the River Shannon to be had as well. If you're very lucky you might even bump into the castle's famously eccentric owner, the Knight of Glin, who likes to be referred to simply as "the Knight."

Limerick-Tarbert rd. (N69), Glin, County Limerick. ℂ **068/34173.** Fax 068/34364. www.glincastle.com. 15 units. €310–€495 ($496–$792) double. 4-course dinner €60 ($96). MC, V. Approx. 40km (25 miles) east of Limerick City. Closed Dec–Feb. **Amenities:** Restaurant (modern European); archery; clay pigeon shooting. *In room:* TV, hair dryer, iron.

Moderate
Dunraven Arms ★ (Value)   On the banks of the River Maigue, this 18th-century inn is a charming country retreat 16km (10 miles) south of Limerick City. The public areas have an old-world ambience, with open fireplaces and antiques, although occasionally the color scheme is a bit startling (vivid green walls and blue upholstery with floral throw pillows and a maroon Oriental rug . . . oh, dear). The rooms, blessedly, are more subtly done in neutral colors. Half are in the original house, half in a new wing, and all are furnished in traditional style, with Victorian accents and period pieces. It's not all old-fashioned style, as there's a thoroughly modern leisure center with a huge pool as well. It's had its share of stars— Gwyneth Paltrow stayed here a few years ago while in Ireland for a friend's wedding.

Main St. (N21), Adare, County Limerick. ℂ **800/447-7462** in the U.S., or 061/605900. Fax 061/396541. www.dunravenhotel.com. 86 units. €195 ($312) double; €260–€335 ($416–$536) suite. Breakfast €18–€23 ($29–$37). AE, DC, MC, V. **Amenities:** Restaurant (international); bar; indoor pool; gym; steam room; room service; massage; beauty treatments. *In room:* TV, radio, Wi-Fi, hair dryer.

The Mustard Seed at Echo Lodge ★★★ (Finds)   Built in 1884 as a parochial house, then converted for use as a convent, this is a lovely place to stay and eat. Owner Daniel Mullane's world travels are evident in the furnishings, colors, and luxurious fabrics, all of which come together in harmony. Beds are comfortable, and guest rooms are designed with subtle flair. The **restaurant** (see below) is a destination in itself, with a menu that presents a creative mix of organic local produce, brilliantly prepared.

13km (8 miles) from Adare, off the Newcastle West rd. from the center of Ballingarry, County Limerick. ℂ **069/68508.** Fax 069/68511. www.mustardseed.ie. 18 units. €180–€240 ($288–$384) double; €330 ($528) suite. Rates include full breakfast. Fixed-price 4-course dinner €62 ($99). AE, MC, V. Dining hours daily 7–9:30pm. Closed Feb 1–15. **Amenities:** Restaurant (modern Continental). *In room:* TV, hair dryer, trouser press.

Impressions

In Ireland, the inevitable never happens and the unexpected constantly occurs.

—Sir John Pentland Mahaffy

Abbey Villa ★ (Value)   This bungalow has a picturesque setting in pretty little Adare. The owners are welcoming and friendly, and more than willing to help you plan an itinerary for your travels in Limerick. The comfortable rooms are tastefully decorated, and all have satellite TV and electric blankets for those chilly nights.

Station Rd., Adare, County Limerick. ℭ **061/396113.** Fax 061/396969. www.abbeyvilla.net. 6 units. €80 ($128) double. 50% discount for children. Rates include full breakfast. MC, V. **Amenities:** Sitting room. *In room:* TV, hair dryer.

Where to Dine Around County Limerick
Expensive

The Mustard Seed ★★★ MODERN INTERNATIONAL   Most food critics place this elegant rural restaurant among the top restaurants in the country. The chef uses fresh, organic herbs and vegetables from the restaurant's own gardens and all meats are sourced from local organic producers, so the food is as fresh as it can possibly be. The cooking style is an intelligent mixture of European styles with an Irish touch. It's evident in dishes such as pan-seared Irish beef on wild mushroom polenta with Parmesan crackling, or breast of Barbary duck on buttered greens with lime-and-vanilla mash and chocolate oil. A dinner here is a memorable event.

13km (8 miles) from Adare, off the Newcastle West rd. from the center of Ballingarry, County Limerick. ℭ **069/68508.** www.mustardseed.ie. Fixed-price 4-course dinner €62 ($99). AE, MC, V. Daily 7–9:30pm. Closed Feb 1–15.

The Wild Geese ★★★ MODERN INTERNATIONAL   County Limerick has two stellar restaurants, the Mustard Seed (above) and the Wild Geese. The emphasis here is simple, but perfect: Start with superb local ingredients and build on that. The cooking is complex and refined, yet always controlled. This is clear in dishes such as the duck confit served on wontons with sesame dressing, the Clare crabmeat soufflé, or grilled salmon with tempura of vegetables. In season, you will find unforgettable dishes such as wild pheasant stuffed with rosemary and currants. Service is impeccable, and because of that, the atmosphere is relaxed and filled with a sense of anticipation.

Rose Cottage, Adare, County Limerick. ℭ **061/396451.** www.thewild-geese.com. Reservations required. 3-course early-bird menu (Tues–Fri 6:30–7:30pm, Sat 6:30–7pm) €35 ($56); main courses €30 ($48). AE, MC, V. May–Sept Tues–Sat 6:30pm–closing, Sun 5:30pm–closing; Oct–Apr Tues–Sat 6:30pm–closing. Closed Dec 24–Jan 2.

Moderate

Inn Between ★ INTERNATIONAL   Although it lines up in a row of charming Adare houses and shops, this thatched-roof brasserie-style restaurant has a surprisingly airy, sky-lit interior and a breezy courtyard for outdoor seating on warm days. The menu is classic and approachable, with homemade soups, steaks with green-peppercorn sauce, wild salmon on leek fondue, and the classic Inn Between burgers with homemade relish.

Main St., Adare, County Limerick. ℭ **061/396633.** Reservations recommended. Main courses €14–€24 ($22–$38). AE, DC, MC, V. Tues–Sat 6:30–10:30pm; June–Aug also 12:30–2:30pm.

Pubs Around County Limerick

Finnegan's   First opened in 1776, this historic alehouse is as old as the U.S. The name is borrowed from *Finnegan's Wake,* which is why the decor has a Joycean theme. There are plenty of picnic tables in the rose garden for summer days, Irish music on most weekends, and good food served year-round. Dublin rd. (N7), about 8km (5 miles) east of Limerick City, Annacotty, County Limerick. © **061/337338.**

Matt the Thrasher About 24km (15 miles) northeast of Limerick—and well worth the drive—is this 19th-century farmers' pub. A rustic, cottagelike atmosphere prevails, with antique furnishings, agricultural memorabilia, and lots of cozy alcoves. There's plenty of pleasant outdoor seating for sunny days, and a small restaurant. This pub is known for traditional music, so there's usually a band playing in the evening. Dublin rd. (N7), Birdhill, County Tipperary. © **061/379227.**

2 COUNTY CLARE

Ennis: 67km (42 miles) S of Galway, 27km (17 miles) NW of Shannon Airport, 37km (23 miles) NW of Limerick, 235km (146 miles) SW of Dublin, 133km (83 miles) NW of Cork

After stepping off the plane at Shannon Airport, your first sight of Ireland will be the rich green fields and rolling hills of County Clare. Perhaps that explains why, to many non-Irish, this is the landscape the world associates with Ireland—it was, for many years, the world's first view of it. From the airport, if you turn left off the main road, the barren, rocky Atlantic coast awaits you; if you continue north, you'll eventually make your way to the charming county town of **Ennis** and then to the gravely beautiful limestone land-scape of the **Burren.**

Like its neighbors Kerry and Galway, Clare has a dramatic stretch of coastline, includ-ing the spectacular **Cliffs of Moher** and darling seaside towns such as **Lahinch** and **Kilkee.** At its southern heart the boating paradise of Lough Derg brings in water cruisers and sailboats, and the surrounding towns and villages—including those in northern Tipperary—are set up to take care of aquatic fanatics. Around the edges of the lake are charming towns including **Killaloe**—a darling village at the foot of the Slieve Bernagh Hills, and home to a picturesque inland marina and a host of watersports. Killaloe Cathe-dral dates from the 13th century, and has extensive carving on its southern doorway. The stone cross near the doorway dates to early Christian times and is carved with Irish ogham scripts and Scandinavian runes. The grounds also hold a 12th-century oratory.

Few counties have more Irish music on heavy rotation than Clare, which is well known for a vibrant traditional music scene, especially in the charming villages of **Doolin, Miltown Malby, Fanore,** and **Ennistymon.** This is also an excellent place for those fascinated by the country's ancient history, as it's littered with historic and prehis-toric sites, from the **Poulnabrone Dolmen** to **Bunratty Castle,** with its better-than-you-probably-expected folk park.

COUNTY CLARE ESSENTIALS

GETTING THERE From the United States, American Airlines, Air France, Aer Lingus, Continental, Delta Airlines, and US Airways all operate regularly scheduled flights into **Shan-non Airport,** off the Limerick-Ennis road (N18), County Clare (© **061/712000;** www.shannonairport.com), 24km (15 miles) west of Limerick. Domestic flights from Dublin and flights from Britain and the Continent are available on carriers including Iberworld, Air France, and Ryanair. (See "Getting There & Getting Around" in chapter 3 for airline details.)

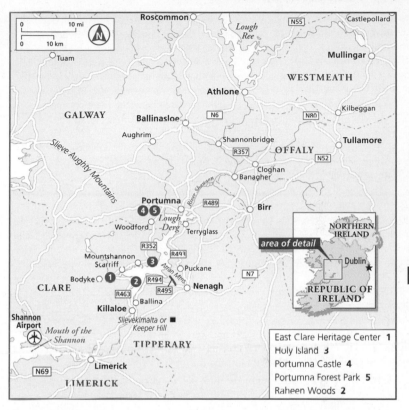

East Clare Heritage Center 1
Holy Island 3
Portumna Castle 4
Portumna Forest Park 5
Raheen Woods 2

Irish Rail provides service to **Ennis Rail Station,** Station Road (✆ **1850/366-222;** www.irishrail.ie), and Limerick's **Colbert Station,** Parnell Street (✆ **061/315555**), 24km (15 miles) from Shannon.

Bus Éireann provides bus services from all parts of Ireland into **Ennis Bus Station,** Station Road (✆ **065/682-4177;** www.buseireann.ie), and other towns in County Clare.

By car, County Clare can be reached on N18. Shannon Airport has offices of the following international firms: **Car Hire** (✆ **061/472633;** www.carhire.ie), **Avis** (✆ **061/715600;** www.avis.ie), **Budget** (✆ **061/471361;** www.budget.ie), and **Hertz** (✆ **061/471369;** www.hertz.ie). Several local firms also maintain desks at the airport; among the most reliable is **Dan Dooley Rent-A-Car** (✆ **061/471098;** www.dan-dooley.ie).

From points south, County Clare can be reached directly, bypassing Limerick, on the **Tarbert-Killimer Car Ferry.** It crosses the Shannon River from Tarbert, County Kerry, to Killimer, County Clare. Trip time for the drive-on/drive-off service is 20 minutes; no reservations are needed. Crossings from Tarbert are on the half-hour; from Killimer, on the hour. Ferries operate year-round except Christmas Day. From Killimer departures are

(Tips) **Don't Drink the Water in Ennis!**

There's definitely something in the water around these parts—and it's not good. Back in 2005, the water supply in Ennis was found to be tainted with *Cryptosporidium,* a parasite that causes intestinal illness. Tediously for visitors (and even more so for residents), everybody in the town is now advised to boil water for cooking and to drink bottled water until a new water plant is built—which at this writing was on target for May 2009. So if you're planning on staying in Ennis, make sure you ask your hotelier about the safety of the water, when you make your reservation *and* when you arrive, and be prepared to buy or bring bottled water.

Other towns in Ireland have been found to have potentially dangerous levels of carcinogens in their water supplies. For more details, see the "Worrisome Water Supply" box in chapter 3.

April to September Monday to Saturday 7am to 9pm and Sunday 9am to 9pm (with additional sailings May–Sept at half past the hour from 10:30am–5:30pm daily), and October to March Monday to Saturday 7am to 7pm and Sunday 9am to 7pm. From Tarbert departures are April to September Monday to Saturday 7:30am to 9:30pm and Sunday 9:30am to 9:30pm (with additional sailings May–Sept at half past the hour from 11am–6pm daily), and October to March Monday to Saturday 7:30am to 7:30pm and Sunday 9:30am to 7:30pm. Summer fares for cars with passengers are €17 ($27) one-way and €28 ($45) round-trip; for foot passengers and cyclists, fares are €5 ($8) one-way and €7 ($11) round-trip. For more information, contact **Shannon Ferry Ltd.,** Killimer/Kilrush, County Clare (© **065/905-3124;** www.shannonferries.com). The Killimer Ferry terminal has a gift shop and restaurant, and daily hours are 9am to 9pm.

VISITOR INFORMATION   A **tourist office** is in the Arrivals Hall of Shannon Airport (© **061/471644**). Hours coincide with flight arrivals and departures.

The **Ennis Tourist Office,** Authors Row, Ennis, County Clare (© **065/682-8366**), is about 1.6km (1 mile) south of town on the main N18 road. It's open year-round Monday to Saturday 9:30am to 1pm and 2 to 5pm, with weekend and extended hours April to October.

Seasonal tourist offices in County Clare are at the Cliffs of Moher (© **065/708-1171**); O'Connell Street, Kilkee (© **065/905-6112**); and Town Hall, Kilrush (© **065/905-1577**). These offices are usually open from May or June until early September.

Because Lough Derg unites three counties (Clare, Galway, and Tipperary), there are several sources of information about that area. They include the **Shannon Development Tourism Group,** Shannon, County Clare (© **061/361555;** www.discoverireland.ie/shannon); **Failte Ireland West,** Forster Street, Galway (© **091/537700;** www.discoverireland.ie/west); and **Tipperary Lake Side & Development,** The Old Church, Mill Street, Borrisokane, County Tipperary (© **067/27155;** www.tipperarylakeside.com). Seasonal information offices include the **Nenagh Tourist Office,** Connolly Street, Nenagh, County Tipperary (© **067/31610**), open early May to early September; and the **Killaloe Tourist Office,** The Lough House, Killaloe, County Clare (© **061/376866**), open May to September. You can also find visitor information at any Limerick tourist office, or online at **www.county-clare.com.**

The 24km (15-mile) road from Shannon Airport to Ennis, a well-signposted section of the main Limerick-Galway road (N18), is a well-traveled route with the feel of a proper highway—something that you didn't encounter previously much in these shores, but which is becoming more and more ubiquitous. On the whole, though, the Irish country-side is still a land of *boreens* (country single-lane roads), so don't get too comfortable.

To reach the village of **Bunratty,** with its 15th-century medieval castle (which is inevitably besieged by tour groups in the summer), turn right on the N18 and proceed for 8km (5 miles). Or you could turn left, heading toward Ennis, and pass through the charming river town of **Newmarket-on-Fergus,** with its grand **Dromoland Castle.**

The county town of Clare, **Ennis** (pop. 19,000) is a busy market town, and one of the largest towns in this part of the country. Unfortunately, it not only sits on the banks of a river—the River Fergus—but on the busy N18, meaning that the traffic congestion is appalling and the exhaust fumes a perpetual menace. Work is currently underway on a bypass that should help alleviate this problem, but for now, expect a traffic jam whenever you pass through town. Ennis is a sprawling place, with lots of unspectacular suburbs, but its center is easily explored on foot, especially if you stop by the tourist office and pick up a walking tour and map before you set out. You can still see the town's medieval layout—its winding narrow lanes date back centuries, as does its 13th-century friary. The statue in the town center is of Daniel O'Connell, a beloved Irish politician whose over-whelming election to the British Parliament in 1828 forced Britain to end its ban of Catholic parliamentarians. The statue near the courthouse is of Eamon de Valera, who represented Clare in the Irish Parliament and later became president of Ireland.

SEEING THE SIGHTS

Bunratty Castle and Folk Park ★★ (Kids)   Long before you reach Bunratty, the gray stone walls of this rugged, 15th-century fortress dominate the views from the main road. Standing fiercely beside the O'Garney River, Bunratty Castle (1425) is an exception-ally complete medieval castle and thus offers a rare perspective on living in a castle in those troubled times. The ancient stronghold has been restored with period-appropriate furni-ture, stained glass, luxurious tapestries, and other art. The castle you see today was the fourth castle built on this spot, and it was largely built by the MacNamara family in 1425, but in an earlier incarnation it was a home of the English royal family, until it was destroyed by the Irish chieftains of Thomond in 1332. After the current structure was completed, it was ultimately taken over by the powerful O'Brien family clan, the largest in North Munster. They ruled from here and lived a life of luxury. In their time, the castle was surrounded by lush gardens in which thrived thousands of deer. After Ireland fell to Cromwell, the castle was taken over by a variety of English families, until the last abandoned it in 1804 and moved into Bunratty House, which is also available for tours.

Today the castle is a kind of historical theme park, crawling with tourists in the high season. By day, the building's inner chambers and grounds are open for tours; at night, the Great Hall serves as a candlelit setting for medieval banquets and entertainment (p. 379).

Around the castle is the 8-hectare (20-acre) theme park, Bunratty Folk Park. While it is, as you might expect, extremely touristy, it's also done well. The re-creation of 19th-century Irish villages includes thatched cottages, farmhouses, and an entire village street, with a school, post office, pub, grocery store, print shop, and hotel—all open for brows-ing and shopping. Fresh scones are baked in the cottages, and craftspeople ply such trades as knitting, weaving, candle making, pottery, and photography. It's all a bit cute, and yet

(Fun Facts) Taking a (Moon) Shine to Potcheen

"Keep your eyes well peeled today, the excise men are on their way, searching for the mountain tay, in the hills of Connemara . . . ."

Potcheen, also known as Irish moonshine whiskey, is a potent drink traditionally brewed from grain or potatoes. It was banned by the English crown in 1661, an act that effectively criminalized thousands of distillers overnight. Unsurprisingly, that didn't stop people from making the stuff, and after 336 years on the wrong side of the law, potcheen was finally made legal again in 1997.

One 17th-century writer said of potcheen that "it enlighteneth ye heart, casts off melancholy, keeps back old age and breaketh ye wind." Its usefulness didn't stop there, evidently, as history records the drink being used as everything from a bath tonic to a substitute for dynamite.

Potcheen has long been used in fiction as a symbol of Irish nationalism, its contraband status rich with rebellious overtones. The traditional folk song "The Hills of Connemara" describes potcheen being secretly distributed under the noses of excise men, and it was a popular subject for Irish poets in the 19th century. Indeed, the first film to be made entirely in the Irish language—*Poitín* (1977)—was a violent tale about a potcheen moonshiner harassed by local ne'er-do-wells.

There are currently just two licensed potcheen distilleries in the world: Bunratty Winery (see above) and Knockeen Hills in Waterford. In 2008, the European Union awarded the drink "Geographical Indicative" protection, which means that only the genuine Irish product is allowed to carry the name (the same status enjoyed by champagne and Parma ham). Like most liquors it can be drunk straight, on the rocks, or with a mixer, but at anything from 80 to a massive 180 proof, newly legal potcheen packs a mean punch, so enjoy . . . cautiously.

it's quite fun, too. In the summer there's a *céilidh* (traditional Irish party) in the folk park nightly. The evening starts with a three-course meal, followed by a 40-minute show featuring storytelling, folk music, and dancing (7pm nightly; €48/$77 adults, €24–€40/$38–$64 children; call ahead to book). You can while away a very enjoyable afternoon exploring the castle, great house, and folk park, and kids will find its living history aspect fascinating.

Limerick-Ennis rd. (N18), Bunratty, County Clare. (© 061/361511. Admission €15 ($24) adults, €10 ($16) students, €6.50 ($10) seniors, €9 ($14) children, €32 ($51) families. June–Aug daily 9am–6pm (last admission 5:15pm); Apr–May and Sept–Oct daily 9am–5:30pm (last admission 5:15pm); Jan–Mar and Nov–Dec daily 9:30am–5:30pm (last admission 4:15pm).

Bunratty Winery   In a coach house dating from 1816, this winery produces traditional medieval wines including mead—a medieval drink made from honey, fermented grape juice, water, matured spirits, and herbs, a historical favorite of the upper classes. The winery is also one of only two distilleries officially licensed to brew Irish potcheen, a heady potato moonshine that was so popular and pernicious, it was banned in 1661—

and was only made legal again in 1997. Most of the products are made for Bunratty
Castle's medieval-style banquets (p. 379), but visitors are welcome at the working winery
to watch the production in progress and taste the brew.

Bunratty, County Clare. © **061/362222.** http://homepage.eircom.net/~bunrattywinery. Free admission.
Daily 9:30am–5:30pm.

Clare Museum   In the same building as the Ennis tourist office, this interesting little
museum does a good job of explaining and illustrating the colorful history of the county.
Through a combination of films, drawings, and artifacts, the exhibition stretches back
6,000 years and can make a good early stop to a first-time tour of the county. The
museum has recently abolished admission charges—an increasingly rare gesture, and a
welcome one.

Arthur's Row, Ennis, County Clare. © **065/682-3382.** Free admission. Oct–May Tues–Sat 9:30am–1pm
and 2–5pm; June–Sept Mon–Sat 9:30am–5pm, Sun 9:30am–1pm.

Craggaunowen Bronze-Age Project   Through an old fortified castle and re-cre-
ations of ancient sites such as a *crannog* (a fortified island) and a ring fort, the Craggaunowen Project seeks to present a timeline of Ireland's past from the Neolithic period to the
Middle Ages. There are reconstructed Bronze Age dwellings (often inhabited by craftspeople demonstrating ancient weaving techniques and the like—in period costume, naturally);
working demonstrations of cooking and farming methods; pottery making; and even a herd
of rare sheep, of a breed native to Ireland since prehistoric times. It's interesting to wander,
and certainly makes up in charm for what it lacks in razzmatazz, although it's not as effective as it might be at conveying any real sense of living history. Still, it's worth a visit,
especially for history buffs and those curious about what such sites looked like.

About 16km (10 miles) from Ennis, signposted off R469, Quin, County Clare. © **061/367178.** Admission
€8.50 ($14) adults, €6.20 ($9.90) seniors and students, €5 ($8) children, €20 ($32) families. Mid-Apr to
mid-Oct daily 10am–6pm (last admission 5pm).

de Valera Library and Museum   This quirky museum is devoted to Ireland's
American-born former president, Eamon de Valera (1882–1975), with a small collection
of memorabilia. Apropos of nothing, it also holds a tiny art collection and random relics,
such as a door from a Spanish Armada galleon that sank off the Clare coast in 1588.

Harmony Row, off Abbey St., Ennis, County Clare. © **065/684-6353.** Free admission. Mon and Wed–
Thurs 10am–5pm; Tues and Fri 10am–8pm; Sat 10am–2pm.

Dysert O'Dea Castle and Clare Archaeology Centre ★★   Built in 1480 by
Diarmaid O'Dea on a rocky outcrop of land, this castle was later badly damaged by
Cromwell's gang. Hundreds of years passed before it was restored and opened to the
public in 1986 as an archaeology center and museum. Today it offers exhibitions on the
history of the area, and forms the starting point for a signposted trail that leads to 25 sites
of historical and archaeological interest within a 3km (2-mile) radius. These include a
church founded by St. Tola in the 8th century, which contains a unique Romanesque
doorway surrounded by a border of 12 heads carved in stone. The O'Deas, the former
chieftains of the area, are buried underneath. There's also a round tower from the 10th
or 12th century, a 12th-century high cross, a holy well, a 14th-century battlefield, and a
stone fort believed to date from the Iron Age.

R476 to Corofin, County Clare. © **065/683-7401.** www.dysertcastle.com. Admission €4.50 ($7.20) adults,
€3.50 ($5.60) seniors and students, €2.50 ($4) children, €10 ($16) families. May–Sept daily 10am–6pm.

The Lough Derg Drive

Often called an inland sea, Lough Derg was the main inland waterway trading route between Dublin and Limerick when canal and river commercial traffic was at its height in the 18th and 19th centuries. It is the Shannon River's largest lake and widest point: 40km (25 miles) long and almost 16km (10 miles) wide. It is a longtime favorite place for the Irish to spend summer weekends.

The road that circles the lake for 153km (95 miles), the **Lough Derg Drive,** is one continuous photo opportunity, where panoramas of hilly farmlands, gentle mountains, and glistening waters are unspoiled by commercialization. The drive is a collage of colorful shoreline towns, starting with **Killaloe** ★, County Clare, and **Ballina,** County Tipperary. They're so close that they are essentially one community—only a splendid 13-arch bridge over the Shannon separates them. It's a favorite stopping point for recreational sailors, and in the summer, its pubs and bars are filled with them.

Kincora, on the highest ground at Killaloe, was the royal settlement of Brian Boru and the other O'Brien kings, but no trace of any building remains. Killaloe is a lovely town with lakeside views at almost every turn and many restaurants and pubs providing outdoor seating on the shore, but don't overlook Ballina's legendary nightlife.

Eight kilometers (5 miles) inland from Lough Derg's lower southeast shores is **Nenagh,** the chief town of north Tipperary. It lies in a fertile valley between the Silvermine and Arra mountains.

On the north shore of the lake in County Galway, **Portumna** is worth a visit for its lovely forest park and castle.

Memorable little towns and harborside villages like **Mountshannon** and **Dromineer** dot the rest of the Lough Derg Drive. Some towns, like **Terryglass** and **Woodford,** are known for atmospheric old pubs where spontaneous sessions of traditional Irish music are likely to occur. Others, like **Puckane** and **Ballinderry,** offer unique crafts or locally made products.

The best way to get to Lough Derg is by car or boat. Although there is limited public transportation in the area, you will need a car to get around the lake. Major roads that lead to Lough Derg are the main Limerick-Dublin road (N7) from points east and south, N6 and N65 from Galway and the west, and N52 from the north. The Lough Derg Drive, which is well signposted, is a combination of R352 on the west bank of the lake and R493, R494, and R495 on the east bank.

East Clare Heritage Centre/Holy Island Tours In the restored 10th-century church of St. Cronan, this center provides genealogical research and explains the heritage and history of the East Clare area through a series of exhibits and an audiovisual presentation. A pier across the road is the starting point for a 15-minute excursion in an eight-seat boat on Lough Derg to nearby Inishcealtra (Holy Island), a 7th-century monastic settlement. The remains include a tall round tower that has long since lost its pointed

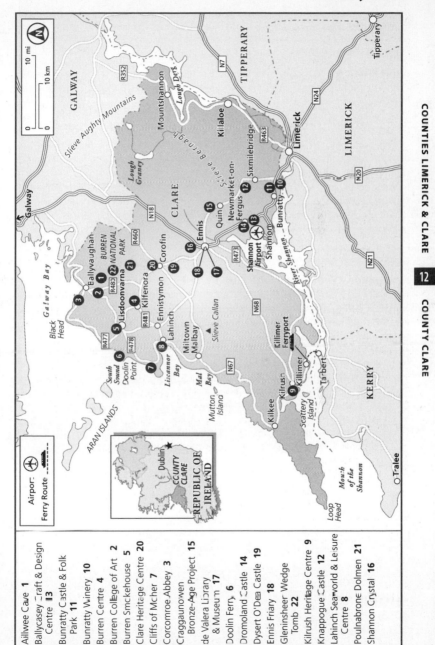

Aillwee Cave **1**
Ballycasey Craft & Design Centre **13**
Bunratty Castle & Folk Park **11**
Bunratty Winery **10**
Burren Centre **4**
Burren College of Art **2**
Burren Smokehouse **5**
Clare Heritage Centre **20**
Cliffs of Moher **7**
Corcomroe Abbey **3**
Craggaunowen Bronze-Age Project **15**
de Valera Library & Museum **17**
Doolin Ferry **6**
Dromoland Castle **14**
Dysert O'Dea Castle **19**
Ennis Friary **18**
Gleninsheer Wedge Tomb **22**
Kilrush Heritage Centre **9**
Knappogue Castle **12**
Lahinch Seaworld & Leisure Centre **8**
Poulnabrone Dolmen **21**
Shannon Crystal **16**

roof, as well as four chapels, hermit cells, and graves that date from the settlement's earliest days.

Off the Portumna-Ennis rd. (R352), Tuamgraney, County Clare. Center $\textcircled{C}$ **061/921351.** Island tours $\textcircled{C}$ **086/874-9710.** www.eastclareheritage.com. Free admission to the center; Holy Island Tours €9 ($14) adults, €5 ($8) seniors and children. Center daily Mon–Fri 10am–5pm; Holy Island Tours June–Sept daily 10am–5pm, weather permitting.

Ennis Friary ★ When you walk around Ennis Friary, it can be hard to get a sense of scale, but if it helps you to understand it, consider that records show that in 1375 it was home and workplace for 350 friars and 600 students. Founded in 1241, this Franciscan abbey, a famous seat of learning in medieval times, made Ennis a focal point of western Europe for many years. It was finally forced to close in 1692 and thereafter fell into ruin, but it's been partly restored, and contains many beautifully sculpted medieval tombs, decorative fragments, and carvings, including the famous McMahon tomb. The nave and chancel are the oldest parts of the friary, but other structures, such as the 15th-century tower, transept, and sacristy, are also rich in architectural detail. It's run by the Irish historical preservation group, Dúchas, which offers entertaining and informative tours in the summer. *Note:* The friary has only limited access for those with mobility problems— call in advance to arrange.

Abbey St., Ennis, County Clare. $\textcircled{C}$ **065/682-9100.** Admission €1.60 ($2.55) adults, €1.10 ($1.75) seniors, €1 ($1.60) children and students, €4.50 ($7.20) families. Easter–Sept daily 10am–6pm; Oct daily 10am–5pm.

Knappogue Castle & Walled Gardens ★★ Midway between Bunratty and Ennis, this regal castle was built in 1467 as the home of the McNamara clan, who, along with the O'Briens, dominated the area for more than 1,000 years. Oliver Cromwell used the castle as a base in the mid–17th century while pillaging the countryside and thus, unlike many castles, it was largely left intact. The original Norman structure includes elaborate late-Georgian and Regency wings added in the mid–19th century. Early in the 20th century, it fell into disrepair, but was rescued by Texan Mark Edwin Andrews, a former U.S. assistant secretary of the navy. He and his wife, Lavone, an architect, worked closely with area historical societies and returned the castle to its former glory, even furnishing it with 15th-century furniture. The Andrewses were the last private owners of the house, as they turned it over to the Shannon Development group in 1996. The restored Victorian walled gardens were opened to the public shortly afterward, and today they supply the castle with fresh herbs for the medieval banquets held nightly during the summer months (p. 379).

Quin, County Clare. $\textcircled{C}$ **061/368103.** Admission €7 ($11) adults; €3.35 ($5.35) children, seniors, and students. May–Sept daily 9:30am–5pm (last admission 4:15pm). Medieval banquets daily Apr–Oct.

Shannon Crystal In the north end of town (on the way to Galway Rd.), this crystal-making enterprise produces hand-cut glassware on the premises. The showroom is open to visitors, who can watch demonstrations by the master cutter in the skill of crystal carving.

Sandfield Rd., Ennis, County Clare. $\textcircled{C}$ **065/682-1250.** Free admission. Daily 9am–6pm.

SHOPPING

Avoca This pink, thatched-roof cottage shop is a branch of the legendary County Wicklow–based Avoca Handweavers. Like its sister shops, this one carries the colorful woolen knit clothes and mohair throws that have made the Avoca line justifiably famous, plus kitchenware, children's clothes, bedding, and knickknacks. The in-house cafe, serving healthy lunch, tea, and fresh cakes, is just as good as the rest of the shop. Limerick-Ennis rd. (N18), Bunratty, County Clare. $\mathcal{C}$ 061/364029. www.avoca.ie.

Bunratty Village Mills   On the grounds of the Bunratty Castle Hotel, dozens of fine shops are laid out like a 19th-century village. This includes a branch of Tipperary Crystal; the wonderful housewares shop, Meadows & Byrne; Linen Shop; Aran Shop, for knit-wear; Celtic Sounds Music & Book Shop; and Bunratty Cottage, for clothing, gifts, and jewelry. Main St., Bunratty, County Clare. $\mathcal{C}$ 061/364321.

Custy's Traditional Music Shop   Bring the melodious sounds of County Clare home with you. The selection here includes a full range of traditional-music tapes and CDs, instruments, books, and photos. Cooks Lane, O'Connell St., Ennis, County Clare. $\mathcal{C}$ 065/682-1727.

Gift Venue   This spacious china store, formerly known as the Belleek Shop, also sells Waterford, Galway, and Tipperary crystal. 36 Abbey St., Ennis, County Clare. $\mathcal{C}$ 065/686-7891. www.giftvenue.com.

McKernan Scarves   A husband-and-wife team, Eugene and Anke McKernan offer a colorful array of distinctive tweed scarves, jackets, vests, and blankets. The couple hand-weave all items on the premises, and you can pop into the workshop and watch the work underway. Open daily 10am to 6pm. Handweavers, Main St., Tuamgraney, County Clare. $\mathcal{C}$ 061/921527. www.mckernanscarves.com.

Puckane Crafts   A rustic, thatched-roof cottage serves as the shop of Adele Starr's artisanal wares. There are Celtic and rural scenes and pieces with heraldic and religious themes. She stocks Jerpoint glass, as well as works by potter Nicholas Mosse and designs by Louise Kennedy. These all make great souvenirs. Open Monday to Saturday from 10am to 6pm, Sundays 2 to 6pm. R493, Puckane, Nenagh, County Tipperary. $\mathcal{C}$ 067/24229. www.puckanecrafts.com.

SPORTS & OUTDOOR PURSUITS

BOATING & OTHER WATERSPORTS   If you enjoy boating, tubing, water-skiing, windsurfing, canoeing, or other water activities, this is the place for you.

River cruising is big business in this part of the country, and there are plenty of ways to do it—if you're an experienced cruiser you can rent a barge or cruiser and make your own way, or you can rent a cruiser or barge complete with crew, or take a cabin on a shared cruiser. It all depends on your level of expertise, and the depth of your pocketbook. Numerous companies rent cabin cruisers along this stretch of the cabin, including **Emerald Star Line,** The Marina, Portumna, County Galway ($\mathcal{C}$ 071/962-7633; www.emeraldstar.ie); and **Shannon Castle Line,** The Marina, Williamstown, County Clare ($\mathcal{C}$ 061/927042; www.shannoncruisers.com).

Whelan's Boat Hire, at the bridge, Killaloe, County Clare ($\mathcal{C}$ 086/376159; whelans@killaloe.ie), rents 20-foot lake boats with outboard engines for sightseeing or fishing in the waters of Lough Derg. Prices include fuel, fishing gear, life jackets, and rainwear. In the summer, Whelan's offers river tours that provide plenty of local history and lore.

GOLF   Shannon may be the only airport in the world with its own championship golf course. The 18-hole, par-72 championship course at the **Shannon Golf Club,** Shannon Airport ($\mathcal{C}$ 061/471849; www.shannongolf.com), may not be the quietest course in

Ireland, but it's the handiest. Greens fees are €55 ($88) weekdays and €65 ($104) weekends, with early and late tee times from €25 ($40). Within 1km (²/₃ mile) of the terminal, it is bounded on one side by the Shannon River, and on the other by busy runways.

More peaceful choices in the area include the par-71 **Dromoland Golf Club,** Newmarket-on-Fergus, County Clare (© 061/368444; www.dromolandgolf.com), with greens fees of €60 to €125 ($96–$200). The par-71 parkland course at the **Ennis Golf Club,** Drumbiggle, Ennis, County Clare (© 065/682-4074; www.ennisgolfclub.com), charges greens fees of €35 to €40 ($56–$64).

The **East Clare Golf Club,** Scariff/Killaloe Road, Bodyke, County Clare (© 061/921322; www.eastclare.com), is an 18-hole championship course. Greens fees are €30 ($48) weekdays, €35 ($56) weekends.

SWIMMING   Lough Derg is known for clear, unpolluted water that's ideal for swimming, particularly at **Castle Lough, Dromineer,** and **Portumna Bay.** Portumna Bay has changing rooms and showers.

WALKING   There are some excellent walks in **Portumna Forest Park,** in **Raheen Woods,** and along the shoreline of **Lough Derg.** For a touch of scenic wilderness, walk a portion of the **Slieve Bloom Way,** a circular 34km (21-mile) signposted trail that begins and ends in Glenbarrow, County Laois.

WHERE TO STAY

Very Expensive

Dromoland Castle ★★   This vision of turrets and towers makes for a fairy-tale night, albeit at prices fit for a king. About 15 minutes' drive from Shannon Airport, the castle dates from 1686, and stands amid extensive parklands and gardens where deer roam freely. The drawing rooms and stately halls have all your heart could desire of splendid wood and stone carvings, medieval suits of armor, rich oak paneling, and oil paintings. The guest rooms are lavishly decorated with designer fabrics and reproduction furniture. Service is excellent, if a bit stiff and self-conscious, although that's not a surprise given that in 2004, George W. Bush stayed here while attending the E.U.-U.S. Summit.

Limerick-Ennis rd. (N18), Newmarket-on-Fergus, County Clare. © **800/346-7007** in the U.S., or 061/368144. Fax 061/363355. www.dromoland.ie. 100 units. €440–€560 ($704–$896) double. Full Irish breakfast €29 ($46). AE, DC, MC, V. **Amenities:** 2 restaurants (French, country club); bar; 18-hole golf course; tennis courts; fishing and boating equipment; concierge; room service; babysitting; laundry service; walking/jogging trails. *In room:* TV, hair dryer, garment press.

Expensive

Bunratty Castle Hotel ★   This manor house adjoining Bunratty Castle isn't a castle at all—instead it's a gracious country-house hotel with a sunny yellow facade, offering comfort and convenience with a touch of elegance. Recently renovated, it's got a fresh new feel. The public rooms are nicely done, with an antique marble altar as a reception desk. The spacious guest rooms have orthopedic king-size beds draped in neutral fabrics with occasional bright touches. There's also a new spa, where you can soak away the cares of world travel.

Bunratty, County Clare. © **061/478-700.** Fax 061/364-891. www.bunrattycastlehotel.com. 80 units. €130–€240 ($208–$384) double. Executive suites also available. Rates include full breakfast. AE, DC, MC, V. **Amenities:** Restaurant (Irish); bar; spa; babysitting. *In room:* A/C, TV, tea/coffeemaker, hair dryer.

Clare Inn Resort Hotel (Kids)   The panoramic views of the River Shannon and the Clare from this contemporary hotel are great here, but the real lure is all the family activities. *Warning:* Do not stay here if you do not like children. There are so many of them in the hallways, pool, and public areas that at times they seem to run the place. The hotel is surrounded by the Dromoland Castle golf course and thousands of acres of woodland. The grounds hold a huge fitness center with a pool, hot tub, sauna, tennis courts, and an 18-hole miniature golf course—all designed with families and kids in mind. The public areas are bright and airy with large picture windows, but a renovation is past due here, and the rooms are looking battered.

Limerick-Ennis rd. (N18), Newmarket-on-Fergus, County Clare. © **800/473-8954** in the U.S., or 065/682-3000. Fax 065/682-3759. www.lynchotels.com. 187 units. €150–€170 ($240–$272) double. Rates include full breakfast. AE, DC, MC, V. **Amenities:** 2 restaurants (international, cafe); bar; indoor swimming pool; 18-hole golf course; 2 tennis courts; gym; Jacuzzi; sauna; supervised children's facilities; jogging track; miniature golf; solarium. *In room:* TV, radio, hair dryer.

Lakeside Hotel (Kids)   On the southern banks of Lough Derg, shaded by ancient trees, this two-story country house–style hotel has a lovely setting. Guest rooms have simple furnishings but are greatly enhanced by wide views of the lake or gardens. Make sure you stipulate a lake view, although these cost extra. The hotel is on the Ballina side of the bridge, on the edge of town next to the marina.

Killaloe, County Clare. © **800/447-7462** in the U.S., or 061/376122. Fax 061/376431. www.lakeside-killaloe.com. 46 units. €140–€150 ($224–$240) double. €20 ($32) supplement for lake views. Rates include full breakfast. AE, MC, V. **Amenities:** Restaurant (Continental); bar; indoor swimming pool; tennis court; snooker (pool table); gym; Jacuzzi; steam room; crèche (staffed nursery for babysitting/child care); nonsmoking rooms. *In room:* TV, tea/coffeemaker.

Old Ground Hotel   Long a focal point in the busy market town of Ennis, this ivy-covered hotel dates from 1749, and was once both the town hall and the jail. It's simply but elegantly decorated, with creamy yellows in the lobby, and neutral tones in the guest rooms, livened by soft, russet bed covers. There are lots of memorable touches—look out for a fireplace dating to 1553; it once warmed Lemaneagh Castle. On summer evenings, cabaret-style entertainment is offered in the pub. Word has reached us of slipping standards at the Old Ground lately, however, with several visitors complaining about the tatty state of some rooms, and even the lingering smell of pre–smoking ban cigarette smoke. Certainly not what one would expect for the price.

O'Connell St., Ennis, County Clare. © **065/682-8127**. Fax 065/682 8112. www.flynnhotels.com. 114 units. €170–€190 ($272–$304) double. Rates include full breakfast. AE, DC, MC, V. **Amenities:** 2 restaurants (international, grill); bar; lounge. *In room:* TV, hair dryer, garment press.

Roundwood House ★★ (Kids)   Roundwood House has an insouciant, put-up-your-feet casual elegance, due in part to the Kennan family's warmth and relaxed approach. Good taste pervades the splendid 18th-century Palladian country villa, set amid secluded woods, pasture, and gardens. The six guest rooms in the main house are spacious and decorated with an eye for charm and simplicity. The two on the second floor share a large central play area ideal for families with children. The Yellow House, across the herb garden and courtyard from the main building, has been tastefully restored to offer four delightful double rooms. Roundwood's soft couches, firm beds, lovely views, and excellent meals all calm the soul. *Note:* The nearest TV is a long walk away.

4.8km (3 miles) northwest of Mountrath, on R440 toward the Slieve Bloom Mountains, Mountrath, County Laois. © **057/873-2120**. Fax 057/873-2711. www.roundwoodhouse.com. 10 units. Main house

€170 ($272) double; Yellow House €150 ($240). 50% reduction for children sharing with parents. Rates include full Irish breakfast. Dinner Tues–Sat (book by 2pm) €50 ($80); Sun–Mon supper €30 ($48); 6pm children's dinner €8 ($13). AE, DC, MC, V. **Amenities:** Croquet; boule; drawing room.

Temple Gate Hotel ★   This modern hotel is very nicely done, as a sort of new interpretation of the old convent that once stood on the site it now occupies. Rooms are big and decorated with a masculine touch, with rich maroons and grays. Beds are firm and there are desks for working, should you be so inclined. The restaurant is candlelit and lovely, and the food is a good take on modern Irish. All in all, it's an attractive, restful place in central Ennis.

The Square, Ennis, County Clare. ⓒ **065/682-3300.** Fax 065/364891. www.templegatehotel.com. 70 units. €130–€190 ($208–$304) double. Children 9 and under stay free in parent's room. Breakfast €11 ($17). AE, DC, MC, V. **Amenities:** Restaurant (bistro); pub. *In room:* A/C, TV, high-speed Internet access, tea/coffeemaker, hair dryer.

Inexpensive

Bunratty Woods ⓥⒶⓁⓤⒺ   If you're looking for peace and tranquillity—but within easy reach of the airport—you might want to try this tasteful guesthouse. At the edge of the titular woods, this place is very nicely done: furnished in antique pine, with bare wood floors and handmade patchwork quilts on the firm beds. Most rooms have views of the rolling Clare countryside. The house breakfast special is pancakes, served however you like them.

Low Rd., Bunratty, County Clare. ⓒ **061/369689.** Fax 061/369454. www.iol.ie/~bunratty. 14 units. €65–€80 ($104–$128) double. Rates include full breakfast. DC, MC, V. Closed mid-Nov to Feb. **Amenities:** Lounge. *In room:* TV, tea/coffeemaker, hair dryer.

Cill Eoin House ★ ⒻⒾⓃⒹⓈ   Just off the main N18 road at the Killadysert Cross, 5 minutes' drive south of Ennis, this two-story yellow guesthouse is a real find. Its bright, comfortable rooms have hotel-quality furnishings, beautiful views of the countryside, and firm beds at a good price, capped by attentive service from the Lucey family.

Killadysert Cross, Clare Rd., Ennis, County Clare. ⓒ **065/684-1668.** Fax 065/684-1669. www.euroka.com/cilleoin. 14 units. €80–€90 ($128–$144) double. Rates include full breakfast. AE, MC, V. Closed Dec 24–Jan 8. **Amenities:** Sunroom; TV lounge. *In room:* TV.

Lantern House   The biggest attraction at this pleasant, unpretentious guesthouse is the sweeping view of Lough Derg. Palm trees grow on the well-tended hilltop grounds, and all the public rooms overlook the Shannon, as do some of the guest rooms (but be sure to ask for a room with a view when booking). Furnishings are homey and comfortable. Guests can gather for drinks around the fireplace in the cozy lounge. The **restaurant** (see below) is quite popular among locals.

9.7km (6 miles) north of Killaloe on the main road, Ogonnelloe, Tuamgraney, County Clare. ⓒ **061/923034.** Fax 061/923139. www.lanternhouse.com. 6 units. €80 ($128) double. Rates include full breakfast. AE, DC, MC, V. Closed Nov–Feb. **Amenities:** Restaurant (Continental); lounge; bar; nonsmoking rooms. *In room:* TV.

Self-Catering

For an area of such popularity, much of County Clare has surprisingly few hotels. In many ways, that's part of its allure—its lakes and forests are unspoiled by condos, motels, and fast-food joints—but it still has left travelers in the lurch over the years.

When the "Rent an Irish Cottage" program was pioneered here almost 30 years ago, the idea was simple: Build small rental cottages designed in traditional style, with exteriors of white stucco, thatched roofs, and half doors. Aside from the turf fireplaces, all of the interior furnishings, plumbing, heating, and kitchen appliances are modern. Built in groups of 8 to 12, the cottages are on picturesque sites in remote villages such as Puckane, Terryglass, and Whitegate, overlooking or close to Lough Derg's shores. As there are no restaurants or bars on-site, you shop in local grocery stores, cook your own meals, and mix with locals in pubs at night. In other words, it's a chance to become part of the community. Rates range from around €350 to €1,500 ($560–$2,400) per cottage per week, depending on the size (one to six bedrooms) and time of year. Rental rates include bed linens and color TV; towels and metered electricity are extra.

One of the loveliest cottage settings belongs to **Mountshannon,** County Clare, a cluster of 12 pastel-toned, one- and two-story cottages on the shores of Lough Derg at Mountshannon Harbour. Grouped like a private village around a garden courtyard, the three-bedroom cottages cost €300 to €725 ($480–$1,160) per week, depending on the time of year. Also on the shores of Lough Derg are 12 cottages in a country village setting in **Puckane,** County Tipperary. Rates for two- and three-bedroom cottages are €290 to €725 ($464–$1,160) per week, depending on season and size.

For more information, contact **Rent an Irish Cottage,** 51 O'Connell St., Limerick, County Limerick (© **061/411109;** fax 061/314821; www.rentacottage.ie).

WHERE TO DINE
Moderate

Brogan's PUB FOOD This place is big but friendly, with plenty of tables, even when it's busy at lunchtime. The food is classic Irish, with lots of stews, meat pies, and fish and chips. It's marginally better for lunch than dinner, as it feels more like a restaurant than a pub.

24 O'Connell St., Ennis, County Clare. © **065/682-9480.** Main courses €8–€22 ($13–$35). No credit cards. Daily 10am–10pm.

The Cherry Tree Restaurant ★★★ (Finds) MODERN CONTINENTAL This lovely waterside restaurant in enchanting Killaloe is the destination restaurant of the midlands, and it has scooped a number of prestigious European awards in the past few years. The dining room is colorful and inviting, and the cooking is sophisticated. Seafood is a strong suit, but everything on the menu begins with fine local ingredients: Tipperary beef, Comeragh lamb, Castletownbere sea mullet, Dinish Island scallops. Then what's added—every hint of cream, every garnish, every side dish—is a well-thought-out complement to the meal.

Lakeside, Ballina, Killaloe, County Clare. © **061/375688.** www.cherrytreerestaurant.ie. Reservations recommended. Main courses €28–€32 ($45–$51); fixed price 3-course dinner €48 ($77). AE, MC, V. Tues–Sat 6–10pm; Sun 12:30–3pm.

Cruise's Pub Restaurant GRILL Another marvelously historic restaurant (dating from 1658), this one has low beamed ceilings, crackling fires in open hearths, lantern lighting, and a rough flagstone floor strewn with sawdust. It's a casual place with a traditional pub menu, including dishes like Irish stew, steaks, and seafood. On warm days, you can sit outside in the courtyard overlooking the friary.

Abbey St., Ennis, County Clare. © **065/684-1800.** Reservations recommended. Main courses €10–€26 ($16–$42). MC, V. Daily 12:30–10pm.

COUNTIES LIMERICK & CLARE

12

COUNTY CLARE

Galloping Hogan's Restaurant ★ CONTINENTAL   In a restored old railway station, this restaurant sits beside Lough Derg, overlooking the water on the Ballina side of the Killaloe bridge. There's a plant-filled conservatory-style room and a patio-terrace for fair-weather dining. The menu is filled with fresh local foods, and the most memorable dishes include the rack of lamb and perfectly grilled steaks. Seafood choices are also plentiful, including pan-fried black sole and a huge baked cod filet. Lighter bar food is available from noon to 10pm.

Ballina, County Clare. ✆ 061/622789. Reservations recommended. Main courses €15–€26 ($24–$42). AE, MC, V. Daily 6:30–10pm.

Goosers ★ SEAFOOD   With a thatched roof and mustard-colored exterior, this popular pub and restaurant sits on the Ballina side of the Shannon, looking out at the river. Its two informal rooms have open fireplaces, stone floors, and beamed ceilings, and you sit on *sugan* chairs (traditional wood chairs with twisted straw rope seats). There's picnic-table seating outside in good weather. The bar-food menu includes traditional dishes such as bacon and cabbage, and Irish stew, while the restaurant focuses on local seafood—lobster, salmon, sole, and monkfish—simply prepared.

Ballina, County Clare. ✆ 061/376791. Reservations recommended for dinner. Bar food €6–€22 ($9.60–$35); dinner main courses €22–€34 ($35–$54). AE, MC, V. Daily 11am–11pm.

Lantern House ★ CONTINENTAL   High on a hillside just north of Killaloe, the biggest draw of this country-house restaurant is its panoramic views of Lough Derg. The owners here extend a warm welcome, and the candlelit dining room exudes old-world charm, with a beamed ceiling, wall lanterns, and lace tablecloths. The menu changes frequently, but good options usually include tender poached local salmon, delicate pan-fried sole, or a particularly juicy sirloin steak.

Ogonnelloe, County Clare. ✆ 061/923034. Reservations recommended. Main courses €10–€24 ($16–$38). AE, MC, V. Daily 6–9pm (closed Mon Nov to mid-Feb).

Inexpensive

Country Choice ★ CAFE   If you're looking for picnic provisions or food for the road, this is the place to find it. You can fill a basket with the sweet local marmalade, rich farmhouse cheeses, and freshly baked loaves of bread. There's a cafe out back where you can linger over a cup of coffee and find out all the local gossip. There's an inexpensive lunch menu, and fresh baked goods are served in the morning.

25 Kenyon St., Nenagh, County Tipperary. ✆ 067/32596. www.countrychoice.ie. Lunch main courses €5–€12 ($8–$19). No credit cards. Mon–Sat 9am–6pm (lunch served after noon).

Molly's Bar and Restaurant CONTINENTAL   Next to the Killaloe bridge, this brightly colored pub and restaurant offers expansive views of Killaloe Harbour. Inside is a cheerful clutter with shelves lined with old plates, vintage clocks, and pine and mahogany furnishings. The food is a similarly casual mix of light fare and heavier dinner selections, and good options on our visit included the fresh local salmon and huge chargrilled steaks. Outdoor seating is available on picnic-style tables. There's live music, traditional and modern, Thursday to Sunday evenings, as well as a disco and sports bar in the basement.

Killaloe/Ballina, County Clare. ✆ 061/376632. Reservations recommended for dinner. All items €7–€22 ($11–$35). AE, MC, V. Daily 12:30–11:30pm.

Medieval Banquets & Traditional Meals with Music

The medieval banquets at Bunratty and Knappogue castles and the traditional evening at Bunratty Folk Park can be booked in the United States through a travel agent or by calling 🕻 **800/CIE-TOUR** (243-8687). They're all undeniably touristy, but fun nevertheless, and even the locals have been known to attend once in a while.

Bunratty Castle ★★ IRISH   Every evening a full medieval banquet is re-created in this sturdy castle, complete with music, song, and merriment. Seated at long tables in the magnificent baronial hall, guests sample chicken with apple and mead sauce, or spareribs with honey and whiskey (nobody minds if you eat with your fingers). Drinks include mulled wine, claret, and flagons of ale and mead. To add to the fun, at each banquet, a "lord and lady" are chosen from the participants to reign over the 3-hour proceedings, and someone else is thrown into the dungeon.

Castle Limerick-Ennis rd. (N18), Bunratty, County Clare. 🕻 **061/360788.** Reservations required. Dinner and entertainment €58 ($93) adults; €43 ($69) children 9–12; €29 ($46) children 6–8. AE, MC, V. Daily 5:30 and 8:45pm.

Knappogue Castle ★ IRISH   Once the stronghold of the McNamara clan, this 15th-century castle is smaller and has a more intimate feel than Bunratty (and, unlike most banquet venues, is wheelchair accessible). However, their assertion that the menu consists of real dishes from the Middle Ages is frankly a little ridiculous, given that it includes such famous medieval fare as Chicken Supreme, roast potatoes, lemon cheesecake, and coffee. Post-dinner entertainment consists of a colorful 35-minute show telling the history of Ireland through music and dance.

Quin, County Clare. 🕻 **061/360788.** Reservations required. Dinner and entertainment €55 ($88) adults; €41 ($66) children 9–12; €28 ($45) children aged 6–8. AE, DC, MC, V. May–Oct daily 6:30pm.

CLARE AFTER DARK

Brandon's Bar   Irish music aficionados will probably already have heard of this place, as it's one of the best places to see traditional music played in the region. Its Monday night sessions have been known to feature more than a dozen musicians, and they tend to turn into classic jam sessions. If you're in town and like Irish music, it's well worth stopping by. O'Connell St., Ennis, County Clare. 🕻 **065/682-8133.**

Cois na hAbhna   This traditional arts center (the name is pronounced *Cush*-na *How*-na) stages lively sessions of music, song, and dance, followed by Irish dancing with audience participation. Snacks are traditional as well—the likes of tea and brown bread. Traditional dance sessions are run seasonally on Wednesdays from 9pn to midnight. Call for the most current schedule of *céilís* and other events. Gort Rd., Ennis, County Clare. 🕻 **065/682-4276.** www.coisnahabhna.ie. Admission around €8 ($13), depending on the event.

The Derg Inn   On the south bank of Lough Derg at the edge of Tipperary, this is one of the lake's better watering holes. The decor is . . . well, everything. There are horse pictures, china plates, books, beer posters, vintage bottles, lanterns, you name it. Find your way through the eclectic mix and you can have a well-poured pint, accompanied by traditional music on Wednesday and Sunday evenings. The menu here is also excellent and not unsophisticated—the pâté with homemade chutney and garlic bread is divine. Terryglass, County Tipperary. 🕻 **067/22037.** www.derginn.ie.

Durty Nellie's Established in 1620 next door to Bunratty Castle, this ramshackle, thatched-roof cottage was originally a watering hole for the castle guards. Now it's a favorite haunt of locals and tourists looking for a pint after the medieval banquets at the castle. It's likely the decor—old lanterns, sawdust on the floors, and open turf fireplaces—hasn't changed much over the centuries. This is a good spot for a substantial pub lunch or a full dinner in one of the two restaurants. Spontaneous Irish music sessions erupt here on most evenings. Limerick-Ennis rd. (N18), Bunratty, County Clare. ✆ **061/364072.**

Paddy's Pub From the harbor on south Lough Derg, it's a short walk up a winding lane to this small, dark pub. A fine display of antiques and nightly traditional music in summer make it a jewel among Lake Derg's pubs. Casual pub food (burgers and sandwiches) makes it a good option. Poker fans may want to come down on Friday, when an intense game of Texas hold 'em is open to anyone with €10 ($16). Terryglass, County Tipperary. ✆ **067/22147.**

THE BURREN ★★★

The extraordinary otherworldly landscape of the region known simply as the Burren is difficult to describe. Carved by nature from bare carboniferous limestone, the view manages to be both desolate and beautiful. Sheets of rock jut and undulate in a kind of moonscape as far as you can see. Amid the rocks, delicate wildflowers somehow find enough dirt to thrive, and ferns curl gently around boulders, moss softens hard edges, orchids flower exotically, and violets brighten the landscape. With the flowers come butterflies that thrive on the rare flora. Even Burren animals are unusual: The pine marten (small weasels), stoat (ermine), and badger, all rare in the rest of Ireland, are common here.

The Burren began to get its strange and unforgettable appearance 300 million years ago when layers of shells and sediment were deposited under a tropical sea. Many millions of years later, those layers were exposed by erosion and poor prehistoric farming methods, and since then, it's all been battered by the Irish rain and winds, producing all that you see today. About 7,000 years ago, when this landscape was already very old indeed, humans first began to leave their mark here, in the form of Stone Age burial monuments, such as the famed **Poulnabrone Dolmen** and **Gleninsheen wedge tomb.**

Lisdoonvarna, on the western edge, is a charmingly old-fashioned spa town that has long been known for its natural mineral springs. Each summer, it draws thousands of people to bathe in its sulfuric streams, iron creeks, and iodine lakes.

One of the best ways to explore the Burren is to take the R480. The corkscrewlike road leads in a series of curves from **Corofin** through gorgeous scenery to **Ballyvaughan,** a delightful little village overlooking the blue waters of Galway Bay.

Exploring the Region

Burren National Park ★★★ spreads across 1,653 hectares (4,083 acres) and continually acquires more land as it becomes available. The remarkable rocky land is dotted with picturesque ruined castles, tumbling cliffs, rushing rivers, lakes, barren rock mountains, and plant life that defies all of nature's conventional rules. The park is particularly rich in archaeological remains from the Neolithic through the medieval periods—dolmens and wedge tombs (approx. 120 of them), ring forts (500 of those), round towers, ancient churches, high crosses, monasteries, and holy wells. The park is centered at Mullaghmore Mountain, but there is, as of yet, no official entrance point and no admission charges or restrictions to access.

> **Fun Facts** **Green Roads**
>
> "Green roads" are former highways that crisscross the Burren landscape in inaccessible areas. Most of these unpaved roads were created during the Great Famine as make-work projects for starving locals, although some are ancient roads of indeterminate origin. These old, unused roads are now popular with amblers and hikers, and some are signposted. They're also famous for harboring rare and beautiful wildflowers, such as orchids and deep blue gentians.

With its unique terrain and meandering walking paths, the Burren lends itself to **walking.** One of the best ways to amble through the limestone pavements and terraces, shale uplands, and lakes is to follow the **Burren Way.** The 42km (26-mile) signposted route stretches from Ballyvaughan to Liscannor, and you can pick it up in the park, walk a stretch of it, and then head back to your car, if you wish. An information sheet outlining the route is available from any tourist office. **Burren Walking Holidays,** in conjunction with the Carrigann Hotel, Lisdoonvarna (© 065/707-4036), offers a wide selection of guided and self-guided walks.

Aillwee Cave ★★   This deep cave was undiscovered for thousands of years until a local farmer followed a dog into it 50 years ago. Inside he found a huge cavern with 1,000m (3,280 ft.) of passages running straight into the heart of a mountain. He kept it to himself for decades before eventually spreading the word. Professional cave explorers later uncovered its magnificent bridged chasms, deep caverns, a frozen waterfall, and bear pits—hollows scraped out by hibernating brown bears. Brown bears have been extinct in Ireland for 10,000 years. Guided tours are excellent here—generally led by geology students from area universities. There's a scary moment when they turn out the lights for a minute so you can experience the depth of the darkness inside. Tours last approximately 30 minutes, and are conducted continuously. On-site, there's also a craft shop, a farm shop, a cheese-making enterprise called Burren Gold Cheese, and the new **Burren Bird of Prey Centre** (© 065/707-7036; www.birdofpreycentre.com), a working aviary designed to mimic the natural habitat of the buzzards, falcons, eagles, and owls that live there. Visitors can observe the birds, learn about the center's breeding program, and watch daily flying demonstrations in an open-air arena.

Ballyvaughan, County Clare. © 065/707-7036. www.aillweecave.ie. Admission €15 ($24) adults (joint ticket with Burren Bird of Prey Centre), €13 ($21) seniors and students, €8 ($13) children, €35 ($56) families. Sept to mid-Nov and Feb–June daily 10am–5:30pm; July–Aug daily 10am–6:30pm.

The Burren Centre   This is a fine place to acquaint yourself with all facets of the area. Using films, landscape models, and interpretive displays, it highlights the local geology, flora, and fauna. There's a tearoom and a shop stocked with locally made crafts and products.

R476 to Kilfenora, County Clare. © 065/708-8030. www.theburrencentre.ie. Admission to exhibition €6 ($9.60) adults, €5 ($8) seniors and students, €4 ($6.40) children, €20 ($32) families. Sept–Oct and mid-Mar to May daily 10am–5pm; June to late Aug daily 9:30am–6pm.

Clare Heritage Centre   If you're named Kelly, Murphy, or Walsh (among others) and researching your family roots, you might want to stop by this genealogical research center. Housed in a former Church of Ireland edifice built in 1718, it also has exhibits on Clare farming, industry, commerce, language, and music, as well as a handy tearoom and gift shop.

R476 to Corofin, County Clare. 🕐 **065/683-7955.** www.clareroots.com. Museum admission €4 ($6.40) adults; €3.50 ($5.60) seniors, students, and children. May–Oct daily 10am–6pm.

Corcomroe Abbey   Set jewel-like in a languid, green valley bounded by rolling hills, the jagged ruins of this Cistercian abbey are breathtaking. The abbey was founded in 1194 by Donal Mór O'Brien, and his grandson, a former king of Thomond, is entombed in the abbey's northern wall. There are some interesting medieval and Romanesque carvings in the stone, including one of a bishop with a crosier.

1.5km (1-mile) walk inland from Bellharbour, County Clare. Free admission.

Poulnabrone Dolmen ★   This portal tomb is an exquisitely preserved prehistoric site. Its dolmen (or stone table) is huge, and surrounded by a natural pavement of stones. The tomb has been dated back 5,000 years. When it was excavated in the 1980s, the remains of 16 people were found. The greatest mystery remains how the gigantic stones were moved and lifted—the capstone alone weighs 5 tons. You'll have no trouble finding this sight—just look for all the tour buses. At times they literally block the road. What must the locals think?

R480 8km (5 miles) south of the Aillwee Caves, County Clare. Free admission. Daily 10am–6pm.

Spa Wells Centre   Nestled in a shady park on Lisdoonvarna, this Victorian spa complex features a massage room, sauna, and mineral baths, all centered on the odiferous sulfur-laced mineral waters, drawn from an illuminated well. The waters were once believed to be good for rheumatic complaints, and you can have a glass if you wish, but be warned: This isn't Evian.

Kincora Rd., Lisdoonvarna, County Clare. 🕐 **065/707-4023.** Free admission; treatment charges vary. June–Oct daily 10am–6pm.

Where to Stay
Expensive
Gregans Castle Hotel ★★★ (Finds)   Not a castle at all, but an ivy-covered, stone manor house, this hotel is filled with light and offers lovely views of the Burren and Galway Bay. Owned and managed by the Hayden family, Gregans demonstrates decades of attention to detail. The drawing room and expansive hallways are filled with heirlooms, and the walls are decorated with Raymond Piper's mural paintings of the Burren. Guest rooms are spacious and elegantly decorated in muted colors with antique touches and comfortable orthopedic beds—some have four-poster or canopied beds. All have expansive views of the countryside. On a sunny day, you can play croquet on the flat lawn or feed the hotel's donkeys and ponies in a nearby pasture. The kitchen is led by a talented chef who turns the freshest local produce and meat into extraordinary meals— it's well worth the cost for dinner here. Afterward, you can linger over drinks around the fire in the cozy lounge—it's hard to believe this peaceful retreat is just an hour's drive from Shannon Airport.

Ballyvaughan-Lisdoonvarna rd. (N67), Ballyvaughan, County Clare. 🕐 **800/323-5463** in the U.S., or 065/707-7005. Fax 065/707-7111. www.gregans.ie. 22 units. €195–€320 ($312–$512) double; suites from €295 ($472). Children 13–17 sharing with parent €50 ($80), 6–13 €30 ($48), 5 and under €20 ($32). Rates include full breakfast. AE, MC, V. Closed Nov–Mar. **Amenities:** Restaurant (seafood); bar; drawing room; library. *In room:* TV, hair dryer.

> **(Fun Facts**   **Falling in Love with Love in Lisdoonvarna**
>
> If you've been looking for love in all the wrong places, clearly you've never been to Lisdoonvarna. This adorable little County Clare town lives for love. There's a Matchmaker Pub on the main street. There are two people in town who still officially call themselves matchmakers (Willie Daly, a horse dealer, and James White, a hotelier—wink, wink).
>
> Every autumn, the entire town gets involved in the matchmaking business, when it throws the month-long Lisdoonvarna Matchmaking Festival. Thousands of lovelorn singletons descend upon the town looking for "the One," and all of Lisdoonvarna cheers them on.
>
> Throughout the town, up and down each street, and in every atmospheric corner, every available space is used for mixers, minglers, and . . . well, more mixers. The locals stir the pot as much as humanly possible, holding romantic breakfasts, romantic dinners, romantic games, romantic dances, romantic horse races (?)—well, it *is* Ireland, after all.
>
> So good are their intentions, and so charming is their belief in true love—in the idea that there really is somebody out there for everybody, and that they should all come together in a far-flung corner of western Ireland to find one another—that they make you believe that they might actually have something there. It's a kind of madness.
>
> To find out more about Lisdoonvarna and its love of love, visit its marvelously kitsch website, **www.matchmakerireland.com**.

Inexpensive

Fergus View ★ (Finds   The views from this lovely, rambling house are extraordinary—rolling hills, undulating green fields, colorful gardens. Inside there's a fire crackling at the hearth, and a warming cup of tea after your long drive. The guest rooms are sweet and not particularly frilly, although they are a bit small. Owner Mary Kelleher goes out of her way to make guests feel at home, and has compiled one of the best local guides to the region that we've seen. She's also converted a small stone lodge nearby into attractive self-catering accommodations for up to five people.

Kilnaboy, Corofin, County Clare. ✆ **065/683-7606.** Fax 065/683-7192. www.fergusview.com. 6 units. €62 ($99) double. Rates include full breakfast. No credit cards. Closed end of Oct to Easter. 3.2km (2 miles) north of Corofin on road to Kilfenora. **Amenities:** Nonsmoking rooms. *In room:* Tea/coffeemaker.

Rusheen Lodge ★   On the main road just south of Ballyvaughan village, this award-winning bungalow-style guesthouse is completely surrounded by flowers. The innkeeper is Karen McGann, whose grandfather, Jacko McGann, discovered the nearby Aillwee Caves. Rooms are simply decorated in blond woods and have firm beds covered in floral fabric. Breakfast, served in a bright, pastel-toned dining room, can include fresh-caught local fish.

Knocknagrough, Ballyvaughan, County Clare. ✆ **065/707-7092.** Fax 065/707-7152. www.rusheenlodge. com. 9 units. €90–€100 ($144–$160) double. Rates include full breakfast. AE, MC, V. Closed Dec–Feb. **Amenities:** Nonsmoking rooms. *In room:* TV, tea/coffeemaker, hair dryer.

Bofey Quinn's SEAFOOD/GRILL   An informal atmosphere prevails at this pub-restaurant in the center of Corofin, where dinner specialties include lobster, fresh wild salmon, and cod, as well as a variety of steaks, chops, and mixed grills. We like the "Smokies"—an unusual and tasty casserole of smoked fish and potatoes. Stick-to-your-ribs pub lunches are available throughout the day.

Main St., Corofin, County Clare. (C) **065/683-7321.** Main courses €12–€20 ($19–$32); lobster €36 ($58). MC, V. Daily noon–9:30pm.

Tri na Cheile IRISH BISTRO   This intimate restaurant in the middle of Bally-vaughan village offers simple, homey meals made with local ingredients. The menu includes sirloin; mussels and linguine; whole crab; beef curry; filet of salmon; roast lamb with anchovies, garlic, and rosemary; and roast chicken. In general, the less adventurous dishes are the best; some vegetarian options are also available.

Main St., Ballyvaughan, County Clare. (C) **065/707-7029.** Reservations recommended. Main courses €10–€18 ($16–$29). MC, V. Mar–Sept Mon–Sat noon–10pm.

After Dark

Vaughn's   This is a music pub with a countrywide reputation for attracting excellent traditional bands and stellar Irish dancing. Summers are the busiest times (things quiet down quite a bit in the off season). The barn next door is used for dancing on Thursday and Sunday. The traditional Irish food is good as well. Main St., Kilfenora, County Clare. (C) **065/708-8004.**

THE CLARE COAST

One of Ireland's most photographed places, the **Cliffs of Moher** ★ draw thousands of visitors to Clare's remote reaches every day of the year—rain or shine. Rising to vertiginous heights 210m (689 ft.) above the Atlantic and stretching along about 8km (5 miles) of coastline, the cliffs are undeniably impressive. In bad weather, access to the cliffs is (understandably) limited, as the wind can blow very hard here and it's a long way down. When the weather is fine, there's a guardrail to offer you a small sense of security as you peek over the edge, although visitors treat it with startling disdain, climbing over it for a better view of the sheer drop (although a fierce new anti-climb policy promises to put a stop to that). It's all well worth a visit, but be aware that in the high season, the crowds can rather spoil the effect.

Farther along the Clare Coast, **Lahinch** is an old-fashioned Victorian seaside resort, with a wide beach and long promenade curving along the horseshoe bay. Golfers will already know all they need to know about this town, as it's renowned for its golf course. Dubbed by fans the "St. Andrews of Ireland," it is the paradigm of Irish links golf and is ranked among the 50 best courses in the world by *Golf* magazine.

Nearby, the secluded fishing village of **Doolin** is the unofficial capital of Irish traditional music. Its quaint old pubs and restaurants ring with the sound of fiddle and accordion all year long. Doolin is also a departure point for the short boat trip to the beautiful and isolated **Aran Islands** (p. 404).

The Clare Coast is dotted with **seaside resorts** with varying degrees of crowds and beauty, and the best include places such as **Kilrush, Kilkee, Miltown Malbay,** and **Ennistymon.** This part of the county is a marvelous place to take amusing pictures of signs denoting the presence of tiny villages and beauty spots with quirky names like Puffing Hole, Intrinsic Bay, Chimney Hill, Elephant's Teeth, Mutton Island, and Lover's Leap.

Irish Spelunking

The area around Doolin is well known among cavers for its many intriguing potholes and caves. The area is riddled with them—the ground underneath your feet may look solid, but it's really like Swiss cheese. If you're interested in joining the spelunkers, you can stop by the tourist office and pick up brochures from local caving guides, as well as maps.

The most extraordinary single cave is **Poll na gColm,** just northeast of Lisdoonvarna. This is one of Ireland's longest caves, and its caverns wander for miles through underground passageways, vaults, and natural wonders.

For divers, there's a cluster of underwater caves just north of Doolin's harbor called the **Green Holes of Doolin** that are said to be simply extraordinary. You can get a peek at what divers will see at an area known as "Hell," where the roof of a cave has worn away, and the water rushes through an open cavern into a series of undersea pathways.

Novices should not go caving on their own without training or guides. To get one or both of those, check out www.cavingireland.org.

Seeing the Sights

Cliffs of Moher ★   These high, undulating cliffs plunging down to the Atlantic offer unforgettable views. This is a dramatic place, where the soundtrack is provided by the roar of waves crashing against the cliff walls far below and the faint cries of nesting seabirds. On a clear day, you can see the Aran Islands in Galway Bay as misty shapes off in the distance. Understandably, this is also dead center on the tourist track, with a constant throng of tour buses and cars clogging the parking lot below. In recent years, a large modern visitor center has opened, changing the landscape and adding little to the wonders wrought by nature. Now there are more souvenir shops and a "Cliffs of Moher Experience" including a film—why this is necessary when the real thing is right outside, we simply do not know. Unsurprisingly, this means the already high price to park at the cliffs (a de facto admission charge since there is no legal free alternative parking) has nearly doubled over the last 2 years, and we fear it will go still higher. As we are talking about a natural wonder here, created by winds and waves, this seems dangerously like naked profiteering. Some clever visitors have begun rejecting the pointless parking charge and finding places to park nearby, then hiking up to the cliffs, but before you try this bear in mind that virtually all roadside parking nearby is illegal. On the other hand, parking enforcement is pretty lax this far out in the countryside. *Tip:* If you visit the cliffs after the visitor center closes, it's much more peaceful. Sunsets are absolutely gorgeous.

R478, 11km (6³/₄ miles) north of Lahinch, County Clare. (*C*) **065/708-6146.** Atlantic Edge exhibition €4 ($6.40) adults, €3.50 ($5.60) seniors and students, €2.50 ($4) children 4–12, free for children 3 and under, €12 ($19) families. Parking €8 ($13). Visitor center daily 9:30am–5:30pm.

Lahinch Seaworld and Leisure Centre (Kids)   This small but well-designed aquarium has all the usual kid pleasers, including slithery conger eels, ferocious sharks, and rubbery rays. There's a touch pool where they can get up close and personal. If you are then inspired to take to the water yourself, the leisure center next door charges very reasonable rates. For extra savings, combination tickets are available.

The Promenade, Lahinch, County Clare. ✆ 065/708-1900. www.lahinchseaworld.com. Admission to aquarium €8 ($13) adults, €6 ($9.60) children. Daily 10am–9pm.

Scattery Island ★   This marvelously named, unspoiled island in the Shannon Estuary near Kilrush holds atmospheric monastic ruins dating from the 6th century. A high, round tower and several churches are all that is left of an extensive settlement that was founded by St. Senan. To visit the island, contact one of the boat operators who arrange the 20-minute ferry rides—frequency depends on demand, and even in summer there may be only one trip per day. Or ask at the Information Centre (in Kilrush, just past the pier) when the next ferry departs.

Merchants Quay, Kilrush, County Clare. ✆ 065/682-9100 or 905-1577. Free admission. Ferry €12 ($19) round-trip. Mid-June to mid-Sept daily 10:30am–6:30pm.

To the Aran Islands
Doolin Ferry Co.   Although the three fabled islands—Inishmore, Inishmaan, and Inisheer—are usually associated with Galway, the isles are actually closer to Doolin (roughly 8km/5 miles, or 30 min. in a boat). Ferries run back and forth to the islands daily during the high season. (For more information about the Aran Islands, see "Side Trips from Galway City" in chapter 13.)

The Pier, Doolin, County Clare. ✆ 065/707-4455. www.doolinferries.com. Innis Mor or Inis Meain round-trip €40 ($64) adults, €20 ($32) children; Inis Oirr round-trip €30 ($48) adults, €15 ($24) children; interisland ferry one-way €20 ($32) adults, €10 ($16) children. Student and family discounts available. Operates Mar–Oct; call for current schedule.

Shopping
Burren Smokehouse   Get all of the smoked salmon you've ever dreamed of at this excellent smokehouse, where the freshest fish is prepared in traditional ways. You can watch the fish being prepared, and then buy some to take home. Doolin Rd., Lisdoonvarna, County Clare. ✆ 065/707-4432. www.burrensmokehouse.ie.

Doolin Crafts Gallery   This shop is the brainchild of two artisans: Matthew O'Connell, who creates batik work with Celtic designs on wall hangings, cushion covers, and scarves; and Mary Gray, who hand fashions gold and silver jewelry inspired by the Burren. There is a good coffee shop on the premises. Ballyvoe, Doolin, County Clare. ✆ 065/707-4688.

Traditional Music Shop   In this town known for its traditional music, this small shop is a center of attention. It offers all types of Irish traditional music on CD, as well as books and instruments. Ballyreen, Doolin, County Clare. ✆ 065/707-4407.

Sports & Outdoor Pursuits
BIRD-WATCHING   The **Bridges of Ross,** on the north side of **Loop Head,** is one of the prime autumn bird-watching sites in Ireland, especially during northwest gales, when several rare species have been seen with some consistency. The **lighthouse** at the tip of the head is also a popular spot for watching seabirds.

DOLPHIN-WATCHING   The Shannon Estuary is home to about 70 bottlenose dolphins, one of four such resident groups of dolphins in Europe. Cruises run by **Dolphinwatch** leave daily May to September from Carrigaholt. Advance booking is essential

(© 065/905-8156; www.dolphinwatch.ie). Fees start at €24 ($38) for adults, €12 ($19) for children 15 and under.

GOLF   Doonbeg Golf Club, Doonbeg (© 065/905-5624; www.doonbeggolfclub. com), has links designed by golf pro Greg Norman in a breathtaking setting. The magnificent 15th hole ends in a funnel-shaped green surrounded by sky-high dunes. With a helipad and a complex that includes a country club, hotel, and deluxe cottages, Doonbeg has quickly become a haunt for the moneyed set, so it should come as no surprise that greens fees are a hefty €200 to €210 ($320–$336) per person.

Also famous, but less pricey, is **Lahinch Golf Club,** Lahinch (© 065/708-1003; www.lahinchgolf.com). It has two attractive 18-hole links courses, and the "Old Course"—the longer championship links course—is the one that has given Lahinch its far-reaching reputation. This course's elevations, especially at the 9th and 13th holes, make for great views, but it also makes wind an integral part of play. Watch the goats, Lahinch's legendary weather forecasters; if they huddle by the clubhouse, it means a storm is approaching. Visitors are welcome to play, especially on weekdays; greens fees are €155 ($248) daily for the Old Course, and €50 ($80) for the newer Castle Course, or €195 ($312) for a round on both courses on the same day.

SURFING   If you've always wanted to try it, here's your chance: **Lahinch Surf School** (© 087/960-9667; www.lahinchsurfschool.com) is set up in a hut on Lahinch promenade, and they specialize in getting people suited up and out on the waves—regardless of whether you surf every weekend, or have never hit a board in your life. Staff are friendly, and surfing is good for you, apparently. Wet suits, surfboards, and lessons included. Rates start at €100 ($160) for private lessons (group lessons are cheaper).

Where to Stay
Expensive
Moy House ★★ Finds   This unusual 19th-century tower house overlooking the bay about 1.6km (1 mile) outside the little town of Lahinch is beautiful inside and out. Rooms have comfortable modern beds covered in crisp Irish linens and are decorated with original paintings and period antiques. Televisions are tastefully hidden inside recessed cabinets. Some rooms have wooden floors, and some bathrooms are beautifully designed (a glass panel in one lets you look down into an old well). Bath products are L'Occitane, and there are lots of thoughtful extra touches: After dinner, bathrobes and chocolates are laid out on your bed. Fresh, local produce is used in the kitchen, and dining in is worthwhile, although it's a bit of a splurge. The front of the house is amiably guarded by Wolf, the house dog, who will also accompany you on your seaside walks. About an hour's drive from Shannon Airport, this makes a good first or last night's stop. *Note:* There are good special offers during the fall and spring.

Miltown Malbay Rd., Lahinch, County Clare. © **065/708-2800.** Fax 065/708-2500. www.moyhouse.com. 9 units. €240–€280 ($384–$448) double; suites from €310 ($496). 4-course dinner €55 ($88). Rates include full breakfast. AE, DC, MC, V. **Amenities:** Drawing room. *In room:* TV, hair dryer.

Moderate
Aran View House Value   Dating from 1736, this rambling three-story stone house stands on a hill surrounded by farmland just north of Doolin. Its prime location affords panoramic views of the gorgeous Clare coastline. Inside the decor is a bit old-fashioned, with colorful carpets and mahogany furnishings, but rooms are big and comfortable, and

some have four-poster beds. There are a handful of self-catering cottages as well, should you require a bit more space or privacy.

Doolin, County Clare. © 065/707-4420. Fax 065/707-4540. www.aranview.com. 19 units. €110–€140 ($176–$224) double. Rates include full breakfast. AE, DC, MC, V. Closed Nov–Mar. **Amenities:** Restaurant (international); bar. *In room:* TV, hair dryer.

Ballinalacken Castle Country House ★   This is a beautifully located hotel, just below the crest of a hill, overlooking the misty Aran Islands. The hotel itself is not a castle, but it sits next to the atmospheric ruins of Ballinalacken Castle. The main hotel building was built in the 1840s, but most of the guest rooms are in a modern wing. If you love architectural detail, ask for a room in the old house, which has high ceilings, marble fireplaces, and, in room no. 16, sweeping views of hill and sea. All rooms are traditionally furnished and quite spacious.

Doolin, County Clare. ©/fax **065/707-4025**. www.ballinalackencastle.com. 12 units. €130–€150 ($208–$240) double, €160 ($256) double with four-poster beds; €190 ($304) suites. Rates include full breakfast. AE, DC, MC, V. Closed Nov–Apr 15. **Amenities:** Restaurant (Continental). *In room:* TV, hair dryer.

Inexpensive
Doonmacfelim Guest House (Value)   On Doolin's main street a few hundred feet from Gus O'Connor's Pub (see below), this modern two-story guesthouse is a great value. Although it's close to the center of everything, the house is surrounded by a farm, and thus marvelously peaceful. Guest rooms have unexceptional furnishings, but nice country views.

Doolin, County Clare. © **087/125-0303**. Fax 065/707-4129. www.doonmacfelim.com. 8 units. €70 ($112) double. Rates include full breakfast. MC, V. **Amenities:** Tennis court; sitting room. *In room:* Tea/coffeemaker, hair dryer.

Self-Catering
Loop Head Lightkeeper's House ★★ (Finds)   Here is yet another of the many splendid new properties run by the Irish Landmark Trust (ILT). This is a comfortingly solid old house next to a lighthouse at the very tip of remote Loop Head, just southwest of Kilkee. Once home to the keeper of the lighthouse, it offers astonishing views and a real historical feel. Downstairs are a kitchen, sitting room, two bathrooms, and a double bedroom. Upstairs are two more bedrooms (one double, one twin) and a small sitting room. Nice touches are everywhere: sturdy mahogany furnishings, brass beds, oversize sofas and armchairs, a fireplace in every room, and deep windowsills. It's perfect for a get-away-from-it-all vacation: as remote as you'd hope for from a lighthouse, and a 20-minute drive from bustling Kilkee, a little seaside resort with old-fashioned appeal. As with all ILT properties, there is no TV, but there is a radio. Guests should bring bottled water for drinking.

Loop Head, about 3 miles from Kibaha, County Clare. Contact the Irish Landmark Trust © **01/670-4733**. Fax 01/670-4887. www.irishlandmark.com. €400 ($640) for 4 nights in low season, going up to €1,000 ($1,600) per week in high season. AE, MC, V at booking.

Where to Dine
Barrtrá Seafood Restaurant ★★ SEAFOOD   With windows overlooking Liscannor Bay, this is a good place to bite into fresh seafood and take in gorgeous views. The food is simple but well prepared. Starters include duck leg confit with black-currant sauce, and mussels in wine and garlic, while main dishes include sirloin steak with

onion-and-pepper sauce, or gnocchi with regatta cheese, tomatoes, and spinach. It's not fancy, but it's friendly and the food is reliably good. Sunset here is a wonder.

Barrtrá, Lahinch, County Clare. ✆ **065/708-1280.** www.barrtra.com. Reservations recommended. Fixed-price dinner €42 ($67); main courses €18–€25 ($29–$40). AE, MC, V. Daily 6–10pm. Closed Jan–Feb; always call ahead during off season.

Seafarer's Restaurant SEAFOOD/CONTINENTAL   This mom-and-pop place is an institution in Lahinch. Simple local foods are prepared with style in dishes such as the pan-fried turbot with a potato crust or scallops in vermouth sauce. Starters, such as the warm St. Tola goat cheese with sesame seeds, are cleverly done, and desserts are good. The atmosphere is bubbly, the service is great, and the crowd is content.

Kettle St., Lahinch, County Clare. ✆ **065/708-1050.** Reservations recommended. Main courses €13–€25 ($21–$40). AE, DC, MC, V. Apr–Oct daily 7–9:30pm.

Doolin's Traditional Music Pubs

Gus O'Connor's Pub   Amid a row of thatched fishermen's cottages and a 10-minute walk from the seafront, this country pub brings people in from miles around. While this keeps the evening buzzing, it also means that it can get very crowded, especially on weekend nights. Along with its historical charm (it dates from 1832), it has a deserved international reputation for its lively Irish traditional-music sessions. If you're hungry, it serves good meals, too. Fisher St., Doolin, County Clare. ✆ **065/707-4168.**

McGann's Finds   Sure, Gus O'Connor's is more famous than this place, but it is also jammed with tourists. On many nights, there are no locals in Gus's at all—they're just up the road, downing pints of Guinness and listening to just-as-wonderful traditional music at this friendly pub. Feel free to join them. Roadford, Doolin, County Clare. ✆ **065/707-4133.**

13

Galway City

Galway, which has an affluent, artsy population of 70,000, is one of Ireland's most prosperous cities and also one of its most appealing. It is a busy workaday town, but it also has a lively art-and-music scene that has made it the unofficial arts capital of the country. The excellent Galway Arts Festival, held every summer, is an accessible, buzzing culture fest. It's not surprising that Galway attracts droves of visitors, but it does so without alienating its long-standing population or losing its character.

Tucked between the Atlantic and the navy-blue waters of Lough Corrib, Galway was founded by fishermen. After an invasion by the Anglo-Norman forces of Richard de Burgo in the early 13th century, it walled itself in, as so many cities did then, although little remains of those old stone walls.

In the center of town, on Shop Street, is **Lynch's Castle,** dating from 1490 and renovated in the 19th century. It's the oldest Irish medieval town house used daily for commercial purposes (it's now a branch of the Allied Irish Bank). The stern exterior is watched over by a handful of amusing gargoyles. Walk northwest 1 block to Market Street and you'll see the **Lynch Memorial Window** in a wall above a built-up Gothic doorway. It commemorates the tragic story of the 16th-century Galway mayor James Lynch FitzStephen, who condemned his own son to death for the murder of a Spanish merchant. After finding no one to carry out the deed, he acted as executioner. The act destroyed him and he retreated into a life of seclusion.

In the 16th and 17th centuries, Galway was wealthy and cosmopolitan, with particularly strong trade links to Spain. Close to the city docks, you can still see the area where Spanish merchants unloaded cargo from their galleons. The **Spanish Arch** was one of four arches built in 1594, and the **Spanish Parade** is a small open square.

Local legend has it that Christopher Columbus attended Mass at Galway's **St. Nicholas Collegiate Church** in 1477, before one of several attempts to circumnavigate the globe. Originally built in 1320, the church has been enlarged, rebuilt, and embellished over the years. It has also changed denominations at least four times.

The hub of the city is a pedestrian park at **Eyre Square** (pronounced *Air* Square), officially called the John F. Kennedy Park in commemoration of his visit here in June 1963, a few months before his assassination. A bust of JFK shares space in the park with a statue of a man sitting on a limestone wall—a depiction of Galway-born hero Padraig O'Conaire, a pioneer in the Irish literary revival of the early 20th century and the epitome of a Galway Renaissance man.

From Eyre Square, it's a minute's walk to the **medieval quarter** with its festive, Left Bank atmosphere. Here it is clear that, despite Galway's population boom, the city core remains strikingly unchanged from the Middle Ages. In fact, a street map from the 1700s would still get you around today. That enticing blend of history and modernity make Galway stand out, even in Ireland.

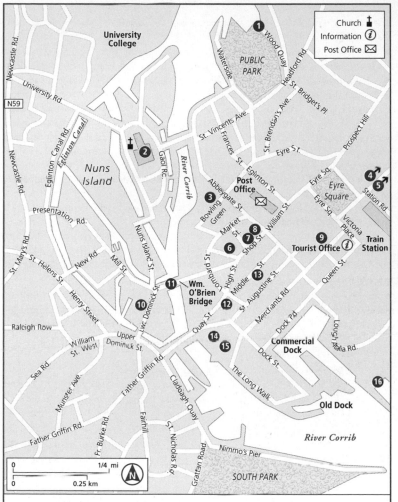

Legend (top right):
- Church ✝
- Information ⓘ
- Post Office ✉

Map labels:

University College

PUBLIC PARK

Wood Quay · Waterside · Headford Rd. · St. Bridget's Pl. · St. Brendan's Ave. · St. Vincents Ave. · Frances St. · Eyre St. · Prospect Hill

Newcastle Rd. · University Rd. · N59 · Eglinton Canal Rd. · Eglinton Canal · Nuns Island · Presentation Rd. · Newcastle Rd.

River Corrib · Gaol Rd. · Nuns Island St. · Eglinton St. · Eyre Sq. · Eyre Square · Station Rd. · Victoria Place · Eyre Sq. · Train Station

Abbeygate St. · Bowling Green · Market St. · Shop St. · William St. · Post Office ✉ · Tourist Office ⓘ

St. Mary's Rd. · St. Helens St. · New Rd. · Mill St. · St. Bridget's · High St. · Lombard St. · Middle St. · St. Augustine St. · Merchants Rd. · Dock Rd. · Queen St. · Lough Atalia Rd.

Henry Street · Raleigh Row · William St. West · Upper Dominick St. · Lwr. Dominick St. · Quay St. · Wm. O'Brien Bridge · Commercial Dock

Sea Rd. · Munster Ave. · Father Griffin Rd. · Fr. Burke Rd. · Fairhill · Claddagh Quay · St. Nicholas Rd. · Grattan Road · Nimmo's Pier · Dock St. · The Long Walk · Old Dock · River Corrib

SOUTH PARK

0 — 1/4 mi
0 — 0.25 km

Numbered markers: 1 2 3 4 5 6 7 8 9 10 11 12 13 14 15 16

NORTHERN IRELAND

Galway City · Dublin ★

REPUBLIC OF IRELAND

Bridge Mills **11**
Corrib Princess **1**
Druid Theatre **12**
Eyre Square Shopping Centre **9**
Ferry to Aran Islands **16**
Galway Arts Centre **10**
Galway Cathedral **2**
Galway City Museum **14**

Galway Irish Crystal Heritage Centre **4**
Lynch Memorial Window **7**
Lynch's Castle **8**
Nora Barnacle House **3**
Royal Tara China **5**
St. Nicholas' Collegiate Church **6**
Spanish Arch **15**
Taibhdhearc Theatre **13**

1 ORIENTATION

92km (57 miles) N of Shannon Airport, 219km (136 miles) W of Dublin, 105km (65 miles) NW of Limerick, 209km (130 miles) NW of Cork, 193km (120 miles) N of Killarney

ARRIVING **Aer Arann** (✆ **011/353-81821-0210** in the U.S., 818/210-210 in Ireland, or 0800/587-23-24 in the U.K.; www.aerarann.ie) flies from Dublin into Galway Airport (Carnmore, about 16km/10 miles east of the city; ✆ **091/755569;** www.galway airport.com) four times daily, two times a day to London. There's also regular service to Cardiff, Liverpool, Manchester, and Edinburgh. The European budget airline **Flybe** (www.flybe.com) is expected to start regular flights to Belfast City airport from Galway sometime in 2008. A taxi to the city center costs about €20 ($32); the occasional bus, if it coincides with your arrival, can be a handy alternative. It costs upwards of €5 ($8) and drops you off at Galway Rail Station.

Irish Rail trains from Dublin and other points arrive daily at **Ceannt Station** (✆ **091/561444;** www.irishrail.ie), off Eyre Square, Galway.

Buses from all parts of Ireland arrive daily at **Bus Éireann Travel Centre,** Ceannt Station, Galway (✆ **091/562000;** www.buseireann.ie).

As the gateway to west Ireland, Galway is the terminus for many national roads. They lead in from all parts of Ireland, including N84 and N17 from the north points, N63 and N6 from the east, and N67 and N18 from the south.

VISITOR INFORMATION For information about Galway and the surrounding areas, contact or visit **Ireland West Tourism (Aras Fáilte),** Foster Street (✆ **091/537700;** www.irelandwest.ie). Hours are May, June, and September daily 9am to 5:45pm; July and August daily 9am to 7:45pm; and October to April Monday to Friday 9am to 5:45pm, Saturday 9am to 12:45pm. For further detailed information on events and news in Galway, consult **www.galway.net**.

CITY LAYOUT The core of downtown Galway lies between Eyre Square on the east and the River Corrib on the west. The main thoroughfare begins west of Eyre Square. Its name changes—from William to Shop, Main Guard, and Bridge—before it crosses the River Corrib and changes again. If that sounds confusing, well, it is a bit. But the streets are all short and well marked, and it's fairly simple to find your way around the city center.

GETTING AROUND Galway has excellent local bus service. Buses run from the **Bus Éireann Travel Centre** (✆ **091/562000**) or Eyre Square to various suburbs, including Salthill and the Galway Bay coastline. The fare starts at €1.50 ($2.40).

There are taxi ranks at Eyre Square and all the major hotels in the city. If you need to call a cab, try **Abby Taxis** (✆ **091/533333**), **Big-O Taxis** (✆ **091/585858**), or **Galway Taxis** (✆ **091/561111**).

ⓕFun Facts **City of Tribes**

By the 15th century, 14 wealthy merchant families ruled the Galway Town, giving it the nickname it still bears today—"City of Tribes." These families, mostly of Welsh and Norman origin, ruled as an oligarchy, and you still see storefronts and businesses bearing these names today: Athy, Blake, Bodkin, Browne, Darcy, Deane, Font, Ffrench, Joyce, Kirwan, Lynch, Martin, Morris, and Skerret.

(**Fun** Facts) **Souvenir Stories: The Claddagh Ring**

The delicate Claddagh (pronounced *Clod*-uh) ring has become synonymous with Ireland and its diaspora. It originated here, or more precisely, just over the Father Griffin Bridge, on the west bank of the River Corrib, in the town of Claddagh. It's now a residential satellite to Galway, but in ancient times it was a kingdom with its own laws, fleet, and customs. The earliest known Claddagh ring was made in the 17th century for a wedding.

The ring features two hands holding a heart topped by a crown. The hands are said to represent friendship, the crown loyalty, and the heart love—the three ingredients of a perfect marriage. Originally, the ring was a wedding band worn facing out for engagement and facing in for marriage. Though no longer widely worn as a wedding band, it is still frequently worn in Ireland by men and women as a friendship ring and makes a lovely memento.

A town of medieval arches, alleyways, and cobblestone lanes, Galway is best explored on foot (wear comfortable shoes). Once you check in at your hotel or guesthouse, park your car and tour by walking. (To see the highlights, follow the signposts on the Tourist Trail of Old Galway. A handy booklet, available at the tourist office and at most bookshops, provides historical and architectural details.) If you must bring your car into the center of town, park it and then walk. There is free parking in front of Galway Cathedral, but most street parking uses a pay-to-park system. It costs €1 ($1.60) for about 1 hour. Multistory parking garages average €1.70 ($2.70) per hour or €12 ($19) per day.

To rent a car, contact one of the following firms: **Avis,** Higgins Garage, Headford Road (© **091/568886;** www.avis.ie); **Budget,** Galway Airport (© **091/556376;** www.budget.ie); or **Murrays Rent-A-Car,** Headford Road (© **091/562222;** www.europcar.ie).

FAST FACTS   If you need a drugstore, try **Flanagan's Pharmacy,** 32 Shop St. (© **091/562924**); **Matt O'Flaherty Chemist,** 16 William St. (© **091/561442,** or after hours 091/525426); or **Whelan's Chemist,** Williamsgate Street (© **091/562291**).

In an emergency, dial © **999. University College Hospital** is on Newcastle Road (© **091/544544**). There's also **Merlin Park Regional Hospital** (© **091/775775**). The local **Garda Station** is on Mill Street (© **091/538000**).

For information, gay and lesbian travelers might contact the **Galway Gay Help Line** (© **091/566134**) Tuesday and Thursday 8 to 10pm, or the **Galway Lesbian Line** (© **091/546611**) Wednesday 8 to 10pm.

For Internet access in Galway, try **Net Access,** in the heart of the city in the Olde Malte Arcade, High Street (© **091/395725;** www.netaccess.ie). **Hotlines,** 4 High St. (© **091/562838**), offers Internet access and low-cost international phone calls and is open 7 days a week. The **Galway Library/An Leabhar,** in the Hynes Building, Augustine Street (© **091/561666**), is open Monday 2 to 5pm, Tuesday to Thursday 11am to 8pm, Friday 11am to 5pm, and Saturday 11am to 1pm and 2 to 5pm.

The **Post Office,** Eglinton Street (© **091/534727**), is open Monday to Saturday 9am to 5:30pm.

2 WHERE TO STAY

VERY EXPENSIVE

The G ★ (**Finds**)   All Galway is talking about this over-the-top place. Designed by the hat designer Philip Treacy, it looks like a cross between *Barbarella* and *My Fair Lady,* which is to say it's an extraordinary-looking place. There are psychedelic touches (the Pink Salon is the color of Pepto-Bismol with a white-and-black spiral carpet and purple sofas) and a love of disco chic (the otherwise subtle taupe-and-white grand salon has masses of huge glass baubles hanging overhead). Rooms are calmer, in soothing white with touches of coffee and cream, and luxuriant beds with soft pillows and lush linens. Bathrooms are sensational, many have showers built for two, and all have excellent bath products. The service is outstanding—a team of butlers attend to your every whim, and the room service menu is long and varied, featuring dishes from the Italian-Irish in-house restaurant. The **ESPA spa** is oh-so-sophisticated, and it's all very Manhattan. It's all about a 15-minute walk from central Galway. It was included in Condé Nast's Hot 100 list for 2007, and there is no place trendier on Ireland's west coast.

Wellpark, Galway, County Galway. ℂ **091/865200.** Fax 091/765293. www.theghotel.ie. 101 units. €260 ($416) double; €320–€380 ($512–$608) suites. Rates include full breakfast. AE, MC, V. **Amenities:** Restaurant (modern Irish/Italian); bar; spa; nonsmoking rooms. *In room:* Satellite TV, DVD/CD player, Wi-Fi, tea/coffeemaker, hair dryer, trouser press, voice mail.

Glenlo Abbey Hotel ★★   About 3km (2 miles) outside of Galway on the main Clifden road, this secluded, sprawling stone hotel overlooks Lough Corrib in a sylvan setting, surrounded by a 9-hole golf course. Dating from 1740, this was originally the ancestral home of the Ffrench and Blake families, 2 of the 14 families who ruled the city for centuries. The building has retained its grandeur in the public areas, with hand-carved wood furnishings, hand-loomed carpets, ornate plasterwork, and an extensive collection of Irish art and antiques. The guest rooms, which have lovely views of Lough Corrib and the countryside, are luxuriously decorated with traditional furnishings, as well as marbled bathrooms.

Bushy Park, Galway, County Galway. ℂ **091/526666.** Fax 091/527800. www.glenlo.com. 46 units. €250–€400 ($400–$640) double; €550–€980 ($880–$1,568) suites. Breakfast €20 ($32). Dinner from around €50 ($80) per person. AE, DC, MC, V. Free parking. **Amenities:** 2 restaurants (international, Continental); 2 bars; 9-hole golf course; concierge; room service; laundry service; drawing room; fishing in Lough Corrib. *In room:* TV, Wi-Fi, hair dryer, garment press, safe.

EXPENSIVE

The House Hotel ★★   This four-story stone building in Galway's historic area, next to the Spanish Arch, was formerly a warehouse, and is now a boutique loft hotel. From its low-key lobby with polished oak floors, columns, and big windows, to its subtle, contemporary rooms, it's a comfortable, modern alternative. Rooms are divided into categories like "comfy," "classy," and "swanky," and they pretty much do what it says on the label. The swanky rooms are definitely the swankiest. All have comfortable beds, soft linens, lots of sunlight, high ceilings, and a refreshing urban feel. Its design has won accolades, and it prides itself on its service. It's a good new option in Galway.

Spanish Parade, Galway, County Galway. ℂ **091/538900.** Fax 091/568262. www.thehousehotel.ie. 45 units. €150–€300 ($240–$480) double. AE, DC, MC, V. **Amenities:** Restaurant (modern Continental); bar. *In room:* TV, broadband Internet, minibar, tea/coffeemaker, hair dryer, laptop safe.

Park House Hotel ★   With a steady, old-fashioned approach to luxury, the Park
House is a reliable option in central Galway. For 30 years, its warmly lit frontage has been
welcoming travelers into the tastefully decorated lobby. Rooms are spacious and classically decorated with plaid bedspreads and colorful throw pillows. Privacy is one of the
things this hotel does especially well—no two rooms directly face each other, ensuring
peace and quiet for all guests. Superior rooms are arranged around a roof garden, which
adds a nice touch. All rooms have free broadband—a relative rarity in Ireland. The **Park
Room Restaurant** is an award-winning, luxurious operation (see below), and its traditional style fits perfectly with this rock-steady hotel's ethos.

Foster St., Eyre Sq., Galway, County Galway. ℂ **091/564924.** Fax 091/569219. www.parkhousehotel.ie.
84 units. €200–€250 ($320–$400) double; €320 ($512) suites. Rates include full breakfast. AE, MC, V.
Amenities: Restaurant (modern Irish); bar; nonsmoking rooms. In room: TV, DVD/CD player, broadband
Internet, tea/coffeemaker, hair dryer, trouser press, voice mail.

The Radisson SAS   This hotel might be a bit bland and international-chainesque,
but it has a great location near Eyre Square, and it has all those handy little perks a big
hotel chain can offer. Its location near the water means that some rooms have scenic bay
views. All rooms are fairly spacious and well equipped with comfortable beds, desks,
modern bathrooms, and plenty of electronic gadgets for business travelers—although the
standard rooms are probably not going to win any design awards. The sun pours into the
in-house bar through huge windows, and the hotel restaurant is popular with locals. You
can chill out in the soothing spa, or work out in the well-equipped fitness club. Upper
rooms are quieter than lower rooms, which can get a bit of street noise, but all in all, this
is a handy option.

Lough Atalia Rd., Galway, County Galway. ℂ **091/538300.** Fax 091/538380. www.radissonhotelgalway.
com. 282 units. €150–€300 ($240–$480) double. AE, DC, MC, V. **Amenities:** Restaurant (modern Continental); bar. In room: TV, Wi-Fi, minibar, tea/coffeemaker, hair dryer, laptop safe.

MODERATE

Galway Harbour Hotel   This modern hotel has borrowed a lot from boutique
hotels, and its design has clean lines, along with lots of blond wood, neutral colors, and
arty touches like cleverly recessed lights above the beds. Rooms are large and quiet, and
it's well located, so it's not at all bad for the price, but there are flaws. Some beds are a
bit uncomfortable, and the bathrooms are unimaginatively designed with painfully
bright lighting. The breakfast dining room looks too chain-hotelish to be comfortable.
In general, although it's still a decent option, this place feels a bit tired, as many hotels
that rely on tour bus traffic inevitably do. *Note:* Keep an eye on the hotel's website—
there are very good deals to be found online.

New Dock Rd., Galway, County Galway. ℂ **091/569466.** Fax 091/569455. www.galwayharbourhotel.
com. 96 units. €130–€180 ($208–$288) double. No service charge. Rates include full breakfast. AE, MC, V.
Free parking at nearby car park. **Amenities:** Restaurant (modern Continental); bar; Internet room; nonsmoking rooms. In room: TV, CD player, dataport, tea/coffeemaker, hair dryer, trouser press, voice mail.

(Tips)   **Service Charges**

A reminder: Unless otherwise noted, room rates don't include service charges
(usually 10%–15% of your bill).

Barnacle's Quay Street House ★ ⟨Value⟩   This cheap and cheerful guesthouse is bright, attractive, and friendly—what more do y ou need? It's a 16th-century house, with marvelous fireplaces and lots of character. Bedrooms are done in sunny yellows, and there's a communal kitchen if you are weary of restaurants. The clientele tends to be young, mostly college students filling the shared dorm rooms, but the four-bed rooms are also good for families traveling on a budget. All are welcome, and the location is handily central. Book early in the high season, as the place tends to fill up quickly.

10 Quay St., Galway, County Galway. ✆ 091/568644. www.barnacles.ie. 10 units. €58–€66 ($93–$106) double. Rates include continental breakfast. No credit cards. **Amenities:** Lounge; kitchen; Internet; TV room.

Clare Villa ★ ⟨Value⟩   This spacious, modern house is steps from the beach and very popular in summer, which is as it should be. Its pleasant rooms all have firm, comfortable beds, and the owners are helpful and friendly. The biggest attraction, though, is its proximity to the seafront and taking in that fresh salt air every morning.

38 Threadneedle Rd. ✆ 091/522520. clarevilla@yahoo.com. 6 units. €70 ($112) double. Rates include full breakfast. No credit cards. **Amenities:** Sitting room. *In room:* TV, hair dryer.

Devondell ★ ⟨Value⟩   You'd be hard-pressed to find a better B&B in Galway than Berna Kelly's much-lauded house in the Lower Salthill residential area, about 2km (1¼ miles) from Galway's city center. It's a modern house, and guest rooms are spacious and done up with period furnishings and crisp Irish linens. Breakfasts are exceptional, with cereal, fresh fruit, yogurt, cheese, hash browns, kippers, eggs, and French toast. Devondell is walking distance from the seafront.

47 Devon Park, Lower Salthill, County Galway. ✆ 091/528306. www.devondell.com. 4 units. €80–€90 ($128–$144) double. Rates include full breakfast. MC, V. Free parking. Closed Nov–Feb. **Amenities:** Sitting room. *In room:* TV.

---

3 WHERE TO DINE

EXPENSIVE

Kirwan's Lane ★★ CONTINENTAL   Chef-owner Michael O'Grady's stylish, inviting restaurant is widely acclaimed, and for good reason. The dining room is rustic chic, with pine furnishings and walls painted warm ocher and vivid red. It's a particularly good value at lunchtime, when the constantly changing menu might include a starter of smoked haddock and clam chowder, or ox tongue pancetta with truffle smokes potatoes. The dinner menu features dishes with fresh local produce and seafood, including crab, guinea fowl, and sautéed fresh monkfish, all beautifully presented.

Kirwan's Lane. ✆ 091/568266. Reservations recommended. Main courses €18–€29 ($29–$46). AE, MC, V. Daily 12:30–2:30pm and 6–10pm. Closed Sun Sept–June.

The Malt House ★★ MODERN IRISH   Barry and Therese Cunningham's cozy place, tucked into a courtyard off one of Galway's main streets, has long been a big hit with the locals. The draw is the creative cooking that turns traditional Irish dishes into modern international cuisine. Seafood is a specialty here; the signature dish is the seafood tower, a huge plate for two including Malbay crab, Irish smoked salmon, and chilled local oysters. Come for the early-bird menu and save a bundle.

6–7:30pm €25 ($40); main courses €20–€38 ($32–$61). AE, MC, V. Mon–Sat 12:30–3pm and 6:30–
10:30pm.

Park Room Restaurant ★SEAFOOD/CONTINENTAL   Half a block east of Eyre
Square, at the back of the Park House Hotel, this fine restaurant has an old-world decor
of stained glass, dark woods, and oil paintings, and a sophisticated cooking approach.
Entrees include grilled prime sirloin steak au poivre, marinated tandoori chicken with
noodles and Thai curry sauce, and pan-fried supreme of sea trout with shrimp and dill
butter. The seafood is exceptional, and the ambience is pleasantly upscale.

Forster St., Eyre Sq. © **091/564924.** Reservations recommended. Main courses €20–€32 ($32–$51). AE,
DC, MC, V. Daily 12:30–3pm and 6–10pm.

MODERATE
Conlon SEAFOOD   If you love seafood, head for this place, as it is the local specialist,
with 20 varieties of fresh fish and shellfish on the menu at any time. You're bound to find
something to choose—the house specialties are wild salmon and oysters, so that's not a
bad place to start. Entrees include grilled wild salmon, steamed Galway Bay mussels, and
fishermen's platters with a bit of everything—smoked salmon, mussels, prawns, oysters,
and crab claws.

Eglinton Court. © **091/562268.** Seafood bar items €4–€10 ($6.40–$16); main courses €8–€27 ($13–$43).
DC, MC, V. Mon–Sat 11am–midnight; Sun 5pm–midnight.

G.B.C. (Galway Bakery Company) ★ BISTRO   With a distinctive Old Galway
shop-front facade, this building is two eateries in one: a ground-level self-service coffee
shop and a full-service bistro upstairs. The restaurant menu lists a straightforward and
unfussy selection of dishes, from steaks, seafood, and burgers to pasta and chicken fajitas.
Baked goods, particularly the homemade brown bread, are an added attraction. The coffee shop serves memorably good breakfasts and light lunches.

7 Williamsgate St. © **091/563087.** www.gbcgalway.com. Coffee-shop items under €8 ($13); dinner main
courses €13–€20 ($21–$32). AE, DC, MC, V. Coffee shop daily 8am–10pm. Restaurant daily noon–10pm.

McDonagh's FISH AND CHIPS/SEAFOOD   For seafood straight off the boats,
served up in an authentic maritime atmosphere, this is Galway's best choice. The place is
divided into three parts: a traditional "chipper" for fish and chips, a smart restaurant in the
back, and a fish market where you can buy raw seafood. The McDonaghs, fishmongers for
more than four generations, buy direct from local fishermen every day, and it shows; crowds
line up every night to get in. The menu includes salmon, trout, lemon or black sole (or
both), turbot, and silver hake, all cooked to order. In the back restaurant, you can crack
your own prawns' tails and crab claws in the shell, or tackle a whole lobster.

22 Quay St. © **091/565809.** Reservations not accepted June–Aug. Main courses €8–€35 ($13–$56). AE,
MC, V. Daily noon–10pm.

Nimmo's ★★ WINE BAR/SEAFOOD   This is one of Galway's trendy tables—a
place to see and be seen that manages to serve fantastic food while constantly admiring
itself. It's ideal for a festive, buzzy meal out. Pass the stone facade, climb a winding stair-
way, and you'll find yourself in a wonderfully romantic dining room, particularly on a
starry night when you can see the moon through the skylights. The menu changes
according to season and tends to feature seafood in the summer and game during the

winter. Start with the soup or the daily fish special, then move on to the delicious Barbary duck confit or grilled filet of sea bass with spring onion mashed potatoes. Save room for dessert, which is brought in by Goya's, the best bakery in Galway. The wines are terrific, too. Make a reservation in advance to be sure of getting a table.

Long Walk, Spanish Arch. ℭ 091/561114. www.nimmos.ie. Reservations recommended. Main courses €17–€26 ($27–$42). MC, V. Tues–Sun 6–10pm.

INEXPENSIVE

Busker Brown's ★ CAFE/BAR   A modern cafe in a medieval building, Busker Brown's is a favorite of locals and travelers for its funky decor that mixes ancient stonework with modern tables and art, as well as for its big breakfasts and homemade, inexpensive lunches and dinners. It offers everything from hamburgers and sandwiches to fresh stews and pasta. It also stays open late—one of a few Galway eateries to do so.

Upper Cross St. ℭ 091/563377. Main courses €6–€15 ($9.60–$24). MC, V. Mon–Sat 10:30am–11:30pm; Sun 12:30–11:30pm.

The Cobblestone ★ VEGETARIAN   Tucked away on a winding medieval lane, this casual eatery is a bright light on Galway's cuisine scene. Proprietor Kate Wright serves up excellent fresh salads, soups, quiches, and pastas. There are plenty of vegetarian dishes (try the "beanie shepherd pie") and fresh croissants, breads, muffins, cakes, and cookies. Head here when you're in the mood for a light meal or snack.

Kirwan's Lane. ℭ 091/567227. Main courses €6–€16 ($9.60–$26). MC, V. Daily 9am–7pm.

4 SEEING THE SIGHTS

Many of Galway's top attractions are outdoors and free of charge—one of its biggest delights is simply strolling around the Spanish Arch and Spanish Parade, through Eyre Square and the John F. Kennedy Park. An afternoon picnicking on the banks of the River Corrib is similarly free and often unforgettable.

Galway Arts Centre ★★   Once the home of W. B. Yeats's patron, Lady Gregory, this attractive town house for many years housed local governmental offices. Today it offers an excellent program of concerts, readings, and exhibitions by Irish and international artists, returning, in a way, to a form Lady Gregory would have appreciated. A second building, used primarily for performances and workshops, is located at 23 Nuns Island (same phone).

47 Dominick St. ℭ 091/565886. www.galwayartscentre.ie. Free admission to exhibits. Mon–Sat 10am–6pm.

Galway Cathedral ★   It's easy to understand why this church's nickname is so short and simple, given that its official name is "Cathedral of Our Lady Assumed into Heaven and St. Nicholas." Its walls are fine-cut limestone from local quarries and its floors are Connemara marble. It's not particularly old, as it was built in the 1960s. Contemporary Irish artisans designed the statues, stained-glass windows, and mosaics.

University and Gaol roads, beside the Salmon Weir Bridge on the river's west bank. ℭ 091/563577. www.galwaycathedral.org. Free admission; donations welcome. Daily 8am–6pm.

Galway City Museum ★ This little museum offers a fine collection of local documents, photographs, city memorabilia, examples of medieval stonework, and revolving exhibits.

Off Spanish Arch. (✆ **091/567641.** Free admission. June–Sept daily 10am–5pm; Oct–May Tues–Sat 10am–5pm.

Galway Irish Crystal Heritage Centre ★★ Visitors to this distinctive crystal manufacturer can watch the craftsmen at work—blowing, shaping, and hand-cutting the glassware—and then go shop for the perfect pieces to take back home. Glassmaking demonstrations are continuous on weekdays. The shop and restaurant are open daily.

East of the city on the main Dublin rd. (N6), Merlin Park, Galway, County Galway. (✆ **091/757311.** Free admission. Mon–Fri 9am–5:30pm; Sat 10am–5:30pm; Sun 11am–5pm.

Nora Barnacle House ★ Just across from the St. Nicholas church clock tower, this restored 19th-century terrace house was once the home of Nora Barnacle, who later would become the wife of James Joyce. It contains letters, photographs, and other exhibits on the lives of the Joyces and their connections with Galway.

Bowling Green. (✆ **091/564743.** www.norabarnacle.com. Admission €2.50 ($4) adults; €2 ($3.20) seniors, students, and children. Mid-May to mid-Sept Mon–Sat 10am–5pm (closed for lunch), and by appointment rest of year.

St. Nicholas' Collegiate Church ★★ This is Galway's oldest church—it's said that Christopher Columbus prayed here in 1477 before sailing away on one of his attempts to reach the New World. Established about 1320, it has changed from Roman Catholic to Church of Ireland and back again at least four times and is currently under the aegis of the latter denomination. Inside are a 12th-century crusader's tomb with a Norman inscription, a carved font from the 16th or 17th century, and a stone lectern with barley-sugar twist columns from the 15th century. Guided tours, conducted by Declan O Mordha, a knowledgeable and enthusiastic church representative, depart from the south porch according to demand, except on Sunday morning.

Lombard St. (✆ **091/564648.** Free admission to church; donations of €2 ($3.20) adults, €1.30 ($2.10) seniors and students requested. Tours €3 ($4.80); reservations required. Mid-Apr to Sept Mon–Sat 9am–5:45pm, Sun 1–5:45pm; Oct to mid-Apr Mon–Sat 10am–4pm, Sun 1–5pm.

CRUISES & TOURS

Corrib Princess This 157-passenger, two-deck boat cruises along the River Corrib, with commentary on points of interest. The trip lasts 90 minutes, passing castles, historical sites, and assorted wildlife. There is a full bar and snack service. You can buy tickets at the dock or at the *Corrib Princess* desk in the tourist office.

Woodquay. (✆ **091/592447.** www.corribprincess.ie. Cruise €14 ($22) adults, €12 ($19) seniors and students, €7 ($11) children, €35 ($56) families. May–June and Sept daily 2:30 and 4:30pm; July–Aug daily 12:30 and 4:30pm.

Galway Panoramic Galway is small enough to be walkable, but these open-top buses are a handy way to explore the highlights. They run on a loop—when you see something you want to explore, you just hop off and hop back on when the next bus comes around.

Grayline/Guide Friday Irish City Tours. (✆ **01/670-8822.** €12 ($19) adults, €11 ($18) students, €5 ($8) children. Apr–Oct daily, with schedule varying according to demand.

5 SPORTS & OUTDOOR PURSUITS

SPECTATOR SPORTS

GREYHOUND RACING The hounds race year-round every Thursday, Friday, and Saturday at the newly redeveloped **Galway Greyhound Track,** College Road, off Eyre Square (© **091/562273**). Doors open 7pm and admission is €10 ($16) adults, €5 ($8) seniors and students, and €.50 (80¢) children.

HORSE RACING This is one of the most famous racetracks in Europe—the subject of fable and song—and when (in July, Sept, and Oct) horses pound the track at the **Galway Racecourse,** Ballybrit (© **091/753870;** www.galwayraces.com), less than 3km (2 miles) east of town, it's an event known simply as the **Galway Races.** It brings in horse lovers and high rollers from around the country, and is well worth catching. Admission is €20 to €35 ($32–$56), depending on the event and day of the week.

OUTDOOR PURSUITS

BICYCLING To rent a bike, contact **Richard Walsh Cycles,** Headford Road, Woodquay (© **091/565710**).

FISHING Set beside the River Corrib, Galway City and nearby Connemara are popular fishing centers for salmon and sea trout. For the latest information on requirements for licenses and local permits, check with the **Western Regional Fisheries Board (WRFB),** Weir Lodge, Earl's Island, Galway (© **091/563118;** www.wrfb.ie). The extraordinarily accessible WRFB also provides free consultation for overseas anglers on where to go at different times of the season for salmon or trout, where to find the best *ghillies* (guides), and which flies and gear to use. Maps and brochures are available on request. For gear and equipment, try **Duffys Fishing,** 5 Main Guard St. (© **091/562367**), **Freeney Sport Shop,** 19 High St. (© **091/568794**), or **Great Outdoors Sports Centre,** Eglinton Street (© **091/562869**).

GOLF Less than 8km (5 miles) east of Galway is the 18-hole, par-72 championship **Galway Bay Golf Resort,** Renville, Oranmore, County Galway (© **091/790711;** www. galwaybaygolfresort.com). At this writing the course was closed for reconstruction but

---

ⓂMoments   **The Galway Races**

Galway horses are famous for their speed, small size, and beauty, so it's no surprise that the races here are the best in Ireland and among the best in Europe. There are records of organized horse racing in Galway as far back as the 13th century, and in 1764 there was a well-known 5-day race at Knockbarron near Loughrea. Almost a century later, the Galway Racecourse opened officially. To this day, races in Galway are extremely popular, and people come from around the country to experience the frivolity (music is usually performed around the racecourse), the pomp (ladies are known to get dressed to the nines), and the exhilaration of the race itself. Tickets aren't expensive and it's a truly Irish event well worth catching if you happen to be in town when the races are on.

was due to reopen in late 2008. Call for details. Less than 3km (2 miles) west of the city is the 18-hole, par-69 seaside course at **Galway Golf Club,** Blackrock, Galway (© **091/522033;** www.galwaygolf.com). Greens fees are €50 ($80) weekdays, €60 ($96) Saturdays (closed to nonmembers Sun).

HORSEBACK RIDING Riding enthusiasts head to **Aille Cross Equestrian Centre,** Aille Cross, Loughrea, County Galway (© **091/841216;** www.aille-cross.com), about 32km (20 miles) east of Galway. Run by personable Willy Leahy (who has appeared often on American television), this facility is one of the largest in Ireland, with 50 horses and 20 Connemara ponies. For about €25 to €40 ($40–$64) an hour, you can ride through nearby farmlands, woodlands, forest trails, and along beaches.

---

6 SHOPPING

Given its status as both a tourist hub and a vibrant arts community, it's unsurprising that Galway has fairly good shopping. Some of the best is in tiny malls of small shops clustered in historic buildings, such as the **Cornstore** on Middle Street, the **Grainstore** on Lower Abbeygate Street, and the **Bridge Mills,** a 430-year-old mill building beside the River Corrib. **Eyre Square Centre,** the downtown area's largest shopping mall, with 50 shops, incorporates a section of Galway's medieval town wall into its complex.

Most shops are open Monday to Saturday 9 or 10am to 5:30 or 6pm. In July and August, many shops stay open late, usually until 9pm on weekdays, and some also open on Sunday from noon to 5pm.

Here's a sampling of some of Galway's best shops.

ANTIQUES & CURIOS

Cobwebs This sweet little shop across from the Spanish Arch offers jewelry, antique toys, curios, and rarities from Ireland and beyond. 7 Quay Lane. © **091/564388.** www.cobwebs.ie.

Connaught Antiques This shop is a wonderful place to rummage through for 18th- and 19th-century antique treasures from France and across Europe. 9 Eyre Sq. © **091/567840.**

The Winding Stair Three floors crammed with antiques—just the place to pick up an Art Nouveau lamp, painted wooden chest, or church pew. 4 Mainguard St. © **091/561682.**

BOOKS

Charlie Byrne's Bookshop This is an atmospheric bookshop, where most of the books are secondhand. There's a good selection of paperbacks, should you need to stock up, and plenty of Irish-interest titles. There are also some surprising finds, with a fair selection of titles in archaeology, art history, the cinema, and music. The Cornstore, Middle St. © **091/561766.** www.charliebyrne.com.

Kenny's Book Shop and Galleries Ltd. A Galway fixture for more than 50 years, this shop is an attraction unto itself. It's a friendly, busy shop with plenty of old maps, prints, engravings, and books on all topics—many on local history, as well as whole sections on Yeats and Joyce—wedged in every available crevice. Kenny's is famous for its antiquarian department, its bookbinding workshop, and an ever-changing gallery of local artworks. Middle and High sts. © **091/709350.** www.kennys.ie.

CRYSTAL, CHINA & SOUVENIRS

Galway Irish Crystal   This factory outlet on the loop (or "ring road") around Galway Town has lots of hand-cut crystal, and a center that explains where it all comes from and how it's made. Dublin rd., Merlin Park. ✆ **091/757311.**

Treasure Chest   With an artful exterior that seems to have stepped straight out of Wedgwood, this is a pleasant one-stop shop for Waterford crystal chandeliers, Royal Tara and Royal Doulton china, Irish Dresden and Lladró figures, and Belleek china. It also carries Irish designer clothing, Aran knitwear, lingerie, and swimwear, not to mention touristy souvenirs. 31–33 William St. and Castle St. ✆ **091/563862.** www.treasurechest.ie.

HANDICRAFTS

Design Concourse   If you're looking for local handicrafts, this is a good choice, as it's filled with the work of dozens of talented Irish craftspeople. Its offerings include woodwork, jewelry, furniture, and glass. Kirwan's Lane. ✆ **091/566927.**

Twice as Nice   A sweet, old-fashioned shop, this little gem is filled with fine white linens and cottons for the bedroom and dining room, as well as antique linens and sumptuous christening gowns. 5 Quay St. ✆ **091/566332.**

JEWELRY

Fallers of Galway   Dating from 1879, Fallers has long been a prime source of Claddagh rings, many of which are made on the premises. It also sells Celtic crosses, some inlaid with Connemara marble, as well as gold and silver jewelry and crystal. Williamsgate St. ✆ **800/229-3892** in the U.S. (for catalogs), or 091/561226. www.fallers.com.

Hartmann & Son Ltd.   The Hartmann family, which started in the jewelry business in the late 1800s in Germany, brought their skills and wares to Ireland in 1895, and opened this shop just off Eyre Square in 1942. They enjoy a far-reaching reputation as watchmakers, goldsmiths, and makers of Claddagh rings. 29 William St. ✆ **091/562063.** www.hartmanns.ie.

MUSIC & MUSICAL INSTRUMENTS

P. Powell and Sons   This family-run shop sells traditional Irish music, instruments, and recordings. The Four Corners, Williams St. ✆ **091/562295.**

TWEEDS, WOOLENS & CLOTHING

Brown Thomas   The local branch of one of Ireland's oldest and most upscale department stores, owned by the same people as London's Selfridges. Galway's best-dressed fashionistas have this place on speed dial. William St. (at Eglinton St.). ✆ **091/565254.** www.brownthomas.com.

Faller's Sweater Shop   This shop has a huge supply of knitwear made by Irish artisans from the wool of Irish sheep. Prices are quite good. 25 High St. ✆ **091/564833.**

Mac Eocagain/Galway Woollen Market   This is an excellent resource if you're shopping for traditional Aran hand-knits and colorful hand-loomed sweaters and capes, as well as linens, lace, and sheepskins. Each item has two prices, one including value-added tax (VAT) and one tax-free for non–European Union (E.U.) residents. 21 High St. ✆ **091/562491.**

O'Máille (O'Malley)   Established in 1938, this shop became famous in the 1950s for outfitting the entire cast of *The Quiet Man* and has done a fabulous business ever since in quality Irish tweeds, knitwear, and traditional Aran knits. 16 High St. ✆ **091/562696.** www.omaille.com.

7 GALWAY CITY AFTER DARK

PUBS

An Pucan   A block east of Eyre Square, this old-fashioned nautical-theme pub hosts good Irish traditional music (daily from 9pm). It's an Irish-language pub, though, so the eavesdropping is terrible if you're not bilingual. 11 Forster St. © 091/561528.

Crane Bar   In the southwestern part of Galway, at the corner of an open market area called "the Small Crane," this rustic pub is known for its nightly musical entertainment. From 9pm every night, there is country-and-western music downstairs and traditional Irish tunes upstairs. 2 Sea Rd. © 091/587419.

Front Door (Finds)   This sunny, laid-back pub is a good place to linger over a pint and newspaper. Its many windows let the sun pour in, and the staff couldn't care less how long you stay. It's a lovely, relaxed place. High St. © 091/563757. www.frontdoorpub.com.

The Quays   If this unusual pub looks a bit theological, that's because its entire interior was imported from a French medieval church—stained glass, carved wood, Gothic arches, pews, and all. Evening music ranges from traditional Irish to '70s retro to Dixieland, and usually starts at 9pm. Quay St. and Chapel Lane. © 091/568347.

Rabbitt's   This place dates from 1872 and hardly appears to have changed since then, with lanterns hanging in the corners and pictures of old Galway on the walls. Run by the fourth generation of the Rabbitt family, it's a block east of Eyre Square. 23–25 Forster St. © 091/566490.

Séhán Ua Neáchtain   This is a proper locals pub, and its interior always appears enveloped in smoke, even now when smoking is forbidden in bars. It's like the haze of time has left its mark. It's got a quirky crowd that defies categorization—artists, farmers, shop owners, and business types—and a cheery, buzzing atmosphere. Come here to make new friends. 17 Cross St. © 091/568820.

CLUBS

Nightclubs in Galway tend to be wastelands until 11pm, and then packed up until 2am when most close. There are plenty of options if you've got dancing on your mind, including **Halo,** 36 Abbeygate St. Upper (© **091/565976**), which attracts an over-20s crowd with its laid-back vibe; **Cuba,** Eyre Square (© **091/565991**), for seriously cool Latin jazz funk Saturday nights; and the **GPO,** Eglinton Street (© **091/563073;** www.gpo.ie). In nearby Salthill, new dance clubs with hot guest DJs are popping up all the time. One reliably good option is **Liquid** (© **091/527155**).

Fridays and Saturdays are gay nights at the **Attic @ Liquid,** Liquid, Salthill (© **091/527155**).

At Galway nightclubs, you'll usually pay cover charges in a range of about €5 to €20 ($8–$32), which doesn't include drinks.

A MEDIEVAL BANQUET

A half-hour drive from Galway, **Dunguaire** is a splendid 16th-century castle where, in the summer, you can attend a medieval banquet with a show featuring works by Irish writers like Synge, Yeats, and Gogarty. Banquets cost €51 ($82) adults, €38 ($61) children 11 and under. Reservations can be made at © **061/361511** (www.shannonheritage.com). Dunguaire is in south County Galway on the Ballyvaughan road (N67), near Kinvara, approximately 26km (16 miles) from Galway. The castle is open to visitors daily from

9:30am to 5pm, after which there are two banquet seatings—one at 5:30pm and one at 8:45pm. Banquets are held every night from May to September.

THEATERS

The creative theater group, **Druid Theatre,** performs in two venues in Galway—in a converted grain warehouse at Chapel Lane (℘ **091/568617**), and at the Town Hall Theatre (℘ **091/569777;** www.druidtheatre.com). Performances are unique and original, focusing on Irish folk dramas and Anglo-Irish classics. This is widely viewed as one of Ireland's best theaters, and so its shows are frequently either sold out or on tour; book well in advance. Tickets run €15 to €40 ($24–$64).

Taibhdhearc Theatre   Pronounced *Thive*-yark, this is a 108-seat, year-round venue for Irish-language plays. In summer, it presents a program of traditional music, song, dance, and folk drama. The box office is open Monday to Saturday from 1 to 6pm (until 8pm on show nights); most shows start at 8pm. Middle St. ℘ **091/563600.** www.antaibhdhearc. com (website in Gaelic). Tickets €10–€15 ($16–$24).

---

13

8 SIDE TRIPS FROM GALWAY CITY

THE ARAN ISLANDS ★

When you see the ghostly shapes of the islands floating 48km (30 miles) out at sea like misty Brigadoons, you instantly understand why the **Aran Islands** have been the subject of fable and song for thousands of years. The islands—**Inis Mór (Inishmore), Inis Meain (Inishmaan),** and **Inis Oirr (Inisheer)**—are outposts of Gaelic culture and language. The islands are physically beautiful and home to protected bird species, with a lovely, deeply isolated landscape. To this day, many of the 1,500 inhabitants of the islands still maintain a somewhat traditional life, fishing from *currachs* (small crafts made of tarred canvas stretched over timber frames), living in stone cottages, relying on pony-drawn wagons to get around, and speaking Gaelic, although they all speak English as well. The classic hand-knit *bainin* sweaters that originated here are still worn, as there's nothing better for keeping out the chill. Sadly, though, the constant flow of tourists has had an impact on island life, and more and more islanders are involved in modern life, running tourist-related businesses. In fact, visiting in the high season—particularly in July and August—can be a disappointment, since the small, rocky islands are not suited to being overrun by crowds, and at that time of year, visitors arrive by the boatload.

Most visitors debark from the ferries at Kilronan, Inishmore's main town and a very easy place in which to arrange or rent transportation. The mode is up to you: Jaunting cars can be hailed like taxis as you step off the boat, minivans stand at the ready, and bicycle-rental shops are within sight.

Of the islands, Inishmore is the largest and easiest to reach from Galway, and the one that best handles the large groups of tourists. Its easy transport means you can escape the crowds if you wish, or, if you play well with others, there are plenty of pubs and restaurants. If that all seems far too noisy, you might prefer Inishmaan or Inisheer, both of which are smaller and quieter, and arguably more beautiful than Inishmore.

All of the islands are physically strange looking, with a ring of rocks around their outer edges and, inside, small farms layered in soft green grass and wildflowers. The most dramatic landscape is to be found on the western sides where huge cliffs plummet dizzily into the frothing sea below.

Impressions

I have heard that, at that time, the ruling proprietor and magistrate of the north island used to give any man who had done wrong a letter to a jailer in Galway, and send him off by himself to serve a term of imprisonment.

—J. M. Synge (1871–1909), *The Aran Islands*

There are some excellent geological sights out here, including the magnificent **Dún Aengus ★★**, a vast, 2,000-year-old stone fortress on Inishmore, on the edge of a cliff that drops 90m (295 ft.) to the sea. Its original purpose is unknown—some think it was a military structure, others say it was a vast ceremonial theater. From the top, there are spectacular views of Galway Bay, the Burren, and Connemara.

Also on Inishmore, a heritage center, **Ionad Árann,** Kilronan (© **099/61355;** www.visitaranislands.com), explores the history and culture of the islands. Exhibits examine the harsh landscape, Iron Age forts, and early churches. In addition, the 1932 film *Man of Aran,* directed by Robert Flaherty, is shown six times daily. The center is open March to May and October daily 10am to 5pm, and from June to September daily 10am to 7pm. Admission to the center is €4.50 ($7.20) for adults, €3 ($4.80) for students, €2.50 ($4) for seniors and children, and €9.25 ($15) for families. Discounted combination tickets to the center and film are available. The cafe serves soups, sandwiches, and pastries throughout the day.

Here are the best ways to arrange an excursion to the Aran Islands from Galway City (for more information about the Aran Islands, including getting there from Doolin in County Clare, see "The Clare Coast" in chapter 12):

Aer Arann Islands The fastest way to get from the mainland to the Aran Islands is on this local airline, which has small planes departing from Connemara Airport, approximately 29km (18 miles) west of Galway City to the islands every day in the high season. Flight time is 10 minutes, and bus service between Galway City and the airport is available. Alternatively, you could try one of the new scenic routes, a 30-minute trip that takes in the islands together with the **Cliffs of Moher** (p. 385). It costs €280 ($448) for an eight-seater aircraft; no individual fares are available. You can book your flight at the Galway Tourist Office or at Aer Arann Reservations. A range of specials are usually offered, combining flights with bus/accommodations, and so forth.

Connemara Airport, Inverin, County Galway. © **091/593034.** Fax 091/593238. www.aerarannislands.ie. Round-trip fare €45 ($72) adults, €37 ($59) students, €25 ($40) children 11 and under. MC, V. Apr–Sept daily 9am, 10:30am, 4pm, and 5pm; Oct–Mar daily 9am, 10:30am, and 3pm.

Aran Island Ferries This company, with a number of offices in Galway center, offers extensive, year-round daily service to all three Aran Islands. Most boats leave from Rossaveal in Connemara, 37km (23 miles) west of the city, for the 40-minute trip. Island Ferries provides bus connection service from its Victoria Place office 90 minutes before sailing time. During peak summer season, there are daily excursions from Galway Dock, which cost up to about €7 ($11) more than tickets from Rossaveal.

Victoria Place, off Eyre Sq., Galway, County Galway. © **091/568903.** Fax 091/568538. www.aranisland ferries.com. Round-trip fare starts at €25 ($40) adults, €20 ($32) seniors and students, €13 ($21) children; family and group rates on request. From Rossaveal Nov–Mar daily 10:30am and 6pm; Apr–Oct daily 10:30am, 1pm, and 6pm. Additional sailings July–Aug according to demand.

The Inishmore tourist office (© **099/61263**), on the waterfront near the ferry pier in Kilronan, can help you book a room if you haven't reserved in advance.

Kilmurvey House ★   This has been *the* place to stay on Inishmore since Dún Aengus fell into ruin. The 18th-century stone family home of the "Ferocious O'Flahertys" forms the core of this most hospitable and pleasant guesthouse, with 12 diverse rooms, all comfortable and impeccably clean. It's a friendly place, where an array of delights awaits you at breakfast. An optional four-course dinner is served with advance reservations. Kilmurvey House lies just below Dún Aengus, Inishmore's prime attraction. A handful of shops, cafes, and restaurants, as well as a Blue Flag (safe to swim) white-sand beach, are within a short stroll.

8km (5 miles) from the ferry on the coast rd., Kilmurvey, Kilronan, Inis Mór, Aran Islands, County Galway. © **099/61218.** Fax 099/61397. www.kilmurveyhouse.com. 12 units. €90–€110 ($144–$176) double. Rates include full breakfast. MC, V. Closed Nov–Easter. **Amenities:** Sitting room.

Man of Aran Cottage   In the traditional thatched seaside cottage constructed in 1934 for the filming of *Man of Aran,* this cozy B&B overlooking Kilmurvey Bay is friendly and unpretentious, with comfortable rooms—decorated with simple pine furniture and white-washed walls—and tranquil views. The biggest draw may well be its first-class **restaurant,** open Monday to Saturday 12:30 to 3pm and 7:30 to 10pm. The menu draws upon the organic vegetables and herbs grown in the cottage garden, and fresh seafood.

Kilmurvey, Kilronan, Aran Islands, County Galway. © **099/61301.** www.manofarancottage.com. 5 units. €80 ($128) double with private bathroom; €77 ($123) double with shared bathroom. Rates include full breakfast. Reservations required for dinner. Fixed-price dinner €35 ($56). No credit cards. **Amenities:** Restaurant; sitting room.

Radharc An Chlair ★ (Finds)   Leaving the ferry and walking onto tiny Inisheer, you're met by Peadar Poil and given a lift up to the house—wait for it—on his tractor. Peadar's wife, Brigid, runs a spit-and-polish B&B operation and the guest rooms are all comfortable and cozy. She is a superb cook and a terrific baker, so even a scone and a cup of tea here are a pleasure.

Inis Oirr, Aran Islands, County Galway. © **099/75019.** 6 units. €70 ($112) double en suite; €64 ($102) double with shared bathroom. Rates include full breakfast. MC, V. Closed Christmas. **Amenities:** Sitting room.

SOUTH OF GALWAY CITY

On the main road south (N18) of Galway are two small fishing villages, **Clarenbridge** and **Kilcolgan.** Each year at the end of September, the villages host the annual **Galway Oyster Festival** ★. Launched in 1954, the 5-day festival is packed with traditional music, song, dancing, sports, art exhibits, and, above all, oyster-tasting events and oyster-opening competitions.

If you continue south on N18 for another 16km (10 miles), you'll see signs to the quietly beautiful **Coole Park National Forest** (© **091/631804**). This was once a country home of the dramatist and arts patron Lady Gregory, who, along with W. B. Yeats and Edward Martyn, founded the Abbey Theatre. Sadly, her house no longer stands, but her influence is memorialized in a tree on the grounds on which the following people carved their initials while visiting with her: George Bernard Shaw, Sean O'Casey, John Masefield, Oliver St. John Gogarty, W. B. Yeats, and Douglas Hyde, the first president of Ireland. Clearly, this is an exceptional place. There's a visitor center, as well as a tearoom, picnic tables, and plenty of nature trails to wander. The visitor center is open daily 10am to 5pm March to September and 10am to 6pm June to August. The last admission is 15 minutes before closing (1 hr. for the audiovisual presentations). Admission is free.

Not too far away from the home of his friend, W. B. Yeats had his own summer home in Gort at **Thoor Ballylee** (© **091/631436;** www.gortonline.com). The restored 16th-century Norman tower house served as the inspiration for his poems "The Winding Stair" and "The Tower." In the interpretive center, an audiovisual presentation examines the poet's life. Also on the grounds are the original Ballylee Mill, partially restored, and a bookshop specializing in Anglo-Irish literature. The site is on the N18 at Gort. Admission is €6 ($9.60) for adults, €5.50 ($8.80) for seniors and students, €2.50 ($4) for children 12 and over, and €1.50 ($2.40) for children 11 and under. It's open from May to September daily 10am to 6pm. There's a **Tourist Information Office** (© **091/ 631436**) open May to September daily 9:30am to 5pm.

Not too far away from Yeats's and Lady Gregory's summer homes, west off the main road, between Gort and Kilcolgan, **Dunguaire Castle,** Kinvara (© **061/360788;** www. shannonheritage.com), sits on the south shore of Galway Bay. Once the royal seat of the 7th-century King Guaire of Connaught, the castle was taken over later by the legendary Oliver St. John Gogarty, Irish surgeon, author, poet, and wit. Together the three must have had a kind of Bloomsbury society west in the summertime, when all of Dublin's greatest literary minds decamped to their manor homes. Today Dunguaire's greatest appeal is the exquisite view from its battlements of the nearby Burren and Galway Bay. Admission is €5.50 ($8.80) for adults, €2.95 ($4.70) for seniors and students, €3.15 ($5.05) for children, and €13 ($21) for families. It's open daily from mid-April through September 9:30am to 5:30pm (last admission 1 hr. before closing). There are **medieval banquets** here on summer evenings (p. 403). Dunguaire is on the N67 just east of Kinvara.

Where to Dine

Moran's Oyster Cottage ★★ SEAFOOD   Presidents, prime ministers, movie stars, and locals all find their way here, because the food is legendary. For six generations, the Morans have been catching salmon and shucking oysters and preparing them to perfection. The wild smoked salmon is exquisite—sheer velvet. Willie Moran believes in a small menu, fresh and wild and with nothing in the way. Ambience? It's a thatched cottage with 36 swans and a blue heron outside the front door.

The Weir, Kilcolgan, County Galway. © **091/796113.** www.moransoystercottage.com. Main courses €15–€25 ($24–$40). AE, MC, V. Mon–Sat 10:30am–11:30pm; Sun noon–11:30pm.

Paddy Burke's ★ SEAFOOD   Platters of local oysters and mussels are served throughout the day at this homey tavern, with its lemon color and thatched roof. You can pick your favorite spot to relax in the half-dozen rooms and alcoves with stone walls, open fireplaces, potbellied stoves, and traditional *sugan* chairs (wood chairs with twisted rope seats). In good weather, there is seating in a back garden. Lunch and snack items range from seafood soups and chowders to sandwiches, salads, and omelets. In the evening, you can also order full meals, with choices such as Atlantic plaice and crab with prawn sauce, and honey roast duck with mead sauce. The tavern is on the main road, 16km (10 miles) south of Galway City.

Ennis-Galway rd. (N18), Clarenbridge, County Galway. © **091/796226.** www.paddyburkesgalway.com. Reservations recommended for dinner. Main courses €16–€27 ($26–$43). AE, DC, MC, V. Mon–Sat 10:30am–10:30pm; Sun noon–9:30pm.

14

Out from Galway

For many travelers to Ireland, Galway is the farthest edge of their journey. Part of the reason they draw the line here is that the county looks so otherworldly—with its bleak bogs; wind-swept, heather-clad moors; and its extraordinary light—they think that it must be the end of all that's worth seeing in Ireland (if not the end of the world). It isn't, of course, as County Mayo has picturesque rocky coasts and Donegal a kind of exquisite isolation, but Galway is just far enough from the madding crowds (3-hr. drive from Dublin) without pushing the limits of some people's comfort. If you've come this far, you've seen the land that drew the ancient settlers to Connemara and seduced the early Christian monks with its isolation. In fact, some went even farther—monastic remains have been found on 17 islands off the Galway coast.

The history of this area—the southernmost portion of the region known as Connaught—is as hard as the rocky soil. In the 17th century, after Oliver Cromwell and his armies mercilessly ravaged the rest of the country, he famously said the Irish could go "to hell or Connaught," and ordered Irish landowners to give up their property and live west of the Shannon River. It was a condemnation to destitution. While English landlords divvied up Ireland's most fertile lands, Connaught seemed so barren and uncultivable that it held no interest for them. And many years later, it was here that the Great Famine of 1845 to 1849 took its largest toll. Entire towns in Connemara became ghost towns as tens of thousands of people either starved or emigrated.

These are happier times, though, and there's virtually nothing left to remind you of the gloomy days gone by. These days, this region is bustling and affluent, its villages brightly painted, and property prices are soaring. The land Cromwell thought nobody could farm is gorgeous in photographs and offers excellent hunting and fishing. Given that, Galway and its surrounding counties are booming from a mix of the tourist trade and international investment. Its natural beauty and wild soul make it an unforgettable place to visit.

1 THE GALWAY BAY COAST

Even for the Irish, who have seen it all many times, driving up the spectacular Galway Bay coast is breathtaking, with the Aran Islands in soft focus and the heather-covered foothills of Connemara beside you. Departing Galway, and certainly once you pass Spiddal, you have the sense of passing through a gateway into Ireland's wild west, a land strikingly remote, melancholy, and moody. Count on it taking about 40 minutes from Galway to Rossaveal, and another 40 minutes to Carna, at the northernmost tip of the bay, and be prepared for every traffic sign to be in Gaelic.

GALWAY BAY COAST ESSENTIALS
GETTING THERE & GETTING AROUND The best way to see the sights along the Galway Bay coast is to drive. From Galway City, follow the coast road (R336). From Galway City to Inverin, it's about 32km (20 miles).

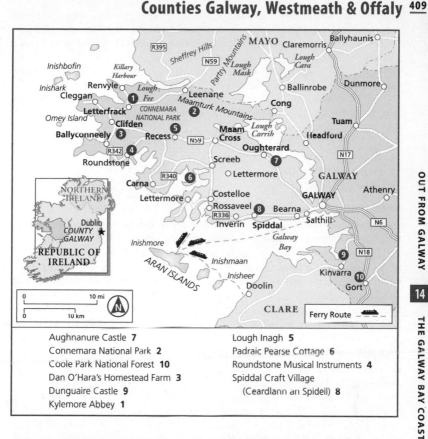

Aughnanure Castle **7**

Connemara National Park **2**

Coole Park National Forest **10**

Dan O'Hara's Homestead Farm **3**

Dunguaire Castle **9**

Kylemore Abbey **1**

Lough Inagh **5**

Padraic Pearse Cottage **6**

Roundstone Musical Instruments **4**

Spiddal Craft Village
  (Ceardlann an Spidéil) **8**

VISITOR INFORMATION   Contact or visit **Ireland West Tourism,** Aras Fáilte, Foster Street, Galway, County Galway (© **091/537700;** www.discoverireland.ie/west). Hours are May, June, and September daily 9am to 5:45pm; July and August daily 9am to 7:45pm; October to April Monday to Friday 9am to 5:45pm, and Saturday 9am to 12:45pm. Seasonal offices, open from late April through September, are at Clifden (© **095/21163**) and Salthill (© **091/520500**).

EXPLORING THE COAST

Head west into Connemara, following signs for the coast road (R336). The road winds its way along the edge of the headland to the busy, unromantic modern beach resort, **Salthill (Bóthar na Trá),** a summer favorite of Irish families, which is somewhat reminiscent of the New Jersey shore in the U.S., or Blackpool in England. It has a boardwalk and a fine beach, plus lots of bars, fast food, amusement rides, and game arcades, which can be good if you've got children looking for an alternative to historic sights. Farther along the scenic road are charming little historic towns including Gaelic-speaking **Spiddal (An Spidéal),** which is also an ideal spot to shop for locally made Aran knit sweaters and other handicrafts.

The road continues as far as **Inverin (Indreabhán),** then turns northward, with signposts for **Rossaveal (Ros an Mhíl).** From Rossaveal, you can make the shortest sea crossing from the Galway mainland to the Aran Islands (see "Side Trips from Galway City" in chapter 13), and on a sunny day, you might want to combine this coastal drive with a trip to the islands.

If you continue on R336, you'll leave the Galway Bay coast and travel past the rocky and remote scenery approaching the center of Connemara. Along the way you'll pass **Ros Muc,** site of the **Padraig Pearse Cottage.** This simple thatched-roof structure served as a retreat for Dublin-based Pearse (1879–1916), who was one of the leaders of Ireland's 1916 Easter Rising. He used his time here to improve his knowledge of the Irish language. Now a national monument, the cottage contains documents, photographs, and other memorabilia. Admission is €1.50 ($2.40) for adults. It's open from mid-June to mid-September daily 9:30am to 5:30pm.

At this point, you can continue north into the heartland of Connemara or retrace your route to Galway.

SHOPPING

Ceardlann an Spidéil/Spiddal Craft Village   Rather than one shop, this is actually a cluster of cottage shops for local craftspeople, and a good place to find unique pottery, woven wool, and jewelry. The art galleries feature hand-carved stone crafts, sculpture, paintings, and posters, and there's a good coffee shop on the premises. For a snack, lunch, or light meal, **Jackie's Bistro,** in a rustic cottage at the Craft Village, serves highly recommended fare. The shops are open Monday to Saturday from 9:30am to 6:30pm and Sunday from 2 to 5:30pm in July and August, and Monday to Saturday from 9:30am to 5:30pm September through June. Coast rd., Spiddal, County Galway. © 091/553041. www.ceardlann.com.

Standún   A fixture on the Connemara coast since 1946, this shop has long been known as a good source for authentic *bainin* sweaters, handcrafted by local women from the Aran Islands and the surrounding Connemara countryside. Along with these chunky white knits, it also offers tweeds, sheepskins, linens, glassware, china, pottery, jewelry, books, and maps. It also has a good cafe with panoramic views of Galway Bay and the Aran Islands. Open from March to December Monday to Saturday from 9:30am to 6:30pm. Coast rd., Spiddal, County Galway. © 091/553108. www.standun.com.

SPORTS & OUTDOOR PURSUITS

FISHING   As you might surmise, this area is prime territory for sea fishing, especially for mackerel, pollock, cod, turbot, and shark. To locate a boat-rental service in the area where you plan to stay, contact the **Western Regional Fisheries Board,** the Weir Lodge, Earl's Island, County Galway (© 091/563118; fax 091/566335; www.wrfb.ie), for recommendations. A fishing license costs around €36 ($58) per day or €50 ($80) for 3 weeks. Rental of rods, reels, and bait is likely to run another €35 to €50 ($56–$80) per day.

Those who prefer trout fishing might want to check out the **Crumlin Lodge Fisheries,** Inverin, County Galway (© 091/593105). This fishery has a lake stocked with sea-reared rainbow trout and allows two fish per person to be taken per day. Prices range from €16 ($26) for fishing from the bank to €50 ($80) for fishing with a boat; *ghillies* (guides) are available for approximately €40 ($64) extra. Fishing starts at 9am daily; reservations must be made at least a day in advance.

SWIMMING   The Silver Strand at Barna and the beach at Spiddal are clean, sandy, and ideal for swimming.

Cloch na Scíth/Kellough Thatched Cottage (Value) The trio of guest rooms in Nancy Hopkins Naughton's centuries-old thatched farmhouse are warm and welcoming, with antique pine furniture, polished wood floors, and patterned quilts. The whole house is open to guests and is full of antiques and keepsakes. Tomas Naughton, Nancy's husband, is both a talented painter and an all-Ireland *sean-nos* (traditional a cappella Gaelic) singer. Nancy bakes a fresh corn cake in the open hearth each day and leaves it out for her guests to have with tea. A small sandy beach is minutes away by foot. In addition, there is an inviting **self-catering thatched stone cottage,** built by Tomas's great-grandfather. It rents for €295 to €560 ($472–$896) per week, depending on the season. It has two bedrooms, a kitchen-dining-living room with a woodstove, a spacious sunroom, and one-and-a-half bathrooms.

15km (9¹/₃ miles) from Galway center, just east of Spiddal, coast rd., Kellough, Spiddal, County Galway. ℂ 091/553364. www.thatchcottage.com. 3 units. €70 ($112) double. Rates include full breakfast. No credit cards. **Amenities:** Nonsmoking rooms. *In room:* No phone.

Connemara Coast Hotel ★ Only 10km (6¹/₄ miles) west of Galway City and with Galway Bay at its back door, this friendly, midsize hotel has a lot going for it. The guest rooms are nicely decorated in neutral colors, but that's not what will lure you here—the big draw is that each room has a picture-window view of the Aran Islands or Clare hills. Some have turf-burning fireplaces and some have private verandas. It's an attractive, laidback seafront hotel that makes a good hub for your journey. There are two restaurants, and the hotel pub, **Sin Sceal Eile** ("That's Another Story"), offers traditional entertainment most nights.

Coast rd., Furbo, County Galway. ℂ 091/592108. Fax 091/592065. www.connemaracoasthotel.com. 112 units. €170–€360 ($272–$576) double. Rates include full breakfast. AE, DC, MC, V. **Amenities:** Restaurant (Continental); bar; Indoor swimming pool; 2 tennis courts; gym; Jacuzzi; steam bath; nonsmoking rooms. *In room:* TV, tea/coffeemaker.

The Twelve Named for the famous Twelve Pins mountain range of Connemara, this old-world roadside inn has revamped itself in recent years into a luxurious, modern, four-star boutique guesthouse. Bedrooms have comfortable king-size or twin beds, and some have fold-out sofa beds for families traveling with children. Beds are covered in fluffy comforters and soft bedspreads; windows have peaceful views. The West Restaurant downstairs is one of the best in the area. Its menu features fresh local seafood and produce; try the marinated salmon carpaccio, or the lobster, crab, and prawn terrine. This is a pet-friendly hotel; just call ahead if you want to bring your dog.

Coast rd., Bearna Village, Barna, County Galway. ℂ 091/597000. Fax 091/597003. www.thetwelvehotel. ie. 48 units. €170–€360 ($272–$576) double. Suites also available. Rates include full breakfast. AE, DC, MC, V. **Amenities:** Restaurant (seafood); bar; room service; nonsmoking rooms. *In room:* TV, DVD player, MP3 dock, minibar, tea/coffeemaker.

(Tips) **Service Charges**

A reminder: Unless otherwise noted, room rates don't include service charges (usually 10%–15% of your bill).

Impressions

I have a total irreverence for anything connected with society except that which makes the roads safer, the beer stronger, the food cheaper, the old men and old women warmer in the winter and happier in the summer.

—Brendan Behan (1923–64)

WHERE TO DINE

Boluisce SEAFOOD This is one of the few restaurants in little Spiddal. In a friendly, homey dining room, locals and visitors fill its seats each night to feast on the freshest possible seafood. Dishes include fresh Galway Bay lobster thermidor, grilled, organic salmon with scallion mashed potatoes, and whole, black sole, cooked on the bone with lemon and butter.

Coast rd., Spiddal, County Galway. © **091/553286.** Reservations recommended. Dinner main courses €12–€25 ($19–$40). AE, MC, V. Daily 12:30–9:30pm.

2 CONNEMARA

If you look for Connemara on road signs, you may be looking forever, because it's not a city or county, but an area or region. Like the Burren in County Clare, the boundaries are a bit hazy, but most agree that Connemara is west of Galway City, starting at Oughterard and continuing toward the Atlantic. You know it when you see it, as it is an area of heartbreaking barrenness and unique beauty, with dark bogs and tall jagged mountains punctuated by curving glassy lakes dotted with green islands.

The desolate landscape is caused, in part, by an absence of trees that were felled and dragged off long ago for building ships, houses, and furniture. Connemara is part of the **Gaeltacht,** or Irish-speaking area, so many signs are in Gaelic only. Traditional music thrives here, as do handicrafts and cottage industries.

It's a varied place—in fact, you could say that there are two Connemaras. South of the Galway-Clifden road is a vast bog-mantled moorland dotted with lakes, and with a low, indented, rocky coastline. North of the Galway-Clifden road, tall quartzite domes and cones form the Maumturks and the Twelve Bens (also called the Twelve Pins), rising toward the breathtaking Killary fiord—the only fiord in the British Isles—near where Mayo takes over from Galway. Oscar Wilde wrote, "Connemara is a savage beauty." Now you can see that for yourself.

CONNEMARA AREA ESSENTIALS

GETTING THERE & GETTING AROUND From Galway City, **Bus Éireann** (© **091/ 562000;** www.buseireann.ie) provides daily service to Clifden and other small towns en route. The best way to get around Connemara is to drive, following N59 from Moycullen and Oughterard. Or you can take a guided tour (see "Sightseeing Tours," below). Clifden is 65km (40 miles) west of Galway City.

VISITOR INFORMATION Contact or visit **Ireland West Tourism,** Aras Fáilte, Foster Street, Galway, County Galway (© **091/537700;** www.discoverireland.ie/west). See "Visitor Information" in section 1 for hours. The **Oughterard Tourist Office,** Main

to 5pm, with extended hours in the summer season. In addition, a **seasonal office,** open
Monday to Saturday 9am to 5pm between March and October, is maintained at Clifden
(© **095/21163**).

EXPLORING THE AREA

The seaside town of **Clifden (An Clochán)** has an enviable location at the edge of the
blue waters of Clifden Bay, where miles of curving, sandy beaches skirt the rugged coastline. It's a small, attractive Victorian town with colorful shop fronts and church steeples
thrusting skyward through a veil of trees. With its plentiful restaurants, shops, hotels, and
pubs, it makes a handy base for exploring the area, so it's quite touristy; if you prefer a
quieter location, you might want to look at one of the many smaller towns and villages
in the area, such as the small fishing port of **Roundstone (Cloch na Rón)** ★ about
24km (15 miles) away, which, while still relatively peaceful, is also equipped with all of
the essentials: pristine beaches, comfortable guesthouses, good restaurants, shops to
explore, and more than its share of natural charm.

From Roundstone, you can head on to the little community of **Letterfrack (Leitir
Fraic)** at the edge of Connemara National Park, close to the glorious Gothic Kylemore
Abbey. The tiny village, founded by Quakers, has a handful of pubs and B&Bs in a
glorious natural setting. It's near the bright white sands of **Glassillaun Beach** and **Let-
tergesh,** where horses raced across the sand in the film *The Quiet Man.*

The Top Attractions

Aughnanure Castle ★ Standing on an outcrop of rock surrounded by forest and
pasture, this sturdy fortress is a well-preserved Irish tower castle, with an unusual double
bawn (a fortified enclosure) and a still-complete watchtower that you can climb. It was
built around A.D. 1500 as a stronghold of the "Fighting" O'Flaherty clan, who dominated the region and terrified its neighbors in its day. One interesting design element:
The castle's fireplaces are so big that you could fit a double bed in them.

32km (20 miles) west of Galway City, signposted off N59, Clifden rd., Oughterard, County Galway.
© **091/552214.** Admission €3.20 ($5.10) adults, €2.20 ($3.50) seniors, €1.50 ($2.40) students and chil-
dren. Mid-June to mid-Sept daily 9:30am–6:30pm.

Connemara National Park ★★★ (Kids) This lovely national park spreads over
2,000 hectares (4,940 acres) of mountains, bogs, and grasslands. There's an excellent
visitor center just south of the crossroads in Letterfrack, which can give you tips and
general information on the park's landscape, population of wild things, and scenic walking trails. It's worth taking one of these up some of the Twelve Bens, or through the
peaceful Gleann Mór (Big Glen), with its River Polladirk. The center also offers sustenance in the form of tea, sandwiches, and freshly baked goods. During July and August,
Tuesday and Thursday are "nature days" for children; on Monday, Wednesday, and Fri-

---

(Fun Facts **What's in a Name?**

Connemara is the Anglicization of *Conmaicne mara,* the "descendants of Conmac
who live by the sea."

day, there are guided walks for the whole family. Call the center for information on these and other special programs.

Clifden-Westport rd. (N59), Letterfrack, County Galway. ✆ **095/41054.** Park open year-round; visitor center Apr–May and Sept to mid-Oct daily 10am–5:30pm, June daily 10am–6:30pm, July–Aug daily 9:30am–6:30pm.

Dan O'Hara's Homestead Farm   If you're intrigued by the unique Connemara landscape and want more insight into how Connemara farmers find soil to till on this rocky land, you may want to head to this small farm. It is set up under prefamine conditions and reflects daily life in the 1840s, with local people using traditional tilling and farming methods. There are also some cleverly designed reconstructions of ancient dwellings and fortifications that give real insight into how things looked then. And, as ever in Ireland, hidden away on the land is an authentic megalithic tomb and a dolmen. For those who like the peace and quiet here too much to tear themselves away, there are a farmhouse B&B and some self-catering cottages.

About 6.5km (4 miles) east of Clifden off N59, Lettershea, Clifden, County Galway. ✆ **095/21246.** Admission €8 ($13) adults, €7 ($11) seniors and students, €4.50 ($7.20) children, €20 ($32) families. Apr–Oct daily 10am–6pm.

Kylemore Abbey ★★   This extraordinary Gothic abbey sits at the base of a heavily wooded hill overlooking the mirrorlike waters of Kylemore Lake. The exterior of the main building—a vast, crenelated 19th-century house—is a splendid example of neo-Gothic architecture. The inside is not so impressive—in 1920, its owners donated it to the Benedictine nuns, and the sisters have run a convent boarding school here ever since, using the building as a utilitarian structure. Only the grounds and a tiny section of the house are open to the public, but the grounds are attraction enough. The highlight is the recently restored Gothic chapel, an exquisite cathedral in miniature with a plain, somber cemetery to one side; a lavish Victorian walled garden; and the breathtaking views of it all from across the lake. The complex includes a decent **restaurant** that serves produce grown on the nuns' farm, as well as tea and good scones, a shop with a working pottery studio, and a visitor center. The abbey is most atmospheric when the bells are rung for midday office or for vespers at 6pm.

Kylemore, County Galway. ✆ **095/41146.** www.kylemoreabbey.com. Admission €12 ($19) adults, €9 ($14) seniors and students. Abbey year-round daily 9am–5:30pm; garden Easter–Sept daily 10:30am–4:30pm.

Ⓕ**un Facts**   **The Bogs**

Connemara's **bog lands** began forming 2,500 years ago. During the Iron Age, the Celts preserved butter in the bog. Today, with one-third of Connemara classified as bog, the turf (or peat) that's cut from the bog remains an important source of fuel. Cutting and drying turf is an integral part of the rhythm of the seasons in Connemara. Cutting requires a special tool, a spade called a *slane,* which slices the turf into bricks about 46 centimeters (18 in.) long. The bricks are first spread out flat to dry, and then stacked in pyramids for further drying. If you spend enough time in Ireland, you'll get used to the strong, smoky smell of burning turf. You can always tell when turf is burning in a home's fireplace—the smoke coming out of the chimney is blue and sweet scented.

> ### Ⓜ Moments   An Excursion to Inishbofin
>
> The island of Inishbofin is a small emerald-green gem that lies 11km (6¾ miles) off the northwest coast of Connemara and offers seclusion and spectacular beauty, provided the skies are clear enough to deliver the unforgettable views of and from its shores. Once the domain of monks, then the lair of pirate queen Grace O'Malley, later Cromwell's infamous priest prison, and currently home to 180 year-round residents, Inishbofin is well worth a day's expedition or even a 2-day stay for those looking for peace and quiet.
>
> Numerous ferries to the island operate from the port of Cleggan (13km/8 miles northwest of Clifden off N59) daily April through October. **Inishbofin Island Tours,** Kings of Cleggan, Cleggan, County Galway (⌀ **095/45819**), operates the largest, newest, and fastest boat, the *Island Discovery*. Tickets cost €16 ($26) per adult and €9 ($14) per child, round-trip, and are available at the company office in Cleggan. ***Note:*** Reservations are *essential*.

Sightseeing Tours

Several companies offer sightseeing tours of Connemara from Galway or Clifden.

Bus Éireann   Departing from the bus station in Galway, this 8-hour tour of Connemara takes in Maam Cross, Recess, Roundstone, and Clifden, as well as Kylemore Abbey, Leenane, and Oughterard. It's available in the summertime only.

Ceannt Station, Galway, County Galway. ⌀ **091/562000.** www.buseireann.ie. €23 ($37) adults; €16 ($26) seniors and students; €12 ($19) children. June–Aug Sun–Fri 10am.

Connemara Walking Centre   This company's expert local guides lead walking tours of Connemara, with an emphasis on history and archaeology, as well as scenery. The walks cover different sections—from the Renvyle Peninsula and Roundstone Bog to the Kylemore Valley, the Maumturk Mountains, and Sky Road. Weeklong walking trips are based at Dun Gibbons, a center dedicated to exploring Connemara's countryside. All walks assemble at Island House in Clifden and include bus transportation to the walking site. Advance reservations are required.

The Island House, Market St., Clifden, County Galway. ⌀ **095/21379.** Tours from €20 ($32). Tours offered Mar–Oct; call for times and a detailed price list.

Corrib Cruises   Departing from the pier at Oughterard, this company's sightseeing boat cruises across Lough Corrib, Ireland's largest lake, stopping at some of its 365 islands. One visits Inchagoill Island, with its 12th-century monastery that was inhabited until the 1940s. Another trip visits the island only, and the other goes to the island and to Cong in County Mayo, site of **Ashford Castle** (p. 439) and the area where the movie *The Quiet Man* was filmed. The Cong-Oughterard round-trip cruise can start at either place. In fact, there are currently four different day cruises on offer, as well as an evening "Irish Hour" (happy hour) cruise.

Oughterard, County Galway. ⌀ **092/46029** or 46292. www.corribcruises.com. 90-min round-trip cruises to island start at €12 ($19) adults, €6 ($9.60) children, €25 ($40) families. Cruises run May–Sept daily. Be sure to book ahead and to confirm times.

Avoca Handweavers   The Connemara branch of the famous Wicklow weavers is in a lovely, isolated location 10km (6¼ miles) north of Clifden on an inlet of the bay, surrounded by colorful flower gardens. Inside are the Irish chain's trademark colorful woven clothes and blankets, as well as locally made marble souvenirs, pottery, jewelry, and music. There's an excellent cafe as well, which makes a good place for lunch. Open April through October daily from 9:30am until at least 6pm. Clifden-Leenane rd. (N59), Dooneen Haven, Letterfrack, County Galway. ℂ 095/41058.

Celtic Shop & Tara Jewelry   This is a good place to pick up souvenirs, including gold and silver Celtic jewelry, hand-woven Irish rugs, knitwear, ceramics, and crystal, as well as a good selection of Irish books. Open daily 9am to 6pm from September through June, and from 9am to 9pm in July and August. Main St., Clifden, County Galway. ℂ 095/21064.

Connemara Marble Visitor Centre   Connemara's unique green marble is quarried, cut, shaped, and polished here. Estimated by geologists to be about 500 million years old, the marble ranges from lime green to dark emerald. On weekdays you'll see craftspeople at work hand-fashioning jewelry, paperweights, ashtrays, Celtic crosses, and other giftware. Open daily from 9am to 5:30pm. 13km (8 miles) west of Galway City on Galway-Clifden rd. (N59), Moycullen, County Galway. ℂ 091/555102.

Fuchsia Craft   Wedged in the center of Oughterard's main thoroughfare, this small shop sells crafts produced throughout Ireland, including handmade fishing flies, products made from pressed Irish peat, bronze sculptures, and recycled art cards of Connemara scenes, as well as the usual pottery, crystal, jewelry, knitwear, and much more. Open daily 9am to 10pm from June through September; daily 9am to 7pm in April, May, and October; and Monday to Saturday 9am to 6pm from November through March. The Square, Oughterard, County Galway. ℂ 091/552644.

Millars Connemara Tweed Ltd.   This is the home of the colorful Connemara tweeds. Although most people just buy skeins of wool or hand-woven materials—plus ready-made ties, hats, caps, scarves, blankets, and bedspreads—there are also rush baskets, Aran *crios* belts, plus an art gallery of regional paintings. Open Monday to Saturday from 9am to 6pm, with extended summer hours. Main St., Clifden, County Galway. ℂ 095/21038.

O'Dalaigh Jeweller   This family-run jewelry shop has handmade, one-of-a-kind pieces with a sophisticated Celtic theme. Along with affordable silver pieces, there is

---

Ⓕun Facts   Connemara Pony

The **donkey** is a trademark of this region, and the long-eared creatures still work on many farms. But more famous is the sturdy little horse known as the **Connemara pony,** the only horse breed native to Ireland (although it's had an infusion of Spanish blood over the centuries). Often raised in tiny fields with limestone pastures, these animals have great stamina and are invaluable for farming and pulling equipment. The Connemara pony is also noted for its gentle temperament, which makes it ideal for children's riding.

some gorgeous gold jewelry, some based on designs found carved on stones at Newgrange, and some truly unique engagement and wedding rings. Main St., Clifden, County Galway. © 095/22119. www.celticimpressions.com.

Síla Mag Aoide Designs (Sheila Magee)   Although inspired by ancient Celtic images and designs, Sheila Magee's work is original and contemporary. In addition to a wide selection of her handmade silver jewelry, her shop offers a range of works, including watercolor prints and art cards of Connemara scenes, baskets, and handmade frames. Open daily from 9am to 9pm May to September, with shorter off-season hours. The Monastery, Michael Killeen Park, Roundstone, County Galway. © 095/35912. www.thehouseof magaoide.com.

SPORTS & OUTDOOR PURSUITS

Endlessly popular with college-aged backpackers, school groups, and families with kids, the **Delphi Adventure Company,** Leenane, County Galway (© 095/42208; www. delphiadventureholidays.ie), is all about activity. Whether it's watersports or mountaineering, pony trekking, tennis, or archery, people here are constantly on the go. You don't have to stay here to take advantage of the activities, but if you choose to, you'll be assigned a bright, simply furnished single or dorm-style room. Weekend prices for room, full board, and activities begin at €200 ($320) for an adult. The nonresidential activities fee for 1 full day is €50 ($80).

BICYCLING   Bicycles can be rented year-round from **Mannion Cycles,** Bridge Street, Clifden, County Galway (© 095/21160). The rate for a regular touring bike in high season starts at around €10 ($16) per day. Mountain bikes can be hired from May through October at the **Little Killary Adventure Company,** Leenane, County Galway (© 095/43411; www.killary.com). They go for €20 ($32) per day, and road bikes for €14 ($22) per day. If you'd like to plan a holiday around cycling in this part of the country, **Irish Cycling Tours** (© 095/42302; www.irishcyclingtours.com) offers guided and self-guided bike tours.

DIVING   You can rent equipment and receive instruction at **Scubadive West,** Renvyle, County Galway (© 095/43922; fax 095/43923; www.scubadivewest.com).

FISHING   Lough Corrib is renowned for brown-trout and salmon fishing. Brown-trout fishing is usually good from the middle of February, and salmon is best from the end of May. The mayfly fishing begins around the middle of May and continues for up to 3 weeks.

Angling on Lough Corrib is free, but a state license is required for salmon. For expert advice and rental equipment, contact the **Cloonnabinnia Angling Centre,** Moycullen, County Galway (© 091/555555).

For salmon and sea trout, the **Ballynahinch Castle Fishery** at Ballynahinch, Recess, County Galway (© 095/31006), is an angler's paradise. State fishing licenses, tackle hire and sales, maps, and advice are available at the hotel.

At **Portarra Lodge,** Tullykyne, Moycullen, County Galway (© 091/555-051; www. portarralodge.com), packages are available, including B&B accommodations in a modern guesthouse on the shores of Lough Corrib, dinners, and boats and tackle. Michael Canney is an avid angler and a great guide to this part of Galway. A double room with full breakfast is €70 ($112) per night. Weekly packages that include half-board, boat, and *ghillie* are also available.

Lough Inagh & the Walk to Maum Ean Oratory

Lough Inagh, nestled between the Maumturk and the Twelve Bens mountains in the heart of Connemara, is in a spectacularly beautiful valley, where mountain slopes rise precipitously from the valley floor and small streams cascade into the lake in a series of sparkling waterfalls. The R344 cuts through the valley, linking Recess to the south and Kylemore Lake to the north.

The **Western Way,** a walking route that traverses the high country of Galway and Mayo, follows a quiet country road above the R344 through the Lough Inagh Valley. To reach the beginning of the walk, drive north on the R344, turning right on a side road—the sign for Maum Ean—about 200m (656 ft.) before the Lough Inagh Lodge Hotel. Continue on this side road for about 6km (3³/₄ miles) to a large gravel parking lot on the left. Park here, and follow the well-worn trail 2km (1.25 miles) to the top of the pass, through glorious mountain scenery.

This short (4km/2.5-mile) walk follows the Western Way to the top of a mountain pass that has long been associated with St. Patrick and is now the site of a small oratory, a hollow in the rock known as **Patrick's Bed,** a life-size statue of the saint, and a series of cairns marking the Stations of the Cross. Together, these monuments make a striking ensemble, strangely eerie when the mists descend and conceal the far slopes in their shifting haze. On a clear day, there are great views, with the Atlantic Ocean and Bertraghboy Bay to the southwest and another range of mountains to the northeast. The round-trip walking time is about 1 hour.

GOLF   Visitors are welcome at the 18-hole, par-72 championship seaside course of the **Connemara Golf Club,** Ballyconneely, Clifden, County Galway (© 095/23502; www.connemaragolflinks.com), nestled in the heart of Connemara and overlooking the Atlantic. Greens fees from May to September are €50 ($80) weekdays, €55 ($88) weekends; from October to April, they're €40 ($64) weekdays, €45 ($72) weekends.

The **Oughterard Golf Club,** Oughterard, County Galway (© 091/552131; www.oughterardgolfclub.com), is an 18-hole, par-70 inland course. Greens fees are €35 ($56).

HORSEBACK RIDING   See the beaches of Connemara from horseback on a trek with the **Cleggan Riding Centre,** Clegan, County Galway (© 095/44746; www.clegganriding centre.com). The center offers beach and mountain treks, and the most popular is a 3-hour ride to Omey Island at low tide. Prices start at €50 ($80). Or explore with **Connemara and Coast Trails,** Loughrea, County Galway (© 091/841216; www.connemara-trails.com). Rides are for experienced and beginning riders alike. Riding starts at €20 ($32) per person per hour.

WALKING   If you feel like stretching your legs, head to the town of **Leenane,** which is the start of any number of exhilarating walks. One of the best takes you to the picturesque Aasleagh Waterfall (Eas Liath) east of the Killary Harbor. Another walk around that harbor, Ireland's only fiord, follows the Green Road. It was once the primary route from the Rinvyle Peninsula to Leenane, and is now largely a sheep track. The path passes a ghost town (an abandoned prefamine village) on the far side of the harbor, where the fields rise at a devilishly steep slope from the ruined cottages clustered at the water's edge. There are excellent walking trails in the **Connemara National Park,** some of which lead up the sides of the Twelve Bens. You can get maps at the park's visitor center.

WATERSPORTS   Hobie Cat sailing and sailboarding can be arranged at the **Little Killary Adventure Company,** Leenane, County Galway (© 095/43411; www.killary.com). Rates start at around €60 ($96) per day (two sessions), which entitles you to use the watersports equipment and participate in all the center's supervised sporting activities, including kayaking, water-skiing, hill and coastal walking, rock climbing, archery, and more.

WHERE TO STAY
Expensive
Cashel House Hotel ★   About 20 minutes outside Clifden in the tiny seaside town of Cashel, this lovely, old-fashioned hotel is a virtual haven of peace. The same family has owned and run the place for years, and the matriarch of the clan is personally responsible for the magical gardens that surround the low, wide-windowed building. Rooms are large, with separate seating areas and picture windows. The king-size beds are firm, and the bathrooms modern. The floral motif is carried from the gardens through to the wallpaper, curtains, and bedding, but it's all tastefully done. Dinner in the big dining room is excellent Continental cuisine, but you will pay (€50/$80 per person) for the privilege of trying it (beware if staff members offer you anything—tea, for example—as nothing comes free and it will all appear on your bill in the end). There's plenty to keep you busy here—a private beach, tennis courts, fishing areas, stables with riding lessons and trekking, and signposted walking paths, but it's still a quiet, mature place for quiet, mature people.

Cashel Bay, Cashel, County Galway. © **800/323-5463** or 800/735-2478 in the U.S., or 095/31001. Fax 095/31077. www.cashel-house-hotel.com. 32 units. €170–€330 ($272–$528) double. Rates include full breakfast. AE, DC, MC, V. Closed Jan. **Amenities:** Restaurant (Continental); bar; tennis court; nonsmoking rooms; library; private beach. *In room:* TV, hair dryer.

Expensive
Abbeyglen Castle ★★   On a hilltop overlooking Clifden and the bay, this is a splendidly informal Irish castle hotel—it's the kind of place where a parrot in reception confuses staff by making the sound of the telephone ringing, and the piano bar brings guests together in a house party atmosphere. The grand public areas have candelabra chandeliers, arched windows, and vintage settees. Guest rooms are large and comfortable, with beautiful fabrics. The personable staff can arrange fishing trips, packed lunches, and local activities. Dinner is part of the fun here (€45/$72 per person) and the food is excellent, with virtually all produce sourced locally.

Sky Rd., Clifden, County Galway. © **800/447-7462** in the U.S., or 095/21201. Fax 095/21797. www.abbey glen.ie. 45 units. €200–€300 ($320–$480) double. Rates include full breakfast. AE, MC, V. Closed early Jan to Feb. **Amenities:** Restaurant (Continental); bar; outdoor swimming pool; tennis court; Jacuzzi; sauna; miniature golf; solarium. *In room:* TV.

Ballynahinch Castle ★★   Set on an enchanting 140-hectare (346-acre) estate at the base of Ben Lettery, one of the Twelve Bens mountains, this turreted, gabled manor house overlooks the Owenmore River. Dating from the 16th century, it has served over the years as a base for the "Fighting" O'Flaherty chieftains and the sea pirate Grace O'Malley. The ambience can be best described as country-house casual; the place feels luxurious, yet there's little stuffiness. The guest rooms are individually decorated, and many have fireplaces and four-poster beds (all with orthopedic mattresses). This is a sportsman's lodge, renowned for top-notch sea trout and salmon fishing. Each evening, the day's catch is weighed in and recorded at the Fishermen's Bar, usually creating a cause for celebration.

Recess, County Galway. 📞 **095/31006.** Fax 095/31085. www.ballynahinch-castle.com. 40 units. €190–€400 ($304–$640) double. Suites also available. Rates include full breakfast. AE, DC, MC, V. Closed Feb. **Amenities:** Restaurant (Continental); bar; tennis courts; limited room service; babysitting; library; private fishing. *In room:* TV, hair dryer.

Lough Inagh Lodge ★★   Standing alone on the shore of the tranquil Lough Inagh, this handsome fishing-and-sporting lodge has an enviable location. Without another building in sight, you can soak up the tranquillity, with only the splashing of fish in the lake to break the silence. Inside, the public rooms strike a note of warm hospitality, with open log fires in the library and oak-paneled bar. Spacious guest rooms have a similarly traditional look, with period furnishings; most have separate dressing rooms. Request a room in the front of the house for views of the lake and the Twelve Bens.

Recess, County Galway. 📞 **800/323-5463** or 800/735-2478 in the U.S., or 095/34706. Fax 095/34708. www.loughinaghlodgehotel.ie. 12 units. €180–€220 ($288–$352) double. Rates include service charge and full breakfast. AE, MC, V. Closed Jan–Feb. **Amenities:** Restaurant (Continental); bar; library. *In room:* TV, hair dryer.

Renvyle House ★★   This grand old house sits on the wild Atlantic shoreline. It was purchased in 1917 by Oliver St. John Gogarty, the famed Irish poet, wit, surgeon, and politician, who fondly called this secluded seascape and mountain setting "the world's end." That's putting it mildly: It really is off the beaten track, about 10 minutes' drive from the Connemara National Park—not ideal for a quick overnight, but perfect for a stay of a few days or longer. Many have found it worth the trek. W. B. Yeats honeymooned here, and Churchill was a frequent guest. Today it retains a turn-of-the-20th-century ambience, particularly in its public areas. Guest rooms vary in size and decor, from grand rooms with balconies to cozy attic rooms with dormer windows. Along with sporting amenities, it hosts event weekends, including murder-mystery weekends, fly-fishing clinics, and painting weekends.

> Ⓕun Facts   **Aran Sweaters**
>
> The distinctive chunky creamy Irish "fisherman's sweaters" known as **Aran knit sweaters** originated in this region. Using the oat-colored wool from the native sheep, the semi-waterproof sweaters were first knit by the women of the nearby Aran Islands for their husbands and sons to wear while out at sea. Each family had a different stitch or pattern. Years ago, the patterns were not only a matter of aesthetics; they served as the chief way to identify men who had drowned in the treacherous waters off the coast. Today these sweaters are hand-knit in the homes of Connemara and the nearby Aran Islands, then sold in the many craft shops throughout the region.

Renvyle, County Galway. ☎ **095/43511.** Fax 095/43515. www.renvyle.com. 65 units. €100–€300 ($160–$480) double. Rates include full Irish breakfast. AE, DC, MC, V. Closed Jan–Feb 15. **Amenities:** Restaurant (Continental); bar; outdoor swimming pool; 9-hole golf course; 2 tennis courts; boating; horseback riding. *In room:* TV.

Zetland Country House Hotel ★   This fine fishing lodge in Cashel, about 20 minutes' drive from Clifden, is another good option for anglers. The unusual building was constructed in 1850 as a sporting lodge for a wealthy family. The guest rooms, many of which look out onto the bay, are lavishly decorated with antique and reproduction furniture and neutral fabrics. The dining room is known for its inventive touch with seafood and lamb dishes, and its vegetables and fruit come from the inn's kitchen garden. The Zetland owns the Gowla Fishery, a private sea-trout fishery with 14 lakes and 6.5km (4 miles) of river, so if you don't catch anything here, you'll have some explaining to do.

Cashel Bay, Cashel, County Galway. ☎ **800/448-8355** in the U.S., or 095/31111. Fax 095/31117. www. zetland.com. 19 units. €190–€290 ($304–$464) double. Rates include full breakfast. AE, MC, V. Closed Nov–Mar. **Amenities:** Tennis court; billiards room; croquet. *In room:* TV, hair dryer.

Moderate

Connemara Gateway   Just outside the village of Oughterard, this contemporary two-story inn sits near the upper shores of Lough Corrib and across the road from an 18-hole golf course. Beyond its rambling modern exterior, a cheery down-to-earth lobby features lots of plants and homey bric-a-brac. Guest rooms have a smart look, with local tweed fabrics and hangings, oak dressers and headboards, and scenes of Connemara. A seemingly endless array of activities can be arranged at the touch of a button—from organized tours to pony treks to fishing trips.

Galway-Clifden rd. (N59), Oughterard, County Galway. ☎ **091/552328.** Fax 091/552332. www.connemara gateway.com. 62 units. €110–€190 ($176–$304) double. Rates include full breakfast. AE, DC, MC, V. **Amenities:** Restaurant (international); bar; indoor swimming pool; tennis court; sauna; nonsmoking rooms; croquet; solarium; walking trails. *In room:* TV, tea/coffeemaker.

Delphi Lodge ★★ (Finds)   A vast country house dwarfed by the mountains that surround it, Delphi Lodge was built in the early 19th century as a sportsman's hideaway, and it was purchased and restored for the same purpose by the current owners in the 1980s. It forms part of an exquisite landscape of crystal lakes and trickling rivers, hardwood forests, and mountain slopes. The rooms are spacious and a bit masculine, furnished with an informally elegant touch, all with peaceful lake and mountain views. Guests are divided evenly between those here for the fishing and those here for the relaxation. Dinners (€50/$80 per person) here are excellent, with an emphasis on the catch of the day, and eaten together at the elegant, long dining table. The library and lounge are warmed by wood-burning fireplaces, there's an honor bar where you make your own cocktails in the evening, and the staff is warm and friendly. Owner Peter Mantle can supply you with everything you need to fish—permits, licenses, and equipment rental. *Note:* Rooms do not have locks, but the staff keeps a close eye on who comes in and out of the building. And all cancellations incur an administration fee of €30 ($48).

The Delphi Estate and Fishery, Leenane, County Galway. ☎ **095/42222.** Fax 095/42296. www.delphi lodge.ie. 12 units, 5 cottages. €200 ($320) double. Rates include full Irish breakfast. 2- and 3-bedroom self-catering cottages €800–€1,200 ($1,280–$1,920) per week. AE, MC, V. Closed Christmas and New Year's holidays. **Amenities:** Restaurant (guests only); sitting room; fishing trips; honor bar; private lake. *In room:* TV.

Dolphin Beach House ★★   This is a stylish, restful place to base yourself about 19km (12 miles) from Clifden. The 19th-century house has been beautifully restored, and the spacious bedrooms have soaring ceilings, heated floors, antique furnishings, pristine bed linens, and spellbinding views. It all combines for a feeling of homespun luxury, with the beach just a stone's throw away. Meals are fashioned mainly from ingredients produced on the estate; you can even collect your own eggs for breakfast on a walk down to the beach. Dinner is available for €40 ($64).

Lower Sky Rd., Clifden, County Galway. ⓒ **095/21204.** Fax 095/22935. www.connemara.net/dolphin beachhouse. 8 units. €130–€180 ($208–$288) double. Rates include full breakfast. MC, V. Closed Nov–Feb. **Amenities:** Restaurant (Continental). *In room:* TV.

Rock Glen Country House Hotel   This restored 18th-century hunting lodge sits amid pleasant gardens a couple of miles south of Clifden. The building is set well back from the road, with rugged views of Ardbear Bay and the Atlantic Ocean. It's a restful spot, with sunny rooms and public areas, but the decor is a bit dated, especially given the price charged. Most rooms, and the restaurant, face the sea.

Ballyconneely rd., Clifden, County Galway. ⓒ **095/21035.** Fax 095/21737. 27 units. €150–€190 ($240–$304) double. Rates include service charge and full breakfast. AE, DC, MC, V. Closed Nov to mid-Mar. **Amenities:** Restaurant (Continental); tennis court; fishing privileges; putting green. *In room:* TV, radio, hair dryer, garment press.

Inexpensive

Doonmore Hotel (Kids)   This seasoned waterfront hotel in a prime location on Inishbofin has stunning views of the sea and of nearby Inishshark and High Island. Small boats dot the bay, and there is a seal colony just beyond the hotel's front doors. The rooms are basic, but the wide range of options is handy for families, as there are plenty of spacious family units with children's bunk beds. The unpretentious rooms in the modern wing are clean, full of light, and furnished with simple pine furniture. The older rooms in the original hotel building are worn but comfortable. The hotel is a short walk from the ferry, and the owners can arrange all you need for sea angling and scuba diving.

Inishbofin Island, County Galway. ⓒ/fax **095/45804.** www.doonmorehotel.com. 25 units. €90–€120 ($144–$192) double. Rates include full breakfast. AE, MC, V. Closed Nov–Mar. **Amenities:** Restaurant (Continental); bar; sitting room. *In room:* TV, tea/coffeemaker.

Errisbeg Lodge ★   Conveniently proximate to Roundstone, yet blessedly ensconced between mountainside and sea, Errisbeg Lodge is a place where you may plan to spend a night and wind up lingering for days. Jackie and Shirley King's family land starts high on Errisbeg Mountain and slopes down to the sea, forming a haven for rare species of wildflowers and birds, while the Atlantic stretches out beyond glorious sandy beaches. Guest rooms are rustic and serenely spare, with stucco walls, light-pine furniture, and pastel floral comforters, with either mountain or ocean views. It's all about tranquillity here and warm, gracious hospitality.

Just over 1.6km (1 mile) outside of Roundstone on Clifden rd., Roundstone, County Galway. ⓒ/fax **095/35807.** www.errisbeglodge.com. 5 units. €70–€80 ($112–$128) double. Rates include full breakfast. No credit cards. Closed Dec–Jan. **Amenities:** Nonsmoking rooms.

Glen Valley House and Stables   At the base of a remote glaciated valley, this award-winning B&B redefines "secluded." The entrance drive follows the base of the valley for over 1.6km (1 mile) before you arrive at the house, which has sweeping views across to the far line of hills. Rooms are simply but pleasantly decorated, and the house is in a serene, restful setting. The spectacular Western Way walking trail passes near the house and follows the hills along Killary Harbour, with unforgettable views of the harbor—there's no better place to watch the sun set.

Signposted 5.6km (3½ miles) west of Leenane on the Clifden rd., Glencroff, Leenane, County Galway. ⓒ 095/42269. Fax 095/42365. www.glenvalleyhouse.com. 4 units, 2 with private bathroom. €76 ($122) double with private bathroom; €72 ($115) double with shared bathroom. MC, V. Closed Nov–Feb. **Amenities:** Sitting room. *In room:* Tea/coffeemaker.

WHERE TO DINE
Moderate
High Moors ★ (Finds) MODERN CONTINENTAL   Just outside of Clifden, a narrow country road leads to this modern bungalow-style restaurant, high on a hill with panoramic views of the Atlantic and the wild countryside. A homey ambience prevails, and the food and menu are simple, based on whatever is fresh at the markets. The dishes include such classics as breast of chicken with basil and tomato, filet of pork with three spices, and roast leg of Connemara lamb with red currant and rosemary. Try to book a table for sunset—the views are incredible.

Off the Ballyconneely rd., Dooneen, Clifden, County Galway. ⓒ **095/21342.** Reservations recommended. Main courses €14–€20 ($22–$32). AE, MC, V. Wed–Sun 6:30–10pm. Closed Nov–Easter.

O'Dowd's Seafood Restaurant SEAFOOD   This homey, traditional restaurant overlooking the harbor has been serving up meals since 1840 and delivers perhaps the best seafood in Roundstone at near-budget prices. The decor is rustic, but nobody minds, as everyone is here for the food: seafood chowder, crab claws in garlic butter, fresh oysters, steamed mussels, lobster served in the shell, and piled-high fishermen's platters.

Roundstone Harbour, Connemara, County Galway. ⓒ **095/35809.** www.odowdsrestaurant.com. Reservations recommended. Main courses €8–€20 ($13–$32). AE, DC, MC, V. Apr–Sept daily noon–10pm; Oct–Mar daily noon–3pm and 6–9pm.

O'Grady's SEAFOOD   Since the 1960s, this restaurant has been drawing seekers of great seafood to Clifden. The menu features all that is freshest from the sea, with choices such as Clifden lobster with lemon or garlic butter, and filet of Cleggan brill. For non–fish eaters, there are usually excellent beef and lamb dishes on the menu.

Market St., Clifden, County Galway. ⓒ **095/21450.** Reservations recommended for dinner. Dinner main courses €15–€25 ($24–$40). AE, MC, V. Apr–Oct Mon–Sat 12:30–2:30pm and 6:30–10pm.

Station House Restaurant ★ MODERN CONTINENTAL   Locals flock to this restaurant, hidden away in the courtyard at the rear of the Clifden Station House Hotel. The draw is the imaginative cooking that manages to infuse even the simplest dish with zest and originality. The chef loves to chargrill and smoke, which heightens the taste of the rich flavors he prefers in dishes like the blackened turbot, served with smoked oysters and grilled mushrooms. Desserts are delectable, too.

At the rear of the Station House Hotel, on the N59, Clifden, Connemara, County Galway. ⓒ **095/22946.** Reservations recommended. Main courses €18–€26 ($29–$42). AE, MC, V. Wed–Sun 6:30–9:30pm. Closed Oct–Apr.

Inexpensive
Two Dog Café MEDITERRANEAN   This bright, smoke-free cafe is a great place to relax and enjoy homemade soups, fresh sandwiches (on baguettes, tortillas, and ciabatta),

salads, pastries, tea, and Italian coffee. The baguette with goat's cheese and grilled red peppers is particularly enticing. Wine is served by the glass or bottle.

There is also an Internet cafe on the second floor. You pay €2 ($2.60) for the first 15 minutes, €.65 ($1.05) for each additional 5 minutes, or €8 ($13) per hour, with discounts for students.

Church St., Clifden, Connemara, County Galway. (℃ **095/22186.** www.twodogcafe.ie. All items €3–€7 ($4.80–$11). MC, V. June–Sept daily 9:30am–10pm; Oct–May Tues–Sun 10:30am–6:30pm.

---

3 EASTERN GALWAY, WESTMEATH & OFFALY

Birr: 24km (15 miles) E of Portumna. Athlone: 97km (60 miles) E of Galway

Eastern Galway segues smoothly into Offaly and Westmeath, and the rugged countryside becomes a bit softer and greener as you head inland. This is farming country, and pastures stretch as far as the eye can see, punctuated by historic sites and small farming communities. The early Christian settlement of **Clonmacnois (Cluain Mhic Nóis)** occupies a beautiful stretch of land by the river, with its stone chapels and mysterious round towers. Farther along, you might want to stop by the town of **Birr (Biorra),** known for its magnificent and historic gardens, and **Banagher (Beannchar na Sionna),** a sleepy river town with a picturesque harbor. Later, the river winds and curls its way to **Athlone (Baile Átha Luain),** a vibrant, colorful university town where the buildings are all brightly painted, and there's plenty to do and see. It also has excellent restaurants, coffee shops, historic pubs, and a popular marina for mooring and hiring boats.

AREA ESSENTIALS

GETTING THERE & GETTING AROUND The best way to get here is by car. Although there's some public transportation, you're still best off with a car in order to see the smaller towns and remote sites. Major roads that lead to this area are the main Galway-Dublin road (N6) from points east and west, N62 from the south, and N55 and N61 from the north. You can also boat through the region along the Shannon River, which cuts a swath through it.

VISITOR INFORMATION Information on this area can be obtained from the **Ireland West Tourism Office,** Foster Street, Galway (℃ **091/537700;** www.discoverireland.ie/west). Hours are May, June, and September daily 9am to 5:45pm; July and August daily 9am to 7:45pm; and October to April Monday to Friday 9am to 5:45pm, Saturday 9am to 12:45pm. The **East Coast & Midlands Tourism Office,** Clonard House, Dublin Road, Mullingar, County Westmeath (℃ **044/48650**), is open Monday to Friday 9am to 5:45pm, plus Saturday during peak season.

Seasonal tourist information points are open from May or June to September at signposted sites in **Athlone,** at the Athlone Castle (℃ **090/649-4630;** www.athlone.ie), **Ballinasloe** (℃ **090/964-2131**), **Birr** (℃ **090/972-0110**), and **Clonmacnois** (℃ **090/967-4134**).

SEEING THE SIGHTS

Athlone Castle ★ Built in 1210 for King John of England, this mighty stone fortress sits on the edge of the Shannon atop the ruins of an earlier fort built in 1129 as the seat of the chiefs of Connaught. Athlone Castle protected the town for centuries. It was besieged for almost 6 months in 1641, and again in 1690, but it fell in 1691 after an intense bombardment by forces sent by William of Orange. The Dutch military commander who took the town, Godard van Glinkel, was rewarded for his efforts with the earldom of Athlone. Today the castle is a national monument, adapted as a visitor center and museum. There are displays on the history of the area, and on the great Irish tenor (and local boy) John McCormack. The castle's original medieval walls have been preserved, as have two large cannons dating from the reign of George II and a pair of 25-centimeter (10-in.) mortars cast in 1856.

Athlone, County Westmeath. © 090/649-2912. Admission €6 ($9.60) adults, €3.60 ($5.75) seniors and students, €1.90 ($3.05) children, €17 ($27) families. May to mid-Oct daily 9:30am–5pm. On the riverbank, signposted from all directions.

Battle of Aughrim Interpretative Centre

Via a high-tech, three-dimensional audiovisual presentation, this center re-creates the Battle of Aughrim, which took place on July 12, 1691. On that day, the army of James II of England confronted the forces of his son-in-law, William of Orange, in a bloody battle. The confrontation involved 45,000 soldiers from eight countries and cost 9,000 lives, changing the course of Irish and European history. (For more about the conflict between William and James, see "Looking Back at Ireland" in chapter 2.) The center, which holds a bookshop, craft shop, and cafe, is in Aughrim village, adjacent to the battlefield, which is signposted. Aughrim is on the main Dublin-Galway road, about 19km (12 miles) west of the Shannonbridge/Clonmacnois area.

Galway-Dublin rd. (N6), Aughrim, near Ballinasloe, County Galway. © 090/967-3939. Admission €5 ($8) adults, €3 ($4.80) children 11 and under. June to mid-Sept Tues–Sat 10am–6pm; Sun 2–6pm.

Birr Castle Demesne ★★

The 17th-century castle is not open to the public, but people come here anyway, just to see the extraordinary gardens. The demesne (or estate) of the Parsons family, now the earls of Rosse, wraps around a peaceful lake and along the banks of the two rivers. The box hedges are featured in the *Guinness Book of Records* as the tallest in the world, and the hornbeam cloisters are lovely. The grounds contain an astronomical exhibit, with a 19th-century reflecting telescope that was once the largest in the world. Recently restored by the Historic Science Centre, the telescope is used twice daily, at noon and 3pm. During the summer, there are often exhibits on the history of Birr Castle and its residents.

Birr, County Offaly. © 0509/20336. www.birrcastle.com. Admission €9 ($14) adults, €7.50 ($12) students and seniors, €5.50 ($8.80) children 5 and over, free for children 4 and under, €25 ($40) families. Daily 9am–6pm. Take N52 37km (23 miles) southwest of Tullamore.

Bog Train Tours ★

Bog-land discoveries are the focus of this tour in the heart of the Irish midlands, on the east bank of the Shannon. Visitors board the narrow-gauge Clonmacnois and West Offaly Railway for an 8km (5-mile) circular ride around the Blackwater bog. The commentary explains how the bog land was formed and became a vital source of fuel. The route includes a firsthand look at turf cutting, stacking, drying, and close-up views of bog plants and wildlife, and you can take a turn at digging the turf or picking bog cotton. For groups who make advance arrangements, a 2- to 4-hour nature trail and field-study tour is available.

Bord na Mona (the Irish Peat Board), Blackwater Works, Shannonbridge, County Offaly. © 090/967-4114. Tours €6.70 ($11) adults, €5.60 ($8.95) seniors and students, €4.50 ($7.20) children, €21 ($34) families. Apr–Oct daily 10am–5pm; tours on the hour. Signposted from Shannonbridge.

Charleville Castle ★   Now, *this* is a castle. Designed in 1798 by Francis Johnston, this spooky, Gothic, crenelated masterpiece took 12 years to build. Today it's considered one of the best of Ireland's early-19th-century castles, with a fine limestone exterior and plenty of towers, turrets, and battlements. The rooms have spectacular plasterwork and hand-carved stairways, as well as secret passageways and dungeons. Admission includes a guided tour. Prices have shot up recently, and although it's an interesting place to see, lovely though it is, it's hard to say that it's worth what they're now asking; however, the money is desperately needed for restoration. On the other hand, Tullynally (see below) is much cheaper.

Off Birr rd. (N52), Tullamore, County Offaly. ℂ **0506/41581.** www.charlevillecastle.com. Guided tour €17 ($27). Free for children 3 and under. Apr–May Sat–Sun 2–5pm; June–Sept Tues–Sun 11am–5pm.

Clonmacnois ★★★   Resting somberly on the east bank of the Shannon, this is one of Ireland's most profound ancient sites. St. Ciaran founded the monastic community of Clonmacnois in A.D. 548 at the crucial intersection of the Shannon and the Dublin-Galway land route, and it soon became one of Europe's great centers of learning and culture. For nearly 1,000 years, Clonmacnois flourished under the patronage of Irish chiefs. The last high king, Rory O'Conor, was buried here in 1198. Clonmacnois was raided repeatedly by native chiefs, Danes, and Anglo-Normans, until it was finally destroyed by English troops in 1552. Always before, the monks had something to rebuild, but the English carried away everything—the roofs from the buildings, the doors, even the panes from the windows. By the time they'd finished, according to a report written by a monk from that time, "There was not left a bell, small or large, an image or an altar, or a book, or a gem, or even glass in a window, from the wall of the church out, which was not carried off." Today you can see what was left of the cathedral, a castle, eight churches, two round towers, three sculpted high crosses, and more than 200 monumental slabs, including some stones on which the old carvings can still be seen with thoughtful messages in ancient Celtic writing saying things like, "A prayer for Daniel." The visitor center has a well-designed exhibition, a slightly childish film, and pleasant tearooms.

On R357, 6.5km (4 miles) north of Shannonbridge, County Offaly. ℂ **090/967-4195.** Admission €5 ($8) adults, €3.50 ($5.70) seniors, €2 ($3.20) students and children 8 and over, free for children 7 and under, €11 ($17) families. Nov to mid-Mar daily 10am–5:30pm; mid-Mar to mid-May and mid-Sept to Oct daily 10am–6pm; mid-May to mid-Sept daily 9am–7pm.

Locke's Distillery Museum   Established in 1757, this 18th- and 19th-century enterprise was one of the oldest licensed pot-still whiskey distilleries in the world. After producing whiskey for almost 200 years, it closed in 1953; over the past 15 years, a local group has restored it as a museum. In 1998, a major exhibition space opened in the restored front grain loft to display a host of distilling artifacts. A 35-minute tour will not only tell you how whiskey was distilled using old techniques and machinery, but also inform you about the area's social history. It's midway between Dublin and Galway, making it a good stop-off point while you're on a cross-country journey or touring in the area. There's an on-site restaurant and craft shop.

On N6, east of Athlone, Kilbeggan, County Westmeath. ℂ **0506/32134.** Admission €5 ($8) adults, €4 ($6.40) seniors and students, €11 ($17) families. Apr–Oct daily 9am–6pm; Nov–Mar daily 10am–4pm.

Portumna Castle ★   Built in 1609 by earl Richard Burke, this massive, noble structure on the northern shores of Lough Derg is a particularly fine manor house. Had it not been gutted by fire in 1826, who knows what billionaire might own it now? The fire spared much of the impressive exterior, including its Dutch-style decorative gables and rows of stone mullioned windows. The ground floor is open to the public, as are the recently restored walled kitchen and gardens.

Off N65, Portumna, County Galway. ✆ **090/974-1658.** Admission to castle €2.20 ($3.50) adults, €1.50 ($2.40) seniors and children 11 and under. Free admission to gardens. Mar–Apr daily 10am–5pm; Apr–Oct daily 10am–6pm.

Portumna Forest Park ★★ On the shores of Lough Derg, this 560-hectare (1,383-acre) park is east of the town, off the main road. It offers trails and signposted walks, plus viewing points and picnic areas.

Off N65, Portumna, County Galway. ✆ **0905/42365.** Free admission. Daily dawn–9pm.

Tullynally Castle and Gardens ★★ A turreted and towered Gothic Revival manor, this creamy white castle home is dazzling. It has been the home of the Pakenham family, the earls of Longford, since 1655. The highlights include a great hall that rises two stories, with a ceiling of plaster Gothic vaulting, filled with family portraits, china, and antique furniture. There's a strangely fascinating collection of workaday 19th-century gadgets. The 12-hectare (30-acre) grounds are an attraction in themselves, with woodland walks, a linear water garden, a Victorian grotto, and an avenue of 200-year-old Irish yew trees. Tullynally is near Lough Derravaragh, an idyllic spot featured in the legendary Irish tale *The Children of Lir.*

About 32km (20 miles) east of Longford and 21km (13 miles) north of Mullingar, off the main Dublin-Sligo rd. (N4), Castlepollard, County Westmeath. ✆ **044/61159.** www.tullynallycastle.com. Admission to gardens €6 ($9.60) adults, €3 ($4.80) children; admission to both castle and gardens €10 ($16) adults, €5 ($8) children. Castle building is only open for prebooked tours—call in advance for information. Garden May–June weekends noon–6pm; July–Aug daily noon–6pm.

Sightseeing Cruises

Viking Tours Head to Clonmacnois on this company's 71-passenger Viking replica ship. The 4¹/₂-hour trip includes a 1-hour stopover at the monastic site. For no particular reason, the crew dress themselves in Viking attire for the journey, and passengers are encouraged to dress up as well—Viking clothing is provided should you be so inclined. Buy tickets at the Strand Fishing Tackle Shop (✆ **090/647-9277**), from where you'll also depart. Advance booking required.

7 St. Mary's Place, Athlone, County Westmeath (office address). ✆ **090/273383.** €20 ($32) adults, €12 ($19) seniors and children. July–Sept daily 9am.

SPORTS & OUTDOOR PURSUITS

BICYCLING Bikes can be rented from **D.B. Cycles,** 23 Connaught St., Athlone, County Westmeath (✆ **090/649-2280**), for around €12 ($19) per day or €70 ($112) per week.

BOATING The following companies rent cabin cruisers, usually for a minimum of 1 week, along this section of the Shannon: **Athlone Cruisers,** Jolly Mariner Marina, Athlone, County Westmeath (✆ **090/647-2892**); **Silverline Cruisers,** The Marina, Banagher, County Offaly (✆ **090/975-1112**); and **Tara Cruiser Ltd.,** Kilfaughna, Knockvicar, County Roscommon (✆ **071/966-7777**). Crafts range from four to six berths; rates average €1,000 to €2,000 ($1,600–$3,200) per week in high season.

GOLF   **Birr Golf Club,** Birr, County Offaly (© **0509/20082;** www.birrgolfclub.com), is an 18-hole course on 45 hectares (111 acres) of parkland countryside; the greens fees are €25 ($40) weekdays, €35 ($56) weekends.

In the Athlone area is the 18-hole **Athlone Golf Club,** Hodson Bay, Athlone, County Westmeath (© **090/649-2073;** www.athlonegolfclub.ie), with greens fees of €30 ($48) weekdays, €35 ($56) weekends; and the 18-hole championship **Mount Temple Golf Club,** Moate, County Westmeath (© **090/648-1841;** www.mounttemplegolfclub.com), 8km (5 miles) east of Athlone, with greens fees of €30 ($48) weekdays, €35 ($56) weekends. The **Glasson Golf Hotel & Country Club,** Glasson, County Westmeath (© **090/648-5120;** www.glassongolf.ie), is on the shores of Lough Ree, 10km (6¼ miles) north of Athlone. Greens fees are €55 ($88) Monday to Thursday, €60 ($96) Friday and Sunday, and €70 ($112) Saturday.

Lovely parkland and woodland golfing in the Lough Derg area is offered at 18-hole clubs such as **Portumna Golf Club,** Portumna, County Galway (© **090/974-1059;** www.portumnagolfclub.ie), with greens fees of €30 ($48) weekdays, €35 ($56) weekends.

HORSE RACING   The horse racing runs from July to September at the **Kilbeggan Racecourse,** Loughnagore, Kilbeggan, County Westmeath (© **0506/32176**), off the main Mullingar road (N52), 1.6km (1 mile) from town. Admission is €12 ($19) for adults, €7 ($11) for students.

WHERE TO STAY
Very Expensive

St. Cleran's Manor House ★★   This stone 17th-century manor house about 24km (15 miles) out of Galway City is a grand evocation of Irish country life. Owned by the Burke family for more than 300 years, it was purchased by the film director John Huston, who owned it for years before it was sold to the entertainer Merv Griffin. He restored it into a luxurious hotel in which each of the 12 bedrooms is individually decorated in a comfortable, elegant style. The public rooms are similarly designed with an eye to upscale tradition, and the richly furnished library is filled with old and new books and chessboards—the perfect place for a whiskey. The house sits on hundreds of acres of pristine gardens and green lawns. The **dining room** is the scene of spectacular Asian-influenced meals, courtesy of chef Hishashi Kumagi, and the whole experience is one of luxurious relaxation.

Craughwell, County Galway. © **091/846070.** Fax 091/846600. www.stclerans.com. 12 units. €325–€415 ($520–$664) double. Rates include full breakfast. AE, MC, V. Free parking. **Amenities:** Restaurant (modern European). *In room:* TV, tea/coffeemaker, hair dryer, trouser press.

Temple Country House & Spa ★★   This 250-year-old manor has recently undergone a wide-ranging renovation, more than doubling the number of rooms, and expanding and improving its famed spa. The result is a clever mix of modern architecture with the historic structure, and even more devotion to peace and relaxation. Days are spent wandering the countryside and indulging in spa treatments (the house has its own line of skin-care products), while at mealtimes Temple's acclaimed low-fat cooking—nothing chaste and deprived here, just rich, tasty food without the fat—allows indulgence without guilt. The spacious rooms are comfortably and attractively appointed, if not overtly luxurious. Weekends at Temple Country House tend to be booked solid about 8 weeks in advance; figure on booking 3 weeks ahead for a midweek stay.

€250–€300 ($400–$480). AE, MC, V. Free parking. **Amenities:** Sauna/steam room; bicycle rental; salon; massage and reflexology treatments; aromatherapy; hydrotherapy tub sitting room. *In room:* TV.

Wineport Lodge ★★★   On weekends, this contemporary cedar lodge on Lough Ree is a haven for stressed-out Dubliners, who travel an hour to get here, and are rewarded with peace and quiet. Every room is named for a wine or wine region (Bollinger, Loire Valley, Tuscany), and all have panoramic views of the lake. The modern decor (sleek walnut furnishings, cream linens) and spacious bathrooms (with heated floors) ensure that you feel cosseted and cared for. To feel even more so, you can indulge in an array of beauty and massage treatments. Dining here is also an event and, as you might imagine, the wine list is excellent.

Glasson, Athlone, County Westmeath. © **090/643-9010.** Fax 090/648-5471. www.wineport.ie. 10 units. €220–€300 ($352–$480). AE, MC, V. Free parking. **Amenities:** Restaurant (modern European). *In room:* TV, tea/coffeemaker, hair dryer, trouser press.

Moderate
Brosna Lodge Hotel (Value)   Although it sits on the main thoroughfare in Banagher, a busy river town near Clonmacnois, this two-story hotel has a warm country atmosphere, thanks to a beautiful, flower-filled front garden and enthusiastic innkeeper-owners Pat and Della Horan. The public areas are furnished with traditional period pieces and antiques, and there's a busy pub and restaurant. Guest rooms are bright and airy with simple decor, and most overlook the gardens or the town. Best of all, it's just a short walk to the riverfront.

Main St., Banagher, County Offaly. © **0509/51350.** Fax 0509/51521. www.brosnalodge.com. 14 units. €105–€110 ($168–$176) double. Rates include full breakfast. MC, V. Free parking. **Amenities:** Restaurant (International); bar; lounge. *In room:* TV.

Dooly's Hotel   Dating from 1747, this three-story Georgian hotel is in the center of Birr. A former coaching inn, its guest rooms have been restored and refurbished in recent years, with antiques and an occasionally startling color scheme. The public areas retain real Georgian charm, there's a good restaurant and handy coffee shop, and the guest rooms are comfortable if not fancy, with views of the town or back garden.

Emmet Sq., Birr, County Offaly. © **0509/20032.** Fax 0509/21332. www.doolyshotel.com. 18 units. €135 ($216) double. Rates include full breakfast. AE, DC, MC, V. Free public parking. **Amenities:** 2 restaurants (international, cafe); bar; nightclub. *In room:* TV, tea/coffeemaker.

Inexpensive
The Bastion ★★   In the heart of Athlone's Left Bank district, surrounded by good restaurants and just up the street from Athlone Castle, the Bastion is a marvelously contradictory place—the outside of the building is brightly painted in red and blue, but inside, it's all sophisticated pale hues, dark-wood floors, minimal furniture, and peace and quiet. Brothers Vinny and Anthony McCay have converted an old draper's shop into a lovely, relaxing place, with crisp white linens, comfortable beds, and modern art. Bathrooms are a bit of a squeeze, but they're perfectly adequate. In the morning, a big buffet breakfast of cereal, fresh bread, Irish cheeses, and fruit is served in the comfortable dining room—a healthy break from the usual B&B eggs and bacon. There are no TVs or telephones in rooms—you're here to relax. *Note:* There are lots of steep staircases here, so it's not for those with mobility issues.

2 Bastion St., Athlone, County Westmeath. ℂ **090/649-4954.** Fax 090/649-3648. www.thebastion.net. 6 units. €55–€70 ($88–$112) double. Rates include continental breakfast. MC, V. *In room:* No phone.

WHERE TO DINE

Most small towns in this area have little in the way of restaurant life. In some villages, the only place in town making food at all is the pub. But **Athlone** has a vibrant restaurant scene, with increasingly sophisticated restaurants and lots of coffee shops on its Left Bank, while **Shannonbridge** is improving as well. Along with the choices below, see the hotels listed above, as most have excellent restaurants.

Expensive

Crookedwood House ★★ MODERN IRISH   An attractive country house with a fine restaurant and rooms to rent, Crookedwood is a good place to know about. Noel Kenny is a terrifically talented chef who delights in giving earthy flavors a bit of a kick. Try the grilled rack of lamb with an herb crust, or the seafood in chardonnay, to get a feel for his culinary talents. The guest rooms are spacious and nicely furnished, and best of all, they allow you to just fall into bed after one of those fabulous meals. Eight overnight accommodations are also available for €140 ($224) double (including full breakfast).

Crookedwood, Mullingar, County Westmeath. ℂ **044/72165.** Fax 044/72166. www.crookedwoodhouse. com. Early dinner Tues–Sat 6:30–7:30pm €26 ($42). Main courses €25–€48 ($40–$77). MC, V. Mon–Sat 6:30–10pm, Sun noon–2pm.

Left Bank Bistro ★★ FUSION   This smart little bistro is as sassy and bright as they come. The menu circles the earth, starting with French filet of beef with mustard butter and moving on to Asia and Italy for grilled Parmesan polenta. You can choose between a French cassoulet and a delicious Thai chicken breast on egg noodles. The food is good, the service cheerful and professional, the crowd happy and buzzing.

Fry Place, Athlone, County Westmeath. ℂ **090/649-4446.** www.leftbankbistro.com. Reservations required. Main courses €18–€26 ($29–$42). AE, MC, V. Tues–Sat 10am–9:30pm.

Moderate

Hatter's Lane ★ (Kids) CONTINENTAL   This warm and friendly restaurant right next to the excellent Gertie Browns pub has just the right casual but attractive Irish country feel. The food is a little of everything, from pasta dishes to seafood to grilled steaks, all served in large enough portions to please the heartiest appetite.

Strand St., Athlone, County Westmeath. ℂ **090/273-077.** Main courses €9–€19 ($14–$30). MC, V. Tues–Sat 6–10pm.

Le Chateau CONTINENTAL   This is one of Athlone's more formal restaurants, inside a former church near the castle, and yet it manages to be friendly, too. Upon arrival, you're taken into a comfortable bar area for an aperitif while you peruse the menu and choose your dinner. You might have the chargrilled medallions of pork, or the locally reared beef filet, or one of several vegetarian options. Once the starters are ready, you're taken to your table. It's a good combination of old formality and new informality, all with a lovely view of the River Shannon.

St. Peter's Port, Athlone, County Westmeath. ℂ **090/649-4517.** Main courses €18–€26 ($29–$42). MC, V. Daily 6:30–10pm.

Slice of Life ★ SANDWICHES   This sunny, welcoming coffee shop just across from the Bastion guesthouse (p. 429) serves breakfast rolls and croissants, sandwiches made to order, lots of vegetarian options, and soups made fresh each day. It's a great place for lunch, or for a cup of tea and a slice of cake. The staff members are so friendly, you'll want to take them home.

Bastion St., Athlone, County Westmeath. ℭ **090/649-3970.** Main courses €3–€6 ($4.80–$9.60). No credit cards. Tues–Sat 8am–8pm.

PUBS

If music is what you're after, Banagher, in County Offaly, is known for the lively Irish-traditional-music sessions at two of its pubs: **J. J. Hough's,** Main Street (no phone), has music every night during the summer and Friday to Sunday the rest of the year, while the **Vine House,** West End (ℭ **0509/51463**), offers music every night during the summer. Here are a couple of more pubs with color and character:

Gertie Browns   This big, rambling pub on Athlone's Right Bank, just off the river, is a friendly place where everybody seems to know everybody else. A fire blazes at the hearth, a band sometimes strikes up an impromptu performance by the door, the Guinness is cold, and the atmosphere is warm. 9 Costume Place, Athlone, County Westmeath. ℭ **090/274848.**

Killeen's   A few miles from Clonmacnois, tucked into the little village of Shannonbridge, this is another good Irish boozer that has outgrown its pub-and-grocery-store origins. Along with a relaxed mood and friendly regulars come turf fires, excellent pints of Guinness, and faultless Irish coffees. Shannonbridge, County Offaly. ℭ **090/967-4112.**

Moran's   Overlooking the Woodford River, this place (correct pronunciation is *Mor*-ins) is a traditional, old-style Irish pub, peddling groceries and pints with equal friendliness. It has plenty of shaded, outdoor seating with lovely views of the water. Woodford, County Galway. ℭ **090/974-9063.**

Sean's (Finds)   There's been a quiet competition underway for years between this humble old pub and the Brazen Head in Dublin over which is the oldest pub in Ireland. The *Guinness Book of World Records* weighed in on Sean's side in 2004, and not long afterward, on an Irish radio program, the owner of the Brazen Head conceded that given its ancient walls and written evidence that it has been a pub through centuries, Sean's won—but only just. So there you have it. This ancient building—long and narrow with low ceilings and a fireplace at one end—has been a public house for more than 400 years. There's live music (usually traditional) here nightly, and a friendly local crowd. 13 Main St., Athlone, County Westmeath. ℭ **090/649-2358.**

15

Mayo, Sligo & the North Shannon Valley

The strikingly beautiful landscape of Galway becomes the strikingly beautiful landscape of southern Mayo without fanfare. Like Galway, Mayo is marked by dramatic scenery, which terminates in rocky cliffs plunging down into the opaque blue waters of the icy sea.

If you head farther north, you'll reach the smooth pastures of County Sligo. The main appeal here is not its towns, which tend to be functional farm communities, but the countryside. This is the landscape that soothed W. B. Yeats's soul and inspired his poetry. Sligo's unspoiled marvels are still a healing tonic. The county is filled with fairy-tale castles and mysterious prehistoric sites, but its biggest gift to you is peace.

Heading inland from Sligo, you'll reach the upper Shannon River valley, with its sprawling lakes, promising fresh trout and salmon, and nearly limitless watersports in the summer.

1 COUNTY MAYO

Ballina: 101km (63 miles) N of Galway, 193km (120 miles) N of Shannon Airport, 246km (153 miles) NW of Dublin, 311km (193 miles) NW of Cork

Serenely beautiful, County Mayo sits in the shadow of its more famous neighbor, Galway, and doesn't seem to mind. For experienced Ireland travelers, Mayo is a kind of Galway Lite—its rugged coastal scenery is similar to that of Galway, but it has less of the traffic or tourist overload from which Galway suffers in the summer. This is peaceful, pleasant Ireland, with striking seascapes and inland scenery that ranges from lush and green to stark, desertlike, and mountainous. It's an unpredictable place, where the terrain changes at the turn of a steering wheel. This region was hit so hard by the potato famine that, in some ways, it's only now recovering. Starvation and emigration emptied it then, and that emptiness is still noticeable. It feels, as you leave Galway, as if it all goes quiet.

For Americans, the county is still identified with the 1951 John Ford film *The Quiet Man,* starring John Wayne and Maureen O'Hara. The setting for the film was the town of **Cong,** which is still the only international tourist attraction in the county. There's little to see there except for the scant remains of the stone cottage used in the film, which has been gradually torn apart over the years by people who want to bring home one of its stones. (We strongly request that you do not take anything except photographs—as do the locals.)

Among Mayo's other attractions are the mysterious 5,000-year-old settlement at **Céide Fields,** the religious shrine at **Knock,** and some of Europe's best fishing waters at **Lough Conn, Lough Mask,** and the **River Moy. Ballina (Béal an Átha),** Mayo's largest town, calls itself the home of the Irish salmon. And **Westport** is a little resort town guaranteed to steal your heart.

Ballintubber Abbey 9	Mayo North Heritage Centre 4
Céide Fields 1	Moyne Abbey 2
Errew Abbey 5	National Shrine of Our Lady of Knock 10
Foxford Woollen Mills 6	Rosserk Abbey 3
Granuaile Centre 7	Westport House 8

COUNTY MAYO ESSENTIALS

GETTING THERE   Several airlines serve **Knock International Airport,** Charlestown, County Mayo (© **1850/67-2222** or 94/936-8100; www.knockairport.com). From Dublin you can fly to Knock on **Aer Arann** (© **011/353-81821-0210** in the U.S., 818/210-210 in Ireland, or 0800/587-23-24 in the U.K.; www.aerarann.ie); **bmibaby** (© **1890/340-122** in Ireland; www.bmibaby.com) serves Knock from Manchester and Birmingham.

Irish Rail (© **096/20229;** www.irishrail.ie) and **Bus Éireann** (© **096/21011;** www. buseireann.ie) provide daily service from Dublin and other cities into Ballina, Westport, and Castlebar, with bus connections into smaller towns. There is also express service from Galway into most Mayo towns.

From Dublin and points east, the main N5 road leads to many points in County Mayo; from Galway, take N84 or N17. From Sligo and points north, take N17 or N59. To get around County Mayo, it's best to rent a car. Three firms with outlets at Knock International Airport are **Casey Auto Rentals, Ltd.** (© **094/932-4618;** www.caseycar. com), **Europcar** (© **094/936-7221;** www.europcar.ie), and **National Car Rental** (© **094/ 936-7252;** www.carhire.ie).

Tips **Irish Only**

Parts of Mayo are in the Gaeltacht—or Irish-language section of the country. In some sections, this means town names are in Irish only, so we'll include the Irish names as well as the English names for the places likely to be affected by this. Confusingly, most maps are still in English only.

VISITOR INFORMATION   For year-round information, visit or contact the **Westport Tourist Office,** The Mall, Westport (© **098/25711;** http://westport.mayo-ireland.ie). It's open September through May Monday to Saturday from 9am to 5:45pm, and June through August Monday to Friday 9am to 7pm.

The **Knock Airport Tourist Office** (© **094/936-7247**) is open June to September at times coinciding with flight arrivals.

Seasonal tourist offices, open from May or June to September or October, are the **Ballina Tourist Office,** Cathedral Road, Ballina, County Mayo (© 096/70848); **Castlebar Tourist Office,** Linenhall Street, Castlebar, County Mayo (© 094/902-1207); **Knock Village Tourist Office,** Knock (© 094/938-8193); **Cong Village Tourist Office** (© 094/954-6542); and **Achill Tourist Office,** Achill Sound (© 098/45384).

EXPLORING THE COUNTY

Because it's a rural county with no major cities or many large towns, County Mayo feels a bit like a place without a center. Towns like Castlebar, Claremorris, Westport, and Ballinrobe in the southern part of the county, and Ballina in the northern reaches, make good places to stop, refill the tank, and have lunch, but they offer little to make you linger. The county's attractions lie in the countryside, and in smaller communities like Knock, Foxford, Ballycastle, Louisburgh, and Newport.

County Mayo's loveliest town, **Westport (Cathair na Mairt)** ★, nestles on the shores of Clew Bay. Once a major port, it was designed by Richard Castle with a tree-lined mall, rows of Georgian buildings, and an octagonal central mall where a vibrant market adds zest to the town on Thursdays.

Southeast of Westport, **Croagh Patrick,** a 750m (2,460-ft.) mountain, dominates the views of western Mayo for miles. St. Patrick is said to have spent the 40 days of Lent praying here in the year 441. To commemorate that, on the last Sunday of July, thousands of Irish people make a pilgrimage to the site, which has become known as St. Patrick's Holy Mountain.

Heading west, the rugged, bog-filled, sparsely populated coast makes for scenic drives to secluded outposts. Leading the list is **Achill Island (An Caol)** ★, a heather-filled bog land with sandy beaches and spectacular views of waves crashing against rocky cliffs. The drive from the mainland and then across the island to the little town of Keel requires patience and skill, but rewards you with a camera filled with photos. **Clare Island,** once the home of Mayo's legendary "Pirate Queen," Grace O'Malley, is another scenic isle, south of Achill in Clew Bay.

Like the drive to Achill Island, the road from Ballina along the edge of the northern coast to Downpatrick Head is breathtaking. It passes through **Killala (Cill Alaidh** or **Cill Ála),** a small, secluded harbor village that came close to changing the course of Ireland's history. In 1798, the French General Amable Humbert landed here with 1,100 troops in an attempt to help the Irish defeat the British forces. After several surprisingly successful fights with troops under British command, particularly a thorough routing at Castlebar, Humbert had attracted thousands of Irish volunteers who fought by his side. At that point, the British sent General Cornwallis (the same general who surrendered to Washington at Yorktown in 1781) to take him on in Longford, with thousands of well-armed troops. The battle lasted only half an hour before Humbert surrendered. The French soldiers were treated honorably, but the Irish volunteers who had fought with Humbert, and anybody suspected of sympathizing with him, were slaughtered.

Outside Killala on the road R314 to **Ballina (Béal an Átha)** are several ruined friaries worth a stop for those who love the blurred beauty of ancient abbeys. **Moyne Abbey** was established in the mid-1400s and destroyed by Richard Bingham, the English governor of Connaught, in the 16th century. It's a peaceful place, and you can see why the monks chose it. The same is true, even more so, of **Rosserk Abbey** about 3km (2 miles) away. Sitting at the edge of the River Rosserk, the abbey is in much better shape than the Moyne: Its chapel windows are well preserved. You can climb a winding stone stair to look out across the bay. The piscina of the church (once used for washing altar vessels) is still here, carved with angels, and on its lower-left-hand column is a delightful detail: a tiny, elegant carving of a round tower that recalls its 23m-tall (75-ft.) counterpart in nearby Killala. The Rosserk Abbey was built at the same time as the Moyne and also destroyed by Bingham's troops.

Ballintubber Abbey ★   This abbey is a survivor—one of few Irish churches in continuous use for almost 800 years. Founded in 1216 by Cathal O'Connor, king of Connaught, it has endured fires, numerous attacks, illnesses, and anti-Catholic pogroms. Although Oliver Cromwell's forces so thoroughly dismantled the abbey that they even carried off its roof in 1653 in an effort to finally suppress it, clerics continued discreetly conducting religious rites. Today it's an impressive church, with 13th-century windows on the right side of the nave and a doorway dating to the 15th century. It was completely restored in 1966. A helpful visitor center tells its troubled and fascinating history.

Off the main Galway-Castlebar rd. (N84), about 32km (20 miles) west of Knock, Ballintubber, County Mayo. (✆) **094/903-0934.** www.ballintubberabbey.ie. Free admission; €2.50 ($4) donation requested. Daily 9am–midnight.

Céide Fields ★★   In a breathtaking setting, above huge chalk cliffs that plunge hundreds of feet down into a deep blue sea, ancient people once lived, worked, and buried their dead—a fact that nobody knew until the 1930s, when a local farmer named Patrick Caulfield noticed stones piled in strange patterns in his fields. More than 40 years later, his son Seamus, by then an archaeologist, explored his father's discovery (he became a scientist in part because he wanted to understand the stones he'd played among as a child). Under the turf, he found Stone Age fields, megalithic tombs, and the foundations of a village. Standing amid it now, you can see a pattern of farm fields as they were laid out 5,000 years ago (predating the construction of the Egyptian pyramids). Preserved for millennia beneath the bog, the site is both fascinating and inscrutable, as, to a casual observer, it's all little more than piles of stones, but the visitor center makes it meaningful in a series of displays, films, and tours. The pyramid-shaped center itself is designed to fit in with the dramatic surroundings—you can see the building for miles. It also contains a **cafeteria,** which comes as a relief since this site is 20 hilly, rocky kilometers (12 miles) of winding roads from anywhere.

On R314, the coastal road north of Ballina, btw. Ballycastle and Belderrig, Ballycastle, County Mayo. (✆) **096/43325.** Admission €3.70 ($5.90) adults, €2.60 ($4.15) seniors, €1.50 ($2.40) students and children, €8.70 ($14) families. Mid-Mar to May and Oct–Nov daily 10am–5pm; June–Sept daily 10am–6pm.

Errew Abbey   This atmospheric, ruined 13th-century Augustinian church sits on a tiny peninsula in Lough Conn. The cloister is well preserved, as is the chancel with altar and piscina. There's also an oratory with massive stone walls in fields adjacent to the abbey—on the site of a church founded in the 6th century, and known locally as Templenagalliaghdoo, or "Church of the Black Nun."

Signposted about 3.2km (2 miles) south of Crossmolina on the Castlebar rd., then 5km (3 miles) down a side road, County Mayo. No phone. Free admission.

Foxford Woollen Mills Visitor Centre   Founded in 1892 by a local nun to provide work for a community ravaged by the effects of the Irish famine, Foxford Woollen Mills brought prosperity to the area through the worldwide sales of beautiful tweeds, rugs, and blankets. Using a multimedia presentation, the center tells the story of this local industry, then offers an on-site tour of the working mills. Tours run every 20 minutes and last approximately 45 minutes. A restaurant, shop, exhibition center, art gallery, heritage room, and other craft units (including a doll-making workshop) are also part of the visit.

Off the Foxford-Ballina rd. (N57), 16km (10 miles) south of Ballina, St. Joseph's Place, Foxford, County Mayo. (C) **094/925-6756.** www.museumsofmayo.com/foxford.htm. Admission €4 ($6.40) adults; €3 ($4.80) seniors, students, and children; €9 ($14) families. May–Oct Mon–Sat 10am–6pm, Sun noon–6pm; Nov–Apr Mon–Sat 10am–6pm, Sun 2–6pm. Last tour at 5:30pm.

Granuaile Centre ★   This interesting center in an old, converted church, is dedicated to the life and story of one of Ireland's great female heroes, Grace O'Malley (Grainne ni Mhaille, 1530–1600). Known as the "Pirate Queen," she led battles against the English and ruled the high seas. Parts of the center also address the Great Famine that killed an estimated 100,000 people in County Mayo.

Louisburgh, County Mayo. (C) **098/66341.** Admission €4 ($6.40) adults, €2 ($3.20) seniors and students. Students and children free if accompanied by parents. June to mid-Sept Mon–Sat 10am–6pm.

Mayo North Heritage Centre   If you're tracing your Mayo family tree, you'll want to stop in here. The data bank includes indexes to church registers of all denominations, plus school records, leases, and wills. There's a somewhat incongruous adjacent museum, with displays of rural household items, farm machinery, and farm implements. The lovely Enniscoe Gardens adjoin the center; combined tickets to the center and gardens are a good deal. There is a handy tearoom on the premises should you need a break.

On Lough Conn, about 3.2km (2 miles) south of Crossmolina, off R315, Enniscoe, Castlehill, Ballina, County Mayo. (C) **096/31809.** Fax 096/31885. www.mayo.irish-roots.net. Admission to museum €5 ($8) adults, €3 ($4.80) children, €8 ($13) families; combined ticket with gardens €6 ($9.60) adults, €4 ($6.40) children, €15 ($24) families. Oct–May Mon–Fri 9am–4pm; June–Sept Mon–Fri 9am–6pm, Sat–Sun 2–6pm.

National Shrine of Our Lady of Knock/Church of the Apparition ★   This is Ireland's version of Lourdes, and Catholic pilgrims (mostly Irish Catholic) come here in droves. It all dates from a day in August 1879 when two young local girls said they saw Joseph, Mary, and St. John standing in bright light in front of the southern tower of the parish church. Soon, 13 other witnesses claimed to have seen the same thing, and the Church declared it a miracle. Before long, miracles were occurring fast and furious, as sick and lame visitors claimed to be healed after visits to the church. Knock came to the world's attention in 1979, when Pope John Paul II visited the shrine. There's not much to the town of Knock on the whole—it sits unspectacularly at the intersection of the N17

Moments A Trip to Clare Island

Floating just about 5km (3 miles) off the Mayo coast, just beyond Clew Bay, Clare Island is a place of unspoiled splendor. Inhabited for 5,000 years and once quite populous—1,700 people lived there in the early 19th century—Clare is now home to 150 year-round islanders, plus perhaps as many sheep. But the island is best known as the haunt of Grace O'Malley, the "Pirate Queen" who controlled the coastal waters 400 years ago. O'Malley's modest castle and the partially restored Cistercian Abbey where she is buried are among the island's few attractions. The rest of the draw is its remote natural beauty. Two ferry services operate out of Roonagh Harbour, 29km (18 miles) south of Westport; fares run about €15 ($24) each way for the 15-minute journey: **O'Malley's Ferry Service**, aboard the *Island Princess* (© **098/25045**), and **Clare Island Ferries**, aboard the *Pirate Queen* (© **098/26307**).

If you want a proper tour of the island, look for Ludwig Timmerman's 1974 Land Rover. Ludwig offers cordial, informative tours from June to August. Otherwise, your transport options are rented mountain bikes or your own feet.

and R323 (it's not even on some maps of Ireland, it's so small)—but it's filled with increasingly large, modern religious structures, including a huge circular basilica seating 7,000 people and containing artifacts or furnishings from every county in Ireland. The grounds also hold a folk museum and a religious bookshop.

On the N17 Galway rd., Knock, County Mayo. © 094/938-8100. www.knock-shrine.ie. Free admission to shrine; museum €4 ($6.40) adults, €3.75 ($6), €3 ($4.80) seniors and children age 5 and over, free for children 4 and under. Shrine and grounds year-round daily 8am–6pm or later; museum May–Oct daily 10am–6pm.

Westport House ★ Kids   At the edge of the town of Westport, this late-18th-century residence is the home of Lord Altamont, the marquis of Sligo, and a descendant, it is said, of "Pirate Queen" Grace O'Malley—thus, the bronze statue of her on the grounds. The work of Richard Cassels and James Wyatt, the house has a graceful staircase of ornate white Sicilian marble, unusual Art Nouveau glass and carvings, family heirlooms, and silver. The grandeur of the residence is undeniable, but purists might be put off by its gardens, which are quite a commercial enterprise these days, with a children's zoo, a log ride, swan-shaped pedal boats on the lake, a kid-size train tooting its way through the gardens, an aviary, and more. Probably because of that, prices are quite high.

Westport, County Mayo. © 098/25430 or 27766. www.westporthouse.ie. Admission to house and children's animal and bird park €21 ($34) adults, €12 ($19) seniors, €20 ($32) students, €17 ($27) seniors and children; to house only €12 ($19) adults, €7.50 ($12) seniors, €9 ($14) students, €6.50 ($10) children. Westport House and gardens mid-Mar to Oct daily 11:30am–5:30pm. Attractions mid- to late Mar daily, May Sun and 1st Sat and Mon only, June–Aug daily 11:30am–5:30pm.

SPORTS & OUTDOOR PURSUITS

FISHING   The waters of the River Moy and loughs Carrowmore and Conn are known for good fishing, particularly for salmon and trout. For general information about fishing in County Mayo, contact the **North Western Regional Fisheries Board,** Ardnaree

House, Abbey Street, Ballina (© **096/22788;** www.cfb.ie). To arrange a day's fishing, contact **Cloonamoyne Fishery** ★, Castlehill, near Crossmolina, Ballina (© **096/51156;** www.cloonamoynefishery.com). Managed by an Irish-born former New Yorker, Barry Segrave, this professional angling service will advise and equip you to fish the local waters—for brown trout on loughs Conn and Cullin; for salmon on loughs Beltra, Furnace, and Feeagh; and for salmon and sea trout on the rivers Moy and Deel. The fishery rents fully equipped boats and tackle, teaches fly-casting, and provides transport to and from all fishing. Daily rates average around €50 ($80) for a rowboat, €70 ($112) for a boat with engine, and €130 ($208) for a boat with engine and *ghillie* (guide).

County Mayo is also home to the **Pontoon Bridge Hotel Fly Fishing School,** Pontoon, County Mayo (© **094/925-6120).** Daily rates are €40 ($64) for a rowboat, €60 ($96) for a boat with engine, and €130 ($208) for a boat with engine and *ghillie*. This school offers a 1-day course in the art of fly-casting, as well as fly-tying, tackle design, and other information necessary for successful game fishing. Fees run from €90 ($144) per person. Courses run daily year-round if there is demand. The newly expanded Pontoon Bridge Hotel also runs painting and cooking classes.

Permits and state fishing licenses can be obtained at the **North Mayo Angling Advice Centre** (Tiernan Bros.), Upper Main Street, Foxford, County Mayo (© **094/945-6731).** It also offers a range of services, including boat hire and *ghillies*.

For fishing tackle, try, **Kingfisher Bates,** Pier Road, Enniscrone, County Mayo (© **096/36733)** or **Walkins Fishing Tackle,** Tone Street, Ballina, County Mayo (© **096/ 22442).** On Achill Island, get sea-angling gear at **O'Malley's Island Sports** on the main road in Keel (© **098/43125).** It will also arrange boat hire and bike hire.

GOLF County Mayo's 18-hole golf courses include a par-72 links course at **Belmullet Golf Course,** Carne, Belmullet, County Mayo (© **097/82292;** www.belmulletgolfclub. ie), with greens fees of €60 ($96) daily. The par-71 inland course at **Castlebar Golf Club,** Rocklands, Castlebar, County Mayo (© **094/902-1649;** www.castlebargolfclub. ie), has greens fees of €25 ($40) weekdays and €35 ($56) weekends. The par-73 championship course at **Westport Golf Club,** County Mayo (© **098/28262;** www.golf westport.com), charges varied greens fees of €40 to €60 ($64–$96) depending on the time of year and day of the week. On the shores of Clew Bay, the challenging and scenic course winds around the slopes of Croagh Patrick Mountain.

KAYAKING Courses for adults and children are at the **Atlantic Adventure Centre,** in Lecanvey, just outside of Westport, County Mayo (© **098/64806).** Most of the kayaking is done at Old Head, Bertra, and Carramore. Very reasonable accommodations rates are available for campers. The adventure center has all you need for a wide range of activities, from canoeing to rock climbing. Call for details.

WALKING The region to the east of the Mullet peninsula has a spectacular array of sheer sea cliffs and craggy islands. The small, secluded beach at **Portacloy,** 14km (8²/₃ miles) north of Glenamoy on the R314, is a good starting point for a dramatic walk. On a sunny day, its aquamarine waters and fine-grained white sand recall the Mediterranean more than the North Atlantic. At its western edge, there is a concrete quay. From here, head north up the steep green slopes of the nearest hill. Don't be too distracted by the fantastic view or adorable little sheep: The boggy slopes on which you are walking end precipitously at an unmarked cliff edge—the walk is not recommended for children. Exercise caution and resist the urge to try to get a better view of the mysterious sea caves or to reach the outermost extent of the coast's promontories. Instead, use a farmer's fence as a guide and head

Local Hero: Pirate Grace O'Malley

Grace O'Malley, the "Pirate Queen," was born in 1530 in Clare Island. She was, by all accounts, ahead of her time. A heroine, adventurer, pirate, gambler, mercenary, traitor, chieftain, and noblewoman, she is remembered now with affection, although at the time she was feared and despised. Even as a child, she was fiercely independent. When her mother refused to let her sail with her father, she cut off her hair and dressed in boys' clothing. Her father called her "Grainne Mhaol," or "Bald Grace," later shortened to Granuaile, a nickname she'd carry all her life.

At 16, Grace married Donal O'Flaherty, second in line to the O'Flaherty clan chieftain, who ruled all of Connacht. A few years later, her career as a pirate began when the city of Galway, one of the largest trade centers in the British Isles, refused to trade with the O'Flahertys. Grace used her fleet of fast galleys to waylay slower vessels on their way into Galway Harbour. She then offered safe passage for a fee in lieu of pillaging the ships.

She is most fondly remembered for refusing to trade her lands in return for an English title, a common practice of the day.

At the age of 56, she was captured by the English, who planned to hang her. Instead, she was released on the condition that she would stop all piracy. She was stripped of her cattle and most of her lands and forced into poverty. In return, she defied authority and continued to sail. To this day, the Irish think of her as a defender of Gaelic life.

west toward the striking profile of **Benwee Head,** about 2.4km (1½ miles) away. Return the same way to have a swim in the chilly, tranquil waters of Portacloy.

WINDSURFING & OTHER WATERSPORTS The constant wind off the Atlantic Ocean means that Achill Island is ideal for windsurfing, hang gliding, or any activities that involve a breeze. If you want to try it out, talk with Richie O'Hara at **McDowell's Hotel** (Slievemore Rd., near Dugort; © 098/43148). He also gives surfing instructions and advice on rock climbing, and rents out canoes and surfboards. For other options, contact the useful Atlantic Adventure Centre (see above).

WHERE TO STAY
Very Expensive

Ashford Castle ★★★   Turrets, towers, drawbridge, and battlements: Ashford has them all. The structure dates from the 13th century, when it was built for the De Burgo (Burke) family. Later it became a country residence of the Guinness clan. A hotel since 1939, it has been enlarged and updated over the years. It drew worldwide media attention in 1984 when President Ronald Reagan stayed here during his visit to Ireland, and in 2001, the Irish actor Pierce Brosnan held his wedding here. Reflected in the glassy waters of Lough Corrib, the castle sits regally amid vast forested, flowering grounds. The fairy tale continues inside with antiques, medieval armor, carved oak paneling, and museum-quality paintings. Bedrooms convey an air of privilege with heavy fabrics, soft carpets, and big, comfortable beds. The restaurant serves respectable European cuisine with a stiffly formal attitude—jacket and tie are required for men after 7pm. There are two bars—the jovial **Dungeon** and the **Prince of Wales Cocktail Bar,** which has the air of a men's club. Check online before booking, as specials are often offered outside of the high season.

Cong, County Mayo. © **800/346-7007** in the U.S., or 092/954-6003. Fax 092/954-6260. www.ashford.ie. 83 units. €450–€860 ($720–$1,376) double. Rates include service charge. AE, DC, MC, V. **Amenities:** Restaurant (Continental, French); 2 bars; 9-hole golf course; tennis court; gym; spa; Jacuzzi; sauna; concierge; room service; babysitting; laundry service; boating (salmon and trout fishing). *In room:* TV, minibar, hair dryer, garment press.

Expensive

Enniscoe House ★★   This is a terrific place for unwinding and escaping the real world. Overlooking Lough Conn and surrounded by an extensive wooded estate, complete with nature walks, this two-story Georgian country inn is owned and run by Susan Kellett, a descendant of a family who settled on the lands in the 1660s. Inside Enniscoe is truly magnificent, with delicate plasterwork, lovely fireplaces, and a grand staircase. Guest rooms are individually furnished; those at the front of the house are particularly impressive, with hand-carved armoires and canopied beds. All rooms have views of parkland or the lake. Meals feature locally caught fish and vegetables and herbs from the adjacent garden. Enniscoe also has its own fishery (see Cloonamoyne Fishery under "Fishing" in "Sports & Outdoor Pursuits," above). Self-catering apartments are available.

3.2km (2 miles) south of Crossmolina, off R315, next to the North Mayo Heritage Centre, Castlehill, near Crossmolina, Ballina, County Mayo. © **800/223-6510** in the U.S., or 096/31112. Fax 096/31773. www. enniscoe.com. 6 units. €180–€232 ($288–$371) double. Self-catering cottages €450–€800 ($720–$1,280) per week. Dinner from €40 ($64). Rates include full breakfast. AE, MC, V. Closed Nov–Mar. **Amenities:** Nonsmoking rooms; drawing room. *In room:* TV.

Mount Falcon Castle ★★   This sternly beautiful gray-stone manor house has a striking setting just south of Ballina amid lush forests and lakes. It was built in 1876 by the same man responsible for the exterior of Ashford Castle, and was renovated in 2006 in luxurious style. The expansion tripled the number of guest rooms and also changed the property from one of near total isolation to a somewhat busier place, by adding three private home developments to the estate. A spa with a heated pool has been added for hotel guests, and the house's kitchen has been turned into a 72-seat **restaurant** with an attractive bar. Given all of that, the fact that the hotel's prices have more than doubled since the renovation should come as no surprise.

Foxford rd. (N57), Ballina, County Mayo. © **800/223-6510** in the U.S., or 096/74472. Fax 096/74473. www.mountfalcon.com. 32 units. €280–€345 ($448–$552) double. Rates include full breakfast. AE, DC, MC, V. Closed Feb–Mar and Christmas week. **Amenities:** Restaurant; bar; pool; tennis court; spa; private salmon and trout fishing. *In room:* TV, hair dryer, safe.

Newport House Hotel ★★   Close to the Clew Bay coast, this ivy-covered Georgian mansion house is a lovely place to stay. Its architectural detail is excellent and includes fine, ornate plasterwork on the soaring ceilings and a sky-lit dome above the cascading central staircase. It all feels a bit like a lavish period film—with heavy antique furnishings and big oil paintings. The guest rooms are divided between the main house and two smaller courtyard buildings. They're spacious and elegant, with sash windows, high ceilings, and original paintings and prints. The **restaurant** is a destination in itself and a place of pilgrimage for food lovers. As the hotel sits at the edge of Newport Town along the Newport River, it's an excellent base for salmon anglers. That said, though, prices are **441** still a bit high for what's on offer here.

Newport, County Mayo. © **800/223-6510** in the U.S., or 098/41222. Fax 098/41613. www.newport house.ie. 18 units. €244–€448 ($390–$717) double. Rates include full breakfast. AE, DC, MC, V. Closed Oct to mid-Mar. **Amenities:** Restaurant (Continental); bar; drawing room; private salmon and sea-trout fishing. *In room:* TV, hair dryer.

Moderate

The Bervie ★★★ (Finds)

Standing strong at the edge of the sea, the Bervie seems to cradle you protectively within its sturdy walls. Once a coast guard station, the whitewashed building has been a hotel for two generations. Owner Elizabeth Barrett was born and raised here, where her mother ran a guesthouse for decades. A few years back, Elizabeth and her husband, John, took over and upgraded the building and made it into what it is today—a snug, relaxing, attractive place to stay. Many rooms have views of the sea (it's just a few feet away), and all are decorated in soothing tones with distinctive, locally made furniture and art. The large, relaxing lounge is filled with tastefully appointed chairs and sofas and is heated by an open fireplace. The sunny breakfast room has dramatic views of the sea and the cliffs across the bay. Breakfasts are out of this world, including homemade cereals, Elizabeth's delectable jams, and a variety of egg options, including light and fluffy scrambled eggs with smoked salmon. Excellent dinners are also available if you book in advance.

From Westport, take the N59 to Achill Island, then the R319 across the island to the village of Keel, where the Bervie is signposted, County Mayo. © **098/43114.** Fax 098/43407. www.bervieachill.com. 14 units. €100–€130 ($160–$208) double. Dinner from €40 ($64). Rates include full breakfast. MC, V. Closed Nov–Mar. **Amenities:** Nonsmoking rooms; drawing room. *In room:* TV.

Rosturk Woods ★

This lovely, cheerfully decorated house is well located on the road between Newport and Achill Island on Clew Bay. You won't realize how beautifully set it is—or how close it is to the sea—until you reach the end of the long driveway. The place is run by Louisa Stoney, a terrific cook with many recommendations about the area. Rooms are spacious, tastefully decorated, and comfortable, with king-size beds and power showers in the bathrooms. There are also two very attractive self-catering cottages (two-bedroom and four-bedroom) that can be rented for €800 to €1,200 ($1,280–$1,920) per week. Writers seeking a literary getaway can take part in the Rosturk writing courses held here regularly.

> ### (Tips) Service Charges
>
> *A reminder:* Unless otherwise noted, room rates don't include service charges (usually 10%–15% of your bill).

Mulranny, Westport, County Mayo. ©/fax **098/36264.** www.rosturk-woods.com. 3 units. €150–€200 ($240–$320) double. 3-course dinner €40 ($64). No credit cards. Closed Dec–Feb. *In room:* Tea/coffeemaker, hair dryer.

Inexpensive

Drom Caoin ★ (Kids)

From Mairin Maguire-Murphy's comfortable home, a short walk from the center of Belmullet, there are panoramic views of Blacksod Bay and Achill Island. Two of the guest rooms have recently been renovated into self-catering apartments that can be rented by the night or by the week, with or without breakfast. It's a great concept—you can cook your own meals and enjoy the extra space of a suite. The other two bedrooms are small, with compact bathrooms. Breakfast is something to look forward to here—omelets, fresh fish, and toasted cheese are offered periodically, and the fresh scones are delicious.

Belmullet, County Mayo. ©/fax 097/81195. 4 units, 2 with shower only. From €70–€80 ($112–$128) double; €450–€550 ($720–$880) apt. by the week (without breakfast). 33% reduction for children. MC, V. In room: TV.

WHERE TO DINE
Expensive
The Quay Cottage ★★ SEAFOOD   This place is known for its freshly caught seafood. In an old stone building overlooking the harbor, Quay Cottage is done up from top to bottom with nautical bric-a-brac. The menu presents fresh, beautifully prepared seafood, such as lemon sole beurre blanc or wild local salmon, with an array of daily specials that often includes steaks. You can take a waterside stroll afterward.

The Quay, Westport, County Mayo. © 098/26412. www.quaycottage.com. Reservations recommended. Main courses €20–€28 ($32–$45). AE, MC, V. May–Oct daily 6–10pm; Nov–Apr Tues–Sat 6–10pm. Closed Christmas.

Moderate
Achill Cliff House SEAFOOD   With sweeping views of the bay and the Minaun Cliffs beyond, the restaurant in the Achill Cliff House hotel in Keel is one of few good options on Achill Island. As it's just a few yards from the sea, the menu leans toward seafood, with fresh mussels and seafood chowder both good options as starters. For main courses, there's grilled plaice, Clew Bay oysters, and fresh Atlantic lobster. All entrees come with generous portions of fresh vegetables, as well as the decadent house garlic-cheese potatoes. Service is relaxed and friendly, and the mood is one of infectious holiday pleasure.

Main St., Keel, Achill Island, County Mayo. © 098/43400. www.achillcliff.com. Fixed-price dinner €26 ($42). MC, V. Daily 6:30–10pm.

Echoes ★ (Finds IRISH   Look out for this lilac-colored, two-story building in the middle of Main Street in Cong, for it's a likable place. Tom Ryan, Jr., gets his meats from his dad's butcher shop, right next door, and the quality of the produce is exceptional. He does all the classics—lamb with rosemary sauce, steak with peppercorns. Tom's fish dishes are likewise fresh and flavorful, be it dreamy scallops with bacon in garlic butter or his prawn scampi with tomato-and-basil sauce. Starters and desserts are good, too (his homemade ice cream is legendary in these parts).

Main St., Cong, County Mayo. © 094/954-6059. Reservations recommended. Dinner main courses €14–€20 ($22–$32). AE, MC, V. Daily 6:30–10pm.

The Lemon Peel ★ MODERN IRISH   If you dine at the Lemon Peel, chef/owner Robbie McMenamin may just arrive table-side to tell you about the specials himself. The dress code is smart casual, and the bistro is stylish and buzzy. McMenamin uses only local produce to concoct tasty "modern Irish" fare (code for traditional Irish dishes updated with the chef's personal touch). Delicious appetizers include baked goat cheese and red-onion tart, or smooth duck liver parfait as starters, while main courses feature the likes of salmon filet stuffed with crabmeat, or roast duck glazed with honey and Grand Marnier. Everything comes with a medley of fresh vegetables on the side, and the cheese sauce on the broccoli is a state secret. An early-bird menu (served 5–7pm) includes appetizer, main course, sides, and coffee or tea, and is priced according to the main course.

The Octagon, Westport, County Mayo. (C) **098/26929.** www.lemonpeel.ie. Reservations required on weekends. Main courses €17–€23 ($27–$37). AE, MC, V. Tues–Sun 5–11pm.

Inexpensive

La Bella Vita ★ ITALIAN   Its name means "the Beautiful Life," and this relaxed feel-good Italian wine bar–cum-restaurant delivers good pasta, risotto, veal, poultry, and game in a romantic atmosphere, with open fires and candlelight. Start with the antipasti or bruschetta, and leave room for one of the homemade desserts. There's a great wine list here, too.

High St., Westport, County Mayo. (C) **098/29771.** Reservations not accepted. Main courses €8–€16 ($13–$26). MC, V. Tues–Sun 6–10pm.

2 SLIGO & YEATS COUNTRY

Sligo Town: 219km (136 miles) NE of Shannon Airport, 217km (135 miles) NW of Dublin, 76km (47 miles) NE of Knock, 60km (37 miles) NE of Ballina, 140km (87 miles) NE of Galway, 118km (73 miles) N of Athlone, 337km (209 miles) N of Cork

Sligo Town (pop. 18,000) is a thriving farm town on the south side of the River Garavogue, surrounded on three sides by mountains, the most famous of which are Ben Bulben to the north and Knocknarea to the south. A gray and somber town, with a mix of historic and less interesting modern architecture, Sligo is in the midst of a major renaissance. Roughly half of the town center has been refurbished in the past 10 years and work is still underway. From a visitor's perspective, the focus of this radical rejuvenation has been Sligo's new "Left Bank," where cafes and restaurants spill onto the waterfront promenade whenever weather permits. It will also affect you in terms of driving, as construction closes streets and requires confusing roadway diversions, but it's a small enough place that it's really impossible to be lost for long.

Sligo Town isn't busy, historic, or pretty enough to require much of your time, but it is a handy place to base yourself if you really want to explore the bucolic farmland that has become, thanks to the impressive energy of the County Sligo tourism offices, "Yeats Country." Although he was born in Dublin, the poet W. B. Yeats spent so much time in County Sligo that it became a part of him, and he a part of it—literally, as he is buried here. As you'll quickly discover, every hill, cottage, vale, and lake seems to bear a plaque indicating its relation to the poet or his works.

When you plan your itinerary, allow plenty of time to explore the countryside that so inspired him.

SLIGO TOWN ESSENTIALS

GETTING THERE   **Aer Arann** ((C) **011/353-81821-0210** in the U.S., 818/210-210 in Ireland, or 0800/587-23-24 in the U.K.; www.aerarann.ie) operates two daily flights from Dublin into little **Sligo Airport,** Strandhill, County Sligo ((C) **071/916-8280;** www.sligoairport.com), 8km (5 miles) southwest of Sligo Town. The flight takes about 40 minutes. The bus to Sligo Town from the airport will cost you around €4 ($6.40), while you can expect a taxi to cost around €15 to €20 ($24–$32).

Irish Rail, with its station on Lord Edward Street (© 071/916-9888; www.irishrail. ie), operates daily service into Sligo from Dublin.

Bus Éireann, also pulling into Lord Edward Street (© 071/916-0066; www.buseireann. ie), operates daily bus service to Sligo from Dublin, Galway, and other points, including Derry in Northern Ireland.

Four major roads lead to Sligo: N4 from Dublin and the east, N17 from Galway and the south, N15 from Donegal to the north, and N16 from County Fermanagh in Northern Ireland.

VISITOR INFORMATION For information about Sligo and the surrounding area, contact the **North West Tourism and Cultural Centre,** Aras Reddan, Temple Street, Sligo (© 071/916-1201; www.discoverireland.ie/northwest). It's open year-round Monday to Friday 9am to 5pm, with weekend and extended hours April to August. The most comprehensive local Internet source for Sligo can be found at **www.sligotourism.ie.**

TOWN LAYOUT Edged by Sligo Bay to the west, Sligo Town is bisected by the Garavogue River, with most of its commercial district on the river's south bank. **O'Connell Street** is the main north-south artery, and the main east-west thoroughfare is **Stephen Street,** which becomes Wine Street and then Lord Edward Street. The **Tourist Office** is in the southwest corner of the town on Temple Street, 2 blocks south of O'Connell Street. Three bridges span the river; the **Douglas Hyde Bridge,** named for Ireland's first president, is the main link between the two sides.

GETTING AROUND There is no public transport in the town of Sligo. During July and August, **Bus Éireann** (© 071/916-0066) runs from Sligo Town to Strandhill and Rosses Point.

Taxis line up at the taxi stand on Quay Street. If you prefer to call for a taxi, try **A&C Taxis** (© 071/913-8333), **ACE Cabs** (© 071/914-4444), **City Cabs** (© 071/914-5577), or **Euroline Cabs** (© 071/914-4044).

You'll need a car to see the sights outside Sligo Town. If you need to hire one, contact **Avis,** Sligo Airport (© 071/916-8280), or **Hertz,** Sligo Airport (© 071/914-4068).

The best way to see the town is on foot. Follow the signposted route of the Tourist Trail. The walk takes approximately 90 minutes. From mid-June to September, the **Tourist Office,** Temple Street, Sligo (© 071/916-1201), offers guided tours; contact the office for details and reservations.

FAST FACTS In an emergency, dial © **999. St. John's Hospital** is at Ballytivan, Sligo (© 071/914-2606), or you can try **Sligo County Hospital,** The Mall (© 071/914-2620). The **Garda Station** is on Pearse Road (© 071/915-7000).

Need to check your e-mail? There are Internet-accessible PCs at the **County Sligo Library,** on Stephen Street (© 071/914-2212), which is open Tuesday to Friday 10am to 5pm, and Saturday 10am to 1pm and 2 to 5pm.

The **Sligo General Post Office,** Wine Street (© 071/915-9273), is open Monday to Friday 9:30am to 5:30pm and Saturday 9am to 1pm.

SEEING THE SIGHTS IN SLIGO TOWN

Model Arts Centre and Niland Gallery The M.A.C. is a popular venue for touring shows and local exhibits by artists, sculptors, writers, and musicians. In the summer, there are often poetry readings and arts lectures (many of which are free) and a varied program of film screenings by the Sligo Film Society. At this writing, the center was closed for a major redevelopment, which we're concerned to discover involves a rather

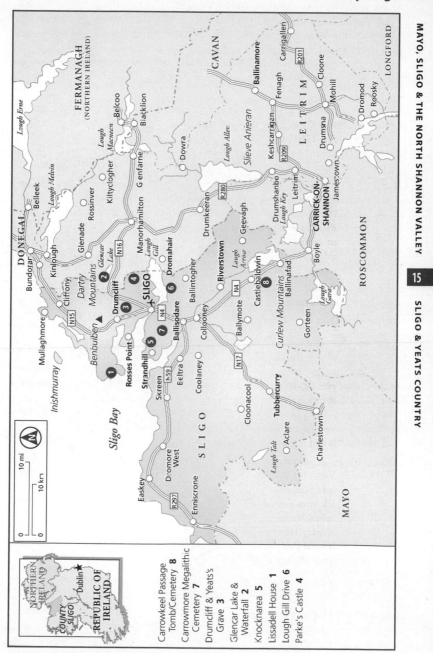

Carrowkeel Passage Tomb/Cemetery **8**
Carrowmore Megalithic Cemetery **7**
Drumcliff & Yeats's Grave **3**
Glencar Lake & Waterfall **2**
Knocknarea **5**
Lissadell House **1**
Lough Gill Drive **6**
Parke's Castle **4**

stark, modernist extension to the 19th-century schoolhouse building in which it all used to take place. Outward appearances aside, however, the plans seem good, with the creation of new performance spaces and galleries, an improved restaurant, and better wheelchair access. It's scheduled to open in early 2009; call ahead for details.

The Mall, Sligo, County Sligo. ℂ **071/914-1405.** www.modelart.ie. Free admission. Readings and lectures free to €10 ($16), depending on artist. Tues–Sun 11am–6pm; evening events 8pm.

Sligo Abbey   Founded as a Dominican house in 1252 by Maurice Fitzgerald, earl of Kildare, Sligo Abbey was the center of early Sligo Town. It thrived for centuries, and flourished in medieval times when it was the burial place of the chiefs and earls of Sligo. But, as with other affluent religious settlements, the abbey was under constant attack, and it was finally destroyed in 1641. Much restoration work has been done in recent years, and the cloisters contain outstanding examples of stone carving; the 15th-century altar is one of few intact medieval altars in Ireland.

Abbey St., Sligo, County Sligo. ℂ **071/914-6406.** Admission €2.10 ($3.35) adults, €1.30 ($2.10) seniors, €1.10 ($1.75) students and children. Mid-Mar to Oct daily 10am–6pm; Nov to mid-Dec Fri–Sun 9:30am–4:30pm.

Sligo County Museum ★   In a 19th-century church mansion, this museum has quite a good exhibit related to Sligo's Stone Age history and archaeological finds in the area. Leaping forward centuries, another section is devoted to the Yeats family, with a display of William Butler Yeats's complete works in first editions, poems on broadsheets, letters, and his Nobel Prize for literature (1923). There's also a collection of oils, watercolors, and drawings by Jack B. Yeats (W. B. Yeats's brother) and John B. Yeats (William and Jack's father). There is a permanent collection of 20th-century Irish art, including works by Paul Henry and Evie Hone.

Stephen St., Sligo, County Sligo. ℂ **071/914-2212.** Free admission. Tues–Sat 10am–noon and 2–4:50pm. Closed Oct–May.

Yeats Memorial Building   In a 19th-century red-brick Victorian building, this memorial contains an extensive library with items of special interest to Yeats scholars. The building is also headquarters of the Yeats International Summer School and the Sligo Art Gallery, which exhibits works by local, national, and international artists. The latest addition is a handy cafe.

Douglas Hyde Bridge, Sligo, County Sligo. ℂ **071/914-2693.** www.yeats-sligo.com. Free admission. Mon–Fri 9:30am–5pm.

Sightseeing Tours & Cruises

Lough Gill Cruises   On this tour, you cruise on Lough Gill and the Garavogue River aboard the 72-passenger *Wild Rose* water bus while listening to the poetry of Yeats. Trips to the Lake Isle of Innisfree are also scheduled. An onboard bar serves refreshments.

Blue Lagoon, Riverside, Sligo, County Sligo. ℂ **071/916-4266.** www.roseofinnisfree.com. Lough Gill cruise from €15 ($24) adults, €7.50 ($12) children 11 and over; Innisfree cruise €17 ($27) adults, €8.50 ($14) children 11 and over. June–Sept Lough Gill cruise daily 2:30 and 4:30pm; Innisfree tour daily 12:30, 3:30, and 6:30pm. Apr–May and Oct (Sun only) cruise and tour schedule subject to demand; call ahead.

SHOPPING IN SLIGO TOWN

Most Sligo shops are open Monday to Saturday 9am to 6pm, and some may have extended hours during July and August.

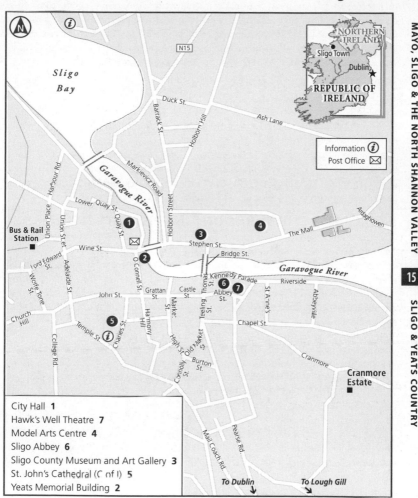

City Hall **1**

Hawk's Well Theatre **7**

Model Arts Centre **4**

Sligo Abbey **6**

Sligo County Museum and Art Gallery **3**

St. John's Cathedral (C of I) **5**

Yeats Memorial Building **2**

The Cat & the Moon   This shop offers uniquely designed crafts from throughout Ireland, ranging from beeswax candles and baskets to modern art, metal and ceramic work, wood turning, hand weaving, Celtic jewelry, and furniture. An expanded gallery displays a large variety of paintings, limited-edition prints, and occasionally sculpture. 4 Castle St., Sligo, County Sligo. © **071/914-3686.**

Kate's Kitchen/Hopper & Pettit   Kate's has an outstanding delicatessen section, with gourmet meats, cheeses, salads, pâtés, and breads baked on the premises, all ideal makings for a picnic. Don't miss the handmade Irish chocolates and preserves. Hopper & Pettit stocks potpourri, soaps, and natural oils, as well as Crabtree & Evelyn products. 3 Castle St., Sligo, County Sligo. © **071/43022.** www.kateskitchensligo.com.

M. Quirke   Michael Quirke started out as a butcher, but a few years ago he traded his cleaver for woodcarving tools and transformed his butcher shop into a craft studio. Step inside and watch as he transforms chunks of native timbers into Ireland's heroes of mythology, from Sligo's Queen Maeve to Cúchulainn, Oisin, and other folklore characters. He also carves chess sets and other Irish-themed wood items. The price of an individual carving averages €90 ($144). Wine St., Sligo, County Sligo. ✆ **071/914-2624.**

Sligo Craft Pottery   This shop features the work of one of Ireland's foremost ceramic artists, Michael Kennedy, who produces pottery and porcelain with layers of textured markings and drawings that form a maze of intricate patterns. He then applies glazes that reflect the strong tones and shades of the Irish countryside in vases, jars, and dishes. Market Yard, Sligo, County Sligo. ✆ **071/914-2586.**

Wehrly Bros. Ltd   Established in 1875, this is one of Sligo's oldest shops, noted for a fine selection of jewelry and watches, as well as cold-cast bronze sculptures of Irish figures, silverware, Claddagh rings, Waterford crystal, Belleek china, and Galway crystal. 3 O'Connell St., Sligo, County Sligo. ✆ **071/914-2252.**

EXPLORING THE SURROUNDING COUNTRYSIDE

The area around Sligo Town is known for its ancient burial grounds and pagan sites, some dating from the Stone Age. As you drive down country lanes, you'll often spy a **dolmen (ancient stone table)** in pastures with sheep or ponies grazing casually around it. The presence of so many burial sites and of the stacked stones of mysterious ancient religions makes this a particularly fascinating section of the country. Some are open to the public, but most are not, and the Irish are passionate about property rights, so don't go clambering over a fence for a better photo without getting permission first.

To plunge in at the deep end of ancient sites, stop by the vast and strangely beautiful **Carrowmore** (see listing below). It's a huge Neolithic cemetery that once contained as many as 200 passage tombs, some predating Newgrange by 500 years. From Carrowmore, you can see the hilltop cairn grave of **Knocknarea** as a lump atop the large hill in the distance. Local legend has it that this is the grave of the "fairy queen" Queen Maeve (Queen Mab in Shakespeare plays). If you have the energy to make the relatively gentle 30-minute climb to the top, the views are extraordinary. (Knocknarea is on the same road as Carrowmore—follow signs for MESCAN MEADHBHA CHAMBERED CAIRN.) From Carrowmore and Knocknarea, it's about an hour's drive to the Neolithic mountaintop cemetery of **Carrowkeel,** which offers an unforgettable experience: After a breathtaking ascent on foot, you'll find yourself alone with the past. The tombs face Carrowmore below and are aligned with the summer solstice.

At the foot of Knocknarea is **Strandhill,** 8km (5 miles) from Sligo Town. This delightful resort area stretches into Sligo Bay, with a sand-duned beach and a patch of land nearby called Coney Island, which is usually credited with lending its name to the New York beach amusement area. Across the bay is another resort, Rosses Point.

Northwest of Sligo Bay, 6km (3³⁄₄ miles) offshore, lies the uninhabited island of **Inishmurray** ★, which contains the haunting ruins of a very early monastic settlement. Founded in the 6th century and destroyed by the Vikings in 807, the monastery of St. Molaise contains in its circular walls the remains of several churches, beehive cells, altars, and an assemblage of "cursing stones" once used to bring ruin on those who presumably deserved it. For transportation to the island, ask at the tourism office, or call **Joe McGowan** (✆ **087/254-0190;** joemcgowan@sligoheritage.com) or **Keith Clarke** (✆ **087/ 667-4522).** Aside from this ancient history and waterfront beauty, most of the rest of

Sligo's attractions are associated in some way with the poet William Butler Yeats, as you'll note below.

Carrowkeel Passage Tomb Cemetery ★★

Atop a hill overlooking Lough Arrow, this ancient cemetery is gorgeous, isolated, and frequently empty. Its 14 cairns, dolmens, and stone circles date from the Stone Age (3000 B.C.), and it's easy to feel that history, standing among the cold, ageless rocks. The walk up from the parking lot takes about 20 minutes, so be ready to get a little exercise. But it's worth the effort. This is a simple site—no visitor center, no tea shop, no admission fee—nothing but ancient mystery.

West off the N4 (signposted on N4), btw. Sligo Town and Boyle, County Sligo. Free admission.

Carrowmore Megalithic Cemetery ★★★

Here, at the dead center of the Coolera Peninsula, sits a massive passage grave that once had a Stonehenge-like stone circle of its own. Encircling that were as many as 200 additional stone circles and passage graves arranged in an intricate and mysterious design. Over the years, some of the stones have been moved, but more than 60 circles and passage graves still exist, although the site spreads out so far that many of them are in adjacent farms. Look out for your first dolmen in a paddock next to the road about a mile before you reach the site. The dolmens were the actual graves, once covered in stones and earth. Some of these are open to visitors—you can get a map to them from the visitor center. On the main site, Tomb 52A (which was only excavated in 1998) is estimated to be 7,400 years old, making it the earliest known piece of free-standing stone architecture in the world. This is one of the great sacred landscapes of the ancient world. It's all well presented, and the excellent visitor center has good exhibits and guided tours.

Carrowmore Visitors Centre (signposted on N4 and N15), County Sligo. ✆ **071/916-1534.** Admission €2.10 ($3.35) adults, €1.30 ($2.10) seniors, €1.10 ($1.75) students and children. Daily 9:30am–6:30pm. Both visitor center and site closed Oct–Apr.

Drumcliff & Yeats's Grave ★

Eight kilometers (5 miles) north of Sligo Town, Drumcliff is a small, stone church that somehow manages to dominate the valley in which it sits—drawing your eye with its tall steeple and its ancient Celtic crosses. When Yeats died in 1939 in France, he asked that, "If I die here, bury me up there on the mountain, and then after a year or so, dig me up and bring me privately to Sligo." True to his wishes, in 1948 his body was moved here, to the church where his great-grandfather had been a rector. As you walk into the graveyard, Yeats's grave is marked with a dark, modest stone just to the left of the church. He's buried alongside his young wife, Georgie Hyde-Lee (when they married in 1917 he was 52 and she was 23). The moving epitaph ("Cast a cold eye on life, on death . . .") comes from his poem "Under Ben Bulben." The church sits atop the 6th-century foundations of the monastery St. Columba, and the round tower on the main road dates from that earlier building. The high cross in the churchyard is from the 11th century, and its faded eastern side shows Christ, Daniel in the lions' den, Adam and Eve, and Cain murdering Abel. On the simpler west side, there's a scene of the crucifixion. The little visitor center has a few gifts and doodads, and an excellent tea shop with marvelous cakes; good, hearty sandwiches; and fresh hot soup.

Drumcliff Churchyard, Drumcliff (off N15), County Sligo.

Lissadell House ★

On the shores of Sligo Bay, this impressive neoclassical building was another of Yeats's favorite haunts. Dating from 1830, it was long the home of the Gore-Booth family, including Yeats's friends Eva Gore-Booth, a fellow poet, and her sister Constance, who became the Countess Markievicz after marrying a Polish count.

She took part in the 1916 Irish Rising and was the first woman elected to the British House of Commons (although she refused to take her seat) and the first woman cabinet member in the Irish Dáil. Lissadell was purchased by a wealthy young family a couple of years ago, and they've certainly been busy since taking over; the house has undergone a complete restoration, including an ambitious conversion of the old gatehouse, which from summer 2008 houses an art gallery and garden museum in addition to the big new reception center. The tearoom serves snacks and light meals, prepared using ingredients from the on-site kitchen gardens, including oysters from their own oyster beds.

Off N15, 13km (8 miles) north of Sligo, Drumcliff, County Sligo. ℂ 071/916-3150; www.lissadellhouse. com. Admission to the house €6 ($9.60) adults, €3 ($4.80) children; house, gardens, and exhibition €12 ($19) adults, €6 ($9.60) children; Victorian Kitchen Garden €5 ($8); Alpine Garden €5 ($8). Daily 10:30am–6pm. Tours take place on the hour.

The Lough Gill Drive ★★   This 42km (26-mile) drive-yourself tour around Lough Gill is well signposted. Head 1.6km (1 mile) south of town and follow the signs for **Lough Gill,** the beautiful lake that figured so prominently in Yeats's writings. Within 3.2km (2 miles) you'll be on the lower edge of the shoreline. Among the sites are **Dooney Rock,** with its own nature trail and lakeside walk (inspiration for the poem "Fiddler of Dooney"); the **Lake Isle of Innisfree,** made famous in Yeats's poetry and in song; and the **Hazelwood Sculpture Trail,** a unique forest walk along the shores of Lough Gill, with 13 wood sculptures.

The storied Innisfree is one of 22 islands in Lough Gill. You can drive the lakeside circuit in less than an hour, or you can stop at the east end and visit **Dromahair ★,** a delightful village on the River Bonet, in County Leitrim. The road along Lough Gill's upper shore brings you back to the northern end of Sligo Town. Continue north on the main road (N15), and you'll see the graceful profile of **Ben Bulben** (519m/1,702 ft.), one of the Dartry Mountains, rising off to your right.

County Sligo and County Leitrim.

Parke's Castle ★   On the north side of the Lough Gill Drive, on the County Leitrim side of the border, Parke's Castle stands out as a lone outpost amid the natural tableau of lake view and woodland scenery. Named after an English family that gained possession of it during the 1620 plantation of Leitrim (when land was confiscated from the Irish and given to favored English families), this castle was originally the stronghold of the O'Rourke clan, rulers of the kingdom of Breffni. Beautifully restored using Irish oak and traditional craftsmanship, it exemplifies the 17th-century fortified manor house. In the visitor center, informative exhibits and a splendid audiovisual show illustrate the history of the castle and introduce visitors to the rich, diverse sites of interest in the surrounding area. The tearoom offers enticing pastries.

Lough Gill Dr., County Leitrim. ℂ **071/916-4149.** Admission €2.90 ($4.65) adults, €2.10 ($3.35) seniors, €1.30 ($2.10) students and children, €7.40 ($12) families. Mid-Mar to Oct Tues–Sun 10am–6pm (last admission 5:15pm).

SPORTS & OUTDOOR PURSUITS

BEACHES   For walking, jogging, or swimming, there are safe sandy beaches with promenades at **Strandhill, Rosses Point,** and **Enniscrone** on the Sligo Bay coast.

BICYCLING   With its lakes and woodlands, Yeats Country is particularly good biking territory. To rent a bike, contact **Flanagans Cycles,** Market Square, Sligo (ℂ **071/ 44477).**

FISHING   For fishing gear and tackle, see **Barton Smith,** Hyde Bridge, Sligo (✆ 071/ 914-6111). For boat rental, see **Kingfisher Bates,** Pier Road, Enniscrone (✆ 096/ 36733).

GOLF   With its seascapes, mountain valleys, and lakesides, County Sligo is known for challenging golf courses. Leading the list is **County Sligo Golf Club ★**, Rosses Point Road, Rosses Point (✆ **071/917-7134;** www.countysligogolfclub.ie), overlooking Sligo Bay under the shadow of Ben Bulben mountain. It's an 18-hole, par-71 championship seaside links famed for its wild, natural terrain and constant winds. Greens fees range from €40 to €125 ($64–$200) weekdays and €50 to €150 ($80–$240) weekends, depending on the time of year.

Eight kilometers (5 miles) west of Sligo Town is **Strandhill Golf Club,** Strandhill (✆ 071/916-8188; www.strandhillgc.com), a seaside par-69 course with greens fees of €40 ($64) weekdays, €50 ($80) weekends. On Mondays from April to October (except Bank Holidays), you can get 18 holes plus coffee and a hearty meal for €30 ($48).

In the southwestern corner of the county, about 40km (25 miles) from Sligo Town and overlooking Sligo Bay, the **Enniscrone Golf Club,** Enniscrone (✆ **096/36297;** www. enniscronegolf.com), is a seaside par-72 course. Greens fees are €60 ($96) weekdays, €75 ($120) weekends.

HORSEBACK RIDING   An hour's or a day's riding on the beach, in the countryside, or over mountain trails can be arranged at **Sligo Riding Centre,** Carrowmore (✆ **071/916-1353**), or at **Woodlands Equestrian Centre,** Loughill, Lavagh, Tubbercurry, County Sligo (✆ **071/918-4207**). Rates average €20 to €30 ($32–$48) per hour.

WHERE TO STAY
Very Expensive
Cromleach Lodge ★★   Thirty-two kilometers (20 miles) south of Sligo Town, this lovely, modern sprawling hotel, nestled in the quiet hills above Lough Arrow, is run by Moira and Christy Tighe. Though not a period house, it's decorated to feel like one. Views from the restaurant, lounges, and most guest rooms deliver a stunning panorama of lake land and mountain scenery. Guest rooms are large by Irish standards and feature sitting areas, oversize orthopedic beds, designer fabrics, and original oil paintings. The hotel was due to open a big extension in 2008, with 60 new rooms and a spa. It wasn't finished in time to visit for this edition, but the biggest attraction will probably remain the award-winning **restaurant** and Moira's fabulous cooking (see below).

Ballindoon, Castlebaldwin, County Sligo. ✆ **071/916-5155.** Fax 071/916-5455. www.cromleach.com. 70 units. €150–€400 ($240–$640) double. Rates include full breakfast. AE, DC, MC, V. Closed Nov–Jan. **Amenities:** Restaurant (modern Continental); 2 lounges; nonsmoking rooms. *In room:* TV, minibar, tea/coffeemaker, safe.

Expensive
Markree Castle   Four stories high, with a forbidding entrance, a monumental stone staircase, and thrusting turrets, Markree is satisfyingly, properly, definitely a castle. It's also family owned—the current owner, Charles Cooper, is the 10th generation of his family to live here. The approach to the castle is impressive—a long drive through smooth, green pastures and past lovely gardens that stretch down to the Unsin River. Climb up the old, stone staircase, and walk through the wooden doors to a hand-carved oak staircase, ornate plasterwork, and a stained-glass window. Once there, though, it all starts to go wrong. The furniture is modern and not well chosen, and much of it has seen better days. Guest rooms are large but quite worn around the edges, and, in our room, the

beds were not at all comfortable. We couldn't help but wonder who chose the vivid and clashing colors and fabrics. Sadly, we found the staff to be less friendly and helpful than we had hoped, but others have said they've had better experiences here. The restaurant (see below) is hit-or-miss—it can be either surprisingly good or startlingly bad. Altogether, this hotel is not for the faint of heart, but many claim to love it, warts and all.

Collooney (13km/8 miles south of Sligo Town), County Sligo. ✆ **800/223-6510** or 800/44-UTELL (448-8355) in the U.S., or 071/916-7800. Fax 071/916-7840. www.markreecastle.ie. 30 units. €165–€230 ($264–$368) double. Rates include full breakfast. AE, MC, V. Closed several days at Christmas. **Amenities:** Restaurant (Continental); horseback riding; salmon fishing. *In room:* TV, tea/coffeemaker, hair dryer.

Moderate

Sligo Park Hotel (Value)   With a glass-fronted facade and sky-lit atrium lobby, this is Sligo's most contemporary hotel, set back from the road amid sprawling parkland, and surrounded by lovely gardens, with distant views of Ben Bulben to the north. The decor in the lobby is modern and creative, with a good use of color, and sleek contemporary furniture. The guest rooms are more generic but inoffensive, with pastel-toned floral fabrics, quilted headboards, and orthopedic beds. The leisure center is a big draw, with a gorgeous indoor pool, and plenty to keep you busy.

Pearse Rd. (just over 1.6km/1 mile south of Sligo on the Dublin rd./N4), Sligo, County Sligo. ✆ **071/919-0400.** Fax 071/916-9556. www.leehotels.ie or www.sligoparkhotel.com. 137 units. €135–€180 ($216–$288) double. Rates include service charge and full breakfast. DC, MC, V. **Amenities:** 2 restaurants (international, cafe); bar; indoor swimming pool; tennis court; gym; Jacuzzi; sauna/steam room; nonsmoking rooms. *In room:* TV, radio, tea/coffeemaker, hair dryer.

Temple House ★★★ (Finds)   A grand manor house tucked away amid pastures, forest, and terraced gardens, Temple House is where you can live out your country house dream. Overlooking a lake and the ruins of a Knights Templar castle, the house impresses with its sheer size and historic authenticity. The Perceval family has lived here since 1665, and recently a new generation, the wonderful Roderick and Helena, have taken over. They artfully juggle raising their two young children with caring for their guests and running their working farm. Guest rooms are enormous—one is so big that it's called "the Half Acre Room"—and filled with heirlooms. Beds are firm and comfortable, and all the bathrooms are modern. The walled garden a short walk from the house supplies the vegetables served with the evening meals, and the fruit offered at breakfast. Book a place for dinner, where the atmosphere is intentionally like a relaxed manor house party—guests meet for drinks around the fire in the drawing room and dine together at the vast table. Breakfast includes homemade cereals, fresh fruit compote, and yogurt. Staying here, even for a night, is a friendly and unique experience. There are now also two charming self-catering guesthouses for those who want a bit more privacy.

> ## Impressions
>
> *Being Irish, I have an abiding sense of tragedy which sustains me through temporary periods of joy.*
>
> —W. B. Yeats

Ballymote, County Sligo. ✆ **071/918-3329.** Fax 071/918-3808. www.templehouse.ie. 6 units. €160–€180 ($256–$288) double. Rates include full breakfast. 4-course dinner €45 ($72). AE, MC, V. Free parking. Closed Dec–Easter. **Amenities:** Wi-Fi; nonsmoking rooms.

Yeats Country Hotel   This hilltop property has sweeping views of Ben Bulben and the sandy beaches of Sligo Bay. Slightly reminiscent of the Edwardian period, the public

rooms are elegant, while guest rooms are blandly traditional in dark woods and floral
bedspreads. However, the rooms are being renovated a few at a time, and those that have
been updated are more tastefully decorated—ask for a renovated room when you book.
There's also a great heated indoor pool and sauna to soak away your cares.

Rosses Point Rd. (8km/5 miles northwest of Sligo Town), Rosses Point, County Sligo. (℗ **800/44-UTELL**
(448-8355) in the U.S., or 071/917-7211. Fax 071/917-7203. www.yeats-country-hotel.com. 79 units.
€150–€190 ($240–$304) double. Rates include service charge and full Irish breakfast. AE, DC, MC, V.
Amenities: Restaurant (international); bar; indoor swimming pool; gym; Jacuzzi; sauna/steam room;
babysitting; dry cleaning. *In room:* TV, tea/coffeemaker, hair dryer.

WHERE TO DINE
Very Expensive
Cromleach Lodge ★★★ MODERN CONTINENTAL   It's worth the drive 32km
(20 miles) south of Sligo Town to dine at this lovely country house overlooking Lough
Arrow. The panoramic views are secondary, however, to Chef Moira Tighe's food, which
has won a fistful of prestigious awards. The menu changes nightly, depending on what is
freshest and best from the sea and garden. It may include such dishes as filet of halibut
with sun-dried tomato beurre blanc, and loin of lamb with garlic and Irish Mist. Desserts
are characterized by an imaginative and expertly judged combination of flavors, such as
warm ginger sponge with apple compote, honey-vanilla ice cream and praline sauce, or
marinated fruits with gin-and-tonic sorbet. The dining room is a delight, with plaster
moldings and chair rails, curio cabinets with figurines and crystal, ruffled valances, pot-
ted palms, and place settings of Rosenthal china and fine Irish linens and silver. If you
love it so much you may want to spend the night here (see above).

Ballindoon, Castlebaldwin, County Sligo. (℗ **071/916-5155.** www.cromleach.com. Reservations required.
Main courses €29 ($46). AE, MC, V. Daily 6:30–9pm. Closed Nov–Jan.

Expensive
Markree Castle Restaurant INTERNATIONAL   This is an extraordinary-looking
restaurant—a regal 60-seat room under lavish 19th-century Louis Philippe–style plasterwork inside a grand, stone castle. You dine like a king here, but unfortunately the food
doesn't always reach royal status. The menu can dazzle with its use of local produce and
game in dishes such as thyme-marinated Irish lamb in Maderia *jus,* or fresh scallops and
crabmeat lasagna, but it can also disappoint with a provincial cooking style and unprofes-
sional staff. As with the castle's hotel (see above), this place has its fans and its enemies.
Some love its unpredictability and localism, and some say they received dreadful service
and worse food. But even many of the latter say it might be worth it just to dine in that
gorgeous room.

Collooney, County Sligo. (℗ **071/916-7800.** Reservations required. Main courses €24–€36 ($38–$58); fixed-
price dinner €45 ($72). AE, DC, MC, V. Daily 7–9pm; Sun 1–2:30pm. Closed several days at Christmas.

Moderate
Austie's Bar and Restaurant SEAFOOD   Set on a hill with lovely views of Sligo
Bay, this pub-restaurant is filled with nautical knickknacks, fishnets, periscopes, and paintings of sailing ships. Substantial pub grub is available during the day—open-faced sandwiches of crab, salmon, or smoked mackerel; crab claw or mixed-seafood salads; and hearty
soups and chowders. The dinner menu offers such fresh seafood choices as pan-fried Dover
sole and crab au gratin, as well as steaks and chicken curry. Lobster is also available, at
market prices. Outdoor seating on picnic tables is available in good weather.

Rosses Point Rd. (6.5km/4 miles northwest of Sligo), Rosses Point, County Sligo. ℭ **071/917-7111.** Reservations recommended. Main courses €10–€27 ($16–$43). MC, V. Daily 5:30–9:30pm; Sun 12:30–3:30pm.

Inexpensive

Cafe Bar Deli ⟨Finds⟩ MEDITERRANEAN   This small Irish chain is always reliable for simple yet sophisticated cuisine in relaxed, attractive surroundings. Good salads include one with goat cheese, beets, and walnuts, while there's a lengthy menu of stone-baked pizzas and plenty of light, healthy pasta dishes. This is just the place for when you need a break from lamb, beef, and the like.

15 Rear Stephen's St., Sligo, County Sligo. ℭ **071/914-0100.** Main courses €10–€13 ($16–$21). MC, V. Wed–Sun 6–10pm.

SLIGO AFTER DARK

Pubs

The Crossbar   In the heart of County Sligo's rich traditional music scene, this bright yellow pub stands at the center of the little village of Gurteen. There's always a lively buzz from the local crowd, drawn by the congeniality of owners Adrian Tansey and Pauline Walsh and the warmth of the open fireplace. This is the preferred hangout of the Sligo Gaelic football team, with the requisite big-screen television to air major sporting events. Gurteen, County Sligo. ℭ **071/918-2203.**

15

Hargadon Brothers   This pub is legendary. The decor is a mélange of dark-wood walls, mahogany counters, stone floors, colored glass, old barrels and bottles, a potbellied stove, and alcoves. There are four snugs, and together they are reminiscent of an old-fashioned railway carriage—a bit cramped, but extremely conducive to conversation. 4 O'Connell St., Sligo, County Sligo. ℭ **071/917-0933.**

Stanford's Village Inn   Five generations of the McGowan family have run this old tavern, and not much has changed over the years. There are several comfortable bars with open fires, and there's a delightful blend of old stone walls, vintage pictures, and oil lamps. If you're driving around Lough Gill from Sligo, this 160-year-old pub is a great midway stop for a drink or a snack. Main St., Dromahair, County Leitrim. ℭ **071/916-4140.**

The Thatch   Established in 1638 as a coaching inn, this pub is about 8km (5 miles) south of Sligo on the main road. Its thatched roof and whitewashed exterior have withstood modernization without losing charm. Irish traditional music usually starts at 9pm on Thursday and Sunday year-round and Tuesday through Sunday in August. Dublin-Sligo rd. (N4), Ballisodare, County Sligo. ℭ **071/916-7288.**

The Performing Arts

Blue Raincoat Theatre   This is Sligo's award-winning theater company. It is one of only three professional Irish acting companies (the Abbey in Dublin and the Druid in Galway are the others) that own their own theaters. During July and August, the Blue Raincoat often presents lunchtime performances of Yeats's plays, as well as other Sligo-related productions. Evening shows usually start at 8pm. Lower Quay St., Sligo, County Sligo. ℭ **071/917-0431.** www.blueraincoat.com. Tickets average €10–€15 ($16–$24).

Hawk's Well Theatre   The premier stage of Ireland's northwest region, this modern 350-seat theater presents a varied program of drama, comedy, ballet, opera, and concerts of modern and traditional music. It derives its name from *At the Hawk's Well,* a one-act play by Yeats. The theater occasionally produces shows, but mostly books visiting profes-sional and local companies. The box office is open Monday to Saturday 10am to 6pm; most shows open at 8pm. Johnston Court, Sligo, County Sligo. © **071/916-1526.** www.hawks well.com. Tickets average €7–€25 ($11–$40).

3 THE NORTH SHANNON VALLEY: ROSCOMMON, LEITRIM & CAVAN

Roscommon: 82km (51 miles) NE of Galway; 147km (91 miles) NW of Dublin; Longford: 129km (80 miles) NW of Dublin, 44km (27 miles) NE of Athlone; Carrick-on-Shannon: 56km (35 miles) SE of Sligo; Cavan: 105km (65 miles) NW of Dublin

The northern region of the Republic sprawls across three counties, with vast green parks and luxurious manor houses dolloped generously across it like clotted cream on a scone. Through it all, the River Shannon pours and rushes and trickles into a series of lakes, canals, and waterways, providing plenty to keep rough-and-ready anglers and sailors happy.

In **County Roscommon** you can spend days wandering through places like the grand Strokestown Park House, which, with its sobering Irish Famine Museum, tells of both the haves and the have-nots of Ireland's recent past. Head to the town of **Boyle** to won-der at the ancient carvings on the worn walls of Boyle Abbey and explore the green and pleasant baths within the wilds of Lough Key Forest Park before heading off to discover the lost worlds of Roscommon Castle.

In **County Leitrim,** above Lough Ree, the river is relatively narrow until it reaches the town of **Carrick-on-Shannon,** which sits beautifully at one of the great ancient crossing places of the Shannon, now the Ballinamore-Ballyconnell Canal, which provides a clear path from the Shannon in the Republic of Ireland all the way to Lough Erne in Ulster. Carrick-on-Shannon is one of the true boating hubs in Ireland, and its vast marina holds dozens of companies that rent or sell cabin cruisers.

Similarly, **County Cavan** is a lovely place to drive through, with thick forests, miles of farmland, and a distinctive form of local crystal that makes a memorable souvenir.

AREA ESSENTIALS
GETTING THERE & GETTING AROUND   The best way to get to and around the Upper Shannon area is by car. Although there is public transportation to major towns, you will need a car to get to most of the attractions. Among the main roads that lead to this area are the main Dublin-Sligo road (N4), the main Dublin-Cavan road (N3), N5 and N63 from Castlebar and the west, and N61 and N55 from the south.

VISITOR INFORMATION   Information on **County Roscommon** is available from the **Ireland West Tourism Office,** Foster Street, Galway (© **091/537700;** www.discover ireland.ie/west). Hours are May, June, and September daily 9am to 5:45pm; July and August daily 9am to 7:45pm; and October to April Monday to Friday 9am to 5:45pm and Saturday 9am to 12:45pm. Information on **County Cavan** is available from the **Cavan Tourist Office,** Farnham Street, Cavan, County Cavan (© **049/437-7200;** www.cavan tourism.com), open May through September Monday to Friday 9am to 6pm, Saturday 10am to 2pm; on **County Leitrim** from the **North-West Tourism Office,** Aras Reddan, Temple Street, Sligo (© **071/916-1201**), open Easter through September Monday to

Friday 9am to 6pm, Saturday 9am to 5pm, and Sunday 9am to 3pm, with extended hours in July and August; and also from the tourist office at **Carrick-on-Shannon** (✆ **071/962-0170**), open May through September Monday to Saturday 9:15am to 5:30pm and Sunday 10am to 2pm.

    Seasonal information points, operating from June to August, are signposted in Boyle (✆ **071/966-2145**), Longford (✆ **043/46566**), and Roscommon (✆ **090/662-6342**).

EXPLORING THE AREA

Boyle Abbey ★   Sitting forlornly in a corner of bustling central Boyle, rugged old Boyle Abbey looks sad and forgotten. Time has truly passed it by. Founded in 1161 by Cistercian monks from Mellifont, and once a large and architecturally beautiful place, the abbey was a haven of otherworldliness for 500 years until it was savagely destroyed in the mid-1600s by English soldiers suppressing Irish Catholicism. As part of their efforts, they murdered the resident monks and converted the structure into a military garrison. After they left it, it was abandoned to decay. Today the ruins form a complex fossil clearly imprinted with both the serene and violent aspects of the abbey's history. The 13th-century nave in the northern section of the structure still has distinctive capitals on its columns, some carved with faces, others with fanciful creatures and dragons. There's a *sheela-na-gig* (an erotic pagan symbol) tucked in one corner of the nave, according to the abbey's own information, but despite enthusiastic searching, we were unable to find the sexy little wench. The interpretive center, housed in the restored gatehouse, is informative and thoughtfully designed.

N4, Boyle, County Roscommon. ✆ **071/966-2604.** Admission €2.10 ($3.35) adults, €1.30 ($2.10) seniors, €1.10 ($1.75) students and children, €5.80 ($9.30) families. Easter–Oct daily 10am–6pm.

Cavan Crystal Craft & Design Centre ★   One of the country's top crystal companies, this establishment is known for its delicate glassware, mouth-blown and hand-cut by skilled craftspeople. Visitors are invited to watch as the master blowers fashion the molten crystal into intricate shapes and designs, which are then finished by master cutters. Handily enough, the completed products are sold in the center's shop. Bring your credit card, but don't make any sudden moves in this fragile place.

Dublin rd. (N3), Cavan, County Cavan. ✆ **049/433-1800.** www.cavancrystaldesign.com. Free admission. Mon–Fri 9:30am–6pm; Sat 10am–5pm; Sun noon–6pm.

Clonalis House ★   This great house stands on land that has belonged to the O'Conor clan for more than 1,500 years. The O'Conors were the kings of Connaught, and this is the current home of the O'Conor Don, a direct descendant of the last high king of Ireland. The house, built in 1880, is a combination of Victorian, Italianate, and Queen Anne architecture, with mostly Louis XV–style furnishings, plus antique lace, horse-drawn farm machinery, and other memorabilia. Its primary attraction, though, is its O'Conor clan collection of portraits, documents, and genealogical tracts 2,000 years old. Displays include an ancient harp said to have belonged to Turlough O'Carolan (1670–1738), a blind Irish bard who composed tunes still played today. The grounds, with terraced and woodland gardens, hold the O'Conor inauguration stone, similar to the Stone of Scone at Westminster Abbey. If you really want to experience Clonalis, stay the night—bed-and-breakfast accommodations are offered from €140 to €170 ($224–$272) per night for a double. There are also self-catering cottages on the grounds at thoroughly reasonable rates.

On the N60 west of Castlerea, County Roscommon. ✆ **094/962-0014.** www.clonalis.com. Admission €7 ($11) adults, €6 ($9.60) students and seniors, €5 ($8) children 7–12. June–Aug Mon–Sat 11am–5pm.

Boyle Abbey **1**
Cavan Crystal **4**
Clonalis House **7**
Irish Famine Museum **6**
Lough Key Forest Park **2**
Lough Rynn Castle **3**
Strokestown Park House **5**

Lough Key Forest Park ★ (Kids   Stretching for miles along the shores of Lough Key, encompassing lush woodlands, a glassy lake, and a dozen islands, this park holds nature walks, ancient monuments, ring forts, a central viewing tower, picnic grounds, a cafe, and a shop. All of it was privately owned until 1957, when it was sold to the Irish Land Commission. Sadly, the manor house designed by John Nash burned long ago, but even without it, there's plenty to see and do. In addition to cypress groves and wildflower meadows, there are bog gardens filled with unusual peat-loving plants and shrubs. Wildlife, including deer, otters, and shy hedgehogs, has the run of the place. The ruins of a 12th-century abbey can be seen on Trinity Island, while on Castle Island, a 19th-century castle stands there, as if taunting you for not living someplace this beautiful. Powerboats and rowboats are available to rent if you want a closer look. Pony and cart rides are a good way to explore the park without breaking a sweat, and there's also an audio tour that takes you through a 9m-high (30-ft.) tree canopy walk and a section of Victorian tunnel. There's plenty for kids here, too, with the **Adventure Kingdom,** a vaguely castle-themed playground, and **Borda Borg,** a rather peculiar indoor problem-solving game—although neither is likely to amuse anyone but the very youngest.

Enter from the main Dublin-Sligo rd. (N4), 3km (2 miles) east of Boyle, County Roscommon. © 071/966-2363. www.loughkey.ie. Admission to park €5 ($8) per car charged Apr–Sept only. Year-round daily dawn–dusk.

Strokestown Park House, Gardens, and Famine Museum ★★★ Strokestown Park House was the seat of the Pakenham-Mahon family from 1600 to 1979, and the vast estate, which stretches for miles in every direction, was granted to Nicholas Mahon by King Charles II after the Restoration in appreciation of his support of the House of Stewart during the bloody English Civil War. It was quite a reward. The original house, completed in 1697, was considered to be too small and unimposing by Nicholas's grandson, Thomas. So he hired Richard Cassels (also known as Richard Castle) to build him something bigger and more impressive. The result is this 45-room Palladian house. The north wing houses Ireland's last existing galleried kitchen (where the lady of the house could observe the culinary activity without being part of it). The south wing is an elaborate vaulted stable so magnificent that it has been described as an "equine cathedral."

To see the other end of the economic scale, head out into the old stable yards to the excellent **Irish Famine Museum** ★★. Anyone who wants to understand the effects and causes of the deadly potato blight of the 1840s will want to visit this exhibition. It chronicles the twists of fate, catastrophic mistakes, and callous disregard that caused widespread starvation and mass deaths. The cruel irresponsibility of the landowners and the British government of Ireland in ignoring the spreading death and disease is exposed in jaw-dropping detail. This has been called one of the most important museums in Ireland, and that is not overstating it.

On the main Dublin-Castlebar rd. (N5), Strokestown Park, Strokestown, County Roscommon. © 071/963-3013. www.strokestownpark.ie. Admission to house, garden, and museum €14 ($22) adults, €13 ($21) seniors and students, €7 ($11) children, €30 ($48) families; separate admission to each sight €9.50 ($15) adults, €5.50 ($8.80) seniors and students. Mar–Oct daily 10am–5:30pm.

SPORTS & OUTDOOR PURSUITS

BOATING There are dozens of companies renting out cabin cruisers on the Shannon. **Carrick Craft,** The Marina, Carrick-on-Shannon, County Leitrim (© 071/962-0236; www.carrickcraft.com), and **Emerald Star Line,** The Marina, Carrick-on-Shannon, County Leitrim (© 071/962-0234), are two that get particularly good word of mouth.

FISHING Head to Roscommon Town and stop by the Tourist Office (John Harrison Hall, The Square; © 090/662-6342; www.discoverireland.ie/west) and ask for a map of the **Suck Valley Way.** The walk along the river passes some of the best fishing in Ireland, according to local fishermen. With the right equipment, you could catch rudd, tench, pike, and perch.

GOLF The **Slieve Russell Hotel Golf Club,** Cranaghan, Ballyconnell, County Cavan (© 049/952-6444; www.quinnhotels.com), charges greens fees of €75 ($120) weekdays and €90 ($144) weekends for nonguests of the hotel. Guests of the hotel (see below) pay €50 ($80) weekdays and €60 ($96) weekends.

Two other 18-hole courses in the area are **County Cavan Golf Club,** Arnmore House, Drumellis, County Cavan (© 049/433-1541; www.cavangolf.ie), with greens fees of €30 ($48) weekdays, €35 ($56) weekends; and **County Longford Golf Club,** Dublin Road, Longford (© 043/46310; www.countylongfordgolfclub.com), with greens fees of €25 ($40) weekdays, €30 ($48) weekends.

Strokestown: A Kind of Atonement

The somber and informative Famine Museum at Strokestown could be seen as a kind of atonement for the behavior of Major Denis Mahon, the landlord at Strokestown in the 1840s. When a blight killed the country's potato crop, setting off widespread famine, Mahon and his land agents could have done many things to help the hundreds of starving peasants who lived and worked on the property, but instead they evicted them as soon as it became clear they would not be able to pay their rent. He even went so far as to charter ships to send them away from Ireland. In 1847 Major Mahon was shot to death near Strokestown, and two men were hastily (and dubiously) convicted of the crime. But it seems clear that many hungry people had motives.

HORSEBACK RIDING **Moorlands Equestrian & Leisure Centre,** Drumshanbo, County Leitrim (✆ **071/964-1500;** www.moorlands.ie), offers lessons, as well as trail rides along Lough Allen and the nearby hills. Children are welcome. During the off season, courses in equestrian science are offered. Book lessons or trail rides at least a day in advance. Mountain walking, watersports, and accommodations are also offered.

WHERE TO STAY & DINE
Expensive

Lough Rynn Castle   Seat of the Clements, the earls of Leitrim, this new hotel is in a grand 19th-century stone castle, surrounded by a vast, sprawling estate of woodland, ornamental gardens, open pastures, and lakes. It will entrance history buffs and garden lovers. Its perfectly restored terraced walled garden dates from 1859, and is designed in the manner of a Victorian pleasure garden. Inside it's all a certain kind of luxury: silk wallpaper, Chippendale chairs, polished antiques, and floral carpets—you get the picture. Beds are big and piled high with cushions and linens; some are four-poster, many are antiques. Views are pastoral, and the mood throughout is formal. There are many handsome guest lounges where you can have tea and relax, and the hotel restaurant is in a simply gorgeous historic room.

South of Carrick-on-Shannon, on the outskirts of Mohill, 5.2km (3¼ miles) from the main Dublin-Sligo rd. (N4), County Leitrim. ✆ **071/963-1427.** www.manorhousehotels.com. 40 units. €165–€290 ($264–$464) double. Rates include full breakfast. AE, MC, V. **Amenities:** Restaurant (modern European); bar; 18-hole golf course; fishing privileges; walking trails. In room: TV, fridge, tea/coffeemaker, hair dryer.

Slieve Russell Hotel ★ (Kids)   Set amid vast parklands, lake land, and gardens, this impressive resort hotel is a popular destination among the Irish. (The easy 2-hr. drive from the capital means it's big with Dubliners.) It's a well-designed modern building with the feel of a historic hotel—the public areas have huge open fireplaces, marble staircases, and wrought-iron trim. Guest rooms vary—some are traditional in style, less attractive, and small, others are modern and bigger. It seems to be random selection of which kind you get, so hope for the best.

Ballyconnell, County Cavan. ✆ **049/952-6444.** Fax 049/952-6474. www.quinnhotels.com. 219 units. €170–€250 ($272–$400) double. Rates include full breakfast. DC, MC, V. Free parking. **Amenities:** 2 restaurants (international, brasserie); 2 bars; indoor swimming pool; 18-hole championship golf course;

4 tennis courts; 2 squash courts; exercise room; spa; Jacuzzi; sauna/steam room; children's playroom; concierge; salon; room service; babysitting; laundry service; dry cleaning; walking trails. *In room:* TV, minibar, tea/coffeemaker, hair dryer, garment press.

Moderate

The Park Hotel ★   Originally known as Deer Park Lodge, a sporting and summer residence of the marquis of Headfort in the mid–18th century, this grand old building has been a hotel since the 1930s. Set on sylvan grounds, with forest walks and trickling streams, it makes a big impact when you first drive up. Over the years, the building itself has undergone a number of renovations and extensions, making for lots of connecting corridors and varying standards of guest rooms; some are sleek, large, and modern, others are less so. The lounge retains an 18th-century charm, with high ceilings, chandeliers, period furnishings, and original oil paintings. The hotel and its kitchen are used as the Irish campus for the Baltimore International (Culinary) College in the off season, so it comes as no surprise that the food in the hotel **restaurant** is excellent modern European cuisine.

Deer Park Lodge, Cavan-Dublin rd. (N3), Virginia, County Cavan. ℂ **049/854-6100.** Fax 049/854-7203. www.parkhotelvirginia.com. 28 units. €150–€200 ($240–$320) double. Rates include full breakfast. AE, MC, V. **Amenities:** Restaurant (modern European); bar; 9-hole golf course; tennis court; fishing privileges; walking trails. *In room:* TV.

Ross Castle and House ★★ (Value   Owners Benita and Sam Walker have turned this family-run farm on Lough Sheelin into one of the nicest hideaways in this affordable corner of Ireland. There are two equally intriguing options amid the bucolic sheep and cow pastures. Ross Castle is a 16th-century fortified tower that's said to be haunted by a lovesick bride-to-be named Sabrina, whose lover, Orwin, drowned in Lough Sheelin en route to their elopement. Along with spirits, it contains four guest rooms, including one family room. Rooms are comfortable, pleasantly decorated, and atmospheric. Nearby, Ross House is a spacious, comfortable manor house with seven lovely guest rooms. The oldest portions of the building date from the mid–17th century. On request, three-course dinners are served, with an excellent small selection of wines, modestly priced. Whether you fish for trout or ghosts, this is a most congenial spot. Fisherfolk take note: The farm is noted for its brown trout and is stocked with pike and perch.

Mount Nugent, County Cavan. Ross Castle ℂ **043/81286.** www.ross-castle.com. 16 units. €110–€130 ($176–$208) double. Breakfast €7 ($11). MC, V. Closed Dec–Feb. **Amenities:** Tennis court; Jacuzzi; sauna; massage treatments; babysitting; drawing room; horseback riding. *In room:* TV (house only).

A PUB

There are many good pubs in this area, but don't miss the **Derragarra Inn,** Butlersbridge, County Cavan (ℂ **049/433-1003**), for a drink or a meal. Relax by the turf fireplace or on the garden patio. It's 6km (3³/₄ miles) north of Cavan Town.

County Donegal

Beyond Sligo, the topography changes and the roads twist and turn through tortuous corkscrews. When the signs change into Gaelic, and the landscape opens up into great sweeping views of rocky hills and barren shores, and a freezing mist blows in off the sea, you've reached Donegal. The austere beauty of this county can be almost too bleak, but it is also unforgettable. On a sunny day, you can stand at the edge of the sea at Malin Head and, despite the sun, the wind and the sea spray will blow a chill right through you—it feels as if you're standing at the edge of the world. Its natural wonders include the magnificent Slieve League cliffs and the remote beaches tucked into the bays and inlets of its sharply indented coast.

The towns of Donegal are perhaps the least developed for tourism in Ireland. Few tourists make it this far. Buildings are made of cold stone and villages perch on the slopes of precipitous hillsides. When you stop to take a wander, you can't help but wonder if the car's brakes will hold. But take that chance. The people in Donegal are as nice as can be, and meeting them is worth the trip in itself. Of course, fewer tourists mean fewer amenities. It's harder to find good restaurants and modern guesthouses. In addition, you'll have to contend with road signs that vary from cryptic to nonexistent. You will spend half your time lost. But it's a small island, and wherever you're headed, you'll get there eventually and you're bound to have adventures along the way.

1 DONEGAL TOWN

222km (138 miles) NW of Dublin, 283km (176 miles) NE of Shannon Airport, 66km (41 miles) NE of Sligo, 69km (43 miles) SW of Derry, 180km (112 miles) W of Belfast, 205km (127 miles) NE of Galway, 403km (250 miles) N of Cork, 407km (253 miles) NE of Killarney

Overseen by a low, gloomy castle at the edge of the picturesque estuary of the River Eske on Donegal Bay, Donegal Town (pop. 3,200) is a small country burg. As recently as the 1940s, the town's central mall (called "the Diamond") was used as a market for trading livestock and goods. Today the marketing is done in the form of tweeds and tourist goods, as the Diamond is surrounded by little crafts shops and somewhat dingy small hotels. Although Donegal Town makes for a pleasant enough stop after miles of empty countryside, it's not the best place to spend the night as most of its hotels are old-fashioned, and there are more interesting hostelries in the surrounding countryside. If you're here at the end of June, you can catch part of the lively Donegal Arts Festival, which fills the town with traditional Irish singing, dancing, and storytelling.

ESSENTIALS

GETTING THERE   **Aer Arann** (*©* **011/353-81821-0210** in the U.S., 818/210-210 in Ireland, or 0800/587-23-24 in the U.K.; www.aerarann.ie) flies twice daily from Dublin to tiny **Donegal Airport,** Carrickfinn, Kincasslagh, County Donegal (*©* **074/954-8284;** www.donegalairport.ie), about 65km (40 miles) northwest of Donegal Town on the Atlantic coast.

Bus Éireann (© 074/912-1309; www.buseireann.ie) operates daily bus service to Donegal Town from Dublin, Derry, Sligo, Galway, and other points. All tickets are issued on the bus. The pickup and boarding point is in front of the Abbey Hotel on the Diamond.

If you're driving from the south, Donegal is reached on N15 from Sligo or A46 or A47 from Northern Ireland; from the east and north, it's N15 and N56; from the west, N56 leads to Donegal Town.

VISITOR INFORMATION The **Donegal Tourist Office,** Quay Street (© 074/972-1148), is open Easter through September Monday to Friday 9am to 5pm, Saturday 10am to 6pm, and Sunday noon to 4pm, with extended hours in July and August. For online tourist information, go to **www.donegaltown.ie.**

TOWN LAYOUT The town is laid out around the triangular central mall called the Diamond, where the roads from Killybegs, Ballyshannon, and Ballybofey converge. **Main Street** and **Upper Main Street,** which form the prime commercial strip, extend northeast from the Diamond.

GETTING AROUND Easily walked, Donegal has no local bus service within the town. Taxis park in the Diamond, or call **Jim Johnston** (© 074/972-1349) or **Brendan McBrearty** (© 074/913-3420).

There is a pay parking lot along the quay beside the tourist office and off Main Street.

A booklet outlining the signposted walking tour of Donegal Town is available at the tourist office and most bookshops.

FAST FACTS In an **emergency,** dial © **999.** Donegal **District Hospital** is on Upper Main Street (© 074/972-1019). The local **Garda Station** is on Quay Street (© 074/972-1021).

Donegal County Library, Mountcharles Road (© 074/972-1705), is open Monday, Wednesday, and Friday 3 to 6pm, and Saturday 11am to 1pm and 2 to 6pm. Internet access is free (for the time being), but there is a limit of 1 hour per session. Book ahead.

The **Donegal Post Office** on Tirconnail Street (© 074/972-1024) is open Monday, Tuesday, and Thursday to Saturday 9am to 5:30pm, Wednesday 9:30am to 5:30pm.

EXPLORING DONEGAL TOWN

The greatest attraction of Donegal Town is the town's layout itself, a happy mix of medieval and modern buildings. Most of the structures are there for you to wander at will, with no audiovisuals, interpretive exhibits, admission charges, or crowds.

The **Diamond** is the triangular market square dominated by an obelisk erected in memory of four early-7th-century Irish clerics from the local abbey who wrote *The Annals of Ireland,* the first recorded history of Gaelic Ireland.

Lough Derg and its many islands lie about 16km (10 miles) east of Donegal. Legend has it that St. Patrick spent 40 days and 40 nights fasting in a cavern at this secluded spot, and since then it has been revered as a place of penance and pilgrimage. From June 1 to August 15, thousands of Irish people take turns coming to Lough Derg to do penance for 3 days at a time, remaining awake and eating nothing but tea and toast. It's considered one of the most rigorous pilgrimages in all of Christendom. To reach the lake, take R232 to Pettigo, then R233 for 8km (5 miles).

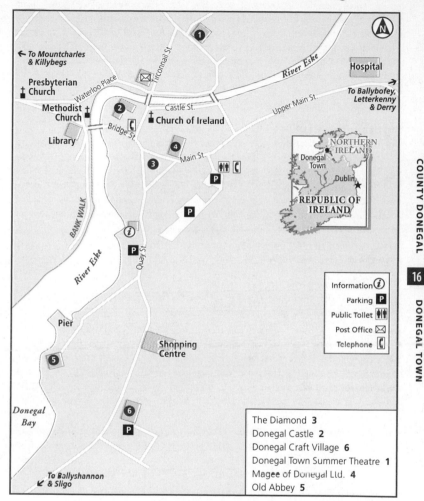

The Diamond **3**
Donegal Castle **2**
Donegal Craft Village **6**
Donegal Town Summer Theatre **1**
Magee of Donegal Ltd. **4**
Old Abbey **5**

Donegal Castle Built in the 15th century on the banks of the River Eske, this stern castle was once the chief stronghold for the O'Donnells, a powerful Donegal clan. In the 17th century, during the Plantation period, it was taken over by Sir Basil Brook, who added an extension with 10 gables, a large bay window, and smaller mullioned windows in Jacobean style. Much of the building has survived the centuries, and both the interior and exterior of the castle were beautifully restored in 1996. Free 25-minute guided tours are available.

Castle St., Donegal. ℂ **074/972-2405.** Admission €3.70 ($5.90) adults, €2.60 ($4.15) seniors, €1.30 ($2.10) students and children. Mid-Mar to Oct daily 10am–5:15pm.

Old Abbey Sitting in a peaceful spot where the River Eske meets Donegal Bay, this ruined Franciscan monastery was founded in 1474 by the first Red Hugh O'Donnell and his wife, Nuala O'Brien of Munster. It was generously endowed by the O'Donnell family and became an important center of religion and learning. Great gatherings of clergy and lay leaders assembled here in 1539. It was from this friary that some of the scholars undertook to salvage old Gaelic manuscripts and compile *The Annals of the Four Masters* (1632–36). Enough remains of its glory—ruins of a church and a cloister—to give you an idea of what once was.

The Quay, Donegal. Free admission.

Sightseeing Cruises

Donegal Bay Waterbus New and improved, this 160-seat boat has replaced the older, smaller version. The new, modern two-deck boat makes daily tours of Donegal Bay. The guided tour lasts 90 minutes and passes the Old Abbey and Seal Island, home to a colony of about 200 noisy seals. (*Warning:* The guide never seems to take a break, and the detailed commentary is nonstop.) The views are wonderful. Sailing times are usually morning and afternoon or evening, but are dependent upon weather and the tides. Tickets can be obtained from the ticket office on the pier.

The Pier, Donegal Town. ℂ 074/972-3666. €15 ($24) adults, €5 ($8) seniors and children 4–12, free for children 3 and under. Closed Oct–Apr.

SHOPPING

Most Donegal shops are open Monday to Saturday from 9am to 6pm, with extended hours in summer and slightly shorter hours in winter.

Donegal Craft Village This cluster of artisans' shops in a rural setting about 1.6km (1 mile) south of town provides a creative environment for an ever-changing group of craftspeople and a range of ancient and modern trades: porcelain, ceramics, weaving, batik, jewelry, and metalwork. You can browse from shop to shop and see the artists at work. The coffee shop serves baked goods, snacks, and lunch in the summer. The studios are open year-round Monday to Saturday 10am to 6pm and Sunday noon to 6pm. Ballyshannon Rd., Donegal. ℂ 074/972-2015.

Forget-Me-Not/The Craft Shop This shop features a wide selection of gifts both usual and unusual. Items include handmade jewelry, Celtic art cards, Donegal county banners and hangings, Irish traditional music figures, tweed paintings, bog oak sculptures, and beaten-copper art. The Diamond, Donegal. ℂ 074/972-1168.

Magee of Donegal Ltd. Established in 1866, this shop is *the* name for fine Donegal hand-woven tweeds, including beautiful suits, jackets, overcoats, hats, ties, and even material on the bolt. The Diamond, Donegal. ℂ 074/972-2660. www.mageedonegal.com.

Melody Maker Music Shop If you're enchanted by the traditional and folk music of Donegal, stop in here for tapes, recordings, and posters. This is also the main ticket agency for the southwestern section of County Donegal, handling tickets for most concerts and sports nationwide. Castle St., Donegal. ℂ 074/972-2326.

William Britton & Sons Established in 1874, this shop stocks antique jewelry, silver, crystal, clocks, sports-related sculptures, pens, and watches. W. J. Britton is a registered appraiser and a fellow of the National Association of Goldsmiths of Great Britain and Ireland. Main St., Donegal. ℂ 071/912-1131.

BICYCLING   The north side of Donegal Bay offers great cycling roads—scenic but very hilly. For long-distance bikers, one good but arduous route from Donegal Town follows the coast roads west to Glencolumbkille (day 1), continues north to Ardara and Dawros Head (day 2), and then returns to Donegal (day 3). It takes in lots of spectacular coastal scenery along the way. Rental bikes are available from **Pat Boyle** (© **074/972-2515**). The cost varies based on the kind of bike, but starts at around €10 ($16) a day, €60 ($96) a week.

FISHING   For advice and equipment for fishing in Lough Eske and other local waters, contact **Doherty's Fishing Tackle,** Main Street (© **074/972-1119**). The shop stocks a wide selection of flies, reels, bait, and fishing poles. It's open Monday to Saturday 9am to 6pm.

WALKING   Crossing Boyce's Bridge on the Killybegs road will bring you to the beginning of the **Bank Walk** to your left. This 2.5km (1¹/₂-mile) walk is delightful, following the west bank of the River Eske as it empties into Donegal Bay. It offers great views of the Old Abbey, Green Island, and Donegal Bay.

WHERE TO STAY
Very Expensive
Harvey's Point Country Hotel ★   About 6km (3³/₄ miles) northwest of town, this modern, rambling, Swiss-style lodge sits in a lovely woodland setting on the shores of Lough Eske at the foot of the Blue Stack Mountains. The large guest rooms, most of which feature views of the lake, are elegantly decorated with mahogany furniture—some with four-poster beds. The excellent **restaurant** was recently expanded down to the edge of the *lough*, so ask for a table by the window and enjoy the sunset on the water.

Lough Eske, Donegal, County Donegal. © **074/972-2208.** Fax 074/972-2352. www.harveyspoint.com. 20 units. €290–€310 ($464–$496) double. Rates include service charge, tax, and full breakfast. AE, DC, MC, V. Closed weekdays Nov–Mar. **Amenities:** Restaurant (French); bar; lounge; bicycle hire; boat hire. *In room:* TV, minibar, tea/coffeemaker, hair dryer.

St. Ernan's Country House ★★   This extraordinary guesthouse is the only structure on a small island in Donegal Bay, connected to the mainland by a causeway. The tiny island, named for a 7th-century Irish monk, is planted with hawthorn and holly bushes that have bloomed for 3 centuries. Inside the Regency country house, the public rooms and the dining room, acclaimed for its cuisine, have all been magnificently restored with delicate plasterwork, high ceilings, crystal chandeliers, gilt-framed oil paintings, heirloom silver, antiques, and working fireplaces. The guest rooms, all decorated by proprietors Brian and Carmel O'Dowd, have tasteful traditional furnishings, dark woods, designer fabrics, and floral art; most have views of the water. It's a delightful spot, a kingdom unto itself, 3km (2 miles) south of town.

St. Ernan's Island, Donegal, County Donegal. © **800/323-5463** in the U.S., or 074/972-1065. Fax 074/972-2098. www.sainternans.com. 12 units. €260–€350 ($416–$560) double. Suites also available. Rates include full breakfast. 2-course dinner €52 ($83). MC, V. Closed Nov–Easter. **Amenities:** Drawing room. *In room:* TV.

Moderate
The Abbey   In the heart of town, with the Diamond at its front door and the River Eske at its back, this vintage three-story hotel is a handy option. The guest rooms, about

half of which are in a newish wing overlooking the river, have standard furnishings and make generous use of bright floral fabrics. The pub has views of the River Eske, and a beer garden and patio also offer waterside views.

The Diamond, Donegal, County Donegal. (*C*) **074/972-1014.** Fax 074/972-3660. www.whites-hotels ireland.com. 112 units. €140–€160 ($224–$256) double. Rates include service charge and full breakfast. AE, MC, V. **Amenities:** Restaurant (international); bar; lounge. *In room:* TV, hair dryer, garment press.

Mill Park Hotel ★ A few minutes' walk from Donegal Town center, this modern hotel and wellness center is a great option in its price range. The large guest rooms are neatly, if a bit colorfully, decorated with modern furnishings and fabrics in red and russet hues. The lobby and lounge are lovely, with polished wood floors and nicely chosen rustic decor. The restaurants (including an upscale traditional Irish restaurant and a modern cafe-bar with lighter Mediterranean-style cuisine) are good options, and the health center is a real bonus, with a beautifully designed pool and gym. There are great deals to be had by booking online.

Killybegs Rd., Donegal, County Donegal. (*C*) 074/972-2880. Fax 074/972-2640. www.millparkhotel.com. 115 units. €110–€170 ($176–$272) double. Rates include full breakfast. AE, DC, MC, V. **Amenities:** 2 restaurants; bar; indoor swimming pool; gym; spa; Jacuzzi; steam room. *In room:* TV, tea/coffeemaker, hair dryer, garment press.

Inexpensive

Rhu-Gorse ★ (Value) Winding your way to this little guesthouse just outside of Donegal Town is an effort well rewarded. A modern home of stature and character, beautifully set at the foot of the Blue Stack Mountains, Rhu-Gorse has a North Woods feel, with a big stone fireplace, open beams, thick duvets on the soft beds, and custom-fitted pine furniture. Best of all are the extraordinary views of Lough Eske and the encircling mountains from the guest rooms.

Lough Eske Dr. (8km/5 miles outside of Donegal), Lough Eske, Donegal, County Donegal. (*C*)/fax **074/ 972-1685.** 3 units. €70–€90 ($112–$144) double. Rates include full breakfast. MC, V. Free parking. Closed Nov–Mar. *In room:* TV.

WHERE TO DINE

As in many towns in northwest Ireland, the best restaurants here are in hotel dining rooms.

The Weaver's Loft CAFETERIA Upstairs from Magee's tweed shop, this 60-seat self-service restaurant with its huge mural of Donegal conveys the feel of times past. The menu changes daily, but usually includes prawn, cheese, and fruit salads, as well as tasty sandwiches, soups, cakes, and tarts.

Magee Shop, The Diamond, Donegal. (*C*) **074/972-2660.** Main courses €5–€10 ($8–$16). AE, MC, V. Mon–Sat 9:45am–5pm.

DONEGAL AFTER DARK

Nightlife in Donegal Town is very low-key, but if you're in town during July and August, try to take in a performance of the Donegal Drama Circle at the **Donegal Town Summer Theatre,** O'Cleary Hall, Tirconaill Street (no phone). Performances are held on Tuesday, Wednesday, and Thursday at 9pm and feature works by Donegal-based playwrights. No reservations are necessary; admission prices start at €5 ($8) for adults, €2.50 ($4) for students.

Pubs

Biddy O'Barnes (Finds) You have to detour into the Blue Stack Mountains and the scenic Barnesmore Gap, 11km (6³/₄ miles) northeast of Donegal Town, to visit this pub, which has been in the same family for four generations. Passing through the front door—with its etched-glass window and iron latch—is like entering a country cottage, with blazing turf fires, stone floors, wooden stools, and benches. On most evenings, there's a spontaneous music session. Donegal-Ballybofey rd. (N15), Barnesmore, County Donegal. ✆ 074/972-1402.

The Olde Castle Bar There is an old-Donegal aura at this little pub, which has a welcoming open fireplace, etched glass, and whitewashed walls. The bartenders are friendly and there's a good menu of pub food. Castle St., Donegal. ✆ 074/972-1062.

The Schooner Inn Given the name, it's somewhat unsurprising that this pub is decorated with model ships and seafaring memorabilia. There is music on most summer evenings, with traditional Irish music on Monday and Saturday, folk music on Wednesday, and singing acts on Thursday, Friday, and Sunday. Upper Main St., Donegal. ✆ 074/972-1671.

---

2 THE DONEGAL BAY COAST

The Donegal Bay coast extends for 80km (50 miles) from Bundoran (32km/20 miles S of Donegal Town) to Glencolumbkille (48km/30 miles W of Donegal Town)

The rugged coastline around Donegal Bay is wild and beautiful. The rocky land careens toward the dark blue Atlantic, where the roads stop just short of the icy water. Roads wind so tightly that it will almost make you dizzy, and the main speed limit is the one you impose on yourself, as speeds much above 55kmph (35 mph) are dangerous. That's just as well, since the spectacular views will cause you to stop again and again to take in the rolling hills, jagged mountains, bright green fields, and sea views. There's plenty to see and do here, as there are excellent beaches and watersports, as well as seaport towns, folk museums, and craft centers.

The towns along the way are varied: To the south of Donegal Town, **Bundoran (Bun Dobhráin)** is a tacky seaside town with little to offer to anyone except the surfers who make the most of its famously rough surf, while **Ballyshannon (Béal Átha Seanaidh)** is a busy, pretty hill town that many use as a base for exploring the surrounding countryside. In the summer, **Rossnowlagh (Ross Neamblach)** is nicer and also has a fine beach. To the north of Donegal Town, the coastal scenery is breathtaking, especially once you pass the little town of **Killybegs (Ceala Beaga).** The mountains reach right to the sea, creating the breathtakingly rugged coastline for which Donegal is famed. Killybegs itself is a fishing town known for its handmade carpets, while nearby, near the foot of the striking Slieve League cliffs, **Kilcar (Cill Chártha)** is a manufacturing center for warm Donegal tweed.

AREA ESSENTIALS

GETTING THERE & GETTING AROUND Aer Arann (✆ 011/353-81821-0210 in the U.S., 818/210-210 in Ireland, or 0800/587-23-24 in the U.K.; www.aerarann.ie) operates regularly scheduled flights from Dublin to Donegal Airport, Carrickfinn, Kincasslagh, County Donegal (✆ 074/954-8284), about 65km (40 miles) north of Killybegs.

Bus Éireann (© 074/912-1309; www.buseireann.ie) runs daily bus service to Killybegs and Glencolumbkille, on the northern half of the bay, and to Ballyshannon and Bundoran, on the southern half of the bay.

The best way to get to and around Donegal Bay is by car. Follow the N15 route on the southern half of the bay, the N56 route on the northern half of the bay.

VISITOR INFORMATION   Contact the **North West Tourism Office,** Aras Reddan, Temple Street, Sligo (© 071/916-1201; www.discoverireland.ie/northwest); the **Letterkenny Tourist Office,** Derry Road, Letterkenny (© 074/912-1160); or **Bundoran Tourist Office,** Main Street, Bundoran, County Donegal (© 071/984-1350). The first two are open daily year-round; the third is open daily from June through August and Thursday to Sunday in September.

SOUTHERN DONEGAL BAY

To reach the southern section of Donegal Bay from Sligo, take the N15 road up the Atlantic coast, and at about 32km (20 miles) north, you'll come to **Bundoran,** the southern tip of County Donegal and a major beach resort. A victim of its own success, Bundoran is littered with tacky amusement arcades, fast-food restaurants, and cheap souvenir stands, and offers little to warm your heart, unless you're toting a surfboard—its waves draw surfers from throughout Europe.

Continuing up the coast, you'll pass **Ballyshannon.** Dating from the 15th century, it has a charming town center with a distinctive clock tower where its two main streets meet; it's another favorite with beachgoers, and is known for its lively pubs and traditional music. In late July or early August, the **Ballyshannon Folk Festival** brings music to the streets day and night.

Two kilometers (just over a mile) northwest of Ballyshannon, **Abbey Mills** is a heritage center inside a restored portion of the grand Cistercian Assaroe Abbey, which was founded in 1184 and mostly lies in ruins. The great mill wheel has been rebuilt and is driven by water from the Abbey River just as in ancient days. Some 50m (164 ft.) away, at the edge of the Abbey River, **Catsby Cave** is a grotto where a rough-hewed altar still stands. Here, Mass was celebrated in secrecy during the so-called "penal years" (17th–19th c.), when Catholic rituals were illegal.

If it's a sunny day, you may want to leave the main road and head for the coastal resort of **Rossnowlagh,** with its Blue Flag beach. At over 3km (2 miles) long and as wide as the tides allow, it's a flat sandy stretch shielded by flower-filled hills and ideal for walking. You'll see horses racing on it occasionally. This spot is a splendid vantage point for watching sunsets over the sea.

Overlooking the beach from a hilltop is the **Donegal Historical Society Museum,** Rossnowlagh (© 071/985-1342), inside a somber Franciscan friary. Its small exhibit on

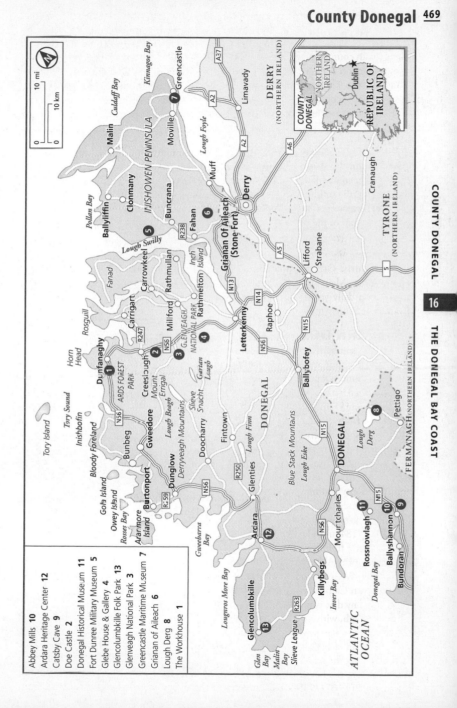

local history is limited in scope, but the place itself—vast gardens overlooking the sea and peaceful woodlands—is extraordinary. There's a tearoom with outdoor seating and a shop with religious objects. It's open daily from 10am to 8pm. There's no admission charge, but donations are welcome.

From Rossnowlagh, return to the main road via the **Donegal Golf Club** (see "Sports & Outdoor Pursuits," below) at Murvagh, a spectacular setting nestled on a rugged sandy peninsula of primeval dune land, surrounded by a wall of dense woodlands. From here, the road curves inland and it's less than 16km (10 miles) to Donegal Town.

Shopping

Britton and Daughters   In a cottage opposite the Sandhouse Hotel, this workshop is a source of unusual crafts. Its wares include mirrors or glass hand-etched with local scenes and Celtic, nautical, and wildlife designs; carved rocks (heads, Celtic designs, dolphins, and so on); and posters. Off the Ballyshannon-Donegal rd., Rossnowlagh, County Donegal. © 071/985-2220.

Donegal Parian China   Established in 1985, this pottery works produces wafer-thin Parian china (thinner even than bone china) and tableware in patterns of the shamrock, rose, hawthorn, and other Irish flora. Free guided tours (every 20 min.) enable visitors to watch as vases, lamps, and coffee and tea sets are shaped, decorated, fired, and polished. There are also an art gallery, a tearoom, and a showroom and shop. Bundoran rd. (N15), Ballyshannon, County Donegal. © 071/985-1826.

Sports & Outdoor Pursuits

BEACHES   Donegal Bay's beaches are wide, sandy, clean, and flat—ideal for walking. The best are **Rossnowlagh** and **Bundoran.**

GOLF   The Donegal Bay coast is home to two outstanding 18-hole championship seaside golf courses. **Donegal Golf Club,** Murvagh, Ballintra, County Donegal (© 074/973-4054; www.donegalgolfclub.ie), is 5km (3 miles) north of Rossnowlagh and 11km (6³/₄ miles) south of Donegal Town. It's a par-73 course with greens fees of €50 ($80) weekdays, €65 ($104) weekends.

The **Bundoran Golf Club,** off the Sligo-Ballyshannon road (N15), Bundoran, County Donegal (© 071/984-1302; www.bundorangolfclub.com), is a par-69 course designed by Harry Vardon. The greens fees are €40 ($64) weekdays, €50 ($80) weekends.

HORSEBACK RIDING   **Stracomer Riding School Ltd.,** off the Sligo-Ballyshannon road (N15), Bundoran, County Donegal (© 071/984-1787), specializes in trail riding on the surrounding farmlands, beaches, dunes, and mountain trails. An hour's ride averages €18 ($29).

SURFING   Bundoran has hosted the European Surfing Championships, and Rossnowlagh also attracts lots of surfers. When the surf is up, you can rent boards and wet suits locally for roughly €5 ($8) per hour per item.

Where to Stay
Expensive
Great Northern Hotel   Set amid vast parklands, sand dunes, and an 18-hole golf course, this sprawling hotel is right on Donegal Bay. The hotel's lounge and lobby have a traditional feel, while rooms have a slightly haphazard design that cheerfully clashes

striped bedcovers with floral curtains. Most rooms have views of the sea or the golf course. A favorite with Irish families, it's on the northern edge of Bundoran.

Sligo-Donegal rd. (N15), Bundoran, County Donegal. ℭ **071/984-1204.** Fax 071/984-1114. www.great northernhotel.com. 111 units. €150–€220 ($240–$352) double. Rates include service charge and full Irish breakfast. AE, MC, V. Closed Dec 24–Jan 2. **Amenities:** 2 restaurants (international, grill); bar; indoor swimming pool; gym; children's playroom; room service. *In room:* TV, tea/coffeemaker, hair dryer.

Sandhouse Hotel   On a crescent of beach overlooking the Atlantic coast, this is a friendly, homey option. Warmed by open fireplaces, the public rooms are decorated with antiques and local art, while a sunlit, plant-filled conservatory offers clear views of the sea. Guest rooms are a bit old-fashioned in style, and vary in size; all are decorated with antiques and replicas, while a few have canopied or four-poster beds. The restaurant specializes in fresh Donegal Bay seafood. There's a small spa offering beauty treatments, or you could just walk along the 3.2km (2 miles) of soft sand outside.

Off the Ballyshannon-Donegal rd. (N15), Rossnowlagh, County Donegal. ℭ **800/44-UTELL** (448-8355) in the U.S., or 071/985-1777. Fax 071/985-2100. www.sandhouse-hotel.ie. 64 units. €170–€300 ($272–$480) double. Rates include full Irish breakfast. AE, MC, V. Closed late Dec to Jan. **Amenities:** Restaurant (seafood); bar; lounge; tennis court; marine spa; Jacuzzi; steam room; conservatory; croquet; private 3.2km (2-mile) beach. *In room:* TV, hair dryer.

Inexpensive

Ard-na-Mara ★★   A beautiful country home nestled between the Blue Stack mountains and Rossnowlagh's Blue Flag beach, Ard-na-Mara is a relaxing getaway with panoramic views of the sea. The hotel is 3 minutes' walk from the beach, so it's perfect in the summertime. Rooms are simply but pleasantly decorated, so this hotel is a good low-cost alternative to the more expensive hotels in the area.

Rossnowlagh Rd., Rossnowlagh, County Donegal. ℭ **071/985-1141.** 7 units. €75 ($120) double. Rates include full Irish breakfast. MC, V. Closed late Dec to Jan. *In room:* TV, hair dryer.

Where to Dine

Smuggler's Creek ★ SEAFOOD   For good food and grand sunset views, head to this little gem perched on a cliff overlooking Donegal Bay. The 1845 stone building was restored and enlarged to include a conservatory-style dining area with open fireplaces and beamed ceilings. Seafood is the main attraction here, with oysters and mussels from local beds. Options include seafood casserole (scallops, salmon, and prawns) and deep-fried squid. More than a dozen B&B **rooms** with private bathrooms are available for around €80 ($128) double.

Rossnowlagh, County Donegal. ℭ **071/985-2366.** Reservations required for dinner. Dinner main courses €12–€24 ($19–$38). DC, MC, V. Daily 12:30–8:30pm. Closed Mon–Tues Oct–Easter.

Southern Donegal Bay After Dark

In summer **Rossnowlagh** is a hub of social activity. People flock to the **Sandhouse Hotel** (see above) on the beach for the nautical atmosphere of the Surfers Bar.

Farther south, **Dorrian's Thatch Bar,** Main Street, Ballyshannon, County Donegal (ℭ **071/985-1147**), holds nightly sessions of Irish traditional music in summer.

NORTHERN DONEGAL BAY

From Donegal Town, follow the main road (N56) for a slow, spectacularly scenic drive along the northern coast of Donegal Bay, where the road winds along past sheer cliffs, craggy rocks, bog land, panoramic mountain and sea views, and green pastures. You'll often see the distinctive thatched-roof cottages typical of this area—with rounded roofs held down by ropes (called *sugans*) fastened beneath the eaves to help the thatch resist the strong sea winds. It's only 48km (30 miles) from Donegal Town to gorgeous Glencolumbkille (Gleann Cholm Cille), the traditional end of the west coast drive, but these are some of the most winding roads you'll ever drive, so it can take an hour.

Your first stop could be at **Killybegs (Ceala Beaga)**—where, if you arrive around sundown, you can watch the fishing boats unloading the day's catch—or at Studio Donegal in **Kilcar (Cill Chártha)** if you're interested in picking up Donegal tweed at a bargain (see "Shopping," below).

Spectacular photo ops await at **Slieve League ★★**, with its perilously high sea cliffs crashing down into the waters below. (Take the turnoff for the Bunglass viewing point at Carrick.) Once at the cliffs, you must decide whether you want to merely gaze at their 300m (984-ft.) splendor or to brave a wind-buffeted walk along the treacherous ridge. This walk should only be for the fearless and fit. Including the climb up and then back down, the hike is about 10km (6¼ miles) and takes 4 or 5 hours.

Just before you come to Killybegs, the N56 road swings inland and northward, and the landscape becomes desolate and wild. Continue on the coastal road west to discover the extraordinary beauty of **Glencolumbkille ★★**, a 5,000-year-old Atlantic outpost. Here the dark bogs disappear, replaced by a lush green valley. It is said that St. Columba established a monastery here in the 6th century and gave his name to the glen (its Gaelic name—Gleann Cholm Cille—means "Glen of Columba's Church"). Those interested in the history of the place will want to stop by the **Glencolumbkille Folk Park ★** (✆ 074/973-0017). Built by the people of Glencolumbkille in the form of a tiny village, or *clachan,* this modest theme park of thatched cottages reflects life in this remote corner over centuries. There are miniature playhouses to entertain the children, while a tearoom serves traditional Irish stews and *brútin* (a stew of hot milk and potatoes). Hearty Guinness cake is a house specialty. In the *sheebeen,* a shop of traditional products, check out the local wines made from fuchsia, heather, seaweed, and tea. Admission and tour are €4 ($6.40) for adults, €2.50 ($4) for seniors and children, and €11 ($17) for families. It's open daily from Easter through September.

To continue touring from Glencolumbkille, follow the signs directing you to the charming, hilly town of Ardara (Árd an Rátha), reached over a mountainous terrain. The road follows one of the most breathtaking drives in Ireland, through **Glengesh Pass,** a narrow, sinuous, scenic roadway that rises to a height of 270m (886 ft.) before plunging, in a tortuously zigzag pattern of hairpin curves, into the valley below. The road leads eventually to **Ardara,** a stone village known for its tweed and woolen craft shops (see section 3, "The Atlantic Highlands," below).

Shopping

Folk Village Shop   Part of Glencolumbkille's folk park mentioned above, this is well worth a visit in its own right for smart shopping. The well-stocked shelves of this whitewashed cottage feature the arts and crafts of members of the local community—handknit sweaters and other woolen items, turf-craft art, books, jewelry, and assorted cottage industry souvenirs. Since the Folk Village operates as a charitable trust, purchases are not subject to VAT (sales tax), so you save some money and help a good cause by shopping here. Glencolumbkille, County Donegal. ✆ 074/973-0017.

Lace House   A combination crafts shop and information bureau, this is where you go for almost everything in Glencolumbkille, including advice and good conversation. It also sells lovely local crafts, including woolen knitted items and the titular lace. Glen- columbkille, County Donegal. ✆ **074/973-0116.**

Studio Donegal Started in 1979, this hand-weaving enterprise is distinguished by its knobby tweed, subtly colored in tones of beige, oat, and ash. You can walk around the craft shop and the mill and see the caps, jackets, and cloaks in the making. Kilcar is on the R263 between Killybegs and Glencolumbkille, about 32km (20 miles) west of Donegal Town. Glebe Mill, Kilcar. ✆ **074/973-8194.** www.studiodonegal.ie.

Taipeis Gael The name "Gaelic Tapestry" refers to a group of artists who create unique Irish tapestries using natural dyeing, carding, spinning, and weaving skills handed down from generation to generation. The completed tapestries are influenced by Gaelic culture, music, and folklore. There are weeklong tapestry-making courses during the summer months, should you want to try it yourself. Malin Beg, Glencolumbkille, County Donegal. ✆ **074/973-0325.**

Sports & Outdoor Pursuits

BEACHES Glencolumbkille has two fine beaches: One is the flat, broad, sandy beach at the end of Glencolumbkille village, where the R263 swings left; the lesser known gem is a tiny beach surrounded by a horseshoe of cliffs, accessible from the small road signposted to Malin More (off the R263) about 1.6km (1 mile) southwest of town.

BICYCLING If you're very fit, the north side of Donegal Bay has great cycling roads— tremendously scenic though very hilly. One good but arduous route from Donegal Town follows the coast roads west to Glencolumbkille (day 1), continues north to Ardara and Dawros Head via Glengesh Pass (day 2), and then returns to Donegal (day 3). It takes in some of the most spectacular coastal scenery in Ireland along the way, but takes place on small winding roads that must be shared with car drivers. Rental bikes are available in Donegal from Pat Boyle (✆ **074/972-2515**) at the **Bike Shop,** Waterloo Place, Donegal, for roughly €10 ($16) per day.

FISHING Surrounded by waters that hold shark, skate, pollock, conger, cod, and mackerel, **Killybegs** is one of the most active centers on the northwest coast for commercial and sport sea fishing. **Brian McGilloway** (✆ **074/973-2444**) operates full-day fishing expeditions on the 12m (39-ft.) MV *Meridian,* from Blackrock Pier. Prices average €55 ($88) per person per day, plus €10 ($16) for rods and tackle, or around €400 ($640) for a party of 8 to 10 (8 is preferable for comfort). The daily schedule and departure times vary according to demand; reservations are required.

WALKING The peninsula to the west of Killybegs boasts some of the most spectacular coastal scenery in Ireland, and much of it is accessible only from the sea or on foot. The grandeur of the **Slieve League** cliffs makes the hills popular with hikers, but only attempt them with a good map, hiking boots, and basic provisions. The best way to visit this natural monument is to hike from the Bunglass lookout point to Trabane Strand in Malin Beg, a few miles southwest of Glencolumbkille. This walk crosses the notorious "One Man's Pass," a vertigo-inducing narrow ridge with steep drops on both sides. The distance from Bunglass to Trabane Strand is 15km (9¹⁄₃ miles), and you will have to arrange a pickup at the end. The summits of the Slieve League, rising almost 600m (1,968 ft.) above the sea, are often capped in clouds, and you should think twice about undertaking the walk if there is danger of losing visibility along the way.

Another lesser known walk that is just as spectacular is the coastal walk between Glencolumbkille and the town of **Maghera** (not so much a town as a small cluster of houses).

Glen Head, topped by a Martello tower, overlooks Glencolumbkille to the north. This walk begins with a climb to the tower and continues along the cliff face for 24km (15 miles), passing only one remote outpost of human habitation along the way, the tiny town of Port. For isolated sea splendor, this is one of the finest walks in Ireland, but only experienced walkers with adequate provisions should undertake the walk, and only in fine weather.

Where to Stay

Bay View Hotel ★ Right on the harbor in the middle of Killybegs, this four-story hotel is as close to the water as you can get without getting wet. Guest rooms vary in decor—some are decorated in contemporary style with light-pine furnishings, bright quilted fabrics, and brass accessories, while others have antiques and even four-posters. All are enhanced by sweeping views of the marina. The **restaurant** does marvelous things with the fresh local seafood.

1–2 Main St., Killybegs, County Donegal. © 074/973-1950. Fax 074/973-1856. www.bayviewhotel.ie. 40 units. €130–€160 ($208–$256) double. Rates include full breakfast. AE, MC, V. **Amenities:** Restaurant (international); 2 bars; indoor swimming pool; gym; Jacuzzi; sauna. *In room:* TV.

Bruckless House ★ Clive and Joan Evans have restored their mid-18th-century farmhouse with such care and taste that every room is a delight. Furniture and art they brought back from their years in Hong Kong add a special elegance. All the guest rooms are smoke-free, spacious, and bright. Joan's gardens have taken first prize in County Donegal's country garden competition at least twice in recent years. Inside and out, Bruckless House is a gem. Be sure to ask Clive to introduce you to his fine Connemara ponies that he raises and treasures.

Signposted on N56, 19km (12 miles) west of Donegal, Bruckless, County Donegal. © 074/973-7071. Fax 074/973-7070. 4 units, 1 with private bathroom. €80 ($128) double with bathroom; €85 ($135) double with shared bathroom. Rates include full Irish breakfast. AE, MC, V. Closed Oct–Mar. **Amenities:** Non-smoking rooms; sitting room. *In room:* No phone.

Dún Ulún House ★ (Value) This is a friendly and diverse hostelry with a B&B and two cottages, each with its own personality. The main building is unremarkable, but the extraordinary beauty of the seaside it overlooks makes it memorable. The rooms (with orthopedic beds) are pleasant and comfortable. Then there's the cottage with an open fire in the kitchen and basic, functional furnishings in the bedrooms; rates are €25 to €27 ($40–$43) per person per night. There's also a separate self-catering cottage across the street, which rents by the week for €250 to €400 ($400–$640) plus electricity. Finally, there's the in-house band made up of five family members who play traditional music. Denis Lyons is a great source of information on the archaeology of the Kilcar region and can direct you to little-known sites.

R263 (1.6km/1 mile west of Kilcar), Kilcar, County Donegal. © 074/973-8137. 10 units, 9 with private bathroom. €55–€60 ($88–$96) double. Rates include full breakfast. MC, V. Free parking. **Amenities:** Sitting room. *In room:* TV.

Where to Dine

The Blue Haven ★ CONTINENTAL On a broad, open sweep of Donegal Bay between Killybegs and Kilcar, this modern sky-lit restaurant offers 180-degree views of the bay from a bank of windows. It's an ideal place to stop for a meal while touring. The bar-food menu, available throughout the day, offers soups, sandwiches, and omelets. The

dinner menu includes filet of rainbow trout, T-bone and sirloin steaks, and savory mush- **475**
room pancakes. You can stay the night in one of 15 bright and sunny rooms, with views
of Donegal Bay and bed-and-breakfast for €80 ($128).

Largymore, Kilcar, County Donegal. ℰ **074/973-8090.** www.bluehaven.ie. Reservations recommended
for dinner. Dinner main courses €9–€16 ($14–$26). MC, V. May–Oct daily 11am–11pm; Nov–Apr weekends only.

Kitty Kelly's ★ Value SEAFOOD/CONTINENTAL   You can't miss this 200-year-
old converted farmhouse on the coastal road out of Killybegs—just look for a bright
fuchsia building with a green door next to Fentra Beach. The exterior may be funky and
modern, but inside the place is packed with old-world charm, and the fresh seafood is
exceptional here.

Largy, Killybegs, County Donegal (5km/3 miles west of Killybegs on coast road). ℰ **074/973-1925.** Dinner main courses €8–€15 ($13–$24). AE, MC, V. Daily 7–9:30pm.

Pubs

Harbour Bar   This popular meeting place in Killybegs holds an Irish-music night on
Tuesdays during July and August. Main St., Killybegs, County Donegal. ℰ **074/973-1049.**

Piper's Rest   This thatched-roof pub heated by a turf fire has stone walls and flagged
floors. Music may erupt at any time and usually does on summer nights. Watch out for
a local band called Dún Ulún (see also Dún Ulún House, above)—their traditional
music brings down the house. Kilcar, County Donegal. ℰ **074/973-8205.**

3 THE ATLANTIC HIGHLANDS

The Atlantic Highlands start at Ardara, 40km (25 miles) NW of Donegal Town, 16km (10 miles) N of Killybegs

This is the most isolated part of Donegal, which is the most isolated county in Ireland,
so it doesn't get much more rugged, exhilarating, and, well, *isolated* than this. There is a
point when you're driving through the highlands, where the signs drop all pretense at
bilingualism and switch to Gaelic. This is disconcerting, because most maps are in English, and the Gaelic names and the English names of places frequently are not even distant relatives. It's disorienting—one minute you know exactly where you are and the next
you haven't a clue. It's as if somebody has stolen your compass. At that moment, which
often occurs on a mountainside by a rushing stream amid rocky terrain where there's no
space to pull the car over and stare more closely at the useless map, it's just possible that
you see Ireland as the locals see it—which is to say, as their own country: a somewhat
private and not always hospitable place. Coming this far would be worth it for that
moment of understanding alone, but there is much more to draw you here. There is the
breathtaking coastal scenery, the mountain ranges, the lunar landscape of the rocky
beaches. If you've gone digital, you'll fill your camera's memory card here.

The best place to start a tour of Donegal's Atlantic Highlands is at **Ardara (Árd an
Rátha)** ★, an adorable village about 40km (25 miles) northwest of Donegal Town. From
there, weave your way up the coast, turning inland when a place lures you to do so. This
drive can take 4 hours or 4 days, depending on your schedule and interests. Our advice
is: Take your time. You may never come this way again, and you will want to remember
every moment.

GETTING THERE & GETTING AROUND   Aer Arann (© 011/353-81821-0210 in the U.S., 818/210-210 in Ireland, or 0800/587-23-24 in the U.K.; www.aerarann.ie) operates regularly scheduled flights from Dublin to **Donegal Airport,** Carrickfinn, Kincasslagh, County Donegal (© 074/954-8284), in the heart of the Atlantic coast.

Bus Éireann (© 074/912-1309; www.buseireann.ie) operates daily bus service to Ardara and Glenties.

The best way to get to and around Donegal's Atlantic Highlands is by **car,** starting on the main N56 route, but don't expect a freeway—at times the N56 is so small, it's difficult for two cars to pass. Signs are infrequent and occasionally in Gaelic, so pay close attention when you pass them. It's easy to miss a turn if you're lulled into complacency.

VISITOR INFORMATION   Contact the **North West Tourism Office,** Aras Reddan, Temple Street, Sligo (© 071/916-1201; www.discoverireland.ie/northwest); the **Letterkenny Tourist Office,** Derry Road, Letterkenny (© 074/912-1160); or the **Donegal Tourist Office,** Quay Street, Donegal (© 074/972-1148). The first two are open year-round; the third is open from May through September.

EXPLORING THE REGION

Looking as if it were carved from stone, charming little **Ardara** is known for its exceptional tweed and wool creations. Astride a narrow river in a steep gulch, it is a pleasant place to stop, chat with the locals, and do a bit of shopping or maybe have a cup of tea in its small but useful heritage center. If you happen to arrive in June, you may be lucky enough to catch the **Ardara Weavers Fair,** which has been going on since the 18th century, and features spectacular works in wool.

Heading north from Ardara, the landscape rolls across green hills and splashes into clear lakes. There are two little resort towns here—**Naran** and **Portnoo**—which are favorites with Irish families in the summer. They have lovely beaches, particularly Naran which has an excellent Blue Flag beach. A little farther along is the neat-as-a-pin little town of **Glenties (Na Gleanta),** which unsurprisingly has been the winner several times of the Irish Tidy Towns competition. It's excellent for fishing and for walks. The playwright Brian Friel set his play *Dancing at Lughnasa* here.

From here, the road curves inland to towns like **Gweedore (Gaoth Dobhair),** where Gaelic is the primary language and the countryside is increasingly desolate, but you're just a few miles from the gorgeous **Glenveagh National Park** and **Mount Errigal,** Donegal's highest mountain. The park is strewn with lakes and thick forest, and is home to rare golden eagles. At the edge of the park, Glenveagh Castle is a good place to meet other travelers, a bit of a relief after a long time driving empty roads.

Out along the coast, the road passes through Dungloe to an area known as the **Rosses,** extending from Gweebarra Bridge as far north as Crolly. It's a hard and rock-strewn land, but strangely beautiful, punctuated by mountains, rivers, and glassy lakes. Along the way, you'll pass **Burtonport (Ailt an Chorrain),** and it's said that more salmon and lobster are landed here than at any other port in the country.

The coastal area north of the Rosses, between Derrybeg and Gortahork, is known as the **Bloody Foreland,** from the fact that its rocks take on a ruddy color when lit by the setting sun. If you can arrange to be driving through such far-flung terrain at sunset on a clear day, you are in for a treat.

Next you'll approach the top rim of Donegal, dominated by a series of small peninsulas like fingers of land jabbing out into the sea. **Horn Head (Corrán Binne)** is the most

extraordinary of these, with breathtaking cliffs towering 180m (590 ft.) above the sea.
But roads on this headland are a bit perilous in places, and definitely not for those uncomfortable with heights. At the base of the peninsula, **Dunfanaghy** is one of the prettiest little towns you'll pass, with a great beach, much favored by Irish families. After Horn Head, the next peninsula to the east is **Rosguill.** The 16km (10-mile) route around this peninsula is much less traumatic than the one around Horn Head, and is called the Atlantic Drive. This leads you to yet another peninsula, the **Fanad,** with a 73km (45-mile) circuit between Mulroy Bay and the glassy waters of Lough Swilly. The village of **Rathmelton (Ráth Mealtain)** is another one of those distinctive Irish villages that seems to have been hewn from the rocky hillside. It is tiny and eminently photographic, with its gray Georgian warehouses reflected in the mirrorlike water of the lake. It was once a bustling place, apparently, but then the rail line was rerouted to Letterkenny, and it all went quiet here. A few miles away, along a winding waterfront road, the village of **Rathmullan (Ráth Maoláin)** is an excellent stopping point, with a couple of good hotels, an evocative ruined abbey, and a beautiful stretch of flat, sandy beach on which to stroll or ride horses.

Ardara Heritage Centre
Ardara has long been a center for weaving, and this center's varied displays represent the history of tweed production in the region. A video provides an outline of nearby places of interest. The staff is eager to help, and the cafe serves inexpensive teas, soups, and simple meals.

On N56 in the center of Ardara, County Donegal. C 074/954-1704. Admission €3 ($4.80) adults, €1.70 ($2.70) seniors and students, €1.20 ($1.90) children 13 and under. Easter–Sept Mon–Sat 10am–6pm; Sun 2–6pm.

Doe Castle
This little tower house is so complete, it looks as if you could move in today and set up well-fortified housekeeping. A battlement wall with round towers at the corners encloses the central tower; the view from the battlements across the bay is superb. Built in the early 16th century, the castle was extensively restored in the 18th century and inhabited until 1843. It's a lovely little place, surrounded on three sides by the waters of Sheep Haven Bay, and on the fourth by a moat carved into the bedrock that forms its foundation. If the entrance is locked, you can get the key from the caretaker in the house nearest the castle.

5.6km (3½ miles) off N56; turnoff signposted just south of Creeslough, County Donegal. Free admission.

Glebe House and Gallery ★ (Finds)
Sitting in woodland gardens on the shores of Lough Gartan, about 6.5km (4 miles) southwest of Glenveagh, this Regency-style house was built as a rectory in the 1820s. It was owned until recently by English artist Derek Hill. Hill donated the house and his art collection to the Irish government. The house is decorated with Donegal folk art, Japanese and Islamic art, Victoriana, and William Morris papers and textiles. The stables were converted into an art gallery housing the 300-item Hill Collection of works by Picasso, Bonnard, Yeats, Annigoni, and Pasmore.

18km (11 miles) northwest of Letterkenny on the Churchill rd. (R251), Church Hill, County Donegal. C 074/913-7071. Admission €2.90 ($4.65) adults, €2.10 ($3.35) seniors, €1.30 ($2.10) students and children, €7.40 ($12) families. Mid-May to Sept Sat–Thurs 11am–6:30pm (last tour at 5:30pm).

Glenveagh National Park and Castle ★★★
This thickly wooded valley is a lush forest paradise, with the lavish Glenveagh Estate at its core. It's beautiful and pleasant now, but its history is dark. This was originally the home of the infamously cruel landlord John George Adair, who evicted scores of struggling tenant farmers in the freezing winter

of 1861, ostensibly because their presence on his estate was ruining his view. If the tale is true, it's a form of divine justice that his estate now belongs to all of the people of Ireland. In keeping with his reputation, Adair didn't donate the property to anybody. He sold it to the distinguished Philadelphia art historian Henry McIlhenny, and then McIlhenny donated the land and house to the Irish nation. Today the fairy-tale setting includes woodlands, herds of red deer, alpine gardens, a sylvan lake, and the highest mountain in Donegal, Mount Errigal. There's a visitor center with a little shop, and a charming tearoom in the castle.

Main entrance on R251, Church Hill, County Donegal. © **074/913-7090.** www.heritageireland.ie. Free admission. Mid-Mar to 1st Sun in Nov daily 10am–6:30pm. Closed Fri in Oct.

The Workhouse ★   This simple stone structure was one of 100,000 workhouses in Ireland during the Great Famine, which killed tens of thousands of people. This one was constructed in 1844, just before the height of the famine, and it provided meals and a roof for more than 300 people. Exhibits here portray the life of workhouse inmates and relate local famine history. There is also information on the history of Dunfanaghy. Perhaps inappropriately given the subject matter, a cozy tea-and-gift shop with an open fire serves tasty baked goods.

Just west of Dunfanaghy on N56, County Donegal. © **074/913-6540.** Admission €4 ($6.40) adults, €2.75 ($4.40) seniors and students, €2 ($3.20) children, €10 ($16) families. Mid-Mar to mid-Oct Mon–Fri 10am–5pm; Sat–Sun noon–5pm.

SHOPPING

Ardara is a hub of tweed and woolen production. Most shops are open Monday to Saturday 9am to 5:30pm, with extended hours in summer. Unless otherwise noted, shops are on the main street of the town (N56).

C. Bonner & Son   With 500 hand-knitters throughout County Donegal and 50 weavers in its factory, C. Bonner & Son produces a wide selection of hand-knit and hand-loomed knitwear, including linen-cotton and colorful sheep-patterned lamb's-wool sweaters, all for sale here in its factory outlet. Also for sale is a broad selection of crafts and gifts, including sheepskins, pottery, wool hangings, linens, crystal, and china. Closed January and February. Glenties Rd., Ardara, County Donegal. © **074/954-1196.** Front St., Ardara, County Donegal. © **074/954-1303.**

C. Kennedy & Sons Ltd.   Established in 1904, this family-owned knitwear company employs about 500 home workers who hand-knit or hand-loom *bainin* sweaters, hats, scarves, and jackets in native Donegal patterns and colors. The shop also sells turf crafts, pottery, and dolls. Ardara, County Donegal. © **074/954-1106.**

Eddie Doherty   A hand-weaver with over 40 years experience, Eddie weaves throws, scarves, caps, and shawls in a variety of colors and designs, some of which reflect the colors of the Donegal landscape. The loom is on display and the weaving is demonstrated to visitors. Ardara, County Donegal. © **074/954-1304.**

Francis O'Donnell   Francis is a weaver who knows just about all there is to know about weaving, Donegal, and Ardara. His work is absolutely beautiful, and while prices are not cheap, they're approachable. Front St., Ardara, County Donegal. © **074/954-1688.**

John Molloy   In the heart of wool and weaving country, this factory shop is well stocked with hand-knits, homespun fashions, sports jackets, tweed scarves and rugs, and all types of caps, from kingfisher to *ghillie* styles. There's even a bargain bin. Factory tours and a shop weaving demonstration are available. Ardara, County Donegal. © **074/954-1133.**

SPORTS & OUTDOOR PURSUITS

BEACHES   The western coast of Donegal has lots of pristine and secluded beaches. If you like populated beaches, several of them spread around Dawros Head, including **Traighmore Strand** in Rossbeg, and the Blue Flag beaches in Portnoo and Navan. **Magheroarty,** near Falcarragh on the northern coast, has a breathtaking beach, unspoiled by crowds or development. The same goes for **Tramore** beach on the western side of Horn Head near Dunfanaghy; you have to hike a short distance, but the rewards are seclusion and miles of creamy sand. Other peaceful sandy beaches ideal for walking and jogging include Carrigart, Downings, Marble Hill, and Port na Blagh.

BIRD-WATCHING   **Horn Head,** a nesting site for many species of seabirds, has a huge nesting population of razorbills. **Malin Head,** at the end of the Inishowen Peninsula, is a good site for watching migrating species in late autumn.

FISHING   The rivers and lakes in this area produce salmon, sea trout, and brown trout, and the coastal waters yield flounder, pollock, and cod. Fishing expeditions are offered by charter boats, fishing boats, and trawlers. For details, contact the **North Western Regional Fisheries Board,** Abbey Street, Ballina, County Mayo (✆ **096/22788;** fax 096/70543; www.northwestfisheries.ie or www.cfb.ie).

GOLF   One of Ireland's most challenging golf courses is the **Rosapenna Golf Club,** Atlantic Drive, Downings, County Donegal (✆ **074/915-5000;** www.rosapenna.ie), an 18-hole championship seaside par-70 links course that was laid out in 1983 by Tom Morris of St. Andrews. Greens fees are €45 ($72) weekdays, €50 ($80) weekends.

Other 18-hole courses in this part of Donegal are **Dunfanaghy Golf Club,** Dunfanaghy, County Donegal (✆ **074/913-6335;** www.dunfanaghygolfclub.com), a seaside par-68 course with greens fees of €28 ($45) weekdays, €33 ($53) weekends; **Narin & Portnoo Golf Club,** Narin-Portnoo, County Donegal (✆ **074/954-5107;** www.narin portnoogolfclub.ie), a par-69 seaside course with greens fees of €30 ($48) weekdays, €35 ($56) weekends; and **Portsalon Golf Club,** Portsalon, County Donegal (✆ **074/915-9459;** www.portsalongolfclub.ie), a seaside par-69 course with greens fees of €35 ($56) weekdays, €40 ($64) weekends.

HORSEBACK RIDING   **Dunfanaghy Stables,** Arnold's Hotel, Dunfanaghy, County Donegal (✆ **074/913-6208**), specializes in trail riding on the surrounding beaches, dunes, and mountain trails. An hour's ride averages €20 ($32).

WALKING   A section of the **Ulster Way** passes through Donegal between the towns of Falcarragh to the north and Pettigo to the south, on the border with Fermanagh. This trail traverses some remote and wild terrain, passing Mount Errigal and Glenveagh Park before heading south into the Blue Stack Mountains, so should not be undertaken without a good map, proper attire, and supplies.

There are some incredible walks on **Hook Head,** signposted off N56 just west of Dunfanaghy. Follow Hook Head Drive to the concrete lookout point. From here you can walk out to a ruined castle on the headland and continue south along a line of impressive quartzite sea cliffs that glitter in the sun as though covered with glass. This is a moderately difficult walk.

The **Ards Forest Park** is on a peninsula jutting out into Sheep Haven Bay, about 5.6km (3¹/₂ miles) south of Dunfanaghy on N56. The park is mostly forested and includes an area of dunes along the water. There are signposted nature trails, and you can buy a guidebook as you enter the park.

Expensive

Rathmullan House ★★★   On the western shores of Lough Swilly, Donegal's great sea lake, just outside of the sweet little village of Rathmullan, this secluded, sprawling country mansion is surrounded by extensive gardens and mature trees. The mostly Georgian (ca. 1760) mansion has lots of beautifully appointed public rooms where you can relax with the newspaper by a crackling fire. Guest rooms vary in size, but all are comfortably and attractively furnished. Rooms in the well-designed new wing are even more desirable than those in the original section, with polished wood floors, elegantly modern decor, gas fireplaces, and big claw-foot tubs in the spacious bathrooms. A number of small cottages are also available for those seeking even more privacy. All rooms have orthopedic beds, and two are wheelchair accessible. The staff is genuinely friendly, and will happily book spa treatments for you in advance. The award-winning breakfast buffet is copious and imaginative, and dinner in the **restaurant** is a memorable event.

Lough Swilly, Rathmullan, County Donegal. ℂ **800/223-6510** in the U.S., or 074/915-8188. Fax 074/915-8200. www.rathmullanhouse.com. 34 units. €180–€390 ($288–$624) double. Rates include full Irish breakfast. Dinner €45 ($72). AE, DC, MC, V. **Amenities:** Restaurant (modern Irish); bar; indoor swimming pool; 2 tennis courts; steam room; massage treatments; drawing room; library; private beach. *In room:* TV, hair dryer.

Moderate

Arnold's Hotel   Right across the road from Sheephaven Bay, this family-run place offers warm hospitality and sweeping views of the Atlantic. Brothers Derek and William Arnold run the place cheerfully, acting as desk clerks, porters, waiters, and whatever else is needed. Rooms are comfortable and attractive, if slightly bland, although those above the restaurant can smell of food. Arnold's is an ideal base for touring northwest Donegal and for exploring Glenveagh National Park. Golf, fishing, and pony trekking can be arranged at the front desk.

Dunfanaghy, County Donegal. ℂ **800/44-UTELL** [448-8355] in the U.S., or 074/913-6208. Fax 074/913-6352. www.arnoldshotel.com. 30 units. €120–€160 ($192–$256) double. Rates include full breakfast. AE, MC, V. Closed Nov–Mar 15. **Amenities:** Restaurant (international). *In room:* TV.

Castle Grove ★   This beautiful white manor house sits like a jewel in a crown of sweeping green grounds originally designed by the famed Lancelot "Capability" Brown in the 18th century. Its public rooms are done in a traditional style, with big fireplaces in the lounges. Guest rooms are large and decorated with antiques; all have peaceful, bucolic views. Breakfasts are grand here, and usually include fresh fish options, as well as homemade breads and cereals. There are boats you can borrow for fishing and rowing on the lake, there are stables with horses for trekking, and the house has an arrangement for guests to use three nearby golf courses.

Ballymaleel, off Ramelton Rd., Letterkenny, County Donegal. ℂ **074/915-1118.** Fax 074/915-1384. www.castlegrove.com. 14 units. €160–€190 ($256–$304) double. Rates include full breakfast. MC, V. **Amenities:** Restaurant (Irish); bar; lounge; golfing; tennis courts; fishing; rowing; stables. *In room:* TV.

Fort Royal Hotel ★   Built in 1819, this rambling, three-story country house sits amid sprawling gardens and woodlands, with a small sandy beach on the western shore of Lough Swilly, just north of the Rathmullan village. Both the public areas and the guest rooms are attractively decorated in an upscale country style, with traditional furnishings, period pieces, and oil paintings of Donegal. Though not as luxurious as Rathmullan House (see above), Fort Royal delivers an extremely comfortable country-house experience.

fortroyalhotel.com. 15 units. €170–€190 ($272–$304) double. Rates include full breakfast. AE, V. Closed Nov–Easter. **Amenities:** Restaurant (Continental); bar; lounge; golf course; tennis court. *In room:* TV.

Ostán Na Rosann/Hotel of the Rosses ⓥⁱⁱᵘᵉ⟩   On a hill overlooking the Atlantic, this modern ranch-style hotel sits in the scenic Gaelic-speaking Rosses overlooking Dungloe Bay. The guest rooms have wide-windowed sea views and comfortable if standard furnishings. Quite frankly, the public rooms and guest rooms are nothing special, but the leisure center and sea views make it a good value. A popular hotel with Irish families, it has a **bar** that's lively in the evenings.

Dungloe, County Donegal. © **074/952-2444.** Fax 074/952-2400. www.ostannarosann.com. 48 units. €114–€126 ($182–$202) double. Rates include full breakfast. AE, MC, V. **Amenities:** Restaurant (Continental); lounge; indoor swimming pool; gym; Jacuzzi; sauna; nonsmoking rooms. *In room:* TV, tea/coffeemaker, hair dryer.

Rosapenna Golf Hotel   Surrounded by Sheephaven Bay and the hills of Donegal, this contemporary two-story hotel is a favorite with golfers, who flock here to enjoy the hotel's 18-hole links course. Nongolfers come for the scenery, the seclusion, and the hotel's proximity to northern Donegal attractions. The guest rooms, dining area, and lounges all have panoramic views of land and sea.

Atlantic Dr., Downings, County Donegal. © **074/915-5301.** Fax 074/915-5128. www.rosapenna.ie. 53 units. €160–€180 ($256–$288) double. Rates include full breakfast. AE, MC, V. Closed late Oct to mid-Mar. **Amenities:** Restaurant (international); bar; indoor swimming pool; 18-hole golf course; 2 tennis courts. *In room:* TV.

Inexpensive

Ardeen ★   This pretty, white country house sits on peaceful grounds at the edge of the town of Ramelton overlooking Lough Swilly. Let the friendly owners know when you're arriving, and they'll have tea and scones waiting when you get there. There's a snug lounge with a fireplace, while guest rooms are spacious and pleasantly decorated with antiques and replicas. Breakfast is served around the antique family dining table, and includes fresh fruits, homemade brown bread, and scones, as well as the usual eggs and bacon. There's also a sweet self-catering cottage with two double bedrooms that rents for €350 to €500 ($560–$800) per week.

Ramelton, County Donegal. ©/fax **074/915-1243.** www.ardeenhouse.com. 5 units. €70 ($112) double. Rates include full breakfast and tax. No credit cards. Closed Oct to mid-Mar. **Amenities:** Nonsmoking rooms; sitting rooms. *In room:* No phone.

Self-Catering

Donegal Thatched Cottages ★★   This cluster of cottages has a spectacular situation on Cruit Island, an enchanting landscape of rock and sand just off the Donegal coast near Dungloe. Accessible by a small bridge, Cruit is a narrow finger of land reaching into the Atlantic, dwarfed by its neighbors Aranmore and Owey islands. The cottages are on the Atlantic side, which alternates rocky headlands with unspoiled beaches; on the lee side, a quiet beach extends for miles. There's a great seaside walk along the western side of the island, which takes in a series of half-moon beaches. Each cottage has three bedrooms and is built according to a traditional plan, resembling many rural homes here, with wooden and tiled floors, high ceilings, and a great loft bedroom on the second floor. Although the location is remote, there are pubs and restaurants within short driving distance.

Cruit Island, c/o Conor and Mary Ward, Rosses Point, County Sligo. Signposted opposite Viking House Hotel on Kincasslagh Rd., 9.5km (6 miles) north of Dungloe, Cruit Island. ℂ **071/917-7197.** Fax 071/917-7500. www.donegalthatchcottages.com. 10 cottages. €325–€950 ($520–$1,520) per cottage per week. Weekend discounts available. MC, V. **Amenities:** Washer/dryer. *In room:* TV, kitchen w/dishwasher, no phone.

Termon House ★★★ (Finds)   The setting of this remote seaside cottage is spectacular, directly on a wind-swept beach that calls out to be explored. Within walking distance of the wee village of Maghery, the house sleeps six people upstairs in three handsome bedrooms; downstairs there's a sitting room, a parlor, and a country-style kitchen with a Stanley range and a big farmhouse table. The house is full of treasures—sturdy mahogany furnishings, oversize sofas and armchairs, stone fireplaces, and deep windowsills with cushioned seats, perfect for relaxing with a book. As with all Irish Landmark Trust properties, there's no TV.

Termon House, Maghery (near Dungloe), County Donegal. Contact the Irish Landmark Trust ℂ **01/670-4733.** Fax 01/670-4887. www.irishlandmark.com. €350 ($560) for 4 nights in low season, going up to €925 ($1,480) per week in high season. MC, V. *In room:* Kitchen, dishwasher, washing machine.

WHERE TO DINE

Dining in hotel restaurants is often a good idea. **Rathmullan House** (see above) has an excellent restaurant if you're in the mood to splurge.

The Mill Restaurant ★★ INTERNATIONAL   This is deservedly one of the hottest dining destinations in this part of Donegal. The draw is the cooking, which is all about pairing ingredients to achieve disarming results. All the seafood dishes are exceptional, especially the Doe Castle mussels. Desserts are simple and elegant, and the wine list is well chosen.

Figart (.8km/¹/₂ mile past village of Dunfanaghy, beside lake), County Donegal. ℂ **074/913-6985.** Reservations recommended for dinner. Fixed-price dinner €34 ($54); dinner main courses €18–€26 ($29–$42). MC, V. Tues–Sat 7–9pm; Sun 12:30–2pm and 7–9pm.

Water's Edge ★ INTERNATIONAL   As its name implies, this restaurant is at the edge of picturesque Lough Swilly. Its modern exterior belies its traditional dining room, with beamed ceilings, an open fireplace, and watercolors of Donegal landscapes. The menu blends Irish dishes with such international favorites as wild salmon in brandy-bisque sauce, and well-cooked steaks. More basic bar food is served all day. Rooms with a view and breakfast are available for €60 ($96) double.

The Ballyboe, Rathmullan, County Donegal. ℂ **074/915-8182.** Reservations recommended for dinner. Dinner main courses €16–€25 ($26–$40). MC, V. Easter–Sept daily noon–10pm; Oct–Easter daily 6:30–10pm.

PUBS

Most of the pubs in this Irish-speaking area are prone to sudden outbreaks of traditional Irish music in summer, which can be a good or bad thing, depending upon your perspective. Two places especially renowned for music are the **Lakeside Centre,** Dunlewey (ℂ **074/953-1699**), and **Leo's Tavern ★**, Meenaleck, Crolly (ℂ **074/954-8143**). The highly successful Irish group Clannad and the vocalist Enya (all part of the talented Brennan family) got their starts at Leo's.

The don't-miss pub in Ardara is **Nancy's ★** (ℂ **074/954-1187**) on Front Street, which has to be one of the smallest pubs in Ireland. It's an old Victorian house with the pub in the sitting room. As the crowd pours in, other rooms open up in hospitality.

4 THE INISHOWEN PENINSULA

Buncrana: 113km (70 miles) NE of Donegal Airport, 84km (52 miles) NE of Donegal Town, 19km (12 miles) NW of Derry, 145km (90 miles) NE of Sligo, 359km (223 miles) NE of Shannon, 259km (161 miles) NW of Dublin

With its exotic name and far-flung locale, it is appropriate that, by popular acclaim, this rarely visited but much admired stretch of land is one of the loveliest sections of the country. To drive around the Inishowen is to traverse desolate seascapes, intimidating mountains, restful valleys, and impenetrable woodlands. This is a world apart, where residents treasure the legends of Ireland and still observe its ancient traditions. If you've made it this far, well done! You join the hardy, lucky few who have discovered the rugged, peaceful beauty of Inishowen.

INISHOWEN PENINSULA ESSENTIALS

GETTING THERE & GETTING AROUND　　North West Busways (© 074/918-2619) offers service between Letterkenny and Moville, via Cardonagh and Buncrana, and there's daily Dublin-Inishowen service on offer by John McGinley (© 074/913-5201).

　　The best way to get to and around the Inishowen Peninsula is by car, following the signposted 161km (100-mile) Inishowen route.

VISITOR INFORMATION　　Contact the **North West Tourism Office,** Aras Reddan, Temple Street, Sligo (© 071/916-1201; www.discoverireland.ie/northwest); the **Letterkenny Tourist Office,** Derry Road, Letterkenny (© 074/912-1173); or the **Inishowen Tourism Society,** Chapel Street, Cardonagh, County Donegal (© 074/937-4933; www.visitinishowen.com). The latter's website has excellent hotel and guesthouse listings if you want more options. All the tourist offices are open year-round Monday to Friday 9:30am to 5:30pm, with extended summer hours.

SEEING THE SIGHTS

To an extent, driving around the northernmost point of Ireland is worth doing just so you can say you did. You stood on Malin Head and felt the icy mist come in on a wind that hit you like a fist, and you balanced yourself on the rocky edge of the country and looked out at the true north. You have felt the satisfaction that comes from knowing there is no farther to go.

　　Luckily, though, there's more to Inishowen than just that metaphysical urge. The Inishowen (Inis Eoghain) Peninsula reaches out from Lough Foyle to the east and Lough Swilly to the west toward Malin Head, its farthest point. Around the edges are ancient sites, beautiful beaches, and charming villages. At its center are gorgeous views, mountains, and quiet, vivid green pastures. If you are looking to get lost, this is a great place to do it.

　　But it won't be easy. Inexplicably, despite its clear need to be off the beaten path, and even with a decided dearth of traffic, the Inishowen Peninsula circuit is very well signposted, with all directions clearly printed in English and Irish, miles and kilometers.

　　To make a loop around the peninsula, start in the bustling little town of **Moville (Bun an Phobail),** which is a good place to stock up on gas and picnic provisions, and after a few miles of coastal road, you'll soon find yourself driving through **Greencastle (An Cáisleá Nua),** which holds the quirky Maritime Museum and Planetarium. From there, it's a short drive to the picturesque Inishowen Head. Follow signs off the main road onto a small side road, which you can take to the end, and then you walk the rest of the way to the headland. It's a bit eerily isolated, but the views are stupendous—on clear days, you can see all the way to the Antrim Coast. Back along the main road, look for a turn-off for **Culdaff (Cúil Dabhcha),** a sleepy waterfront village with a pretty beach. On its main street, the Clonca Church is a solid 17th-century structure with a high cross carved on one side with the biblical tale of loaves and fishes, and on the other with Celtic designs.

From Culdaff, it's about a 20-minute drive north to the pretty town of **Malin (Málainn),** with its stone bridge and village green. From Malin, it's another 20-minute drive to **Malin Head (Cionn Mhélanna),** a satisfyingly remote place at the end of the road where, even on a sunny day, the wind often howls and the temperature can be 10 degrees colder than it is 20 miles south. The farther north you go, the tinier the road becomes, the hillier and wilder the terrain, and the fewer the signs; a few corkscrew turns later and you'll be wondering where you are, but persevere. There are not really many places to go here, so follow your instincts and the few signs, and meander past the small cluster of houses until you reach rocky **Banba's Crown (Fíorcheann Éireann),** the far-thest point of the headland. Here, winds permitting, you can wander down to the rocky edge of the land and catch a glimpse of some old concrete huts built in World War II as lookout points. To the west of them is **Hell's Hole,** a natural land formation where waves crash deafeningly against the craggy shore. To the east, a path leads to a hermit's cave known as the **Wee House of Malin.**

Finding your way back to the main road without any signs is half the battle, and once you've done it, you're soon around the top of the peninsula and headed down the other side, through the **Gap of Mamore,** a mountain pass that rises 240m (787 ft.), then slowly descends on a corkscrew path to sea level, past a series of small, scenic villages to busy **Buncrana,** an excellent place to rest and have a meal. From the northern end of the seafront, you can find the old stone Castle Bridge that leads to **O'Doherty's Keep,** a simple, ruined tower house that served as the headquarters of the O'Doherty clan from the 15th century until it was destroyed by the English 300 years later. The ruins next to it are all that's left of the castle that the English built to replace it. Appropriately, they are privately owned and inaccessible to the public; the O'Doherty grounds, on the other hand, can be explored for free.

One of the peninsula's most impressive monuments is about 16km (10 miles) south of Buncrana. The hilltop fort known as **Grianan of Aileach** is an excellent example of a ring fort. It was built as a temple of the sun around 1700 B.C., and from the mid–5th century A.D. to the early 12th century A.D., it was the royal residence of the O'Neills, the chiefs of this area.

After you've toured the Inishowen, head south through **Letterkenny (Leitir Cean-ainn;** pop. 5,000). The largest town in the county, it's on a hillside overlooking the River Swilly. There you can pick up the N56, the main road, and drive to the twin towns of **Ballybofey** and **Stranorlar.** Change here to N15, which takes you to yet another scenic Donegal drive, the **Barnesmore Gap,** a vast open stretch through the Blue Stack Moun-tains, which leads you into Donegal Town and points south.

Fort Dunree Military Museum   Perched on a cliff overlooking Lough Swilly, Fort Dunree is a military and naval museum that incorporates a Napoleonic Martello tower into more recent World War I defenses. It features a wide range of exhibitions, an audio-visual center, and a cafeteria housed in a restored forge. Even if you have no interest in military history, it's worth a trip for the extraordinary views.

Signposted on the coast road north of Buncrana, County Donegal. ℭ **074/936-1817** or 932-1173. Admission €4 ($6.40) adults, €2 ($3.20) seniors and children. June–Sept Tues–Sat 10:30am–6pm, Sun 12:30–8pm; Oct–May Tues–Sat 10:30am–4:30pm.

Greencastle Maritime Museum and Planetarium This compact maritime museum, in the harbor home of a busy fishing fleet, is housed in the old 1857 coast-guard station. Outside are grand views of Lough Foyle above a monument to those lost while working at sea. The museum's modest rambling exhibits focus on the everyday struggles, as well as the historical events, from armada wrecks and famine-era emigration to the heroism of the Irish lifeboat-rescue teams. There's even an incongruous Mesolithic exhibit. A small coffee, craft, and souvenir shop is at hand. Proving there's a little bit of everything here, a planetarium has three shows daily; call ahead to confirm times.

Harbour, Greencastle, County Donegal. ℭ **074/938-1363.** www.inishowenmaritime.com. Admission to museum €5 ($8) adults; €3 ($4.80) seniors, children, and students. Admission to museum and planetarium €10 ($16) adults; €6 ($9.60) seniors, children, and students. Easter–Oct Mon–Fri 10am–6pm, Sat–Sun noon–6pm; Nov–Easter Mon–Fri 10am–5pm.

SPORTS & OUTDOOR PURSUITS

BEACHES **Ballyliffin, Buncrana, Greencastle,** and **Moville** have safe, sandy beaches ideal for swimming or strolling.

GOLF The Inishowen is the traditional home for golf in Ireland, and it has four 18-hole golf courses. Two are at the **Ballyliffin Golf Club,** Ballyliffin, County Donegal (ℭ **074/937-6119;** www.ballyliffingolfclub.com). The "Old Links" is a par-71 course with greens fees of €45 ($72) weekdays, €50 ($80) weekends. The "New Links" course costs €60 ($96) weekdays, €70 ($112) weekends. The **North West Golf Club,** Fahan, Buncrana, County Donegal (ℭ **074/936-1027**), founded in 1890, is a par-69 seaside course with greens fees of €25 ($40) weekdays, €30 ($48) weekends. **Greencastle Golf Course,** Greencastle, County Donegal (ℭ **074/938-1013**), is a par-69 parkland course with greens fees of €25 ($40) weekdays, €35 ($56) weekends.

WATERSPORTS The Inishowen's long coastline, sandy beaches, and combination of open ocean and sheltered coves provide great opportunities for watersports. The north-west coast presents some of the most challenging surfing conditions in Europe. For advice and specific information, contact the **Irish Surfing Association,** Tirconaill Street, Donegal (ℭ **074/972-1053;** www.isasurf.ie).

WHERE TO STAY
Expensive/Moderate
Carlton Redcastle Hotel & Spa ★★ On the shores of Lough Foyle on the Inishowen's eastern coast, this country inn–style hotel recently underwent a major renovation that doubled the number of rooms and gave the place a more luxurious feel. But it still offers a combination of old-world charm and modern comforts. The guest rooms are done up in subtle modern style, with designer fabrics, dark wood, orthopedic beds, and marble bathrooms. Rooms all have views of either the lake or the adjacent golf course. There's now an elegant **spa,** as well as an elaborate gym for those who need to work off some steam. If you'd prefer to just steam off some work, there's a lovely sauna.

Redcastle, Moville, County Donegal. ℭ **074/938-2073.** Fax 074/938-2214. www.redcastlehotel.com. 71 units. €100–€200 ($160–$320) double. Rates include full breakfast. AE, MC, V. **Amenities:** 2 restaurants (international, cafe); bar; 9-hole golf course; tennis court; gym; spa; Jacuzzi; sauna/steam room. *In room:* TV, broadband, tea/coffeemaker, hair dryer.

Mount Errigal ★   South of Lough Swilly and less than .8km (¹/₂ mile) east of Letterkenny, this contemporary two-story hotel is a handy place to stay. It's midway between the Inishowen Peninsula and Donegal Town, within 32km (20 miles) of Glenveagh National Park. Although it has a rather ordinary gray facade, the inside is bright and airy, with skylights, light woods, hanging plants, colored and etched glass, and brass fixtures. The guest rooms are outfitted in contemporary style, with cheerful colors and modern art, and good reading lights over the beds.

Derry Rd., Ballyraine, Letterkenny, County Donegal. ℂ **074/912-2700.** Fax 074/912-5085. www.mount errigal.com. 82 units. €130 ($208) double. Rates include full breakfast. AE, DC, MC, V. **Amenities:** 2 restaurants (international, cafe); bar; indoor swimming pool; gym; sauna/steam room; massage treatments. *In room:* TV, tea/coffeemaker, hair dryer, garment press.

Inexpensive

The Strand   On a hillside overlooking Pollen Strand, with views of nearby Malin Head, this small family-run hotel is on the edge of town, set apart in its palm tree–lined gardens. The decor throughout the hotel is contemporary, with wide windows and traditional touches. Guest rooms are neatly, though not imaginatively, appointed with beech furnishings, patterned fabrics, and neutral carpets. Bathrooms are modern but smallish. Still, if you're looking for a slightly old-style family hotel, it's hard to beat the price. The bar is known for its local entertainment.

Ballyliffin, Clonmany, County Donegal. ℂ **074/937-6107.** Fax 074/937-6486. www.ballyliffin.com/strand. 21 units. €90–€100 ($144–$160) double. Rates include full breakfast. MC, V. **Amenities:** Restaurant (international); bar. *In room:* TV, tea/coffeemaker, hair dryer.

Self-Catering

Ballyliffin Self Catering ★★   Ballyliffin is a tiny seaside village on the west coast of Inishowen, with two golf courses in proximity. This group of cottages is situated along the main road through town, a 10-minute walk from the fine sand and clear waters of Pollan Bay. The six connected cottages are all built in stone and pine, with lofty vaulted ceilings in the living rooms and massive central fireplaces that the stairs circle on their way to the second floor. Each cottage has three bedrooms and two bathrooms—two of the bedrooms have a double bed and an attached bathroom, while the third bedroom has three single beds. In some cottages, second-floor bedrooms overlook the living room, where a foldout couch provides yet more sleeping space. The well-equipped kitchen includes a microwave, an electric stove, a dishwasher, and a washing machine and dryer.

Rossaor House, Ballyliffin, County Donegal. ℂ/fax **074/937-6498.** 6 cottages. €475–€695 ($760–$1,112) per week. Rates include oil-fired heat and electricity. MC, V. **Amenities:** Washer/dryer. *In room:* TV, kitchen w/dishwasher and microwave, no phone.

WHERE TO DINE

The Corncrake ★★ MODERN CONTINENTAL   A restaurant like the Corncrake is as rare as the endangered bird from which it takes its name. The freshest of ingredients are sought out by Brid McCartney and Noreen Lynch and then transformed using herbs grown in their own gardens in a way that is nothing short of sublime. Meat and fish dishes are coupled with sauces and seasonings so masterful that they seem to give lamb a new tenderness and monkfish an unanticipated delicacy. Vegetarians need to book a day in advance, but will be rewarded by delectable dishes.

Malin St., Carndonagh, County Donegal. ℂ **074/937-4534.** Reservations recommended. Dinner main courses €17–€21 ($27–$34). No credit cards. Mar–June and Oct–Dec Sat–Sun 6–9pm; July–Sept daily 6–9pm. Closed St. Patrick's Day.

Kealy's Seafood Bar ★ SEAFOOD   Right across the road from the pier in Green-castle, Tricia Kealy's always-buzzing little fish house is a terrific place to know about. Tricia knows what to pair with just-off-the-boat fish—poached hake in saffron sauce, plaice in anchovy butter, cod with Stilton—which makes dining here a surprisingly refined experience. If you prefer, sidle up to the bar for an afternoon bite, and you can have a simple bowl of chowder or smoked salmon on brown bread.

Greencastle, County Donegal. ℭ **074/938-1010.** Reservations recommended for dinner. Fixed-price dinner €35 ($56); dinner main courses €23–€50 ($37–$80). MC, V. Daily 12:30–3pm and 7–9:30pm; bar snacks 3–5pm. Closed Mon–Wed in off season (usually Oct–Easter).

St. John's Country House and Restaurant ★ CONTINENTAL   On vast grounds overlooking Lough Swilly, this Georgian house has two cozy but elegant dining rooms. Open turf fireplaces, Waterford crystal, embroidered linens, and richly textured wallpaper add to the ambience. The food is dependably good, with dishes like baked Swilly salmon with lemon sauce and roast duck with port-and-orange sauce. B&B is available for €110 to €190 ($176–$304) double.

Fahan, County Donegal. ℭ **074/936-0289.** Fax 074/936-0612. Reservations required. Fixed-price 6-course dinner €38 ($61). AE, DC, MC, V. Mar–Sept Tues–Sat 6–10pm.

17

Northern Ireland

The terms Ulster, Northern Ireland, "the six counties," and "the North" are used interchangeably in Ireland for this small, ruggedly beautiful, and historically troubled land. The fact that nobody knows quite what to call it is appropriate given the seemingly endless struggle that has gone on for the soul of this place.

For many years, visitors to Ireland avoided the North, for obvious reasons. In fact, the vast majority of Irish people have never crossed the border into Ulster, and that's a pity. This is a colorful, exciting region, with vibrant towns and a countryside of breathtaking beauty. The way the locals treat you may come as a surprise—in fact, we'll go out on a limb and say that rural Northern Ireland is, in many ways, friendlier to visitors than the Republic. In part because of its relatively low tourism numbers, you'll find you are very welcome here, whereas, in the southern counties, the overwhelming flow of visitors has taken a toll on that famous Irish *fáilte* (courtesy).

Belfast and **Derry,** the North's only cities of any size, are both quite manageable, with complex political situations and grand historical monuments. But the main draw here is the magnificent countryside: the cool greens of the **Glens of Antrim,** the rugged **Mourne Mountains,** and the famously craggy coastline culminating in the lunar **Giant's Causeway.**

Still, the Troubles are obviously the elephant in the Northern Irish living room. It would be a unique visit that ignored politics entirely, whether it's the unforgiving murals in west Belfast or the strident graffiti that startles you in even the most bucolic village. Everybody picks a side in the Sisyphean effort to claim this rocky soil for God and country. But whose God and which country? You may as well have a quick rundown of the history of it all, if only so that you can tell your UFFs from your IRAs.

The strife in Northern Ireland can be traced back 800 years. In fact, there's an apocryphal story about a phone call between two friends—an Irish politician and an English parliamentarian—at the start of the Irish civil war in the 1920s. According to lore, the Englishman asked his Irish friend, "Is it true that there's an uprising in Ireland?" and the Irishman replied, "Aye, 'tis true." "When did it start?" the Englishman asked. "When Strongbow invaded Ireland," the Irishman said. "When will it end?" asked the Englishman. "When Cromwell gets out of hell," came the reply. The story alludes to the fact that when the English first invaded Ireland in the 12th century, they were led by the earl of Pembroke, nicknamed "Strongbow." They never really left, and the Irish never quit trying to get rid of them.

Over the centuries, the British waged a largely futile effort to make Ireland, and the Irish, British. Their tactics included outlawing the Irish language, banning Catholicism, and barring Catholics from landownership; finally, Oliver Cromwell's New Model Army went for the more basic approach of killing them in droves. British families were brought over to take their land—essentially, physically replacing Irish Catholics with British Protestants—in a process the Irish called "planting." The descendants of those British settlers, generally speaking, form the Protestant population of Northern Ireland today.

After centuries of struggle, Ireland finally won independence of a sort from Britain in 1921, in the aftermath of the 1916 rebellion. After much arguing, it was decided that the

Tips **Keeping Your Irish Up**

If you want to brush up on your knowledge of Northern Ireland, **Newshound** (www.nuzhound.com) is an indispensable resource. Run by American expat John Fay, this is an extremely well-organized catalog of news articles culled from international newspapers, covering everything from the Troubles to dining and shopping in Belfast. A vast array of articles about the Republic (click "NewsoftheIrish") includes culture, travel, and even dining reviews from Dublin to Donegal. The site is intelligent, user-friendly, and searchable.

island would be divided. Twenty-six Irish counties would form an independent, free state (now the Republic of Ireland), while six counties in the Ulster province with predominantly Protestant populations would become Northern Ireland and remain a part of the United Kingdom.

When the six counties were detached from the rest of the island, two conflicting ideological bodies emerged: Unionists, associated with the Protestant majority, who want to remain a part of the United Kingdom, and Nationalists, associated with the Catholic minority, who want the whole of Ireland united as one independent nation. Of course, being a Unionist or a Nationalist doesn't imply approval of the violence. In fact, the overwhelming majority of Northern Irish people, regardless of whether they want British rule or Irish rule, oppose the use of violence.

After the division, the British police and government in Ulster were quite brutal toward the Catholic minority. Things came to a head in the late 1960s when the minority Catholic population began an intense civil rights campaign. Their marches and demonstrations were crushed by the authorities, sometimes with disproportionate levels of violence, thus setting the stage for the re-emergence of the Irish Republican Army, a violent paramilitary Nationalist group that first appeared early in the 20th century. This modern battle between the British authorities and the Irish resistance that became known as the Troubles began in

1969 and would not end for nearly 30 years. Throughout the 1970s, violence was a fact of everyday life in Northern Ireland. By the 1980s, the violence was sporadic, if still shocking, and in the 1990s, the Northern Irish people—stunned by the sheer horror of an IRA bombing in the town of Omagh that killed 29 civilians on a busy shopping street—had had enough.

With the personal involvement of U.S. President Bill Clinton urging them to find a peaceful solution to their disagreements, on May 22, 1998, Northerners and their fellow islanders in the Republic voted to accept the Belfast Agreement, universally known as the "Good Friday Agreement." It dismantled the claims of both Ireland and Britain to the North and acknowledged the sovereign right of the people of Northern Ireland to take charge of their political destiny, effectively separating their government from London.

Since then, there has been little violence and virtually none of the kinds of terrorism that once shattered the peace.

From a visitor's perspective, the violence has always been remarkably contained. Like diplomats, foreigners have a kind of immunity. Derry and Belfast at their worst have always been safer for visitors than almost any comparable American city, and the Ulster countryside was then, and is now, as idyllic and serene as Vermont. When we've marveled at this, more than one Northern Irish person has told us, "It isn't your fight."

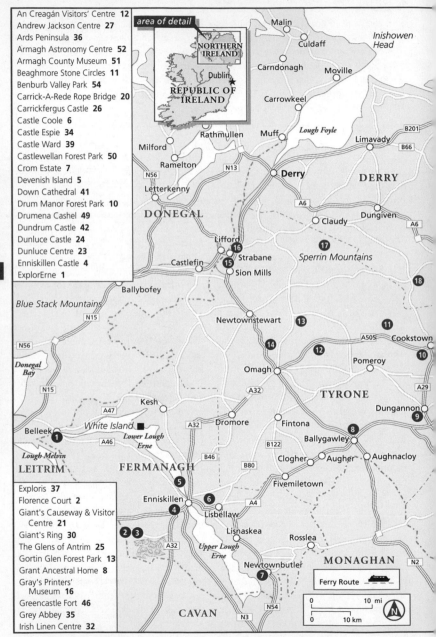

NORTHERN IRELAND

17

NORTHERN IRELAND ESSENTIALS

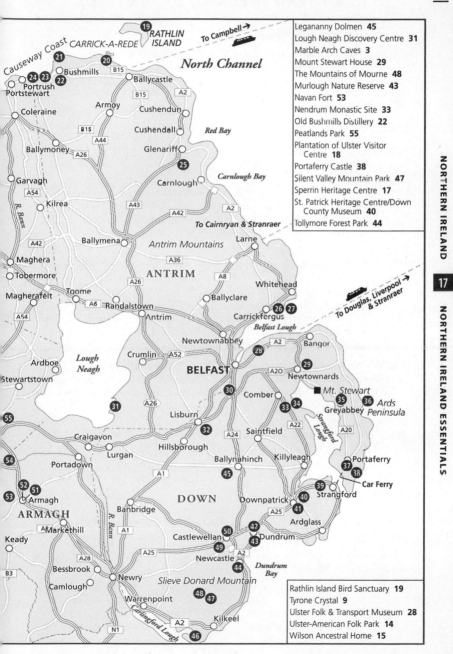

Leganany Dolmen **45**
Lough Neagh Discovery Centre **31**
Marble Arch Caves **3**
Mount Stewart House **29**
The Mountains of Mourne **48**
Murlough Nature Reserve **43**
Navan Fort **53**
Nendrum Monastic Site **33**
Old Bushmills Distillery **22**
Peatlands Park **55**
Plantation of Ulster Visitor
  Centre **18**
Portaferry Castle **38**
Silent Valley Mountain Park **47**
Sperrin Heritage Centre **17**
St. Patrick Heritage Centre/Down
  County Museum **40**
Tollymore Forest Park **44**

Rathlin Island Bird Sanctuary **19**
Tyrone Crystal **9**
Ulster Folk & Transport Museum **28**
Ulster-American Folk Park **14**
Wilson Ancestral Home **15**

1 NORTHERN IRELAND ESSENTIALS

VISITOR INFORMATION

The **Belfast Visitor & Convention Bureau** welcome center is at 47 Donegall Place, Belfast (© **028/9024-6609;** www.discovernorthernireland.com or www.gotobelfast. com). In addition, there are more than 30 tourist information centers (TICs) scattered around the province, most of which are open year-round. The obliging personnel will make sure you see the highlights. Local accommodations may be booked in any TIC, and most are hooked up to online reservations systems that can secure reservations throughout all of Ireland and the United Kingdom. To make your own reservations anywhere in Ireland using a credit card, you can call the free-phone number (© **0800/6686-6866**).

GETTING TO THE NORTH

BY AIR   Belfast has two airports—**Belfast International Airport** (© **028/9448-4848;** www.belfastairport.com) and **Belfast City Airport** (© **028/9093-9093;** www.belfast cityairport.com). **Continental** (© **800/231-0856;** www.continental.com) offers scheduled flights from New York to Belfast International.

There is service into both airports by a range of carriers, including **British Airways** (© **800/403-0882;** www.ba.com) from Birmingham, Edinburgh, London/Heathrow, and Manchester; **bmibaby** (© **08702/642229** in Britain; www.flybmi.com) from London Heathrow; and **easyJet** (© **0871/244-2366** in Britain; www.easyjet.com) from Liverpool, London, and many cities in continental Europe.

Service to **City of Derry Airport** (© **028/7181-0784;** www.cityofderryairport.com) is provided by **British Airways** from Glasgow, Dublin, and Liverpool; and by **Ryanair** (© **0871/246-0000;** www.ryanair.com) from London Stansted.

BY FERRY   Ferry services into Belfast include **Norfolk Line Irish Ferries** (© **0870/8 70-1020** in Britain, or 01/819-2999 in Ireland; www.norfolkline.com), which takes 8 hours from Liverpool, and the **Isle of Man Steam Packet Co.** (© **0162/466-1661;** www.steam-packet.com), which takes 2 hours and 45 minutes from Douglas, on the Isle of Man (summer service only). In addition, **Stena Sealink** (© **08705/707070;** www. stenaline.com) operates fast craft (105 min.) and ferry service (3 hr., 15 min.) from Stranraer, Scotland, to Belfast, and from Larne to the port of Fleetwood in the north of England; **P&O European Ferries** (© **08716/645-645;** www.poferries.com) from Fleetwood, Troon, and the Scottish port of Cairnryan to Larne.

BY CRUISE SHIP   Cruise ships call at the deepwater facilities at Lisahally or at Queen's Quay in the city center. For the latest information on cruises to Derry Port, contact the **Cruise Development Officer,** Derry City Council, 98 Strand Rd., Derry BT48 7NN (© **028/7136-5151;** fax 028/7126-4858), or contact the tourist office.

BY TRAIN   Trains on the **Irish Rail** (© **1850/366222;** www.irishrail.ie) and **Northern Ireland Railways** (© **028/9024-6485**) systems travel into Northern Ireland from Dublin's Connolly Station daily. They arrive at Belfast's **Central Station,** East Bridge Street (© **028/ 9089-9411**). Monday to Saturday, eight trains a day connect Dublin and Belfast; on Sunday, it's five. The trip takes about 2 hours. Trains for Derry, Larne, Bangor, and Portadown depart from **Great Victoria Street Station** (Glengall St.; © **028/9043-4424**).

BY BUS   **Ulsterbus** (© **028/9066-6630;** www.translink.co.uk) runs buses from the Republic to Belfast and towns across Northern Ireland. Belfast has two bus stations: The main **Europa Bus Centre** is behind the Europa Hotel and near the Great Victoria Street Station, while the **Laganside Bus Centre,** mainly used for buses into the surrounding counties, is on Oxford Street. The express bus from Dublin to Belfast takes under 3 hours and runs hourly Monday to Saturday, less frequently Sunday.

BY CAR You can easily reach Northern Ireland from the Republic of Ireland. Odds are you'll find it hard to identify the border at all since the big border crossings are long gone. Main roads to Northern Ireland from the Republic include N1 from Dublin (which is regularly under extensive construction), N2 from Monaghan, N3 from Cavan, N14 and N15 from Donegal, and N16 from Sligo. *Important note:* If you are renting a car and taking it across the border, make certain that all your insurance coverage is equally valid in the North and in the Republic. Don't forget to check any coverage provided by your credit card as well.

GETTING AROUND IN THE NORTH

BY TRAIN Belfast is the hub for **Northern Ireland Railways** (also known as Translink; © 028/9066-6630), with two principal rail stations: **Great Victoria Street Station,** on Great Victoria Street, and **Belfast Central Station,** on East Bridge Street. Most trains depart from Belfast Central. The three main routes in the North's rail system are north and west from Belfast to Derry via Ballymena; east to Bangor, tracing the shores of Belfast Lough; and south to Dublin via Newry.

BY BUS Ulsterbus (© 028/9033-3000; www.ulsterbus.co.uk) runs daily scheduled service from Belfast to major cities and towns throughout Northern Ireland. From the **Laganside Bus Centre,** Donegall Quay, Belfast (© 028/9032-0011), buses leave for destinations in the North, including Belfast International Airport and the Larne ferries, as well as the Republic. Bus service in the North is thorough and will get you to most towns of any size, although small villages are less well served.

BY SIGHTSEEING TOUR From June to August, **Ulsterbus** operates full- and half-day coach tours from the Europa Bus Centre, Glengall Street, Belfast. The tours run to places such as the Glens of Antrim, Causeway Coast, Fermanagh Lakelands, Sperrin Mountains, the Mountains of Mourne, and Armagh. There are also tours to specific attractions, such as the Giant's Causeway, Old Bushmills Distillery, Navan Centre in Armagh, and the Ulster-American Folk Park in Omagh. For more information, visit or phone the Ulsterbus/Translink tourism office at the Europa Bus Centre, Glengall Street (© 028/9066-6630).

BY CAR The best way to travel around the Northern Ireland countryside is by car. The roads are not always in great condition (although this is largely the result of ongoing construction programs that will ultimately improve them), but they are well signposted. Your biggest problem will be other drivers—Northern Ireland has an appalling record of road accidents, and many people drive far too fast here—but the same attention to safety that you exhibit when driving at home will bear similar rewards here. Generally speaking,

NORTHERN IRELAND ESSENTIALS

Ⓣ**ips** **Watch Where You Light Up**

As in the Republic of Ireland, smoking has been banned in public places, including restaurants and bars, in Northern Ireland.

distances between towns and villages here are quite small. If you want to rent a car, **Avis** (✆ **028/9024-0404**), **Budget** (✆ **028/9023-0700**), **Europcar** (✆ **028/9031-3500**), and **Hertz** (✆ **028/9073-2451**) have offices in Belfast, and most have branches at the airports. If you rent a car in the Republic, you can drive it in the North as long as you arrange the proper insurance.

(*Fast Facts*)   Northern Ireland

Area Code   The area code for all of Northern Ireland is **028.** Drop the "0" when dialing from within Northern Ireland.

Business Hours   Banks are generally open Monday to Friday 10am to 12:30pm and 1:30 to 3 or 4pm; they're closed on holidays. In Belfast and Derry City, banks tend not to close for lunch. Most shops are open Monday to Saturday 9 or 9:30am to 5 or 5:30pm, with one early-closing day a week, usually Wednesday or Thursday. Shops in tourist areas are likely to be open Sunday and to have extended hours, especially in the summer months.

Currency   Since Northern Ireland is a part of the United Kingdom, it uses the **pound sterling,** not the euro.

Electricity   The electrical current (220 volts/AC) and outlets (requiring three-pin flat, fused plugs) are the same in the North as in the Republic, and in the U.K. Note that they are not the two-pin round plugs standard throughout Europe.

Embassies & Consulates   The **U.S. Consulate General** is at Danesfort House, 223 Stranmillis Rd., Belfast BT9 5GR (✆ **028/9038-6100;** www.usembassy.org.uk/ nireland). Other foreign offices include the **Australian High Commission,** Australia House, Strand, London WC2 B4L (✆ **020/7379-4334); Canadian High Commission,** Macdonald House, Grosvenor Square, London W1X 0AB (✆ **020/ 7499-9000);** and **New Zealand High Commission,** New Zealand House, 80 Haymarket Sq., London SW1Y 4TQ (✆ **020/7930-8422).**

Emergencies   Dial ✆ **999** for fire, police, and ambulance.

Gas (Petrol)   Filling up the tank is far cheaper in the Republic, so do it before you cross the border. In the North, the approximate price of 1 liter of unleaded gas is £1.20 sterling ($2.40). There are approximately 4 liters to the U.S. gallon, which makes the price of a gallon of unleaded gas a whopping £4.80 ($9.60).

Mail   United Kingdom postal rates apply, and mailboxes are painted red. Most post offices are open weekdays 9am to 5pm, and Saturday 9am to 1pm.

Newspapers & Magazines   For listings of upcoming cultural events throughout Northern Ireland, check the free bimonthly *Arts Link* brochure, published by the Arts Council of Northern Ireland and available at any Northern Ireland Tourist Board office.

Parking   Because of long-standing security concerns, parking regulations are more restrictive and more relentlessly enforced in the North than in the Republic. Look out for signs warning you where to park and not park. Never park on double red or double yellow lines.

Police   To reach the **Police Service of Northern Ireland (PSNI),** as the Northern Irish police force is known, dial ✆ **999** anywhere in the North.

Safety Contrary to the media image, the North has one of the lowest levels of crime in western Europe. Historically, serious crimes such as homicide and robbery have been associated with terrorism and the Troubles. Nonetheless, there are crime problems in cities, so use care to avoid pickpockets in crowded areas, and follow other basic rules of safety.

Taxes **VAT (value-added tax)** of 17.5% is included in the price of almost everything, except B&B accommodations. The percentages vary with the category of the services and purchases. It is usually already included in the prices you're quoted by hotels and the prices you see marked on merchandise tags. VAT is included in the hotel prices we've quoted in this guide. Many shops offer tax-free shopping options, such as "Cashback," and are pleased to explain the details. Vouchers from the North can be presented at the Dublin or Shannon airports before departure from Ireland. For further information, contact HM Revenue and Customs, Belfast International Airport (© **028/9441-3439** or 9442-3439; www.hmrc.gov.uk).

Telephone To reach Northern Ireland from anywhere but the Republic of Ireland or Great Britain, dial the U.K. country code (44) and then 28 (the area code minus the initial 0) and finally the local eight-digit number. From the Republic of Ireland, omit the country code; dial 048 and then the local eight-digit number. From Great Britain, dial 028 and the eight-digit number. For local calls within Northern Ireland, simply dial the eight-digit local number.

2 BELFAST

166km (103 miles) N of Dublin, 340km (211 miles) NE of Shannon, 201km (125 miles) E of Sligo, 422km (262 miles) NE of Cork

For those who grew up in the '70s and '80s when Belfast was plagued by violence and political unrest, to think of it now in terms of tourism rather than terrorism requires some mental calisthenics. But try. Because this is an extraordinary time to visit this city, as it is still in the process of picking itself up and dusting itself off after years of strife. Nearly half a million people, a third of Northern Ireland's population, live in Belfast, most of them in neighborhoods segregated by religion. Yet, you really see little sign of any residual religious tension in the city center. In recent years, the center has been polished up, and it is a pleasure to wander its pedestrianized lanes, to shop in the upscale arcades lined with glittering jewelry stores and colorful boutiques, to linger in the historic pubs, and to dine in the Michelin-starred restaurants.

The city is easily divided into walkable quarters: The **City Center** spreads out from around the impressive, domed City Hall building and bustling Donegall Square. This is the best place for shopping, particularly along Donegall Place, which extends north from the square, onto Royal Avenue. Bedford Street, which travels south from the Donegall Square, becomes Dublin Road, which, in turn, leads south to the **University Quarter,** the leafy area around Queen's University. This is where you'll find the Botanic Gardens, art galleries, and museums, as well as a buzzing nightlife scene. Heading north from Donegall Place, it's a short distance to the **Cathedral Quarter,** which surrounds Donegall Street, and holds, as the name implies, the city's most important cathedrals, as well as many vast Victorian warehouses. Finally there's the **Golden Mile**—the area around Great Victoria Street beyond Bradbury Place. It's considered the city's best address for restaurants and pubs, although it's a bit hyperbolically named. As one local said to us, "It's not a mile and it's not golden. But it's nice enough."

It's easiest to start in the center and then branch out from there. Perhaps tour the City Hall, then spend some time shopping for linen and china, then a walk to the Cathedral Quarter to take in the architecture, and finally dinner and drinks on the Golden Mile.

The sectarian areas, with the famous IRA and Protestant murals, are just to the west of the city center. The most famous of these are on the Shankill and Falls roads. It's perfectly safe to drive the roads and take photos yourself (locals are quite proud of the murals), or you could take one of the Black Cab tours (p. 500) if you want a guide to explain what it all means.

ESSENTIALS

GETTING THERE   For details, see "Getting to the North," in section 1, above. Belfast has two airports—Belfast International and Belfast City—and gets considerable sea traffic at Belfast Harbour and at Larne (30 min. from Belfast by train, bus, or car).

From Belfast International Airport, nearly 31km (19 miles) north of the city, your best option is the **Translink Airbus** to the city center. It leaves every half-hour, and costs around £6.50 ($13) per person for a one-way ticket and £10 ($20) for a round-trip. A taxi will run closer to £25 to £30 ($50–$60).

Belfast City Airport is 6km (3³/₄ miles) from the city center, and is affordably reached by taxi, which should cost roughly £7 ($14) to get into the city. You can also take Citybus no. 21 from the airport terminal or the Sydenham Halt train from the station directly across from the airport, both for £2 ($4).

VISITOR INFORMATION   Brochures, maps, and other data on Belfast and the North are available from the **Belfast Welcome Centre,** at 47 Donegall Place (© **028/9024-6609;** www.gotobelfast.com). It's open June through September Monday to Saturday 9am to 7pm and Sunday noon to 5pm; October through May, hours are Monday to Saturday 9am to 5:30pm. The tourist information desk at **Belfast City Airport** (© **028/ 9045-7745**) is open year-round Monday to Friday 5:30am to 10pm, Saturday 5:30am to 9pm, and Sunday 5:30am to 10pm. The desk at **Belfast International Airport** (© **028/ 9442-2888**) is open March to September daily whenever the airport is open, October to February daily 6:30am to 11pm. Also check **www.belfast.net**, a comprehensive guide to the city, featuring tourism, news, accommodations, events, and nightlife listings.

GETTING AROUND   **Metro,** Donegall Square West, Belfast (© **028/9066-6630;** www. translink.co.uk), is the recently renamed local bus service provider in Belfast. Buses depart from Donegall Square East, West, and North, plus Upper Queen Street, Wellington Place, Chichester Street, and Castle Street, and from bus stops throughout the city. There is an information kiosk on Donegall Square West, and you can download timetables from their website. Fares are determined by the number of zones traversed. The maximum fare for city-center travel is £1.10 ($2.20). Multiple-trip tickets, day tickets, and 7-day passes offer significant savings.

If you've brought a **car** into Belfast, it's best to leave it parked and take public transportation or walk around the city. If you must drive and want to park your car downtown, look for a blue P sign that shows a parking lot or a parking area. Belfast has a number of "control zones," indicated by a pink-and-yellow sign, where no parking is

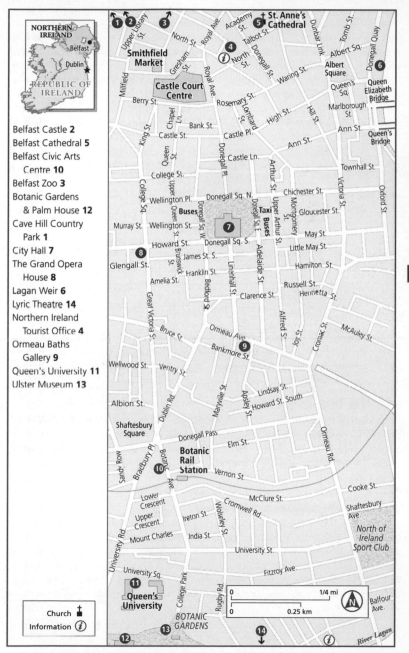

Belfast Castle **2**
Belfast Cathedral **5**
Belfast Civic Arts
  Centre **10**
Belfast Zoo **3**
Botanic Gardens
  & Palm House **12**
Cave Hill Country
  Park **1**
City Hall **7**
The Grand Opera
  House **8**
Lagan Weir **6**
Lyric Theatre **14**
Northern Ireland
  Tourist Office **4**
Ormeau Baths
  Gallery **9**
Queen's University **11**
Ulster Museum **13**

Church †
Information ⓘ

NORTHERN IRELAND   **17**   BELFAST

permitted. In general, on-street parking is limited to an area behind City Hall (south side), St. Anne's Cathedral (north side), and around Queen's University and Ulster Museum.

Taxis are available at all main rail stations, ports, and airports, and in front of City Hall. Most metered taxis are London-type black cabs with a yellow disc on the window. Other taxis may not have meters, so you should ask about the fare to your destination in advance. Except for reasonably inexpensive service down the Shankill Road and the Falls Road, Belfast taxi fares are on the high side, with a £2.20 ($4.40) minimum and an additional £1.10 ($2.20) per mile.

Belfast is a good city for **walking.** To guide visitors on the best and safest areas for a stroll, the Belfast City Council offers leaflets for five self-guided walking tours. They are city center south to Shaftesbury Square, city center north to the Irish News office, Shaftesbury Square south to the university area, city center northeast to the port area, and Donegall Square south to Donegall Pass. Each walk is about a mile and lasts an hour. Ask for a leaflet for the walk that interests you at the Belfast Welcome Centre.

FAST FACTS The **U.S. consulate general** is at Danesfort House, 223 Stranmillis Rd., Belfast BT9 5GR (✆ **028/9038-6100;** www.usembassy.org.uk/nireland). For other embassies and consulates, see "Fast Facts: Northern Ireland," above.

In an **emergency,** dial ✆ **999** for fire, police, and ambulance. Central hospitals include Belfast City Hospital (✆ **028/9032-9241**) on Lisburn Road, and Mater Hospital (✆ **028/9074-1211**) on Crumlin Road near Antrim Road.

For Internet access, head to the **Belfast Welcome Centre,** 47 Donegall Place (✆ **028/9024-6609;** www.gotobelfast.com), which has an Internet cafe where connections cost around £2 ($4) per hour. Or try the **Friends Café** (✆ **028/9024-1096**) at 109–113 Royal Ave., where Internet connection is £2 ($4) an hour and you can have a nice cup of joe while you're at it.

The main post office, the **Belfast GPO (General Post Office)** is at Castle Place, at the intersection of Royal Avenue and Donegall Place. It's open Monday to Friday 9am to 5:30pm, and Saturday 9am to 7pm.

SEEING THE SIGHTS

To discover the most historic parts of Belfast, you might try **Old Town: 1660-1685** (✆ **028/9024-6609**), which traces the old city walls and explores the oldest part of the city at 2pm Saturdays (£5/$10). From May to September, the **Historical Pub Tours of Belfast** (✆ **028/9268-3665**) departs twice a week from the Crown Liquor Saloon on Great Victoria Street and then travels on to six of the city's pubs. Tours are Thursday at 7pm and Saturday at 4pm, take 2 hours, and cost £6 ($12), not including drinks.

Belfast Botanic Gardens & Palm House Dating from 1828, these gardens were established by the Belfast Botanic and Horticultural Society. Ten years later, they gained a glass house, or conservatory, designed by noted Belfast architect Charles Lanyon. Now known as the Palm House, this unique building is one of the earliest examples of curvilinear cast-iron glass-house construction. It contains a good variety of tropical plants, including sugar cane, coffee, cinnamon, banana, aloe, ivory nut, rubber, bamboo, guava, and spindly birds of paradise. If the weather's fine, stroll in the outdoor rose gardens, first established in 1927.

Signposted from M1/M2 (Balmoral exit), Stranmillis Rd., County Antrim. ✆ **028/9032-4902.** Free admission. Palm House and Tropical Ravine Apr–Sept Mon–Fri 10am–noon, daily 1–5pm; Oct–Mar Mon–Fri 10am–noon, daily 1–4pm. Gardens daily 8am–sunset. Bus: 61, 71, 84, or 85.

Belfast Castle Northwest of downtown and 120m (394 ft.) above sea level stands
Belfast Castle, whose 80-hectare (198-acre) estate spreads down the slopes of Cave Hill.
Dating from 1870, this was the family residence of the third marquis of Donegall, and it
was built in the style of Britain's Balmoral castle. After a relatively brief life in private ownership, in 1934 it was given to the city, which used it largely for private functions for more
than 50 years before opening it to the public in 1988. It's a lovely place to visit, with sweeping views of Belfast and the lough. Its cellars contain a nifty Victorian arcade, with a bar, a
bistro, and a shop selling antiques and crafts. According to legend, a white cat was meant
to bring the castle residents luck, so look around for carvings featuring the creature.

Signposted off the Antrim Rd., 4km (2½ miles) north of the city center, County Antrim. © **028/9077-6925.**
www.belfastcastle.co.uk. Free admission and parking. Castle Mon–Sat 9am–10pm; Sun 9am–6pm.

Belfast Cathedral The foundation stone on this monumental cathedral was laid in
1899, but it would be more than a century later before it was finally completed, and even
now it awaits a steeple. Crisscrossing architectural genres from Romanesque to Victorian
to modern, the huge structure is more attractive inside than out. In the nave, the ceiling
soars above the black-and-white marble walls and stone floors, and elaborate stained-glass
windows fill it with color. Carvings representing life in Belfast top the 10 pillars in the
nave. Its most impressive features, though, are the delicate mosaic ceilings of the tympa-
num and the baptistery, both designed by sisters Gertrude and Mary Martin over the
course of 7 years, and made of thousands of pieces of glass.

Donegall St., Belfast, County Antrim. © **028/9033-2328.** Free admission (donations accepted). Mon–Fri
10am–4pm.

Belfast Zoo (Kids) In a picturesque mountain park on the slopes of Cave Hill overlooking the city, this zoo was founded in 1920 as Bellevue Gardens and has been modernized completely in recent years. It emphasizes conservation and education, and
focuses on breeding rare species, including Hawaiian geese, Indian lions, red lechwe (a
kind of antelope), and golden lion tamarins.

8km (5 miles) north of the city on A6, Antrim Rd., County Antrim. © **028/9077-6277.** www.belfastzoo.
co.uk. There are 2 price tiers; lower prices apply Oct–Mar. Admission £6.70–£8.10 ($13–$16) adults,
£3.40–£4.30 ($6.80–$8.60) children 4–18. Free for seniors and children 3 and under. Apr–Sept daily
10am–7pm; Oct–Mar daily 10am–4pm. Bus: 9, 45, 46, 47, 48, 49, 50, or 51.

Cave Hill Country Park (Kids) This park atop a 360m (1,181-ft.) basalt cliff offers
panoramic views, walking trails, and a number of interesting archaeological and historical
sights. There are the Neolithic caves that gave the hill its name, and MacArt's Fort, an
ancient earthwork built against the Vikings. In this fort, in 1795, Wolfe Tone and fellow
United Irishmen planned the 1798 rebellion. On a lighter note, there's an adventure
playground for the kids.

Off Antrim rd., 6.5km (4 miles) north of city center, County Antrim. Parking at Belfast Castle or Belfast Zoo
(above).

City Hall ★ Standing as a symbol to Belfast's Industrial Revolution preeminence, this
is a glorious explosion of granite, marble, and stained glass. It was built in classical
Renaissance style in 1906. Its creamy white walls are Portland stone and its soft green
dome is copper. There are several statues on the grounds—a grim-faced statue of Queen
Victoria stands in front of it, looking as if she wishes she were anyplace else. Bronze
figures around her represent the textile and ship-building industries that powered Belfast's success. There's also a memorial to the victims of the *Titanic* disaster. Inside the

(Tips) **Tour the Troubles**

For many years, Belfast was best known for its most conflicted neighborhoods, where in the 1970s protests occurred daily, and in the 1980s violence was the norm. Now that peace has grudgingly descended upon the Catholic Falls Road and its nearby parallel, the Protestant Shankill Road, there's a growing industry around exploring the city's most infamous sectarian neighborhoods. The best tours are given by the various "Black Cabs," which take groups of one to five people in London-style cabs through the neighborhoods, past the barbed wire, towering fences, and partisan murals, as guides explain their significance. There are a number of these tour groups, and quality varies considerably, but the 2-hour **Black Taxi Tour** (© **0800/052-3914;** www.belfasttours.com) is highly recommended. Its drivers are relaxed, patient, and amazingly unbiased (our driver let us guess at the end of the tour whether he was Catholic or Protestant . . . we guessed wrong). The fare is £25 ($50) for the first two passengers, or £8 ($16) per person for three or more passengers.

building is even better, with an elaborate entry hall heavy with marble, but lightened by stained glass, and a rotunda with a soaring painted ceiling—and it all somehow manages not to be tacky. There are often exhibitions upstairs. To learn all the building's details, take a free guided tour—ask in the lobby.

Donegall Sq., Belfast, County Antrim. © **028/9027-0456.** Free admission. Guided tours June–Sept Mon–Fri 11am, 2pm, and 3pm, Sat 2:30pm; Oct–May Mon–Sat 11am and 2:30pm. Otherwise by arrangement. Reservations required.

Cultúrlann Macadam Óflaich ★ This warm and welcoming place is the center for Irish language and culture. Inside a red-brick former church, it holds a tourist information desk, but the biggest attraction is the shop, which sells a good selection of books about Ireland, as well as Irish crafts and CDs of Irish music. Its pleasant cafe is a good place to stop for a cup of coffee.

216 Falls Rd., Belfast, County Antrim. © **028/9023-9303.** Free admission. Mon–Fri 9am–5:30pm; Sat 10am–5:30pm.

Falls Road ★★ Scarred by decades of conflict, the Catholic Falls Road is a compelling place, as are all political hotbeds. It is quite safe—the residents are used to sightseers wandering through to photograph the political murals, and most people are welcoming. It's an ordinary enough *looking* neighborhood—houses have flowers in the windows and kids play in the streets. The big skyscraper you can see down the road is the Divis Tower—it's all residential save for the top two floors, which were taken over by the British military in the 1970s, and are still used as a watchtower. Just past the tower begins the long, tall, imposing wall of wood, concrete, and metal that has become known as the "Peace Line." It has divided the Catholics of Falls Road from the Protestants of Shankill Road for 30 years. Its huge metal gates are open during the day, but some are still closed at night. In some sections, the fence is more than 6m (20 ft.) tall. It has become a sort of Berlin Wall of Ireland, and locals and visitors draw pictures and write messages of peace on it. On the corner of Falls and Sevastopol Street is the surprisingly small Sinn

Fein headquarters—at one end of the building is a mural of the late hunger striker Bobby Sands, arguably the most famous political mural in Belfast.

From Donegall Sq., travel north along Donegall Place and turn left on Castle St., then head straight ahead on Divis St. across the busy Westlink to the Falls Rd.

Fernhill House: The People's Museum ★   An educational museum (if not an unbiased one) on Glencairn Road, beyond the end of Shankill Road, this is a re-creation of a Protestant Belfast house as it would have looked in the 1930s. Its exhibitions trace the history of the area through Home Rule, war, and the continuing tensions, and thus may answer many questions you might have.

Glencairn Rd., Belfast, County Antrim. ✆ **028/9071-5599.** www.fernhillhouse.co.uk. Admission £2 ($4) adults, £1 ($2) children. Mon–Sat 10am–4pm; Sun 1–4pm.

Choosing Sides

To understand Northern Ireland, you first must understand who is involved in the sectarian game, because the battle between Republicans (those who believe the North should become part of the Republic of Ireland; also called Nationalists or "the Catholics," depending on who's talking), and the loyalists (those who are loyal to the British crown and think the North should stay, as it is now, part of the United Kingdom; also called Unionists or "the Protestants") defines this region to this day. The problem is that both sides have splintered over the last decade, and so it's hard to keep up with who's who.

The Republicans are now divided among devotees of the IRA (the Irish Republican Army), the "Real" IRA (a rebellious faction formerly part of the IRA), and Sinn Fein (also splintered from the IRA, and now its political face). Supporters for this side have the green, white, and orange Irish flag hanging from their homes and businesses.

The loyalists are divided among a variety of paramilitary groups, including the UDA (Ulster Defence Association), the UDF (Ulster Defence Force), and the UVF (Ulster Volunteer Force). Much of the violence in the last decade has been the result of turf wars between those Protestant groups. Supporters of that side have the British Union Jack flag flying from their homes and businesses.

These days, most, if not all, of these groups are more involved in organized crime than political struggle, and all of them have been lumped together by pundits under the new term "Irish mafia." Massive bank robberies (all of Northern Ireland's currency was withdrawn and reissued within 1 week in 2005 after a gang suspected to be connected with the IRA stole £22 million in a bank heist), importation and sales of illegal weaponry, and drugs are all blamed on the same factions that once battled for political power here. Most Irish people will tell you that they're sick of the lot of them—however, don't ask unless you know the person you're talking to. It's an extremely sensitive subject that should not be brought up casually. If curiosity is killing the cat, take one of the Black Cab tours and you can ask your driver questions to your heart's content.

Lagan Weir & Visitors Center (Kids)   By the 1980s, decades of pollution had left the River Lagan, once the center of Belfast life, a filthy mess. In the 1990s, a cleanup program and the addition of the Lagan Weir gradually brought the river back to life, and today it is a healthy ecosystem, home to eels, salmon, and sea trout. The change is commemorated in the ceramic statue *Bigfish*, a giant salmon covered in tiles that tell the history of the city and its river. The Lagan Lookout Visitor Center offers an up-close and entertaining look at how the weir works. The hands-on center has computers and interactive activities to tell the tale.

1 Donegall Quay, Belfast, County Antrim. ✆ **028/9031-5444.** Admission £2 ($4). Apr–Sept Mon–Fri 11am–5pm, Sat noon–5pm, Sun 2–5pm; Oct–Mar Tues–Fri 11am–3:30pm, Sat 1–4:30pm, Sun 2–4:30pm.

Odyssey Complex (Kids)   This enormous entertainment, education, and sports center on the east bank of the river is bursting with activities and has been popular since it opened in 2001. For kids, its hands-on science center—W5—is a hypermodern, interactive learning environment where children can compose their own music on an air harp, create tornadoes, learn how robots are built, and try to make one of their own. Also in the complex are an arena where the Belfast Giants ice hockey team plays, an IMAX cinema, video-game arcades, and lots of bars, restaurants, and cafes. On a rainy day, there's probably no better place to go to keep everyone amused and dry.

5-min. walk across the weir from the Lagan Lookout, Belfast, County Antrim. ✆ **028/9046-7700.** www.theodyssey.co.uk. Admission to W5 £6 ($12) adults, £4 ($8) children 4–18, £17 ($34) families. Mon–Sat 10am–6pm; Sun noon–6pm.

Ormeau Baths Gallery ★   Occupying the site of, and partly incorporating, the old Victorian swimming baths designed by Robert Watt, Ormeau Baths Gallery opened in 1995 as the city's principal exhibition space for contemporary visual art. This striking and versatile facility can program multiple simultaneous exhibitions in a variety of mediums, and has become the premier showcase for the best of Northern Irish contemporary art.

18A Ormeau Ave., Belfast, County Antrim. ✆ **028/9032-1402.** www.ormeaubaths.co.uk. Free admission. Tues–Sat 10am–6pm.

Queen's University   This is Northern Ireland's most prestigious university, founded by Queen Victoria in 1845 to provide nondenominational higher education. The main, 19th-century Tudor Revival building may remind you of England's Oxford, as its design was based on that of the Founder's Tower at Magdalen College. But that's hardly all there is to this university, which sprawls through 250 buildings, where 17,500 students are studying at any given time. Most of the buildings are of interest only for those rushing to chemistry class, but the whole neighborhood around the university is a quiet, attractive place to wander, and University Square on the north side of campus is simply beautiful. At one end of

Impressions

We make out of the quarrel with others, rhetoric, but of the quarrel with ourselves, poetry.

—W. B. Yeats

the square is the Union Theological College, which dates to 1853 and housed the Northern Ireland Parliament after the partition of Ireland.

Visitor Centre, University Rd., Belfast, County Antrim. © **028/9033-5252**. www.qub.ac.uk/vcentre. Free admission. May–Sept Mon–Sat 10am–4pm; Oct–Apr Mon–Fri 10am–4pm. Bus: 61, 71, 84, or 85.

Shankill Road ★★   Almost as soon as you turn onto Protestant Shankill Road, you pass a building that has been entirely painted with the Union Jack flag. A few blocks down the road, and off to the right, you'll see a cluster of enormous murals, including one celebrating Oliver Cromwell, who massacred Irish Catholics in an effort to conquer the island. Across a field from that mural is one of a man in a ski mask pointing a machine gun at the street. Locals say it's the Belfast version of Mona Lisa's eyes, which are said to follow you around the room—no matter where you go in the area, that gun is always pointing at you. Shankill is indefinably grimmer than the Falls Road—it's more down at heel and you'll see more boarded-up shops, but the people are just as friendly and you're just as welcome here. Shankill murals seem to be darker than those on the Falls, where many murals are about solidarity with the downtrodden; here, they're all about the corruption of Catholics, with a display of painted weaponry.

The Shankill Rd. runs parallel to the Falls Rd. To reach it from Donegall Sq., head north along Donegall Place and Royal Ave., then turn left on Peter's Hill and cross the Westlink rd.

Ulster Museum ★★   Built in the grand Classical Renaissance style, with an Italian marble interior, this excellent museum crams in 9,000 years of Irish history with exhibits on art, furniture, ceramics, costume, industrial heritage, and a permanent display of products "made in Belfast." One of the best-known exhibits is the collection of gold and silver jewelry recovered by divers in 1968 off the Antrim coast from the 1588 wreckage of the armada treasure ship *Girona*. Check out the "Early Ireland" gallery, which has an extensive, cleverly displayed collection of prehistoric artifacts of stone and bronze from Northern Ireland's many ancient archaeological sites.

Signposted from M1/M2 (Balmoral exit); next to the Botanic Gardens, Stranmillis Rd., Belfast, County Antrim. © **028/9038-3000**. Free admission, except to major special exhibitions. Mon–Fri 10am–5pm; Sat 1–5pm; Sun 2–5pm. Bus: 61, 71, 84, or 85.

SHOPPING

Belfast is a surprisingly good place to shop. We recommend starting at Donegall Place, where the streets are lined with shops, and the Victorian arcades are filled with gift shops and jewelry stores. Good buys are to be had on Belleek china, linen, and crystal from County Tyrone. Continue your spree at **Craftworks Gallery,** Bedford House, Bedford Street (© **028/9024-4465**), a one-stop shop for crafts from throughout the region. The gallery can supply a free copy of the brochure "Crafts in Northern Ireland," detailing local crafts and where to find them. It is just behind Belfast City Hall. Or you could head to the excellent **Wicker Man** in the Donegall Arcade (© **028/9024-3550**), which has a good stock of crafts. You'll find both Irish crafts and traditional Irish music at **Cultúrlann MacAdam Ó Fiaich** (216 Falls Rd.; © **028/9023-9303**).

The main shopping street is **Royal Avenue,** home of well-known chains such as Waterstone's bookstore, Jaeger clothing store, and Virgin Music Megastore. The **Castlecourt Shopping Centre** on Royal Avenue is Belfast's main downtown multistory shopping mall—the largest in Northern Ireland—with more than 70 boutiques and shops.

Red Hand of Ulster

Around Belfast, and all of Northern Ireland, you'll frequently come across representations of a red hand. It's carved in door frames, painted on walls and ceilings, and even planted in red flowers in gardens. Known as the Red Hand of Ulster, it is one of the symbols of the region. According to one version of the old tale, the hand can trace its history from a battle between two men competing to be king of Ulster. They held a race (some say by boat, others say it took place on horseback) and agreed that the first man to touch Ulster soil would win. As one man fell behind, he pulled his sword and cut off his right hand, then with his left, flung the bloody hand ahead of his competitor, winning the right to rule.

Belfast's leading department stores are **Anderson & McAuley** and **Marks & Spencer,** both on Donegall Place, and **Debenham's** in the Castlecourt Shopping Centre on Royal Avenue. Other shops to look for include the following:

Archive's Antiques Centre   This labyrinth of collectibles sprawls across three floors filled with military memorabilia, books, Irish silver, and china. Open Monday to Friday 10:30am to 5:30pm, Saturday 10am to 6pm. 88 Donegall Pass. Belfast, County Antrim. ✆ 028/9023-2383.

Oakland Antiques   On Belfast's antiques row, Donegall Pass, this is the biggest shop of them all, with an impressive array of Edwardian, Georgian, and Victorian silver, porcelain, and more. Open Monday to Saturday 10am to 5:30pm. 135 Donegall Pass. Belfast, County Antrim. ✆ 028/9023-0176.

St. George's Market   This is Belfast's original "variety market," dating from the 19th century and now standing across from the new Waterfront Hall. The market was completely restored in 1999 and is a colorful outlet for fresh fruit, flowers, fish, vegetables, clothing, crafts, and lots more. Open Tuesday and Friday starting at 8am. May St. at Oxford St. Belfast, County Antrim. ✆ 028/9043-5704.

Smyth's Irish Linens   If you want to stock up on fine Irish linen damask tablecloths, napkins, and handkerchiefs, head for this shop in the heart of the city's prime shopping thoroughfare. It also stocks other traditional gift items and offers VAT-free export. 65 Royal Ave. Belfast, County Antrim. ✆ 028/9024-2232.

The Steensons   This is the main showroom of Bill and Christina Steenson, two of the most celebrated goldsmiths in Ireland. On display and for sale is the widest collection anywhere of the Steensons' unique gold and silver jewelry, as well as work by a select number of top designers from afar. Bedford St. (behind Belfast City Hall). Belfast, County Antrim. ✆ 028/9024-8269. www.thesteensons.com.

Tom Caldwell Gallery   Come here for a selection of paintings, sculptures, and ceramics by living artists, as well as handcrafted furnishings, rugs, and cast-iron candelabras. Open Monday to Friday from 9:30am to 5pm, Saturday from 10am to 1pm. 40 Bradbury Place. Belfast, County Antrim. ✆ 028/9032-3226. www.tomcaldwellgallery.com.

Utopia   This is where you go for a wide range of gifts from Ireland and around the world, including locally designed jewelry and ceramics. Open Monday to Friday from 10am to 5pm, Saturday from 10am to 1pm. Fountain Centre, College St. Belfast, County Antrim. ✆ 028/9024-1342. www.utopiaonline.co.uk.

Workshops Collective A clearinghouse of sorts for local artists, this shop in the University Quarter allows you to purchase paintings, sculpture, crafts, and furniture directly from the artists who made them. The works are ever-changing and range from the interesting to the I-wouldn't-have-that-in-my-house. 1a Lawrence St. Belfast, County Antrim. © **028/9020-0707.**

SPORTS & OUTDOOR PURSUITS

FISHING The 9km (5½-mile) stretch of the Lagan River from Stranmillis weir to Shaw's Bridge offers decent coarse fishing, especially on summer evenings. From May to July, Lough Neagh has good shore and boat fishing. For fishing equipment and contacts try **Get Hooked,** 49 Suffolk Rd., Belfast (© **028/9062-3431**). For info, tackle, and bait, try the **Village Tackle Shop,** 55a Newtownbreda Rd., Belfast (© **028/9049-1916**).

GOLF The Belfast area offers four 18-hole courses within 6km (3¾ miles) of the city center. Some 5km (3 miles) southwest of the city, there's the **Balmoral Golf Club,** 518 Lisburn Rd., Belfast (© **028/9038-1514;** www.balmoralgolf.com), with greens fees of £27 ($54) weekdays (except Wed), £40 ($80) weekends and Wednesdays. About 6km (3¾ miles) southwest of the city center the **Dunmurry Golf Club,** 91 Dunmurry Lane, Dunmurry, Belfast (© **028/9061-0834;** www.dunmurrygolfclub.co.uk), costs £27 ($54) weekdays, £37 ($74) weekends. About 4.8km (3 miles) south of the city center is the **Belvoir Park Golf Club,** 73 Church Rd., Newtownbreda, Belfast (© **028/9049-1693;** www.belvoirparkgolfclub.com), £65 ($130) weekdays, £75 ($150) weekends; and 4.8km (3 miles) north, the **Fortwilliam Golf Club,** Downview Avenue, Belfast (© **028/9037-0770;** www.fortwilliam.co.uk), £22 ($44) weekdays, £29 ($58) weekends. Weekdays are usually better for visitors, and each club has preferred weekdays. Phone ahead. Club pros offer lessons, usually for about £25 ($50) per hour; book at least 2 days ahead.

HORSEBACK RIDING Saddle up at the **Drumgooland House Equestrian Centre,** 29 Dunnanew Rd., Seaforde, Downpatrick, County Down (© **028/4481-1956**). It offers half- and full-day forest treks and beach rides starting at £35 ($70). Full equestrian holidays are available.

WHERE TO STAY
Expensive
Merchant Hotel ★★ Perhaps nothing symbolizes the North's rebirth more than this place—a luxurious, elegant hotel draped in rich fabrics and equipped with the latest business technology. They don't build hotels like this unless there are customers demanding it, so the Merchant's spacious rooms, flatscreen televisions, and wireless Internet access indicate that Belfast's star is rising. In this former bank converted into a hotel with exquisite attention to detail, the Great Room restaurant is the most beautiful space in the building. Its soaring ceilings, gilded plasterwork frieze, Corinthian columns, and marble floors make a breakfast of eggs and bacon seem entirely wrong, and champagne and caviar seem so right. Guest rooms will horrify minimalists, with silk wallpaper, designer carpets in vivid colors, and king-size beds draped in the softest, thickest blankets. Well-chosen antiques round up the look, creating a warm, comfortable feeling. This place is all about service and luxury, so for a mere £70 ($140) you can be taken to or picked up at the airport in style— in the hotel's chauffeur-driven Bentley Arnage. It's new, and so still offering excellent rates online, in advance. Check its website for discounted bargains.

35–39 Waring St., Belfast, County Antrim. © **028/9023-4888.** Fax 028/9024-7775. www.themerchant hotel.com. 26 units. £220 ($440) deluxe double. Rates include breakfast. AE, DC, MC, V. Free valet parking.

Amenities: 2 restaurants (Continental, brasserie); bar; room service; concierge; laundry service. *In room:* TV, Wi-Fi, tea/coffeemaker, hair dryer.

Ten Square ★   This funky boutique hotel is Belfast's hippest place to stay. It aims to emulate the exotic luxury of Shanghai's Pudong district with small bedrooms and low-slung beds, white linens and dark headboards, and cream coir carpet. Armoires, shutters, and double doors are all inlaid with white opal glass. The overall feel is one of elegant minimalism. The hotel's **Grill Room & Bar** serves modern Irish cuisine in a lavishly designed contemporary setting.

10 Donegall Sq., Belfast, County Antrim. © **028/9024-1001.** Fax 028/9024-3210. www.ten-sq.com. 23 units. £160–£240 ($320–$480) double. Rates include breakfast. AE, MC, V. Street parking only. **Amenities:** 2 restaurants (fusion, deli); 2 bars; concierge. *In room:* TV, broadband, minibar, tea/coffeemaker, hair dryer, garment press.

Moderate

Culloden Hotel ★   Not in the city itself, this elegant hotel is 8km (5 miles) east on the shore of Belfast Lough, in County Down. Sprawling across acres of secluded gardens and woodlands, the manor house was originally built as a palace for the bishops of Down. Later, it was sold and remained a private home until it was converted into a hotel in 1963. It has grand style, with fine antiques, plasterwork and paintings, Louis XV chandeliers, an unexpectedly modern spa, and exceptional service.

142 Bangor Rd., Holywood, County Down. © **028/9042-1066.** Fax 028/9042-6777. www.hastingshotels. com. 79 units. £110–£120 ($220–$240) double. Full breakfast £18 ($36). AE, DC, MC, V. Free valet parking. **Amenities:** Restaurant (Continental); bar; indoor swimming pool; tennis court; gym; spa; beauty treatments; Jacuzzi; steam room; bicycle rental; room service; babysitting; concierge; laundry service. *In room:* TV, hair dryer, garment press.

Europa Hotel ★   Once the IRA's favorite hotel target in Belfast, the Europa is the city's best hotel. Former U.S. President Bill Clinton stays here when he's in town, and for good reason—the lobby is warm and welcoming, with Irish art on the walls and a fire crackling in the hearth. Hotel workers are as friendly as Belfastians get. An ongoing renovation has left the hotel modern but not soulless. The guest rooms are spacious and filled with mahogany furnishings, rich fabrics, and marble bathrooms. The downsides are the restaurant and bar, which lack the style displayed effortlessly in the rest of the hotel. But there are excellent restaurants on the Golden Mile (as the street out front is known), and one of the city's best historic pubs, the Crown Liquor Saloon, is just across the street.

Great Victoria St., Belfast, County Antrim. © **028/9027-1066.** Fax 028/9032-7800. www.hastingshotels. com. 240 units. £115–£170 ($230–$340) double. Luxury suites available. Continental breakfast £15 ($30); full breakfast £18 ($36). AE, DC, MC, V. Free valet parking. **Amenities:** 2 restaurants (Continental, brasserie); bar; access to nearby health club; room service; babysitting; concierge; laundry service. *In room:* TV, tea/coffeemaker, hair dryer.

Malmaison Belfast ★★   This hotel—part of the sophisticated British Malmaison chain—is cool, sleek, and modern. It's so decked out in eggplant-and-black hues that one

---

Ⓣ **Tips**   **Price Swings**

A reminder: Prices change frequently at hotels, and your rate is likely to be slightly different than those listed here.

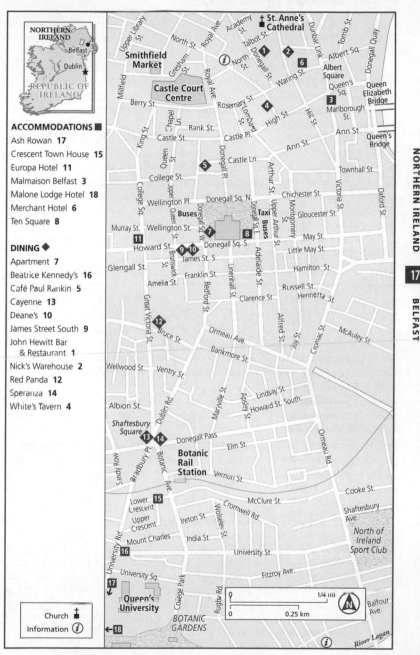

NORTHERN
IRELAND
Belfast
Dublin
REPUBLIC OF
IRELAND

St. Anne's
Cathedral

Smithfield
Market

Castle Court
Centre

ACCOMMODATIONS ■

Ash Rowan **17**
Crescent Town House **15**
Europa Hotel **11**
Malmaison Belfast **3**
Malone Lodge Hotel **18**
Merchant Hotel **6**
Ten Square **8**

DINING ◆

Apartment **7**
Beatrice Kennedy's **16**
Café Paul Rankin **5**
Cayenne **13**
Deane's **10**
James Street South **9**
John Hewitt Bar
  & Restaurant **1**
Nick's Warehouse **2**
Red Panda **12**
Speranza **14**
White's Tavern **4**

Church ✝
Information ⓘ

NORTHERN IRELAND

17

BELFAST

Tips **Your Own Private Hideaway**

Hoping to stay somewhere off the beaten path? The **Irish Landmark Trust** (in the Republic © **01/670-4733;** www.irishlandmark.com), our favorite source of unique rental accommodations on the Emerald Isle, has just the ticket. The charming **Ballealy Cottage** sits just 8km (5 miles) from Belfast International Airport in Ballealy, in County Antrim. It was built as the lodge for the castle's gamekeeper and is tucked deep in the Randalstown Forest on the magnificent Shanes Castle Estate. The house has an endearingly irregular architectural style in high Victorian folly tradition, with octagonal chimney pots, hipped rooflines, mullioned transom windows, and countless gables. Inside, there is a hodgepodge of half-landings, shuttered windows, mahogany antiques, and enough books and interesting *objets* to keep even the most curious guest engaged for weeks. The house sleeps five to seven people in three bedrooms with lovely old brass beds. It is surrounded by the forest and its wildlife (deer regularly visit the cottage yards). The dining room features a Stanley range that heats the entire house (there's also a modern electric oven range in the kitchen, along with a washing machine). But the best room in the house is the enormous bathroom where a giant claw-foot tub takes center stage. Rates change month to month, but average around £350 ($700) per week.

British newspaper described it as looking like "Dracula's living room." Created from two classically ornate Italianate warehouses (which were designed by William Hastings in the mid-1850s), it manages to offer a kind of cozy sophistication. Rooms are not huge, but will be home sweet home to those who think modern is the way to go. The color scheme includes neutral walls with black touches and blood-red crushed-velvet covers on the firm orthopedic beds. All the latest gadgetry awaits your moments of idleness, including plasma TVs, DVDs, and free Internet service. The bar and brasserie are (surprise, surprise) sleek and modern in design, with an emphasis on black (it makes everybody look thinner, you know).

34–38 Victoria St., Belfast, County Antrim. © **800/525-4800** in the U.S., or 028/9022-0200. Fax 028/9022-0220. www.malmaison-belfast.com. 59 units. £100–£140 ($200–$280) double. AE, DC, MC, V. **Amenities:** Brasserie (modern Irish); bar; health club; 24-hr. room service; nonsmoking rooms; foreign-currency exchange. *In room:* TV w/DVD, CD player, Wi-Fi, minibar, tea/coffeemaker, hair dryer, garment press.

Inexpensive

Ash Rowan ★★   On a quiet, tree-lined street in a residential neighborhood, this four-story Victorian house near Queen's University was once the home of Thomas Andrews, a designer of the *Titanic* who went down with the ship. Owner Evelyn Hazlett has outfitted it with country-style furnishings, family heirlooms, and antiques, along with bouquets of fresh flowers from the garden. Beds are exceptionally firm and dressed in fine Irish linens. The mood here is relaxed, with morning papers and late breakfasts. The rates include a choice of nine breakfasts, including the Ulster Fry (scrambled eggs, smoked salmon, kippers), or vegetarian options, such as flambéed mushrooms. The location is a short stroll into the city center.

12 Windsor Ave. (btw. Lisburn and Malone roads), Belfast, County Antrim. ℭ **028/9066-1758.** Fax 028/9066-3227. 5 units. £90–£100 ($180–$200) double. Rates include full breakfast. MC, V. Free parking. *In room:* TV.

Crescent Town House   As the name implies, this stylish hotel fills a huge converted Victorian town house just south of the city center. Using deep purple as an accent color, the rooms have a modern decor, with chrome and leather touches alongside blonde wood and neutral fabrics. Basic doubles are more simply equipped, but deluxe doubles have plasma-screen TVs, modem points, and other extras. The brasserie serves modern Irish cuisine, while **Bar Twelve** has a laid-back, publike atmosphere, and attracts locals as well as guests.

13 Lower Crescent, Belfast, County Antrim. ℭ **028/9032-3349.** Fax 028/9032-0646. www.crescenttown house.com. 17 units. £95–£110 ($190–$220) double. Rates include full breakfast. AE, MC, V. **Amenities:** Restaurant (modern Irish); bar. *In room:* TV, hair dryer.

Malone Lodge Hotel   Tucked away in the leafy university neighborhood south of the city center, the Malone Lodge has plenty of fans drawn by its unfussy but efficient style. Rooms are large and decor varies—most are relatively tame, with cream wallpaper and traditional wood furniture. Generally, the rooms have everything you need—televisions, power showers, Wi-Fi—and there's a handy restaurant and bar as well. The staff is reliably friendly and helpful.

60 Eglantine Ave., Belfast, County Antrim. ℭ **028/9038-8000.** Fax 028/9038-8088. www.malonelodgehotel. com. 50 units. £90–£125 ($180–$250) double. Rates include breakfast. AE, MC, V. Free parking. **Amenities:** Restaurant (international); bar. *In room:* Satellite TV, Wi-Fi, tea/coffeemaker, hair dryer, trouser press.

The Old Inn ★★★   When the author C. S. Lewis wrote about this historic coaching inn of North County Down, about 10 minutes' drive from central Belfast, it was already very old. Records date it from 1614, and those hoping for a historic place to stay should look no further. Its **Parlour Bar and Lounge** are still topped by thatched roofs, and its crackling fire has warmed the toes of former president George H. W. Bush. You can stay in one of the large, beautifully decorated rooms, many with polished wood floors and some with excellent antiques, or isolate yourself in the private cottage, which comes with its own fireplace. The food in its restaurant, **1614,** has won plaudits, and there's cheaper fare in the relaxing bistro and Parlour Bar.

Main St., Crawfordsburn, County Down. ℭ **028/9185-3255.** Fax 028/9185-2775. www.theoldinn.com. 32 units. £100–£125 ($200–$250) double; £225 ($450) for the cottage. Rates include full Irish breakfast. AE, MC, V. **Amenities:** 2 restaurants (modern Irish, bistro); bar. *In room:* TV, hair dryer.

WHERE TO DINE

Belfast is not famed for its cuisine, but over the last 5 years, the restaurant scene has changed considerably—expanding from a longtime reliance on traditional meat-and-potatoes meals to more international cuisine, and even a Michelin-starred chef (Michael Deane). There's no particular restaurant quarter, although there are plenty of eateries on the Golden Mile, and the **Odyssey Complex** holds a dozen or so eating places, many of which are geared to families with kids.

The Odyssey Complex (ℭ **028/9046-7700;** www.theodyssey.co.uk) is a 5-minute walk across the weir from the Lagan Lookout in Belfast. It's open Monday to Saturday 10am to 6pm, and Sunday noon to 6pm.

Alden's ★★ MODERN IRISH   Alden's is one of the most consistently good restaurants in Belfast. The cooking is full of punch and yet thoughtfully restrained, while the atmosphere is low-key elegance. Start with something suitably complex to put you in the right frame of mind—perhaps the steamed mussels with white wine and garlic to start, then the roast breast of chicken with Parma ham and mushrooms. Desserts are wonderful, the wine list intelligent, the staff eager to please.

229 Upper Newtownards Rd., Belfast. ✆ **028/9065-0079**. www.aldensrestaurant.com. Reservations recommended. Main courses £12–£16 ($24–$32). AE, DC, MC, V. Mon–Fri noon–2:30pm; Mon–Thurs 6–10pm; Fri–Sat 6–11pm.

Beatrice Kennedy's ★★ TRADITIONAL IRISH   This is a sweet place in the University Quarter, with bare wood floors and neatly folded white linens. The menu is rich with traditional dishes, including roasted lamb and tasty stews, all served with home-baked bread by the friendly staff.

44 University Rd., Belfast. ✆ **028/9020-2290**. www.beatricekennedy.co.uk. Main courses £14–£18 ($28–$36). MC, V. Tues–Sat 5–10:30pm; Sun 12:30–2:30pm and 5–8:30pm.

Cayenne ★★ MODERN IRISH   Owned by the people behind Alden's, Cayenne's chef-owner Paul Rankin is known for pairing the best local produce with exotic ingredients. The wide-ranging menu offers everything from crispy aromatic pork belly (with squid and arugula) to the braised shoulder and roast pepper haunch of Finnebrogue venison. Save room for the warm chocolate tart.

7 Lesley House, Shaftesbury Sq., Belfast. ✆ **028/9033-1532**. www.rankingroup.co.uk. Reservations required. Main courses £11–£18 ($22–$36). AE, DC, MC, V. Mon–Fri noon–2:15pm; Mon–Thurs 6–10pm; Fri–Sat 6–11pm; Sun 5–8:45pm.

Deane's ★★★ FUSION   The titular Michelin star–winning chef Michael Deane presides over the stove at this sleek modern restaurant for dinner from Wednesday to Sunday, and the once very formal dining space has been taken down a notch so that it focuses on food rather than the knot in your (no-longer-required) tie. Deane's cooking is modern and sublime, a hip pairing of Asian ingredients with classic French methods. For a starter, try the red mullet in crisp couscous. For a main course, you could have the Irish venison with baked potato purée.

38–40 Howard Place, Belfast. ✆ **028/9033-1134**. Reservations required. www.michaeldeane.co.uk. Main courses £14–£20 ($28–$40). AE, DC, MC, V. Mon–Sat noon–3pm and 5:30–11pm.

James Street South ★★★ MODERN IRISH   With its chic, minimalist interior, decorated with modern artwork and narrow mirrors on cream walls and brightened by the floor-to-ceiling arched windows overlooking James Street South, this is one of the city's hot restaurants. The terrific cooking delivers modern classics with an Irish twist. Try the saddle of lamb with crispy lamb cutlet in red-wine *jus*, after you savor the butternut squash–and–prawn soup with crème fraîche, or maybe the oysters on ice with chili-and-vodka dressing. Don't pass on a side order of champ—mashed potatoes with spring onions and lots of butter. Portions are generous, the wine list excellent.

21 James St. S., Belfast. ✆ **028/9043-4310**. www.jamesstreetsouth.co.uk. Reservations required. Main courses £12–£20 ($24–$40). AE, MC, V. Mon–Fri noon–2:45pm; Mon–Sat 5:45–10:45pm.

Apartment ★ INTERNATIONAL   This is one for the trendy crowd. Calling itself Belfast's "only style bar," this hot spot is filled with all the brushed chrome and brown leather your stylish heart desires. It's more bar than restaurant by night, but by day it's the reverse. The menu is an affordable list of rib-eye steak with peppercorn-and-thyme sauce, penne with zucchini (called *courgette* on this side of the Atlantic), and confit of duck with sweet-potato cakes. The food is good, but wear your Manolos.

2 Donegall Sq. W., Belfast. ℂ **028/9050-9777.** www.apartmentbelfast.com. Main courses £7–£9 ($14–$18). MC, V. Mon–Sat noon–9pm; Sun noon–6pm.

Nick's Warehouse ★★ MODERN IRISH   In an old warehouse between St. Anne's Cathedral and the tourist office, this extremely popular place offers a world-spanning menu of rib-sticking, soulful, hearty food. Nick Price gets his influence from everywhere—you might see Scandinavian dishes on the menu alongside Mediterranean ones—but he is clearheaded enough to be true to each individual dish. There's a relaxed wine bar downstairs and a classy dining room upstairs, with brick walls and an open kitchen. Appetizers include smoked salmon with potatoes and creamed horseradish. Main courses include sirloin steaks, lamb chops with honey-and-ginger sauce, and dill-and-black-pepper-marinated salmon.

35 Hill St., Belfast. ℂ **028/9043-9690.** www.nickswarehouse.co.uk. Reservations recommended. Main courses £7–£19 ($14–$38). AE, DC, MC, V. Mon–Fri noon–2:30pm; Mon–Sat 6–9:30pm (drinks until midnight).

Speranza ITALIAN   This huge Italian restaurant on the Golden Mile is a bit of a Belfast institution. It's been around for decades, although its modern look is relatively new. It's known for traditional pizzas and pasta. They don't take reservations and, although the two-story dining area holds 200 people noisily, there's usually a wait, so be prepared. Avoid the peak time of 7:30 to 9pm.

16–19 Shaftesbury Sq., Belfast. ℂ **028/9023-0213.** Main courses £8–£10 ($16–$20). MC, V. Mon–Sat 5–11:30pm; Sun 3–10pm.

Inexpensive

Café Paul Rankin ★★ CAFE   This casual cafe makes a great place to stop for lunch or just coffee and a snack in the afternoon. As the name alerts you, it's owned by Chef Paul Rankin of Cayenne fame (see above), Northern Ireland's first celebrity chef. Food served includes fresh focaccia bread sandwiches, soups, pasta, salads, and cakes, and there's plenty of room to relax. There's a second cafe in the Castlecourt shopping center in central Belfast.

27–29 Fountain St., Belfast. ℂ **028/9031-5090.** Main courses £2–£5 ($4–$10). MC, V. Mon–Wed and Fri–Sat 7:30am–6pm; Thurs 7:30am–9pm.

John Hewitt Bar & Restaurant ★ MODERN IRISH   This centrally located bar is always buzzing, as its well-dressed, young crowd finds time to hang out, day and night. It's a good place for lunch, as the menu leans toward upscale Irish traditional pub food with dishes like the wild mushroom–and–sweet corn fritters, and the grilled salmon and cod cakes, served with mashed potatoes. It also has some of the best Guinness in town. Happily, as it aims to be true to the socialist principles of its namesake Irish politico, prices are extremely reasonable.

51 Donegall St., Belfast. ℭ **028/9023-3768.** www.thejohnhewitt.com. Main courses £5–£8 ($10–$16). MC, V. Mon–Sat noon–3pm; Fri noon–6pm (drinks until midnight).

Red Panda CHINESE   This small chain of upscale Chinese restaurants is relentlessly popular, and this restaurant, on the Golden Mile, may be the busiest of all. The attraction is the authentic food in bright, pleasant surroundings. The menu has all the usual favorites, and it's a great break from the hearty local fare.

60 Great Victoria St., Belfast. ℭ **028/9080-8700.** Main courses £6–£8 ($12–$16). MC, V. Mon–Sat noon–3pm and 6–10pm.

White's Tavern ★ TRADITIONAL IRISH   This may well be Belfast's favorite place to have lunch. One of the city's many historic pubs, White's is tucked away on a lane between Rosemary and High streets. It's hard to find, but worth ferreting out as it's got all the low beams and wood floors you might hope for. The food is warming, traditional dishes like Irish stew, sausage and mashed potatoes, and fish and chips.

2–12 Wine Cellar Entry, Belfast. ℭ **028/9024-3080.** Main courses £5–£8 ($10–$16). No credit cards. Mon–Sat noon–6pm (drinks until midnight).

BELFAST AFTER DARK
Pubs & Clubs

Belfast has a plethora of historic pubs where the crowds tend to be local and friendly, but the big news here in recent years has been its fast-growing new generation of hip modern bars geared at the young and trendy. The late-night places are mostly clustered in the University Quarter, while the pubs are spread around town. If you're drawn to traditional pubs, several of the best are hidden away in the pedestrian lanes off Donegall Place.

Pub hours are Monday to Saturday from 11:30am to 11pm and Sunday from 12:30 to 2:30pm and from 7 to 10pm. Bars stay open later, and nightclubs tend not to get busy until after the pubs close; admission ranges from £3 to £10 ($6–$20).

Apartment   If you feel like a good cocktail in sophisticated surrounds with a 20- to 30-something crowd of Belfast's beautiful people, then this is the place. It has dubbed itself Belfast's "only style bar," and its smooth, sophisticated style clearly appeals to Belfast's best DJs, as they are regularly at the turntables. Upscale, city-center style is the name of the game here. 2 Donegall Sq., Belfast. ℭ **028/9050-9777.** www.apartmentbelfast.com.

Bar Bacca/La Lea   Essentially two bars in one, this has been Belfast's most stylish nightclub for several years now. It's a sensory experience, with classic architecture, soaring ceilings, and an Eastern bent—a huge Buddha head hangs above the dance floor, incense burns, and bodies dance the night away. The private bar evokes a decadent Bedouin tent. There's a strict door policy—you'll have a better chance of getting in if you're dressed to kill. 43 Franklin St., Belfast. ℭ **028/9023-0200.** www.lalea.com or www.barbacca.com.

Crown Liquor Saloon (Finds)   Dating from 1826, this is the jewel in Northern Ireland's crown of pubs. Opposite the Europa Hotel and the Grand Opera House, this gas-lit old alehouse has what many architecture buffs believe to be the finest example of Victorian Gothic decor in the country. Owned by the National Trust and run by Bass Ireland, it has it all: stained-glass windows, pounded tin ceiling, elaborate tile floor, etched and smoked glass dividing the wooden cubicle seating, a beveled mirror with floral and wildlife decorations, scalloped lamps, and a long bar with inlaid colored glass and marble trim. Don't even get us started on the gorgeous mosaic exterior. The 10 dark-wood private rooms are guarded by mythological beasts with shields. There are gunmetal plates for striking matches, little windows to peep discreetly through, and an antique system of bells that once summoned service. Great Victoria St., Belfast. ℭ 028/9027-9901. www.crownbar.com.

Empire Music Hall   This is a grand place—a converted Victorian church that has become legendary on the Irish music and bar scenes. It has three floors of bars and music, with different styles represented on different nights—jazz on Tuesday, Irish traditional on Wednesday, blues Thursday, and rock Friday and Saturday nights. 42 Botanic Ave., Belfast. ℭ 028/9024-9276. www.thebelfastempire.com.

Irene & Nan's   The young and trendy crowd into this elaborately decorated bar every night. Its name is a homage to two glamorous retirees who hung out in a nearby pub. Taking their style to heart, this place drowns in designer chic, with a slight 1950s retro theme. The mezzanine floor is the most sumptuous, but the music is excellent on all levels. If you're hungry, the in-house bistro is not bad at all. 12 Brunswick St., Belfast. ℭ 028/9023-9123. www.ireneandnans.com.

John Hewitt Bar & Restaurant   This centrally located joint—named after a local socialist hero—is an exquisitely rare thing: a modern bar with no televisions and no gaming machines. During the day and early in the evening, the low rumble of conversation is the loudest thing you'll hear here. In the evening, there's often music, including folk several nights a week and jazz on Fridays. The food is good here, too. This one is for the grown-ups. 51 Donegall St., Belfast. ℭ 028/9023-3768. www.thejohnhewitt.com.

Limelight & Katy Daly's   This is where pub and club morph into one venue. Rock bands regularly perform in its music club space, while the stripped-down pub is one of the best places in Belfast to hang out, take in the music, and down a few pints. The crowd is youngish, and the mood is usually friendly and untrendy. 17–19 Ormeau Ave., Belfast. ℭ 028/9032-5942. www.thelimelightbelfast.com.

Mezza(nine) at Robinson's   This trendy, modern bar next door to the Crown Liquor Saloon attracts Belfast's young and beautiful, with two floors of bars, pounding live music, and top local and national DJs spinning tunes late into the night. 38–42 Great Victoria St., Belfast. ℭ 028/9024-7447.

Milk Bar Club   In the city's Cathedral Quarter, this is one of Belfast's hottest clubs, with music 7 nights a week and a devoted 20-something clientele. Inside, you'll find a riot of color, energy, and noise—everything from house and disco to R&B. 10–14 Tomb St., Belfast. ℭ 028/9027-8876. www.clubmilk.com.

Morning Star   This beautifully restored old pub tucked away in Pottinger's Entry arcade is a nice, traditional pub. It dates from 1810, and may be even older. It was once the final stop of the Dublin-to-Belfast stagecoach; its horseshoe-shaped bar may be a result of that history. It still has its original facade and the wooden snugs in which weary stagecoach travelers once rested. Along with evening drinking, it's a good place for lunch as well. 17–19 Pottinger's Entry, Belfast. ℭ 028/9023-5986. www.themorningstarbar.com.

Pat's Bar   For a taste of Belfast's harbor atmosphere, join the sailors, dockers, and businesspeople at this pub at the gates of Prince's Dock. Cross its red-tile floor to the antique hand-carved beech bar, and then relax in its pinewood surroundings. There's an interesting collection of memorabilia—much of it given to the bar's owner by sailors—clogs, swords, a telescope, and a bayonet. There's traditional Irish music on Friday and Saturday night at 9pm. 19 Prince's Dock St., Belfast. ℭ 028/9074 4524.

Rotterdam This small, traditional place in the Cathedral Quarter eschews modern annoyances—you'll find no TVs above the bar here. Instead, there are roaring fires and good pub food, as well as excellent pints of Guinness. This is one of the better music pubs in town, so expect jazz on Tuesdays, blues on Wednesdays, acoustic on Thursdays, and a mix of good sounds on the weekend. 54 Pilot St., Belfast. ✆ **028/9074-6021.** www.rotterdambar.com.

White's Tavern Tucked into a historic cobblestone trading lane in the city center, this old tavern was established in 1630 as a wine shop. It's full of old barrels and hoists, ornate snugs, brick arches, large copper measures, framed newspaper clippings of 200-year-old vintage, quill pens, and other memorabilia. It's a good pub for conversation and browsing, and it features traditional music as well as quiz nights, darts, and theme nights. 2–4 Winecellar Entry (btw. High and Rosemary sts.), Belfast. ✆ **028/9033-0988.**

The Performing Arts

For up-to-date listings of shows and concerts, there are several sources. *That's Entertainment* is free and widely available at tourist offices and pubs, as are the *Big List* and *Artslink*. There's always the *Belfast Daily Telegraph* and the *Irish News*. You could also try www.gotobelfast.com and www.belfast.net.

With its distinctive bronze dome, the **Waterfront Hall** dominates the Lagan skyline (Oxford St., Laganside; ✆ **028/9033-4455** for credit card reservations, or 9033-4400 for program information; www.waterfront.co.uk). The state-of-the-art conference center and concert venue attracts international performers. On the Golden Mile near the Europa Hotel, the **Grand Opera House** (Great Victoria St.; ✆ **028/9024-1919;** www.goh.co.uk) first opened its doors in 1895. A central part of Belfast's cultural scene, it offers the finest opera, drama, and musicals in town. The **Ulster Hall** (Bedford St.; ✆ **028/9032-3900;** www.ulsterhall.co.uk) hosts touring music groups, comedy, and drama, and is home to the Ulster Orchestra. The **Odyssey** (2 Queen's Quay; ✆ **028/9073-9074;** www.odysseyarena.com) is the latest addition to the city's crowded performing arts roster. The massive complex on the waterfront has a 10,000-seat arena where touring rock groups from Oasis to Destiny's Child have performed. The complex also holds dozens of restaurants and bars, so there's plenty to keep you busy before the show.

Theaters include the **Lyric Theatre** (Ridgeway St.; ✆ **028/9038-1081;** www.lyrictheatre.co.uk) for new plays by Irish and international playwrights; and the **Group Theatre,** part of Ulster Hall on Bedford Street (✆ **028/9032-9685**), for performances by local drama societies.

For stand-up comedy, head for the basement of the **Empire Music Hall,** 42 Botanic (✆ **028/9032-8110**). It's home every Tuesday at 9pm to *The Empire Laughs Back*. If you'd rather sit down than stand up, get there at least an hour early.

Tickets, which cost £8 to £30 ($16–$60) for most events, can be purchased in advance from www.ticketmaster.ie. (You can always arrange to have tickets purchased online delivered to your hotel.)

The Gay & Lesbian Scene

The gay and lesbian scene in Belfast is very low-key and always has been. The handful of gay pubs and bars are generally friendly places, though; once you've been around a bit and people recognize you, you'll find a welcome. The scene is getting more cosmopolitan all the time.

Widely viewed as the heart of the scene is **Kremlin** (Donegall St.; ✆ **1232/809-700;** www.kremlin-belfast.com), a clever, Soviet-themed bar open 7 nights a week but best known for its Saturday-night party, "Revolution." The gay scene goes public each year in late July or early August for Belfast's small but enthusiastic Pride celebration (**www. belfastpride.com**). For general information about GLBT life in Belfast check out the **Gay Belfast** website (**www.gaybelfast.net**), or search for Northern Ireland on the **Gay Ireland** website (**www.gay-ireland.com**).

3 SIDE TRIPS FROM BELFAST

CARRICKFERGUS

19km (12 miles) NE of Belfast

Just outside Belfast off the M3 motorway, the castle town of Carrickfergus offers a nice break from the hustle and bustle of the city, and some fresh sea air. Locals like to say that Carrickfergus was thriving when Belfast was a sandbank, and looking around its winding medieval streets at the edge of the sea, it's easy to believe. In 1180 John de Courcy, a Norman, built a massive keep at Carrickfergus, the first real Irish castle, to guard the approach to the strategically critical Belfast Lough. Even today, although the town spreads for several miles in each direction along the shore, the huge, forbidding castle is still its center. The narrow streets across from the castle follow the historic winding pattern of medieval roads, and you can still find some of the old city walls.

Stop into the **Carrickfergus Tourist Information Office,** Heritage Plaza, Antrim Street, Carrickfergus, County Antrim (© **028/9336-6455**). It's open all year Monday to Friday 9am to 5pm.

Andrew Jackson Centre   This one-story cottage with earthen floor and open fireplace was the ancestral home of Andrew Jackson, seventh president of the United States. His parents emigrated to the United States in 1765. The house now contains a display on Jackson's life and career and Ulster's connections with America.

Boneybefore, Carrickfergus, County Antrim. © **028/9336-6455**. Free admission. June–Sept Mon–Fri 10am–1pm, daily 2–6pm; reduced hours in Apr–May and Oct.

Carrickfergus Castle ★ **(Kids)**   This impressive Norman castle looms darkly over the entrance to Belfast Lough, where William of Orange landed on June 14, 1690, en route to the Battle of the Boyne. The central keep inside dates to the 12th century, the thick outer walls were completed 100 years later, and the gun ports are a relatively new addition, only 400 years old. The castle has withstood sieges by Edward the Bruce in 1315 and King John in 1210, though it was temporarily captured by the French in 1760. The outside is more impressive than the inside, which has been largely dedicated to inspiring the imagination of children. The use of waxwork figures inside (riding horses, threatening to shoot people over the walls) is a bit over-the-top, and it's a shame that, in the interest of safety, the keep's upper windows are glassed in, making it impossible to photograph the lovely view (or even to see it properly). Much of the remains of the castle walls were closed to the public on our visit, so we couldn't take in the view from there. Still, kids will love it, although those without little ones may want to take a photo and drive on. In the summer, medieval banquets, a medieval fair, and a crafts market are held, adding a touch of play and pageantry.

Marine Hwy., Antrim St., Carrickfergus, County Antrim. © **028/9335-1273**. Admission £4 ($8) adults, £3 ($6) seniors and children, £11 ($22) families. Apr–Sept Mon–Sat 10am–6pm, Sun noon–6pm; Oct–Mar Mon–Sat 10am–1pm, Sun 2–4pm.

11km (6¾ miles) E of Belfast

Ulster Folk & Transport Museum ★ (Kids) This 70-hectare (173-acre) site brings together many parts of Ulster's past in a sprawling outdoor folk museum. The museum includes a collection of 19th-century buildings saved from the bulldozer's path and moved here intact from their original sites. You walk among farmhouses, mills, and churches; and explore rural schools, a forge, a bank, a print shop, and more. Actors in period dress reenact tasks of daily life—cooking over an open hearth, plowing the fields with horses, thatching roofs, and practicing traditional Ulster crafts such as textile making, spinning, quilting, lace making, printing, spade making, and shoemaking. The transport museum's collection ranges from donkey carts to De Loreans, and there is a permanent exhibition on the *Titanic*.

153 Bangor Rd. (11km/6¾ miles northeast of Belfast on the A2), Cultra, Holywood, County Down. ℂ 028/9042-8428, or 9042-1444 for 24-hr. information. www.uftm.org.uk. Day ticket to both museums £7 ($14) adults; £4 ($8) seniors, students, and children; £19 ($38) families. Mar–June Mon–Fri 10am–5pm, Sat 10am–6pm, Sun 11am–6pm; July–Sept Mon–Sat 10am–6pm, Sun 11am–6pm; Oct–Feb Mon–Fri 10am–4pm, Sat 10am–5pm, Sun 11am–5pm.

THE ARDS PENINSULA

The Ards Peninsula, beginning about 16km (10 miles) east of Belfast, curls around the western shore of **Strangford Lough** ★. This is a place of great natural beauty, as well as a bird sanctuary and wildlife reserve. Two roads traverse the peninsula: A20 (the Lough road) and A2 (the coast road). The Lough road is the more scenic.

At the southern tip of the Lough, car ferry service connects Portaferry with the Strangford Ferry Terminal (ℂ 028/4488-1637), in Strangford, on the mainland side. It runs every half-hour, weekdays 7:30am to 10:30pm, Saturday 8am to 11pm, Sunday 9:30am to 10:30pm. No reservations are needed. A one-way trip takes 5 minutes and costs £5 ($10) for a car and driver, £1 ($2) for each additional passenger.

The **Portaferry Tourist Information Office,** The Stables, Castle Street (ℂ 028/4272-9882; www.ards-council.gov.uk), is open Monday to Saturday 10am to 5:30pm, Sunday 1 to 6pm. There are two National Trust properties in this area, one on the Ards Peninsula and the other just across the lough at Portaferry. For information about where to stay, eat, and play on the peninsula, visit the region's website at **www.armaghanddown.com**.

Castle Espie ★ (Kids) This marvelous wildlife center, owned and managed by the Wildlife and Wetlands Trust, is home to a virtual UN of rare migratory geese, ducks, and swans. Some are so accustomed to visitors that they will eat grain from their hands, so children can have the disarming experience of meeting Hooper swans eye to eye. Guided trails are designed for children and families, and the center sponsors activities and events year-round. A favorite of bird-watchers in search of waterfowl, the center has thousands of pale-bellied brents in early winter. The book and gift shop is enticing, and the restaurant serves good lunches and home-baked cakes.

78 Ballydrain Rd., Comber, County Down. ℂ 028/9187-4146. Admission £5.50 ($11) adults, £4 ($8) seniors and students, £2.85 ($5.70) children. Mar–Sept Mon–Fri 10:30am–5:30pm, Sat–Sun 11am–5:30pm; Oct–Feb Mon–Fri 11am–4pm, Sat–Sun 11am–4:30pm. 21km (13 miles) southeast of Belfast, signposted from the A22 Comber-Killyleagh-Downpatrick rd.

Castle Ward (Kids) About 2km (1¼ miles) west of Strangford village is this grand manor house dating from 1760. A hybrid of architectural styles melding Gothic with classical, it sits on a 280-hectare (692-acre) country estate of formal gardens, woodlands, lake lands, and seashore. Inside, kids can dress up in period clothes and play with period toys, or they can ride a tractor-trailer out to see the farm animals. There's a theater in the stable yard that hosts operatic performances in summer. *Note:* If you don't mind skipping the inside of the house, you can visit the grounds for about half the house ticket price.

Strangford, County Down. (C) **028/4488-1204.** www.nationaltrust.org.uk. Admission to house, gardens, and grounds £6 ($12) adults, £3 ($6) children. House Sept–June Sat–Sun 1–6pm; July–Aug daily 1–6pm.

Exploris (**Kids**) This cheery, kid-friendly aquarium concentrates on sea life native to Strangford Lough and the Irish Sea. Inside, the mixture of displays ranges from the educational-but-arguably-dull (models of the Strangford Lough ecosystem) to the more lively (giant aquariums filled with local and regional sea life) to the downright fun (the seal sanctuary). Along with its splashy occupants, the aquarium complex contains a cafe where you can rest and a gift shop where you can buy fish-related key rings, as well as a park, picnic area, children's playground, bowling green, tennis courts, and woodlands.

Castle St., Portaferry, County Down. (C) **028/4272-8062.** www.exploris.org.uk. Admission £7 ($14) adults, £4 ($8) children. Apr–Aug Mon–Fri 10am–6pm, Sat 11am–6pm, Sun 1–6pm; Sept–Mar Mon–Fri 10am–5pm, Sat 11am–5pm, Sun 1–5pm.

Giant's Ring (**Finds**) This massive, mysterious, prehistoric earthwork, 180m (590 ft.) in diameter, has at its center a megalithic chamber with a single capstone. Ancient burial rings like this one were long thought to be protected by fairies, and thus were left untouched, but this one was quite an exception—in the 19th century, it was used as a racetrack, with the high embankment around it serving as grandstands. Today, its dignity has been restored and it is a place of wonder for the few who visit; sadly, it is largely neglected by tourists.

Ballynahatty, County Down. 6km (3¾ miles) southwest of Belfast center, west off A24; or 1.6km (1 mile) south of Shaw's Bridge, off B23. Free admission.

Grey Abbey The impressive ruins of Grey Abbey sit amid a beautifully landscaped setting, perfect for a picnic. Founded in 1193 by the Cistercians, it contained one of the earliest Gothic churches in Ireland. This is a particularly plain Cistercian ruin (some of their abbeys were quite elaborate). Amid the ruined choirs, there is a fragmented stone effigy of a knight in armor, possibly a likeness of John de Courcy, husband of the abbey's founder, Affrica of Cumbria. There's also a small visitor center.

Greyabbey, County Down. No phone. Admission £1 ($2) adults, 50p ($1) children. Apr–Sept Tues–Sat 10am–7pm; Sun 2–7pm. On the east side of Greyabbey, 3.2km (2 miles) southeast of Mt. Stewart.

Legananny Dolmen This renowned, impressive granite dolmen (Neolithic tomb) on the southern slope of Slieve Croob looks, in the words of archaeologist Peter Harbison, like "a coffin on stilts." This must be one of the most photographed dolmens in Ireland, and you must see it up close to fully appreciate its size. The massive capstone seems weightlessly poised on its supporting uprights.

Slieve Croob, County Down. Take A24 from Belfast to Ballynahinch, B7 to Dromara, and then ask directions.

Mount Stewart House Once the home of Lord Castlereagh, this 18th-century house sits on the eastern shore of Strangford Lough. Its lush gardens hold an impressive array of rare and unusual plants. Inside, the art collection is excellent, including the *Hambletonian* by George Stubbs and family portraits by Batoni, Mengs, and Lazlo. The Temple of the Winds, a rare 18th-century banqueting house, is also on the estate, but is only open on public holidays.

On the east shore of Strangford Lough, southeast of Newtownards, 24km (15 miles) southeast of Belfast, on A20, Newtownards, County Down. ℭ **028/4278-8387**. www.nationaltrust.org.uk. House and garden admission £6 ($12) adults, £3 ($6) children. House Mar–Apr and Oct (except Easter Week) Sat–Sun noon–6pm; Easter Week daily noon–6pm; May Wed–Mon 1–6pm; June–Aug daily 1–6pm; Sept Wed–Mon noon–6pm. Bus: 9, 9A, or 10 from Laganside Bus Centre (Mon–Sat).

Nendrum Monastic Site   Hidden away on an isolated island, this site dates from the 5th century, when it was founded by St. Mochaoi (St. Mahee). This site is much older than Grey Abbey across the water, and the remains of the ancient community are fascinating. Foundations show the outline of ancient churches, a round tower, and beehive cells. There are concentric stone ramparts and a sundial, reconstructed from long-broken pieces. Its visitor center shows informative videos and has informative exhibits. The road to Mahee Island crosses a causeway to Reagh Island and a bridge still protected by the 15th-century Mahee Castle.

Signposted from Lisbane, on the A20 south of Comber, County Down. ℭ **028/9754-2547**. Free admission. Site 24 hr. Visitor center Apr–Sept Tues–Sat 10am–7pm, Sun 2–7pm; Oct–Mar Sat 10am–4pm, Sun 2–4pm.

Portaferry Castle   This is little more than a small, 16th-century tower house, but, together with another tower house in Strangford, it once controlled the ship traffic through the Narrows. It's a piece of history right beside the visitor center, so it's worth popping your head in for a peek.

Castle St., Portaferry, County Down. Free admission. Easter–Sept Mon–Sat 10am–5pm; Sun 2–6pm.

Sports & Outdoor Pursuits

BICYCLING   If you want to explore the area on two wheels, you can rent bicycles for roughly £10 to £15 ($20–$30) a day. Cycle rental by the day or week, and delivery in the North Down/Ards area, are available from **Mike the Bike,** 53 Frances St., Newtownards (ℭ **028/9181-1311**). He also rents kayaks, if you feel like a splash. If you want some guidance and companionship, contact Tony Boyd at **Iron Donkey,** 15 Ballyknocken Rd., Saintfield (ℭ **028/9081-3200;** www.emeraldtrail.com).

DIVING   The nearby loughs and offshore waters are a diver's dream—remarkably clear and littered with wrecks. To charter a diving expedition in Strangford Lough, contact **Des Rogers** (ℭ **028/4272-8297**). **Norsemaid Charters,** 152 Portaferry Rd., Newtownards, County Down (ℭ **028/9181-2081;** www.salutay.com), caters 4- to 10-day diving parties along the Northern Irish coast, in Belfast Lough and Strangford Lough, amid the St. Kilda Isles, and along the coast of Scotland. One of Europe's finest training centers, **DV Diving,** 138 Mountstewart Rd., Newtownards, County Down (ℭ **028/9146-4671;** www.dvdiving.co.uk), offers diving courses.

FISHING   For info, tackle, and bait, try the **Village Tackle Shop,** 55a Newtownbreda Rd., Belfast (ℭ **028/9049-1916**), or **H. W. Kelly,** 54 Market St., Downpatrick, County Down (ℭ **028/4461-2193**). Sea-fishing trips from Portaferry into the waters of Strangford Lough and along the County Down coast are organized by Peter and Iris Wright at **Norsemaid Sea Enterprises,** 152 Portaferry Rd., Newtownards, County Down (ℭ **028/9181-2081**). Reservations are required. To outfit yourself and fish for rainbow trout year-round, visit **Ballygrangee Trout Fishery,** Mountstewart Road, Carrowdore, County Down (ℭ **028/4278-8883**).

GOLF   There are several well-established courses a short drive from Belfast in north County Down. They include the **Bangor Golf Club,** Broadway, Bangor (ℭ **028/9127-0922;**

www.bangorgolfclubni.co.uk), with greens fees of £27 ($54) weekdays, £33 ($66) weekends; **Downpatrick Golf Club,** 43 Saul Rd., Downpatrick (© **028/4461-5947;** www.downpatrickgolfclub.org.uk), with greens fees of £19 ($38) weekdays, £24 ($48) weekends; and the 71-par **Scrabo Golf Club,** 233 Scrabo Rd., Newtownards (© **028/9181-2355;** www.scrabo-golf-club.org), with greens fees of £30 ($60) weekdays, £25 ($50) weekends.

Where to Stay in the Area
Moderate
Portaferry Hotel ★ Set in a designated conservation area and incorporating a terrace dating from the mid–18th century, the Portaferry Hotel retains the charm of a seasoned waterside inn while providing all the amenities of a modern hotel. A recent renovation brought in more sleek, neutral color schemes, along with higher prices that are somewhat hard to justify. Many rooms have excellent views of the lough, though, and if you can get a deal by booking online, it's a pleasant place to stay.

The Strand, Portaferry (47km/29 miles from Belfast), County Down. © **028/4272-8231.** Fax 028/4272-8999. www.portaferryhotel.com. 14 units. £130 ($260) double. Rates include full breakfast. AE, DC, MC, V. **Amenities:** Restaurant (seafood); bar; nonsmoking rooms. *In room:* TV, radio, hair dryer.

Inexpensive
Ballycastle House ★ Mrs. Margaret Deering's home is a beautiful 300-year-old farmhouse that has been elegantly refurbished. The guest rooms are nicely appointed with pretty floral bedspreads and dark woods, and offer restful rural views. A two-bedroom self-catering cottage is also available for £320 ($640) per week.

20 Mountstewart Rd. (8km/5 miles southeast of town on A20), Newtownards, County Down. ©/fax **028/4278-8357.** 3 units. £55 ($110) double. Children's and senior discounts available. Rates include full breakfast. No credit cards. **Amenities:** Laundry facilities; nonsmoking rooms; sitting room. *In room:* Tea/coffeemaker, hair dryer.

Edenvale House Just down the road from Mount Stewart House, with distant views of Strangford Lough and the Mourne Mountains, this welcoming Georgian country house is run by Gordon and Diane Whyte. Request one of the two front guest rooms, since they are the most spacious—with either a four-poster or king-size bed, good-size bathrooms, large dressing rooms, and far-reaching views across the lough. The other guest room is smaller but extremely attractive, with garden views and a shower-only bathroom. Breakfasts are excellent, and the entire house is nonsmoking.

130 Portaferry Rd., Newtownards, County Down (3.2km/2 miles from Newtownards on A20). © **028/9181-1881.** Fax 028/9181-6192. www.edenvalehouse.com. 3 units, 1 with shower only. £85 ($170) double. Rates include full breakfast. MC, V. Closed Christmas. **Amenities:** Drawing room; gardens. *In room:* TV, tea/coffeemaker, hair dryer.

Killyleagh Castle Towers ★★ This is for those people who always wanted to spend more time in a castle. These three gatehouse towers in the small, picturesque town of Killyleagh rent by the week. The fanciful stone towers have spiral staircases and roof terraces. The two smaller towers sleep four; the larger tower sleeps five. Rooms range from small and snug to barely more spacious.

High St., Killyleagh, County Down. © **028/4482-8261.** 3 units. £250–£450 ($500–$900) per week. MC, V.

Old School House Inn ★ This handy guesthouse just south of Castle Espie near Nendrum is a personable establishment with rooms that border on luxurious, a friendly staff, and good restaurants. Relax in your well-appointed room before heading downstairs to sample fresh oysters from the inn's oyster farm.

Ballydrain Rd., Comber (on the road to Nendrum), County Down. ⓒ **028/9754-1182.** www.theold schoolhouseinn.com. 12 units. £75 ($150) double. Rates include full breakfast. MC, V. **Amenities:** Restaurant (seafood). *In room:* TV, hair dryer.

Where to Dine in the Area

Cornstore SEAFOOD   This is a friendly place, handily located near the Portaferry visitor center, and one of the best places in the area for sampling the local seafood. Try raw oysters, grilled prawns, or fried cod in relaxed environs.

2 Castle St., Portaferry, County Down. ⓒ **028/4272-9779.** Main courses £5–£7 ($10–$14). MC, V. Wed–Thurs and Sun noon–7pm; Fri–Sat noon–8:30pm.

The Narrows ★★ ⓕ**Finds** MEDITERRANEAN   If you'd travel anywhere to discover a good restaurant, then set your compass for the sleepy waterside hamlet of Portaferry. Here, Andrew Gargan peppers his menu with Mediterranean touches and uses the best local seafood. The food is excellent and the mood is relaxed. After dinner here, it's heavenly to amble upstairs to one of the chic, white-on-beige guest rooms, priced at £140 ($280) for a double.

8 Shore Rd., Portaferry, County Down. ⓒ **028/4272-8148.** Dinner main courses £10–£17 ($20–$34). AE, MC, V. Mon–Fri noon–3pm; daily 5–11pm.

Primrose Bar and Restaurant PUB GRUB   The Primrose—an erstwhile blacksmith shop—is known locally for its steak casseroles, open-faced prawn sandwiches, and fresh-baked bread. Other offerings include chicken dishes, pizza, and a variety of salads. There's a nice fire blazing, and, as the locals say, the *craic* is good (there's a good time to be had). The adjacent Primrose Tea Room serves good quiches and pies Monday to Saturday 9am to 4:30pm.

30 Main St., Ballynahinch, County Down. ⓒ **028/9756-3177.** Dinner main courses £6–£12 ($12–$24). AE, MC, V. Bar daily noon–11pm. Restaurant Fri–Sun noon–2:30pm and 5–9pm.

DOWNPATRICK

37km (23 miles) SE of Belfast

The charming town of Downpatrick is closely identified with St. Patrick. Legend has it that when Patrick came to Ireland in A.D. 432 to begin his missionary work, strong winds blew his boat here. He'd meant to sail up the coast to County Antrim, where as a young slave he had tended flocks on Slemish Mountain. Instead, he settled here and converted the local chieftain Dichu and his followers to Christianity. Over the next 30 years, Patrick roamed through Ireland carrying out his work, but this is where he died, and some believe he is buried in the graveyard of Downpatrick Cathedral, although there's no proof. Because of all of this, the town tends to be crowded, largely with Catholic pilgrims, around St. Patrick's Day, but the constant activities and religious fervor are worth witnessing.

For information in the Down District, stop into the **St. Patrick Visitor Centre,** 53A Market St., Downpatrick, County Down (ⓒ **028/4461-2233**). It's open October to March Monday to Saturday 10am to 5pm; April to September, hours are Monday to Saturday 9:30am to 6pm and Sunday 1 to 6pm. A "St. Patrick's Country" bus tour is offered according to demand and can be booked through this office.

Down Cathedral Excavations show that Downpatrick was a *dún* (or fort), perhaps as early as the Bronze Age, and its earliest structures were built on the site where this church now sits. Ancient fortifications ultimately gave way to a series of churches, each built atop the ruins of the previous incarnation, over 1,800 years. The current cathedral is an 18th- and 19th-century reconstruction of its 13th- and 16th-century predecessors. Just south of the cathedral stands a relatively recent monolith inscribed with the name *Patric*. By some accounts, it roughly marks the grave of the saint, who is said to have died at Saul, 3km (2 miles) northeast. The tradition identifying this site as Patrick's grave seems to go back no further than the 12th century, though, when John de Courcy reputedly transferred the bones of saints Brigit and Columba here to lie beside those of St. Patrick.

The Mall, Downpatrick, County Down. ☎ **028/4461-4922.** Mon–Sat 9:30am–5pm; Sat–Sun 2–5pm.

St. Patrick Heritage Centre/Down County Museum (Kids) Next to the cathedral and sharing an extensive 18th-century jail complex, the St. Patrick Centre and the County Museum provide some intriguing glimpses into the rich history of this area. You'll also be introduced to some of the county's more notorious figures, from St. Patrick to a handful of prisoners sent off to Australia in the 19th century.

The Mall, Downpatrick, County Down. ☎ **028/4461-5218.** Free admission, except for some special events. June–Aug Mon–Fri 10am–5pm, Sat–Sun 1–5pm; Sept–May Tues–Fri 10am–5pm, Sat 1–5pm.

LISBURN
16km (10 miles) SE of Belfast

There's a nice museum in this small town a short distance from Belfast.

Irish Linen Centre and Lisburn Museum Using multimedia presentations to recreate historic factory scenes, this museum traces the history of Irish linen. Given the rather stodgy subject matter, it's surprisingly interesting. There are opportunities to see linen in all stages of production, and to watch skilled weavers at work on restored 19th-century looms in the workshop. If you're a big fan of linen and want to give over a whole day to it, you can book a place on an **Irish Linen Tour** (£10/$20 per person) by calling the Banbridge Gateway Tourist Information Centre (☎ **028/4062-3322**).

Market Sq., Lisburn, County Antrim. ☎ **028/9266-3377.** Free admission. Mon–Sat 9am–5pm.

LOUGH NEAGH
16km (10 miles) W of Belfast

Lough Neagh, at 396 sq. km (153 sq. miles), is the largest lake in the British Isles. Ancient Irish lore maintains the lake was created by the mighty giant Fionn MacCumhail (Finn McCool) when he flung a chunk of earth into the sea to create the Isle of Man. But before you think about taking a dip, consider this: The lake's claim to fame is its eels. Yep, the waters are positively infested with the slimy creatures. Hundreds of tons of eels are taken from Lough Neagh and exported each year, mainly to Germany and Holland. The ages-old eel-extraction method involves "long lines," baited with up to 100 hooks. As many as 200 boats trailing these lines are on the lake each night (the best time to go fishing for eels).

If you're not entirely creeped out by that, you can take a **boat trip** on the lovely lake. Boats depart regularly from the nearby **Kinnego Marina** (☎ **0374/811248** mobile), signposted from the main road. They last about 45 minutes and cost about £10 ($20) for adults, £7 ($14) for children.

Lough Neagh Discovery Centre ★ Midway between Belfast and Armagh city, this center on the southern shore of the lake at Oxford Island is a sprawling nature reserve with lush reed beds, verdant woodlands, and gorgeous wildflower meadows. The center has historical and geographic exhibits, walking trails, bird-watching observation points, and bucolic picnic areas. For a closer look at everything in sight, the center has binoculars for hire.

Oxford Island, Craigavon, County Armagh. © **028/3832-2205.** Free admission. Apr–Sept daily 10am–6pm; Oct–Mar Wed–Sun 10am–5pm.

ARMAGH
65km (40 miles) SW of Belfast

County Armagh is a green rolling stretch of gentle hills and small villages. It is also one of Northern Ireland's most rebellious Republican regions—there are police watchtowers atop some hills, occasional barracks (mostly empty these days), and until a couple of years ago, you could expect to hear the rhythmic thumping of military helicopters flying over. Peace or no peace, the sectarian graffiti is omnipresent, but that said, it's not directed at visitors, and these days there's no reason to avoid this scenic, forested county.

Small and manageable **Armagh City** is a handsome cathedral city. Its name, from the Irish *ard Macha* (Macha's height) refers to the pagan queen Macha who is said to have built a fortress here. It's no coincidence that St. Patrick chose to base himself here when he was spreading Christianity—it was a bold challenge to the native paganism. The simple stone church that he built in the 5th century is now the giant Church of Ireland cathedral—clearly, his plan worked, at least to some extent. There are actually two St. Patrick cathedrals in Armagh City—one Catholic and one Protestant—and each is the seat of its primate.

The town has the kind of dignity you might expect in a seat of religion, with grand public buildings, huge churches, and big Georgian town houses along the Mall. Buildings, doorsteps, and sidewalks are made of delightful pink, yellow, and red local limestone that make the city glow even on a dull day.

Stop into the **Armagh Tourist Information Centre,** the Old Bank Building, 40 English St., Armagh (© **028/3752-1800**). It's open all year, Monday to Saturday 9am to 5pm and Sunday 2 to 5pm.

A short distance outside the city, the small town of Bessbrook has historic cottages, the forests of Slieve Gullion, and ancient Navan Fort, the most important archaeological site in Ulster.

Armagh Astronomy Centre and Planetarium (Kids) On your way up College Hill from the Mall, you'll pass the 200-year-old Armagh Observatory, still in service but closed to the public. Farther up the hill stands the Astronomy Centre and Planetarium complex, whose Astropark (a scale model of the universe kids can walk through), and Digital Theatre offer an array of exhibits and shows, with hands-on learning opportunities for kids. After a renovation in 2006, though, prices doubled, and it's hard to say it's worth the money.

College Hill, Armagh, County Armagh. © **028/3752-3689.** www.armaghplanet.com. Admission to show and exhibition area £6 ($12) adults, £5 ($10) seniors and children. June–Aug daily 11:30am–5pm; Sept–May Mon–Fri 1–5pm, Sat 11:30am–5pm.

Armagh County Museum The Armagh museum is in a building that looks like a diminutive Greek temple. Its collection documents local life across the millennia, and ranges from prehistoric ax heads to wedding dresses to a grim cast-iron skull that once rested atop the Armagh gallows. In addition to natural history specimens and folklore items, the museum also has an art collection, with works by George Russell and John Luke, as well as maps, photographs, and a research library.

The Mall East, Armagh. ✆ **028/3752-3070.** Free admission. Mon–Fri 10am–5pm; Sat 10am–1pm and 2–5pm.

Armagh Public Library   Founded in 1771 by Archbishop Richard Robinson, the library has an inscription in Greek above its door that translates as "the Medicine Shop for the Soul." As small-town libraries go, this one is exceptional, as it contains Robinson's collection of 17th- and 18th-century books, engravings, and maps, as well as a 1726 first edition of *Gulliver's Travels* annotated by Swift himself. It was stolen in a robbery in 1999, but recovered 2 years later and returned to its rightful home.

43 Abbey St., Armagh. ✆ **028/3752-3142.** Free admission. Mon–Fri 10am–1pm and 2–4pm.

Benburb Valley Park, Castle, and Heritage Centre ★   The sweet village of Benburb sits on the dramatic banks of the River Blackwater, a favorite for canoeists and anglers. The park at the edge of town follows the river to a tree-lined gorge where a partially restored 17th-century castle high on a cliff keeps an eye on the scene. From there, a half-mile walk brings you to the Benburb Valley Heritage Centre, a restored linen mill, and the Benburb Castle, all within the grounds of a Servite monastery. It's a historical smorgasbord.

89 Milltown Rd., Benburb, County Armagh. ✆ **028/3754-8170.** Park free admission. Castle and heritage center admission £2.70 ($5.40). Park daily until dusk. Castle and Heritage Center Apr–Sept Mon–Sat 10am–5pm. 11km (6³⁄₄ miles) northwest of Armagh; take B128 off A29.

The Mall   Just to the east of the town center, this park has an interesting history. It was used for such low activities as horse racing and cock fighting until the 18th century, when an archbishop converted it into a lush park surrounded by Georgian buildings. The courthouse at its northern end was destroyed by an IRA bomb in 1993, but then rebuilt. It dates from 1809, and was designed by a local architect, Francis Johnston, who went on to create much of Dublin's famous Georgian architecture. Opposite the courthouse, the gloomy Armagh Gaol (jail), was built in 1780 and remained in use until 1988.

The Mall, east of the town center, Armagh.

Navan Fort ★   Believed to have been the royal and religious capital of Ulster from 1150 B.C. until the spread of Christianity, the Navan Fort is a mysterious place. Its central circular earthwork enclosure holds a smaller circular structure, and it all encloses an Iron Age burial mound. Even today, scientists do not really know what it was used for, although they know that it was all set on fire around 95 B.C., possibly as part of a ritual. Unfortunately, the extremely useful interpretive center at the site is frequently closed due to lack of funding. However, if you happen to catch it open, it's an excellent resource with exhibits and multimedia presentations to explain the history and prehistory of the site. A book, gift shop, and cafe are also on hand.

The Navan Centre, 81 Killylea Rd., Armagh. ✆ **028/3752-5550.** Fax 028/3752-2323. Admission £5 ($10) adults, £3 ($6) children. Mon–Sat 10am–5pm; Sun noon–5pm. 3.2km (2 miles) from Armagh on A28, signposted from Armagh center.

Peatlands Park   As the name implies, Peatlands Park is a park filled with peat. It's a big park—more than 240 hectares (593 acres)—and the peat bogs and small lakes are

524 quite lovely. The whole thing is a nature reserve, so you wander through it on a well-designed system of walking paths, or, slightly more fun on rainy days, you ride through it on a narrow-gauge railway. Nature walks and events are offered through the year.

33 Derryhubbert Rd. (11km/6¾ miles southeast of Dungannon, at exit 13 off M1), The Birches, County Armagh. © 028/3885-1102. Free admission to park. Rail ride £1 ($2). Vehicle access to park daily 9am-dusk. Railway Easter–Aug daily 1–6pm.

St. Patrick's Church of Ireland Cathedral ★

Built on the site of St. Patrick's 5th-century church, the Anglican cathedral dates back to the 13th century, although much of the structure was built in the 1830s. Inside the church are the remains of an 11th-century Celtic cross, and a strange granite carved figure known as the Tandragee Idol, which dates from the Iron Age. A stone slab on the exterior wall of the north transept marks the spot where Brian Boru, the high king of Ireland who died in the last great battle with the Vikings in 1014, is buried.

Cathedral Close, Armagh. © 028/3752-3142. Free admission (donations accepted). Apr–Oct daily 10am–5pm; Nov–Mar daily 10am–4pm. Guided tours June–Aug Mon–Sat 11:30am and 2:30pm.

St. Patrick's Roman Catholic Cathedral ★

Built at the same time as the current structure of the Anglican church—in the mid-1800s—the cathedral is a grand Gothic Revival building dominating its portion of the town. It stands on a hill and is reached via stone stairs. Outside it's gray and hulking, but inside is another story, as vividly painted mosaics bathe it in color. Unfortunately, a renovation in the 1980s added some modern touches that stand out starkly against its otherwise perfect 19th-century authenticity.

Cathedral Rd., Armagh. © 028/3752-2802. Free admission (donations accepted). Daily 8am–dusk.

St. Patrick's Trian Visitor Complex ★

In the old Second Presbyterian Church in the heart of Armagh, this modern visitor complex provides an informative and engaging introduction to Armagh, the "motherhouse" of Irish Christianity. Its dramatic presentations, including the *Armagh Story* and *The Land of Lilliput* (complete with a giant Gulliver beset by Lilliputians), are entertaining for the whole family. This is a good first stop to get your bearings in local history and culture. There are a craft courtyard and a cafe, as well as a visitor genealogical service, if you have local roots.

40 English St. (off Friary Rd., a 10-min. walk from town), Armagh. © 028/3752-1801. www.saintpatrickstrian.com. Admission £4 ($8) adults, £2.25 ($4.50) children. Mon–Sat 10am–5pm; Sun 2–5pm. Closed Jan 1 and Dec 25–26.

4 THE CAUSEWAY COAST & THE GLENS OF ANTRIM

106km (66 miles) from Larne to Portstewart on the coastal A2; Larne: 40km (25 miles) from Belfast

The most extraordinary stretch of countryside in Northern Ireland, the evocatively named Glens of Antrim are really nine green valleys stretching north and west from Belfast, and curving around toward Donegal. The names of the glens are all based on local legends, and although the meanings are largely lost to the ages, the popular translations are: Glenarm (glen of the army), Glencloy (glen of the hedges), Glenariff (ploughman's glen), Glenballyeamon (Edwardstown glen), Glenaan (glen of the rush lights), Glencorp (glen of the slaughter), Glendun (brown glen), Glenshesk (sedgy glen), and Glentaisie (Taisie's glen).

Many modern residents of this region are descendants of the ancient Irish and the Hebridean Scots, so this is one of the strongholds in Northern Ireland of the Gaelic tongue. To this day, the glen people are known to be great storytellers.

The area's attractions are formidable, and include the awe-inspiring **Giant's Causeway**, the picturesque **Carrick-A-Rede Rope Bridge,** and **Old Bushmills Distillery.** For bird-watchers, the coastal moors and cliffs and the offshore nature reserve on **Rathlin Island** are prime destinations. Each August, the seaside town of **Ballycastle** plays host to one of Ireland's oldest traditional gatherings, the Oul' Lammas Fair.

VISITOR INFORMATION The principal **tourist information centers** in North Antrim are at Narrow Gauge Road, **Larne** (✆ **028/2826-0088**); Sheskburn House, 7 Mary St., **Ballycastle** (✆ **028/2076-2024**); 44 Causeway Rd., **Giant's Causeway Information Centre** (✆ **028/2073-1855**); and Dunluce Centre, Sandhill Drive, **Portrush** (✆ **028/7082-3333**). All but the Dunluce Centre are open year-round; hours vary seasonally. Summer hours, at the minimum, are Monday to Friday 9:30am to 5pm, Saturday 10am to 4pm, and Sunday 2 to 6pm.

EXPLORING THE COAST

The Antrim Coast is 97km (60 miles) long, stretching north of **Larne** and west past Bushmills and the Giant's Causeway to **Portrush.** If you start in gorgeous **Glenarm,** with its castle walls and barbican gate, and head north along the coast from there, the route takes in sweeping views of midnight-blue sea against gray unforgiving cliffs and deep green hillsides. As you arc around the northern headlands, the road passes through the National Trust village of **Cushendun** ★, with its tea shops and perfect Cornish-style cottages, and a string of bustling beach towns at the foot of rocky cliffs (**Portstewart, Portballintrae, Portrush, Ballycastle).** Along the way the coastal drive meanders under bridges and stone arches, passing crescent bays, sandy beaches, harbors, and huge rock formations. The ocean gleams beside you as you curve along its craggy shoreline, and the light creates intense colors. In the spring and autumn, you can often have the road all to yourself. In **Carnlough,** a quiet village with a glassy harbor, you can climb the white stone bridge and walk along a path for about a mile to the Cranny Falls waterfall. Later, for spectacular views, turn off the main coastal road at Cushendun onto the **Torr Head Scenic Road** (it's signposted), although note that this narrow, rugged, cliff-side road is not for those with fears of heights. It climbs in seemingly perilous fashion to the tops of hills that are bigger than you might think, and on a clear day, you can see all the way to the Mull of Kintyre in Scotland. Arguably the best views are to be had at **Murlough Bay** (follow the signs off the scenic road). In the late spring and summer, you can take a ferry from **Ballycastle** to **Rathlin Island,** where seals and nesting birds make their homes at the **Kebble National Reserve.** Near Ballycastle, the town of **Ballintoy** is a picture postcard waiting to happen, stretched out at the edge of **White Park Bay,** with its wide, sandy beach at the foot of rocky hills. Finally, you can take in the eerily lunar **Giant's Causeway**—a true natural wonder.

SEEING THE SIGHTS

Carrick-A-Rede Rope Bridge ★★★ (Moments) Eight kilometers (5 miles) west of
Ballycastle off the A2 road, this open rope bridge spans a chasm 18m (59 ft.) wide and 24m (79 ft.) above the sea between the mainland and a small island. Local fishermen put up the bridge each spring to allow access to the island's salmon fishery, but visitors can use it for a thrilling walk and the chance to call out to each other, "Don't look down!"

(By the way, that is excellent advice.) If you are acrophobic, stay clear; if you don't know whether you are, this is not the place to find out. *Note:* The 19km (12-mile) coastal cliff path from the Giant's Causeway to the rope bridge is always open and is worth the exhaustion.

Larrybane, County Antrim. ✆ **028/2073-1582.** Free admission. Bridge, center, and tearoom Apr–June and early Sept daily 10am–6pm; July–Aug 10am–8pm. Parking £5 ($10).

Dunluce Castle ★   Between the Giant's Causeway and the bustling seaside town of Portrush, the coastline is dominated by the hulking skeletal outline of what must have been a glorious castle. This site was the main fort of the Irish MacDonnells, chiefs of Antrim. From the 14th to the 17th century, it was the largest and most sophisticated castle in the North, with a series of fortifications built on rocky outcrops extending into the sea. This was the power base of the north coast for 400 years. In 1639, part of the castle fell into the sea, taking some of the servants with it; soon after, it was allowed to fall into ruin. The site incorporates two of the original Norman towers dating from 1305. The visitor center shows an audiovisual presentation with background on the site.

87 Dunluce Rd. (5.6km/3¹/₂ miles east of Portrush off A2), Bushmills, County Antrim. ✆ **028/2073-1938.** www.northantrim.com/dunlucecastle.htm. Admission £2.80 ($5.60). Apr–May and Sept Mon–Sat 10am–6pm, Sun 2–6pm; June–Aug Mon–Sat 10am–6pm, Sun noon–6pm; Oct–Mar Mon–Sat 10am–4pm, Sun 2–4pm. Last admission 30 min. before closing.

Dunluce Centre ★ (Kids)   Rainy days do happen, and when they do, this is where you take the kids. This family-oriented entertainment complex will keep them busy all day with a multimedia show, *Myths & Legends,* illustrating the folklore of the Antrim coast; "Turbo Tours," a thrill ride simulating space; and "Earthquest," an interactive display on the wonders of nature. There are also a viewing tower with panoramic views of the coast, a Victorian-style arcade of shops, and a restaurant with a children's play area.

Dunluce Rd., Bushmills, Country Antrim. ✆ **028/7082-3333.** Admission £5 ($10).

Giant's Causeway ★★★   A World Heritage Site, this natural rock formation is extraordinary. Sitting at the foot of steep cliffs, and stretching out into the sea, it is a natural formation of thousands of tightly packed basalt columns. The tops of the columns form flat steppingstones the size of dinner plates, but the strangest thing about them is that they are almost perfectly hexagonal. They are all about 12 inches in diameter, and some are as tall as 12m (39 ft.). Scientists believe they were formed 60 or 70 million years ago by volcanic eruptions and cooling lava. The ancients, on the other hand, believed the rock formation to be the work of giants. To reach the causeway, you walk from the parking area down a steep path for nearly 1.6km (1 mile), past amphitheaters of stone columns and formations with fanciful names like Honeycomb, Wishing Well, Giant's Granny, King and his Nobles, and Lover's Leap. If you wish, you can then climb up a wooden staircase to Benbane Head to take in the views, and then walk back along the cliff top. There is a regular shuttle service down from the helpful visitor center for those who can't face such a long hike. *Note:* The causeway itself is never closed—even after the visitor center shuts down, you can still walk down the path on your own. Also, they make a lot of money through parking in the causeway parking lot, but you can park for free on the street.

Causeway Rd., Bushmills, County Antrim. ✆ **028/2073-1582.** www.giantscausewayofficialguide.com. Free admission (parking £5/$10). Visitor center daily 10am–5pm.

Moments **Going to the Birds: A Trip to Rathlin Island**

Want to get close to nature? Plan a trip to **Rathlin Island** ★, 9.7km (6 miles) off the coast north of Ballycastle. The tiny island is 6km (3³/₄ miles) long, and less than 1.5km (1 mile) wide and almost completely treeless, with a rugged coast of 60m-high (197-ft.) cliffs, a small beach, and crowds of seals and seabirds in spring and summer. Once you get there you'll realize that it's not quite as isolated as it seems—it has a resident population of 100, and there are even a pub, a restaurant, and several guesthouses, should you miss the last boat to shore. This is a favorite bird-watching spot, especially in spring and early to midsummer when the birds are nesting, and given that there's little else to do here except to take in the scenery, it's no surprise that the island's biggest draw is bird-watching at the **Kebble National Nature Reserve** on the western side of the island, and the **RSPB West Lighthouse Viewpoint** (✆ **028/2076-3948;** free admission, by arrangement Apr–Aug), where you can spot guillemots, kittiwakes, razorbills, and colorful puffins.

Boat trips operate daily from Ballycastle pier; crossing time is 50 minutes. The round-trip fare is £9 ($18) for adults; £4.50 ($9) for seniors, students, and children (those 4 and under travel free). The number and schedule of crossings vary from season to season and from year to year, and are always subject to weather, but there are usually several crossings a day. It's best to book well in advance by phoning the **Caledonian MacBrayne** ticket office (✆ **028/2076-9299;** www.calmac.co.uk).

On the island, a minibus (summer only) will take you from Church Bay to the West Light Platform and the Kebble Nature Reserve for roughly £3.50 ($7) adults, £3 ($6) children, round-trip. Bicycles can be rented from **Soerneog View Hostel** (✆ **028/2076-3954**) for £10 ($20) per day.

For more information, call ✆ **028/2076-3948.**

Old Bushmills Distillery ★★ Licensed to distill spirits in 1608, but with historical references dating from as far back as 1276, this ancient distillery is endlessly popular. Visitors can tour the working sections and watch the whiskey-making process, starting with fresh water from the adjacent River Bush and continuing through distilling, fermenting, and bottling. At the end of the tour, you can sample the wares in the Potstill Bar, where you can learn more about the history of the distillery. Tours last about 25 minutes. The Bushmills coffee shop serves tea, coffee, homemade snacks, and lunches.

Main St., Bushmills, County Antrim. ✆ **028/2073-1521.** www.bushmills.com. Admission £6 ($12) adults, £5 ($10) seniors and students, £3 ($6) children 8–17, £17 ($34) families; children 7 and under not allowed on tours. Apr–Oct tours offered frequently throughout the day Mon–Sat 9:30am–5:30pm, Sun noon–5:30pm (last tour leaves 4pm); Nov–Mar tours offered Mon–Sat at 10:30am, 11:30am, 1:30, 2:30, and 3:30pm, Sun at 1:30, 2:30, and 3:30pm. Closed Good Friday, July 12, Christmas, and New Year's Day.

NORTHERN IRELAND

17

THE CAUSEWAY COAST & THE GLENS OF ANTRIM

The Steensons   This is the workshop-showroom of Bill and Christina Steenson, two of the most celebrated goldsmiths in Ireland. On display and for sale is a small, impressive selection of their pieces, as well as a sampling of the work of other distinguished Irish goldsmiths and silversmiths with a similar contemporary eye. Toberwine St., Glenarm, County Antrim. © 028/2884-1445. www.thesteensons.com.

SPORTS & OUTDOOR PURSUITS

ADVENTURE SPORTS   The **Ardclinis Activity Centre,** High Street, Cushendall, County Antrim (© **028/2177-1340;** www.ardclinis.com), offers a range of year-round outdoor programs and courses. They include everything from rock climbing and mountain biking to windsurfing and rafting. Half-day, full-day, and weeklong activities for ages 8 and older are provided, as well as 5- and 6-night scenic walking and cycling tours. It's best to book at least several weeks ahead. The center will arrange local B&B or hostel accommodations.

FISHING   The best time to fish in the North Antrim Glens is July to October, both for salmon and for sea trout. The rivers of choice are the Margy, Glenshesk, Carey, and Dun. The **Marine Hotel** (see below) in Ballycastle offers an array of services to the game angler. For locally arranged game fishing, contact **Gillaroo Angles,** 7 Cooleen Park, Jordanstown, Newtownabbey, County Antrim (© **028/9086-2419**). For info, tackle, and bait, try **Red Bay Boats,** Coast Road, Cushendall (© **028/2177-1331**).

GOLF   North Antrim boasts several notable courses, including champion pro golfer Darren Clarke's home course, the **Royal Portrush Golf Club,** Dunluce Road, Portrush (© **028/7082-2311;** www.royalportrushgolfclub.com). Royal Portrush has three links courses, including the celebrated Dunluce Course, ranked number three in the United Kingdom. Greens fees are £95 ($190) weekdays and £110 ($220) weekends. Just over the border in County Londonderry is the **Portstewart Golf Club,** 117 Strand Rd., Portstewart (© **028/7083-2015;** www.portstewartgc.co.uk). Of its three links courses, the par-72 Strand Course is the celebrated one here. Some days and times are more accessible than others for visitors, so it's advisable to call ahead for times and fees, which range from £10 to £90 ($20–$180) for 18 holes, depending on the course you choose and the day of the week.

PONY TREKKING   **Watertop Farm Family Activity Centre,** 188 Cushendall Rd., Ballycastle (© **028/2076-2576**), offers pony trekking and other outdoor activities, daily in July and August and weekends in late June and early September. In the Portrush area, contact **Maddybenny Riding Centre** (© **028/7082-3394;** www.maddybenny.com), also offering accommodations, which won the "Farmhouse of the Year" award for Ireland in 1999. B&B accommodations run around £65 ($130) for a double. Also, in Castlerock, there's **Hillfarm Riding and Trekking Centre** (© **028/7084-8629**). Fees are typically around £15 ($30) per hour-long trek.

WALKING   The **Ulster Way,** 904km (560 miles) of marked trail, follows the North Antrim Coast from Glenarm to Portstewart. The **Moyle Way** offers a spectacular detour from Ballycastle south to Glenariff. Maps and accommodations listings for both ways are in the free NITB booklet *The Ulster Way: Accommodation for Walkers.* Or pick up a copy of *Walking the Ulster Way,* by Alan Warner (Appletree Press, 1989). The NITB also offers *An Information Guide to Walking,* full of useful information for avid pedestrians.

Last but far from least is the **Causeway Coast Path.** It stretches from Bushfoot Strand, near Bushmills, in the west to Ballintoy Harbour in the east. Short of sprouting wings, this is the best way to take in the full splendor of the North Antrim coast.

Expensive

Bushmills Inn ★★   In the center of the famous whiskey-making village of the same name, this inn dates from the 17th century. Some of the guest rooms are in the original coaching inn and the others are in the newer mill house. The interior of the coaching inn has old-world charm, with open turf fireplaces, gas lamps, and antique furnishings. Guest rooms here are comfortable, with country-pine furniture, floral wallpaper, and vintage prints. The mill house rooms have less character, but they are considerably more spacious and modernized.

9 Dunluce Rd., Bushmills, County Antrim. ℂ **028/2073-2339.** Fax 028/2073-2048. www.bushmills-inn. com. 32 units, 26 with private bathroom. £100–£230 ($200–$460) double. Family rooms available. Rates include full breakfast. MC, V. **Amenities:** Restaurant (Continental); bar; babysitting; baby-monitoring service; nonsmoking rooms; drawing room. *In room:* TV, dataport, hair dryer, iron, garment press.

Moderate

Londonderry Arms Hotel   At the foot of Glencloy, one of the nine Antrim glens, this ivy-covered former coaching inn dates from 1848; at one point Sir Winston Churchill owned it through a family inheritance. (He slept in room no. 114.) It has been in the hands of the O'Neill family since 1947. It sits in the heart of a delightful coastal town with views of the harbor across the street. The hotel recently expanded and a surprising degree of tasteful continuity was achieved between the original Georgian structure and the newer wing. Each room has its own character, but all are done in traditional style.

20 Harbour Rd., Carnlough, County Antrim. ℂ **800/44-PRIMA** [447-7462] in the U.S., or 028/2888-5255. Fax 028/2888-5263. www.glensofantrim.com. 35 units. £85 ($160) double. Rates include full breakfast. High tea £14 ($28); dinner £22 ($44). AE, DC, MC, V. **Amenities:** Restaurant (seafood); bar. *In room:* TV, radio, tea/coffeemaker.

Magherabuoy House Hotel   Nestled amid gardens at the edge of Portrush, this beautiful country-manor hotel offers panoramic views of the seacoast, while staying well away from the town's hubbub. The traditional decor of the public rooms—dark woods, gilded mirrors, and open fireplaces—is brought down a notch in the guest rooms, which are comfortable and homey, with frilly fabrics, brass fittings, and watercolors of seascapes on the walls.

41 Magheraboy Rd., Portrush, County Antrim. ℂ **028/7082-3507.** Fax 028/7082-4687. www. magherabuoy.co.uk. 40 units. £100 ($200) double. Rates include full breakfast. AE, DC, MC, V. **Amenities:** 2 restaurants (Continental, cafe); bar/nightclub; gym; Jacuzzi. *In room:* TV.

Marine Hotel ★ (Value)   Right on the harbor at Ballycastle, a 10-minute drive from the Giant's Causeway, this refurbished three-story, contemporary-style hotel is a favorite with Irish vacationers. The guest rooms have bright modern furnishings, king-size beds, plenty of amenities, and views of the sea. Many of its rooms are fully accessible to those with mobility issues.

1 North St., Ballycastle, County Antrim. ℂ **028/2076-2222.** Fax 028/7076-9507. www.marinehotel.net. 55 units. £60–£100 ($120–$200) double. Rates include full breakfast. AE, DC, MC, V. **Amenities:** Restaurant (Continental); bar; nightclub; indoor swimming pool; gym; spa; sauna; nonsmoking rooms. *In room:* Cable TV, broadband, tea/coffeemaker.

Whitepark House ★★   Sitting above gorgeous Whitepark Bay, this is a unique, warm, and welcoming place to stay. Owners Bob and Siobhán Isles have filled their 18th-century home with art and pictures from their travels around the world, but their hearts are clearly right here. The bedrooms are luxuriously decorated with rich fabrics and good, firm mattresses. Rooms are spacious and have sweeping views of the sea. All rooms have new bathrooms. Guests can chat in the pleasant living room by the warming fireplace, in the new, light-filled conservatory, or at the breakfast table over one of Bob's excellent Irish breakfasts. No wonder the inn has received a number of prestigious awards.

A2 coast rd. to Whitepark Bay, Ballintoy, County Antrim. ✆ **028/2073-1482.** www.whiteparkhouse.com. 3 units. £95 ($190) double. Rates include full Irish breakfast. MC, V. **Amenities:** Nonsmoking rooms; lounge w/fireplace.

Inexpensive

The Meadows ★ This modern guesthouse, a 10-minute walk from Cushendall, provides spacious, well-designed rooms in a lovely coastal setting. The views of the sea (even of Scotland off in the distance on clear days) are splendid. There's a family room, and one unit is fully adapted for travelers with disabilities. Anne Carey, your host, will gladly arrange for you to eat at the private boat club across the road.

81 Coast Rd., Cushendall, County Antrim. ✆ **028/2177-2020.** 6 units, all with shower only. £50 ($100) double. Family rates negotiable. Rates include service charge and full Irish breakfast. V. **Amenities:** Nonsmoking rooms; sitting room. *In room:* TV, tea/coffeemaker.

Sanda ★ Perched high at the mouth of Glenariff, the "Queen of the Glens," Sanda affords spectacular views. The two guest rooms are modest and immaculate. The beds are very firm, and a pleasant lounge, complete with TV and a stack of books about the area, is available to guests. Host Donnell O'Loan is quite knowledgeable and articulate about the region's ancient sites, as well as its current attractions.

29 Kilmore Rd., Glenariff, County Antrim. ✆ **028/2177-1785.** 2 units, both with shower only. £50 ($100) double. Family rates negotiable. Rates include service charge and full Irish breakfast. No credit cards. Closed Dec–Feb. **Amenities:** Nonsmoking rooms; TV lounge.

Self-Catering

Bellair Cottage ★ (Value) This century-old whitewashed farmhouse and attached barn have been converted into an inviting traditional home away from home. The three-bedroom house occupies a secluded setting high on Glenarm Glen, with a stone-walled garden. The kitchen has its original open fireplace, and the master bedroom is lovely. For an extended working holiday or summer break, Bellair is a good size for two people, giving each a private workplace. The nearby North Antrim Coast is all the inspiration any writer, painter, photographer, or gazer could ask for. You can book activities through **Rural Cottage Holidays (RCH)**—horseback riding, day boats, trekking, rock climbing, or bicycling. This cottage is very popular, so check the Cottages in Ireland website for other options—many of them more affordable and just as beautiful—in the area.

Glenarm, County Antrim. Contact RCH at ✆ **028/9024-1100.** Fax 028/9024-1198. www.cottagesin ireland.com. 1 cottage. £300–£420 ($600–$840) per week. Also available for 2- or 3-day stays. MC, V. **Amenities:** Full kitchen; fridge; microwave; oven/stove; washing machine. *In room:* TV, no phone.

Tully Cottage ★ This old farm cottage has been lovingly restored and tastefully appointed. Although it has two bedrooms and is just large enough to accommodate four people quite comfortably, it is the perfect love nest or honeymoon nook. Elevated and secluded, it affords spectacular views of Glenarm Glen and the North Channel down to the Mull of Galloway. The beds are firm, the tub is spacious, the fireplace works, and the kitchen is well equipped. Glenarm makes a good base for exploring the North Antrim

coast. Horse riding, day boats, trekking, and rock climbing can be arranged in advance;
bicycles can be waiting for you at the cottage, all through RCH.

Glenarm, County Antrim. Contact RCH at ✆ **028/9024-1100.** Fax 028/9024-1198. www.cottagesin
ireland.com. 1 cottage. £250–£350 ($500–$700) per week. Also available for 2- to 3-day stays. MC, V.
Amenities: Kitchen; fridge; microwave; oven/stove; washing machine. *In room:* TV.

WHERE TO DINE

Coast Italiano ITALIAN   This big, boisterous Italian joint offers all the usual Italian
fare, big plates of pasta, and fresh, crisp, stone-baked pizzas. It also has a selection of steak
and seafood dishes if you just aren't in the mood for Italian food and everybody else is.
Prices are very reasonable.

6 Harbour Rd., Portrush, County Antrim. ✆ **028/7082-3311.** Main courses £7–£16 ($14–$32). AE, MC, V.
Mon and Wed–Fri 12:30–2:30pm and 5–10pm; Sat 12:30–10:30pm; Sun 12:30–10pm.

The Harbour Bar SEAFOOD   The menu at this cacophonous restaurant and bar
leans heavily toward seafood, but also offers steaks and other meat dishes. It's almost
always crowded, sometimes overwhelmingly so. Still, the food is good, and the atmosphere is buzzy.

6 Harbour Rd., Portrush, County Antrim. ✆ **028/7082-2430.** Main courses £7–£16 ($14–$32). AE, MC, V.
Bar Mon–Fri 12:30–2:30pm and 5–10pm; Sat 12:30–10:30pm; Sun 12:30–10pm. Bistro Mon–Sat 12:15–
2:15pm and 5–10pm; Sun 12:30–3pm and 5–9pm.

Londonderry Arms Hotel ★ IRISH   This rambling old hotel in Carnlough sits
right on the waterfront and is beloved for its home-style Irish food. Stews, roasts, baked
chicken, and soups are all freshly made, and sold at thoroughly reasonable prices (£4–£9/
$8–$18). That's why this rustic, amiable place in the middle of nowhere gets so crowded
at lunchtime.

20 Harbour Rd., Carnlough, County Antrim. ✆ **028/2888-5255.** Main courses £7–£14 ($14–$28). MC, V.
Daily 7:30–8:30am, 11:30am–3pm, and 5–9pm.

The Ramore Restaurant and Wine Bar INTERNATIONAL   This big restaurant
is really two eateries in one—there's a big, noisy restaurant/wine bar on the lower floor,
and a more expensive fine-dining restaurant upstairs. The menu in the lower restaurant
is wide-ranging and features contemporary international food ranging from nachos to
steaks to salads. Upstairs the cuisine features local seafood, cooked with a French touch.

6 Harbour Rd., Portrush, County Antrim. ✆ **028/7082-6969.** Main courses £10–16 ($20–$32). AE, MC,
V. Restaurant Wed–Sun 5–10pm. Wine bar Mon–Fri 12:30–2:30pm and 5–10pm; Sat 12:30–10:30pm; Sun
12:30–10pm.

Smuggler's Inn Country House ★ IRISH   Surrounded by lovely gardens and across
from the entrance to the Giant's Causeway, this restaurant has wide-windowed views of the
coast, which are particularly beautiful at sunset. The menu emphasizes local ingredients and
creative sauces: baked salmon, grilled venison, and roast North Antrim duck with peach
brandy. Bed-and-breakfast is also available for £80 ($160) for a double.

306 Whitepark Rd., Giant's Causeway, County Antrim. ✆ **028/2073-1577.** Reservations required. Main
courses £8–£15 ($16–$30). MC, V. Daily noon–2:30pm and 4–9pm.

Sweeney's Wine Bar ★ PUB GRUB   This is a popular, informal spot on the coast,
with a conservatory-style extension and outdoor seating in good weather. The menu offers
good pub grub—burgers, pasta, seafood plates, steak-and-kidney pie, and stir-fry vegetables.

6b Seaport Ave., Portballintrae, County Antrim. ℭ **028/2073-2405.** Reservations recommended for dinner. Main courses £6–£14 ($12–$28). No credit cards. Mon–Sat 12:30–8pm; Sun 12:30–2:30pm and 5–8pm.

PUBS

J. McCollam   Known to locals as John Joe's or McCollam's Bar, this has been the hottest scene in Cushendall for traditional music and Antrim atmosphere for nearly a century. You have to be willing to wedge yourself in, but you're not likely to have any regrets. There's a trad session every Friday night year-round. Mill St., Cushendall, County Antrim. ℭ **028/2177-1992.**

M. McBride's   Opened in 1840, Mary McBride's was the smallest pub or bar in Europe until it expanded to include a bistro and restaurant. The old record-holding pub is still intact, so squeeze in and partake of the legend. Traditional music tends to break out in the pub's conservatory, while the Riverside Bistro serves light lunches and dinners (noon–9pm). The Waterside Restaurant, specializing in seafood, has a dinner menu (6–9pm) that features Torr Head lobster and Cushendun salmon; main courses run £6 to £17 ($12–$34). 2 Main St., Cushendun Village, County Antrim. ℭ **028/2176-1511.**

O'Malley's Ⓕ**inds**   This is a favored fisherman's haunt and a great place to have a drink and kick back without being up to your elbows in tourists. The bar is off the wood-paneled lobby of the Edgewater Hotel, facing the magnificent beach at Portstewart. The Edgewater Hotel, 88 Strand Rd., Portstewart, County Derry. ℭ **028/7083-3314.**

5 THE MOURNE MOUNTAINS

48km (30 miles) SW of Belfast

South and west from Downpatrick, the rolling foothills of the Mournes make a promise that the mountains beyond fulfill. These are the highest mountains in Northern Ireland and the rocky landscape here is breathtaking—all gray granite, yellow gorse, purple heather, and white stone cottages. Remote and traversed by few roads, the mountains—complete with barren, wind-swept moors—are left to hikers and walkers. The ancestral home of the Brontës is here, in ruins. But it's not desolate. There are forest parks, sandy beaches, lush gardens, and, of course, pubs.

The region is dominated by the massive cold, barren peak of **Slieve Donard** (839m/ 2,752 ft.). From the top, the view takes in the full length of Strangford Lough, Lough Neagh, the Isle of Man, and, on a crystalline day, the west coasts of Wales and Scotland. (The recommended ascent of Slieve Donard is from Donard Park on the south side of Newcastle.) If that's too high for you, head to the heart of the Mournes, to the exquisite **Silent Valley Reservoir** (Silent Valley; ℭ **028/9074-6581;** car/motorcycle £3.50/$7; May–Sept daily 10am–6:30pm, Oct–Apr daily 10am–4pm), where there are easy, well-marked paths around the lake and a coffee shop with an information center to keep it all from feeling too far from civilization.

Besides walking and climbing and sighing at the wuthering splendor of it all, there's **Newcastle,** a lively, traditional seaside resort with a golden sand beach and one of the finest golf courses in Ireland. It makes a good base for exploring the area, but if it's too urban for you (pop. 7,200), there are small coastal towns strung along the A2—**Kilkeel, Rostrevor,** and **Warrenpoint**—that have more bucolic charms. If you make it to the town of **Dundrum** in mid-August, you could find the streets filled with musicians, fire-eaters, and jugglers, all drawn by the annual **All Ireland Busking Competition.**

Wherever you stay, the mountains are the main attraction, and in Ireland you can't have cliffs and sea without soaring birds, fairy-tale castles, and mysterious dolmens. Finally, if your idea of nightlife has much to do with the stars, the Mourne Mountains provide a luminous getaway.

ESSENTIALS

GETTING THERE   If you're driving up from Dublin, turn east off the Dublin-Belfast road at Newry and take A2, following the north shore of Carlingford Lough, between the mountains and the sea. It's a drive you won't soon forget.

VISITOR INFORMATION   For information in the Down District, stop into the **St. Patrick Visitor Centre,** 53A Market St., Downpatrick, County Down (© **028/4461-2233**), open October to June, Monday to Friday 9am to 5:30pm, Saturday 9:30am to 5pm; July to September Monday to Saturday 9:30am to 6pm and Sunday 2 to 6pm. (Downpatrick, covered in section 3 of this chapter, "Side Trips from Belfast," is a good gateway stop as you head into the Mourne Mountains from Belfast.)

There's also the **Newcastle Tourist Information Centre,** 10–14 Central Promenade, Newcastle, County Down (© **028/4372-2222**). It's open Monday to Saturday 10am to 5pm and Sunday 2 to 6pm, with extended hours (daily 10am–7pm) in the summer. A coach tour of the Mournes, offered according to demand, can be booked here. Or get information and maps at the **Mourne Heritage Trust Centre,** 87 Central Promenade, Newcastle, County Down (© **028/4372-4059**), open all year Monday to Friday 9am to 5pm. It offers guided mountain walks Mondays and Saturdays when the weather cooperates.

SEEING THE SIGHTS

Castlewellan Forest Park ★   Surrounding a fine trout lake and watched over by a magnificent private castle, this forest park just begs for picnics and outdoor activities. Woodland walks, a lakeside sculpture trail, formal walled gardens, and excellent trout fishing (brown and rainbow) await. The real draw is the National Arboretum, begun in 1740 and now grown to 10 times its original size. The largest of its three greenhouses features aquatic plants and a collection of free-flying tropical birds. The town of Castlewellan, elegantly laid out around two squares, is a short distance away.

6.5km (4 miles) northwest of Newcastle on A50, The Grange, Castlewellan Forest Park, Castlewellan, County Down. © **028/4377-8664.** Free admission. Parking £4.50 ($9). Daily 10am–dusk; coffeehouse summer 10am–5pm.

Drumena Cashel (Stone Fort)   The walls of this irregularly shaped ancient stone-ring fort—a farmstead dating from the early Christian period—were partially rebuilt in the mid-1920s and measure 2.7m (9 ft.) to 3.6m (12 ft.) thick. The *souterrain* (underground stone tunnel) is T-shaped and was likely used in ancient times for cold storage. In the extreme, it likely provided some protection from Viking raiders. There were once thousands of such fortifications in Ireland and this is one of the better-preserved examples in this region.

3km (2 miles) southwest of Castlewellan, off A25, County Down.

Dundrum Castle ★   The site of an early Irish fortification (of which nothing is visible now), the oldest visible portions of this castle's striking and extensive ruins date from the 12th century. The enormous keep was built in the 13th century, as was the gatehouse. It was the home of the Maginnis family until the 17th century, when it was captured by Oliver Cromwell's army, which destroyed it in 1652. The hilltop setting is lovely, and the views from the keep's parapet are panoramic. This was once one of the mightiest of the Norman castles in Northern Ireland (second only to Carrickfergus), and it still commands the imagination, if nothing else.

6.5km (4 miles) east of Newcastle, off A2, Dundrum, County Down. No phone. Admission £1 ($2). Apr–Sept Tues–Sat 10am–1pm and 1:30–7pm, Sun 2–7pm; Oct–Mar Tues–Sat 10am–1pm and 1:30–4pm, Sun 2–4pm.

Greencastle Fort   The first castle on this site, built in 1261, faced its companion, Carlingford Castle, across the lough. It was a two-story rectangular tower surrounded by a curtain wall with corner towers. Very little survives. Most of what you see is from the 14th century. It served as a royal garrison until it was destroyed by Cromwell's forces in 1652.

6.5km (4 miles) southwest of Kilkeel, Greencastle, Cranfield Point, Mouth of Carlingford Lough, County Down. No phone. Admission £1 ($2). Apr–Sept Tues–Sat 10am–1pm and 1:30–7pm, Sun 2–7pm; Oct–Mar Tues–Sat 10am–1pm and 1:30–4pm, Sun 2–4pm.

Murlough Nature Reserve   Sand dunes, heath land, and forest, surrounded by estuary and sea, make for a lovely outing on a clear, bright day, but you'll want to bring a windbreaker and some binoculars; this is a prime habitat for a host of waders and seabirds. Take a picnic, and you may find your dessert on the dunes, which are strewn with wild strawberries in the summertime.

On the main Dundrum-Newcastle rd. (A2), southeast of Dundrum, County Down. ✆ **028/4375-1467.** Free admission. Parking £3 ($6). Open year-round. Facilities available Mar 17–May 28 Sat–Sun 10am–6pm (daily Easter week); June 1–Sept 15 daily 10am–6pm.

Silent Valley Mountain Park (Kids)   More than 90 years ago, the 36km (22-mile) dry-stone Mourne Wall was built to enclose Silent Valley, which was dammed to create the Silent Valley Reservoir, to this day the major source of water for County Down. The 36km (22-mile) **Mourne Wall trek** ★★ follows the Mourne Wall, a 2.4m (8-ft.) granite fence built over 18 years between 1904 and 1922, which threads together 15 of the range's main peaks. The steep path is more than most hikers want to take on, and certainly shouldn't be attempted in a single day, but it is a fine, long walk for experienced ramblers, and offers wonderful views. A good alternative is the more modest walk from the fishing port of Kilkeel to the Silent Valley and Lough Shannagh. An even less strenuous alternative is to drive to the Silent Valley Information Centre and take the shuttle bus to the top of nearby Ben Crom. The bus runs daily in July and August, weekends only in May, June, and September, and costs £2.50 ($5) round-trip, £1 ($2) for children. There are also a restaurant, gift shop, children's playground, and picnic area.

6km (3³⁄₄ miles) north of Kilkeel on Head Rd., Silent Valley, County Down. ✆ **028/9074-6581.** Admission £3 ($6) per car. Information Centre Easter–Sept daily 10am–6:30pm; Oct–Easter daily 10am–4:30pm.

Tollymore Forest Park   All that's left of the once-glorious Tollymore House is a delightful 480-hectare (1,186-acre) wildlife and forest park. The park offers a number of walks along the Shimna River, noted for its salmon, or up into the north slopes of the Mournes. The forest is a nature preserve inhabited by a host of local wildlife, including badgers, foxes, otters, and pine martens. Don't miss the trees for the forest—there are some exotic species here, including magnificent Himalayan cedars and a 30m-tall (98-ft.) sequoia in the arboretum.

Off B180, 3.2km (2 miles) northwest of Newcastle, Tullybrannigan Rd., Newcastle, County Down. ✆ **028/ 4372-2428.** Free admission. Parking £4 ($8). Daily 10am–dusk.

BICYCLING   The Mourne roads are narrow and often bordered by 1.7m-high (5¹/₂-ft.) dry-stone walls. The foothills of the Mournes around Castlewellan are ideal for cycling, with panoramic vistas and very little traffic. In these parts, the perfect year-round outfitter is **Ross Cycles,** 44 Clarkhill Rd., signposted from the Clough-Castlewellan road, .8km (¹/₂ mile) out of Castlewellan (℃ **028/4377-8029**), which has light-frame, highly geared mountain bikes for the whole family, with helmets and children's seats. All cycles are fully insured, as are their riders. You can park and ride, or request local delivery. Daily rates are £7 to £10 ($14–$20). Family and weekly rates are available.

FISHING   The best time to fish for trout and salmon is August to October. Some sizable sea trout can be seen on the Whitewater River in the Mournes, and not all of them get away. The **Burrendale Hotel** in Newcastle (℃ **028/4372-2599**) and the **Kilmorey Arms Hotel** in Kilkeel (℃ **028/4176-2220**) offer special holiday breaks for game anglers. For further information, as well as tackle, bait, and outfitting needs, try **Four Seasons,** 47 Main St., Newcastle (℃ **028/4372-5078**).

GOLF   **Royal County Down ★**, Newcastle, County Down (℃ **028/4372-3314;** www.royalcountydown.org), is nestled in huge sand dunes with the Mountains of Mourne in the background. This 18-hole, par-71 championship course was created in 1889 and is considered one of the best in the British Isles, and there are also the Annesley links to try. Greens fees are £25 to £55 ($50–$110) weekdays, £30 to £65 ($60–$130) weekends. Not too far away, the **Kilkeel Golf Club,** Mourne Park, Ballyardle, Kilkeel (℃ **028/ 4176-5095;** www.kilkeelgolfclub.org), is a beautiful parkland course on the historic Kilmorey Estate. The best days for visitors are weekdays except Tuesday, and greens fees are £20 ($40) weekdays, £25 ($50) weekends.

HORSEBACK RIDING   The **Mount Pleasant Trekking and Horse Riding Centre** (℃ **028/4377-8651**) offers group trekking tours into Castlewellan Forest Park for around £11 ($22) an hour. For riding in the Tollymore Forest Park or on local trails, contact the **Mourne Trail Riding Centre,** 96 Castlewellan Rd., Newcastle (℃ **028/ 4372-4315**). It has quality horses and offers beach rides for highly skilled riders. The **Drumgooland House Equestrian Centre,** 29 Dunnanew Rd., Seaforde, Downpatrick, County Down (℃ **028/4481-1956**), also offers trail riding in the Mournes, including 2¹/₂-hour trekking around Tollymore and Castlewellan Forest Parks from £30 ($60). Full equestrian holidays are also available.

SAILING   For leisure sailing cruises—from sightseeing to a meal afloat   contact Pamela or Aidan Reilly at **Leisure Sailing Cruises,** 5 Coastguard Villas, Newcastle (℃ **028/4372-2882**).

WHERE TO STAY
Expensive
The Slieve Donard Hotel ★★   From this turreted, red-brick Victorian hotel on the seafront, you look across Dundrum Bay to where the Mountains of Mourne sweep down to the sea. Outside, you can walk along the 6.5km (4-mile) sandy strand to the foot of them. When the hotel was built in 1897, there were coal fires in every bathroom. These days, the renovated public areas and well-appointed guest rooms incorporate every modern convenience. Front rooms overlooking the sea are especially appealing. Others look out onto the mountains or Royal County Down Golf Course.

Downs Rd., Newcastle, County Down. © **028/4372-1066.** Fax 028/4372-4830. www.hastingshotels.com. 178 units. £180 ($360) double. Children's discount available. Rates include full breakfast. AE, DC, MC, V. **Amenities:** Restaurant (Continental); bar; indoor swimming pool; gym; spa; Jacuzzi; steam room; salon. *In room:* TV, minibar, hair dryer.

Moderate

Burrendale Hotel and Country Club ★★ (Kids)

This meticulously maintained, modern hotel enjoys a fine location between the Mournes and the shore, and is a 15-minute walk from Newcastle Centre and the Royal County Down Golf Course. The gracious, contemporary rooms are spotless and spacious. In addition, so much attention has been paid to the needs of guests with limited mobility that the Burrendale is a past recipient of the British Airways award for disabled access and amenities, both in the hotel and in the country club. If you're traveling with kids, the spacious family rooms are the way to go.

51 Castlewellan Rd., Newcastle, County Down. © **028/4372-2599.** Fax 028/4372-2328. www.burrendale. com. 69 units. £110 ($220) double. Rates include full buffet breakfast. AE, DC, MC, V. **Amenities:** Restaurant (seafood, vegetarian); bar; indoor swimming pool; gym; beauty treatments; room service; massage; babysitting; laundry service; nonsmoking rooms. *In room:* TV, radio, tea/coffeemaker, hair dryer, iron, trouser press.

Glassdrumman Lodge Country House and Restaurant ★★

"Simple elegance" is the mark Graeme and Joan Hall set in establishing this extraordinary place, and they have achieved just that. Poised between sea and mountains, with splendid views of each, Glassdrumman Lodge is encrusted with awards for fine dining and gracious accommodations. Here is a place that knows what good service is all about: Shoes are shined and cars cleaned overnight. Some of the light-filled rooms have working fireplaces, and room no. 4 has a grand view of the sea. Fabrics are floral, and the attitude is old-fashioned grace. Note that the lodge is only 3km (2 miles) from the Silent Valley. The restaurant specializes in organic, natural produce and ingredients, and is an attraction in itself.

85 Mill Rd., Annalong, County Down. © **028/4376-8451.** Fax 028/4376-7041. www.glassdrummanlodge. com. 10 units. £120 ($240) double. Rates include full breakfast. MC, V. **Amenities:** Restaurant (organic); bar; room service; nonsmoking rooms; valet service. *In room:* TV, hair dryer.

Inexpensive

Briers Country House ★ (Value)

Mary Bowater has lovingly converted her 200-year-old house into an award-winning B&B, keeping its old-world charm. The house is surrounded by acres of gardens, where the Bowaters grow most of their own fruit and vegetables. They also make the breads and preserves served in their full-service **restaurant,** where breakfasts are excellent. The home-style guest rooms are relaxing and have good views. The house is in the foothills of the Mourne Mountains, beside the Tollymore Forest Park.

39 Middle Tollymore Rd. (2.5km/1½ miles from the beach at Newcastle, off B180), Newcastle, County Down. © **028/4372-4347.** Fax 028/4372-6633. www.thebriers.co.uk. 8 units. £60 ($120) double. Rates include full breakfast. 3-day and weekly rates available. MC, V. **Amenities:** Restaurant (seafood); nonsmoking rooms; sitting room. *In room:* TV, hair dryer.

Dufferin Coaching Inn ★★

The brightly painted former bank is a good indication of the cheery personalities of the owners, Morris and Kitty Crawford, who run this place with infectious enthusiasm. The bedrooms have four-poster beds and other furniture handmade by Kitty of wood, metal, and marble. Walls are bedecked with William Morris prints, and beds have matching covers. Bathrooms are spacious and carefully decorated. If you **537** feel like a pint, the Dufferin Arms next door is lively.

31 High St., Killyleagh, County Down. © **028/4482-8229.** Fax 028/4482-8755. www.dufferincoaching inn.com. 6 units. £65 ($130) double. Rates include full breakfast. No credit cards.

Kilmorey Arms Hotel ★ (Value) In this pleasant seaside resort, the Kilmorey Arms was a delightful 200-year-old inn, but after a recent renovation it's now a delightful *modern* hotel, with a colorful, contemporary look. Rooms are spacious, simply decorated, and well equipped. The hotel bar is a popular local hangout, so it's a good place to mix and mingle with nontourists. However, it can be a bit loud at night, so if noise bothers you, ask for a room away from the bar. In their favor, after a wide-ranging renovation, prices were not raised, and it offers real value for money.

41 Greencastle St., Kilkeel, County Down. © **028/4176-2220.** Fax 028/4176-5399. www.kilmoreyarms hotel.co.uk. 26 units. £70 ($140) double. Children's and senior discounts available. Rates include full breakfast. MC, V. **Amenities:** Restaurant (international); bar; nightclub; nonsmoking rooms. *In room:* TV.

Slieve Croob Inn ★ (Value) This small, family resort has a lovely setting in a patch-work of Drumlin pastureland just shy of the Mournes's peaks with panoramic views of Slieve Croob, Newcastle Bay, and the Isle of Man. This is a rambler's fantasy, with good trails on Slieve Croob and lots of lazy mountain lanes to explore. The spotless inn is outfitted in a homey, mountain-lodge style with simple pine furniture. Nothing fancy, but all that you need. Along with standard doubles, there's a three-bedroom family apart-ment. There are also 10 one- to three-bedroom self-catering cottages—appealingly rustic in decor, yet fitted with the conveniences of modern life, that rent by the week.

Seeconnell Centre, 119 Clanvaraghan Rd. (signposted 1.6km/1 mile out of Castlewellan on the A25), Castlewellan-Clough Rd., Castlewellan, County Down. © **028/4377-1412.** Fax 028/4377-1162. 7 units in the inn; 10 1- to 3-bedroom self-catering cottages. Inn £75 ($150) double; cottages start at £350 ($700) per week. AE, MC, V. **Amenities:** Restaurant (international); bar; 18-hole golf course; laundry facilities; horseback riding. *In room:* TV, tea/coffeemaker, garment press.

Self-Catering

Hannas Close ★★ (Kids) Hannas Close is a meticulously restored *clachan,* or medi-eval-style extended-family settlement, founded in 1640 and restored in 1997. On a low bluff over a lovely shallow stream, facing the spectacular Mountains of Mourne, this born-again *clachan* is so quiet that there's little to wake you other than singing birds. The cottages, which sleep from two to seven, have everything you'll need, including central heating, open fireplaces, and a wood-burning stove. They are ideal for families with kids 4 years and over, though the steep steps and rustic character of the cottages won't suit everyone.

Aughnahoory Rd., Kilkeel, County Down. Contact RCH at © **028/9024-1100.** Fax 028/9024-1198. www. cottagesinireland.com. 7 cottages. £300–£500 ($600–$1,000) per week. Also available for 2- to 3-day stays. Additional charge for heat and electricity. V. **Amenities:** Kitchen; fridge; microwave; oven/stove; washing machine.

WHERE TO DINE

Most of the dining in the Mournes, with or without frills, gourmet or generic, happens in hotels, guesthouses, and pubs. When your stomach growls, in addition to the sugges-tions here, you may also consider the accommodations listed above and the pubs listed below.

The Duke Restaurant ★ Ⓥalue MODERN   Chef Ciaran Gallagher has been making a name for himself in this excellent restaurant above the Duke Bar in Warrenpoint, garnering critical acclaim and customers galore. He's a creative cook who uses restraint and wonderful ingredients to come up with scintillating tastes. His starter of seared chili beef with crunchy veggies and Thai rice is a winner; so is the filet of turbot with butternut squash risotto drizzled with balsamic vinegar. Seafood is a particular strong point, as Gallagher makes good use of his proximity to Kilkeel's fishing port. The steaks are fabulous, too. The midweek three-course dinner special, offering four choices at each course, is one of the great dining values on this island. Speaking of value, the wine list offers one white and one red under £8 ($16) a bottle, along with pricier options.

Above the Duke Bar, 7 Duke St., Warrenpoint (9.7km/6 miles on A2 from Newry), County Down. Reservations recommended. Ⓒ **028/4175-2084.** Dinner main courses £12–£14 ($24–$28). MC, V. Tues–Sat 6–10pm; Sun 5:30–9pm.

Seasalt Ⓥalue IRISH/ECLECTIC   This bright and cheerful Newcastle bistro is a good place to go when you don't know what you want. During the day, it's a casual place with organic soups and steak-and-Guinness pie made from local livestock. On weekend nights, though, you must book in advance, and things go upscale with a fusion menu. *Note:* As this book went to press, word came that the Seasalt had a new owner, so things could change by the time you make your trip.

51 Central Promenade, Newcastle, County Down. Ⓒ **028/4372-5027.** Reservations recommended weekends. Main courses £5–£7 ($10–$14). MC, V. Tues–Sun 10am–6pm; dinner Fri–Sat 7 and 9pm.

PUBS

Harbour Inn   You won't find a quainter "wee" harbor on the Down Coast than Annalong, and the Harbour Inn, as its name suggests, is right on the dock. The black guillemots tend to outnumber the people here, and on a warm day, picnic tables sit out front for the dockside happy hour. There's an inviting lounge and full restaurant serving lunch, tea, dinner, and snacks. A local band plays every Saturday night. 6 Harbour Dr., Annalong Harbour, Annalong, County Down. Ⓒ **028/4376-8678.**

Jacob Halls   If there's a chill in the air, you'll leave it behind in Jacob Halls, with its three massive fires blazing at the first suggestion of frost. This well-worn pub is a hub of hospitality. There's live music Thursday to Sunday, and pub grub from lunch on. Greencastle St., Kilkeel, County Down. Ⓒ **028/4176-4751.**

The Percy French   The Percy French has stood watch over the gates of the Slieve Donard Hotel for a century. It's named after the famed Irish composer who died in 1920, leaving behind these words as an epitaph:

> *Remember me is all I ask—and yet*
> *If remembrance proves a task—forget.*

Forgetting is not a real option, however, as long as this fine old faux-Tudor pub pours a good pint and serves hearty fare. The same beamed roof encloses both the lounge and a full-service restaurant with a traditional Irish menu. There's a band playing oldies (1960s–1980s) music on Saturday, and a disco every Friday. Downs Rd., Newcastle, County Down. Ⓒ **028/4372-3175.**

6 DERRY CITY

118km (73 miles) NW of Belfast, 63km (39 miles) SW of Portrush, 113km (70 miles) NW of Armagh, 98km (61 miles) NE of Enniskillen, 232km (144 miles) NW of Dublin, 354km (220 miles) NE of Shannon

Standing on a hill on the banks of the Foyle estuary, strategically close to the open sea, Derry was long a favorite Irish target for invaders: In 1566, Queen Elizabeth I sent English troops to take the town, and Derry was nearly destroyed in 1608 by Sir Cahir O'Doherty. Always, the city resisted ferociously. In 1609, King James I decided to settle the problem once and for all by giving much of Derry to Protestant English and Scottish families, casting out the native Catholics. At the same time, London workers' guilds sent over hundreds of builders to reconstruct the ruined medieval town (and, not coincidentally, add even more Protestant residents, thus changing the religious mix once and for all). Subsequently the town changed its name from "Derry" to "Londonderry"—a move that has kept the city's true identity a source of controversy ever since. Londonderry remains the official name of the city in Ulster, but it's called Derry a few miles away in the Republic of Ireland and by most residents. Over the years, those not wanting to step on toes have come to write the town's name as "Derry/Londonderry," and to say it as "Derry-stroke-Londonderry." That led a local radio DJ to coin the nickname "Stroke City," a bit of a double-entendre (get it wrong and someone will have a stroke).

The fact that even its name is controversial is excellent symbolism of the city's tenuous position, all but straddling the border between Ulster and the Republic of Ireland. Drive into the suburbs and suddenly the currency changes to euro—but that's the only way you can tell that you are in a different country.

The city's greatest beauty—aside from its setting amid rolling green hills—is its noble 17th-century **walls,** about 1.6km (1 mile) in circumference and more than 5m (16 ft.) thick. You can climb the steps to the top of the walls and walk all the way around the town center. Although they were the focus of attacks and repeated sieges, the walls remain solid and unbroken to this day. Derry is a pretty, vibrant, hill town—a pleasure to walk and easy to traverse. Historians believe the town's design was modeled on the French Renaissance community Vitry-Le-Francois, which is similarly designed like a Roman military camp—with two main streets forming a central cross and ending in four city gates. The architecture within the walls is largely medieval, while the rest of the city's architecture is Georgian, with big, brick-fronted town houses and imposing public buildings.

Within Ireland, though, Derry is not known for its architecture, but for the fact that, in the 1960s and 1970s, the North's civil rights movement was born here, and baptized in blood on the streets. The "Bloody Sunday" massacre in 1972, in which British troops opened fire on a peaceful civil rights march, killing 14, shocked the world and led to years of violent unrest. In the **Bogside,** as the neighborhood at the bottom of the hill

---

Tips   **Coin of the Realm**

When we're in the Derry area (on the border between Ulster and the Republic of Ireland), we carry two change purses—one for euros and one for pence—you never know which you'll need.

The Apprentice Boys

Changing Derry's name and planting it with Protestants didn't immediately end the city's troubles. In December 1688, after backing the British Parliament during the civil war, Derry was attacked by Catholic forces led by the earl of Antrim. At one point in the battle, messengers from the earl were sent into the city, ostensibly for talks, but it was a trick to distract the city leaders as the earl's troops prepared to attack. At the last minute, some of the town's apprentice boys saw the ruse for what it was, and locked the city gates—thus saving the town, but setting off the Great Siege of Derry. For months, the town's population endured attacks, disease, and starvation as the earl's troops waited them out. By the time they were rescued, nearly a quarter of the city's residents had died.

The apprentice boys were seen as Protestant heroes, and have been celebrated by the town ever since in marches and parades held every summer, although these have been widely associated with conflict between Protestants and Catholics.

west of the walled section is known, the famed mural reading "You Are Now Entering Free Derry" remains as a symbol of those times.

Happily, much of that sectarian strife seems to be behind Derry now, and it is emerging as a promising center of culture and commerce. Symbolic of the changes in Derry is the *Hands Across the Divide* sculpture that you pass as you cross the Craigavon Bridge into town. Erected 20 years after Bloody Sunday, it is a bronze sculpture of two men reaching across a divide toward one another.

For travelers, Derry is strategically located at the edge of the picturesque Inishowen Peninsula, while the Giant's Causeway and the North Antrim Coast, the Northwest Passage and the Sperrins, and Glenveagh National Park in Donegal are all within an hour's drive. This makes the town an ideal base of operations from which to explore one of Ireland's most unspoiled regions.

ESSENTIALS

GETTING THERE **By Plane** Service to **City of Derry Airport** (✆ **028/7181-0784;** www.cityofderryairport.com) is provided by **British Airways** (✆ **0345/222111;** www. ba.com) from Glasgow and Manchester, and by **Ryanair** (✆ **0541/569569** in Britain; www.ryanair.com) from London Stansted. **Aer Arann** (✆ **011/353-81821-0210** in the U.S., 818/210-210 in Ireland, or 0800/587-23-24 in the U.K.; www.aerarann.com) operates flights between Derry and other cities in Ireland. The no. 43 Limavady **bus** stops at the airport. A **taxi** for the 13km (8-mile) journey to the city center costs about £10 ($20). If you're landing in either of the Belfast airports, without a connection to Derry, the **Airporter** coach can take you straight to Derry. Call ✆ **028/7126-9996** for information.

By Cruise Ship Derry City is a port of call for an increasing number of cruise ships, including six-star luxury liners, which call at the deepwater facilities at Lisahally or at the city center's Queen's Quay. For the latest information on cruises to Derry Port, contact

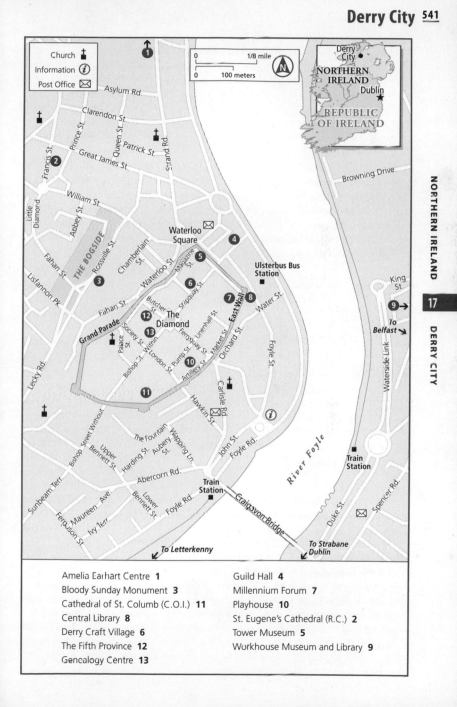

Amelia Earhart Centre **1**

Bloody Sunday Monument **3**

Cathedral of St. Columb (C.O.I.) **11**

Central Library **8**

Derry Craft Village **6**

The Fifth Province **12**

Genealogy Centre **13**

Guild Hall **4**

Millennium Forum **7**

Playhouse **10**

St. Eugene's Cathedral (R.C.) **2**

Tower Museum **5**

Workhouse Museum and Library **9**

the **Cruise Development Officer,** Derry City Council, 98 Strand Rd., Derry (℃ **028/ 7136-5151**).

By Train   **Northern Ireland Railways** (℃ **888/BRITRAIL** [274-8724] or 028/9089-9411) operates frequent trains from Belfast and Portrush, which arrive at the **Northern Ireland Railways Station** (℃ **028/7134-2228**), on the east side of the Foyle River. A free Linkline bus brings passengers from the train station to the city center.

It's possible to travel by train from Dublin, but you'd have to take the train to Belfast and transfer. The whole journey costs about £40 ($80) one-way, and takes about 4 hours, depending on the transfers. For more information, contact **Irish Rail/Iarnród Éireann** (℃ **1850/366222** or 01/836-6222; www.irishrail.ie).

By Bus   The fastest bus between Belfast and Derry, the no. 212 Maiden City Flyer, operated by **Ulsterbus** (℃ **028/7126-2261** in Derry; www.translink.co.uk), takes a little over 90 minutes. **Ulsterbus** also has service from Portrush and Portstewart. From the Republic, **Bus Éireann** offers three buses a day from Galway's **Bus Éireann Travel Centre,** Ceannt Station, Galway (℃ **091/562000;** www.buseireann.ie), via Sligo and Donegal; and there's one bus daily to and from Cork. **Lough Swilly Bus Service** (℃ **028/ 7126-2017**) serves Derry from a number of towns in County Donegal, including Dunfanaghy and Letterkenny.

VISITOR INFORMATION   The **Derry Visitor and Convention Bureau and Tourist Information Centre** is at 44 Foyle St., Derry (℃ **028/7126-7284**). It's open October to March Monday to Friday 9am to 5pm; April to June Monday to Friday 9am to 5pm, Saturday 10am to 5pm; and July to September Monday to Friday 9am to 7pm, Saturday 10am to 7pm, and Sunday 10am to 5pm. For all you ever wanted to know about Derry, consult **www.derryvisitor.com.**

GETTING AROUND   **Ulsterbus,** Foyle Street Depot, Derry (℃ **028/7126-2261;** www.translink.co.uk), operates local bus service to the suburbs. There is no bus service within the walls of the small, easily walkable city. The black London-style taxis you'll see are known in Derry and Belfast as "people's taxis," and they pick up multiple passengers going in the same direction for very cheap fares (they first appeared during the Troubles when buses would not serve the violence-prone areas and are now local institutions). However, they primarily serve nationalist areas outside the walls and will not go to most areas of interest to tourists. Use any of the other taxis available throughout the city, which are plentiful and reasonably priced.

There are taxi stands at the **Ulsterbus Depot,** Foyle Street (℃ **028/7126-2262**), and at the **Northern Ireland Railways Station,** Duke Street, Waterside (℃ **028/7134-2228**). To call a cab, contact **Co-Op Taxis** (℃ **028/7137-1666**), **Derry Taxi Association** (℃ **028/7126-0247**), or **Foyle Taxis** (℃ **028/7126-3905**).

Local car-rental offices include **Europcar** (℃ **028/9031-3500**) and **Argus Car Rentals** (℃ **353-1/490-4444**) at the City of Derry Airport.

The focal point of Derry is the **Diamond,** a large square holding a war memorial in the center of the city. Four streets radiate out from the Diamond: Bishop, Ferryquay, Shipquay, and Butcher. Each extends for several blocks and ends at a gateway (Bishop's Gate, Ferryquay Gate, Shipquay Gate, and Butcher's Gate) cut into the thick city walls.

Two bridges connect the east and west banks of the River Foyle. The Craigavon Bridge, built in 1933, is one of the few examples of a double-decker bridge in the British Isles. The Foyle Bridge, Ireland's longest bridge, opened in 1984 and provides a dual-lane highway about 3.2km (2 miles) north of the Craigavon Bridge. West of the river are two

major areas: the walled inner city and, beyond that, the area known as the Bogside. The **543**
streets near the waterfront are known as Waterside, and it's where most of the better
hotels and many restaurants are located. Also in Waterside is a small grassy viewing point
called the **"Top of the Hill,"** where you can enjoy spectacular eagle's-eye views of the city
and its splendid environs. You'll never find your own way there, so take a taxi and bring
your map. Short of a helicopter tour, this is the best way to get your initial bearings.

FAST FACTS   In the city center, the **Bank of Ireland** (✆ **028/7126-4992**) is on
Shipquay Street, and the **Ulster Bank** (✆ **028/7126-1882**) is at Waterloo Place. Both
are open Monday to Friday 9:30am (10am on Wed) to 4:30pm. The **Northern Bank**
(✆ **028/7126-5333**) at Shipquay Place is open Saturday 9:30am to 12:30pm, in addition to the typical weekday hours.

In an emergency, dial ✆ **999** for fire, police, and ambulance. **Altnagevin Hospital** is
on Glenshane Road (✆ **028/7134-5171**). The main **police station** is on Strand Road
(✆ **028/7136-7337**).

Internet access is available at the **Central Library,** 35 Foyle St. in the city center
(✆ **028/7127-2300**), for £3 ($6) per hour. There are also several Internet cafes to be
found around town, but their prices tend to be slightly higher.

The main **post office,** 3 Custom House St. (✆ **028/7136-2563**), is open Monday
8:30am to 5:30pm, Tuesday to Friday 9am to 5:30pm, and Saturday 9am to 12:30pm.

SEEING THE SIGHTS

The Derry Visitor and Convention Bureau sponsors **Inner City Walking Tours,** June to
September Monday to Friday. They depart at 10:30am and 2:30pm from the Tourist Information Centre, 44 Foyle St. The price is £4 ($8) adults, £3 ($6) seniors and children.
Alternatively, Martin McCrossan's colorful **City Tours** (✆ **028/7127-1996/7**) group offers
informative walking tours year-round. Tours set out from 11 Carlisle Rd. daily at 10am,
noon, and 2pm, but call ahead to book a place. The cost is £5 ($10) adults.

Finally, if you're tired of walking, Martin McGowan will take you by horse-drawn
carriage through the old city and unravel its history as you go. Excursions cost around
£35 ($70) for 90 minutes. Call **Charabanc Tours** (✆ **028/7127-1886**) for details and
reservations from May to October.

Amelia Earhart Centre   Located 5km (3 miles) north of Derry off the A2 road, this
cottage commemorates Amelia Earhart's landing here in 1932 on her successful attempt to
be the first woman to fly across the Atlantic solo. The grounds encompass the Ballyarnett
Community Farm and Wildlife Centre, with a range of farmyard animals and wildlife.

Ballyarnett, County Derry. ✆ **028/7135-4040.** Free admission. Cottage Mon–Thurs 10am–4pm, Fri
10am–1pm; farm and sanctuary daily 10am–dusk.

The Bogside ★★   Just outside the walled city center, the Bogside developed in the
19th and early 20th centuries as a home to Catholic workers. By the 1960s, it was over-
crowded and rife with poverty and unemployment, making it ripe for revolution. In the
late 1960s and 1970s, protests were regular events here as Derry became the center of the
Catholic civil rights movement. In 1969, protests morphed into riots, and the "Battle of
the Bogside" unfolded over the course of 3 days, while fires burned and rocks were hurled
at local police officers. At the end of it, the British government decided to base armed
soldiers in Derry to keep the peace. By then, relations between Catholics and the Protestant local government had broken down entirely. The 30,000 residents of the neighborhood declared their area as "Free Derry," independent of British and local government.

NORTHERN IRELAND

17

DERRY CITY

(Tips) **Climbing the Walls**

One of the best ways to explore Derry is via its old stone walls. Climb to the top and you can circle the entire walled city in about 30 minutes. Steps off of the parapets are frequent, so you'll never get stuck up there. If you start at the **Diamond,** as the square in the center of the walled section is called, and walk down Butcher Street, you can climb the steps at **Butcher's Gate,** which, during the Troubles, was a security checkpoint between the Bogside and the city. Walk to the right across **Castle Gate,** which was built in 1865, and on to **Magazine Gate,** which was once near a powder magazine. Shortly afterward you'll pass **O'Doherty's Tower,** which houses the worthwhile Tower Museum. From there you can see the brick walls of the Guildhall. Farther along, you'll pass **Shipquay Gate,** which once was very near the port, back when the waters passed closer to the center. The walls turn uphill from there, past the Millennium Forum concert hall, and up to **Ferryquay Gate,** where in 1688, local apprentice boys, anticipating an attack, barred the gate against attacking forces, thus saving the town. Next you'll pass **Bishop's Gate,** and notice a tall brick tower just outside the gate—it's all that remains of the **Old Gaol** (jail), where the rebel Wolfe Tone was imprisoned after the unsuccessful uprising in 1798. Farther along, the **Double Bastion** holds a military tower with elaborate equipment used to keep an eye on the Bogside—it's usually splashed by paint hurled at it by Republicans. From there you can easily access the serene churchyard of **St. Columb's Cathedral.** From the next stretch of wall, you have a good view over the political murals of the Bogside down the hill. A bit farther along the wall, an empty plinth stands where once there was a statue of Rev. George Walker, a governor of the city during the siege of 1699. It was blown up by the IRA in 1973. The small chapel nearby is the **Chapel of St. Augustine** (1872), and the building across the street from it with metal grates over the windows is the **Apprentice Boys' Memorial Hall.** Walk but a short way farther, and you're back to Butcher's Gate.

They painted murals arguing their cause on the walls of their houses and barricaded the soldiers and police out of the area. The Bogside was so dangerous for outsiders that even the military wouldn't go there without armored vehicles. Thus, on a Sunday in January 1972, the civil rights march that attracted 20,000 marchers shouldn't have attracted particular attention, but for reasons still not fully understood, British troops opened fire on the marchers, killing 14, in one of the worst atrocities of the Troubles. The soldiers later said they'd been fired upon and only returned fire, but subsequent investigations found little or no evidence of that. Relations between soldiers and residents remained very low for some time. The day of the incident was known as "Bloody Sunday," and it galvanized the IRA into further acts of violence throughout the region. Tensions remained through the 1970s and 1980s, but calmed in the 1990s.

Most of the Bogside has been redeveloped, with modern buildings replacing the old Victorian structures, and most who lived there in the 1960s have moved elsewhere. But the Free Derry corner remains near the house painted with the mural reading "You Are hunger strikes in the 1970s. On Rossville Street, where the Bloody Sunday shootings happened, a memorial has been erected commemorating those killed.

The Bogside, Derry.

Cathedral of St. Columb ★

Within the city walls, near the Bishop's Gate, this cathedral, built as a Church of Ireland edifice between 1628 and 1633, is a prime example of the so-called "Planters Gothic" style of architecture. It was the first cathedral built in Europe after the Reformation, although several sections were added afterward, including the impressive spire and stained-glass windows depicting scenes from the siege of 1688 and 1689. The chapter house contains a display of city relics, including the four massive original padlocks for the city gates, and an audiovisual presentation that provides background on the history of the building and the city. On the porch, a small stone inscribed *"In Templo Verus Deus Est Vereo Colendus"* (The true God is in His temple and is to be truly worshiped) is part of the original church built on this site in 1164. There's an old mortar shell on the porch as well—it was fired into the churchyard during the great siege; in its hollow core it held proposed terms of surrender. The flags around the chancel window were captured during the siege.

London St., Derry. ℂ **028/7126-7313.** £1 ($2) donation requested. Mar–Oct Mon–Sat 9am–5pm; Nov–Feb Mon–Sat 9am–1pm and 2–4pm.

Fifth Province ★ (Kids)

This multimedia exhibition takes you through the history of Ireland's "Fifth Province," as it calls the world of the Celts. Starting with a brief history of Derry, you travel in a "chariot" as the surprisingly sexy Celtic warrior Calgach tells you the story of the Celts and of famous Irish people who emigrated. By the end of all that enthusiastic brainwashing, you are thoroughly assimilated and profoundly believe that all the Irish must be geniuses.

4–22 Butcher St., Derry. ℂ **028/7137-3177.** Admission £3.50 ($7) adults. Mon–Sat 9:30am–5pm.

Genealogy Centre

If you're of Irish ancestry and are wondering about your family's Derry links, this is the place to go to find out the truth. Derry was one of the main ports for the exodus of thousands of emigrants for the New World in the 18th and 19th centuries; records show that Ulster men and women became the second-most-numerous group in the colonial population and played an important role in the settlement of the West. This heritage library and Genealogy Centre, in the heart of the old walled city, can help you research your Derry roots.

Heritage Library, 14 Bishop St., Derry. ℂ **028/7126-9792.** Fax 028/7136-0921. www.irish-roots.net/derry. asp. €30 ($60) initial search fee. Mon–Fri 9am–5pm.

Guild Hall ★

Just outside the city walls, between Shipquay Gate and the River Foyle, this Tudor Gothic–style building looks much like its counterpart in London. The site's original structure was built in 1890, but it was rebuilt after a fire in 1908 and after a series of sectarian bombings in 1972. The hall is distinguished by its huge, four-faced clock and its stained-glass windows, made by Ulster craftsmen, that illustrate almost every episode of note in the city's history. The hall is used as a civic center for concerts, plays, and exhibitions.

Shipquay Place, Derry. ℂ **028/7137-7335.** Free admission. Mon–Fri 9am–5pm; Sat–Sun by appointment. Free guided tours July–Aug.

Fun Facts   **Oh, Danny Boy . . .**

About 19km (12 miles) east of Derry is another Georgian enclave, the town of **Limavady** in the Roe Valley. It was here that Jane Ross wrote down the tune of a lovely song she heard played by a fiddler passing through town. It became the famous "Londonderry Air," otherwise known as "Danny Boy."

St. Eugene's Cathedral ★★   Designed in the Gothic Revival style, this is Derry's Catholic cathedral, in the heart of the Bogside district just beyond the city walls. The foundation was laid in 1851, but work continued until 1873. The spire was added in 1902. It's built of local sandstone and is known for stained-glass windows by the famed makers of stained glass, Meyer and Co. of Munich, depicting the Crucifixion.

Fransic St., Derry. Free admission. Mon–Sat 7am–9pm; Sun 7am–6:30pm.

Tower Museum ★★   In O'Doherty Tower, a medieval-style fort, this award-winning museum presents the history of the city, from its geological formation to the present day. Visitors are invited to walk through time, and a series of exhibits and audiovisual presentations provoke their imaginations along the way. The tower's collection of historical artifacts includes items salvaged from the Spanish Armada, ravaged by storms off the Irish coast in 1588. The Tower Museum, a must for all visitors to Derry, is just inside the city walls next to Shipquay Gate and now includes a new Spanish Armada museum that opened in 2005.

Union Hall Place, Derry. ℂ **028/7137-2411.** Admission £4.50 ($9) adults; £2.50 ($5) seniors, students, and children. July–Aug Mon–Sat 10am–5pm, Sun 2–5pm; Sept–June Tues–Sat 10am–4:30pm.

The Workhouse Museum and Library ★★   This splendid, compact museum on the Waterside, only minutes from central Derry, sits inside a building that was one of the much-feared 19th-century workhouses. In their day, they were notorious for disease, misery, and death. The story told here is both grim and moving. Built to keep the poor from starving to death, workhouses were actually little more than concentration camps. Along with explaining the role of the facilities in Irish history, the museum also presents intriguing multimedia exhibitions on two moments in Derry's history: the Great Famine and the Battle of the Atlantic, when Derry played a major role in the defeat of the *Kriegsmarine*—a German U-boat that surrendered at Derry in May 1945. On the latter, the museum's reach seems to exceed its grasp, as the display seems a bit oxymoronic in a museum ostensibly about one serious issue. Put it down to overenthusiasm.

23 Glendermott Rd., Waterside, Derry. ℂ **028/7131-8328.** Free admission. Mon–Thurs and Sat 10am–4:30pm.

SHOPPING

The city center offers the best shopping options, including two modern multistory malls: the **Richmond Centre,** facing the Diamond at the corner of Shipquay and Ferryquay streets; and the new **Foyleside Shopping Centre,** just outside the walls. **London Street,** beside St. Columb's Cathedral, is Derry's antiques row, where most of the city's antiques and curio shops cluster.

In general, shops are open Monday to Saturday 9am to 5:30pm. Shops in the two large shopping centers are open Monday to Wednesday and Saturday 9am to 5:30pm, Thursday and Friday 9am to 9pm. In the summer, some shops are open on Sunday.

Austin & Co., Ltd.   This is the city's landmark three-story, Victorian-style department store, specializing in fashions, perfumes, china, crystal, and linens. It's the island of Ireland's oldest department store, established in 1839. The coffee shop on the third floor looks out on a panorama of the city. The Diamond, Derry. ✆ **028/7126-1817.**

Derry Craft Village   In the heart of the inner city near the Tower, this shopping complex reflects Old Derry, with architecture of the 16th to 19th centuries. It houses crafts shops, artists' workshops, and a tearoom. Shipquay St. (enter on Shipquay or Magazine St.), Derry. ✆ **028/7126-0329.**

The Donegal Shop   For those not traveling on to Donegal, which is known for its wool and knitted textiles, this is a good place to stock up on colorful sweaters, blankets, hats, and other fine wool products. 8 Shipquay St., Derry. ✆ **028/7126-6928.**

MTM   Whether you've left home without your favorite music or are looking for the latest music from the Irish traditional scene, you're likely to find it here. You can book tickets for major concerts and plays throughout the island. Richmond Centre, Derry. ✆ **028/7137-1970.**

SPORTS & OUTDOOR PURSUITS

BICYCLING   Whether you want to rent a bike and do your own exploring or sign up for a cycling tour of County Derry and County Donegal, **An Mointean Rent-a-Bike and Cycle Tours,** 245 Lone Moor Rd., Derry (✆ **028/7128-7128**), offers excellent service. Rental of mountain or touring bikes costs £15 ($30) a day, £50 ($100) a week. Package tours with bed-and-breakfast included are also available.

FISHING   The Foyle System of rivers makes this a promising area for snagging brown and sea trout (Apr to early July and Sept) and a variety of salmon (Mar–Sept). In addition, there is a stocked lake at Glenowen. Call **Glenowen Fisheries Co-operative** (✆ **028/7137-1544**) for bookings. You can outfit yourself and get useful information at **Rod and Line,** 1 Clarendon St., Derry (✆ **028/7126-2877**). If you're looking for an experienced local *ghillie* (guide) or boatman, contact **Glenowen Fisheries Co-operative** (✆ **028/7137-1544**), or the **Faughan Angler's Association,** 26a Carlisle Rd., Derry (✆ **028/7126-7781**). For a game-fishing rod license (around £15/$30 per season), contact the **Foyle and Carlingford Locks Agency,** 8 Victoria Rd., Derry (✆ **028/7134-2100**).

GOLF   Derry has two 18-hole parkland courses: the **City of Derry Golf Club,** 49 Victoria Rd. (✆ **028/7134-6369;** www.cityofderrygolfclub.com), with greens fees of £25 ($50) weekdays, £30 ($60) weekends; and the very inexpensive **Foyle International Golf Centre,** 12 Alder Rd., Derry (✆ **028/7135-2222;** www.foylegolfcentre.co.uk), which charges greens fees of £15 ($30) weekdays, £18 ($36) weekends. It is always best to phone ahead.

HORSEBACK RIDING   **Ardmore Stables,** 8 Rushall Rd., Ardmore (✆ **028/7134-5187**), offers lessons, trail rides, and pony trekking. Across the border, only 6.5km (4 miles) from Derry in County Donegal, **Lenamore Stables,** Muff, Inishowen (✆ **077/84022**), also offers lessons and trekking, and has guest accommodations.

WALKING   Just outside the city, off the main Derry-Belfast road, the **Ness Woods** have scenic walks, nature trails, and the North's highest waterfall.

WHERE TO STAY
Expensive
Beech Hill Country House Hotel ★   In a residential area southeast of the city, this country-house hotel dates from 1729. Antiques and marble fireplaces decorate the public

areas, and some of the pleasant guest rooms have four-poster beds with frilly floral covers. The hotel restaurant is the elegant **Ardmore,** which is all nonsmoking. The wooded grounds around the house are great to wander.

32 Ardmore Rd., Derry, County Derry. ℂ **800/44-PRIMA** (447-7462) in the U.S., or 028/7134-9279. Fax 028/7134-5366. www.beech-hill.com. 27 units. £130–£140 ($260–$280) double. Rates include full breakfast. AE, MC, V. Free parking. **Amenities:** Restaurant (Continental); bar; lounge; minigym; Jacuzzi; sauna/steam room. In room: TV, tea/coffeemaker, hair dryer, garment press.

Moderate

Broomhill Hotel ★   Views of Lough Foyle are a feature of this modern hotel, on its own grounds in a residential area 2.4km (1½ miles) east of the city, on the main road near the Foyle Bridge. Rooms are modern, with standard furnishings, welcome trays, and garment presses. The **Garden Restaurant** offers views of the river and the city.

Limavady Rd., Derry, County Derry. ℂ **028/7134-7995.** Fax 028/7134-9304. 42 units. £65 ($130) double. Rates include full breakfast. MC, V. Free parking. **Amenities:** Restaurant (international); bar. In room: TV, tea/coffeemaker, garment press.

City Hotel ★   The newest modern hotel in the town center, the City Hotel overlooks the waters of the River Foyle and has good-size rooms with neutral, modern decor. It offers all the conveniences you might hope for, including restaurants, a bar, and a leisure center with a swimming pool.

Queens Quay, Derry, County Derry. ℂ **028/7136-5800.** Fax 028/7136-5801. www.cityhotelderry.com. 145 units. £85 ($170) double. Rates include full breakfast. MC, V. Free parking. **Amenities:** Restaurant (international); bar. In room: TV, tea/coffeemaker, garment press.

Clarence House ★   This well-kept brick Victorian guesthouse is great for families, as it has rooms of all sizes—from twins to doubles to family rooms. Guest rooms are comfortable, and the owner, Michael Slevin, is friendly enough that he has a loyal group of regular visitors—it's a favorite of British and Irish television crews.

15 Northland Rd., Derry, County Derry. ℂ/fax **028/7126-5342.** 11 units, 7 with private bathroom. £65 ($130) double with bathroom; £60 ($120) double with shared bathroom. Children's discount available. Rates include full breakfast. MC, V. Limited free parking available. **Amenities:** Babysitting; laundry facilities; sitting room. In room: TV, tea/coffeemaker, hair dryer, iron.

Everglades Hotel ★★ (Value   On a hill overlooking the east bank of Lough Foyle in the prosperous Waterside district, this three-story contemporary hotel takes its name from Florida's Everglades, with the tenuous connection that, like much of Florida, the hotel is built on reclaimed waterfront land. Guest rooms are luxuriously decorated in quality contemporary furnishings and smart designer fabrics. The tasteful **Library Bar** features live jazz on weekends.

Prehen Rd., Derry, County Derry. ℂ **028/7132-1066.** www.hastingshotels.com. 64 units. £80–£110 ($160–$220) double. Rates include full breakfast. High tea £10 ($20). AE, DC, V. Free parking. **Amenities:** Restaurant (international); bar; room service; laundry service; nonsmoking rooms. In room: TV, tea/coffeemaker, hair dryer, garment press.

Tower Hotel   It doesn't get much more central than this—this modern hostelry is the only hotel inside the old city walls. Its rooms are a sleek turn on the usual modern chain hotel, with well-chosen furnishings, comfortable beds, neutral linens, and quite a few bells and whistles. There's a handy Mediterranean-style bistro, as well as a cafe and bar and a workout facility.

> **(Value)** **A Note on Prices**
>
> Derry prices for both accommodations and dining are exceptionally reasonable. The fact that Derry has hardly any expensive hotels or restaurants does not mean that it lacks quality lodging or dining. The city simply offers more for less and is, for the foreseeable future, a real bargain.

The Diamond, Butcher St., Derry, County Derry. ℰ **028/7137-1000.** Fax 028/7137-1234. www.tower hoteldery.com. 93 units. £70–£110 ($140–$220) double. Rates include full breakfast. MC, V. Free parking. **Amenities:** Restaurant (Mediterranean); cafe/bar. *In room:* TV, tea/coffeemaker, garment press.

Inexpensive

The Saddlers House and the Merchant's House ★★ (Value)   Peter and Joan
Pyne have beautifully restored two architectural gems into award-winning B&Bs. The Saddlers House is a rambling Victorian mansion with spacious rooms, simply but tastefully decorated. The elegant Merchant's House is a grand late-Georgian structure revived with such care that it's won conservation awards. The pair also own a couple of self-catering cottages (starting at £90/$180 per night). Joan and Peter are cheerful hosts—their door is (literally) always open—and their sweet bulldog, Bertie, greets everyone at the front door. A full Irish breakfast is served in both Saddlers House and the Merchant's House, as well as a more healthy cereal, yogurt, and homemade fruit compote. Both houses are just a few minutes' walk from the walled city center.

Saddlers House, 36 Great James St., Derry, County Derry. ℰ **028/7126-9691.** Fax 028/7126-6913. www. thesaddlershouse.com. 7 units, 3 with private bathroom. £55 ($110) double with bathroom; £50 ($100) double with shared bathroom. Merchant's House, 16 Queen St., Derry. ℰ **028/7126-4223.** Fax 028/ 7126-6913. 5 units, 1 with private bathroom. £55 ($110) double with bathroom; £50 ($100) double with shared bathroom. Children's and senior discounts available. Rates include full breakfast. No credit cards. **Amenities:** Sitting room. *In room:* TV, tea/coffeemaker.

Travelodge (Value) (Kids)   This chain hotel may lack character, but it's a reliable affordable option. The spacious rooms are decorated in warm tones with basic modern furniture. Its family rooms—which easily hold two adults and two children—are a blessing for those traveling with little ones.

22–24 Strand Rd., Derry, County Derry. ℰ **028/7127-1271.** Fax 028/7127-1277. www.travelodgederry. co.uk. 40 units. £55 ($110) double. Continental breakfast £5 ($10). AE, MC, V. Free parking. **Amenities:** 2 restaurants (international, bistro); bar; complimentary access to nearby fitness center; foreign-currency exchange. *In room:* TV, tea/coffeemaker, hair dryer, garment press.

White Horse Hotel (Value)   This hotel, once an old inn and now part of the Best Western chain, is a favorite of tour operators. Its countryside setting 6km (3³/₄ miles) northeast of the city on the Limavady road, is peaceful, and there's frequent bus service into Derry. Rooms are spacious and well appointed in a homey style.

68 Clooney Rd., Campsie, County Derry. ℰ **028/7186-0606.** Fax 028/7186-0371. www.bestwestern.com or www.whitehorsehotel.biz. 56 units. £60 ($120) double. Rates include full breakfast. Weekly and weekend discounts available. AE, DC, MC, V. Free parking. **Amenities:** Restaurant (international); bar; laundry facilities. *In room:* TV, tea/coffeemaker.

Expensive

Ardmore Room Restaurant ★ CONTINENTAL Lunch in this pretty dining room draws many business types, who relax in what was once a billiard room overlooking gardens, while enjoying a superb meal. In the evening, there's a soft, romantic ambience. Seafood is one of the menu specialties, and it is expertly prepared. There's an extensive international wine list, as well as a selection of excellent home-baked specialty breads.

Beech Hill Country House Hotel, 32 Ardmore Rd. ℂ **028/7134-9279.** Reservations recommended. Main courses £13–£19 ($26–$38). MC, V. Daily noon–2:30pm and 6–9:30pm.

La Sosta ITALIAN This family-run Italian restaurant is an excellent choice when you have spaghetti on your mind. The menu carries all the usual pasta suspects, and there are also fresh salads and good meat dishes. The sauces are particularly tasty and betray the chef's Italian roots. Service is friendly and the atmosphere is relaxed.

45a Carlisle Rd., Derry. ℂ **028/7137-4817.** Main courses £12–£20 ($24–$40). AE, MC, V. Mon–Sat 5:30–9:30pm; Sun noon–2:30pm and 5:30–9pm.

Satchmo's Restaurant ★ INTERNATIONAL One of Derry's most upscale restaurants, Satchmo's combines the best local produce with classical cooking styles to produce excellent fish and roasted meat. Like the Everglades Hotel in which it sits, the ambience here is formal, and the dress code seems to be mostly suit and tie for men. It's a good way to treat yourself after a hard day's sightseeing.

Everglades Hotel, Prehen Rd., Derry. ℂ **028/7134-6722.** Reservations recommended. Main courses £11–£22 ($22–$44). AE, DC, MC, V. Mon–Sat 5:30–9:30pm; Sun noon–2:30pm and 5:30–9pm.

Moderate

Brown's Bar and Brasserie ★ FUSION Behind the unassuming exterior of this Waterside area row house, you will find some of the finest food in Derry. The decor is warm, streamlined, and minimalist—conducive to quiet conversation. The innovative menu blends the best of modern Irish, Italian, and Thai influences with an emphasis on fresh and, when possible, organic ingredients. Dishes include marinated loin of lamb on a warm noodle salad, or supreme of chicken with parsnip purée and tiger prawn–coconut sauce.

1–2 Bond's Hill, Waterside, Derry. ℂ **028/7134-5180.** www.brownsrestaurant.com. Reservations recommended. Main courses £10–£15 ($20–$30). MC, V. Tues–Fri noon–2:30pm; Tues–Thurs 5:30–10pm; Fri–Sat 5:30–10:30pm.

Da Vinci's Grill Room INTERNATIONAL The glow of candlelight and rich Renaissance reds and blues romantically warm the rough stone walls and arched door-ways here, but it's the food that will coax you a short distance (5 min.) from Derry center. Choose from delights such as grilled sea bass with tikka crust and lime-cherry relish, or pesto cream over tender chicken breast stuffed with sun-dried tomatoes. Stop in to see the magnificent mahogany central bar and its towering three-faced clock. Da Vinci's also has good, affordable **rooms** at £45 ($90) per night.

15 Culmore Rd., Derry, County Derry. ℂ **028/7127-9111.** Reservations recommended. Main courses £11–£16 ($22–$32). AE, MC, V. Mon–Sat 5:30–9:30pm; Sun noon–2:30pm and 5:30–9pm.

Mange 2 ★ FUSION A family-owned restaurant that colors outside all the lines most restaurants stay in between, Mange 2 is both romantic and relaxed, bright by day and candlelit at night, friendly but not intrusive. Its mixed-bag menu of Continental cuisine changes regularly, but is reliably good and made with fresh local produce. Think braised duck with warm apple chutney, mussels marinara, or cider glazed salmon. This is one of the best restaurants in Derry.

2 Clarendon St., Derry. ℭ **028/7136-1222.** www.mange2derry.com. Main courses £11–£17 ($22–$34). AE, MC, V. Mon–Fri 11:30am–3pm and 5:30–10pm; Sat–Sun 10:30am–3pm and 5:30–10pm.

O'Brien's American Steakhouse & Grill ★ ⓥalue STEAKS This is a loud, bright, extroverted piece of Americana in the middle of central Derry. Big TVs blast music videos or sports, staff are young and cheerful, clientele are known to drink a bit, and the food is cheap and very good. Considering what you get—huge steaks served on sizzling platters with large salads and gigantic mounds of potatoes—prices are beyond reasonable. This place is a steal.

59 Strand Rd., Derry. ℭ **028/7136-1527.** Reservations not accepted. Main courses £7–£17 ($14–$34). AE, MC, V. Mon–Fri noon–10pm; Sat 4–11pm; Sun 2–10pm.

Quaywest Wine Bar & Restaurant INTERNATIONAL This is one of the trendier options in Derry—you might want to wear your high heels to this one. The mix of bar and restaurant leans more heavily toward bar as the night goes on, but the food is always excellent, and the international menu travels from Morocco to Mexico and back again.

28 Boating Club Lane, Derry. ℭ **028/7137-0977.** www.quaywestrestaurant.com. Reservations recommended. Main courses £9–£15 ($18–$30). MC, V. Mon–Sat 5–11pm; Sun noon–10:30pm.

Spice Restaurant INTERNATIONAL It bodes well that this place is always crowded with locals, even on weeknights. The vast menu features Thai, Portuguese, Caribbean, Indian, and Irish entrees, such as coconut-crusted chicken with coriander and prawns or seared salmon with mango-and-chili sauce with fresh linguine. The modest wine list is well selected and affordable.

Spencer Rd., Waterside, Derry. ℭ **028/7134-4875.** Reservations recommended. Main courses £10–£15 ($20–$30). MC, V. Tues–Fri 12:30–2:30pm; Tues–Sat 5:30–10:30pm; Sun 5–9pm.

Inexpensive

Badger's PUB GRUB This comfortable corner pub and restaurant is just the place to enjoy a simple, satisfying dinner before the theater, or to settle into after your day's adventures for a drink and a chat. With stained glass and wood paneling, the two levels have a Victorian feel, but were designed with a modern appreciation of light and openness. It's a popular meeting spot for locals who come for both the friendly service, the steak-and-Guinness pie, and the hot sandwiches known as "damper melts."

16–18 Orchard St., Derry. ℭ **028/7136-0763.** Reservations not accepted. Dinner main courses £5–£10 ($10–$20). MC, V. Mon noon–3pm; Tues–Thurs noon–7pm; Fri–Sat noon–9:30pm.

Fitzroy's BRASSERIE This laid-back, brightly colored bistro is open all day and is a great option for a quick, easy meal at reasonable prices. It tends to have a buzzing crowd of regulars, and it's easy to see why. Food is a casual mix of cultures, from chicken and bacon ciabatta sandwiches to Cajun chicken to pasta, along with plenty of vegetarian options.

2–4 Bridge St., Derry. ℭ **028/7126-6211.** www.fitzroysrestaurant.com. Reservations recommended. Main courses £5–£6 ($10–$12) lunch, £7–£10 ($14–$20) dinner. MC, V. Mon–Tues 10am–8pm; Thurs–Sat 9:30am–10pm; Wed 10am–10pm; Sun noon–8pm.

One thing to keep in mind as you're sketching out your after-dark plans is that Derry is a youthful city—roughly 40% of its population is under 30. This fact, coupled with a legal drinking age of 18, means that the night scene is driven by the young. On weekends, after 1 or 2am when the clubs empty, the city center can seem a rather loud and volatile place.

The Performing Arts

Derry has long been associated with the arts, especially theater, poetry, and music. While its financial resources have been modest, its commitment remains inventive and tenacious. The **Millennium Forum,** Newmarket Street (✆ **028/7126-4455** box office), inside the city walls, has added a cultural meeting place and superb theater space to the local mix.

Other principal venues for concerts, plays, and poetry readings are the **Guild Hall,** Shipquay Place (✆ **028/7136-5151**), and the **Playhouse,** 5–7 Artillery St. (✆ **028/7126-8027**), as well as the **Nerve Centre,** 7–8 Magazine St. (✆ **028/7126-0562;** www.nerve-centre.org.uk), which has a cinema and two concert and theater amphitheaters. The **Verbal Arts Centre,** Stable Lane and Mall Wall, Bishop Street Within (✆ **028/7126-6946;** www.verbalartscentre.co.uk), is devoted to promoting literature through readings and spoken-word events. Ticket prices for most performances range from £5 to £15 ($10–$30).

Pubs

Derry pubs are an important part of the local fabric, and hanging out in one is a good way to meet locals. Boozers are tied into the local music scene, so you'll frequently find bands playing. There are even pub debating contests, in the midst of which you'll hear Irish eloquence at its well-lubricated best. Here's a small sampling of Derry's more-than-ample pub options.

Along **Waterloo Street,** just outside the city walls, is a handful of Derry's most traditional and popular pubs, known for their live music and simply as the place to be. The **Dungloe,** the **Gweedore,** and **Peador O'Donnells** are three well-established hot spots. Walk from one end of Waterloo to the other—an act that will take you all of 2 minutes—and you'll likely find the bar for you.

The Clarendon   This inviting bar offers more quiet and calm than most of Derry's bars. It's a congenial pub for those who are past 30 and are somewhere beyond the sonic boom. You can have a conversation here, as well as a drink. 48 Strand Rd., Derry. ✆ **028/7126-3705.**

Mullan's Bar   This is not only a good place to down a pint, it's also a great place to hear local music. Bands play most nights, and the music varies from jazz to blues and traditional Irish sessions during the week. There's often a DJ on weekends. The interior is all traditional pub, with stained glass, brass, and wood polished until it shines. You wouldn't know by looking at it, but the whole place was rebuilt after being bombed during the Troubles. 13 Little James St., Derry. ✆ **028/7126-5300.**

River Inn   Two adjoining bars combine to form the oldest pub in Derry. The downstairs River Inn inhabits cellars opened to the thirsty public in 1684. Thursday is cocktail night. Shipquay St., Derry. ✆ **028/7136-7463.**

Sandino's Cafe Bar   This tiny place is quite trendy, and is where many of the city's more literary folk settle in for the evening. Its "South of the Border" theme refers to the

United States' Mexican border, not to the North's border on the Republic. Bands play most nights. Water St., Derry. ✆ **028/7130-9297.**

The Club Scene

Provided you're under 25, there are several places where you'll want to be seen if not heard. Two multi-entertainment complexes stand out; the first is **Sugar Night Club,** 33 Shipquay St. (✆ **028/7126-6017**), behind the Townsman bar. Once you pay the cover charge, usually £4 to £5 ($8–$10), you can make your way up to the VIP room or farther back to the 1,200-capacity **Voxbox.** Then there's the **Strand,** 31–35 Strand Rd. (✆ **028/ 7126-0494**), with a classy bar serving mostly pub grub and an open venue for bands. On weekend nights, the tables in the bar are moved aside and the Strand morphs into a nightclub for the 20-plus crowd. **Earth,** 1 College Terrace (✆ **028/7136-0556**), has long been the city's main nightclub. It's near the university, so expect a young crowd.

---

7 THE SPERRIN MOUNTAINS

65km (40 miles) E to W along the Derry-Tyrone border

Southeast of Derry, the Sperrin Mountains rise up out of County Tyrone, reaching their highest point at Sawel, from which you can see as far as the Foyle Estuary and across the Northern Ireland countryside to Lough Neagh and the Mournes. This is splendid, wide-open, walking country, home to golden plover, red grouse, and thousands upon thousands of fluffy white sheep.

In the Sperrins, you won't be likely to find the tallest, oldest, or most famous anything. Even the highest peak in the range—Sawel, at 661m (2,168 ft.)—is an easy climb. This is Ireland in a minor key. It is a corner of Ireland largely unsung and unspoiled. You'll see mostly wildflowers here, rather than formal gardens, and cottages rather than castles. All the same, gold has been found in these mountains. Poetry, too. The Nobel-winning poet Seamus Heaney grew up on the edge of the Sperrins and found words to suit their subtle splendor.

Unless you come to farm, chances are you'll spend your time exploring the dark-russet blanket bogs and purple heathland, the gorse-covered hillsides, and the forest parks, whether on foot, cycle, or horseback. There are salmon and trout to be fished from Foyle. There are also a few historical museums. As for minor destinations for a morning walk or an afternoon drive, there's no shortage of standing stones (about 1,000 have been counted), high crosses, dolmens, and hill forts—more reminders that every last bit of bog on this island has its own slew of stories, if only we could hear them told.

VISITOR INFORMATION   There are four nationally networked tourist information centers in County Tyrone. The **Cookstown Centre,** 48 Molesworth St., Cookstown (✆ **028/ 8676-6727**), is open weekdays 9am to 5:30pm, with weekend and extended hours Easter to September. The **Killymaddy Centre,** Ballygawley Road (off A4), Dungannon (✆ **028/ 8776-7259**), is open Monday to Friday 9am to 5pm, Saturday 10am to 4pm. The **Omagh Centre,** 1 Market St., Omagh (✆ **028/8224-7831**), is open Easter to September Monday to Saturday 9am to 5pm, and from October to Easter Monday to Friday 9am to 5pm. The **Strabane Centre,** Abercorn Square, Strabane (✆ **028/7188-3735**), is open April to October Monday to Saturday 9:30am to 5pm.

An Creagán Visitors' Centre Beautifully designed to fit in with the craggy country-side around, this visitor center is an excellent place to get your bearings when you first arrive in the Sperrins. Besides viewing interpretive exhibitions on the region, you can find cycling and trekking routes, rent bicycles, and have a meal in the restaurant. The center owns self-catering cottages nearby, which could make a great base. Call for more information.

A505 (20km/13 miles east of Omagh), Creggan, County Tyrone. ✆ **028/8076-1112**. www.an-creagan. com. Admission £1.50 ($3) adults, £1 ($2) children. Apr–Sept daily 11am–6:30pm; Oct–Mar Mon–Fri 11am–4:30pm.

Beaghmore Stone Circles In 1945, six stone circles and a complex assembly of cairns and alignments were uncovered here, in remote moorland north of Evishbrack Mountain and near Davagh Forest Park on the southern edge of the Sperrins. The precise function of this intriguing concentration of Bronze Age stonework is unknown, but it may have involved astronomical observation and calculation.

17km (11 miles) northwest of Cookstown, signposted from A505 to Omagh, County Tyrone.

Drum Manor Forest Park Once a private estate, this extensive park and woodland has numerous trails and three old walled gardens, one of which has been designed as a butterfly garden. There are also a pond that attracts a variety of wildfowl, a heronry, and a visitor center with exhibits on local wildlife.

4km (2¹/₂ miles) west of Cookstown on A505, County Tyrone. ✆ **028/8676-2774**. Admission £3 ($6) per car; pedestrians £1 ($2) adults, 50p ($1) children. Daily 10am–dusk.

Gortin Glen Forest Park ★★ Nearly 400 hectares (988 acres) of conifers make up this nature park. The woodlands are a habitat to a variety of wildlife, including a herd of Japanese silka deer. A forest drive offers splendid views of the Sperrins. There are also a nature center, wildlife enclosures, trails, and a cafe. For those planning to arrive on foot, the Ulster Way passes through the park.

B48 (11km/6³/₄ miles north of Omagh), Cullion, County Tyrone. ✆ **028/8164-8217**. Free admission. Parking £3 ($6). Daily 9am to 1 hr. before sunset.

Grant Ancestral Home This farm cottage was the home of the ancestors of Ulysses S. Grant, 18th president of the United States. Grant's maternal great-grandfather, John Simpson, was born here and emigrated to Pennsylvania in 1738 at the age of 22. The cottage has two rooms with mud floors and has been restored and furnished with period pieces. The site includes a visitor center with an audiovisual presentation, a tearoom, and various exhibits, including a collection of typical 18th-century agricultural implements.

32km (20 miles) southeast of Omagh off A4, Dergina, Ballygawley, County Tyrone. ✆ **028/7188-3735**. Admission £1 ($2) adults, 50p ($1) seniors and children. Apr–Sept Mon–Sat noon–5pm; Sun 2–6pm.

Gray's Printers' Museum Although a museum and print shop are housed together here, the two are unrelated. The shop, maintained by the National Trust, dates from 1760 and holds an exhibit of 19th-century hand-operated printing presses. John Dunlop, founder of the first daily newspaper in the U.S. and printer of the American Declaration of Independence, learned his trade here. An audiovisual show provides insight into how the presses operated and the part Dunlop played in America's early days. The museum, operated by the local district council, is a venue for changing exhibits germane to the history and culture of the region. Access to the printing press is through the museum.

Plantation of Ulster Visitor Centre ★   This interpretive center tells the story of the Ulster plantation of 1610, which marked the completion of the Elizabethan conquest of Ireland, with an array of graphic images, audiovisual presentations, and interactive displays. Anyone wanting to understand the divisions that to this day define Irish geography and disrupt Irish life would do well to consider the center's informative and moving exhibits. The restaurant serves homemade meals, and the gift shop stocks a selection of local crafts.

50 High St., Draperstown, County Derry. ℭ **028/7962-7800.** Admission £3.50 ($7) adults, £3 ($6) seniors and students, £2 ($4) children. July–Sept Mon–Sat 10am–4pm, Sun 11am–4pm; Oct–June Mon–Fri 10am–4pm.

Sperrin Heritage Centre ★ (Kids)   A range of computerized presentations and other exhibits introduce the history, culture, geology, and wildlife of the region. This is a gold-mining area, and for a small additional fee (around 70p/$1.40) you'll get a chance to try your hand at panning for gold. A cafeteria, craft shop, and nature trail share the grounds.

274 Glenelly Rd. (east of Plumbridge off B47), Cranagh, County Tyrone. ℭ **028/8164-8142.** Admission £3 ($6) adults, £2 ($4) children. Apr–Sept Mon–Fri 11:30am–5:30pm; Sat 11:30am–6pm; Sun 2–6pm.

Ulster American Folk Park ★★   This outdoor museum presents the story of emigration from this part of rural Ireland to America in the 18th and 19th centuries. There are reconstructions of the thatched cottages that emigrants left behind and replicas of the log cabins that became their homes on the American frontier. The park developed around the homestead where Thomas Mellon was born in 1813. He emigrated to Pittsburgh and prospered to the point where his son Andrew became one of the world's richest men. The Mellon family donated part of the funding to build this excellent park. Walk-through exhibits include a forge, weaver's cottage, schoolhouse, famine cabin, and full-scale replica of an emigrant ship with original buildings from the ports of Derry, Belfast, and Newry. A self-guided tour of all the exhibits, which are staffed by interpreters in period costume, takes about 2 hours. Musical events tie in with the Ulster-American theme, such as a bluegrass music festival in September.

Mellon Rd. (4.8km/3 miles north of Omagh on A5), Castletown, Camphill, Omagh, County Tyrone. ℭ **028/8224-3292.** www.folkpark.com. Admission £5.50 ($11) adults, £3.50 ($7) seniors and children 5–16. Oct–Easter Mon–Fri 10:30am–5pm; Easter–Sept Mon–Sat 10:30am–6pm, Sun 11am–6:30pm. Last admission 1 hr. before closing.

Wilson Ancestral Home   This small thatched, whitewashed cottage on the slopes of the Sperrin Mountains was the home of Judge James Wilson, grandfather of Woodrow Wilson, 28th president of the United States. James Wilson left the house in 1807 at the age of 20. It contains some of the family's original furniture, including a tiny out-shot bed (sleeping nook) in the kitchen close to the fire, larger curtained beds, and a portrait of the president's grandfather over the fireplace. Wilsons still occupy the farmhouse next door. *Note:* Opening hours are subject to change; phone in advance.

Off Plumbridge Rd., Dergalt, Strabane, County Tyrone. ℭ **028/8224-3292.** Free admission. Apr–Sept daily 2–6pm.

SPORTS & OUTDOOR PURSUITS

BICYCLING   The Sperrin countryside is ideal for cycling. Bicycles can be rented by the day or week from the **An Creagán Visitors' Centre** (see above). Bike rentals run roughly £10 ($20) a day or £35 ($70) a week.

BIRD-WATCHING   The Sperrins are home to golden plovers, peregrines, ravens, grouse, and hen harriers. **Sawel Mountain,** the highest of the Sperrins, is a great place to take out your binoculars and field guide.

FISHING   The **Foyle System** of rivers, from Derry to Omagh and Limavady to Dungiven, makes this a promising area for brown and sea trout (Apr to early July and Sept) and a variety of salmon (Mar–Sept). There's also some good coarse fishing available north and west of Omagh, on the Baronscourt Lakes and on the Strule and Fairy Water rivers. The necessary permits, equipment, and good advice are available from **C. A. Anderson & Co.,** 64 Market St., Omagh (© **028/8224-2311**); **Mourne Valley Tackle,** 50 Main St., Newtownstewart (© **028/8166-1543**); and **Floyd's Fish and Tackle,** 28 Melmount Villas, Strabane (© **028/7188-3981**). In fact, if you're in the market for an experienced *ghillie* (guide), ask at Floyd's for Martin Floyd.

GOLF   There are several 18-hole courses in County Tyrone within a modest drive from the heart of the Sperrins: **Strabane Golf Club,** 33 Ballycolman Rd., Strabane (© **028/7138-2007**), with greens fees of £15 ($30) weekdays, £17 ($34) on weekends; **Newtownstewart Golf Club,** 38 Golf Course Rd., Newtownstewart (© **028/8166-1466**), with greens fees of £14 ($28) weekdays, £19 ($38) weekends; **Omagh Golf Club,** 83a Dublin Rd., Omagh (© **028/8224-3160**), with greens fees of £15 ($30) weekdays, £20 ($40) weekends; and **Killymoon Golf Club,** 200 Killymoon Rd., Cookstown (© **028/8676-3762**), with greens fees of £15 ($30) Mondays, £20 ($40) other weekdays, and £25 ($50) weekends.

HORSEBACK RIDING   To rent by the hour or take a multiday journey through the mountains, contact the **Edergole Riding Centre,** 70 Moneymore Rd., Cookstown (© **028/8676-1133**).

WALKING   Whether you're on foot, wheels, or horseback, be sure to traverse the **Glenshane Pass** between Mullaghmore (545m/1,788 ft.) and Carntogher (455m/1,492 ft.), and the **Sawel Mountain Drive** along the east face of the mountain. The vistas along these routes through the Sperrins will remind you of why you've gone out of your way to spend time in Tyrone.

WHERE TO STAY
Moderate

Grange Lodge ★   Norah and Ralph Brown are the gracious hosts of this handsome Georgian guesthouse, which began life as a 17th-century settler's hall. Set high on a hill atop an 8-hectare (20-acre) estate, it's a classy, tranquil retreat and a good base for day trips throughout County Tyrone. Guest rooms are attractive and comfortable, but everyone stays here for the food. Norah has won all sorts of culinary awards, and her lovingly prepared, home-style meals have achieved near-cult status in this otherwise gastronomically challenged part of the North. At breakfast, don't miss the house specialty: porridge infused with Bushmills Whiskey and cream. And book a place for dinner, too (£28/$56). Unfortunately for nonguests, Norah only cooks for residents of Grange Lodge.

7 Grange Rd. (signposted 1.6km/1 mile south of M1, Junction 15), Moy, Dungannon, County Tyrone.
C **028/8778-4212.** Fax 028/8778-4313. 5 units. £80 ($160) double. Rates include full breakfast. MC, V.
Closed Dec 20–Feb 1. **Amenities:** Nonsmoking rooms; sitting room. *In room:* TV.

Inexpensive
Greenmount Lodge (Kids)   This large, first-rate guesthouse is set on a 60-hectare
(148-acre) farm. All the rooms are nicely appointed; four are family units. Mrs. Frances
Reid, the friendly hostess, is a superb cook; both breakfasts and evening meals are a
home-style delight.

58 Greenmount Rd. (13km/8 miles southeast of Omagh on A5), Gortaclare, Omagh, County Tyrone.
C **028/8284-1325.** Fax 028/8284-0019. 8 units. £55 ($110) double. Children's discount available. Rates
include full breakfast. Dinner £16 ($32). MC, V. **Amenities:** Guest laundry room; sitting room. *In room:* TV.

Self-Catering
Sperrin Clachan ★   This restored *clachan,* or family cottage compound, sits beside
the Sperrin Heritage Centre in the beautiful Glenelly Valley. It makes an ideal base for
exploring the natural riches and cultural legacy of the Sperrin region, as well as the city
of Derry, only 40km (25 miles) to the north. Each cottage has everything you'll need to
set up house, including central heating and an open fireplace. There are four cottages in
all; each sleeps two to five people. In addition to these, Rural Cottage Holidays offers a
wide array of other traditional cottages in the region, including the award-winning, four-
star Glenelly Cottages.

Glenelly Valley, Cranagh, County Tyrone. Contact RCH at *C* **028/9024-1100.** Fax 028/9024-1198. www.
cottagesinireland.com. 4 cottages. £110–£200 ($220–$400) per week. Also available for 2- or 3-day stays.
No credit cards. Free parking. **Amenities:** Kitchen; fridge; dishwasher; microwave; oven/stove; washing
machine. *In room:* TV.

WHERE TO DINE
Mellon Country Inn ★ INTERNATIONAL   Just over 1km (²/₃ mile) north of the
Ulster-American Folk Park, this old-world country inn has had a modern makeover, and
now has a sleek new interior. Its handy restaurant offers simple, hearty fare—burgers,
soup, salads, and ploughman's platters—as well as classic casseroles and seafood dishes.
The house specialty is Tyrone black steak, a locally bred hormone-free beef. Food is available all day on a hot and cold buffet, and you can also order a late breakfast or afternoon
tea. There are a few nicely decorated rooms, should you choose to stay the night, starting
at £50 ($100).

134 Beltany Rd., Omagh, County Tyrone. *C* **028/8166-1224.** Dinner main courses £8–£14 ($16–$28). AE,
MC, V. Daily 8am–9pm.

---

8 THE FERMANAGH LAKELANDS

Enniskillen: 134km (83 miles) SW of Belfast, 98km (61 miles) SW of Derry, 84km (52 miles) W of Armagh,
44km (27 miles) SW of Omagh, 174km (108 miles) NW of Dublin, 271km (168 miles) NE of Shannon

In the extreme southwest corner of Northern Ireland, County Fermanagh is a resort area
dominated by **Lough Erne,** a long, narrow lake with 154 islands and countless coves and
inlets.

   The **Shannon-Erne Waterway,** linking the lough to the Shannon system, enhances
the lure of Lough Erne as a boating destination. Were you to cruise the whole length of

the waterway between the village of Leitrim and Lough Erne, you'd travel 65km (40 miles), past 16 lochs, three lakes, and the Woodford River, all of which are ripe for aquatic exploring.

The hub of this lake-land paradise, wedged between the upper and lower branches of Lough Erne, is **Enniskillen,** a delightful resort town that was the medieval seat of the Maguire clan and a major crossroads between Ulster and Connaught. Both Oscar Wilde and Samuel Beckett were once students here at the royal school.

At the northern tip of the lake is **Belleek,** sitting right across the border in the Republic of Ireland, and known the world over for its trademark delicate bone chinaware. At the southern end of the lake is County Cavan and another slice of border with the Irish Republic. The surrounding countryside holds diverse attractions, from stately homes at Florence Court and Castle Coole to the Marble Arch Caves.

In medieval times, a chain of island monasteries stretched across the waters of Lough Erne, establishing it as a haven for contemplatives. Even allowing for less lofty minds, the Fermanagh Lakelands are still a peaceful place to get away from it all and to gaze, in a phrase from Hopkins, at the "pied beauty" of it all.

VISITOR INFORMATION   Contact the **Fermanagh Tourist Information Centre,** Wellington Road, Enniskillen, County Fermanagh (© **028/6632-3110**). It's open weekdays year-round from 9am to 5:30pm (until 7pm July–Aug). From Easter to September, it's also open Saturday 10am to 6pm and Sunday 11am to 5pm. For an introduction to the Fermanagh Lakelands on the Web, take a look at **www.fermanaghlakelands.com**.

EXPLORING THE LAKELANDS
Touring the Lakes & Islands

Erne Tours Ltd., Enniskillen (© **028/6632-2882**), operates cruises on Lower Lough Erne. The MV *Kestrel,* a 56-seat cruiser, departs from the Round "O" Jetty, Brook Park, Enniskillen. Trips, including a stop at Devenish Island, last just under 2 hours. They operate daily in July and August at 10:30am and 2:15 and 4:15pm; in May and June on Sunday at 2:30pm; and in September on Tuesday, Saturday, and Sunday at 2:30pm. Call for reservations and to confirm times. The fare starts at £10 ($20) for adults, £7 ($14) for seniors, and £5 ($10) for children 13 and under.

The **Share Holiday Village,** Smith's Strand, Lisnaskea (© **028/6772-2122**), operates cruises on Upper Lough Erne. These 1¹/₂-hour trips are conducted onboard the *Inishcruiser,* a 57-passenger ship. Sailings are scheduled Easter through September on Sunday at 2:30pm (July–Aug also Thurs–Sat at 2:30pm). The fares are about the same as those for Erne Tours. Share Holiday Village also offers other watersports activities and self-catering chalets.

There are lots of charter boat companies in the area, which will allow you to travel privately for a day or a week on narrow boats, barges, or yachts. Prices vary from a few hundred pounds to much more, for the more elegant options. For a good list of options, go to **www.fermanaghlakelands.com** and click on "Find Something To Do," or call the tourist office and request a brochure.

Independent boatmen offer ferry crossings to some of the many islands in Lough Erne. White Island, Devenish Island, and Boa Island are all rich in archaeological and early Christian remains. Devenish Island has Lough Erne's most important island monastery, founded in the 6th century by St. Molaise. The extensive remains include a 12th-century round tower, which you can climb to take in the view and get a feel for the tiny

---

ⓘ Tips **Buying Belleek**

If you're not a china expert, but you still want to bring back some Belleek pieces from your trip, here are a few tips to ensure that your purchases become heirlooms.

- The Belleek Heirloom Centre has the best selection of patterns from which to choose, giving you lots of options and a wide price range.
- At the center, all the china is displayed around the room. You walk around looking at all the pieces, then note the item numbers of those pieces you like. You take the numbers to the central counter, and they bring boxed china pieces to you.
- Make sure they pull the pieces out of the boxes so you can be sure they are what you expected.
- Take the pieces from the sales assistant and look at them closely. This is delicate china, and it can have tiny imperfections that you can only see by getting up close and personal.
- Be particularly conscious of the bottom of the piece—look for tiny hairline cracks. We bought a lovely Belleek vase recently, but it leaks through a nearly invisible crack.
- If it looks good to you and you love it—buy it!

---

space inside. From April to September, a ferry runs to Devenish Island from Trory Point, 6km (3¾ miles) from Enniskillen on A32; journey time is about 12 minutes.

On White Island, seven stone figures remain from a vanished 10th-century monastery inside a ruined 12th-century church. From April through August, a ferry runs to White Island, departing from Castle Archdale Marina (for times, call Mr. Bradshaw at ⓒ **028/ 6862-1892,** or 0836/787123 mobile), 16km (10 miles) from Enniskillen on the Kesh road; journey time is about 18 minutes. Departures April through June are on weekends only, every hour on the hour from 11am to 6pm with the exception of 1pm. In July and August, the ferry runs daily, with the same sailing times. The round-trip fare is £4 ($8) for adults and £3 ($6) for children. In the cemetery at the west end of Boa Island, there are two ancient Janus (looking both ways) idols, which are thought to date from the 1st century. Boa Island is connected to the shore by bridges.

Though it's possible to visit all three islands in a single day, it's a bit ambitious. Begin with Devenish, then visit White, and, if time permits, finish up with Boa.

Seeing the Sights

Belleek Visitor Center ★★   The fine Parian china produced in the tiny village of Belleek is recognized worldwide for its quality. While you'll find pieces in shops all over the north of Ireland, this is the flagship store. In the visitor center, in a Victorian-era china-making factory, you can browse to your heart's content in the spacious shop, or head to the free museum and learn the history of this china-making town and see its best works. Depending on the exchange rate, prices are generally considerably less than you'll find elsewhere, and shipping by UPS is available. If you want to learn even more about Belleek, take one of the informative 30-minute tours of the china factory. If you prefer to relax and ponder the china in peace, you might spend that same time lingering over a cup of tea and a slice of cake in the cheery tearoom. *Note:* Belleek is just inside the Ulster border, so prices will be in British pounds.

Follow signs in Belleek, County Fermanagh. ✆ **028/6865-8501.** www.belleek.ie. Free admission; tours £4 ($8) adults, £3 ($6) children. Apr–June and Sept Mon–Sat 9am–5:30pm; July–Aug Mon–Sat 9am–6pm, Sun noon–6pm; Oct–Dec Mon–Sat 9am–5pm; Jan–Mar Mon–Fri 9am–5pm.

Castle Coole ★   On the east bank of Lower Lough Erne, this quintessential neoclassical mansion was designed by James Wyatt for the earl of Belmore and completed in 1796. Its rooms include a lavish state bedroom hung with crimson silk, said to have been prepared for George IV. Other features include a Chinese-style sitting room, magnificent woodwork, fireplaces, and furniture dating from the 1830s. A nearly 600-hectare (1,482-acre) woodland estate surrounds the house. A classical music series runs from May to October.

2.4km (1½ miles) southeast of Enniskillen on the main Belfast-Enniskillen rd. (A4), County Fermanagh. ✆ **028/6632-2690.** www.nationaltrust.org.uk. House admission £4.50 ($9) adults, £2 ($4) children; grounds £2 ($4) per car. House Easter–May and Sept Sat–Sun 1–6pm; June–Aug daily 1–6pm (last tour 5:15pm). Grounds daily 10am—4pm.

Crom Estate ★★   This nearly 800-hectare (1,976-acre) nature reserve is a splendid National Trust property, with forest, parks, wetlands, fen meadows, and an award-winning lakeshore visitor center. There are numerous trails, with concealed places for observing birds and wildlife, as well as a heronry and boat rental. The estate is also a great place to fish for bream and roach. Permits and day tickets are available at the gate lodge. During the summer, there are frequently special programs and guided nature walks on weekends.

Newtownbutler, County Fermanagh. ✆ **028/6773-8118.** www.nationaltrust.org.uk. Admission £5 ($10) per car or boat. Apr–Sept Mon–Sat 10am–6pm; Sun noon–6pm. 34km (21 miles) south of Enniskillen. Take A4 and A34 from Enniskillen to Newtownbutler, then take the signposted right turn onto a minor road.

Devenish Island ★★   This is the most extensive of the ancient Christian sites in Lough Erne. In the 6th century, St. Molaise founded a monastic community here, to which the Augustinian Abbey of St. Mary was added in the 12th century. In other words, this is hallowed ground, hallowed all the more by the legend that the prophet Jeremiah is buried somewhere nearby—if you can figure that one out. The jewel of Devenish is the perfectly intact, 12th-century round tower, which was erected with Vikings in mind. The island is a marvelous mélange of remnants and ruins, providing a glimpse into the lake's mystical past. While you're in the spirit, be sure to explore Boa and White islands, with their extraordinary carved stone figures, and bring your camera (see the introduction to this section for details on island hopping).

2.4km (1½ miles) downstream from Enniskillen. ✆ **028/6862-1588.** Admission to round tower £2.25 ($4.50). Ferry from Trory Point (6.5km/4 miles from Enniskillen on A32) Apr–Sept at 10am, 1pm, 3pm, and 5pm. Round-trip fare £3 ($6) adults, £2 ($4) children.

Enniskillen Castle ★★   Dating from the 15th century, this magnificent stone fortress sits overlooking Lough Erne on the western edge of Enniskillen. It incorporates three museums: the medieval castle, with its unique twin-turreted Watergate tower, once the seat of the Maguires, chieftains of Fermanagh; the county museum, with exhibits on the area's history, wildlife, and landscape; and the museum of the famous Royal Inniskilling Fusiliers, with a collection of uniforms, weapons, and medals dating from the 17th century. Other exhibits include life-size figurines and 3-D models of old-time castle life.

Castle Barracks, Enniskillen, County Fermanagh. ✆ **028/6632-5000.** Admission £2.75 ($5.50) adults, £1.80 ($3.60) children. May–June and Sept Mon and Sat 2–5pm; Tues–Fri 10am–5pm; July–Aug Tues–Fri 10am–5pm, Sat–Mon 2–5pm; Oct–Apr Mon 2–5pm, Tues–Fri 10am–5pm.

ExplorErne ★ (Kids) Just outside Belleek village, this exhibition offers an engaging multimedia introduction to Lough Erne. It covers its geologic formation and the lives, ancient and modern, lived along its reedy banks. Science, myth, and history blend to tell the story of this legendary, alluring lake.

Erne Gateway Centre, off main Enniskillen-Belleek rd., Corry, Belleek, County Fermanagh. ℂ **028/6865-8866.** Admission £1 ($2) adults. June–Sept daily 11am–5pm.

Florence Court ★★ One of the most beautifully situated houses in Northern Ireland, this 18th-century Palladian mansion is set among dramatic hills, 13km (8 miles) southwest of Upper Lough Erne and Enniskillen. Originally the seat of the earls of Enniskillen, its interior is rich in rococo plasterwork and antique Irish furniture, while its exterior has a fine walled garden, an icehouse, and a water-wheel-driven sawmill. The forest park offers a number of trails, one leading to the top of Mount Cuilcagh (nearly 660m/2,165 ft.). There's also a tearoom.

Florence Court, off A32, County Fermanagh. ℂ **028/6634-8249.** Admission £4.50 ($9) adults, £2.50 ($5) children, £11 ($22) families. June Mon–Fri 1–6pm, Sat–Sun noon–6pm; July–Aug daily noon–6pm; Sept–May Sat–Sun noon–6pm.

Marble Arch Caves ★★★ (Kids) West of Upper Lough Erne and 19km (12 miles) from Enniskillen near the Florence Court estate, these caves are among the finest in Europe for exploring underground rivers, winding passages, and hidden chambers. Electrically powered boat tours take visitors underground, and knowledgeable guides explain the origins of the amazing stalactites and stalagmites. Tours last 75 minutes and leave at 15-minute intervals. The caves are occasionally closed after heavy rains, so phone ahead before making the trip.

Marlbank, Florence Court, off A32, County Fermanagh. ℂ **028/6634-8855.** Admission £8 ($16) adults, £5.50 ($11) seniors and students, £5 ($10) children 17 and under. Reservations recommended. Late Mar to June and Sept daily 10am–4:30pm (last tour at 4:30pm); July–Aug daily 10am–5pm (last tour at 5pm).

SHOPPING

Enniskillen has fine shops along its main street, which changes its name five times (East Bridge, Townhall, High, Church, Darling, Ann) as it runs the length of the town. Most shops are open Monday to Saturday 9:30am to 5:30pm.

The largest shopping complex in Enniskillen is the **Erneside Shopping Center,** a modern bi-level mall on Shore Road, just off Wellington Road. It stays open until 9pm on Thursday and Friday. The other principal towns for shopping in the area are **Irvinestown** and **Lisnaskea.**

The town's former butter market offers a nifty shopping experience. Dating from 1835, it has been restored and transformed into the **Buttermarket, Enniskillen Craft and Design Centre,** Down Street (ℂ **028/6632-3837**). It offers craft workshops and retail outlets, with occasional traditional music, craft fairs, and street theater to enliven the atmosphere.

SPORTS & OUTDOOR PURSUITS

BICYCLING Several of the watersports and activity centers in the area, such as **Lakeland Canoe Center** (see "Watersports," below), also rent bicycles. Bicycles are also available from **Corralea Activity Centre,** Belcoo (ℂ **028/6638-6668**), and **Out & Out Activities,** 501 Rosscor, Belleek (ℂ **028/6865-8105**). Daily bike rental runs £7 to £10 ($14–$20). For cycle tours with **Kingfisher Cycle Trail,** contact Pat Collum at the Tourist Information Centre, Wellington Road, Enniskillen (ℂ **028/6632-0121;** www.kingfishercycletrail.com)

BIRD-WATCHING These lake lands are prime bird-watching territory. To mention a few, you'll find whooper swans, great-crested grebes, golden plovers, curlews, corncrakes, kingfishers, herons, merlins, peregrines, kestrels, and sparrow hawks. On Upper Lough Erne, the primary habitats are the reed swamps, flooded drumlins, and fen; on the lower lake, the habitats of choice are the less visited islands and the hay meadows. Two important preserves are at the Crom Estate (see "Seeing the Sights," above) and the Castle-caldwell Forest and Islands.

BOATING Lough Erne is an explorer's dream, and you can take that dream all the way to the Atlantic if you want. The price range for fully equipped, four- to eight-berth cruisers is £700 to £1,135 ($1,400–$2,270) per week, including VAT, depending on the season and the size of the boat. The many local cruiser-hire companies include **Belleek Charter Cruising,** Belleek (② 028/6865-8027); **Erne Marine,** Bellanaleck (② 028/6634-8267); and **Carrickcraft,** Lurgan (② 028/3834-4993; www.cruise-ireland.com).

On Lower Lough Erne, north of town, you can hire motorboats from **Manor House Marine,** Killadeas (② 028/6862-8100). Charges average £60 ($120) for a half-day, and £100 ($200) for a full day. You'll have to pay a refundable deposit before heading out.

FISHING The **Fermanagh Lakes** are an angler's heaven. If you can't catch a fish here, you will really have to question your technique. The best time for salmon is February to mid-June; for trout, mid-March to June or mid-August until late September. As for coarse fishing, about a dozen species await your line in the area's lakes and rivers. If you've left time for advance planning and consultation, contact the **Fisheries Conservancy Board,** 1 Mahon Rd., Portadown (② 028/3833-4666). For on-the-spot info, tackle, and bait, try **Trevor Kingston,** 18 Church St., Enniskillen (② 028/6632-2114). For locally arranged game fishing, call or drop in on **Melvin Tackle,** Main Street, Garrison, County Fermanagh (② 028/6865-8194). All necessary permits and licenses are available at the **Fermanagh Tourist Information Centre** (see "Visitor Information," above).

GOLF There are two 18-hole courses in the Lakelands, both in Enniskillen. The **Enniskillen Golf Club,** in the Castle Coole estate (② 028/6632-5250; www.enniskillengolf club.com), charges greens fees of £20 ($40) weekdays, £25 ($50) weekends. The **Castle Hume Golf Club,** Castle Hume (② 028/6632-7077; www.castlehumegolf.com), is 5km (3 miles) north of Enniskillen, with greens fees of £25 ($50) weekdays, £30 ($60) weekends.

HORSEBACK RIDING The **Ulster Lakeland Equestrian Centre,** Necarne Castle, Irvinestown (② 028/6862-1919), is an international center that offers full equestrian holidays. Pony trekking and riding lessons are available from **Drumhoney Stables,** Lisnarick (② 028/6862-1892).

WALKING The southwestern branch of the **Ulster Way** follows the western shores of Lough Erne, between the lake and the border. The area is full of great walks. One excellent 11km (6.75-mile; 3–7 hr.) hike is from a starting point near Florence Court and the Marble Arch Caves (see "Seeing the Sights," above) to the summit of **Mount Cuilcagh** (656m/2,152 ft.). A trail map is included in the Northern Ireland Tourist Board's *Information Guide to Walking.*

WATERSPORTS The **Lakeland Canoe Centre,** Castle Island, Enniskillen (② 028/6632-4250), is a watersports center based on an island west of downtown. For a full day of canoeing and other sports, including archery, cycling, dinghy sailing, and windsurfing, prices start roughly at £15 ($30) per day. Camping and simple accommodations are also available at a modest cost. The **Share Holiday Village,** Smith's Strand, Lisnaskea

(© 028/6772-2122; www.sharevillage.org), offers sailing, canoeing, windsurfing, and
banana skiing. Costs start at around £8 ($16) per person. Other watersports centers
include the **Boa Island Activity Centre,** Tudor Farm, Kesh (© 028/6863-1943).

WHERE TO STAY
Very Expensive
Castle Leslie ★★ (Finds)   This majestic place is where Sir Paul McCartney married
Heather Mills in June 2002. W. B. Yeats, Winston Churchill, and Mick Jagger also loved
Castle Leslie, a quintessential Victorian retreat just across the border in County Monaghan. A stay here is one of Ireland's unique surprises, an experience well worth whatever
detour it necessitates. The sprawling estate stretches over hundreds of acres, with three
lakes and ancient hardwood forests casting a relaxing spell. The manor house is as comfortable as an old slipper. This is a place of hidden treasures—Wordsworth's harp, the
Bechstein grand on which Wagner composed *Tristan and Isolde,* and Winston Churchill's
baby clothes, to mention only a few. Each guest room has special features—a claw-foot
tub in an alcove near the bed, a spectacular view in a bay window, or perhaps a beefy
four-poster bed. The meals are memorable. If you prefer more privacy, you can rent one
of the cottages on the grounds, or the old hunting lodge. If the excellent cuisine inspires
you, there's a **cooking school** on-site. The castle has recently changed into an all-inclusive venue, with membership packages. If you choose to purchase a membership (starting
at €3,000/$4,800), room rates are considerably lower. The all-inclusive fees, as the name
implies, cover everything—your room, three meals a day, all activities.

Glaslough, County Monaghan. © **047/88109.** Fax 047/88256. www.castleleslie.com. 14 units, 4 with
shower only. Members €300 ($480) per person per night; nonmembers €500 ($800) per person per night.
Rates include all meals and most activities. MC, V. **Amenities:** Restaurant (Continental); tennis courts; spa;
cooking school; cinema; fishing; boating; hunting; drawing room. *In room:* TV, hair dryer.

Expensive
Manor House Country Hotel ★ (Kids)   Dating from 1860, this three-story Victorian mansion has a varied history that includes a stint as a base for American forces during World War II. The public areas are decorated with antiques and ornate plasterwork,
and from the windows you have lovely views of Lough Erne. Rooms are a bit dull but
nice enough, furnished in traditional style, with dark-wood furniture and big beds; a few
have four-posters or half-canopy beds. This is a good option for families with children,
as it has kid-friendly facilities including family rooms, a swimming pool, minigolf, and a
supervised playroom.

Killadeas, Irvinestown, Enniskillen, County Fermanagh. © **028/6862-1561.** Fax 028/6862-1545. www.
manor-house-hotel.com. 81 units. £125 ($250) double. Rates include full breakfast. AE, MC, V. **Amenities:**
Restaurant (Continental); 2 bars; indoor swimming pool; tennis court; gym; beauty treatments; sauna/
steam room; supervised children's playroom; marina; miniature golf. *In room:* TV, tea/coffeemaker, garment press.

Inexpensive
Belmore Court Motel ★ (Value)   If you're just looking for a bed on which to crash,
this three-story motel has a variety of options at rock-bottom prices. It's the same motel
principle as in the United States: bland decor, no amenities, but rates that you really can't
beat. Most rooms have kitchenettes, and about a third of the units have two bedrooms
or a suite setup of bedroom and sitting room. Some have kitchens. Guest rooms are
nondescript but inoffensive, done in pastel colors, with standard furnishings in light

564 wood, and writing desks. The motel is on the eastern edge of town, within walking distance of all the major sights and shops.

Temp Rd., Enniskillen, County Fermanagh. (℃ **028/6632-6633.** Fax 028/6632-6362. www.motel.co.uk. 31 units. £45 ($90) double; £50 ($100) double with kitchenette; £70 ($140) family room (sleeps 5). Full breakfast £5 ($10); continental breakfast £3 ($6). AE, MC, V. *In room:* TV, kitchenette, tea/coffeemaker.

WHERE TO DINE

Castle Leslie ★★★ CONTINENTAL   Dinner at Castle Leslie (see above) offers all the relaxed graciousness—and drama—of a prewar dinner party. The dining rooms in the great house look out on one of the estate's lovely lakes and on ancient hardwood forests. The view alone is a perfect appetizer. The cuisine is classic and French influenced, with a well-chosen wine list. The menu is constantly changing, but you could start with the likes of local smoked salmon with lemon and capers, then proceed to roasted Irish lamb, and finish with white-chocolate crème brûlée. The order of service is formal—guests gather before the meal for champagne, and then proceed to the dining room. But such luxury does not come cheap.

Glaslough, County Monaghan. Drive through the center of Glaslough to castle gates. (℃ **047/88109.** Reservations required. Fixed-price dinner €130 ($208); a la carte menu available. MC, V. Daily 6–9:30pm.

Franco's ★ INTERNATIONAL   Next to the Buttermarket in three converted and restored buildings once part of Enniskillen's working waterfront, this casual restaurant blends old-world ambience and the legacy of the sea with contemporary recipes and fresh local ingredients. The Italian-American menu includes plenty of pasta and pizza options, as well as alternatives including barbecue dishes and shish kabob.

Queen Elizabeth Rd., Enniskillen, County Fermanagh. (℃ **028/6632-4424.** Reservations not accepted. Dinner main courses £8–£18 ($16–$36). AE, MC, V. Daily noon–11pm.

ENNISKILLEN AFTER DARK

Many or even most of the pubs and hotels in the area offer live entertainment, especially in the summer and on weekends.

If you're looking for Victorian style, try **Blakes of the Hollow ★**, 6 Church St., Enniskillen (℃ **028/6632-2143**). The pub opened in 1887 and has been in the Blake family ever since, retaining its original Victorian decor and ambience, with a long marble-topped mahogany bar and pinewood alcoves.

Check out what's on at the **Ardhowen Theatre,** Dublin Road, Enniskillen (℃ **028/6632-3233**). Also known as the Theatre by the Lakes because of its enviable position overlooking Upper Lough Erne, this 300-seat theater presents a varied program of concerts, drama, cabarets, jazz, gospel, blues, and other modern music. Tickets run from £9 to £17 ($18–$34) for most performances; curtain time is usually 8pm.

Appendix: Fast Facts, Toll-Free Numbers & Websites

1 FAST FACTS: IRELAND

AMERICAN EXPRESS There is no full-service **American Express** office in Dublin. Keith Prowse Travel, Lower Abbey Street, Irish Life Mall, Dublin 1 (① **01/878-3500**), offers limited services to card-holders. It is open Monday to Friday 9:30am to 5:30pm. There are no longer branches in the North. In an emergency, traveler's checks can be reported lost or stolen by dialing collect (to the U.S.) ① **00-1-336-393-1111.**

AREA CODES Area codes in Ireland range from one number (the Dublin area code is "1") to three. Area codes are included in all listings in this guide. Within Ireland, you dial 0 before the area code. It's like dialing "1" before the number in the U.S. Outside of Ireland, however, you do not dial 0 before the area code.

ATM NETWORKS & CASHPOINTS See "Money & Costs" in chapter 3.

BUSINESS HOURS Banks are open 10am to 4pm Monday to Wednesday and Friday, and 10am to 5pm Thursday.

Post offices (also known as **An Post**) in city centers are open from 9am to 5:30pm Monday to Friday and 9am to 1:30pm Saturday. The GPO on O'Connell Street in Dublin is open 8am to 8pm Monday to Saturday, and 10:30am to 6:30pm Sunday (for stamps only). Post offices in small towns often close for lunch from 1 to 2:30pm.

Museums and sights are generally open 10am to 5pm Tuesday to Saturday and 2 to 5pm Sunday.

Shops generally open 9am to 6pm Monday to Friday, with late opening on Thursday until 7 or 8pm. In Dublin's city center, most department stores and many shops are open noon to 6pm Sunday.

In **Northern Ireland,** bank hours are Monday to Friday 9:30am to 4:30pm. Post offices are open 9:30am to 5:30pm Monday to Friday and Saturday 9am to 1pm. Some in smaller towns close for an hour at lunchtime. Shopping hours are much the same as in the Republic, with some smaller shops closing for an hour at lunchtime.

CAR RENTALS See "Car-Rental Agencies" under "Toll-Free Numbers & Websites," later in the appendix.

DRINKING LAWS Individuals must be age 18 or over to be served alcoholic beverages in Ireland. For pub hours, see "Eating & Drinking in Ireland," in chapter 2. Restaurants with liquor licenses are permitted to serve alcohol during the hours when meals are served. Hotels and guesthouses with licenses can serve during normal hours to the public; overnight guests, referred to as "residents," can be served after closing hours. Alcoholic beverages by the bottle can be purchased at stores displaying OFF-LICENSE signs and at most supermarkets, but only during legal drinking hours. Ireland has very severe laws and penalties regarding driving while intoxicated, so don't even think about it.

DRIVING RULES See "Getting There & Getting Around" in chapter 3.

DRUGSTORES Drugstores are called "chemist shops" and are found in every city, town, and village. Look under "Chemists—Pharmaceutical" in the Golden Pages of the Irish telephone book or "Chemists—Dispensing" in the Yellow Pages of the Northern Ireland telephone book.

ELECTRICITY Wherever you go, bring a **connection kit** of the right power and phone adapters, a spare phone cord, and a spare Ethernet network cable—or find out whether your hotel supplies them to guests. The Irish electric system operates on 220 volts with a plug bearing three rectangular prongs. The Northern Irish system operates on 250 volts. To use standard American 110-volt appliances, you'll need both a transformer and a plug adapter. Most new laptops have built-in transformers, but some do not, so beware. Attempting to use only a plug adapter is a sure way to fry your appliance or, worse, cause a fire.

EMBASSIES & CONSULATES The **American Embassy** is at 42 Elgin Rd., Ballsbridge, Dublin 4 (✆ 01/668-8777); the **Canadian Embassy** is at 7–8 Wilton Terrace, 3rd Floor, Dublin 2 (✆ 01/417-4100); the **British Embassy** is at 29 Merrion Rd., Dublin 2 (✆ 01/205-3700); and the **Australian Embassy** is at Fitzwilton House, 7th Floor, Wilton Terrace, Dublin 2 (✆ 01/664-5300). In addition, there is an **American Consulate** at Danesfort House, 223 Stranmillis Rd., Belfast BT9 5GR (✆ 028/9038-6100).

EMERGENCIES For the **Garda (police)**, fire, ambulance, or other emergencies, dial ✆ **999.**

GASOLINE (PETROL) In Ireland, gas is called petrol and it is sold by the liter. At press time, the cost of a gallon of gas was around €5 ($8).

HOLIDAYS See "When to Go," in chapter 3.

INSURANCE Medical Insurance For travel overseas, most U.S. health plans (including Medicare and Medicaid) do not provide coverage, and the ones that do often require you to pay for services upfront and reimburse you only after you return home.

As a safety net, you may want to buy travel medical insurance, particularly if you're traveling to a remote or high-risk area where emergency evacuation might be necessary. If you require additional medical insurance, try **MEDEX Assistance** (✆ 410/453-6300; www.medexassist.com) or **Travel Assistance International** (✆ 800/821-2828; www.travelassistance.com; for general information on services, call the company's **Worldwide Assistance Services, Inc.,** at ✆ 800/777-8710).

Canadians should check with their provincial health plan offices or call **Health Canada** (✆ 866/225-0709; www.hc-sc.gc.ca) to find out the extent of their coverage and what documentation and receipts they must take home in case they are treated overseas.

Travelers from the U.K. should carry their European Health Insurance Card (EHIC), which replaced the E111 form as proof of entitlement to free/reduced cost medical treatment abroad (✆ 0845/606-2030; www.ehic.org.uk). Note, however, that the EHIC only covers "necessary medical treatment," and for repatriation costs, lost money, baggage, or cancellation, travel insurance from a reputable company should always be sought (www.travelinsuranceweb.com).

Travel Insurance The cost of travel insurance varies widely, depending on the destination, the cost and length of your trip, your age and health, and the type of trip you're taking, but expect to pay between 5% and 8% of the vacation itself.

You can get estimates from various providers through **InsureMyTrip.com.** Enter your trip cost and dates, your age, and other information, for prices from more than a dozen companies.

U.K. citizens and their families who make more than one trip abroad per year may find an annual travel insurance policy works out cheaper. Check **www.money supermarket.com**, which compares prices across a wide range of providers for single- and multitrip policies.

Most big travel agents offer their own insurance and will probably try to sell you their package when you book a holiday. Think before you sign. **Britain's Consumers' Association** recommends that you insist on seeing the policy and reading the fine print before buying travel insurance. The **Association of British Insurers** (© 020/7600-3333; www.abi.org.uk) gives advice by phone and publishes "Holiday Insurance," a free guide to policy provisions and prices. You might also shop around for better deals: Try **Columbus Direct** (© 0870/033-9988; www.columbusdirect.net).

Trip-Cancellation Insurance   Trip-cancellation insurance will help retrieve your money if you have to back out of a trip or depart early, or if your travel supplier goes bankrupt. Trip cancellation traditionally covers such events as sickness, natural disasters, and State Department advisories. The latest news in trip-cancellation insurance is the availability of **expanded hurricane coverage** and the **"any-reason"** cancellation coverage—which costs more but covers cancellations made for any reason. You won't get back 100% of your prepaid trip cost, but you'll be refunded a substantial portion. **TravelSafe** (© 888/885-7233;   www.travelsafe.com) offers both types of coverage. Expedia also offers any-reason cancellation coverage for its air-hotel packages. For details, you can also contact one of the following recommended insurers: **Access America** (© 866/807-3982;   www.accessamerica.com);

Travel Guard International (© 800/826-4919;   www.travelguard.com);   **Travel Insured International** (© 800/243-3174; www.travelinsured.com); and **Travelex Insurance Services** (© 888/457-4602; www.travelex-insurance.com).

INTERNET ACCESS   Public access terminals are no longer hard to find in Ireland; they're now in shopping malls, hotels, and even hostels, especially in the larger towns and more tourist-centered areas. Virtually every town with a public library offers free Internet access, though you may have to call ahead to reserve time on a PC. (For a list of public libraries in Ireland, visit **www.libdex.com/country/Ireland.html**.) Additionally, there are an increasing number of Internet cafes sprouting up across the island. We list many of these in the chapters that follow.

LANGUAGE   Ireland has two official languages: English and Gaelic (also known as Irish). All native Irish can speak English, however. Gaelic is growing in popularity, and there is a strong national movement to preserve and expand use of the language. Areas of the country where Gaelic is protected are known as the Gaeltacht and include Donegal, Galway, and parts of Kerry. In these regions, signs are in Gaelic, which is a complex and ancient language that you will not be able to figure out on your own. Ask for help if you get lost—despite the government's best efforts, everybody in Gaeltacht regions speaks English.

LOST & FOUND   Be sure to tell all of your credit card companies the minute you discover your wallet has been lost or stolen and file a report at the nearest police precinct. Your credit card company or insurer may require a police report number or record of the loss. Most credit card companies have an emergency toll-free number to call if your card is lost or stolen; they may be able to wire you a cash advance immediately or deliver an emergency credit card in a day or two.

For American Express, call ℂ **1850/ 882-028** in Ireland, ℂ **01273/696-993** in Northern Ireland; for MasterCard, call ℂ **1800/557378** toll-free in Ireland, ℂ **0800/964-767** in Northern Ireland; and for Visa, call ℂ **1800/558002** toll-free in Ireland, ℂ **0800/891-725** in Northern Ireland.

If you need emergency cash over the weekend when all banks and American Express offices are closed, you can have money wired to you via **Western Union** (ℂ **800/325-6000;** www.westernunion. com).

Identity theft or fraud are potential complications of losing your wallet, especially if you've lost your driver's license along with your cash and credit cards. Notify the major credit-reporting bureaus immediately; placing a fraud alert on your records may protect you against liability for criminal activity. The three major U.S. credit-reporting agencies are **Equifax** (ℂ **800/766-0008;** www.equifax. com), **Experian** (ℂ **888/397-3742;** www. experian.com), and **TransUnion** (ℂ **800/ 680-7289;** www.transunion.com). Finally, if you've lost all forms of photo ID, call your airline and explain the situation; they might allow you to board the plane if you have a copy of your passport or birth certificate and a copy of the police report you've filed.

MAIL   In Ireland, mailboxes are painted green with the word POST on top. In Northern Ireland, they usually look the same but are painted red, with a royal coat of arms symbol. From the Republic, an airmail letter or postcard to the United States or Canada, not exceeding 25 grams, costs €.90 ($1.45) and takes 5 to 7 days to arrive. From Northern Ireland to the United States or Canada, airmail letters not exceeding 20 grams cost 81p ($1.60) and postcards 50p ($1). Delivery takes about 5 to 7 days.

MEASUREMENTS   The metric system of measurement is used in Ireland, with nonmetric equivalents as follows. Temperature: 32°F = 0°C. Liquid volume: 1 liter = .26 U.S. gallon; 1 U.S. gallon = 3.8 liters. Distance: 1 foot = .30m; 1m = 3.3 feet; 1 mile = 1.6km; 1km = .62 mile. Weight: 1 ounce = 28 grams; 1 pound = .4555 kilogram; 1 gram = .04 ounce; 1 kilogram = 2.2 pounds.

NEWSPAPERS & MAGAZINES   *The Irish Independent* is the country's best-selling newspaper, and it's published daily (www.independent.ie).

Other major daily newspapers include *The Irish Examiner* and *The Irish Times.*

The Dubliner Magazine is a slick, monthly news and entertainment magazine with listings, arts and culture information, and a useful website (www. thedubliner.ie).

In Dublin Magazine (www.indublin.ie) is a popular arts-and-entertainment listings magazine.

PASSPORTS   Allow plenty of time before your trip to apply for a passport; processing normally takes 4 weeks but can take longer during busy periods (especially spring). And keep in mind that if you need a passport in a hurry, you'll pay a higher processing fee.

For Residents of Australia: You can pick up an application from your local post office or any branch of Passports Australia, but you must schedule an interview at the passport office to present your application materials. Call the **Australian Passport Information Service** at ℂ **131- 232,** or visit the government website at www.passports.gov.au.

For Residents of Canada: Passport applications are available at travel agencies throughout Canada or from the central **Passport Office,** Department of Foreign Affairs and International Trade, Ottawa, ON K1A 0G3 (ℂ **800/567-6868;** www. ppt.gc.ca).

For Residents of New Zealand: You can pick up a passport application at any New Zealand Passports Office or download it from their website. Contact the **Passports Office** at © **0800/225-050** in New Zealand, or 04/474-8100, or log on to www. passports.govt.nz.

For Residents of the United Kingdom: To pick up an application for a standard 10-year passport (5-year passport for children 15 and under), visit your nearest passport office, major post office, or travel agency; or contact the **United Kingdom Passport Service** at © **0870/ 521-0410** or search its website at www. ips.gov.uk.

For Residents of the United States: Whether you're applying in person or by mail, you can download passport applications from the U.S. State Department website at **http://travel.state.gov**. To find your regional passport office, either check the U.S. State Department website or call the **National Passport Information Center** toll-free number (© **877/487-2778**) for automated information.

POLICE In the Republic of Ireland, a law enforcement officer is called a **Garda,** a member of the Garda Síochána ("Guardian of the Peace"); in the plural, it's Gardaí (pronounced *Gar*-dee) or simply "the Guards." Dial © **999** to reach the Gardaí in an emergency. Except for special detachments, Irish police are unarmed and wear dark blue uniforms. In Northern Ireland you can also reach the police by dialing © **999.**

SMOKING Ireland has a broad antismoking law that bans smoking in all public places, including bars, restaurants, and hotel lobbies. Most restaurants and pubs have covered indoor smoking areas these days.

TAXES As in many European countries, sales tax is called VAT (value-added tax) and is often already included in the price quoted to you or shown on price tags. In the Republic, VAT rates vary—for hotels, restaurants, and car rentals, it is 13.5%; for souvenirs and gifts, it is 21%. In Northern Ireland, the VAT is 17.5%

across-the-board. VAT charged on services such as hotel stays, meals, car rentals, and entertainment cannot be refunded to visitors, but the VAT on products such as souvenirs is refundable.

TELEPHONES See "Staying Connected," in chapter 3.

TIME Ireland follows Greenwich Mean Time (1 hr. earlier than Central European Time) from November to March, and British Standard Time (the same as Central European Time) from April to October. Ireland is 5 hours ahead of the eastern United States.

Ireland's latitude makes for longer days and shorter nights in the summer, and the reverse in the winter. In June, the sun doesn't fully set until around 11pm, but in December, it is dark by 4pm.

TIPPING Most hotels and guesthouses add a service charge to the bill, usually 12.5% to 15%, although some smaller places add only 10% or nothing at all. Always check to see what amount, if any, has been added to your bill. If it is 12.5% to 15%, and you feel this is sufficient, then there is no need for more gratuities. However, if a smaller amount has been added or if staff members have provided exceptional service, it is appropriate to give additional cash gratuities. For porters or bellhops, tip €1 ($1.60) per piece of luggage. For taxi drivers, hairdressers, and other providers of service, tip as you would at home, an average of 10% to 15%.

For restaurants, the policy is usually printed on the menu—either a gratuity of 10% to 15% is automatically added to your bill or it's left up to you. Always ask if you are in doubt. As a rule, bartenders do not expect a tip, except when table service is provided.

TOILETS Public restrooms are usually simply called "toilets" or are marked with international symbols. In the Republic of Ireland, some of the older ones still carry the Gaelic words *fir* (MEN) and *mna*

(WOMEN). Among the newest and best-kept restrooms are those found at shopping malls and at multistory parking lots. Free restrooms are available to customers of sightseeing attractions, museums, hotels, restaurants, pubs, shops, theaters, and department stores. Most of the newer gas stations (called "petrol stations" in Ireland) have public toilets, and a few have baby-changing facilities.

USEFUL PHONE NUMBERS

U.S. Dept. of State Travel Advisory 📞 202/647-5225 (manned 24 hr.)

U.S. Passport Agency 📞 202/647-0518

U.S. Centers for Disease Control International Traveler's Hotline: 📞 404/332-4559

WATER Tap water throughout the island of Ireland is generally safe. However, some areas in the west of Ireland have been battling with out-of-date water purification systems. If, for example, you'll be visiting the town of Ennis, you will not be able to drink the tap water there. Other towns have also had problems, and whenever we learn of a community with water purification problems, we have detailed it in the appropriate chapter of this guide. Keep an eye out for signs warning you that water is not drinkable, and consider always carrying a large bottle of water with you.

2 TOLL-FREE NUMBERS & WEBSITES

MAJOR U.S. AIRLINES
(*flies internationally as well)

American Airlines*
📞 800/433-7300 (in U.S. or Canada)
📞 020/7365-0777 (in U.K.)
www.aa.com

Continental Airlines*
📞 800/523-3273 (in U.S. or Canada)
📞 084/5607-6760 (in U.K.)
www.continental.com

Delta Air Lines*
📞 800/221-1212 (in U.S. or Canada)
📞 084/5600-0950 (in U.K.)
www.delta.com

Northwest Airlines
📞 800/225-2525 (in U.S. or Canada)
📞 870/0507-4074 (in U.K.)
www.nwa.com

United Airlines*
📞 800/864-8331 (in U.S. or Canada)
📞 084/5844-4777 (in U.K.)
www.united.com

US Airways*
📞 800/428-4322 (in U.S. or Canada)
📞 084/5600-3300 (in U.K.)
www.usairways.com

Virgin America*
📞 877/359-8474
www.virginamerica.com

MAJOR INTERNATIONAL AIRLINES

Air France
📞 800/237-2747 (in U.S.)
📞 800/375-8723 (in U.S. or Canada)
📞 087/0142-4343 (in U.K.)
www.airfrance.com

Air New Zealand
📞 800/262-1234 (in U.S.)
📞 800/663-5494 (in Canada)
📞 0800/028-4149 (in U.K.)
www.airnewzealand.com

Alitalia
📞 800/223-5730 (in U.S.)
📞 800/361-8336 (in Canada)
📞 087/0608-6003 (in U.K.)
www.alitalia.com

British Airways
📞 800/247-9297 (in U.S. or Canada)
📞 087/0850-9850 (in U.K.)
www.ba.com

Lufthansa

- ✆ 800/399-5838 (in U.S.)
- ✆ 800/563-5954 (in Canada)
- ✆ 087/0837-7747 (in U.K.)

www.lufthansa.com

Virgin Atlantic Airways

- ✆ 800/821-5438 (in U.S. or Canada)
- ✆ 087/0574-7747 (in U.K.)

www.virgin-atlantic.com

BUDGET AIRLINES

Aer Lingus

- ✆ 800/474-7424 (in U.S. or Canada)
- ✆ 087/0876-5000 (in U.K.)

www.aerlingus.com

bmibaby

- ✆ 870/126-6726 (in U.S. or Canada)
- ✆ 087/1224-0224 (in U.K.)

www.bmibaby.com

easyJet

- ✆ 870/600-0000 (in U.S. or Canada)
- ✆ 090/5560-7777 (in U.K.)

www.easyjet.com

Ryanair

- ✆ 353/01-249-7791 (in U.S. or Canada)
- ✆ 081/830-3030 (in Ireland)
- ✆ 087/1246-0000 (in U.K.)

www.ryanair.com

CAR-RENTAL AGENCIES

Alamo

- ✆ 800/GO-ALAMO (462-5266)

www.alamo.com

Auto Europe

- ✆ 888/223-5555 (in U.S. or Canada)
- ✆ 0800/2235-5555 (in U.K.)

www.autoeurope.com

Avis

- ✆ 800/331-1212 (in U.S. or Canada)
- ✆ 084/4581-8181 (in U.K.)

www.avis.com

Budget

- ✆ 800/527-0700 (in U.S.)
- ✆ 800/268-8900 (in Canada)
- ✆ 087/0156-5656 (in U.K.)

www.budget.com

Enterprise

- ✆ 800/261-7331 (in U.S.)
- ✆ 514/355-4028 (in Canada)
- ✆ 012/9360-9090 (in U.K.)

www.enterprise.com

Hertz

- ✆ 800/654-3131
- ✆ 800/654-3001 (for international reservations)

www.hertz.com

MAJOR HOTEL & MOTEL CHAINS

Best Western International

- ✆ 800/780-7234 (in U.S. or Canada)
- ✆ 0800/393-130 (in U.K.)

www.bestwestern.com

Clarion Hotels

- ✆ 800/CLARION (252-7466) or 877/424-6423 (in U.S. or Canada)
- ✆ 0800/444-444 (in U.K.)

www.choicehotels.com

Comfort Inns

- ✆ 800/228-5150
- ✆ 0800/444-444 (in U.K.)

www.choicehotels.com

Four Seasons

- ✆ 800/819-5053 (in U.S. or Canada)
- ✆ 0800/6488-6488 (in U.K.)

www.fourseasons.com

Hilton Hotels

- ✆ 800/HILTONS (445-8667) (in U.S. or Canada)
- ✆ 087/0590-9090 (in U.K.)

www.hilton.com

Holiday Inn

- ✆ 800/315-2621 (in U.S. or Canada)
- ✆ 0800/405-060 (in U.K.)

www.holidayinn.com

Hyatt

- ✆ 888/591-1234 (in U.S. or Canada)
- ✆ 084/5888-1234 (in U.K.)

www.hyatt.com

InterContinental Hotels & Resorts
- ✆ 800/424-6835 (in U.S. or Canada)
- ✆ 0800/1800-1800 (in U.K.)
- www.ichotelsgroup.com

Marriott
- ✆ 877/236-2427 (in U.S. or Canada)
- ✆ 0800/221-222 (in U.K.)
- www.marriott.com

Omni Hotels
- ✆ 888/444-OMNI (444-6664)
- www.omnihotels.com

Radisson Hotels & Resorts
- ✆ 888/201-1718 (in U.S. or Canada)
- ✆ 0800/374-411 (in U.K.)
- www.radisson.com

Ramada Worldwide
- ✆ 888/2-RAMADA (272-6232) (in U.S. or Canada)
- ✆ 080/8100-0783 (in U.K.)
- www.ramada.com

Renaissance
- ✆ 888/236-2427
- www.marriott.com

Sheraton Hotels & Resorts
- ✆ 800/325-3535 (in U.S.)
- ✆ 800/543-4300 (in Canada)
- ✆ 0800/3253-5353 (in U.K.)
- www.starwoodhotels.com/sheraton

Travelodge
- ✆ 800/578-7878
- www.travelodge.com

Westin Hotels & Resorts
- ✆ 800/937-8461 (in U.S. or Canada)
- ✆ 0800/3259-5959 (in U.K.)
- www.starwoodhotels.com/westin

Wyndham Hotels & Resorts
- ✆ 877/999-3223 (in U.S. or Canada)
- ✆ 050/6638-4899 (in U.K.)
- www.wyndham.com

INDEX

See also Accommodations, Restaurants, and Pubs indexes, below.

FROMMER'S® COMPLETE TRAVEL GUIDES

Alaska
Amalfi Coast
American Southwest
Amsterdam
Argentina
Arizona
Atlanta
Australia
Austria
Bahamas
Barcelona
Beijing
Belgium· Holland & Luxembourg
Belize
Bermuda
Boston
Brazil
British Columbia & the Canadian
 Rockies
Brussels & Bruges
Budapest & the Best of Hungary
Buenos Aires
Calgary
California
Canada
Cancún· Cozumel & the Yucatán
Cape Cod· Nantucket & Martha's
 Vineyard
Caribbean
Caribbean Ports of Call
Carolinas & Georgia
Chicago
Chile & Easter Island
China
Colorado
Costa Rica
Croatia
Cuba
Denmark
Denver· Boulder & Colorado Springs
Eastern Europe
Ecuador & the Galapagos Islands
Edinburgh & Glasgow
England
Europe
Europe by Rail

Florence· Tuscany & Umbria
Florida
France
Germany
Greece
Greek Islands
Guatemala
Hawaii
Hong Kong
Honolulu· Waikiki & Oahu
India
Ireland
Israel
Italy
Jamaica
Japan
Kauai
Las Vegas
London
Los Angeles
Los Cabos & Baja
Madrid
Maine Coast
Maryland & Delaware
Maui
Mexico
Montana & Wyoming
Montréal & Québec City
Morocco
Moscow & St· Petersburg
Munich & the Bavarian Alps
Nashville & Memphis
New England
Newfoundland & Labrador
New Mexico
New Orleans
New York City
New York State
New Zealand
Northern Italy
Norway
Nova Scotia· New Brunswick &
 Prince Edward Island
Oregon
Paris
Peru

Philadelphia & the Amish Country
Portugal
Prague & the Best of the Czech
 Republic
Provence & the Riviera
Puerto Rico
Rome
San Antonio & Austin
San Diego
San Francisco
Santa Fe· Taos & Albuquerque
Scandinavia
Scotland
Seattle
Seville· Granada & the Best of
 Andalusia
Shanghai
Sicily
Singapore & Malaysia
South Africa
South America
South Florida
South Korea
South Pacific
Southeast Asia
Spain
Sweden
Switzerland
Tahiti & French Polynesia
Texas
Thailand
Tokyo
Toronto
Turkey
USA
Utah
Vancouver & Victoria
Vermont· New Hampshire & Maine
Vienna & the Danube Valley
Vietnam
Virgin Islands
Virginia
Walt Disney World· & Orlando
Washington· D·C·
Washington State

FROMMER'S® DAY BY DAY GUIDES

Amsterdam
Barcelona
Beijing
Boston
Cancún & the Yucatan
Chicago
Florence & Tuscany

Hong Kong
Honolulu & Oahu
London
Maui
Montréal
Napa & Sonoma
New York City

Paris
Provence & the Riviera
Rome
San Francisco
Venice
Washington D·C·

PAULINE FROMMER'S GUIDES: SEE MORE. SPEND LESS.

Alaska
Hawaii
Italy

Las Vegas
London
New York City

Paris
Walt Disney World·
Washington D·C·

A Guide for Every Type of Traveler

Frommer's Complete Guides

For those who value complete coverage, candid advice, and lots of choices in all price ranges.

Pauline Frommer's Guides

For those who want to experience a culture, meet locals, and save money along the way.

MTV Guides

For hip, youthful travelers who want a fresh perspective on today's hottest cities and destinations.

Day by Day Guides

For leisure or business travelers who want to organize their time to get the most out of a trip.

Frommer's With Kids Guides

For families traveling with children ages 2 to 14 seeking kid-friendly hotels, restaurants, and activities.

Unofficial Guides

For honeymooners, families, business travelers, and others who value no-nonsense, *Consumer Reports*–style advice.

For Dummies Travel Guides

For curious, independent travelers looking for a fun and easy way to plan a trip.

Visit Frommers.com

WILEY

Now you know.